PENGUIN BOOKS

The Grammys

Thomas O'Neil is a freelance writer who lives in New York City where he has channeled his twin obsessions with pop culture and who won what entertainment award into writing books about them. His first book, also published by Penguin, was *The Emmys: Star Wars, Showdowns, and the Supreme Test of TV's Best*. His articles have appeared in such leading publications as *The New York Times*, *The Boston Globe*, *The Chicago Sun-Times,* and *Good Housekeeping*.

THE GRAMMYS®

For the Record

Thomas O'Neil

Penguin Books

A WEXFORD PRESS BOOK

PENGUIN BOOKS
Published by the Penguin Group
Penguin Books USA Inc., 375 Hudson Street,
New York, New York 10014, U.S.A.
Penguin Books Ltd, 27 Wrights Lane,
London W8 5TZ, England
Penguin Books Australia Ltd, Ringwood,
Victoria, Australia
Penguin Books Canada Ltd, 10 Alcorn Avenue,
Toronto, Ontario, Canada M4V 3B2
Penguin Books (N.Z.) Ltd, 182–190 Wairau Road,
Auckland 10, New Zealand

Penguin Books Ltd, Registered Offices:
Harmondsworth, Middlesex, England

First published in Penguin Books 1993

1   3   5   7   9   10   8   6   4   2

A Wexford Press Book
Design by Louis Cruz Creative Group, Inc.

"Grammy" is a registered trademark of the
National Academy of Recording Arts and Sciences.
Grammy statuette copyright N.A.R.A.S. This book
is not authorized or endorsed by N.A.R.A.S.

ISBN 0 14 01.6657 2
(CIP data available)

Printed in the United States of America
Set in Times Roman

To the memory

of Brian Mangum,

who brought harmony

to so many lives

Contents

Acknowledgments

Compiling this book sometimes seemed like conducting a vast orchestra, all the members of which performed at peak skill and now deserve their bows and bouquets.

Both go to the gifted design team of Louis and Pilar Cruz, who made this fact-filled reference volume easily accessible and aesthetically beautiful. The difficult task of keeping track of all these facts belonged to two expert (and unflappable) copy editors — Hilary Marsh and Sue Dahlinger. Bravo to all of you.

Dawn Reel performed every task — from list compilation to editing and layout assistance — with true professional panache and her typical cheerful ease.

Research was headed by three industrious sleuths: the late Edwin Gardner, who canvassed the libraries of New York and Washington, and Sherie Van Sanford and Paula Petrie, who unearthed invaluable archival material out in Los Angeles. The awesome task of compiling this volume's index was performed by Jerry Ralya.

Caroline Kozo and her staff in the photo department at the L.A. Public Library provided this book with much of its visual accompaniment. Thanks for your patient follow-up to my many harried requests by fax.

Ray Whelan at Globe Photos and Paula Vogel at Wide World also came up with invaluable pictures. Kudos go, too, to the many record companies that also provided vital visual material: A&M, Bagdasarian Productions, CBS Columbia, C.E.M.A., Fantasy, Deutsche Grammophon, Island, Motown, MCA, and RCA. Special thanks go to Bob Kaus at Atlantic, Bob Bernstein at Capitol, and Sue Satriano at Sony.

A chorus of other talent contributed hard work and long hours, including Dick Kagan, Lara Davidson, Karen Clay, and Timothy Marek. Other thanks go to Jeff Miles (who knows why), Syd and Miriam Cassyd, Lynn Dunn, Ty Wilson, Chandler Warren, Jules Warshaw, Curtiss Anderson, Doris Ramirez, and Margaret Beall. Penguin Books publicist Joyce Goldberg also deserves immense credit for her long hours and enthusiastic work on this project and the previous book on the Emmy Awards.

I am much indebted as well to the many people who helped out in other ways, including Catherine Miller (who lit the spark), the late Fred Birmingham and his darling wife Franny, and especially the warm-hearted Mangum family (Nancy, Dianne, Kathy, Ovis, Rodney, and Michael), who were supportive and loving during a tragic time that coincided with the compilation of this book. I give you the Irish salute: *Salante*.

Among the many people who contributed time for interviews were N.A.R.A.S. founding father Jim Conkling; Priscilla Dunn, wife of cofounder Lloyd Dunn; and Grammy-winning artists such as Henry Mancini, Herb Alpert, Marvin Hamlisch, and others.

Throughout this editorial performance we were all guided by the inspired baton of our maestro at Penguin Books, associate editor Caroline White, who deserves the deepest bow — and our deepest gratitude.

Facing the Music:
How the Grammys Measure Up

"Glamour! Excitement! The most star-studded musical-variety show of the year!" is how *TV Guide* once described the annual ceremony surrounding America's leading music awards. "In the end," wrote *The New York Times*, "there's no outguessing the Grammys. They're mysterious, puzzling, and rarely less than entertaining."

The Grammys' entertainment value can be staggering. Everyone from Prince to Placido Domingo shows up once a year for a spectacle that includes musical extravaganzas, backstage intrigues, flash, glitter, outrageous acceptance speeches and — given the Grammys' notorious eccentricities — suspense that usually proves *anything* is possible.

It's also the most audacious fashion show of the year. At the Oscars, by comparison, flamboyant couture is usually defined by what Cher wears in a given year. At the Grammys, viewers see a bizarre runway display of torn T-shirts, antique prom dresses, tuxedo travesties, underwear-as-outerwear, and gowns that Giorgio Armani might design if he were addicted to eating magic mushrooms. Wrote *Time* magazine columnist Lance Morrow in 1983: "Stevie Wonder, for example, wore a cumulously quilted white satin tuxedo whose upswept lapels formed great angel wings. The costume had the curious effect of making him look like a Puritan headstone." And speaking of heads, Bette Midler once wore something on top of hers that constituted one of the most ingenious Grammy fashion statements ever: a 45-r.p.m. record. "It's 'Come Go with Me' by the Dell-Vikings," she informed the audience. "It

was a great record, but it's a better *hat!*"

When the Oscars do a musical number, you usually get safe and workman-like productions that are full of Vegas-style spectacle but short on heart and soul. At the Grammys you get Michael Jackson storming the stage, as he did at the 1987 awards, with a nine-minute jam session of "Man in the Mirror" that is as exhilarating as performance art can get. Jackson then returned to his seat in the audience that year and watched one of Grammy's real dramas begin as his *Bad* album, which had been expected to sweep the awards, suffered defeat after defeat all night. Only its engineers ended up with a Grammy. Jackson — who, just four years earlier, had set a record for the most victories won in a single year — came up with scratch. The *L.A. Times* observed, "He couldn't have looked any more heartbroken if someone had just run away with his pet chimp."

The Grammys matter because all these dramas are *real* — not just a music video tale of boy-meets-award, boy-loses-award, but boy-wins-award-*next*-year-when-no-one-expects-it! (Michael actually had to wait two more years till he picked up his next one — and his most recent so far — the short form music video prize for "Leave Me Alone.") The central conflict over who will win what pits the likes of Prince against "the Boss" Bruce Springsteen and Bobby McFerrin against Mel Tormé — revealing music's most gifted megastars locked in a heated struggle for the most valued prize of their profession. How it all ends is often controversial, but always fun.

And what is it like to win? "It's finger bitin' time," Count Basie once told *Grammy Pulse*, the membership magazine of the recording academy. "If your name is called, a lot of things happen in a few seconds. You're numb, there's an explosion, you're with it, you smile, you think this is the impossible dream come true .... For a minute or so you're on a par with all those Oscar winners and those cats who went home with Emmys. It's national television on one hand and a room full of friends and acquaintances on the other."

Dionne Warwick told the same source: "Being voted 'the best' by one's peers in this profession is the greatest honor that one can hope to receive. With all of the other music awards that have sprung up in recent years, the Grammy is still *the* award. It was the first and original, and when you receive one, you know you did it right." *The Washington Post* has been one of the honor's most cynical detractors over the years, but even it once begrudgingly described them as "the recording industry's only truly prestigious awards." *Rolling Stone* once dismissed them as "the laughing stock, the spitting spittoon of the business," but it also admitted, in a separate article, that "the Grammy affair is the granddaddy of them all and the one that commands the most respect within the music industry."

What gives Grammy its detractors — and there are many of them — is its assertion that it recognizes "the best." *L.A. Times* music critic Robert Hilburn is among those who think that's absurd. "I mean, how many times can you sit by and watch nondescript singles like [the Captain & Tennille's] 'Love Will Keep

> **"The Grammys celebrate the best of the broad but conservative pop mainstream."**

Us Together' walk away with top Grammy honors without asking yourself: Do these people actually listen to the records?" he asked in 1984. The winners are chosen (after being listened to, presumably) by the 6,000 full members of the National Academy of Recording Arts and Sciences, who are veterans of the creative side of the music industry. Older people already established within their fields tend to be the ones who join professional organizations like N.A.R.A.S., of course (the record academy seldom gets membership applications from teenage street rappers in Harlem), so the voters tend to like music more similar to that which was popular when they were young. Given the members' professional expertise, it certainly matters what they think is the best in American music, even if those views have an obvious bias toward more conservative tastes. The American Music Awards, by comparison, make no such claims. Their prizes go simply to the "favorite" music and artists of the year, which are determined by sales figures, the amount of radio air time a song gets, and polls conducted of frequent music buyers. Which is better? The *L.A. Times* once gave this answer: "Dick Clark's American Music Awards make the Grammys seem like the Nobel Prize for literature in comparison."

For the most part, the Grammys tend to reward hummable popular music such as past — and deserving — Record of the Year winners "Moon River" by Henry Mancini in 1961 and "Bridge Over Troubled Water" by Simon & Garfunkel in 1970. "Members of the Recording Academy tend to favor the hits," critic Paul Grein once wrote in the *L.A Times*, "and they like their music right down the middle — not too hard, too funky nor too adventurous. The Grammys celebrate the best of the broad but conservative pop mainstream."

That voting preference has led to some pretty puffy choices over the years when songs like the 5th Dimension's "Up, Up and Away" and Christopher Cross's "Sailing" swept the highest honors. But the Grammys have also made some courageous selections in the top categories like Album of the Year winners *Sgt. Pepper's Lonely Hearts Club Band* by the Beatles, Paul Simon's *Graceland*, and U2's *The Joshua Tree*. It doesn't happen often enough for critics with progressive tastes, but when it does, it goes a long way toward dispelling the accusation that the Grammys are really "the Grannys," as they've often been labeled in the past.

Grammy pantheon members, from left: Art Garfunkel, Paul Simon, Yoko Ono, John Lennon, and Roberta Flack gathered backstage at the 1974 awards ceremony.

WIDE WORLD PHOTO

awards in one swoop. In the intervening and subsequent years, Jones has demonstrated extraordinary talent, amazing diversity, and incredible staying power. Everybody wants to be a citizen in the country where Quincy Jones rules, and

"When figures like Stevie Wonder and Paul Simon combine substance and craft within the mainstream tradition, academy members frequently respond with an armful of awards," the *L.A. Times* said. "But the mavericks, from Presley and Dylan to Bowie and Hendrix, have generally been ignored because their work fell outside that neat tradition."

To arrive at a fair estimation of the awards, one should consider, first, who has won the most. In the nonclassical fields, with 25, it's Quincy Jones, the man who not only has the most impressive Rolodex in the music industry, but one who has the most talent in all of music's many aspects. No one is more important on the music scene today than the gentleman who was an arranger for Count Basie as early as 1963 (winning a Grammy for "I Can't Stop Loving You") and collaborated with Michael Jackson as a producer of *Thriller* 20 years later to pick up an impressive four

so in Grammyland the citizenry is content to sing "Hail to the Chief" to a class act that reflects well on them.

When Michael Jackson set the record for reaping the most Grammys in a year at the 1983 awards, he picked up eight, seven of them for *Thriller*. The Chicago Symphony Orchestra's conductor, Georg Solti, has received more throughout an entire career (29), which puts Quincy Jones in second place overall. Solti also holds the record for the longest continuous winning streak, prevailing for 10 years in a row from 1974 to 1983. The second-longest winning streak was achieved by Aretha Franklin, who monopolized the female r&b vocal award for eight years (1967–84) and has picked up an additional seven statuettes as of this writing, making her the most honored woman in the awards' history.

The artist who has won Grammy's biggest prize, Record of the Year, the most is three-time champ Paul Simon for two Simon & Garfunkel singles, "Mrs. Robinson" in 1968 and "Bridge Over Troubled Water" in 1970, as well as his own "Graceland" in 1987. For winning Album of the Year the most times (three), Simon is tied with Stevie Wonder and Frank Sinatra. Sinatra has the most nominations for Album of the Year (eight), followed by Barbra Streisand's seven. Sinatra also has the most nominations for Record of the Year (seven), followed by a tie for second place between Streisand and Paul McCartney with five each. (Paul Simon comes in third place with four; McCartney's record bids include his work both with, and after, the Beatles). Grammy's pantheon may not represent the most daring and pioneering artists of the day, but the biggest winners certainly rank as some of music's most divine talent.

Lesser-known greats have benefitted tremendously from victories in the top categories, which often transformed them suddenly into superstars. "Had I been asked three years ago to evaluate the chances of Bonnie Raitt winning four Grammys," *The New York Times* reviewer Stephen Holden wrote about the 1989 awards, "I would have shaken my head and said impossible." The impossible happened when Raitt's *Nick of Time* won Album of the Year after picking up its three earlier honors, causing its obviously overwhelmed artist to gasp at the Grammycast, "Wake me when it's over!" The awards spotted another real winner in Bette Midler as far back as 1973 when it hailed her as Best New Artist, thereby boosting her fledgling career. At the 1986 awards show, Sting was generous in acknowledging the role his victories played in his and his group finding a wider audience. "The Grammys gave recognition to the Police before we really broke in America," he said. "That gave us a lot of respectability."

When the Grammys are at their best, the choices can be a true credit to our remembrance of America's greatest music. Who could quarrel with the selection of Sinatra's "Strangers in the Night" as the best record of any year? Not even knowing what its competition was in 1966, any rational person would have to believe that such a classic was unbeatable. (It topped, among others, "Monday, Monday" by the Mamas & the Papas and "Winchester Cathedral" by the New Vaudeville Band.) Consider, too, some of the other early and memorable winners: Bobby Darin's "Mack the Knife" (1959), Tony Bennett's "I Left My Heart in San Francisco" (1963), and Herb Alpert's "A Taste of Honey" (1965).

Who and what wins Grammys often reveal things about ourselves and our times. When Americans experienced the disillusionment of the late 1960s and early 1970s and Simon & Garfunkel yearned for a "Bridge Over Troubled Water," the duo reached out and touched a national spirit — and won the Record, Song, and Album of the Year awards. Hollywood was once the one place in the country where harsh realities like Vietnam and Watergate didn't seem to affect the fantasy American lifestyle at its most overindulgent, but in 1977 the Eagles won the top Grammy for revealing what it was really like to live it up in "Hotel California." Life just wasn't the same anywhere anymore throughout the decade and it could be lonely, as the Doobie Brothers confessed in their 1979 Record of the Year soul-searcher "What a Fool Believes." When the booming 1980s arrived, everything seemed to change for the better, however, and Steve Winwood was honored for the joyous new spirit found in "Higher Love."

It's amazing how often sad songs win

in the record category, though. Logic might suggest that voters would want to embrace more upbeat music, giving them something to feel good about like they did in 1988 when hailing Bobby McFerrin's "Don't Worry, Be Happy." Simon & Garfunkel's "Bridge" is the best case in point, since it was the first Grammy record winner to muse so publicly and painfully about the disillusionments of life. When Roberta Flack won back-to-back trophies in 1972 and 1973 for "The First Time Ever I Saw Your Face" and "Killing Me Softly with His Song" that same slowly sung anguish took on a soulful note, and a black artist won in the top categories for the first time, reflecting the changing times in society, too. Picking Flack — twice — was a courageous thing, especially considering that voters could have favored the more feelgood "You Are the Sunshine of My Life" by Stevie Wonder in 1973 or had their pain, if they really wanted it, the old-fashioned way with "Song Sung Blue" by Neil Diamond in 1972.

A decade later, the Grammys continued to show courage in picking such other bittersweet choices as Tina Turner's "What's Love Got to Do with It" in 1985 when Bruce Springsteen's uplifting "Dancing in the Dark" might have been a more popular choice with young, fun-loving record buyers. They, after all, are the ones that the record industry insiders (read N.A.R.A.S. members) are accused of pandering to on the job whenever they crank out more feelgood music for the dance clubs. It's interesting to know that, when it comes down to voting privately for the Grammys during their off hours, these same insiders often forsake what's popular and upbeat in favor of such curious but laudable choices as "What's Love Got to Do with It." During that same year, by contrast, the American Music Awards gave their prize for Best Single

to "Dancing in the Dark," hardly Springsteen's best artistic work — or his best pop single, even of that year.

The Grammys may be star-studded, mysterious, exciting, and include one of the most outrageous fashion shows of the year, but, unfortunately, the awards themselves aren't especially fashionable. Popular, yes, but not hip to those, you know, who *really know* what the best music of the year is. Rock's mavericks are the harshest with their opinions since they're usually the ones that the awards overlook. Shortly before Frank Zappa won the rock instrumental performance award for his *Jazz from Hell* album in 1987, he told *The Cleveland Plain Dealer*, "I have no ambiguous feelings about the Grammys at all. I know they're fake. I find it difficult to believe that Whitney Houston is the answer to all of America's music needs." After he won, Zappa issued no press release to counter his earlier comment. Not surprisingly, he didn't attend the awards ceremony either.

"The American Music Awards make the Grammys seem like the Nobel Prize for literature in comparison."

The list of Grammy sins are many. Ballads almost always sweep the honors for Record and Song of the Year (examples: Bette Midler's "Wind Beneath My Wings" in 1989; "I Honestly Love You" by Olivia Newton-John in 1974), making most music critics groan in their yearly post-Grammy newspaper and magazine columns. West Coast artists usually have an edge. "The Grammys are famous for a pro-California bias," the *L.A. Times* once wrote, citing examples like Toto's sweep in 1982. (Defenders counter, saying: Yes, but most pop music stars now *live* in Hollywood.) Country music almost never wins the top trophies. (Among the five exceptions so far are Glen Campbell's 1968 Album of the Year *By the Time I Get to Phoenix* and 1982 Song of the Year "Always on My Mind.") Jazz has fared just as poorly. Its few victories include the first Album of the Year, Henry Mancini's *The Music from Peter Gunn,* 1964 Album of the Year *Getz/Gilberto,* and Bobby McFerrin's 1988 Record and Song of the Year "Don't Worry, Be Happy." Classical music — like religious, polka, and other genres of less broad appeal — has *never* won in the top categories, which prompted N.A.R.A.S. to introduce a special Classical Album of the Year award in 1962. Nominees with a social cause attached — like the 1972 Album of the Year *The Concert for Bangla Desh* or the 1985 Record of the Year "We Are the World" — almost *always* win. The grumbling is quiet on that point, though. Few critics want to take on the hungry half a world away just to stress such an obvious truth.

> *The bottom line is that, by a score of six to five, the 5th Dimension has won more awards than the Beatles.*

Outside of the top pop and rock categories, winners frequently repeat from year to year. "Once the academy has a winner's name lodged in its collective consciousness (and hasn't drawn too much scorn for that name), it likes to keep on doling out awards," the *L.A. Times* once observed. That may be how Chicago Symphony conductor Sir Georg Solti has racked up the most victories of

anyone and how Aretha Franklin came to dominate the r&b vocal awards the same way Ella Fitzgerald once reigned over the jazz singing prizes.

Rewarding such classic veteran talent is always safe and easy. The true challenge comes when Grammy voters have to pick the year's Best New Artist, one of its four highest honors. Except for Midler and other sensible past selections like Bobby Darin, winners tend to be featherweight choices like the Starland Vocal Band and A Taste of Honey — or, worse, made-for-MTV pop hunks like Milli Vanilli. The record academy was publicly humiliated by choosing the last group when the duo was unmasked as lip-synching frontmen soon after their victory. N.A.R.A.S. stripped Milli Vanilli of its award for 1989 after the truth was learned, but it seems like the academy will still never live down the embarrassment. It may be no consolation to N.A.R.A.S., but it's interesting to note that the American Music Awards gave their equivalent prize that same year to Milli Vanilli. Nobody seems to care, though.

The American Music Awards are proud of the fact that their winners are the most popular artists in the country, but when Grammys happen to go the top pop talent, as they often do, it's not something that academy leaders boast about. The trophies were designed to recognize high artistic achievement. ("Sales and mass popularity are the yardsticks of the record industry," the N.A.R.A.S. credo reads. "They are not the yardsticks of this academy.") Still, more than three-quarters of the winners of Record and Album of the Year were number one at one time or another in the singles or LP charts. Nearly all of them at least have made the Top 10.

Notable exceptions include "the biggest longshot in Grammy history," according to the *L.A. Times* in 1979:

Henry Mancini's Record of the Year in 1963, "Days of Wine and Roses," which only reached number 33 at its peak. "Graceland" surpassed that failing record in 1987 when it won the same award after having never climbed higher than 81st in the rankings. (The Album of the Year category, by contrast, is less accessible to the non-hit makers. Only one winner has failed to reach a Top 10 position: Glen Campbell's *By the Time I Get to Phoenix* in 1968.) One of the most convincing and ironic other pieces of evidence one can use to counter the pop sales claim (unfortunately, for N.A.R.A.S.) is that, throughout the 1960s when Motown was shaking up the Top 10 chart with a steady stream of hits, it reaped only one award. And that was slid in, too, just at the decade's end in 1969 (for the 1968 awards) when the Temptations won the best r&b group vocals prize for "Cloud Nine."

Throughout the Grammys' history, the most stinging indictment against them has been the accusation that they took forever to recognize rock & roll adequately. And, unfortunately, on this most serious charge of all, the Grammys are clearly guilty. After several half-hearted attempts to do so earlier, it wasn't until 1979 that N.A.R.A.S. permanently gave rock & roll its own categories, which jazz, rhythm & blues, and classical had from the very first awards for 1958 when Frank Sinatra and friends were so terrified that Elvis Presley might be nominated. (He wasn't.) Angry rockers have always suspected that there has been a conspiracy to stop rock & roll from the minute it first twisted and shouted outside the awards ceremony door. And they — plus countless music critics and other progressive Grammy watchers — have never forgiven N.A.R.A.S.

Responding to all the criticism that the awards have fielded over the years,

N.A.R.A.S. president Michael Greene once more or less conceded that there really is a little bit of Granny in the Grammy after all when he told *Rolling Stone*: "We're a fat old lady walking down the street and it's easy to throw things at us." But he also seemed to be asking: Doesn't Granny, after all, deserve some respect, too? "Grammy bashing is one of the easiest sports in the world," he once told *The New York Times*.

Greene, in particular, has made some impressive changes while at N.A.R.A.S. The *L.A. Times* wrote, "Since Greene came on board as chairman in 1985, academy membership has grown from 5,000 to 8,000 [including 2,000 non-voting members] with most of the new members drawn from the younger rock and pop worlds." Greene told the *L.A. Times* in 1990, referring to the increase in both voting and non-voting members: "The academy has so long been looked at as an institutional stick-in-the-mud organization that people weren't comfortable participating. Now we've broadened it so much that we really do have a lot of those people in, and it's OK to be rebellious within the context of the academy. We can still have our big band and polka and Hispanic people right there alongside the bad boys and girls."

The perplexing aspect of all this is why the Grammys get singled out for such enormous abuse at all when compared to the other prime entertainment awards. No one bashes the Oscars for picking picture-postcard movies like *Out of Africa* and *Dances with Wolves* as the year's finest. The Emmys still maintain their reputation as the most accurate and fair of all the top show-biz prizes despite having named *Get Smart* and *The Monkees* as past best shows on TV. The Tonys once hailed *Cats* as the best piece of musical theater on Broadway and it didn't even have a *plot*. All four awards frequently honor work that is mostly entertaining and beautiful to look at.

Grammy grousers love to point out that some of the music's most illustrious talents like Diana Ross, the Beach Boys, and Rod Stewart have never won. True, but a comparison to other leading show business awards is appropriate here. Richard Burton went to his grave without an Oscar; TV's "Great One" Jackie Gleason found the Emmys just as elusive throughout his lifetime; and some of Broadway's most stellar talent — including Lynn Fontanne and Ian McKellan — have never taken their bows on the Tonys' stage. (Fontanne at least won an Emmy.)

> *Winning a top Grammy can increase album sales by half a million to two million copies.*

One of the most frequently quoted bits of Grammy trivia is the fact that the Beatles never won Record of the Year, which is also true, leading many to believe that therefore the Grammys must really be *hopeless*. But the Fab Four were victorious in the other top three categories: They were the Best New Artists of 1964 and won Song of the Year i n 1 9 6 6 f o r McCartney's "Michelle" in addition to the Album of the Year prize for *Sgt. Pepper* one year later.

What the people who quote that trivia fact are really trying to say, though, is that often the most obvious and deserving winners get scooped by noncontroversial, mainstream favorites, like what happened to the Beatles in 1965 when they lost the group vocals award — in one of the most notorious upsets in Grammy history — to Nashville's Anita Kerr Quartet. The Beatles lost the Record of the Year award on four occasions, but Barbra Streisand, who is just the sort of talented mainstream pop artist that N.A.R.A.S. voters adore, lost it five times. Streisand has nonetheless won an impressive eight Grammys to date.

Still, the criticism is weighted with some additional, hard-hitting evidence. Elvis Presley was nominated for Record of the Year twice — for "A Fool Such as I" in 1959 and "Are You Lonesome Tonight?" in 1960 — but the only Grammys that rock & roll's "king" ever won were in the categories for religious recordings (three times).

Bob Dylan finally won a Grammy in 1972 when he shared the laurels for Album of the Year *The Concert for Bangla Desh*, but he didn't win his own award till 1979. Dylan, appropriately, was one of the first recipients of the newly reinstated rock & roll Grammys, but, like Presley, he was honored for singing religious music ("Gotta Serve Somebody"). Bruce Springsteen still hadn't won a Grammy as of 1981, but then, when it looked like he might finally pull off a victory, he got clobbered in the rock vocal category by pop singer and soap opera heartthrob Rick Springfield. Three years later, Springsteen's *Born in the U.S.A.* was beaten for Album of the Year by Lionel Richie's *Can't Slow Down*. But, again, comparisons to other awards are relevant. Arguably the greatest and most innovative film ever made, *Citizen Kane*, lost the Best Picture Oscar in 1941 to the safe-but-good *How Green Was My Valley*. In short, the Grammys are just as guilty as the next show-biz award — and whole civilizations, historically, for that matter — of not recognizing artistic innovation when it's introduced in a revolutionary — and sometimes threatening — form.

One has to ask: Does it all matter?

Marvin Hamlisch, Grammy's choice for Best New Artist of 1974, doesn't think so, at least as it pertains to his profession. "Awards like this don't really help musical artists," he says. "That's been my experience. They do seem to help actors and writers sometimes." Hamlisch may or may not be right in terms of artistic recognition, but, at the very least, winning Grammys seems to perk up record sales, thereby helping out musical artists a lot. Tina Turner's "What's Love Got to Do with It" leapt back into the Top 10 for an additional 12 weeks after winning Record of the Year. Quincy Jones's *The Dude* entered the Top 10 only after it swept up five awards for 1981. Bonnie Raitt's *Nick of Time* peaked at only number 22 just before winning 1989's Album of the Year, then zoomed to number 1.

"The public has come to look to the Grammys as a signal that a star has really arrived, and the impact can be enormous," Tommy Mottola, president of Sony Records, recently told *The New York Times*. "Depending on the timing, a Grammy win can increase the sales of an album by anywhere from half a million to two million albums."

The difference between the Grammys and the other leading entertainment awards can be found in the music industry itself. It's vast. Rap and heavy metal music are only part of contemporary culture because they were able to find outlets on a daring handful of the thousands of alternative radio stations across the country. Film, TV, and Broadway producers are powerless, by comparison, to champion such new and radical art forms or artists given the limited room on screen and stage. Those harmless Monkees may have had their own TV show in the 1960s (the group, in fact, was formed specifically *for* the series), but no one, not even Norman Lear, could have sold Hollywood on giving the Rolling Stones

Bob Dylan's frustrating quest for a Grammy dramatized N.A.R.A.S.'s on-going reluctance to reward mavericks.

their own half-hour in prime time. The parallel helps to explain why the Stones never won a Grammy in a competitive category, although they eventually were given a Lifetime Achievement Award. We expect revolutions in our music industry and therefore, looking back over the winners of America's highest music award, we expect the past winners to have been the vanguards. Usually, they weren't.

The Grammys have made some bold exceptions to that rule, though, such as John Lennon and Yoko Ono's 1981 Album of the Year *Double Fantasy*. But the truth of the matter is that, when Grammy historians draw the bottom line, it turns out the 5th Dimension, by a score of six to five, has won more awards than the Beatles. That says a lot about the Grammys and the kind of music they love. It's also a reminder of Noel Coward's famous line from *Private Lives*, "Extraordinary how potent cheap music is." But then one might ask: What did Noel Coward know anyway? He once put down the Beatles, saying, "Delightful lads, absolutely no talent."

There are some occasions when the Grammys are perfectly in tune with the times, as in 1983 when Michael Jackson's *Thriller* seized both the national consciousness and the top Grammy categories, but there are other times when they seem to be hopelessly out of touch and behind the times. The latter phenomenon occurred again as recently as the 1991 awards — and offered a fascinating insight into what the Grammys are really all about.

> *Paul Simon has won the Grammys' highest honor, Record of the Year, the most times (three).*

Only one year before "Unforgettable" won Record, Album, and Song of the Year, the Grammys proved just how hip they could be by picking Quincy Jones's *Back on the Block* as the top LP. Then, for the 1991 awards, came the return of Grammy's Best New Artist of 1975 — Natalie Cole. She was back with the ultimate in fuddy-duddy fare: an overtly sentimental duet with her long-dead father, Nat "King" Cole, that interposed an old tape of him crooning one of his classic tunes with a new one of her singing along with a daughter's Daddy-I-love-you smile that can be seen on the video. When the song pulled off a landslide at the awards ceremony, Grammy bashers everywhere rose up to denounce the "Unforgettable" sweep as unforgivable.

Everybody who knows the Grammys' voting patterns knew ahead of time that "Unforgettable" was invincible, even though Cole's competition for the record and album laurels included Paul Simon, Bonnie Raitt, Bryan Adams, R.E.M., and Amy Grant. "Unforgettable" had it all in terms of the criteria used by Grammy voters. The music was a tuneful ballad and sold well in the stores. It also featured two generations of Grammy greats in one piece of music (Nat "King" Cole won Best Performance by a "Top 40" Artist in 1959), thereby appealing to young and old N.A.R.A.S. voters alike while also offering them the chance to reward past winners again, which they love to do.

Despite what Grammy bashers have to say about its awards sweep, "Unforgettable" was a magical combination of mood, nostalgia, musical agility, and family bonding so intimate that, when listeners heard the song for the first time, they invariably felt that they had stumbled accidentally onto a private moment from which they could only escape by leaving the room or turning down the sound. The song reveals Natalie longing openly for her father far away in body but still close to her in spirit and on tape. When Daddy Nat sings back to his little girl, now all grown up and hitting the charts just like he used to, we know why Natalie is smiling. All family moments should be this harmonious, tender — and classy, too. Nat "King" Cole personified class. Blacks everywhere today have benifitted from the respect that his talents once commanded from the white-dominated music industry of America. When Natalie puts on a silk gown and sings back to him on the music video version of the song, it looks just right, not like when her father dressed up in tight-fitting coat and tie only to look awkward performing on those equally all-white variety TV shows of the 1950s and '60s. It's reasonable to assume that Nat "King" Cole made a difference between then and now. His work certainly did so in terms of music history. Street rappers might maintain that it's all just pure corn —

and it is — especially at a time today when R.E.M. is out there losing its religion and Amy Grant is forsaking gospel music to make it in the heathen pop industry. Those old values just aren't hip in an industry that idolizes the Beastie Boys and scorns Debby Boone (Grammy's Best New Artist of 1977). But if it's OK for Frank Sinatra to win Record of the Year for "Strangers in the Night" at a time when the Beatles were rocking America's sports stadiums and an angry young Bob Dylan was running loose in the land with no Grammy in hand, it's probably OK to find faith and comfort in the Grammys' — sometimes delightful — eccentricities. The "Unforgettable" triumph certainly proves that they sometimes have class, too — and, if nothing else, continuing courage.

*****

The Grammys were born in Hollywood in the 1950s. Tinsel Town was losing some of its sparkle in those days, at least along the main stretch of Hollywood Boulevard where more and more lackluster shops like hardware stores were springing up to remind tourists that even Bing Crosby had a leaky faucet now and then. A Hollywood Beautification Committee was formed to dress up the area by putting stars in the sidewalks to honor the leading talents in film, TV, and music. Five top executives from the five leading record labels where tapped to contribute the names of music's finest. In 1955, they gathered together one day in a back room of the Brown Derby restaurant: Paul Weston of Columbia Records, Lloyd Dunn of Capitol, Sonny Burke of Decca, Jesse Kaye of MGM, and Dennis Farnon of RCA. As Weston once told *Grammy Pulse*, "There was no thought of an academy at that time."

"One day, the man [from the Holly-wood Beautification Committee] who was supposed to be with us was late, and we were talking among ourselves," Jesse Kaye told the same source. "And it was Sonny [Burke] who came up with the idea. He said there were Academy Awards for the movies and the TV industry had already organized its own academy. He felt that the record business was getting of age and we ought to be thinking about the same thing. We all agreed that it was a great idea. A little starry eyed, but it was a good idea. So, after that, [at] every meeting for that other purpose, we would talk about forming an academy."

By 1957, the group approached a mutual friend to help them organize the effort, Jim Conkling, who had been president of Columbia Records and the Record Industry Association of Commerce, but who was now semi-retired. According to *Variety*, Conkling "agreed to serve in a temporary organizational capacity to launch a national organization which would include reps of vocalists, leaders, conductors, art directors, engineers, arrangers, orchestrators, composers, producers, directors, and instrumentalists." In short, the founding fathers were after the best creative people, or as Conkling says today, "We wanted it to be on a higher level." On May 28, 1957, the National Academy of Recording Arts and Sciences was officially formed at the Brown Derby with Conkling named as the academy chairman.

N.A.R.A.S.'s first regular meeting was held on June 26, 1957, at the Beverly Hilton Hotel, where a board of governors was elected, which included songwriter Sammy Cahn and Nat "King" Cole in addition to Burke, Weston, and others. The board stressed the rule that only creative persons in the industry were allowed to become members. The record academy wanted to remain truly academic in nature, free from all commercial pressures, and functioning as an institution where its members could discuss and pursue — and reward — great music as it *should* be. "That eliminated record companies from participating," Weston told *Grammy Pulse.* "That kept out disc jockeys, promotional people, and publishers." In August, 1957, the academy's Los Angeles chapter was incorporated with Weston serving as its first president. A New York chapter followed early the next year with Guy Lombardo waving his baton at the top. In 1961, a chapter was formed in Chicago, too, followed by other outlying cities like Nashville, Memphis, and Atlanta.

"There weren't any secrets" about who won in the early years.

It was a member of the academy's Awards and Nominations Committee, Val Valentin, who came up with the idea of what the new music award should look like: a composite design of the old gramophones once made by Columbia, Edison, and Victor. The academy then decided to hold a contest to determine what to call it, offering 25 albums to the person who came up with the winning name. The Associated Press spread the word. About half of the letters that came back in response suggested "Grammy," so the committee took the hint and made it official. (None of the entries, to anyone's recollection, proposed the alternative shortening of "phonograph.") Grammy's first award — those 25 LPs — was thus given to the first person who proposed the right answer: a Mrs. Jay Danna of New Orleans.

The premiere awards ceremony was held in the Grand Ballroom of the Beverly Hilton Hotel where 500 people paid $15 each for a nontelevised dinner gala *Down Beat* was calling "*the* big night for the recording industry." A few snafus occurred when there turned out to be a shortage of both statuettes and presenters. ("I was still lining up presenters while people were eating their dinner," Weston told *Grammy Pulse.*) But otherwise things went smoothly as the new golden gramophones were given out to Henry Mancini, Ella Fitzgerald, Perry Como, and others who represented the best of the melodic music of the day.

Presenters included André Previn, Frank Sinatra, Milton Berle, Sammy Davis, Jr., Peggy Lee, and Weston's wife, singer Jo Stafford. Noticeably missing were leading rock & rollers like Elvis Presley and Little Richard, but this was an industry insiders' party, not a frat house bash. And "it was fun," says Conkling's wife, Donna, who was then a member of the King Sisters, "because it was small and you knew everybody [in] this cozy little group." It wasn't fun for Sinatra, though. His music was nominated 12 times and only ended up winning an award for Best Album Cover. The fun went to victors like Henry Mancini, who told *Grammy Pulse*, "When I think back, I guess the first one was kind of historic although at the time I didn't realize where the Grammys were going. I didn't know it was going to become such a world-wide enterprise."

Sinatra boycotted the second awards celebration and, of course, ended up winning big. This time there were two ceremonies, held simultaneously in both Los Angeles and New York, which were followed by a live L.A.–based TV show that featured winners such as Ella Fitzgerald, Van Cliburn, Jimmy Driftwood, Shelley Berman, and the 350-member Mormon Tabernacle Choir. Duke Ellington and Nat "King" Cole couldn't make it but sent taped performances instead. Several newspapers gave the show bad reviews, but *Variety* insisted that it "was handled with savvy and imagination." Whatever the case, the Grammys didn't go back on TV until 1963 (for the 1962 awards) when "Best on Record" was born, featuring performances by the artists who had actually won a few months earlier.

N.A.R.A.S. wanted a live awards telecast like the Oscars and Emmys had, but the TV network executives weren't convinced the Grammys could attract the necessary superstar participants needed to draw viewers in large numbers. The execs weren't convinced that they wanted to continue the "Best on Record" show either, but it was tried again in 1965 (for the 1964 awards) and, when the reviews stayed positive, the program stayed on the air until 1971 when at last the ceremony itself was broadcast live. The first Grammycast, as we know it today, was also the hardest to pull off. Producer Pierre Cossette told *TV Guide*, "We literally had to go out on the street to get people to fill up the seats in front." By the late 1970s and early 1980s, the Grammys became the second-highest rated awards show on TV, after the Oscars. "For the 1986 telecast," Cossette asserted, "we could fill Yankee Stadium."

The networks may have been right about an embarrassing shortage of stars occurring in the Grammys' early days. The Beatles failed to show up at the 1965 awards ceremony (for the 1964 awards) and also skipped making a live performance on that year's "Best on Record" show, although they did prepare a taped segment on which they accepted their award for Best New Artist from actor Peter Sellers and performed "I'm So Happy Just to Dance with You." Years later, however, once the Grammys were an established force and the first live show was aired, they were there, more or less. The Beatles had bro-

ken up, but Paul McCartney — dressed casually in a blue suit, unbuttoned flower shirt, and white tennis shoes — appeared to "shrieks of surprise" to accept the best film score award for the Fab Four's *Let It Be*, saying only, "Thank you."

In those early years, N.A.R.A.S. leaders were caught in a frustrating catch-22. Without the excitement of a live telecast, they had a difficult time rounding up stars for the comparatively sedate awards ceremonies. One of the founding fathers, Jim Conkling, is surprisingly candid about what they had to do in the early years as a result: let the winners know that they'd won before the results were announced. "There weren't any surprises like you have today," he says. "We had to tell the people because they were on the road and we had to bring them in. There weren't any secrets, but the public didn't know that. [But] we told [the winners], 'If it leaks, we might have to take you out of it,' so nobody talked."

The first song to win Record of the Year was "Nel Blu Dipinto di Blu (Volare)," and some critics say that things haven't changed since as ballads continue to prevail in the top category. But some pretty daring work has won, too. It was Henry Mancini's offbeat and jazzy score to the TV series *Peter Gunn* that beat out Sinatra's *Come Fly with Me* and *Only the Lonely* for the first Album of the Year award. For the most part, though, in those days the predictable giants of mainstream music reigned in the other leading categories: Ella Fitzgerald, Count Basie, Perry Como, Ray Charles, and Judy Garland. The boldest departure N.A.R.A.S. voters made in the early days was picking Bob Newhart's comedy LP *Button Down Mind* as winner of Album of the Year in 1960. Otherwise, safe, mainstream songs like Percy Faith's "Theme from *A Summer Place*" and powerful vocal albums like Garland's *Judy at*

Carnegie Hall took the highest honors.

Jazz was the one adventurous sound that N.A.R.A.S. voters were comfortable with so another exception occurred at the 1964 awards when Stan Getz and Astrud Gilberto shook up the Grammys (with Record of the Year "The Girl from Ipanema" and Album of the Year *Getz/Gilberto*) just as they were shaking up America with their new bossa nova sound. A breakthrough came for pop rock finally in 1966 when McCartney and John Lennon reaped Song of the Year for "Michelle." The first winners of the two highest honors, Record and Album of the Year, that can be considered victories for the younger sound occurred one year later when the 5th Dimension won for "Up, Up and Away" (an ironic triumph, considering that such a radical breakthrough was accomplished by a song now regarded as the epitome of lightweight pop; back in 1967, though, it was *groovy*) and the Beatles *really* scored a triumph with *Sgt. Pepper's Lonely Hearts Club Band.*

Grammy's reluctance to recognize r&r was evident from the very first year. *Variety* wrote about the debut ceremony, "Over the pomp and circumstance of the festivities hung a cloud. The record academy has sharply snubbed the rock." The academy considered introducing an r&r category the next year, but changed its mind at the last minute and instead created Best Performance by a "Top 40" Artist. Nat "King" Cole won for "Midnight Flyer," which never actually made it into the Top 40 and, of course, wasn't a rock tune.

In 1961, the academy finally introduced a prize for Best Rock & Roll Recording, which went to Chubby Checker's "Let's Twist Again." (N.A.R.A.S. had overlooked the original "The Twist" when it topped the charts a year earlier.) The subsequent winners weren't especially radical choices and weren't really rock music either, but at least the academy was earnest in its attempt to recognize the popular sound of the day, giving the prize to "Alley Cat" by Bent Fabric (1962), "Deep Purple" by Nino Tempo and April Stevens (1963), and "Downtown" by Petula Clark (1964).

After that, the awards' title changed to "Best Contemporary (R&R)" and they were bestowed to Petula Clark (again), the Statler Brothers, Roger Miller, Paul McCartney, and the Mamas & the Papas. In 1967, the category kept its "Contemporary" label, but lost the "R&R" designation. New winners included Glen Campbell, Dionne Warwick, and Peggy Lee. And the younger generation was continuing to make inroads. One year later *Variety* wrote that "a host of youths have overthrown the elders in the field .... The recording industry has virtually shucked off its past. The Grammy Awards gave an indication of how far the rebellion of the young has gone. There was rarely a prize in the pop field to anyone over 30." Works by young artists may have been winning more awards, but r&r was still faring poorly. The *L.A. Times* asked in a headline as late as 1976: "Is Grammy Boycotting Rock?" Finally, in 1979, rock & roll got its own awards again, apparently for good.

Rock isn't the only music genre singled out for oversight. It wasn't until 1975 that *Billboard* ran the headline, "N.A.R.A.S. Says 'Sí' to Latin Grammy, Wins Loud Olé." Reggae wasn't added until 1984. Polka joined the lineup one year later. Rock has certainly been the biggest sound in America, though, in addition to being the loudest, so it seems strange that the Grammys chose for so long to turn a deaf ear.

But they did, right from the beginning, because N.A.R.A.S. leaders were afraid of where this new call of the wild might take them. The late N.A.R.A.S. founding father Lloyd Dunn was a senior executive at Capitol Records when the Grammys were born. His wife, Priscilla, says, "He just didn't understand the music. In fact, he hated it! The music he knew was from Gilbert and Sullivan and Irving Berlin and on and on through all the great musicals of the '20s to the '50s. He loved all that, but he just couldn't understand all this banging and shrieking. He came into work one day and there was this group with their guitars and things. They were all pimply faced kids with their hair dyed green and he went over to the reception desk and said, 'What the heck is that over there?' and [the receptionist] said, 'Wait till I tell you what they call themselves!' He said, 'What? I'm afraid to ask,' and she said, 'They call themselves the Underarm Deodorants!' Lloyd went 'Oh, my God!' and went upstairs and wrote out his resignation, asking 'Where are we going?!'" Dunn, it turned out, didn't go anywhere. He stuck with Capitol — like deodorant — and would eventually help introduce the Beatles to America.

In time, the entire music industry would yield, of course, to the revolutionary new sound, but not before becoming engaged in a battle that consumed American culture and blasted the generation gap further apart with each new r&r hit single played on the airwaves. As the Grammys were being born, Frank Sinatra was denouncing rock & roll as "the most brutal, ugly, degenerate, vicious form of expression it has been my displeasure to hear." He not only didn't understand the appeal of the amazing new sound, he and his contemporaries, surprisingly, could never appreciate its true musical artistry either. From its earliest days as an organization, N.A.R.A.S. was thereafter used as a fortress by the most conservative elements of the music industry in their battle against the new music — and the angry young rockers, in turn, used the academy as a target for their rage and frustration over not being recognized as artists. As a result, the entire historic battle over rock & roll — at its rockiest and sometimes even its most ridiculous — ended up getting played out at the Grammys.

The 1969 awards ceremony is a good example of the absurd heights that the battle could reach as the older generation continued to show signs of distrust and paranoia long after they had really lost their fight. Host Merv Griffin introduced a mellow pop/folk group with the half jest, "Here's Peter and Mary. It's Paul's night at home to work on the dynamite caps."

The Grammys' credibility has been challenged outside of rock & roll, too. Sizing them up in 1987, critic Jon Pareles wrote, "Results range from passable (r&b awards) to tacky (the jazz awards) to out-of-it (the Latin awards).

"In jazz, Grammy awards have been piled onto Ella Fitzgerald, George Benson, Bill Evans, Manhattan Transfer and, lately, Wynton Marsalis, to the virtual exclusion of Sarah Vaughan, Keith Jarrett, Weather Report .... It's a long list. The logic seems to be that once you get one Grammy, like Wynton Marsalis, who's deserving but hardly the only good young jazz musician, you get more. In blues, the great

The whole historic battle over rock & roll — at its rockiest and sometimes its most ridiculous — ended up being played out at the Grammys.

Muddy Waters got six Grammys during the '70s; Howlin' Wolf, equally influential, never had one."

Pareles was exaggerating. Sarah Vaughan and Weather Report had each won one award at the time he wrote of their "virtual exclusion." Weather Report's quest for its eventual victory was particularly anguished, though, since the group was so often held up by *Down Beat* and other industry leaders as the prime example of slighted genius until it finally won a 1979 fusion prize for its *8:30* album. Vaughan's single vocal honor for her 1982 album *Gershwin Live!* is a humble dose of kudos when compared to the 13 awards that fellow jazz diva Ella Fitzgerald has received.

It's surprising to learn that the Grammys weren't taken very seriously until as late as the mid-1970s.

In the classical categories, the awards are the victim of "celebrity-itis," according to Don Vroon, editor of the classical music magazine *American Record Guide*. "Grammys tend to go to the artists with the most name recognition," he says. "The awards have recognized some beautiful music in the past, but, in nine cases out of ten, I wouldn't even consider those records as nominees for being called the year's best."

The problem with the jazz and classical awards is the same one that plagues the religious, comedy, and some other categories: repeat winners. *The Washington Post* once quoted a classical music critic as claiming the honors even seem to go to "the same artists playing the same repertoire by the same composers." (It's less true of the r&b, spoken word, and, to some extent, the country awards, which have been more open to newcomers.) Previously unrecognized classical talent does get nominated. Grammy voters, like everybody else, just happen to have their favorites. The Oscars and Tonys have the same problem — and the Emmys even more so, since TV shows stay on for years while movies, musicals, and plays come and go. Beyond that, the only other explanation for the Grammys overlooking additional deserving talent is an understanding of the fact that it's the right hemisphere of the human brain that processes the beauty and mysteries of music — the same half that absorbs emotion and intuition, not logic.

*****

The Grammy Awards are such an established and formidable force today that it's surprising to learn how long it took them, following that uneasy birth, to reach adulthood — at least in the sense that they were regarded on an equal basis with the Oscars, Emmys, and Tonys. Probably because the Grammys weren't given an annual telecast till 1971, they spent more than a decade in relative obscurity.

As late as 1966, the *L.A. Times* covered the results of the Eighth Annual (1965) awards in an article that can be found on page 2 of Part II of that day's paper (March 16). The National Book Awards were announced the same day — on the *front* page of another section.

Even after the Grammys got on live TV in 1971, it still took time for the aura to build. *The Hollywood Reporter* was obviously impressed enough by the awards' new prominence to give the 1972 voting result a banner headline: "Roberta Flack Wins Grammy." Unfortunately, though, it was the second line in a double-decker that was topped with the news: "Coppola Named Top Director." Apparently, the outcome of the Directors Guild of America Awards (Francis Ford Coppola triumphed for *The Godfather*) was more important.

In 1976, *The New York Times* ran a brief roundup piece on the winners of the 1975 awards on its inside TV page. The article was dwarfed by another one that reviewed a new, and now forgotten, pilot film for a proposed TV series called *Young Pioneers*. The review said the show was lousy.

Even if it wasn't reflected in the pages of the *Times*, the Grammys started to be taken very seriously about then. The big winners were names that actually made music not only cool enough for rockers to listen to and popular enough for everyone else to appreciate, too — they made music that could live for the ages. Stevie Wonder swept the awards more than once in the mid-to-late '70s. Other top winners included the Eagles, Billy Joel, the Doobie Brothers, Paul Simon, and George Benson. When disco reigned supreme, some years before it became a joke, the Bee Gees ruled the Grammys, too. By 1976, critic Robert Hilburn of the *L.A. Times* expressed high praise for all of the Album of the Year nominees, saying they reflected "the academy's most impressive collective judgment" so far. (Stevie Wonder's *Songs in the Key of Life* was the winner.) By the 1979 awards, when the rock & roll categories were reinstated for good and the Doobie Brothers' "What a Fool Believes" took Record of the Year, even the awards' most cynical onlookers, like rock critic Dave Marsh, conceded, "For once the Grammys spent its accolades where they were deserved."

The N.A.R.A.S. awards were clearly onto something and were commanding more respect. By the 1980s, the newspaper articles were more prominent and more extensive. The photos that accom-panied them suddenly got bigger, too, and more numerous. On Feb. 28, 1985, a headline in *The New York Times* boldly proclaimed,"Grammy Awards Show Finally Comes of Age."

"The Grammys have reached the stage of being a television 'event,'" the article by reviewer John J. O'Connor said. "In the beginning, they were just another awards show, heavily weighted to middle-of-the-road easy-listening music. By around 1970, it became something of a scandal that the music industry was giving so little, and so reluctant, attention to such vital music areas as rock .... Fortunately, that silliness changed, especially as the recording establishment realized where the bulk of its sales were coming from. The Grammys began attracting a younger audience and last year's ceremonies, the Michael Jackson Festival, got one of the biggest ratings of the season, second only to football's Super Bowl. Now the event is covered extensively, before and after, on the local and national news shows and on such syndicated series as *Entertainment Tonight*, which this week even managed to sneak in some speculation about who would be nominated for 1986's awards (Madonna, for one). The hype machine is humming furiously."

*****

"Whatever the inevitable disappointments in any awards procedure," Robert Hilburn once wrote in the *L.A. Times*, "the Grammys do matter. As with film's Oscars and TV's Emmys, the awards reflect the judgment of the professionals in the field. That gives the Grammys a credibility that none of the other, mostly hapless music awards can match."

"A Grammy does mean something," columnist David Hinckley said in *The*

New York Daily News. "You win an American Music Award and you put it with your baby pictures. Tell people you won a Grammy and they're impressed."

"The acknowledgment of a job well done from fellow performers: That's what the Grammy is all about," José Feliciano once said. When Shabba Ranks accepted the statuette for 1991's Best Reggae Recording (*As Raw as Ever*), he addressed what the Grammy is all about to those who win one when he said, beaming, "I'm a star now!"

The Grammys

Debut

"It was *the* big night for the recording industry," *Down Beat* wrote, reporting the launch of the first awards. "In the Grand Ballroom of Beverly Hills' plush Beverly Hilton Hotel, the mahoffs, bigwigs and toppers of Recordom were assembled May 4 [1959] for the first annual awards ceremony in the history of the record business, and the debut in the public eye of the National Academy of Recording Arts and Sciences."

Comedian Mort Sahl emceed the formal dinner banquet, which began at 8:30 p.m. and attracted more than 500 people who paid $15 each to attend. Entertainment included a satiric skit, "How South was My Pacific," starring band leader Billy May. Among the celebrity presenters were Frank Sinatra, Dean Martin, Peggy Lee, Jo Stafford (wife of N.A.R.A.S. head Paul Weston), Henry Mancini, Sammy Davis, Jr., André Previn, Johnny Mercer, and Milton Berle. Not enough people had been formally scheduled ahead of time, though ("I was still lining up presenters while people were eating their dinner," Weston later recalled to *Grammy Pulse*), while the only other glitch that occurred was a shortage of statuettes when a preponderance of groups ended up winning. Pepsi-Cola

Domenico Modugno singing "Volare," the precedent for ballads and other safe music winning best record.

wanted to sponsor a TV broadcast, but couldn't put the show together in time for the ceremony.

The balloting was done by N.A.R.A.S.'s 700 members who could vote for the nominees and winners in all 28 categories. The results were huge surprises. Jazz and pop tunes fared extremely well while rock and roll, claimed *Variety* in a banner headline, got the "Brush Off." In the recent past, for example, nearly half of all of RCA's record sales resulted from tunes by Elvis Presley, but he wasn't nominated.

Grammy insiders predicted a sweep for Frank Sinatra, who loathed the new rock revolution in general and Elvis in particular. In an article he wrote in 1957 for *Western World* magazine, Sinatra called the new sound "the most brutal, ugly, degenerate, vicious form of expression it has been my displeasure to hear" and described Elvis's music as "deplorable, a rancid-smelling aphrodisiac."

But the first annual Grammy show was deliberate fanfare for the kind of music Sinatra championed. He and his work started out with more than twice as many nominations as his closest rival (Henry Mancini, whose musical score for the TV detective series *Peter Gunn* had five bids). "Sinatra's overwhelming leadership in number of nominations is explained by the fact that he swept the field in both singles and albums," *Billboard* explained. The 12 nods his music received included some of his recent recordings with arranger Nelson Riddle, with whom Sinatra had worked at Capitol Records since 1953. The duo had two LPs contending for Album of the Year (*Come Fly with Me*, and *Only the Lonely*) and one single up for Record of the Year ("Witchcraft").

Leading nominee Frank Sinatra suffered a near shut-out.

The suspense of the night was expected to center on which LP would win, just as it was presumed that Sinatra would take the laurels for best male vocalist, an honor for which he was also nominated twice (for "Witchcraft" and the "Come Fly with Me" single).

The multiple nominations backfired, however, causing a split in Sinatra's votes that invited dark horse victories. "Sinatra won only for best album cover of his *Only the Lonely* album," noted the *L.A. Mirror News*, "and he acknowledged that the honor should have gone to artist Nick Volpe, who drew the sad clown face picture that adorned the cover."

Sinatra was "so upset about not winning a music award," his date for the evening, actress Sandra Giles, later told biographer Kitty Kelley, "that he refused to let any of the photographers take our picture that night. He was very moody and drank a lot afterwards .... I guess I should've been grateful that Elvis didn't win anything."

Instead, the top honors mostly went to the non-rock music that topped the pop charts. The double winner of the awards for Record of the Year and Song of the Year was also *Billboard*'s number-seven single of 1958: "(Nel Blu Dipinto di Blu) Volare," sung by its cowriter, the romantic Italian balladeer Domenico Modugno, who since then has never won, or even been nominated for, another Grammy. The song title was inspired by an illustration on the back of a pack of cigarettes that once caught the eye of co-lyricist Franco Migliacci. "Volare" means "to fly." The rest of the title is an intentionally nonsensical phrase referring to the whimsical dream of a man who paints his hands blue and flies through the sky — or "the blue painted in blue."

"Volare" was such a huge hit that *Billboard* reviewed seven versions of the tune in just one issue (July 21, 1958), including renditions by Dean Martin and Nelson Riddle. Martin's version had English lyrics written by Mitchell Parish and was extremely popular, too, peaking at number 12 on *Billboard*'s charts.

The first soundtrack for a TV series to sell more than a million copies became Grammy's first Album of the Year. *The*

Music from Peter Gunn was the country's number one LP for 10 weeks and also won a best arrangement Grammy for Henry Mancini, who had previously distinguished himself as an arranger and composer for Hollywood films such as *The Glenn Miller Story* and *A Touch of Evil*. When he was asked to work in television by producer Blake Edwards (after they ran into each other one day outside the Universal Studios barber shop), Mancini used the opportunity to experiment with an innovative jazz beat that ultimately became more successful than the action scenes it underscored.

Henry Mancini dominated many of the early years starting with the first Album of the Year prize, which went to his jazzy TV score The Music from Peter Gunn.

"The idea of using jazz in the *Gunn* score was never even discussed. It was implicit in the story," Mancini says in his autobiography *Did They Mention the Music?* "Peter Gunn hangs out in a jazz roadhouse called Mother's — the name was Blake's way of tweaking the noses of the censors — where there is a five-piece jazz group .... The title theme actually derives more from rock and roll than from jazz. I used guitar and piano in unison, playing what is known in music as an *ostinato*, which means obstinate. It was sustained throughout the piece, giving it a sinister effect, with some frightened saxophone sounds and some shouting brass."

More Music from Peter Gunn would bring the composer six more nominations next year, and *Gunn* would even prove to have a longer life. Emerson, Lake & Palmer's interpretation would score a nomination in 1981; the Art of Noise featuring Duane Eddy would win Best Rock Instrumental Performance for 1986 for its own shot at *Peter Gunn*. By 1992, Mancini would become such a long-standing Grammy favorite that his total of 20 Grammys established him as the fourth biggest winner of all time.

Other top award champs of 1958 included the first winners of best rhythm & blues performance, the Champs, a throw-together group invented out of the musicians present when guitarist Dave Burgess recorded a "B" side to his "Train to Nowhere" release for Gene Autry's new Challenge label. (Autry's famous horse was named Champion, thus suggesting their band's name.) When the single came out and "Train to Nowhere" went nowhere, the Champs nonetheless became the first instrumental group in music history to zoom to *Billboard*'s number one position for their first single release after "Tequila" was discovered on the flip side of "Nowhere" by admiring DJs. It ended the year as *Billboard*'s fifth-best selling single.

A controversy erupted over the prize for best country & western performance, which went to the Kingston Trio for the year's number six–ranked "Tom Dooley," a traditional Blue Ridge Mountains folk song about a man hanged for murder in 1868. (Critics maintained that its *folk* quality didn't necessarily make it a *country* song.) Perry Como created a bit of a buzz, too, when he beat out Sinatra, Modugno, and Andy Williams in the category of Best Male Vocal Performance. It was considered the upset of the night, even though "Star" was Como's 16th single to sell a million copies and the year's 17th-ranked disc.

Broadway's *The Music Man* (Best Original Cast Album, Broadway or TV) was the year's number three best-selling album. When sixth-ranked *Gigi* won Best Film Soundtrack, an awkward moment of confusion followed. One of N.A.R.A.S.'s founding fathers, Jesse Kaye, was seated at the same table with André Previn, who composed the movie's score, but not its songs, which were penned by the Broadway team of Alan Jay Lerner and Frederick Loewe. Kaye told *Grammy Pulse*: "We didn't know who should be the one to go up and get it. There was no clear-cut decision at that time, who gets what!" (It was Previn who was finally designated to accept as the winner.)

In terms of sales, however, nothing topped the winner of three awards, "The Chipmunk Song," which became the fastest-selling record of all time in 1958. It sold three and half million copies in five weeks — and seven million in all.

The Chipmunks were the creation of a failed California raisin farmer who established himself as a hit composer and singer when his song "Witch Doctor" became number one for a week in 1958. "Witch Doctor" had a bewitching, novel quality about it: David Seville (born Ross Bagdasarian) had recorded the title character's voice at half speed and then played it back at regular tempo, giving the song an eerie but comical quality.

After driving through California's Yosemite Park a few months later and encountering a stubborn chipmunk who refused to budge off the road, he came up with the fanciful idea of a new singing trio. He again employed his tape recorder tricks to simulate their voices by distorting his own at different speeds. For fun, he named his three Chipmunks Alvin, Simon, and Theodore after three executives at Liberty Records (Alvin Bennett, Sy Waronker, and Ted Keep) and then set out to write a Christmas novelty song. The result won Best Recording for Children, Best Comedy Performance, and Best Engineered Record (Other Than Classical). The Chipmunks later became a popular TV cartoon series and inspired further songs that sold more than 30 million copies by the time Seville died of a heart attack in 1972.

Among the other multiple winners of the night was Ella Fitzgerald, who, like Mancini, would come to dominate the early Grammy ceremonies. In the first five years of the awards, in fact, Fitzgerald won an impressive tally of seven statuettes. By 1958, Fitzgerald was already considered the nation's reigning jazz diva. Her "A-Tisket A-Tasket" recording with Chick Webb and his band made her a star in 1938 (and would be inducted into the N.A.R.A.S. Hall of Fame in 1986). Fitzgerald was one of the lead vocalists of the swing movement, but with its decline branched out by taking career chances such as teaming up with the Ink Spots, making mainstream hits like 1946's "Stone Cold Dead in the Market," and by starring in films like *Pete Kelly's Blues.*

In an especially ambitious gesture, she also wanted to take on the best work of some of America's top songwriters and give it her own signature interpretation, which she was encouraged to do after switching from Decca records to the newly formed Verve label in the late 1950s. The results were astounding: Fitzgerald won 1958's best female vocal performance Grammy for *Ella Fitzgerald Sings the Irving Berlin Song*

Book (also nominated for Album of the Year) and the year's best individual jazz performance prize for *Ella Fitzgerald Sings the Duke Ellington Songbook*, which was the first in her "songbook" series. To celebrate the launch of the Ellington collection, she and the Duke gave a joint concert at Carnegie Hall in April, 1958, which turned out to be a historic performance.

Another elder statesman of jazz, Count Basie (whose 1955 recording of "April in Paris" would be inducted into the Hall of Fame in 1985), also won two awards, both for his musical collection *Basie,* which was voted Best Performance by a Dance Band and Best Group Jazz Performance. Basie's and Fitzgerald's wins, however, caused some discord. "In the jazz categories, N.A.R.A.S. was charged with riding a few particular hobby horses ... and ignoring the mainstream of current jazz creativity," *Variety* wrote. "Where, one jazz expert asked, were names like Charles Mingus, Miles Davis, Thelonius Monk, or Gerry Milligan?" One lesser-known, Billy May, did receive a statuette for Best Performance by an Orchestra. May had been freelancing solo as a trumpet player and arranger around Hollywood for several years after dropping out of a band in 1954, but he reassembled a group a few years later to pull off the winning *Billy May's Big Fat Brass.*

The *L.A. Mirror* hinted at provinciality in the classical music competitions, noting, "Local artists made a strong showing in the seven classical categories, winning four trophies: *Gaîté Parisienne* by the Hollywood Bowl Symphony, under Felix Slatkin, for best classical orchestral performance; the Hollywood String Quartet's *Beethoven Quartet No. 13,* for Best Classical Chamber Music Performance, giving Slatkin a second award; *Virtuoso* by the Roger Wagner Chorale, Best Operatic or Choral Classi-

cal Performance; and Laurindo Almeida's *Duets with Spanish Guitar* Best Engineered Classical Record."

Critics were mixed on whether or not the prizes were deserved. "These performances by the Hollywood Quartet are not profound," *High Fidelity* magazine had written about the Beethoven collection, "but they are accessible, and to a remarkable degree." The magazine much preferred *Gaîté Parisienne*: "There have been a number of glittering *Gaîtés* before, but none that shine as brightly as this from one end of the tonal spectrum to the other."

Fifty years earlier, in Granada, guitarist Andrés Segovia gave his first concert performance. Now in honor of his *Golden Jubilee*, Decca released a three-disc tribute that expressed his versatility by including works spanning 17th-century masters such as Roncalli to 20th century composers like Manuel Ponce, who wrote specifically for Segovia. The reviews were ecstatic. "Nothing can be more alive or humanly expressive than the guitar in Segovia's hands," wrote *High Fidelity*. The magazine also embraced the choice for the vocal soloist award: Renata Tebaldi, whose *Recital of Songs and Arias* included 13 Italian works and one Spanish tune. Said *High Fidelity*: "Those who maintain that Renata Tebaldi possesses the most beautiful tone of any present-day soprano will find their most potent argument in this recital."

For the next 20 years, the Grammys would be engulfed in a controversy that

> *Nearly half of RCA's record sales resulted from songs by Elvis Presley, who wasn't nominated.*

actually had its origins at the very first awards ceremony: N.A.R.A.S.'s failure to recognize rock & roll's importance in the music world. "Over the pomp and circumstance of the festivities hung a cloud," said *Variety*. "The record academy [has] sharply snubbed the rock. Not one R & R record was nominated in the 28 categories submitted to members."

Lew Chudd, president of Liberty Records (label for Fats Domino, Ricky Nelson, and, of course, the Chipmunks), was the most vociferous. "N.A.R.A.S. is obviously headed by a group which is outdated for today's recording market," Chudd told *Down Beat*. "It isn't accepting the reality of rock & roll."

N.A.R.A.S. president Weston told the magazine in response: "We do not honor commercial success. Our purpose is to recognize artistic achievement by the creative persons in the industry. Record sales is not the factor that governs our awards." Weston said that rock and roll might have a better chance in the voting if more people joined the academy, which he urged them to do.

Capitol had the most wins among record manufacturers, taking 10 of the 28 awards. RCA received 4 statuettes, Decca and Liberty 3 each. *Variety* said, "Some of the major disc company execs, whose labels were shut out of all categories, voiced some complaints about the voting system, but they, too, will still stick with N.A.R.A.S., hoping the kinks will be ironed out by the time it gets around to voting again next year."

"The Grammy Awards came to be a real party from the start," Mancini says in his memoirs. But the famed composer and arranger adds that many of the early participants, like himself, failed to realize the full importance of Grammy's debut night. "There was this little award that no one had had in their hands before, no one had ever seen before," he wrote. "I thought, that's nice and took [the statuettes] home ... and they sat there until next year when their brothers arrived .... When I think back, I guess the first one was kind of historic although at the time I didn't realize where the Grammys were going. I didn't know it was going to become such a world-wide enterprise."

1958

Awards bestowed at the Beverly Hilton Hotel in Los Angeles on May 4, 1959, for music released during 1958.

ALBUM OF THE YEAR
• *The Music from Peter Gunn*, Henry Mancini. RCA.
Ella Fitzgerald Sings the Irving Berlin Song Book, Ella Fitzgerald. Verve.
Come Fly with Me, Frank Sinatra. Capitol.
✓*Only the Lonely*, Frank Sinatra. Capitol.
Tchaikovsky: Concerto No. 1 in B Flat Minor, Op. 23, Van Cliburn. RCA.

RECORD OF THE YEAR
• "Nel Blu Dipinto Di Blu (Volare)," Domenico Modugno. Decca.
"Catch a Falling Star," Perry Como. RCA.
"The Chipmunk Song," David Seville. Liberty.
"Fever," Peggy Lee. Capitol.
✓"Witchcraft," Frank Sinatra. Capitol.

SONG OF THE YEAR
(Songwriter's Award)
• "Nel Blu Dipinto Di Blu (Volare)," Domenico Modugno (lyrics collaborator Franco Migliacci not noted by N.A.R.A.S.). Decca.
"Catch a Falling Star," Paul Vance, Lee Pockriss. RCA.
"Fever," Johnny Davenport, Eddie Cooley. Capitol.
"Gigi," Alan J. Lerner, Frederick Loewe. MGM.
✓"Witchcraft," Cy Coleman, Carolyn Leigh. Capitol.

BEST VOCAL PERFORMANCE, MALE
• Perry Como, "Catch a Falling Star." RCA.
Domenico Modugno, "Nel Blu Dipinto Di Blu (Volare)." Decca.
✓Frank Sinatra, "Come Fly with Me." Capitol.

Frank Sinatra, "Witchcraft." Capitol.
Andy Williams, "Hawaiian Wedding
 Song." Cadence.

BEST VOCAL PERFORMANCE, FEMALE
• Ella Fitzgerald, *Ella Fitzgerald Sings the
 Irving Berlin Song Book*. Verve.
Doris Day, "Everybody Loves a Lover."
 Columbia.
Eydie Gormé, *Eydie in Love*. ABC-
 Paramount.
Peggy Lee, "Fever." Capitol.
Keely Smith, "I Wish You Love." Capitol.

BEST PERFORMANCE BY A VOCAL GROUP OR CHORUS
• Louis Prima, Keely Smith, "That Old
 Black Magic." Capitol.
King Sisters, "Imagination." Capitol.
✓Kingston Trio, "Tom Dooley." Capitol.
Kirby Stone Four, "Baubles, Bangles &
 Beads." Columbia.
Lambert, Hendricks & Ross, *Sing a Song
 of Basie*. ABC-Paramount.

BEST PERFORMANCE BY A DANCE BAND
• Count Basie, *Basie*. Roulette.
Ray Anthony, *The Music from Peter Gunn*.
 Capitol.
Warren Covington & the Tommy Dorsey
 Orchestra, *Tea for Two Cha Cha*.
 Decca.
Jonah Jones, "Baubles, Bangles & Beads."
 Capitol.
Perez Prado, "Patricia." RCA.

BEST PERFORMANCE BY AN ORCHESTRA
• Billy May, *Billy May's Big Fat Brass*.
 Capitol.
Buddy Defranco, "Cross Country Suite."
 Dot.
Esquivel, *Other Worlds, Other Sounds*.
 RCA.
Jack Kane, *Kane Is Able*. Coral.
Henry Mancini, *The Music from Peter
 Gunn*. RCA.
Johnny Mandel, *I Want to Live*. United
 Artists.
David Rose and his Orchestra with André
 Previn, *Young Man's Lament*. MGM.
George Shearing, *Burnished Brass*. Capitol.

BEST COUNTRY & WESTERN PERFORMANCE
✓• Kingston Trio, "Tom Dooley." Capitol.
Everly Brothers, "All I Have to Do Is
 Dream." Cadence.
Everly Brothers, "Bird Dog." Cadence.

*Perry Como won the male vocals award
for "Catch a Falling Star" in an upset
over Frank Sinatra and Andy Williams.*

Don Gibson, "Oh Lonesome Me." RCA.
Jimmie Rodgers, "Oh, Oh, I'm Falling in
 Love Again." Roulette.

BEST COMPOSITION, OVER 5 MINUTES' DURATION
• "Cross Country Suite," Nelson Riddle. Dot.
"Vanessa," Samuel Barber. RCA.
I Want to Live, Johnny Mandel. United
 Artists.
Victory at Sea, Vol. III, Richard Rodgers.
 RCA.
"Mahagonny," Kurt Weill. Columbia.

BEST ORIGINAL CAST ALBUM, BROADWAY OR TV
• *The Music Man* (original Broadway
 cast), Meredith Willson. Capitol.
Flower Drum Song (original cast album),
 Salvatore dell'Isola, musical director.
 Richard Rodgers, music. Columbia.
Sound of Jazz, from CBS TV *Seven Lively
 Arts* with Basie, Giuffre, Holliday, and
 others. Columbia.
Victory at Sea, Vol. II, from NBC TV
 production, RCA Victor Symphony
 Orchestra, Richard Rodgers. RCA.
The Music from Peter Gunn, Henry
 Mancini. RCA.

BEST SOUND TRACK ALBUM, DRAMATIC PICTURE SCORE OR ORIGINAL CAST

• *Gigi*, original motion picture sound track, André Previn. MGM.

Auntie Mame, sound track, Ray Heindorf Orchestra. Warner Bros.

The Bridge on the River Kwai, Malcolm Arnold. Columbia.

I Want to Live, Johnny Mandel. United Artists.

South Pacific, original sound track, orchestra conductor Alfred Newman. RCA.

BEST ARRANGEMENT

• Henry Mancini, *The Music from Peter Gunn* (Henry Mancini). RCA.

Billy May, *Come Fly with Me* (Frank Sinatra). Capitol.

Jack Marshall, "Fever" (Peggy Lee). Capitol.

Billy May, *Billy May's Big Fat Brass* (Billy May). Capitol.

✓Nelson Riddle, "Witchcraft" (Frank Sinatra). Capitol.

BEST RHYTHM & BLUES PERFORMANCE

• Champs, "Tequila." Challenge.

Harry Belafonte, *Belafonte Sings the Blues*. RCA.

Nat "King" Cole, *Looking Back*. Capitol.

Earl Grant, *The End*. Decca.

Perez Prado, "Patricia." RCA.

BEST JAZZ PERFORMANCE, INDIVIDUAL

• Ella Fitzgerald, *Ella Fitzgerald Sings the Duke Ellington Song Book*. Verve.

Jonah Jones, "Baubles, Bangles & Beads." Capitol.

George Shearing, *Burnished Brass*. Capitol.

Matty Mattock, "Dixieland Story." Warner Bros.

Jonah Jones, *Jumpin' with Jonah*. Capitol.

BEST JAZZ PERFORMANCE, GROUP

• Count Basie, *Basie*. Roulette.

Jonah Jones, "Baubles, Bangles & Beads." Capitol.

George Shearing, *Burnished Brass*. Capitol.

Four Freshmen, *The Four Freshmen in Person*. Capitol.

Basie Rhythm Section, Dave Lambert Singers, *Sing a Song of Basie*. ABC-Paramount.

BEST CLASSICAL PERFORMANCE, ORCHESTRA
(Conductor's Award)

• Felix Slatkin conducting Hollywood Bowl Symphony, *Gaîté Parisienne*. Capitol.

Leonard Bernstein conducting New York Philharmonic, *Stravinsky: Le Sacre du Printemps*. Columbia.

Pierre Monteux conducting London Symphony, *Rimsky-Korsakoff: Scheherezade*. RCA.

Charles Munch conducting Boston Symphony, *Barber: Meditation and Dance of Vengeance*. RCA.

Eugene Ormandy conducting Philadelphia Orchestra, *Prokofiev: Symphony No. 5 in B Flat Major*. Columbia.

Bruno Walter conducting Columbia Symphony Orchestra, *Beethoven: Symphony No. 6 in F Major*. Columbia.

Bruno Walter conducting New York Philharmonic (Westminster Choir; solos: Emilia Cundari, Maureen Forrester,), *Mahler: Symphony No. 2 in C Minor*. Columbia.

BEST CLASSICAL PERFORMANCE, CHAMBER MUSIC (INCLUDING CHAMBER ORCHESTRA)

• Hollywood String Quartet, *Beethoven: Quartet 130*. Capitol.

Budapest String Quartet, *Ravel: Quartet in F Major; Debussy: Quartet in G Minor*. Columbia.

Pablo Casals, Eugene Istomin, Fuchs, *Beethoven: Trio in E Flat Major; Trio in D Major*. Columbia.

Jascha Heifetz, William Primrose, Gregor Piatigorsky, *Beethoven: Trio in E Flat, Op. 3*. RCA.

Jascha Heifetz, William Primrose, Gregor Piatigorsky, *Beethoven: Trio in G, Op. 9, No. 1; Trio in C Minor, Op. 9, No. 3*. RCA.

BEST CLASSICAL PERFORMANCE, INSTRUMENTAL (WITH CONCERTO SCALE ACCOMPANIMENT)

• Van Cliburn (Kondrashin Symphony), *Tchaikovsky: Concerto No. 1 in B Flat Minor, Op. 23*. RCA.

Andrés Segovia, *Segovia Golden Jubilee* (last record in set). Decca.

Emil Gilels (Fritz Reiner conducting Chicago Symphony), *Brahms: Piano Concerto No. 2*. RCA.

"The Chipmunk Song," winner of three statuettes, became the fastest-selling record of all time as of 1958, eventually selling as many as seven million copies.

Leonard Pennario, *Rachmaninoff: Rhapsody on a Theme of Paganini.* Capitol.

Artur Rubinstein (Wallenstein conducting Symphony of the Air), *Saint-Saëns: Piano Concerto No. 2.* RCA.

Isaac Stern, (Leonard Bernstein conducting New York Philharmonic), *Bartók: Concerto for Violin.* Columbia.

BEST CLASSICAL PERFORMANCE, INSTRUMENTAL (OTHER THAN CONCERTO SCALE ACCOMPANIMENT)

• Andrés Segovia, *Segovia Golden Jubilee.* Decca.

Marcel Grandjany, *Music for the Harp.* Capitol.

Vladimir Horowitz, *Horowitz Plays Chopin.* RCA.

Wanda Landowska, *Art of the Harpsichord.* RCA.

Nathan Milstein, *Beethoven Sonata No. 9 and Sonata No. 8.* Capitol.

BEST CLASSICAL PERFORMANCE, OPERATIC OR CHORAL

• Roger Wagner Chorale, *Virtuoso.* Capitol.

Maria Callas, Tito Gobbi, *Rossini: Barber of Seville.* Angel.

Erich Leinsdorf conducting Rome Opera House Chorus & Orchestra (solos: Peters, Pace, Carlin, Paima, Peerce, Maero, Tozzi), *Donizetti: Lucia di Lammermoor.* RCA.

Erich Leinsdorf conducting Rome Opera House Chorus & Orchestra (solos: Cifferi, Mattioli, Moffo, Zeri, Elias, Pace, Carlin, Valletti, Catalani Cesari, Mineo, Corena [Monreale]), *Puccini: Madame Butterfly.* RCA.

Dimitri Mitropoulos, Metropolitan Opera Chorus and Orchestra (solos: Steber, Elias, Resnick, Gedda, Nagy, Cehanovsky, Tozzi), *Barber: Vanessa.* RCA.

Dom David Nicholson directing Choir of the Abbey of Mt. Angel & C. Robert Zimmerman, directing Portland Symphony Choir, *Victoria: Requiem Mass.* RCA.

BEST CLASSICAL PERFORMANCE, VOCAL SOLOIST (WITH OR WITHOUT ORCHESTRA)

• Renata Tebaidi, *Recital of Songs and Arias.* London.

Maria Callas, *Cherubini: Medea.* Mercury.

Salli Terri, *Duets for Spanish Guitar.* Capitol.

Eileen Farrell, *Eileen Farrell as Medea.* Columbia.

Eileen Farrell (Charles Munch conducting Boston Symphony), *Wagner: Prelude & Liebestod/ (Tristan & Isolde), Brunn-Hilde's Immolation (Die Gotterdamerung).* RCA.

BEST ENGINEERED RECORD, CLASSICAL

• Sherwood Hall III, *Duets with a Spanish Guitar* (Almeida & Terri). Capitol.

Sherwood Hall III, *Gaîté Parisienne* (Felix Slatkin). Capitol.

Prokofiev: Lieutenant Kiji; Stravinsky: Song of the Nightingale (Fritz Reiner). RCA.

Stravinsky: Rite of Spring (Leonard Bernstein). Columbia.

BEST DOCUMENTARY OR SPOKEN WORD RECORDING

• *The Best of the Stan Freberg Shows,* Stan Freberg. Capitol.

Great American Speeches, Melvyn Douglas, Vincent Price, Carl Sandburg, Ed Begley. Caedmon.

Green Christmas, Stan Freberg. Capitol.
Improvisations to Music, Mike Nichols,
　Elaine May. Mercury.
The Lady from Philadelphia, Marion
　Anderson (Rupp, Morrow). RCA.
Two Interviews of Our Time, Henry
　Jacobs, Woody Leafer. Fantasy.

BEST COMEDY PERFORMANCE
• David Seville, "The Chipmunk Song."
　Liberty.
Stan Freberg, *The Best of the Stan Freberg
　Shows.* Capitol.
Stan Freberg, *Green Christmas.* Capitol.
Mike Nichols and Elaine May,
　Improvisations to Music. Mercury.
Mort Sahl, *The Future Lies Ahead.* Verve.

BEST RECORDING FOR CHILDREN
• "The Chipmunk Song," David Seville.
　Liberty.
"Children's Marching Song," Cyril
　Stapleton. London.
Fun in Shariland, Shari Lewis. Victor.
Mommy, Give Me a Drinka Water, Danny
　Kaye. Capitol.
Tubby the Tuba, Jose Ferrer. MGM.
"Witch Doctor," David Seville. Liberty.

BEST ENGINEERED RECORDING, OTHER THAN CLASSICAL
• Ted Keep, "The Chipmunk Song" (David
　Seville). Liberty.
Hugh Davies, *Billy May's Big Fat Brass*
　(Billy May). Capitol.
Luis P. Valentin, *Come Fly with Me*
　(Frank Sinatra). Capitol.
✓Luis P. Valentin, "Witchcraft" (Frank
　Sinatra), Capitol.
Rafael O. Valentin, *Other Worlds, Other
　Sounds* (Esquivel). RCA.

BEST ALBUM COVER
✓• Frank Sinatra, *Only the Lonely* (Frank
　Sinatra). Capitol.
Ray Heindorf, photographer. Paramount
　Pictures, Ray Rennahan, A.S.C., *For
　Whom the Bells Toll.* Warner Bros.
David Rose, *Ira Ironstrings Plays Music
　for People with $3.98.* Warner Bros.
Marvin Schwartz, *Come Fly with Me*
　(Frank Sinatra). Capitol.
Charles Ward, *Julie* (Julie London).
　Liberty.

Sinatra's Revenge

Following the modest success of the first Grammys, N.A.R.A.S. was so eager to move on to the next set of prizes that the second annual Grammy Awards were held just six months after the first. The eligibility period for contending nominees was only eight months long, but it was a time span that included releases of important new music by such big winners from the first Grammys as Ella Fitzgerald and Henry Mancini. And losers, too. The heavily nominated Frank Sinatra suffered a near shut-out last time, but now he was back with new nods that didn't compete against each other within the same categories, as they did in 1958. For the most important prize of all, however — Record of the Year — Sinatra was up against two nominees he considered particularly irksome: teen idol Bobby Darin, who was often likened to a young Sinatra (much to the elder's dismay), and the greasy-haired "King" of rock & roll whom the "Chairman of the Board" so openly despised: Elvis Presley.

Presley's three nominations (the same number as Sinatra, coincidentally) represented a serious new effort on N.A.R.A.S.'s part to acknowledge the cutting edge of the growing rock revolution, just as it seemed to ignore it deliberately only six months earlier. N.A.R.A.S. was also serious about reaching out beyond California to the easterners who were vital to the record industry and the future success of the Grammy Awards. In what would become a tradition for a decade in the future, the West Coast ceremony was held in concert with an East Coast party simultaneously conducted at the Wal-

Frank Sinatra bounced back from his humiliating defeats last year with 1959's Album of the Year *Come Dance with Me.*

dorf-Astoria Hotel in New York City.

But most of the action was out in L.A. where the Grammys received an impressive birthday present on the occasion of its second set of prizes: its own TV show. The live NBC broadcast took place at the network's Burbank studios immediately following the awards banquet at the Beverly Hilton Hotel. Ten of the year's 34 winners were announced a month earlier so they could be on hand for the program. Seven showed up. Duke Ellington and Nat "King" Cole were missing, but they had performed on tape in New York a few weeks earlier so they could still be part of the telecast. Frank Sinatra was unavailable altogether, but the show put on by the remaining nine performers was good enough to merit the release of a special LP that bore a N.A.R.A.S. label and was under-written and distributed by the show's sponsor, Watchmakers of Switzerland. Emcee of both the L.A. awards ceremony and TV broadcast was the winner for last year's Best Original Cast Album, Meredith Willson, composer of *The Music Man*.

Reviews of the TV show were widely mixed. "Willson proved to be a stiff and uneasy host, who contributed nothing to enliven what was basically an inept and amateurish production," groused *Down Beat*. "Only the [Ella] Fitzgerald and [Bobby] Darin segments were up to professional standards." The *L.A. Examiner* said the show "revealed both the best and worst sides of the platter." *Variety*

Jazz diva Ella Fitzergald proved a big winner again when she was lauded for "But Not for Me" and Ella Swings Lightly.

was unequivocal in liking it: "The overall approach was handled with savvy and imagination, adding up to a fairly solid hour of entertainment."

Although Frank Sinatra wasn't on hand for the ceremony (the music industry rumor mill asserted he was still miffed over his humiliating losses at the first awards night), he nonetheless remained a formidable presence in the awards competition. Sinatra's recent work with Capitol Records, begun in 1953, marked his professional comeback as he made the career changeover from teen idol of the war-torn 1940s to seasoned "saloon singer" and screen star of the quieter and safer Eisenhower '50s. Record buyers had discovered him again, but acknowledgment from his industry peers was still elusive.

Sinatra wanted a big Grammy victory badly. At the first awards show, his two top LPs *Come Fly with Me* and *Only the Lonely* came up with only one prize between them — best album cover, which was mistakenly awarded to Ol' Blue Eyes instead of the album's art director, much to everyone's embarrassment. This time Sinatra implored his fans to *Come Dance with Me* instead and his luck changed dramatically.

Come Dance with Me earned for Sinatra what proved to be so elusive at Grammy's debut ceremony — the high honor of Album of the Year. He was also lauded for giving the year's Best Male Vocal Performance, a title he lost last year in a major upset to Perry Como. *Come Dance* had the year's Best Arrangement, too, a prize that went to Billy May, who conducted last year's Best Performance by an Orchestra. Sinatra's championship LP was a bona fide winner in many respects. It featured such hit tunes as "Dancing in the Dark" and "Cheek to Cheek" and ended up ranked 11th for the year.

By virtue of his absence, however, Sinatra was literally upstaged by the young "imitator" whose music, complained the *L.A. Herald & Express*, was so popular that it was "super-charging the air around any given juke-box" in America.

"I'd like to be a legend by the time I'm 25 years old," Bobby Darin once told *Life* magazine. By 1958, at age 22 and after watching his first half-dozen singles turn out to be flops, Darin finally got his first break: "Splish, Splash" hit number three in the nation. But Darin didn't want to be known just for rock & roll. "In night clubs I lean to other things," he told *Billboard*, proudly. "I even do 'Mack the Knife' from *The Threepenny Opera*," the Kurt Weill–Bertolt Brecht musical.

Darin based his version of "Mack the Knife" on an earlier rendition by Louis Armstrong and included it in his album *That's All* as an example of his musical versatility. He opposed its release as a 45, but Atco proceeded to distribute it anyway and "Mack" ended up ruling the charts for nine weeks at number one, becoming the best-selling single of the year. It also became Darin's signature song — and the Grammy's Record of the Year. By the end of 1959, "Mack" shared the Top 10 with another Darin hit, "Dream Lover," and N.A.R.A.S. acknowledged him with its first Best New Artist award (even though he was really a "new artist" when "Splish Splash" was released a year earlier). The popularity of "Mack the Knife" continues to cut across time: *Billboard* hailed it as number seven in its 1991 list of the top 3,000 songs of the rock era.

The Grammys' Song of the Year turned out to be the year's number-two hit tune, much "to everyone's surprise," noted the *L.A. Examiner*, since the choice was a country & western song. "The Battle of New Orleans" described the final fight of the War of 1812, which saw U.S. General Andrew Jackson defeat the British on January 8, 1815, two weeks after the war was declared over in faraway London and Washington. To celebrate the victory, fiddlers across America played a catchy new tune called "The Eighth of January."

One hundred and forty years later,

Jimmy Driftwood, a schoolteacher from Snowball, Arkansas, penned lyrics to a song that subsequently came to the attention of country singer Johnny Horton. Horton had been struggling for professional kudos since 1951, but had so far failed to score a pop hit. With "New Orleans," his battle would be over. While the trophy for songwriting went to Driftwood, Horton won the prize for giving the year's best country & western performance. It was Driftwood, however, not Horton, who was asked to perform the song on the Grammy telecast.

Duke Ellington

Duke Ellington was honored for his first film score, **Anatomy of a Murder.**

Duke Ellington won the first three of his 11 eventual Grammys, not for some of his typical after-hours club classics like "Mood Indigo" or the more jumpy "Take the 'A' Train," but for his first attempt at scoring a motion picture. *Anatomy of a Murder* was a gripping courtroom drama, directed by Otto Preminger and starring James Stewart, Lee Remick, George C. Scott, and the Duke himself in a cameo appearance. Ellington's score was voted best sound track album as well as Best Performance by a Dance Band and Best Musical Composition First Recorded and Released in 1959 (Over 5 Minutes).

After a stellar career that first brought Ellington to prominence in 1927 when he performed at New York's Cotton Club, the Duke's popularity had reached a low ebb by the mid-1950s. It experienced a resurgence, however, thanks partly to Ella Fitzgerald's *Song Book* salute to his considerable *oeuvre* (to date) that thrilled the critics, rallied record buyers, and won her a Grammy at the first awards show. This time Fitzgerald was back winning two again: best solo jazz performance for her album *Ella Swings Lightly* and best female vocal performance for her single "But Not for Me." Trumpet player Jonah Jones and his quartet gave the year's best group performance on *I Dig Chicks*. Dinah Washington was acclaimed for giving the best Rhythm & Blues Performance for her classic version of "What a Diff'rence a Day Makes," which beat out Elvis Presley and his "A Big Hunk O'Love." Veteran Hollywood bandleader David Rose won the orchestral honors for his work with André Previn on the latter's hit *Like Young* LP.

Artur Rubinstein won two classical awards for his Beethoven Sonatas Nos. 21 and 18 (the recording has "moments of delicacy and quiet beauty that merit commendation," said *High Fidelity*). The Boston Symphony Orchestra's salute to Debussy was called "sumptuous" by the critics and won the award for classical orchestra performance. Pianist Van Cliburn had a best-selling album in *Billboard*'s Top 20 of 1959 (Tchaikovsky's *Piano Concerto No. 1*), but he won his Grammy (Best Classical Performance — Concerto) for his rendition of Rachmaninoff's Piano Concerto No. 3, the composer's favorite and, according to many pianists, his most difficult concerto to play. It was recorded at Van Cliburn's Carnegie Hall concert of May 19, 1958, which came just two days after he returned from the Soviet Union where he had made world headlines after triumphing at the Tchaikovsky competition.

The opera awards went to Swedish tenor Jussi Bjoerling and to the recording of Mozart's *The Marriage of Figaro* by the Vienna Philharmonic with Erich Leinsdorf conducting.

"An amateur musical group of 350 singers walked away with the award for best performance by a chorus," noted the *L.A. Herald & Express*. "It was the Mormon Tabernacle Choir from Salt Lake City out-polling such professionals as the Ames Brothers, the Kingston Trio, and the Robert Shaw Chorale to win with its rendition of 'Battle Hymn of the Republic.'" The Kingston Trio did end up with the new award for best folk performance — for their album *The Kingston Trio at Large*—which was the fifth-best selling LP of the year.

There was a tie for Best Broadway Show Album between *Gypsy* (starring Ethel Merman, with music by Jule Styne and lyrics by Stephen Sondheim) and *Redhead* (starring Gwen Verdon, with music by Albert Hague and lyrics by Dorothy Fields), while André Previn and Ken Darby's rendition of Gershwin's *Porgy and Bess* won the honors for best film sound track. The first filmed version of *Porgy and Bess* featured Sidney Poitier, Dorothy Dandridge, and Pearl Bailey in the lead roles and was the last movie produced by studio mogul Samuel Goldwyn.

Last year Capitol won the most awards, taking 10 of the 28 categories. This year the sweepstakes champ was RCA, which nabbed 11 trophies in the year's 34 categories, followed by Columbia with 9, Capitol 7, Atco 3, and Verve 3. Clearly, a pattern was already developing: Large companies had an obvious advantage over the smaller record labels. The big firms often paid the annual $15 membership fee for large numbers of employees to join N.A.R.A.S. and then benefitted from their staffers voting — out of loyalty or as a result of corporate pressure — for their own company's music.

In 1959, *Saturday Review* was among the critics crying foul. "Of the 40-odd nominations ... in the eight categories involving jazz and classical performances," it noted, "a total of 30 (or some 80 percent of the whole) are products of RCA." RCA's dominance of the year's competition was actually worse than that: It scored almost 100 nominations, a sum larger than the bids earned by all other record companies combined. The magazine accused N.A.R.A.S. of tolerating "stuffed ballot boxes" and added, "Whatever the causes, the results, plainly, are awards without distinction, to which no well-informed record buyer or critic would attach any significance."

Columbia president Goddard Lieberson agreed and delivered "a hot blast" in an open letter, published in *Variety*, to N.A.R.A.S.'s West Coast and East Coast chapter presidents. The nominations, he said, "in no way reflect either the status, the quality, or the scope of the record industry .... There is no merit in self-served awards won by the sort of electioneering and lobbying which I believe must invariably accompany the N.A.R.A.S. method of balloting." N.A.R.A.S. said it would investigate the problem and try to take corrective action by next year.

Some critics accused voters of determining the top prizes on the basis of record sales. "The N.A.R.A.S. membership still seems to be using the best-seller charts to determine Record of the Year," said *Variety*. It also resurrected a complaint from last year: "and it still has to come to terms with rock & roll."

Rock & roll, however, did somewhat better this year than last. At least its "King," Elvis Presley (who was then serving in the U.S. Army as a jeep driver in Germany), was nominated in the Record of the Year lineup for "A Fool Such as I," even though the tune ranked only a distant 50 in *Billboard*'s year-end rankings. Presley's musical output was sparse in 1959 because of his military obligations. It was the first time since 1957, in fact, that he didn't have a hit in the Top 10.

N.A.R.A.S., furthermore, was also concerned enough about rock's representation to come up with a new category that was originally to be called Best Rock & Roll Performance. In the end, however, it was switched to Best Performance by a "Top 40" Artist and the difference was significant enough to create a loophole that caused the Grammys, for their second year in a row, not to recognize r&r in an official way. The new award went instead to another "King" — Nat Cole — for "Midnight Flyer," which not only didn't rock, it never even made it into *Billboard*'s Top 40. The victory is considered one of Grammy's most embarrassing vote results, especially since Cole beat Elvis Presley and his "A Big Hunk O'Love," which charted at number 39 for the year.

The year 1959 was a tragic time for rock & roll, seeing the deaths of Buddy Holly, Ritchie Valens, and the "Big Bopper" (J.P. Richardson) in a plane crash after their concert at Clear Lake, Iowa. The sound was still having trouble gaining popular acceptance, too, particularly from listeners of the bovine kind. A story on page one of the *L.A. Mirror* on the same day that the Grammy results were announced (on an inside page) reported that dairy cows now joined the ranks of rock detractors. "Rock 'n' Roll Makes Cows Tighten Up," said the paper's grabber headline. "That music tightens the cow's glandular system and deters milking," said a spokesman for the American Dairy Association in the article. "Waltz music produces much better milking conditions."

> *The Grammy,* said **Variety,** *"still has to come to terms with rock & roll."*

Awards bestowed on November 29, 1959, at ceremonies held simultaneously at the Beverly Hilton Hotel in Los Angeles and the Waldorf-Astoria Hotel in New York for the eligibility period January 1 to August 31, 1959. A post-Grammy show was broadcast live by NBC.

ALBUM OF THE YEAR
• *Come Dance with Me*, Frank Sinatra. Capitol.
Belafonte at Carnegie Hall, Harry Belafonte. RCA.
More Music from Peter Gunn, Henry Mancini. RCA.
Rachmaninoff Piano Concerto No. 3, Van Cliburn, Kiril Kondrashin. RCA.
Victory at Sea, Vol. I, Robert Russell Bennett. RCA.

RECORD OF THE YEAR
✓• "Mack the Knife," Bobby Darin. Atco.
"A Fool Such as I," Elvis Presley. RCA.
✓"High Hopes," Frank Sinatra. Capitol.
"Like Young," André Previn. MGM.
"The Three Bells," Browns. RCA.

SONG OF THE YEAR
(Songwriter's Award)
• "The Battle of New Orleans," Jimmy Driftwood. Columbia.
✓"High Hopes," Sammy Cahn, Jimmy Van Heusen. Capitol.
"I Know," Karl Stutz, Edith Lindeman. AFO.
"Like Young," Paul Francis Webster, André Previn. MGM.
"Small World," Jule Styne, Stephen Sondheim.

BEST NEW ARTIST
• Bobby Darin. Atco.
Edd Byrnes. Warner Bros.
Mark Murphy. Capitol.
Johnny Restivo.
Mavis Rivers.

BEST VOCAL PERFORMANCE, MALE
• Frank Sinatra, *Come Dance with Me*. Capitol.
Harry Belafonte, *Belafonte at Carnegie Hall*. RCA.
Jesse Belvin, "Guess Who." RCA.
✓Bobby Darin, "Mack the Knife." Atco.
Robert Merrill, *An Evening with Lerner and Loewe*. RCA.

BEST VOCAL PERFORMANCE, FEMALE
• Ella Fitzgerald, "But Not for Me." Verve.
Lena Horne, *Porgy and Bess*. RCA.
Peggy Lee, "Alright, Okay." Capitol.
Pat Suzuki, *Broadway '59*. RCA.
Caterina Valente, *La Strada del Amore*. RCA.

BEST PERFORMANCE BY A VOCAL GROUP OR CHORUS
• Mormon Tabernacle Choir, Richard Condi conducting, "Battle Hymn of the Republic." Columbia.
Ames Brothers, *Ames Brothers Sing Famous Hits of Famous Quartets*. RCA.
Browns, "The Three Bells." RCA.
Kingston Trio, *The Kingston Trio at Large*. Capitol.
Robert Shaw Chorale, *The Stephen Foster Song Book*. RCA.

BEST PERFORMANCE BY A "TOP 40" ARTIST
• Nat "King" Cole, "Midnight Flyer." Capitol.
Coasters, "Charlie Brown." Atco.
Elvis Presley, "A Big Hunk O'Love." RCA.
Floyd Robinson, "Makin' Love." RCA.
Neil Sedaka, *Neil Sedaka*. RCA.
Sarah Vaughan, "Broken Hearted Melody." Mercury.

SECURITY PACIFIC COLLECTION/ L.A. PUBLIC LIBRARY

Nat "King" Cole's only Grammy was a "Top 40" award for "Midnight Flyer," which never made it into the Top 40.

Best Rhythm & Blues Performance
- Dinah Washington, "What a Diff'rence a Day Makes." Mercury.
Jesse Belvin, "Guess Who." RCA.
The Coasters, "Charlie Brown." Atco.
Nat "King" Cole, "Midnight Flyer." Capitol.
Elvis Presley, "A Big Hunk O'Love." RCA.

Best Jazz Performance, Soloist
- Ella Fitzgerald, *Ella Swings Lightly*. Verve.
Ruby Braff, *Easy Now*. RCA.
Urbie Green, *Best of New Broadway Show Hits*. RCA.
Red Norvo, *Red Norvo in Hi-Fi*. RCA.
André Previn, *Like Young*. MGM.
Bobby Troup, *Bobby Troup and his Stars of Jazz*. RCA.

Best Jazz Performance, Group
- Jonah Jones, *I Dig Chicks*. Capitol.
Duke Ellington, *Ellington Jazz Party*. Columbia.
Henry Mancini, *More Music from Peter Gunn*. RCA.
Red Norvo, *Red Norvo in Hi-Fi*. RCA.
Shorty Rogers, *Chances Are It Swings*. RCA.

Best Country & Western Performance
- Johnny Horton, "Battle of New Orleans." Columbia.
Eddy Arnold, "Tennessee Stud." RCA.
Skeeter Davis, "Set Him Free." RCA.
Don Gibson, "Don't Tell Me Your Troubles." RCA.
Jim Reeves, "Home." RCA.

Best Performance, Folk
- Kingston Trio, *The Kingston Trio at Large*. Capitol.
Eddy Arnold, "Tennessee Stud." RCA.
Harry Belafonte, *Belafonte at Carnegie Hall*. RCA.
Jimmy Driftwood, *The Wilderness Road*. RCA.
Ralph Hunter Choir, *The Wild Wild West*. RCA.

Best Performance by a Dance Band
- Duke Ellington, *Anatomy of a Murder*. Columbia.
Ray Anthony, *Sound Spectacular*. Capitol.
Count Basie, *Breakfast Dance and Barbecue*. Roulette.

Larry Elgart, *New Sounds at the Roosevelt*. RCA.
Glenn Miller, *For the Very First Time*. RCA.
Perez Prado, *Pops and Prado*. RCA.

Best Performance by an Orchestra
- David Rose and His Orchestra with André Previn, *Like Young*. MGM.
Esquivel, *Strings Aflame*. RCA.
Henry Mancini, *More Music from Peter Gunn*. RCA.
Bob Thompson and Orchestra, *Just for Kicks*. RCA.
Stanley Wilson, *Music from M Squad*. RCA.
Hugo Winterhalter, *Two Sides of Winterhalter*. RCA.

Best Musical Composition First Recorded and Released in 1959 (Over 5 Minutes)
- *Anatomy of a Murder*, Duke Ellington.
More Music from Peter Gunn, Henry Mancini.
Prokofiev: The Overture Russe, Op. 72, Serge Prokofiev.
St. Lawrence Suite, Morton Gould.
Shostakovitch: Concerto No. 2 for Piano and Orchestra, OP. 101, Dmitri Shostakovitch.

Best Broadway Show Album
(Tie)
- *Gypsy*, Ethel Merman. Columbia.
- *Redhead*, Gwen Verdon. RCA.
A Party with Betty Comden and Adolph Green, Betty Comden, Adolph Green. Capitol.
Ages of Man, Sir John Gielgud. Columbia.
Once Upon a Mattress, Hal Hastings, conductor. Kapp.

Best Sound Track Album—Original Cast, Motion Picture or Television
- *Porgy and Bess*, André Previn, Ken Darby. Columbia.
The Five Pennies. Dot.
For the First Time, Mario Lanza. RCA.
Sleeping Beauty. Disneyland.
Some Like it Hot. United Artists.

Best Sound Track Album— Background Score from Motion Picture or Television
- *Anatomy of a Murder*, Duke Ellington. Columbia.
More Music from Peter Gunn, Henry Mancini. RCA.

Best New Artist Bobby Darin wanted to be "a legend" by his 25th birthday.

Pete Kelly's Blues, Dick Cathcart. Warner Bros.
The Music from M Squad, Stanley Wilson. RCA.
The Nun's Story, Franz Waxman. Warner Bros.

BEST ARRANGEMENT
• Billy May, *Come Dance with Me* (Frank Sinatra). Capitol.
Johnny Green, *An Evening with Lerner and Loewe*. RCA.
✓Richard Wess, "Mack the Knife" (Bobby Darin). Atco.
More Music from Peter Gunn (Henry Mancini). RCA.
Strings Aflame (Esquivel). RCA.
Victory at Sea, Vol. 1, (Robert Russell Bennett conducting RCA Victor Symphony Orchestra). RCA.

BEST CLASSICAL PERFORMANCE, ORCHESTRA
(Conductor's Award)
• Charles Munch conducting Boston Symphony, *Debussy: Images for Orchestra*. RCA.
Morton Gould and His Orchestra, *Tchaikovsky: 1812 Overture; Ravel: Bolero*. RCA.
Kiril Kondrashin conducting RCA Victor Symphony Orchestra, *Tchaikovsky: Capriccio Italien; Rimsky-Korsakov: Capriccio Espagnol*. RCA.

Pierre Monteux conducting Vienna Philharmonic, *Beethoven: Symphony No. 6*. RCA.
Fritz Reiner conducting Chicago Symphony, *Rossini: Overtures*. RCA.

BEST CLASSICAL PERFORMANCE, CHAMBER MUSIC (INCLUDING CHAMBER ORCHESTRA)
• Artur Rubinstein, *Beethoven: Sonata No. 21, in C, Op. 53; "Waldstein" Sonata No. 18 in E Flat, Op. 53, No. 3*. RCA.
Festival Quartet, *Beethoven: Piano Quartet in E Flat Op, 16; Schumann Piano Quartet in E Flat Op. 47*. RCA.
Nathan Milstein, *Four Italian Sonatas*. Capitol.
Felix Slatkin, *Cello Galaxy*. Capitol.
Felix Slatkin, *Villa Lobos: String Quartet*. Capitol.

BEST CLASSICAL PERFORMANCE, CONCERTO OR INSTRUMENTAL SOLOIST (FULL ORCHESTRA)
• Van Cliburn (Kondrashin conducting Symphony of the Air), *Rachmaninoff: Piano Concerto No. 3*. RCA.
Jascha Heifetz (Munch conducting Boston Symphony), *Mendelssohn: Violin Concerto No. 2 in E Minor, Op. 64; Prokofiev: Violin Concerto No. 2 in G Minor*. RCA.
Vladimir Horowitz (Toscanini conducting NBC Symphony), *Tchaikovsky: Piano Concerto No. 1*. RCA.
Artur Rubinstein (Krips conducting RCA Victor Symphony), *Brahms: Piano Concerto No. 2*. RCA.
Henryk Szeryng (Monteux conducting London Symphony), *Brahms: Violin Concerto in D*. RCA.

BEST CLASSICAL PERFORMANCE, INSTRUMENTAL SOLOIST (WITHOUT ORCHESTRAL ACCOMPANIMENT)
• Artur Rubinstein, *Beethoven: Sonata No. 21 in C, Op. 53, "Waldstein" Sonata No. 18 in E Flat, Op. 53, No. 3*. RCA.
Laurindo Almeida, *Danzas*. Capitol.
Glenn Gould, *Berg: Sonata for Piano, Op. 1; Krenek: Sonata No. 3, Op. 92, No 4; Schönberg: Three Piano Pieces, Op. 11*. Columbia.
Jaime Laredo, *Presenting Jaime Laredo*. RCA.
Nathan Milstein, *Four Italian Sonatas*. Capitol.
Leonard Pennario, *Pennario Plays*. Capitol.

BEST CLASSICAL PERFORMANCE, OPERA CAST OR CHORAL

- Erich Leinsdorf conducting Vienna Philharmonic (solos: Peters, London, Della, Casa), *Mozart: The Marriage of Figaro*. RCA.

Fausto Cleva conducting Metropolitan Opera Orchestra and Chorus (solos: Stevens, Del Monago), *Saint-Saëns: Sampson and Delilah*. RCA.

Richard Condie conducting Mormon Tabernacle Choir, *The Beloved Choruses*. Columbia.

Erich Leinsdorf conducting Metropolitan Orchestra and Chorus (solos: Peters, Valetti, Merrill, Tozzi), *Rossini: The Barber of Seville*. RCA.

Fernado Previtali conducting Accademia de Santa Cecilia, Rome, Orchestra and Chorus (solos: Milanov, Tozzi), *Verdi: La Farza del Destino*. RCA.

BEST CLASSICAL PERFORMANCE, VOCAL SOLOIST
(WITH OR WITHOUT ORCHESTRA)

- Jussi Björling, *Björling in Opera*. London.

Maria Callas, *Maria Callas Portrays Verdi Heroines*. Angel.

Maureen Forrester, *A Brahms/Schumann Recital*. Decca.

Zinka Milanov, *Milanov Operatic Arias*. RCA.

Cesare Valletti, *The Art of Song*. RCA.

BEST ENGINEERED RECORDING, CLASSICAL

- Lewis W. Layton, *Victory at Sea, Vol. 1*, (Robert Russell Bennett). RCA.

Lewis W. Layton, *Doubling in Brass* (Morton Gould). RCA.

Lewis W. Layton, *Rossini Overtures* (Fritz Reiner). RCA.

Lewis W. Layton, *Tchaikovsky: Capriccio Italien; Rimsky-Korsakov: Capriccio Espagnol*, (Kiril Kondrashin). RCA.

Lewis W. Layton, *Tchaikovsky: 1812 Overture; Ravel: Bolero* (Morton Gould). RCA.

BEST DOCUMENTARY OR SPOKEN WORD RECORDING

- *A Lincoln Portrait*, Carl Sandburg. Columbia.

Ages of Man, Sir John Gielgud. Columbia.

New York Taxi Driver, Tony Schwartz. Columbia.

Basil Rathbone Reads Sherlock Holmes, Basil Rathbone. Audio Book.

Mark Twain Tonight, Hal Holbrook. Columbia.

BEST COMEDY PERFORMANCE, SPOKEN WORD

- Shelley Berman, *Inside Shelley Berman*. Verve.

Lenny Bruce, *Sick Humor*. Fantasy.

Stan Freberg, *Stan Freberg with Original Cast*. Capitol.

Andy Griffith, *Hamlet*. Capitol.

Mort Sahl, *Look Forward in Anger*. Verve.

BEST COMEDY PERFORMANCE, MUSICAL

- Homer & Jethro, *The Battle of Kookamonga*. RCA.

Cliff Arquette, *Charlie Weaver Sings for His People*. Columbia.

Betty Comden, Adolph Green, *A Party with Betty Comden and Adolph Green*. Capitol.

Hans Conreid, Alice Pearce, *Monster Rally*. RCA.

Bernie Green, *Musically Mad*. RCA.

BEST RECORDING FOR CHILDREN

- *Peter and the Wolf*, Peter Ustinov (von Karajan conducting Philharmonia Orchestra). Angel.

The Arabian Nights, Maria Ray. RCA.

Hansel and Gretel, Franz Allers. RCA.

Popeye's Favorite Sea Chanties, Captain Allen Swift. RCA.

Three to Make Music/ Cinderella, Mary Martin. RCA.

BEST ENGINEERING, NOVELTY RECORDING

- Ted Keep, *Alvin's Harmonica* (David Seville). Liberty.

Thorne Nogar, *Orienta* (Markko Polo Adventurers). RCA.

Robert Simpson, *Supersonics in Flight* (Billy Mure). RCA.

Robert Simpson, *The Wild Wild West* (Ralph Hunter Choir). RCA.

Luis P. Valentin, *The Bat* (Alvino Rey). Capitol.

BEST ENGINEERING CONTRIBUTION, OTHER THAN CLASSICAL OR NOVELTY

- Robert Simpson, *Belafonte at Carnegie Hall*. (Harry Belafonte). RCA.

Ernest Oelrich, *Strings Aflame* (Esquivel). RCA.

Robert Simpson, *Big Band Guitar* (Buddy Morrow). RCA.

Robert Simpson, *Compulsion to Swing* (Henri René). RCA.

Robert Simpson, *New Sounds at the Roosevelt* (Larry Elgart). RCA.

BEST ALBUM COVER

• Robert M. Jones, *Shostakovich: Symphony No. 5* (Howard Mitchell). RCA.

Saul Bass, *Anatomy of a Murder* (Duke Ellington). Columbia.

Acy R. Lehmann, *Porgy and Bess* (Lena Horne, Harry Belafonte). RCA.

Col. Tom Parker, *For LP Fans Only* (Elvis Presley). RCA.

Robert L. Yorke, Acy R. Lehmann, *The South Shall Rise Again* (Phil Harris). RCA.

SPECIAL TRUSTEES AWARDS FOR ARTISTS & REPERTOIRE CONTRIBUTION

Record of the Year, "Mack the Knife," Bobby Darin. Ahmet Ertegun, A&R producer. Atco.

Album of the Year, *Come Dance with Me*, Frank Sinatra. Dave Cavanaugh, A&R producer. Capitol.

Grammy's Night at the Movies

By introducing new changes in the award categories, N.A.R.A.S. meant to address a growing chorus of complaints in the music industry. The best vocal performance awards were separated into honors for albums and single cuts for males and females (although, coincidentally, both were won this year by the same man and woman). In jazz, a new slot was created for best composition, while the jazz performance prizes were split into categories for large and small groups, with vocal soloists being bunched with small groups. Nearly all of the Top 10 best-selling singles of 1960 were rock & roll tunes (Elvis had three of the top five, including, ironically, "It's Now or Never"), but — again — none would win an award. Rock was finally granted its own category this year — Best Performance by a Pop Single Artist (changed from "Top 40 Artist" last year) — but the award went to a new recording of a 1930 Hoagy Carmichael song.

N.A.R.A.S. voters were stubbornly loyal either to "serious" music (read jazz or classical) or to the melodic, instrumental variety that tended to dominate the album charts just as rock & roll ruled the singles lineup. Typically, the top LPs of the day were Broadway cast albums, such as *The Sound of Music*, which was the number-one seller of 1960 (and Grammy's Best Show Album), or hit film scores — the more romantic the better.

Record of the Year was also the year's number one–ranked single (selling two million copies), the only all-instrumental disc to hold that position in the rock era. "Theme from *A Summer Place*," performed by Percy Faith & His Orchestra, was from Max Steiner's score for the romance melodrama set at a resort on the coast of Maine, starring Dorothy McGuire, Sandra Dee, and Troy Donahue. (Faith would later record a disco version of the music shortly before his death from cancer in 1976, but it failed to catch on in the record stores.)

The 1960 awards looked like a class of 1958 reunion when past champs like Count Basie repeated their wins.

Song of the Year turned out to be from a movie score, too: the "Theme from *Exodus*," which was written by Ernest Gold and also won the film score honors. *Exodus* was director Otto Preminger's film adaptation of the Leon Uris novel about the struggle of two Jewish refugees, played by Paul Newman and Eva Marie Saint, to reach the newly formed state of Israel. Several versions of the lead theme became popular in 1960, including the original film score recording and ones by Ferrante & Teicher and Mantovani & His Orchestra. Other movie music winners included André Previn's interpretation of Leonard Bernstein's *West Side Story* score, which was voted Best Jazz Performance, Solo or Small Group.

On only two occasions in Grammy history has the Album of the Year award gone to a comedy LP, in this case one that was also significant for launching the career of the low-key satirist Bob Newhart, previously known chiefly to nightclub audiences. And just like the choice for Record of the Year, the Album of the Year *Button Down Mind* was a big seller, too, at number three in *Billboard*'s LP rankings of 1960. Its success helped fuel critics' accusations that N.A.R.A.S. still favored commercially popular recordings. Newhart's huge disc sales also proved that he had a universally appealing touch. In *Button Down Mind,* he poked fun at such diverse working people as bus drivers, real-estate salesmen, and a particular Madison Avenue ad executive who gives Abraham Lincoln ridiculous advice on how to buff up his public image just prior to giving the Gettysburg Address. Strangely, the album was not acclaimed for the Best Comedy Performance. That went to its sequel, *Button Down Mind Strikes Back,* released six months after the original. Newhart was also voted Best New Artist — the only time the prize has gone to a comedian.

The winner of Grammy's first Album of the Year award, Henry Mancini, returned to claim two new awards (best performance by an orchestra and best arrangement) for the short-lived TV series, *Mr. Lucky,* about a professional gambler, and another for giving the Best Jazz Performance (Large Group) for *The Blues and the Beat.* Another alumnus of the 1958 awards came back, too, when Count Basie reprised his win for the best dance band performance, this time for *Dance with Basie.* When the Chipmunks burrowed back as well, this Grammy show started to look like a reunion of the class of 1958. *Let's All Sing with the Chipmunks* became 1960's Best Album Created for Children.

For the third year in a row, Ella Fitzgerald took the best female vocalist award, thereby monopolizing the category since its inception. (A good argument could be made for the fact that she deserved the honor: One smitten reviewer once said Fitzgerald "could sing the Van Nuys telephone directory with a broken jaw and make it sound good.") This year she resurrected the music from 1959's Record of the Year — "Mack the Knife" — and gave it her own signature lilt to win Best Vocal Performance (Single Record or Track) while its parent album, *Ella in Berlin,* took the equivalent LP kudos.

The recipient of the dual male vocal prizes, Ray Charles, was the clear champ on Grammys night, taking four top trophies. His version of the 1930 Hoagy Carmichael classic "Georgia on

Record and Song of the Year ("Summer Place" and "Exodus") were both from hit films.

My Mind" reaped the performance award for best single record or track; its album, *The Genius of Ray Charles*, nabbed the LP statuette. Charles also won Best Performance by a Pop Single Artist for "Georgia," which he recorded after being urged to do so by his driver who heard him sing it often while they were on the road together. (Charles was born in Georgia and lived for many of his early years just over the state line, in Florida.) When he eventually made the recording in New York, he tossed it off in just four takes, compared to the 10 to 12 that he usually made. "Georgia" turned out to be his sec-

Best New Artist Bob Newhart's Button Down Mind *won Album of the Year over LPs by Sinatra and Belafonte.*

ond million-selling single, his first being last year's "What'd I Say." His fourth Grammy of 1960 was for giving the Best Rhythm & Blues Performance in "Let the Good Times Roll."

The year's Best Country & Western Performance was given by Marty Robbins, for "El Paso," the 10th best-selling single of the year. Robbins was accustomed to crossover success. Many of his earlier hit country tunes also made it onto the pop charts, such as "Singing the Blues" and "A White Sport Coat (and a Pink Carnation)."

The classical awards were mostly dominated by the works of Brazilian-born guitarist Laurindo Almeida, who emigrated to the U.S. in 1947 at the age of 30, played as a soloist with Stan Kenton's Orchestra, and then made his mark in the field of film music. Almeida's *Conversations with the Guitar*

was chosen as Best Classical Performance, Vocal or Instrumental Chamber Music. *The Spanish Guitars of Laurindo Almeida* reaped him the honor for instrumental soloist and also won the classical engineering award.

Aaron Copland's *The Tender Land* was chosen Best Contemporary Classical Composition and was hailed as his "most important opera to date" by *High Fidelity*. The magazine added: "This is Copland, the composer of folkloric lyricism, at his most eloquent, luminous, delicate, and restrained." The selection of Handel's *Messiah*, performed by the Royal Philharmonic Orchestra and Chorus, under the baton of Sir Thomas Beecham, as best choral performance was less popular with the same source: "Sir Thomas went off here on a musical spree. He produced an orchestration in the style of — *Die Meistersinger!* ... It would be hard to imagine anything less suited to Handel."

The Best Classical Opera Production was Puccini's unfinished *Turandot* performed by Erich Leinsdorf leading the Chorus and Orchestra of the Rome Opera House with accompanying vocals by Birgit Nilsson and Renata Tebaldi. "The presentation as a whole is fine indeed," *High Fidelity* wrote. "The soloists are simply the best that could be found today for their roles. Nilsson sails through the altitudinous title role with even, powerful tone."

> **Best classical composition, Copland's The Tender Land, was hailed as "his most important opera to date."**

When Bob Newhart was named Best New Artist, he beat out the formidable American soprano Leontyne Price, who was just then coming to the serious attention of critics after impressive debuts in San Francisco in 1957 and Vienna in 1958 (where she triumphed as Aida at the Vienna State Opera). Price nonetheless earned a Grammy for Best Classical Performance for a Vocal Soloist for her *A Program of Song*, which included works by Gabriel Fauré, Francis Poulenc, and Richard Strauss. "Miss Price's voice is one of real stature — steady, effulgent, and controlled," *High Fidelity* said.

Because last year's TV show got such mixed reviews, a telecast was not attempted this year, although again simultaneous ceremonies were held in Los Angeles (at the Beverly Hills Hotel) and New York (at the Hotel Astor where corporate patrons paid $400 per table to attend). Presenters included Leonard Bernstein, André Previn, Rudy Vallee, Margaret Whiting, Louella Parsons, and Lawrence Welk (whose *Calcutta* was number one on *Variety*'s album chart that same week; the Grammy-winning *Exodus* soundtrack was number two). In the past, the crowds at each ceremony heard what was happening — and who was winning — on the opposite coast via a phone hookup that was broadcast to the audiences. This year, however, the telephone line went dead just as the proceedings were about to begin and confusion reigned until the faraway victors were simply announced by reading from N.A.R.A.S.'s secret winners list.

"RCA walked away with the third annual N.A.R.A.S. Grammy awards," *Variety* reported afterward, adding, "and the Artia label walked out of the organization." Artia's beef was that small record companies continued to fare poorly and it wanted to register its complaint dramatically. Artia had a strong case when considering who won the most. RCA ended up with 11 awards, Capitol and Columbia with 6 each, and Warner Bros. and Verve with 3. *Down Beat* howled: "The voting system is fundamentally inequitous [sic]."

N.A.R.A.S. had revamped the nomination process considerably this year in an effort to quell such criticism. As in the past, nominations were submitted by individual academy members (and five entries each were permitted from record companies), but now the academy nominating committee was also allowed to recommend contenders. The change ended up complicating the voting procedure considerably, but the bulk of electoral power stayed in members' hands while the committee presumably gave worthy musical works by the smaller producers a better chance.

The fundamental balloting problem, however, was still not corrected. The behemoth record firms kept their advantage by purchasing memberships for their employees who in turn voted for their own companies' music. "Some N.A.R.A.S. board members from RCA proposed that a bylaw be added which would not allow members to vote for their company's product," *Variety* reported. "The proposition was passed by the N.Y. chapter, but failed to go through a vote at a combined N.Y.–L.A. meet."

There were also some quarrels with the artistic merit of some of the winners. "Some of this year's awards are funny, and some are merely sad," *Down Beat* groused about the jazz awards. "It is amusing to see Henry Mancini's *Mr. Lucky* chosen over Gerry Mulligan's *The Concert Jazz Band* as best performance by an orchestra. It is sad to see André Previn's *West Side Story* called the best jazz performance, solo or small group, when John Coltrane's significant LP *Giant Steps* didn't even reach the final nominations stage, and the fair-minded Previn would probably be the first to admit it....

"But, to keep things in perspective," the magazine added, "we should also note how much more meaningful the awards were this year than last year. Some progress seems to have been made."

1960

Awards bestowed on April 12, 1961, at ceremonies held simultaneously at the Beverly Hills Hotel in Los Angeles and the Hotel Astor in New York for the eligibility period September 1, 1959, to November 30, 1960. No telecast.

ALBUM OF THE YEAR
• *Button Down Mind*, Bob Newhart. Warner Bros.
Belafonte Returns to Carnegie Hall, Harry Belafonte. RCA.
Brahms: Concerto No. 2 in B Flat, Sviatoslav Richter. RCA.
Nice 'n' Easy, Frank Sinatra. Capitol.
Puccini: Turandot, Erich Leinsdorf. RCA.
Wild Is Love, Nat "King" Cole. Capitol.

RECORD OF THE YEAR
• "Theme from *A Summer Place*," Percy Faith. Columbia.
"Are You Lonesome Tonight?" Elvis Presley. RCA.
"Georgia on My Mind," Ray Charles. ABC.
"Mack the Knife," Ella Fitzgerald. Verve.
✓"Nice 'n' Easy," Frank Sinatra. Capitol.

SONG OF THE YEAR
(Songwriter's Award)
• "Theme from *Exodus*," Ernest Gold.
"He'll Have to Go," Charles Green, Joe Allison, Audrey Allison.
✓ "Nice 'n' Easy," Lew Spence, Marilyn Keith, Alan Bergman.

"Second Time Around," Sammy Cahn, Jimmy Van Heusen.
"Theme from *A Summer Place*," Max Steiner.

BEST NEW ARTIST
• Bob Newhart. Warner Bros.
Brothers Four. Columbia.
Miriam Makeba. RCA.
Leontyne Price. RCA.
Joanie Sommers. Warner Bros.

BEST VOCAL PERFORMANCE, ALBUM, MALE
• Ray Charles, *Genius of Ray Charles*. Atlantic.
Harry Belafonte, *Belafonte Returns to Carnegie Hall*. RCA.
Nat "King" Cole, *Wild Is Love*. Capitol.
Elvis Presley, *G.I. Blues*. RCA.
Frank Sinatra, *Nice 'n' Easy*. Capitol.

BEST VOCAL PERFORMANCE, SINGLE OR TRACK, MALE
• Ray Charles, "Georgia on My Mind." ABC.
Johnny Mathis, "Misty." Columbia.
Elvis Presley, "Are You Lonesome Tonight?" RCA.
Jim Reeves, "He'll Have to Go." RCA.
✓Frank Sinatra, "Nice 'n' Easy." Capitol.

The year's biggest champ nabbed four trophies with The Genius of Ray Charles.

BEST VOCAL PERFORMANCE, ALBUM, FEMALE
• Ella Fitzgerald, *Mack the Knife, Ella in Berlin.* Verve.
Rosemary Clooney, *Clap Hands, Here Comes Rosie.* Columbia.
Peggy Lee, *Latin a la Lee.* Capitol.
Miriam Makeba, *Miriam Makeba.* RCA.
Della Reese, *Della.* RCA.

BEST VOCAL PERFORMANCE, SINGLE RECORD OR TRACK, FEMALE
• Ella Fitzgerald, "Mack the Knife." Verve.
Doris Day, "Sound of Music." Columbia.
Eileen Farrell, "I've Gotta Right to Sing the Blues." Columbia.
Brenda Lee, "I'm Sorry." Decca.
Peggy Lee, "I'm Gonna Go Fishin'." Capitol.

BEST PERFORMANCE BY A POP SINGLE ARTIST
• Ray Charles, "Georgia on My Mind." ABC.
Ella Fitzgerald, "Mack the Knife." Verve.
Peggy Lee, "Heart." Capitol.
Elvis Presley, "Are You Lonesome Tonight?" RCA.
√ Frank Sinatra, "Nice 'n' Easy." Capitol.

BEST PERFORMANCE BY A VOCAL GROUP
• Eydie Gormé, Steve Lawrence, "We Got Us." ABC.
Brothers Four, "Greenfields." Columbia.
Hi-Los, "All Over the Place." Columbia.
Kingston Trio, "Here We Go Again." Capitol.
Swe-Danes, "Scandinavian Shuffle." Warner Bros.

BEST PERFORMANCE BY A CHORUS
• Norman Luboff Choir, *Songs of the Cowboy.* Columbia.
Belafonte Folk Singers, *Belafonte Returns to Carnegie Hall.* RCA.
Ray Charles Singers, *Deep Night.* Decca.
Pete King Chorale, *My Favorite Things.* Kapp.
Robert Shaw Chorale, *What Wondrous Love.* RCA.

BEST PERFORMANCE BY A BAND FOR DANCING
• Count Basie, *Dance with Basie.* Roulette.
Les Brown, *Bandland.* Columbia.
Henry Mancini, *The Blues and the Beat.* RCA.
Billy May, *Girls & Boys on Broadway.* Capitol.
Perez Prado, *Big Hits by Prado.* RCA.

BEST PERFORMANCE BY AN ORCHESTRA
• Henry Mancini, *Mr. Lucky.* RCA.
Count Basie, *Count Basie Story.* Roulette.
Esquivel, *Infinity in Sound.* RCA.
Percy Faith, "Theme from *A Summer Place.*" Columbia.
Gerry Mulligan, *The Concert Jazz Band.* Verve.

BEST COUNTRY & WESTERN PERFORMANCE
• Marty Robbins, "El Paso." Columbia.
Johnny Horton, "North to Alaska." Columbia.
Ferlin Husky, "Wings of a Dove." Capitol.
Hank Locklin, "Please Help Me, I'm Falling." RCA.
Jim Reeves, "He'll Have to Go." RCA.

BEST PERFORMANCE, FOLK
• Harry Belafonte, "Swing Dat Hammer." RCA.
Belafonte Singers, "Cheers." RCA.
Brothers Four, "Greenfields." Columbia.

Jimmy Driftwood, *Songs of Billy Yank and Johnny Reb*. RCA.

Kingston Trio, "Here We Go Again." Capitol.

Alan Lomax, *Southern Folk Heritage Series*. Atlantic.

Ewan MacColl, *Songs of Robert Burns*. Folkways.

Miriam Makeba, *Miriam Makeba*. RCA.

BEST RHYTHM & BLUES PERFORMANCE
• Ray Charles, "Let the Good Times Roll." Atlantic.

LaVerne Baker, "Shake a Hand." Atlantic.

Hank Ballard, "Finger Poppin' Time." King.

Bo Diddley, "Walkin' and Talkin'." Checker.

John Lee Hooker, "Travelin'." VeeJay.

Etta James, "All I Could Do Was Cry." Argo.

Muddy Waters, "Got My Mojo Working." Chess.

Jackie Wilson, "Lonely Teardrops." Brunswick.

BEST JAZZ COMPOSITION, MORE THAN 5 MINUTES
(Composer's Award)
• *Sketches of Spain*, Miles Davis, Gil Evans. Columbia.

"Blues Suite," Bob Brookmeyer. Atlantic.

"Blue Rondo à la Turk," Dave Brubeck. Columbia.

Idiom '59 (Festival Session), Duke Ellington. Columbia.

"Newport Suite," Maynard Ferguson. Roulette.

"Western Suite," Jimmy Giuffre. Atlantic.

Sketch from Third Stream Music John Lewis. Atlantic.

BEST JAZZ PERFORMANCE, SOLO OR SMALL GROUP
• André Previn, *West Side Story*. Contempo.

Miles Davis, *Jazz Track*. Columbia.

Duke Ellington, Johnny Hodges, *Back to Back*. Verve.

Dizzy Gillespie and His Octet, *The Greatest Trumpet of Them All*. Verve.

Lambert, Hendricks & Ross, *The Hottest New Group in Jazz*. Columbia.

Modern Jazz Quartet, *Pyramid*. Atlantic.

George Shearing, *White Satin*. Capitol.

Art Tatum, *Greatest Piano of Them All*. Verve.

BEST JAZZ PERFORMANCE, LARGE GROUP
• Henry Mancini, *The Blues and the Beat*. RCA.

Count Basie, *The Count Basie Story*. Roulette.

Miles Davis, Gil Evans, *Sketches of Spain*. Columbia.

Quincy Jones, *The Great Wide World of Quincy Jones*. Mercury.

Gerry Mulligan, *I'm Gonna Go Fishin'*. Verve.

Recording Artists, *Spirituals to Swing Concert*. Vanguard.

BEST CLASSICAL PERFORMANCE, ORCHESTRA
(Conductor's Award)
• Fritz Reiner conducting Chicago Symphony, *Bartók: Music for Strings, Percussion and Celeste*. RCA.

Sir Thomas Beecham conducting Royal Philharmonic, *Haydn: Solomon Symphonies Volume 2*. Capitol.

Leonard Bernstein conducting New York Philharmonic, *Ives: Symphony No. 2*. Columbia.

Aaron Copland conducting Boston Symphony, *Copland: Appalachian Spring*. RCA.

Morton Gould conducting Morton Gould Orchestra, *Grofé: Grand Canyon Suite*. RCA.

Josef Krips conducting London Symphony, *Schubert: Symphony No. 9*. London.

Pierre Monteux conducting Boston Symphony, *Stravinsky: Petruchka*. RCA.

Eugene Ormandy conducting Philadelphia Symphony, *Tchaikovsky: Sixth Symphony*. Columbia.

BEST CLASSICAL PERFORMANCE, VOCAL OR INSTRUMENTAL, CHAMBER MUSIC
• Laurindo Almeida, *Conversations with the Guitar*. Capitol.

Clifford Curzon and Vienna Octet, *Schubert: "Trout" Quintet*. London.

Joseph Eger, Henryk Szeryng, Victor Babin, *Brahms: Horn Trio; Beethoven: Sonata for Horn and Piano*. RCA.

Griller Quartet, *Haydn: Quartets, Op. 71 and 74*. Vanguard.

Juilliard Quartet, *Debussy and Ravel Quartets*. RCA.

Yehudi Menuhin and Bach Festival Chamber Orchestra, *Bach: The Complete Brandenburg Concerti*. Capitol.

Robert Shaw Chorale, *Bach: Cantata No. 4; Christ Lag in Todesbaden*. RCA.

Smetana Quartet, *Janacek String Quartets, Nos. 1 and 2*. Artia.

BEST CLASSICAL PERFORMANCE, CONCERTO OR INSTRUMENTAL SOLOIST

• Sviatoslav Richter (Leinsdorf conducting Chicago Symphony), *Brahms: Piano Concerto No. 2 in B Flat*. RCA.

Gervase De Peyer (Maag conducting London Symphony), *Mozart: Clarinet Concerto*. London.

Malcolm Frager (Leibowitz conducting Paris Conservatoire), *Prokofiev: Concerto No. 2*. RCA.

Zino Francescatti, Pierre Fournier (Bruno Walter conducting Columbia Symphony), *Brahms: Double Concerto (Concerto for Violin and Cello in A Minor)*. Columbia.

Glenn Gould (Vladimir Golschmann conducting Columbia Symphony), *Bach: Concerto No. 5*. Columbia.

Jascha Heifetz (Walter Hendl conducting Chicago Symphony), *Sibelius: Violin Concerto in D*. RCA.

Rudolf Serkin (Eugene Ormandy conducting Philadelphia Symphony), *Brahms: Piano Concerto No. 2*. Columbia.

Van Cliburn (Fritz Reiner conducting Chicago Symphony), *Schumann: Piano Concerto in A*. RCA.

BEST CLASSICAL PERFORMANCE, INSTRUMENTAL SOLOIST OR DUO (OTHER THAN ORCHESTRA)

• Laurindo Almeida, *The Spanish Guitars of Laurindo Almeida*. Capitol.

Julian Bream, *The Art of Julian Bream*. RCA.

Vladimir Horowitz, *Pictures at an Exhibition*. RCA.

Wanda Landowska, *Haydn ... Landowska*. RCA.

Jaime Laredo, *Bach: Partita No. 3 in E; Brahms: Sonata No. 3 in D Minor*. RCA.

Paul Maynard, *Brahms: Keyboard Music of the French Court*. American Society of Concerts in Home.

Sviatoslav Richter, *Prokofiev: Sonata No. 7 and Pictures at an Exhibition*. Artia.

Artur Rubinstein, *Chopin: Ballades*. RCA.

BEST CLASSICAL PERFORMANCE, CHORAL (INCLUDING ORATORIO)

• Sir Thomas Beecham conducting Royal Philharmonic and Chorus (solos: Vyvyan, Sinclair, Vicki, Tozzi), *Handel: The Messiah*. RCA.

Moravian Festival Chorus, *Arias, Anthems and Chorales of American Moravians, Vol. 1*. Columbia.

Charles Munch and New England Conservatory Chorus, *Berlioz: Requiem*. RCA.

Fritz Reiner, Vienna Philharmonic Society of Friends of Music of Vienna, *Verdi: Requiem*. RCA.

Robert Shaw Chorale, *Bach: Motet No. 3 "Jesu Meine Freude."* RCA.

Maria Stader, Sieglinde Wagner, Hans Ernst Haefliger, Kim Borg, *Dvorak: Requiem*. DGG.

Roger Wagner Chorale, *Vaughan Williams: Mass in G Minor; Bach: Christ Lay in the Bonds of Death*. Capitol.

BEST CLASSICAL OPERA PRODUCTION

• *Puccini: Turandot*, Erich Leinsdorf, Rome Opera House Chorus and Orchestra (solos: Tebaldi, Nilsson, Björling, Tozzi). RCA.

Boito: Mefistofele, Tullio Serafin (solos: Siepi, Tebaldi, Del Monaco). London.

Britten: Peter Grimes, Benjamin Britten conducting Royal Opera Chorus and Orchestra (solos: Pears, Pease, Watson). London.

Mozart: Don Giovanni, Josef Krips (solos: Siepi, Danco, Dermote, Corena). London.

Poulenc, Cocteau: La Voix Humaine, Georges Pretre conducting Paris Opera Comique and National Theatre Orchestra (solo: Duval). RCA.

Puccini: La Bóhème, Tullio Serafin conducting L' Accademia di Santa Cecilia (solos: Tebaldi, Bergonzi, Bastianini, Corena). London.

Verdi: Aida, Herbert von Karajan conducting Vienna Singverim & Vienna Philharmonic (solos: Tebaldi, Bergonzi, Simionato, Corena). London.

Verdi: La Traviata, Tullio Serafin conducting Rome Opera Chorus and Orchestra (solos: de los Angeles, Del Monte, Sereni). Capitol.

Verdi: Macbeth, Erich Leinsdorf conducting Metropolitan Opera Chorus and Orchestra (solos: Warren, Hines, Rysanek, Bergonzi). RCA.

BEST CLASSICAL PERFORMANCE, VOCAL SOLOIST
- Leontyne Price, *A Program of Song*. RCA.

Eileen Farrell, *Arias in Great Tradition*. Columbia.

Dietrich Fischer-Dieskau, *Schubert: Songs, Album 3*. Angel.

Maureen Forrester, *Mahler: Kindertotenlieder*. RCA.

Peter Pears, *Britten: Nocturne*. London.

Joan Sutherland, *Handel: Arias*. Oiseau-Lyre.

Salli Terri, *Conversations with the Guitar*. Capitol.

Cesare Valletti, *Schumann: Dichterliebe*. RCA.

BEST CONTEMPORARY CLASSICAL COMPOSITION
- *Orchestral Suite from* Tender Land, Aaron Copland. RCA.

Symphony No. 1, Easley Blackwood. RCA.

Sonata for Cello and Piano, Paul Hindemith. RCA.

Symphony No. 2, Charles Ives. Columbia.

La Voix Humaine, Francois Poulenc. RCA.

Symphony No. 1, Roger Sessions. Composition.

Threni, Igor Stravinsky. Columbia.

Density 21.5, Edgard Varese. Columbia.

BEST ENGINEERING CONTRIBUTION, CLASSICAL RECORDING
- Hugh Davies, *The Spanish Guitars of Laurindo Almeida*. Capitol.

John Kraus, *The Two Pianos of Leonard Pennario*. Capitol.

Lewis Layton, *Bartók: Music for Strings, Percussion and Celeste* (Reiner conducting Chicago Symphony). RCA.

Lewis Layton, *Berlioz: Requiem* (Charles Munch conducting New England Conservatory Chorus and Boston Symphony). RCA.

Lewis Layton, *Prokofiev: Alexander Nevsky* (Fritz Reiner conducting Chicago Symphony Orchestra). RCA.

Lewis Layton, *Puccini: Turandot* (Erich Leinsdorf conducting Rome Opera Chorus and Orchestra; solos: Tebaldi, Nilsson, Bjoerling, Tozzi). RCA.

Lewis Layton, *R. Strauss: Don Quixote* (Fritz Reiner conducting Chicago Symphony). RCA.

Leontyne Price's soprano was a "voice of real stature," said High Fidelity.

BEST SHOW ALBUM, ORIGINAL CAST
(Composer's Award)
- *The Sound of Music*, Richard Rodgers, Oscar Hammerstein. Columbia.

Bye Bye Birdie, Charles Strouse, Lee Adams. Columbia.

Camelot, Alan Jay Lerner, Frederick Loewe. Columbia.

Fiorello! Jerry Bock, Sheldon Harnick. Capitol.

The Unsinkable Molly Brown, Meredith Willson. Capitol.

BEST SOUND TRACK ALBUM OR RECORDING OF ORIGINAL CAST FROM A MOTION PICTURE OR TELEVISION
(Composer's Award)
- *Can-Can*, Cole Porter (film cast with Frank Sinatra). Capitol.

Bells are Ringing, Betty Comden, Adolph Green, Jule Styne (film cast with Judy Holliday, Dean Martin). Capitol.

G.I. Blues, Elvis Presley. RCA.

Li'l Abner, Nelson Riddle. Columbia.

BEST SOUND TRACK ALBUM OR RECORDING OF MUSIC SCORE FROM A MOTION PICTURE OR TELEVISION
(Composer's Award)
- *Exodus*, Ernest Gold. RCA.

The Apartment, Adolph Deutsch. United Artists.

Ben-Hur, Dr. Miklos Rozsa. MGM.

Mr. Lucky, Henry Mancini. RCA.

The Untouchables, Nelson Riddle. Capitol.

BEST ARRANGEMENT
• Henry Mancini, *Mr. Lucky*. RCA.
Don Costa, "Theme from *The Apartment*" (Ferrante & Teicher). United Artists.
Percy Faith, "Theme from *A Summer Place*" (Percy Faith and His Orchestra). Columbia.
Bill Holman, "I'm Gonna Go Fishing" (Gerry Mulligan). Verve.
Quincy Jones, "Let the Good Times Roll" (Ray Charles). Atlantic.
Nelson Riddle, "Nice 'n' Easy" (Frank Sinatra). Capitol.
Dick Schory, "Wild Percussion and Horns A'Plenty" (Dick Schory). RCA.
George Shearing, Billy May, "Honeysuckle Rose" (George Shearing). Capitol.

BEST PERFORMANCE, DOCUMENTARY OR SPOKEN WORD (OTHER THAN COMEDY)
• Franklin Delano Roosevelt, *F.D.R. Speaks*. Robert Bialek, A&R Productions. Washington.
Henry Fonda, *Voices of the Twentieth Century*. Decca.
Sir John Gielgud, *Ages of Man, Vol. 2 (One Man in His Time) Part Two — Shakespeare*. Columbia.
Archibald MacLeish, *J.B*. RCA.

BEST COMEDY PERFORMANCE, SPOKEN WORD
• Bob Newhart, *Button Down Mind Strikes Back*. Warner Bros.
Shelley Berman, *The Edge of Shelley Berman*. Verve.
Carl Reiner, Mel Brooks, *2,000 Year Old Man*. World Pacific.
Jonathan Winters, *The Wonderful World of Jonathan Winters*. Verve.

BEST COMEDY PERFORMANCE, MUSICAL
• Paul Weston, Jo Stafford, *Jonathan and Darlene Edwards in Paris*. Columbia.
Stan Freberg, *The Old Payola Roll Blues*. Capitol.
Homer and Jethro, *Homer and Jethro at the Country Club*. RCA.
Tom Lehrer, *An Evening Wasted with Tom Lehrer*. Lehrer.
David Seville, *Alvin for President*. Liberty.

BEST ALBUM CREATED FOR CHILDREN
• *Let's All Sing with the Chipmunks*, David Seville. Liberty.
Adventures in Music, Grade 3, Volume 1, Howard Mitchell. RCA.
Dr. Seuss Presents: Bartholomew and the Oobleck, Dr. Seuss. Camden.
Folk Songs for Young People, Pete Seeger. Folkways.
Mother Goose Nursery Rhymes, Sterling Holloway. Disneyland.
Stories and Songs of the Civil War, Ralph Bellamy. RCA.

BEST ENGINEERING CONTRIBUTION, POPULAR RECORDING
• Luis P. Valentin, *Ella Fitzgerald Sings the George and Ira Gershwin Songbook*. Verve.
Robert Fine, *Persuasive Percussion No. 2*. Commodore.
John Kraus, *Wild Is Love* (Nat "King" Cole). Capitol.
John Norman, *Infinity in Sound* (Esquivel). RCA.
Robert Simpson, *Belafonte Returns to Carnegie Hall* (Harry Belafonte). RCA.
Robert Simpson, *Wild Percussion and Horns A'Plenty* (Dick Schory). RCA.
Luis P. Valentin, *Louis Bellson Swings Jule Styne*. Verve.

BEST ENGINEERING CONTRIBUTION, NOVELTY
• John Kraus, *The Old Payola Roll Blues* (Stan Freberg). Capitol.
George Fernandez, *Mr. Custer* (Larry Verne). Era.
Ted Keep, *Alvin for President* (David Seville & the Chipmunks). Liberty.
Ted Keep, *Let's All Sing with the Chipmunks* (David Seville and the Chipmunks). Liberty.
John Kraus, *June Night* (Jack Cookerly). Capitol.
Thorne Nogar, *Spike Jones in Hi-Fi*. Warner Bros.
Robert Simpson, John Crawford, Tony Salvatore, *New Sounds America Loves Best* (John Klein). RCA.

BEST ALBUM COVER
(Art Director's Award)

- Marvin Schwartz, *Latin a la Lee* (Peggy Lee). Capitol.

Marvin Israel, *Bean Bags* (Milt Jackson). Atlantic.

Bob Jones, *Carlos Montoya*. RCA.

Bob Jones, *Prokofiev: Alexander Nevsky* (Reiner conducting Chicago Symphony). RCA.

Bob Jones, *Stravinsky: Petruchka* (Monteux conducting Boston Symphony). RCA.

Bob Jones, *Tchaikovsky: Nutcracker Suite Excerpts* (Reiner conducting Chicago Symphony). RCA.

Bob Jones, *Wild Percussion and Horns A' Plenty* (Dick Schory). RCA.

Sheldon Marks, *Ella Fitzgerald Sings the George and Ira Gershwin Songbook*. Verve.

Irving Werbin, *Now! Fred Astaire*. Kapp.

"Moon" Walks — and Rock Finally Rolls

At last, at the very formal awards ceremonies held in New York, Los Angeles, and Chicago, there no longer seemed to be any blatant "conspiracy" to keep those rock & roll ruffians from the door. In fact, the entryway was even cracked open for them by a welcome new category — Best Rock & Roll Recording — which was overseen by a specially appointed panel that was determined to get the selection right. The award went to Chubby Checkers's "Let's Twist Again," which ranked 42 in *Billboard*'s Hot 100. Last year N.A.R.A.S. voters failed even to nominate the original "Twist" when it was in the Top 10.

In New York, 500 people packed the Waldorf-Astoria ballroom where the entertainment included Tony Bennett, Buddy Hackett (who, in an unscheduled appearance, "offered a bit of fast and funny patter that broke the place up," said *Variety*), and Si Zentner & His Orchestra (who won the Best Performance by an Orchestra for Dancing Grammy for *Up a Lazy River*). Presenters included Burl Ives, Steve Lawrence, Leslie Uggams, George Shearing, and Jimmy Dean. Out west, at the Beverly Hills Hotel, 700 gathered to enjoy entertainment by the Dave Pell Octet and last year's multiple winning Best New Artist Bob Newhart. Among the presenters were Vic Damone, Connie Stevens, Percy Faith, Gordon and Sheila MacRae, and André Previn, who reaped a jazz statuette for *André Previn Plays Harold Arlen*. The Chicago N.A.R.A.S. chapter hosted a cocktail party at the Sheraton-Chicago Hotel while its members kept track of the proceedings out east and west via telephone.

Chubby Checker's "Let's Twist Again" won the first r&r award after N.A.R.A.S. bypassed the original "Twist" last year.

As in three out of the past four years, the big winner was Henry Mancini, who took an unprecedented five awards in one night, bringing his career tally so far to nine. He would go on to win 11 more by 1993, making him the fourth most honored artist in Grammy history.

All of Mancini's new prizes were for his film score to *Breakfast at Tiffany's*, Truman Capote's tale of a small-town girl (played by Audrey Hepburn) who becomes recklessly hip when she moves to New York City. The movie was directed by Blake Edwards, who had hired Mancini several years earlier to score his new TV show *Peter Gunn*.

Mancini's collection of jazzy tunes from that series won him Grammy's first Album of the Year award.

Now Mancini was back to claim the other two top prizes: Song of the Year, with lyricst Johnny Mercer, and Record of the Year, both for "Moon River." The same cut from his soundtrack LP also brought him the Best Arrangement prize (for a third time) while the disc won best soundtrack album and best non-dance orchestral performance, too. Earlier in the year, *Breakfast at Tiffany's* and "Moon River" won two equivalent awards at the Oscars — Best Original Score and Best Song. "This is the year of Henry Mancini," *Variety* announced.

In his memoirs, Mancini recalls creating "Moon River": "That song was one of the toughest I have ever had to write. It took me a month to think it through." After finally coming up with melody, he and Mercer met in the ballroom of the Beverly Wilshire Hotel to join the music with words. "Every once in a while you hear something so right that it gives you chills, and when he sang that 'huckleberry friend' line, I got them," Mancini adds. "It made you think of Mark Twain and Huckleberry Finn's trip down the Mississippi. It had such echoes of America. It was the clincher."

The choice of Album of the Year marked a dramatic professional resurrection. Judy Garland's career in the 1950s had endured a series of peaks and valleys, but by the early '60s was at its lowest point ever while Garland privately battled addictions to drugs and alcohol. Her hopes for a comeback hung on a concert at Carnegie Hall that would distinguish her as one of the first popular artists ever to take the stage at America's reigning showcase of classical music. On the night of April 23, 1961, show biz's glitterati filled the auditorium to witness the result. In the audience were Richard Burton, Rock Hudson, Harold Arlen, Myrna Loy, Henry Fonda, and Julie Andrews.

The performance they beheld was transcendent. "She was bringing down the house with every song," claimed critic Richard Schickel. "Never saw the like in my life," Hedda Hopper added. "We laughed, cried and split our gloves applauding .... She was sensational as she clowned, talked, danced a bit and used the mike as though it were a trumpet." After the two-and-a-half-hour performance of 26 songs, including "The Man That Got Away," "Swanee," "Chicago," and "Over the Rainbow," *The New York World Telegram* concluded, "This kid is still a killer." Capitol's two-disc live recording of her performance topped the LP charts for 13 weeks (and was still in *Variety*'s Top 10 lineup a year later during the week of the Grammy Awards). In addition to the Album of the Year trophy, *Judy at Carnegie Hall* won three other honors: Best Female Solo Vocal Performance, best engineering, and Best Album Cover.

The best male vocal laurels went to Jack Jones, who was hailed by his promoters as the "Sinatra of the Sixties." Jones's clean good looks and melodic light baritone made him something of an anachronism in the burgeoning loud and scruffy rock era as he crooned such hits as "Lollipops and Roses," which earned him the Grammy and even more swooning fans among the female record-buying set. But Jones was successful at demonstrating his serious vocal ability, too, and critics

A record five awards for **Breakfast at Tiffany's** *made it "the year of Henry Mancini."*

The first concert LP to win Album of the Year marked a dramatic comeback for Garland. "This kid is still a killer," one critic declared.

by and large regarded him as no mere junior imitator of Ol' Blue Eyes. Another tribute to old-fashioned pop music came with the selection of the year's Best New Artist — pianist Peter Nero — whose signature sound was safe, but jazzy.

In 1961, singer Jimmy Dean had his own weekly TV series featuring popular country music, but it wasn't until he recorded "Big Bad John" that he had his own first million-selling song and the number-four platter of the year. The success of "Big Bad John" was something of a fluke. Dean needed a tune to fill up the "B" side of a new single he had coming out and wrote it in an hour and a half while on a plane ride to Nashville. The song told the tale of a supposedly sinister fellow who dies while saving others from a mining accident, and apparently it touched just the right chord among both record buyers and N.A.R.A.S. voters. "Big Bad John" began the Grammy race with four nominations and ended up with the big prize for Best Country & Western Recording.

Last year's winner of the best male

vocal honors (the two awards for album and single performance were combined this year) returned with the Best Rhythm & Blues Recording — "Hit the Road, Jack," Ray Charles's third million-selling single. André Previn came back, too, repeating the same award he got last year (Best Jazz Performance, Soloist or Small Group) for his tribute to composer Harold Arlen. Last year Previn won it for his recording of Leonard Bernstein's *West Side Story* score. Stan Kenton and his band gave the same music their own interpretation this year and won the jazz award for large groups. The most sought-after singers in the jazz world — Lambert, Hendricks & Ross — were honored for giving the Best Performance by a Vocal Group in *High Flying*. It was Galt MacDermot, who ended up with the most prizes, though, by taking two statuettes (for Best Instrumental Theme and Best Original Jazz Composition), both for "African Waltz."

A new award was added this year for Best Gospel or Other Religious Recording; it went to Mahalia Jackson for her hallelujah vocals on "Every Time I Feel the Spirit." (Jackson scored another professional triumph earlier in the year when she sang at John F. Kennedy's inauguration ceremony.) N.A.R.A.S. also introduced a new Classical Album of the Year award, which went to one of the truly classic LPs of recent times, even though some purists still grumble about occasional sound imperfections of its taping. The winner was *Stravinsky Conducts, 1960: Le Sacre du Printemps; Petruchka. Printemps* and *Petruchka* were two ballets written by Igor Stravinsky for Diaghilev's Ballets Russes. Stravinsky himself conducted the Columbia Symphony Orchestra in what are now considered the definitive performances.

Last year's winner of two Grammys, Brazilian-born American guitarist Laurindo Almeida, returned to take two more, stirring up some controversy, since Almeida was a popular member of the academy's board of governors in addition to being a frequent nominee. In a tie with Movements for Piano and Orchestra, composed by Stravinsky, Almeida shared the award for Best Contemporary Classical Composition for *Discantus*. Beating out Vladimir Horowitz and Andrés Segovia, he was also acknowledged for giving the best solo instrumental performance on *Reverie for Spanish Guitars*, in which Almeida played as many as three guitars at once (on overlapping tapes) while performing such works as Maurice Ravel's "Pavanne for a Dead Princess." The Boston Symphony Orchestra, under the baton of Charles Munch, also played Ravel, resulting in two Grammys, both for *Daphnis et Chloë*: Best Classical Performance by an Orchestra and best engineering.

In opera, reviewers of Grammy's choices were in sound agreement. *High Fidelity* said of Puccini's *Madama Butterfly* performed by the Rome Opera Chorus and Orchestra with Gabriele Santini conducting (Best Opera Recording and Best Classical Album Cover): "Capitol's new version of *Madama Butterfly* is especially welcome, for it offers not only Victoria de los Angeles as Cio-Cio-San, but Jussi Björling as Pinkerton and Mario Sereni as Sharpless, making this the best sung *Butterfly* in the catalog."

The best classical performance by a vocal soloist was given by Australian soprano Joan Sutherland, who became famous in 1959 after singing the title role in Donizetti's *Lucia di Lammermoor* at Covent Garden in London, a role she reprised in 1961 in her New York debut at the Metropolitan. About her *The Art of the Prima Donna*, in which she sang works by George Handel and Thomas Arne, *High Fidelity* wrote: "This album exhilarates ... Joan Sutherland takes 16 tests in Advanced Vocalism, and sails through them with startling freedom, scattering *grupetti* and *volate* as she goes."

Jack Jones won best male vocalist and women's hearts, too, with his hit "Lollipops and Roses."

"RCA went ahead of the field to cop 12 Grammys," *Variety* wrote, reporting on the winners from the industry viewpoint. It was the third year in a row that RCA won so big, triggering further complaints from smaller record companies. "Capitol (and its Angel subsidiary) ran second with 10 prizes and Columbia took show money with eight awards."

1961

Awards bestowed on May 29, 1962, at ceremonies held simultaneously at the Beverly Hills Hotel in Los Angeles and the Waldorf-Astoria Hotel in New York for the eligibility period December 1, 1960, to November 30, 1961. The N.A.R.A.S. Chicago chapter held a concurrent cocktail party at the Sheraton-Chicago Hotel. No telecast.

ALBUM OF THE YEAR
• *Judy at Carnegie Hall*, Judy Garland. Capitol.
Breakfast at Tiffany's, Henry Mancini. RCA.
Genius + Soul = Jazz, Ray Charles. Impulse.
Great Band with Great Voices, Si Zentner, Johnny Mann Singers. Liberty.

The Nat Cole Story, Nat "King" Cole. Capitol.

West Side Story (Soundtrack), Johnny Green, music director. Columbia.

RECORD OF THE YEAR
• "Moon River," Henry Mancini. RCA.

"Big Bad John," Jimmy Dean. Columbia.

"The Second Time Around," Frank Sinatra. Reprise.

"Take Five," Dave Brubeck. Columbia.

"Up a Lazy River," Si Zentner. Liberty.

SONG OF THE YEAR
(Songwriter's Award)
• "Moon River," Henry Mancini, Johnny Mercer. RCA.

"A Little Bitty Tear," Hank Cochran. Decca.

"Big Bad John," Jimmy Dean. Columbia.

"Lollipops and Roses," Tony Velona. Kapp.

"Make Someone Happy," Jule Styne, Betty Comden, Adolph Green. RCA.

BEST NEW ARTIST
• Peter Nero. RCA.

Ann-Margret. RCA.

Dick Gregory. Colpix.

Lettermen. Capitol.

Timi Yuro. Liberty.

BEST SOLO VOCAL PERFORMANCE, MALE
• Jack Jones, "Lollipops and Roses." Kapp.

Jimmy Dean, "Big Bad John." Columbia.

Burl Ives, "A Little Bitty Tear." Decca.

Steve Lawrence, "Portrait of My Love." United Artists.

Andy Williams, "Danny Boy." Columbia.

BEST SOLO VOCAL PERFORMANCE, FEMALE
• Judy Garland, *Judy at Carnegie Hall*. Capitol.

Ella Fitzgerald, *Mr. Paganini*. Verve.

Billie Holiday, *The Essential Billie Holiday (Carnegie Hall Concert)*. Verve.

Lena Horne, *Lena at the Sands*. RCA.

Peggy Lee, *Basin Street East*. Capitol.

BEST PERFORMANCE BY A VOCAL GROUP
• Lambert, Hendricks & Ross, *High Flying*. Columbia.

Four Freshmen, *Voices in Fun*. Capitol.

Kingston Trio, *Close Up*. Capitol.

Lettermen, *The Way You Look Tonight*. Capitol.

Limeliters, *The Slightly Fabulous Limeliters*. RCA.

BEST PERFORMANCE BY A CHORUS
• Johnny Mann Singers (Si Zentner Orchestra), *Great Band with Great Voices*. Liberty.

Belafonte Folk Singers, *Belafonte Folk Singers at Home and Abroad*. RCA.

Norman Luboff Choir, *This Is Norman Luboff*. RCA.

Pete King Chorale, *Hey, Look Me Over*. Kapp.

Roger Wagner Chorale, *A Song at Twilight*. Capitol.

BEST ROCK & ROLL RECORDING
• "Let's Twist Again," Chubby Checker. Parkway.

"Goodbye Cruel World," James Darren. Colpix.

"I Like It Like That," Chris Kenner. Instant.

"It's Gonna Work Out Fine," Ike & Tina Turner. Sue.

"The Lion Sleeps Tonight," Tokens. RCA.

BEST RHYTHM & BLUES RECORDING
• "Hit the Road, Jack," Ray Charles. ABC-Paramount.

"Bright Lights, Big City," Jimmy Reed. Vee Jay.

"Fool That I Am," Etta James. Argo.

"Mother in Law," Ernie K-Doe. Minit.

"Saved," Laverne Baker. Atlantic.

BEST ORIGINAL JAZZ COMPOSITION
(Composer's Award)
• "African Waltz," Galt MacDermot. Riverside.

"A Touch of Elegance," André Previn. Columbia.

"Gillespiana," Lalo Schifrin. Verve.

"Perceptions," J.J. Johnson. Verve.

"Unsquare Dance," Dave Brubeck. Columbia.

BEST JAZZ PERFORMANCE, SOLOIST OR SMALL GROUP (INSTRUMENTAL)
• André Previn, *André Previn Plays Harold Arlen*. Contemporary.

Bill Evans Trio, *Bill Evans at the Village Vanguard*. Riverside.

Erroll Garner. *Dreamstreet*. ABC-Paramount.

Al Hirt, *The Greatest Horn in the World*. RCA.

Modern Jazz Quartet, *European Concert*. Atlantic.

Best Jazz Performance, Large Group (Instrumental)
• Stan Kenton, *West Side Story*. Capitol.
Count Basie & Orchestra, *Basie at Birdland*. Roulette.
Gil Evans, *Out of the Cool*. ABC.
Dizzy Gillespie, *Gillespiana*. Verve.
André Previn, *A Touch of Elegance*. Columbia.

Best Country and Western Recording
• "Big Bad John," Jimmy Dean. Columbia.
"A Little Bitty Tear," Burl Ives. Decca.
"Hello Walls," Faron Young. Capitol.
"Hillbilly Heaven," Tex Ritter. Capitol.
"Walk On By," Leroy Van Dyke. Mercury.

Best Folk Recording
• *Belafonte Folk Singers at Home and Abroad*, Belafonte Folk Singers. RCA.
The Big Bill Broonzy Story, Bill Broonzy. Verve.
The Clancy Brothers and Tommy Makem, Clancy Brothers and Tommy Makem. Columbia.
Folk Songs of Britain, Vol. 1, Alan Lomax. Caedmon.
The Slightly Fabulous Limeliters, Limeliters. RCA.

Best Gospel or Other Religious Recording
• "Everytime I Feel the Spirit," Mahalia Jackson. Columbia.
Hymns at Home, Tennessee Ernie Ford. Capitol.
Jesus Keep Me Near the Cross, Prof. Alex Bradford. Choice.
Lincoln Hymns, Tex Ritter. Capitol.
Swing Low, Staple Singers. Veejay.

Best Performance by an Orchestra, for Dancing
• Si Zentner, *Up a Lazy River*. Liberty.
Les Brown, *The Lerner and Loewe Bandbook*. Columbia.
Glen Gray, Billy May, *Shall We Swing?* Capitol.
Quincy Jones, *I Dig Dancers*. Mercury.
Henry Mancini, *Mr. Lucky Goes Latin*. RCA.
Lawrence Welk, *Calcutta*. Dot.

Best Performance by an Orchestra, for Other Than Dancing
• Henry Mancini, *Breakfast at Tiffany's*. RCA.
Al Hirt, *The Greatest Horn in the World*. RCA.
Stan Kenton, *West Side Story*. Capitol.
Gerry Mulligan, *A Concert in Jazz*. Verve.
André Previn, *A Touch of Elegance*. Columbia.

The success of Jimmy Dean's Best Country & Western Recording "Big Bad John" was something of a fluke.

Best Instrumental Theme or Instrumental Version of Song (Composer's Award)
• "African Waltz," Galt MacDermot. Roulette.
"La Dolce Vita," Nino Rota. RCA.
"Paris Blues," Duke Ellington. Columbia.
"The Guns of Navarone," Dimitri Tiomkin. Columbia.
"Theme from *Carnival*," Robert Merrill. MGM.

Best Original Cast Show Album (Composer's Award)
• *How to Succeed in Business without Really Trying*, Frank Loesser. RCA.
Carnival, Robert Merrill. MGM.
Do Re Mi, Jule Styne, Betty Comden, Adolph Green. RCA.
Milk and Honey, Jerry Herman. RCA.
Wildcat, Cy Coleman, Carolyn Leigh. RCA.

Best Sound Track Album or Recording of Original Cast from Motion Picture or Television

• *West Side Story*, Johnny Green, Saul Chaplin, Sid Ramin, Irwin Kostal. Columbia.
Babes in Toyland, Tutti Camarata. Buena Vista.
Blue Hawaii, Elvis Presley. RCA.
Flower Drum Song, Alfred Newman, Ken Darby. Decca.
The Parent Trap, Tutti Camarata. Buena Vista.

Best Sound Track Album or Recording of Score from Motion Picture or Television

• *Breakfast at Tiffany's*, Henry Mancini. RCA.
Checkmate, Johnny Williams. Columbia.
The Guns of Navarone, Dimitri Tiomkin. Columbia.
La Dolce Vita, Nino Rota. RCA.
Paris Blues, Duke Ellington, Louis Armstrong. United Artists.

Best Arrangement

• Henry Mancini, "Moon River." RCA.
Bob Florence , "Up a Lazy River" (Si Zentner). Liberty.
J.J. Johnson, "Perceptions" (Dizzy Gillespie). Verve.
Peter Nero, "New Piano in Town." RCA.
George Russell, "All About Rosie" (Gerry Mulligan). Verve.

Album of the Year, Classical

• *Stravinsky Conducts, 1960: Le Sacre du Printemps; Petruchka*, Igor Stravinsky conducting Columbia Symphony. Columbia.
The Art of the Prima Donna, Joan Sutherland (Molinari - Pradelli, Royal Opera House Orchestra). London.
Block: Sacred Service, Leonard Bernstein, New York Philharmonic. Columbia.
Brahms: Symphony No. 2, William Steinberg, Pittsburgh Symphony. Command.
Reverie for Spanish Guitars, Laurindo Almeida. Capitol.

Best Contemporary Classical Composition
(Composer's Award—Tie)

• *Discantos*, Laurindo Almeida. Capitol.
• Movements for Piano and Orchestra, Igor Stravinsky. Columbia.

Gloria in G Major, Francois Poulenc. Angel.
Music for Brass Quintet, Gunther Schuller. Comp. Recordings.
String Quartet No. 2, Elliott Carter. RCA.

Best Classical Performance, Orchestra
(Conductor's Award)

• Charles Munch conducting Boston Symphony, *Ravel: Daphnis et Chloë*. RCA.
Herbert von Karajan conducting Philharmonia, *Bartók: Music for String Instruments, Percussion & Celesta; Hindemith: Mathis der Mahler*. Angel.
Fritz Reiner conducting Chicago Symphony, *R. Strauss: Don Juan; Debussy: La Mer*, RCA.
George Szell conducting Cleveland Orchestra, *R. Strauss: Don Quixote*, Epic.
Bruno Walter conducting Boston Symphony. *Bruckner: Symphony No. 4 in E Flat Major; Wagner: Tannhäuser Overture & Venusberg Music*. Columbia.

Best Classical Performance, Chamber Music

• Jascha Heifetz, Gregor Piatigorsky, William Primrose, *Beethoven: Serenade, Op. 8; Kodaly: Duo for Violin & Cello, Op. 7*. RCA.
Juilliard String Quartet, *Berg: Lyric Suite; Sebern: 5 Pieces for String Quartet, Op. 5, 6 Bagatelles, Op. 9*. RCA.
Leonard Pennario, Eudice Shapiro, Sanford Schonbach, Victor Gottlieb, *Fauré: First Quartet, Op. 15; Schumann: Clavier Quartet, Op. 47*. Capitol.
Gary Graffman, Berl Senofsky, *Fauré: Sonata No. 1; Debussy: Sonata No. 3*. RCA.
Erica Morini, Rudolf Firkusny, *Franck and Mozart Sonatas*. Decca.

Best Classical Performance, Instrumental Soloist
(with Orchestra)

• Isaac Stern (Ormandy conducting Philadelphia Orchestra), *Bartók: Concerto No. 1 for Violin & Orchestra*. Columbia.
Leon Fleisher (Szell conducting Cleveland Orchestra), *Beethoven: Emperor Concerto*. Epic.

Pierre Fournier (Szell conducting
Cleveland Orchestra), *R. Strauss: Don
Quixote*. Epic.
Jascha Heifetz, Gregor Piatigorsky
(Wallenstein conducting), *Brahms:
Double Concerto (Concerto in A for
Violin & Cello)*. RCA.
Andrés Segovia (Jorda conducting
Symphony of Air), *Boccherini,
Cassado: Concerto for Guitar*. Decca.

CLASSICAL PERFORMANCE, INSTRUMENTAL SOLOIST (WITHOUT ORCHESTRA)
• Laurindo Almeida, *Reverie for Spanish
Guitars*. Capitol.
Vladimir Horowitz, *Homage to Liszt*.
RCA.
Ruggerio Ricci, Bartók, Hindemith,
Prokofiev: Solo Violin Sonatas.
London.
Sviatoslav Richter, *Beethoven:
Appassionata Sonatas, Funeral March
Sonata*. RCA.
Andrés Segovia, *Bach: Suite No. 3*. Decca.

BEST OPERA RECORDING
(Conductor's Award)
• *Puccini: Madama Butterfly*, Gabriele
Santini conducting Rome Opera Chorus
and Orchestra (solos: de Los Angeles,
Bjoering, Pirazzini, Sereni). Capitol.
Donizetti: Lucia di Lammermoor, John
Pritchard conducting Chorus and
Orchestra of L'Accademia di Santa
Cecilia. (solos: Sutherland, Cioni,
Merrill, Siepi). London.
Mozart: The Marriage of Figaro, Carlo
Maria Giulini conducting Philharmonic
Orchestra and Chorus (solos:
Schwarzkopf, Moffo, Taddei, Wachter,
Cossotto). Angel.
R. Strauss: Elektra, Karl Bohm conducting
Orchestra and Chorus of Dresden State
Opera (solos: Borkh, Schech, Madeira,
Fischer-Dieskau, Uhl). Deutsche
Grammophon.
Wagner: The Flying Dutchman, Antal
Dorati conducting Royal Opera House
Orchestra (solos: London, Rysanek,
Tozzi, Enas, Liebl, Lewis). RCA.

BEST CLASSICAL PERFORMANCE, CHORAL (OTHER THAN OPERA)
• Robert Shaw Chorale (Robert Shaw
conducting), *Bach: B Minor Mass*.
RCA.

*Was N.A.R.A.S. favoring its own when
academy insider Laurindo Almeida
picked up two more classical awards?*

French National Radio-TV Chorus &
Orchestra (Yvonne Gouverne, director.
Georges Pretre, conducting), *Poulenc:
Gloria in G Major for Soprano Solo,
Chorus and Orchestra*. Angel.
Roger Wagner Chorale (Roger Wagner,
director. Alfred Wallenstein conducting
Los Angeles Philharmonic), *Respighi:
Laud to the Nativity; Monteverdi:
Magnificat*. Capitol.
Rutgers University Choir (F. Austin
Walter, director. Eugene Ormandy
conducting the Philadelphia Orchestra),
Walton: Belshazzar's Feast. Columbia.
St. Anthony Singers with Pears, Morrison
(Goldsbrough Orchestra, Colin Davis,
conducting), *Berlioz: L'Enfance Du
Christ*. Oiseau-Lyre.
Westminster Choir (Warren Martin,
director, Leonard Bernstein, conducting
the New York Philharmonic),
Beethoven: Missa Solemnis. Columbia.

BEST CLASSICAL PERFORMANCE, VOCAL SOLOIST

• Joan Sutherland (Molinari-Pradelli conducting Royal Opera House Orchestra), *The Art of the Prima Donna*. London.

Adele Addison (Conant, Russo, Orenstein), *Trimble: Four Fragments from the Canterbury Tales*. Columbia.

Victoria de los Angeles (Moore, pianist), *The Fabulous Victoria de los Angeles*. Angel.

Eileen Farrell (Bach Aria Group Orchestra), *Bach: Cantatas No. 58 & No. 202*. Decca.

Leontyne Price (Defabrutis conducting Rome Opera House Orchestra), *Operatic Arias*. RCA.

BEST ALBUM COVER, CLASSICAL
(Art Director's Award)

• Marvin Schwartz, Puccini: *Madama Butterfly* (solos: de los Angeles, Björling, Pirazzini, Sereni; Gabriele Santini conducting Rome Opera Chorus and Orchestra). RCA.

Robert Jones, *Albeniz: Iberia;* Ravel: *Rapsodie Espagnole* (Morel conducting Paris Conservatory Orchestra). RCA.

Robert Jones, *Gould Ballet Music: Fall River Legend, Interplay, Latin American Symphonette* (Gould & his Orchestra). RCA.

Meyer Miller, *Golden Age of English Lute Music* (Julian Bream). RCA.

Marvin Schwartz, *Beethoven: Nine Symphonies* (Klemperer conducting Philharmonia Orchestra). Angel.

BEST ENGINEERING CONTRIBUTION, CLASSICAL RECORDING

• Lewis W. Layton, *Ravel: Daphnis et Chloë* (Munch conducting Boston Symphony). RCA.

Robert Fine, *Brahms: Symphony No. 2* (Steinberg conducting Pittsburgh Symphony). Command.

Heinrich Keiholtz, *R. Strauss: Elektra*, (solos: Borkh, Schech, Madeira, Fischer-Dieskau, Uhl; Bohm conducting Orchestra and Chorus of Dresden State Opera). Deutsche Grammophon.

Chris Parker, *Prokofiev: Concerto No. 3* (solo: Browning; Leinsdorf conducting Philharmonia Orchestra). Capitol.

Paul Vavasseur, Walter Ruhlmann, *Poulenc: Concerto in G for Organ, Strings and Timpani*, (solo: Duruflé; Pretre conducting French National Radio-TV Orchestra). Angel.

BEST DOCUMENTARY OR SPOKEN WORD RECORDING, OTHER THAN COMEDY

• *Humor in Music*, Leonard Bernstein conducting New York Philharmonic. Columbia.

The Coming of Christ, Alexander Scourby. Robert Russell Bennett, conducting Decca.

More of Hal Holbrook in Mark Twain Tonight!, Hal Holbrook. Columbia.

Wisdom, Vol. I, Milt Gabler, producer. (Sandburg, Shapley, Nehru, Lipschitz). Decca.

The World of Dorothy Parker, Dorothy Parker. Verve.

BEST COMEDY PERFORMANCE

• Mike Nichols, Elaine May, *An Evening with Mike Nichols and Elaine May*. Mercury.

Bill Dana, *José Jimenez the Astronaut*. Kapp.

Stan Freberg, *Stan Freberg Presents the United States of America*. Capitol.

Carl Reiner, Mel Brooks, *2,001 Years with Carl Reiner and Mel Brooks*. Capitol.

Jonathan Winters. *Here's Jonathan*. Verve.

BEST RECORDING FOR CHILDREN

• *Prokofiev: Peter and the Wolf*, Leonard Bernstein, New York Philharmonic. Columbia.

Golden Treasury of Great Music and Literature, Arthur Shimkin, producer. Golden.

101 Dalmations, Tutti Carmarata, producer. Disney.

The Soupy Sales Show, Soupy Sales. Reprise.

Young Abe Lincoln (Original Broadway Cast), Arthur Shimkin, producer. Golden.

BEST ENGINEERING CONTRIBUTION, NOVELTY RECORDING

• John Kraus, *Stan Freberg Presents the United States of America*. Capitol.

Eddie Brackett, *The Soupy Sales Show*. Reprise.

Ted Keep, *The Alvin Show* (David Seville). Liberty.

Rafael O. Valentin, *X-15 and Other Sounds: Rockets Missiles & Jets.* Reprise.

Bruno Vineis, *Cartoons in Stereo* (Bob Prescott). Audio Fld.

BEST ENGINEERING CONTRIBUTION, POPULAR RECORDING

• Robert Arnold, *Judy at Carnegie Hall* (Judy Garland). Capitol.

Al Schmitt, *Breakfast at Tiffany's* (Henry Mancini). RCA.

Bill MacMeekin, *Cozy* (Steve Lawrence, Eydie Gormé). United Artists.

Al Schmitt, *Great Band with Great Voices* (Johnny Mann Singers). Liberty.

Robert Fine, *Stereo 35/MM* (Enoch Light). Command.

BEST ALBUM COVER
(Art Director's Award)

• Jim Silke, *Judy at Carnegie Hall* (Judy Garland). Capitol.

Bob Cato, *A Touch of Elegance* (André Previn). Columbia.

Ken Deardoff, *New Orleans—The Living Legend* (Peter Bocage). Riverside.

Robert Jones, *Breakfast at Tiffany's* (Henry Mancini). RCA.

Reid Miles, *Jackie's Bag* (Jackie McLean). Blue Note.

Of Hearts, Fools, and Kennedys

For the first time since the Grammys began, the music competition seemed to be proceeding harmoniously. "With a fairly large spread of record companies represented with nominations," *Variety* wrote, "the squawks that have hounded the Academy in the past years have been virtually eliminated." Rock & roll was still downplayed compared to its prominence on American jukeboxes and in record stores, but otherwise the nominations demonstrated a solid and fair mix of talent. Even *Down Beat* was upbeat: "Jazz recordings have never been as well represented as they are this year."

Vaughn Meader's Album of the Year The First Family *spoofed life in the Kennedy White House.*

The winner of the Record of the Year award was the trademark song of a performer Frank Sinatra once called "the greatest singer in the world." Tony Bennett has recorded more than 1,000 tunes on 100 albums over the course of his career, but it was "I Left My Heart in San Francisco" that became his professional anthem. Bennett's 1961 recording of it scored five nominations, including nods for Song, Record, and Album of the Year. It won three: Best Male Solo Performance and Best Background Arrangement, in addition to the top platter prize. It also sold more than two million copies in the early 1960s. In 1970, in a presentation made to Mayor Joseph Alioto in City Hall, Bennett gave the gold record he received as a result of its sales to the people of San Francisco, thereby leaving more than just his heart in the city often known as Baghdad by the Bay.

Song of the Year was "'What Kind of Fool Am I' from the Leslie Bricusse-Anthony Newley Broadway musical *Stop the World — I Want to Get Off*. Newley's single recording of "Fool" was up for the best male vocals honor, as was Sammy Davis, Jr.'s album of the same name. It was also Davis's single rendition that was contending for Record of the Year.

As it had two years earlier when Bob Newhart proved that the recording business was comprised of more than just music, the Album of the Year trophy went to a comedy LP for a second and,

WIDE WORLD PHOTO

as of this writing, last time. "President Kennedy's family held the top spot at the Grammys," *Variety* reported, "when one [award] was presented to comic Vaughn Meader for *The First Family*." Meader also received the prize for best comedy performance of the year.

Meader is remembered in comedy circles today as one of its most tragic figures. He was clearly America's leading political parodist of his day, but one whose career was wrongfully shot down the same day that gunfire made history in Dallas on November 22, 1963.

Meader's *The First Family* album was a breakthrough in humor recordings, being one of the first audio sitcoms on vinyl instead of yet another stand-up routine. When *The First Family* was released in 1962, it was a phenomenal success certified by the folks at the *Guinness Book of World Records* as the fastest-selling album of all time.

The LP was a gentle spoof of the Kennedy clan that included such silly scenes of life in the White House as young Caroline and little John taking a bath together and fighting over their floatable toys, screaming, "The rubber swan is mine!" When French president Charles De Gaulle comes to visit, a budget-conscious Kennedy orders out for sandwiches instead of giving the French general what he really wants: duck under glass. Meader chose to tweak the First Family more on a cute personal basis than a biting political one. (President Kennedy even tweaked back once, saying, "I listened to Mr. Meader's record, but I thought it sounded more like Teddy than it did me.") When Kennedy was assassinated in Dallas, the album was tossed out of homes and record stores across America. While other comics like Mort Sahl also lampooned Kennedy in the past and were able to prevail professionally after his death, Meader was unable to

rescue his career, despite countless comeback tries that even included him changing his name.

The choice of the top rock & roll recording was Bent Fabric's "Alley Cat," which beat out "Big Girls Don't Cry" by the Four Seasons and Neil Sedaka's "Breaking Up Is Hard to Do." Fabric was a notable Danish TV personality, musician, and record executive whose real name was Bent Fabricus Bjerre. "Alley Cat" was his only American hit, but it sold better than a million copies and marked the first time that a Danish tune became an American best seller, which it did for 18 weeks, peaking at number 12.

Peter, Paul & Mary burst onto the popular music scene in a big way in 1962. The folk troupe had a hip, cool style that caused one critic to label them "the Kingston Trio with sex appeal," and often landed them in the pop singles charts. ("Puff the Magic Dragon" was in *Variety*'s Top 10 the week of the 1962 Grammys, held in 1963.) They were nomi-

> *President Kennedy kidded Meader back, saying his comedy LP "sounded more like Teddy than it did me."*

nated for several awards, including Best New Artist, and reaped two (Best Vocal Group and Best Folk Recording), both for their recording of Pete Seeger's "If I Had a Hammer," which was the year's tenth-best selling single. Another folk group that became famous in 1962 (and was also up for the new artist honor) won the trophy for choral performance: the New Christy Minstrels, honored for their debut album.

The Best New Artist distinction

ended up going to Robert Goulet, the handsome 28-year-old baritone whom Judy Garland once called "a living eight-by-ten glossy." Goulet's matinee-star looks were literal: He gained renown on Broadway in 1960 as Lancelot in Lerner and Loewe's *Camelot,* also starring Richard Burton and Julie Andrews. Goulet had an album in the Top 20 for the year, *Two of Us,* but it was overlooked by the Grammys. *Variety* therefore called his prize one of the "odd bits" of the awards outcome. "Goulet copped the Best New Artist honor, but there was no record award to substantiate that accolade," it wrote. "In fact, Goulet didn't even have a disc nomination among the 240 platters in the competition."

Among industry veterans, several came back from past competitions to claim even more Grammys. Ella Fitzgerald nabbed her seventh for giving the best female vocal performance on her album salute to composer/arranger/conductor Nelson Riddle. *Great Songs of Love and Faith* won gospel contralto Mahalia Jackson her second consecutive Best Religious Recording award.

Ray Charles received his sixth career Grammy for the year's best r&b recording, "I Can't Stop Loving You," which he included on his first country & western album. In an interview with *Rolling Stone* years later, Charles recalled people warning him against making the LP. He recounted their admonishments: "'Hey, man, gee whiz, Ray, you got all these fans, you can't do no country-western things. You gonna lose all your fans!'" His *Modern Sounds in Country & Western Music* disc became the first million-seller for ABC-Paramount. "I Can't Stop Loving You" made it to number two in *Billboard*'s Hot 100 of 1962 and was nominated for five Grammys, three for Charles personally.

As *Down Beat* noted, jazz was get-ting better representation throughout the awards recently. The reason was largely that because N.A.R.A.S. had decided to redress "such misunderstandings in jazz and other music on the part of the membership," the magazine added. "One should note in passing that even the nominations for these awards are usually made in an open, preliminary balloting of the full membership," *Down Beat* said, but noted that for the past two years the recording academy had polled a number of jazz journalists among its membership for nomination recommendations.

"This is the first year that a jazz artist, Stan Getz, has been associated in eight categories of nominations," *Down Beat* noted in discussing the result of the changes. "Most of the Getz-associated nominations are for 'Desafinado' and *Jazz Samba,* the album from which the former came, both culled by the tenorist and guitarist Charlie Byrd. The 'Desafinado' performance or the album are nominated for record of the year, album of the year, best jazz performance by a soloist or small group, and best album cover. Getz's album *Focus,* written by Eddie Sauter, was nominated for best original jazz composition and best instrumental arrangement."

By 1962, Getz had become known as a "musician's musician" and the leading tenor sax player of the last decade. His frequent collaborator Byrd had recently traveled to Brazil, was impressed by the indigenous music he heard, and brought back seven songs he thought might work well to a jazz beat. Together he and Getz produced one of the top-selling albums in jazz lore and one that was singly responsible for popularizing the bossa nova sound (bossa nova means "new wave" or "new wrinkle") that would soon engulf the U.S. — and the Grammys. "Getz was established as the first American soloist to incorporate the idiom effectively into American jazz," critic Leonard Feather once wrote, "and to enrich it with rhythmic improvisational qualities that created a perfect marriage."

While Getz would snag three more awards in 1964, he won just one this year — the performance prize for "Desafinado." The composition award went to pianist Vince Guaraldi for "Cast Your Fate to the Winds." Henry Mancini had been nominated in four categories, but won only the Best Arrangement trophy for "Baby Elephant Walk."

The Classical Album of the Year was *Columbia Records Presents Vladimir Horowitz*, which also won the virtuoso pianist the solo instrumental award for performing works such as Chopin's *Sonata for Piano No. 2 in B Flat Minor* and Robert Schumann's *Arabeske in C, Opus 18*. Columbia's name was prominent in the title because the album was the artist's first release since his break with RCA. After 1953, Horowitz performed only on recordings (he returned to making live performances in 1965), so they were considered particularly valuable, not only for the rare chance to hear the artist play, but for his unique interpretation of the classics. "It's the silence that matters," he once told *Newsweek* about his approach, "the silence before and during the play, that is everything."

As of 1962, Columbia had recorded more than 40 compositions by Igor Stravinsky and now, in honor of the maestro turning 80, released seven more. Stravinsky's work dominated three of the other classical prizes. He had won Classical Album of the Year last year for new recordings of two dance scores he once wrote for the Ballets Russes, (*Petruchka* and *Le Sacre du Printemps*). This year he again conducted the Columbia Symphony Orchestra in another of his Ballets Russes scores, *The Firebird,* which earned him 1962's Best Classical Performance by an Orchestra. The maestro was also honored for Best Classical Composition for *The Flood*, a new musical theater work *High Fidelity* called "a kind of Mystery play." With Stravinsky again conducting the Columbia orchestra, Isaac Stern played his Concerto in D for Violin and won the solo instrumental prize for orchestral accompaniment.

Violinist Jascha Heifetz shared the chamber music award with cellist Gregor Piatigorsky for a recording of their four joint concerts with violinist William Primrose held at Hollywood's Pilgrimage Theater. For the winner of the choral accolade, *High Fidelity* had only the highest praise. Bach's *St. Matthew Passion,* as performed by a stellar cast including tenor Peter Pears, soprano Elisabeth Schwarzkopf, and bass Walter Berry, was, it said, "an overwhelming performance, with no weak spots." Soprano Eileen Farrell took the

Both Sammy Davis, Jr., and Anthony Newley recorded Song of the Year "What Kind of Fool Am I."

solo vocalist kudos for *Brunnhilde's Immolation Scene* by Wagner, with Leonard Bernstein conducting the New York Philharmonic. (She had performed it once before with Charles Munch and the Boston Symphony.) Sir Georg Solti, the person who has won more Grammys than anyone else as of this writing, garnered the first of his career for Verdi's *Aida,* which was sung by Leontyne Price. "The proportions are beautifully judged," *High Fidelity* said, although "Solti occasionally throws in a highly personal, almost eccentric note .... Price's *Aida* is nothing less than a revelation."

Tony Bennett's classic anthem "I Left My Heart in San Francisco" garnered three Grammys, including Record of the Year.

In other award categories, Burl Ives won the only Grammy of his long singing career for "Funny Way of Laughin'," which was judged best country & western platter. The theme song to the film *A Taste of Honey*, about a homely white girl who gets pregnant by a black sailor, would come back strong at the 1965 Grammys as Herb Alpert's Record of the Year, but this year won its first award, for Best Instrumental Theme, for writers Bobby Scott and Ric Marlow.

WNEW radio broadcast the New York end of the ceremonies, which was held at the Hotel Astor and emceed by the radio station's William B. Williams. Out on the west coast, Soupy Sales did the honors at the Beverly Hilton Hotel. Presenters included Henry Mancini, Les Brown, Connie Stevens, Nelson Riddle, and Johnny Mathis. The night's most touching moment involved the bestowal of the price for Best Spoken Word Recording. "An emotional scene was presented when actress Elsa Lanchester accepted the award for her late husband Charles Laughton, for his recording of *The Story Teller*," *Variety* reported. "This album makes Charles's life a little longer in a way," Lanchester said, "especially for his friends and family."

For the first time since 1959, the Grammys were back on television, but with a difference. Its "Best on Record" roundup show featured winners of the top prizes singing on sequences actually taped months after their victories were announced. N.A.R.A.S. had been lobbying the TV networks aggressively for a live show, but since it couldn't guarantee that celebrity winners would show up, the "Best on Record" was the best it could do.

The program had an ominous beginning. It was set to air on November 24, 1963 — just two days after the assassination of President Kennedy. Luckily for the academy, the program was moved to more than a week afterward, giving viewers a chance to cope with the shocking news. The "Best on Record" failed, however, to feature the person who won the best album prize. Kennedy impersonator Vaughn Meader was nixed from the program, even though he offered to substitute his usual Kennedy spoof with a serious personal tribute.

Awards bestowed on May 15, 1963, at ceremonies held simultaneously at the Beverly Hilton Hotel in Los Angeles and the Hotel Astor in New York for the eligibility period December 1, 1961, to November 30, 1962.

ALBUM OF THE YEAR
• *The First Family*, Vaughn Meader. Cadence.
I Left My Heart in San Francisco, Tony Bennett. Columbia.
Jazz Samba, Stan Getz, Charlie Byrd. Verve.
Modern Sounds in Country & Western Music, Ray Charles. ABC-Paramount.
My Son, the Folk Singer, Allan Sherman. Warner Bros.

RECORD OF THE YEAR
✓ • "I Left My Heart in San Francisco," Tony Bennett. Columbia.
"Desafinado," Stan Getz, Charlie Byrd. Verve.
"Fly Me to the Moon Bossa Nova," Joe Harnell and His Orchestra. Kapp.
"I Can't Stop Loving You," Ray Charles. ABC-Paramount.
✓ "Ramblin' Rose," Nat "King" Cole. Capitol.
"What Kind of Fool Am I," Sammy Davis, Jr. Reprise.

SONG OF THE YEAR
(Songwriter's Award)
• "What Kind of Fool Am I," Leslie Bricusse, Anthony Newley. London.
"As Long as He Needs Me," Lionel Bart. RCA.
✓ "I Left My Heart in San Francisco," Douglass Cross, George Cory. Columbia.
"My Coloring Book," John Kander, Fred Ebb. Colpix.
"The Sweetest Sounds," Richard Rodgers. Capitol.

BEST NEW ARTIST
• Robert Goulet. Columbia.
Four Seasons. Vee-Jay.
Vaughn Meader. Cadence.
New Christy Minstrels. Columbia.
Peter, Paul & Mary. Warner Bros.
Allan Sherman. Warner Bros.

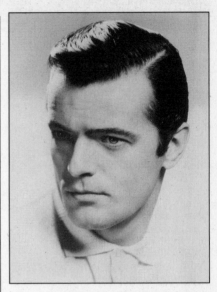

Judy Garland once called Grammy's Best New Artist of 1962 Robert Goulet "a living eight-by-ten glossy."

BEST SOLO VOCAL PERFORMANCE, MALE
✓ • Tony Bennett, "I Left My Heart in San Francisco." Columbia.
Ray Charles, "I Can't Stop Loving You." ABC-Paramount.
Sammy Davis, Jr., "What Kind of Fool Am I." Reprise.
Anthony Newley. "What Kind of Fool Am I." London.
Mel Tormé, "Comin' Home Baby." Atlantic.

BEST SOLO VOCAL PERFORMANCE, FEMALE
• Ella Fitzgerald, *Ella Swings Brightly with Nelson Riddle*. Verve.
Diahann Carroll, *No Strings*. Capitol.
Lena Horne, *Lena ... Lovely and Alive*. RCA.
Peggy Lee, "I'm a Woman." Capitol.
Ketty Lester, *Love Letters*. Era.
Sandy Stewart, "My Coloring Book." Colpix.
Pat Thomas, "Slightly Out of Tune, (Desafinado)." Verve.

BEST PERFORMANCE BY A VOCAL GROUP
• Peter, Paul & Mary, "If I Had a Hammer." Warner Bros.
Four Freshmen, *The Swingers*. Capitol.
Hi-Lo's, *The Hi-Lo's Happen to Folk Songs*. Reprise.
Lettermen, *A Song for Young Love*. Capitol.
Limeliters, *Through Children's Eyes*. RCA.

BEST PERFORMANCE BY A CHORUS
• New Christy Minstrels, *Presenting the New Christy Minstrels*. Columbia.
Pete King Chorale, *Consider Yourself*. Kapp.
Norman Luboff, *A Choral Spectacular*. RCA.
Johnny Mann Singers, (Si Zentner Orchestra), *Great Band with Great Voices Swing the Great Voices of the Great Bands*. Liberty.
Fred Waring & the Pennsylvanians, *The Waring Blend*. Capitol.

BEST ROCK & ROLL RECORDING
• "Alley Cat," Bent Fabric. Atco
"Big Girls Don't Cry," Four Seasons. Vee-Jay.
"Breaking Up Is Hard to Do," Neil Sedaka. RCA.
"Twistin' the Night Away," Sam Cooke. RCA.
"Up on the Roof," Drifters. Atlantic.
"You Beat Me to the Punch," Mary Wells. Motown.

BEST RHYTHM & BLUES RECORDING
• "I Can't Stop Loving You," Ray Charles. ABC-Paramount.
"Bring It on Home to Me," Sam Cooke. RCA.
"Comin' Home Baby," Mel Tormé. Atlantic.
"Loco-Motion," Little Eva. Dimension.
"Nut Rocker," B. Bumble and the Stingers. Rendezvous.
"What'd I Say," Bobby Darin. Atco.

BEST ORIGINAL JAZZ COMPOSITION
(Composer's Award)
• Vince Guaraldi, "Cast Your Fate to the Winds." Fantasy.
Paul Desmond, "Desmond Blue." RCA.
Quincy Jones, "Quintessence." Impulse.
Henry Mancini, "Sounds of *Hatari!*" RCA.

Stan Getz and Charlie Byrd's Jazz Samba *launched a nationwide bossa nova craze.*

Charlie Mingus, "Tijuana Moods." RCA.
Eddie Sauter, "Focus." Verve.
Lalo Schifrin, "Tunisian Fantasy." Verve.

BEST JAZZ PERFORMANCE, SOLOIST OR SMALL GROUP (INSTRUMENTAL)
• Stan Getz, "Desafinado." Verve.
Laurindo Almeida, *Viva Bossa Nova!* Capitol.
Eddie Cano, *A Taste of Honey*. Reprise.
Bill Evans, Jim Hall, *Undercurrent*. United Artists.
Charlie Mingus, *Tijuana Moods*. RCA.
Oscar Peterson Trio, *West Side Story*. Verve.
George Shearing Quintet, *Nat "King" Cole Sings, George Shearing Plays*. Capitol.

BEST JAZZ PERFORMANCE, LARGE GROUP (INSTRUMENTAL)
• Stan Kenton, *Adventures in Jazz*. Capitol.
Count Basie, *The Legend*. Roulette.
Miles Davis, Gil Evans (Orchestra), *Miles Davis at Carnegie Hall*. Columbia.
Duke Ellington, Count Basie, *First Time!* Columbia.
Stan Getz, Gary McFarland, *Big Band Bossa Nova*. Verve.
Dizzy Gillespie, *Carnegie Hall Concert*. Verve.
Jimmy Smith, *Walk on the Wild Side*. Verve.

BEST COUNTRY & WESTERN RECORDING
• "Funny Way of Laughin'," Burl Ives. Decca.
"Devil Woman," Marty Robbins. Columbia.
"It Keeps Right on A-Hurtin'," Johnny Tillotson. Cadence.
"P.T. 109," Jimmy Dean. Columbia.
"She Still Thinks I Care," George Jones. United Artists.
"Wolverton Mountain," Claude King. Columbia.

BEST FOLK RECORDING
• "If I Had a Hammer," Peter, Paul & Mary. Warner Bros.
"The Ballad of Jed Clampett," Flatt & Scruggs. Columbia.
Bob Dylan, Bob Dylan. Columbia.
Joan Baez in Concert, Joan Baez. Vanguard.
The Midnight Special, Harry Belafonte. RCA.
Presenting the New Christy Minstrels, New Christy Minstrels. Columbia.
Something Special, Kingston Trio. Capitol.

BEST GOSPEL OR OTHER RELIGIOUS RECORDING
• *Great Songs of Love and Faith*, Mahalia Jackson. Columbia.
Black Nativity, Prof. Alex Bradford (Marion Williams & Stars of Faith). Vee-Jay.
Hymns at Sunset, Ralph Carmichael. Capitol.
I Love to Tell the Story, Tennessee Ernie Ford. Capitol.
Inspiration—Great Music for Chorus & Orchestra, Norman Luboff Choir (Leopold Stokowki conducting the New Symphony Orchestra of London). RCA.
Marian Anderson—He's Got the Whole World in His Hands, and 18 Other Spirituals, Marian Anderson (Franz Rupp, piano). RCA.
Same Me, Clefs of Calvary. True Sound.

BEST PERFORMANCE BY AN ORCHESTRA FOR DANCING
• Joe Harnell, *Fly Me to the Moon Bossa Nova*. Kapp.
Laurindo Almeida, *Viva Bossa Nova!* Capitol.

Stan Getz, Gary McFarland, *Big Band Bossa Nova*. Verve.
Neal Hefti, *Jazz Pops*. Reprise.
Quincy Jones, *Big Band Bossa Nova*. Mercury.
David Rose, *The Stripper*. MGM.

BEST PERFORMANCE BY AN ORCHESTRA OR INSTRUMENTALIST WITH ORCHESTRA, NOT JAZZ OR DANCING
• Peter Nero, *The Colorful Peter Nero*. RCA.
Elmer Bernstein, *Walk on the Wild Side*. Ava.
Acker Bilk, *Stranger on the Shore*. Atco.
Henry Mancini, *Hatari!* RCA.
Felix Slatkin, *Hoedown!* Liberty.

BEST INSTRUMENTAL THEME
(Composer's Award)
• "A Taste of Honey," Bobby Scott, Ric Marlow. Reprise.
"Baby Elephant Walk," Henry Mancini. RCA.
"*Route 66* Theme," Nelson Riddle. Capitol.
"Stranger on the Shore," Acker Bilk, Robert Mellin. Atco.
"The Stripper," David Rose. MGM.
"Walk on the Wild Side," Elmer Bernstein, Mack David. Ava.

BEST INSTRUMENTAL ARRANGEMENT
• Henry Mancini, "Baby Elephant Walk." RCA.
Robert Farnon, *Sensuous Strings of Robert Farnon*. Mercury.
Joe Harnell, *Fly Me to the Moon Bossa Nova*. Kapp.
Quincy Jones, "Quintessence." Impulse.
Nelson Riddle, "*Route 66* Theme." Capitol.
David Rose, "The Stripper." MGM.
Eddie Sauter, "Focus" (Stan Getz). Verve.

BEST ORIGINAL CAST SHOW ALBUM
(Composer's Award)
• *No Strings*, Richard Rodgers (Original Broadway cast). Capitol.
A Funny Thing Happened on the Way to the Forum, Stephen Sondheim (Original Broadway cast). Capitol.
Beyond the Fringe, Dudley Moore (Alan Bennett, Peter Cook, Jonathan Miller, Dudley Moore). Capitol.
Oliver!, Lionel Bart (Original Broadway cast recording). RCA.

Stop the World—I Want to Get Off, Leslie Bricusse, Anthony Newley (Anthony Newley, Anna Quayle, and cast). London.

BEST BACKGROUND ARRANGEMENT
• Marty Manning, "I Left My Heart in San Francisco" (Tony Bennett). Columbia.
Marion Evans, "Go Away Little Girl" (Steve Lawrence). Columbia.
Bill Finegan, "My Ship" (Carol Sloane). Columbia.
Antonio Carlos Jobim, *Joao Gilberto* (Joao Gilberto). Capitol.
Marty Paich, "Born to Lose" (Ray Charles). ABC-Paramount.
Marty Paich, "I Can't Stop Loving You" (Ray Charles). ABC-Paramount.
Marty Paich, "What Kind of Fool Am I" (Sammy Davis, Jr.). Reprise.

ALBUM OF THE YEAR, CLASSICAL
• *Columbia Records Presents Vladimir Horowitz*, Vladimir Horowitz. Columbia.
Bach: St. Matthew Passion, Otto Klemperer conducting Philharmonia Orchestra and Choir. Angel.
The Heifetz–Piatigorsky Concerts with Primrose, Pennario and Guests, Jascha Heifetz, Gregor Piatigorsky, William Primrose. RCA.
Mahler: Symphony No. 9 in D Minor, Bruno Walter conducting Columbia Symphony. Columbia.
Stravinsky: The Firebird Ballet, Igor Stravinsky conducting Columbia Symphony. Columbia.

BEST CLASSICAL COMPOSITION BY A CONTEMPORARY COMPOSER
• Igor Stravinsky, *The Flood*. Columbia.
Benjamin Britten, *Noye's Fludde*. London.
Aaron Copland, *Connotations for Orchestra*. Columbia.
Lukas Foss, *Song of Songs*. Columbia.
Lukas Foss, *Time Cycle*. Columbia.
Edgard Varese, *Arcana*. Columbia.
Sir William Walton, *Symphony No. 2*. Epic.

BEST CLASSICAL PERFORMANCE, ORCHESTRA
(Conductor's Award)
• Igor Stravinsky conducting Columbia Symphony, *Stravinsky: The Firebird Ballet*. Columbia.

Leonard Bernstein conducting New York Philharmonic, *Mahler: Symphony No. 3 in D Minor*. Columbia.
Otto Klemperer conducting Philharmonia Orchestra, *Bruckner: Symphony No. 7 in E Major*. Angel.
Fritz Reiner conducting Chicago Symphony, *R. Strauss: Also Sprach Zarathustra, Op. 30*. RCA.
Bruno Walter conducting Columbia Symphony, *Mahler: Symphony No. 9 in D Minor*. Columbia.

BEST CLASSICAL PERFORMANCE, CHAMBER MUSIC
• Jascha Heifetz, Gregor Piatigorsky, William Primrose, *The Heifetz–Piatigorsky Concerts with Primrose, Pennario and Guests*. RCA.
Laurindo Almeida, Virginia Majewski, Vincent De Rosa, *The Intimate Bach*. Capitol.
Budapest String Quartet. *Beethoven: The Late Quartets*. Columbia.
Hungarian Quartet, *Bartók: Complete Quartets*. Deutsche Grammophon.
Yehudi Menuhin, George Malcolm, *Bach: Sonatas for Violin & Harpsichord*. Angel.
Artur Rubinstein, Henryk Szeryng, *Rubinstein and Szeryng Violin Sonatas, Brahms: Sonata No. 1; Beethoven: Sonata No. 8, Op. 30, No. 3*. RCA.

BEST CLASSICAL PERFORMANCE, INSTRUMENTAL SOLOIST(S) (WITH ORCHESTRA)
• Isaac Stern (Stravinsky conducting Columbia Symphony), *Stravinsky: Concerto in D for Violin*. Columbia.
Jascha Heifetz (Sargent conducting New Symphony Orchestra of London), *Bruch: Scottish Fantasy; Vieuxtemps: Concerto No. 5*. RCA.
David Oistrakh (Klemperer conducting French National Radio Orchestra), *Brahms: Concerto in D for Violin*. Angel.
Sviatoslav Richter (Kondrashin conducting London Symphony), *Liszt: Concertos 1 and 2 for Piano & Orchestra*. Mercury.
Van Cliburn (Reiner conducting Chicago Symphony), *Rachmaninoff: Concerto No. 2*. RCA.

Best Classical Performance, Instrumental Soloist or Duo (without Orchestra)

- Vladimir Horowitz, *Columbia Records Presents Vladimir Horowitz*. Columbia.
Leon Goossens, *The Art of Leon Goossens*. Angel.
Robert and Gaby Casadesus, *French Piano Music—Four Hands*. Columbia.
Glenn Gould, *Bach: The Art of the Fugue, Vol. I*. Columbia.
Sviatoslav Richter, *Beethoven: Sonata No. 22 for Piano*. RCA.
Artur Rubinstein, *Highlights of Rubinstein at Carnegie Hall Recorded During the Historic Ten Recitals of 1961*. RCA.
Andrés Segovia, *Five Pieces from Platero and I*. Decca.
Joseph Szigeti, *Bach: The Six Sonatas & Partitas for Violin Unaccompanied*. Vanguard.

Best Opera Recording
(Conductor's Award)

- *Verdi: Aida*, Georg Solti conducting Rome Opera House Orchestra and Chorus (solos: Price, Vickers, Gorr, Merrill, Tozzi). RCA.
Beethoven: Fidelio, Otto Klemperer conducting Philharmonia Orchestra and Chorus (solos: Ludwig, Vickers, Frick, Hallstein, Berry). Angel.
Bizet: The Pearl Fishers, Pierre Dervaux conducting Chorus and Orchestra of Theatre National de l'Opera Comique (solos: Micheau, Gedda). Angel.
Puccini: La Bohème, Erich Leinsdorf conducting Rome Opera House Orchestra and Chorus (solos: Moffo, Tucker, Costa, Merrill, Tozzi, Maero). RCA.
R. Strauss: Salome, Georg Solti conducting Vienna Philharmonic (solos: Nilsson, Wachter, Stolze). London.
Wagner: Die Walküre, Erich Leinsdorf conducting London Symphony (solos: Nilsson, Brouwenstien, Gorr, Vickers, London, Ward). RCA.

Best Classical Performance, Choral (Other Than Opera)

- Philharmonia Choir, Wilhelm Pitz, choral director. Otto Klemperer conducting Philharmonia Orchestra, *Bach: St. Matthew Passion*. Angel.
New England Conservatory Chorus, Lorna Cooke de Varon, director. Charles Munch conducting Boston Symphony, *Berlioz: Romeo and Juliet*. RCA.

University of Utah Chorus, Ardean Watts, director. Maurice Abravanel conducting Utah Symphony, *Honegger: King David (Le Roi David)*. Vanguard.
Roger Wagner Chorale, Orchestra de la Societe des Concerts du Conservatoire de Paris, Roger Wagner, conductor, *Fauré: Requiem*. Capitol.
Westminster Choir, Warren Martin, director; Thomas Schippers conducting New York Philharmonic, *Prokofiev: Alexander Nevsky, Op. 78*. Columbia.
Women's Chorus of Schola Cantorum. Hugh Ross, director of Boy's Choir. Church of Transfiguration, Stuart Gardner, director. Leonard Bernstein conducting New York Philharmonic, *Mahler: Symphony No. 3 in D Minor*. Columbia.

Best Classical Performance, Vocal Soloist (with or without Orchestra)

- Eileen Farrell (Bernstein conducting New York Philharmonic), *Wagner: Götterdämmerung, Brunnhilde's Immolation Scene; Wesendonck: Songs*. Columbia.
Adele Addison (Bernstein conducting New York Philharmonic), *Foss: Time Cycle*. Columbia.
Victoria de los Angeles (Soriano, piano), *Spanish Songs of the 20th Century*. Angel.
Maria Callas (Pretre conducting Orchestra National de la Radio Diffusion Francaise), *Great Arias from French Opera*. Angel.
Dietrich Fischer-Dieskau (Moore, piano), *Schubert: Die Schöne Müllerin*. Angel.
Birgit Nilsson (Solti conducting Vienna Philharmonic), *R. Strauss: Salome*. London.

Best Album Cover, Classical
(Art Director's Award)

- Marvin Schwartz, *The Intimate Bach* (solos: Almeida, Majewski, De Rosa). Capitol.
Marvin Schwartz, *Beethoven: Fidelio* (Klemperer conducting Philharmonia Orchestra & Chorus). Angel.
Marvin Schwartz, *Fauré: Requiem* (Wagner conducting Roger Wagner Chorale and Orchestra de la Société des Conservatoire de Paris). Capitol.

Marvin Schwartz, *Otto Klemperer Conducts* (*Weill: Threepenny Opera Suite* and others) (Klemperer conducting Philharmonia Orchestra). Angel.

Marvin Schwartz, *Wagner: Prelude and Love Death; R. Strauss: Death and Transfiguration* (Leinsdorf conducting Los Angeles Philharmonic). Capitol.

Jim Silke, *Bartók: The Miraculous Mandarin; Shostakovich: The Age of Gold* (Irving conducting Philharmonia Orchestra). Capitol.

BEST ENGINEERING CONTRIBUTION, CLASSICAL RECORDING

• Lewis W. Layton, *Strauss: Also Sprach Zarathustra, Op. 30* (Reiner conducting Chicago Symphony). RCA.

William Britten, *Mahler: Symphony No. 9 in D Minor* (Walter conducting Columbia Symphony Orchestra). Columbia.

Robert Fine, *Copland: Billy the Kid; Appalachian Spring* (Dorati conducting London Symphony). Mercury.

Robert Fine, *Prokofiev: Concerto No. 3 for Piano; Rachmaninoff: Concerto No. 1 for Piano* (Janis, piano; Kondrashin conducting Moscow Philharmonic). Mercury.

London Recording Team, *Holst: The Planets* (von Karajan conducting Vienna Philharmonic). Columbia.

Fred Plaut, *Mahler: Symphony No. 3 in D Minor* (Bernstein conducting New York Philharmonic). Columbia.

Fred Plaut, *Columbia Records Presents Vladimir Horowitz.* Columbia.

BEST DOCUMENTARY OR SPOKEN WORD RECORDING (OTHER THAN COMEDY)

• *The Story-Teller: A Session with Charles Laughton*, Charles Laughton. Capitol.

Carl Sandburg Reading his Poetry, Carl Sandburg. Caedmon.

Enoch Arden (Music by R. Strauss; Poem by Alfred Tennyson), Claude Rains, reader, Glenn Gould, pianist. Columbia.

First Performance: Lincoln Center for the Performing Arts, Leonard Bernstein conducting New York Philharmonic. Columbia.

Mama Sang a Song, Stan Kenton. Capitol.

Sir Michael Redgrave Reads "The Harmfulness of Tobacco," "A Transgression." "The First Class Passenger" by Anton Chekhov, Sir Michael Redgrave. Spoken Arts.

Six Million Accuse, Yehuda Lev, narrator. United Artists.

This Is My Beloved, Laurence Harvey. Atlantic.

BEST COMEDY PERFORMANCE

• Vaughn Meader, *The First Family.* Cadence.

Alan Bennett, Peter Cook, Jonathan Miller, Dudley Moore, *Beyond the Fringe.* Capitol.

Elaine May, Mike Nichols, *Nichols and May Examine Doctors.* Mercury.

Allan Sherman, *My Son, the Folk Singer.* Warner Bros.

Jonathan Winters, *Another Day, Another World.* Verve.

BEST RECORDING FOR CHILDREN

• *Saint-Saëns: Carnival of the Animals; Britten: Young Person's Guide to the Orchestra*, Leonard Bernstein. Columbia.

The Cat Who Walked by Herself, Boris Karloff. Caedmon.

The Chipmunk Songbook, David Seville. Liberty.

Grimm's Fairy Tales, Danny Kaye. Golden.

Shari in Storyland, Shari Lewis. RCA.

Through Children's Eyes, Limeliters. RCA.

You Read to Me, I'll Read to You, John Ciardi. Spoken.

BEST ENGINEERING CONTRIBUTION, NOVELTY

• Robert Fine, *The Civil War, Vol. 1* (Fennell conducting Eastman Wind Ensemble; Martin Gabel, narrator). Mercury.

Lowell Frank, *My Son, the Folk Singer* (Allan Sherman). Warner Bros.

John Quinn, *The First Family* (Vaughn Meader). Cadence.

Al Schmitt, *The Chipmunk Songbook* (David Seville). Liberty.

Eddie Smith. *Pepino, the Italian Mouse* (Lou Monte). Reprise.

BEST ENGINEERING CONTRIBUTION, OTHER THAN NOVELTY OR CLASSICAL
• Al Schmitt, *Hatari!* (Henry Mancini). RCA.
Hugh Davies, *Jonah Jones and Glen Gray.* Capitol.
William Hamilton, *Stereo Spectacular* (Various Artists). Audio Fidelity.
John Kraus, "*Route 66* Theme" (Nelson Riddle). Capitol.
Bill Putnam, *I Can't Stop Loving You* (Ray Charles). ABC-Paramount.
Al Schmitt, *Great Band with Great Voices Swing the Great Voices of the Great Bands* (Si Zentner Orchestra, Johnny Mann Singers). Liberty.
Carson C. Taylor, *Adventures in Jazz* (Stan Kenton). Capitol.

BEST ALBUM COVER (OTHER THAN CLASSICAL)
(Art Director's Award)
• Robert Jones, *Lena ... Lovely and Alive* (Lena Horne). RCA.
Loring Eutemey, *The Comedy* (Modern Jazz Quartet). Atlantic.
Loring Eutemey, *Lonely Woman* (Modern Jazz Quartet). Atlantic.
Ken Kim, *My Son, the Folk Singer* (Allan Sherman). Warner Bros.
Bill Longcore, *The First Family* (Vaughn Meader). Cadence.
John Murello, *Jazz Samba* (Stan Getz). Verve.
Jim Silke, *The Great Years* (Frank Sinatra). Capitol.
Ed Thrasher, *Potpourri Par Piaf* (Edith Piaf). Capitol.

Happy Days
for Mancini and Streisand

In 1961, the last time that both the Record and Song of the Year awards were given to one artist, they went to the same artist they did this year: Henry Mancini, who was back to claim three more Grammys to bring his career total to an astounding 14. Mancini's success also marked his fourth year of a five-year, record-setting winning streak that would go unsurpassed until 1969.

Mancini also won an Oscar once again for the same music for which he won a Grammy, too. It had happened just two years earlier with "Moon River" when he last teamed up with Johnny Mercer. This time he and Mercer triumphed for "The Days of Wine and Roses," which they composed for Blake Edwards, the same

The youngest artist ever to win Album of the Year was Barbra Streisand, who was only 22 years old.

GLOBE PHOTO

director Mancini worked with on the TV series *Peter Gunn* (earning him two Grammys) and the film *Breakfast at Tiffany's* (five more, one shared with Mercer). Whereas it took Mancini more than a month to write "Moon River," he penned "Days of Wine and Roses" in about half an hour. "It just came, it rolled out," he says in his memoirs. It was Mercer who took his time, often stalling things. "There was no point in prompting him," Mancini writes.

The movie *The Days of Wine and Roses* was adapted from a *Playhouse 90* teleplay and starred Jack Lemmon and Lee Remick as a married couple engulfed by the horrors of alcoholism. On vinyl, the theme was recorded sepa-

rately by both Mancini (who also won Best Background Arrangement) and Andy Williams. Mancini's victory in the record category has been called "the biggest long shot in Grammy history," given that the single received the academy's highest honor even though Mancini's single reached only number 33 in the weekly charts. The soundtrack was also nominated for Album of the Year.

Before Barbra Streisand became famous for the stage and film versions of *Funny Girl*, she was already, at the age of 19, a middling Broadway actress known for her large nose and "delicatessen accent" in the role of Miss Marmelstein in the Harold Rome musical *I Can Get It for You Wholesale*. Streisand's rave critical notices and the success of the cast album convinced Columbia that she might be due for her first solo LP. The result was a standout for her renditions of Cole Porter's "Come to the Supermarket (in Old Peking)" and the slow, ballad version of "Happy Days Are Here Again" that was nominated for Record of the Year and would eventually become one of her trademark songs. *The Barbra Streisand Album* won three Grammys, including Album of the Year and Best Female Vocal Performance for Streisand as well as Best Album Cover. At age 22, Streisand thus became — and still is, as of this writing — the youngest artist ever to win the top LP prize.

The best male vocalist honor went to the singer of "Wives and Lovers," Jack Jones, who, like Mancini, last won in 1961. Another return winner from years past was Count Basie, who was acknowledged for *This Time by Basie! Hits of the '50s and '60s,* which earned him the dance orchestra award for a third time, bringing his total career tally to four statuettes. Quincy Jones won the first statuette of his many-Grammyed career for his instrumental arrangement of "I Can't Stop Loving You."

Last year's winner of Best Performance by a Vocal Group and Best Folk Recording came back to claim both prizes again, this time for their rendition of Bob Dylan's "Blowin' in the Wind." Peter, Paul & Mary had a banner year. Their eponymous album was 1963's number-five best seller while "Blowin' in the Wind" landed at number 36 in *Billboard*'s Hot 100 and "Puff the Magic Dragon" surpassed it at 22.

The choice of best rock & roll platter came as a surprise when it beat out Lesley Gore's "It's My Party," Sam Cooke's "Another Saturday Night," Little Peggy March's "I Will Follow Him," and "Our Day Will Come" by Ruby & the Romantics. "Deep Purple" had been a last-minute, desperation release by Atlantic Records, which had been trying for years to popularize the brother-sister team of Nino Tempo and April Stevens. When "Purple" topped the charts for a week in November, it became the crowning record of the combo's career.

Belgium's Singing Nun had only one huge hit in her career, too— "Dominique," a paean to St. Dominic that was the year's top religious recording and a nominee for Record of the Year. The Singing Nun was really Sister Luc-Gabrielle (Jeanine Deckers in lay life; dubbed Soeur Sourire, or "Sister Smile," by Philips Records). Prior to her professional recording career, she had pressed Philips executives into letting her use their studios to tape some religious songs that were favorites with the students at her convent. The execs were so impressed by the result that they gave her music a commercial release. At one point in 1963, and for the first time in *Billboard*'s chart-keeping history, "Dominique" and *The Singing Nun* album from which it came were simultaneously number one on the singles and album lineups. *The Singing Nun* ended up ranked eighth for the year. Then came the vocalist's fall, in a sense, from grace. A 1966 movie based on her life starring Debbie Reynolds enjoyed only marginal commercial success and was panned by the critics. Soon thereafter, Sister Luc-Gabrielle left the convent. In 1985, she committed suicide.

Bobby Bare had the year's best country & western song. He first gained renown with his surprise hit of 1959, "The All-American Boy," but then vanished from the music scene for a few years while he

"Dominique" was the Singing Nun's only hit. She committed suicide in 1985.

served in the military. Soon after being discharged, Bare wrote and recorded the Grammy-winning "Detroit City" and went on to croon more than 50 other c&w hits such as "500 Miles from Home" and "Come Sundown."

Allan Sherman gave the comedy performance of the year in his number-one single "Hello Muddah, Hello Faddah," a recitation of a boy's letter to his parents from summer camp, set to the music of Amilcare Ponchielli's "Dance of the Hours." One of the funniest aspects of the win is that Sherman triumphed over a man who took himself very seriously and was not accustomed to losing (Cassius Clay, later known as Muhammed Ali) and another one who would come to dominate the category for six years (Bill Cosby) after Sherman introduced him to record executives.

Comedian Steve Allen pulled off an amazing upset to win the jazz writing award for "Gravy Waltz."

"Several surprises rocked" the evening presentations, according to the *Hollywood Citizen News*. Jazz diehards were rooting for Charlie Mingus and his "Black Saint and the Sinner Lady" for the best composition prize, but instead it went, in a major upset, to musician/composer Ray Brown and comedian and occasional songwriter and pianist Steve Allen for "Gravy Waltz." "The virtually unknown Swingle Singers" were named Best New Artists over Vikki Carr (who would finally win a Grammy in 1985) and Trini Lopez (who never did win, but at least had a half-dozen singles in the Top 40, including "Kansas City" and "If I Had a Hammer"). The Swingle Singers were a French pop vocal group formed by singer/arranger Ward Lamar Swingle. They became one of the pioneers of jazzing up classical music by scat-singing Bach and Mozart. Their *Bach's Greatest Hits* LP won the chorus award over such formidable past winners as the New Christy Minstrels and the Mormon Tabernacle Choir.

In another surprise outcome, the orchestra trophy went to "Java," a work that marked a move into the big time for the 6'2", 300-pound bandleader and trumpet player known in the jazz world as "The Monster," Al Hirt. "Java," Hirt's first million-selling single, was a track from *Honey in the Horn,* his first million-selling album. The jazz solo acknowledgment went to *Conversations with Myself* by Bill Evans, who "plays the piano the way it should be played," Miles Davis once said to jazz writer Leonard Feather (who won a Grammy this year himself for the album notes to *The Ellington Era*). The renowned Woody Herman Band garnered the large group jazz statuette for *Encore*.

The choice of the Classical Album of the Year was Benjamin Britten's recording of his *War Requiem*, one of the most critically acclaimed and popular classical compositions of modern times. Britten wrote the piece for the rededication of England's Coventry Cathedral, which had been damaged severely during World War II. The result was an unconventional music work mingling elements of the *Latin Mass for the Dead* with the inspired antiwar poems of Wilfred Owen, a 25-year-old British soldier who died in battle just days before the armistice was signed. *Requiem* was also named Best Classical Composition by a Contemporary Composer and took the choral honors.

The winner of last year's Classical Album of the Year, Vladimir Horowitz, returned for more prizes and snared one for best instrumental soloist for his new *Sound of Horowitz* album. Conductor

Erich Leinsdorf figured prominently in the other classical categories: He led the Boston Symphony Orchestra in Bartok's *Concerto for Orchestra* (best classical orchestra performance) and he and the orchestra backed up Artur Rubinstein in Tchaikovsky's *Concerto No. 1 in B Flat Minor for Piano and Orchestra* (best instrumental soloist with orchestra). "Passion rather than frenzy predominates in this splendid performance," *High Fidelity* wrote of the Tchaikovsky work. Rubinstein, it added, "admirably resists the temptation to blow the spark into a conflagration."

Leinsdorf also conducted the RCA Italiana Opera Orchestra and Chorus in the year's top operatic recording, Puccini's *Madama Butterfly*, sung by Leontyne Price (who won the vocal soloist award for *Great Scenes from Gershwin's Porgy and Bess*). About Leinsdorf, *High Fidelity* said: "He must share praise with his orchestra, which is every bit as good as hoped." About Price, the magazine's reviewer wrote, "This is beautiful, thrilling singing ... I don't think there's a wrong note within hailing distance of this recording."

N.A.R.A.S. added a new accolade this year meant to be a classical equivalent of Best New Artist and one that would last only a few years. The first of the few Most Promising New Classical Recording Artist awards (the word "Classical" would be eliminated next year) went to André Watts, the young pianist who had made his celebrated debut with the New York Philharmonic in a televised program in 1962 when

The victory of Henry Mancini's "The Days of Wine and Roses" as Record of the Year was called "the biggest longshot" in Grammy Awards history.

he was only 16 years old.

The Grammy ceremony in Los Angeles "was handled deftly by [comic] Stan Freberg as emcee," said the *Citizen News*, "but the entire presentation might have been labeled 'In Abstentia' inasmuch as about 80 percent of the winners were not on hand to pick up their awards. The bulk of the prizes, particularly in the classical categories, were carried off by performers or groups in New York" at the Waldorf-Astoria Hotel.

Presenters included André Previn, Bill Cosby, Margaret Whiting, Johnny Mercer, and Steve Allen. Because of the problem of the headline winners not being on hand for the show, it offered a chance for the losing Best New Artists to take the spotlight. Vikki Carr and John Gary were part of the night's entertainment and "scored well with the hip audience," said the *Citizen-News*, "in singing the five Song of the Year nominees."

Awards bestowed on May 12, 1964, at ceremonies held at the Beverly Hilton Hotel in Los Angeles, the Waldorf-Astoria Hotel in New York City, and the Knickerbocker Hotel in Chicago for the eligibility period December 1, 1962, to November 30, 1963.

ALBUM OF THE YEAR
• *The Barbra Streisand Album*, Barbra Streisand. Columbia.
Bach's Greatest Hits, Swingle Singers. Philips.
The Days of Wine and Roses, Andy Williams. Columbia.
Honey in the Horn, Al Hirt. RCA.
The Singing Nun, Soeur Sourire (Singing Nun). Philips.

RECORD OF THE YEAR
• "The Days of Wine and Roses," Henry Mancini. RCA.
"Dominique," Soeur Sourire (Singing Nun). Philips.
"Happy Days Are Here Again," Barbra Streisand. Columbia.
✓"I Wanna Be Around," Tony Bennett. Columbia.
"Wives and Lovers," Jack Jones. Kapp.

SONG OF THE YEAR
(Composer's Award)
• "The Days of Wine and Roses," Johnny Mercer, Henry Mancini. RCA
"Call Me Irresponsible," Sammy Cahn, Jimmy Van Heusen. Reprise.
✓"The Good Life," Sacha Distel, Jack Reardon. Jay Gee.
✓"I Wanna Be Around," Sadie Vimmerstedt, Johnny Mercer. Columbia.
"Wives and Lovers," Burt Bacharach, Hal David. Kapp.

BEST NEW ARTIST
• Swingle Singers. Philips.
Vikki Carr. Liberty.
John Gary. RCA.
J's with Jamie. Columbia.
Trini Lopez. Reprise.

BEST VOCAL PERFORMANCE, MALE
✓• Jack Jones, "Wives and Lovers." Kapp.
✓Tony Bennett, "I Wanna Be Around." Columbia.

Ray Charles, "Busted." ABC-Paramount.
John Gary, "Catch a Rising Star." RCA.
Andy Williams, "The Days of Wine and Roses." Columbia.

BEST VOCAL PERFORMANCE, FEMALE
• Barbra Streisand, *The Barbra Streisand Album*. Columbia.
Eydie Gorme, "Blame It on the Bossa Nova." Columbia.
Peggy Lee, *I'm a Woman*. Capitol.
Miriam Makeba, *The World of Miriam Makeba*. RCA.
Soeur Sourire (The Singing Nun), "Dominique." Philips.

BEST PERFORMANCE BY A VOCAL GROUP
• Peter, Paul & Mary, "Blowin' in the Wind." Warner Bros.
Hi-Lo's, *The Hi-Lo's Happen to Bossa Nova*. Reprise.
J's with Jamie, *Hey Look Us Over!* Columbia.
Anita Kerr Quartet, *Waitin' for the Evening Train*. RCA.
Jackie and Roy Kral, *Like Sing—Jackie and Roy Kral*. Columbia.

BEST PERFORMANCE BY A CHORUS
• Swingle Singers, *Bach's Greatest Hits*. Philips.
Henry Mancini & his Orchestra with Chorus, *Charade*. RCA.
Mormon Tabernacle Choir (Richard P. Condie, director; Leonard Bernstein conducting New York Philharmonic), *The Joy of Christmas*. Columbia.
New Christy Minstrels, *Green, Green*. Columbia.
Robert Shaw Chorale (Robert Shaw conducting RCA Orchestra), *The Many Moods of Christmas*. RCA.

BEST ROCK & ROLL RECORDING
• "Deep Purple," Nino Tempo, April Stevens. Atco.
"Another Saturday Night," Sam Cooke. RCA.
"I Will Follow Him," Little Peggy March. RCA.
"It's My Party," Lesley Gore. Mercury.
"Our Day Will Come," Ruby & the Romantics. Kapp.
"Teen Scene," Chet Atkins. RCA.

Best Rhythm & Blues Recording
- "Busted," Ray Charles. ABC-Paramount.
"Frankie and Johnny," Sam Cooke. RCA.
"(Love Is Like a) Heat Wave," Martha & the Vandellas. Gordy/Motown.
"Hey, Little Girl," Major Lance. Okeh.
"Hello Stranger," Barbara Lewis. Atlantic.
"Part Time Love," Little Johnny Taylor. Galaxy.
"Since I Fell for You," Lenny Welch. Cadence.

Best Original Jazz Composition
(Composer's Award)
- Ray Brown, Steve Allen, "Gravy Waltz." Dot.
Paul Desmond, "Take Ten." RCA.
Dick Grove, Pete Jolly, Tommy Wolf, "Little Bird." Ava.
Kenyon Hopkins, "East Side-West Side." Backbone Hill.
Newton Mendonco, Antonio Carlos Jobim, "Meditation." Riverside.
Charlie Mingus, "Black Saint and the Sinner Lady." Impulse.

Best Instrumental Jazz Performance, Soloist or Small Group
- Bill Evans, *Conversations with Myself.* Verve.
Dave Brubeck Quartet, *Dave Brubeck at Carnegie Hall.* Columbia.
Miles Davis, *Seven Steps to Heaven.* Columbia.
Al Hirt, *Our Man in New Orleans.* RCA.
Thelonious Monk, *Criss-Cross.* Columbia.
Peter Nero, *Peter Nero in Person.* RCA.
André Previn, with Ray Brown, Herb Ellis, Shelly Manne, *4 to Go!* Columbia.

Best Instrumental Jazz Performance, Large Group
- Woody Herman Band, *Encore: Woody Herman, 1963.* Philips.
Miles Davis, *Seven Steps to Heaven.* Columbia.
Al Hirt, *Our Man in New Orleans.* RCA.
Quincy Jones, *Quincy Jones Plays the Hip Hits.* Mercury.
Gerry Mulligan Concert Jazz Band, *Gerry Mulligan '63.* Verve.
Oliver Nelson Orchestra, *Full Nelson.* Verve.

Best Country & Western Recording
- "Detroit City," Bobby Bare. RCA.
Flatt & Scruggs at Carnegie Hall, Flatt & Scruggs. Columbia.
"Love's Gonna Live Here," Buck Owens. Capitol.
"Ninety Miles an Hour (Down a Dead End Street)," Hank Snow. RCA.
The Porter Wagoner Show, Porter Wagoner. RCA.
✓"Ring of Fire," Johnny Cash. Columbia.
"Saginaw, Michigan," Lefty Frizzell. Columbia.

Best Folk Recording
- "Blowin' in the Wind," Peter, Paul & Mary. Warner Bros.
Green, Green, New Christy Minstrels. Columbia.
Judy Collins No. 3, Judy Collins. Elektra.
Odetta Sings Folk Songs, Odetta. RCA.
Walk Right In, Rooftop Singers. Vanguard.
We Shall Overcome, Pete Seeger. Columbia.
The World of Miriam Makeba, Miriam Makeba. RCA.

Gospel or Other Religious Recording (Musical)
- "Dominique," Soeur Sourire (Singing Nun). Philips.
The Earth Is the Lord's (and the Fullness Thereof), George Beverly Shea. RCA.
Make a Joyful Noise, Mahalia Jackson. Columbia.
Makin' a Joyful Noise, Limeliters. RCA.
Piano in Concert, Charles Magnuson, Fred Bock. Sacred.
Recorded Live! Bessie Griffin and the Gospel Pearls. Epic.
Steppin' Right In, Kings of Harmony. Kings of Harmony.
The Story of Christmas, Tennessee Ernie Ford, Roger Wagner Chorale. Columbia.

Best Performance by an Orchestra for Dancing
- Count Basie, *This Time by Basie! Hits of the 50's and 60's.* Reprise.
Les Brown, *Richard Rodgers Bandbook.* Columbia.
Page Cavanaugh, *The Page 7... An Explosion in Pop Music.* RCA.

Joe Harnell, *Fly Me to the Moon and the Bossa Nova Pops*. Kapp.

Woody Herman, *Encore: Woody Herman, 1963*. Philips.

Quincy Jones, *Quincy Jones Plays the Hip Hits*. Mercury.

BEST PERFORMANCE BY AN ORCHESTRA OR INSTRUMENTALIST WITH ORCHESTRA—NOT JAZZ OR DANCING

• Al Hirt, "Java." RCA.

Percy Faith, *Themes for Young Lovers*. Columbia.

Henry Mancini, *Our Man in Hollywood*. RCA.

Peter Nero, *Hail the Conquering Nero*. RCA.

André Previn, *André Previn in Hollywood*. Columbia.

Kai Winding, *More*. Verve.

BEST INSTRUMENTAL THEME
(Composer's Award)

• "More (Theme from *Mondo Cane*)," Riz Ortolani, Nino Oliviero, (Norman Newell). United Artists.

"Bluesette," Jean "Toots" Theilmans. ABC-Paramount.

"Gravy Waltz," Ray Brown, Steve Allen. Dot.

"Lawrence of Arabia," Maurice Jarre. Colpix.

"Washington Square," Bob Goldstein, David Shire. Epic.

BEST SCORE FROM AN ORIGINAL CAST SHOW ALBUM
(Composer's Award)

• *She Loves Me*, Jerry Bock, Sheldon Harnick (Original cast with Barbara Cook, Daniel Massey, Jack Cassidy). MGM.

Here's Love, Meredith Willson (Original cast with Janis Paige, Craig Stevens, Laurence Naismith; Elliot Lawrence, musical director). Columbia.

Jennie, Arthur Schwartz, Howard Deitz (Original cast with Mary Martin Ethel Shutta, George Wallace, Jack DeLon, Robbin Bailey). RCA.

110 in the Shade, Harvey Schmidt, Tom Jones (Original cast with Robert Horton, Inga Swenson, Stephen Douglass, Will Peer, Steve Roland, Scooter Teague, Lesley Warren; orchestra conducted by Donald W. Pippin). RCA.

Tovarich, Lee Pockriss, Anne Cromwell (Original cast with Vivien Leigh, Jean-Pierre Aumont). Capitol.

BEST ORIGINAL SCORE WRITTEN FOR MOTION PICTURE OR TELEVISION
(Composer's Award)

• *Tom Jones*, John Addison. United Artists.

Cleopatra, Alex North. 20th Century Fox.

Lawrence of Arabia, Maurice Jarre. Colpix.

Mondo Cane, Riz Ortolani, Nino Oliviero. United Artists.

BEST INSTRUMENTAL ARRANGEMENT

• Quincy Jones, "I Can't Stop Loving You" (Count Basie). Reprise.

Robert N. Enevoldsen, "Gravy Waltz" (Steve Allen). Dot.

Peter Nero, Marty Gold, "Mountain Greenery" (Peter Nero). RCA.

Claus Ogerman, "More" (Kai Winding). Verve.

Joe Sherman, "Washington Square" (Village Stompers). Epic.

BEST BACKGROUND ARRANGEMENT

• Henry Mancini, "The Days of Wine and Roses" (Henry Mancini). RCA.

Benny Carter, "Busted" (Ray Charles). ABC-Paramount.

Marion Evans, "Blame It on the Bossa Nova" (Eydie Gormé). Columbia.

Pete King, "Wives and Lovers" (Jack Jones). Kapp.

Nelson Riddle, "Call Me Irresponsible" (Frank Sinatra). Reprise.

Gerald Wilson, "Tell Me the Truth" (Nancy Wilson). Capitol.

ALBUM OF THE YEAR, CLASSICAL

• *Britten: War Requiem*, Benjamin Britten conducting London Symphony Orchestra and Chorus (solos: Vishnevskaya, Pears, Fischer-Dieskau), David Willocks directing Bach Choir. Edward Chapman directing Highgate School Choir. London.

Debussy: La Mer; Ravel: Daphnis and Chloë, George Szell conducting Cleveland Orchestra. Epic.

Great Scenes from Gershwin's Porgy & Bess, Skitch Henderson conducting RCA Symphonic Orchestra and Chorus (solos: Leontyne Price and William Warfield). RCA.

Puccini: Madama Butterfly, Erich
   Leinsdorf conducting RCA Italiana
   Opera Orchestra and Chorus (solos:
   Price, Tucker, Elias). RCA.
*The Sound of Horowitz (works of
   Schumann, Scarlatti, Schubert,
   Scriabin)*, (solo: Vladimir Horowitz).
   Columbia.

BEST CLASSICAL COMPOSITION
BY A CONTEMPORARY COMPOSER
• Benjamin Britten, *War Requiem*.
   London.
Samuel Barber, *Andromache's Farewell,
   Op. 39*. Columbia.
John LaMontaine, *Concerto for Piano*.
   Composers Recordings.
Dmitri Shostakovich, *Symphony No. 4, Op.
   43*. Columbia.
William Schuman, *Symphony No. 8*.
   Columbia.
Heitor Villa-Lobos, *Concerto No. 2 for
   Cello & Orchestra*. Westminster.

BEST CLASSICAL PERFORMANCE,
ORCHESTRA
(Conductor's Award)
• Erich Leinsdorf conducting Boston
   Symphonic Orchestra, *Bartók:
   Concerto for Orchestra*. RCA.
Herbert von Karajan conducting Berlin
   Philharmonic, *Beethoven: The Nine
   Symphonies (Complete)*. Deutsche
   Grammophon.
Fritz Reiner conducting Chicago
   Symphony, *Beethoven: Symphony No.
   6 in F Major, Op. 68 ("Pastorale")*.
   RCA.
George Szell conducting Cleveland
   Orchestra, *Ravel: Daphnis and Chloë*.
   Epic.
Arturo Toscanini conducting Philadelphia
   Symphony, *Schubert: Symphony No. 9
   in C Major ("The Great")*. RCA.
Bruno Walter conducting Columbia
   Symphony, *Mahler: Symphony No. 1
   in D Major ("The Titan")*.
   Columbia.

MOST PROMISING NEW CLASSICAL
ARTIST
• André Watts, pianist. Columbia.
Abbey Singers, vocalists. Decca.
Regine Crespin, vocalist. London.
Colin Davis, conductor. Angel.
Alirio Diaz, guitarist. Vanguard.

John Ogdon, pianist. Angel.
Fou Ts'Ong, pianist. Westminster.

BEST CLASSICAL PERFORMANCE,
CHAMBER MUSIC
• Julian Bream Consort, *An Evening of
   Elizabethan Music*. RCA.
Members of Budapest String Quartet with
   Mieczyslaw Horszowski and Julius
   Levine, *Schubert: Quintet in A Major
   for Piano & Strings, Op. 114
   ("Trout")*. Columbia.
Zino Francescatti, violinist; Robert
   Casadesus, pianist, *Beethoven: Sonatas
   for Violin & Piano (Nos. 3, 4 & 5)*.
   Columbia.
Arthur Gold, Robert Fizdale (with
   vocalists), *Brahms: Liebeslieder
   Waltzes; Schumann: Spanische
   Liebeslieder*. Columbia.
Juilliard String Quartet, *Beethoven:
   Quartet No. 11 in F Minor, Op. 95;
   Quartet No. 16 in F Major, Op. 135*.
   RCA.
London Wind Soloists, *Mozart: Wind
   Music, Vols. 1–5*. London.

BEST CLASSICAL PERFORMANCE,
INSTRUMENTAL SOLOIST(S)
(WITH ORCHESTRA)
• Artur Rubinstein (Leinsdorf conducting
   Boston Symphony), *Tchaikovsky:
   Concerto No. 1 in B Flat Minor for
   Piano & Orchestra*. RCA.
Vladimir Ashkenazy (Fistoulari
   conducting London Symphony),
   *Rachmaninoff: Concerto No. 3 in D
   Minor for Piano*. London.
Jascha Heifetz (Sargent conducting New
   Symphony Orchestra of London),
   *Bruch: Concerto No. 1 in G Minor for
   Violin, Op. 26; Mozart: Concerto No. 4
   in D Major, for Violin, K 218*. RCA.
Lorin Hollander (Leinsdorf conducting
   Boston Symphony), *Ravel: Concerto in
   G for Piano & Orchestra; Dello Joio:
   Fantasy & Variations for Piano &
   Orchestra*. RCA.
David Oistrakh (Hindemith conducting
   London Symphony), *Hindemith:
   Concerto for Violin*. London.
Rudolf Serkin (Szell conducting Columbia
   Symphony), B*artók: Concerto No. 1 for
   Piano & Orchestra*. Columbia.

André Watts (Bernstein conducting New
York Philharmonic), *Liszt: Concerto
No. 1 for Piano & Orchestra.*
Columbia.

**BEST CLASSICAL PERFORMANCE,
INSTRUMENTAL SOLOIST
OR DUO (WITHOUT ORCHESTRA)**
• Vladimir Horowitz, *The Sound of
Horowitz* (works of Schumann,
Scarlatti, Schubert, Scriabin).
Columbia.
Glenn Gould, *Bach: The Six Partitas.*
Columbia.
Artur Rubinstein, *Schumann: Carnaval
Fantasiestüke.* RCA.
Andrés Segovia, *Granada (Albeniz:
"Granada"; Granados: "Spanish Dance
in E Minor"; Ponce, Tansman, Aguado:
"Eight Lessons for the Guitar"; Sor:
"Four Studies").* Decca.
Rudolf Serkin, *Beethoven: Three Favorite
Sonatas (Sonata No. 8 "Pathétique";
Sonata No. 14 "Moonlight"; Sonata
No. 23 "Appassionata").* Columbia.

BEST OPERA RECORDING
• *Puccini: Madama Butterfly,* Erich
Leinsdorf conducting RCA Italiana
Orchestra and Chorus (solos: Price,
Tucker, Elias). RCA.
Bartók: Bluebeard's Castle, Eugene
Ormandy conducting Philadelphia
Orchestra (solos: Elias, Hines).
Columbia.
Mozart: Cosí fan tutte, Eugen Jochum
conducting RIAS Chamber Chorus,
Berlin Philharmonic (solos: Seefried,
Merriman, Koth, Haefliger, Prey,
Fischer-Dieskau). Deutsche
Grammophon.
Mussorgsky: Boris Godounov, André
Cluytens conducting Paris
Conservatoire Orchestra and Chorus of
National Opera of Sofia (soloist:
Christoff). Angel.
Puccini: Tosca, Herbert von Karajan
conducting Vienna Philharmonic
(solos: Price, DiStefano, Taddei). RCA.
Wagner: Siegfried, Georg Solti conducting
Vienna Philharmonic (solos: Nilsson,
Windgassen, Hotter, Stolze, Hoffgen,
Neidlinger, Sutherland). London.

*Conductor Erich Leinsdorf's reading of
Puccini's* Madama Butterfly *was hailed
as the year's Best Opera Recording.*

**BEST CLASSICAL PERFORMANCE, CHORAL
(OTHER THAN OPERA)**
• David Willcocks directing Bach Choir.
Edward Chapman directing Highgate
School Choir. Benjamin Britten
conducting London Symphony
Orchestra and Chorus, *Britten: War
Requiem.* London.
Richard Condie directing Mormon
Tabernacle Choir. Eugene Ormandy
conducting Philadelphia Orchestra,
Brahms: A German Requiem.
Columbia.
Abraham Kaplan directing Collegiate
Chorale. Stuart Gardner directing
Boy's Choir, Church of
Transfiguration. Leonard Bernstein
conducting New York Philharmonic,
Bach: St. Matthew Passion. Columbia.

Hugh Ross directing Schola Cantorum of New York. Leonard Bernstein conducting New York Philharmonic, *Milhaud: Les Choephores*. Columbia.

Robert Shaw conducting Robert Shaw Chorale and Orchestra, *Robert Shaw Chorale "On Tour"* (Ives, Schönberg, Mozart, Ravel). RCA.

Igor Stravinsky conducting Chorus and Orchestra of Washington Opera Society, *Stravinsky: Oedipus Rex*. Columbia.

David Willcocks conducting Choir of King's College and London Symphony, *Haydn: "Nelson Mass" (Mass No. 9 in D Minor, Missa Solemnis)*. London.

Best Classical Performance, Vocal Soloist

• Leontyne Price, *Great Scenes from Gershwin's Porgy & Bess*. RCA.

Netania Davrath (Orchestra conducted by Pierre de la Roche), *Canteloube: Songs of the Auvergne, Vol. 2*. Vanguard.

Victoria de los Angeles (Pretre conducting Paris Conservatoire Orchestra), *Melodies de France* (Ravel, Debussy, Duparc). Angel.

Dietrich Fischer-Dieskau (Moore, pianist), *Schubert: Schwanengesang*. Columbia.

Maureen Forrester (Prohaska conducting Symphony Orchestra of Vienna Festival), *Mahler: Des Knaben Wunderhorn*. Vanguard.

Anna Moffo (Ferrara conducting RCA Italiana Symphonic Orchestra), *A Verdi Collaboration*. RCA.

Joan Sutherland (Bonynge conducting London Symphony), *Command Performance*. London.

Jennie Tourel (Bernstein conducting New York Philharmonic), *Ravel: Scheherazade; Berlioz: Cleopatre (Scene Lyrique)*. Columbia.

Shirley Verrett (Stravinsky conducting Chorus and Orchestra of Washington Opera Society), *Stravinsky: Oedipus Rex*. Columbia.

Best Album Cover, Classical
(Art Director's Award)

• Robert Jones, *Puccini: Madama Butterfly* (Leinsdorf conducting RCA Italiana Orchestra and Chorus). RCA.

John Berg, *Beethoven: Symphony No. 5 in C Minor, Op. 67* (Bernstein conducting New York Philharmonic). Columbia.

Vladimir Bobri, *Granada (Albeniz: "Granada"; Granados: "Spanish Dance in E Minor"; Ponce, Tansman, Aguado: "8 Lessons for Guitar"; Sor: "Four Studies")* (Andrés Segovia). Decca.

Bob Cato, *R. Strauss: Don Quixote* (Ormandy conducting Philadelphia Orchestra). Columbia.

Robert Jones, *Beethoven: Symphony No. 6 in F Major, Op. 68 ("Pastorale")* (Reiner conducting Chicago Symphonic Orchestra). RCA.

Dorle Soria, *An Evening of Elizabethan Music* (Julian Bream Consort). RCA.

Dorle Soria, *Puccini: Tosca* (von Karajan conducting Vienna Philharmonic Orchestra). RCA.

Best Engineered Recording, Classical

• Lewis Layton, *Puccini: Madama Butterfly* (Leinsdorf conducting RCA Italiana Orchestra & Chorus; solos: Price, Tucker, Elias). RCA.

Lewis Layton, *Great Scenes from Gershwin's Porgy & Bess* (solos: Price, Warfield). RCA.

Lewis Layton, *Mahler: Symphony No. 1 in D ("The Titan")* (Leinsdorf conducting Boston Symphony). RCA.

Gordon Parry, *Wagner: Siegfried* (Solti conducting Vienna Philharmonic; solos: Nilsson, Windgassen, Hotter, Stolze, Hoffgen, Neidlinger, Sutherland). London.

Fred Plaut, *Bernstein Conducts Tchaikovsky* (Bernstein conducting New York Philharmonic). Columbia.

Kenneth Wilkenson, *Britten: War Requiem* (Britten conducting London Symphony Orchestra and Chorus). London.

Best Documentary, Spoken Word, or Drama Recording (Other Than Comedy)

• *Who's Afraid of Virginia Woolf?* Edward Albee, playwright. (Original Cast: Uta Hagen, Arthur Hill, George Grizzard, with Melinda Dillon). Warner Bros.

The Badmen, Goddard Lieberson, producer. (Pete Seeger and others). Columbia.

Brecht on Brecht, Bertolt Brecht, playwright (Original cast with Dane Clark, Anne Jackson, Lotte Lenya, Viveca Lindfors, George Voskovec, Michael Wager). Columbia.

John F. Kennedy—The Presidential Years, Norman Weiser, producer. (David Teig, narrator). Four Corners.

Strange Interlude, Eugene O'Neill, playwright (Original Broadway cast: Betty Field, Jane Fonda, Ben Gazzara, Pat Hingle, Geoff Horne, William Prince, Geraldine Page, Richard Thomas, Franchot Tone). Columbia.

We Shall Overcome (The March on Washington, August 28, 1963), Dr. Martin Luther King, Jr. (with Joan Baez, Marian Anderson, Odetta, Rabbi Joachim Prinz, Bob Dylan, Whitney M. Young, Jr., John Lewis, Roy Wilkins, Walter Reuther, Peter, Paul & Mary, Bayard Rustin, A. Philip Randolph). United Civil Rights.

BEST COMEDY PERFORMANCE

• Allan Sherman, *Hello Mudduh, Hello Faddah*. Warner Brothers.

Cassius Clay, *I Am the Greatest!* Columbia.

Bill Cosby, *Bill Cosby is a Very Funny Fellow, Right!* Warner Bros.

Carl Reiner, Mel Brooks, *Carl Reiner and Mel Brooks at the Cannes Film Festival*. Capitol.

Smothers Brothers, *Think Ethnic*. Mercury.

BEST RECORDING FOR CHILDREN

• *Bernstein Conducts for Young People*, Leonard Bernstein conducting the New York Philharmonic. Columbia.

Addition and Subtraction, Rica Owen Moore. Disney.

Children's Concert, Pete Seeger. Columbia.

Let's Go to the Zoo, Fred V. Grunfeld, producer (Various artists). Decca.

On Top of Spaghetti, Tom Glazer (and the Do Re Mi Children's Chorus). Kapp.

"Puff the Magic Dragon," Peter, Paul & Mary. Warner Bros.

Winnie the Pooh, Jack Gilford. Golden.

BEST ENGINEERED RECORDING, SPECIAL OR NOVEL EFFECTS

• Robert Fine, *Civil War Vol. 2* (Frederick Fennell). Mercury.

William Hamilton, *Fast, Fast, Fast Relief from TV Commercials* (Bill McFadden, Bryna Rayburn). Audio Fidelity.

John Kraus, *Cheyenne Frontier Days* (Hank Thompson). Capitol.

John Kraus, *Zounds! What Sounds* (Dean Elliott). Capitol.

John Kraus, Hugh B. Davies, *Heartstrings* (Dean Elliott). Capitol.

Phil Macy, Al Weintraub, *Pepino's Friend Pasquale* (Lou Monte). Reprise.

Scotty Shackner, Bob MacMeekin, *Four in the Floor* (Shut Downs). Dimension.

BEST ENGINEERED RECORDING, OTHER THAN CLASSICAL

• James A. Malloy, *Charade* (Henry Mancini Orchestra and Chorus). RCA.

Harold Chapman, *Exotic Sounds of Bali* (Mantle Hood, director). Columbia.

Frank Laico, *The Barbra Streisand Album* (Barbra Streisand). Columbia.

Frank Laico, *The Second Barbra Streisand Album* (Barbra Streisand). Columbia.

Anthony J. Salvatore, *The Many Moods of Christmas* (Robert Shaw Chorale). RCA.

Albert H. Schmitt, *Our Man in Hollywood* (Henry Mancini). RCA.

Ronald A. Steele, *Politely Percussive* (Dick Schory). RCA.

Ronald A. Steele, *Supercussion* (Dick Schory). RCA.

Luis P. Valentin, *Ella and Basie*. (Ella Fitzgerald, Count Basie). Verve.

BEST ALBUM COVER, OTHER THAN CLASSICAL
(Art Director's Award)

• John Berg, *The Barbra Streisand Album* (Barbra Streisand). Columbia.

Robert Jones, *Aloha from Norman Luboff* (The Norman Luboff Choir). RCA.

Robert Jones, *Honey in the Horn* (Al Hirt). RCA.

Jim Ladwig, *Bach's Greatest Hits* (Swingle Singers). Philips.

John Murello, *Night Train* (Oscar Peterson). Verve.

Jim Silke, *Hollywood My Way* (Nancy Wilson). Capitol.

Edward L. Thrasher, *Carl Reiner and Mel Brooks at the Cannes Film Festival* (Carl Reiner, Mel Brooks). Warner Bros.

BEST ALBUM NOTES
(Annotator's Award)
- Leonard Feather, Stanley Dance, *The Ellington Era* (Duke Ellington). Columbia.

Edward Albee, Harold Clurman, *Who's Afraid of Virginia Woolf?* (Original Cast). Columbia.

Harold Arlen, *The Barbra Streisand Album* (Barbra Streisand). Columbia.

Sidney Bock, *An Evening of Elizabethan Music* (Julian Bream Consort). RCA.

Bob Bollard, *The Amazing Amanda Ambrose* (Amanda Ambrose). RCA.

B.A. Botkin, Sylvester L. Vigilante, Harold Preece, James L. Horan, *The Badmen* (Pete Seeger and others). Columbia.

A "Hard Night" for the Beatles

Grammy detractors have long perpetuated a myth that the Beatles, like Elvis Presley, were slighted by N.A.R.A.S. throughout their mutual association (noting that the Fab Four, for example, never won Record of the Year, which is true). But in their first year at the Grammys, the long-haired lads from Liverpool actually led the contest with their music up for nine prizes. "The three B's — Barbra, the Beatles, and Bossa Nova — have dominated the nomina-

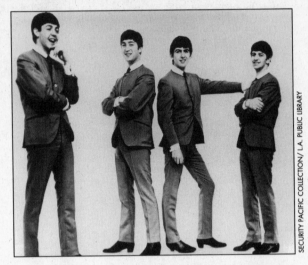

The Beatles had the most nominations (nine), but won only two awards: Best New Artist and best group vocals.

SECURITY PACIFIC COLLECTION/ L.A. PUBLIC LIBRARY

tions," *Variety* remarked after the year's contenders were announced.

Three of the Beatles' bids were for their music performed by other groups. The rest were all the Beatles' own, including nods for Record of the Year ("I Want to Hold Your Hand") and Song of the Year ("A Hard Day's Night," also nominated for Best Rock & Roll Recording), best film score, best group vocal performance, and Best New Artist.

The Beatles nabbed the Best New Artist honors easily, having spawned a new sound as well as a new word in 1964: "Beatlemania." When they arrived in America on February 7th, screaming mobs greeted them at New York's Kennedy Airport. Seventy million people then watched their two performances on *The Ed Sullivan Show* on February 9th and 16th, although little of the music could be heard above the screeching of

fans in the audience. By April, the Beatles established a *Billboard* record that still stands: Their music held all five top positions on the singles chart — "Can't Buy Me Love," "I Want to Hold Your Hand," "Twist and Shout," "She Loves You," and "Please, Please Me." "Hold Your Hand" held the number-one spot on *Billboard*'s annual Hot 100, a ranking that combines data such as record sales along with the frequency with which songs are requested by listeners and played on the radio.

Most of the Beatles' nominations were for music from their first movie, *A Hard Day's Night*, which was released in August and grossed an amazing $1.3 million in its first week. *The Village Voice* called it "the *Citizen Kane* of juke box musicals" because of its daring zaniness as it followed the foursome through two fictitious days of gearing up to perform a rock concert. Even their worst critics like *The London Daily Mirror* declared their film effort "cheeky, irreverent, funny, irresistible." Within two weeks of the movie's release, its title song leapt to the top of the U.S. charts, too. The LP recording ended up as the top seller of 1964.

Hard Day lost the prize for Best Original Score Written for a Motion Picture or TV Show to *Mary Poppins*, also a winner for Best Recording for Children. (All of *Hard Day*'s singles were also eligible for Best Song at the Oscars, but none were nominated. What took the prize was "Chim Chim Cheree" from *Mary Poppins*, the number one LP of 1965.) How they fared with the rest of their N.A.R.A.S. nods was another matter: "Beatles Play 2d Fiddle in Grammys," said *Variety*'s headline after the ceremony. The Fab Four did well, but less than fabulously. In addition to Best New Artist, they reaped Best Performance by a Vocal Group for "A Hard Day's Night," but that was all. The Beatles, however, hardly felt slighted. At Grammy's after-the-fact "Best on Record" TV show, the revolutionary rockers appeared on a segment taped at London's Twickenham Studios where they were filming *Help!* They performed "I'm So Happy Just to Dance with You," and accepted their trophies, quite happily, from actor Peter Sellers.

What the Beatles played second fiddle to was the bossa nova sound introduced to America by 1962 Grammy winner Stan Getz and collaborator Charlie Byrd, whose *Jazz Samba* album became one of the biggest sellers in jazz history and launched a music craze that soon found followers in Eydie Gormé, Dizzy Gillespie,and Frank Sinatra.

"In his lifetime, Stan Getz got under our skins," wrote *Esquire* of the famed tenor sax player soon after his death from cancer in 1991. Getz was, added *Time*, "the master of cool riffs and sultry melodic lines." He was also the first person in Grammy history to win both Record and Album of the Year.

The bossa nova ("new wave" or "new wrinkle") craze, begun two years earlier, was at a low ebb by 1964. Getz considered it time for a renaissance and teamed up for a new album effort with Brazil's leading performer of the genre, guitar player/singer Joao Gilberto. But their *Getz/Gilberto* collaboration included occasional vocals in addition to instrumental music, presenting the twosome with a problem. Gilberto could sing only in Portugese. Getz's solution was to ask Gilberto's English-speaking wife, Astrud — a capable singer who had never performed professionally before — to do the album's "Girl from Ipanema" track in both languages. The result: "Ipanema" reigned for two weeks at number five on *Billboard*'s lineup and was voted Record of the Year. *Getz/Gilberto* also won Album of the Year — plus prizes for instrumental jazz performance and engineering. (Astrud Gilberto lost her bid for Best New Artist.)

Past multiple winner and classical guitarist Laurindo Almeida was among those who got caught up in the new bossa nova wave that followed. Almeida recorded *Guitar from Ipanema* in 1964 and won a jazz instrumental gramophone.

For Song of the Year, N.A.R.A.S. voters again expressed their appreciation for traditional American melodies when they honored "Hello, Dolly!" by Jerry Herman, which became the third-

> **The Village Voice** *called* **A Hard Day's Night** *"The* **Citizen Kane** *of juke box musicals."*

show tune to win one of the top three Grammys. *Hello, Dolly!*'s title song was so popular that it was "covered" (re-recorded by different artists) more than 200 times within two years of the show's premiere.

The tune pulled off another amazing coup. Three Beatles songs ruled the number-one slot on *Billboard*'s singles list for 14 consecutive weeks up until May 9, 1964. The Fab Four were then dislodged by an unlikely contender: Louis "Satchmo" Armstrong, the legendary 63-year-old trumpet player and sometime singer, who, ironically, wasn't even familiar with the song when he

Stan Getz became the first artist to win both Record and Album of the Year when Getz/Gilberto *took four awards.*

decided to record it. Armstrong had been compiling a tribute to Broadway show tunes when he was approached by an associate of songwriter Herman and asked to include "Dolly" in the album. The result was one of the three show tunes to rank number one in the rock era, the other two being Bobby Darin's "Mack the Knife" (Grammy Record of the Year, 1959) and "Aquarius/Let the Sun Shine In" from *Hair* (Grammy Record of the Year, 1969).

Satchmo did "Hello, Dolly!" with raspish gusto and a jazzy beat, earning

him the best male vocalist award. Later Grammy winner Herb Alpert remembers Armstrong's private reaction to his victory then. "He couldn't believe it," Alpert says. "He told me, 'I've been playing for 50 years and now I've got a f---ing number-one record! I don't know what happened to all those other records. But I'm singin' on this one!'" His success with "Dolly" even helped to boost the musical's Broadway attendance and also helped Armstrong land a part in the 1969 film version, which starred Barbra Streisand.

Streisand's newest LP release was *People*, the year's number six best seller. The title song came from her long-running Broadway musical *Funny Girl*, winner of this year's Grammy for Best Score from an Original Cast Show Album despite strong competition from *Hello, Dolly!* and *Fiddler on the Roof*. "People" was nominated for both Record and Song of the Year, but, having failed to take either, it at least won a trophy for vocal accompaniment arrangement and the Best Female Vocal Performance prize for Streisand for a second year in a row. The LP took Best Album Notes, too.

A loser for the female vocalist honor, Petula Clark, managed to score a surprise victory over the Beatles, Roy Orbison, and the Righteous Brothers for 1964's Best Rock & Roll Recording. Prior to 1964, Clark had a solid career as a singer back in her native England where she first performed on radio in 1941 at the age of nine. Now, 23 years later, her upbeat "Downtown" established her as an international star and one of the first British women ever to have a rock hit in America.

But while the Brits, Brazilians, and Broadway's best did well at this year's Grammys (the event carried, according to *The Los Angeles Times*, "a heavily but not exclusively British accent"),

VERVE

the ceremony night really belonged to country singer Roger Miller, who tied Henry Mancini's 1961 record of winning the most Grammys in a single year — five. Moreover, he would return next year to top it.

After several years of difficult negotiations, an eager N.A.R.A.S. finally set up a chapter in Nashville in 1964. Critical observers said the academy gave away too many concessions in the bargain: Country & western music now had six categories of its own (more than jazz, rock, and rhythm & blues put together), up from only one last year. And Miller, along with his funny and folksy tune "Dang Me," dang near swept all of them — the sole exception being the one for which Miller wasn't qualified due to gender, the best c&w female vocalist prize, which went to Dottie West for "Here Comes My Baby."

Among Miller's five prizes was one for Best New Country & Western Artist. His sudden ascendancy was the stuff of story books: He had once been a bellboy at Nashville's now demolished Andrew Jackson Hotel when a record company executive heard him sing and gave him a contract on the spot. What made Miller special was a lighthearted touch (typical of his early songwriting efforts was "You Can't Roller Skate in a Buffalo Herd") that struck a universal chord. "Dang Me" had whole choruses of humorous lines and, when it sold a million copies, Miller became one of the first country-to-pop crossover stars in music history. At the Grammys, "Dang Me" was named country's best song and best single and won Miller the prize for giving the Best Male Country & Western Vocal Performance. The *Dang Me/Chug-a-Lug* LP (the latter being his "goofy" musical toast to moonshine) was also hailed as Country & Western Album of the Year, a category that would be dropped after Miller

won it a second time next year.

In the comedy category, a historic winning streak was begun when a losing nominee of last year — Bill Cosby for *Bill Cosby Is a Very Funny Fellow, Right!* — returned to topple the same comic (Allan Sherman) who bested him in 1963. (A fitting victory, since it was Sherman who introduced Cosby to Warner Bros. record executives soon after Cosby proved himself in Greenwich Village nightclubs.) By the time the 1964 Grammys were bestowed in 1965, Cosby had distinguished himself as the first black leading actor in a TV drama series when he starred opposite Robert Culp on *I Spy*. But he stayed active in the comedy field. It was his second album, *I Started Out as a Child*, that brought him his first of six Grammy Awards in a row — a record that would not be broken until Aretha Franklin won eight consecutive trophies as best female r&b vocalist from 1967 to 1974. In *Child*, Cosby recalled

Bill Cosby snatched the comedy laurels from the same person who helped to discover him: Allan Sherman.

such childhood scenes as playing street football with his pals and being told by the quarterback, "Cosby, you go down to 3rd Street, catch the J bus, have him open the doors at 19th Street — I'll take it to ya."

After Miller, Stan Getz, and Joao Gilberto, the biggest winner on Grammy night was veteran champ Henry Mancini, "a repeat winner every year," said the mistaken *L.A. Herald Examiner*. (Mancini's amazing winning streak actually skipped one year — 1959 — but otherwise set a new five-year record, from 1960 to 1964, that no one would surpass until Bill Cosby did so in 1969.) Mancini's classic *Pink Panther* film score was the result of his teaming up yet again with film and TV director Blake Edwards and won him three instrumental awards: for composition, performance, and arrangement.

Mancini's three trophies were matched by three bestowed on the work of English composer Benjamin Britten, whose *War Requiem* garnered several statuettes last year, including Classical Album of the Year. Britten's *Ceremony of Carols,* performed by the Robert Shaw Chorale, now won the choral performance award while his *Young Person's Guide to the Orchestra* nabbed the prizes for best engineering and best album cover.

> *Roger Miller scored an amazing five Grammys for his humorous hit "Dang Me."*

This year's Classical Album of the Year award went to Leonard Bernstein's Symphony No. 3 (*Kaddish* — the traditional Hebrew prayer for the dead), performed by the New York Philharmonic. *High Fidelity* called it "a powerful artistic statement," adding, "Bernstein has built many high, dramatic peaks, and much of the music does show his original touch." The reviewer also added, however, "What we have here is a major expression by a minor composer."

Samuel Barber's Concerto was named best original composition. "Barber has written a big, splashy, old-fashioned concerto," *High Fidelity* opined. "All the work really lacks, and the lack is only relative to some of Barber's other scores, is distinctive melodic substance." Vladimir Horowitz continued his three-year winning streak by picking up a performance prize for instrumental soloist. Four-time past victor and double-champ of last year, conductor Erich Leinsdorf of the Boston Symphony, returned again to win the orchestral performance kudos for works by Gustav Mahler (*Symphony No. 5 in C Sharp Minor*) and Alban Berg (the opera *Wozzeck*).

American mezzo-soprano Marilyn Horne had supplied the vocals for Dorothy Dandridge in the movie of *Carmen Jones,* but it wasn't until the early 1960s — when she teamed up periodically with diva Joan Sutherland, toured Europe, and perfected her coloratura style — that critics and serious operagoers took equally serious note of her. Horne was a rising star in 1964 (her debut at New York's Metropolitan Opera was still six years off) when she was named Grammy's Most Promising New Recording Artist. Opera superstar and two-time past winner Leontyne Price (1960 and 1963) again took the vocalist's laurels, this time for singing Berlioz with the Chicago Symphony.

Price also performed the lead in the Best Opera Recording, Georges Bizet's *Carmen,* recorded by the Vienna Philharmonic with Herbert von Karajan conducting. Price had not yet played the role on stage, but of her first recording of the music, *High Fidelity* said, "From a verbal standpoint, she copes, she handles it smartly."

The *Herald Examiner* noted "a star-filled crowd at the Beverly Hilton Hotel" on the night of the Grammy festivities. On hand were 750 people, including winners Henry Mancini, Robert and Richard Sherman (composers of *Mary Poppins*), and songbird Nancy Wilson (winner of Best Rhythm & Blues Performance for "How Glad I Am"). In New York, Louis Armstrong, Allan Sherman, and Woody Herman entertained 800 at the Grand Ballroom of the Astor Hotel. The Chicago and Nashville chapters also held dinners.

Variety judged the year's awards to be "the most successful to date." Over the course of seven years, the Grammys had come a long way in their quest to gain the respect of the entertainment industry. In its article summing up the 1964 prizes, *The New York Times* informed its readers that a Grammy "carries the same meaning for the record industry as the Oscar does for the film world."

1964

Awards were bestowed on April 13, 1965, for the eligibility period December 1, 1963, to November 30, 1964, at ceremonies held at the Beverly Hilton Hotel in Los Angeles, the Astor Hotel in New York, and at dinners held in Nashville and Chicago.

Song of the Year "Hello, Dolly!" was recorded by 200 artists, including best male vocalist Louis Armstrong.

ALBUM OF THE YEAR
• *Getz/Gilberto*, Stan Getz, Joao Gilberto. Verve.
Cotton Candy, Al Hirt. RCA.
Funny Girl, Robert Merrill, Jule Styne. Capitol.
People, Barbra Streisand. Columbia.
The Pink Panther, Henry Mancini. RCA.

RECORD OF THE YEAR
• "The Girl from Ipanema," Stan Getz, Astrud Gilberto. Verve.
"Downtown," Petula Clark. Warner Bros.
"Hello, Dolly!" Louis Armstrong. Kapp.
"I Want to Hold Your Hand," Beatles. Capitol.
"People," Barbra Streisand. Columbia.

SONG OF THE YEAR
(Songwriter's Award)
• "Hello, Dolly!" Jerry Herman. Kapp.
"A Hard Day's Night," John Lennon, Paul McCartney. Capitol.
"Dear Heart," Henry Mancini, Ray Evans, Jay Livingston. RCA.
"People," Jule Styne, Bob Merrill. Columbia.
"Who Can I Turn To?" Leslie Bricusse, Anthony Newley. Columbia.

BEST NEW ARTIST
• Beatles. Capitol.
Petula Clark. Warner Bros.
Astrud Gilberto. Verve.
Antonio Carlos Jobim. Warner Bros.
Morgana King. Mainstream.

BEST VOCAL PERFORMANCE, MALE
• Louis Armstrong, "Hello, Dolly!" Kapp.
Tony Bennett, "Who Can I Turn To?" Columbia.
Joao Gilberto, *Getz/Gilberto*. Verve.
Dean Martin, "Everybody Loves Somebody." Reprise.
Andy Williams, *Call Me Irresponsible*. Columbia.

BEST VOCAL PERFORMANCE, FEMALE
• Barbra Streisand, "People." Columbia.
Petula Clark, "Downtown." Warner Bros.
Gale Garnett, "We'll Sing in the Sunshine." RCA.
Astrud Gilberto, "The Girl from Ipanema." Verve.
Nancy Wilson, "How Glad I Am." Capitol.

BEST PERFORMANCE BY A VOCAL GROUP
• Beatles, *A Hard Day's Night*. Capitol.
Browns, *Grand Ole Opry Favorites*. RCA.
Double Six of Paris, *The Double Six Sing Ray Charles*. Philips.

Four Freshmen, *More Four Freshmen and Five Trombones*. Capitol.

Peter, Paul & Mary, *Peter Paul & Mary in Concert*. Warner Bros.

BEST PERFORMANCE BY A CHORUS
• Swingle Singers, *The Swingle Singers Going Baroque*. Philips.

Ray Charles Singers, *Love Me with All Your Heart*. Columbia.

Stan Kenton Orchestra: Chorus by Pete Rugolo, *Artistry in Voices & Brass*. Capitol.

Henry Mancini Orchestra and Chorus, *Dear Heart*. RCA.

Serendipity Singers, *Don't Let the Rain Come Down (Crooked Little Man)*. Philips.

BEST ROCK & ROLL RECORDING
• "Downtown," Petula Clark. Warner Bros.

"A Hard Day's Night," Beatles. Capitol.

"Mr. Lonely," Bobby Vinton. Epic.

"Oh, Pretty Woman," Roy Orbison. Monument.

"You've Lost That Lovin' Feeling," Righteous Brothers. Philles.

BEST RHYTHM & BLUES RECORDING
• "How Glad I Am," Nancy Wilson. Capitol.

"Baby Love," Supremes. Motown.

"Good Times," Sam Cooke. RCA.

"Hold What You've Got," Joe Tex. Dial.

"Keep On Pushing," Impressions. ABC.

"Walk On By," Dionne Warwick. Sceptre.

BEST ORIGINAL JAZZ COMPOSITION
(Composer's Award)
• Lalo Schifrin, "The Cat." Verve.

Dave Brubeck, "Theme from *Mr. Broadway*." Columbia.

Duke Ellington, "Night Creature." Reprise.

Bob Florence, "Here and Now," Liberty.

Quincy Jones, "The Witching Hour." Mercury.

Gerald Wilson, "Paco." World Pacific.

BEST INSTRUMENTAL JAZZ PERFORMANCE, SMALL GROUP OR SOLOIST WITH SMALL GROUP
• Stan Getz, *Getz/Gilberto*. Verve.

Miles Davis, *Miles Davis in Europe*. Columbia.

Modern Jazz Quartet with Laurindo Almeida, *Collaboration*. Atlantic.

Pete Jolly, *Sweet September*. Ava.

Oscar Peterson, Clark Terry, *Mumbles*. Mercury.

André Previn, *My Fair Lady*. Columbia.

BEST INSTRUMENTAL JAZZ PERFORMANCE, LARGE GROUP OR SOLOIST WITH LARGE GROUP
• Laurindo Almeida, *Guitar from Ipanema*. Capitol.

Miles Davis, Gil Evans, *Quiet Nights*. Columbia.

Gil Evans, *The Individualism of Gil Evans*. Verve.

Woody Herman, *Woody Herman '64*. Phillips.

Quincy Jones, *Quincy Jones Explores the Music of Henry Mancini*. Mercury.

Rod Levitt, *Dynamic Sound Patterns of the Rod Levitt Orchestra*. Riverside.

Shelly Manne, *My Fair Lady with the Unoriginal Cast*. Capitol.

Oscar Peterson, Nelson Riddle, *Oscar Peterson—Nelson Riddle*. Verve.

BEST COUNTRY & WESTERN ALBUM
• *Dang Me/Chug-a-Lug*, Roger Miller. Smash.

The Best of Buck Owens, Buck Owens. Capitol.

The Best of Jim Reeves, Jim Reeves. RCA.

Bitter Tears, Johnny Cash. Columbia.

Guitar Country, Chet Atkins. RCA.

Hank Williams, Jr., Sings Songs of Hank Williams, Hank Williams, Jr. MGM.

BEST COUNTRY & WESTERN SINGLE
• "Dang Me," Roger Miller. Smash.

"Four Strong Winds," Bobby Bare. RCA.

"Here Comes My Baby," Dottie West. RCA.

"Once a Day," Connie Smith. RCA.

"You're the Only World I Know," Sonny James. Capitol.

BEST COUNTRY & WESTERN SONG
(Songwriter's Award)
• "Dang Me," Roger Miller. Smash.
"Here Comes My Baby," Dottie West, Bill West. RCA.
"Once a Day," Bill Anderson. RCA.
"Wine, Women and Song," Betty Sue Perry. Decca.
"You're the Only World I Know," Sonny James, Bob Tubert. Capitol.

BEST NEW COUNTRY & WESTERN ARTIST
• Roger Miller. Smash.
Charlie Louvin. Capitol.
Connie Smith. RCA.
Dottie West. RCA.
Hank Williams, Jr. MGM.

BEST COUNTRY & WESTERN VOCAL PERFORMANCE, MALE
• Roger Miller, "Dang Me." Smash.
Bobby Bare, "Four Strong Winds." RCA.
Johnny Cash, "I Walk the Line." Columbia.
George Hamilton IV, *Fort Worth, Dallas or Houston*. RCA.
Sonny James, *You're the Only World I Know*. Capitol.
Hank Locklin, *Hank Locklin Sings Hank Williams*. RCA.
Buck Owens, *My Heart Skips a Beat*. Capitol.

BEST COUNTRY & WESTERN VOCAL PERFORMANCE, FEMALE
• Dottie West, "Here Comes My Baby." RCA.
Skeeter Davis, "He Says the Same Thing to Me." RCA.
Wanda Jackson, *Two Sides of Wanda Jackson*. Capitol.
Jean Shepard, "Second Fiddle." Capitol.
Connie Smith, "Once a Day." RCA.

BEST FOLK RECORDING
• *We'll Sing in the Sunshine*, Gale Garnett. RCA.
Belafonte at the Greek Theatre, Harry Belafonte. RCA.
Peter, Paul & Mary in Concert, Peter, Paul & Mary. RCA.
The Times, They Are A-Changin', Bob Dylan. Columbia.
Today, New Christy Minstrels. Columbia.
The Voice of Africa, Miriam Makeba. RCA.
Woody Guthrie: Library of Congress Recordings, Woody Guthrie. Nonesuch.

BEST GOSPEL OR OTHER RELIGIOUS RECORDING (MUSICAL)
• *Great Gospel Songs*, Tennessee Ernie Ford. Capitol.
Family Album of Hymns, Roger Williams. Kapp.
Gregorian Chant, Dominican Nuns of Fichermont. Philips.
George Beverly Shea Sings Hymns of Sunrise and Sunset, George Beverly Shea. RCA.
Sweet Hour of Prayer, Jo Stafford. Capitol.
Standin' on the Banks of the River, James Cleveland and the Angelic Choir. Savoy.
This I Believe, Fred Waring. Capitol.

BEST INSTRUMENTAL COMPOSITION (OTHER THAN JAZZ)
(Composer's Award)
• Henry Mancini, *"The Pink Panther Theme."* RCA.
Russ Daymon, "Cotton Candy." RCA.
Buddy Killen, Billy Sherrill, "Sugar Lips." RCA.
Jack Marshall, "Theme from *The Munsters*." Capitol.
Charles Strouse, Lee Adams, "Theme from *Golden Boy*." Decca.

BEST INSTRUMENTAL PERFORMANCE, NON-JAZZ
• Henry Mancini, *"The Pink Panther Theme."* RCA.
Al Hirt, "Cotton Candy." RCA.
Quincy Jones, "Golden Boy" (string version). Mercury.
Peter Nero, "As Long as He Needs Me." RCA.
Stu Phillips, *The Beatles Song Book*. (Hollyridge Strings). Capitol.

BEST INSTRUMENTAL ARRANGEMENT
• Henry Mancini, *"The Pink Panther Theme."* RCA.
Bob Florence, "The Song Is You." Liberty.
Quincy Jones, "Golden Boy" (string version). Mercury.
Richard Hayman, "I Want to Hold Your Hand" (Arthur Fiedler & the Boston Pops). RCA.
Anita Kerr, "Sugar Lips" (Al Hirt). RCA.
Hugo Montenegro, "Theme from *The Long Ships*." RCA
Billy Strayhorn, "A Spoonful of Sugar" (Duke Ellington). Reprise.

BEST ACCOMPANIMENT ARRANGEMENT FOR VOCALIST(S) OR INSTRUMENTALIST(S)
• Peter Matz, "People" (Barbra Streisand). Columbia.
Sid Bass, "We'll Sing in the Sunshine" (Gale Garnett). RCA.
Pete King, "Where Love Has Gone" (Jack Jones). Kapp.
Oliver Nelson, "How Glad I Am" (Nancy Wilson). Capitol.
Don Ralke, "Ringo" (Lorne Green). RCA.
George Siravo, "Who Can I Turn To?" (Tony Bennett). Columbia.

BEST SCORE FROM AN ORIGINAL CAST SHOW ALBUM
(Composer's Award)
• *Funny Girl*, Jule Styne, Bob Merrill (Original cast with Barbra Streisand). Capitol.
Fiddler on the Roof, Jerry Bock, Sheldon Harnick (Original cast with Zero Mostel, Tanya Everett, Joanna Merlin). RCA.
Hello, Dolly! Jerry Herman (Original cast with Carol Channing). RCA.
High Spirits, Hugh Martin, Timothy Gray (Original cast with Beatrice Lillie, Tammy Grimes, Edward Woodward). ABC.
What Makes Sammy Run? Ervin Drake (Original cast with Steve Lawrence). Columbia.

BEST ORIGINAL SCORE WRITTEN FOR A MOTION PICTURE OR TV SHOW
(Composer's Award)
• *Mary Poppins*, Richard M. Sherman, Robert B. Sherman (Julie Andrews, Dick Van Dyke, with David Tomlinson, Glynis Johns, Ed Wynn). Buena Vista.
A Hard Day's Night, John Lennon, Paul McCartney (Beatles). United Artists.
Goldfinger, John Barry (John Barry, conductor). United Artists.
The Pink Panther, Henry Mancini (Henry Mancini, conductor). RCA.
Robin and the Seven Hoods, Sammy Cahn, Jimmy Van Heusen (Frank Sinatra, Dean Martin, Bing Crosby, Sammy Davis, Jr.). Reprise.

ALBUM OF THE YEAR, CLASSICAL
• *Bernstein: Symphony No. 3 ("Kaddish")*, Leonard Bernstein conducting New York Philharmonic. Columbia.

Bizet: Carmen, Herbert von Karajan conducting Vienna Philharmonic (solos: Price, Corelli, Merrill, Freni). RCA.
Mahler: Symphony No. 5; Berg: Wozzeck Excerpts, Erich Leinsdorf conducting Boston Symphony (solo: Phyllis Curtin). RCA.
Verdi: Falstaff, Georg Solti conducting RCA Italiana Opera Orchestra and Chorus (solos: Evans, Merrill, Kraus, Simionato, Ligabue, Elias, others). RCA.
Verdi: Requiem Mass, Carlo Maria Giulini conducting Philharmonia Orchestra (solos: Schwarzkopf, Gedda, Ludwig, Ghiaurov). Angel.

BEST CLASSICAL COMPOSITION BY A CONTEMPORARY COMPOSER
• Samuel Barber, *Piano Concerto*. Columbia.
Leonard Bernstein, *Symphony No. 3 ("Kaddish")*. Columbia.
Charles E. Ives, *New England Holidays*.
Darius Milhaud, *A Frenchman in New York*. RCA.
Igor Stravinsky, *Sermon, Narrative and Prayer*. Columbia.

BEST CLASSICAL PERFORMANCE, ORCHESTRA
(Conductor's Award)
• Erich Leinsdorf conducting Boston Symphony, *Mahler: Symphony No. 5 in C Sharp Minor; Berg: Wozzeck Excerpts* (solo: Phyllis Curtin). RCA.
Leonard Bernstein conducting New York Philharmonic, *Mahler: Symphony No. 2 in C ("Resurrection")*. Columbia.
Yehudi Menuhin conducting Bath Festival Chamber Orchestra, *Handel: Concerti Grossi (12), Op. 6*. Angel.
Eugene Ormandy conducting Philadelphia Orchestra, *Bartók: Concerto for Orchestra*. Columbia.
Fritz Reiner conducting Chicago Symphony, *Haydn: Symphony No. 95 in C Minor, Symphony No. 101 in D Major ("Clock")*. RCA.
George Szell conducting Cleveland Orchestra, *R. Strauss: Symphonia Domestica*. Columbia.
Bruno Walter conducting Columbia Symphony, *Mozart: Last Six Symphonies*. Columbia.

Six years before her debut at New York's Metropolitan Opera, Marilyn Horne was voted Most Promising New Artist.

MOST PROMISING NEW CLASSICAL ARTIST

• Marilyn Horne, mezzo-soprano. London.
Mirella Freni, soprano. Angel.
Igor Kipnis, harpsichord. Epic.
Judith Raskin, soprano. Decca.
Jess Thomas, tenor. Deutsche Grammophon.

BEST OPERA RECORDING
(Conductor's Award)

• *Bizet: Carmen*, Herbert von Karajan conducting Vienna Philharmonic Orchestra and Chorus (solos: Price, Corelli, Merrill, Freni). RCA.
Mussorgsky: Boris Godounov, Alexander Melik-Pachaev conducting Orchestra and Chorus of Bolshoi Theatre. (solos: London, Arkhipova). Columbia.
Puccini: La Bohème, Thomas Schippers conducting Orchestra and Chorus of Opera House, Rome. (solos: Freni, Gedda, Adani, Sereni). Angel.
Smetana: The Bartered Bride, Rudolf Kempe conducting Bamberg Symphony. (soloists: Lorengar, Wunderlich, Frick). Angel.
Wagner: Lohengrin, Rudolf Kempe conducting Vienna Philharmonic, Chorus of Vienna State Opera. (solos: Thomas, Gummer, Fischer-Dieskau, Ludwig). Angel.
Verdi: Falstaff, Georg Solti conducting RCA Italiana Opera Orchestra and Chorus (solos: Evan, Merrill, Kraus, Simionato, Ligabue, Elias, Freni). RCA.

BEST CLASSICAL PERFORMANCE, INSTRUMENTAL SOLOIST(S) (WITH ORCHESTRA)

• Isaac Stern (Ormandy conducting Philadelphia Orchestra), *Prokofiev: Concerto No. 1 in D Major for Violin.* Columbia.
Julian Bream (Davis conducting Melos Chamber Orchestra), *Rodrigo: Concierto de Aranjuez for Guitar & Orchestra; Vivaldi: Concerto in D for Lute & Strings.* RCA.
John Browning (Szell conducting Cleveland Orchestra), *Barber: Concerto for Piano & Orchestra, Op. 38.* Columbia.
Rafael Druian, Abraham Skernick (Szell conducting Cleveland Orchestra), *Mozart: Sinfonia Concertante in E Flat Major for Violin, Viola & Orchestra.* Columbia.
Yehudi Menuhin (Kletzki conducting Philharmonia Orchestra), *Bloch: Concerto for Violin.* Angel.
Artur Rubinstein (Leinsdorf conducting Boston Symphony), *Beethoven: Concerto No. 5 in E Flat.* RCA.
Van Cliburn (Leinsdorf conducting Boston Symphony), *Brahms: Concerto No. 1 in D Minor for Piano.* RCA.

BEST CLASSICAL PERFORMANCE, INSTRUMENTAL SOLOIST(S) (WITHOUT ORCHESTRA)

• Vladimir Horowitz, *Vladimir Horowitz Plays Beethoven, Debussy, Chopin (Beethoven: Sonata No. 8 "Pathétique"; Debussy: Preludes; Chopin: Etudes & Scherzos 1 through 4).* Columbia.
Julian Bream, *Popular Classics for Spanish Guitar* (Villa-Lobos, Falla, etc.). RCA.
Glenn Gould, *Bach: Two and Three Part Inventions.* Columbia.
Igor Kipnis, *French Baroque Music for Harpsichord* (Couperin, Rameau, Boismortier). Epic.
Sviatoslav Richter, *Richter Plays Schubert (Sonata in A Major for Piano, "Wanderer" Fantasia for Piano).* Angel.
Artur Rubinstein, *A French Program* (Ravel, Poulenc, Fauré, Chabrier). RCA.

BEST CLASSICAL VOCAL SOLOIST PERFORMANCE
(WITH OR WITHOUT ORCHESTRA)
- Leontyne Price (Reiner conducting Chicago Symphony), *Berlioz: Nuits d'Ete; Falla: El Amor Brujo*. RCA.

Maria Callas (Rescigno conducting Paris Conservatoire), *Callas Sings Verdi*. Angel.

Boris Christoff (Cluytens conducting Paris Conservatoire Orchestra), *Tsars and Kings (Opera Arias)*. Angel.

Regine Crespin (Ansermet conducting Suisse Romande Orchestra), *Berlioz: Nuits d'Ete*. London.

Dietrich Fischer-Dieskau, *Shubert: die Winterreise*. Angel.

Peter Pears (Britten conducting London Symphony), *Britten: Serenade for Tenor, Horn & Strings*. London.

Joan Sutherland (Bonygne conducting London Symphony and New Symphony of London), *The Age of Bel Canto: Operatic Scenes*.

BEST CHAMBER PERFORMANCE, INSTRUMENTAL
- Jascha Heifetz, Gregor Piatigorsky (Jacob Lateiner, piano), *Beethoven: Trio No. 1 in E Flat, Op. 1, No. 1.* RCA.

Juilliard String Quartet, *Beethoven: Quartet No. 15 in A Minor Op. 132.* RCA.

Igor Markevich conducting Chamber Group (with narrators Jean Cocteau, Peter Ustinov, Jean-Marie Fertey, Anne Tonietti), *Stravinsky: L'Histoire du Soldat*. Philips.

Jean-Pierre Rampal, Robert Veyron-Lacroix, *Mozart: The Complete Flute Sonatas*. Epic.

Sviatoslav Richter, Mstislav Rostropovich, *Beethoven: Sonatas (5) for Piano & Cello (Complete)*. Philips.

Rudolph Serkin with Budapest String Quartet, *Brahms: Quintet in F Minor for Piano and Strings*. Columbia.

BEST CHAMBER MUSIC PERFORMANCE, VOCAL
- New York Pro Musica (Noah Greenberg conducting), *It Was a Lover and his Lass* (Morley, Byrd, and Others). Decca.

Deller Consort, *Music of Medieval France, 1200–1400, Sacred and Secular*. Vanguard.

Hermione Gingold, Russell Oberlin (Dunn conducting), *Walton: Façade*. Decca.

Golden Age Singers, *Music for Voices and Violins in the Time of Shakespeare*. Westminster.

Le Petit Ensemble Vocal de Montreal, *Dufay Motets*. Vox.

Vocal Arts Ensemble, *Music of the Renaissance (Des Prez, Morley)*. Counterpoint.

BEST CHORAL PERFORMANCE, OTHER THAN OPERA
- Robert Shaw conducting Robert Shaw Chorale, *Britten: A Ceremony of Carols*. RCA.

Rene Duclos conducting Rene Duclos Chorus. Georges Pretre conducting Paris Conservatoire, *Poulenc: Stabat Matter*. Angel.

Elliott Forbes conducting Harvard Glee Club, Radcliffe Choral Society. Alfred Nash Patterson conducting Chorus Pro Musica. Lorna Cooke De Varon conducting New England Conservatory Chorus. Rt. Rev. Russell H. Davis conducting St. John's Seminary Choir. Erich Leinsdorf conducting Boston Symphony, *Mozart: Requiem Mass in D Minor*. RCA.

Elmer Iseler conducting Toronto Festival Chorus. Igor Stravinsky conducting Canadian Broadcasting Corp. Orchestra, *Stravinsky: Symphony of Psalms*. Columbia.

George Lynn directing Westminster Choir. Eugene Ormandy conducting Philadelphia Orchestra, *Verdi: Requiem Mass*. Columbia.

Wilhelm Pitz directing Philharmonia Chorus. Carlo Maria Giulini conducting Philharmonia Orchestra, *Verdi: Requiem Mass*. Angel.

BEST ALBUM COVER, CLASSICAL
(Art Director's Award)
- Robert Jones. Jan Balet, graphic artist, *Saint-Saëns: Carnival of the Animals; Britten: Young Person's Guide to the Orchestra* (Fiedler conducting Boston Pops). RCA.

John Berg. Henrietta Condak, designer, *R. Strauss: Also Sprach Zarathustra* (Ormandy conducting Philadelphia Orchestra). Columbia.

Robert Cato, *Mexico: (Legacy Collection)* (Carlos Chavez). Columbia.

Bill Harvey; Lionel Kalish, graphic artist, *Court and Ceremonial Music of the 16th Century* (Roger Blanchard Ensemble with the Poulteau Consort). Nonesuch.

Robert Jones. David Hecht, photographer, *Mahler: Symphony No. 5 in C Sharp Minor* (Leinsdorf conducting Boston Symphony). RCA.

Marvin Schwartz, *Verdi: Requiem Mass* (Giulini conducting Philharmonia Orchestra). Angel.

BEST ENGINEERED RECORDING, CLASSICAL
• Douglas Larter, *Britten: Young Person's Guide to the Orchestra* (Carlo Maria Giulini conducting Philharmonia Orchestra). Angel.

Lewis Layton, *Mahler: Symphony No. 5 in C Sharp Minor* (Leinsdorf conducting Boston Symphony). RCA.

Lewis Layton, *Prokofiev: Symphony No. 5, Op. 100* (Leinsdorf conducting Boston Symphony). RCA.

Fred Plaut, *Mahler: Symphony No. 2 in C Minor ("Resurrection")* (Bernstein conducting New York Philharmonic). Columbia.

Fred Plaut, *Vladimir Horowitz Plays Beethoven, Debussy, Chopin* (solo: Vladimir Horowitz). Columbia.

BEST DOCUMENTARY, SPOKEN WORD, OR DRAMA RECORDING (OTHER THAN COMEDY)
• *BBC Tribute to John F. Kennedy*, "That Was the Week That Was" Cast. Decca.

Dialogue Highlights from "Becket," Richard Burton, Peter O'Toole. RCA.

Dylan, Original Cast with Sir Alec Guinness, Kate Reid.

The Kennedy Wit, John F. Kennedy, narrated by David Brinkley, introduction by Adlai Stevenson. RCA.

Shakespeare: Hamlet, Richard Burton (Original Cast: Hume Cronyn, John Gielgud, Alfred Drake, George Voskovec, Eileen Herlie, William Redfield, George Ross). Columbia.

Shakespeare: Othello, National Theatre of Great Britain, producers (Sir Laurence Olivier with Maggie Smith, Joyce Redman, Frank Finlay). RCA.

BEST COMEDY PERFORMANCE
• Bill Cosby, *I Started Out as a Child*. Warner Bros.

Woody Allen, *Woody Allen*. Colpix.

Godfrey Cambridge, *Ready or Not, Here Comes Godfrey Cambridge*. Epic.

Allan Sherman, *For Swingin' Livers Only!* Warner Bros.

Jonathan Winters, *Whistle Stopping*. Verve.

BEST RECORDING FOR CHILDREN
• *Mary Poppins*, Julie Andrews, Dick Van Dyke with David Tomlinson, Glynis Johns, Ed Wynn. Buena Vista.

Britten: Young Person's Guide to the Orchestra, Hugh Downs, narrator (Arthur Fiedler conducting Boston Pops Orchestra). RCA.

Burl Ives Chim Chim Cheree and Other Children's Choices, Burl Ives and Children's Chorus. Buena Vista.

Daniel Boone, Fess Parker. RCA.

A Spoonful of Sugar, Mary Martin and Do-Re-Mi Children's Chorus. Kapp.

BEST ENGINEERED RECORDING, SPECIAL OR NOVEL EFFECTS
• Dave Hassinger, *The Chipmunks Sing the Beatles* (the Chipmunks). Liberty.

Bill Robinson, *The Big Sounds of the Sport Cars*.

Larry Levine, *Walkin' in the Rain* (the Ronettes). Phillies.

James Malloy, "Main Theme: *"The Addams Family."* (Vic Mizzy). RCA.

John Norman, *Les Poupees de Paris* (Various artists). RCA.

BEST ENGINEERED RECORDING
• Phil Ramone, *Getz/Gilberto* (Stan Getz, Joao Gilberto). Verve.

Bernie Keville, *Pops Goes the Trumpet* (Al Hirt, Arthur Fiedler & Boston Pops). RCA.

George Kneurr, Frank Laico, *Who Can I Turn To?* (Tony Bennett). Columbia.

John Kraus, *Artistry in Voices & Brass* (Stan Kenton). Capitol.

James Malloy, *The Pink Panther* (Henry Mancini). RCA.

Chuck Seitz, *Sugar Lips* (Al Hirt). RCA.

BEST ALBUM COVER
(Art Director's Award)
- Robert Cato; Don Bronstein, photographer, *People* (Barbra Streisand). Columbia.

Robert Cato. Milton Glaser, graphic artist, *The Sound of Harlem* (Various Artists). Columbia.

Acy Lehman. Olga Albizu, graphic artist, *Getz/Gilberto* (Stan Getz, Joao Gilberto). Verve.

Acy Lehman. Tom Daly, graphic artist, *Oscar Peterson Plays My Fair Lady* (Oscar Peterson). Verve.

George Osak. George Jerman, photographer, *Guitar from Ipanema* (Laurindo Almeida). Capitol.

Ed Thrasher, *Poitier Meets Plato*. Warner Bros.

BEST ALBUM NOTES
(Annotator's Award)
- Stanton Catlin, Carleton Beals, *Mexico (Legacy Collection)* (Carlos Chavez). Columbia.

Neville Cardus, *Mahler: Symphony No. 5; Berg: Wozzeck Excerpts* (Phyllis Curtin) (Leinsdorf conducting Boston Symphony). RCA.

Alexander Cohen, *Beyond the Fringe '64* (Original Cast). Capitol.

Stan Getz, Joao Gilberto, Gene Lees, *Getz/Gilberto* (Stan Getz, Joao Gilberto). Verve.

Rory Guy, *The Definitive Piaf* (Edith Piaf). Capitol.

George Sponholtz, *The Young Chevalier* (Maurice Chevalier). Capitol.

Jack Tracy, *Quincy Jones Explores the Music of Henry Mancini* (Quincy Jones). Mercury.

It Was a Very Good Year ... for a Confederate Coup

It was one of the most controversial—and, some critics say, embarrassing—years in Grammy history.

The awards contest began, as *Variety* noted in a headline, with "lotsa beefs." The nominations "touched off another brouhaha this year," the publication added, pointing to "glaring omissions" from the lineup. The Beach Boys and Rolling Stones ruled the top of the charts in 1965, but, in terms of their quests for recognition from within the music industry, got no satisfaction from the record academy. The most glaring oversight, though, was noted in a different — and sassy — *Variety* headline: "Wha' Hoppen to Folk-Rock Hero Bob Dylan in Grammy Nominations?" The trade paper said, "The failure of Bob Dylan, the single most influential figure in the pop field since Elvis Presley, to receive a single mention has raised eyebrows over the judgment of the electorate of the academy."

The list of contenders wasn't a total fiasco. The academy continued its generous recognition of the Beatles by giving them nine nods for "Yesterday" and the music from their latest film, *Help!* (although it would give them a shocking "brushoff," noted *Variety*, once the awards were given out). All of the following were also nominated: the

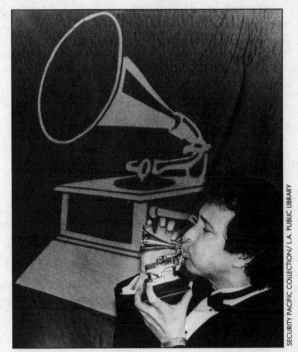

Ex-army bugler Herb Alpert won Record of the Year after rearranging the film song "A Taste of Honey" : "It was written as a waltz and I did it as a shuffle."

Supremes ("Stop! In the Name of Love"), Herman's Hermits ("Mrs. Brown, You've Got a Lovely Daughter"), Glen Yarbrough ("Baby the Rain Must Fall"), and Sam the Sham & the Pharaohs ("Wooly Bully"). Yarbrough and Herman's Hermits were up for Best New Artist, as were the Byrds and Sonny & Cher.

But the chief problem of the year's contest involved *who else* was nominated in the rock & roll categories: country & western artists, who had six slots of their own to compete in, a number many critics thought was excessive enough. The folksy country artists obviously didn't belong in the same lineup as mopheaded rockers from *another* country (like England, as in the case of Beatle Paul McCartney), but they landed bids nonetheless thanks to the considerable sway of the huge new block of faithful voters in Nashville.

A number of industry insiders believed that the academy made too many concessions when it negotiated to bring Nashville into the fold last year. Among the irate was Jerry Wexler, executive vice president of Atlantic Records, who, *Variety* said, "sent off a hot note to N.A.R.A.S. prexy Francis M. Scott, protesting the disproportion between the six categories allocated to country & western music and the one category given to rhythm & blues disks." Wexler added, "One is to wonder at the nature of the pressure to which [the academy] obviously succumbed when they subscribed to this weird alignment of categories."

Nashville's influence was so great that country artists even swept the rock awards.

Nashville used its clout to shower its record-setting star of last year, Roger Miller, with more nominations than it ever bestowed to one artist or group before: 10. The king of the Grammys was up for his classic "King of the Road" disc, a huge hit that sold more than half a million copies in 18 days. Considering its enormous pop success, the large block of Nashville voters judged it a worthy entry in the top rock categories, and, when it came time to vote for who would take home the golden gramophones, they again rallied behind their own golden boy.

Miller ended up with six Grammys, thereby topping the record he set last year when he tied Henry Mancini for reaping the most awards in a single year,

and established a new one that would not be overtaken until Michael Jackson's *Thriller* album enthralled both disc buyers and N.A.R.A.S. voters alike in 1983 when it won eight Grammys. "King of the Road" took five of the six for Miller: for best contemporary (r&r) single and male vocal performance as well as top country & western single, song, and male vocal performance. *The Return of Roger Miller* reaped the prize for Best Country & Western Album. A good-natured spoof of Miller's tune won the c&w female vocal honors for Jody Miller (no relation) for "Queen of the House."

Among those Roger Miller trounced was the Beatles' Paul McCartney (for "Yesterday") in the r&r single and male vocalist categories. The entire Fab Four in turn lost their nod for *Help!* in the r&r group performance slot to Nashville boys, the Statler Brothers ("Flowers on the Wall"), who were neither Statlers nor brothers, but a harmony group discovered by Johnny Cash that was also voted Best New Country & Western Artist. It was a defeat the Beatles suffered at the hands of other Nashville talent, though, that triggered the biggest "beef" of all and amounted to what is still considered one of the sourest notes in the history of music's highest honor.

Of their nine bids, the one award the Beatles seemed sure to get was one of the two prizes they took easily last year — Best Performance by a Vocal Group, a category in which they were now up against the Statler Brothers, Herman's Hermits, We Five, and the Anita Kerr Quartet.

Anita Kerr was a songstress of moderate success, who had a minor hit with "Joey Baby" in 1962 and was one of the first women to produce c&w albums. She was also a darling of the Grammy crowd, being vice president of the Nashville chapter and extremely active in the Los Angeles and New York academy branches. Due to her popularity among N.A.R.A.S. voters, no one dismissed her group's nomination for *We Dig Mancini* as lightweight, but when it prevailed over the Beatles' *Help!* the critics cried "foul!"

So did many of the other Grammy contenders who were at the ceremony. "I felt the same," says multiple nominee Herb Alpert, who recalls his surprise and dismay when Kerr was announced as the winner. "The Beatles made such an unusual statement and touched so many people musically and intellectually that we all felt at the time that they deserved to be recognized."

Not everyone was unhappy about the outcome. Some Beatle-bashing was still in vogue as late as 1965. "American musical tastes are finally creeping upward," jazz critic Leonard Feather wrote in the *L.A. Times*. "Any organization that presents 47 Grammys for 'artistic merit' without acknowledging the Beatles can't be all bad."

After the Confederate forage into pop territory was over, and the smoke cleared, some of pop's top talents were still left with considerable turf of their own. The Best New Artist honors were wrested from the Statler Brothers (who still held on to their Best New Country & Western Artists designation) by Tom Jones, the overtly sexy Welsh crooner who got his first big break in the big time when he recorded "It's Not Unusual" after it had been turned down by British singer Sandie Shaw. Another British vocalist, Petula Clark, whose "Downtown" was last year's Best Rock & Roll Recording, returned to claim the trophy for Best Contemporary (R&R) Female Vocal Performance for her latest release "I Know a Place." Barbra Streisand came back, too, to seize the laurels for Best Female Vocal Performance for a third year in a row, this time for her *My Name Is Barbra* album,

which had just won five Emmy Awards as a TV special.

Another returning champ, Bill Cosby, took the comedy prize for a second year in a row for *Why Is There Air?*, about a nervous father-to-be who frets over what lies ahead for him as a family man. Recalling his own childhood, he said on the LP, "I was playing with my navel [and] my mother said, 'All right, keep playin' with your navel, pretty soon you're gonna break it wide open, the air's gonna come right out of your body, you'll fly around the room backwards for 30 seconds, and land flat as a piece of paper, nothin' but your little eyes buggin' out.' I used to carry Band-Aids in case I had an accident." It remained a best seller for an astounding 152 weeks.

Among all the homecomers, none was greeted more generously than Frank Sinatra, winner of the Album of the Year award over Streisand, Herb Alpert & the Tijuana Brass, *The Sound of Music*'s film soundtrack — and, again, the Beatles. Sinatra hadn't been heard from at the Grammys since 1959 when he won the same prize for *Come Dance with Me*. Now the "Chairman of the Board" was 50 years old and, showing surprising sensitivity to his advancing age, chose to muse candidly about growing older in the winning LP *September of My Years*. *September* included "Last Night When We Were Young" and the tune that also won him the trophy for Best Male Vocal Performance, "It Was a Very Good Year."

1965 was a very good year for Sinatra for another reason: He was finally singing his own tune on a new label — his own. Back in the late 1950s, during his earlier Grammy reign, Sinatra felt confined by his contract with Capitol Records and wanted to break free. In January 1961, he started up the Reprise label and announced in the trade papers: "Now — a newer, happier, emancipated

Sinatra ... untrammeled, unfettered, unconfined." Two years later, and after signing up such pals as Dean Martin, Sammy Davis, Jr., Bing Crosby, and Rosemary Clooney, he sold two-thirds of his stock to Warner Bros. in exchange for several million dollars and various film commitments. Since he still held a sizeable stake in the firm, however, his return to the Grammys, for music on his Reprise label, marked an important career triumph for him. (*September* won Best Album Notes, too.)

Nashville's Anita Kerr Quartet scored one of the most notorious upsets in Grammy history by trouncing the Beatles for the group vocals prize.

Herb Alpert & the Tijuana Brass made up for their loss of the LP honors by nabbing three others, the second-highest tally of the night, after Roger Miller. "The mariachi band with the north-of-the-border sound" (as the *L.A. Herald Examiner* described them) reaped Record of the Year for "A Taste of Honey," in addition to statuettes for Best Non-Jazz Instrumental Performance and Best Instrumental Arrangement.

Alpert, a former Army bugler who played taps for as many as 19 funerals a day, once described his band, saying, "The seven who made up the Tijuana Brass sound were not of Spanish-American descent. We were four salamis, two bagels, and an American cheese."

Alpert was one of the "bagels," the product of Hungarian-Russian ancestry. He was born and raised in L.A. and often went down to the Mexican border town of Tijuana to watch bullfights for recreation. "That's where it hit me," he later said. "Something in the excitement of the crowd, the traditional mariachi music, it all clicked." The spectacle inspired Alpert to write "The Lonely Bull," but he wasn't well enough connected in the music business to snare a producer, so he and a friend, Jerry Moss, kicked in $100 apiece to produce it themselves. Their collaboration not only created a hit — it followed Sinatra's formula for success and launched a major new label. A&M record company subsequently signed up headliners Sergio Mendes and Brazil '66, Quincy Jones, Carole King, and the Police.

For "A Taste of Honey," Alpert rearranged the title song from the score of the 1961 British-produced film about a homely white girl who becomes pregnant by a black sailor. There were a number of recordings already extant, including one by the Beatles and another, Latin version that inspired Alpert to try his own interpretation. "I thought it was a wonderful melody," he says. "It was written as a waltz and I did it as a shuffle, which I thought was unique and would have an interesting, original flair to it." Record buyers and critics agreed: The parent album of "Honey," *Whipped Cream and Other Delights,* was so successful that it was still ranked number two by *Variety* on Grammy night, a year after its release. The only LP that surpassed it was Alpert's latest disc, *Going Places.* Today *Whipped Cream* holds the number 10 spot on *Billboard*'s 1991 list of the all-time Albums of Longevity.

The source of the Song of the Year winner was another motion picture, *The Sandpiper*, an ordinary sudser about a sordid love triangle that featured extraordinary talent, including Elizabeth Taylor, Richard Burton, Eva Marie Saint, and director Vincent Minnelli. Its equally exceptional love theme, "The Shadow of Your Smile," was written by lyricist Paul Webster and by composer Johnny Mandel, the latter of whom also won the Grammy for Best Original Score Written for a Motion Picture or a Television Show. Four weeks after its Grammy victory, "The Shadow of Your Smile" was hailed as the Song of the Year at the Oscars, too.

Like Frank Sinatra, Duke Ellington hadn't reaped gold at the Grammys since 1959, but now he was back for the large-group jazz instrumental performance salute to his *Ellington '66* collection. The jazz instrumental kudos for small groups went to the Ramsey Lewis Trio, whose *The "In" Crowd* at last catapulted them to fame after nine years of jamming in smoke-filled basement clubs. ("This group could hit the heights of acclaim achieved by such as Shearing, Brubeck and Garner," *Down Beat* predicted). The best jazz composition of 1965 was "Jazz Suite on the Mass Texts" by Lalo Schifrin. In the sole rhythm & blues category — best recording — James Brown snagged his first career Grammy for "Papa's Got a Brand New Bag," which he also wrote.

After pianist Vladimir Horowitz returned to Carnegie Hall in 1965 following a 12-year, self-imposed retirement from public appearances (he made his debut there in 1928), *The New York Times* called the evening "one of the most dramatic events in music history." He performed works by Schumann, Scriabin, Chopin, Debussy, and others. *High Fidelity* commented: "The way Horowitz energizes and characterizes a new idea in the second section of the *Fantasia*, his spacing and coloring of subordinate inner-notes in the Bach-Busoni Adagio, the almost Scriabin-esque mysteriousness he imparts to the end of that same Adagio by discreetly adjusting the balance of his chord progressions — all these feats represent pianism of the first order." The album recording (called "priceless" by the same magazine) won three awards (thus tying Herb Alpert & the Tijuana Brass for garnering the second-most trophies): Classical Album of the Year, Best Engineered Classical Recording, and Best Classical Performance — Instrumental Soloist (without Orchestra).

When the nominations came out, **Variety** *asked,* **"Wha' Hoppen to Folk-Rock Hero Bob Dylan?"**

The Grammy for best composition by a contemporary classical composer was awarded to Charles Ives for Symphony No. 4. Ives died in 1954, but "finished the symphony between 1910 and 1916," *The New York Times* noted. "It received its first performance, however, last spring." The reason, added *High Fidelity*, was that "for years people have said [it] was unplayable." The challenge was taken up by the American Symphony Orchestra under the direction of Leopold Stokowski, winner of the statuette for Best Classical Orchestra Performance. Artur Rubinstein won the instrumental soloist prize for Beethoven's Concerto No. 4 in G Major for Piano and Orchestra.

The year's best opera recording was Alban Berg's *Wozzeck*, performed by the Orchestra of German Opera (with Karl Böhn conducting), American soprano Evelyn Lear, German baritone Dietrich Fischer-Dieskau, and German tenor Fritz Wunderlich. ("Brilliant," *High Fidelity* declared, "a near essential recording.") Three-time past winner Leontyne Price returned to take the vocal honors for her *Salome* by Richard Strauss. "She is in excellent voice," *High Fidelity* said.

The Most Promising New Recording Artist laurel went to Peter Serkin, a pianist with a mostly modern repertory, who was a student of his famous pianist father, Rudolf.

When the winnings were tallied, they triggered renewed carping in the industry: RCA had 12 awards, Columbia 10, Mercury and its subsidiaries 9, and Warner Bros.-Reprise 7. "MGM Records, one of the hottest pop labels in the business during 1965," *Variety* said, "received no awards outside of a Grammy for *Wozzeck* opera on the Deutsche Grammophon label distributed by MGM." In addition to what some music critics were calling Nashville's "Confederate invasion" this year and what *Variety* was terming "the brush of the Beatles," N.A.R.A.S. was dogged with another problem: the old issue of block voting, which would persist for years to come.

"Capitol execs were particularly bitter" over receiving only one award, *Variety* added. "One company exec said that Capitol should walk out of the Academy."

N.A.R.A.S. had its biggest turnout ever for the ceremonies held in Los Angeles, New York, Chicago, and Nashville. In Los Angeles, the event took place, as it did the previous year, at the Beverly Hilton, while in New York the academy added some of the glitzy trappings that are traditionally part of other show business events. As *Variety* noted, "The presentation at the Hotel Astor was glamorized with a kleig-lighted entrance for the guests as they stepped out of limousines into the hotel."

1965

A wards were bestowed on March 15, 1966, for the eligibility period December 1, 1964, to November 30, 1965, at ceremonies held at the Beverly Hilton Hotel in Los Angeles, the Hotel Astor in New York, and at dinners held in Nashville and Chicago.

ALBUM OF THE YEAR
• *September of My Years*, Frank Sinatra. Sonny Burke, A&R producer. Reprise.
Help! Beatles. George Martin, A&R producer. Capitol.
My Name Is Barbra, Barbra Streisand. Bob Mersey, A&R producer. Columbia.
My World, Eddy Arnold. Chet Atkins, A&R producer. RCA.
The Sound of Music, Julie Andrews and cast. Neely Plumb, A&R producer. RCA.

Whipped Cream and Other Delights, Herb Alpert & the Tijuana Brass. Herb Alpert, Jerry Moss, A&R producers. A&M.

RECORD OF THE YEAR
• "A Taste of Honey," Herb Alpert & Tijuana Brass. Herb Alpert, Jerry Moss, A&R producers. A&M.
"The 'In' Crowd," Ramsey Lewis Trio. Esmond Edwards, A&R producer. Cadet.
"King of the Road," Roger Miller. Jerry Kennedy, A&R producer. Smash.
"The Shadow of Your Smile (Love Theme from *The Sandpiper*)," Tony Bennett. Ernie Altschuler, Al Stanton, A&R producers. Columbia.
"Yesterday," Paul McCartney. George Martin, A&R producer. Capitol.

SONG OF THE YEAR
(Songwriter's Award)
• "The Shadow of Your Smile (Love Theme from *The Sandpiper*)," Paul Francis Webster, Johnny Mandel. Mercury.
"I Will Wait for You (Theme from *Umbrellas of Cherbourg*)," Michel Legrand, Norman Gimbel, Jacques Demy. Philips.
"King of the Road," Roger Miller. Smash.
"September of My Years," Jimmy Van Heusen, Sammy Cahn. Reprise.
"Yesterday," John Lennon, Paul McCartney. Capitol.

BEST NEW ARTIST
• Tom Jones. Parrot.
Byrds. Columbia.
Herman's Hermits. MGM.
Horst Jankowski. Mercury.
Marilyn Maye. RCA.
Sonny & Cher. Atco.
Glenn Yarbrough. RCA.

BEST VOCAL PERFORMANCE, MALE
• Frank Sinatra, "It Was a Very Good Year." Reprise.
Tony Bennett, "The Shadow of Your Smile (Love Theme from *The Sandpiper*)." Columbia.
Paul McCartney, "Yesterday." Capitol.
Roger Miller, "King of the Road." Smash.
Glenn Yarbrough, "Baby the Rain Must Fall." RCA.

BEST VOCAL PERFORMANCE, FEMALE
• Barbra Streisand, *My Name Is Barbra*. Columbia.
Petula Clark, "Downtown." Warner Bros.
Jackie DeShannon, "What the World Needs Now Is Love." Imperial.
Astrud Gilberto, *The Astrud Gilberto Album*. Verve.
Nancy Wilson, *Gentle Is My Love*. Capitol.

BEST PERFORMANCE BY A VOCAL GROUP
• Anita Kerr Quartet, *We Dig Mancini*. RCA.
Beatles, "Help!" Capitol.
Herman's Hermits, "Mrs. Brown, You've Got a Lovely Daughter." MGM.
Statler Brothers, "Flowers on the Wall." Columbia.
We Five, "You Were on My Mind." A&M.

BEST PERFORMANCE BY A CHORUS
• Swingle Singers, *Anyone for Mozart?* Philips.
Paul Horn and Chorus, *Jazz Suite on the Mass Texts*. RCA.
Henry Mancini Chorus and Orchestra, *Dear Heart & Other Songs About Love*. RCA.
New Christy Minstrels, *Chim Chim Cher-ee & Other Happy Songs*. Columbia.
Robert Shaw Chorale and Orchestra, *Robert Shaw Chorale & Orchestra on Broadway*. RCA.

SECURITY PACIFIC COLLECTION/ L.A. PUBLIC LIBRARY

Roger Miller's six victories in a single year set a Grammy record. Michael Jackson would "beat it" in 1983.

BEST CONTEMPORARY (R&R) SINGLE
• "King of the Road," Roger Miller. Smash.
"Baby the Rain Must Fall," Glenn Yarbrough. RCA.
"It's Not Unusual," Tom Jones. Parrot.
"What the World Needs Now Is Love," Jackie DeShannon. Imperial.
"Yesterday," Paul McCartney. Capitol.

BEST CONTEMPORARY (R&R) VOCAL PERFORMANCE, MALE
• Roger Miller, "King of the Road." Smash.
Len Barry, "1-2-3." Decca.

Tom Jones, "What's New, Pussycat?" Parrot.

Paul McCartney, "Yesterday." Capitol.

Johnny Tillotson, "Heartaches by the Number." MGM.

BEST CONTEMPORARY (R&R) VOCAL PERFORMANCE, FEMALE
• Petula Clark, "I Know a Place." Warner Bros.

Fontella Bass, "Rescue Me." Chess.

Jackie DeShannon, "What the World Needs Now Is Love." Imperial.

Lesley Gore, "Sunshine, Lollipops and Rainbows." Mercury.

Barbara Lewis, "Baby I'm Yours." Atlantic.

BEST CONTEMPORARY (R&R) PERFORMANCE BY A GROUP (VOCAL OR INSTRUMENTAL)
• Statler Brothers, "Flowers on the Wall." Columbia.

Beatles, "Help!" Capitol.

Herman's Hermits, "Mrs. Brown, You've Got a Lovely Daughter." MGM.

Sam the Sham & the Pharaohs, "Woolly Bully." MGM.

The Supremes, "Stop in the Name of Love." Motown.

BEST RHYTHM & BLUES RECORDING
• "Papa's Got a Brand New Bag," James Brown. King.

"In the Midnight Hour," Wilson Pickett. Atlantic.

"My Girl," the Temptations. Motown.

"Shake," Sam Cooke. RCA.

"Shotgun," Jr. Walker & the All Stars. Soul.

BEST ORIGINAL JAZZ COMPOSITION
(Composer's Award)
• Lalo Schifrin, *Jazz Suite on the Mass Texts*. RCA.

John Coltrane, *A Love Supreme*. Impulse.

Duke Ellington, Billy Strayhorn, "Virgin Islands Suite." Reprise.

Wes Montgomery, *Bumpin'*. Verve.

Oscar Peterson, "Canadiana Suite." Limelite.

Eddie Sauter, *Mickey One*. MGM.

BEST JAZZ PERFORMANCE, SMALL GROUP OR SOLOIST WITH SMALL GROUP
• Ramsey Lewis Trio, *The "In" Crowd*. Cadet.

John Coltrane, *A Love Supreme*. Impulse.

Paul Desmond, Jim Hall, *Glad to be Unhappy*. RCA.

Bill Evans Trio, *Trio '65*. Verve.

Paul Horn, *Cycle*. RCA.

Gary McFarland Group, *Soft Samba*. Verve.

Clark Terry, Bob Brookmeyer Quintet, *The Power of Positive Swinging*. Mainstream.

Cal Tjader, *Soul Sauce*. Verve.

BEST JAZZ PERFORMANCE, LARGE GROUP OR SOLOIST WITH LARGE GROUP
• Duke Ellington Orchestra, *Ellington '66*. Reprise

Kenny Burrell, Gil Evans Orchestra, *Kenny Burrell: Guitar Forms*. Verve.

Stan Getz, *Mickey One*. Verve.

Dizzy Gillespie (Fuller, Monterey Jazz Festival), "Love Theme from *The Sandpiper*." World Pacific.

Paul Horn, *Jazz Suite on the Mass Texts*. RCA.

Rod Levitt, *Insight*. RCA.

Wes Montgomery with String Orchestra, *Bumpin'*. Verve.

BEST COUNTRY & WESTERN ALBUM
• *The Return of Roger Miller*, Roger Miller. Smash.

Father & Son: Hank Williams & Hank Williams, Jr., Hank Williams & Hank Williams, Jr. MGM.

The Jim Reeves Way, Jim Reeves. RCA.

More of That Guitar Country, Chet Atkins. RCA.

My World, Eddy Arnold. RCA.

BEST COUNTRY & WESTERN SINGLE
• "King of the Road," Roger Miller. Smash.

"Flowers on the Wall," the Statler Brothers. Columbia.

"Is It Really Over," Jim Reeves. RCA.

"Make the World Go Away," Eddy Arnold. RCA.

"May the Bird of Paradise Fly Up Your Nose," "Little" Jimmy Dickens. Columbia.

"Yakety Axe," Chet Atkins. RCA.

BEST COUNTRY & WESTERN SONG
(Songwriter's Award)
• "King of the Road," Roger Miller. Smash.

"Crystal Chandelier," Ted Harris. RCA.

"Flowers on the Wall," Lewis Dewitt. Columbia.

"May the Bird of Paradise Fly Up Your Nose," Neal Merritt. Columbia.
"What's He Doing in My World," Carl Belew, B.J. Moore, Eddie Busch. RCA.

BEST NEW COUNTRY & WESTERN ARTIST
• Statler Brothers. Columbia.
Wilma Burgess. Decca.
Norma Jean. RCA.
Jody Miller. Capitol.
Del Reeves. United Artists.

BEST COUNTRY & WESTERN VOCAL PERFORMANCE, MALE
• Roger Miller, "King of the Road." Smash.
Eddy Arnold, "Make the World Go Away." RCA.
Bobby Bare, "Talk Me Some Sense." RCA.
Carl Belew, "Crystal Chandelier," RCA.
Jim Reeves, "Is It Really Over." RCA.

BEST COUNTRY & WESTERN VOCAL PERFORMANCE, FEMALE
• Jody Miller, "Queen of the House." Capitol.
Molly Bee, "Single Girl Again." MGM.
Wilma Burgess, "Baby." Decca.
Skeeter Davis, "Sunglasses." RCA.
Dottie West, "Before the Ring on Your Finger Turns Green." RCA.

BEST FOLK RECORDING
• *An Evening with Belafonte/Makeba,* Harry Belafonte, Miriam Makeba. RCA.
A Song Will Rise, Peter, Paul & Mary. Warner Bros.
Makeba Sings, Miriam Makeba. RCA.
Roscoe Holcomb: The High Lonesome Sound, Roscoe Holcomb. Folkways.
Strangers and Cousins, Pete Seeger. Columbia.
There But for Fortune, Joan Baez. Vanguard.
The Womenfolk at the Hungry 1, Womenfolk. RCA.

BEST GOSPEL OR OTHER RELIGIOUS RECORDING
• *Southland Favorites*, George Beverly Shea and Anita Kerr Quartet. RCA.
All Day Sing and Dinner on the Ground, Statesmen Quartet with Hovie Lister. RCA
Bob Ashton's Songs of Living Faith, Ralph Carmichael Singers and Orchestra. Stylist.

How Great Thou Art, Kate Smith. RCA.
Just Keep on Singing, Marian Anderson. RCA.
Let Me Walk with Thee, Tennessee Ernie Ford. Capitol.
Something Old, Something New, Blackwood Brothers. RCA.
What a Happy Time, Happy Goodman Family. Word.

BEST INSTRUMENTAL ARRANGEMENT
• Herb Alpert, "A Taste of Honey" (Herb Alpert & the Tijuana Brass). A&M.
Bob Florence, "Mission to Moscow" (Si Zentner Orchestra). RCA.
Neal Hefti, "Girl Talk" (Neal Hefti). Columbia.
Horst Jankowski, "Walk in the Black Forest" (Jankowski Orchestra). Mercury.
Johnny Mandel, "The Shadow of Your Smile" (Armbruster Orchestra). Mercury.
Jack Mason, "A Hard Day's Night" (Fiedler conducting Boston Pops). RCA.

BEST ARRANGEMENT ACCOMPANYING A VOCALIST OR INSTRUMENTALIST
• Gordon Jenkins, "It Was a Very Good Year" (Frank Sinatra). Reprise.
Burt Bacharach, "What the World Needs Now Is Love" (Jackie DeShannon). Imperial.
Don Costa, "He Touched Me" (Barbra Streisand). Columbia.
Gil Evans, "Greensleeves" (Kenny Burrell). Verve.
Bob Florence, "Everything I've Got" (Vikki Carr). Liberty.
George Martin, "Yesterday" (Beatles). Capitol.
Claus Ogerman, "Day By Day" (Astrud Gilberto). Verve.
Les Reed, "It's Not Unusual" (Tom Jones). Parrot.

BEST INSTRUMENTAL PERFORMANCE, NON-JAZZ
• Herb Alpert & the Tijuana Brass, "A Taste of Honey." A&M.
Chet Atkins, "Yakety Axe." RCA.
Neal Hefti, "Girl Talk." Columbia.
Horst Jankowski, "Walk in the Black Forest." Mercury.
Henry Mancini, "The Great Race." RCA.

BEST SCORE FROM AN ORIGINAL CAST SHOW

• *On a Clear Day You Can See Forever*, Alan Jay Lerner, Burton Lane. RCA.
Bajour, Walter Marks. Columbia.
Baker Street, Marian Grudeff, Raymond Jessell. MGM.
Do I Hear a Waltz? Richard Rodgers, Stephen Sondheim. Columbia.
Half a Sixpence, David Heneker. RCA.

BEST ORIGINAL SCORE, MOTION PICTURE OR TV SHOW
(Composer's Award)

• *The Sandpiper* (Robert Armbruster Orchestra), Johnny Mandel. Mercury.
Help! (Beatles), John Lennon, Paul McCartney, George Harrison, Ken Thorne. Capitol.
The Man from U.N.C.L.E. (Hugo Montenegro Orchestra), Lalo Schifrin, Mort Stevens, Walter Scharf, Jerry Goldsmith. RCA.
The Umbrellas of Cherbourg (Michel Legrand Orchestra), Michel Legrand, Jacques Demy. Philips.
Zorba the Greek (Mikis Theodorakis Orchestra), Mikis Theodorakis. 20th Century-Fox.

ALBUM OF THE YEAR, CLASSICAL

• *Horowitz at Carnegie Hall, An Historic Return*, Vladimir Horowitz. Thomas Frost, A&R producer. Columbia.
Berg: Wozzeck, Karl Bohm conducting Orchestra of German Opera, Berlin. Otto Gerdes, A&R producer. Deutsche Grammophon.
Chopin: 8 Polonaises, 4 Impromptus, Artur Rubinstein. Max Wilcox, A&R producer. RCA.
Ives: Symphony No. 4, Leopold Stokowski conducting American Symphony. John McClure, A&R producer. Columbia.
Strauss: Salome ("Dance of the Seven Veils," Interlude & Final Scene); The Egyptian Helen (Awakening Scene), Erich Leinsdorf conducting Boston Symphony (solo: Leontyne Price). Richard Mohr, A&R producer. RCA.

BEST COMPOSITION BY A CONTEMPORARY CLASSICAL COMPOSER
(Composer's Award)

• Charles Ives, *Symphony No. 4*. Columbia.
Benjamin Britten, *Cantata Misericordium*. London.

Leonard Bernstein, *Chichester Psalms*. London.
David Diamond, *String Quartet No. 4*. Epic.
Morton Gould, *World War I Suite*. RCA.
William Walton, *Variations on a Theme by Hindemith*. Columbia.

BEST CLASSICAL PERFORMANCE, ORCHESTRA
(Conductor's Award)

• Leopold Stokowski conducting American Symphony, *Ives: Symphony No. 4*. Columbia.
Morton Gould conducting Chicago Symphony, *Gould: Spirituals for Orchestra; Copland: Dance Symphony*. RCA.
Herbert von Karajan conducting Berlin Philharmonic, *Bach: Brandenburg Concertos*. Deutsche Grammophon.
Erich Leinsdorf conducting Boston Symphony, *Prokofiev: Symphony No. 6 in E Flat Minor*. RCA.
Jean Martinon conducting Chicago Symphony, *Ravel: Daphnis et Chloë Suite No. 2/ Roussel: Bacchus and Ariadne, Suite No. 2*. RCA.
Arturo Toscanini conducting NBC Symphony, *Berlioz: Romeo and Juliet*. RCA.

MOST PROMISING NEW CLASSICAL ARTIST

• Peter Serkin, pianist. RCA.
Nicolai Ghiaurov, bass. London.
Evelyn Lear, soprano. Deutsche Grammophon.
Raymond Lewenthal, pianist. RCA.
Shirley Verrett, mezzo. RCA.

BEST CLASSICAL CHAMBER MUSIC PERFORMANCE, INSTRUMENTAL OR VOCAL

• Juilliard String Quartet, *Bartók: The Six String Quartets*. Columbia.
Vladimir Ashkenazy, Malcolm Frager, *Mozart/Schumann Recital*. London.
Erick Friedman, Bruce Prince-Joseph, *Bach: The Six Sonatas for Violin & Harpsichord*. RCA.
Yehudi Menuhin and Members of Bath Festival Orchestra, *A Purcell Anthology*. Angel.
Isaac Stern, Eugene Istomin, Leonard Rose, *Schubert: Trio No. 1 in B Flat for Piano*. Columbia.
Joseph Szigeti, Bela Bartók, *Sonata Recital by Szigeti & Bartók* (Bartók/ Beethoven/ Debussy). Vanguard.

BEST CLASSICAL PERFORMANCE, INSTRUMENTAL SOLOIST(S) (WITH ORCHESTRA)

- Artur Rubinstein (Leinsdorf conducting Boston Symphony), *Beethoven: Concerto No. 4 in G Major for Piano and Orchestra*. RCA.

Gary Graffman (Ormandy conducting Philadelphia Orchestra), *Tchaikovsky: Concerto No. 2 in G Major for Piano & Orchestra; Concerto No. 3 in E Flat Major for Piano & Orchestra*. Columbia.

Leonard Pennario (Previn conducting Royal Philharmonic), *Rachmaninoff: Concerto No. 1 in F Sharp for Piano; Concerto No. 4 in G Minor for Piano*. RCA.

Rudolf Serkin (Toscanini conducting NBC Symphony), *Beethoven: Concerto No. 4 in G Major for Piano and Orchestra*. RCA.

Isaac Stern (Bernstein conducting New York Philharmonic), *Barber: Concerto for Violin & Orchestra; Hindemith: Concerto for Violin & Orchestra*. Columbia.

Isaac Stern, Leonard Rose, Eugene Istomin (Ormandy conducting Philadelphia Orchestra), *Beethoven: Triple Concerto*. Columbia.

BEST CLASSICAL PERFORMANCE, INSTRUMENTAL SOLOIST(S) (WITHOUT ORCHESTRA)

- Vladimir Horowitz, *Horowitz at Carnegie Hall, An Historic Return*. Columbia.

Vladimir Ashkenazy, *Chopin Ballades (1, 2, 3, 4)*. London.

Julian Bream, *Julian Bream in Concert*. RCA.

Glenn Gould, *Bach: Well Tempered Clavier, Book 1, Vol. 3 (17–24)*. Columbia.

Raymond Lewenthal, *Alkan: Piano Music*. RCA.

Artur Rubinstein, *Chopin: 8 Polonaises and 4 Impromptus*. RCA.

BEST OPERA RECORDING
(Conductor's Award)

- *Berg: Wozzeck*, Karl Bohm conducting Orchestra of German Opera, Berlin (solos: Fischer-Dieskau, Lear, Wunderlich). Deutsche Grammophon.

Bellini: Norma, Richard Bonynge conducting London Symphony and Chorus (solos: Sutherland, Horne, Alexander, Cross). RCA.

Artur Rubinstein was honored for his mastery of Beethoven's Concerto No. 4.

Verdi: La Forza Del Destino, Thomas Schippers conducting RCA Italiana Opera Orchestra and Chorus (solos: Price, Tucker, Verrett, Merrill, Tozzi, Flagello). RCA.

Verdi: Luisa Miller, Fausto Cleva conducting RCA Italiana Opera Orchestra & Chorus (solos: Moffo, Bergonzi, Verrett, MacNeil, Tozzi, Flagello). RCA.

Wagner: Götterdämmerung, Georg Solti conducting Vienna Philharmonic (solos: Nilsson, Windgassen, Fischer-Dieskau). London.

BEST CLASSICAL CHORAL PERFORMANCE, OTHER THAN OPERA

- Robert Shaw conducting Robert Shaw Chorale, RCA Victor Symphony, *Stravinsky: Symphony of Psalms; Poulenc: Gloria*. RCA.

Benjamin Britten conducting London Symphony Chorus and Orchestra, *Britten: Cantata Misericordium*. London.

Herbert von Karajan conducting Vienna Singverein and Berlin Philharmonic, *Brahms: A German Requiem*. Deutsche Grammophon.

Robert Page conducting Temple University Choir; Eugene Ormandy conducting Philadelphia Orchestra, *Berlioz: Requiem*. Columbia.

Wilhelm Pitz, chorus master, Philharmonia Chorus. Otto Klemperer conducting Philharmonia Orchestra, *Handel: Messiah*. Angel.

Wolfgang Schubert conducting Bavarian Radio Symphony Chorus. Rafael Kubelik conducting Bavarian Radio Symphony, *Schönberg: Gurrelieder*. Deutsche Grammophon.

BEST CLASSICAL VOCAL PERFORMANCE (WITH OR WITHOUT ORCHESTRA)

• Leontyne Price (Leinsdorf conducting Boston Symphony), *Strauss: Salome ("Dance of the Seven Veils," Interlude, Final Scene); The Egyptian Helen (Awakening Scene)*. RCA.

Dietrich Fischer-Dieskau (Moore, pianist), *Schumann: Liederkreis*. Angel.

Mirella Freni (Ferraris conducting Rome Opera House Orchestra), *Mirella Freni—Operatic Arias*. Angel.

Nicolai Ghiaurov (Downes conducting London Symphony), *Russian & French Arias*. London.

Anna Moffo (Stokowski conducting American Symphony), *Canteloube: Songs of the Auvergne; Rachmaninoff: Vocalise; Villa Lobos: Bachianas Brasileiras No. 5*. RCA.

Shirley Verrett, *Falla: Seven Popular Spanish Songs*. RCA.

Galina Vishnevskaya (Markevitch conducting Russian State Symphony), *Mussorgsky: Songs*.

BEST ENGINEERED RECORDING, CLASSICAL

• Fred Plaut, *Horowitz at Carnegie Hall, An Historic Return* (Vladimir Horowitz). Columbia.

Edward T. Graham, *Ives: Symphony No. 4* (Stokowski conducting American Symphony Orchestra). Columbia.

Bernard Keville, *Gould: Spirituals for Orchestra; Copland: Dance Symphony* (Gould conducting Chicago Symphony). RCA.

Bernard Keville, *Stravinsky: Symphony of Psalms* (Robert Shaw Chorale, RCA Symphony). RCA.

Anthony Salvatore, *Strauss: Salome; The Egyptian Helen* (Leinsdorf conducting Boston Symphony; solo: Leontyne Price). RCA.

BEST SPOKEN WORD OR DRAMA RECORDING

• *John F. Kennedy: As We Remember Him*, produced by Goddard Lieberson. Columbia.

The Brontës, Margaret Webster. Vanguard.

Much Ado About Nothing, National Theatre of Great Britain. RCA.

A Personal Choice, Sir Alec Guinness. RCA.

A Time to Keep: 1964, Chet Huntley, David Brinkley. RCA.

The Voice of the Uncommon Man, Adlai Stevenson (produced by Mort Nasatir). MGM.

BEST COMEDY PERFORMANCE

• Bill Cosby, *Why Is There Air?* Warner Bros.

Godfrey Cambridge, *Them Cotton Pickin' Days is Over*. Epic.

Earl Doud, Allen Robin, *Welcome to the L.B.J. Ranch*. Capitol.

Smothers Brothers, *Mom Always Liked You Best*. Mercury.

Various artists, written by Bob Booker & George Foster, *You Don't Have to Be Jewish*. Kapp.

BEST RECORDING FOR CHILDREN

• *Dr. Seuss Presents "Fox in Sox" and "Green Eggs and Ham,"* Marvin Miller. RCA.

Love Songs for Children: "A" You're Adorable, Diahann Carroll. Golden.

Patrick Muldoon & His Magic Balloon, Carmel Quinn. RCA.

Supercalifragelistic Expialidocious, Chipmunks (David Seville). Liberty.

Winnie the Pooh & the Honey Tree, Sterling Holloway, Sebastian Cabot. Disney.

BEST ENGINEERED RECORDING

• Larry Levine, "A Taste of Honey" (Herb Alpert & the Tijuana Brass). A&M.

Richard Bogert, James Malloy, *Latin Sound of Henry Mancini* (Henry Mancini). RCA.

Lowell Frank, *September of My Years* (Frank Sinatra). Reprise.

Frank Laico, *My Name Is Barbra* (Barbra Streisand). Columbia.

Al Pachucki, Chuck Seitz, *More of That Guitar Country* (Chet Atkins). RCA.

Chuck Seitz, William Vandevort, *That Honey Horn Sound* (Al Hirt). RCA.

BEST ALBUM COVER, PHOTOGRAPHY
(Art Director's Award)
• Bob Jones; Ken Whitmore, photographer, *Jazz Suite on the Mass Texts* (Paul Horn). RCA.
John Berg; Dan Kramer, photographer, *Bringing It All Back Home* (Bob Dylan). Columbia.
Robert Cat;. Sheldon Streisand, photographer, *My Name is Barbra* (Barbra Streisand). Columbia.
Ed Thrasher; Sherman Weisburd, photographer, *The Aznavour Story* (Charles Aznavour). Reprise.
Acy Lehman; Rudolph Regname, photographer, *Kenny Burrell: Guitar Forms* (Kenny Burrell & Gil Evans Orchestra). Verve.
Jerry Smokler; W. Eugene Smith, photographer, *Monk* (Thelonious Monk). Columbia.
Peter Whorf, art director/photographer, *Whipped Cream and Other Delights* (Herb Alpert & the Tijuana Brass). A&M.

BEST ALBUM COVER, GRAPHIC ARTS
(Art Director's Award)
• George Estes; James Alexander, graphic artist, *Bartók: Concerto No. 2 for Violin; Stravinsky: Concerto for Violin* (Silverstein, Leinsdorf, Boston Symphony). RCA.

John Berg, art director/graphic artist, *Horowitz at Carnegie Hall* (Horowitz). Columbia.
John Berg, art director/graphic artist, *William Tell & Other Favorite Overtures* (Bernstein conducting New York Philharmonic). Columbia.
George Estes; Charles White, graphic artist, *Gould: Spirituals for Orchestra; Copland: Dance Symphony* (Gould conducting Chicago Symphony). RCA.
Jerry Smokler; Paul Davis, graphic artist, *Solo Monk* (Thelonious Monk). Columbia.
Ed Thrasher; Patrick Blackwell, graphic artist, *Concert in the Virgin Islands* (Duke Ellington). Reprise.

BEST ALBUM NOTES
• Stan Cornyn, *September of My Years* (Frank Sinatra). Reprise.
Dom Cerulli, *The Voice of the Uncommon Man* (Adlai Stevenson). MGM.
Stanley Dance, *Grand Terrace Band* (Earl Hines). RCA.
Charles Lamb, *Father & Son: Hank Williams & Hank Williams, Jr.* MGM.
Gustav Rudolf Sellner, Otto Gerdes, *Berg: Wozzeck* (Karl Böhm conducting Orchestra of German Opera). Deutsche Grammophon.

"Ol' Blue Eyes" Is Back

The big winner of 1966 was certainly no stranger on Grammy night. Frank Sinatra had five awards so far — including Albums of the Year *Come Dance with Me* in 1959 and last year's *September of My Years*. 1966 would mark his swan song at the Grammys — Ol' Blue Eyes has not picked up another award since — but his last triumph so far was another show-stopper. "The old pro with the receding hairline left the mop-top, guitar-strumming set at the starting gate," noted UPI, "when he walked off with three top Grammy Awards."

"For Sinatra, it was the most memorable Grammy ceremony in the nine-year history of the awards," *The Los Angeles Herald Examiner* said, declaring him "still King of the Swingers." He held onto the LP category when *Sinatra: A Man & His Music* took Album of the Year honors. His other two victories were for "Strangers in the Night" (from the album of the same name), which reaped Record of the Year, and a third best male vocal performance trophy for the self-styled saloon singer. "Strangers" also snagged arrangement and engineering trophies. *Sinatra at the Sands* took Best Album Notes.

Frank Sinatra has had more Top 10 albums than any other singer in the rock

Sinatra continued to reign as "King of the Swingers" when "Strangers in the Night" won Record of the Year and Sinatra: A Man & His Music *was voted best LP.*

era (31, a number tied only by the Rolling Stones, who have never won a competitive Grammy) and the most in the Top 40: 49. (Elvis Presley is second with 48.) *A Man & His Music* was an anthology of Sinatra's biggest career hits that included overview narration by the singer. *Strangers in the Night* was one of his four albums to reach number one (the other three being *Come Fly with Me, Nice 'n' Easy,* and *Sinatra Sings for Only the Lonely*).

Strangers' title song was by German composer Bert Kaempfert from the score for a forgettable James Garner spy film called *A Man Could Get Killed*. Music industry insiders knew early on that it was a hit tune, though, and a rush ensued, involving Sinatra, Bobby Darrin, and Jack Jones, to record it as a single as soon as English lyrics were written. When Sinatra discovered that Jones's version was due out in three days, an orchestra and arrangement were thrown together over the next 48 hours. On the third day, Sinatra stepped into a Reprise recording studio at 8 p.m., finished the taping session by 9, and the song was on the nation's airwaves 24 hours later.

"Strangers" turned out to be the first of Sinatra's two number-one singles in the rock era, a pinnacle he hit just 18 weeks after his daughter Nancy was there with "These Boots Are Made for Walkin'" (a losing nominee for two vocal performance Grammys). Nine months later, he and Nancy teamed up for his second chart-topper, "Somethin' Stupid" (a losing contender for 1967 Record of the Year), the only father-daughter duet ever to hold that status. *Billboard* now ranks Sinatra as the number-three singer in its list of the Top 100 Artists of the Rock Era, after the Beatles and Sinatra's old nemesis Elvis Presley.

The only defeat Ol' Blue Eyes and his music suffered was for Song of the Year, which went to John Lennon and Paul McCartney for "Michelle," thereby redressing the "brushoff" the Beatles got from the Grammys last year. (The Liverpool lads nonetheless got the brush off from *The New York Times*, which, strangely, failed to note the historic win in its roundup Grammy coverage.) The Beatles and their music were up for seven prizes in all, including Album of the Year (for *Revolver*), and won two more prizes in addition to top song: Best Album Cover (for art director

Klaus Voormann) and Best Contemporary (R&R) Solo Vocal Performance—Male or Female for McCartney for "Eleanor Rigby." (The r&r vocal honors had been split by gender last year, but were combined for 1966.) Curiously, on the same day that McCartney's ode to loneliness reigned as the number-one platter in America — August 29, 1966 — the Beatles performed their last paid public concert at Candlestick Park in San Francisco.

The success of "Michelle" was historic because it marked a major shift in Grammy voting preferences. For the first time ever, one of the top award choices was in tune with the front-line music of the day, which, strangely, came during another tribute year to Sinatra, who was clearly the champion of the old sound. Even better, "Michelle" prevailed over four songs — all stage and screen tunes — that typified the

Sinatra's only loss came when "Strangers" bowed to the Beatles' winning Song of the Year "Michelle."

kind of music that usually won: "Born Free," "The Impossible Dream," "Somewhere, My Love," and even Sinatra's "Strangers in the Night."

The breakthrough came at time when N.A.R.A.S. was actively reaching out for more young blood to join the academy. The "hip" Rev. Norman O'Connor, a noted author and musicologist, was the newly elected head of the New York chapter, and, although a cleric, was apparently less worried about the Rock of Ages than he was about the Grammys' performance in the rock age. "Father O'Connor Tosses Out

N.A.R.A.S. Welcome Mat to 'Vital' Rock Makers," said a headline in *Variety*. The priest told the trade paper, "Up till now we have reached too few of these very productive people." Apparently, he was not as flustered as others were by John Lennon's recent remark that shocked the religiously devout and caused a furor in the press. "The Beatles are probably bigger then Jesus," Lennon had boasted.

But the vital rock makers were still needed as voting academy members in order to correct the Grammys' ongoing failure, despite occasional exceptions, to acknowledge r&r adequately. Again this year, the choice for Best Contemporary (R&R) Recording was controversial: "Winchester Cathedral" by the New Vaudeville Band.

"Winchester Cathedral" was deliberately *anti*-rock. Its composer/producer/singer Geoff Stephens was attempting to recreate the sound of a bygone time when he came up with the idea for the song one day when he spied a calendar photo of the famed medieval church while working as a songwriter at a small British music publisher. Stephens wanted to bring back the bouncy spirit of old vaudeville. When setting up the recording, he had musicians play the same band instruments popular during the late 1920s and sang the lead vocals himself, Rudy Vallee–style, by shouting them through a megaphone. The novelty sparked a megaphone fad across America and helped land the song at number two in the year's Hot 100. Within four years, it was covered by 400 artists, including Frank Sinatra.

Another victory that triggered an outcry was the return of the Anita Kerr Quartet, whose triumph over the Beatles last year for Best Performance by a Vocal Group is still considered one of the most shocking results in Grammy vote history. This time the Fab Four wasn't even among the nominees when Kerr, a popular N.A.R.A.S. insider, reclaimed the same trophy for "A Man and a Woman." The latest losers were the Beach Boys, the Association, the Sandpipers, and the Mamas & the Papas.

The Mamas & the Papas were the perfect mix of pop talent for their time: four mellow hippies whose soaring old-style harmonies made rock, by their folksy interpretation of it, palatable both to real everyday mamas and papas and to their record-buying teens. Rock's Mamas and Papas were also the first group to include an equal balance between the sexes, being comprised of two women (Cass Elliott and Michelle Phillips) and two men (John Phillips and Dennis Doherty). Although they lost the vocal group honors to Kerr, they did take the prize for Best Contemporary (R&R) Group Performance, Vocal or Instrumental for a track from their first album, *If You Can Believe Your Eyes and Ears*. "Monday, Monday," a losing nominee for Record of the Year, was so popular that radio deejays started playing it even before its release as a single, creating a clamor for the song that resulted in its selling 150,000 copies on the first day that it was finally available in record stores.

Many of the other Grammy wins went to the kind of MOR (middle of the road) music that N.A.R.A.S. voters embraced in the past. Eydie Gorme ("If He Walked into My Life" from the Broadway musical *Mame*) managed to break the lock on the Best Female Vocal Performance category held since the Grammys' inception by Ella Fitzgerald and Barbra Streisand (both of whom were nominated again this time), and interrupted only by Judy Garland in 1961. Herb Alpert & the Tijuana Brass ("a perennial winner," said the *Herald Examiner*, noting their impressive three victories last year) picked up two instrumental trophies (performance and arrangement) for "What Now My Love."

"I got the idea for doing it while we [the Tijuana Brass] were doing a concert in Hawaii," Alpert says about the familiar song. "I heard some car horns honking while I was walking down the beach at Waikiki. I heard one horn go 'doo-doo' and a taxi picking up the next notes and I started to fill in the rest. Prior to [my new arrangement] it was just kind of a torch song, but I put a little lift and a lilt to it."

Best contemporary group vocalists the Mamas & the Papas were four mellow hippies who made rock & roll palatable to real mamas and papas as well as their teens.

The song from the TV show *Batman* reaped Best Instrumental Theme. Past Grammy champ Jerry Herman (for 1964's Song of the Year "Hello, Dolly!") won Best Score from on Original Cast Show Album for *Mame* (beating out *Man of La Mancha* and *Sweet Charity*). The theme music to *Dr. Zhivago* had won the Oscar for best film score and now garnered the equivalent accolade from the record academy, topping close contender *Born Free.*

Dr. Zhivago snagged a second prize when "Somewhere, My Love (Lara's Theme)" won Best Performance by a Chorus for Ray Coniff & Singers. Coniff and his troupe specialized in what Grammy voters loved: sweeping, instrumental mood music accompanied by equally soaring vocals. Coniff's fare dominated the easy-listening FM channels of the mid to late '60s, although "Somewhere" turned out to be his only Top 40 hit and only Grammy victory.

Bill Cosby continued his dominance of the comedy category when he won for a third year in a row. *Wonderfulness* was only his fourth LP, but it contained some of his most wonderfully funny routines such as "Tonsils," "Chicken Heart," "Go Carts," and "The Playground." (In "Chicken Heart," he recalls being so frightened by a popular radio drama as a child that he smeared Jell-O — a product for which he'd become a spokesman in future years — all over the floor in order to keep the program's monster at bay.) When it was released, *Wonderfulness* set a new record for most comedy albums sold in a day — 200,000 — and remained in the *Billboard* Hot 100 for 106 weeks.

One of the most curious — and least comical — wins of the year involved the Best Folk Recording, which went to a blind street singer who panhandled in downtown Nashville for a living. Cortelia Clark's sole LP, *Blues in the Street,* had been a financial disaster, so he couldn't afford to attend the Nashville Grammy show because of the prohibitive cost of renting a tuxedo. Worse, his moment of glory would be short-lived. Despite his award success and the subsequent and extensive news coverage that followed, Clark was never again asked to perform on record. The day after the Grammy ceremony, he was seen still hustling spare change on the sidewalks of the honky-tonk capital. Two years later he died when a kerosene stove exploded in his trailer home. He has since been immortalized in a Mickey Newberry song called "Cortelia Clark," a popular tune in Newberry's concert repertoire.

Seven-time past winner Ray Charles received a standing ovation on Grammys night when he made a triumphant return to claim two statuettes for his bitter-sweet "Crying Time," including Best R&B Recording. Charles had dominated the category from 1961–63 after it replaced the earlier r&b performance award, which Charles won in 1960.

> **Ray Charles reaped two Grammys and a standing ovation for "Crying Time."**

Since the start of the Grammys, the genre had had only one annual category, but after the jealous turmoil that followed Nashville copping six country & western categories when it joined the recording academy in 1964, a comprehensive awards revamping ensued. Charles's second award was for the reinstated performance prize. A new r&b category for group performance (vocal or instrumental) was nabbed by last year's jazz group winner Ramsey Lewis for "Hold It Right There."

Jazz ended up losing one of its three categories in the overhaul, leaving only Best Original Jazz Composition (claimed by Duke Ellington for "In the Beginning God") and the instrumental performance slot, which went to Wes Montgomery. (Previously, the category was split between prizes for large groups and small group or soloist. Now all performers competed for a single honor.) Ellington's fifth Grammy came with a heartfelt bonus. On the after-the-fact "Best on Record" Grammy TV show, which showcased performances by some of the winning artists, "the Duke" was given a Lifetime Achievement Award. He accepted it telling the audience and the academy, "We do love you madly."

Wes Montgomery's Grammy success was a welcome win to his fans, but a disappointment to some critics. He was the reigning jazz guitarist of the 1950s and early '60s, having, in the words of *Rolling Stone*, "demonstrated a fluid single-note style brilliantly interfaced with a subtle use of chords." Some critics and musicians turned away from him in the mid-1960s, however, when he pursued more commercial music like his Grammy-honored "Goin' Out of My Head," which they dismissed as light pop fare.

Country & western was cut back to only four categories, three of which were claimed by David Houston and his "Almost Persuaded" disc about "the charms of honky-tonk temptresses," in the words of journalist Bill Malone.

"Almost Persuaded" almost didn't make it. Houston was looking for a "B" side to his "We Got Love" single even up to the night before the 45 was due to be wrapped up. Songwriters Billy Sherrill and Glenn Sutton worked on it till midnight. The next morning Houston recorded the tune, which was subsequently discovered by an Atlanta deejay and went on to top the country charts for nine weeks. Sherrill and Sutton prevailed over 11-time (over two years) winner Roger Miller and his "Husbands and Wives" platter for Best Country & Western Song. Houston won Best Country & Western Recording and the c&w male vocal performance prize.

Jeannie Seely took the equivalent female honors for "Don't Touch Me," a pioneering Hank Cochran song that epitomized the new soul-searing, woeful tunes that were just then replacing the traditional storytelling c&w music of the past. Country's two-year-old best new artist award was dropped entirely, just as the overall Best New Artist prize was, too — the only time in Grammy history that the category was skipped after it was introduced in 1959.

The choice of Classical Album of the Year was the first recording of Charles Ives's *Symphony No. 1 in D Minor*, which the adventurous American composer wrote while he was still a student at Yale. (His Symphony No. 4 was voted best contemporary classical composition last year.) Performed by the Chicago Symphony Orchestra under the baton of conductor/composer Morton Gould, Ives's first symphony was "the highest point of Gould's conducting career," in the words of critic Arthur Cohn, who added, "No one has thus far matched the caressing sweetness of his interpretation." Conductor Gregg Smith and the Columbia Chamber Orchestra were among the winners tied for Best Classical Choral Performance (Other than Opera) for Ives's *Music for Chorus*, which included works such as "General William Booth Enters into Heaven." The honors were shared with Robert Shaw and his chorale and orchestra for their rendition of Handel's *Messiah*.

Five-time past Grammy winner Erich Leinsdorf reaped the orchestral performance trophy for the Boston Symphony's *Symphony No. 6 in A Minor* by Mahler. Classical guitarist Julian Bream won the instrumental soloist award for his *Baroque Guitar*, which incorporated works by Bach, Sanz, and Weiss. "Bream's art does beautifully by them," *High Fidelity* wrote, "and vice versa."

Leontyne Price stretched her winning streak to four years by holding on to the laurels for vocal soloist, this time for *Prima Donna*, an assortment of arias by Verdi, Purcell, and Barber. The Best Opera Recording went to Sir Georg

Solti for conducting the Vienna Philharmonic in the first of Wagner's *Ring* operas, *Die Walküre*. *High Fidelity* called it "his best work on records," and said soprano Birgit Nilsson as Brünnhilde "does a wonderful job." Regine Crespin as Sieglinde, it added, "is magnificent." The principal soloists, including Nilsson, Crespin, Christa Ludwin, James King, and Hans Hotter received their own special plaques.

The Grammy ceremonies again took place in New York, L.A., Nashville, and Chicago. In L.A., the ceremony was held at the Beverly Hilton with Bill Dana acting as master of ceremonies and Les Brown's orchestra providing the entertainment. In New York, the festivities were shifted this year from the Hotel Astor to the Hilton where Tony Randall acted as host before a crowd of 500. 1963 Grammy winner Woody Herman and his band provided the entertainment, while presenters included songwriter Harold Arlen, bandleader Skitch Henderson, and singer Steve Lawrence. But the presenters didn't have many opportunities to pass out the gold gramophones as planned. Lawrence's wife and frequent vocal partner turned out to be the single highlight of the gala by default. *Variety* noted: "The only winning artist accepting an award at the New York affair was Eydie Gormé.

"The most popular refrain as the prizes were announced was that 'the winner of this award will accept it in Hollywood' or, in the same degree, Nashville," *Variety* continued. "Frank Sinatra's domination of the ceremonies by copping accolades in six of the 42 categories was symptomatic of the shift in accent to the coast." Out in Los Angeles, noted the *Herald Examiner*, "an enthusiastic and natty throng of diners applauded the results at the Beverly Hilton International Ballroom" where most of the action was. Key victories by those "California Dreamers" the Mamas & the Papas (who would have been the likely winners of Best New Artist) and other L.A. heroes such as Herb Alpert & the Tijuana Brass confirmed that the west coast–based N.A.R.A.S. had reclaimed control over the newly humbled rebels in Nashville and the once all-powerful titans of Tin Pan Alley in New York.

1966

Awards were bestowed on March 2, 1967, for the eligibility period November 2, 1965, to November 1, 1966, at ceremonies held at the Beverly Hilton Hotel in Los Angeles, the Hilton Hotel in New York, and at dinners held in Nashville and Chicago.

ALBUM OF THE YEAR
• *Sinatra: A Man & His Music*, Frank Sinatra. Sonny Burke, A&R producer. Reprise.
Color Me Barbra, Barbra Streisand. Bob Mersey, A&R producer. Columbia.
Dr. Zhivago (soundtrack), Maurice Jarre. Jesse Kaye, A&R producer. MGM.
Revolver, Beatles. George Martin, A&R producer. Capitol.
What Now My Love, Herb Alpert & the Tijuana Brass. Herb Alpert, Jerry Moss, A&R producers. A&M.

RECORD OF THE YEAR
• "Strangers in the Night," Frank Sinatra. Jimmy Bowen, A&R producer. Reprise.
"Almost Persuaded," David Houston. Billy Sherrill, A&R producer. Epic.
"Monday, Monday," Mamas & the Papas. Lou Adler, A&R producer. Dunhill.
"What Now My Love," Herb Alpert & the Tijuana Brass. Herb Alpert, Jerry Moss, A&R producers. A&M.
"Winchester Cathedral," New Vaudeville Band. Geoff Stephens, A&R producer. Fontana.

SONG OF THE YEAR
(Songwriter's Award)
• "Michelle," John Lennon, Paul McCartney. Capitol.
"Born Free," John Barry, Don Black. MGM.
"The Impossible Dream," Mitch Leigh, Joe Darion. Kapp.
"Somewhere, My Love (Lara's Theme from *Dr. Zhivago*)," Paul Francis Webster, Maurice Jarre. MGM.

"Strangers in the Night," Bert Kaempfert, Charles Singleton, Eddie Snyder. Reprise.

BEST VOCAL PERFORMANCE, MALE
• Frank Sinatra, "Strangers in the Night." Reprise.
David Houston, "Almost Persuaded." Epic.
Jack Jones, "The Impossible Dream." Kapp.
Paul McCartney, "Eleanor Rigby." Capitol.
Jim Reeves, "Distant Drums." RCA.
Andy Williams, *The Shadow of Your Smile*. Columbia.

BEST VOCAL PERFORMANCE, FEMALE
• Eydie Gormé, "If He Walked into My Life." Columbia.
Ella Fitzgerald, *Ella at Duke's Place*. Verve.
Sandy Posey, "Born a Woman." MGM.
Nancy Sinatra, "These Boots Are Made for Walkin'." Reprise.
Barbra Streisand, *Color Me Barbra*. Columbia.

BEST PERFORMANCE BY A VOCAL GROUP
• Anita Kerr Quartet, "A Man and a Woman." Warner Bros.
Association, "Cherish." Valiant.
Beach Boys, "Good Vibrations." Capitol.
Mamas & the Papas, "Monday, Monday." Dunhill.
Sandpipers, "Guantanamera." A&M.

BEST PERFORMANCE BY A CHORUS
• Ray Conniff & Singers, "Somewhere, My Love (Lara's Theme from *Dr. Zhivago*)." Columbia.
Alan Copeland Singers with Count Basie, *Basie Swingin', Voices Singin'*. ABC-Paramount.
Henry Mancini, Orchestra and Chorus, *Henry Mancini Presents the Academy Award Songs*. RCA.
Johnny Mann Singers, *A Man and a Woman*. Liberty.
Swingle Singers, *Rococo A'Go Go*. Philips.

1966

Best Contemporary (R&R) Recording

- "Winchester Cathedral," New Vaudeville Band. Fontana.
"Cherish," Association. Valiant.
"Eleanor Rigby," Paul McCartney. Capitol.
"Good Vibrations," Beach Boys. Capitol.
"Last Train to Clarksville," Monkees. Colgems.
"Monday, Monday," Mamas & the Papas. Dunhill.

Best Contemporary (R&R) Solo Vocal Performance, Male or Female

- Paul McCartney, "Eleanor Rigby." Capitol.
Bobby Darin, "If I Were a Carpenter." Atlantic.
Sandy Posey, "Born a Woman." MGM.
Nancy Sinatra, "These Boots Are Made for Walkin'." Reprise.
Dusty Springfield, "You Don't Have to Say You Love Me." Philips.

Best Contemporary (R&R) Group Performance, Vocal or Instrumental

- Mamas & the Papas, "Monday, Monday." Dunhill.
Association, "Cherish." Valiant.
Beach Boys, "Good Vibrations." Capitol.
Monkees, "Last Train to Clarksville." Colgems.
Sandpipers, "Guantanamera." A&M.

Best Rhythm & Blues Recording

- "Crying Time," Ray Charles. ABC-Paramount.
"It's a Man's Man's Man's World," James Brown. King.
"Love Is a Hurtin' Thing," Lou Rawls. Capitol.
"Uptight," Stevie Wonder. Tamla.
"When a Man Loves a Woman," Percy Sledge. Atlantic.

Best Rhythm & Blues Solo Vocal Performance, Male or Female

- Ray Charles, "Crying Time." ABC-Paramount.
James Brown, "It's a Man's Man's Man's World." King.
Lou Rawls, "Love Is a Hurtin' Thing." Capitol.
Percy Sledge, "When a Man Loves a Woman." Atlantic.
Stevie Wonder, "Uptight." Tamla.

Best Rhythm & Blues Group, Vocal or Instrumental

- Ramsey Lewis, "Hold It Right There." Cadet.
Capitols, "Cool Jerk." Atco.
King Curtis, "Spanish Harlem." Atco.
James & Bobby Purify, "I'm Your Puppet." Bell.
Sam & Dave, "Hold On, I'm Comin'." Stax.

Best Original Jazz Composition (Composer's Award)

- Duke Ellington, "In the Beginning God." RCA.
Bob Brookmeyer, "ABC Blues." Solid State.
Bill Evans, "Time Remembered." Riverside.
John Handy, "If Only We Knew." Columbia.
Claus Ogerman, "Jazz Samba." Verve.
Lalo Schifrin, "Marquis de Sade." Verve.

Best Instrumental Jazz Performance, Group or Soloist with Group

- Wes Montgomery, "Goin' Out of My Head." Verve.
Ornette Coleman Trio, At the "Golden Circle." Blue Note.
Duke Ellington Orchestra, Concert of Sacred Music. RCA.
Bill Evans, Jim Hall, Intermodulation. Verve.
John Handy Quintet, John Handy Recorded Live at the Monterey Jazz Festival. Columbia.
Woody Herman Orchestra, Woody's Winners. Columbia.
Stan Kenton, Stan Kenton Conducts the Los Angeles Neophonic Orchestra. Capitol.

Best Sacred Recording (Musical)

- Grand Old Gospel, Porter Wagoner and the Blackwood Brothers. RCA.
Bigger 'N' Better, Happy Goodman Family. Canaan.
Connie Smith Sings Great Sacred Songs, Connie Smith. RCA.
How Big Is God, Blackwood Brothers. RCA.
The Oak Ridge Boys at Their Best, Oak Ridge Boys. United Artists.
Southland Songs That Lift the Heart, George Beverly Shea. RCA.

BEST COUNTRY & WESTERN RECORDING
• "Almost Persuaded," David Houston. Epic.
"Distant Drums," Jim Reeves. RCA.
"Don't Touch Me," Jeannie Seely. Monument.
"I'm a Nut," Leroy Pullins. Kapp.
"There Goes My Everything," Jack Greene. Decca.

BEST COUNTRY & WESTERN VOCAL PERFORMANCE, FEMALE
• Jeannie Seely, "Don't Touch Me." Monument.
Jan Howard, "Evil on Your Mind." Decca.
Loretta Lynn, "Don't Come Home a Drinkin'." Decca.
Connie Smith, "Ain't Had No Loving." RCA.
Dottie West, "Would You Hold It Against Me." RCA.

BEST COUNTRY & WESTERN VOCAL PERFORMANCE, MALE
• David Houston, "Almost Persuaded." Epic.
Ben Colder, "Almost Persuaded No. 2." Verve.
Jack Greene, "There Goes My Everything." Decca.
Charley Pride, "Just Between You and Me." RCA.
Jim Reeves, "Distant Drums." RCA.

BEST COUNTRY & WESTERN SONG
(Songwriter's Award)
• "Almost Persuaded," Billy Sherrill, Glenn Sutton. Epic.
"Don't Touch Me," Hank Cochran. Monument.
"Husbands and Wives," Roger Miller. Smash.
"Streets of Baltimore," Tompall Glaser, Harlan Howard. RCA.
"There Goes My Everything," Dallas Frazier. Decca.

BEST FOLK RECORDING
• *Blues in the Street*, Cortelia Clark. RCA.
God Bless the Grass, Pete Seeger. Columbia.
"Hurry Sundown," Peter, Paul & Mary. Warner Bros.
Leadbelly, Leadbelly. Elektra.
Oliver Smith, Oliver Smith. Elektra.
Reflections in a Crystal Wind, Mimi & Richard Farina. Vanguard.
Sound of the Sitar, Ravi Shankar. World Pacific.
Violets of Dawn, Mitchell Trio. Mercury.

BEST INSTRUMENTAL THEME
(Composer's Award)
• *"Batman* Theme," Neal Hefti. RCA.
"Arabesque," Henry Mancini. RCA.
"Prissy," Priscilla Hubbard. RCA.
"Trumpet Pickin'," D.J. Edwards. RCA.
"Who's Afraid," Alex North. Warner Bros.

BEST INSTRUMENTAL PERFORMANCE
(Other Than Jazz)
• Herb Alpert & the Tijuana Brass, "What Now My Love." A&M.
Chet Atkins, *Chet Atkins Picks on the Beatles*. RCA.
Neal Hefti, *"Batman* Theme." RCA.
Maurice Jarre, *Dr. Zhivago* (soundtrack). MGM.
Roger Williams, "Born Free." Kapp.

BEST INSTRUMENTAL ARRANGEMENT
• Herb Alpert, "What Now My Love" (Herb Alpert & the Tijuana Brass). A&M.
John Barry, "Born Free" (John Barry). MGM.
Bob Florence, "Michelle" (Bud Shank). World Pacific.
Neal Hefti, *"Batman* Theme" (Neal Hefti). RCA.
Henry Mancini, "Arabesque" (Henry Mancini). RCA.

BEST ARRANGEMENT ACCOMPANYING VOCALIST OR INSTRUMENTALIST
• Ernie Freeman, "Strangers in the Night" (Frank Sinatra). Reprise.
Don Costa, "If He Walked into My Life" (Eydie Gorme). Columbia.
George Martin, "Eleanor Rigby" (Paul McCartney). Capitol.
Oliver Nelson, "Goin' Out of My Head" (Wes Montgomery). Verve.
Billy Strange, "These Boots Are Made for Walkin'" (Nancy Sinatra). Reprise.
Brian Wilson, "Good Vibrations" (the Beach Boys). Capitol.

BEST SCORE FROM AN ORIGINAL CAST SHOW ALBUM
(Composer's Award)
• *Mame*, Jerry Herman. Columbia.
The Apple Tree, Jerry Bock, Sheldon Harnick. Columbia.
Man of La Mancha, Mitch Leigh, Joe Darion. Kapp.
Skyscraper, Jimmy Van Heusen, Sammy Cahn. Capitol.
Sweet Charity, Cy Coleman, Dorothy Fields. Columbia.

**BEST ORIGINAL SCORE WRITTEN
FOR A MOTION PICTURE OR TELEVISION SHOW
(Composer's Award)**
• *Dr. Zhivago*, Maurice Jarre. MGM.
Arabesque, Henry Mancini. RCA.
Born Free, John Barry. MGM.
Original Music from the Score "Alfie,"
Sonny Rollins. Impulse.
Who's Afraid of Virginia Woolf? Alex
North. Warner Bros.

ALBUM OF THE YEAR, CLASSICAL
• *Ives: Symphony No. 1 in D Minor*,
Morton Gould conducting Chicago
Symphony. Howard Scott, A&R
producer. RCA.
Aaron Copland Conducts ("Music for a
Great City," "Statements"), Aaron
Copland conducting London Symphony.
John McClure, A&R producer.
Columbia.
Handel: Messiah, Colin Davis conducting
London Symphony Orchestra and
Choir. Harold Lawrence, A&R
producer. Philips.
Henze: Symphonies (1 through 5), H.W.
Henze conducting Berlin Philharmonic.
Otto Gerdes, A&R producer. Deutsche
Grammophon.
Mahler: Symphony No. 6 in A Minor,
Erich Leinsdorf conducting Boston
Symphony. Richard Mohr, A&R
producer. RCA.
Mahler: Symphony No. 10, Eugene
Ormandy conducting Philadelphia
Orchestra. Thomas Frost, A&R
producer. Columbia.
Opening Nights at the Met, Various Artists.
Peter Dellhelm, A&R producer. RCA.
Presenting Montserrat Caballé (Bellini and
Donizetti arias), Montserrat Caballé. C.
Gerhardt, A&R producer. RCA.
Wagner: Die Walküre, Georg Solti
conducting Vienna Philharmonic
(solos: Nilsson, Crespin, Ludwig, King,
Hotter, Frick). John Culshaw, A&R
producer. London.

**BEST CLASSICAL PERFORMANCE,
ORCHESTRA
(A Conductor's Award)**
• Erich Leinsdorf conducting Boston
Symphony, *Mahler: Symphony No. 6 in
A Minor*. RCA.
Ernest Ansermet conducting L'Orchestre
de la Suisse Romande, *Ravel: Daphnis
et Chloë*. London.

Leonard Bernstein conducting New York
Philharmonic, *Ives: Fourth of July*.
Columbia.
Pierre Boulez, Antal Dorati conducting
BBC Symphony, *Boulez: Le Soleil des
Eaux; Messiaen: Chronochromie;
Koechlin: Les Bandar-Log*. Angel.
Morton Gould conducting Chicago
Symphony, *Ives: Symphony No. 1 in D
Minor*. RCA.
Jean Martinon conducting Chicago
Symphony, *Varese: Arcana; Martin:
Concerto for Seven Wind Instruments,
Timpani, Percussion and String
Orchestra*. RCA.
Eugene Ormandy conducting Philadelphia
Orchestra, *Mahler: Symphony No. 10*.
Columbia.
George Szell conducting Cleveland
Orchestra, *Bartók: Concerto for
Orchestra*. Columbia.

**BEST CHAMBER MUSIC PERFORMANCE,
INSTRUMENTAL OR VOCAL**
• Boston Symphony Chamber Players,
Boston Symphony Chamber Players
(selections by Mozart, Brahms,
Beethoven, Fine, Copland, Carter,
Piston). RCA.
Erick Friedman, André Previn, *Franck:
Sonata in A Major for Violin and
Piano; Debussy: Sonata in G Minor for
Violin and Piano*. RCA.
Jascha Heifetz, Gregor Piatigorsky with
Leonard Pennario, *Arensky: Trio in D
Minor for Violin, Cello and Piano;
Martinu: Duo for Violin and Cello*. RCA.
Eugene Istomin, Isaac Stern, Leonard
Rose, *Beethoven: Trio No. 6 in B Flat,
Op. 97 ("Archduke")*. Columbia.
Gregor Piatigorsky, Rudolf Firkusny,
*Prokofiev: Sonata for Cello and Piano,
Op. 119; Chopin: Sonata in G Minor
for Piano and Cello, Op. 65*. RCA.
Walter Trampler and Budapest Quartet,
*Mozart: The Six Quintets for String
Quartet and Viola*. Columbia.
Vienna Philharmonic Quartet, *Schubert:
Quintet in C Major*. London.
Weller Quartet, *Haydn: Quartets (Op. 33)*.
London.

Best Classical Performance, Instrumental Soloist(s) (With or Without Orchestra)

• Julian Bream, *Baroque Guitar* (Bach, Sanz, Weiss, etc.). RCA.

John Browning (Leinsdorf conducting Boston Symphony), *Prokofiev: Concerto No. 1 in D Flat Major for Piano; Concerto No. 2 in G Minor for Piano.* RCA.

Raymond Lewenthal, *Operatic Liszt.* RCA.

Yehudi Menuhin (Boult conducting New Philharmonia Orchestra), *Elgar: Concerto for Violin.* Angel.

Ivan Moravec, *Chopin: Nocturnes.* Connoisseur Society.

Artur Rubinstein, *Rubinstein and Chopin* ("Bolero," "Tarentelle," "Fantasia in F Minor Barcarolle," "Bercuse," and 3 Nouvelles Etudes). RCA.

Isaac Stern (Ormandy conducting Philadelphia Orchestra), *Dvorak: Concerto in A Minor for Violin.* Columbia.

John Williams (Eugene Ormandy conducting Philadelphia Orchestra), *Rodrigo: Concierto de Aranjuez for Guitar and Orchestra; Castelnuovo, Tedesco: Concerto in D Major for Guitar.* Columbia.

Best Opera Recording
(Conductor's Award)

• *Wagner: Die Walküre*, Georg Solti conducting Vienna Philharmonic (solos: Nilsson, Crespin, Ludwig, King, Hotter). London.

Bartók: Bluebeard's Castle, Istvan Kertesz conducting London Symphony (solos: Ludwig, Berry). London.

Copland: The Tender Land, Aaron Copland conducting Choral Arts Society and New York Philharmonic (solos: Clements, Turner, Cassilly, Treigle, Fredericks). Columbia.

Puccini: Turandot, Francesco Molinari-Pradelli conducting Rome Opera Chorus and Orchestra (solos: Nilsson, Corelli). Angel.

Wagner: Lohengrin, Erich Leinsdorf conducting Boston Symphony (solos: Konya, Amarca, Gorr, Dooley). RCA.

Best Classical Choral Performance, Other Than Opera
(Tie)

• Robert Shaw conducting Robert Shaw Chorale and Orchestra, *Handel: Messiah.* RCA.

• Gregg Smith conducting Columbia Chamber Orchestra, Gregg Smith Singers, Ithaca College Concert Choir. George Bragg conducting Texas Boys Choir, *Ives: Music for Chorus* ("General William Booth Enters into Heaven," "Serenity," "The Circus Band," etc.). Columbia.

Richard Condie directing Mormon Tabernacle Choir. Eugene Ormandy conducting Philadelphia Orchestra, *Bless This House.* Columbia.

Colin Davis conducting soloists, London Symphony Orchestra and Choir, *Handel: Messiah.* Philips.

Alfred Nash Patterson directing Boston Symphony Chorus. Erich Leinsdorf conducting Boston Symphony Orchestra, *Verdi: Requiem.* RCA.

Wilhelm Pitz conducting New Philharmonia Chorus. Otto Klemperer conducting New Philharmonia Orchestra, *Beethoven: Missa Solemnis in D Major.* Angel.

Wilhelm Pitz conducting New Philharmonia Chorus. Rafael Fruhbeck de Burgos conducting New Philharmonia Orchestra, *Orff: Carmina Burana.* Angel.

David Willcocks conducting Bach Choir and Choristers of Westminster Abbey and London Symphony, *Vaughan Williams: Hodie.* Angel.

Best Classical Vocal Soloist Performance

• Leontyne Price (Molinari-Pradelli conducting RCA Italiana Opera Orchestra; solos: Barber, Purcell, etc.), *Prima Donna.* RCA.

Janet Baker (Morris conducting London Philharmonic), *Mahler: The Youth's Magic Horn* (Das Knaben Wunderhorn). Angel.

Dietrich Fischer-Dieskau, *Schumann: Dichterliebe.* Deutsche Grammophon.

Montserrat Caballé (Cilario, conductor), *Presenting Montserrat Caballé* (Bellini and Donizetti arias). RCA.

Judith Raskin (Szell conducting Cleveland Orchestra), *Mahler: Symphony No. 4 in G Major.* Columbia.

Elisabeth Schwarzkopf (Szell conducting
Berlin Radio Symphony), *Strauss:
Four Last Songs*. Angel.

**BEST ENGINEERED RECORDING,
CLASSICAL**
• Anthony Salvatore, *Wagner: Lohengrin*
(Leinsdorf conducting Boston
Symphony Pro Musica Chorus and
soloists). RCA.
Bernard Keville, *Ives: Symphony No. 1 in
D Minor* (Gould conducting Chicago
Symphony). RCA.
Bernard Keville, *Varese: Arcana*
(Martinon conducting Chicago
Symphony). RCA.
Ernest Oelrich, *Vivaldi: Gloria in D* (Robert
Shaw Orchestra and Chorus). RCA.
Anthony Salvatore, *Mahler: Symphony No.
6 in A Minor* (Leinsdorf conducting
Boston Symphony). RCA.

**BEST SPOKEN WORD, DOCUMENTARY,
OR DRAMA RECORDING**
• *Edward R. Murrow, A Reporter
Remembers—Vol. I, The War Years,*
Edward R. Murrow. Columbia.
Day for Decision, Johnny Sea. Warner
Bros.
Death of a Salesman, Lee J. Cobb, Mildred
Dunnock. Caedmon.
History Repeats Itself, Buddy Starcher.
Decca.
The Stevenson Wit, Adlai Stevenson.
David Brinkley, narrator. RCA.

BEST COMEDY PERFORMANCE
• Bill Cosby, *Wonderfulness.* Warner Bros.
Don Bowman, *Funny Way to Make an
Album.* RCA.
Archie Campbell, *Have a Laugh on Me.*
RCA.
Homer & Jethro, *Wanted for Murder.*
RCA.
Mrs. Miller, *Downtown.* Capitol.

BEST RECORDING FOR CHILDREN
• *Dr. Seuss Presents: "If I Ran the Zoo"
and "Sleep Book,"* Marvin Miller.
RCA.
Alice Through the Looking Glass, original
cast. Moose Charlap, Elsie Simmons,
score. RCA.
The Christmas That Almost Wasn't, Paul
Tripp and cast. RCA.
*For the Children of the World Art
Linkletter Narrates "The Bible,"* Art
Linkletter. RCA.

*The 1966 choral laurels were shared by
Robert Shaw (above) and Gregg Smith.*

Happiness Is, Marty Gold conducting Do-
Re-Mi Children's Chorus. Kapp.

**BEST ENGINEERED RECORDING,
NON-CLASSICAL**
• Eddie Brackett, Lee Herschberg,
Strangers in the Night (Frank Sinatra).
Reprise.
Dick Bogert, "Arabesque" (Henry
Mancini). RCA.
James Malloy, *The Last Word in
Lonesome Is Me* (Eddy Arnold). RCA.
Phil Ramone, *Presenting Thad Jones* (Mel
Lewis and the Jazz Orchestra). Sid. St.
Phil Ramone, *Joe Williams and Thad
Jones* (Mel Lewis and the Jazz
Orchestra). Sid. St.

BEST ALBUM COVER, PHOTOGRAPHY

• Robert Jones, art director. Les Leverette, photographer, *Confessions of a Broken Man* (Porter Wagoner). RCA.

Bob Cato, John Berg, art directors. Gerald Schatsberg, photographer, *Blonde on Blonde* (Bob Dylan). Columbia.

Bob Cato, John Berg, art directors. Guy Webster, photographer, *Turn! Turn! Turn!* (Byrds). Columbia.

Robert Jones, art director. Tom Zimmerman, photographer, *The Time Machine* (Gary Burton). RCA.

Ed Thrasher, art director. Tom Tucker, photographer, *Sammy Davis, Jr. Sings, Laurindo Almeida Plays*. Reprise.

Peter Whorf, art director and photographer, *Guantanamera* (Sandpipers) A&M.

Peter Whorf, art director. George Jerman, photographer, *What Now My Love* (Herb Alpert & the Tijuana Brass). A&M.

BEST ALBUM COVER, GRAPHIC ARTS

• Klaus Voormann, graphic artist, *Revolver* (the Beatles). Capitol.

Elinor Bunin, graphic artist. Bob Cato, John Berg, art directors, *Color Me Barbra* (Barbra Streisand). Columbia.

Rod Dyer, graphic artist. George Osaki, art director, *Stan Kenton Conducts Los Angeles Neophonic Orchestra*. Capitol.

Gordon Kibbee, graphic artist. William S. Harvey, art director, *Baroque Fanfares and Sonatas for Brass* (Rifkin directing London Brass Players). Nonesuch.

Mozelle Thompson, graphic artist. George Estes, art director, *Ives: Symphony No. 1 in D Minor* (Gould conducting Chicago Symphony). RCA.

Allen Weinberg, graphic artist. Bob Cato, John Berg, art directors, *Charlie Byrd Christmas Carols for Solo Guitar*. Columbia.

Peter Whorf, graphic artist. Woody Woodward, art director, *Talk That Talk* (Jazz Crusaders). Pacific Jazz.

BEST ALBUM NOTES

• Stan Cornyn, *Sinatra at the Sands*. Reprise.

Harvey Cowen, *Ben Colder Strikes Again*. MGM.

Stanley Dance, Ralph Gleason, *The Ellington Era, Vol. II*. Columbia.

Fred Friendly, *Edward R. Murrow, A Reporter Remembers—Vol. I, The War Years*. Columbia.

Nelson Lyon, *Dr. Zhivago* (Maurice Jarre). MGM.

Sgt. Pepper Breaks Through

No major Grammy triumph has generated more hot air than the 5th Dimension's "Up, Up and Away," the Jimmy Webb Song and Record of the Year about a fanciful balloon ride that soared up the singles charts for 12 weeks, peaking at number 4. N.A.R.A.S. voters were trying hard in 1967 to keep their picks in tune with the times, but once again they embraced an easy-listening choice despite the academy's insistence that the awards were becoming more hip.

To critics, "Up, Up and Away" represented the height of sentimentality in music as well as consider-

The Beatles' Album of the Year Sgt. Pepper's Lonely Hearts Club Band *led the charge as music by younger artists swept the top awards for the first time ever.*

CAPITOL RECORDS

able proof that N.A.R.A.S.'s Sinatra-loving old guard still held sway, even though the song's victory as Record of the Year marked the first time that the Grammys' highest honor went to music written for the younger generation. But just as last year when "Ol' Blue Eyes" and the Beatles split the top awards, the Grammys were again headed toward a schizophrenic outcome.

"Up, Up and Away" was unabashedly cute and breezy. Its obvious appeal to N.A.R.A.S. voters resulted in the 5th Dimension receiving the most nominations of the year — seven, a number tied by Bobbie Gentry. (The Beatles and Glen Campbell followed with six nods each.) The group ended up winning four Grammys. N.A.R.A.S. dropped the "Contemporary (R&R)" awards this

year in favor of simply "Contemporary" ones (a slap at r&r that still has many Grammy detractors smarting). In addition to the prizes for best song and record, the 5th Dimension also nabbed Best Contemporary Group Performance as well as Best Contemporary Single, a new category that would vanish into the stratosphere next year. An even *easier*-listening version of "Up, Up and Away" recorded by the Johnny Mann Singers just as easily took the prize for Best Performance by a Chorus.

Like Best Contemporary Single, a new Best Contemporary Album award was also dropped after 1967, but not before being caught by the winners of the Album of the Year honors. The Beatles' victories of 1967 were a milestone in Grammy history. The Fab Four had won only one of the top three awards in the past — for last year's Song of the Year "Michelle," a platter well suited to N.A.R.A.S. voters' long-standing preference for strong, safe melodies and romantic lyrics. *Sgt. Pepper's Lonely Hearts Club Band*, by comparison, was everything but safe: Its experimental electronic sound was revolutionary and utilized the latest technological devices like the four-track tape recorder, making it the Grammys' Best Engineered Recording, too. Lyrics to songs like "Lucy in the Sky with Diamonds" and "A Day in the Life" were psychedelic and deliberately nonsensical, causing fans to scrutinize them carefully for hidden meaning. Its brightly colored, hallucinogenic cover (featuring images of Marlene Dietrich, W.C. Fields, and a flower patch spelling out "Beatles") earned it the Best Album Cover award. N.A.R.A.S.'s bold acknowledgment of *Sgt. Pepper*'s importance, however, did not represent a future trend. The Beatles, as a group, would reap only one more Grammy in subsequent years despite having such other breakthrough releases as *Abbey Road*. Their final bow would come in 1970, for the film score to *Let It Be*, released after they broke up.

> To critics, Record and Song of the Year "Up, Up and Away" represented the height of sentimentality in music.

Tied with the 5th Dimension for the most awards of the night — four — was the perfect N.A.R.A.S. music hero. Glen Campbell was squeaky-clean cool. Even better, he had lots of talent and loved a good melody. Campbell may have repre- sented more of the western influence in country & western, but Nashville voters, at least for now, considered him their own and ensured his triumph with a wave of votes. His first hit record, "Gentle on My Mind," was the easy victor of Best Country & Western Recording and also brought him c&w's male vocal performance trophy.

But Campbell's support stretched far beyond Nashville. He'd worked in the Hollywood film studios, stood in for Brian Wilson of the Beach Boys for a few months on tour, and performed as a loyal session man for Eydie Gormé, Nat "King" Cole, and Frank Sinatra, among others. His many N.A.R.A.S. friends also voted him the overall best male vocal performance prize and the performance award allotted to the new "Contemporary" categories, both of them for his second hit, "By the Time I Get to Phoenix," which he originally opposed as a single release. (Pat Boone, he argued, had recorded it earlier without much success. Luckily for Campbell, he was overruled by Capitol record executives.) When he accepted his first award of the night at the Grammy ceremony, the *L.A. Times* noted, Campbell "thanked all the people he had backed up on guitar for their votes."

"By the Time I Get to Phoenix" was written by Jimmy Webb, who was nominated for Song of the Year for both "Phoenix" and the winning "Up, Up and Away." "Gentle on My Mind" was the work of John Hartford, who took the prize for Best Folk Performance, for his own rendition of his hit tune, as well as Best Country & Western Song.

The Best New Artist award was reinstated this year and went, for the first time ever, to a country & western artist. Bobbie Gentry was a Mississippi Delta lass who was born Roberta Lee Streeter and changed her name after seeing the Jennifer Jones film *Ruby Gentry*. She began writing music at the age of 7 (her first tune was "My Dog Sergeant is a Good Dog") and made her first public appearance at age 11. By the time she was 23, her "Ode to Billie Joe," number 4 in the year's Hot 100, had nominations for Grammy's Record and Song of the Year.

"The song is a sort of study in unconscious cruelty," Gentry told *Billboard* about the tune she both wrote and performed. The "Ode" tells the story of Billie Joe McCallister, who jumps off the Tallahatchie Bridge, a suicide noted only casually by onlookers and even Billie Joe's own family. The song

Aretha Franklin with one of her two Grammys for "Respect": She would continue to prevail in the female r&b category for a record-setting eight years in a row.

took less than an hour to record, with Gentry doing her own guitar playing (violins and cellos were added later) and earned her the Best Female Vocal Performance award and the equivalent honor in the new contemporary categories. "Ode" also won an arrangement prize for Jimmie Haskell.

"How the times have changed was shown by the award for Best Sacred Performance," *Variety* wrote. It was also the most curious victory of the year and, in a sense, the most sacrilegious. Elvis Presley not only had never won a Grammy before, but many of his fans and N.A.R.A.S. critics believed there was a clear conspiracy to keep him at bay while he reigned as "King" of the rock & roll heathens. That he'd finally win one was probably inevitable, but that he'd win the prize for a religious recording was certainly ironic. It was "not so many

years ago [that Presley] was a dubious moral item on TV because of his swivel hips," *Variety* pointed out. "That, however, was long before them twist and other sundry exhibitionist dances." It was also long before Presley settled down. In 1967, he married Priscilla Beaulieu; their only child, Lisa Marie, was born four weeks before Grammy night. It was now safe for the conservative N.A.R.A.S. to acknowledge the "King" at last, particularly if it was for his obvious and sincere religious faith. Presley would take two more of music's top awards before his death in 1977 — both of those for religious discs, too. His first and last were for two versions of *How Great Thou Art*, recorded first as a studio album and later as a live performance LP.

Johnny Cash had also settled down by the time the 1967 Grammys were awarded in 1968. He and singer June

Carter were to be married within a few weeks and Cash was enjoying success in his private battle against pill addiction. Cash and Carter went on to have five hit duets together, the first of which, "Jackson," earned them the 1967 C&W Duet, Trio, or Group vocal honor. Their mutual reading of it, wrote *Rolling Stone*, was "inspired."

Tammy Wynette had only been recording since 1966, but she climbed the charts quickly with such sassy tunes as "Your Good Girl's Gonna Go Bad." The former hairdresser from Tupelo, Mississippi, won her first Grammy (Best Female C&W Vocal Performance) for "I Don't Wanna Play House," an interesting choice since Wynette once walked away from her young marriage that resulted in three children.

Bernstein and Boulez scored a tie for the best classical album award.

Members of a Mississippi sharecropping family, the Blackwood Brothers, shared the trophy for Best Gospel Performance with country singer/ guitarist/songwriter Porter Wagoner. *More Grand Old Gospel* marked the first of three collaborative works that would bring them three awards, too.

Aretha Franklin had been signed up with Columbia Records since 1961, but she was primarily given show tunes to sing and was "produced by a series of white pop producers who tried to make her a black version of Barbra Streisand," wrote rock critic Dave Marsh. "This approach was generally disastrous." In 1967, she switched to Atlantic where producer Jerry Wexler finally gave her the professional respect she craved by letting the former church singer perform the blues and soul music she loved. Her

"Respect" single (written and first recorded by Otis Redding) followed (number 14 in *Billboard*'s Hot 100), along with Grammys for Best Rhythm & Blues Recording and best r&b vocal performance. The single was from *I Never Loved a Man (The Way I Love You)*, which is considered one of the greatest LPs in the history of soul.

The r&b male vocal honors went to another gospel-trained singer, Lou Rawls, for "Dead End Street," which became one of his most successful platters of the decade. The group performance honors were bestowed on Sam & Dave for "Soul Man," one of the two 1960s hits enjoyed by the dual champions of Memphis soul, Sam Moore and Dave Prater. "In the seventies," however, *Rolling Stone* wrote, "the pair all but disappeared."

Duke Ellington and his band experienced a renaissance in the 1960s, even though the Duke's personal compositions were generally considered inferior to his work from the 1930s and '40s, which then included "Mood Indigo" and *Black, Brown and Beige*. The "Far East Suite" was inspired by a recent world tour and showed him back in high style, though, earning him the large group jazz performance trophy. (The Duke would also likely have won the jazz composition prize for a second year in a row, too, but the category was dropped by N.A.R.A.S.) He also accepted an honorary award on behalf of his late arranger Billy Strayhorn, who had been with him since 1939 and contributed to, and in many cases composed, such classics as 1941's "Take the 'A' Train."

Sax player Cannonball Adderly suffered a slump in the 1960s as his celebrated bluesy jazz style took on a more soulful sound, causing jazz diehards to turn away. When he and his quintet recorded "Mercy, Mercy, Mercy," however, they welcomed a whole host of new fans as it zoomed to number 11 in the pop singles charts and to 14th in the LP rankings. It also garnered them the instrumental jazz performance Grammy for a small group.

Meanwhile, Bill Cosby knew no interruption in his successful string of album hits in the 1960s. His five LPs so far had grossed $30 million for Warner Bros., a record for spoken-word discs. His latest (and fourth-in-a-row Grammy winner) was *Revenge*, which followed his quest for retribution from a childhood bully who once hit him in the face with a slushball. (The young Cosby keeps one of his own, hidden in the freezer until after winter passes in order to ambush his nemesis come summer.) *Revenge* also introduced one of Cosby's most popular childhood pals, Fat Albert, the "two thousand pound" boy who causes the ground to quake while playing the street game "Buck-Buck."

For the first time since the category was introduced in 1961, an opera recording was named Classical Album of the Year — and took Best Opera Recording, too: Berg's *Wozzeck*, performed by conductor Pierre Boulez with the Paris National Opera and recorded in stereo for the first time. (Karl Böhm and the Orchestra of German Opera won Best Opera Recording two years earlier for a monaural version of *Wozzeck*.) "If Böhm's commands the last degree of one's admiration and respect," wrote *High Fidelity* of the two versions, "Boulez's may finally engender a more personal sort of attachment" because of "its romantic emotions and moods." In another first, Boulez's *Wozzeck* tied for the album prize with Mahler's Symphony No. 8 in E Flat Major ("Symphony of a Thousand") with Leonard Bernstein conducting the London Symphony Orchestra. And in yet another Grammy tie, Bernstein's Mahler recording took the laurels for Best Classical Choral Per-

formance along with Carl Orff's *Catulli Carmina* (one of his stage works that Orff called "scenic cantatas") performed by the Temple University Chorus (Robert Page conducting) and the Philadelphia Orchestra (Eugene Ormandy conducting).

Like *Wozzeck*, another Grammy victor of yore returned for more recognition in the form of the 1967 orchestra performance award: Igor Stravinsky conducting the Columbia Symphony in his *Firebird* and *Petrouchka* suites. (His earlier *Petrouchka* recording, paired with *Le Sacre du Printemps*, was Classical Album of the Year in 1961). American soprano Leontyne Price also came back, reprising her *Prima Donna* victory of last year for best vocal soloist with one for *Prima Donna, Volume 2*, another collection of her favorite arias. Winner of the instrumental soloist award was Vladimir Horowitz for a two-disc album of works by Haydn, Chopin, Mozart, and Liszt that he had performed recently at Carnegie Hall. The Liszt selections were "breath-taking" and "fiery," wrote *High Fidelity*, while the Chopin nocturne was "serenely beautiful in its fluid pacing."

When a tally of the year's winning discs was taken, Capitol "ran away with the Grammy sweepstakes," *Variety* wrote, "paced by Bobbie Gentry, the Beatles and Glen Campbell." Capitol's 14 trophies were followed by runners-up Columbia with 12 and RCA with 8. The biggest losers among performers were Vikki Carr and Ray Charles, with four failed nominations each. "Nominations ignored among the rock groups," noted the *L.A. Times*, included "the Bee Gees, Cream, the Rolling Stones, Jimi Hendrix, Donovan, and the Buffalo Springfield."

1958 Grammy-winning comic Stan Freberg served as master of Grammy ceremonies in Los Angeles where one of the trans-America events was held at the Century Plaza Hotel. "The West Coast was the focus of the activities," the *Times* reported, also acknowledging ceremonies in New York, Nashville, and Chicago. "Glen Campbell, Bobbie Gentry, the 5th Dimension, and Ed Ames sang the songs for which they were nominated."

In New York, the Grammy party relied more on comic entertainment. In a humorous sidebar article accompanying its Grammy coverage, *Variety* reported the results of the new "Allen Awards,"

saying, "Steve Allen, emcee of the Grammy Awards dinner at the N.Y. Hilton, took one look at the 48 categories in which the awards were to be made and thought that the list omitted some worthy causes. He suggested awards in the following categories:

"1. For the longest sideburns.

"2. For the longest delay by a diskery in paying royalties.

"3. For the longest beating caused by switching jukebox distributors."

1967

Awards were bestowed on February 29, 1968, for the eligibility period November 2, 1966, to November 1, 1967, at ceremonies held at the Century Plaza Hotel in Los Angeles and the New York Hilton Hotel, and at dinners held in Nashville and Chicago.

ALBUM OF THE YEAR
• *Sgt. Pepper's Lonely Hearts Club Band*, Beatles. George Martin, A&R producer. Capitol.
Francis Albert Sinatra/Antonio Carlos Jobim, Frank Sinatra, Antonio Carlos Jobim. Sonny Burke, A&R producer. Reprise.
It Must Be Him, Vikki Carr. Dave Pell, Tommy Oliver, A&R producers. Liberty.
My Cup Runneth Over, Ed Ames. Jim Fogelsong, A&R producer. RCA.
Ode to Billie Joe, Bobbie Gentry. Bobby Paris, Kelly Gordon, A&R producers. Capitol.

RECORD OF THE YEAR
• "Up, Up and Away," 5th Dimension. Marc Gordon, Johnny Rivers, A&R producers. Soul City.
"By the Time I Get to Phoenix," Glen Campbell. Al de Lory, A&R producer. Capitol.
"My Cup Runneth Over," Ed Ames. Jim Fogelsong, Joe Reisman, A&R producers. RCA.
"Ode to Billie Joe," Bobbie Gentry. Bobby Paris, Kelly Gordon, A&R producers. Capitol.

"Somethin' Stupid," Nancy and Frank Sinatra. Jimmy Bowen, Lee Hazelwood, A&R producers. Reprise.

SONG OF THE YEAR
(Songwriter's Award)
• "Up, Up and Away," Jimmy Webb. Soul City.
"By the Time I Get to Phoenix," Jimmy Webb. Capitol.
"Gentle on My Mind," John Hartford. RCA.
"My Cup Runneth Over," Tom Jones, Harvey Schmidt. RCA.
"Ode to Billie Joe," Bobbie Gentry. Capitol.

BEST NEW ARTIST
• Bobbie Gentry. Capitol.
Lana Cantrell. RCA.
5th Dimension. Soul City.
Harpers Bizarre. Warner Bros.
Jefferson Airplane. RCA.

BEST VOCAL PERFORMANCE, MALE
• Glen Campbell, "By the Time I Get to Phoenix." Capitol.
Ed Ames, *My Cup Runneth Over*. RCA.
Ray Charles, "Yesterday." ABC.
Frank Sinatra, *Francis Albert Sinatra/Antonio Carlos Jobim*. Reprise.
Joe South, "Can't Take My Eyes Off You." Philips.

BEST VOCAL PERFORMANCE, FEMALE
• Bobbie Gentry, "Ode to Billie Joe." Capitol.
Vikki Carr, "It Must Be Him." Liberty.
Petula Clark, "Don't Sleep in the Subway." Warner Bros.

Aretha Franklin, "Respect." Atlantic.
Dionne Warwick, "Alfie." Scepter.

BEST PERFORMANCE BY A VOCAL GROUP
• 5th Dimension, "Up, Up and Away."
  Soul City.
Association, "Never My Love." Warner
  Bros.
Beatles, "Sgt. Pepper's Lonely Hearts
  Club Band." Capitol.
Box Tops, "The Letter." Bell.
Monkees, "I'm a Believer." Colgems.

BEST PERFORMANCE BY A CHORUS
• Johnny Mann Singers, "Up, Up and
  Away." Liberty.
Ray Charles Singers, "Blame It on Me."
  Command.
Living Voices; Ethel Gabriel, conductor,
  "Wish Me a Rainbow." RCA.
Percy Faith Chorus & Orchestra, "Windy."
  Columbia.
Swingle Singers with Modern Jazz
  Quartet, "Encounter." Philips.

BEST CONTEMPORARY SINGLE
• "Up, Up and Away," 5th Dimension.
  Marc Gordon, Johnny Rivers, A&R
  producers. Soul City.
✓ "By the Time I Get to Phoenix," Glen
  Campbell. Al de Lory, A&R producer.
  Capitol.
"Don't Sleep in the Subway," Petula
  Clark. Tony Hatch, A&R producer.
  Warner Bros.
"Ode to Billie Joe," Bobbie Gentry. Bobby
  Paris, Kelly Gordon, A&R producers.
  Capitol.
"Yesterday," Ray Charles. Sid Feller,
  Tangerine Records, A&R producers.
  ABC.

BEST CONTEMPORARY ALBUM
• *Sgt. Pepper's Lonely Hearts Club Band*,
  the Beatles. George Martin, A&R
  producer. Capitol.
Insight Out, Association. Bones Howe,
  A&R producer. Warner Bros.
It Must Be Him, Vikki Carr. Dave Pell,
  Tommy Oliver, A&R producer.
  Liberty.
Ode to Billie Joe, Bobbie Gentry. Bobby
  Paris, Kelly Gordon, A&R producers.
  Capitol.
Up, Up and Away, 5th Dimension. Marc
  Gordon, Johnny Rivers, A&R
  producers. Soul City.

*Glen Campbell with two of his four
Grammys: N.A.R.A.S. voters proved
loyal to the former backup guitarist.*

BEST CONTEMPORARY MALE SOLO VOCAL PERFORMANCE
✓• Glen Campbell, "By the Time I Get to
  Phoenix." Capitol.
Ray Charles, "Yesterday." ABC.
Scott McKenzie, "San Francisco (Be Sure
  to Wear Some Flowers in Your Hair)."
  Columbia.
Jimmie Rodgers, "Child of Clay." A&M.
Frankie Valli, "Can't Take My Eyes Off
  You." Philips.

BEST CONTEMPORARY FEMALE SOLO VOCAL PERFORMANCE
• Bobbie Gentry, "Ode to Billie Joe."
  Capitol.
Vikki Carr, "It Must Be Him." Liberty.
Petula Clark, "Don't Sleep in the
  Subway." Warner Bros.
Aretha Franklin, "A Natural Woman."
  Atlantic.
Dionne Warwick, "I Say a Little Prayer."
  Scepter.

BEST CONTEMPORARY GROUP PERFORMANCE, VOCAL OR INSTRUMENTAL
• 5th Dimension, "Up, Up and Away."
  Soul City.
Association, "Windy." Warner Bros.
Beatles, "Sgt. Pepper's Lonely Hearts
  Club Band." Capitol.

Box Tops, "The Letter." Bell.
Monkees, "I'm a Believer." Colgems.
Procol Harum, "A Whiter Shade of Pale."
   Deram.

BEST RHYTHM & BLUES RECORDING
• "Respect," Aretha Franklin. Jerry
   Wexler, A&R producer. Atlantic.
"Dead End Street," Lou Rawls. David
   Axelrod, A&R producer. Capitol.
"Skinny Legs and All," Joe Tex. Buddy
   Killen, A&R producer. Dial.
"Soul Man," Sam & Dave. David Porter,
   Isaac Hayes, A&R producers. Stax.
"Try a Little Tenderness," Otis Redding.
   Steve Cropper, A&R producer. Atco.

BEST RHYTHM & BLUES SOLO VOCAL PERFORMANCE, MALE
• Lou Rawls, "Dead End Street." Capitol.
Wilson Pickett, "Funky Broadway."
   Atlantic.
Otis Redding, "Try a Little Tenderness."
   Atco.
Joe Tex, "Skinny Legs and All." Dial.
Jackie Wilson, "Higher and Higher."
   Brunswick.

BEST RHYTHM & BLUES SOLO VOCAL PERFORMANCE, FEMALE
• Aretha Franklin, "Respect." Atlantic.
Etta James, "Tell Mama." Cadet.
Gladys Knight, "I Heard It Through the
   Grapevine." Soul.
Nina Simone, "(You'll) Go to Hell." RCA.
Carla Thomas, "The Queen Alone." Stax.

BEST RHYTHM & BLUES GROUP PERFORMANCE, VOCAL OR INSTRUMENTAL
• Sam & Dave, "Soul Man." Stax.
Marvin Gaye, Tammi Terrell, "Ain't No
   Mountain High Enough." Tamla.
Smokey Robinson & the Miracles, "I
   Second That Emotion." Tamla.
Booker T. & the M.G.'s, "Hip Hug-Her."
   Stax.
Carla Thomas, Otis Redding, "The King
   and Queen." Stax.

BEST INSTRUMENTAL JAZZ PERFORMANCE, SMALL GROUP OR SOLOIST WITH SMALL GROUP (7 or Fewer Persons)
• Cannonball Adderley Quintet, Mercy,
   Mercy, Mercy. Capitol.
Gary Burton Quartet, Duster. RCA.
Miles Davis, Miles Smiles. Columbia.

Bill Evans, Further Conversations with
   Myself. Verve.
Stan Getz, Sweet Rain. Verve.
Bobby Hutcherson, Happenings. Blue Note.

BEST INSTRUMENTAL JAZZ PERFORMANCE, LARGE GROUP OR SOLOIST WITH LARGE GROUP (8 or More Persons)
• Duke Ellington, "Far East Suite." RCA.
Don Ellis Big Band, Live at Monterey.
   Pacific Jazz.
Woody Herman, Woody Live, East and
   West. Columbia.
Thad Jones, Mel Lewis, Live at the Village
   Vanguard. United Artists.
Buddy Rich, Big Swing Face. Pacific Jazz.

BEST SACRED PERFORMANCE
• Elvis Presley, How Great Thou Art. RCA.
Browns, The Old Country Church. RCA.
Red Foley, Songs for the Soul. Decca.
George Beverly Shea, the Blackwood
   Brothers Quartet, Surely Goodness and
   Mercy. RCA.
Dottie West, Dottie West Sings Sacred
   Ballads. RCA.

BEST GOSPEL PERFORMANCE
• Porter Wagoner, the Blackwood Brothers
   Quartet, More Grand Old Gospel.
   RCA.
Blackwood Brothers Quartet, The
   Blackwood Brothers Quartet Sings for
   Joy. RCA.
Happy Goodman Family, Good 'n' Happy.
   Canaan.
Oak Ridge Boys, Oak Ridge Boys.
   Heartwarming.
Singing Rambos, Singing Rambos, Gospel
   Ballads. Heartwarming.

BEST COUNTRY & WESTERN RECORDING
• "Gentle on My Mind," Glen Campbell.
   Al de Lory, A&R producer. Capitol.
"Cold Hard Facts of Life," Porter
   Wagoner. Bob Ferguson, A&R
   producer. RCA.
"Does My Ring Hurt Your Finger,"
   Charley Pride. Chet Atkins, Jack
   Clement, Felton Jarvis, A&R
   producers. RCA.
"Pop a Top," Jim Ed Brown. Felton Jarvis,
   A&R producer. RCA.
"Through the Eyes of Love," Tompall &
   the Glaser Brothers. Jack Clement,
   A&R producer. MGM.

BEST COUNTRY & WESTERN SOLO VOCAL PERFORMANCE, FEMALE
• Tammy Wynette, "I Don't Wanna Play House." Epic.
Liz Anderson, "Mama Spank." RCA.
Skeeter Davis, "What Does It Take." RCA.
Connie Smith, "Cincinnati, Ohio." RCA.
Dottie West, "Paper Mansions." RCA.

BEST COUNTRY & WESTERN SOLO VOCAL PERFORMANCE, MALE
√ • Glen Campbell, "Gentle on My Mind." Capitol.
Jim Ed Brown, "Pop a Top." RCA.
Jack Greene, "All the Time." Decca.
Charley Pride, "Does My Ring Hurt Your Finger." RCA.
Porter Wagoner, "Cold Hard Facts of Life." RCA.

BEST COUNTRY & WESTERN PERFORMANCE DUET, TRIO, OR GROUP (VOCAL OR INSTRUMENTAL)
• Johnny Cash, June Carter, "Jackson." Columbia.
Liz Anderson, Bobby Bare, and Norma Jean, "Game of Triangles." RCA.
Blue Boys, "My Cup Runneth Over." RCA.
Bobby Goldsboro, Del Reeves, "Our Way of Life." United Artists.
David Houston and Tammy Wynette, "My Elusive Dreams." Epic.
Lonesome Rhodes, "The Lonesome Rhodes." RCA.
Some of Chet's Friends, "Chet's Tune." RCA.
Tompall & the Glaser Brothers, "Through the Eyes of Love." MGM.

BEST COUNTRY & WESTERN SONG (Songwriter's Award)
√ • "Gentle on My Mind," John Hartford. RCA.
"Break My Mind," John Loudermilk. RCA.
"Cold Hard Facts of Life," Bill Anderson. RCA.
"Does My Ring Hurt Your Finger," Don Robertson, John Crutchfield, Doris Clement. RCA.
"It's Such a Pretty World Today," Dale Noe. Capitol.

BEST FOLK PERFORMANCE
• John Hartford, "Gentle on My Mind." RCA.
Judy Collins, In My Life. Elektra.

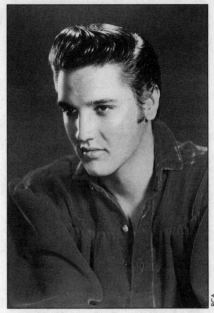

Elvis Presley's only Grammys were for religious works like How Great Thou Art, *the Best Sacred Performance of 1967.*

Arlo Guthrie, *Alice's Restaurant.* Reprise.
Janis Ian, *Janis Ian.* Verve.
Peter, Paul & Mary, *Album 1700.* Warner Bros.
Pete Seeger, "Waist Deep in the Big Muddy." Columbia.

BEST INSTRUMENTAL THEME (Composer's Award)
• "Mission: Impossible," Lalo Schifrin. Dot.
"A Banda," Chico Buarque De Hollanda. A&M.
"Casino Royale," Burt Bacharach, Hal David. A&M.
"Hurry Sundown," Hugo Montenegro. MGM.
"Mercy, Mercy, Mercy," Joe Zawinul. Capitol.

BEST INSTRUMENTAL ARRANGEMENT
• Burt Bacharach, *Alfie* (Burt Bacharach Orchestra). A&M.
Burt Bacharach, *Casino Royale* (Herb Alpert & the Tijuana Brass). A&M.
Hutch Davie, *Music to Watch Girls By* (Bob Crewe Generation). Philips.
Bill Holman, *Norwegian Wood* (Buddy Rich Orchestra). Pacific Jazz.

Claus Ogerman, *Wave* (Antonio Carlos Jobim). A&M.

Bill Reddie, *West Side Medley* (Buddy Rich Orchestra). Pacific Jazz.

BEST INSTRUMENTAL PERFORMANCE

• Chet Atkins, *Chet Atkins Picks the Best.* RCA.

Herb Alpert & the Tijuana Brass, "Casino Royale." A&M.

Cannonball Adderley Quintet, *Mercy, Mercy, Mercy.* Capitol.

Bob Crewe Generation, *Music to Watch Girls By.* Philips.

Lalo Schifrin, "Mission: Impossible." Dot.

BEST SCORE FROM AN ORIGINAL CAST SHOW ALBUM
(Composer's Award)

• *Cabaret*, Fred Ebb, John Kander. Goddard Lieberson, A&R producer. Columbia.

Hallelujah, Baby, Jule Styne, Betty Comden, Adolph Green. Edward Kleban, A&R producer. Columbia.

I Do! I Do! Harvey Schmidt, Tom Jones. Andy Wiswell, A&R producer. RCA.

Walking Happy, Sammy Cahn, Jimmy Van Heusen. Richard C. Jones, A&R producer. Capitol.

You're a Good Man, Charlie Brown, Clark Gesner. Bob Morgan, Herb Galewitz, A&R producers. MGM.

BEST ORIGINAL SCORE WRITTEN FOR A MOTION PICTURE OR TV SHOW

• *Mission: Impossible* (Lalo Schifrin Orchestra), Lalo Schifrin. Dot.

Casino Royale (Various artists, Burt Bacharach, conductor), Burt Bacharach. RCA.

Doctor Doolittle (Rex Harrison and motion picture cast, Lionel Newman, conductor), Leslie Bricusse. 20th.

In the Heat of the Night (Quincy Jones, conductor), Quincy Jones. United Artists.

To Sir with Love (soundtrack with Lulu and the Mindbenders), Ron Grainer, Don Black, Mark London. Fontana.

BEST ARRANGEMENT ACCOMPANYING VOCALIST(S) OR INSTRUMENTALIST(S)

• Jimmie Haskell, "Ode to Billie Joe" (Bobbie Gentry). Capitol.

Beatles, George Martin, "A Day in the Life" (Beatles). Capitol.

Tony Hatch, "Don't Sleep in the Subway" (Petula Clark). Warner Bros./Seven Artists.

Bill Holman, Bones Howe, Ray Pohlman, "Windy" (the Association). Warner Bros./Seven Artists.

Al de Lory, "By the Time I Get to Phoenix" (Glen Campbell). Capitol.

ALBUM OF THE YEAR, CLASSICAL
(Tie)

• *Berg: Wozzeck*, Pierre Boulez conducting orchestra and chorus of Paris National Opera (solos: Berry, Strauss, Uhl, Doench). Thomas Shepard, A&R producer. Columbia.

• *Mahler: Symphony No. 8 in E Flat Major ("Symphony of a Thousand")*, Leonard Bernstein conducting London Symphony with soloists and choruses. John McClure, A&R producer. Columbia.

Horowitz in Concert, Vladimir Horowitz. Thomas Frost, A&R producer. Columbia.

Mahler: Das Lied von der Erde, Leonard Bernstein conducting Vienna Philharmonic (solos: King, Fischer-Dieskau). John Culshaw, A&R producer. London.

Puccini: La Rondine, Francesco Molinari-Pradelli conducting RCA Italiana Opera Orchestra and Chorus (solos: Moffo, Barioni, Sereni, Sciutti, De Palma). Richard Mohr, A&R producer. RCA.

The World of Charles Ives, "Robert Browning Overture," Leopold Stokowski conducting American Symphony; "Washington's Birthday," Leonard Bernstein conducting New York Philharmonic. John McClure, Thomas Frost, A&R producers. Columbia.

BEST CLASSICAL PERFORMANCE, ORCHESTRA
(Conductor's Award)

• Igor Stravinsky conducting Columbia Symphony, *Stravinsky: Firebird and Petrouchka Suites.* Columbia.

Leonard Bernstein conducting Vienna Philharmonic (solos: King, Fischer-Dieskau), *Mahler: Das Lied von der Erde.* London.

Sir Adrian Boult conducting New Philharmonia Orchestra, *Holst: The Planets.* Angel.

Morton Gould conducting Chicago Symphony, *Ives: Orchestral Set No. 2; Robert Browning Overture; Putnam's Camp*. RCA.

Herbert von Karajan conducting Berlin Philharmonic, *Shostakovich: Symphony No. 10 in E Minor*. Deutsche Grammophon.

Georg Solti conducting London Symphony, *Mahler: Symphony No. 2 in C Minor ("Resurrection")*. London.

BEST CHAMBER MUSIC PERFORMANCE
• Ravi Shankar, Yehudi Menuhin, *West Meets East*. Angel.

Eugene Istomin, Isaac Stern, Leonard Rose, *Brahms: Trios for Piano, Violin and Cello (Nos. 1, 2, & 3)*. Columbia.

Juilliard Quartet, *Ives: Quartets Nos.1 and 3*. Columbia.

Philadelphia Brass Ensemble, *The Glorious Sound of Brass*. Columbia.

Artur Rubinstein, Guarneri Quartet, *Brahms: Quintet in F Minor for Piano, Op. 34*. RCA.

Yale Quartet, *Beethoven: Quartet No. 15 in A Minor, Op. 132*. Vanguard.

BEST CLASSICAL PERFORMANCE, INSTRUMENTAL SOLOIST(S) (WITH OR WITHOUT ORCHESTRA)
• Vladimir Horowitz, *Horowitz in Concert*. Columbia.

Julian Bream, *20th Century Guitar* (works by Brindle, Britten, Villa-Lobos, Martin, Henze). RCA.

Alicia de Larrocha, *Granados: Goyescas Complete/Escenas Romanticas*. Epic.

William Masselos, *Ives: Sonata No. 1 for Piano*. RCA.

Artur Rubinstein, *Chopin: Nocturnes*. RCA.

Andrés Segovia, *Segovia on Stage*. Decca.

BEST OPERA RECORDING
• *Berg: Wozzeck*, Pierre Boulez conducting Orchestra and Chorus of Paris National Opera (solos: Berry, Strauss, Uhl, Doench). Thomas Shepard, A&R producer. Columbia.

Handel: Julius Caesar, Julius Rudel conducting New York City Opera Chorus and Orchestra (solos: Treigle, Sills, Forrester, Wolff). Peter Dellheim, A&R producer. RCA.

Puccini: La Rondine, Francesco Molinari-Pradelli conducting RCA Italiana Opera Orchestra and Chorus (solos: Moffo, Barioni, Sereni Sciutti, De Palma). Richard Mohr, A&R producer. RCA.

Puccini: Madama Butterfly, Sir John Barbirolli conducting Rome Opera Orchestra and Chorus (solos: Scotto, Bergonzi). Kinloch Anderson, A&R producer. Angel.

Verdi: Falstaff, Leonard Bernstein conducting Vienna Philharmonic Orchestra and Chorus (solos: Fischer-Dieskau, Ligabue, Sciutti, Resnik). Erik Smith, A&R producer. Columbia.

Wagner: Die Walküre, Herbert von Karajan conducting Berlin Philharmonic (solos: Crespin, Janowitz, Veasey, Vickers, Stewart, Talvela). Otto Gerdes, A&R producer. Deutsche Grammophon.

Wagner: Tristan and Isolde "Live," Karl Böhm conducting Bayreuth Festival Chorus and Orchestra (solos: Nilsson, Windgassen, Ludwig, Talvela, Wachter). Otto Gerdes, Hans Hirsch, A&R producers. Deutsche Grammophon.

BEST CLASSICAL CHORAL PERFORMANCE, OTHER THAN OPERA (Tie)
• Leonard Bernstein conducting London Symphony Chorus and Orchestra with soloists and choruses, *Mahler: Symphony No. 8 in E Flat Major ("Symphony of a Thousand")*. Columbia.

• Robert Page conducting Temple Univ. Chorus. Eugene Ormandy conducting Philadelphia Orchestra, *Orff: Catulli Carmina*. Columbia.

Karl Böhm conducting Vienna Singverein and Vienna Symphony, *Haydn: The Seasons*. Deutsche Grammophon.

Aaron Copland conducting New England Conservatory Chorus, *Copland: In the Beginning, Lark, Las Agachadas*. CBS.

John McCarthy conducting Ambrosian Singers. Charles MacKerras conducting English Chamber Orchestra, *Handel: Messiah*. Angel.

Janusz Przybylski and Jozef Suwara conducting Boys Chorus of Cracow. Henryk Czyz conducting Cracow Philharmonic, *Penderecki: Passion According to St. Luke*. Philips.

Gregg Smith Singers, *The Choral Music of Arnold Schoenberg*. Everest.

Best Classical Vocal Soloist Performance

• Leontyne Price (Molinari-Pradelli conducting RCA Italiana Opera Orchestra), *Prima Donna, Volume 2.* RCA.

Adele Addison (Aaron Copland, pianist), *Copland: 12 Poems of Emily Dickinson.* CBS.

Victoria de los Angeles (Gonzalo Soriano, pianist), *Victoria de los Angeles Sings Debussy and Ravel and other French Songs.* Angel.

Dietrich Fischer-Dieskau (Jorg Demus, pianist), *Beethoven: Songs.* Deutsche Grammophon.

Christa Ludwig (with instrumental ensemble), *Shepherd on the Rock and Other Songs.* Angel.

Peter Pears (Benjamin Britten, pianist), *Schubert: Die Winterreise.* London.

Elisabeth Schwarzkopf (Gerald Moore, pianist), *An Elisabeth Schwarzkopf Songbook.* Angel.

Fritz Wunderlich (Hubert Giesen, pianist), *Schubert: Die Schöne Müllerin.* Deutsche Grammophon.

Best Engineered Recording, Classical

• Edward T. Graham, *The Glorious Sound of Brass* (Philadelphia Brass Ensemble). Columbia.

Edwin Begley, *Mahler: Symphony No. 3 in D Minor* (Leinsdorf conducting Boston Symphony). RCA Red Seal.

Edward T. Graham, *Rachmaninoff: Symphony No. 1 in D* (Ormandy conducting Philadelphia Orchestra). Columbia.

Gunter Hermanns, *Wagner: Tristan and Isolde "Live"* (Böhm conducting Bayreuth Festival Orchestra; solos: Nilsson, Windgassen). Deutsche Grammophon.

Hellmuth Kolbe, *Mahler: Symphony No. 8 in E Flat* (Bernstein conducting London Symphony). Columbia.

Gordon Parry, *Mahler: Symphony No. 2 in C Minor ("Resurrection")* (Solti conducting London Symphony Chorus and Orchestra; solos: Harper, Watts). London.

Gordon Parry, *Mahler: Das Lied von der Erde* (Bernstein conducting Vienna Philharmonic and soloists). London.

Best Spoken Word, Documentary, or Drama Recording

• *Gallant Men,* Sen. Everett M. Dirksen. Capitol.

The Balcony, Patrick Magee, Cyril Cusack. Caedmon.

The Earth, Rod McKuen. Warner Bros.

A Man for All Seasons, Paul Scofield, Wendy Hiller, Robert Shaw. RCA.

Mark Twain Tonight, Vol. 3, Hal Holbrook. Columbia.

An Open Letter to My Teenage Son, Victor Lundberg. Liberty.

Poems of James Dickey, James Dickey. Spoken Arts.

Best Comedy Recording

• *Revenge,* Bill Cosby. Warner Bros.

The Cockfight and Other Tall Tales, Archie Campbell. RCA.

Cowboys and Colored People, Flip Wilson. Atlantic.

Lenny Bruce in Concert, Lenny Bruce. United Artists.

Take-Offs and Put-Ons, George Carlin. RCA.

Best Recording for Children

• *Dr. Seuss: How the Grinch Stole Christmas* (TV soundtrack), Boris Karloff. MGM.

The Carnival of the Animals, verses by Ogden Nash, narrated by Tutti Camarata (Symphonie-Orchester Graunke). Buena Vista.

A Happy Birthday Party with Winnie the Pooh, Sterling Holloway. Disneyland.

The Jungle Book, motion picture cast, including Phil Harris, Louis Prima, Sterling Holloway, Sebastian Cabot, George Saunders. Tutti Camarata, A&R producer. Disney.

Jungle Books, Richard Kiley. MGM.

Magic Fishbone/Happy Prince/Potted Princess, Julie Harris, Richard Kiley. MGM.

Best Engineered Recording, Non-Classical

• G.E. Emerick, *Sgt. Pepper's Lonely Hearts Club Band* (Beatles). Capitol.

Hank Cicalo, *Mission: Impossible* (Lalo Schifrin). Dot.

James Malloy, *How Great Thou Art* (Elvis Presley). RCA.

Joe Polito, *Ode to Billie Joe* (Bobbie Gentry). Capitol.

William Vandevort, *Chet's Tune* (Some of Chet's Friends). RCA.

BEST ALBUM COVER, PHOTOGRAPHY

• John Berg, Bob Cato, art directors. Roland Scherman, photographer, *Dylan's Greatest Hits* (Bob Dylan). Columbia.

Bill Harvey, art director. Guy Webster, Joel Brodsky, photographers, *The Doors* (Doors). Elektra.

Bob Jones, art director. Jimmy Moore, photographer, *Suburban Attitudes in Country Verse* (John Loudermilk). RCA.

Robert Jones, art director. New World Photography, photography, *Earthwords and Music* (John Harford). RCA.

Robert Jones, art director. Howard Cooper, photographer, *From Mexico with Laughs* (Don Bowman). RCA.

Ken Kim, art director and photographer, *Bravo, Bravo, Aznavour* (Charles Aznavour). Monument.

Ken Kim, art director and photographer, *That Man, Robert Mitchum, Sings*. Monument.

BEST ALBUM COVER, GRAPHIC ARTS

• Peter Blake, Jann Haworth, art directors, *Sgt. Pepper's Lonely Hearts Club Band* (Beatles). Capitol.

John Berg, Bob Cato, art directors. Henrietta Condak, graphic artist, *Haydn: Symphony No. 84 in E Flat Major; Symphony No. 85 in B Flat Major ("La Reine")* (Bernstein conducting New York Philharmonic). Columbia.

John Berg, Bob Cato, art directors. Lasio Kubinyi, graphic artist, *Monk: Straight, No Chaser* (Thelonious Monk). Columbia.

Robert Jones, art director. Jack Davis, graphic artist, *Nashville Cats* (Homer & Jethro). RCA.

Ed Thrasher, art director. Charles White, graphic artist, *The Gold Standard Collection* (Hank Thompson). Warner Bros./Seven Artists.

Woody Woodward, art director. Wayne Kimball, graphic artist, *Up, Up and Away* (5th Dimension). Soul City.

BEST ALBUM NOTES
(Annotator's Award)

• John D. Loudermilk, *Suburban Attitudes in Country Verse* (John Loudermilk). RCA.

Stan Cornyn, *Francis Albert Sinatra/ Antonio Carlos Jobim*. Reprise.

Stanley Dance, *Far East Suite* (Duke Ellington). RCA.

Rory Guy, *Extra Special* (Peggy Lee). Capitol.

Rod McKuen, *The Earth* (Rod McKuen, music by Anita Kerr). Warner Bros.

Richard Oliver, *Listen!* (Gary Lewis & the Playboys). Liberty.

A Smooth Triumph
for the New Generation

"The recording industry," wrote *Variety*, "has virtually shucked off its past. It's doing its own thing with a roster of youths who have overthrown the elders in the field .... The Grammy Awards gave an indication of how far the rebellion of the young has gone. There was rarely a prize in the pop field to anyone over 30."

The spirited new generation of artists may at long last have won their battle against Sinatra & Co., but they suddenly found themselves locked in a different struggle that saw their numbers divided into two

The cool, flamenco-flavored singing of Best New Artist José Feliciano made him a favorite of young lovers.

camps: smooth pop and cutting edge rock. The fight, in short, was the same as in the old days (easy listening vs. adventurous rock), but at least they had the consolation that, for the most part, the larger revolution was won and the graybeards — for now — were gone.

The new showdown was over Record of the Year pitting the Beatles' "Hey Jude" against Simon & Garfunkel's "Mrs. Robinson." "Jude" had the advantage of being the best-selling single of the year, but "Mrs. Robinson" better represented the MOR (middle-of-the-road) pop music N.A.R.A.S. voters hailed in the past. Also to the folk/pop duo's credit was that they were fairly new on the scene, having had only one top single, "The Sounds of Silence," in addition to smaller successes like "Homeward Bound." The Beatles, on the other hand,

warned *Variety*, "may be old hat." Still, the Fab Four had proved their popularity with Grammy voters last year when they took Album of the Year honors for *Sgt. Pepper's Lonely Hearts Club Band*.

The suspense dragged on even beyond Grammy night. N.A.R.A.S. executives decided to delay naming the Record of the Year winner so it could be revealed during the modestly rated, after-the-fact "Best on Record" telecast that was once reserved exclusively for performances by the winners. (For more than a decade, TV network executives refused to air the awards ceremony because they didn't think the top nominated talent would show up.) The Beatles showed up for "Best on Record," but performed mechanically. Simon & Garfunkel chose to perform "Mrs. Robinson" on tape and submitted an energetic precursor of the modern music video that showed them romping around Yankee Stadium as the song's lyrics asked "Where have you gone, Joe DiMaggio?" in voiceover.

Simon & Garfunkel had the most nominations of the year (five), compared to four each for the Beatles (and Glen Campbell). The duo ended up with three awards, including Record of the Year and the group vocals prize for best contemporary-pop performance for "Mrs. Robinson." (The Beatles got zip.) "Pop" was added to the title of the contemporary categories after N.A.R.A.S. again made drastic changes in the awards line-up, even cutting the categories back from 48 to 40 in a streamlining effort. Gone were last year's laurels for Best Contemporary Single and Album (one or both of which the Beatles might have received as a consolation prize) as well as Classical Album of the Year and the general vocal performance honors, among others.

"Mrs. Robinson" was written by Paul Simon for the Mike Nichols film *The Graduate,* starring Dustin Hoffman and Anne Bancroft in the story of a young man who is seduced by his girlfriend's mother. Bridging the generation gap was a specialty of Simon & Garfunkel's. Their mellow folk/rock sound and poetic lyrics were appreciated by both the vanquished Sinatra crowd as well as young hipsters. The duo's third Grammy was for *The Graduate*'s film score, which included, and helped popularize, much of their earlier material such as "Scarborough Fair." Among their unsuccessful nods was an Album of the Year bid for their latest LP, *Bookends,* which also included the song "Mrs. Robinson."

Bookends and the Beatles' *Magical Mystery Tour* were the early favorites to win Album of the Year, but both were overtaken by a choice that confused many Grammy watchers — Glen Campbell's *By the Time I Get to Phoenix,* the title song of which won two awards for the c&w troubador last year. The reason for the delayed album honor was that the LP was released after the "Phoenix" single and landed on the other side of Grammy's next eligibility period, a phenomenon that would occur occasionally in the future (like when Simon's *Graceland* would win Album of the year in 1986 and Record of the Year in 1987). But it was a first in 1968 and caused a minor furor. Campbell's latest victory only underscored his enormous popularity at the time of the 1968 awards ceremony on March 12, 1969. The former regular on TV's *The Smothers Brothers Comedy Hour* had his own hit variety series and new best-selling records like "Wichita Lineman" (Best Engineered Recording) and "Galveston" (ranked number 12 on *Variety*'s chart on Grammy day).

Safe, smooth pop continued its winning streak when the recipient of Song of the Year was named — "Little Green Apples," written by Bobby Russell, who was also nominated in the category for Bobby Goldsboro's "Honey" (number five in 1968's Hot 100 and a contender for Record of the Year). "Apples" was popularized by pop/soul singer O.C. Smith, although it had also been recorded earlier by Roger Miller and Patti Page. The tune's past association with Nashville brought it the prize for Best Country Song, too. (Older songs can compete as long as they've never before been nominated.) "& Western" was dropped from the country prize titles this year as part

> *Simon & Garfunkel made Record of the Year "Mrs. Robinson" into one of the first music videos.*

of the larger awards revamping. Some critics speculated that the real reason for the change was because of western star Glen Campbell's victories over Nashville country artists last year.

The smoothest music of 1968 was recorded by Best New Artist José Feliciano, whose *Feliciano!* was then the favorite "make-out" album among teen lovers and a strong nominee for Album of the Year. Born blind, Feliciano was raised in New York's Spanish Harlem and championed an impassioned form of flamenco-flavored singing that made him popular in Greenwich Village coffee houses where he was discovered one day by an RCA record executive. (He performed there with his 12-string guitar "not for coins, just for the hell of it," he once said.) By 1968, he was renowned throughout the Spanish-speaking world, but he didn't reach the American pop music market till he covered a recent hit by the Doors. For his own interpretation of "Light My Fire," he combined influences of Latin, soul, folk, and rock music, earning him the Grammy for Best Contemporary Pop Vocal Performance, Male.

The female vocalist prize went to Dionne Warwick, the signature singer of the melodic tunes of Burt Bacharach and Hal David. Their latest collaboration was "Do You Know the Way to San Jose," which followed earlier hits including "I Say a Little Prayer" and "Walk On By."

Mason Williams's "Classical Gas" won three Grammy Awards, thereby tying Simon & Garfunkel for the evening's most wins: best contemporary, pop instrumental performance, Best Instrumental Theme, and Best Instrumental Arrangement. But "Classical Gas" was more than classical in nature: It also combined elements of rock, bluegrass, and Latin music to achieve a sound Williams once described as "half

flamenco, half Flatt & Scruggs, and half classical."

Motown and its affiliated Gordy and Tamla labels made a formidable impact on the pop scene of the 1960s with such talent as the Supremes, "Little Stevie Wonder," the Four Tops, and Gladys Knight & the Pips, but the only Grammy the company won in the entire decade went to the Temptations for "Cloud Nine," winner of the rhythm & blues group vocal award. The song marked a key turning point for one of the most successful male singing groups of the decade. Shortly before recording "Cloud Nine," the Temptations decided to shake off the old pop style of their earlier hits like "My Girl" and "You're My Everything" to pursue the same "funk" terrain being explored by Sly & the Family Stone. "Cloud Nine" became the first cerebral soul recording in history. It represented the best of the underground sound of the day and had a daring, two-level narrative that fans were left wondering if the tune was about drug addiction or a dream.

At the heart of the 1960s drug culture was the new hippie movement, which was portrayed with fanciful idealism in 1968's Best Cast Show Album, *Hair*, written by Galt MacDermot, Gerome Ragni, and James Rado. *Hair* spent 59 weeks in the LP charts, 13 of the them at number one, and spawned a number of single hits, one of which would win the top Grammy of 1969.

Dual award winner of last year, Aretha Franklin, was at her professional peak in 1968, having scored nine Top 10 singles over the previous two years, and now returned to reclaim the r&b vocal laurels for "Chain of Fools." The recording was from her *Lady Soul* album, which was such a milestone in contemporary music that she was crowned with the title "Lady Soul" herself and made the cover of *Time* magazine. In "Chain of

Fools," Franklin pitched all the passion and unbridled angst she could muster, trademarks of her emotional range and talent that have brought her more million-selling records than any other woman in music history.

The writer of the single that earned Franklin her first two Grammys, "Respect," was awarded the male vocal r&b vocal honors for "(Sittin' on) The Dock of the Bay," the number-six song in the year's Hot 100. By the late 1960s, Otis Redding commanded considerable respect as a singer and songwriter and was famous in France and England for his grainy, gutsy style. In 1967, he finally came to the attention of the mainstream American music world when he wowed a dozing audience at the Monterey Pop Festival, the first major rock fête ever held. With Steve Cropper, Redding wrote "Dock of the Bay" in gratitude for the response he received in California, but three days after he taped it in a Memphis recording studio, he died at the age of 26 when his private twin-engine plane crashed into a frozen lake near Madison, Wisconsin, killing four members of his backup group, in addition to Redding, his valet, and the pilot. The tune spent 16 weeks on the charts, reaching number one for four weeks, the first time that an artist ever held that rank posthumously.

It was aboard a plane that Johnny Cash once wrote his hit 1955 single "Folsom Prison Blues." Cash had been killing time while waiting for the flight out of Memphis one day when he ducked into a movie theater and saw a

In "Folsom Prison Blues," best male country vocalist Johnny Cash reached out to inmates to let them know somebody "cared for them as human beings."

stirring documentary about the jailhouse. Soon after he recorded his bluesy salute, the tune took off to number four on the country charts and Cash went to the prison to perform for its inmates. The response was such a popular and critical success that he returned in 1968 to make a live album recording. In a nostalgic remembrance of the historic session, *The New York Times* wrote years later, "The prisoners in the audience holler every time Mr. Cash makes explicit reference to their situation: 'I hear that train a-coming, it's rolling round the bend/ And I ain't seen the sunshine since I don't know when/ I'm stuck in Folsom prison.'"

"By doing a prison concert, we were letting inmates know that somewhere in the free world was somebody who cared for them as human beings," Cash wrote in his autobiography *Man in Black. Johnny Cash at Folsom Prison* became the number-one country album for 10 weeks and earned him the Best Male

Country Vocal Performance Grammy. (*Folsom* also took Best Album Notes.) He followed it up, in 1969, with *Johnny Cash at San Quentin*.

The trophy for best female vocal performance went to Jeannie C. Riley, a former Nashville secretary and demo singer who was unknown to music buyers prior to the success of "Harper Valley P.T.A." The song by journeyman deejay Tom T. Hall was nominated for Record and Song of the Year and was based on an actual showdown he once witnessed between a Southern widow and the P.T.A. board in her small town over her short skirts and independent ways. The recording premiered at number 81 in the pop rankings, then zoomed up to number seven a week later — the largest leap in the history of the charts. After it settled in at number one, Riley was suddenly a star, if a short-lived one. The losing nominee for Grammy's Best New Artist once told journalists Bob Gilbert and Gary Theroux, "I soon found out people thought that's what I was really like," referring to the saucy heroine of her song. "I was just tryin' to tell a story." After failing to get into the Top 40 again, Riley eventually quit the pop field in favor of the gospel circuit. "Harper Valley P.T.A.," however, continued to survive in pop culture — as a 1980 TV film starring Barbara Eden and a brief weekly TV series the following year.

A hit feature movie that incorporated

> *Triple winner "Classical Gas" was described as "half flamenco, half Flatt & Scruggs, and half classical."*

existing music into its score helped to bring singer Lester Flatt and banjo player Earl Scruggs into the popular mainstream. Flatt & Scruggs had been a favorite of country audiences since the 1940s when they first recorded "Foggy Mountain Breakdown," but when it was revived for the Warren Beatty/Faye Dunaway movie *Bonnie and Clyde*, it introduced the song to a whole new generation of music lovers and brought the duo the prize for best country group performance.

Miles Davis once said of Bill Evans (1963 Grammy winner for *Conversations with Myself*), "He plays the piano the way it should be played." Evans and his trio took a romantic approach to jazz, emphasizing strong harmonies interrupted by innovative improvisations. The first recording of their many performances at the Montreux Jazz Festival in Switzerland became a quick success and earned them the honor for small group instrumental performance.

Duke Ellington acknowledged a special Grammy tribute last year to his late arranger/composer, Billy Strayhorn. This year he accepted a large group jazz performance award for *And His Mother Called Him Bill*, Ellington's salute to the memory of the man with whom he had worked since 1939 and wrote such memorable music as *Perfume Suite*. The Duke's latest LP included Strayhorn's final composition, "Blood Count."

In the comedy category, Bill Cosby won the laugh laurels for a fifth year in a row for *To Russell, My Brother, Whom I Slept With* in which Cosby taunts his sibling bed partner, saying, "I don't want you touchin' my body because you're not really my brother anyway. You were brought here by the police. They said, 'Take care of this boy until he starts lying.' And I'm gonna tell the police that you have *lied* and you'll go back to jail!" After the squabble intensifies in the recording, the boys break the bed and tell their angry father, "Some man came in here, started jumpin' on the bed, dad .... We told him, 'You better cut it out!' and he broke it and ran out the window laughin'."

While there was no Classical Album of the Year award this year, there were still several standout LPs, including conductor Pierre Boulez's first recording with the Cleveland Orchestra, which nabbed the orchestral performance award. "This is the most lucid and illuminating performance of [Debussy's] *Images* that I know," wrote a reviewer in *High Fidelity*, "and the *Danses* are equally accomplished." The chamber music performance prize went to conductor Vittorio Negri and others behind a two-set recording of works by two innovative Italian composers. *High Fidelity* wrote: "The music recorded on both discs brilliantly recaptures the excitement that must have been in the air when the two galleries of the basilica of St. Mark's resounded to the bold new creations of Andrea Gabrieli and his even more illustrious nephew Giovanni."

Vladimir Horowitz garnered his eighth career Grammy for a recording of a recent TV special ("one of television's finest moments," commented *High Fidelity*) during which he performed works by Chopin, Schumann, and Scriabin.

The award for Best Opera Recording went for a performance of a work Stendhal once called "the union of an exquisite ear with an impassioned heart" — Mozart's *Cosi fan tutte*. "It is the first truly comprehensive recording," *High Fidelity* noted, offering special praise to its American cast of vocalists that included Leontyne Price. Together they demonstrated, it said, "how far American singers have come in our time." This was the first occasion in six years, however, that Price would not win a Grammy. Instead, the vocalist award went to Spanish soprano Montserrat Caballé for her renditions of arias by Rossini.

While "smooth" music reigned at the Grammy Awards this year, the ceremonies in New York, Los Angles, Nashville, and Chicago were also "smoothly functioning affairs," wrote *Variety*, adding, "the prize winners were just as frequently in Nashville or the Coast as New York, and various indications point to an even more complete departure in the future." The fact that N.A.R.A.S. delayed the announcement of the winner of Grammy's most esteemed trophy — Record of the Year — till the "Best on Record" broadcast outraged many, particularly the crowd out in L.A.

"Dumb? You bet it is," commented *The Los Angeles Times*. "The audience booed" the announcement of the delay, the paper reported, adding, "fortunately, nobody threw anything. This was probably because the waiters had wisely cleared the tables." The *L.A. Times*'s reporter, Wayne Warga, also noted that a number of the banquet attendees knew who the recipients were going to be before the voting results were announced. "In my pocket — and quite a few others judging from the men's room chatter," Warga wrote, "was the list of winners, handed me before the show began."

The broadcast of "Best on Record" also sparked criticism when it was aired nearly two months later. According to *Variety*, it was a "weakly produced and unimaginative anticlimax to the in-person Grammy Awards earlier this year." While performers Dionne Warwick and the Los Angeles company of *Hair* "were able to project artistry," the Beatles were dismissed as "wooden" by the trade paper, the Temptations were "lacking [their] normal spontaneity," and the creativity demonstrated by all the performers "wasn't mixed with the smallest degree of musical astuteness."

Jazz winner Bill Evans was among

those who pointed to some of the show's "shameful omissions." In a letter written to *Down Beat* columnist Leonard Feather, he said, "As the date of the TV show approached and I wasn't called to appear, I was well satisfied to assume that Duke [Ellington] would represent jazz on the show. But when I checked the listings, I was at first disappointed, then progressively angry, to realize that jazz as well as classical music was to be ignored entirely in favor of the 'sure' commercial categories. I was under the impression that N.A.R.A.S. was trying to build a meaningful award, but apparently they gave way to the wishes of the network or sponsor."

"N.A.R.A.S. is still, after a decade of honest attempts to improve itself, little more than a popularity poll," Feather answered in his column. (Feather was a longtime critic of the academy but had recently accepted the elected post of secretary of its L.A. branch.) "For the TV program, the academy was caught in a conflict of interest between presenting what was really the best on record and assuring a good rating for the sponsor (Timex) and a continuance of sponsorship next year. Clearly, it opted for the latter alternative.

"This is not essentially the fault of N.A.R.A.S.," he added, "but of a whole system affecting the entire American musical scene that imposes irreconcilable difference between music as art and music as a means of making money .... Until [something changes], the 'Best on Record' will still be represented by Jeannie C. Riley singing 'Harper Valley P.T.A.' and classical music by Mason Williams playing 'Classical Gas.'"

1968

Awards were bestowed on March 12, 1969, for the eligibility period of November 2, 1967, to November 1, 1968, at the Beverly Hilton Hotel in Los Angeles, the Hotel Astor in New York, and at dinners held in Nashville and Chicago.

ALBUM OF THE YEAR
• *By the Time I Get to Phoenix*, Glen Campbell. Al de Lory, A&R producer. Capitol.
Bookends, Simon & Garfunkel. Paul Simon, Art Garfunkel, Roy Halee, A&R producers. Columbia.
Feliciano! José Feliciano. Rick Jarrard, A&R producer. RCA.
Magical Mystery Tour, Beatles. George Martin, A&R producer. Capitol.
A Tramp Shining, Richard Harris. Jim Webb, A&R producer. Dunhill.

RECORD OF THE YEAR
• "Mrs. Robinson," Simon & Garfunkel. Paul Simon, Art Garfunkel, Roy Halee, A&R producers. Columbia.
"Harper Valley P.T.A.," Jeannie C. Riley. Shelby S. Singleton, Jr., A&R producer. Plantation.

"Hey Jude," Beatles. George Martin, A&R producer. Capitol.
"Honey," Bobby Goldsboro. Bob Montgomery, Bobby Goldsboro, A&R producers. United Artists.
"Wichita Lineman," Glen Campbell. Al de Lory, A&R producer. Capitol.

SONG OF THE YEAR
(Songwriter's Award)
• "Little Green Apples," Bobby Russell. Columbia.
"Harper Valley P.T.A.," Tom T. Hall. Plantation.
"Honey," Bobby Russell. United Artists.
"Hey Jude," John Lennon, Paul McCartney. Capitol.
"Mrs. Robinson," Paul Simon. Columbia.

BEST NEW ARTIST
• José Feliciano. RCA.
Cream. Atco.
Gary Puckett & the Union Gap. Columbia.
Jeannie C. Riley. Plantation.
O.C. Smith. Columbia.

BEST CONTEMPORARY, POP VOCAL PERFORMANCE, MALE

- José Feliciano, "Light My Fire." RCA.
- ✓ Glen Campbell, "Wichita Lineman." Capitol.
- Bobby Goldsboro, "Honey." United Artists.
- Richard Harris, "MacArthur Park." Dunhill.
- O.C. Smith, "Little Green Apples." Columbia.

BEST CONTEMPORARY, POP VOCAL PERFORMANCE, FEMALE

- Dionne Warwick, "Do You Know the Way to San Jose." Scepter.
- Aretha Franklin, "I Say a Little Prayer." Atlantic.
- Mary Hopkins, "Those Were the Days." Capitol.
- Merrilee Rush, "Angel of the Morning." Bell.
- Barbra Streisand, *Funny Girl*. Columbia.

BEST CONTEMPORARY, POP VOCAL PERFORMANCE, DUO OR GROUP

- Simon & Garfunkel, "Mrs. Robinson." Columbia.
- Beatles, "Hey Jude." Capitol.
- Blood, Sweat & Tears, "Child Is Father to the Man." Columbia.
- Lettermen, "Goin' Out of My Head/Can't Take My Eyes Off You" (medley). Capitol.
- Sergio Mendes & Brasil '66, "Fool on the Hill." A&M.
- Gary Puckett & the Union Gap, *Woman, Woman*. Columbia.

BEST CONTEMPORARY, POP PERFORMANCE BY A CHORUS

- Alan Copeland Singers, "Mission Impossible/Norwegian Wood" (medley). ABC.
- Ray Charles Singers, "MacArthur Park." Command.
- Ray Conniff Singers, "Honey." Columbia.
- Percy Faith Chorus and Orchestra, "Angel of the Morning." Columbia.
- Johnny Mann Singers, "This Guy's in Love with You." Liberty.

BEST CONTEMPORARY, POP PERFORMANCE, INSTRUMENTAL

- Mason Williams, "Classical Gas." Warner Brothers.
- José Feliciano, "Here, There and Everywhere." RCA.
- Hugh Masekela, "Grazing in the Grass." Uni.

Hugo Montenegro, "The Good, the Bad and the Ugly." RCA.
Wes Montgomery, "Eleanor Rigby." A&M.

BEST RHYTHM & BLUES VOCAL PERFORMANCE, MALE

- Otis Redding, "(Sittin' On) The Dock of the Bay." Volt.
- Marvin Gaye, "I Heard It Through the Grapevine." Tamla/Motown.
- Joe Simon, "(You Keep Me) Hangin' On." Sound Stage 7.
- Johnnie Taylor, "Who's Making Love." Stax.
- Stevie Wonder, "For Once in My Life." Tamla/Motown.

Motown's only Grammy throughout the 1960s was for the Temptations singing "Cloud Nine," from All Directions

BEST RHYTHM & BLUES VOCAL PERFORMANCE, FEMALE

- Aretha Franklin, "Chain of Fools." Atlantic.
- Barbara Acklin, "Love Makes a Woman." Brunswick.
- Erma Franklin, "Piece of My Heart." Shout.
- Etta James, "Security." Cadet.
- Ella Washington, "He Called Me Baby." Sound Stage 7.

BEST RHYTHM & BLUES PERFORMANCE BY A DUO OR GROUP, VOCAL OR INSTRUMENTAL

- The Temptations, "Cloud Nine." Gordy.
- Archie Bell & the Drells, "Tighten Up." Atlantic.
- Sam & Dave, "I Thank You," Stax.

Peggy Scott, Jo Jo Benson, "Pickin' Wild Mountain Berries." Plantation.

Sweet Inspiration, "Sweet Inspiration." Atlantic.

Best Rhythm & Blues Song
(Songwriter's Award)

• "(Sittin' On) The Dock of the Bay," Otis Redding, Steve Cropper. Volt.

"Chain of Fools," Don Lovay. Atlantic.

"I Wish It Would Rain," Norman Whitfield, Barrett Strong, Roger Penzabene. Gordy/Motown.

"Pickin' Wild Mountain Berries," Edward Thomas, Bob McRee, Clifton Thomas. Plantation.

"Who's Making Love," Homer Banks, Bettye Crutcher, Raymond Jackson, Donald Davis. Stax.

Best Instrumental Jazz Performance, Small Group or Soloist with Small Group

• Bill Evans Trio, *Bill Evans at the Montreux Jazz Festival*. Verve.

Dave Brubeck, Gerry Mulligan, *Compadres*. Columbia.

Gary Burton, *Gary Burton Quartet in Concert*. RCA.

Miles Davis, Herbie Hancock, *Miles in the Sky*. Columbia.

Eddie Harris, *The Electrifying ... Eddie Harris*. Atlantic.

Jazz for a Sunday Afternoon, Vol. 1, produced by Sonny Lester (Various artists). Solid State.

Best Instrumental Jazz Performance, Large Group or Soloist with Large Group

• Duke Ellington, "And His Mother Called Him Bill." RCA.

Don Ellis, *Electric Bath*. Columbia.

Erroll Garner, "Up in Erroll's Room." Verve.

Woody Herman, *Concerto for Herd*. Verve.

Wes Montgomery, *Down Here on the Ground*. A&M.

Buddy Rich, "Mercy, Mercy." World Pacific.

Best Country Solo Vocal, Male

• Johnny Cash, "Folsom Prison Blues." Columbia.

Glen Campbell, "I Wanna Live." Capitol.

Henson Cargill, "Skip a Rope." Monument.

Roger Miller, "Little Green Apples." Smash.

Porter Wagoner, "The Carroll County Accident." RCA.

Best Country Solo Vocal, Female

• Jeannie C. Riley, "Harper Valley P.T.A." Plantation.

Lynn Anderson, "Big Girls Don't Cry." Chart.

Jan Howard, "My Son." Decca.

Dottie West, "Country Girl." RCA.

Tammy Wynette, "D-I-V-O-R-C-E." Epic.

Best Country Performance, Duo or Group, Vocal or Instrumental

• Flatt & Scruggs, "Foggy Mountain Breakdown." Columbia.

Everly Brothers, "It's My Time." Warner Bros.

Bill Wilbourne, Kathy Morrison, "The Lovers." United Artists.

Nashville Brass, "Mountain Dew." RCA.

Tompall & The Glaser Brothers, "Through the Eyes of Love." MGM.

Best Country Song
(Songwriter's Award)

• "Little Green Apples," Bobby Russell. Smash.

"D-I-V-O-R-C-E," Curly Putman, Bobby Braddock. Columbia.

"Harper Valley P.T.A.," Tom T. Hall. Plantation.

"Honey," Bobby Russell. Verve.

"Skip a Rope," Glenn Tubb, Jack Moran. Monument.

Best Sacred Performance

• Jake Hess, "Beautiful Isle of Somewhere." RCA.

Anita Bryant, "How Great Thou Art." Columbia.

Jim Bohi, "I'll Fly Away." Supreme.

Ralph Carmichael, *102 Strings, Vol. 2*. Word.

George Beverly Shea, "Whispering Hope." RCA.

Elvis Presley, *You'll Never Walk Alone*. RCA.

Best Gospel Performance

• Happy Goodman Family, *The Happy Gospel of the Happy Goodmans*. Word.

Blackwood Brothers Quartet, *Yours Faithfully*. RCA.

Florida Boys Quartet, *The Florida Boys Sing Kinda Country*. Word.

Oak Ridge Boys, *A Great Day.*
Heartwarming.
Thrasher Brothers, *For Goodness Sake.*
Anchor.

BEST SOUL GOSPEL PERFORMANCE
• Dottie Rambo, "The Soul of Me."
Heartwarming.
James Cleveland & Angelic Choir, "Bread
of Heaven," Parts 1 & 2. Savoy.
Staple Singers, "Long Walk to D.C." Stax.
Swan Silvertones, "Only Believe."
Scepter.
Davis Sisters, "Wait a Little Longer."
Savoy.
Willa Dorsey, "Willa Dorsey: The World's
Most Exciting Gospel Singer." Word.

BEST FOLK PERFORMANCE
• Judy Collins, "Both Sides Now." Elektra.
Bob Dylan, "John Wesley Harding."
Columbia.
Incredible String Band, "The Hangman's
Beautiful Daughter." Elektra.
Irish Rovers, "The Unicorn." Decca.
Gordon Lightfoot, "Did She Mention My
Name." United Artists.
Peter, Paul & Mary, "Late Again." Warner
Bros.

BEST INSTRUMENTAL THEME
(Composer's Award)
• "Classical Gas," Mason Williams.
Warner Bros.
"The Good, the Bad and the Ugly," Hugo
Montenegro, Ennio Morricone. RCA.
"The Odd Couple," Neal Hefti. Dot.
"Rosemary's Baby," Christopher Komeda.
Dot.
"Theme from *The Fox*," Lalo Schifrin.
Warner Bros./Seven Artists.

BEST INSTRUMENTAL ARRANGEMENT
• Mike Post, "Classical Gas" (Mason
Williams). Warner Bros.
Al Capps, "Baroque-A-Nova" (Mason
Williams). Warner Bros.
Michel Legrand, "The Windmills of Your
Mind" (Michel Legrand). United
Artists.
Hugo Montenegro, "The Good, the Bad
and the Ugly" (Hugo Montenegro).
RCA.
Don Sebesky, "Scarborough Fair" (Wes
Montgomery). A&M.

RCA

*Music from the best cast show album
of 1968,* Hair, *would return to the
Grammys next year for bigger rewards.*

BEST SCORE FROM AN ORIGINAL CAST SHOW ALBUM
• *Hair,* Gerome Ragni, James Rado, Galt
MacDermot. Andy Wiswell, A&R
producer. RCA.
George M! George M. Cohan. Thomas
Shepard, A&R producer. Columbia.
The Happy Time, Fred Ebb, John Kander.
George R. Marek, Andy Wiswell, A&R
producers. RCA.
*Jacques Brel Is Alive and Well and Living
in Paris,* Jacques Brel. Ed Kleban,
A&R producer. Columbia.
Your Own Thing, Hal Hester, Danny
Apolinar. George R. Marek, Andy
Wiswell, A&R producer. RCA.

BEST ORIGINAL SCORE WRITTEN FOR A MOTION PICTURE OR TV SPECIAL
(Composer's Award)
• *The Graduate,* Paul Simon, Dave Grusin.
Columbia.
Bonnie and Clyde, Charles Strouse.
Warner Bros./Seven Artists.
The Fox, Lalo Schifrin. Warner
Bros./Seven Artists.
The Odd Couple, Neal Hefti. Dot.
Valley of the Dolls, André Previn. 20th.

BEST ARRANGEMENT ACCOMPANYING VOCALIST(S)
• Jim Webb, "Mac Arthur Park" (Richard
Harris). Dunhill.
Dave Grusin, "Fool on the Hill" (Sergio
Mendes & Brasil '66). A&M.
Al de Lory, "Wichita Lineman "(Glen
Campbell). Capitol.

George Tipton, "Light My Fire" (José Feliciano). RCA.

Torrie Zito, "Yesterday I Heard the Rain" (Tony Bennett). Columbia.

BEST CLASSICAL PERFORMANCE, ORCHESTRA
(Conductor's Award)

• Pierre Boulez conducting New Philharmonia Orchestra, *Boulez Conducts Debussy*. Columbia.

Leonard Bernstein conducting New York Philharmonic, *Mahler: Symphony No.6 in A Minor and Symphony No. 9 in D Major*. Columbia.

Nikolaus Harnoncourt conducting Concentus Musicus of Vienna, *Bach: Four Suites for Orchestra*. Telef.

Erich Leinsdorf conducting Boston Symphony, *Prokofiev: Romeo & Juliet*. RCA.

Seiji Ozawa conducting Toronto Symphony, *Messiaen: Turangalila; Takemitsu: November Steps*. RCA.

Seiji Ozawa conducting Chicago Symphony, *Stravinsky: Rite of Spring*. RCA.

André Previn conducting London Symphony, *Rimsky-Korsakov: Scheherazade*. RCA.

BEST CHAMBER MUSIC PERFORMANCE

• E. Power Biggs with Edward Tarr Brass Ensemble and Gabrieli Consort. Vittorio Negri, conductor, *Gabrieli: Canzoni for Brass, Winds, Strings and Organ*. Columbia.

Boston Symphony Chamber Players, *Works by Mozart, Brahms, Schubert, Poulenc, Haieff, Villa-Lobos, Colgrass*. RCA.

Julian Bream and Cremona String Quartet, *Julian Bream and His Friends*. RCA.

Guarneri Quartet, *Beethoven: The Five Middle Quartets*. RCA.

Jascha Heifetz, Gregor Piatigorsky, William Primrose, Leonard Pennario, *Mozart: Quintet K. 515; Mendelssohn: Trio No. 2 in C Minor*. RCA.

Eugene Istomin, Isaac Stern, Leonard Rose, *Beethoven: Trio No. 3 in C Minor; Mendelssohn: Trio No. 1 in D Minor*. Columbia.

Walter Trampler, Ronald Turini, *Hindemith: Sonata for Viola and Piano*. RCA.

BEST CLASSICAL PERFORMANCE, INSTRUMENTAL SOLOIST(S), WITH OR WITHOUT ORCHESTRA

• Vladimir Horowitz, *Horowitz on Television*. Columbia.

Arthur Grumiaux (Markevitch conducting Concertgebouw Orchestra), *Berg: Concerto for Violin and Orchestra*. Philips.

Julian Bream, *Dances of Dowland*. RCA.

Jacob Lateiner (Leinsdorf conducting Boston Symphony), *Carter: Concerto for Piano*. RCA.

John Ogdon (Revenaugh conducting Royal Philharmonic), *Busoni: Concerto for Piano With Male Chorus*. Angel.

Artur Rubinstein (Giulini conducting Chicago Symphony), *Schumann: Concerto in A Minor for Piano and Orchestra*. RCA.

Alexis Weissenberg (Pretre conducting Chicago Symphony), *Rachmaninoff: Concerto No. 3 in D Minor for Piano and Orchestra*. RCA.

BEST OPERA RECORDING

• *Mozart: Cosi fan tutte*, Erich Leinsdorf conducting New Philharmonia Orchestra and Ambrosian Opera Chorus (solos: Price, Troyanos, Raskin, Milnes, Shirley, Flagello). Richard Mohr, A&R producer. RCA.

Berg: Lulu, Karl Böhm conducting Orchestra of German Opera, Berlin (solos: Lear, Fischer-Dieskau). Dr. Hans Hirsch, A&R producer. Deutsche Grammophon.

Ginastera: Bomarzo, Julius Rudel conducting Opera Society of Washington (solos: Novoa, Turner, Penagos, Simon). Thomas Shepard, A&R producer. Columbia.

Strauss: Elektra, Georg Solti conducting Vienna Philharmonic (solos: Nilsson, Resnik, Collier, Krause, Stolze). John Culshaw, A&R producer. London.

Wagner: Das Rheingold, Herbert von Karajan conducting Berlin Philharmonic (solos: Fischer-Dieskau, Stolze, Mitalvela, Veasey, Grobe, Keleman, Dominguez). Otto Gerdes, A&R producer. Deutsche Grammophon.

Best Choral Performance, Other Than Opera

- Vittorio Negri conducting Gregg Smith Singers; Texas Boys' Choir. George Bragg, director, Edward Tarr Ensemble (with E. Power Biggs), *The Glory of Gabrieli*. Columbia.
- Colin Davis conducting John Alldis Choir and B.B.C. Symphony, *Mozart: Requiem*. Philips.
- Eugen Jochum conducting Schoenberg Children's Chorus; Chorus and Orchestra of German Opera, Berlin, *Orff: Carmina Burana*. Deutsche Grammophon.
- Abraham Kaplan conducting Camerata Singers. Leonard Bernstein conducting New York Philharmonic, *Haydn: The Creation*. Columbia.
- Joseph Keilberth conducting Bavarian Symphony Chorus and Orchestra, *Pfitzner: Von Deutscher Seele*. Deutsche Grammophon.
- John McCarthy conducting Ambrosian Singers. Morton Gould conducting Royal Philharmonia, *Shostakovich: Symphony No. 2 in C Major; Symphony No. 3 in E Flat Major*. RCA.
- Charles Munch conducting Bavarian Radio Chorus and Symphony, *Berlioz: Requiem*. Deutsche Grammophon.
- Stephen Simon conducting Vienna Jeunesse Chorus and Vienna Volksoper Orchestra (solos: Shirley-Quirk, Endich, Brooks, Young), *Handel: Solomon*. RCA.

Best Classical Vocal Soloist Performance

- Montserrat Caballé (Cillario conducting RCA Italiana Opera Orchestra and Chorus), *Rossini Rarities*. RCA.
- Janet Baker (Barbirolli conducting Halle Orchestra), *Mahler: Kindertotenlieder and Songs of a Wayfarer*. Angel.
- Victoria de los Angeles (ARS Musicae Ensemble of Barcelona), *Songs of Andalucia*. Angel.
- Dietrich Fischer-Dieskau (Jorg Demus, pianist), *Schumann: Songs*. Deutsche Grammophon.
- Gerard Souzay (Dalton Baldwin, pianist), *Songs of Poulenc*. RCA.
- Shirley Verrett (Pretre conducting RCA Italiana Opera Orchestra), *Verrett in Opera*. RCA.

Best Engineered Recording, Classical

- Gordon Parry, *Mahler: Symphony No. 9 in D Major* (Solti conducting London Symphony). London.
- Bernard Keville, *Messiaen: Turangalila; Takemitsu: November Steps* (Ozawa conducting Toronto Symphony). RCA.
- Bernard Kevill, *Stravinsky: Rite of Spring* (Ozawa conducting Chicago Symphony). RCA.
- Michael Moran, *Rachmaninoff: Concerto No. 3 in D Minor for Piano and Orchestra* (Weissenberg/Pretre conducting Chicago Symphony). RCA.
- Gordon Parry, Kenneth Wilkenson, *Britten: Billy Budd* (Britten conducting London Symphony; solos: Glossop, Pears, Shirley-Quirk, Brannigan). London.
- Anthony Salvatore, *Prokofiev: Romeo & Juliet* (Leinsdorf conducting Boston Symphony). RCA.
- Anthony Salvatore, *Verdi: Ernani* (Schippers conducting RCA Italiana Opera Orchestra and Chorus). RCA.

Best Comedy Recording

- *To Russell, My Brother, Whom I Slept With*, Bill Cosby. Warner Bros.
- *W.C. Fields Original Voice Tracks from Great Movies*, produced by Gil Rodin. Decca.
- *Flip Wilson, You Devil You*, Flip Wilson. Atlantic.
- *Hello Dummy!* Don Rickles. Warner Bros.
- *Rowan and Martin's Laugh-In*, Dan Rowan, Dick Martin. Epic.

Best Spoken Word Recording

- *Lonesome Cities*, Rod McKuen. Warner Bros.
- *The Canterbury Pilgrims*, Martin Starkie. Deutsche Grammophon.
- *I Have A Dream*, Rev. Martin Luther King, Jr. 20th.
- *Kennedy-Nixon: The Great Debates, 1960*, produced by Joel Heller. Columbia.
- *Murder in the Cathedral*, Paul Scofield. Caedmon.

Best Engineered Recording (Other Than Classical)

- Joe Polito, Hugh Davies, "Wichita Lineman" (Glen Campbell). Capitol.
- Richard Bogert, *The Good, the Bad and the Ugly* (Hugo Montenegro). RCA.

Jerry Boys, Peter Vince, *Man of La Mancha* (Original London Cast). Decca.

Doug Brand, *Rotary Connection Trip 1* (Rotary Connection). Concept.

Dave Wiechman, *Daktari* (Shelly Manne). Atlantic.

BEST ALBUM COVER

• John Berg, Richard Mantel, art directors. Horn/Griner Studio, photography, *Underground* (Thelonius Monk). Columbia.

Sam Antupit, art director. Pete Turner, photography, *Road Song* (Wes Montgomery). A&M.

John Berg, Bob Cato, art directors. Ron Coro, designer. Don Huntstein, photographer, *Ives: Holidays Symphony* (Bernstein conducting New York Philharmonic). CBS

Bob Cato, art director and graphic design, *Wow* (Moby Grape). Columbia.

William S. Harvey, art director. Gene Szafran, graphic design, *Rhinoceros* (Rhinoceros). Elektra.

BEST ALBUM NOTES
(Annotator's Award)

• Johnny Cash, *Johnny Cash at Folsom Prison* (Johnny Cash). Columbia.

Stan Cornyn, *Francis A. and Edward K.* (Francis Albert Sinatra, Edward Kennedy Ellington). Reprise.

Miles Krueger, *Ethel Waters on Stage and Screen 1925–40*. Columbia.

Richard Oliver, *Anthology of Indian Music, Volume One* (Ravi Shankar, Ali Akbar Khan, Balachander). World Pacific.

Pete Seeger, *Pete Seeger's Greatest Hits* (Pete Seeger). Columbia.

Aquarius: Sign of the Times

In the final year of the turbulent 1960s, Woodstock rocked, Paul McCartney and John Lennon got married (to Linda Eastman and Yoko Ono, respectively), George Harrison and Jim Morrison got arrested (for marijuana possession and indecent exposure, respectively), and a vanguard of the old music sound, Peggy Lee, was back in the Top 10, asking, "Is That All There Is"?

1967's Record of the Year champs, the 5th Dimension, returned to claim the prize again for "Aquarius/Let the Sunshine In," a medley from Hair *that was the year's best-selling single.*

Peggy Lee and Led Zeppelin were among the unlikely array of Grammy nominees. The *L.A. Times* commented that the awards "reflected something of a tug-of-war between the traditional and contemporary segments of the record industry" — just as they had since 1958, and despite last year's optimistic pronouncements that the new generation was now in complete control of the Grammys.

"Is That All There Is" was up for the Record of the Year honors along with Henry Mancini's version of "A Time for Us (Love Theme from *Romeo & Juliet*)" — both reflecting traditional N.A.R.A.S. tastes. The "contemporary" segment was represented by "Spinning Wheel," performed by Blood, Sweat & Tears, one of the two Grammy-winning groups of 1969 that also participated in Wood-

stock (Crosby, Stills & Nash did, too). Johnny Cash's "A Boy Named Sue" was evidence of Nashville's continued voting clout. None would take the top prize, however, because, towering above all of them, was an invincible fifth nominee — the 5th Dimension — the perfect N.A.R.A.S. compromise choice that last proved its might when the group swept the awards in 1967 with Record of the Year "Up, Up and Away."

The 5th Dimension was now at its professional apogee. When two of its most celebrated singers — Marilyn McCoo and Billy Davis — decided, like McCartney and Lennon, to settle down by getting married (to each other), the wedding ceremony became a media event that took place, of course, aboard a floating hot-air balloon (apropos of their 1967 Record of the Year "Up, Up and Away").. The group's

"Aquarius/ Let the Sunshine In" single was the number-one song of the year on *Billboard*'s Hot 100, and proved the easy victor of Record of the Year honors, in addition to earning its singers the award for Best Contemporary Vocal Performance by a Group.

The record was a medley of two songs from last year's Grammy-winning best original cast show album *Hair*, an idealized interpretation of the Sixties hippie movement and its simple people-are-groovy message. *Hair* was nonetheless beloved by the record-buying public (becoming the top-selling LP of 1969) and spawned several successful singles. On May 10, 1969, the Hot 100 had the 5th Dimension's "Aquarius/Let the Sunshine In" at number one, followed by the Cowsills' rendition of the "Hair" single at number two. The show's other pop hits were "Good Morning Starshine," sung by Oliver, and "Easy to Be Hard" by Three Dog Night.

> As its name suggested, Album of the Year winner Blood, Sweat & Tears represented a mature new sound.

"Aquarius/Let the Sunshine In" was from the 5th Dimension's *Age of Aquarius* LP, which spent 30 weeks in the best-sellers and included such other hits as "Wedding Bell Blues" (which topped the charts for three weeks the same month that McCoo and Davis were married). It was also a strong contender for Album of the Year in a tight race involving the Beatles' *Abbey Road*, *Johnny Cash at San Quentin* (with Cash's humorous megahit "A Boy Named Sue"), one of the most eagerly awaited debut album releases ever (*Crosby, Stills & Nash*), and one of the most critically acclaimed rock & roll discs of the decade, *Blood, Sweat & Tears*.

Blood, Sweat & Tears was the early front-runner. The *L.A. Times* identified its artists as "a jazz-rock outfit that has wide appeal among both a younger, rock-oriented audience and the older, big band-oriented members of N.A.R.A.S." As its name suggested, Blood, Sweat & Tears was a mature music group whose sound was serious, full of bluesy horns, intricate arrangements, and vocals that tapped underground influences such as 19th-century black spirituals. The group's first album, *Child Is Father to the Man*, debuted in 1968 and was a brilliant artistic effort spearheaded by lead singer Al Kooper. When Kooper quit the troupe in 1969, he was replaced by David Clayton-Thomas, who contributed works such as "Spinning Wheel," which was nominated for Record and Song of the Year. The band's subsequent *BS&T* LP ("one of the all-time best-selling albums on the Columbia label," noted *Variety*) also included innovative works like the instrumental "Variations on a Theme by Eric Satie" as well as hits like "And When I Die" and "You've Made Me So Very Happy."

Blood, Sweat & Tears headed into the Grammys ceremony *very* happy, having 10 nominations, four more than its nearest rival, the 5th Dimension. (Burt Bacharach and Quincy Jones came in third with five nods each.) "There were no stunning upsets in the Grammy winners," *Variety* said, reporting that *BS&T* easily took the album laurels and Best Contemporary Instrumental Performance for "Variations." "Spinning Wheel" garnered the prize for Best Arrangement Accompanying Vocalists.

What eclipsed "Spinning Wheel" for Song of the Year was "Games People

Play" by Joe South, a leading session guitarist and songwriter who would also pen such popular songs during his career as "Walk a Mile in My Shoes" and "Rose Garden." "In 'Games People Play,'" the *L.A. Times* reported, "South, a 27-year-old singer-writer from Atlanta, weaves a timely, almost universal message in language that is as straightforward as its rock accompaniment: 'Oh, the games people play, now/ Every night and every day, now/ Never meaning what they say, now/ Never saying what they mean.'" Although South was a losing nominee for a best contemporary vocal performance award for his own version of the song that he recorded for Capitol; King Curtis's rendition took Best Rhythm & Blues Instrumental Performance. "Games" also won the newly reinstated award for Best Contemporary Song.

Realizing that it had cut back too many awards last year, N.A.R.A.S. reinstated five of them, including best song honors for contemporary and r&b works, Best Recording for Children, Classical Album of the Year, and separate prizes for country group vocal and instrumental performances, which had been combined in 1968. The contemporary-pop categories now dropped the "pop" designation and then, strangely, welcomed back an old-style singer who was hardly in tune with the newest music sound, but who still had a pop hit.

"The N.A.R.A.S. balloting went with traditional, mainline pop music," said the *L.A. Times*, "in naming Peggy Lee as best female vocal performer" for "Is That All There Is," which was also a strong nominee for Record of the Year. Peggy Lee's victory was a swan song for the Grammy tastes of yore — and a final volley from the old guard that reminded the young hooligans that they were still around, even if their traditional music was regulated to the FM dial (back in the days when AM stations broadcast the top pop tunes almost exclusively.)

Peggy Lee was old guard *establishment*. She had performed with Benny Goodman ("I Got It Bad and That Ain't Good"), written music with Duke Ellington ("I'm Gonna Go Fishin'"), and crooned in classic old movies like *Pete Kelly's Blues*, for which she was Oscar-nominated in 1955. But her win wasn't just another rally for easy-listening music by older record academy voters. "Is That All There Is" had been a Top 40 success, too.

Also a Top 40, easy-listening winner of one of the contemporary trophies was "A Time for Us (Love Theme from *Romeo & Juliet*)," the popular and critically acclaimed film adaptation of the Shakespearean classic by director Franco Zeffirelli. The contemporary choral performance honors went to the Percy Faith Orchestra and Chorus's version of the lead theme song. Henry Mancini's rendition was up for three Grammys, including Record of the Year. It ended up with only one — for Best Instrumental Arrangement, bringing Mancini his 18th Grammy, the most any artist had earned up to that point. Since "A Time for Us" was written by Larry Kusik, Eddie Snyder, and Nino Rota — and not Mancini — it's ironic that it has turned out to be the composer/arranger's only number-one career hit as of this writing. (His 1961 Record of the Year, "Moon River," only reached number 11 at its peak.). "A Time for Us" ended 1969 at number 15 in the Hot 100, an impressive achievement considering the resistance it initially experienced in the pop world. "It was very soft for its time," Mancini once told *Billboard* writer Fred Bronson. "Some of the big [radio stations] refused to put it on until it became number one, because it wasn't a hard rocker."

The old guard's "chairman," Frank Sinatra, was nominated for best contem-

Crosby, Stills & Nash lost their bid for Album of the Year, but won Best New Artist over Led Zeppelin, Chicago, and Oliver.

stretched her winning streak to a third year when she took a vocal performance award for "Share Your Love with Me." The male r&b singing prize went to Joe Simon for "The Chokin' Kind," his first million-seller after a career of lesser hits like "Teenager's Prayer" and "Nine Pound Steel." One of soul's longest-lasting troupes, the Isley Brothers, won

porary male vocal performance for "My Way," but lost to singer/songwriter Harry Nilsson ("My favorite American singer," John Lennon once said), who was also the author of such hits as "One" for Three Dog Night and "Cuddly Toy" for the Monkees. Nilsson won his Grammy for his version of Fred Neil's "Everybody's Talkin'," which was used in the Oscars' Best Picture of 1969, *Midnight Cowboy,* and won the Best Instrumental Theme award for British composer John Barry — at both the Oscars and the Grammys.

Crosby, Stills & Nash's premiere LP was eagerly awaited because the new artistic trio was made up of proven talent: David Crosby had formerly been with the Byrds, Stephen Stills with Buffalo Springfield, and Graham Nash with the Hollies. Together they achieved a seasoned sound that was distinguished by perfect-pitch harmonies. Their eponymous LP lost the Album of the Year contest, but the group still nabbed Best New Artist over such weighty competition as Chicago, Led Zeppelin, Oliver, and the Neon Philharmonic.

In the r&b category, Aretha Franklin

their one and only Grammy (Best R&B Vocal Performance by a Group or Duo) for "It's Your Thing." The Isley Brothers had been recording on the Tamla/Motown label prior to 1969, but had now revived their own T-Neck label and added some of their younger brothers to the act. "Color Him Father" was hailed as Best R&B Song. Written by Richard Spencer, it was recorded by the Winstons (a group that came and went in less than a year) and reached number seven on the pop charts and number two in the r&b rankings.

"A Boy Named Sue," written by Shel Silverstein, was the winner of the revived Best Country Song award. "Sue" was a ditty about a boy cursed with a girl's name that Johnny Cash added at the last minute to his concert act being recorded at San Quentin prison, a follow-up to his popular Folsom Prison session that earned him two Grammys last year. As a single release, "Sue" was an instant number-one hit on both the pop and c&w charts and also earned the country crooner a Grammy for Best Male Vocal Country Performance. Cash won a prize for Best

Album Notes, too, although not for his latest jailhouse jamboree LP, but for Bob Dylan's *Nashville Skyline*. Cash and Dylan were close friends. Dylan, in fact, came to a "guitar pull" at Cash's home a week before the San Quentin concert to help Cash prepare for the event. During his prison gig, Cash performed Dylan's "Wanted Man."

"A Boy Named Sue" beat another classic for Best Country Song — a tune co-written by Tammy Wynette that would become her signature song. Wynette had been popular in the past for her feminist anthems "I Don't Wanna Play House" and "D-I-V-O-R-C-E," but in 1969 she married legendary country singer George Jones and suddenly seemed to have a change of heart about female independence. Her latest hit was "Stand By Your Man," which she co-wrote with her producer at Epic, Billy Sherrill (1966 Grammy winner for "Almost Persuaded"). Its new, back-stepping message caused an uproar in the women's rights movement, but Wynette stood by her work, too, which quickly became the biggest-selling single ever recorded by a country artist and earned her the Grammy for Best Country Vocal Performance, Female. She did not stand by her man forever, however. Jones had a drinking problem (he once drove 10 miles on a lawn mower to buy a bottle of liquor after Wynette hid his car keys), and "Mr. and Mrs. Country Music" divorced in 1975.

The Best Country Instrumental Performance went to the Nashville Brass and its trumpet player/leader Danny Davis, who formed the group as a country equivalent to Herb Alpert & the Tijuana Brass. Waylon Jennings & the Kimberleys covered the Richard Harris hit of last year, "MacArthur Park," to take the prize for Best Country Performance by a Duo or Group.

Joni Mitchell gave the year's Best Folk Performance on her *Clouds* LP, which she recorded, troubador-style, with only her guitar for accompaniment. The newly reinstated category for Best Recording for Children went to folk performers Peter, Paul & Mary for *Peter, Paul & Mommy*. The 42 winners of Best Soul Gospel prize, the Edwin Hawkins Singers, were known as the Northern California State Youth Choir before they recorded "Oh Happy Day" for an upcoming religious congress in Cleveland. It was then discovered by a San Francisco deejay, who introduced the tune to the airwaves.

Burt Bacharach entered the Grammy race with two nominations for Song of the Year — for "I'll Never Fall in Love

The humorous classic "A Boy Named Sue" claimed the reinstated Best Country Song award.

Again" and his Oscar-winning tune from *Butch Cassidy and the Sundance Kid,* "Raindrops Keep Fallin' on My Head." "Raindrops," recorded by B.J. Thomas, lost the top Grammy prize, but *Butch Cassidy* still took Best Original Score Written for a Motion Picture or a TV Special. Bacharach's latest Broadway musical, *Promises, Promises*, won him the laurels for Best Cast Show Album.

1966 Grammy winner Wes Montgomery returned to claim one more for *Willow Weep for Me*, which was voted best large group jazz performance. The small group honors went to Quincy Jones, "one of the youngest and most brilliant arranger-composers to make his mark in jazz," according to critic Leonard Feather. Jones was inspired to write his victorious "Walking in Space" work by the breakthroughs then occurring in the N.A.S.A. space program. (Astronaut Neil

Armstrong made his historic walk on the moon on July 21, 1969.)

In the classical categories, Walter Carlos snared three Grammys for his controversial *Switched-On Bach* LP, which introduced the popular Moog synthesizer to the music industry. Carlos was a friend of its creator, Dr. Robert A. Moog, and was largely responsible for convincing the inventor to attach his name to it. The Moog not only made synthetic imitations of all kinds of instrumental sounds, it created new ones, too. "Purists are going to blast hell out of it," *High Fidelity* predicted when its reviewer first heard the Moog interpretations of such Bach selections as *The Well-Tempered Clavier* and the third Brandenburg Concerto.

> **The hugely successful and highly controversial Switched-On Bach *snagged* three honors.**

A blast from the purists came as expected, but the outcry was accompanied by an astounding commercial reaction, too. *Switched-On Bach* became the number-one selling classical album for 94 weeks and remained on the charts for 310 weeks. As of 1972, only one other classical album had ever sold more copies: Van Cliburn's recording of Tchaikovsky's First Piano Concerto. *Switched-On Bach* was the easy victor of the Classical Album of the Year award and also earned Best Performance by an Instrumental Soloist and Best Engineered Recording.

Pierre Boulez and the Cleveland Orchestra won the orchestral performance honors for Debussy's *Images pour Orchestre* ("an exceptional record by any standard," said *High Fidelity*). The magazine also approved of the winner of the chamber music laurels: "a triple-star brass ensemble drawn from three of the leading American symphony orchestras," wrote *High Fidelity*, "five Clevelanders, seven Philadelphians and seven Chicagoans," who performed works by Giovanni Gabrielli. Pianist Artur Rubinstein had also been nominated in the chamber music lineup, but noticed a mistake on the Grammy ballot when he received his in the mail. He fired off a heated letter to N.A.R.A.S., saying, "I'm flattered to be nominated year after year, but the next time your Trustees select me as nominee, I would appreciate it if you would instruct the proper department to spell my name correctly."

The choral honors went to four-time past Grammy winners the Swingle Singers, for a work written by Luciano Berio with them in mind ("expertly played and brilliantly recorded," wrote *High Fidelity* of *Sinfonia*). The magazine was less enthusiastic about the winner of Best Opera Recording, saying "there are things to praise and curse" about Herbert von Karajan and the Berlin Philharmonic's five-LP stereo version of Wagner's *Siegfried* segment of the *Ring* cycle. The vocalist performance award went to Leontyne Price, who sang a range of works by Samuel Barber, though "the record is not successful," *High Fidelity* wrote, claiming that the selections just didn't "add up to much of a statement."

Price was tied with Henry Mancini and Bill Cosby for having had the longest winning streak in Grammy history prior to 1969: five years (1963–67 for Price, 1960–64 for Mancini, and 1964–68 for Cosby). This year Cosby surpassed the other two by taking a sixth in a row. (His record would later be topped by Aretha Franklin and Sir Georg Solti). Appropriately, his precedent-setting win was for Best Comedy

Recording *The Best of Bill Cosby*, which included such classic routines as "Noah and the Ark," "Revenge," and a visit with a drunken "Lone Ranger."

It was appropriate for Cosby to make Grammy history this year since he was the emcee of the Los Angeles ceremony held at the Century Plaza Hotel where he was joined by winners Harry Nilsson, Burt Bacharach, and Peggy Lee. Cosby, said the *L.A. Times*, "kept things moving and made his humor fit the evening. He also avoided the temptation of making himself rather than the awards presentation the star of the evening. Some of his best jokes involved his own ill-fated attempt at starting a record company."

At the New York ceremony, *Down Beat* reported "a total disaster" at Alice Tully Hall. A dinner of "processed turkey buffet featuring plastic plates" was followed by musical numbers plagued with production problems. "Poor little Brenda Lee," *Down Beat* added. "Her mike went absolutely dead in the middle of her set. After several minutes, an intermission was called to attend to the problem, during which about half the audience decided to split. We've seen more professionalism at high school variety shows."

Variety was much more diplomatic when reporting on the New York show, noting just "a bad case of the gremlins."

1969

Awards were bestowed on March 11, 1970, for the eligibility period of November 2, 1968, to November 1, 1969, at ceremonies held at the Century Plaza Hotel in Los Angeles, Alice Tully Hall in New York, and at dinners held in Nashville and Chicago.

ALBUM OF THE YEAR
• *Blood, Sweat & Tears*, Blood, Sweat & Tears. James William Guercio, A&R producer. Columbia.
Abbey Road, Beatles. George Martin, A&R producer. Apple.
The Age of Aquarius, 5th Dimension. Bones Howe, A&R producer. Soul City.
Crosby, Stills & Nash, Crosby, Stills & Nash. David Crosby, Stephen Stills, Graham Nash, A&R producers. Atlantic.
Johnny Cash at San Quentin, Johnny Cash. Bob Johnston, A&R producer. Columbia.

RECORD OF THE YEAR
• "Aquarius/Let the Sunshine In," 5th Dimension. Bones Howe, A&R producer. Soul City.
"A Boy Named Sue," Johnny Cash. Bob Johnston, A&R producer. Columbia.
"Is That All There Is," Peggy Lee. Jerry Leiber, Mike Stoller, A&R producers. Capitol.

"A Time for Us (Love Theme from *Romeo & Juliet*)," Henry Mancini. Joe Reisman, A&R producer. RCA.
"Spinning Wheel," Blood, Sweat & Tears. James William Guercio, A&R producer. Columbia.

SONG OF THE YEAR
(Songwriter's Award)
• "Games People Play," Joe South.
"I'll Never Fall in Love Again," Burt Bacharach, Hal David.
"Raindrops Keep Fallin' on My Head," Burt Bacharach, Hal David.
"Spinning Wheel," David Clayton Thomas.
"A Time for Us (Love Theme from *Romeo & Juliet*)," Larry Kusik, Eddie Snyder, Nino Rota.

BEST NEW ARTIST
• Crosby, Stills & Nash. Atlantic.
Chicago. Columbia.
Led Zeppelin. Atlantic.
Oliver. Crewe.
Neon Philharmonic. Warner Bros.

BEST CONTEMPORARY VOCAL PERFORMANCE, MALE
• "Everybody's Talkin'," Harry Nilsson. United Artists.
"Games People Play," Joe South. Capitol.
"Guitarzan," Ray Stevens. Monument.

The Grammys answered Peggy Lee's question "Is That All There Is" with a trophy for best contemporary vocals.

✓"My Way," Frank Sinatra. Warner Bros.
"Raindrops Keep Fallin' on My Head," B.J. Thomas. Scepter.

BEST CONTEMPORARY VOCAL PERFORMANCE, FEMALE
• "Is That All There Is," Peggy Lee. Capitol.
"Johnny One Time," Brenda Lee. Decca.
"Put a Little Love in Your Heart," Jackie DeShannon. Liberty/United Artists.
✓ "Son of a Preacher Man," Dusty Springfield. Atlantic.
"This Girl's in Love With You," Dionne Warwick. Scepter.
"With Pen in Hand," Vikki Carr. Liberty.

BEST CONTEMPORARY VOCAL PERFORMANCE, GROUP
• 5th Dimension, "Aquarius/Let the Sunshine In." Soul City.
Beatles, *Abbey Road.* Apple.
Blood, Sweat & Tears, *Blood, Sweat & Tears.* Columbia.
Crosby, Stills & Nash, *Crosby, Stills & Nash.* Atlantic.

Neon Philharmonic, *Morning Girl.* Warner Bros.

BEST CONTEMPORARY PERFORMANCE, CHORUS
• Percy Faith Orchestra and Chorus, "Love Theme from *Romeo & Juliet.*" Columbia.
Brooks Arthur Ensemble, "MacArthur Park." Verve.
Ray Charles Singers, "Slices of Life." Command.
Ray Conniff & the Singers, "Jean." Columbia.
Living Voices, "Angel of the Morning." RCA.

BEST CONTEMPORARY SONG
(Songwriter's Award)
• "Games People Play," Joe South.
✓"In the Ghetto," Mac Davis.
"Jean," Rod McKuen.
"Raindrops Keep Fallin' on My Head," Burt Bacharach, Hal David.
"Spinning Wheel," David Clayton Thomas.

BEST CONTEMPORARY INSTRUMENTAL PERFORMANCE
• "Variations on a Theme by Erik Satie," Blood, Sweat & Tears. Columbia.
"Area Code 615," Area Code 615. Polydor.
"A Time for Us (Love Theme from *Romeo & Juliet*)," Henry Mancini. RCA.
Midnight Cowboy, Ferrante & Teicher. Liberty/United Aritists.
"With Love," Boots Randolph. Monument.

BEST RHYTHM & BLUES SONG
(Songwriter's Award)
• "Color Him Father," Richard Spencer.
"Backfield in Motion," Herbert McPherson, Melvin Harden.
"I'd Rather Be an Old Man's Sweetheart," Clarence Carter, George Jackson, Raymond Moore.
"It's Your Thing," Rudolph Isley, O. Kelly Isley, Jr., Ronnie Isley.
"Only the Strong Survive," Kenny Gamble, Leon Huff, Jerry Butler.

BEST RHYTHM & BLUES VOCAL PERFORMANCE, MALE
• "The Chokin' Kind," Joe Simon. Sound Stage.
"Doing His Thing," Ray Charles. Tangerine.

Ice Man Cometh, Jerry Butler. Mercury.
Live and Well, B.B. King. ABC.
"Your Good Thing (Is About to End),"
   Lou Rawls. Capitol.

BEST RHYTHM & BLUES VOCAL PERFORMANCE, FEMALE
• Aretha Franklin, "Share Your Love with
   Me." Atlantic.
Ruth Brown, "Yesterday." Skye.
Gloria Taylor, "You Gotta Pay the Price."
   Silver Fox.
Tina Turner, *The Hunter*. Blue Thumb.
Dee Dee Warwick, "Foolish Fool."
   Mercury.

BEST RHYTHM & BLUES VOCAL PERFORMANCE, DUO OR GROUP
√ • Isley Brothers, "It's Your Thing." T-
   Neck.
√ Gladys Knight & the Pips, "Friendship
   Train." Motown.
Mel & Tim, "Backfield in Motion." Scepter.
Peggy Scott, Jo Jo Benson, "Soulshake."
   SSS.
Winstons, "Color Him Father."
   Metromedia.

BEST RHYTHM & BLUES INSTRUMENTAL PERFORMANCE
• King Curtis, "Games People Play." Atco.
Albert Collins, "Trash Talkin'." Imperial.
Richard "Groove" Holmes, "Workin' on a
   Groovy Thing." World Pacific.
Ike Turner, "A Black Man's Soul."
   Pompeii.
Junior Walker & the All Stars, "What
   Does It Take." Soul.

BEST INSTRUMENTAL JAZZ PERFORMANCE, SMALL GROUP OR SOLOIST WITH SMALL GROUP
(7 or less)
• Wes Montgomery, *Willow Weep for Me*.
   Verve.
Eubie Blake, *The 86 Years of Eubie Blake*.
   Columbia.
Miles Davis, *In a Silent Way*. Columbia.
Bill Evans, Jeremy Steig, *What's New*.
   Verve.
Stephane Grappelli, Stuff Smith, Sven
   Asmussen, Jean Luc-Ponty, *Violin
   Summit*. Prestige.
Herbie Mann, *Memphis Underground*.
   Atlantic.
Oscar Peterson, *The Great Oscar Peterson
   on Prestige*. Prestige.

BEST INSTRUMENTAL JAZZ PERFORMANCE, LARGE GROUP OR SOLIST WITH LARGE GROUP
(8 or more)
• Quincy Jones, "Walking in Space." A&M.
Count Basie, *Standing Ovation*. Paramont.
Don Ellis, *The New Don Ellis Band Goes
   Underground*. Columbia.
Woody Herman, *Light My Fire*. Cadet.
Thad Jones, Mel Lewis, *Central Park
   North*. Solid State.
Gary McFarland, *America the Beautiful*.
   Skye.
Buddy Rich Orchestra, *Buddy & Soul*.
   World Pacific.
Bob Wilber, *The Music of Hoagy
   Carmichael*. Monmouth.

BEST COUNTRY SONG
(Songwriter's Award)
• "A Boy Named Sue," Shel Silverstein.
"All I Have to Offer You Is Me," Dallas
   Frazier, A.L. Owens.
√ "Stand By Your Man," Tammy Wynette,
   Billy Sherrill.
"The Things That Matter," Don Sumner.
"You Gave Me a Mountain," Marty
   Robbins.

BEST COUNTRY VOCAL PERFORMANCE, MALE
• Johnny Cash, "A Boy Named Sue."
   Columbia.
Clay Hart, "Spring." Metromedia.
Bobby Lewis, "From Heaven to
   Heartache." United Artists.
Charley Pride, "All I Have to Offer You Is
   Me." RCA.
Jerry Reed, "Are You from Dixie." RCA.

BEST COUNTRY VOCAL PERFORMANCE, FEMALE
√ • Tammy Wynette, "Stand By Your Man."
   Epic.
Lynn Anderson, "That's a No No." Chart.
Jeannie C. Riley, "Back Side of Dallas."
   Plantation.
Connie Smith, "Ribbon of Darkness."
   RCA.
Diana Trask, "I Fall to Pieces." ABC-
   Paramount.

BEST COUNTRY PERFORMANCE, DUO OR GROUP
• Waylon Jennings, the Kimberlys,
   "MacArthur Park." RCA.
Jack Greene, Jeanie Seely, "Wish I Didn't
   Have to Miss You." Decca.

Best female country vocalist Tammy Wynette co-wrote "Stand By Your Man," which broke previous c&w sales records.

Tompall & the Glaser Brothers, "California Girl." MGM

Porter Wagoner, Dolly Parton, "Just Someone I Used to Know." RCA.

Dottie West, Don Gibson, "Rings of Gold." RCA.

BEST COUNTRY INSTRUMENAL PERFORMANCE

• Danny Davis & the Nashville Brass, *The Nashville Brass Featuring Danny Davis Play More Nashville Sounds.* RCA.

Tommy Allsup & the Nashville Survey, *The Hits of Charley Pride.* Metromedia.

Floyd Cramer, "Lovin' Season." RCA.

Bob Dylan, "Nashville Skyline Rag." Columbia.

Chet Atkins, *Solid Gold '69.* RCA.

BEST SACRED PERFORMANCE (NON-CLASSICAL)

• Jake Hess, "Ain't That Beautiful Singing." RCA.

Tennessee Ernie Ford, "Holy, Holy, Holy." Capital.

Bill Gaither Trio, "He Touched Me." Heartwarming.

George Beverly Shea, "I Believe." RCA.

Connie Smith, Nat Stuckey, "Whispering Hope." RCA.

BEST GOSPEL PERFORMANCE

• Porter Wagoner, Blackwood Brothers, "In Gospel Country." RCA.

Happy Goodman Family, "This Happy House." Word.

LeFevres, "The Best Is Yet to Come." Canaan.

Oak Ridge Boys, "It's Happening." Heartwarming.

Singing Rambos, "This Is My Valley." Heartwarming.

BEST SOUL GOSPEL PERFORMANCE

• Edwin Hawkins Singers, *Oh Happy Day.* Buddah.

James Cleveland, the Southern California Choir, *Come On and See About Me.* Savoy.

Cassietta George, *Cassietta.* Audio Gospel.

Mahalia Jackson, *Guide Me, O Thou Great Jehovah.* Columbia.

Sister Rosetta Tharpe, *Precious Memories.* Savoy.

BEST FOLK PERFORMANCE

• Joni Mitchell, *Clouds.* Warner Bros.

Joan Baez, "Any Day Now." Vanguard.

Judy Collins, "Bird on a Wire." Elektra.

Donovan, "Atlantis." Epic.

Peter, Paul & Mary, "Day Is Done." Warner Bros.

Pete Seeger, "Young vs. Old." Columbia.

BEST INSTRUMENTAL ARRANGEMENT (Arranger's Award)

• Henry Mancini, "A Time for Us (Love Theme from *Romeo & Juliet)*" (Mancini). RCA.

Arthur Ferrante, Lou Teicher, "Midnight Cowboy" (Ferrante & Teicher). Liberty.

Dick Halligan, "Variations on a Theme by Eric Satie" (Blood, Sweat & Tears). Columbia.

Quincy Jones, "Walking in Space" (Quincy Jones). A&M.

BEST INSTRUMENTAL THEME (Composer's Award)

• *Midnight Cowboy,* John Barry.

"Groovy Grubworm," Harlow Wilcox, Bobby Warren.

"MacKenna's Gold," Quincy Jones.

"Memphis Underground," Herbie Mann.

"Quentin's Theme," Robert Cobert.

BEST SCORE FROM AN ORIGINAL CAST SHOW ALBUM

• *Promises, Promises*, Burt Bacharach, Hal David. Henry Jerome, Phil Ramone, A&R producers. Liberty.

Dames at Sea, George Haimsohn, Robin Miller, Jim J. Wise. Thomas Shepard, A&R producer. Columbia.

Oh, Calcutta! Robert Dennis, Stanley Walden, Peter Schickle. Henry Jerome, A&R producer. Aidart.

1776, Herman Edwards. Thomas Shepard, A&R producer. Columbia.

Zorba, John Kander, Fred Ebb. Richard C. Jones, A&R producer. Capitol.

BEST ORIGINAL SCORE WRITTEN FOR A MOTION PICTURE OR TV SPECIAL
(Composer's Award)

• *Butch Cassidy and the Sundance Kid*, Burt Bacharach. A&M.

The Lost Man, Quincy Jones. Uni.

MacKenna's Gold, Quincy Jones. RCA.

Me, Natalie, Henry Mancini. Columbia.

Yellow Submarine, John Lennon, Paul McCartney, George Harrison, George Martin. Capitol.

BEST ARRANGEMENT ACCOMPANYING VOCALIST(S)

• Fred Lipsius, "Spinning Wheel" (Blood, Sweat & Tears). Columbia.

Bill Holman, Bob Alcivar, Bones Howe, "Aquarius/Let the Sunshine In" (5th Dimension). Soul City.

Al Kooper, Fred Lipsius, "You've Made Me So Very Happy" (Blood, Sweat & Tears). Columbia.

Randy Newman, "Is That All There Is" (Peggy Lee). Capitol.

Torrie Zito, "I've Gotta Be Me" (Tony Bennett). Columbia.

ALBUM OF THE YEAR, CLASSICAL

• *Switched-On Bach* (*Virtuoso Electronic Performance of Branden Concerto No. 3; Air on a G String; Jesu, Joy of Man's Destiny, etc.*, performed on Moog Synthesizer), Walter Carlos. Rachel Elkind, A&R producer. Columbia.

Berio: Sinfonia, Luciano Berio conducting New York Philharmonic & Swingle Singers. Thomas Z. Shepard, A&R producer. Columbia.

Boulez Conducts Berg (Three Pieces for Orchestra; Chamber Concerto; Altenberg Lieder), Pierre Boulez conducting BBC Symphony (solos: Barenboim, Gawriloff, Lukomska). Thomas Z. Shepard, A&R producer. Columbia.

Boulez Conducts Debussy, Vol. 2, "Images pour Orchestre," Pierre Boulez conducting Cleveland Orchestra. Thomas Z. Shepard, A&R producer. Columbia.

Gabrieli: Antiphonal Music of Gabrieli (Canzoni for Brass Choirs), Philadelphia, Cleveland, and Chicago Brass Ensembles. Andrew Kazdin, A&R producer. Columbia.

Strauss: Also Sprach Zarathustra, Zubin Mehta conducting Los Angeles Philharmonic. Raymond Minshull, A&R producer. London.

BEST CLASSICAL PERFORMANCE, ORCHESTRA
(Conductor's Award)

• Pierre Boulez conducting Cleveland Orchestra, *Boulez Conducts Debussy, Vol. 2, "Images pour Orchestre."* Columbia.

Pierre Boulez conducting BBC Symphony, *Bartók: Music for Strings, Percussion & Celesta*. Columbia.

Jean Martinon conducting Chicago Symphony, *Ravel: Rapsodie Espagnole; Mother Goose Suite; Alborada del Gracioso; Introduction & Allegro*. RCA.

Zubin Mehta conducting Los Angeles Philharmonic, *Strauss: Also Sprach Zarathustra*. London.

George Szell conducting Cleveland Orchestra, *Wagner: Great Orchestral Highlights from "The Ring of the Nibelungs."* Columbia.

BEST CHAMBER MUSIC PERFORMANCE

• The Philadelphia, Cleveland, and Chicago Brass Ensembles, *Gabrieli: Antiphonal Music of Gabrieli (Canzoni for Brass Choirs)*. Columbia.

Julian Bream, George Malcolm, *Bach & Vivaldi Sonatas for Lute & Harpsichord*. RCA.

Borodin Quartet, *Shostakovich: String Quartets (Complete)*. Seraphim.

Jacqueline De Pre, Daniel Barenboim, *Brahms: Sonatas in E Minor & F Major for Cello and Piano*. Angel.

Grumiaux Trio, *Beethoven: Trios for Strings*. Philips.

Itzhak Perlman, Vladimir Ashkenazy, *Prokofiev: Sonatas for Violin & Piano.* RCA.

Artur Rubinstein and Guarneri Quartet, *Brahms: Quartets for Piano & Strings (3); Schumann: Quintet in E Flat Major for Piano & Strings.* RCA.

BEST CLASSICAL PERFORMANCE, INSTRUMENTAL SOLOISTS(S) (WITH OR WITHOUT ORCHESTRA)

• Walter Carlos, Moog Synthesizer, *Switched-On Bach.* Columbia.

Edward Druzinsky, harp. Martinon conducting Chicago Symphony, *Ravel: Introduction & Allegro for Harp & Strings.* RCA.

Emil Gilels, *Gilels at Carnegie Hall.* Melyd.

John Kirkpatrick, *Ives: Sonata No 2 "Concord Mass."* Columbia.

Mstislav Rostropovich, cello (von Karajan conducting Berlin Philharmonic), *Dvorak: Concerto in B Minor for Cello.* Deutsche Grammophon.

Henryk Szeryng, *Bach: Sonatas & Partitas for Solo Violin.* Deutsche Grammophon.

BEST OPERA RECORDING

• *Wagner: Siegfried,* Herbert von Karajan conducting Berlin Philharmonic (solos: Thomas, Stewart, Stolze, Dernesch, Keleman, Dominguez, Gayer, Ridderbush). Otto Gerdes, A&R producer. Deutsche Grammophon.

Cavalli: L'Ormindo, Raymond Leppard conducting London Philharmonic (solos: Wakefield, van Bork, Howells, Berbie, Cuenod; Glyndebourne Festival Opera). Michael Bremner, A&R producer. Argo.

Mozart: The Marriage of Figaro, Karl Böhm conducting Chorus and Orchestra of German Opera (solos: Prey, Mathis, Janowitz, Fischer-Dieskau). Gustav Rudolf Sellner, A&R producer. Deutsche Grammophon.

Strauss: Ariadne Auf Naxos, Rudolf Kempe conducting Dresden State Opera (solos: Janowitz, King, Zylis-Gara, Geszty, Adam). R. Kinloch Anderson, Eberhard Geiler, A&R producers. Angel.

Strauss: Salome, Erich Leinsdorf conducting London Symphony (solos: Caballé, Milnes, Lewis, Resnik, King). Richard Mohr, A&R producer. RCA.

Verdi: Otello, Sir John Barbirolli conducting New Philharmonia Orchestra and Chorus (soloists: McCracken, Fischer-Dieskau, Jones, Di Stasio). R. Kinloch Anderson, A&R producer. Angel.

Verdi: La Traviata, Lorin Maazel conducting Orchestra and Chorus of Deutsche Opera Berlin (solos: Lorengar, Aragall, Fischer-Dieskau). John Mordler, A&R producer. London.

BEST CHORAL PERFORMANCE, OTHER THAN OPERA

• Ward Swingle, choral master. Luciano Berio conducting New York Philharmonic. Swingle Singers, *Berio: Sinfonia.* Columbia.

Colin Davis conducting John Aldis Choir and London Symphony Orchestra and Chorus, *Berlioz: Romeo et Juliette.* Philips.

Hans Gillesberger conducting Vienna Boys Choir and Chorus Viennensis. Nikolaus Harnoncourt conducting Concentus Musicus, *Bach: Mass in B Minor.* Telefunken.

Hans Werner Henze conducting Choirs of North German Radio/Berlin Radio/Boy's Chorus of St. Nicolai and North German Radio Symphony, *Henze: The Raft of the Frigate "Medusa."* Deutsche Grammophon.

Frederick Jackson, choral master for London Philharmonic Choir. Adrian Boult conducting London Philharmonic, *Vaughan Williams: Symphony No. 1 (A Sea Symphony).* Angel.

Gregg Smith conducting Gregg Smith Singers, *Billings: The Continental Harmony.* Columbia.

Edmund Walters conducting Royal Liverpool Philharmonic Choir. Charles Groves conducting Royal Liverpool Philharmonic Orchestra, *Delius: Songs of Sunset.* Angel.

BEST VOCAL SOLOIST PERFORMANCE, CLASSICAL

• Leontyne Price (Schippers conducting New Philharmonia), *Barber: Two Scenes from "Antony & Cleopatra"; Knoxville: Summer of 1915.* RCA.

Dietrich Fischer-Dieskau (Gerald Moore, accompanist), *Richard Strauss: Nineteen Early Songs.* Angel.

Marilyn Horne (Lewis conducting Vienna
Cantata Orchestra), *Bach & Handel
Arias* (excerpts from *Magnificat,
Christmas Oratorio, St. Matthew
Passion, Messiah, Rodelinda*). London.
Christa Ludwig, Walter Berry (Moore,
accompanist), *A Most Unusual Song
Recital* (Beethoven, Rossini, Brahms,
Reger, R. Strauss). Seraphim.
Halina Lukomska (from *Boulez Conducts
Berg,* Boulez conducting London
Symphony), *Berg: Altenberg Lieder.*
Columbia.
Sherrill Milnes (from *Brahms: Requiem,*
Erich Leinsdorf conducting Boston
Symphony), *Brahms: Four Serious
Songs.* RCA.
Peter Pears, Dietrich Fischer-Dieskau,
*Britten: Holy Sonnets of Donne, Songs
& Proverbs of Blake.* London.
Elisabeth Schwarzkopf, Dietrich Fischer-
Dieskau (Szell conducting London
Symphony), *Mahler: Des Knaben
Wunderhorn.* Angel.
Beverly Sills (Mackerras conducting Royal
Philharmonic), *Scenes & Arias from
French Opera.* Westminster.

BEST ENGINEERED RECORDING, CLASSICAL
• Walter Carlos, *Switched-On Bach*
(Walter Carlos). Columbia.
Edwin Begley, *Mahler: Symphony No. 1*
(Ormandy conducting Philadelphia
Symphony). RCA.
Edward T. Graham, Arthur Kendy, *Boulez
Conducts Debussy, Vol.2 "Images Pour
Orchestre"* (Boulez conducting
Cleveland Orchestra). Columbia.
Edward T. Graham, Milton Cherin,
*Gabrieli: Antiphonal Music of Gabrieli
(Canzoni for Brass Choirs)*
(Philadelphia, Cleveland, and Chicago
Brass Ensembles). Columbia/Odyssey.
Paul Goodman, *Khachaturian: Symphony
No.3; Rimsky-Korsakov: Russian
Easter Overture* (Stokowski conducting
Chicago Symphony). RCA.
Fred Plaut, Ed Michalski, *Berio: Sinfonia*
(Berio conducting New York
Philharmonic and Swingle Singers).
Columbia.

BEST COMEDY RECORDING
• *The Best of Bill Cosby,* Bill Cosby. Uni.
Berkeley Concert, Lenny Bruce. Warner
Bros.

*Bill Cosby's sixth victory in a row gave
him Grammy's longest winning streak.
Aretha Franklin would top him in 1973.*

Don Rickles Speaks! Don Rickles. Warner
Bros.
Laugh-In '69, Carolyn Raskin, producer.
Warner Bros.
W.C. Fields on Radio, Bruce Lundvall,
A&R producer. Columbia.

BEST RECORDING FOR CHILDREN
• *Peter, Paul & Mommy,* Peter, Paul &
Mary. Warner Bros.
Yellow Submarine, Richard Wolfe
Children's Chorus. RCA.
Chitty Chitty Bang Bang, Do-Re-Mi
Chorus. Kapp.
Folk Tales of the Tribes of Africa, Eartha
Kitt. Caedmon.
For All My Little Friends, Tiny Tim.
Warner Bros.

BEST SPOKEN WORD RECORDING
• *We Love You, Call Collect,* Art Linkletter
& Diane. Word/Capitol.
The Great White Hope, James Earl Jones.
Tetra.
Home to the Sea, Jesse Pearson, narrator.
Warner Bros.
Man on the Moon, Walter Cronkite.
Warner Bros.
Robert F. Kennedy: A Memorial, Thomas
Shepard, Joel Heller, A&R producers.
Columbia.

BEST ENGINEERED RECORDING (OTHER THAN CLASSICAL)
- Geoff Emerick, Phillip McDonald, *Abbey Road* (the Beatles). Apple.

Roy Halee, Fred Catero, *Blood, Sweat & Tears* (Blood, Sweat & Tears). Columbia.

Lee Herschberg, Larry Cox, Chuck Britz, *Velvet Voices & Bold Brass* (Anita Kerr Quartet). Para.

Bones Howe, *Age of Aquarius* (5th Dimension). Soul City.

Bruce Swedien, Doug Brand, Hans Wurman, Chuck Lishon, *Moog Groove* (Electronic Concept Orchestra). Limelight.

BEST ALBUM COVER
- Evelyn J. Kelbish, painting. David Stahlberg, graphics, *America the Beautiful* (Gary McFarland). Skye.

Gary Burden, art director. Henry Diltz, photographer, *Richard Pryor* (Richard Pryor). Dove.

David Juniper, art director, *Led Zeppelin II* (Led Zeppelin). Atlantic.

Tom Lazarus, art director. Gene Brownell, photographer. Bill Gordon, design, *Pidgeon* (Pidgeon). Decca.

Bob Seideman, art director and photographer, *Blind Faith* (Blind Faith). Atco.

BEST ALBUM NOTES
(Annotator's Award)
- Johnny Cash, *Nashville Skyline* (Bob Dylan). Columbia.

Joan Baez, *David's Album* (Joan Baez). Vanguard.

John Dodds II, *Chicago Mess Around* (Johnny Dodds). Milestone.

John Hartford, *John Hartford* (J. Hartford). RCA.

Rex Reed, *Mabel Mercer and Bobby Short at Town Hall*. Atlantic.

Troubled Times

The first complete sweep of the top prizes occurred on a Grammy night that was also historic for a second reason — the award ceremony was broadcast live on national television for the first time ever.

The ABC telecast originated from the Hollywood Palladium where Andy Williams presided over the on-air presentation of 17 of the year's 43 awards, the balance having been bestowed at a special off-the-air ceremony held earlier in the day. Two revolving stages were installed to accommodate Grammy's first prime-time TV spectacle, and a host of celebrity talent pitched in to act as presenters, including Herb Alpert, Burt Bacharach, Duke Ellington, Three Dog Night, Tammy Wynette, the 5th Dimension, Henry Mancini, and Bobby Sherman. The Grammys, said America's leading music critics, were now officially in the same league as the Oscars, Emmys, and Tonys, and the record academy wanted to put on a show to prove it.

The Grammycast did not disappoint, at least in terms of the drama surrounding the award results. It was, by now, a fairly common occurrence for two of the three top categories — Record, Song, and Album of the Year — to go to the same artist (it happened in 6 of

GLOBE PHOTO

Simon & Garfunkel's Bridge Over Troubled Water *addressed an era of disillusionment. "I burst into tears when I wrote and first sang" the song, Simon once said.*

the past 12 years), but never before had anyone won the Triple Crown. Then came the folky rock team of Simon & Garfunkel, who last proved their favored status with N.A.R.A.S. voters in 1968 by winning Record of the Year for "Mrs. Robinson." Their latest collaboration — and one that would be remembered as the duo's last LP of studio recordings as a duo act — was the milestone album and single release *Bridge Over Troubled Water*.

Bridge began the night with the most nominations — seven — and won six awards, incuding Record, Album, and Song of the Year (Simon alone won the prize for songwriting). *Bridge* also garnered the statuettes for Best Contemporary Song, Best Arrangement Accompanying Vocalist, and Best Engineered Recording.

Bridge was the early favorite to sweep the awards since the LP was the number-one seller of the year and the single ended up number four in the year's Hot 100. *Bridge* was also embraced as an anthem of the equally troubled times. The year 1970 marked the student killings at Kent State University and Janis Joplin's drug overdose. "I'm embarrassed to say I burst into tears when I wrote and first sang the line 'Like a bridge over troubled water, I will lay me down,'" Paul Simon later told *Playboy* magazine, remembering the song's sentimental importance in 1970. "Now it's been sung so many times I have no feeling whatsoever for it." The year was an equally troubling time for Simon & Garfunkel. Although they would periodically team up for special concerts and charity benefits in the future, the duo ended their artistic partnership soon after *Bridge*'s release.

> Paul Simon became the first winner of Grammy's Triple Crown: Record, Song, and Album of the Year.

"Bridge [may have] swept the top honors," wrote the *L.A. Times*, "but it was ex-Beatle Paul McCartney, in a rare public appearance, who created the most excitement" at the ceremony. "Though the event was strictly black tie, McCartney strolled in wearing a blue suit, red flower shirt open at the neck, and white tennis shoes."

Like Simon & Garfunkel, the Beatles broke up in 1970 but still had a bounty of nominations (six) for their farewell LP *Let It Be*. They won only one award — for Best Original Score, Motion Picture or TV Special — after losing Record and Song of the Year nods (in a close contest, according to *The Washington Post*) to "Bridge." But "there were shrieks of surprise" from the audience when the winner of best film score was announced, the *Times* reported. "With Linda at his side, McCartney raced up to the podium to accept the award from actor John Wayne, saying only, 'Thank you.'"

John Lennon once said about *Let It Be*: "This is us with our trousers off." The album was from the Beatles' film that documented the group's breakup and included such hit singles as "Get Back." The movie ended with their last public concert — held on the rooftop of their Apple Records headquarters in London (the neighbors called the cops to break it up) — and with Lennon's parting words, "I'd like to say thank you very much on behalf of the group and myself, and I hope we passed the audition."

The Beatles and Simon & Garfunkel were up for Best Contemporary Vocal Performance by a Group, but lost to Grammy's Best New Artists, the Carpenters, who first came to fame after covering the Beatles' "Ticket to Ride" in 1969. The brother and sister act of Richard and Karen Carpenter were often criticized for lacking passion in their singing, but they were nonetheless expert voicesmiths who specialized in melodic ballads such as their winning "Close to You," also a Record of the Year nominee that came in number five in the year's Hot 100 (just behind "Bridge Over Troubled Water"). *Close to You* was also a best-selling LP for an impressive 53 weeks, although it proved a loser as an Album of the Year nominee.

"Close to You" was written by Burt Bacharach and Hal David for Dionne Warwick, who recorded it first, but without much success. Warwick still reigned in the pop charts, though, with another Bacharach/David tune, "I'll Never Fall in Love Again" — from the Broadway musical *Promises, Promises*, which won last year's Grammy for best cast show album. "I'll Never Fall in Love Again" also earned Warwick the laurels for Best Female Contemporary Vocal Performance, a prize she won once before, in 1968, for singing Bacharach and David's "Do You Know the Way to San Jose." Of her first 37 singles, Bacharach and David wrote all but four and produced all but two. In 1971, however, she made a break with them to jump to Warner Bros. where she knew only periodic success after that.

Winner of the best contemporary male vocal performance award was Ray Stevens, who had turned down the chance to make the first recording of Bacharach/David's "Raindrops Keep Fallin' on My Head" (which B.J. Thomas took to number one in 1970's Hot 100). Stevens was a pop country singer known for humorous ditties like 1962's "Ahab the Arab." When he wrote his Grammy-winning "Everything Is Beautiful," he accentuated its seriousness by adding a chorus that sounded like a church choir. "Everything Is Beautiful" won a second Grammy when gospel singer Jake Hess gave it an even more religious lilt, earning him Best Sacred Performance.

Gospel-trained Aretha Franklin picked up her fourth Grammy in a row for best r&b vocal performance for "Don't Play That Song," which ended up number 11 in the year's Hot 100, the exact same ranking it had when it was performed in 1962 by Ben E. King. But in this version, the newly dubbed "Lady Soul" (a name Franklin acquired from

GLOBE PHOTO

Miles Davis was honored for Bitches Brew, *his classic of jazz/rock fusion.*

the title of an earlier LP) gave it her signature eruptions of joy, rage, pain, and sorrow. The swings of feeling must have been easy for her to muster in 1970, considering the personal tragedies she suffered in private life. Her marriage to manager Ted White had just broken up and she had recently been arrested for drunk driving and disorderly conduct.

When B.B. ("Blues Boy") King took the equivalent r&b vocal honors for men for "The Thrill Is Gone," it was a crowning achievement. For 20 years, King had been known primarily to black audiences. In 1969, however, he was the toast of the Newport Jazz Festival, appeared on the *Tonight Show*, toured with the Rolling Stones, and then ventured across Europe and Australia with his own band.

The r&b group vocal prize went to the Delfonics for what *Rolling Stone* once called their "landmark" hit "Didn't I (Blow Your Mind This Time)," which was written by Thom Bell, its producer, and William Hart, one of the three members of the pop/soul vocal trio from Pennsylvania. "Didn't I" was up for Best R&B Song along with other such heavy hitters as Stevie Wonder's "Signed, Sealed, Delivered," but both lost to "Patches," by Ronald Dunbar and General Johnson, "the ultimate soul soap opera," according to music critic David Marsh.

The two jazz categories welcomed back two past winners this year, including pianist and composer Bill Evans (Grammy victor in 1963 for *Conversations with Myself* and in 1968 for *Bill Evans at the Montreux Jazz Festival*). His latest work, *Alone*, reaped him Best Jazz Performance, Small Group or Soloist with Small Group. Miles Davis had won once before, too — in 1960 for *Sketches of Spain*. He now took the prize for large-group performance for *Bitches Brew*, the most commercially successful work of his career and one that also finally achieved what Davis had been attempting for years: the first near-perfect fusion of jazz and rock, which astonished the critics with its novelty and brilliance.

The Best Country Song of the year was the one ranked highest on the c&w charts: "My Woman, My Woman, My Wife" by Marty Robbins, who last won a Grammy in 1960 for his performance of "El Paso." He wrote "My Woman" for his wife of 15 years, Marizona Baldwin. It soon became one of the 50 Top 10 country hits of his career and one of the 14 that reached number one. (Twenty-four crossed over to the pop charts. Only Johnny Cash, Kenny Rogers, and Glen Campbell have bettered his record.) Six weeks after its release, Robbins was named the 1960s' Artist of the Decade by the Country Music Association.

Last year's winner of Song of the Year, Joe South ("Games People Play")

had another crossover hit this year with "Rose Garden," which was also known as "I Never Promised You a Rose Garden." The song landed at number one in the pop charts for a week and spent five weeks at number one on the country rankings. Its success was due in large part to its crystal-voiced, guitar-strumming singer Lynn Anderson, who easily took the prize for Best Female Country Vocal Performance. Anderson was the daughter of Liz Anderson, a notable c&w vocalist for RCA and the wife of producer Glenn Sutton, who was also the coauthor of the 1966 Grammy-sweeper "Almost Persuaded." She credits her success not with talent or connections, however, but with the message of the song. "'Rose Garden' was perfectly timed," she told the Associated Press. "We were just coming out of the Vietnam years and a lot of people were trying to recover. The song's message was that you can make something out of nothing. You can take it and go ahead."

The male vocal country performance prize went to Ray Price, who won for a tune that would become one of his trademark songs, "For the Good Times." Price had had more than 50 hits in the Top 10 on the country charts — 11 of which crossed over to land in the Hot 100 — but "Good Times" was his first song to reach number one in the pop lineup. It also represented a brief period of his career during which he dropped the honky-tonk trappings of country music (including fiddle, banjo, and steel guitar) in favor of violins and a more symphonic sound.

Winners of the prize for best duo or group vocal performance were husband and wife Johnny Cash and June Carter, for "If I Were a Carpenter," one of their five joint Top 40 hits. (Another was "Jackson," for which they won their last Grammy together in 1967.)

In 1970, Chet Atkins declared in an ad in *Billboard* that renowned session guitarist Jerry Reed was "one of the greatest undeveloped talents I have ever known." Atkins was vice-president of the country music division of RCA Records at the time and hoped to make Reed a star. "If Jerry doesn't make it big in the near future," he continued, "I will probably quit my job, because if that is true, I do not know talent." Atkins's job was secure thanks in large part to his own initiative. In 1970, he and "Guitar Man" Reed teamed up for a popular LP *Me & Jerry*, which earned them the Grammy for best instrumental performance, which Atkins had last won in 1967.

The Best Gospel Performance went to the controversial Oak Ridge Boys for *Talk About the Good Times*. The Tennessee quartet may have been approved by Grammy voters, but they were losing popularity with the broader spectrum of the religiously devout in 1970 as they added po/rock qualities to their sound, let their hair grow long, and made sexually suggestive movements on stage.

Texas blues guitarist Aaron "T-Bone" Walker, who helped to modernize country music by introducing more jazzy and electric elements, garnered Best Ethnic or Traditional Recording for "Good Feelin'."

Flip Wilson finally ended Bill Cosby's six-year reign over the comedy category when his *The Devil Made Me Buy This Dress* bested the champ's latest nominated LP *Live at Madison Square Garden*. Wilson was the star of his own hit variety series that premiered on TV in 1970, and he produced popular humor albums like *Flippin'* and *Flip Wilson, You Devil You*. Typical of his routines on record was his version of Christopher Columbus's discovery of America, in which Spain's Queen Isabella, a Ray Charles fan, hands Columbus a traveler's check to get him to America. "You gonna find Ray Charles? He in America?" she asks. "Damn right," Columbus answers. "That's where all those records come from."

Only once before, in 1967, did the same LP win both Classical Album of the Year and Best Opera Recording. Now the honors were shared by the first complete version of Berlioz's *Les Troyens*, with Colin Davis conducting the Chorus and Orchestra of the Royal Opera House and featuring tenor Jon Vickers and soprano Berit Lindholm (neither of whom was nominated for the vocalist's laurel, although both received rave notices; mezzo-soprano Janet Baker *was* nominated for her excerpts from the same work in a separate recording). During his lifetime, Berlioz had been forced to scale back his four-hour opera into two parts before its first performance. In 1969, the halves were combined and carefully reintegrated. "Now, more than a hundred years after its completion," wrote *High Fidelity*, "the opera's fortunes have clearly turned for the better" thanks to this "marvelous" recording.

John Lennon said about the Beatles' farewell album Let It Be: *"This is us with our trousers off."*

Germany's most famous baritone, Dietrich Fischer-Dieskau, ended up taking the vocal honors for the most ambitious accomplishment of his career: a 25-disc, two-volume set of 400 songs by Schubert. "The result is, without question," *High Fidelity* said, "an extraordinary panorama of Schubert's achievements as a Lied composer."

Among the losing nominees for best album was the winner of the orchestral honors: conductor Pierre Boulez and the Cleveland Orchestra's performance of Stravinsky's latest (1967) rendition of *Le Sacre du Printemps*. *High Fidelity* called it "a reading of great authority and panache that Boulez gives us, and a worthy replacement for his earlier version in the front line of *Rite* recordings."

Another losing nominee for best classical LP was a winner of the soloists' award for violinist David Oistrakh and cellist Mstislav Rostropovich — Brahms's Double Concerto, the first concerto in music history to pair those two musical instruments. The teaming of the artists was hailed as "heaven-ordained" by critics. Violinist Isaac Stern teamed up with cellist Leonard Rose and pianist Eugene Istomin for their Best Chamber Music Performance of Beethoven's complete piano trios. *High Fidelity*'s reviewer called their interpretation "occasionally touched by Romantic nuances, but more classical than anything else, hence the closest to what I take to be the style Beethoven himself intended for this music."

The recipient of the choral laurels were the Gregg Smith Singers and Columbia Chamber Ensemble perform-

Colin Davis's reading of Berlioz's **Les Troyens** *reaped both* **Best Opera Recording** *and top classical LP.*

ing *New Music of Charles Ives*, which included "Duty" and "Vita" among what *High Fidelity* called the "masterpieces made available here in superb performances, superbly recorded."

Even though the Grammys show proved to be historic because its live broadcast, the 13th annual ceremony still had an unlucky outcome. "It wasn't worth bothering about," griped *Variety*, even though the trade paper admitted the program had a number of "spirited moments." The show, it claimed, "made nobody happy except Columbia Records," which won nearly half of the awards (18), compared to 4 for its nearest rival, RCA.

Other "raps were also heard from the classical disc departments," *Variety* added. "They point out that not a single Grammy Award in a classical category was made on the national TV hookup."

Variety had predicted that music "pace-setter" James Taylor would do well this year, but was clearly disappointed when he won none, despite five nominations, including ones for Record, Song, and Album of the Year. "This omission," it said, "was ascribed to the failure of the young members of the industry to participate in the work of N.A.R.A.S. Efforts to bring new talent into N.A.R.A.S. have not resulted in much success. In one case, a representative of the new generation was placed on the N.A.R.A.S. council, but he never showed up. These types, it's been pointed out, are distinctly anti-organizational."

1970

The first live telecast of the awards was aired by ABC from the Hollywood Palladium in Los Angeles on March 16, 1971, for the awards eligibility period of November 2, 1969, to October 15, 1970.

ALBUM OF THE YEAR
• *Bridge Over Troubled Water,* Simon & Garfunkel. Paul Simon, Art Garfunkel, Roy Halee, A&R producers. Columbia.

Chicago, Chicago. James William Guercio, A&R producer. Columbia.
Close to You, Carpenters. Jack Daugherty, A&R producer. A&M.
Déja Vu, Crosby, Stills, Nash & Young. Crosby, Stills, Nash & Young, A&R producers. A&M.
Elton John, Elton John. Gus Dudgeon, A&R producer. Uni.
Sweet Baby James, James Taylor. Peter Asher, A&R producer. Warner Bros.

RECORD OF THE YEAR

- "Bridge Over Troubled Water," Simon & Garfunkel. Paul Simon, Art Garfunkel, Roy Halee, A&R producers. Columbia.

"Close to You," Carpenters. Jack Daugherty, A&R producer. A&M.

"Everything Is Beautiful," Ray Stevens. Ray Stevens, A&R producer. Barnaby.

"Fire and Rain," James Taylor. Peter Asher, A&R producer. Warner Bros.

"Let It Be," the Beatles. George Martin, A&R producer. Apple.

Best New Artists the Carpenters beat the Beatles and Simon & Garfunkel for the contemporary vocals kudos.

SONG OF THE YEAR
(Songwriter's Award)

- "Bridge Over Troubled Water," Paul Simon.

"Everything Is Beautiful," Ray Stevens.

"Fire and Rain," James Taylor.

"Let It Be," John Lennon, Paul McCartney.

"We've Only Just Begun," Roger Nichols, Paul Williams.

BEST NEW ARTIST

- Carpenters. A&M.

Elton John. Uni.

Melba Moore. Mercury.

Anne Murray. Capitol.

Partridge Family. Bell.

BEST CONTEMPORARY VOCAL PERFORMANCE, MALE

- Ray Stevens, "Everything Is Beautiful." Barnaby.

Joe Cocker, *Mad Dogs and Englishmen.* A&M.

Brook Benton, "Rainy Night in Georgia." Cotillion.

Elton John, *Elton John.* Uni.

James Taylor, *Sweet Baby James.* Warner Bros.

BEST CONTEMPORARY VOCAL PERFORMANCE, FEMALE

- Dionne Warwick, "I'll Never Fall in Love Again." Scepter.

Bobbie Gentry, *Fancy.* Capitol.

Anne Murray, "Snowbird." Capitol.

Linda Ronstadt, *Long Long Time.* Capitol.

Diana Ross, "Ain't No Mountain High Enough." Motown.

BEST CONTEMPORARY VOCAL PERFORMANCE BY A DUO, GROUP, OR CHORUS

- Carpenters, "Close to You." A&M.

Beatles, "Let It Be." Apple.

Chicago, *Chicago.* Columbia.

Jackson 5, "ABC." Motown.

Simon & Garfunkel, "Bridge Over Troubled Water." Columbia.

BEST CONTEMPORARY SONG
(Songwriter's Award)

- "Bridge Over Troubled Water," Paul Simon.

"Everything Is Beautiful," Ray Stevens.

"Fire and Rain," James Taylor.

"Let It Be," John Lennon, Paul McCartney.

"We've Only Just Begun," Roger Nichols, Paul Williams.

BEST CONTEMPORARY INSTRUMENTAL PERFORMANCE

- Henry Mancini, *Theme from "Z" and Other Film Music.* RCA.

Assembled Multitude, "Overture from *Tommy.*" Atlantic.

Vincent Bell, *"Airport* Love Theme." Decca.

Jimi Hendrix, "Star Spangled Banner." Cotillion.

Quincy Jones, "Soul Flower." United Artists.

Best Rhythm & Blues Song
(Songwriter's Award)
- "Patches," Ronald Dunbar, General Johnson. Atlantic.
- "Didn't I (Blow Your Mind This Time)," Thom Bell, William Hart. Philly Groove.
- "Groovy Situation," Russell Lewis, Herman Davis. Mercury.
- "Signed, Sealed, Delivered," Stevie Wonder, Lee Garrett, Syreeta Wright, Lulu Hardaway. Tamla.
- "Somebody's Been Sleeping in My Bed," Greg Perry, General Johnson, Angelo Bond. Buddah.

Best Rhythm & Blues Vocal Performance, Male
- B.B. King, "The Thrill Is Gone." ABC.
- Clarence Carter, "Patches." Atlantic.
- Wilson Pickett, "Engine No. 9." Atlantic.
- Edwin Starr, "War." Gordy.
- Stevie Wonder, "Signed, Sealed, Delivered." Tamla/Motown.

Best Rhythm & Blues Vocal Performance, Female
- Aretha Franklin, "Don't Play That Song." Atlantic.
- Esther Phillips, "Set Me Free." Atlantic.
- Nina Simone, *Black Gold*. RCA.
- Candi Staton, "Stand By Your Man." Fame.
- Dee Dee Warwick, "She Didn't Know." Atco.

Best Rhythm & Blues Vocal or Instrumental Performance by a Duo or Group
- Delfonics, "Didn't I (Blow Your Mind This Time)." Philly Groove.
- Four Tops, "It's All in the Game." Motown.
- 100 Proof, "Somebody's Been Sleeping in My Bed." Buddah.
- Presidents, "5-10-15-20 (25-30 Years of Love)." Buddah.
- Charles Wright & the Watts 103rd Street Rhythm Band, "Express Yourself." Warner Bros.

Best Jazz Performance, Small Group or Soloist with Small Group
(7 or less)
- Bill Evans, *Alone*. MGM.
- Gary Burton, *Good-Vibes*. Atlantic.
- John Coltrane, *Coltrane Legacy*. Atlantic.
- Erroll Garner, *Feeling Is Believing*. Octave.
- Herbie Hancock, *Fat Albert Rotunda*. Warner Bros.
- Milt Jackson Quintet with Ray Brown, *That's the Way It Is*. Impulse.
- Les McCann, Eddie Harris, *Swiss Movement*. Atlantic.

Best Jazz Performance, Large Group or Soloist with Large Group
(8 or More)
- Miles Davis, *Bitches Brew*. Columbia.
- Paul Desmond, *Bridge Over Troubled Water*. A&R.
- Duke Ellington, *Duke Ellington, 70th Birthday Concert*. Solid State.
- Don Ellis, *Don Ellis at Fillmore*. Columbia.
- Johnny Hodges, *Three Shades of Blue*. Flying Dutchman.
- Quincy Jones, *Gula Matari*. A&M.
- Thad Jones, Mel Lewis, *Consummation*. Blue Note.
- World's Greatest Jazzband, *Live at the Roosevelt Grill*. Atlantic.

Best Country Song
(Songwriter's Award)
- "My Woman, My Woman, My Wife," Marty Robbins. Columbia.
- "The Fightin' Side of Me," Merle Haggard. Capitol.
- "Hello Darlin'," Conway Twitty. Decca.
- "Is Anybody Goin' to San Antone," Glenn Martin, Dave Kirby. RCA.
- "Wonder Could I Live There Anymore," Bill Rice. RCA.

Best Country Instrumental Performance
- Chet Atkins, Jerry Reed, *Me & Jerry*. RCA.
- Chet Atkins, "Yestergroovin'." RCA.
- Danny Davis & the Nashville Brass, "You Ain't Heard Nothin' Yet." RCA.
- Merle Haggard & the Stranger, "Street Singer." Capitol.
- Jerry Smith, "Drivin' Home." Decca.

Best Country Vocal Performance, Male
- Ray Price, "For the Good Times." Columbia.
- Johnny Cash, "Sunday Morning Coming Down." Columbia.
- Merle Haggard, *Okie from Muskogee*. Capitol.

Charley Pride, *Charley Pride's 10th Album*. Columbia.
Jerry Reed, "Amos Moses." RCA.

BEST COUNTRY VOCAL PERFORMANCE, FEMALE
• Lynn Anderson, "Rose Garden." Columbia.
Wanda Jackson, "A Woman Lives for Love." Capitol.
Dolly Parton, "Mule Skinner Blues." RCA.
Jean Shepard, "Then He Touched Me." Capitol.
Tammy Wynette, "Run, Woman, Run." Epic.

BEST COUNTRY VOCAL PERFORMANCE BY A DUO OR GROUP
• Johnny Cash, June Carter, "If I Were a Carpenter." Columbia.
Jack Blanchard, Misty Morgan, "Tennessee Birdwalk." Wayside.
Statler Brothers, "Bed of Roses." Mercury.
Waylon Jennings, Jessi Colter, "Suspicious Minds." RCA.
Porter Wagoner, Dolly Parton, "Daddy Was an Old-Time Preacher Man." RCA.

BEST SACRED PERFORMANCE, MUSICAL
• Jake Hess, "Everything Is Beautiful." RCA.
Pat Boone, "Rapture." Supreme.
Ralph Carmichael Orchestra and Chorus, "The Centurion." Light.
Mormon Tabernacle Choir, Richard Condie conducting, "God of Our Fathers." Columbia.
George Beverly Shea, "There Is More to Life." RCA.

BEST GOSPEL PERFORMANCE (OTHER THAN SOUL GOSPEL)
• Oak Ridge Boys, "Talk About the Good Times." Heartwarming.
Wendy Bagwell & the Sunliters, "Talk About the Good Times." Canaan.
Florida Boys, *The Many Moods of the Florida Boys*. Canaan.
LeFevres, "The LeFevres/Moving Up." Canaan.
Thrasher Brothers, "Fantastic Thrashers at Fantastic Caverns." Canaan.

BEST SOUL GOSPEL PERFORMANCE
• Edwin Hawkins Singers, "Every Man Wants to Be Free." Buddah.
James Cleveland, "Amazing Grace." Savoy.
Andrae Crouch, "Christian People." Liberty.
Jessy Dixon, "Hello Sunshine." Savoy.
Myrna Summers, "God Gave Me a Song." Cotillion.

BEST ETHNIC OR TRADITIONAL RECORDING (INCLUDING TRADITIONAL BLUES)
• "Good Feelin'," T-Bone Walker. Polydor.
Black Music of South America, David Lewisohn. Nonesuch.
Folk Fiddling from Sweden, Bjorn Stabi, Ole Hjorth. Nonesuch.
I Do Not Play No Rock and Roll, Mississippi Fred McDowell. Capitol.
Sail On, Muddy Waters. Chess.
"Shree Rag," Ali Akbar Khan, accompanied by Shankar Ghosh. Tabla. Connoisseur Society.

BEST INSTRUMENTAL ARRANGEMENT
• Henry Mancini, "Theme from *Z*" (Mancini). RCA.
Miles Davis, *Bitches Brew* (Miles Davis). Columbia.
Quincy Jones, "Gula Matari" (Quincy Jones). A&M.
Fred Selden, "The Magic Bus Ate My Donut" (Don Ellis). Columbia.
Tom Sellers, "Overture from *Tommy*" (Assembled Multitude). Atlantic.
Lalo Schifrin, "Theme from *Medical Center*" (Lalo Schifrin). MGM.

BEST INSTRUMENTAL COMPOSITION (Composer's Award)
• Alfred Newman, *"Airport* Love Theme." Decca.
Miles Davis, "Bitches Brew." Columbia.
Quincy Jones, "Gula Matari," A&M.
Henry Mancini, "Love Theme from *Sunflower*." RCA.
Lalo Schifrin, "Theme from *Medical Center*." MGM.

BEST SCORE FROM AN ORIGINAL CAST SHOW ALBUM
• *Company*, Stephen Sondheim, composer. Thomas Z. Shepard, A&R producer. Columbia.

Critics cheered Pierre Boulez's reading of Stravinsky's Le Sacre du Printemps *for its "great authority and panache."*

Applause, Charles Strouse, Lee Adams, composers. Bob Arnold, A&R producer. ABC.

Coco, Alan Jay Lerner, André Previn, composers. Andy Wiswell, A&R producer. Para.

Joy, Oscar Brown, Jr., Jean Pace, Sivuca, composers. Ernie Altschuler, A&R producer. RCA.

Purlie, Gary Geld, Peter Udell, composers. Andy Wiswell, A&R producer. Ampex.

BEST ORIGINAL SCORE WRITTEN FOR A MOTION PICTURE OR TV SPECIAL
(Composer's Award)

• *Let It Be*, John Lennon, Paul McCartney, George Harrison, Ringo Starr. Apple.

Airport, Alfred Newman. Decca.

Darling Lili, Johnny Mercer, Henry Mancini. RCA.

M*A*S*H, Johnny Mandel. Columbia.

The Sterile Cuckoo, Fred Karlin. Paramount.

BEST ARRANGEMENT ACCOMPANYING VOCALIST(S)

• Paul Simon, Art Garfunkel, Jimmie Haskell, Ernie Freeman, Larry Knechtel, "Bridge Over Troubled Water" (Simon & Garfunkel). Columbia.

Richard Carpenter, "Close to You" (Carpenters). A&M.

Dick Halligan, "Lucretia MacEvil" (Blood, Sweat & Tears). Columbia.

Ray Stevens, "Everything Is Beautiful" (Ray Stevens). Barnaby.

ALBUM OF THE YEAR, CLASSICAL

• *Berlioz: Les Troyens*, Colin Davis conducting Royal Opera House Orchestra and Chorus (solos: Vickers, Veasey, Lindholm). Erik Smith, A&R producer. Philips.

Beethoven Edition 1970, Herbert von Karajan conducting Berlin Philharmonic (solos: Oistrakh, Anda, Kempf, Goossens, Leitner, etc.). Dr. Wilfried Daenicke, A&R producer. Deutsche Grammophon.

Brahms: Double Concerto (Concerto in A Minor for Violin and Cello) Szell conducting Cleveland Orchestra (solos: David Oistrakh, Mstislav Rostropovich). Peter Andry, A&R producer. Angel.

Ives: Three Places in New England; Ruggles: Sun Treader, Michael Tilson Thomas conducting Boston Symphony. Tom Mowrey, A&R producer. Deutsche Grammophon.

Shostakovich: Symphony No. 13, Eugene Ormandy conducting Philadelphia Symphony (R. Page directing Male Chorus of Mendelssohn Club of Philadelphia; solo: Krause, baritone). Peter Dellheim, A&R producer. RCA.

Stravinsky: Le Sacre du Printemps, Pierre Boulez conducting Cleveland Orchestra. Thomas Z. Shepard, A&R producer. Columbia.

BEST CLASSICAL PERFORMANCE, ORCHESTRA
(Conductor's Award)

• Pierre Boulez conducting Cleveland Orchestra, *Stravinsky: Le Sacre du Printemps*. Columbia.

Carlo Maria Giulini conducting Chicago Symphony, *Berlioz: Romeo & Juliet*. Angel.

Eugene Ormandy conducting Philadelphia Symphony, *Mahler: Symphony No. 2 in C Minor, "Resurrection."* RCA.

Seiji Ozawa conducting Chicago Symphony, *Bartók: Concerto for Orchestra*. Angel.

Georg Solti conducting Chicago Symphony, *Mahler: Symphony No. 6 in A Minor*. London.

George Szell conducting Cleveland Orchestra, *Bruckner: Symphony No. 8 in C Minor*. Columbia.

George Szell conducting Cleveland Orchestra, *Dvorak: Symphony No. 8 in G Major*. Angel.

Michael Tilson Thomas conducting Boston Symphony, *Ives: Three Places in New England; Ruggles: Sun Treader*. Deutsche Grammophon.

BEST CLASSICAL PERFORMANCE, CHAMBER MUSIC (INCLUDING CHAMBER ORCHESTRA)
• Eugene Istomin, Isaac Stern, Leonard Rose, *Beethoven: The Complete Piano Trios*. Columbia.
Boston Symphony Chamber Players, *Schubert: Trio No. 1 in B Flat Major; Milhaud: Pastorale for Oboe, Clarinet & Bassoon; Hindemith: Kleine Lammer-Musik*. RCA.
Benjamin Britten conducting English Chamber Orchestra and Ambrosian Singers, *Salute to Percy Grainger*. London.
Composers Quartet, *Carter: Quartets Nos. 1 & 2 for Strings*. Nonesuch.
Guarneri Quartet, *Beethoven: The Five Late Quartets*. RCA.
Sviatoslav Richter, David Oistrakh, *Franck: Sonata in A Major for Violin & Piano; Brahms: Sonata No. 3 in D Minor*. Angel.
Gunther Schuller, *Ives: Calcium Light Night*. CBS.

BEST CLASSICAL PERFORMANCE, INSTRUMENTAL SOLOIST(S) (WITH OR WITHOUT ORCHESTRA)
• David Oistrakh, Mstislav Rostropovich (Szell conducting Cleveland Orchestra), *Brahms: Double Concerto (Concerto in A Minor for Violin and Cello)*. Angel.
Walter Carlos, *Well-Tempered Synthesizer*. Columbia.
Glenn Gould, *Bach: The Well Tempered Clavier Book 2*, Nos. 9–16. CBS.
Vladimir Horowitz, *Schumann: Kreisleriana*. Columbia.
Ivan Moravec, *Beethoven: Sonatas No. 26 Op. 81a ("Les Adieux") and No. 15, Op. 28 ("Pastoral")*. Connoisseur Society.
David Oistrakh (Szell conducting Cleveland Orchestra), *Brahms: Concerto in D Major for Violin*. Angel.
Mstislav Rostropovich (Britten, conductor), *Britten: Suites for Cello (2)*. London.

Van Cliburn (Ormandy conducting Philadelphia Symphony), *Chopin: Concerto No. 1 in E Minor for Piano*. RCA.
Alexis Weissenberg (Ormandy conducting Philadelphia Symphony), *Bartók: Concerto No. 2 for Piano*. RCA.

BEST OPERA RECORDING
Berlioz: Les Troyens, Colin Davis conducting Royal Opera House Orchestra and Chorus (solos: Vickers, Veasey, Lindholm). Erik Smith, A&R producer. Philips.
Debussy: Pelleas et Melisande, Pierre Boulez conducting Orchestra of Royal Opera House (solos: McIntyre, Shirley, Soederstroem, David, Ward, etc.). Paul Myers, A&R producer. Columbia.
R. Strauss: Der Rosenkavalier, Georg Solti conducting Vienna Philharmonic (solos: Crespin, Minton, Donath, Jungwirth). Christopher Raeburn, A&R producer. London.
Verdi: Il Trovatore, Zubin Mehta conducting New Philharmonia Orchestra, Ambrosian Opera Chorus (solos: Price, Domingo, Milnes, Cossotto). Richard Mohr, A&R producer. RCA.
Wagner: Gotterdammerung, Herbert von Karajan conducting Berlin Philharmonic, Deutsche Opera Chorus (solos: Brilioth, Stewart, Keleman, Dernesch, Janowitz, Ludwig, Chookasian). Otto Gerdes, A&R producer. Deutsche Grammophon.

BEST CHORAL PERFORMANCE, OTHER THAN OPERA
• Gregg Smith conducting Gregg Smith Singers and Columbia Chamber Ensemble, *New Music of Charles Ives*. Columbia.
Arthur Oldham conducting London Symphony Orchestra Chorus. Pierre Boulez conducting London Symphony, *Mahler: Das Klagende Lied*. Columbia.
Robert E. Page directing Male Chorus of Mendelssohn Club of Philadelphia. Eugene Ormandy conducting Philadelphia Symphony, *Shostakovich: Symphony No. 13*. RCA.
Reinhold Schmid, Helmut Froschauer conducting Vienna Singverien. Herbert von Karajan conducting Berlin Philharmonic, *Haydn: The Creation*. Deutsche Grammophon.

Martin Luther King Jr.'s impassioned LP Why I Oppose the War in Vietnam *was voted Best Spoken Word Recording.*

Gregg Smith conducting Ithaca College Concert Choir. Robert Craft conducting Columbia Symphony, *The New Stravinsky*. Columbia.

Lorna Cooke de Varon directing New England Conservatory Chorus. Katherine Edmonds Pusztai conducting Children's Chorus of New England Conservatory. Seiji Ozawa conducting Boston Symphony, *Orff: Carmina Burana*. RCA.

David Willcocks conducting Bach Choir and New Philharmonia, *Vaughan Williams: Five Tudor Portraits*. Angel.

Best Vocal Soloist Performance, Classical

• Dietrich Fischer-Dieskau (Gerald Moore, accompanist), *Schubert: Lieder*. Deutsche Grammophon.

Janet Baker (Gibson conducting London Symphony), Final scenes, "Death of Cleopatra," *Berlioz: The Trojans*. Angel.

Marilyn Horn (Lewis, conductor), *Mahler: Kindertotenlieder; Wagner: Wesendonck Lieder*. London.

Christa Ludwig, Walter Berry (Bernstein conducting New York Philharmonic), *Mahler: Des Knaben Wunderhorn*. Columbia.

Leontyne Price (Downes conducting London Symphony), *Prima Donna, Volume 3*. RCA.

Beverly Sills (Ceccato conducting London Philharmonic), *Mozart and Strauss Arias*. Audio Treasury.

Best Engineered Recording, Classical

• Fred Plaut, Ray Moore, Arthur Kendy, *Stravinsky: Le Sacre du Printemps* (Boulez conducting Cleveland Orchestra). Columbia.

Walter Carlos, *The Well-Tempered Synthesizer* (Walter Carlos). Columbia.

Paul Goodman, *Shostakovich: Symphony No. 6 and Age of Gold* (Stokowski conducting Chicago Symphony). RCA.

Gunter Hermanns, *Ives: Three Places in New England; Ruggles: Sun Treader* (Thomas conducting Boston Symphony). Deutsche Grammophon.

Bernard Keville, *Shostakovich: Symphony No. 13* (Ormandy conducting Philadelphia Symphony). RCA.

Gordon Parry, James Locke, *R. Strauss: Der Rosenkavalier* (Solti conducting Vienna Philharmonic; solos: Crespin, Minton). London.

Carson C. Taylor, *Brahms: Double Concerto: Concerto in A Minor for Violin and Cello* (solos: Oistrakh, Rostropovich; Szell conducting Cleveland Orchestra). Angel.

Best Comedy Recording

• *The Devil Made Me Buy This Dress*, Flip Wilson. Little David.

The Begatting of the President, Orson Welles. Mediarts.

Daddy Played First Base, Homer & Jethro. RCA.

I Am the President, David Frye. Elektra.

Live at Madison Square Garden, Bill Cosby. Uni.

Best Spoken Word Recording

• *Why I Oppose the War in Vietnam*, Rev. Martin Luther King, Jr. Black Forum.

Everett Dirksen's America, Everett Dirksen. Bell.

Grover Henson Feels Forgotten, Bill Cosby. Uni.

In the Beginning, Robert Cotterell, A&R producer. (Apollo 8, 11, 12 Astronauts, Presidents Kennedy and Nixon). Creative Sound.

Poems and Ballads from 100-Plus American Poets, Paul Molloy, A&R producer. (Ambrose, Dryden, Hecht, Molloy, Seeger). Scholastic.

The Soft Sea, Jesse Pearson. Warner Bros.

BEST RECORDING FOR CHILDREN
• *Sesame Street* (*Sesame Street* TV Cast), Children's Television Workshop. Joan Cooney, producer. Columbia.

Aristocats, Tutti Camarata, musical producer. (Camarata, Holloway, Harris, Lester, Mike Sammes Singers). Disneyland.

A Boy Named Charlie Brown (soundtrack). John Scott Trotter, A&R producer and musical director. Columbia.

Rubber Duckie, Jim Henson. Columbia.

Susan Sings Songs from Sesame Street, Loretta Long. Scepter.

BEST ENGINEERED RECORDING
• Roy Halee, *Bridge Over Troubled Water* (Simon & Garfunkel). Columbia.

Ray Gerhardt, Dick Bogert, *Close to You* (Carpenters). A&M.

Peter Klemt, *The Kaempfert Touch* (B. Kaempfert and Orchestra). Decca.

Armin Steiner, *Tap Root Manuscript* (Neil Diamond). Uni.

Derek Vernals, Adrian Martins, Robin Thompson, *To Our Children's Children's Children* (the Moody Blues). Threshold.

BEST ALBUM COVER
• Robert Lockart, design. Ivan Nagy, photography, *Indianola Mississippi Seeds* (B.B. King). ABC.

John Berg, cover. Nick Fasciano, cover art, *Chicago* (Chicago). Columbia.

John Berg, art director. Philip Hays, cover art. Lloyd Ziff, album design, *The World's Greatest Blues Singer* (Bessie Smith). Columbia.

Ed Thrasher, art director. Dave Bhang, design, *Hand Made* (Mason Williams). Warner Bros.

Desmond Strobel, art director. John Craig, design, *The Naked Carmen* (various). Mercury.

Peter Whorf, photographer. Martin Donald, designer. Christopher Whorf, art director, *Mason Proffit* (Mason Proffit). Paper Tiger.

Peter Whorf, art director. Christopher Whorf, design. Fred Poore, album design, *Schubert "Unfinished" Symphony; Beethoven Fifth Symphony* (Rodzinski conducting Philharmonic Symphony Orchestra of London). Westminster Gold.

Woody Woodward, art director. William E. McEuen, photographer. Dean O. Torrance, album design, *Uncle Charlie & His Dog Teddy* (Nitty Gritty Dirt Band). United Artists.

BEST ALBUM NOTES
(Annotator's Award)
• Chris Albertson, *The World's Greatest Blues Singer* (Bessie Smith). Columbia.

Billy Edd Wheeler, *As I See It* (Jack Moran). Athena.

Ralph J. Gleason, *Bitches Brew* (Miles Davis). Columbia.

Rod McKuen, *Hold Back the World* (Alexander's Greyhound Brass). Stanyan.

Anthony d'Oberoff, *I Do Not Play No Rock and Roll* (Mississippi Fred McDowell). Capitol.

Rex Reed, *Judy. London. 1969.* (Judy Garland). Juno.

James Goodfriend, *Sixteen All Time Greatest Hits* (Bill Monroe & the Blue Grass Boys). Columbia.

Arthur Knight, *They Shoot Horses, Don't They?* (John Green Orchestra). ABC.

Carole King, Grammy Queen

It was, wrote the *L.A. Times*, "the greatest single-year dominance by a singer-songwriter in the history of the record industry awards program. Though Paul Simon and Art Garfunkel were honored last year for best album, single record, and song (all for 'Bridge Over Troubled Water'), they lost in the best group duo vocal category to the Carpenters."

Simon & Garfunkel's Triple Crown victory last year was actually Paul Simon's accomplishment alone, since Art Garfunkel, who did share in the best record and album honors, did not participate in the writing of "Bridge," which was also voted best song. But Simon's milestone achievement was quickly eclipsed this year by a gifted artist who was little known to the public before producing one of the most lauded LPs of the era. Carole King's *Tapestry* turned out to be not only the top-selling album of 1971, but *Billboard*'s number three LP of the decade,

GLOBE PHOTO

Carole King surpassed Paul Simon's Triple Crown victory of last year when Tapestry *won an additional pop vocals performance prize.*

surpassed only by Fleetwood Mac's *Rumours* (Grammy's 1977 Album of the Year) and *Saturday Night Fever* by the Bee Gees et al. (Album of the Year, 1978). At the 1971 awards, *Tapestry* won the Triple Crown *plus* the female pop vocals performance award — thereby establishing a new record that has not been tied or topped since. (Strangely, however, King has since failed to win another Grammy.)

Prior to her new stature as a vocalist, Carole King had already proven herself the most successful female songwriter in music history, having composed eight number-one hit records, including "Will You Love Me Tomorrow?" for the Shirelles and "Hi-De-Ho" for Blood, Sweat & Tears. She wrote or co-wrote all 12 numbers on *Tapestry*, including "It's Too Late" (Record of the Year), "You've Got a Friend" (Song of the Year), and "Tapestry" (vocal performance award).

The new queen of the Grammys could not, however, be on hand for her big night at the Felt Forum at New York's Madison Square Garden where the ceremony was broadcast on ABC-

TV to a national audience for the second year in a row. Instead, King remained in Los Angeles while her producer Lou Adler accepted her four trophies (one for each of four nominations) on her behalf. "The reason Carole is not here is that she just had a baby and is home learning to be mother of the year," he told audience cheerfully.

King was not nominated for Record of the Year for "You've Got a Friend" because she never released it as a single. Roberta Flack and Donny Hathaway did, however, and were now up for Grammy's best r&b duo performance prize for their own version of it. King's real-life friend James Taylor recorded it, too (on *Mud Slide Slim and the Blue Horizon*), and was nominated for Record of the Year as well as the one trophy he would take this year: Best Pop Vocal Performance, Male (changed from the "contemporary" classification last year). As good friends as King and Taylor were, though (she played piano on his *Sweet Baby James* album and toured 27 cities with him as his opening act in early 1971), she has always insisted that "Friend" was not Taylor-made. "'You've Got a Friend' was not written for James," she once told *Billboard*. "It was one of those moments when I sat down at the piano and it wrote itself from some place other than me."

Winner of the year's Best New Artist prize, Carly Simon, was similar in spirit and music style to Taylor and King and also happened to be personally close to them (she would become Mrs. James Taylor just eight months after the Grammycast). Simon had two hit albums out in 1971 — *Carly Simon* (with its number 10–ranked single "That's the Way I've Always Heard It Should Be") and *Anticipation* (the title track of which reached number 13 as a single). Together, she, Taylor, and King were leaders of the new Seventies sound. The counterculture rev-olution of the 1960s youth movement had championed music that was usually loud, electric, and shocking — just like its performers. King, Taylor, and Simon represented a more mature and introspective approach, producing guitar-strumming tunes full of longing, love, and a new adult sense of disillusionment.

The loud, harsher rock music was still in vogue and was also expected to do well at the Grammys, but it suffered a defeat for the group vocal honors when last year's champs, Richard and Karen Carpenter, returned to reclaim the category. "We were really surprised," Richard said, picking up the award. "We both felt [Three Dog Night's] 'Joy to the World' would be the easy winner." The duo won for their eponymous album that included such hits as "For All We Know" and "Rainy Days and Mondays."

Hard rock was vindicated when Isaac Hayes and his score to the film *Shaft* picked up the second most prizes of the night (three): Best Original Score Written for a Motion Picture (beating *Love Story*, much to the surprise of N.A.R.A.S.'s rock critics), Best Instrumental Arrangement, and Best Engineered Recording. When Hayes picked up his first of the three, the audience at the Felt Forum ceremony gave him a one-minute standing ovation.

Shaft had started out with the most Grammy nominations of the year (eight), a number that amounted to a generous reflection of what music industry insiders thought of Hayes. He was clearly one of their own. As a session sax and piano player, he'd worked for Otis Redding

> *King insisted that Song of the Year "You've Got a Friend" was not (James) Taylor-made.*

Bill Withers (left) accepted his Grammy from Isaac Hayes (center) for Best Rhythm & Blues Song "Ain't No Sunshine."

and other soul greats in the 1960s. He was also an accomplished songwriter, penning "Soul Man" and "Hold On, I'm Comin'" for Sam and Dave, and "B-A-B-Y" for Carla Thomas. Hayes started singing his own material in 1967, but it wasn't until his *Hot Buttered Soul* LP (1969) that he became widely known as a performer. *Shaft* turned him into a superstar. Backstage at the Grammys, he told reporters that winning "made all the hard work worthwhile." Four weeks later, the "Theme from *Shaft*" won Best Song at the Oscars, too.

One of the five Grammys that Hayes lost went to Lou Rawls, who caused what the *L.A. Herald Examiner* called one of the biggest surprises on awards night when he claimed the male vocal r&b honors for "A Natural Man." The three-time past Grammy winner was up against tough competition that also included B.B. King, Marvin Gaye, and Stevie Wonder. Clasping his fourth statuette, Rawls said in grateful acknowledgment, "There was some heavy, heavy competition and I'm real surprised and

truly honored."

After Ike and Tina Turner recorded "Proud Mary," Tina announced that she was now a rock & roll singer instead of an r&b vocalist. She did not, however, refuse the r&b award for best vocal performance by a group when it went to her and Ike for the same single, a cut from the last album they did for Liberty Records, *Workin' Together*.

There was no surprise over the winner of the year's Best Rhythm & Blues Song, "Ain't No Sunshine," which had reached number three at its peak on the pop singles charts in 1971. "Sunshine" was written by the same artist who sang it — Bill Withers, a losing nominee for Best New Artist. The soul singer from West Virginia had moved to California in 1967 to pursue a recording career, started making music for Sussex records in 1970, and made his first professional appearance in 1971 at the age of 33.

"Lady Soul" Aretha Franklin held onto the laurels for Best Female R&B Vocal Performance for the fifth year in a row when she covered Simon & Garfunkel's "Bridge Over Troubled Water." The one-time gospel singer gave the 1970 Grammy-winning tune an inspired reading, too, that included a two-minute intro of just instrumental mood-setting music and Franklin's call-and-response interchange with her backup singers. (It's usually cut out by radio stations wanting to shorten the full five-and-a-half minute version.)

Another repeat winner from last year

was Paul McCartney, who claimed Best Arrangement Accompanying Vocalist for "Uncle Albert/Admiral Halsey" from his second solo album, *Ram*. (McCartney once told interviewer Paul Gambaccini that he actually did have an Uncle Albert, "who used to quote the Bible to everyone when he got drunk. It was the only time he ever read the Bible .... He was a good man.")

Chicago bluesman Muddy Waters, who had made a profound influence on McCartney and the other Beatles back in the early '60s, was now demonstrating how rock 'n' roll in turn affected his creative work on *They Call Me Muddy Waters*, winner of the year's best Ethnic or Traditional Recording. Waters's real name was McKinley Morganfield. He acquired the nickname because he liked to play in the muddy creeks back on the Mississippi Delta farm where he grew up.

Three-time past Grammy winner Bill Evans returned from last year to claim two more, both for *The Bill Evans Album*, a two-disk set that featured the jazz pianist and composer's original works. Evans's career was on the upswing in 1971, buoyed by the additions in his private life of a new wife and child. He formed a new trio, too, which included Eddie Gomez on bass and Marty Morrell on drums. Previously, the jazz Grammys were separated into categories for large and small groups (or soloist with large or small group), but when a third slot was added by N.A.R.A.S., it caused the honors to be split into three areas — soloist, group, and big band performance — the first two of which were won by Evans.

The big band prize went to Duke Ellington and his orchestra for their performance of one of the Duke's late masterpieces, "New Orleans Suite," his tribute to such greats as Louis Armstrong, Sidney Bechet, Wellman Braud, and Mahalia Jackson.

Singer/songwriter Kris Kristofferson was a newcomer to the country and pop charts when he began the Grammy race with the second most nominations of the year (five). Three were for writing three contenders for Best Country Song: "Help Me Make It Through the Night," "Me & Bobby McGee," and "For the Good Times." The winner: "Help Me," which was also a nominee for Song of the Year, as was "Bobby McGee." Kristofferson was inspired to write "Help Me" after reading an interview with Frank Sinatra in which Ol' Blue Eyes talked candidly about using the comforts of a woman or a bottle to get through the darkest hours of a day. "Help Me" became a brilliant success. It was named Single of the Year by the Country Music Association and sold more than two million copies when it was recorded by Sammi Smith, who beat former Grammy winners Tammy Wynette, Jody Miller, and Lynn Anderson (plus future winner Dolly Parton) for the Best Female Country Vocal Performance award.

> ### They Call Me Muddy Waters
> *demonstrated rock & roll's influence on modern blues.*

Kristofferson recorded "Help Me" on his 1971 debut album as well as "Me & Bobby McGee," which was covered — and immortalized — by Janis Joplin, a losing nominee (posthumously) for Best Female Pop Vocal Performance. Joplin had died from a heroin overdose in October, 1970.

The other two country categories went to two winners from last year: Chet Atkins and Jerry Reed. Atkins took the instrumental performance prize for his album *Snowbird* as his third Grammy. Reed took the male vocal performance laurels for singing a song of his own that was written as a fluke. In the early 1970s, Reed was a popular supporting TV star on *The Glen Campbell Goodtime Hour*. One day when he couldn't remember his next line on the program, he ad-libbed, saying, "When you're hot, you're hot!" The audience roared with approval and Reed had a song idea that would become a classic party tune.

Singer Charley Pride was not only one of the first blacks to break the color barrier in country & western music, he was voted Entertainer of the Year (and Male Vocalist of the Year) by the Country Music Association in 1971 in addition to being honored for Grammy's Best Sacred Performance for *Did You Think to Pray* as well as the year's Best Gospel Performance with "Let Me Live." The Best Soul Gospel Performance was given by Shirley Caesar, who scored a country and pop hit as well with her *Put Your Hand in the Hand of the Man from Galilee.*

Kristofferson's first Grammy was for writing Best Country Song "Help Me Make It Through the Night."

Bill Cosby was nominated again in the comedy album category (*When I Was a Kid*), but again failed to reclaim the prize that went instead to Lily Tomlin's *This Is a Recording*. Cosby still kidded around, however, in more serious way to win Best Recording for Children for *Bill Cosby Talks to Kids About Drugs*.

The choice for Classical Album of the Year and for best instrumental solo performance was *Horowitz Plays Rachmaninoff*, the now 10-time Grammy winner's tribute to the composer who once promised never again to play his

Third Concerto after hearing a young Vladimir Horowitz perform it to perfection in the early '20s (a vow Rachmaninoff nonetheless broke in 1939). In this recording, which included Études Tableaux Op. 33 and 39 plus Preludes for Piano Op. 23 and 32, "Horowitz's extra voltage and insight are manifest in innumerable ways," said *High Fidelity*. The same magazine was less kind about the winner of the orchestral laurels, guest conductor Carlo Maria Giulini and the Chicago Symphony for Mahler's *Symphony No. 1 in D*. "Giulini views the world from a narrow, Italian viewpoint that tends to reduce nearly everything to theatrics and to the strong display of rudimentary emotions," it said. "This is a position quite at odds with the personality of Mahler."

The fact that conductor Colin Davis and the London Symphony Orchestra would someday perform Berlioz's *Requiem* was considered "inevitable" by *High Fidelity*, which applauded the outcome: "This performance elucidates more dimensions of the work than any to date," it said, "and it has been recorded with considerable success by Philips engineers" at London's Westminster Cathedral. The album was awarded the engineering prize as a result, as well as the choral honors for the Wandsworth School Boys Choir and the London Symphony Chorus. The Juilliard Quartet received the chamber music award for two quartets by Ravel. "There will always be competing ideas about how to play these two quartets, but in this release the Juilliard once again establishes itself as the leading proponent of the objective approach," said *High Fidelity*.

In 1962, when Leontyne Price recorded *Aida* with Sir Georg Solti and the Rome Opera House Orchestra and Chorus, the LP was named Grammy's Classical Album of the Year. In honor of the opera's 100th anniversary, Price

Best New Artist Carly Simon (with James Taylor in background) typified what Variety *called music's "new generation."*

again recorded it, this time with Erich Leinsdorf and the London Symphony Orchestra (as well as Placido Domingo singing Radames), reprising the top opera album honors. "The new RCA set captures her somewhere near peak form," *High Fidelity* said, "singing with memorable beauty and relevance. Comparing her present performance with the one she made nine years ago, one notes a definite maturing of the voice, a certain caution now and then where she was formerly more free; but there is a compensating degree of command, of mastery not always present in the earlier version." Price, however, failed to be nominated for the vocal honors for her portrayal of the Ethiopian princess. Instead, she was nominated — and triumphed — for her tribute to Robert Schumann, including his *Widmung* and *Frauenliebe und Leben*.

"The disc industry Grammy Awards shows are getting better," *Variety* said in its wrap-up coverage article of the awards ceremony. The program "was marked by solid entertainment, attractive production values, sharp timing and an ingratiating emcee stint by Andy Williams .... The only sour note in the show was a nasty remark by Leonard Bernstein, who said he was leaving the precedings to go home and watch *West Side Story* on another network."

West Side Story was being shown at the same time on NBC that the Grammys were being aired on ABC. "The film figured to swamp the Grammy Awards show in the ratings anyway," said *Variety*, "and did."

Fifteen hundred people packed the Felt Forum to be on hand to witness the awards despite having to battle a horrid New York night of rain and sleet. Presenters included Ed Sullivan, the Temptations, Richard Harris, the Carpenters, Roberta Flack, and the 5th Dimension. In Los Angeles, 1,200 people watched the ceremony on closed circuit TV at a party held at the Century Plaza Hotel.

Some complaints were also heard. "Once again there was a notable absence of rock music in the major citations," *The New York Times* observed. "If anything, both the nominees and the winners were dominated by representatives from what can best be described as the music business Establishment."

Variety concurred: "As usual, the N.A.R.A.S. vote completely brushed off the hard rock sound. Such acts as the Rolling Stones, Grand Funk Railroad, Rod Stewart and the Faces, Elton John, Cat Stevens, Allman Bros., Emerson, Lake & Palmer, Alice Cooper, Traffic, Sly and the Family Stone, Jefferson Airplane, were not even in contention." (The charge was partially erroneous: Emerson, Lake & Palmer *were* nominated for Best New Artist.)

Nonetheless, this year's award did usher in what *Variety* called "a new generation of artists, typified by such names as Carole King, James Taylor, the Carpenters, Isaac Hayes and Kris Kristofferson." Lily Tomlin was another example of emerging new talent carrying the day, as was composer Stephen Schwartz, who reaped the Best Original Cast Show Album award for *Godspell*, beating such "Establishment" veterans as Richard Rodgers and Stephen Sondheim. *Godspell* represented the perfect marriage of the popular light folk/rock tastes of "the new generation" and conservative (religious) values of the older one.

1971

The awards ceremony was broadcast on ABC from New York's Felt Forum at Madison Square Garden on March 14, 1972, for the awards eligibility period of October 16, 1970, to October 15, 1971.

ALBUM OF THE YEAR
• *Tapestry*, Carole King. Lou Adler, A&R producer. Ode.
All Things Must Pass, George Harrison. George Harrison, Phil Spector, A&R producers. Apple.
Carpenters, Carpenters. Jack Daugherty, A&R producer. A&M.
Jesus Christ Superstar, London Production. Andrew Lloyd Webber, Tim Rice, A&R producers. Decca.
Shaft, Isaac Hayes. Isaac Hayes, A&R producer. Enterprise.

RECORD OF THE YEAR
• "It's Too Late," Carole King. Lou Adler, A&R producer. Ode.
"Joy to the World," Three Dog Night. Richard Podolor, A&R producer. Dunhill.
"My Sweet Lord," George Harrison. George Harrison, Phil Spector, A&R producers. Apple.
"Theme from *Shaft*," Isaac Hayes. Isaac Hayes, A&R producer. Enterprise.
"You've Got a Friend," James Taylor. Peter Asher, A&R producer. Warner Bros.

SONG OF THE YEAR
(Songwriter's Award)
• "You've Got a Friend," Carole King
"Help Me Make It Through the Night," Kris Kristofferson.
"It's Impossible," Sid Wayne, Armando Manzanero.
"Me & Bobby McGee," Kris Kristofferson, Fred Foster.
"Rose Garden," Joe South.

BEST NEW ARTIST
• Carly Simon. Elektra.
Chase. Epic.
Emerson, Lake & Palmer. Cotillion.
Hamilton, Joe Frank & Reynolds. Dunhill.
Bill Withers. Sussex.

BEST POP VOCAL PERFORMANCE, MALE
• James Taylor, "You've Got a Friend." Warner Bros.
Perry Como, "It's Impossible." RCA.
Neil Diamond, "I Am ... I Said." Uni.
Gordon Lightfoot, "If You Could Read My Mind." Reprise.
Bill Withers, "Ain't No Sunshine." Sussex.

BEST POP VOCAL PERFORMANCE, FEMALE
• Carole King, "Tapestry." Ode.
Joan Baez, "The Night They Drove Old Dixie Down." Vanguard.
Cher, "Gypsys, Tramps & Thieves." Kapp.
Janis Joplin, "Me & Bobby McGee." Columbia.
Carly Simon, "That's the Way I've Always Heard It Should Be." Elektra.

BEST POP VOCAL PERFORMANCE, DUO, GROUP, OR CHORUS
• Carpenters, *Carpenters*. A&M.
Bee Gees, "How Can You Mend a Broken Heart." Atco.
London stage cast, *Jesus Christ Superstar* (Andrew Lloyd Webber, Geoffrey Mitchell, Alan Doggett, Horace James). Decca.
Sonny & Cher, "All I Ever Need Is You." Kapp.
Three Dog Night, "Joy to the World." Dunhill.

BEST POP INSTRUMENTAL PERFORMANCE
• Quincy Jones, *Smackwater Jack*. A&M.
Burt Bacharach, *Burt Bacharach*. A&M.
Michel Legrand, "Theme from *Summer of '42*." Warner Bros.
Henry Mancini, "Theme from *Love Story*." RCA.

Peter Nero, "Theme from *Summer of '42*." Columbia.

BEST RHYTHM & BLUES SONG
(Songwriter's Award)
• "Ain't No Sunshine," Bill Withers.
"If I Were Your Woman," Clay McMurray, Laverne Ware, Pamela Sawyer.
"Mr. Big Stuff," Joseph Broussard, Ralph Williams, Carol Washington.
"Never Can Say Goodbye," Clifton Davis.
"Smiling Faces Sometimes," Norman Whitfield, Barrett Strong.

BEST RHYTHM & BLUES VOCAL PERFORMANCE, MALE
• Lou Rawls, "A Natural Man." MGM.
Marvin Gaye, "Inner City Blues (Make Me Wanna Holler)." Tamla/Motown.
Isaac Hayes, "Never Can Say Goodbye." Enterprise.
B.B. King, "Ain't Nobody Home." ABC.
Stevie Wonder, "We Can Work It Out." Tamla/Motown.

BEST RHYTHM & BLUES VOCAL PERFORMANCE, FEMALE
• Aretha Franklin, "Bridge Over Troubled Water." Atlantic.
Janis Joplin, *Pearl*. Columbia.
Jean Knight, "Mr. Big Stuff." Stax.
Freda Payne, *Contact*. Invictus.
Diana Ross, "I Love You (Call Me)." Motown.

BEST RHYTHM & BLUES PERFORMANCE, DUO OR GROUP, VOCAL OR INSTRUMENTAL
• Ike & Tina Turner, "Proud Mary." United Artists.
Roberta Flack, Donny Hathaway, "You've Got a Friend." Atlantic.
Isaac Hayes, "Theme from *Shaft*." Enterprise.
Gladys Knight & the Pips, "If I Were Your Woman." Soul.
Staple Singers, "Respect Yourself." Stax.

BEST JAZZ PERFORMANCE BY A SOLOIST
• Bill Evans, *The Bill Evans Album*. Columbia.
Larry Coryell, *Gypsy Queen*. Flying Dutchman.
Dizzy Gillespie, *Portrait of Jenny*. Perception.
Earl Hines, *Quintessential Recording Session*. Chiaroscuro.

Carmen McRae, *Carmen McRae*. Mainstream.
Jimmy Rushing, *The You and Me That Used to Be*. RCA.
Phil Woods, *Phil Woods & His European Rhythm Machine at the Frankfurt Jazz Festival*. Embryo.

Bill Evans's twin Grammy triumphs reflected his strong career comeback.

BEST JAZZ PERFORMANCE BY A GROUP
• Bill Evans Trio, *The Bill Evans Album*. Columbia.
Gary Burton, Keith Jarrett, *Gary Burton & Keith Jarrett*. Atlantic.
Miles Davis, *Miles Davis at the Fillmore*. Columbia.
Roy Eldridge, *The Nifty Cat*. Master Jazz.
Dizzy Gillespie, Bobby Hackett, Mary Lou Williams, *Giants*. Perception.
Herbie Hancock, *Mwandishi*. Warner Bros.
Phil Woods, *Phil Woods & his European Rhythm Machine at the Frankfurt Jazz Festival*. Embryo.

BEST JAZZ PERFORMANCE BY A BIG BAND
• Duke Ellington, "New Orleans Suite." Atlantic.
Count Basie, *Afrique*. Flying Dutchman.
Buddy Rich, *A Different Drummer*. RCA.
Maynard Ferguson, *Maynard Ferguson — M.F. Horn*. Columbia.
Woody Herman, *Woody*. Cadet.

Charley Pride was doubly blessed when he received the statuettes for both Best Sacred and Best Gospel Performances.

BEST COUNTRY SONG
(Songwriter's Award)
• "Help Me Make It Through the Night," Kris Kristofferson.
"Easy Loving," Freddie Hart.
"For the Good Times," Kris Kristofferson.
"Me & Bobby McGee," Kris Kristofferson, Fred Foster.
"Rose Garden," Joe South.

BEST COUNTRY VOCAL PERFORMANCE, MALE
• Jerry Reed, "When You're Hot, You're Hot." RCA.
Freddie Hart, "Easy Loving." Capitol.
Johnny Paycheck, "She's All I Got." Columbia.
Ray Price, "I Won't Mention It Again." Columbia.
Charley Pride, "Kiss an Angel Good Mornin'." RCA.

BEST COUNTRY VOCAL PERFORMANCE, FEMALE
• Sammi Smith, "Help Me Make It Through the Night." Mega.
Lynn Anderson, "How Can I Unlove You." Columbia.
Jody Miller, "He's So Fine." Epic.

Dolly Parton, "Joshua." RCA.
Tammy Wynette, "Good Lovin'." Epic.

BEST COUNTRY VOCAL PERFORMANCE, DUO OR GROUP
• Conway Twitty, Loretta Lynn, "After the Fire Is Gone." Decca.
Roy Acuff with the Nitty Gritty Dirt Band, "I Saw the Light." United Artists. .
Johnny Cash, June Carter, "No Need to Worry." Columbia.
Tompall & the Glaser Brothers, "Rings." MGM.
Porter Wagoner, Dolly Parton, "Better Move It on Home." RCA.

BEST COUNTRY INSTRUMENTAL
• Chet Atkins, "Snowbird." RCA.
Bakersfield Brass, *Rose Garden*. Capitol.
Floyd Cramer, *For the Good Times*. RCA.
Danny Davis & the Nashville Brass, *Ruby, Don't Take Your Love to Town*. RCA.
Jerry Kennedy, *Jerry Kennedy Plays: With All Due Respect to Kris Kristofferson*. Mercury.

BEST SACRED PERFORMANCE (MUSICAL)
• Charley Pride, *Did You Think to Pray*. RCA.
Pat Boone Family, *Pat Boone Family*. Word.
Anita Bryant, *Abide With Me*. Word.
Dolly Parton, *Golden Streets of Glory*. RCA.
George Beverly Shea, "Amazing Grace." RCA.

BEST SOUL GOSPEL PERFORMANCE
• Shirley Caesar, *Put Your Hand in the Hand of the Man from Galilee*. Hob.
Blind Boys of Alabarria, *The Five Blind Boys of Alabama*. Hob.
Dottie Rambo, *Pass Me Not*. Heartwarming.
Valerie Simpson, *There Is a God*. Tamla/Motown.
Clara Ward, *Great Moments in Gospel*. Hob.

BEST GOSPEL PERFORMANCE, OTHER THAN SOUL GOSPEL
• Charley Pride, "Let Me Live." RCA.
Blackwood Brothers, *He's Still King of Kings*. RCA.
Imperials, *Time to Get It Together*. Impact.
Hovie Lister with the Statesmen, *Put Your Hand in the Hand*. Skylite.
Oak Ridge Boys, *Jesus Christ, What a Man*. Impact.

BEST ETHNIC OR TRADITIONAL RECORDING (INCLUDING TRADITIONAL BLUES)

• *They Call Me Muddy Waters*, Muddy Waters. Chess.
18th Century Traditional Music of Japan, Keiko Matsuo. Everest.
The Esso Trinidad Steel Band, Esso Trinidad Steel Band. Warner Bros.
Javanese Court Gamelan, Javanese Players. Robert E. Brown, producer. Nonesuch.
Message to the Young, Howlin' Wolf. Chess.
Mississippi Fred McDowell, Mississippi Fred McDowell. Everest.
Stormy Monday Blues, T-Bone Walker. Blues-Time.

BEST INSTRUMENTAL COMPOSITION
(Composer's Award)

• Michel Legrand, "Theme from *Summer of '42*." Warner Bros.
Duke Ellington, "New Orleans Suite." Atlantic.
Isaac Hayes, "Theme from *Shaft*." Enterprise.
Francis Lai, "Theme from *Love Story*." Paramount.
Chuck Mangione, "Hill Where the Lord Hides." Mercury.

BEST SCORE FROM AN ORIGINAL CAST SHOW ALBUM

• *Godspell*, composed and produced by Stephen Schwartz. Bell.
Follies, Stephen Sondheim. Richard C. Jones, A&R producer. Capitol.
The Rothschilds, Jerry Bock, Sheldon Harnick. Thomas Z. Shepard, A&R producer. Columbia.
Touch, Kenn Long, Jim Crazier. Glenn Osser, A&R producer. Ampex.
Two by Two, Richard Rodgers, Martin Charnin. Thomas Z. Shepard, A&R producer. Columbia.

BEST ORIGINAL SCORE, MOTION PICTURE OR A TELEVISION SPECIAL
(Composer's Award)

• *Shaft*, Isaac Hayes. Stax.
Bless the Beasts & Children, Barry DeVorzon, Perry Botkin, Jr. A&M.
Friends, Elton John, Bernie Taupin. Paramount.
Love Story, Francis Lai. Paramount.
Ryan's Daughter, Maurice Jarre. MGM.

BEST INSTRUMENTAL ARRANGEMENT

• Isaac Hayes, Johnny Allen, "Theme from *Shaft*." Enterprise.
Michel Colombier, "Earth." A&M.
Michel Legrand, "Theme from *Summer of '42*." Warner Bros.
Joshua Rifkin, "Nightingale II." Elektra.
Don Sebesky, "The Rite of Spring" (Hubert Laws). CTI.

When he scored three awards for Shaft, *sudden superstar Isaac Hayes said they made "all the hard work worthwhile."*

BEST ARRANGEMENT ACCOMPANYING VOCALIST(S)

• Paul McCartney, "Uncle Albert/Admiral Halsey" (Paul & Linda McCartney). Apple.
Burt Bacharach, Pat Williams, "Long Ago Tomorrow" (B.J. Thomas). Scepter.
Richard Carpenter, "Superstar" (Carpenters). A&M.
Michel Colombier, "Freedom and Fear" (Bill Medley). A&M.
David Van Depitte, "What's Going On" (Marvin Gaye). Tamla/Motown.

ALBUM OF THE YEAR, CLASSICAL

• *Horowitz Plays Rachmaninoff* (Etudes—Tableaux, Piano Music, Sonatas), (solo: Vladimir Horowitz). Richard Killough, Thomas Frost, A&R producers. Columbia.
Berlioz: Requiem, Colin Davis conducting London Symphony; Russell Burgess conducting Wandsworth School Boys' Choir; Arthur Oldham conducting London Symphony Chorus. Vittorio Negri, A&R producer. Philips.

Boulez Conducts Boulez: Pli Selon Pli, Pierre Boulez conducting BBC Symphony. Paul Myers, A&R producer. Columbia.

Crumb: Ancient Voices of Children, Arthur Weisberg conducting Contemporary Chamber Ensemble (solos: Degaetani, Dash). Teresa Sterne, A&R producer. Nonesuch.

Haydn: Symphonies Nos. 65–72 (Vol. 1), Antal Dorati conducting Philharmonia Hungarica. James Mallinson, A&R producer. London.

Janácek: Sinfonietta; Lutoslavski: Concerto for Orchestra, Seiji Ozawa conducting Chicago Symphony. Peter Andry, A&R producer. Angel.

Mahler: Symphony No. 1 in D Major, Carlo Maria Giulini conducting Chicago Symphony. Christopher Bishop, A&R producer. Angel.

Penderecki: Utrenja, the Entombment of Christ, Eugene Ormandy conducting Philadelphia Orchestra. Robert Page directing Temple University Choirs. Peter Dellheim, A&R producer. RCA.

Shostakovich: Symphony No. 14, Eugene Ormandy conducting Philadelphia Orchestra (solos: Curtin, Estes). Max Wilcox, A&R producer. RCA.

Tippett: The Midsummer Marriage, Colin Davis conducting Royal Opera House Orchestra, Covent Garden. Erik Smith, A&R producer. Philips.

BEST CLASSICAL PERFORMANCE, ORCHESTRA
(Conductor's Award)

• Carlo Maria Giulini conducting Chicago Symphony, *Mahler: Symphony No. 1 in D Major*. Angel.

Pierre Boulez conducting BBC Symphony, *Boulez Conducts Boulez: Pli Selon Pli*. Columbia.

Pierre Boulez conducting Cleveland Orchestra, *Boulez Conducts Ravel*. Columbia.

Antal Dorati conducting Philharmonia Hungarica, *Haydn: Symphonies Nos. 65–72 (Vol. 1)*. London.

Bernard Haitink conducting London Philharmonic, *Holst: The Planets*. Philips.

Jascha Horenstein conducting London Symphony, *Mahler: Symphony No. 3 in D Minor*. Nonesuch.

Eugene Ormandy conducting Philadelphia Orchestra, *Respighi: The Fountains of Rome; The Pines of Rome*. Columbia.

André Previn conducting London Symphony, *Vaughan Williams: Symphony No. 4 in F Minor*. RCA.

BEST CLASSICAL PERFORMANCE, INSTRUMENTAL SOLOIST(S) (WITH ORCHESTRA)

• Julian Bream (Previn conducting London Symphony), *Villa-Lobos: Concerto for Guitar*. RCA.

Kyung-Wha Chung (Previn conducting London Symphony), *Sibelius: Concerto in D Minor for Violin; Tchaikovsky: Concerto in D Major for Violin*. London.

Van Cliburn (Ormandy conducting Philadelphia Orchestra), *Rachmaninoff: Rhapsody on a Theme of Paganini; Liszt: Concerto No. 2 in A Major*. RCA.

Jacqueline du Pre (Barenboim conducting Chicago Symphony), *Dvorak: Concerto in B Minor for Cello*. Angel.

Igor Kipnis (Marriner conducting London Strings), *Bach: Complete Concertos for Harpsichord & Orchestra*. Columbia.

Yehudi Menuhin (Walton conducting New Philharmonia), *Walton: Concerto for Violin & Orchestra; Concerto for Viola & Orchestra*. Angel.

David Oistrakh, Mstislav Rostropovich, Sviatoslav Richter (von Karajan conducting Berlin Philharmonic), *Beethoven: Triple Concerto (Concerto in C Major for Violin, Piano & Cello, Op. 56)*. Angel.

Henryk Szeryng (Kubelik conducting Bavarian Symphony), *Berg: Concerto for Violin & Orchestra; Martinon: Concerto for Violin*. Deutsche Grammophon.

Paul Zukofsky (Thomas conducting Boston Symphony), *William Schuman: Concerto for Violin*. Deutsche Grammophon.

BEST CLASSICAL PERFORMANCE, INSTRUMENTAL SOLOIST(S) (WITHOUT ORCHESTRA)

• Vladimir Horowitz, *Horowitz Plays Rachmaninoff* (Etudes—Tableaux, Piano Music, Sonatas). Columbia.

Stephen Bishop, *Bartók: Mikrokosmos, Vol. 6; Out of Doors Suite; Sonatina*. Philips.

Aldo Ciccolini, *Satie: Piano Music of Erik Satie*, Vol. 5. Angel.

Van Cliburn, *Barber: Sonata for Piano; Prokofiev: Sonata No. 6 in A Major*. RCA.

Alicia de Larrocha, *Alicia de Larrocha Plays Spanish Piano Music of the 20th Century*. London.

Glenn Gould, *Bach: Well-Tempered Clavier, Book 2, Vol. 3 Preludes & Fugues 17–24*. Columbia.

Joshua Rifkin, *Piano Rags by Scott Joplin*. Nonesuch.

Artur Rubinstein, *The Brahms I Love*. RCA.

Rudolf Serkin, *Beethoven: Sonata No. 29 in B Flat Op. 106 "Hammerklavier."* Columbia.

BEST CHAMBER MUSIC PERFORMANCE

• Juilliard Quartet, *Debussy: Quartet in G Minor; Ravel: Quartet in F Major*. Columbia.

Beaux Arts Trio, *Dvorak: Piano Trios (Complete)*. Philips.

Jan DeGaitani, Michael M. Dash (Arthur Weisberg conducting Contemporary Chamber Ensemble), *Crumb: Ancient Voices of Children*. Nonesuch.

Nikolaus Harnoncourt conducting Concentus Musicus, *Fux-Schmelzer: Music in the Hapsburg Palace*. Telefunken.

Jascha Heifetz, Brooks Smith, *Schubert: Fantaisie in C Major for Violin (& Piano), Op. 159*. RCA.

Jean-Pierre Rampal, Isaac Stern, Alexander Schneider, Leonard Rose, *The Mozart Quartets for Flute*. Columbia.

Paul Zukofsky, Gilbert Kalish, Charles Russo, Robert Sylvester (New York String Quartet), *Ives: Chamber Music*. Columbia.

BEST OPERA RECORDING

• *Verdi: Aida*, Erich Leinsdorf conducting London Symphony, John Alldis Choir (solos: Price, Domingo, Milnes, Bumbry, Raimondi). Richard Mohr, A&R producer. RCA.

Massenet: Manon, Julius Rudel conducting New Philharmonia & Ambrosian Opera Chorus (solos: Sills, Gedda, Souzay, Bacquier). Michael Williamson, A&R producer. Audio Treasury.

Mozart: The Magic Flute, Georg Solti conducting Vienna Philharmonic (solos: Prey, Lorengar, Burrows, Fischer-Dieskau, Deutekom, Talvela). Christopher Raeburn, A&R producer. London.

Puccini: Il Tabarro, Erich Leinsdorf conducting New Philharmonia; John Aldis Choir (solos: Price, Domingo, Milnes). Richard Mohr, A&R producer. RCA.

Tippett: The Midsummer Marriage, Colin Davis conducting Royal Opera House, Covent Garden (solos: Remedios, Carlyle, Burrows, Harwood) Erik Smith, A&R producer. Philips.

Verdi: Don Carlo, Carlo Maria Giulini conducting Orchestra of Royal Opera House. Covent Garden & Ambrosian Opera Chorus (solos: Domingo, Caballe, Raimondi, Milnes, Verrett). Christopher Bishop, A&R producer. Angel.

Wagner: Die Meistersinger Von Nurnberg, Herbert von Karajan conducting Dresden State Opera Orchestra and Choruses of Dresden State Opera and Leipzig Radio (solos: Adam, Donath, Kollo, Evans, Schreider). R. Kinloch Anderson, Diether Gerhardt Worm, A&R producers. Angel.

Wagner: Parsifal, Pierre Boulez conducting Bayreuth Festival Orchestra and Chorus (solos: Stewart, Ridderbusch, Crass, King, Jones, McIntyre). Dr. Hans Hirsch, A&R producer. Deutsche Grammophon.

BEST CLASSICAL PERFORMANCE, VOCAL SOLOIST

• Leontyne Price (Garvey, accompanist), *Leontyne Price Sings Robert Schumann*. RCA.

Janet Baker, Dietrich Fischer-Dieskau, *An Evening of Duets*. Angel.

Cathy Berberian (Berio conducting BBC Symphony), *Berio: Epifanie*. RCA.

Phyllis Curtin, Simon Estes (Ormandy conducting Philadelphia Orchestra), *Shostakovich: Symphony No. 14*. RCA.

Dietrich Fischer-Dieskau (Peters conducting Vienna Haydn Orchestra), *Haydn & Mozart Arias*. London.

Evelyn Lear, Thomas Stewart, *Ives: American Scenes/American Poets*. Columbia.

Elisabeth Schwarzkopf (Furtwangler, accompanist), *Wolf: Songs (Salzburg Festival 1953)*. Seraphim.

BEST CHORAL PERFORMANCE, OTHER THAN OPERA

• Colin Davis conducting London Symphony; Russell Burgess conducting Wandsworth School Boys' Choir. Arthur Oldham conducting London Symphony Chorus, *Berlioz: Requiem*. Philips.

Wolfgang Fromme conducting Collegium Vocale of Cologne, *Stockhausen: Stimmung.* Deutsche Grammophon.

Robert Page directing Temple University Choirs. Eugene Ormandy conducting Philadelphia Orchestra, *Penderecki: Utrenja, the Entombment of Christ.* RCA.

Ensti Pohjola conducting Helsinki University Men's Choir. Paavo Berglund conducting Bournemout Symphony, *Sibelius: Kullervo,* Op. 7. Angel.

Gennady Rozhdestvensky conducting Moscow Radio Chorus and Moscow Radio Symphony, *Prokofiev: Seven, They Are Seven.* Melodia/Angel.

Roger Wagner conducting Los Angeles Master Chorale. Zubin Mehta conducting Los Angeles Philharmonic, *Verdi: Four Sacred Pieces.* London.

BEST ENGINEERED RECORDING, CLASSICAL

• Vittorio Negri, *Berlioz: Requiem* (Davis conducting London Symphony; Burgess conducting Wandsworth School Boys' Choir; Oldham conducting London Symphony). Philips.

Marc J. Aubort, *Crumb: Ancient Voices of Children* (Weisberg conducting Contemporary Chamber Ensemble; solos: Jan de Gaetani, Michael Dash). Nonesuch.

Paul Goodman, *Tchaikovsky: 1812 Overture; Beethoven: Wellington's Victory* (Ormandy conducting Philadelphia Orchestra). RCA.

Gunter Hermanns, *Holst: The Planets* (Steinberg conducting Boston Symphony). Deutsche Grammophon.

Gordon Parry, *Beethoven: Egmont—Complete Incidental Music* (Szell conducting Vienna Philharmonic). London.

Carson C. Taylor, *Janácek: Sinfonietta* (Ozawa conducting Chicago Symphony). Angel.

Carson C. Taylor, *Mahler: Symphony No. 1 in D Major* (Giulini conducting Chicago Symphony). Angel.

BEST SPOKEN WORD RECORDING

• *Desiderata*, Les Crane. Warner Bros.

Hamlet, Richard Chamberlain. RCA.

I Can Hear It Now—The Sixties, Walter Cronkite. Columbia.

Long Day's Journey Into Night, Stacy Keach, Robert Ryan, Geraldine Fitzgerald. Caedmon.

Will Rogers' U.S.A. James Whitmore. Columbia.

BEST COMEDY RECORDING

• *This Is a Recording*, Lily Tomlin. Polydor.

Ajax Liquor Store, Hudson & Landry. Dore.

Cheech & Chong, Cheech & Chong. Ode.

Flip: The Flip Wilson Show, Flip Wilson. Little David.

When I Was a Kid, Bill Cosby. Uni.

BEST RECORDING FOR CHILDREN

• *Bill Cosby Talks to Kids About Drugs*, Bill Cosby. Uni.

Sesame Street, Rubber Duckie & Other Songs from Sesame Street, Richard Wolfe Children's Chorus. Camden.

Sex Explained for Children, Dr. Stanley Daniels. Carapan.

The Story of Scheherazade, Julie Harris. Caedmon.

Willy Wonka & the Chocolate Factory, Golden Orchestra and Chorus (Peter Moore, conductor). Golden.

BEST ENGINEERED RECORDING, NON-CLASSICAL

• Dave Purple, Henry Bush, Ron Capone, "Theme from *Shaft*" (Isaac Hayes). Enterprise.

Ray Gerhardt, Dick Bogert, *Carpenters* (Carpenters). A&M.

Bones Howe, *The 5th Dimension Live!* (5th Dimension). Bell.

Larry Levine, Roger Roche, *Wings* (Michel Colombier). A&M.

Armin Steiner, "Stones" (Neil Diamond). Uni.

BEST ALBUM COVER

• Gene Brownell, art director. Dean O. Torrance, designer, *Pollution* (Pollution). Prophesy.

John Berg, art director. Robert Lockart, design. Norman Seeff, photos and art, *B, S & T 4* (Blood, Sweat & Tears). Columbia.

Vincent J. Biondi, art director. Susan Obrant, illustration, *The Music of Erik Satie: Through a Looking Glass* (Camarata Contemporary Chamber Orchestra). Dream.

Acy Lehman, concept and design. Nick Sangiamo, photographer, *Bark* (Jefferson Airplane). Grunt.

Norman Seeff, art director. John Van Hamersveld, cover, *Black Pearl* (Jimmy McGriff). United Artists.

Ed Thrasher, art director. John Van Hamersveld, design, *Hot Platters* (Various). Warner Bros.

Ed Thrasher, art director. Terry Paul, photographer, *Sharepickers* (Mason Williams). Warner Bros.

Andy Warhol, photographer. Craig Braun, graphics, *Sticky Fingers* (Rolling Stones). Rolling Stones.

ALBUM NOTES
(Anotator's Award)
• Sam Samudio, *Sam Hard and Heavy* (Samudio). Atlantic.

Colman Andrews, *Miles Davis*. United Artists.

Don Demicheal, *The Genius of Louis Armstrong*. Columbia.

Nat Hentoff, *Louis Armstrong July 4, 1900–July 6, 1971*. RCA.

James Lyons, *Music of Varese* (Simonovitch conducting Paris Instrumental Ensemble). Angel.

Joshua Rifkin, *Piano Rags by Scott Joplin* (Rifkin). Nonesuch.

George T. Simon, *This Is Benny Goodman*. RCA.

Tom West, *Honky Tonkin' with Charlie Walker*. Epic.

Saving *Face* and *Bangla Desh*

"The [N.A.R.A.S.] voting membership is getting younger and younger," academy national manager Chris Farnon announced prior to the Grammycast when she revealed the results of a recent membership study, "and each year the nominations get more with it." When the results were in, Warner Bros. Records president Joe Smith agreed: "The records and artists that won were outstanding as far as both artistic contributions and sales."

Don McLean ("American Pie") and Aretha Franklin (with several strong recordings) were the early front runners with four nominations each, followed by Neil Diamond, Roberta Flack, Nilsson, Donna Fargo, and Michel Legrand, all with three bids apiece. The top prizes were expected to be split between "American Pie" and Diamond's "Song Sung Blue," although Gilbert O'Sullivan's "Alone Again (Naturally)" and Flack's "The First Time Ever I Saw Your Face" were also given a strong chance. All four tunes were up for both Record and Song of the Year. In the contest for Album of the Year, the conclusion seemed foregone: Surely, went the prevailing industry wisdom, the phenomenally successful *American Pie* LP would get its just desserts.

"American Pie" was McLean's musical elegy to what he perceived as the decline of rock & roll. It was so successful, in fact, that it ended the year at number one in *Billboard*'s Hot 100 and had a passionate following among tuned-in young music lovers who studied its cryp-

Record of the Year "The First Time Ever I Saw Your Face," from Roberta Flack's debut album, was popularized by the hit film Play Misty for Me.

tic lyrics for hidden meaning. Had it pulled off its expected Grammy sweep, the victory would have reflected well on N.A.R.A.S.'s renewed hipness, but when it failed to win *any* awards, the shock was only surpassed by the surprise of what won Album of the Year instead: a three-disc LP that showcased serious rockers shunned in the past (Bob Dylan and Eric Clapton among them) and had received only a single nomination.

The Concert for Bangla Desh set another Grammy precedent: It was the first of the cause-oriented, fund-raising works that would involve a host of name artists and take high honors in future years, such as Record and Song of the Year in 1985 "We Are the World" (famine relief for Africa) and Song of the Year in 1986 "That's What Friends Are For" (AIDS research and awareness).

Bangla Desh was the first rock-concert benefit of its kind ever held and was organized by ex-Beatle George Harrison to raise relief money for the war-torn and famine-plagued Asian nation (although subsequent tax problems, legal battles, and distribution foul-ups would tie up the funds for nearly a decade). The show employed the talents of Dylan (in his first U.S. appearance in three years; he was greeted by a screaming, 10-minute ovation), Clapton, Leon Russell, Ringo Starr, Billy Preston, Klaus Voormann, and Ravi Shankar (Harrison's sitar instructor during his flirtation with Eastern religion) in a historic U.N.I.C.E.F. benefit at New York City's Madison Square Garden. The other two Beatles were also invited, but Paul McCartney refused because of a lawsuit he had pending to dissolve the Beatles officially, and John Lennon declined on the basis that his invitation clearly excluded a performance by his wife, Yoko Ono. Highlights of the concert included Dylan singing "Just Like a Woman" and "Blowin' in the Wind" and Harrison and Clapton's rendition of the Beatles' "While My Guitar Gently Weeps."

That Dylan finally won a Grammy (along with other first-timers Clapton, Russell, Preston, and producer Phil Spector) should have been cause for jubilation in the press, but *The Hollywood Reporter* was among those who groused nonetheless, noting that "Dylan won for the first time for his appearance on 25 percent of the album, Leon Russell won his first for 9 minutes, and Ringo Starr received one for 2 and a half minutes." Starr acknowledged the victory on behalf of them all and, according to the *Herald Examiner*, "was in fine form as he picked up a sackful of the miniature gramophone statuettes."

The ceremony took place at the Tennessee Auditorium in Nashville, triggering the biggest controversy of all. ABC had broadcast the first two live Grammy shows, which had taken place in Los Angeles and New York, but disapproved of the choice of venue this year and refused to participate. NBC declined, too, but CBS picked up the option, reluctantly, and only after considerable prodding. When the telecast received favorable notices in the press once again and, even more important to network executives, pulled an amazing 53 percent TV audience share, ABC realized its mistake too late. CBS would thereafter hold onto Grammys' broadcast rights and ABC, while claiming to hold no grudge, set about establishing the new American Music Awards, overseen by producer Dick Clark, who was also the host of the television series *American Bandstand*.

In addition to the staging of another polished ceremony and the triumph of *Bangla Desh*, what made the Grammys so "with it" this year was the winner of both Record and Song of the Year — a tune that was rescued from near-obscurity after it was recorded three years earlier. "The

Everyone expected Album and Record of the Year nominee **American Pie** *to get its just desserts.*

First Time Ever I Saw Your Face" was a track from Roberta Flack's 1969 debut album *First Take*, appropriately named since all eight songs were recorded in only 10 hours. Long after the album's release, Flack was still crooning a living in Washington, D.C., night spots when she got a phone call one day from Clint Eastwood, who was filming *Play Misty for Me* and needed a haunting love melody to underscore the film's eerie theme of an obsessed fan stalking a radio deejay. "Film fans ran from the theaters to record stores asking for the song," *Billboard* noted, "which Atlantic quickly rushed into their hands after slicing 66 seconds from its five minute, 21 second length to accommodate Top 40 radio airplay. At 33 years old, after being involved with music for 24 years, Roberta Flack scored her first commercial success." "First Time" ended up at number two in 1972's Hot 100, just behind losing Record of the Year nominee "American Pie."

Roberta Flack picked up another Grammy when the ballad "Where Is the Love" (number five–ranked single for two weeks) won Best Pop Vocal Performance by a Duo, Group, or Chorus for her and Donny Hathaway, who was once billed as "the nation's youngest gospel singer" when he made his debut public performance in Chicago at the age of three. "Miss Flack was not in Nashville," however, *The Washington Post* noted, because she was back in Washington "conducting a program of Hall Johnson spirituals by the Frederick Wilkerson Choir at the Kennedy Center Concert Hall."

In the running for Best New Artist was an impressive lineup this year — America, Harry Chapin, the Eagles, Loggins & Messina, and John Prine. After losing the pop vocal prize to Flack and Hathaway, America won the new artist award. The folk/rock trio of expatriates met in a school for children of U.S. servicemen stationed in London. They had a huge British following thanks to their popular performances at London's Roadhouse club, but were unknown back home before their "A Horse with No Name" reached number one for three weeks on the U.S. singles charts and ended up ranked number nine for the year.

The most famous acceptance speech in the history of the Grammys was given this year by Helen Reddy when she picked up the trophy for Best Female Pop Vocal Performance for "I Am Woman," her spirited celebration of womanhood that became an anthem for feminists. The Australian-born vocalist co-wrote the "chest-beating song of pride" herself with Ray Burton after searching for a tune "that reflected the positive sense of self that I felt I'd gained from the women's movement," she once told *Billboard*. When she was rewarded with the Grammy, she said, "I want to thank everyone concerned at Capitol Records, my husband and manager Jeff Wald, because he makes my success possible, and God because She makes everything possible." Following the broadcast, Reddy was flooded with protest letters from religious fundamentalists.

The 1969 Grammy winner for "Everybody's Talkin'," Nilsson (who had dropped his first name Harry in professional circles) returned to take the male pop vocal performance award again, this time for his number four hit in 1972's Hot 100 "Without You." *Bangla Desh*'s Billy Preston won a second trophy when the one-time gospel singer snagged the laurels for best pop instrumental performance for "Outa-Space." A second instrumental prize was introduced this year for performances "with vocal coloring," and went to Isaac Hayes, the singer and sax and piano player of *Black Moses* who had picked up two Grammys last year for his *Shaft* soundtrack.

In the 10 years that the Temptations

> *Miffed over CBS's success airing the Grammys, ABC created the American Music Awards.*

had been performing, they had won one Grammy (in 1968 for "Cloud Nine — Motown's only victory for the decade) and had three number-one hits, including "My Girl," "Just My Imagination," and "I Can't Get Next to You." Their fourth and last chart-topper to date, "Papa Was a Rolling Stone," "proved lucky for everyone connected with it," said the *Herald Examiner*. It reaped Best R&B Vocal Performance by a Group, Best R&B Instrumental Performance, and Best R&B Song — thereby becoming 1972's biggest Grammy-winning single. "Yet it missed the Record of the Year award," *The Hollywood Reporter* griped. "It wasn't even nominated."

A song that displaced "I Am Woman" at number one on the pop singles chart garnered the R&B male vocals prize for Billy Paul, but not without causing some "rumblings" according to the *Herald Examiner*. "Me and Mrs. Jones," a soul tune called "middle of the road (almost 1940s style)" by *Variety*, was challenged for being classified as an R&B single. "Why?" *Variety* was among those asking. "Because the singer of the record, Billy Paul, is black?"

Aretha Franklin was nominated in three different categories — r&b, soul gospel, and pop — losing only the laurels for pop muisc when they went to Helen Reddy. Franklin nabbed the soul gospel prize for her classic rendition of "Amazing Grace" (Aretha at her most amazing, said the critics), which she performed with the Rev. James Cleveland acting as pianist plus conductor of the Southern California Community Choir. She also held onto the r&b female vocal category for an equally amazing sixth year in a row, this time for her LP *Young, Gifted & Black*. The Blackwood Brothers returned for their fourth miniature gramophone for *L-O-V-E*, named Best Gospel Performance. Also returning was Elvis Presley, who took the

instrumental kudos for another of his religious albums, *He Touched Me*. (He won for the first time in 1967.)

Despite failing health, Duke Ellington, at the age of 72, continued to record and was honored with a ninth Grammy for his big band performance of "Togo Brava Suite." It was the last that the esteemed Duke would win in his lifetime, although he would be awarded two more, posthumously, in 1976 and 1979.

Two Grammy first-timers took the other two jazz accolades. Classically trained vibraphone player Gary Burton garnered the soloist honors for *Alone at Last,* an LP recording of his 1971 performance at Switzerland's Montreux Jazz Festival. Trumpeter Freddie Hubbard and his troupe took the group prize for *First Light*, which contained several of Hubbard's lyrical ballad renditions in addition to his controversial jazz interpretations of such pop hits as Paul McCartney's "Uncle Albert/ Admiral Halsey."

The Best Country Song of the year was a number one c&w hit for five weeks that subsequently crossed over to the weekly pop Hot 100. "Kiss an Angel Good Mornin'" was written by Ben Peters (about his newborn daughter Angela) and was sung by the double Grammy winner of last year Charley Pride, who this year returned to take one more for Best Country Male Vocal Performance for his LP *Charley Pride Sings Heart Songs*.

It was the year's top-selling country song that reaped the female vocal prize for Donna Fargo, who also wrote "Happiest Girl in the Whole U.S.A.," winner of the Single of the Year accolades from both the Country Music Association and the Academy of Country Music. ("Happiest Girl" and Fargo's "Funny Face" were both losers of the Grammy country song award.) "I only became a writer so I could become a singer," the former schoolteacher once told *Billboard*. After

The Chicago Symphony Orchestra, under the baton of Sir Georg Solti, performed Mahler's Symphony No. 8, winner of three awards, including best classical album.

she recorded a demo of her song, however, "Happiest Girl" was rejected by more than a half-dozen record companies before it was finally picked up by Dot Records, which made it a hit.

This was the third year in a row that the Country Music Association named the Statler Brothers the Vocal Group of the Year. The previous winners of two Grammys in 1965 came back to claim further honors when their "Class of '57" (about a graduating class facing the disillusionment of early adulthood) brought them N.A.R.A.S.'s group vocal prize, too. The instrumental trophy went to the harmonica and guitar player Charlie McCoy, for *The Real McCoy*.

Comedian George Carlin first gained popularity as a frequent *Tonight Show* guest in the late 1960s, but, as the 1970s dawned, he became more irreverent, grew his hair long (some said so that he could look like a *Doonesbury* comic strip character) and even got arrested in 1972 for giving a public performance of his infamous "Seven Words You Can Never Use on Television" routine. (The charges were later dropped.) His overdue Grammy for Best Comedy Recording went to *FM & AM*, which included a parody of the TV show *Let's Make a Deal*, an impression of Ed Sullivan, and a skit called "The 11 O'Clock News" in which Carlin delivered such grabber headlines as "Good Humor Man Slays 10," "Pen Pal Stabs Pal with Pen," and "Jacques Cousteau Dies in Bathtub Accident."

"The happiest by-product of this year's balloting involved the actual choices among the classical winners," the *L.A. Times* reported. Mahler's *Symphony No. 8*, with Sir Georg Solti conducting the Chicago Symphony, swept three of them and was, the *Times* added, an "eminently defensible choice": Classical Album of the Year, Best Choral Performance, and Best Engineered Recording. The orchestra traveled to Austria to tape the symphony at Vienna's Sofiensaal. "And Solti?" asked *High Fidelity*. "He carries it to the highest pitch of exaltation and excitement."

Solti also recorded Mahler's Symphony No. 7 this year (traveling only 150 miles from Chicago to do so, to the Krannert Center at the University of Illinois at Champaign-Urbana) and picked up the Grammy for orchestral honors that eluded him for Mahler's Eighth for which he was not even nominated. The result was an achievement in "clarity and refinement" that amounted, said *High Fidelity*, in "the best-sounding Mahler Seventh we have."

"The grand old man of the keyboard did take the predictable laurels," the *Times* said of Artur Rubinstein when he seized his fifth career Grammy for Brahms's *Concerto No. 2*. "If Rubinstein wins one prize, [Vladimir] Horowitz cannot be far behind," the paper added. "True to form, he defeated all potential threats in the recital category with his all-Chopin album" that included Polonaise No. 6 in A Flat and *Polonaise-Fantaisie*. (It was Horowitz's eleventh win.) The chamber music honors went to guitarists Julian Bream and John Williams for their selections by Sor, Ravel, and Falla.

The year's best opera prize was claimed by conductor Colin Davis, the BBC Symphony, and the Chorus of Covent Garden for *Benvenuto Cellini*, Berlioz's first opera and his last to be recorded on disc. "Davis is, of course, the premier Berlioz conductor of his day, and his sense of pacing, his ability to achieve orchestra clarity, his eye for the long-range shape are much in evidence," said *High Fidelity*. Tenor Nicholai Gedda performed the lead role, but the vocalist award went to baritone

Dietrich Fischer-Dieskau for *Die Schöne Magelone* by Brahms.

When the year's awards ceremony was over, *The Hollywood Reporter* said "it was a well done show," adding, "there were several standouts such as the pairing of Moms Mabley and Johnny Mann as presenters, the 5th Dimension singing a medley of songs during the presenting time, the performances of the Staple Singers and Don McLean, and the simultaneous cue card reading of Ringo Starr and Nilsson." Other highlights included Charley Pride singing "Kiss an Angel Good Mornin'," Helen Reddy doing "I Am Woman," and Donna Fargo's performance of "Happiest Girl in the Whole U.S.A." "On the negative side," added the *Reporter*, "the special effects of dancing girls behind Mac Davis's number and [emcee] Andy Williams' medley were distracting, and the smoke machine was so overpowering in Curtis Mayfield's number that he couldn't even be seen."

"I Am Woman" winner Helen Reddy thanked God "because She makes everything possible."

The program also had other dramatic moments. "We lost power eight minutes before air time," producer Pierre Cossette remembered years later in an interview with *TV Guide*. "I got on the phone with Joe Hamilton (Carol Burnett's husband and producer of the Grammy show) and asked him what *Carol Burnett Show* he wanted to rerun. Then a minute before air time, the power went on."

The broadcast out of Nashville included time for only 11 winners, "leaving the other 36 to a $25 roast beef dinner crowd in Los Angeles, which plodded through dozens of no-shows, then sat down or left for a two-color (purple and green) closed-circuit TV feed from Nashville," complained *Rolling Stone.*

While the award results were certainly more "with it" this year, there were still the usual oversights that caused the predicted "chorus of complaints." Among the artists who were passed up for nominations was Sarah Vaughan (who sang two Michel Legrand hits, including his Song of the Year nominee "The Summer Knows" and his Grammy-winning "What Are You Doing the Rest of Your Life"; Legrand also won a second award for his theme to the hit TV film *Brian's Song*). Also overlooked were Al Green ("the top selling singles artist of 1972," said the *L.A. Times*), previous winners Paul Simon and Carole King (both of whom had more hit music this year) and "some of the rock artists whose work was widely acclaimed in 1972 — including David Bowie, Procol Harum and Cat Stevens," the *Times* added.

N.A.R.A.S. had made a serious effort to improve the nominee lineup in advance of the voting by forming an advisory committee of sixteen record company presidents in addition to a National Screening Committee that "met in a New York hotel suite and spent nine hours trying to sort out the 4,000 'pre-nominations' and place them in proper categories before the ballot for final nominations," *Rolling Stone* pointed out. "But by the nature of the business (last year, as one example, over 4,200 albums were released), and by the nature of popular music, the committee had an impossible job ....

"Aside from the omissions," *Rolling Stone* added, "the most embarrassing aspect of this year's balloting was the Album of the Year nomination received by the *Jesus Christ Superstar* Broadway cast album. It was the original London [studio] cast album that received both the sales and critical attention. The obvious assumption is that lots of N.A.R.A.S. voters confused this album with the original."

The jazz awards also suffered the blues, particularly since jazz was not performed on the ceremony telecast. Furthermore, "a hassle over the definition of jazz has led to jazz flutist Herbie Mann's resignation" from the record academy, *Variety* reported. "Mann was unhappy over the jazz category for N.A.R.A.S.'s Grammy Awards in which the music was to be judged by the 'intention' of the performer."

1972

The awards ceremony was broadcast on CBS from Nashville's Tennessee Auditorium on March 3, 1973, for the awards eligibility period of October 16, 1971, to October 15, 1972.

ALBUM OF THE YEAR

• *The Concert for Bangla Desh*, George Harrison & Friends (Ravi Shankar, Bob Dylan, Leon Russell, Ringo Starr, Billy Preston, Eric Clapton, Klaus Voormann, others). George Harrison, Phil Spector, A&R producers. Apple.

American Pie, Don McLean. Ed Freeman, A&R producer. United Artists.

Jesus Christ Superstar, Orginal Broadway Cast. Andrew Lloyd Webber, Tim Rice, composers. Tom Morgan, A&R producer. Decca.

Moods, Neil Diamond. Tom Catalano, Neil Diamond, producers. Uni.

Nilsson Schmilsson, Nilsson. Richard Perry, A&R producer. RCA.

RECORD OF THE YEAR)

• "The First Time Ever I Saw Your Face," Roberta Flack. Joel Dorn, A&R producer. Atlantic.

"Alone Again (Naturally)," Gilbert O'Sullivan. Gordon Mills, A&R producer. MAM/London.

"American Pie," Don McLean. Ed Freeman, A&R producers. United Artists.
"Song Sung Blue," Neil Diamond. Tom Catalano, Neil Diamond, A&R producer. Uni.
"Without You," Nilsson. Richard Perry, A&R producer. RCA.

SONG OF THE YEAR
(Songwriter's Award)
• "The First Time Ever I Saw Your Face," Ewan MacColl.
"Alone Again (Naturally)," Gilbert O'Sullivan.
"American Pie," Don McLean.
"Song Sung Blue," Neil Diamond.
"The Summer Knows," Marilyn & Alan Bergman, Michel Legrand.

BEST NEW ARTIST
• America. Warner Bros.
Harry Chapin. Elektra.
Eagles. Asylum.
Loggins & Messina. Columbia.
John Prine. Atlantic.

BEST POP VOCAL PERFORMANCE, MALE
• Nilsson, "Without You." RCA.
Mac Davis, "Baby, Don't Get Hooked on Me." Columbia.
Sammy Davis, Jr., "Candy Man." MGM.
Don McLean, "American Pie." United Artists.
Gilbert O'Sullivan, "Alone Again (Naturally)." MAM/London.

BEST POP VOCAL PERFORMANCE, FEMALE
• Helen Reddy, "I Am Woman." Capitol.
Roberta Flack, *Quiet Fire*. Atlantic.
Aretha Franklin, "Day Dreaming." Atlantic.
Carly Simon, *Anticipation*. Elektra.
Barbra Streisand, "Sweet Inspiration/ Where You Lead." Columbia.

BEST POP VOCAL PERFORMANCE
BY A DUO, GROUP, OR CHORUS
• Roberta Flack, Donny Hathaway, "Where Is the Love." Atlantic.
America, "A Horse With No Name." Warner Bros.
Bread, *Baby I'm-a Want You*. Elektra.
New Seekers, "I'd Like to Teach the World to Sing (in Perfect Harmony)." Elektra.
Seals & Crofts, "Summer Breeze." Warner Bros.

APPLE RECORDS

Album of the Year The Concert for Bangla Desh *featured a host of star talent in the first major rock concert benefit.*

BEST POP INSTRUMENTAL PERFORMANCE BY AN INSTRUMENTAL PERFORMER
• Billy Preston, "Outa-Space." A&M.
Apollo 100, "Joy." Mega.
Doc Severinsen, *Doc*. RCA.
Pipes & Drums & Military Band of the Royal Scots Dragoon Guards, *Amazing Grace*. RCA.
Mahavishnu Orchestra with John McLaughlin, *The Inner Mounting Flame*. Columbia.

BEST POP INSTRUMENTAL PERFORMANCE BY AN ARRANGER, COMPOSER, ORCHESTRA, AND/OR CHORAL LEADER
• Isaac Hayes, *Black Moses*. Enterprise.
Cy Coleman, "Theme from *The Garden of the Finzi Continis*." London.
Emerson, Lake & Palmer, *Pictures at an Exhibition*. Cotillion/Atlantic.
Quincy Jones, "Money Runner." Reprise.
Henry Mancini, Doc Severinsen, *Brass on Ivory*. RCA.
Santana, *Caravanserai*. Columbia.

BEST RHYTHM & BLUES SONG
(Songwriter's Award)
• "Papa Was a Rolling Stone," Barrett Strong, Norman Whitfield.
"Back Stabbers," Leon Huff, Gene McFadden, John Whitehead.
"Everybody Plays the Fool," Rudy Clark, J.R. Bailey, Kenny Williams.
"Freddie's Dead," Curtis Mayfield.
"Me and Mrs. Jones," Ken Gamble, Leon Huff, Cary Gilbert.

Best Rhythm & Blues Vocal Performance, Male

• Billy Paul, "Me and Mrs. Jones." Philadelphia International.
Ray Charles, "What Have They Done to My Song Ma." Tangerine.
Curtis Mayfield, "Freddie's Dead." Curtom.
Joe Simon, "Drowning in the Sea of Love." Spring.
Joe Tex, "I Gotcha." Dial/Mercury.

Best Rhythm & Blues Vocal Performance, Female

• Aretha Franklin, *Young, Gifted & Black*. Atlantic.
Merry Clayton, "Oh, No Not My Baby." Ode.
Esther Phillips, *From a Whisper to a Scream*. Kudu/CTI.
Candi Staton, "In the Ghetto." Fame.
Betty Wright, "Clean Up Woman." Alston/Atlantic.

Best Rhythm & Blues Vocal Performance by a Duo, Group, or Chorus

• Temptations, "Papa Was a Rolling Stone." Gordy/Motown.
Gladys Knight & the Pips, "Help Me Make It Through the Night." Soul/Motown.
Harold Melvin & the Blue Notes, "If You Don't Know Me By Now." Philadelphia International.
Spinners, "I'll Be Around." Atlantic.
Staple Singers, "I'll Take You There." Stax.

Best Rhythm & Blues Instrumental Performance

• Temptations & Paul Riser, conducting, "Papa Was a Rolling Stone." Gordy/Motown.
Crusaders, *Crusaders I*. Blue Thumb.
King Curtis, "Everybody's Talkin'." Atco.
Isaac Hayes, "Let's Stay Together," Enterprise.
Curtis Mayfield, "Junkie Chase" (track). Curtom.

Best Jazz Performance by a Soloist

• Gary Burton, *Alone at Last*. Atlantic.
Freddie Hubbard, *The Hub of Hubbard*. MPS/BASF.
Tom Scott, *Great Scott*. A&M.
Sonny Stitt, *Tune-Up!* Cobblestone.
McCoy Tyner, *Sahara*. Milestone.

Best Jazz Performance by a Group

• Freddie Hubbard, *First Light*. CTI.
George Benson, *White Rabbit*. CTI.
Joe Farrell, *Outback*. CTI.
Chuck Mangione, *The Chuck Mangione Quartet*. Mercury.
McCoy Tyner, *Sahara*. Milestone.
Weather Report, *I Sing the Body Electric*. Columbia.

Best Jazz Performance by a Big Band

• Duke Ellington, "Togo Brava Suite." United Artists.
Kenny Clark, Francy Boland Big Band, *All Smiles*. MPS/BASF.
Don Ellis, *Connection*. Columbia.
Maynard Ferguson, *M.F. Horn Two*. Columbia.
Gerry Mulligan, *The Age of Steam*. A&M.

Best Country Song
(Songwriter's Award)

• "Kiss an Angel Good Mornin'," Ben Peters.
"Delta Dawn," Alex Harvey, Larry Collins.
"Funny Face," Donna Fargo.
"Happiest Girl in the Whole U.S.A.," Donna Fargo.
"Woman (Sensuous Woman)," Gary S. Paxton.

Best Country Vocal Performance, Male

• Charley Pride, *Charley Pride Sings Heart Songs*. RCA.
Merle Haggard, "It's Not Love (But It's Not Bad)." Capitol.
Waylon Jennings, "Good Hearted Woman." RCA.
Jerry Lee Lewis, "Chantilly Lace." Mercury.
Charlie Rich, "I Take It on Home." Epic.

Best Country Vocal Performance, Female

• Donna Fargo, "Happiest Girl in the Whole U.S.A." Dot.
Skeeter Davis, "One Tin Soldier." RCA.
Loretta Lynn, "One's on the Way." Decca.
Dolly Parton, "Touch Your Woman." RCA.
Tanya Tucker, "Delta Dawn." Columbia.
Tammy Wynette, "My Man." Epic.

BEST COUNTRY VOCAL PERFORMANCE BY A DUO OR GROUP
• Statler Brothers, "Class of '57." Mercury.
Mother Maybelle Carter, Earl Scruggs, Doc Watson, Roy Acuff, Merle Travis, Jimmy Martin, Nitty Gritty Dirt Band, *Will the Circle Be Unbroken*. United Artists.
Johnny Cash, June Carter, "If I Had a Hammer." Columbia.
George Jones, Tammy Wynette, "Take Me." Epic.
Conway Twitty, Loretta Lynn, *Lead Me On*. Decca.

BEST COUNTRY INSTRUMENTAL PERFORMANCE
• Charlie McCoy, *The Real McCoy*. Monument.
Chet Atkins, *Chet Atkins Picks on the Hits*. RCA.
Chet Atkins, Jerry Reed, *Me and Chet*. RCA.
Danny Davis & the Nashville Brass, *Flowers on the Wall*. RCA.
Lester Flatt, "Foggy Mountain Breakdown." RCA.

BEST INSPIRATIONAL PERFORMANCE
• Elvis Presley, *He Touched Me*. RCA.
Little Jimmy Dempsey, *Award Winning Guitar*. Skylite.
Merle Haggard, *Land of Many Churches*. Capitol.
Danny Lee & the Children of Truth, *Spread a Little Love Around*. RCA.
Eugene Ormandy conducting Philadelphia Orchestra and Chorus, *The Greatest Hits of Christmas*. RCA.
Pipes & Drums & Military Band of the Royal Scots Dragoon Guards, "Amazing Grace," track. RCA.
Ray Stevens, "Love Lifted Me." Barnaby.

BEST SOUL GOSPEL PERFORMANCE
• Aretha Franklin, "Amazing Grace." Atlantic.
B.C. & M. Choir, *My Sweet Lord*. Creed.
Aretha Franklin, James Cleveland, "Precious Memories," track. Atlantic.
Edwin Hawkins Singers, "Jesu." Buddah.
Clara Ward, "Last Mile of the Way." Nashboro.

BEST GOSPEL PERFORMANCE (OTHER THAN SOUL GOSPEL)
• Blackwood Brothers, *L-O-V-E*. RCA.
Wendy Bagwell & the Sunliters, *By Your Request*. Canaan.
Oak Ridge Boys, *Light*. Heartwarming.
Rambos, *Soul in the Family*. Heartwarming.
Thrasher Brothers, *America Sings*. Canaan.

BEST ETHNIC OR TRADITIONAL RECORDING (INCLUDING TRADITIONAL BLUES)
• *The London Muddy Waters Session*, Muddy Waters. Chess.
Blues Piano Orgy, Little Brother Montgomery, Roosevelt Sykes, Sunnyland Slim, Speckled Red, Otis Spann, Curtis Jones. Robert G. Koester, producer. Delmark.
Lightnin' Strikes, Lightnin' Hopkins. Tradition/Everest.
Live at Soledad Prison, John Lee Hooker. ABC.
Walking the Blues, Otis Spann. Barnaby.

BEST INSTRUMENTAL COMPOSITION
(Composer's Award)
• Michel Legrand, "Brian's Song." Bell.
Don Ellis, "Theme from *The French Connection*." Columbia.
Henry Mancini, "Brass on Ivory." RCA.
Billy Preston, Joe Greene, "Outa-Space." A&M.
Nino Rota, "Theme from *The Godfather*." Paramount.

BEST INSTRUMENTAL ARRANGEMENT
• Don Ellis, "Theme from *The French Connection*" (Don Ellis). Columbia.
Richard Carpenter, "Flat Baroque" (Carpenters). A&M.
Quincy Jones, "Money Runner" (Quincy Jones. Reprise.
Henry Mancini, "Theme from *the Mancini Generation*" (Henry Mancini). RCA.
Don Sebesky, "Lonely Town" (Freddie Hubbard). CTI.

BEST SCORE FROM AN ORIGINAL CAST SHOW ALBUM
• *Don't Bother Me I Can't Cope*, Micki Grant, composer. Jerry Ragavoy, producer. Polydor.
Ain't Supposed to Die a Natural Death, Melvin Van Peebles, composer and producer. A&M.

Grease, Warren Casey, Jim Jacobs, com-
posers. Arnold Maxin, producer.
MGM.
Sugar, Jule Styne, Bob Merrill, composers.
Mitch Miller, producer. United Artists.
Two Gentlemen of Verona, John Guare,
Galt MacDermott, composers. Harold
Wheeler, Galt MacDermott, Lee
Young, producers. ABC.

BEST ORIGINAL SCORE WRITTEN FOR A MOTION PICTURE OR A TELEVISION SPECIAL
(Composer's Award)
• *The Godfather*, Nino Rota. Paramount.
"$" Soundtrack, Quincy Jones. Reprise.
The Garden of the Finzi Continis, Manuel
DeSica. RCA.
Nicholas and Alexandra, Richard Rodney
Bennett. Bell.
Superfly, Curtis Mayfield. Curtom.

BEST ARRANGEMENT ACCOMPANYING VOCALIST(S)
• Michel Legrand, "What Are You Doing
the Rest of Your Life" (Sarah Vaugh-
an). Mainstream.
Thom Bell, "Betcha By Golly, Wow"
(Stylistics). Avco.
Michel Legrand, "The Summer Knows"
(Sarah Vaughan). Mainstream.
Don Sebesky, "Day by Day" (Jackie &
Roy). CTI.
Don Sebesky, "Lazy Afternoon" (Jackie &
Roy). CTI.

ALBUM OF THE YEAR, CLASSICAL
• *Mahler: Symphony No. 8 in E Flat Major
(Symphony of a Thousand)*, Georg
Solti conducting Chicago Symphony,
Vienna Boys Choir, Vienna State
Opera Chorus, Vienna Singverein Cho-
rus and soloists. David Harvey, pro-
ducer. London.
Berlioz: Benvenuto Cellini, Colin Davis
conducting BBC Symphony Chorus of
Covent Garden (solos: Gedda, Eda-
Pierre, Soyer, Berbie). Erik Smith, pro-
ducer. Philips.
Bernstein: Mass, Leonard Bernstein con-
ducting Choirs and Orchestra. John
McClure, Richard Killough, producers.
Columbia.
*Brahms: Concerto No. 2 in B Flat Major
for Piano*, Eugene Ormandy conduct-
ing Philadelphia Orchestra.(solo: Artur
Rubinstein). Max Wilcox, producer.
RCA.

*Horowitz Plays Chopin (Polonaise in A
Flat Major Intro & Rondo, Op. 16,
etc.)* (solo: Horowitz). Richard Kil-
lough, Thomas Frost, producers.
Columbia.
Wagner: Tannhauser, Georg Solti con-
ducting Vienna Philharmonic (solos:
Kolio, Dernesch, Ludwig, Braun,
Sotin). Ray Minshull, producer.
London.

BEST CLASSICAL PERFORMANCE, ORCHESTRA
(Conductor's Award)
• Georg Solti conducting Chicago Sym-
phony, *Mahler: Symphony No. 7 in E
Minor*. London.
Pierre Boulez conducting New York Phil-
harmonic, *Boulez Conducts Bartók:
The Miraculous Mandarin & Dance
Suite*. Columbia.
Antal Dorati conducting Philharmonia
Hungarica, *Haydn: Symphonies (Com-
plete) Vol. 4 & 5*. London.
Eugene Ormandy conducting Philadelphia
Orchestra, *Gliere: Ilya Murometz
(Symphony No. 3)*. RCA.
Maksim Shostakovich conducting Moscow
Radio Symphony, *Shostakovich: Sym-
phony No. 15*. Melodiya/Angel.
Leopold Stokowski conducting London
Symphony, *Ives: Orchestral Set No. 2*.
London.
Michael Tilson Thomas conducting Boston
Symphony, *Stravinsky: Rite of Spring
(Sacre du Printemps)*. Deutsche Gram-
mophon.
Herbert von Karajan conducting Berlin
Philharmonic, *Schumann: Symphonies
(4)*. Deutsche Grammophon.

BEST CHAMBER MUSIC PERFORMANCE
• Julian Bream, John Williams, *Julian &
John* (selections by Lawes, Carulli,
Albéniz, Granados). RCA.
Guarneri Quartet, *Schubert: Quartet No.
13 in A Minor*. RCA.
Igor Kipnis, Thurston Dart, *Music for Two
Harpsichords* (Mozart, Byrd, Farnably,
etc.). Columbia.
La Salle Quartet, *String Quartets of the
New Viennese School*. Deutsche Gram-
mophon.
David Oistrakh, Sviatoslav Richter,
*Shostakovich: Sonata for Violin &
Piano*. Melodiya/Angel.
Artur Rubinstein, Guarneri Quartet, *Dvorak:
Quintet in A Major for Piano*. RCA.

Isaac Stern, Alexander Zakin, *Bartók: Sonatas No. 1 & 2 for Violin and Piano*. Columbia.

John Williams, Rafael Puyana, *Music for Guitar & Harpsichord* (works by Straube, Ponce, Dodgson). Columbia.

BEST INSTRUMENTAL SOLOIST PERFORMANCE, CLASSICAL (WITH ORCHESTRA)

• Artur Rubinstein (Ormandy conducting Philadelphia Orchestra), *Brahms: Concerto No. 2 in B Flat Major for Piano*. RCA.

Philippe Entremont (Boulez conducting Cleveland Orchestra), *Ravel: Concerto in D Major for Left Hand*. Columbia.

Heinz Holliger (DeWaart conducting New Philharmonia), *Strauss: Concerto in D Major for Oboe*. Philips.

David Oistrakh (Berlin Philharmonic), *Mozart: Complete Works for Violin & Orchestra.* Angel.

E. Power Biggs (Peress conducting Columbia Brass Percussion Ensemble), *Music for Organ, Brass & Percussion*. Columbia.

Barry Tuckwell (Marriner conducting Academy of St. Martin-in-Fields), *Mozart: The Four Horn Concertos*. Angel.

BEST INSTRUMENTAL SOLOIST PERFORMANCE, CLASSICAL (WITHOUT ORCHESTRA)

• Vladimir Horowitz, *Horowitz Plays Chopin*. Columbia.

Laurindo Almeida, *The Art of Laurindo Almeida*. Orion.

Rudolf Firkusny, *Janácek: Piano Works (Complete)*. Deutsche Grammophon.

William Masselos, *Schumann: Davidsbundlertanze; Brahms: Sonata No. 1.* RCA.

Arturo Beneditti Michelangeli, *Debussy: Images, Books 1 & 2 Children's Corner Suite*. Deutsche Grammophon.

Itzhak Perlman, *Paganini: The 24 Caprices*. Angel.

Rafael Puyana, *Couperin: Harpsichord Pieces*. Philips.

Charles Rosen, *Beethoven: The Late Sonatas for Piano*. Columbia.

BEST OPERA RECORDING

• *Berlioz: Benvenuto Cellini*, Colin Davis conducting BBC Symphony; Chorus of Covent Garden (solos: Gedda, Eda-Pierre, Soyer, Berbie). Erik Smith, producer. Philips.

Britten: Owen Wingrave, Benjamin Britten conducting English Chamber Orchestra (solos: Baker, Pears, Luson, Harper). David Harvey, producer. London.

Mussorgsky: Boris Godunov, Herbert von Karajan conducting Vienna Philharmonic Vienna Boys Choir, Vienna State Opera Chorus (solos: Ghaiurov, Vishnevskaya, Spiess, Talvela, Maslennikov). Ray Minshull, producer. London.

Strauss: Der Rosenkavalier, Leonard Bernstein conducting Vienna State Opera Chorus; Vienna Philharmonic (solos: Ludwig, Berry, Popp, Jones). John Culshaw, producer. Columbia.

Wagner: The Ring of the Nibelung, Wilhelm Furtwangler conducting Rome Symphony; RAI Chorus (solos: Modl, Suthaus, Frantz). Bicknell, Radiotelevisione Italiana, producers. Seraphim.

Wagner: Tannhauser, Georg Solti conducting Vienna Philharmonic (solos: Kollo, Dernesch, Ludwig, Braun, Sotin). Ray Minshull, producer. London.

BEST CHORAL PERFORMANCE, CLASSICAL (OTHER THAN OPERA)

• Georg Solti conducting Vienna State Opera chorus, Vienna Singverein Chorus, Vienna Boys Choir, Chicago Symphony, Soloists, *Mahler: Symphony No. 8 in E Flat Major (Symphony of a Thousand)*. London.

Leonard Bernstein conducting Orchestra and Norman Scribner and Berkshire Boys Choirs, *Bernstein: Mass*. Columbia.

Charles Groves conducting London Philharmonic Choir and Orchestra, *Delius: A Mass of Life*. Angel.

Raymond Leppard conducting Glyndebourne Opera Chorus, Ambrosian Singers, English Chamber Orchestra, *Monteverdi: Madrigals, Books 8, 9 and 10*. Philips.

E. Power Biggs, Gregg Smith Singers, Texas Boys Choir, Gregg Smith. Vittorio Negri conducting Tarr Brass Ensemble, *The Glory of Venice*

(Gabrielli in San Marco—Music for Multiple Choirs, Brass & Organ). Columbia.

André Previn conducting London Symphony Chorus and Orchestra, *Prokofiev: Alexander Nevsky*. Angel.

Best Vocal Soloist Performance, Classical

• Dietrich Fischer-Dieskau (Richter, accompaniment), *Brahms: Die Schöne Magelone*. Angel.

Janet Baker (Barbirolli conducting London Symphony), *Elgar: Sea Pictures*. Angel.

Jan de Gaetani (Kalish, accompaniment), *Songs by Stephen Foster*. Nonesuch.

Anna Moffo (Robert Casadesus, accompaniment), *Songs of Debussy*. RCA.

Birgit Nilsson (Davis conducting London Symphony), *Wagner: Wesendonck Lieder*. Philips.

Leontyne Price (Cleva conducting London Symphony), *Five Great Operatic Scenes (Verdi: La Traviata, Don Carlo; Tchaikovsky: Onegin; Strauss: Ariadne, etc.)*. RCA.

Best Engineered Recording, Classical

• Gordon Parry, Kenneth Wilkinson, *Mahler: Symphony No. 8 (Symphony of a Thousand)* (Solti conducting Chicago Symphony). London.

Paul Goodman, *Gliere: Ilya Murometz (Symphony No. 3)* (Ormandy conducting Philadelphia Orchestra). RCA.

Edward Graham, Raymond Moore, *Boulez Conducts Bartók; The Miraculous Mandarin (Complete) & Dance Suite* (Boulez conducting New York Philharmonic; Hugh Ross directing Schola Cantorum). Columbia.

Hans Lauterslager, *Berlioz: Benvenuto Cellini* (Davis conducting BBC Symphony, Chorus of Covent Garden). Philips.

Raymond Moore, Edward Graham, *Boulez Conducts Stravinsky (Petrushka)* (Boulez conducting New York Philharmonic). Columbia.

Gordon Parry, James Lock, Colin Moorfoot, *Wagner: Tannhauser* (Solti conducting Vienna Philharmonic). London.

Don Puluse, *Bernstein: Mass* (Bernstein conducting Choirs and Orchestra). Columbia.

Best Spoken Word Recording

• *Lenny*, Original cast. Bruce Botnick, producer. Blue Thumb.

Angela Davis Speaks, Angela Davis. Folkways.

Cannonball Adderley Presents Soul Zodiac, Rick Holmes, narrator. Capitol.

The Word, Rod McKuen. Discus/Stanyan.

Yevtushenko, Yevtushenko. Columbia.

Best Comedy Recording

• *FM & AM*, George Carlin. Little David.

All in the Family, the Bunkers (Carroll O'Connor, Jean Stapleton, Sally Struthers, Robert Reiner). Atlantic.

Big Bambu, Cheech & Chong. Ode.

Geraldine, Flip Wilson. Little David.

Best Recording for Children

• *The Electric Company*, Lee Chamberlin, Bill Cosby, Rita Moreno. Warner Bros.

Kukla, Fran & Ollie, Kukla, Fran & Ollie. RCA/Camden.

The Muppet Alphabet Album, Muppets (Jim Henson). Columbia Children's Album.

Sesame Street II, Original TV Cast. Joe Raposo, Jeffrey Moss, producers. Warner Bros

Snoopy, Come Home, Original Cast. Robert B. & Richard M. Sherman, composers. Columbia.

Best Engineered Recording

• Armin Steiner, *Moods* (Neil Diamond). Uni.

Robin Cable, Ken Scott, Phillip Mac Donald, *Son of Schmilsson* (Nilsson). RCA.

Eddy Offord, *Fragile* (Yes). Atlantic.

Ken Scott, *Honky Chateau* (Elton John). Uni.

Armin Steiner, *Baby I'm-a Want You* (Bread). Elektra.

Best Album Cover

• Acy Lehman, art director. Harvey Dinnerstein, artist, *The Siegel-Schwall Band* (Siegel-Schwall Band). Wooden Nickel.

Hipgnosis, art direction & design. Poe, photographer, *Flash* (Flash). Capitol.

Ron Levine, art director. Pacific Eye & Ear, concept & design. Robert Rodriguez, illustrations, *Five Dollar Shoes* (Five Dollar Shoes). Neighborhood/Famous.

Bill Levy, art director. Fred Marcellino, design, *Virgin (The Mission)*. Paramount.

Aaron Schumaker for Tumbleweed Graphics, album design & cover art, *Chief* (Dewey Terry). Tumbleweed.

Norman Seeff, art director & cover photographer, *Historical Figures and Ancient Heads* (Canned Heat). United Artists.

Ed Thrasher, Chris Wolf, art directors. Dave Willardson, illustrator. John & Barbara Casado, graphics, *Sunset Ride* (Zephyr). Warner Bros.

Wilkes & Braun, Inc., album design. Robert Otter, photographer. Sound Packaging Corp., jacket concept, *School's Out* (Alice Cooper). Warner Bros.

BEST ALBUM NOTES, CLASSICAL
(Annotator's Award)
• James Lyons, *Vaughan Williams: Symphony No. 2 (A London Symphony)* (Previn conducting London Symphony). RCA.

David Cairns, *Berlioz: Benvenuto Cellini* (Davis conducting BBC Symphony). Philips.

Tom Eastwood, *Julian & John* (Julian Bream, John Williams). RCA.

Karolynne Gee, *Michael Rabin—in Memoriam* (Michael Rabin). Seraphim.

H. C. Robbins Landon, *Haydn: Symphonies (Complete) Vols. 4 & 5* (Dorati conducting Philharmonia Hungarica). London.

Sacheverell Sitwell, *John Ogdon Plays Alkan* (John Ogdon). RCA.

Dr. Ursula Von Rauchhaupt, *String Quartets of the New Viennese School* (la Salle Quartet) Deutsche Grammophon.

BEST ALBUM NOTES
(Annotator's Award)
• Tom T. Hall, *Tom T. Hall's Greatest Hits* (Tom T. Hall). Mercury.

Michael Brooks, *Super Chief* (Count Basie). Columbia.

Albert Goldman, *Lenny Bruce/Carnegie Hall* (Lenny Bruce). United Artists.

Charles Mingus, *Let My Children Hear Music* (Charles Mingus). Columbia.

Dan Morgenstern, *Bunny Berigan, His Trumpet & His Orchestra, Volume 1* (Bunny Berigan). Vintage.

A Comeback for Flack

The excitement surrounding what would turn out to be a "dynamite" Grammycast (so decreed the *The Hollywood Reporter*) could be seen in the early scramble for tickets. The Hollywood Palladium was oversold before the show and the *L.A. Times* even publicly bemoaned N.A.R.A.S.'s "delicate, ego-bruising" plight of having to decide who would get in, and then, once inside — and even more important — who would be seated at the front tables. (That was decided by lottery.) "This year's turnout is expected to be the most star-studded in the Grammy's 16-year history," the paper promised.

The hoopla was really about another scramble — for the top honor of Record of the Year, which was a surprisingly close race involving all five nominees. Last year's victor Roberta Flack was back, this time with her latest ultra-hit "Killing Me Softly with His Song." 1971's Best New Artist, Carly Simon, had just scored with "You're So Vain," and Charlie Rich's first country hit, "Behind Closed Doors," was considered a close contender, not just because of Nashville's predictable backing, but also because of its crossover success from the country to pop charts. Jim Croce, who had died in a plane crash the previous September, had the sentimental vote locked up for his "Bad, Bad Leroy Brown." And all of them were up against the artist with the most nominations of the night (six), Stevie Wonder ("You Are the Sunshine of My Life"), who was long overdue for a Grammy, having lost on four occasions in the past.

Four of the tunes were also up for Song of the Year, the one exception

Last year's winner of Record of the Year, Roberta Flack, returned triumphant with "Killing Me Softly with His Song."

being "Leroy Brown," which was replaced on the songwriter's line-up by the number-one platter in the year's Hot 100, Tony Orlando & Dawn's "Tie a Yellow Ribbon Round the Ole Oak Tree" (normally a shoo-in, said N.A.R.A.S. critics, considering academy's historic love of "easy listening" standards). But the winner of both Song and Record of the Year turned out to be "Killing Me Softly with His Song."

Never before had the recipient of Grammy's highest honor returned the following year to claim Record of the Year again, nor has it been repeated since. "Killing Me Softly" was another huge hit for Flack (number eight in *Billboard*'s 1973 Hot 100), earning her the Best Pop Female Vocal Performance award, too. Flack was still riding high from her Grammy triumphs of last year when one day, on a TWA flight from Los Angeles to New York, she was flipping through the pages of the in-flight magazine. Her eye fell on the title of a Lori Leiberman song that was listed as one of the music selections on board and it intrigued her enough to plug in her headphones to hear it. "By the time I got to New York I knew I had to do that song and I knew I'd be able to add something to it," Flack once told *High Fidelity*. "My classical background made it possible for me to try a number of things with it. I changed parts of the chord structure and chose to end on a major chord. It wasn't written that way."

Flack worked to perfect her recording for three arduous months in the studio, a sharp contrast to the circumstances surrounding the taping of last year's victorious "The First Time Ever I Saw Your Face," which had been recorded in about an hour. While clutching her ultimate reward on stage at the Palladium on Grammy night, Flack chose to thank Atlantic Records "for having the good sense to sign me."

Roberta Flack may have snatched the top laurels, but it turned out to be Stevie Wonder who took the most bows at the awards ceremony. Like Croce, Wonder had sentiment on his side because of a tragedy he'd suffered just months before the votes were tallied. The Motown star had been in a car crash near Winston-Salem, North Carolina, while making a concert tour of the South, and received multiple head injuries that left him in a coma for four days. He had been sleeping in the passenger seat when the car collided with a truck loaded down with logs, a few of which tumbled off and crashed into the car's windshield. Frankly, said the doctors, it was a wonder that he was still among the living. The artist's mother, Lula Hardaway, was with him on Grammy night and helped her blind son up to the podium to accept his trophies. She told the ceremony crowd, "I can only thank God he's alive to accept these awards."

Wonder dedicated his first victory of the night to her. "I would like for you all not to give this to me, but to my mother," he said in his acceptance remarks, also thanking his brother Calvin, who rescued him from the wrecked car. The trophy was one of his two Rhythm & Blues prizes (Best R&B Song and Best R&B Male Vocal Performance) for the chart-topping single "Superstition." Wonder had written it originally for ex-Yardbird guitarist Jeff Beck, who did record it — in a bluesy style — but not for single release. A frustrated Wonder then went ahead and made his own pop-rock version for the radio airwaves and record stores.

Wonder won a third Grammy when he received the honors for Best Pop Male Vocal Performance for "You Are the Sunshine of My Life," a million-selling single on which he performed most of the instrumentals in addition to

Best New Artist Bette Midler billed herself as "Trash with Flash."

doing the singing. Accepting the golden gramophone for his work, he said, "I would like to thank all of you for making this night the sunshine of my life."

"Superstition" and "Sunshine" were both from his hit *Talking Book* LP, which, strangely, was not nominated for Album of the Year. Wonder's follow-up album, *Innervisions*, was, however, and included such classics as "Higher Ground," "Living for the City," and "Don't You Worry 'Bout a Thing." When *Innervisions* nabbed both the LP prize and Best Engineered Recording, it crowned a night of success that was a vindication for Wonder, who recently had become the first headliner to produce his own albums for Motown. It was also his first LP to feature work exclusively written and sung by him. At age 23, Wonder's victory came close to making another breakthrough, too: He was now the second youngest artist to receive the Album of the Year award. (Barbra Streisand was 22 when she won in 1963.) "I hope that all of you know I am fantastically grateful," he said in his thank-you remarks.

The late jazz great Art Tatum was hailed for his jam sessions on **God Is in the House.**

Gladys Knight & the Pips also proved their crossover appeal from r&b to pop when they, like Wonder, reaped Grammys in both fields. Also, like Wonder, the group had been working for Motown for more than a decade and its members felt they didn't have enough control over their careers. Knight and the Pips made their break from the Detroit label in 1973, but not before scoring one last (and ironically titled) single success with "Neither One of Us (Wants to Be the First to Say Goodbye)," about two people in a relationship who are reluctant to walk away. The disc hit number two in the best sellers and earned them the prize for Best Pop Vocal Performance by a Group. Rock critic Dave Marsh once wrote of the recording: "The aching husk in Knight's voice, so dry she might have been sucking lemons, proves the perfect device for breaking the ice, and her languid phrasing embodies the emotional inertia still holding such lives in thrall to one another."

After saying goodbye to Motown, Knight and the Pips signed up with Buddah Records and had their first chart-topper since 1967's "I Heard It Through the Grapevine" with their release of "Midnight Train to Georgia." The troupe's latest number-one single was from their new *Imagination* album, which Knight coproduced, and it brought them the r&b group vocals prize, too. In later years with Buddah, they would score such further Top 10 hits as "Best Thing That Ever Happened to Me" and "On and On."

Another of the r&b awards went to jazz great Ramsey Lewis, whose keyboard cover of the 1965 pop song "Hang On Sloopy" (originally performed by the McCoys, who never had a follow-up hit) earned him the r&b instrumental performance trophy. The r&b prize for female vocals went — just as it had for the previous six years — to Aretha Franklin for "Master of Eyes." Lady Soul was now officially Lady Grammy, too. Franklin's victory set the new record for having the longest winning streak in the music award's history, toppling the six-year reign of comedian Bill Cosby (1964–69).

Aretha Franklin's latest recordings were being produced by three-time past Grammy champ Quincy Jones, who picked up yet another Grammy Award this year, Best Instrumental Arrangement, for "Summer in the City," his hit single that he also sang. The instrumental performance statuette for pop music was claimed by Brazilian-born pianist Eumir Deodato for *Also Sprach Zarathustra*, his hipped-up interpretation of the Richard Strauss masterwork that was used — in its original, more tame version — in the 1968 blockbuster movie *2001: A Space Odyssey*.

The victories by Flack, Wonder, Knight, Lewis, Franklin, and Jones were popular with even the grumpiest of

Grammy critics because all of the winners were long-time artists who possessed enormous talent as well as the respect of the music industry. The choice of Grammy's Best New Artist, on the other hand, represented the "Trash with Flash" contingent of musicdom: a "broad" who proudly labeled herself "the last of the truly tacky ladies." But the bawdy Bette Midler also had lots of talent that lifted her to celebrity status when her *The Divine Miss M* album soared up the charts in 1973. Her

Presenter Alice Cooper, left, posed backstage with Stevie Wonder, who had survived a recent car crash to emerge victorious at the Grammys with a total of four awards.

tackiness would catch up with her on Grammy night, however. The award was bestowed to an obviously embarrassed Midler by, of all people, Karen Carpenter, whom the winner often lampooned in her outrageous concert and comedy skits. (Midler trashed Carpenter again in '74 while presenting Grammy's Album of the Year award.)

Class prevailed in the jazz lineup when Woody Herman heard huzzahs for *Giant Steps*, winner of Best Jazz Performance by a Big Band. *Steps* had been performed masterfully once before — by the same sax-playing legend who wrote it, John Coltrane — but Herman and his backup players gave it a new interpretation when they added such enhancements as a heavy dose of tenor clarinet. In the group performance category, Supersax, a new band known for its sassy interpretations of Charlie "Yardbird" Parker compositions, was acknowledged for its debut album, *Supersax Plays Bird*.

Art Tatum, who died in 1956, left behind some private tapes of 1941 Harlem jam sessions. The tapes were discovered and put on vinyl, making Tatum eligible for his posthumous prize for Best Jazz Performance by a Soloist. Tatum's *God Is in the House* LP also garnered Best Album Notes.

British-born, Australian-raised Olivia Newton-John was a serious fan of country music, having spent countless hours as a child listening to her father's Tennessee Ernie Ford albums. When the unlikely country singer reaped a c&w performance Grammy, however, for "Let Me Be There" (her first American hit, which reached number six in the weekly Hot 100), the victory was somewhat controversial. Newton-John conceded in her acceptance remarks, "It's probably the first time an English person won an award over Nashville people." But it would not be the last.

N.A.R.A.S. and the Country Music Association agreed on several picks this year: Both honored Charlie Rich and his hit song "Behind Closed Doors" with multiple wins, including best male singer and Best Country Song. The kudos had big protest potential, too. Rich had been recording for Epic for five years, but failed to find an audience. Producer Billy Sherrill told *Billboard*: "The jocks had been complaining that he was too bluesy for country, and others said he was too country for anything else. We just needed the right song." It came when songwriter Kenny O'Dell penned "Closed Doors" for Rich, who took it to number one on the country charts and to the fifth rung of *Billboard*'s annual Hot 100 — a considerable achievement, since some radio stations refused to play the song because they thought it was "dirty."

Country music's Rhodes scholar was quickly gaining a national pop audience in the early 70s, too. Kris Kristofferson (1971 Grammy winner for Best Country Song "Help Me Make It Through the Night") had lately crossed over from the country to pop charts and then from music to acting when he was cast, along with Bob Dylan, in the Sam Peckinpah film *Pat Garrett and Billy the Kid*. (Kristofferson played the Kid; Dylan did a cameo bit and contributed "Knocking on Heaven's Door" to the score.) Kristofferson, who once had a serious drinking problem, teamed up with his new wife, Rita Coolidge, for his Grammy booty this year: best duo performance for "From the Bottle to the Bottom."

Part of the score to another big movie, *Deliverance*, "Dueling Banjos," won the instrumental trophy for its performers. The bluegrass pop hit actually pitted a guitar, played by Steve Mandell, against a banjo handled Earl Scruggs--style by Eric Weissberg.

Guitarist Doc Watson had been celebrated during his career for his agile flat-picking of the blues on the Folkways label, but he switched to United Artists records in 1973 and released "Then and Now," winner of Best Ethnic or Traditional Recording.

Best Instrumental Composition was awarded to the score of the Bernardo Bertolucci film *Last Tango in Paris*, which was composed by the Argentina-born music writer and sax/clarinet player Gato Barbieri (who also appeared in the movie). *Last Tango* was not up for the Best Original Score Written for a Motion Picture prize, however, which went to Neil Diamond (his first and only Grammy as of this writing) for *Jonathan Livingston Seagull*, the film adaptation of the Richard Bach mega-selling book of pop philosophy about an independently minded seagull who flies against the flock. Diamond had a hit single ("Be") from the score that took him a year to write. Actor Richard Harris lost the Grammy he was expected to win in 1968 for "MacArthur Park," but made up for it this year with 1973's Best Spoken Word Recording of the book version of *Jonathan Livingston Seagull*.

Stephen Sondheim, who had won a golden gramophone statuette in 1970 for the year's best stage score (*Company*), reprised his win with *A Little Night Music*, a musical based on the Ingmar Bergman film *Smiles of a Summer Night*. *Hello, Dolly!* composer Jerry Herman once spoke of Sondheim to *Time* magazine on behalf of all his colleagues, commenting, "We would all agree that Steve is the genius of the group, the only one who keeps on taking the musical theater to new places."

The outrageous, pot-puffing comic duo Cheech & Chong topped nominees such as past victors Bill Cosby and George Carlin for the comedy laurels with their *Los Cochinos* album, which charted for 29 weeks (climbing to number two at its highest point). Cheech &

Chong openly celebrated a lazy, "who cares?" attitude about even the most serious issues of the day, including venereal disease, a major health problem since the advent of the sexual revolution in the '60s. Typical of their humor was a *Los Cochinos* parody of a radio commercial hyping the latest treatment, which intentionally sounded similar to a well-known ad for cleaning out household sewage pipes: "Hey, there, swinging bachelors! Tired of the steady drip, drip, drip of gonorrhea? Then Peter-Rooter could be just the thing you're looking for!" A jingle followed: "Peter Rooter, that's the name, ya just flush your troubles down the drain!"

When the engineers at Columbia Records went about recording Grammy's Classical Album of the Year, Bela Bartók's *Concerto for Orchestra* (performed by the New York Philharmonic under the baton of Pierre Boulez), they did so "in the round." Twenty-six microphones were placed in a circular performance space in order to catch each note and nuance for a stereo disc intended to be technologically state-of-the-art. The feat succeeded brilliantly, earning the sound staff an engineering Grammy and Boulez the orchestral performance prize. *High Fidelity* reported: "Here, the music's textures are subtly emphasized, enhanced, and clarified by the manner in which Boulez deploys his forces, and the interweaving thematic lines gain much from the fact that they can be related to precise sources in the surrounding space."

Vladimir Horowitz returned for a third year in a row to retake the soloist honors (without orchestra). His latest recital recording was of music by Alexander Scriabin, including two Op. 69 *Poems* and *Etudes*: Op. 8, Nos. 2, 8, 10, and 11. "This is certainly one of the finest performances available of any Scriabin work," *High Fidelity* said. The award for soloist with orchestral accompaniment went to Vladimir Ashkenazy (his first) for his inspired reading of Beethoven's *Concerti (5) for Piano and Orchestra*. During the span of his career, the Russian-born pianist demonstrated a special flair for performing Beethoven, Mozart, and Chopin. On this disc, "he is sensational," said *High Fidelity*, "with a sheen, a clarity in passagework, superlative articulation, deliciously fluent trills and turns."

The same publication was less enchanted with Grammy's choice for the choral laurels: André Previn and Arthur Oldham conducting the London Symphony Orchestra in Sir William Walton's *Belshazzar's Feast*. While the magazine claimed it was "a rousing, brilliant performance," it backstepped in adding slights at both

"Sondheim is the genius who keeps taking musical theater to new places."

Walton and Previn: "It is the kind of work that makes a great impression on one hearing, but leaves nothing for the second and that is precisely the kind of music in which André Previn excels." Gunther Schuller and the New England Conservatory Ragtime Ensemble gave the year's Best Chamber Music Performance with Scott Joplin's *The Red Back Book*.

The year's best Opera Recording turned out to be *Carmen*, with Leonard Bernstein conducting Marilyn Horne and the Metropolitan Opera Orchestra. "Not since 1959, when RCA recorded the new production of Verdi's *Macbeth* have the forces of the Metropolitan Opera taken part in a complete studio recording," *High Fidelity* wrote. "However, Deutsche Grammophon's increasing activity on the American scene, and their particular interest in the Met ... found a logical continuation in a complete *Carmen*" — a "big" performance, it added, that was "newsworthy and freshly studied."

Leontyne Price had been the voice on a version of *Carmen* in 1964. Price proved herself again this year by winning Grammy number nine for an album of Puccini arias singing "with a freedom and a radiance that precious few other sopranos today could match," *High Fidelity* said.

Just prior to the Grammycast, the artist with the most awards so far, Henry Mancini, gave away five awards that had never before been bestowed: classic entries into N.A.R.A.S.'s newly established Hall of Fame. The purpose of the Hall of Fame was to salute music and recordings made before the Grammys were first given away for 1958. (Five more songs would be inducted every year.) The first admissions were Coleman Hawkins's "Body and Soul," Nat "King" Cole's "The Christmas Song," Paul Whiteman and George Gershwin's recording of "Rhapsody in Blue," Louis Armstrong's "West End Blues," and Bing Crosby's "White Christmas."

"Last year's Grammy Awards show from Nashville was great," wrote *The Hollywood Reporter* when the Grammycast was over. "This year's from the Palladium in Hollywood was even better. There was hit music by the artists who actually made the hit. There was the emotionalism of all the awards for Stevie Wonder and the obvious audience approval. There was also a nicely done tribute to Jim Croce. As for the presenters, Helen Reddy and Alice Cooper had clever double-meaning dialogue. Moms Mabley broke up Kris Kristofferson by taking out her false teeth.

"There were some intermittent audio problems during the reading of the nom-

inees, but that was almost forgettable in the barrage of split screen, rear projection graphics, and other opticals used to make the show wonderful to look at. This first-class production ran like clockwork."

Variety said, "It was a flashy, name-splashed layout originating from the Hollywood Palladium, which was rigged like one of the old Busby Berkeley sound stages .... Andy Williams was back as host and handled his assignment with his customary ingratiating casualness, including his vocalizing of the five songs nominated for the best song of the year."

The Grammycast, though, had a major — and brand-new — problem. "Many of the awards and the winning artists were seen just a couple of weeks ago on the [first] American Music Awards show" on ABC, *Variety* added. "Stevie Wonder, Roberta Flack, and Tony Orlando & Dawn were among those on both shows, so the Grammy Awards couldn't escape that *déjà vu* feeling."

The American Music Awards were established, in part, because when ABC refused to televise last year's Nashville show, CBS picked up the broadcast option and scored a huge ratings hit.

But there was actually more to it than that. Various members of the music industry thought N.A.R.A.S. did a poor job of naming each year's best music and wanted an alternative accolade. Few of Grammy's choices, critics claimed, were in tune with what the public obviously loved — and bought (an ironic accusation, since the Grammys had been plagued from 1958 on with allegations that they deferred too often to the pop charts). The American Music Awards, however, would rely on the rankings in a large way to determine America's "favorite" artists and recordings, while N.A.R.A.S. chose to name the year's "best" talent and recordings.

How did the results compare? Most of the A.M.A. choices were different but still reflected N.A.R.A.S. opinions of the past: Helen Reddy, the Carpenters, Charley Pride, and Lynn Anderson were all big winners at the first awards ceremony that was televised, of course, by ABC. Other initial winners: Stevie Wonder and Roberta Flack (Favorite Male and Female Artists, Soul and R&B), "Superstition" (Favorite Soul/ R&B Single), and "Behind Closed Doors" (Favorite Country Single). The Grammys and the American Music Awards were now at war and both of them, strangely, were fighting for the same music.

1973

The ceremony was broadcast on CBS from the Hollywood Palladium on March 2, 1974, for the awards eligibility period of October 16, 1972, through October 15, 1973.

ALBUM OF THE YEAR
• *Innervisions*, Stevie Wonder. Stevie Wonder, A&R producer. Tamla/Motown.
Behind Closed Doors, Charlie Rich. Billy Sherrill, A&R producer. Epic/Columbia.
The Divine Miss M, Bette Midler. Joel Dorn, Barry Manilow, Geoffrey Haslam, Ahmet Ertegun, A&R producers. Atlantic.
Killing Me Softly, Roberta Flack. Joel Dorn, A&R producer. Atlantic.
There Goes Rhymin' Simon, Paul Simon. Paul Simon, Phil Ramone, Paul Samwell-Smith, Roy Halee, M.S.S. Rhythm Studio, A&R producers. Columbia.

RECORD OF THE YEAR
• "Killing Me Softly with His Song," Roberta Flack. Joel Dorn, A&R producer. Atlantic.
"Bad, Bad Leroy Brown," Jim Croce. Terry Cashman, Tommy West, A&R producers. ABC.
"Behind Closed Doors," Charlie Rich. Bill Sherrill, A&R producer. Epic/Columbia.
"You Are the Sunshine of My Life," Stevie Wonder. Stevie Wonder, A&R producer. Tamla/Motown.
"You're So Vain," Carly Simon. Richard Perry, A&R producer. Elektra.

SONG OF THE YEAR
(Songwriter's Award)
• "Killing Me Softly with His Song," Norman Gimbel, Charles Fox.
"Behind Closed Doors," Kenny O'Dell.
"Tie a Yellow Ribbon Round the Ole Oak Tree," Irwin Levine, L. Russell Brown.
"You Are the Sunshine of My Life," Stevie Wonder.
"You're So Vain," Carly Simon.

BEST NEW ARTIST
• Bette Midler. Atlantic.
Eumir Deodato. CTI.
Maureen McGovern. 20th Century.
Marie Osmond. MGM.
Barry White. 20th Century.

BEST POP VOCAL PERFORMANCE, MALE
• Stevie Wonder, "You Are the Sunshine of My Life." Tamla/Motown.
Perry Como, "And I Love You So." RCA.
Jim Croce, "Bad, Bad Leroy Brown." ABC.
Elton John, "Daniel." MCA.
Paul Simon, *There Goes Rhymin' Simon*. Columbia.

BEST POP VOCAL PERFORMANCE, FEMALE
• Roberta Flack, "Killing Me Softly with His Song." Atlantic.
Bette Midler, "Boogie Woogie Bugle Boy." Atlantic.
Anne Murray, "Danny's Song." Capitol.
Diana Ross, "Touch Me in the Morning." Motown.
Carly Simon, "You're So Vain." Elektra.

BEST POP VOCAL PERFORMANCE DUO, GROUP, OR CHORUS
• Gladys Knight & the Pips, "Neither One of Us (Wants to Be the First to Say Goodbye)." Soul/Motown.
Carpenters, "Sing." A&M.
Dawn Featuring Tony Orlando, "Tie a Yellow Ribbon Round the Ole Oak Tree." Bell.
Paul McCartney & Wings, "Live and Let Die." Apple/Capitol.
Seals & Crofts, "Diamond Girl." Warner Bros.

BEST POP INSTRUMENTAL PERFORMANCE
• Eumir Deodato,"Also Sprach Zarathustra (*2001*)." CTI.
Quincy Jones, *You've Got It Bad Girl*. A&M.
Mahavishnu Orchestra, "Bird of Fire." Columbia.
Billy Preston, "Space Race." A&M.
Edgar Winter, "Frankenstein." Epic/Columbia.

BEST RHYTHM & BLUES VOCAL PERFORMANCE, MALE
• Stevie Wonder, "Superstition." Tamla/Motown.
✓ Marvin Gaye, *Let's Get It On*. Motown.
✓ Al Green, "Call Me (Come Back Home)." Hi/London.
Eddie Kendricks, "Keep on Truckin'." Tamla/Motown.
✓ Barry White, "I'm Gonna Love You Just a Little More Baby." 20th Century.

BEST RHYTHM & BLUES VOCAL PERFORMANCE, FEMALE
• Aretha Franklin, "Master of Eyes." Atlantic.
Etta James, *Etta James*. Chess.
Ann Peebles, "I Can't Stand the Rain." Hi/London.
Esther Phillips, *Alone Again (Naturally)*. Kudu/CTI.
Sylvia, "Pillow Talk." Vibration.

BEST RHYTHM & BLUES VOCAL PERFORMANCE BY A DUO, GROUP, OR CHORUS
• Gladys Knight & the Pips, "Midnight Train to Georgia." Buddah.
✓ O'Jays, "Love Train." Philadelphia International/Columbia.
Spinners, "Could It Be I'm Falling in Love." Atlantic.
Staple Singers, "Be What You Are." Stax.
War, "The Cisco Kid." United Artists.

BEST RHYTHM & BLUES INSTRUMENTAL PERFORMANCE
• Ramsey Lewis, "Hang on Sloopy." Columbia.
Donald Byrd, *Black Byrd*. Blue Note/United Artists.
Crusaders, *2nd Crusade*. Blue Thumb.
Manu Dibango, *Soul Makossa*. Atlantic.
Young-Holt Unlimited, "Yes We Can Can." Atlantic.

BEST RHYTHM & BLUES SONG
(Songwriter's Award)
• "Superstition," Stevie Wonder.
"The Cisco Kid," War.
"Family Affair," Sylvester Stewart.
✓ "Love Train," Ken Gamble, Leon Huff.
"Midnight Train to Georgia," Jim Weatherly.

BEST JAZZ PERFORMANCE BY A SOLOIST
• Art Tatum, *God Is in the House*. Onyx.
Clifford Brown, *The Beginning and the End*. Columbia.
Ray Brown (Milt Jackson Quintet), "The Very Thought of You." Impulse/ABC.
Freddie Hubbard, "In a Mist." CTI.
Hubert Laws, *Morning Star*. CTI.

BEST JAZZ PERFORMANCE BY A GROUP
• Supersax, *Supersax Plays Bird*. Capitol.
Cannonball Adderley Quintet, *Inside Straight*. Fantasy.
Chick Corea, Return to Forever, *Light as a Feather*. Polydor.
Jim Hall, Ron Carter, *Alone Together*. Milestone.
Oregon, *Music of Another Present Era*. Vanguard.

BEST JAZZ PERFORMANCE BY A BIG BAND
• Woody Herman, *Giant Steps*. Fantasy.
Don Ellis, *Soaring*. MPS/BASF.
Gil Evans, *Svengali*. Atlantic.
Oliver Nelson, *Swiss Suite*. Flying Dutchman.
Randy Weston, *Tanjah*. Polydor.

BEST COUNTRY VOCAL PERFORMANCE, MALE
• Charlie Rich, "Behind Closed Doors." Epic/Columbia.
Tom T. Hall, "(Old Dogs . . . Children and) Watermelon Wine." Mercury.
Kris Kristofferson, "Why Me." Monument.
Charley Pride, "Amazing Love." RCA.
Johnny Russell, "Rednecks, White Socks & Blue Ribbon Beer." RCA.

BEST COUNTRY VOCAL PERFORMANCE, FEMALE
✓ • Olivia Newton-John, "Let Me Be There." MCA.
Barbara Fairchild, "Teddy Bear Song." Columbia.
Marie Osmond, "Paper Roses." MGM.
Dottie West, "Country Sunshine." RCA.
Tammy Wynette, "Kids Say the Darndest Things." Epic/Columbia.

BEST COUNTRY VOCAL PERFORMANCE BY A DUO OR GROUP
- Kris Kristofferson, Rita Coolidge, "From the Bottle to the Bottom." A&M.

Dolly Parton, Porter Wagoner, "If Teardrops Were Pennies." RCA.

Statler Brothers, *Carry Me Back*. Mercury.

Conway Twitty, Loretta Lynn, "Louisiana Woman, Mississippi Man." MCA.

Tammy Wynette, George Jones, "We're Gonna Hold On." Epic/Columbia.

Woody Herman snared a jazz performance prize for his new interpretation of John Coltrane's Giant Steps.

GLOBE PHOTO

BEST COUNTRY INSTRUMENTAL PERFORMANCE
- Eric Weissberg, Steve Mandell, "Dueling Banjos." Warner Bros.

Chet Atkins, "Fiddlin' Around." RCA.

Chet Atkins, *Superpickers*. RCA.

Danny Davis & the Nashville Brass, *I'll Fly Away*. RCA.

Charlie McCoy, *Good Time Charlie*. Monument.

BEST COUNTRY SONG
(Songwriter's Award)
- "Behind Closed Doors," Kenny O'Dell.

"Country Sunshine," Billy Davis, Dottie West.

"The Most Beautiful Girl," Rory Bourke, Billy Sherill, Norris Wilson.

"(Old Dogs ..., Children and) Watermelon Wine," Tom T. Hall.

"Why Me," Kris Kristofferson.

BEST INSPIRATIONAL PERFORMANCE
- Bill Gaither Trio, *Let's Just Praise the Lord*. Impact/Heartwarming.

Anita Bryant, *Anita Bryant ... Naturally*. Myrrh/Word.

Roy Rogers & Dale Evans, *In the Sweet By and By*. Word.

George Beverly Shea, *There's Something About That Name*. RCA.

Connie Smith, *All the Praises*. RCA.

BEST SOUL GOSPEL PERFORMANCE
- Dixie Hummingbirds, "Loves Me Like a Rock." ABC.

James Cleveland, "Down Memory Lane." Savoy.

Jessy Dixon, "He Ain't Heavy." Gospel/Savoy.

Edwin Hawkins Singers, *New World*. Buddah.

Swan Silvertones, *You've Got a Friend*. Hob/Scepter.

BEST GOSPEL PERFORMANCE (OTHER THAN SOUL GOSPEL)
- Blackwood Brothers, *Release Me (from My Sin)*. Skylite.

Andrae Crouch, *Just Andrae*. Light/Word.

The Imperials, *Live*. Impact/Heartwarming.

Oak Ridge Boys, *Street Gospel*. Heartwarming.

Statesmen, *I Believe in Jesus*. Artistic.

BEST ETHNIC OR TRADITIONAL RECORDING
- *Then and Now*, Doc Watson. United Artists.

Blues at Montreux, King Curtis, Champion Jack Dupree. Atlantic.

Can't Get No Grindin', Muddy Waters. Chess.

John Lee Hooker's Detroit (1948–1952), John Lee Hooker. United Artists.

Leadbelly (Live in Concert), Leadbelly. Playboy.

BEST INSTRUMENTAL COMPOSITION
(Composer's Award)
- Gato Barbieri, "Last Tango in Paris."

Manu Dibango, "Soul Makossa."

Billy Preston, "Space Race."

Thus van Leer, Jan Akkerman, "Hocus Pocus."
Edgar Winter, "Frankenstein."

BEST INSTRUMENTAL ARRANGEMENT
• Quincy Jones, "Summer in the City" (Quincy Jones). A&M.
Chick Corea, "Spain" (Chick Corea, Return to Forever). Polydor.
Lee Holdridge, "Prologue/Crunchy Granola Suite" (Neil Diamond). MCA.
Bill Holman, "The Daily Dance" (Stan Kenton & his Orchestra). Creative World.
Bob James, "Easy Living/Ain't Nobody's Business If I Do (Medley)" (Grover Washington, Jr.). Kudu/CTI.

BEST ARRANGEMENT ACCOMPANYING VOCALIST
• George Martin, "Live and Let Die" (Paul McCartney & Wings). Apple/Capitol.
Tom Baird, Gene Page, "Touch Me in the Morning" (Diana Ross). Motown.
Richard Carpenter, "Sing" (Carpenters). A&M.
Dave Grusin, "Lady Love" (Jon Lucien). RCA.
Dave Grusin, "Rashida" (Jon Lucien). RCA.
Gene Puerling, "Michelle" (Singers Unlimited). MPS/BASF.

BEST SCORE FROM THE ORIGINAL CAST SHOW ALBUM
• *A Little Night Music*, Stephen Sondheim, composer. Goddard Lieberson, producer. Columbia.
Cyrano, Anthony Burgess, Michael J. Lewis, composers. Jerry Moss, Phil Ramone, producers. A&M.
Man from the East, Stomu Yamashita, composer. Stomu Yamashita, producer. Island/Capitol.
Pippin, Stephen Schwartz, composer. Stephen Schwartz, Phil Ramone, producers. Motown.
Seesaw, Cy Coleman, Dorothy Fields, composers. Cy Coleman, producer. Buddah.

BEST ORIGINAL SCORE WRITTEN FOR A MOTION PICTURE OR A TELEVISION SPECIAL
(Composer's Award)
• *Jonathan Livingston Seagull*, Neil Diamond. Columbia.
Last Tango in Paris, Gato Barbieri. United Artists.

Live and Let Die, Paul & Linda McCartney, George Martin. United Artists.
Pat Garrett and Billy the Kid, Bob Dylan. Columbia.
Sounder, Taj Mahal. Columbia.

ALBUM OF THE YEAR, CLASSICAL
• *Bartók: Concerto for Orchestra*, Pierre Boulez conducting New York Philharmonic. Thomas Z. Shepard, producer. Columbia.
Beethoven: Concerti (5) for Piano & Orchestra, Georg Solti conducting Chicago Symphony (solo: Vladimir Ashkenazy). David Harvey, producer. London.
Bizet: Carmen, Leonard Bernstein conducting Metropolitan Opera Orchestra, Manhattan Opera Chorus (solos: Horne, McCracken, Maliponte, Krause). Thomas W. Mowrey, producer. Deutsche Grammophon/Polydor.
Joplin: The Red Back Book, Gunther Schuller conducting Conservatory Ragtime Ensemble. George Sponhaltz, producer. Angel/Capitol.
Prokofiev: Romeo and Juliet, Lorin Maazel conducting Cleveland Orchestra. Michael Woolcock, producer. London.
Puccini: Heroines (La Bohème, La Rondine, Tosca, Manon, Lescaut), Downes conducting New Philharmonia (solo: Leontyne Price). Richard Mohr, producer. RCA.
Rachmaninoff: The Complete Rachmaninoff—Vols. 1, 2, 3, (solo: Sergei Rachmaninoff). John Preiffer, Greg Benko, producers. RCA.
Rachmaninoff: Concerto No. 2 in C Minor for Piano, Eugene Ormandy conducting Philadelphia Orchestra (solo: Artur Rubinstein). Max Wilcox, producer. RCA.

BEST CLASSICAL PERFORMANCE, ORCHESTRA
(Conductor's Award)
• Pierre Boulez conducting New York Philharmonic, *Bartók: Concerto for Orchestra*. Columbia.
Leonard Bernstein conducting New York Philharmonic, *Holst: The Planets*. Columbia.
Lorin Maazel conducting Cleveland Orchestra, *Prokofiev: Romeo and Juliet*. London.

Eugene Ormandy conducting Philadelphia Orchestra, *Sibelius: Symphony No. 2 in D Major*. RCA.

Seiji Ozawa conducting Boston Symphony, *Berlioz: Symphonie Fantastique*. Deutsche Grammophon/ Polydor.

Seiji Ozawa conducting San Francisco Symphony (Seigel-Schwall Band), *Russo: Three Pieces for Blues Band and Orchestra*. Deutsche Grammophon/Polydor.

André Previn conducting London Symphony, *Prokofiev: Romeo and Juliet (Complete Ballet)*. Angel/ Capitol.

Georg Solti conducting Chicago Symphony, *Beethoven: Symphony No. 9 in D Minor*. London.

BEST CHAMBER MUSIC PERFORMANCE
• Gunther Schuller, New England Ragtime Ensemble, *Joplin: The Red Back Book*. Angel/Capitol.

Janet Baker, Dietrich Fischer-Dieskau, *Schubert: Duets*. Deutsche Grammophon/Polydor.

Julian Bream, Melos Ensemble of London, David Atherton, *Bennett: Concerto for Guitar & Chamber Ensemble*. RCA.

Cleveland Quartet, *Brahms: Quartets for Strings (Complete)*. RCA.

Concord String Quartet, *Rochberg: Quartet No. 3 for Strings*. Nonesuch.

Artur Rubinstein, Guarneri Quartet, *Dvorak: Piano Quartet in E Flat Major, Op. 87*. RCA.

Western Wind Vocal Ensemble, *Early American Vocal Music*. Nonesuch.

BEST CLASSICAL PERFORMANCE, INSTRUMENTAL SOLOIST(S) (WITH ORCHESTRA)
• Vladimir Ashkenazy (Solti conducting Chicago Symphony), *Beethoven: Concerti (5) for Piano & Orchestra*. London.

Stephen Bishop (Davis conducting London Symphony), *Mozart: Concerto No. 21 in C Major & Concerto No. 25 in C Major*. Philips/Mercury.

Aldo Ciccolini (Baudo conducting Orchestre de Paris), *Saint-Saëns: Concerti for Piano (Complete)*. Seraphim/Capitol.

Emil Gilels (Jochum conducting Berlin Philharmonic), *Brahms: Concerto No. 1 in D Minor for Piano & Orchestra &*

André Previn took a critical lashing for his choral winner, Belshazzar's Feast.

Concerto No. 2 in B Flat Major for Piano & Orchestra. Deutsche Grammophon/Polydor.

Artur Rubinstein (Ormandy conducting Philadelphia Orchestra), *Rachmaninoff: Concerto No. 2 in C Minor for Piano*. RCA.

John Williams (Previn conducting London Symphony), *Previn: Concerto for Guitar & Orchestra; Ponce: Concierto Del Sur for Guitar & Orchestra*. Columbia.

Pinchas Zukerman (Zukerman conducting English Chamber Orchestra), *Vivaldi: The Four Seasons*. Columbia.

BEST CLASSICAL PERFORMANCE, INSTRUMENTAL SOLOIST(S) (WITHOUT ORCHESTRA)
• Vladimir Horowitz, *Scriabin: Horowitz Plays Scriabin*. Columbia.

Julian Bream, *The Woods So Wild*. RCA.

Alfred Brendel, *Schubert: Sonata in B Flat, Op. 960*. Philips/Mercury.

Virgil Fox, *Heavy Organ at Carnegie Hall*. RCA.

Glenn Gould, *Bach: French Suites 1–4*. Columbia.

Maurizio Pollini, *Chopin: Etudes*. Deutsche Grammmphon/Polydor.

Sviatoslav Richter, *Bach: Well-Tempered Klavier*. Melodiya/Angel.

BEST OPERA RECORDING
• *Bizet: Carmen*, Leonard Bernstein conducting Metropolitan Opera Orchestra and Manhattan Opera Chorus (solos: Horne, McCracken, Maliponte, Krause). Thomas W. Mowrey, producer. Deutsche Grammophon/Polydor.

Delius: A Village Romeo and Juliet, Meredith Davies conducting Royal Philharmonic and John Alldis Choir (solos: Tear, Harwood). Christopher Bishop, producer. Angel/Capitol.

Puccini: Turandot, Zubin Mehta conducting London Philharmonic; John Alldis Choir and Wandsworth School Choir (solos: Sutherland, Pavarotti, Caballe, Ghaiurov, Krause, Pears). Ray Minshull, producer. London.

Wagner: Der Ring Des Nibelungen, Karl Bohm conducting Bayreuth Festival Orchestra (solos: Nilsson, Rysanek, Burmaister, Windgassen, King, Wohlfart, Adam, Stewart, Talvela, Greindl, Neidlinger). Wolfgang Lohse, producer. Philips/Mercury.

Wagner: Parsifal, Georg Solti conducting Vienna Philharmonic, Vienna State Opera Chorus, Vienna Boys Choir (solos: Kollo, Ludwig, Fischer-Dieskau, Frick, Keleman, Hotter). Christopher Raeburn, producer. London.

Wagner: Tristan Und Isolde, Herbert von Karajan conducting Berlin Philharmonic (solos: Vickers, Dernesch). Michael Glotz, producer. Angel/Capitol.

BEST CHORAL PERFORMANCE, CLASSICAL
• Arthur Oldham conducting London Symphony Orchestra Chorus. André Previn conducting London Symphony, *Walton: Belshazzar's Feast*. Angel/Capitol.

Helmuth Froschauer conducting Vienna Singverein. Herbert von Karajan conducting Berlin Philharmonic, *Bach: St. Matthew Passion*. Deutsche Grammophon/Polydor.

Eugen Jochum conducting Netherlands Radio Chorus and Concertgebouw Orchestra (solos: Giebel, Hoffgen, Haefliger, Ridderbusch), *Beethoven: Missa Solemnis*. Philips.

Raymond Leppard conducting Glyndebourne Opera Chorus, *Monteverdi: Madrigals*, Books 3 & 4. Philips.

Norman Scribner directing Norman Scribner Choir. Leonard Bernstein conducting Orchestra, *Haydn: Mass in Time of War (Leonard Bernstein's Concert for Peace)*. Columbia.

Herbert von Karajan conducting Chorus of the Deutsche Opera, Berlin and Berlin Philharmonic, *Haydn: The Season*. Angel/Capitol.

David Willcocks conducting Choir of King's College, Cambridge. Benjamin Britten conducting London Symphony, *Elgar: The Dream of Gerontius*. London.

BEST CLASSICAL VOCAL SOLOIST PERFORMANCE
• Leontyne Price (Downes conducting New Philharmonia), *Puccini: Heroines (La Bohème, La Rondine, Tosca, Manon, Lescaut)*. RCA.

Janet Baker (Gerald Moore, accompaniment), *Schubert: Songs*. Seraphim/Capitol.

Cathy Berberian (Berio conducting London Sinfonietta), *Berio: Recital I (For Cathy)*. RCA.

Placido Domingo (Santi conducting New Philharmonia), *La Voce D'Oro*. RCA.

Heather Harper (Boulez conducting BBC Symphony), *Berg: Seven Early Songs*. Columbia.

Marilyn Horne (Lewis conducting Royal Philharmonic), *Marilyn Horne Sings Rossini (Excerpts from Siege of Corinth & La Donna del Lago)*. London.

Yvonne Minton, Rene Kollo (Solti conducting Chicago Symphony), *Mahler: Das Lied von der Erde*. London.

Martti Talvela (Irwin Gage, accompaniment), *Martti Talvela—A Lieder Recital (Schumann)*. London.

BEST ENGINEERED RECORDING, CLASSICAL
• Edward T. Graham, Raymond Moore, *Bartók: Concerto for Orchestra* (Boulez conducting New York Philharmonic). Columbia.

Paul Goodman, *Bach's Greatest Fugues* (Ormandy conducting Philadelphia Orchestra). RCA.

Edward T. Graham, Larry Keyes, *Holst: The Planets* (Bernstein conducting New York Philharmonic). Columbia.

Gunther Hermanns, *Bizet: Carmen* (Bernstein conducting Metropolitan Opera Orchestra, soloists). Deutsche Grammophon/Polydor.

Jack Law, Colin Moortoot, Gordon Parry, *Prokofiev: Romeo and Juliet* (Maazel conducting Cleveland Orchestra). London.

Tony Salvatore, *Puccini: Heroines* (Downes conducting New Philharmonia; solo: Leontyne Price). RCA.

Hans Schweigmann, *Berlioz: Symphonie Fantastique* (Ozawa conducting Boston Symphony). Deutsche Grammmphon/Polydor.

Kenneth Wilkinson, Gordon Parry. *Wagner: Parsifal* (Solti conducting Vienna Philharmonic, soloists). London.

BEST ALBUM NOTES, CLASSICAL
(Annotator's Award)
• Glenn Gould, *Hindemith: Sonatas for Piano (Complete)* (Glenn Gould). Columbia.

Misha Donat, *Berio: Recital 1 (For Cathy)* (Berio conducting London Sinfonietta; solo: Berberian). RCA.

Tom Eastwood, *The Woods So Wild* (Julian Bream). RCA.

Irving Kolodin, *Dvorak: Piano Quartet in E Flat Major, Op. 87* (Guarneri Quartet; solo: Artur Rubinstein). RCA.

Harvey Phillips, *Bizet: Carmen* (Bernstein conducting Metropolitan Opera Orchestra; solos: Horne, McCracken, Maliponte, Krause). Deutsche Grammophon.

Alan Rich, *Rachmaninoff: Concerto No. 2 in C Minor for Piano* (Rubinstein; Ormandy conducting Philadelphia Orchestra). RCA.

H.C. Robbins Landon, *Haydn: Symphony No. 36, Symphony No. 48* (Dorati conducting Philharmonica Hungarica). London.

H.C. Robbins Landon, *Haydn: Symphony No. 20 in C Major to Symphony No. 35 in B Flat Major* (Dorati conducting Philharmonica Hungarica). London.

Erik Smith, *Bach: Brandenburg Concerti* (Marriner conducting Academy of St. Martin-in-the Fields). Philips/Mercury.

Cavalier, pot-puffing Cheech & Chong won the comedy kudos for Los Cochinos.

Clair Van Ausdall, *Debussy: La Mer/Prelude a L'Apres Midi D'un Faune*; *Ravel: Daphnis & Chloë Suite No. 2* (Ormandy conducting Philadelphia Orchestra). RCA.

BEST SPOKEN WORD RECORDING
• *Jonathan Livingston Seagull,* Richard Harris. Dunhill/ABC.

America, Why I Love Her, John Wayne. RCA.

Slaughterhouse Five, Kurt Vonnegut, Jr. Caedmon.

Songs & Conversations, Billie Holiday. Paramount.

Witches, Ghosts & Goblins, Vincent Price. Caedmon.

BEST COMEDY RECORDING
• *Los Cochinos*, Cheech & Chong. Ode/A&M.

Fat Albert, Bill Cosby. MCA.

Occupation: Foole, George Carlin. Little David/Atlantic.

Richard Nixon: A Fantasy, David Frye. Buddah.

Lemmings, National Lampoon. Banana/
   Blue Thumb.
Child of the 50's, Robert Klein. Brut/
   Buddah.

BEST RECORDING FOR CHILDREN
• *Sesame Street Live*, Sesame Street Cast.
   Joe Raposo, producer. Columbia.
Free to Be . . . You and Me, Marlo Thomas
   and Friends. Bell.
The Little Prince, Peter Ustinov. Argo.
Multiplication Rock, Bob Dorough, Grady
   Tate, Blossom Dearie. Capitol.
Songs from The Electric Company *TV
   Show*, conducted by Buddy Baker, with
   vocalists. Disneyland.

BEST ENGINEERED RECORDING,
NON-CLASSICAL
• Robert Margouleff, Malcolm Cecil,
   Innervisions (Stevie Wonder).
   Tamla/Motown.
Alan Parsons, *The Dark Side of the Moon*
   (Pink Floyd). Harvest/Capitol.
David Hentschel, *Goodbye Yellow Brick
   Road* (Elton John). MCA.
Donn Landee, "Long Train Runnin'"
   (Doobie Brothers). Warner Bros.
Robin Geoffrey Cable, Bill Schnee, *No
   Secrets* (Carly Simon). Elektra.

BEST ALBUM PACKAGE
(Art Director's Award)
Wilkes & Braun, Inc., *Tommy* (London
   Symphony/Chambre Choir). Ode/
   A&M.
John Berg, *Chicago VI* (Chicago).
   Columbia.
Hipgnosis, *Houses of the Holy* (Led
   Zeppelin). Atlantic.
Jim Ladwig/AGI, *Ooh La La* (Faces).
   Warner Bros.
Ode Visuals, Inc., *Los Cochinos* (Cheech
   & Chong). Ode/A&M.
Pacific Eye and Ear, *Billion Dollar Babies*
   (Alice Cooper). Warner Bros.
Mike Salisbury, *The World of Ike & Tina*
   (Ike & Tina Turner). United Artists.
Al Steckler, *Chubby Checker's Greatest
   Hits* (Chubby Checker). Abkco.

BEST ALBUM NOTES
(OTHER THAN CLASSICAL)
(Annotator's Award)
• Dan Morgenstern, *God Is in the House*
   (Art Tatum). Onyx.
Stan Cornyn, *Ol' Blue Eyes Is Back* (Frank
   Sinatra). Reprise/Warner Bros.
Chet Flippo, *Lonesome, On'ry and Mean*
   (Waylon Jennings). RCA.
William Ivey, *This Is Jimmie Rodgers*
   (Jimmie Rodgers). RCA.
Lionel Newman, *Remember Marilyn*
   (Marilyn Monroe). 20th Century.

Honestly, Marvin!

Roberta Flack was back *again* as a Record of the Year nominee ("Feel Like Makin' Love"). Joni Mitchell ("Help Me," she crooned, like she meant it) and Elton John ("Don't Let the Sun Go Down on Me") were also in the race and long overdue for the honor. Other contenders were Maria Muldaur's "Midnight at the Oasis" (number 29 in the year's Hot 100), plus an irresistible valentine from one of the most wholesome beauties with one of the most crystalline voices in modern music — Olivia Newton-John, who wooed voters with "I Honestly Love You."

"White bread" and black soul: Record of the Year champ Olivia Newton-John and Album of the Year victor for a second year in a row, Stevie Wonder (with wife, right).

"Honestly," written by Peter Allen and Jeffrey Barry, was also up for Song of the Year. Allen, a Vegas-style performer as well as a composer, originally intended to record it himself, but A&M Records wasn't convinced the combination would produce a hit and the project lost momentum. Then "somebody at the publishing office was going to see Olivia with new material," Barry once told *Billboard*, "and she loved it and wanted to record it." A&M at first resisted its release as a single when she included it in her *If You Love Me, Let Me Know* LP, but, as Barry also pointed out, pretty soon "radio demanded it."

The Australian Newton-John, when she won a 1973 Grammy in a country category, caused a lot of hootin' and hollerin' down in Nashville. It was hard to believe that the Barbie doll-faced vocalist could cause *any* ruckus: One critic once compared her to white bread "if white bread could sing." But this time she staved off any potential outcry by claiming the two top awards at both the Grammys and the American Music Awards — for Record of the Year and best female pop vocalist.

The win that "raised the most eyebrows," *Variety* said, and "was a bit shaky," was the selection of Best New Artist — Marvin Hamlisch. The trade paper added, "Hamlisch has emerged as one of the top film score writers and also plays excellent piano, but his name doesn't have the b.o. [box office] charisma of the other contenders." These included Phoebe Snow and Bad Company. The voting result, noted *Rolling Stone*, "drew disapproving grumbles from those among the 2,000 people assembled in the Uris [Theater in New York] who felt that the industry old guard was trying to play it safe." The Best New Artist award had traditionally gone to winners known primarily as performance artists. Hamlisch was regarded first as a composer, but his piano-playing single, "The Entertainer," was number 40 in *Billboard*'s annual Hot 100. Record of the Year "I Honestly Love you," by comparison, came in at number 50.

At the previous year's Oscars, Hamlisch won an unprecedented three music awards for contributing to the scores of two Robert Redford films, *The Way We Were* (the Sydney Pollack sudser, costarring past Grammy winner Barbra Streisand, about a doomed couple who go through college, marriage, and more together) and Oscar's Best Picture *The Sting*, which teamed Redford with Paul Newman as con men who swindle a visiting, out-of-town gangster. Streisand's single release of "The Way We Were" came out on top of 1974's Hot 100, while the score to *The Sting* launched a nationwide revival of interest in the music of ragtime composer Scott Joplin, who wrote "The Entertainer."

> ### The omission of fusion artists caused "considerable discontent in the jazz groove."

At the Grammys, Hamlisch picked up two prizes for "The Way We Were": Song of the Year and best film score. A single release of "The Entertainer" from *The Sting* also earned him the Best Pop Instrumental Performance laurels. When he also accepted the statuette for Best New Artist, Hamlisch thanked Joplin, calling him "the real new artist of the year."

The Grammy "grumbles" over Hamlisch seem surprising in retrospect, given that he was enjoying an amazing awards romp in the mid-1970s thanks to his crossover success in most areas of show business. His *A Chorus Line* musical opened in New York at Joe Papp's Public Theater a few months after this year's Grammys ceremony, then, by summertime, was moved to Broadway where it would reap a staggering nine trophies at the Tony Awards. *A Chorus Line* would also nab a Pulitzer Prize and eventually become the longest-running musical in the history of the Great White Way.

Tied with Hamlisch for the most victories was last year's Grammy sweeper Stevie Wonder, who took the Album of the Year and best pop male vocalist prizes for *Fulfillingness' First Finale*, his first number one–ranked LP since *Little Stevie Wonder — The 10-Year-Old Genius* in 1963. Wonder received a standing ovation when he received the pop vocals honors, his first award of the night, and said he planned to give it to Mercer Ellington in honor of his late father, Duke, "since Mr. Ellington contributed more music than I ever could in a thousand years," Wonder said. "A gallant gesture!" commented *Rolling Stone*.

Among *Fullfillingness*'s hit singles was "Boogie on Reggae Woman," which also earned him the r&b vocal trophy. His fourth Grammy was for Best Rhythm & Blues Song "Living for the City," a late-breaking release from last year's Album of the Year *Innervisions*. "Living for the City" dealt hauntingly with black oppression in urban areas. "This place is cruel," one lyric reads. "Nowhere could be much colder."

The Album of the Year award was bestowed on Wonder by last year's Best New Artist, Bette Milder, who strolled out on stage on Grammy night wearing a mischievous grin, a skimpy dress, and a 45-r.p.m. record for a hat. "It's 'Come

Go with Me' by the Dell-Vikings," she said. "It was a great record, but it's a better *hat*."

Midler then tossed out one more of her ongoing barbs at longtime target Karen Carpenter. "A year ago, Miss Karen Carpenter crowned me Best New Artist," said Midler, who hadn't worked much in the past year, "and if that ain't the kiss of death, I don't know what is!" When Wonder accepted his award from her, he said, graciously acknowledging their first meeting, "I've been listening to your records for some time, and I've been trying to figure out how to get to you."

Paul McCartney, who won seven previous Grammys for his work with the Beatles, plus one for his work with Wings, came soaring back to reclaim the pop group vocal honor for the single "Band on the Run." The album (of the same name) was recorded in Nigeria under dire conditions. Two of Wings's musicians failed to show up for the taping, leaving McCartney alone with his vocalist wife Linda (who didn't play an instrument) and guitarist Denny Laine. "I took control on that album," McCartney once told *Musician* magazine. "I played the drums myself, the bass myself, a lot of guitar with Denny, did a lot of the vocals myself. So it was almost a solo album." The dedicated Wings technicians who also showed up received Grammy's Best Engineered Recording award.

In 1972, Grammy's greatest stalwart, Aretha Franklin, established a winning streak that surpassed Bill Cosby's earlier

Marvin Hamlisch's victory as Best New Artist "drew disapproving grumbles" at the show, said Rolling Stone. "The old guard was trying to play it safe."

record of six consecutive wins. This year Lady Soul added one more — an r&b vocals award for her cover of the 1968 Marvin Gaye and Tammi Terrell hit "Ain't Nothing Like the Real Thing" — but then ended her string of consecutive triumphs. (Sir Georg Solti overtook her Grammy record by winning 10 straight times in the classical categories from 1974 to 1983.) Franklin had monopolized the female r&b vocal category ever since it was established in 1967.

In the other r&b slots, Stevie Wonder wrote the Best Rhythm & Blues Song of the year, which was also the tune that earned the group vocal trophy for Rufus (featuring Chaka Khan): "Tell Me

Something Good." Rock critic Dave Marsh once wrote of Wonder's contribution to the troupe: "What he gave them wasn't just a son-of-'Superstition' hit, it was role defining, establishing, in one fell swoop, Chaka as a demanding, tough 'n' sultry siren, and Rufus as one of the premier black rock bands of the Seventies, designations to which they've devoted the rest of their careers."

When the TV program *Soul Train* asked a group of session musicians at Philadelphia's Sigma Sound Studios to come up with a theme song, they were dealing with professionals who had contributed to such hits as the O'Jays' "Love Train" and Billy Paul's 1972 Grammy winner "Me and Mrs. Jones." The group called themselves MFSB (Mother, Father, Sister, Brother) and gave the TV show producers "TSOP (The Sound of Philadelphia)," which ranked number seven in the year's Hot 100 and was named winner of the r&b instrumental performance award. "The Sound of Philadelphia" was meant to rival the thunder out of Detroit's Motown and was spearheaded by Thom Bell, winner of the newly introduced Grammy for Producer of the Year. Bell had previously overseen works by the Stylistics and the Spinners and had more Top 10 singles (11) in 1974 than any other producer.

When the Grammy nominations came out this year, *Variety* reported "considerable discontent in the jazz groove .... Missing from the nominations are such exponents of 'fusion jazz,' a blend of rock and jazz, as Chick Corea, Mahavishnu Orchestra, Weather Report, Bill Cobham, and Herbie Hancock." The accusation was somewhat unfair — fusionist Chuck Mangione *was* in the line-up — but *Variety* insisted that "the 'new' jazz practitioners ... are consistently passed over in favor of the traditionalists."

The soloist performance award went this year to a man who was not only one of jazz's foremost traditionalists (having been one of its pioneers), but also one of its long-deceased icons, topping newer talent such as fellow nominees Freddie Hubbard and Keith Jarrett. The prize lauded alto sax legend Charlie "Yardbird" Parker, who died in 1955 of a heart seizure one week after performing at Birdland, the famed Manhattan club named after him. The award acknowledged his early "Bird" recordings, never before released, which included works with Jay McShann's 1940 Kansas City band as well as a 1942 Harlem jam session. The victory gave the Grammys this year a special "note of dignity," said *Rolling Stone*.

The magazine added: "In the pretelecast award ceremony, the late Charlie Parker was finally named [a] winner ... for the album *First Recordings* .... His daughter Kim delivered a short but emotional acceptance speech that drew a few gasps. 'This is *very* weird,' she said. 'Bird's still getting awards and somebody else is still getting all his money!'"

Another jazz great, keyboardist Oscar Peterson, received his first Grammy (best group performance), sharing it with guitarist Joe Pass and Danish bass player Niels Pedersen for their LP *The Trio*. A winner from last year, Woody Herman, returned to reclaim the big band laurels for *Thundering Herd*. Herman had had a series of "Herd" bands throughout his career, the first of which was Herman's Herd, then came First, Second, and Third Herd.

In the country categories, the recipient of last year's best male country vocalist prize, Charlie Rich, took this year's winner of Best Country Song to the top of the c&w chart. "A Very Special Love Song" was written for him by Billy Sherrill (writer of 1966's Best Country Song "Almost Persuaded") and

Norris Wilson. Following the success of his "Behind Closed Doors" release last year (also named Best Country Song) the singer was enjoying one of the most successful periods of his career. Wilson told *Billboard* about the genesis of the tune: "We needed something for Charlie and he [Sherrill] said, 'Let's write for him a very special love song.'" On April 20, 1974, Rich held all three top rungs in the country rankings, with "There Won't Be Anymore" at number one, followed by "Behind Closed Doors" and "A Very Special Love Song."

Three-time past Grammy champ Chet Atkins teamed up with fellow guitarist Merle Travis for this year's instrumental performance trophy, which they won for *The Atkins-Travis Traveling Show*. Atkins first heard Travis play years earlier on a radio broadcast out of Cincinnati and was inspired by his amazing two-finger technique, now known as "Travis picking." Atkins developed a three-finger style (between them, noted pundits, they had one whole hand) and the twosome often paired up for concert appearances.

Although the jazz awards were criticized this year for going to traditionalists, "the country music awards," noted *Variety*, "are criticized for ignoring the traditionalists. Current winners — Anne Murray, Ronnie Milsap, and the Pointer Sisters — are still considered outsiders in Nashville."

The Pointer Sisters are known today primarily for their pop singles, but in 1974 they made their first attempt at country music and won their first Grammy (best country group vocals) for "Fairytale," beating such other name nominees as the Statler Brothers, Willie Nelson and Tracy Nelson (no relation), Bobby Bare and son, and last year's championship team of Kris Kristofferson and Rita Coolidge. *Variety* identified them as "a black group specializing in campy versions of vintage material," but Nashville suddenly took the Pointer Sisters seriously enough after their Grammy triumph to invite them to be the first black women's group to perform at the Grand Ole Opry.

"There are only two things I know about Canada," Elton John once said. "Hockey and Anne Murray. (John came up with scratch at the Grammys again this year, despite three nods, including Record and Album of the Year.) Murray, the singer of the 1969 hit single "Snowbird" was raised in Nova Scotia where she often listened to what she called the country-flavored music of Brenda Lee, Elvis Presley, and Buddy Knox on the radio. Now she overtook Nashville divas Dolly Parton, Dottie West, Tammy Wynette, and Tanya Tucker for the vocals award for "Love Song."

Ronnie Milsap was another relative newcomer when he beat out such headliners as Charley Pride, Glen Campbell, Roy Clark, and Waylon Jennings for the male vocalist honors. (Milsap was so new to the business that he heard his name mispronounced "Mislap"— "repeatedly," whined *Rolling Stone* — by presenter Burl Ives at the Grammy ceremony.) "Please Don't Tell Me How the Story Ends" was written for him by Kris Kristofferson, who penned it one night while mulling over a love relationship that he knew was doomed. Milsap had come to prominence only one year earlier with his hit single "I Hate You." Previous to that, he was a backup artist for Elvis Presley, playing piano for Presley's

> *Sir Georg Solti launched a record-breaking winning streak with the year's best classical LP,* **Symphonie Fantastique.**

"Gentle on My Mind" and singing harmony on "Kentucky Rain." In honor of his mentor, Milsap taped "Please Don't Tell Me" on Elvis's birthday, in a recording studio that the King used often.

Presley had won his first Grammy in 1967 for giving the year's Best Sacred Performance on his *How Great Thou Art* LP and also won in 1972 for Best Inspirational Performance with *He Touched Me*. In what *Rolling Stone* and others now called "a strange twist," Presley came back to take the inspirational performance award again, this time for a live performance album recording (rather than a studio taping) of *How Great Thou Art*. The Oak Ridge Boys won Best Gospel Performance for "The Baptism of Jessie Taylor," while the backup talent for Aretha Franklin's 1972 Best Soul Gospel Performance of "Amazing Grace" — James Cleveland & the Southern California Community Choir — won the soul gospel trophy all for themselves this year for their cover of Elvis Presley's classic "In the Ghetto."

Richard Pryor had been known to black club audiences for some time, but he was suddenly catching on with liberal whites by the mid-1970s when Grammy's laugh laurels took a notable shift in preference. Previous winners were usually sassy but sweet (Bill Cosby and Vaughn Meader, to name just two, took pleasure in tweaking their targets), but now the Grammys were suddenly applauding the kind of biting political punishment and gross scatological humor that came into the mainstream soon after Lenny Bruce first ranted and raved before a microphone in the late 1950s. Pryor was a master at it, and particularly skillful at rages strung with a shocking onslaught of four-letter words. He has won five Grammys as of this writing (second only to Cosby in the category), but his first came for *That Nig-ger's Crazy*, a send-up of black and white lifestyles that lampooned the ways that whites flee burning houses (they "just panic," he says, "fall over each other, choke to death and shit") and blacks make love ("Niggers make noise. 'God damn! Move now, bitch!'").

Just like in 1972, conductor Georg Solti was the sweepstakes winner in the classical categories, again reaping three awards, and thus began a 10-year winning streak, a record that is still unrivaled as of this writing. Two were for the Classical Album of the Year, Berlioz's *Symphonie Fantastique*, performed under Solti's baton by the Chicago Symphony, which shared the LP honors in addition to the kudos for best orchestral performance. "No other performance of this much-played score moves more surely, more forcefully, more eloquently than this," said *High Fidelity*. The recording was made at the University of Illinois at Champaign-Urbana and achieved such audio perfection that it also earned the engineering honors. "The sound is fully as spectacular as the performance," the magazine added.

High Fidelity was less moved by the year's Best Opera Recording, which brought Solti his third golden gramophone of the year (and the eighth of his career). Solti led tenor Placido Domingo, soprano Montserrat Caballé, and the London Philharmonic in Puccini's *La Bohème*, a feat of "technical mastery," it said, but added, "Those who love this score on account of its emotional generosity will find themselves fobbed off with good taste instead." The reviewer dismissed Caballé's performance as "chilling in its impersonality and unspontaneousness" and noted that Domingo "sounds tired." Neither singer was nominated for the soloist salute, which went to last year's winner, Leontyne Price (bringing her a 10th Grammy), for her tribute to Richard Strauss, including operatic excerpts from *Guntram* and *Der Rosenkavalier* as well as his *Four Last Songs*. Again, *High Fidelity* was not pleased: Price, it said, "is not at home in this music."

As in the Album of the Year category, music by Berlioz was the source of another classical Grammy win: the choral laurels for *The Damnation of Faust*, conducted by Colin Davis and sung by the London Symphony Orchestra Chorus, the Ambrosian Singers, and the Wandsworth School Boys' Choir ("not entirely homogenous in sound," said *High Fidelity*). Cellist Pierre Fournier, violinist Henryk Szeryng, and pianist Artur Rubinstein shared the prize for chamber music for their execution of several trios by Brahms and Schumann.

The soloist performance kudos went to Russian musician David Oistrakh, who died in 1974, for Shostakovich's Violin Concerto No. 1, a performance that came about through Oistrakh's close collaboration with the composer's son. The world-renowned pianist Madame Alicia de Larrocha won the soloist prize (without orchestra) for her rendition of Isaac Albéniz's magnum opus *Iberia*, a high note in music that *High Fidelity* said "cannot be minimized .... This is proportioned playing, pretty wonderful to experience."

"For the 17th consecutive year, Latin music was ignored at the N.A.R.A.S. awards ceremonies," *Billboard* reported when the Grammy ceremonies were over, noting, "Latin music on discs consistently outsells jazz, classical and most recordings of the spoken word, categories that have their own competition." (The issue was then being explored by the record academy and would result in the creation of a Best Latin Recording prize the next year.)

Other complaints about this year's contest came from *Variety*, which said that the "Grammy Awards gave rock only one major award" (McCartney's "Band on the Run"), and added that "wins by Stevie Wonder, Aretha Franklin, and Olivia Newton-John were expected." "Jackson Browne and Bruce Springsteen continued to go unnoticed," *Rolling Stone* groused.

"In all, some 2,000 turned out to honor their own in an evening full of standing ovations and black-tie color," *Billboard* said, describing the twin galas held in New York at Broadway's Uris Theater (from which the ceremony was broadcast) and the Americana Hotel. The Uris was no doubt chosen for the TV show because it was the site of the first full production of the Scott Joplin ("The Entertainer") opera *Treemonisha*, produced in 1974 by the Houston Grand Opera company. Andy Williams again acted as Grammycast host, with awards presentations made by Ann-Margret, John Lennon, Paul Simon, Rudy Vallee, David Bowie, Kate Smith, and Sarah Vaughan.

> *"It began to get ugly out on the street. Even venerable old Kate Smith narrowly escaped with her makeup intact."*

"Nobody could argue with Wonder's four awards (one less than last year)," the often quarrelsome *Rolling Stone* said afterward, also noting that Wonder's limo was stormed by jubilant fans after the ceremony was over. "It began to get ugly out on the street," the magazine observed. "Even venerable old Kate Smith narrowly escaped with her makeup intact."

The awards ceremony was broadcast by CBS from the Uris Theater in New York on March 1, 1975. An additional ceremony was held in New York at the Americana Hotel. The 17th annual Grammy Awards were bestowed for the eligibility period October 16, 1973, to October 15, 1974.

ALBUM OF THE YEAR
• *Fulfillingness' First Finale*, Stevie Wonder. Stevie Wonder, A&R producer. Tamla/Motown.
Back Home Again, John Denver. Milton Okun, A&R producer. RCA.
Band on the Run, Paul McCartney & Wings. Paul McCartney, A&R producer. Apple/Capitol.
Caribou, Elton John. Gus Dudgeon, A&R producer. MCA.
Court and Spark, Joni Mitchell. Joni Mitchell, Henry Lewy, A&R producers. Asylum.

RECORD OF THE YEAR
• "I Honestly Love You," Olivia Newton-John. John Farrar, A&R producer. MCA.
"Don't Let the Sun Go Down on Me," Elton John. Gus Dudgeon, A&R producer. MCA.
"Feel Like Makin' Love," Roberta Flack. Roberta Flack, A&R producer. Atlantic.
"Help Me," Joni Mitchell. Joni Mitchell, Henry Lewy, A&R producers. Asylum.
"Midnight at the Oasis," Maria Muldaur. Lenny Waronker, Joe Boyd, A&R producers. Reprise/Warner Bros.

SONG OF THE YEAR
(Songwriter's Award)
• "The Way We Were," Marilyn & Alan Bergman, Marvin Hamlisch.
"Feel Like Makin' Love," Eugene McDaniels.
"I Honestly Love You," Jeff Barry, Peter Allen.
"Midnight at the Oasis," David Nichtern.
"You and Me Against the World," Paul Williams, Ken Ascher.

BEST NEW ARTIST
• Marvin Hamlisch. MCA.
Bad Company. Swan Song.
Johnny Bristol. MGM.
David Essex. Columbia.
Graham Central Station. Warner Bros.
Phoebe Snow. Shelter.

BEST POP VOCAL PERFORMANCE, MALE
• Steve Wonder, *Fulfllingness' First Finale*. Tamla/ Motown.
Harry Chapin, "Cat's in the Cradle." Elektra.
Elton John, "Don't Let the Sun Go Down on Me." MCA.
Dave Loggins, "Please Come to Boston." Epic/Columbia.
Billy Preston, "Nothing from Nothing." A&M.

BEST POP VOCAL PERFORMANCE, FEMALE
• Olivia Newton-John, "I Honestly Love You." MCA.
Roberta Flack, "Feel Like Makin' Love." Atlantic.
Carole King, "Jazzman." Ode.
Cleo Laine, *Cleo Laine Live at Carnegie Hall*. RCA.
Joni Mitchell, "Court and Spark." Asylum.

BEST POP VOCAL BY A DUO, GROUP, OR CHORUS
• Paul McCartney & Wings, "Band on the Run." Apple/Capitol.
Quincy Jones, "Body Heat." A&M.
Steely Dan, "Rikki Don't Lose That Number." ABC.
Stylistics, "You Make Me Feel Brand New." Avco.
Dionne Warwick, Spinners, "Then Came You." Atlantic.

BEST POP INSTRUMENTAL PERFORMANCE
• Marvin Hamlisch, "The Entertainer." MCA.
Herbie Hancock, *Head Hunters*. Columbia.
Quincy Jones, "Along Came Betty." A&M.
Love Unlimited Orchestra, *Rhapsody in White*. 20th Century.
Rick Wakeman, *Journey to the Center of the Earth*. A&M.

Best Rhythm & Blues Song
(Songwriter's Award)
- "Living for the City," Stevie Wonder.

"Dancing Machine," Harold Davis, Don Fletcher, Dean Parts.

"For the Love of Money," Ken Gamble, Leon Huff, Anthony Jackson.

"Rock Your Baby," Henry Wayne Casey, Richard Finch.

Best Rhythm & Blues Vocal Performance, Male
- Stevie Wonder, "Boogie on Reggae Woman." Tamla/Motown.

Johnny Bristol, "Hang on in There Baby." MGM.

Marvin Gaye, *Marvin Gaye— Live*. Tamla/Motown.

Eddie Kendricks, "Boogie Down." Tamla/Motown.

George McCrae, "Rock Your Baby." T.K.

Best Rhythm & Blues Vocal Performance, Female
- Aretha Franklin, "Ain't Nothing Like the Real Thing." Atlantic.

Shirley Brown, "Woman to Woman." Truth/Stax.

Thelma Houston, "You've Been Doing Wrong for So Long." Motown.

Millie Jackson, "If Loving You Is Wrong I Don't Want to Be Right." Spring.

Etta James, "St. Louis Blues." Chess.

Ann Peebles, "(You Keep Me) Hangin' On." Hi/London.

Tina Turner, *Tina Turns the Country On!* United Artists.

Rhythm & Blues Vocal Performance, Duo, Group, or Chorus
- Rufus, "Tell Me Something Good." ABC.

Jackson 5, "Dancing Machine." Motown.

Gladys Knight & the Pips, "I Feel a Song (In My Heart)." Buddah.

O'Jays, "For the Love of Money." Philadelphia International/Epic.

Spinners, "Mighty Love." Atlantic.

"Band on the Run" earned Paul McCartney & Wings a pop vocals award for a second time.

Best Rhythm & Blues Instrumental Performance
- MFSB, "TSOP (The Sound of Philadelphia)." Philadelphia International/Epic.

Average White Band, "Pick Up the Pieces." Atlantic.

Crusaders, *Scratch*. Blue Thumb.

Kool & the Gang, *Light of Worlds*. De-Lite.

Billy Preston, "Struttin'." A&M.

Best Jazz Performance by a Soloist
- Charlie Parker, *First Recordings!* Onyx.

Freddie Hubbard, *High Energy*. Columbia.

Keith Jarrett, *Solo Concerts*. ECM/Polydor.

Hubert Laws, *In the Beginning*. CTI.

McCoy Tyner, *Naima*. Milestone.

BEST JAZZ PERFORMANCE BY A GROUP
• Oscar Peterson, Joe Pass, Niels Pedersen, *The Trio*. Pablo.
Bill Evans, *The Tokyo Concert*. Fantasy.
Freddie Hubbard, *High Energy*. Columbia.
Supersax, *Salt Peanuts*. Capitol.
McCoy Tyner, *Sama Layuca*. Milestone.

BEST JAZZ PERFORMANCE BY A BIG BAND
• Woody Herman, *Thundering Herd*. Fantasy.
Les Hooper Big Band, *Look What They've Done*. Creative World.
Chuck Mangione (with Hamilton Philharmonic Orchestra), *Land of Make Believe*. Mercury.
Don Sebesky, *Giant Box*. CTI.
Pat Williams, *Threshold*. Capitol.

BEST COUNTRY SONG
(Songwriter's Award)
• "A Very Special Love Song," Norris Wilson, Billy Sherrill.
"Fairytale," Anita Pointer, Bonnie Pointer.
"If We Make It Through December," Merle Haggard.
"I'm a Ramblin' Man," Ray Pennington.
"Paper Roses," Janice Torre, Fred Spielman.

BEST COUNTRY VOCAL PERFORMANCE, MALE
• Ronnie Milsap, "Please Don't Tell Me How the Story Ends." RCA.
Glen Campbell, "Bonaparte's Retreat." Capitol.
Roy Clark, *The Entertainer*. Dot.
Waylon Jennings, "I'm a Ramblin' Man." RCA.
Charley Pride, *Country Feelin'*. RCA.

BEST COUNTRY VOCAL PERFORMANCE, FEMALE
• Anne Murray, "Love Song." Capitol.
Dolly Parton, "Jolene." RCA.
Tanya Tucker, "Would You Lay With Me (In a Field of Stone)." Columbia.
Dottie West, "Last Time I Saw Him." RCA.
Tammy Wynette, "Woman to Woman." Epic.

BEST COUNTRY VOCAL PERFORMANCE, DUO OR GROUP
• Pointer Sisters, "Fairytale." Blue Thumb.

Bobby Bare, Bobby Bare Jr., "Daddy What If." RCA.
Kris Kristofferson, Rita Coolidge, "Loving Arms." A&M.
Willie Nelson, Tracy Nelson, "After the Fire Is Gone." Atlantic.
Statler Brothers, "Whatever Happened to Randolph Scott." Mercury.

BEST COUNTRY INSTRUMENTAL PERFORMANCE
• Chet Atkins, Merle Travis, *The Atkins–Travis Traveling Show*. RCA.
Floyd Cramer, *The Young & the Restless*. RCA.
Danny Davis & the Nashville Brass, *Nashville Brass in Blue Grass Country*. RCA.
Charlie McCoy, *The Nashville Hit Man*. Monument.
Charlie McCoy, Barefoot Jerry, "Boogie Woogie (a/k/a T.D.'S Boogie Woogie)." Monument.

BEST INSPIRATIONAL PERFORMANCE (NON-CLASSICAL)
• Elvis Presley, *How Great Thou Art*. RCA.
Tennessee Ernie Ford, *Make a Joyful Noise*. Capitol.
Bill Gaither Trio, *Thanks for Sunshine*. Impact.
Sister Janet Mead, "The Lord's Prayer." A&M.
Bill Pursell, *Listen*. Word.

BEST GOSPEL PERFORMANCE (OTHER THAN SOUL GOSPEL)
• Oak Ridge Boys, "The Baptism of Jesse Taylor." Columbia.
Wendy Bagwell & the Sunliters, *The Carpenter's Tool*. Canaan.
Blackwood Brothers, *There He Goes*. Skylite.
Imperials, *Follow the Man with the Music*. Impact.
LeFevres, *Stepping on the Clouds*. Canaan.

BEST SOUL GOSPEL PERFORMANCE
• James Cleveland & the Southern California Community Choir, *In the Ghetto*. Savoy.
Five Blind Boys, *My Desire*. Peacock/ABC.
Edwin Hawkins Singers, *Edwin Hawkins Singers Live*. Buddah.
Ike Turner, "Father Alone." United Artists.

Ike & Tina Turner, *The Gospel According to Ike and Tina*. United Artists.

BEST ETHNIC OR TRADITIONAL RECORDING (INCLUDING TRADITIONAL BLUES AND PURE FOLK)
• *Two Days in November*, Doc & Merle Watson. United Artists.
The Back Door Wolf, Howlin' Wolf. Chess.
Big Daddy, Bukka White. Biograph.
Catalyst, Willie Dixon. Ovation.
London Revisited, Muddy Waters, Howlin' Wolf. Chess.

BEST INSTRUMENTAL ARRANGEMENT
• Pat Williams, "Threshold" (Pat Williams). Capitol.
Les Hooper, "Circumvent" (Les Hooper Big Band). Creative World.
Les Hooper, "Look What They've Done" (Les Hooper Big Band). Creative World.
Bob James, "Night on Bald Mountain" (Bob James). CTI.
Don Sebesky, "Firebird/Birds of Fire" (Don Sebesky). CTI.

BEST INSTRUMENTAL COMPOSITION
(Composer's Award)
• Mike Oldfield, "Tubular Bells" Theme from *The Exorcist*)".
Benny Golson, "Along Came Betty."
Herbie Hancock, Paul Jackson, Bernie Maupin, Harvey Mason,"Chameleon."
Barry White, "Barry's Theme."
Barry White, "Rhapsody in White."

BEST SCORE FROM AN ORIGINAL CAST SHOW ALBUM
• *Raisin*, Judd Woldin, Robert Brittan, composers. Thomas Z. Shepard, producer. Columbia.
Let My People Come, Earl Wilson, Jr., Phil Oesterman, composers. Henry Jerome, producer. Libra.
The Magic Show, Stephen Schwartz, composer. Phil Ramone, Stephen Schwartz, producers. Bell.
Over Here, Richard M. Sherman,& Robert B. Sherman, composers. Charles Koppelman, Teo Macero, producers. Columbia.
The Rocky Horror Show, Richard O'Brien, composer. Lou Adler, producer. Ode.

BEST ORIGINAL SCORE WRITTEN FOR A MOTION PICTURE OR A TELEVISION SPECIAL
(Composer's Award)
• *The Way We Were*, Marvin Hamlisch, Alan and Marilyn Bergman. Columbia.
Death Wish, Herbie Hancock. Columbia.
QB VII, Jerry Goldsmith. ABC.
Serpico, Mikis Theodorakis. Paramount/ABC.
The Three Musketeers, Michel Legrand. Bell.

BEST ARRANGEMENT ACCOMPANYING VOCALISTS
• Joni Mitchell, Tom Scott, "Down to You" (Joni Mitchell). Asylum.
Michael Gibbs, "Smile of the Beyond" (Carol Shive; Mahavishnu Orchestra with London Symphony). Columbia.
Chuck Mangione, "Land of Make Believe" (Esther Satterfield; Chuck Mangione, Hamilton Philharmonic). Mercury.
Gene Puerling, Les Hooper, "We've Only Just Begun" (the Singers Unlimited). MPS/BASF.
Gene Puerling, "Where Is Love" (the Singers Unlimited). MPS/BASF.

ALBUM OF THE YEAR—CLASSICAL
• *Berlioz: Symphonie Fantastique*, Georg Solti conducting Chicago Symphony. David Harvey, producer. London.
Berlioz: The Damnation of Faust, Colin Davis conducting London Symphony Orchestra and Chorus; Ambrosian Singers; Wandsworth School Boys' Choir (solos: Gedda, Bastin, Veasey, Van Allan). Erik Smith, producer. Philips.
Ives: The 100th Anniversary, Various Orchestras, Conductors, Soloists, etc. Leroy Parkins, Vivian Perlis, producers. Columbia.
Mahler: Symphony No. 2 in C Minor ("Resurrection"), Leonard Bernstein conducting London Symphony. Edinburgh Festival Chorus (solos: Baker, Armstrong). John McClure, producer. Columbia.
Schumann: Faust, Benjamin Britten conducting English Chamber Orchestra (solos: Fischer-Dieskau, Pears, Shirley Quirk). Christopher Raeburn. Michael Woolcock, producers. London.
Snowflakes Are Dancing, Isao Tomita. Isao Tomita, producer. RCA.

Weber: Der Freischutz, Carlos Kleiber conducting Dresden State Orchestra. Leipzig Radio Chorus (solos: Mathis, Janowitz, Schreier, Adam, etc.). Dr. Ellen Hickmann, producer. Deutsche Grammophon.

BEST CLASSICAL PERFORMANCE, ORCHESTRA
(Conductor's Award)
• Georg Solti conducting Chicago Symphony, *Berlioz: Symphonie Fantastique*. London.
Leonard Bernstein conducting New York Philharmonic, *Bernstein Conducts Ravel*. Columbia.
Leonard Bernstein conducting London Symphony, *Mahler: Symphony No. 2 in C Minor*. Columbia.
André Previn conducting London Symphony, *Holst: The Planets*. Angel.
José Serebrier conducting London Philharmonic, *Ives: Symphony No. 4*. RCA.
Herbert von Karajan conducting Berlin Philharmonic, *Bartók: Concerto for Orchestra*. Angel.

BEST CHAMBER MUSIC PERFORMANCE, INSTRUMENTAL OR VOCAL
• Artur Rubinstein, Henryk Szeryng, Pierre Fournier, *Brahms: Trios (complete); Schumann: Trio No. 1 in D Minor*. RCA.
Julian Bream, John Williams, *Julian & John, Vol. 2 (Albéniz, Giuliani, Granados, etc.)*. RCA.
Aaron Copland conducting Columbia Chamber Orchestra, *Copland: Appalachian Spring*. Columbia.
Ralph Grierson with George Sponholtz & the Southland Stingers, *Joplin: Palm Leaf Rag*. Angel.
Juilliard Quartet, *Beethoven: Late Quartets*. Columbia.
Tokyo String Quartet, *Haydn: String Quartets, Op. 50 Nos. 1 & 2*. Deutsche Grammophon.
Paul Zukofsky, Gilbert Kalish, *Ives: Violin Sonatas Nos. 1–4*. Nonesuch.

BEST CLASSICAL PERFORMANCE, INSTRUMENTAL SOLOIST(S)
(WITH ORCHESTRA)
• David Oistrakh (M. Shostakovich conducting New Philharmonic), *Shostakovich: Violin Concerto No. 1*. Angel.
Claudio Arrau (Inbal conducting London Philharmonic), *Chopin: Variations on "La ci darem la mano"; Fantasy on Polish Airs, Op. 13; Andante Spianato & Grande Polonaise Brillante in E Flat, Op. 22*. Philips.
Alfred Brendel (Haitink conducting Concertgebouw Orchestra), *Brahms: Piano Concerto No. 2 in B Flat Major*. Philips.
Norbert Hauptmann (von Karajan conducting Berlin Philharmonic), *Strauss: Horn Concerto No. 2 in E Flat Major*. Deutsche Grammophon.
Kyung-Wha Chung (Previn conducting London Symphony), *Walton: Violin Concerto; Stravinsky: Violin Concerto in D Major*. London.
Itzhak Perlman (Previn conducting London Symphony), *Bartók: Violin Concerto No. 2*. Angel.
Barry Tuckwell (Marriner conducting Academy of St. Martin-in-the-Fields), *Weber: Concertino in E Minor for Horn and Orchestra*. Angel.
André Watts (Leinsdorf conducting London Symphony), *Liszt: Todtentanz for Piano & Orchestra; Franck: Symphonic Variations for Piano & Orchestra*. Columbia.

BEST CLASSICAL PERFORMANCE, INSTRUMENTAL SOLOIST(S)
(WITHOUT ORCHESTRA)
• Alicia de Larrocha, *Albéniz: Iberia*. London.
David Burge, *Crumb: Makro Kosmos*. Nonesuch.
Glenn Gould, *Bach: French Suites, Vol. 2 Nos. 5 & 6*. Columbia.
Vladimir Horowitz, *Beethoven: Piano Sonatas Nos. 21 in C Major ("Waldstein") & 23 in F Minor ("Appassionata")*. Columbia.
Alfons and Aloys Kontarsky, *Ravel & Debussy: Music for Two Pianos/4 Hands*. Deutsche Grammophon.
Itzhak Perlman, *Perpetual Motion*. Angel.
Isao Tomita, *Snowflakes Are Dancing*. RCA.

BEST OPERA RECORDING
• *Puccini: La Bohème*, Georg Solti conducting London Philharmonic (solos: Caballé, Domingo, Milnes, Blegen, Raimondi). Richard Mohr, producer. RCA.
Humperdinck: Hänsel und Gretel, Kurt Eichhorn conducting Bavarian Radio Orchestra (solos: Moffo, Ludwig,

Fischer-Dieskau). Fritz Ganss, Theodor Hoizinger, producers. RCA.

Mozart: Cosi fan tutte, Georg Solti conducting London Philharmonic (solos: Lorengar, Berganza, Berbie, Davies, Krause, Bacquier). Christopher Raeburn, producer. London.

Mozart: Don Giovanni, Colin Davis conducting Chorus and Orchestra Royal Opera House, Covent Garden (solos: Wixell, Ganzarolli, Arroyo, Te Kanawa, Freni, Burrows). Erik Smith, producer. Philips.

Pfitzner: Palestrina, Rafael Kubelik conducting Bavarian Radio Chorus and Orchestra (solos: Donath, Fassbaender, Gedda, Fischer-Dieskau, Prey). Dr. Rudolf Werner, producer. Deutsche Grammophon.

Verdi: I Vespri Siciliani, James Levine conducting New Philharmonia; John Alldis Choir (solos: Arroyo, Domingo, Milnes, Raimondi). Richard Mohr, producer. RCA.

Weber: Der Freischütz, Carlos Kleiber conducting Dresden State Orchestra; Leipzig Radio Chorus (solos: Mathis, Janowitz, Schreier, Adam, Crass, Weikl). Dr. Ellen Hickman, producer. Deutsche Grammophon.

BEST CHORAL PERFORMANCE, OTHER THAN OPERA

• Colin Davis conducting London Symphony Orchestra and Chorus, Ambrosian Singers, Wandsworth School Boys' Choir (solos: Gedda, Bastin, Veasey, Van Allan), *Berlioz: The Damnation of Faust*. Philips.

John Alldis, chorus master, London Philharmonic Choir. Sir Adrian Boult conducting Orchestra, *Vaughan Williams: Dona Nobis Pacem*. Angel.

Sir Adrian Boult conducting London Philharmonic Choir and Orchestra, *Holst: Choral Symphony*. Angel.

Jozef Bok, chorus master, Chorus of National Philharmonic Warsaw. Wladyslaw Skoraczewski, chorus master, Pioneer Choir. Andrzej Markowski conducting Symphony Orchestra of National Philharmonic, *Penderecki: Utrenja*. Philips.

Russell Burgess conducting Aldeburgh Festival Singers; Wandsworth School Choir. Benjamin Britten conducting English Chamber Orchestra, *Schumann: Faust*. London.

Rudolf Kempe conducting Royal Philharmonic and Brighton Festival Chorus, *Janácek: Glagolitic Mass* (Slavonic Mass). London.

Eugene Ormandy conducting Philadelphia Orchestra; Robert Page directing Temple University Choirs, *Rachmaninoff: The Bells*. RCA.

Aleksander Sveshnikov conducting U.S.S.R. Russian Chorus, *Rachmaninoff: Vespers (Mass) Op. 37*. Melodiya/Angel.

BEST CLASSICAL PERFORMANCE, VOCAL SOLOIST

• Leontyne Price, *Leontyne Price Sings Richard Strauss*. RCA.

Elly Ameling, *Schubert: Goethe-Lieder*. Philips.

Martina Arroyo, *There's a Meeting Here Tonight*. Angel.

Janet Baker, *Brahms: Alto Rhapsody*. Angel.

Cathy Berberian, *Cathy Berberian at the Edinburgh Festival*. RCA.

Jan Degaetani, *Crumb: Night of the Four Moons*. Columbia.

Julius Eastman, *Davies: Eight Songs for a Mad King*. Nonesuch.

Marilyn Horne, *French and Spanish Songs*. London.

Sherrill Milnes, *Amazing Grace (Agnus Dei, Bless the Lord, O My Soul, etc.)*. RCA.

Birgit Nilsson, Helge Brilioth, *Wagner: Duets from Parsifal & Die Walküre*. Philips.

BEST ENGINEERED RECORDING, CLASSICAL

• Kenneth Wilkinson, *Berlioz: Symphonie Fantastique* (Solti conducting Chicago Symphony). London.

Marc Aubort, Joanna Nickrenz, *Percussion Music* (New Jersey Percussion Ensemble). Nonesuch.

Paul Goodman, Robert Auger, *Ives: Symphony No. 4* (Serebrier conducting London Philharmonic). RCA.

Bud Graham, Ray Moore, *Bernstein: Candide* (Original Cast). Columbia.

Anthony Salvatore, *Puccini: La Bohème* (Solti conducting London Philharmonic; solos: Domingo, Caballe). RCA.

Isao Tomita, *Snowflakes Are Dancing*
(Isao Tomita). RCA.
Stanley Tonkel, Ray Moore, Milt Cherin,
Copland: Appalachian Spring
(Copland conducting Columbia
Chamber Players). Columbia.

BEST ALBUM NOTES, CLASSICAL
• Rory Guy, *Korngold: The Classic Erich
Wolfgang Korngold*. (solo: Hoeischer;
Mattes, conductor). Angel.
David Cairns, *Berlioz: The Damnation of
Faust* (Davis conducting London
Symphony). Philips.
Deryck Cooke, *Mahler: Symphony No. 10*
(Morris conducting New Philharmonia
Orchestra). Philips.
Donald Garvelmann, *Scriabin: Piano
Music (Comp.) Vol. II* (Ponti). Vox.
George Jellinek, *Humperdinck: Hänsel
und Gretel* (Eichhorn conducting
Bavarian Radio; Moffo, Donath). RCA.
Irving Kolodin, *Verdi: I Vespri Siciliani*
(Levine conducting New
Philharmonia). RCA.
Christopher Palmer, *Herrmann: Citizen
Kane* (Gerhardt conducting National
Philharmonic). RCA.
Wolfram Schwinger, *Weber: Der
Freischütz* (Kleiber conducting Mathis,
Janowitz, etc). Deutsche Grammophon.
Erik Smith, *Mozart: Don Giovanni* (Davis
conducting Royal Opera House Chorus
and Orchestra). Philips.
Clair W. Van Ausdall, *Rachmaninoff: The
Bells & Three Russian Songs*
(Ormandy conducting; Curtin, Shirley,
Devin; Temple University Choirs,
Page). RCA.

BEST COMEDY RECORDING
• *That Nigger's Crazy*, Richard Pryor.
Partee/Stax.
Booga! Booga! David Steinberg. Columbia.
Cheech & Chong's Wedding Album,
Cheech & Chong. Ode.
Mind Over Matter, Robert Klein.
Brut/Buddah.
Missing White House Tapes, National
Lampoon. Blue Thumb.

BEST SPOKEN WORD RECORDING
• *Good Evening*, Peter Cook, Dudley
Moore. Island.
An Ear to the Sounds of Our History, Eric
Sevareid. Columbia.
"Autumn," Rod McKuen. Stanyan/Warner
Bros.

Senator Sam at Home, Sam Ervin. Columbia.
Watergate Volume Three: "I Hope the
President Is Forgiven" (John W. Dean
III Testifies), compiled by Don Molner.
Folkways.

BEST RECORDING FOR CHILDREN
• *Winnie the Pooh & Tigger Too*,
Sebastian Cabot, Sterling Holloway,
Paul Winchell. Disneyland.
America Sings, Burl Ives, Others,
Orchestra and Chorus, Buddy Baker
conducting. Disneyland.
Eli Wallach Reads Isaac Bashevis Singer,
Eli Wallach. Newbery.
New Adventures of Bugs Bunny Volume II,
Mel Blanc. Peter Pan.
Robin Hood, Various Artists, narrated by
Roger Miller. Disneyland.

BEST ENGINEERED RECORDING,
NON-CLASSICAL
• Geoff Emerick, *Band on the Run* (Paul
McCartney & Wings). Apple/Capitol.
Rik Pekkonen, Peter Granet, *Southern
Comfort* (Crusaders). Blue Thumb.
Bill Schnee, *Lincoln Mayorga and
Distinguished Colleagues Volume III*
(Lincoln Mayorga). Sheffield.
Ken Scott, John Jansen, *Crime of the
Century* (Supertramp). A&M.
Tommy Vicari, Larry Forkner, *Powerful
People* (Gino Vannelli). A&M.

BEST ALBUM PACKAGE
(Art Director's Award)
• Ed Thrasher, Christopher Whorf, *Come
& Gone* (Mason Proffit). Warner Bros.
John Berg, *Santana's Greatest Hits*
(Santana). Columbia.
Eddie Biscoe, *Ride 'em Cowboy* (Paul
Davis). Bang.
Ron Coro, *On Stage* (Loggins &
Messina). Columbia.
Bob Defrin, Basil Pao, *Is It In* (Eddie
Harris). Atlantic.
Herb Greene, *That's a Plenty* (Pointer
Sisters). Blue Thumb.
Ode Visuals, *Cheech & Chong's Wedding
Album* (Cheech & Chong). Ode.
Ethan A. Russell, *Quadrophenia* (the
Who). MCA.

BEST ALBUM NOTES
(Annotator' Award)
• Charles R. Townsend, *For the Last Time* (Bob Wills & his Texas Playboys). United Artists.
• Dan Morgenstern, *The Hawk Flies* (Coleman Hawkins). Milestone.
Rudy Behlmer, *50 Years of Film Music* (Original Motion Picture Soundtrack Recordings). Warner Bros.

Ralph J. Gleason, *The Pianist* (Duke Ellington). Fantasy.
J.R. Young, *The World Is Still Waiting for the Sunrise* (Les Paul, Mary Ford). Capitol.

PRODUCER OF THE YEAR
• Thom Bell
Rick Hall
Billy Sherrill
Lenny Waronker
Stevie Wonder

Homecoming Night as Disco Dawns

As the rock era reached the mid-1970s, American and European youths were shaking it up in new discos full of swirling lights, pulsing bodies, and music that exhorted them to forget their woes, join the Big Party, and dance, dance, dance till dawn. The rock music of the recent past had been daring — but not danceable. Now a new hit sound with a rolling beat was pervading the airwaves and downtown dance clubs, while also introducing a new generation of musical artists like LaBelle, the Blackbyrds, and Gloria Gaynor.

LP victor Paul Simon (Still Crazy After All These Years) *with producer Phil Ramone (left): "I'd like to thank Stevie Wonder for not releasing an album this year."*

Some disco acts would do especially well at this year's Grammys, including Earth, Wind & Fire, the Silver Connection, Van McCoy & the Soul City Symphony, and K.C. & the Sunshine Band, the artists who would lead with the most nominations (five).

A few of rock's past music heroes, determined to keep the old (and more "serious") sound alive, considered it the perfect time for a comeback. Singer-songwriter Janis Ian had retired in 1967 at the age of 19 after she gave away the fortune she made from her hit protest song "Society's Child (Baby I've Been Thinking)" to needy friends and charities. Her 1975 album, *Between the Lines*, marked a triumphant return for her and brought Ian the second most Grammy nominations — four — including nods

for Record, Album, and Song of the Year. Sources like *The Los Angeles Herald Examiner* considered her the Grammy derby's clear front runner.

Judy Collins was back, too, singing more mournfully than ever (Stephen Sondheim's "Send in the Clowns," which was up for Song of the Year and brought Collins a bid for best female pop vocalist). But no one was more mournful, more melancholy — or more determined, for that matter — than a suddenly matured Paul Simon, who was no longer pining in his music after the faded icons of his boyhood ("Where have you gone, Joe DiMaggio?") or hanging out in the schoolyard with Julio. Simon's marriage to his first wife, Peggy, had just broken up and suddenly the 34-year-old artist was singing about "50 Ways to Leave Your Lover," while also wanting to prove to the crazed teenage disco set that he, too, was *Still Crazy After All These Years*.

Simon had won seven Grammys as part of the Simon & Garfunkel duo, which broke up in 1970 (after sweeping the Grammys with Album, Record, and Song of the Year *Bridge Over Troubled Water*), but now he was back with three nods, including one for Album of the Year and two for best pop vocals. In the LP contest, Simon was pitted against Janis Ian (the sentimental favorite), the Eagles (the hottest pop band in America), Elton John (who was *still* hot and long overdue for *any* Grammy), and Linda Ronstadt (a darling of N.A.R.A.S. voters who appreciated safe rock with lots of vocal craftsmanship). "As an artist, rather than a commercial force or a pleasant entertainer," wrote *Rolling Stone* rock critic Dave Marsh about the competition, "Paul Simon stands out like Kareem Abdul Jabbar in a kindergarten. But I'll bet he doesn't win."

Simon shocked everyone — and pulled off his rock resurrection officially — when he seized the LP laurels and told the crowd gathered at the Hollywood Palladium for the Grammycast, "I'd like to thank Stevie Wonder for not releasing an album this year."

Still Crazy represented an artistic departure for Simon. It had a jazzy beat, more complex themes, and a collaboration with a new emerging artist (Phoebe Snow on "Gone at Last") as well as an old colleague (Art Garfunkel on "My Little Town," which Garfunkel also included in his 1975 album, interestingly entitled *Breakaway*). The former duo still had their creative differences, but teamed up now and then for events like a presidential fund-raiser for George McGovern in 1972. Together they were up for the pop duo/group honors for "My Little Town" but lost to the Eagles, who had been usurped in 1972 for the

Best New Artist award by America. Simon nonetheless took a ninth Grammy for Best Male Pop Vocal Performance for his *Still Crazy* album.

There was no greater shocker, however, than the outcome of the race for Song of the Year, which proved, according to the *L.A. Herald Examiner*, that "artistic quality took precedence over commercial success" on Grammy night. What *Variety* called the evening's "surprising choice" was "Send in the Clowns," the Stephen Sondheim song from his musical *A Little Night Music* that Judy Collins rendered in folksy soprano on her critically acclaimed comeback album *Judith*. The good news came with some bad for the victorious Sondheim: Whereas the original Broadway recording of *A Little Night Music* was voted Best Original Cast Show Album in 1973, the London cast version lost the same award this year to *The Wiz*, written by Charlie Smalls (who also — quite surprisingly — beat out last year's Grammy grabber Marvin Hamlisch for *A Chorus Line*, which would become the most successful musical in Broadway history).

> *Revitalized '60s singer Janis Ian was the Grammy derby's early front runner.*

Janis Ian had attempted a comeback in 1974 with her *Stars* LP, which did reach the bottom rungs of the album charts, but none of its individual songs caught on. When *Between the Lines* was released one year later, its "At Seventeen" single soared up the rankings (to number 25 in the year's Hot 100), having been discovered by young female record buyers who adopted it as their anthem of teenage angst. Ian ended up losing her bids for Record, Song, and

Album of the Year, but she still picked up the prize for Best Female Pop Vocal Performance. The *Herald Examiner* may have believed Ian was poised for a Grammy sweep, but the paper never said it approved, commenting: "How the Academy chose to pit a mere single like Ian's 'At Seventeen,' a nice song but surely not indicative of her best, against a whole album like Linda Ronstadt's stunning *Heart Like a Wheel* album is, to say the least, strange." Moreover, Ian's return to the spotlight would be short-lived. Despite several more album releases after winning her Grammy —

Written by Neil Sedaka and Howard Greenfield, "Love Will Keep Us Together" was the top-selling single of 1975 (and ranked number three in *Billboard*'s annual Hot 100, which took into account poll results from record buyers and the frequency of a song's radio airplay, in addition to sales figures). The Captain & Tennille's debut album of the same name was number four in the year's LP charts and also included their first hit single, "The Way I Want to Touch You," which they produced, manufactured, and distributed themselves in order to break into the pop field.

GLOBE PHOTO

Critics called the Captain & Tennille's "Love Will Keep Us Together" single "a nice, well produced and highly listenable little record, but hardly the best of the year."

The Captain & Tennille were married to each other and bore a passing resemblance to the Carpenters, a comparison that made them bristle noticeably. They had both worked together for a while as side artists for the Beach Boys (Toni Tennille was the group's only "Beach Girl," playing the piano and doing backup vocals; the Captain — whose real name was Daryl Dragon and who was the son of famed orchestra conductor Carmen Dragon — did arrangements) before striking out on their own with "Touch You." When they ended up with the top Grammy of 1975, the *Herald Tribune* was *really* miffed: "Giving 'Love Will Keep Us Together' the Record of the Year award was almost ridiculous. It is a nice, well produced and highly listenable little record, but hardly the best of the year."

including *Night Rains*, her paean to disco in 1979 — she failed to reach the Top 10 again.

Grammy grousers considered this year's contest for Record of the Year to be one of the weakest in memory. "At Seventeen" was pitted against Barry Manilow's "Mandy," Glen Campbell's "Rhinestone Cowboy," "Lyin' Eyes" by the Eagles, and "Love Will Keep Us Together" by the Captain & Tennille. (Paul Simon, surprisingly was overlooked in the runoff.)

"Touch You" came out in 1974, so the Captain & Tennille were not considered for the Best New Artist prize. But the night's leader in total Grammy nominations — K.C. & the Sunshine Band — was and was also expected to take the award easily.

Twenty-five-year-old Natalie Cole ended up causing the second major surprise of awards night when she became the first black ever voted Best New Artist. Her 1975 debut album, *Inseparable*, was released exactly 10 years after the death of her father, the legendary Grammy-winning Nat "King" Cole, and included the song for which she would also win Best Female Rhythm & Blues Vocal Performance "This Will Be." By winning the r&b award, Cole officially ended Aretha Franklin's eight-year monopoly of the category, a fitting victory since Cole's producers had been hyping her around the music world as "the next Aretha Franklin."

The victories, noted *The Washington Post*, "gave her budding show business career an auspicious boost," even though Cole's success, like Ian's, would prove to be temporary. Despite the fact that Cole continued to produce LPs that brushed the bottom rungs of the album charts through the rest of the 1970s, her career went into decline during the 1980s as she battled problems with alcohol and drugs, only to rebound in the early 1990s when she returned to the Grammys, sober and triumphant, with victories for best record and album.

The winners of the pop vocals group honors, the Eagles, had three songs in the year's Hot 100: "One of These Nights" (#9), "Best of My Love" (#26), and "Lyin' Eyes" (#84). They also had considerable professional experience behind them when they first banded together. All five Eagles had been members of notable groups in the past, including the Dillard and Clark Expedition, Poco, Rick Nelson's Stone Canyon Band, and the Flying Burrito Brothers. Since their debut in 1972, the new act had three successful albums (*The Eagles*, *Desperado*, and *On the Border*), but it wasn't until the 1975 release of *One of These Nights* that the Eagles were finally flying high as the most popular rockers on the charts. The difference: They shucked off the country accent of their earlier work and with it, unfortunately, lost band member Bernie Leadon, who quit in protest .

For the male r&b vocal award, Ray Charles came back with "Living in the City" to claim his tenth trophy. Noted the *L.A. Times*: "He thus trails only Henry Mancini (20 Grammys), Vladimir Horowitz (12), and Roger Miller (11) on the all-time list," adding, "Stevie Wonder and Aretha Franklin also have 10." Like other winners this year, Charles was experiencing a comeback of sorts. He toured 12 European cities in 1975, in addition to making his yearly sweep of the U.S.,

"As an artist, Paul Simon stands out like Kareem Abdul Jabbar in a kindergarten."

and, said the critics approvingly, he seemed to have had recaptured his old sense of humor in his music.

The swinging disco set may have had their collective feet knocked out from under them in the top award categories, but they took the rest of the r&b slots like they took America's dance floors of the era — by storm. Of K.C. & the Sunshine Band's five nominations, three ("Where Is the Love," "Get Down Tonight," and "That's the Way (I Like It)," all written by Harry "K.C." Casey and his sunny compatriots) were for Best Rhythm & Blues Song. Two of the tunes were in the annual Hot 100 ("That's the Way" at #7 and "Get Down Tonight" at #81). When "Where Is the

Love" prevailed, critics like *Rolling Stone*'s editors may have wept into their poisoned inkwells, but other press sources, like *The New York Times*, applauded: "In person, they are one of the most exciting groups performing today .... This is no insecure Caucasian kid mimicking black inflections, exhorting a crowd to 'put your hands together.' Raised in the Pentecostal Church, K.C. has assimilated black music as if he were born to it."

The New York Times once called "The Hustle" by Van McCoy & the Soul City Symphony (winner, Best Pop Instrumental Performance) "the biggest dance record of the 1970s." The song, in fact, was named after a popular club dance of the day. "It was completely different from the you-do-your-thing-and-I-do-mine dances," McCoy once told *Essence*. "It was people dancing together again." In early 1975, the step was just catching on among the disco set and McCoy wanted to give them something tailor-made. He wrote the tune in less than a hour and added it at the last minute to his *Disco Baby* LP. New York's club deejays discovered it, a single was released, and it zoomed to number one. After that, McCoy tried to recapture the success of "The Hustle" with more disco works and then by branching out into other music dimensions, but without luck. "It's tough to follow a record like 'The Hustle,'" he told *Billboard*. "It sold 10 million copies and was a complete accident. How do you top it?" He never did. McCoy died in 1979 of a heart attack at the age of 35.

The r&b instrumental award went to

> *Eddie Palmieri won the new Latin award for his daring mix of salsa and disco.*

the newly formed Silver Convention, for "Fly, Robin, Fly." The Convention was an invention of famed disco producer Michael Kunze, who worked in Munich where he also developed other such rising stars as Donna Summer. "Silver" was short for the name of the band's leader, songwriter, and arranger, Silvester Levay. When Levay penned "Fly, Robin, Fly," it was originally entitled "Run, Rabbit, Run." A half hour before his troupe was to tape it, however, he heard a song called "Run Rabbit" on Armed Forces Network Radio and made the word changes at the last minute. "Robin" then flew up the U.S. charts to number one after seven weeks.

Earth, Wind & Fire was a r&b group led by Maurice White, a former drummer for the Ramsey Lewis Trio, who was fast becoming a new dean of disco now that he and his band abandoned their jazz-flavored efforts of the late 1960s and early '70s for a funky new beat. By 1975, White had a message for the young movers and shakers tearing up the dance floors downtown: You, too, can be a star — or, even a "Shining Star," the title of Earth, Wind & Fire's first dance hit that also earned them the r&b group performance Grammy. The group beat out not only K.C. & the Sunshine Band (for "Get Down Tonight"), but also the Pointer Sisters (who had won a Grammy last year in the *country* category — where they were losing nominess this year) and the Average White Band.

It was the producer behind the Average White Band who won Grammy's second annual Producer of the Year prize. Arif Mardin was actually having a better than average year on the job: He also produced Judy Collins's *Judith* LP, "Jive Talkin'" by the Bee Gees, and Richard Harris's reading of Kahlil Gibran's *The Prophet,* which was up for Best Spoken Word Recording. (Harris, however, lost to James Whitmore as

Harry Truman in *Give 'Em Hell Harry*, which Whitmore performed often to critical raves on the stage.)

Chicago bluesman Muddy Waters had remained loyal to the Chess record label since the days of his earliest hits such as "I'm Ready" and "Rolling Stone" (after which the rock band took its name) in the late 1940s and early '50s. But in 1973, he broke away from Chess, sued for back royalties, and switched to Blue Sky where his work took on more of a rock & roll sound. His latest LP, *The Muddy Waters Woodstock Album*, won him the category of Best Ethnic or Traditional Recording for a third time.

Dizzy Gillespie had never won a Grammy before, but he made up for it this year when he claimed the soloist honors for finessing his trumpet on *Oscar Peterson and Dizzy Gillespie*. Gillespie was also nominated in the group category, but lost to Chick Corea and his Return to Forever band for one of their less critically regarded LPs. (*No Mystery*, griped *Rolling Stone*, "is no pleasure either.") But Corea's win was an important victory for the jazz fusion genre. When he and other fusion vanguards like Weather Report and Herbie Hancock failed to be nominated last year, *Variety* had reported "considerable discontent in the jazz groove."

Two jazzmen who had worked for Gillespie in the past shared the trophy for big band performance: alto sax player and onetime Gillespie sideman Phil Woods and Michel Legrand (former Gillespie arranger) and his Orchestra. Their winning work, "Images," also earned Legrand the Best Instrumental Composition award. Besides being a jazz artist, Legrand was known for writing popular film scores to such hits as *Summer of '42* (1971) and the TV movie *Brian's Song* (1972), both of which earned him Grammys. This year the cat-

egory prize for original score went to a victor who would claim it more than a dozen times in the future — John Williams, composer of the music from *Jaws*. Williams beat out the man who had won more Grammys than anyone else: Henry Mancini, who was up for *The Return of the Pink Panther*.

For the past several years a consensus was forming within the record academy for the addition of a new category for Latin music. Finally, a *Billboard* headline proclaimed: "N.A.R.A.S. says 'Sí' to Latin Grammy, Wins Loud Olé." The eventual award recipient was Eddie Palmieri, one of salsa's leading and most innovative artists. His victorious *Sun of Latin Music* LP had a daring mix of both south- and north-of-the-border sounds, including Palmieri's interpretation of the new disco beat using trumpets, trombones, violins, flutes, and baritone sax.

Every year since 1969, Dolly Parton had been nominated for a Grammy (four times as best female country vocalist, twice for group performances) and now was up again for the female singing honor. But she lost again, this time to the Arizona-born Linda Ronstadt for "I Can't Help It (If I'm Still in Love with You)," thus offering further evidence to N.A.R.A.S.'s country contingent that Nashville outsiders were still showing considerable pull, just like last year when the Pointer Sisters took the group vocals prize.

Ronstadt was less of an outsider, though, than many believed. Her first hits may have been mainstream pop singles like 1966's "Different Drum," written by Mike Nesmith of the Monkees, and her first Grammy nomination was in 1970 for best female contemporary vocal performance for "Long, Long Time," but during lulls in her early career she explored country music, too, with singing engagements at the Grand Ole Opry and appearances on Johnny

Cash's television show.

B.J. Thomas had never been on *Billboard*'s country charts before landing there with Grammy's Best Country Song of 1975, "(Hey, Won't You Play) Another Somebody Done Somebody Wrong Song," which turned out to be both a country and pop chart-topper, ending the year at number 12 in the annual Hot 100. It was written in 20 minutes by producers Chips Moman and Larry Butler, the latter of whom objected strongly to Moman's desire to have the Oklahoma-born Thomas record it. Once the song leapt up the charts, Butler told *Billboard* about his objection, "I'm glad Chips talked me out of it."

Willie Nelson lost his bid for a Grammy last year but now claimed the male singing laurels for "Blue Eyes Crying in the Rain," which almost didn't get released when it was included in his self-produced *Red Headed Stranger* LP. Columbia Records "thought it was underproduced, too sparse, all those things," Nelson told *Billboard*. "Even though they didn't like it, they had already paid me a bunch of money for it, so they had to release it under my contract." Soon thereafter, its "Blue Eyes" single hit number one on the country chart and crossed over to become ranked number 21 in the annual Hot 100. To win his Grammy, Nelson beat John Denver, Ray Stevens, Freddy Fender, and Glen Campbell. Campbell had three nominations this year (and five Grammy wins under his belt from 1967 and '68), but came up with scratch.

The Pointer Sisters were again up for the group prize (for "Live Your Life Before You Die"), but lost to a duo they surpassed last year — Kris Kristofferson and Rita Coolidge, who rallied in 1975 with "Lover Please." Kristofferson had won Grammys twice before: for performing with Coolidge in 1973 for "From the Bottle to the Bottom" and for

writing 1971's Best Country Song "Help Me Make It Through the Night." Four-time past winner Chet Atkins held on to the instrumental category (he won it last year with Merle Travis) for his own guitar rendition of Scott Joplin's "The Entertainer," which had earned pianist Marvin Hamlisch the pop instrumental prize in 1974.

For a second year in a row, Richard Pryor had the Best Comedy Recording. In his latest winning LP, *Is It Something I Said?* he said his fair share of objectionable things in skits like "When Your Woman Leaves You" and lampooned cocaine abuse (a problem dogging Pryor's personal life at the time), insisting, "I must've snorted up Peru. I could've bought Peru, all the shit I snorted!"

Just as in other categories on Grammy night, there was a homecoming quality to the classical field. The triple winner of last year, conductor Sir Georg Solti, returned to reclaim the Classical Album of the Year award for his and the Chicago Symphony's recording of all nine Beethoven symphonies. *High Fidelity* gave the musical effort a mixed review. Symphony No. 1, it said, "is one of the better Firsts on modern records," also approving of this version of the Fourth ("the playing throughout has wonderful spirit and solidarity") and Seventh ("the prize of the cycle"). However, "Solti makes some serious errors of judgment" on the others, it added, asserting, for example, that his Symphony No. 9 is "for people who prefer a sonic blast to music."

Also returning were pianist Artur Rubinstein, violinist Henryk Szeryng, and cellist Pierre Fournier, who took the chamber music category last year with their renditions of Brahms and Schumann trios and this year were lauded for their trios by Schubert. ("This set is even better," *High Fidelity* wrote, adding that their joint accomplishment "definitely qualifies as one of the phonograph's classic achievements.") In the soloist categories, pianist Alicia de Larrocha came back for a second consecutive Grammy for performing two Ravel concertos and Fauré's *Fantaisie for Piano and Orchestra* (*High Fidelity*'s reviewer called it "marvelous ... a major release.") Seven-time past winner Pierre Boulez and the New York Philharmonic reaped the orchestral honors for their critically praised rendition of Ravel's ballet *Daphnis et Chloë*.

Violinist Nathan Milstein last recorded Bach's solo

Natalie Cole, the 25-year-old daughter of Nat "King" Cole, became the first black to win Best New Artist when she prevailed over K.C. & the Sunshine Band.

sonatas and partitas 20 years earlier, but when he attempted them again, he told *Musical America*, "This time I must make them as good as I can. I will never do them again." "He has done them colossally," *High Fidelity* said upon his completion of the task that also earned him his only career Grammy. The choral performance award went to the Cleveland Orchestra Chorus and Boys Choir under the choral direction of Michael Tilson Thomas for what the same publication called their "extraordinary" and "first rate" performance of Carl Orff's *Carmina Burana*.

On one occasion in the past a version of Mozart's *Così fan tutte* won Best Opera Recording — in 1968 with Erich Leinsdorf conducting the New Philharmonia Orchestra and Ambrosian Opera Chorus. Now it was back as the year's top opera with last year's Grammy winner Colin Davis conducting the Chorus and Orchestra of the Royal Opera House in London's Covent Garden, with soprano Montserrat Caballé as Fiordiligi and

mezzo-soprano Janet Baker as Dorabella. Davis, said *High Fidelity*, gave Mozart's classic "a sense of theatrical pulse" while Caballé's voice "has never been more ravishing," although Baker proved "disappointing." Neither diva was nominated for her Mozart performance, but Baker nonetheless "refined her singing in certain details" enough to take the vocalist solo honors for Mahler's *Kindertotenlieder,* despite heavy competition from Placido Domingo and the winner of the award for the past two years, Leontyne Price, both of whom were nominated together for their *Verdi & Puccini Duets*.

"As award shows go, this was a good one," *Variety* said in its review of the Grammycast. The ceremony at the Hollywood Palladium again employed Andy Williams as host ("Williams had the good nature to kid about his own less than daring, commercially bent image," said the *L.A. Times*) and included performances by Natalie Cole, Paul Simon, Janis Ian, and Barry Manilow. "Despite the inevitable grumbling, this year's Grammy ceremony was a well-paced, intelligently designed, satisfying production," the *Times* added. "At eighteen, then, the Grammy has definitely come of age."

The *Times*, however, still had some "inevitable grumbling" of its own to do just prior to the show. In an article titled "Is Grammy Boycotting Rock?" music columnist Robert Hilburn wrote, "Any group that nominates Captain & Tennille and ignores Bob Dylan — again — deserves a bit of scolding. And you'd think that a system that gives five nominations to K.C. & the Sunshine Band could find room for at least one for Bruce

Springsteen in a year in which he was clearly the most discussed and stirring new force in contemporary pop music ....

"Because a Latin music category was added this year, N.A.R.A.S. is obviously not averse to altering its awards structure .... It is time to establish a category to honor contemporary/rock artists .... The alternative is simply a continued inability to recognize artistry in a field that represents the heartbeat of pop music. If N.A.R.A.S. can find a place among its 48 categories for the man who wrote the liner notes for [Dylan's] *Blood on the Tracks*, you'd think it could find a way to at least consider the man who made the album."

1975

The awards ceremony was broadcast on CBS from the Hollywood Palladium on February 28, 1976, for the eligibility period October 16, 1974, to October 15, 1975.

ALBUM OF THE YEAR
• *Still Crazy After All These Years*, Paul Simon. Paul Simon, Phil Ramone, A&R producers. Columbia.
Between the Lines, Janis Ian. Brooks Arthur, A&R producer. Columbia.
Captain Fantastic and the Brown Dirt Cowboy, Elton John. Gus Dudgeon, A&R producer. MCA.
Heart Like a Wheel, Linda Ronstadt. Peter Asher, A&R producer. Capitol.
√ *One of These Nights*, Eagles. Bill Szymczyk, A&R producer. Asylum.

RECORD OF THE YEAR
• "Love Will Keep Us Together," Captain & Tennille. Daryl Dragon, A&R producer. A&M.
"At Seventeen," Janis Ian. Brooks Arthur, A&R producer. Columbia.
√ "Lyin' Eyes," Eagles. Bill Szymczyk, A&R producer. Asylum.
√ "Mandy," Barry Manilow. Clive Davis, Barry Manilow, Ron Dante, A&R producers. Arista.

√ "Rhinestone Cowboy," Glen Campbell. Dennis Lambert, Brian Potter, A&R producers. Capitol.

SONG OF THE YEAR
(Songwriter's Award)
• "Send in the Clowns," Stephen Sondheim.
"At Seventeen," Janis Ian.
√ "Feelings," Morris Albert.
"Love Will Keep Us Together," Neil Sedaka, Howard Greenfield.
√ "Rhinestone Cowboy," Larry Weiss.

BEST NEW ARTIST
• Natalie Cole. Capitol.
Morris Albert. RCA.
Amazing Rhythm Aces. RCA.
Brecker Brothers. Arista.
K.C. & the Sunshine Band. T.K.

BEST POP VOCAL PERFORMANCE, MALE
• Paul Simon, *Still Crazy After All These Years*. Columbia.
√ Morris Albert, "Feelings." RCA.
Elton John, *Captain Fantastic and the Brown Dirt Cowboy*. MCA.
√ Glen Campbell, "Rhinestone Cowboy." Capitol.
Neil Sedaka, "Bad Blood." Rocket/MCA.

Best Pop Vocal Performance, Female
• Janis Ian, "At Seventeen." Columbia.
Judy Collins, "Send in the Clowns."
  Elektra.
√ Olivia Newton-John, "Have You Never
  Been Mellow." MCA.
√ Helen Reddy, "Ain't No Way to Treat a
  Lady." Capitol.
Linda Ronstadt, *Heart Like a Wheel*.
  Capitol.

Best Pop Vocal Performance, Duo, Group, or Chorus
√ • Eagles, "Lyin' Eyes." Asylum.
Captain & Tennille, "Love Will Keep Us
  Together." A&M.
Gladys Knight & the Pips, "The Way We
  Were/Try to Remember." Buddah.
√ Simon & Garfunkel, "My Little Town."
  Columbia.
Singers Unlimited, *A Capella 2*. MPS.

Best Pop Instrumental Performance
• Van McCoy & the Soul City Symphony,
  "The Hustle." Avco.
Chuck Mangione, *Chase the Clouds Away*.
  A&M.
Mike Post, "The Rockford Files." MGM.
The Ritchie Family, "Brazil." 20th
  Century.
Tom Scott & the L.A. Express, *Tom Cat*.
  Ode.

Best Rhythm & Blues Song
(Songwriter's Award)
• "Where Is the Love," H.W. Casey,
  Richard Finch, Willie Clarke, Betty
  Wright.
"Ease on Down the Road," Charlie Smalls.
"Get Down Tonight," H.W. Casey,
  Richard Finch.
"That's the Way (I Like It)," H.W. Casey,
  Richard Finch.
"Walking in Rhythm," Barney Perry.

Best Rhythm & Blues Vocal Performance, Male
• Ray Charles, "Living for the City."
  Crossover.
Al Green, "L-O-V-E (Love)." Hi/London.
Major Harris, "Love Won't Let Me Wait."
  Atlantic.
Isaac Hayes, *Chocolate Chip*. Hot Buttered
  Soul.
Ben E. King, "Supernatural Thin, Part
  I."Atlantic.

Best Rhythm & Blues Vocal Performance, Female
• Natalie Cole, "This Will Be." Capitol.
Gloria Gaynor, *Never Can Say Goodbye*.
  MGM.
Gwen McCrae, "Rockin' Chair." Cat/T.K.
Esther Phillips, *What A Diff'rence a Day
  Makes*. Kudo/ CTI.
Shirley (and Company), "Shame, Shame,
  Shame." Vibration.

Best Rhythm & Blues Vocal Performance, Duo, Group, or Chorus
• Earth, Wind & Fire, "Shining Star."
  Columbia.
Average White Band, *Cut the Cake*.
  Atlantic.
K.C. & the Sunshine Band, "Get Down
  Tonight." T.K.
Ohio Players, *Fire*. Mercury.
Pointer Sisters, "How Long (Betcha' Got a
  Chick on the Side)." Blue Thumb.

Best Rhythm & Blues Instrumental Performance
• Silver Convention, "Fly, Robin, Fly."
  Midland/RCA.
Brecker Brothers, "Sneakin' Up Behind
  You." Arista.
B. T. Express, "Express." Scepter.
Herbie Hancock, "Hang Up Your
  Hangups." Columbia.
Van McCoy & the Soul City Symphony,
  Disco Baby. Avco.

Best Jazz Performance, Soloist
• Dizzy Gillespie, *Oscar Peterson and
  Dizzy Gillespie*. Pablo.
John Coltrane, "Giant Steps." Atlantic.
Jim Hall, *Concierto*. CTI.
Phineas Newborn, Jr., *Solo Piano*.
  Atlantic.
Phil Woods, *Images*. Gryphon/RCA.

Best Jazz Performance, Group
• Return to Forever featuring Chick Corea,
  No Mystery. Polydor.
Count Basie, *Basie Jam*. Pablo.
John Coltrane Quartet, "Giant Steps."
  Atlantic.
Dizzy Gillespie Quartet, *Dizzy Gillespie's
  Big 4*. Pablo.
Supersax, *Supersax Plays Bird with
  Strings*. Capitol.

Best Jazz Performance, Big Band
• Phil Woods with Michel Legrand & His Orchestra, *Images*. Gryphon/RCA.
Thad Jones, Mel Lewis, *Potpourri*. Philadelphia International.
Clark Terry, *Clark Terry's Big B-A-D Band Live at the Wichita Jazz Festival*. Vanguard.
North Texas State University Lab Band. Leon Breeden, director, *Lab '75*. NTSU.
Bill Watrous & the Manhattan Wildlife Refuge, *The Tiger of San Pedro*. Columbia.

Best Country Song
(Songwriter's Award)
• "(Hey Won't You Play) Another Somebody Done Somebody Wrong Song," Chips Moman, Larry Butler.
"Before the Next Teardrop Falls," Vivian Keith, Ben Peters.
√"Blue Eyes Crying in the Rain," Fred Rose.
"I'm Not Lisa," Jessi Colter.
√"Thank God I'm a Country Boy," John Martin Sommers.

Best Country Vocal Performance, Male
√• Willie Nelson, "Blue Eyes Crying in the Rain." Columbia.
√Glen Campbell, "Country Boy (You Got Your Feet in L.A.)." Capitol.
√John Denver, "Thank God I'm a Country Boy." RCA.
Freddy Fender, "Before the Next Teardrop Falls." Dot/ABC.
Waylon Jennings, "Are You Sure Hank Done It This Way?" RCA.
Ray Stevens, "Misty." Barnaby.

Best Country Vocal Performance, Female
• Linda Ronstadt, "I Can't Help It (If I'm Still in Love With You)." Capitol.
Jessi Colter, "I'm Not Lisa." Capitol.
Emmylou Harris, "If I Could Only Win Your Love." Reprise.
Loretta Lynn, "The Pill." MCA.
Dolly Parton, "Jolene," track from *In Concert*. RCA.

Best Country Vocal Performance, Duo or Group
• Kris Kristofferson, Rita Coolidge, "Lover Please." Monument.
Asleep at the Wheel, *Texas Gold*. Capitol.
Pointer Sisters, "Live Your Life Before You Die." Blue Thumb.
Statler Brothers, "I'll Go to My Grave Loving You." Mercury.
Conway Twitty, Loretta Lynn, "Feelins.'" MCA.

Best Country Instrumental Performance
• Chet Atkins, "The Entertainer." RCA.
Asleep at the Wheel, "Fat Boy Rag." Capitol.
Chet Atkins, Jerry Reed, "Colonel Bogey." RCA.
Vassar Clements, *Vassar Clements*. Mercury.
Charlie McCoy, *Charlie My Boy*. Monument.

Inspirational Performance
• Bill Gaither Trio, *Jesus, We Just Want to Thank You*. Impact.
Larry Hart, "Amazing Grace." Cam.
Anita Kerr, *Gentle As Morning*. Word.
Ray Price, *This Time Lord*. Myrrh.
The Speers, *Something Good Is About to Happen*. Heartwarming.

Best Gospel Performance (Other Than Soul Gospel)
• Imperials, *No Shortage*. Impact.
Johnny Cash, *Johnny Cash Sings Precious Memories*. Columbia.
Happy Goodman Family, *Happy Goodman Family Hour*. Canaan.
Connie Smith, *Connie Smith Sings Hank Williams Gospel*. Columbia.
Statler Brothers, *Holy Bible—New Testament*. Mercury.

Best Soul Gospel Performance
• Andrae Crouch & the Disciples, *Take Me Back*. Light.
James Cleveland, Chas. Fold Singers, "Jesus Is the Best Thing." Savoy.
James Cleveland, Southern California Community Choir, *To the Glory of God*. Savoy.

James Cleveland with Voices of
Tabernacle, *God Has Smiled on Me*.
Savoy.
21st Century, *The Storm Is Passing Over*.
Creed.

ETHNIC OR TRADITIONAL RECORDING (INCLUDING TRADITIONAL BLUES AND PURE FOLK)
• *The Muddy Waters Woodstock Album*,
Muddy Waters. Chess.
I Got What It Takes, Koko Taylor.
Alligator.
Memphis Blues, Memphis Slim. Olympic.
Music of Guatemala, San Lucas Band.
Kathryn King, producer.
ABC/Command.
Wake Up Dead Man, Black Convict Work
Songs. Recorded & edited by Bruce
Jackson. Rounder.

BEST LATIN RECORDING
• *Sun of Latin Music,* Eddie Palmieri.
Coco.
Afro-Indio, Mongo Santamaria. Fania.
Barretto, Ray Barretto. Fania.
*Fania All-Stars Live at Yankee Stadium,
Vol. 1*, Fania All-Stars. Fania.
The Good, the Bad & the Ugly, Willie
Colon. Fania.
Paunetto's Point, Bobby Paunetto.
Pathfinder.
"Quieres Ser Mi Amante," Camilo Sesto.
Pronto.

BEST INSTRUMENTAL ARRANGEMENT
• Mike Post, Pete Carpenter, "The
Rockford Files" (Mike Post). MGM.
Randy Brecker, "Some Skunk Funk"
(Brecker Brothers). Arista.
Alan Broadbent, "Children of Lima"
(Woody Herman). Fantasy.
Thad Jones, "Living for the City" (Thad
Jones, Mel Lewis). Philadelphia
International.
Ron McClure, "No Show" (Blood, Sweat
& Tears). Columbia.
Herbert Spencer, "Theme from *Jaws*"
(John Williams). MCA.

INSTRUMENTAL COMPOSITION (Composer's Award)
• Michel Legrand, "Images."
Silvester Levay, Stephan Praeger, "Fly,
Robin, Fly."
Chuck Mangione, "Chase the Clouds
Away."
Van McCoy, "The Hustle."
Mike Post, Pete Carpenter, "The Rockford
Files."

BEST CAST SHOW ALBUM
• *The Wiz*, Charlie Smalls, composer. Jerry
Wexler, A&R producer. Atlantic.
Chicago, John Kander, Fred Ebb,
composers. Phil Ramone, A&R
producer. Artist.
A Chorus Line, Marvin Hamlisch, Edward
Kleban, composers. Goddard
Lieberson, A&R producer. Columbia.
A Little Night Music (Original London
Cast), Stephen Sondheim, composer.
Thomas Z. Shepard, A&R producer.
RCA.
Shenandoah, Gary Geld, Peter Udell,
composers. Gary Geld, Peter Udell,
Philip Rose, A&R producers. RCA.

BEST ORIGINAL SCORE WRITTEN FOR A MOTION PICTURE OR A TELEVISION SPECIAL (Composer's Award)
• *Jaws*, John Williams. MCA.
Murder on the Orient Express, Richard
Rodney Bennett. Capitol.
Nashville, Carradine, Blakley, Baskin,
Reicheg, Gibson, Black. ABC.
The Return of the Pink Panther, Henry
Mancini. RCA.
The Wind and the Lion, Jerry Goldsmith.
Artista.

BEST ARRANGEMENT ACCOMPANYING VOCALISTS
• Ray Stevens, "Misty" (Ray Stevens).
Barnaby.
Gene Puerling, "April in Paris" (Singers
Unlimited). MPS.
Gene Puerling, "Autumn in New York"
(Singers Unlimited). MPS.
Gene Puerling, "Killing Me Softly With
His Song" (Singers Unlimited). MPS.
Mel Tormé, "Gershwin Medley" (Mel
Tormé). Atlantic.

High Fidelity *said conductor Colin Davis gave Best Opera Recording* Cosí fan tutte *by Mozart "a sense of theatrical pulse."*

ALBUM OF THE YEAR, CLASSICAL
• *Beethoven: Symphonies (9) Complete*, Sir Georg Solti conducting Chicago Symphony. Ray Minshull, producer. London.

Beethoven: Symphony No. 5 in C Minor, Carlos Kleiber conducting Vienna Philharmonic. Werner Mayer, producer. Deutsche Grammophon.

Mozart: Cosí fan tutte, Colin Davis conducting Royal Opera House, Covent Garden (solos: Caballé, Baker, Gedda, Ganzarolli, Cotrubas, Van Allen). Erik Smith, producer. Philips.

Orff: Carmina Burana, Michael Tilson Thomas conducting Cleveland Orchestra. Robert Page directing Cleveland Orchestra Chorus and Boys' Choir (solos: Blegen, Riegel, Bindery). Andrew Kazdin, producer. Columbia.

Penderecki: Magnificat, Kryzysztof Penderecki conducting Polish Radio National Symphony and Chorus. David Mottley, producer. Angel.

Ravel: Daphnis et Chloë (complete ballet), Pierre Boulez conducting New York Philharmonic; Camarata Singers. Andrew Kazdin, producer. Columbia.

Rossini: The Siege of Corinth, Thomas Schippers conducting London Symphony and Ambrosian Opera Chorus (solos: Sills, Verrett, Diaz, Theyard). John Mordler, producer. Angel.

BEST CLASSICAL PERFORMANCE, ORCHESTRA
(Conductor's Award)
• Pierre Boulez conducting New York Philharmonic, *Ravel: Daphnis et Chloë* (Complete Ballet). Columbia.

Colin Davis conducting Concertgebouw Orchestra, Amsterdam, *Berlioz: Symphonie Fantastique*. Philips.

Carlos Kleiber conducting Vienna Philharmonic, *Beethoven: Symphony No. 5 in C Minor*. Deutsche Grammophon.

Rafael Kubelik conducting Boston Symphony, *Bartók: Concerto for Orchestra*. Deutsche Grammophon.

James Levine conducting Chicago Symphony, *Mahler: Symphony No. 4 in G Major*. RCA.

Seiji Ozawa conducting New Philharmonic Orchestra, *Beethoven: Symphony No. 9 in D Minor*. Philips.

Sir Georg Solti conducting Chicago Symphony, *Beethoven: Symphonies (9) Complete*. London.

Herbert von Karajan conducting Berlin Philharmonic, *Mahler: Symphony No. 5 in C Sharp Minor*. Deutsche Grammophon.

BEST OPERA RECORDING
• *Mozart: Cosi fan tutte*, Colin Davis conducting Royal Opera House, Covent Garden (solos: Caballé, Baker, Gedda, Ganzarolli, Van Allen, Cotrubas). Erik Smith, producer. Philips.

Dallapiccola: Il Prigioniero, Antal Dorati conducting National Symphony Orchestra of Washington, D.C. Paul Traver directing University of Maryland Chorus (solos: Mazzieri, Barrers, Emili). James Mallinson, producer. London.

Korngold: Die Tote Stadt, Erich Leinsdorf conducting Munich Radio Orchestra, Bavarian Radio Chorus (solos: Kollo, Neblett, Prey, Luxon). Charles Gerhardt, producer. RCA.

Rossini: The Barber of Seville, James Levine conducting London Symphony & John Alldis Choir (solos: Sills, Milnes, Gedda). Christopher Bishop, producer. Angel.

Rossini: The Siege of Corinth, Thomas Schippers conducting London Symphony Orchestra & Ambrosian Opera Chorus (solos: Sills, Verrett, Diaz). The Yard/John Mordler, producer. Angel.

Schoenberg: Moses and Aaron, Michael Gielen conducting Orchestra and Chorus of the Austrian Radio (solos: Reich, Devos, Csapo, Obrowsky, Lucas). Abkauf Von Orf, producer. Philips.

Vaughan Williams: Sir John in Love, Meredith Davis conducting New Philharmonia Orchestra; John Alldis Choir (solos: Herincx, Palmer, Tear). Christopher Bishop, producer. Angel.

BEST CHORAL PERFORMANCE, OTHER THAN OPERA

• Robert Page directing Cleveland Orchestra Chorus and Boys' Choir, Michael Tilson Thomas conducting Cleveland Orchestra (solos: Blegen, Binder, Riegel), *Orff: Carmina Burana*. Columbia.

Leonard Bernstein, conducting Westminster Choir & New York Philharmonic, *Haydn: Harmoniemesse*. Columbia.

Pierre Boulez conducting BBC Symphony Chorus, Goldsmith's Choral Union, Gentlemen of London Philharmonic Choir, BBC Symphony (solos: Napier, Minton Thomas), *Schoenberg: Gurrelieder*. Columbia.

Tadeusz Dobrzanski, chorus master, Polish Radio Chorus of Krakow; Palka & Wietrzny, chorus masters, Soloists & Boys Chorus from Krakow; Krzysztof Penderecki conducting Philharmonic Chorus, Polish Radio National Symphony, *Penderecki: Magnificat*. Angel.

John McCarthy directing Ambrosian Singers, Riccardo Muti conducting New Philharmonia Orchestra, *Cherubini: Requiem in D Minor for Male Chorus & Orchestra*. Angel.

John Oliver, chorus master, Tanglewood Festival Chorus; Theodore Marier, chorus master, Boston Boy Choir; Seiji Ozawa conducting Boston Symphony Orchestra, *Berlioz: La Damnation De Faust*. Deutsche Grammophon.

Herbert von Karajan conducting Vienna Singverein & Berlin Philharmonic, *Beethoven: Missa Solemnis*. Angel.

BEST CHAMBER MUSIC PERFORMANCE (INSTRUMENTAL OR VOCAL)

• Artur Rubinstein, Henryk Szeryng, Pierre Fournier, *Schubert: Trios Nos. 1 in B Flat Major Opp. 99 & 2 in E Flat Major, Op. 100 (The Trios)*. RCA.

Concord Quartet, *Ives: Quartets Nos. 1 & 2*. Nonesuch.

Ralph Grierson, Artie Kane, *Gershwin: "Gershwin's Wonderful"* (Side 1: "American in Paris", *3 Preludes*). Angel.

Heinz Holliger, Christiane Jaccottet, Marcal Cervera, *Baroque Oboe Recital: Works by Bach, Couperin & Marais*. Philips.

Jaime Laredo, Ruth Laredo, Jeffery Solow, *Ravel: Trio for Violin, Cello and Piano*. Columbia.

Itzhak Perlman, André Previn, *Joplin: The Easy Winners & Other Ragtime Music of Scott Joplin*. Angel.

Jean Pierre Rampal, Claude Bolling, *Bolling: Suite for Flute & Piano*. Columbia.

Mstislav Rostropovich, Vasso Devetzi, *R. Strauss: Sonata in F for Cello & Piano*. Angel.

BEST CLASSICAL PERFORMANCE, INSTRUMENTAL SOLOIST(S) (WITH ORCHESTRA)

• Alicia de Larrocha (De Burgos conducting London Philharmonic (Fauré). Foster conducting London Philharmonic (Ravel)), *Ravel: Concerto for Left Hand, Concerto for Piano in G Major; Fauré: Fantaisie for Piano and Orchestra*. London.

Maurice Andre (von Karajan conducting Berlin Philharmonic), *Four Trumpet Concertos by Vivaldi, Telemann, Mozart, Hummel*. Angel.

Julian Bream (Gardiner conducting Monteverdi Orchestra), *Berkeley: Guitar Concerto; Rodrigo: Concierto de Aranjuez for Guitar*. RCA.

Alfred Brendel (Marriner conducting Academy of St. Martin-in-the-Fields), *Mozart: Concertos Nos. 18 in B Flat Major & 27 in B Flat Major for Piano & Orchestra*. Philips.

Lynn Harrell (Levine conducting London Symphony), *Dvorak: Concerto in B Minor for Cello*. RCA.

Murray Perahia (Marriner conducting Academy of St. Martin-in-the-Fields), *Mendelssohn: Concerto No. 1 in G Minor for Piano & No. 2 in D Minor for Piano*. Columbia.

Itzhak Perlman (Martinon conducting Orchestre de Paris), *Saint-Saëns: Introduction & Rondo Capriccioso, Havanaise; Chausson: Poeme; Ravel: Tzigane*. Angel.

Peter Serkin (Schneider conducting English Chamber Orchestra), *Mozart: Concertos for Piano and Orchestra Composed in 1784 (6) (Nos. 14–19)*. RCA.

BEST CLASSICAL PERFORMANCE, INSTRUMENTAL SOLOIST(S) (WITHOUT ORCHESTRA)

• Nathan Milstein, *Bach: Sonatas & Partitas for Violin Unaccompanied*. Deutsche Grammophon.

Vladimir Ashkenazy, *Chopin: Etudes, Opp. 10 & 25*. London.

Alicia de Larrocha, *Falla: Music of Falla* ("Three Cornered Hat," "El Amor Brujo," etc.). London.

Arturo Benedetti Michelangeli, *Schuman: Carnaval*, Op. 9. Angel.

Peter Serkin, *Messiaen: Vingt Regards Sur L'Enfant Jesus*. RCA.

John Williams, *Bach: Suites for Lute*. Columbia.

BEST CLASSICAL PERFORMANCE, VOCAL SOLOIST

• Janet Baker (Bernstein conducting Israel Philhamonic), *Mahler: Kindertotenlieder*. Columbia.

Elly Ameling (Baldwin, accompaniment), *Schumann: Frauenliebe und Leben*. Philips.

Victoria de los Angeles (Jacquillat conducting Lamoureux Concerts Orchestra), *Canteloube: Songs of the Auvergne, Album 2*. Angel.

Cleo Laine (Nash Ensemble, Howarth/ Hymas, piano), *Cleo Laine Sings Pierrot Lunaire & Songs by Ives*. RCA.

Joan Morris (Bolcom, accompaniment), *After the Ball (A Treasury of Turn-of-the-Century Popular Songs)*.

Leontyne Price, Placido Domingo (Santi conducting New Philharmonic), *Verdi & Puccini Duets (Othello, Ballo en Maschera, Manon Lescaut, Madame Butterfly)*. RCA.

Elisabeth Schwarzkopf (Parsons, accompaniment), *Schumann: Frauenliebe und Leben*, Op. 42. Angel.

BEST ENGINEERED RECORDING, CLASSICAL

• Gordon Parry, Colin Moorfoot, *Ravel: Daphnis & Chloe* (Maazel conducting Cleveland Orchestra). London.

Bud Graham, Ray Moore, Milton Cherin, *Ravel: Daphnis et Chloë* (Complete Ballet) (Boulez conducting New York Philharmonic). Columbia.

Edward Graham, Raymond Moore, *Orff: Carmina Burana* (Thomas conducting Cleveland Orchestra, Cleveland Chorus & Boys Choir, Page; solos: Blegen, Riegel, Binder). Columbia.

James Lock, Kenneth Wilkinson, *Stravinsky: Rite of Spring* (Solti conducting Chicago Symphony). London.

H.P. Schweigmann, *Beethoven: Symphony No. 5 in C Minor* (Kleiber conducting Vienna Philharmonic). Deutsche Grammophon.

Heinz Wildhagen, *Bartók: Concerto for Orchestra* (Kubelik conducting Boston Symphony). Deutsche Grammophon.

Kenneth Wilkinson, *Beethoven: Symphonies (9) Complete* (Solti conducting Chicago Symphony). London.

BEST ALBUM NOTES, CLASSICAL (Annotator's Award)

• Gunther Schuller, *Footlifters* (A Century of American Marches—Sousa, Joplin, Ives) (Gunther Schuller conducting All-Star Band). Columbia.

Rudi Blesh, *Joplin: The Complete Works of Scott Joplin* (Dick Hyman). RCA.

Laszlo Eosze, *Kodaly: Orchestral Works* (complete) (Antal Dorati conducting Hungarian Philharmonic). London.

Rory Guy, Itzhak Perlman, *Joplin: The Easy Winners* (solos: Itzhak Perlman, André Previn). Angel.

Rory Guy, *Gershwin: "Gershwin's Wonderful"* (solos: Ralph Grierson, Artie Kane). Angel.

James H. Moore, *Gagliano: La Dafne* (Vorwerk conducting Musica Pacifica). ABC/Command.

Christopher Palmer, *Korngold: Die Tote Stadt* (Leinsdorf conducting Munich Radio Orchestra; solos: Kollo, Neblett, Prey, Luxon). RCA.

Judith Robison, *The English Harpsichord* (Byrd, Farnaby, etc.) (solo: Igor Kipnis). Angel.

H.C. Robbins-Landon, *Haydn: Symphonies 93–104* (Dorati conducting Philharmonia Hungarica). London.

Best Comedy Recording

• *Is It Something I Said?* Richard Pryor. Reprise.

An Evening With Wally Londo Featuring Bill Slaszo, George Carlin. Little David.

Matching Tie & Handkerchief, Monty Python. Arista.

Modern Scream, Lily Tomlin. Polydor.

A Star Is Bought, Albert Brooks. Asylum.

Best Spoken Word, Documentary, or Drama Recording

• *Give 'Em Hell Harry*, James Whitmore. United Artists.

The Autobiography of Miss Jane Pittman, Claudia McNeil. Caedmon.

Immortal Sherlock Holmes Mercury Theater on the Air, Orson Welles. Radiola.

The Prophet, Richard Harris. Atlantic.

Talk About America, Alistair Cooke. Pye.

To Kill a Mockingbird, Maureen Stapleton. Miller-Brody.

Best Recording for Children

• *The Little Prince*, Richard Burton, narrator (featuring Jonathan Winters, Billy Simpson). Pip.

Bert & Ernie Sing-Along, Bert & Ernie. Cra.

Merry Christmas from Sesame Street, Sesame Street Cast. Cra.

Mr. Popper's Penguins, Jim Backus. Newbery Award.

Really Rosie, Carole King. Ode.

Sesame Street Monsters, Jim Henson's Sesame Street Monsters. Cra.

Best Engineered Recording, Non-Classical

• Brooks Arthur, Larry Alexander, Russ Payne, *Between the Lines* (Janis Ian). Columbia.

Chuck Johnson, Freddie Piro, Billy Taylor, Tom Trefethen, Alan Parson, *Ambrosia* (Ambrosia). 20th Century.

Bill Schnee, *I've Got the Music in Me* (Thelma Houston, Pressure Cooker). Sheffield.

Eric Stewart, *The Original Soundtrack* (10cc). Mercury.

Tommy Vicari, *Storm at Sun-Up* (Gino Vannelli). A&M.

Best Album Package

• Jim Ladwig, art director, *Honey* (Ohio Players). Mercury.

Agi, art director, *Physical Graffiti* (Led Zeppelin). Swan Song/Atlantic.

Gary Burden, art director, *One of These Nights* (Eagles). Asylum.

Gene Christensen, art director, *Playing Possum* (Carly Simon). Elektra.

Bob Defrin, art director, *Solo Piano* (Phineas Newborn, Jr.). Atlantic.

Mick Haggerty, art director, *Steppin'* (the Pointer Sisters). Blue Thumb.

Hipgnosis, art director, *Wish You Were Here* (Pink Floyd). Columbia.

John Kosh, art director, *Atlantic Crossing* (Rod Stewart). Warner Bros.

William E. McEuen, art director, *Dream* (Nitty Gritty Dirt Band). United Artists.

Best Album Notes
(Annotator's Award)

• Pete Hamill, *Blood on the Tracks* (Bob Dylan). Columbia.

Ralph J. Gleason, *The Real Lenny Bruce* (Lenny Bruce). Fantasy.

Benny Green, *The Tatum Solo Masterpieces* (Art Tatum). Pablo.

Tom T. Hall, *Greatest Hits, Vol. 2* (Tom T. Hall). Mercury.

George T. Simon, *A Legendary Performer* (Glenn Miller & His Orchestra). RCA.

PRODUCER OF THE YEAR
• Arif Mardin
Peter Asher.
Gus Dudgeon
Dennis Lambert, Brian Potter
Bill Szymczyk

Still a Wonder

When Paul Simon accepted the Grammy last year for 1975's top LP, *Still Crazy After All These Years*, and thanked "Stevie Wonder for not releasing an album this year," the half-jest turned out to be prophetically ironic.

Stevie Wonder's previous two albums *Innervisions* (1973) and *Fulfillingness' First Finale* (1974) had both won Album of the Year. His next LP, *Songs in the Key of Life*, took more than two years to make and was causing such frenzied anticipation throughout the music industry that Wonder took to wearing

Stevie Wonder tied Frank Sinatra's record for having the most Album of the Year awards (three) when, as critics predicted, Songs in the Key of Life *proved victorious.*

a T-shirt in public that read "We're almost finished!" When *Songs in the Key of Life* finally came out in 1976, it became only the third album in chart-keeping history to debut at number one (following the lead set by Elton John's *Captain Fantastic* and *Rock of the Westies*). It also came in first in the *Village Voice*'s annual survey of music critics judging the year's best albums and then scored seven Grammy nominations — the record that year.

L.A. Times critic Robert Hilburn wrote just before the awards telecast: "If Stevie Wonder's *Songs in the Key of Life* wins the Grammy that it deserves tonight as the year's best album, Wonder will have brought the nation's normally

feuding pop critics and the Grammy voters together in a rare alliance. While critics often ridicule the Grammy Awards as too conservative, Grammy voters frequently dismiss the critics as too esoteric and rock-oriented. But a Wonder victory will soften the arguments. At least momentarily."

As predicted, it turned out to be another Wonder-ous year at the Grammys. Stevie Wonder actually received two awards for Album of the Year (as both its singer-songwriter and its producer) and became only the second artist in Grammy history to win the LP prize three times (Sinatra won in 1959, 1965, and 1966; Paul Simon would pull even with them in 1986, having also won in

1970 and 1975). No one other than Wonder, however, has been thus honored for three *consecutive* albums.

"Stevie Wonder may be nipping at Horowitz's heels in total awards won," *TV Guide* warned before the evening ceremony. "The leader of the almost 20-year-old Grammy derby is composer-conductor Henry Mancini, who tops all contenders with 20 awards. Vladimir Horowitz is second with 12, Roger Miller third with 11. Ray Charles, Aretha Franklin, Leontyne Price, Paul Simon, and Stevie Wonder have won 10 each." After Wonder picked up a total of five Grammys in 1976, his tally not only put him ahead of Horowitz, but the *L.A. Times* declared that, "Wonder's 15 honors represent the most impressive concentrated show in the history of the awards."

> Strangely, album winner Stevie Wonder wasn't nominated for Record of the Year.

Songs in the Key of Life also snagged the artist prizes for Producer of the Year and Best Male Pop Vocal Performance. The album's first single release, "I Wish," brought him the statuette for Best R&B Male Vocal Performance. N.A.R.A.S. may have given Motown artists only one award throughout the entire decade of the 1960s (for the Temptations' "Cloud Nine" in 1968), but the academy was now burying one of its most supreme talents under an avalanche of them. "While Mancini has been accumulating his Grammys since the record industry competition was initiated in 1958," the *L.A. Times* noted, "Wonder's awards have all come in the last four years."

Wonder couldn't be on hand at the Grammy show at the Hollywood Palladium because he was attending a music festival in Lagos, Nigeria, but the producers arranged for a live satellite hookup that would enable him to perform for the TV audience and accept his prizes with live thank-you remarks beamed from Africa. "Wonder's popularity was marred," however, noted *The Hollywood Reporter*, "by a misfired live broadcast via the Telstar satellite." *Billboard* added, "The transmission was garbled beyond intelligibility in both the audio and video."

The snafu caused an embarrassing delay on the Grammycast as technicians scrambled to solve the problem and host Andy Williams tried to determine whether *any* connection was being made. The confusion built to such a frenzy that an obviously frazzled Williams ended up committing the worst gaffe in Grammycast history when, in ultimate desperation, he asked the blind artist at one point, "Can you *see* us?!" (It was a bad year for Williams. He had been scheduled to appear at the off-air ceremony to announce the Grammy nominations nearly two months earlier, but was replaced by Natalie Cole when he was called out of town to attend the manslaughter trial of his ex-wife Claudine Longet in Aspen, Colorado. Williams was the only host the awards ceremony had known since it was first aired in 1971 [for the 1970 prizes], but he would not be invited back next year. The official explanation: The singer no longer represented the mainstream of American music.)

Strangely, not one of Stevie Wonder's seven nominations was for Record of the Year, although *Songs in the Key of Life*'s two number one–ranked single releases, "I Wish" and "Sir Duke," were both considered strong possibilities. Instead, the contest turned out to be a tight one involving Paul Simon's "50

Ways to Leave Your Lover" (from his 1975 Album of the Year, *Still Crazy After All These Years*; "50 Ways" was released as a single after last year's eligibility period); "Afternoon Delight" by the hottest new pop group in the country, Starland Vocal Band; Barry Manilow's "I Write the Songs" (number six in the year's Hot 100); "If You Leave Me Now" by Chicago (which had been recording hit singles since 1969, but had never won a Grammy despite three earlier nominations); and "This Masquerade" by jazz guitarist George Benson, who was considered a long shot since the platter barely made it into the annual Hot 100, having ended up at number 94.

When "This Masquerade" prevailed, the announcement was met with "an accompanying burst of boisterous approval from the star-studded Palladium audience," *Billboard* noted. Part of the reason for the jubilant response was that its win marked the first time since the victory of "Up, Up and Away" in 1967 that the Record of the Year choice was not a number one–ranked pop single. ("Up, Up and Away" only got up the weekly charts as far as number seven; "This Masquerade" reached number 10.) N.A.R.A.S. voters had been smarting for years from the accusation that they picked winners based purely on popular success, and now Benson's triumph disproved that. The outpouring also expressed voters' sincere regard for a great artist who had toiled in the jazz and r&b fields since the 1950s without broad recognition. Some of his most recent, low-profile work, in fact, had

George Benson's "This Masquerade" was the first Record of the Year in nearly a decade not to top the charts. The Grammy crowd cheered its victory.

been with Stevie Wonder on *Songs in the Key of Life*. (Obviously, Wonder's influence rubbed off. When "This Masquerade" was released, more than one critic commented that it sounded like a Stevie Wonder ballad.) Not everyone was in tune with its selection as the year's top platter, though. *L.A. Times* music critic Robert Hilburn is among those who has dismissed it as a lightweight, "misguided" choice.

"This Masquerade" was from Benson's *Breezin'* LP, a losing nominee for Album of the Year that nonetheless became the biggest-selling jazz album ever, going platinum (marking a million in sales) soon after its release and eventually selling nearly four million copies. It scored big at the Grammys, too. In addition to its Record of the Year single,

Breezin' took the prize for Best Pop Instrumental Performance, while its "Theme from *Good King Bad*" track earned Benson Best R&B Instrumental Performance. *Breezin'* was also hailed as the Best Engineered Recording.

While "I Write the Songs" lost as Record of the Year, it prevailed as Song of the Year. The tune was written by former Beach Boy Bruce Johnston and not, as is commonly assumed, by the vocalist who took it to the Top 10, singer-songwriter Barry Manilow, who also performed it on the Grammycast. Manilow was not even the first artist to record it. The Captain & Tennille (last year's big Grammy winners, who reaped no nominations this year) had included the song on their debut album but never released it as a single.

> *A victorious Linda Ronstadt insisted, "Competition is for race horses, not artists," but she kept her award.*

The choice of Best New Artist is remembered today as one of those Grammy regrettables — a group that would score only one memorable song and then fade from the limelight soon afterward.

The Starland Vocal Band was called a clone of the Mamas & the Papas because both were comprised of two men and two women who displayed an obvious mastery of four-part harmonies. The band's initial two members, Bill and Taffy Danoff, had toured with John Denver (Bill Danoff and Denver wrote "Take Me Home, Country Roads" together) and so had solid music backgrounds, as did fellow band members singer-pianist Jon Carroll and vocalist Margot Chapman, both of whom had worked with the Danoffs years before they signed up with Starland. It was Bill Danoff who wrote the group's first and only number-one hit — "Afternoon Delight," which was a losing contender for both Record and Song of the Year. The song had a sexually suggestive quality that helped it become so popular, but the lyrics had actually been inspired by the nickname of a memorable gourmet lunch that Danoff had one day in Washington, D.C. "So Bill ate it — the food that is," his wife Taffy once told a concert audience, "and went home and explained to me what an 'Afternoon Delight' *should* be!"

Starland Vocal Band began the Grammy contest with five nominations, the same number as Benson, and ended up with one prize in addition to Best New Artist, an arranging award for "Afternoon Delight." The group received no further nods after 1976. It did have two moderately successful singles in the late 1970s ("Hail! Hail! Rock and Roll" and "Loving You with My Eyes") but disbanded in 1980. Soon thereafter, Bill and Taffy Danoff got divorced and Carroll and Chapman got married.

The jazz-rock band Chicago had had five number one–ranked albums in the seven years it had been on the scene, but had never won a Grammy, a point that astonished many since Chicago seemed like perfect N.A.R.A.S. fare: With their strong melodies and an older-jazz sound, they were slightly hip — without being barbaric — and extremely talented. This year they had five nominations, including Record of the Year contender "If You Leave Me Now," which ended up bringing them the prizes for Best Pop Vocal Performance by a Group and Best Arrangement Accompanying Vocalists. The group's LP, *Chicago X*, won Best Album Package.

When Linda Ronstadt won her first Grammy last year, it was in a c&w category, but now she confused Grammy voters with her newest LP, *Hasten Down the Wind,* which included both country and pop-rock selections. The voters opted to put her in the pop line-up this time where she was competing — just like last year, ironically — against country music's newest queen, Emmylou Harris (for "Here, There and Everywhere"). When she beat Harris a second time, Ronstadt obviously felt bad about it. "Competition is for race horses, not artists," she said backstage after receiving her Grammy, quoting George Bernard Shaw. "It doesn't mean I'm the best. It just means I won. I think Emmylou Harris is best. I'm not going to give [the Grammy] back, though."

Ronstadt also topped last year's Best New Artist Natalie Cole in the pop vocal category, but, for a second year in a row, Cole snagged the laurels for Best Female R&B Vocal Performance. Suddenly, it looked like Cole could be launching another winning streak in the category that Aretha Franklin had ruled for eight years before her. Cole's "Sophisticated Lady (She's a Different Lady)" overtook Franklin's "Something He Can Feel" this year and also beat out "Love Hangover" by Diana Ross, who had been nominated for a Grammy three times in the past as a soloist and twice as a member of the Supremes, but never won.

After studying est in the mid-1970s, the husband and wife vocal team of Marilyn McCoo and Billy Davis, Jr., decided to break away from the phenomenally successful (and six-time Grammy winning) 5th Dimension in 1975 to try to make it on their own as a duo. Est "freed me to do what I really wanted," McCoo told *Essence* magazine. "Like Billy, I wanted to try new things." Their first single release, "I Hope We Get to Love on Time," only reached number 91 in the weekly Hot 100, but their second single, "You Don't Have to Be a Star (To Be in My Show)" topped the rankings for two weeks and

Losing nominee Sarah Vaughan (right) congratulated Ella Fitzgerald backstage on her first jazz win since 1962.

SECURITY PACIFIC COLLECTION/L.A. PUBLIC LIBRARY

earned them the r&b group vocals honor. Soon after the Grammycast, McCoo and Davis had their own weekly variety TV show. When it went off the air after just six weeks, however, McCoo signed up to be the host of *Solid Gold* in its second season.

Rock vocalist Boz Scaggs had been active in the music business since the late 1950s when he worked with the young Steve Miller's band, the Marksmen. He veered after that between singing and writing rock and r&b ballads, but then he finally experienced his first pop success with his 1976 album *Silk Degrees*, which ultimately sold five million copies. *Silk Degrees* was nominated in four categories, but Scaggs emerged as victor only once — when he was named with David Paich as the writing talent behind the Best Rhythm & Blues Song, "Lowdown," a hit single from the album.

Two jazz greats who hadn't been heard from at the Grammys since the early 1960s both came back with strong victories. Ella Fitzgerald had won awards as a vocalist in the jazz soloist or individual categories in 1958 and 1959, but then the jazz prizes were reserved for instrumental performers after the 1960 awards. In 1976, N.A.R.A.S. introduced a new prize exclusively for jazz singers and Fitzgerald made a dramatic comeback to claim it over Sarah Vaughan and Ray Charles for her duet album with jazz guitarist Joe Pass, thus marking her first Grammy win since 1962. Count Basie's last Grammy was in 1963, but he returned to seize the Best Jazz Performance by a Soloist trophy for his keyboard virtuosity on his collaborative LP with sax player Zoot Sims. Duke Ellington, another big Grammy winner from the early N.A.R.A.S. days, died of lung cancer in May 1974, but was honored posthumously for best big band performance for a collection of his famous *Suites*.

Fusionists had done poorly in the jazz line-up until a few years ago, but now they seemed to hold sway as Chick Corea's overhauled Return to Forever band came back to reclaim the group performance honors that it won last year for the first time. Its 1975 LP *No Mys-*

tery had fared poorly with the critics, but the latest, *The Leprechaun*, got gushing reviews as Corea tested his new team's talents with an enormous range of sounds. "My own personal ideal is combining all the most beautiful forms of music — classical, rock, and jazz — into a form that doesn't go over people's heads," Corea told *Rolling Stone*. "I guess you could call it a contemporary hybrid." Corea also won Best Instrumental Arrangement for one of its best tracks, "Leprechaun's Dream." Fusionist composer and trumpet player Chuck Mangione had been nominated on six earlier occasions, but finally picked up his first trophy for Best Instrumental Composition, *Bellavia*.

Country singer Emmylou Harris may have been trounced twice in two years by Linda Ronstadt, but she topped seven-time past loser Dolly Parton and two-time past champ Tammy Wynette to be named best female country vocalist for her *Elite Hotel* LP, which included a three-song tribute to her mentor, singer/bandleader Gram Parsons, for whom she had worked as a backup vocalist till his death in 1973. 1974 Grammy winner Ronnie Milsap had recently been named the Country Music Association's Male Vocalist of the Year for a second time and now snagged his second N.A.R.A.S. award for his male response to Tammy's Wynette's 1969 Grammy-winning "Stand By Your Man." "(I'm a) Stand By My Woman Man" hit the top of the country charts the previous August, but it was dangerously close in musical notes to the Wynette classic and incurred a lawsuit. ("The rule of thumb [for parody music used to be]: If every four bars is different, you're okay," producer Tom Collins, the lawsuit's target, told *Billboard*. "Of course, that's never been in writing.")

Milsap beat Larry Gatlin in the male vocalist category, but Gatlin rebounded when his "Broken Lady" was named Best Country Song (topping one of the all-time country classics, "Dropkick Me, Jesus" by Paul Craft). For a third year in a row, Chet Atkins held onto the instrumental performance laurels when he won for his collaboration with fellow guitarist Les Paul. Their *Chester & Lester* LP was hailed by the critics for its fun spirit, chatty interludes, and a superb jazz-country quality that Atkins has not attempted on record since. Also championing an experimental sound was the winner of the group vocal honors, the Amazing Rhythm Aces, the Memphis band with the heavy r&b lilt that was honored for "The End Is Not in Sight (The Cowboy Tune)." John Hartford, a former banjo player for Glen Campbell and the winner of Grammy's Best Country Song of 1967 for "Gentle on My Mind," reaped Best Ethnic or Traditional Recording for his *Mark Twang* LP.

Two-time past winner of the gospel laurels, Mahalia Jackson, died in 1972, but received one last Grammy for *How I Got Over*, a posthumous collection of some of her 1954 radio performances and songs she sang before a black church congregation on a TV show in 1963. ("How I Got Over" was one of the classic songs in Jackson's repertoire.) Also winning a third Grammy were the Oak Ridge Boys for their single "Where the Soul Never Dies." Eddie Palmieri held onto the Best Latin Recording prize, created only one year earlier, for his *Unfinished Masterpieces* album.

Comedian Richard Pryor made a separate and triumphant return this year. Pryor once said that Bill Cosby's success had inspired him to move to New York from Peoria, Illinois, where he grew up, and try to make it in the comedy field. Now it looked like Pryor was challenging Cosby's six-year-winning streak by scoring his third straight win. This one was for *Bicentennial Nigger*, which admiring critics called his masterpiece and detractors labeled his most obscene and humorless LP yet. Pryor taped it in front of a live audience full of celebrities whom the comedian singled out for barbs, including Natalie Cole ("She can sing her ass off!" the comic cries). His six-minute salute to the nation's bicentennial was full of ire over black people's lot in contemporary America: "We're celebrating 200 years of white folks kickin' ass," he says. "How long will this bullshit go on?"

Shortly before his 90th birthday, Artur Rubinstein took on a Herculean task: a five-disc recording of Beethoven's five Concertos for Piano and Orchestra that not only claimed Classical Album of the Year, but earned him a third instrumental soloist award in a row. "It seemed a fitting tribute to a great artist in the twilight of his active career," *Billboard* said.

"It came as no surprise," *Billboard* added, when Vladimir Horowitz reaped the other soloist instrumental prize, bringing his Grammy total to 13 awards (now a third-place rank in the tally of all-time winners thanks to Stevie Wonder's bonanza this year). Horowitz was lauded for the recording of some of his concerts from 1975–76 that included sonatas by Schumann and Scriabin. "They sound marvelously true," wrote *High Fidelity*, "quite exceptional."

The late *Mahalia Jackson* was hailed for How I Got Over.

The orchestral honors went to Sir Georg Solti and the Chicago Symphony for their rendition of Richard Strauss's *Also Sprach Zarathustra*, "a distinctively individual, unexpectedly romantic interpretation," said *High Fidelity*, "with the Chicagoans at their Solti-led best."

High Fidelity gave its Prix Mondial Award this year to the same recipient of the Grammy for chamber music, the late David Munrow, who conducted the Early Music Consort in a three-disc set, titled *The Art of Courtly Love*, of works by the 14th century French composer and poet Guillaume de Machaut and his musical followers. The choral laurels were bestowed to director Arthur Oldham of the London Symphony Chorus and André Previn for leading that orchestra in Rachmaninoff's *The Bells*. Singing in Russian, the chorus, said *High Fidelity* "is in splendid form," but added that Previn's conducting "doesn't run away with the field."

For the first time ever, the Grammy for Best Opera Recording went to an American work when conductor Lorin Maazel led the Cleveland Orchestra and Chorus in the first complete recording of George Gershwin's *Porgy and Bess*, with baritone Willard White as Porgy and soprano Leona Mitchell as Bess. "Nearly all the voices are good, the pacing is lively, the execution meticulous," opined *High Fidelity*. "There's no doubt that all of this makes the opera too long, that cuts should be made (and were, even in the first production) — but for once we should hear it all." The operatic vocal category included some unlikely contenders this year — among them, Barbra Streisand singing works by Debussy and Canteloube and veteran movie-star ghost singer Marni Nixon (who, among other accomplishments, sang the vocals for Audrey Hepburn in the 1964 film version of *My Fair Lady*) tackling Schöenberg — but the prize was claimed by another American diva, Beverly Sills, for *Music of Victor Herbert*.

"Overall, the show was well-paced," said *The Hollywood Reporter* about the Grammycast. It included musical performances by Barry Manilow, Sarah Vaughan, Wild Cherry (a losing nominee for Best New Artist), the Starland Vocal Band, and Marilyn McCoo and Billy Davis, Jr. Some of its better comic interludes came when presenter Bette Milder admonished the audience: "In the music business, you're as good as your last 2-point-40 minutes." The fiasco of losing the satellite hookup to Stevie Wonder in Africa was almost made up for by successful live satellite transmissions of the award ceremony for the first time ever to viewers overseas in the Far East.

1976

The awards ceremony was broadcast on CBS from the Hollywood Palladium on February 19, 1977, for the awards eligibility period of October 16, 1975, to September 30, 1976.

ALBUM OF THE YEAR
• *Songs in the Key of Life*, Stevie Wonder. Stevie Wonder, producer. Tamla.
Breezin', George Benson. Tommy Lipuma, producer. Warner Bros.
Chicago X, Chicago. James William Guercio, producer. Columbia.
Frampton Comes Alive, Peter Frampton. Peter Frampton, producer. A&M.
Silk Degrees, Boz Scaggs. Joe Wissert, producer. Columbia.

RECORD OF THE YEAR
• "This Masquerade," George Benson. Tommy Lipuma, producer. Warner Bros.
"Afternoon Delight," Starland Vocal Band. Milt Okun, producer. Windsong/RCA.
"50 Ways to Leave Your Lover," Paul Simon. Paul Simon, Phil Ramone, producers. Columbia.
"I Write the Songs," Barry Manilow. Ron Dante, Barry Manilow, producers. Arista.
"If You Leave Me Now," Chicago. James William Guercio, producer. Columbia.

SONG OF THE YEAR
(Songwriter's Award)
- "I Write the Songs," Bruce Johnston.
"Afternoon Delight," Bill Danoff.
"Breaking Up Is Hard to Do," Neil Sedaka, Howard Greenfield.
"This Masquerade," Leon Russell.
"The Wreck of the Edmund Fitzgerald," Gordon Lightfoot.

BEST NEW ARTIST
- Starland Vocal Band. Windsong/RCA.
Boston. Epic.
Dr. Buzzard's Original "Savannah" Band. RCA.
Brothers Johnson. A&M.
Wild Cherry. Epic.

BEST POP VOCAL PERFORMANCE, MALE
- Stevie Wonder, *Songs in the Key of Life*. Tamla/Motown.
George Benson, "This Masquerade," track. Warner Bros.
Gordon Lightfoot, "The Wreck of the Edmund Fitzgerald." Reprise.
Lou Rawls, "You'll Never Find Another Love Like Mine." Philadelphia International.
Boz Scaggs, *Silk Degrees*. Columbia.

BEST POP VOCAL PERFORMANCE, FEMALE
- Linda Ronstadt, *Hasten Down the Wind*. Asylum.
Natalie Cole, *Natalie*. Capitol.
Emmylou Harris, "Here, There and Everywhere." Reprise.
Joni Mitchell, *The Hissing of Summer Lawns*. Asylum.
Vicki Sue Robinson, "Turn the Beat Around." RCA.

BEST POP VOCAL PERFORMANCE BY A DUO, GROUP, OR CHORUS
- Chicago, "If You Leave Me Now." Columbia.
Elton John, Kiki Dee, "Don't Go Breaking My Heart." Rocket/MCA.
England Dan & John Ford Coley, "I'd Really Love to See You Tonight." Big Tree.
Starland Vocal Band, "Afternoon Delight." Windsong/RCA.
Queen, "Bohemian Rhapsody." Elektra.

BEST POP INSTRUMENTAL PERFORMANCE
- George Benson, *Breezin'*. Warner Bros.
Jeff Beck, *Wired*. Epic.
Brecker Brothers Band, *Back to Back*. Arista.
Walter Murphy & the Big Apple Band, *A Fifth of Beethoven*. Private Stock.
Stevie Wonder, "Contusion." Tamla/Motown.

BEST RHYTHM & BLUES SONG
(Songwriter's Award.)
- "Lowdown," Boz Scaggs, David Paich.
"Disco Lady," Harvey Scales, Al Vance, Don Davis.
"Love Hangover," Pam Sawyer, Marilyn McLeod.
"Misty Blue," Bob Montgomery.
"(Shake, Shake, Shake) Shake Your Booty," H.W. Casey, Richard Finch.

BEST RHYTHM & BLUES VOCAL PERFORMANCE, MALE
- Stevie Wonder, "I Wish." Tamla/Motown.
Marvin Gaye, *I Want You*. Tamla/Motown.
Lou Rawls, "Groovy People." Philadelphia International.
Boz Scaggs, "Lowdown." Columbia.
Joe Simon, "I Need You, You Need Me." Spring.
Johnnie Taylor, "Disco Lady." Columbia.

BEST RHYTHM & BLUES VOCAL PERFORMANCE, FEMALE
- Natalie Cole, "Sophisticated Lady (She's a Different Lady)." Capitol.
Aretha Franklin, "Something He Can Feel." Atlantic.
Dorothy Moore, "Misty Blue." Malaco.
Melba Moore, "Lean On Me." Buddah.
Diana Ross, "Love Hangover." Motown.

BEST RHYTHM & BLUES VOCAL PERFORMANCE BY A DUO, GROUP, OR CHORUS
- Marilyn McCoo, Billy Davis Jr., "You Don't Have to Be a Star (To Be in My Show)." ABC.
Earth, Wind & Fire, *Gratitude*. Columbia.
K.C. & the Sunshine Band, "(Shake, Shake, Shake) Shake Your Booty." TK.
Spinners, "Rubberband Man." Atlantic.
Wild Cherry, "Play That Funky Music." Epic.

BEST RHYTHM & BLUES INSTRUMENTAL PERFORMANCE
• George Benson, "Theme from *Good King Bad*." CTI.
Brass Construction, *Brass Construction*. United Artists.
Crusaders, "Keep That Same Old Feeling." Blue Thumb.
Marvin Gaye, "After the Dance." Tamla.
Herbie Hancock, "Doin' It." Columbia.
Stanley Turrentine, "Hope That We Can Be Together Soon." Fantasy.

BEST JAZZ VOCAL PERFORMANCE
• Ella Fitzgerald, *Fitzgerald & Pass . . . Again*. Pablo.
Ray Charles, Cleo Laine, *Porgy and Bess*. RCA.
Irene Kral, *Where Is Love?* Choice.
Quire, *Quire*. RCA.
Sarah Vaughan, *More Sarah Vaughan Live in Japan*. Mainstream.

BEST JAZZ PERFORMANCE BY A SOLOIST
• Count Basie, *Basie & Zoot*. Pablo.
Jim Hall, *Commitment*. Horizon/A&M.
Jaco Pastorius, "Donna Lee." Epic.
Art Tatum, *Works of Art*. Jazz.
Clark Terry, *Clark Terry and His Jolly Giants*. Vanguard.
Phil Woods, *The New Phil Woods Album*. RCA.

BEST JAZZ PERFORMANCE BY A GROUP
• Chick Corea, *The Leprechaun*. Polydor.
Count Basie, Zoot Sims, *Basie & Zoot*. Pablo.
Paul Desmond Quartet , *The Paul Desmond Quartet Live*. Horizon/A&M.
Bill Evans Trio, *Since We Met*. Fantasy.
Jaco Pastorius, *Jaco Pastorius*. Epic.

BEST JAZZ PERFORMANCE BY A BIG BAND
• Duke Ellington, *The Ellington Suites*. Pablo.
Toshiko Akiyoshi–Lew Tabackin Big Band, *Long Yellow Road*. RCA.
Dizzy Gillespie, Machito, *Afro-Cuban Jazz Moods*. Pablo.
Thad Jones, Mel Lewis, *New Life*. Horizon/A&M.
Phil Woods, *The New Phil Woods Album*. RCA.

BEST COUNTRY SONG
(Songwriter's Award)
• "Broken Lady," Larry Gatlin.
"The Door Is Always Open," Bob McDill, Dickey Lees.
"Dropkick Me, Jesus," Paul Craft.
"Every Time You Touch Me (I Get High)," Charlie Rich, Billy Sherrill.
"Hank Williams, You Wrote My Life," Paul Craft.

BEST COUNTRY VOCAL PERFORMANCE, MALE
• Ronnie Milsap, "(I'm a) Stand By My Woman Man." RCA.
Mac Davis, *Forever Lovers*. Columbia.
Larry Gatlin, "Broken Lady." Monument.
Waylon Jennings, *Are You Ready for the Country*. RCA.
Willie Nelson, "I'd Have to Be Crazy." Columbia.

BEST COUNTRY VOCAL PERFORMANCE, FEMALE
• Emmylou Harris, *Elite Hotel*. Reprise.
Crystal Gayle, "I'll Get Over You." United Artists.
Dolly Parton, *All I Can Do*. RCA.
Mary Kay Place, *Tonite! At the Capri Lounge Loretta Naggers*. Columbia.
Tammy Wynette, "'Til I Can Make It on My Own." Epic.

BEST COUNTRY VOCAL PERFORMANCE BY A DUO OR GROUP
• Amazing Rhythm Aces, "The End Is Not in Sight (The Cowboy Tune)." ABC.
Asleep at the Wheel, "Route 66." Capitol.
George Jones, Tammy Wynette, "Golden Ring." Epic.
Loretta Lynn, Conway Twitty, "The Letter." MCA.
Statler Brothers, "Your Picture in the Paper." Mercury.

BEST COUNTRY INSTRUMENTAL PERFORMANCE
• Chet Atkins, Les Paul, *Chester & Lester*. RCA.
Ace Cannon, "Blue Eyes Crying in the Rain." Hi.
Floyd Cramer, "I'm Thinking Tonight of My Blue Eyes." RCA.
Danny Davis & the Nashville Brass, *Texas*. RCA.
Marshall Tucker Band, "Long Hard Ride." Capricorn.

1976

BEST INSPIRATIONAL PERFORMANCE
• Gary S. Paxton, *The Astonishing, Outrageous, Amazing, Incredible, Unbelievable, Different World of Gary S. Paxton*. Newpax.
Pat Boone, *Something Super Natural*. Lamb & Lion.
Sonny James, "Just a Closer Walk with Thee." Columbia.
Willie Nelson, "Amazing Grace." Columbia.
Ray Price, *Precious Memories*. Word.
Charley Pride, *Sunday Morning with Charley Pride*. RCA.
Charlie Rich, *Silver Linings*. Epic.
Stevie Wonder, "Have a Talk With God." Tamla/Motown.

BEST GOSPEL PERFORMANCE (OTHER THAN SOUL GOSPEL)
• Oak Ridge Boys, "Where the Soul Never Dies." Columbia.
Blackwood Brothers, *Learning to Lean*. Skylight.
Florida Boys, *Here They Come*. Canaan.
Imperials, *Just Because*. Impact.
Speers, *Between the Cross and Heaven (There's a Whole Lot of Living Going On)*. Heartwarming.

BEST SOUL GOSPEL PERFORMANCE
• Mahalia Jackson, *How I Got Over*. Columbia.
Inez Andrews, *War on Sin*. Songbird.
James Cleveland & the Charles Fold Singers, *Touch Me, Volume II*. Savoy.
James Cleveland & the Southern California Community Choir, *Give It to Me*. Savoy.
Andrae Crouch & the Disciples, *This Is Another Day*. Light.

BEST ETHNIC OR TRADITIONAL RECORDING
• *Mark Twang*, John Hartford. Flying Fish.
Bagpipe Marches and Music of Scotland, Shotts & Dykehead Caledonia Pipe Band. Olympic.
Beware of the Dog, Hound Dog Taylor. Alligator.
If You Love These Blues, Play 'em as You Please, Michael Bloomfield. Guitar Player.
Proud Earth, Chief Dan George, Arliene Nofchissey Williams, Rick Brosseau. Salt City.

BEST LATIN RECORDING
• *Unfinished Masterpiece*, Eddie Palmieri. Coco.
Cocinando La Salsa, Joe Cuba. Tico.
El Maestro, Johnny Pacheco. Fania.
La Gormé, Eydie Gormé. Gala.
"Salsa" Soundtrack, Fania All-Stars. Fania.
Sofrito, Mongo Santamaria. Vaya.

BEST INSTRUMENTAL ARRANGEMENT
• Chick Corea, "Leprechaun's Dream" (Chick Corea). Polydor.
Stanley Clarke, "Life Is Just a Game" (Stanley Clarke). Emperor/Atlantic.
Bob James, "Westchester Lady" (Bob James). CTI.
Henry Mancini, John Williams, Herb Spencer, Al Woodbury, "The Disaster Movie Suite" (Henry Mancini conducting London Symphony). RCA.
Claus Ogerman, "Saudade Do Brazil" (Antonio Carlos Jobim). Warner Bros.

BEST ARRANGEMENT ACCOMPANYING VOCALISTS
• Jimmie Haskell, James William Guercio, "If You Leave Me Now" (Chicago). Columbia.
Robert Farnon, "Sentimental Journey" (Singers Unlimited.) MPS.
Clare Fischer, "Green Dolphin Street" (Singers Unlimited). MPS.
Paul McCartney, "Let 'em In" (Wings). Capitol.
Claus Ogerman, "Boto (Porpoise)" (Antonio Carlos Jobim). Warner Bros.

BEST ARRANGEMENT FOR VOICES
• Starland Vocal Band, "Afternoon Delight" (Starland Vocal Band). Windsong/RCA.
Christian Chevallier, "Ain't Misbehavin'" (Quire). RCA.
Earth, Wind & Fire, "Can't Hide Love" (Earth, Wind & Fire). Columbia.
Gene Puerling, "I Get Along without You Very Well" (Singers Unlimited). MPS.
Queen, "Bohemian Rhapsody" (Queen). Elektra.

BEST INSTRUMENTAL COMPOSITION
• *Bellavia*, Chuck Mangione.
"Contusion," Stevie Wonder.
Earth, Wind & Fire, Maurice White, Skip
    Scarbrough.
"Leprechaun's Dream," Chick Corea.
"Midnight Soul Patrol," Quincy Jones,
    Louis Johnson, Dave Grusin.
"The White Dawn," Henry Mancini.

BEST CAST SHOW ALBUM
• *Bubbling Brown Sugar*, Razaf,
    Goodman, Sampson, Webb, Strayhorn,
    Holgate, Kemp, Lopez, Rogers,
    Williams, Mills, Parish, Ellington,
    Hines, Sissle, Blake, Pinkard, Waller,
    Overstreet, Higgins, Herzog, Webster,
    Holiday, composers. Hugo and Luigi,
    producers. H&L.
My Fair Lady, 20th anniversary
    production, Alan Jay Lerner, Frederick
    Loewe, composers. Goddard Lieberson,
    producer. Columbia.
Pacific Overtures, Stephen Sondheim,
    composer. Thomas Z. Shepard,
    producer. RCA.
Rex, Richard Rodgers, Sheldon Harnick,
    composers. Thomas Z. Shepard,
    producer. RCA.
Side by Side by Sondheim, Stephen
    Sondheim, composer. Thomas Z.
    Shepard, producer. RCA.

**ALBUM OF BEST ORIGINAL SCORE
WRITTEN FOR A MOTION PICTURE
OR A TELEVISION SPECIAL**
• *Car Wash*, Norman Whitfield. MCA.
The Omen, Jerry Goldsmith. Tattoo/RCA.
One Flew Over the Cuckoo's Nest, Jack
    Nitzsche. Fantasy.
Rich Man, Poor Man, Alex North. MCA.
Taxi Driver, Bernard Herrmann. Arista.
Three Days of the Condor, Dave Grusin.
    Capitol.

ALBUM OF THE YEAR, CLASSICAL
• *Beethoven: The Five Piano Concertos*,
    Daniel Barenboim conducting London
    Philharmonic (solo: Artur Rubinstein).
    Max Wilcox, producer. RCA.
The Art of Courtly Love (music by
    Machaut & his contemporaries), David
    Munrow conducting Early Music
    Consort of London. Christopher
    Bishop, producer. Seraphim.

*Artur Rubinstein's ambitious, five-disc
set of Beethoven concertos brought him
"a fitting tribute" — best classical LP.*

Bizet: Carmen, Sir Georg Solti conducting
    London Philharmonic (solos: Troyanos,
    Domingo, Kanawa, Van Dam).
    Christopher Raeburn, producer.
    London.
Gershwin: Porgy & Bess, Lorin Maazel
    conducting Cleveland Orchestra (solos:
    Mitchell, White). Michael Woolcock,
    producer. London.
Gershwin: Rhapsody in Blue (with 1925
    piano roll), Michael Tilson Thomas
    conducting Columbia Jazz Band;
    Gershwin: An American in Paris,
    Michael Tilson Thomas conducting
    New York Philharmonic. Andrew
    Kazdin, producer. Columbia.
Horowitz Concerts 1975/76 (Schumann,
    Scriabin) (solo: Vladimir Horowitz).
    John Pfeiffer, producer. RCA.
Joplin: Treemonisha, Gunther Schuller
    conducting the original cast orchestra
    and chorus (solos: Balthrop, Allen,
    White). Tom Mowrey, producer.
    Deutsche Grammophon.
*Arturo Toscanini, The Philadelphia
    Orchestra* (first release of the historic
    1941–42 recording, Schubert, Debussy,
    Berlioz, Respighi, etc.), Arturo
    Toscanini conducting Philadelphia
    Orchestra. John Pfeiffer, producer.
    RCA.

BEST CLASSICAL ORCHESTRAL PERFORMANCE
(Conductor's Award)

• Sir Georg Solti conducting Chicago Symphony, *Strauss: Also Sprach Zarathustra*. Ray Minshull, producer. London.
Pierre Boulez conducting New York Philharmonic, *Falla: Three Cornered Hat (Boulez Conducts Falla)*. Andrew Kazdin, producer. Columbia.
James Levine conducting Chicago Symphony, *Brahms: Symphony No. 1 in C Minor*. Thomas Z. Shepard & Jay David Saks, producers. RCA.
Jean Martinon conducting Orchestre de Paris, *Ravel: Daphnis et Chloë* (complete ballet). Rene Challan, producer. Angel.
Jean Martinon conducting Orchestra National of the Orft, *Berlioz: Symphonie Fantastique*. Rene Challan, producer. Angel.
Zubin Mehta conducting Los Angeles Philharmonic, *The Fourth of July! Ives: Symphony No. 2, variation on America; Copland: Appalachian Spring; Bernstein: Overture to Candide; Gershwin: American in Paris*. Ray Minshull, producer. London.
Sir Georg Solti conducting London Philharmonic, *Elgar: Symphony No. 2 in E Flat Major*. Ray Minshull, producer. London.
Michael Tilson Thomas conducting Columbia Jazz Band (with Gershwin 1925 piano roll), *Gershwin: Rhapsody in Blue*. Andrew Kazdin, producer. Columbia.

BEST CHAMBER MUSIC PERFORMANCE
(INSTRUMENTAL OR VOCAL)

• David Munrow conducting Early Music Consort of London, *The Art of Courtly Love* (Machaut and his contempories). Seraphim.
The Cleveland Quartet, *Barber: Quartet for Strings, Op. 11, Ives: Quartet No. 2 for Strings (Two American Masterpieces)*. RCA.
Glenn Gould, Philadelphia Brass Ensemble, *Hindemith: Sonatas for Brass & Piano (Complete)*. Columbia.
Jascha Heifetz, Gregor Piatigorsky, *The Heifetz Piatigorsky Concerts* (Dvorak: Trio in F Min. for Piano with Leonard Pennario; Stravinsky: Suite Italienne

for Violin & Cello; Gliere: Duo for Violin & Cello, etc.). Columbia.
Thomas Igloi, Alberni Quartet, *Schubert: Quintet in C, Op. 163*. CRD.
Fitzwilliam Quartet, *Shostakovich: Quartet No. 14 in F Sharp Major*. Oiseau Lyre.
Prague String Quartet, *Dvorak: Quartets, Opp. 96 & 105*. Deutsche Grammophon.
Jacqueline du Pre, Daniel Barenboim, *Beethoven: Sonatas for Cello (complete)*. Angel.
Tashi (Peter Serkin, Fred Sherry, Ida Kavafian, Richard Stoltzman), *Messiaen: Quartet for the End of Time*. RCA.

BEST CLASSICAL PERFORMANCE, INSTRUMENTAL SOLOIST(S)
(WITH ORCHESTRA)

• Artur Rubinstein, piano (Barenboim conducting London Philharmonic), *Beethoven: The Five Piano Concertos*. RCA.
Vladimir Ashkenazy, piano (Previn conducting London Symphony), *Prokofiev: The Five Piano Concertos*. London.
Stephen Bishop, piano (David conducting London Symphony), *Bartók: Concerti for Piano Nos. 1 & 3*. Philips.
Aldo Ciecolini, piano (Martinon conducting Orchestre de Paris), *Ravel: Concerto in G Major for Piano & Orchestra & Concerto in D Major for Left Hand*. Angel.
Nathan Milstein, violin (Jochum conducting Vienna Philharmonic), *Brahms: Concerto in D Major for Violin*. Deutsche Grammophon.
Mstislav Rostropovich, cello (von Karajan conducting Berlin Philharmonic), *Strauss: Don Quixote*. Angel.

BEST CLASSICAL PERFORMANCE, INSTRUMENTAL SOLOIST(S)
(WITHOUT ORCHESTRA)

• Vladimir Horowitz, piano, *Horowitz Concerts 1975/76* (Schumann, Scriabin). RCA.
Vladimir Ashkenazy, piano, *Rachmaninoff: 23 Preludes*. London.
Lazar Berman, piano, *Liszt: Legendary Soviet Pianist, Lazar Berman Plays Liszt*. Everest.
Alfred Brendel, piano, *Schubert: Sonata in A Minor, Op. 42, Hungarian Melody in B Minor (D 817)*. Philips.

Itzhak Perlman, violin (Kreisler), *Itzhak Perlman Plays Fritz Kreisler*. Angel.

Maurizio Pollini, piano, *Chopin: Preludes, Op. 28*. Deutsche Grammophon.

Andrés Segovia, guitar, *The Intimate Guitar – 2* (Bach, Sor, Albéniz, Molleds, San Sebastian, Samazeuilh). RCA.

André Watts, piano, *Watts By George: André Watts Plays George Gershwin* ("Rhapsody in Blue," Preludes for Piano (3), 13 Songs from Gershwin Songbook). Columbia.

BEST OPERA RECORDING

• *Gershwin: Porgy & Bess,* Lorin Maazel conducting Cleveland Orchestra and Chorus (solos: Mitchell, White). Michael Woolcock, producer. London.

Bizet: Carmen, Sir Georg Solti conducting London Philharmonic (solos: Troyanos, Domingo, Te Kanawa, Van Dam). Christopher Raeburn, producer. London.

Joplin: Treemonisha, Gunther Schuller conducting Original Cast Orchestra & Chorus (solos: Balthrop, Allen, White). Tom Mowrey, producer. Deutsche Grammophon.

Massenet: Thais, Lorin Maazel conducting New Philharmonia Orchestra, John Alldis Choir (solos: Sills, Milnes, Gedda). Christopher Bishop, producer. Angel.

Schönberg: Moses and Aaron, Pierre Boulez conducting BBC Symphony, BBC Symphony Singers, Orpheus Boys Choir (solos: Reich, Cassilly, Angus, Palmer, Hermann). Paul Myers, producer. Columbia.

Verdi: Macbeth, Claudio Abbado conducting Chorus and Orchestra of La Scala (solos: Verrett, Domingo, Ghiaurov). Rainer Brock, producer. Deutsche Grammophon.

BEST CHORAL PERFORMANCE, CLASSICAL

• Arthur Oldham, chorus master, London Symphony Chorus. André Previn conducting London Symphony, *Rachmaninoff: The Bells*. Angel.

Leonard Bernstein conducting Choeurs de Radio France, Orchestre National de France and Orchestre Philharmonique de Radio France (Burrows, tenor), *Berlioz: Requiem*. Columbia.

Sir Adrian Boult conducting London Philharmonic Chorus and London Philharmonic Orchestra, *Elgar: The Kingdom, Op. 51*. Connoisseur Society.

Dom Jean Claire conducting Choir of the Monks of Saint-Pierre de Solesmes Abbey, *Gregorian Chant*. London.

Colin Davis conducting BBC Singers and Choral Society and BBC Symphony, *Tippett: A Child of Our Time*. Philips.

Romano Gandolfi, chorus master, Chorus of La Scala, Milan. Claudio Abbado conducting Orchestra of La Scala, Milan, *Verdi: Opera Choruses* (from *Nabucco, II Trovatore, Otello, Aida*, etc.). Deutsche Grammophon.

Walter Hagen-Groll, chorus master, New Philharmonia Chorus. Carlo Maria Giulini conducting London Philharmonic, *Beethoven: Missa Solemnis*. Angel.

Phillip Ledger conducting Kings College Choir, Cambridge, *Bernstein: Chichester Psalms*; *Britten: Rejoice in the Lamb*. Angel.

Franz Müller, chorus master, Netherlands Radio Chorus. Jean Fournet conducting Rotterdam Philharmonic, *Fauré: Requiem*. Philips.

BEST CLASSICAL VOCAL SOLOIST PERFORMANCE

• Beverly Sills (Kostelanetz conducting London Symphony), *Music of Victor Herbert* ("Kiss in the Dark," "Italian Street Song," "Kiss Me Again," etc.). Angel.

Janet Baker, James King (Haitink conducting Concertgebouw Orchestra), *Mahler: Das Lied von der Erde*. Philips.

Carlo Bergonzi (Santi conducting New Philharmonia, Gardelli conducting Royal Philharmonic), *Carlo Bergonzi Sings Verdi*. Philips.

Dietrich Fischer-Dieskau (Sviatoslav Richter, accompanist), *Wolf: Morike Lieder*. Deutsche Grammophon.

Jan de Gaetani (Gilbert Kalish, accompanist), *Ives: Songs*. Nonesuch.

Margaret Price, (Lockhart conducting English Chamber Orchestra), *Mozart: Arias* (La Clemenza di Tito, Die Entfuhrung aus dem Serail, Nozze di Figaro, etc.). RCA.

Marni Nixon (Leonard Stein, accompanist), *Schöenberg: Nine Early Songs; The Cabaret Songs of Arnold Schoenberg*. RCA.

Barbra Streisand (Ogerman conducting Columbia Symphony), *Classical Barbra* (Debussy: *Beau Soir*, Canteloube: *Berceuse*, Wolf: *Verschwiegene*, etc.). Columbia.

BEST ENGINEERED RECORDING, CLASSICAL

• E. T. (Bud) Graham, Ray Moore, Milt Cherin, *Gershwin: Rhapsody in Blue*, George Gershwin (1925 Piano Roll) & Thomas conducting Columbia Jazz Band. Columbia.

Patrick Gleason, Skip Shimmin, Neil Schwartz, Seth Dworken, *Beyond the Sun: An Electronic Portrait of Holst's "The Planets."* Mercury.

Paul Goodman, *Brahms: Symphony No. 1 in C Minor,* James Levine conducting Chicago Symphony. RCA.

E.T. (Bud) Graham, Ray Moore, Milton Cherin, *Falla: Three Cornered Hat (Boulez Conducts Falla)*, Boulez conducting New York Philharmonic (solo: de Gaetani). Columbia.

James Lock, Arthur Lilley, Colin Moorfoot, Michael Mailes, *Gershwin: Porgy & Bess*, Maazel conducting Cleveland Orchestra (solos: Mitchell, White). London.

James Lock, Colin Moorfoot, Jack Law, *Mahler: Symphony No. 2 in C Minor ("Resurrection")*, Mehta conducting Vienna Philharmonic. London.

James Lock, *Strauss: An Alpine Symphony*, Mehta conducting Los Angeles Philharmonic. London.

Christopher Parker, *Britten: Four Sea Interludes & Passacaglia from "Peter Grimes,"* Previn conducting London Symphony. Angel.

Klaus Scheibe, *Saint-Saëns: Symphony No. 3 in C Minor ("Organ")*, Barenboim conducting Chicago Symphony. Deutsche Grammophon.

BEST COMEDY RECORDING

• *Bicentennial Nigger*, Richard Pryor. Warner Bros.

Critics called Richard Pryor's best comedy LP Bicentennial Nigger *either brilliant or obscene and humorless.*

Bill Cosby Is Not Himself These Days, Rat Own, Rat Own, Rat Own, Bill Cosby. Capitol.

Goodbye Pop, National Lampoon. Epic.

Sleeping Beauty, Cheech & Chong. Ode.

You Gotta Wash Your Ass, Redd Foxx. Atlantic.

BEST SPOKEN WORD RECORDING

• *Great American Documents*, Orson Welles, Henry Fonda, Helen Hayes, James Earl Jones. CBS.

Asimov: Foundation, The Psychohistorians, William Shatner. Caedmon.

Dickens: A Tale of Two Cities, James Mason. Caedmon.

Fahrenheit 451, Ray Bradbury. Listening Library.

Hemingway: The Old Man and the Sea, Charlton Heston. Caedmon.

BEST RECORDING FOR CHILDREN

• *Prokofiev: Peter and the Wolf; Saint Saëns: Carnival of the Animals*, Hermione Gingold, narrator; Bohm conducting Vienna Philharmonic. Deutsche Grammophon.

The Adventures of Ali and His Gang vs. Mr. Tooth Decay, Muhammed Ali & his Gang. St. John's Fruits & Vegetables.

Dickens' Christmas Carol, Mickey Mouse and Scrooge McDuck. Disneyland.

Snow White and the Seven Dwarfs, original soundtrack. Buena Vista.

"Winnie the Pooh for President (Campaign Song)," Sterling Holloway, Larry Groce. Disneyland.

BEST BEST ENGINEERED RECORDING, NON-CLASSICAL

• Al Schmitt. *Breezin'* (George Benson). Warner Bros.

Jay Lewis, *The Dream Weaver* (Gary Wright). Warner Bros.

Ron Hitchcock, *The King James Version*, (Harry James & His Big Band). Sheffield Lab.

Alan Parsons, Tom Trefethen, *Somewhere I've Never Travelled* (Ambrosia). 20th Century.

Alan Parsons, *Tales of Mystery and Imagination, Edgar Allan Poe* (Alan Parsons Project). 20th Century.

BEST ALBUM PACKAGE

• John Berg, art director, *Chicago X* (Chicago). Columbia.

Ron Coro, Nancy Donald, art directors, *Silk Degrees* (Boz Scaggs). Columbia.

Hipgnosis, Hardie, art directors, *Presence* (Led Zeppelin). Swan Song.

Acy Lehman, art director, *Coney Island Baby* (Lou Reed). RCA.

J. Stelmach, art director, *Schumann: Symphony No. 1 in B Flat, Op. 38; Manfred: Overture, Op. 115* (Charles Munch conducting Boston Symphony). RCA.

Roland Young, art director, *Bellavia* (Chuck Mangione). A&M.

Roland Young, art director, *The End of the Beginning* (Richie Havens). A&M.

Roland Young, art director, *Mirrors* (Peggy Lee). A&M.

BEST ALBUM NOTES
(Annotator's Award)

• Dan Morgenstern, *The Changing Face of Harlem*, Savoy Sessions (various artists). Savoy.

George R. Marek, *Beethoven: The Five Piano Concertos* (Baremboim conducting London Philharmonic; solo: Rubinstein). RCA.

Douglas B. Green, *The Blue Sky Boys* (Bill & Earl Bolick). RCA.

Francis Robinson, *Caruso, A Legendary Performer* (Enrico Caruso). RCA.

Mort Goode, *The Complete Tommy Dorsey, Volume I – 1935*. RCA.

PRODUCER OF THE YEAR

• Stevie Wonder

Richard Perry

Lennie Waronker

Joe Wissert

Pop Goes California

The recent changes in the pop/rock scene were profoundly evident in 1977. In August, the King of Rock & Roll, Elvis Presley, was found dead and bloated on his bathroom floor at his Graceland estate in Memphis, while in New York City, Studio 54, the queen of all discos, opened its doors to a sea of young and anxious faces.

The faces that made up the new music hierarchy were changing, too, in terms of identity, gender, and color. Half of the Top 10 songs in the year's Hot 100 featured female lead vocalists, the most ever. *Variety* noted the color difference when the Grammy bids came out: "The most striking thing about the pop nominations is the complete absence of black performers." Music's geography also seemed to be shifting: All of the winners of the top awards would turn out either to be based in California or tied in to Hollywood films.

Typical were the winners of Record of the Year. Critic Robert Hilburn of the *L.A. Times* said that on *Hotel California* the Eagles used California "as a metaphor for the nation [when singer and drummer Don Henley and vocalist Glen Frey] wrote about the pursuit of the American dream, '70s style, using their own experiences in rock to convey the innocence ('New Kid in Town'), temptations ('One of These Nights'), and disillusionments ('The Sad Cafe') of that pursuit."

The Eagles won two Grammys in 1977: Record of the Year for "Hotel

GLOBE PHOTO

"We can't even try to top" Rumours' *amazing success, said a Fleetwood Mac member of* Billboard's *album of the decade and Grammy's choice for LP of the year.*

California" and Best Arrangement for Voices for "New Kid in Town." Despite their earlier assurance that they would be on hand for the Grammycast at Los Angeles's Shrine Auditorium, the Eagles skipped it at the very last minute, causing considerable confusion backstage when it came time for them to perform on the show. When the *Times*'s Hilburn reached the group later by phone in Malibu where they were rehearsing their next album, *The Long Run*, Henley told him with typical Californian flipness, "The whole idea of a contest to see who is 'best' just doesn't appeal to us. It's all a matter of personal taste."

All the top winners were either based in California or tied in to Hollywood movies.

Fleetwood Mac was the other leading purveyor of California rock and easily took the Album of the Year award as predicted by most Grammy watchers, including Hilburn, who was nonetheless rooting publicly for the Eagles' *Hotel California* LP. It was, he wrote in the *Times*, "the strongest nominee [because it] contributed well to the overall theme of disillusionment in the symbolic promised land of Southern California."

Fleetwood Mac's *Rumours* has been ranked by *Billboard* as the number one album of the 1970s and number five in its list of all-time top 100 albums of the rock era. It sold a staggering 10 million copies, spent an unprecedented 31 weeks at number one in the charts, and was the first group album to have four Top 10 hits: "Go Your Own Way," "Dreams," "Don't Stop," and "You Make Loving Fun." "We can't even try to top what we've done with *Rumours*,"

guitarist Lindsey Buckingham told reporters backstage at the Grammys.

The LP prize was bestowed on them by the recently reunited Crosby, Stills & Nash, who were also leaders of the California pop movement and past winners of Grammy's Best New Artist award in 1969. (This time the trio appeared on the Grammycast dressed in conformist coats and ties in sharp contrast to the scruffy garb they wore back in 1969. "We were jive then ... in our hippie phase," Graham Nash told the *Times* later. "I think it's different now. There's nothing wrong with putting on a suit.") Fleetwood Mac's award was accepted by Buckingham, who expressed his pleasure by reminiscing with the viewing audience: "I can remember being 11 years old and watching the Grammys on TV."

For the first time in Grammy history, there was a tie for Song of the Year, and both winners happened to be related to recent Hollywood films. Interestingly, both tunes would also win Best Original Song in different years at the Oscars thanks to a difference in eligibility periods between the two awards.

Barbra Streisand launched her career as a songwriter while receiving a guitar lesson on the set of *A Star Is Born*, the film she was making with Kris Kristofferson. "I just started to fool around with chords," she told biographer James Spada. "Instead of 'A Star Is Born,' a song was born! It just came out of absolute impatience."

Singer-songwriter Paul Williams wrote the lyrics to "Love Theme from *A Star Is Born* (Evergreen)," and Streisand recorded it soon thereafter for both the film score and a single version that ended up ranked number five in the year's Hot 100, Streisand's best showing since she topped the chart in 1974 with "The Way We Were" (which was also Grammy's Song of the Year).

"Miss Streisand also was the surprise

victor in the pop female singer category," noted *The New York Times* when she overtook rival nominees Linda Ronstadt, Dolly Parton, Carly Simon, and Debby Boone ("easily the best-matched field" among this year's Grammys, said the *L.A. Times*'s Hilburn). The California newspaper added: "The awards broke a long Grammy dry spell for Streisand, perhaps the most respected female singer in pop. They were her first since 1965 when she was named best singer for *My Name Is Barbra*."

"Love Theme from *A Star Is Born* (Evergreen)" had been released in early 1977 so it was not considered a strong contender at the time of the ceremony one year later. "I thought we were forgotten," Streisand said, accepting the best song honor, "so I really am shocked." The nervous, first-time winner Paul Williams joined her at the podium and thanked his "doctor for giving me the fantastic Valium."

The second winner of Song of the Year was the top-selling song of 1977, the biggest seller in the history of Warner Bros. Records, and the first single since Guy Mitchell's "Singing the Blues" in 1956 to spend 10 weeks ranked number one in the weekly charts. The song was "You Light Up My Life," written by Joe Brooks. Brooks penned it for the highly forgettable film of the same name that he produced, directed, and wrote about a disillusioned young woman trying to make it as a singer in Hollywood. Brooks accepted his songwriter's prize with obvious relish, saying, "This song was

Barbra Streisand was "shocked" to win the female pop vocal award for "Evergreen," which tied for Song of the Year with "You Light Up My Life."

turned down by every [record] firm that is out there tonight. Some turned it down twice .... This is so sweet."

The mega-hit single version of "You Light Up My Life" was sung by the winner of Grammy's Best New Artist award, Debby Boone, daughter of crooner Pat Boone. Debby Boone was only 20 years old when she topped the year's chart, just as her father had done with "Two Hearts," at exactly same age. "You Light Up My Life" was written as a love ballad, but Boone, who was then the lead singer of a family gospel quartet comprised of her and her sisters, decided to sing it like a prayer. "It wasn't a Christian song, although many people thought it was," she told *Billboard*. "However, mainly because the lyrics really lent themselves to how I felt about

WIDE WORLD PHOTO

my relationship with the Lord, that's the way I chose to sing it. I never really thought anyone would know."

Among the singers Boone beat for Best New Artist was 19-year-old heartthrob Andy Gibb, whose older brothers, the Bee Gees, were Grammy nominees for the pop group vocal honors. When they won it, the victory proved a virtual omen for the Grammy Awards of next year.

Best New Artist Debby Boone sang Song of the Year co-winner "You Light Up My Life" like it was a love song to God: "I never thought anyone would know."

The Bee Gees had the number two song in the year's Hot 100, "How Deep Is Your Love," (followed at number three by brother Andy's "I Just Want to Be Your Everything" — never before had brothers occupied two of the top three slots in the year-end lineup). "How Deep" stayed in the Top 10 for an unprecedented 17 continuous weeks and

was an advance release from the Bee Gees' songs included in the definitive film about disco delirium, *Saturday Night Fever*. The *Saturday Night Fever* LP would earn the Bee Gees an impressive tally of five awards at next year's Grammys, including the coveted Album of the Year.

In the pop male vocals category, the prize went to the 1971 winner for "You've Got a Friend," James Taylor, whose latest hit (called "sly, sultry" by the *L.A. Times*) was a cover of "Handy Man," written in part by Otis Blackwell, who also penned "Don't Be Cruel" and "Return to Sender" for Elvis Presley. Taylor's producer, Peter Asher, who was also the behind the recent surge in Linda Ronstadt's career, took the Producer of the Year award.

Disco ruled the r&b awards when several other dance hits from the Hot 100's Top 10 figured in Grammy triumphs. Thelma Houston had been toiling at Dunhill and then at Motown for nearly 10 years before she finally reached the top of the charts. ("You release a record and you say, 'this is it,' but it isn't," she once told the *L.A. Times*, describing her frustration during her early career.) Then producer Hal Davis suggested she remake a onetime middling hit for Harold Melvin & the Blue Notes. "Don't Leave Me This Way" ended up number eight in the year-end rankings and earned her the female r&b vocal award.

Success was also a long time coming for the victor of the group vocals prize, the Emotions, a trio of sisters who had been performing since the 1950s, initially as a gospel group called the Hutchinsons (Wanda, Sheila, and Jeanette), then the Heavenly Sunbeams. The sisters turned to recording secular songs in the 1960s, but their record company, Stax/Volt, folded within a few years. They were rescued professionally by Maurice White of Earth, Wind & Fire, who co-wrote and produced the song that proved a five-week chart-topper for them as well as a dance club standard, "Best of My Love."

Singer-songwriter Leo Sayer kept the discos hopping with the year's Best Rhythm & Blues Song, "You Make Me Feel Like Dancing," which he wrote with Vini Poncia, who had previously penned "Do I Love You" for the Ronettes. "Dancing" was from Sayer's fourth album, *Endless Flight*, but it was his first number one–ranked single. Also adept at making the young set boogie were the Brothers Johnson, who had been discovered by Quincy Jones, the producer of the group's next four albums. The first of the lot, *Look Out for No. 1*, sold a million copies in 1976, followed by 1977's *Right on Time*, which was certified gold (marking one-half million in sales) three days after its release. (Single hits include "I'll Be Good to You," written by Jones.) *Right on Time* included the brothers' grateful salute to Jones, a track called "Q," that earned them the r&b instrumental performance prize.

The sole r&b champ who was not a disco champion was an artist who twice before captured the male vocal award. Lou Rawls had won in 1967 for "Dead End Street" and again in 1971 for "Natural Man." Rawls's career had been at low ebb during the early 1970s before he signed up with Philadelphia International Records (a division of Epic) in 1976 and scored a string of hits beginning with "You'll Never Find Another

Love Like Mine" the same year. His latest r&b award was for his 1977 Philadelphia International album *Unmistakably Lou.*

The biggest champ in terms of the most Grammys won this year was John Williams, composer of the score to *Star Wars*, the highest-grossing film in the history of Hollywood, having earned a record $200 million at the box office by the end of 1977. ("There wasn't much doubt of the *Star Wars* phenomenon spreading to the record industry," the *L.A. Herald Tribune* commented in its Grammy coverage.) Williams's outer space symphonics were performed under his baton by the London Symphony Orchestra and garnered him three awards: Best Instrumental Composition, Best Pop Instrumental Performance, and Best Original Score Written for a Motion Picture. Adding to its success, Williams's score performed amazingly well on the album charts for orchestra music, spending two weeks at number two and selling more than two million copies. A single release made it into the weekly Hot 100, too, but was surpassed in rank by a separate disco version by Meco (Monardo) that topped the lineup for two weeks and lost the pop instrumental Grammy to Williams.

Record of the Year champs, the Eagles, snubbed the Grammy show at the last minute.

The big band laurels in jazz were claimed by last year's winner of the soloist award, Count Basie, for his and his orchestra's latest LP, *Prime Time*. Alto sax player Phil Woods had won the big band award with Michel Legrand in 1975 for their *Images* album and now returned for the group performance prize for *The Phil Woods Six — Live from the Showboat*. Oscar Peterson had won the group honor in 1974 for his collaboration with Joe Pass and Niels Pedersen, but now he took the soloist award for *The Giants*. Fusion singer Al Jarreau (*Look to the Rainbow*) garnered the new prize for jazz vocals that was introduced in 1976 and won that year by the diva of the older-style jazz singing, Ella Fitzgerald.

"Don't It Make My Brown Eyes Blue" dominated the country music field in 1977, taking the Grammy's Best Country Song award as well as the equivalent prize from the Country Music Association. "Brown Eyes Blue" was written by Richard Leigh, who literally had his inspiration at his feet when he scripted it — his brown-eyed dog Amanda who, ironically, would actually end up with one blue eye years later when she developed a cataract after being hit in the head with a rock hurled by a frightened garbage collector.

"Brown Eyes Blue" made its vocalist an overnight sensation when the song crossed over from the country charts to the number two slot in the pop line-up. Crystal Gayle, who actually had blue eyes, had only minor success before that. She toured the honky-tonk circuit with her sister, Loretta Lynn, in the early 1970s and finally scored a minor hit with "I'll Get Over You" (Gayle's first Grammy nod in 1976) after she signed with United Artists. But it wasn't until the release of her *We Must Believe in Magic* LP and its "Brown Eyes Blue" single in 1977 that she achieved nearly the same celebrity status as her sister. *Magic* became the first country album to be certified platinum (marking a million copies in sales), and "Brown Eyes Blue" earned Gayle the best female country vocalist Grammy as well as the Female Vocalist of the Year designation from both the Country Music Association and the Academy of Country Music. "I was in a category with four great singers," Gayle said backstage at the Grammycast, referring to fellow nominees Janie Fricke, Emmylou Harris, Barbara Mandrell, and Dolly Parton. "But I knew it was a special song from the first time I heard it."

A losing nominee for Song of the Year, "Lucille," still made its performer, Kenny Rogers, Grammy's best male country vocalist. Rogers had been the leader of the First Edition, but when the group disbanded in 1975, he struck out on a solo career. A few minor hits followed. Then the singer was wrapping up his *Kenny Rogers* album one day when he learned that he still had 15 minutes of studio time left. "Lucille" was added at the last minute — and made Rogers a country/pop superstar.

Serendipity also played a part in the success of the Kendalls, winners of the country group vocals prize. "Heaven's Just a Sin Away" was released as the throwaway "B" side to only the second single issued by the harmony-singing father and daughter team of Royce and Jeannie Kendall. Hargus "Pig" Robbins spent more than a decade as an obscure session pianist for Chet Atkins at RCA's country division and working with other artists like Bob Dylan (*Blonde on Blonde*, 1966). When he won the instrumental performance Grammy for his *Country Instrumentalist of the Year* LP, Robbins ironically beat his boss Atkins, who had won the award in the previous three years and was nominated twice this year.

Nearly all of the winners of the religious awards were repeats from previous years, including the Imperials (*Sail On*), the Oak Ridge Boys ("Just a Little Talk with Jesus"), and the San Francisco gospel group the Edwin Hawkins Singers (*Wonderful!*). Pianist-singer James Cleveland had won before, too, and now reaped a new award for the recording of his recent concert at Carnegie Hall. Cleveland performed one of the concert selections on the Grammycast and thus became the first gospel artist to be featured on the show. B.J. Thomas had been nominated for a pop vocalist Grammy in 1968 and sang 1975's Country Song of the Year "(Hey, Won't You Play) Another Somebody Done Somebody Wrong Song," but he finally claimed his first trophy for 1977's Best Inspirational Performance for his all-gospel LP *Home Where I Belong*. Thomas started recording gospel extensively in 1976 after having a religious experience that he claimed saved him from his earlier life of drug abuse.

Ever since the Latin category was introduced in 1975, it had been dominated by salsa artist Eddie Palmieri. Palmieri wasn't nominated this year, but Latin music's "El Rey" ("The King") Tito Puente was and was clearly the odds-on favorite to win. Instead, the award went to one of his former band members, Mongo Santamaria (for *Dawn*), the Afro-Cuban percussionist, bandleader, and composer who became one of the leading Latin musicians of the 1960s when he first gained notice for fusing the Latin beat with jazz and r&b sounds.

Richard Pryor's three-year winning streak in the comedy category came to an end when the prize was claimed by the wild and crazy Steve Martin, who was fast becoming the hottest comedian in the country thanks to his frequent appearances on TV's *Saturday Night Live*. On his victorious *Let's Get Small* LP, which went platinum despite crushing reviews from the critics, Martin bordered on tastelessness when he described a visit to the Turd Museum ("They got some real great shit there") and insulted female smokers ("Virginia Slims, that's a woman's cigarette. What do they have, little breasts on 'em or

something?"). Martin was actually at his funniest when he received his Grammy at the Shrine Auditorium. For his acceptance speech, he sang a few bars of "The Impossible Dream."

Grammy's Classical Album of the Year involved a host of celebrity talent in a fête held on May 18, 1976, that was billed as the "Concert of the Century" to mark the 85th anniversary of Carnegie Hall. The two-disc live recording included performances by Leonard Bernstein and the New York Philharmonic (Beethoven's Leonore Overture No. 3), Yehudi Menuhin and Isaac Stern (Bach's Concerto in D Minor for Two Violins), and Vladimir Horowitz and Dietrich Fischer-Dieskau (Schumann's *Dichterliebe*). It also featured the Philharmonic's Oratorio Society, as well as the Carnegie Hall audience itself, when, at the end of the evening, everyone was asked to join in singing the joyous "Hallelujah Chorus" from Handel's *Messiah*.

"Brown Eyes Blue" finally made the blue-eyed Crystal Gayle a superstar.

Carlo Maria Giulini won his only previous Grammy in 1971 when he conducted the Chicago Symphony Orchestra in *Mahler: Symphony No. 1*. He reclaimed the orchestra honors again now for another guest appearance with the Chicago players, this time performing Mahler's Symphony No. 9 in a recording "with a rich and characterful sound," said *High Fidelity*. It was also nominated for Classical Album of the Year. Pianist Artur Rubinstein won a Grammy for the fourth consecutive year for his third career recording of Beethoven's Sonata for Piano, No. 18 and Schumann's *Fantasiestücke*. In his latest version, actually taped in 1976, the maestro "displays certain frailties," said *High Fidelity*, "as indeed he always has, but few are traceable to advanced age. In the Beethoven sonata there were actually more finger slips in his previous recording," taped in 1963. Itzhak Perlman reaped the honors for soloist with orchestra accompaniment for his rendition of Vivaldi's *The Four Seasons*, which the critics called "pure magic."

In the early 1950s, the Juilliard Quartet taped Schöenberg's Quartets for Strings and then repeated its effort in 1977 to win the chamber music laurels. "Intensity certainly was the keynote of those earlier Juilliard performances," said *High Fidelity*, "and the remarkable, wonderful thing about the new ones is that they have relaxed (and, in places, broadened) without becoming in any way less propulsive or committed." The magazine was less taken with Sir Georg Solti's latest Grammy-winning album, Verdi's *Requiem* (Best Classical Choral Performance), which he and the Chicago Symphony Chorus and Orchestra had last recorded a decade earlier. Both versions, said *High Fidelity*, lacked "a sense of unfolding spiritual drama."

Janet Baker joined Leontyne Price for the vocals on Solti's *Requiem*, but she received an equally bad review from *High Fidelity*. But when she won the vocal soloist prize for a collection of arias by Bach, the magazine said she "sounds far more solid and secure than she has on recent recordings." For a second year in a row, Gershwin's *Porgy & Bess* won Best Opera Recording, a version (also complete) executed by the Houston Grand Opera company. The troupe took its production to New York in July 1977, then on a 16-week national tour. *High Fidelity* called it "a lively, moving, theatrically vivid re-creation of Catfish Row."

"As a production, the 20th anniversary of the Grammys proved a colorful and moving two-hour show," said *The Hollywood Reporter* in its wrap-up coverage of the ceremony that included performances by Debby Boone, Crystal Gayle, Ronnie Milsap, Dancing Machine, and host John Denver. "It was particularly well written and tightly directed. From its opening, which focused on Grammy winners over the past 20 years, the show's momentum was never lost."

The New York Times, however, took issue with some of its interludes of weak humor, production flubs, and more: "The awards telecast was fraught with mistakes, clumsiness and vulgarity. Halfway through the proceedings the audience had stopped even trying to laugh at the jokes John Denver, the host, was asked to recite, and the cameras kept making furtive sorties to celebrities in the hall, several of whom were caught with expressions on their faces that denoted horror, embarrassment or cynicism."

On the occasion of its historic 20th ceremony, the Grammys gave its fans a precedent-setting present. For the first time ever, the ceremony was open to the general public. *The L.A. Herald Tribune* noted, "Half of the 6,000 Shrine Auditorium seats were occupied by non-music industry people."

The ceremony was broadcast on CBS from the Los Angeles Shrine Auditorium on February 23, 1978, for the awards eligibility period of October 1, 1976, to September 30, 1977.

ALBUM OF THE YEAR
• *Rumours*, Fleetwood Mac. Fleetwood Mac, Richard Dashut, Ken Caillat, A&R producers. Warner Bros.
Aja, Steely Dan. Gary Katz, A&R producer. ABC.
Hotel California, Eagles. Bill Szymczyk, A&R producer. Asylum.
J T, James Taylor. Peter Asher, A&R producer. Columbia.
Star Wars, John Williams conducting London Symphony. George Lucas, A&R producer. 20th Century.

RECORD OF THE YEAR
• "Hotel California," Eagles. Bill Szymczyk, A&R producer. Asylum.
"Blue Bayou," Linda Ronstadt. Peter Asher, A&R producer. Asylum.
"Don't It Make My Brown Eyes Blue," Crystal Gayle. Allen Reynolds, A&R producer. United Artists.
"Love Theme from *A Star Is Born* (Evergreen)," Barbra Streisand. Barbra Streisand, Phil Ramone, A&R producers. Columbia.
"You Light Up My Life," Debby Boone. Joe Brooks, A&R producer. Warner Bros./Curb.

SONG OF THE YEAR
(Songwriter's Award—Tie)
• "Love Theme from *A Star Is Born* (Evergreen)," Barbra Streisand, Paul Williams.
• "You Light Up My Life," Joe Brooks.
"Don't It Make My Brown Eyes Blue," Richard Leigh.
"Hotel California," Don Felder, Don Henley, Glenn Frey.
"Nobody Does It Better," Marvin Hamlisch, Carole Bayer Sager.
"Southern Nights," Allen Toussaint.

BEST NEW ARTIST OF THE YEAR
• Debby Boone. Warner Bros./Curb.
Stephen Bishop. ABC.
Shaun Cassidy. Warner Bros./Curb.
Foreigner. Atlantic.
Andy Gibb. RSO.

BEST POP VOCAL PERFORMANCE, MALE
• James Taylor, "Handy Man." Columbia.
Stephen Bishop, "On and On." ABC.
Andy Gibb, "I Just Want to Be Your Everything." RSO.
Engelbert Humperdinck, "After the Lovin'." Epic.
Leo Sayer, "When I Need You." Warner Bros.

BEST POP VOCAL PERFORMANCE, FEMALE
• Barbra Streisand, "Love Theme from *A Star Is Born* (Evergreen)." Columbia.
Debby Boone, "You Light Up My Life." Warner Bros./Curb.
Dolly Parton, "Here You Come Again." RCA.
Linda Ronstadt, "Blue Bayou." Asylum.
Carly Simon, "Nobody Does It Better." Elektra.

BEST POP PERFORMANCE BY A DUO, GROUP, OR CHORUS WITH VOCAL
• Bee Gees, "How Deep Is Your Love." RSO.
Crosby, Stills & Nash, *CSN*. Atlantic.
Eagles, *Hotel California*. Asylum.
Fleetwood Mac, *Rumours*. Warner Bros.
Steely Dan, *Aja*. ABC.

BEST POP INSTRUMENTAL PERFORMANCE
• London Symphony, John Williams, conductor, *Star Wars*. 20th Century.
Bill Conti, "Gonna Fly Now (Theme from *Rocky*)." United Artists.
Barry De Vorzon, "Nadia's Theme (*The Young and the Restless*)." Arista.
Maynard Ferguson, "Gonna Fly Now (Theme from *Rocky*)." Columbia.
Meco, "*Star Wars* Theme/Cantina Band." Millennium.

BEST RHYTHM & BLUES SONG
(Songwriter's Award)
• "You Make Me Feel Like Dancing," Leo Sayer, Vini Poncia.
"Best of My Love," Maurice White, Al McKay.

"Brick House," Milan Williams, Walter Orange, Thomas McClary, William King, Lionel Richie, Ronald LaPread.

"Don't Leave Me This Way," Kenny Gamble, Leon Huff, Carry Gilbert.

"Easy," Lionel Richie.

Best Rhythm & Blues Vocal Performance, Male

• Lou Rawls, *Unmistakably Lou*. Philadelphia International/Epic.

Marvin Gaye, "Got to Give It Up" (Part 1). Motown.

B. B. King, "It's Just a Matter of Time." ABC.

Joe Tex, "Ain't Gonna Bump No More (With No Big Fat Woman)." Epic.

Johnny "Guitar" Watson, "A Real Mother For Ya." DJM.

Best Rhythm & Blues Vocal Performance, Female

• Thelma Houston, "Don't Leave Me This Way." Motown.

Natalie Cole, "I've Got Love on My Mind." Capitol.

Aretha Franklin, "Break It to Me Gently." Atlantic.

Dorothy Moore, "I Believe You." Malaco.

Diana Ross, "Your Love Is So Good for Me," track. Motown.

Best Rhythm & Blues Performance by a Duo, Group, or Chorus with Vocal

• Emotions, "Best of My Love," track. Columbia.

Commodores, "Easy." Motown.

Heatwave, "Boogie Nights." Epic.

Gladys Knight & the Pips, "Baby Don't Change Your Mind," track. Buddah.

Rufus featuring Chaka Khan, *Ask Rufus*. ABC.

Best Rhythm & Blues Instrumental Performance

• Brothers Johnson, "Q," track. A&M.

Blackbyrds, "The Unfinished Business," track. Fantasy.

Brecker Brothers, "Funky Sea, Funky Dew." Arista.

Salsoul Orchestra, "Getaway." Salsoul.

Stuff, *More Stuff*. Warner Bros.

Best Jazz Vocal Performance

• Al Jarreau, *Look to the Rainbow*. Warner Bros.

Joao Gilberto, *Amoroso*. Warner Bros.

Irene Kral, *Kral Space*. Catalyst.

Carmen McRae, *Carmen McRae at the Great American Music Hall*. Blue Note/United Artists.

Helen Merrill, *Helen Merrill–John Lewis*. Mercury.

Best Jazz Instrumental Performance, Soloist

• Oscar Peterson, *The Giants*. Pablo.

John Coltrane, *Afro Blue Impressions*. Pablo.

Hank Jones, *'Bop Redux*. Muse.

Jaco Pastorius, *Heavy Weather*. Columbia

Phil Woods, *The Phil Woods Six—Live from the Showboat*. RCA.

Best Jazz Instrumental Performance, Group

• Phil Woods, *The Phil Woods Six—Live from the Showboat*. RCA.

John Coltrane, *Afro Blue Impressions*. Pablo.

Tommy Flanagan Trio, *Eclypso*. Inner City.

Dexter Gordon, *Homecoming, Live at the Village Vanguard*. Columbia.

Mel Lewis, *Mel Lewis & Friends*. Horizon/A&M.

Best Jazz Performance, Big Band

• Count Basie and his Orchestra, *Prime Time*. Pablo.

Woody Herman, *The 40th Anniversary, Carnegie Hall Concert*. RCA.

North Texas State University Lab Band, Leon Breeden, director, *Lab '76*. NTSU Lab Jazz.

Buddy Rich, *Buddy Rich Plays and Plays and Plays*. RCA/ Gryphon.

Toshiko Akiyoshi–Lew Tabackin Big Band, *Road Time*. RCA.

Best Country Song
(Songwriter's Award)

• "Don't It Make My Brown Eyes Blue," Richard Leigh.

"Desperado," Glenn Frey, Don Henley.

"It Was Almost Like a Song," Archie Jordan, Hal David.

"Lucille," Roger Bowling, Hal Bynum.

"Luckenbach, Texas," Bobby Emmons, Chips Moman.

BEST COUNTRY VOCAL PERFORMANCE, MALE
• Kenny Rogers, "Lucille." United Artists.
Larry Gatlin, "I Don't Wanna Cry." Monument.
Waylon Jennings, "Luckenbach, Texas." RCA.
Ronnie Milsap, "It Was Almost Like a Song." RCA.
Jerry Jeff Walker, "Mr. Bojangles." MCA.

BEST COUNTRY VOCAL PERFORMANCE, FEMALE
• Crystal Gayle, "Don't It Make My Brown Eyes Blue." United Artists.
Janie Fricke, "What're You Doing Tonight." Columbia.
Emmylou Harris, "Making Believe." Warner Bros.
Barbara Mandrell, "After the Lovin'," track. ABC/Dot.
Dolly Parton, "(Your Love Has Lifted Me) Higher and Higher," track. RCA.

BEST COUNTRY PERFORMANCE BY A DUO OR GROUP WITH VOCAL
• The Kendalls, "Heaven's Just a Sin Away." Ovation.
Asleep at the Wheel, *The Wheel*. Capitol.
George Jones, Tammy Wynette, "Near You." Epic.
Loretta Lynn, Conway Twitty, *Dynamic Duo*. MCA.
Oak Ridge Boys, *Y'All Come Back Saloon*. ABC/Dot.

BEST COUNTRY INSTRUMENTAL PERFORMANCE
• Hargus "Pig" Robbins, *Country Instrumentalist of the Year*. Elektra.
Asleep at the Wheel, "Ragtime Annie," track. Capitol.
Chet Atkins, *Me & My Guitar*. RCA.
Chet Atkins, Floyd Cramer, Danny Davis, *Chet, Floyd & Danny*. RCA.
Jerry Reed, "West Bound and Down," track. MCA.

BEST GOSPEL PERFORMANCE, CONTEMPORARY OR INSPIRATIONAL
• Imperials, *Sail On*. Dayspring/Word.
Reba Rambo Gardner, *Reba/Lady*. Greentree.
Larry Hart & the Soul Singers, *Hart and Soul*. Genesis.
Michael Omartian, *Adam Again*. Myrrh/Word.

Gary S. Paxton, *More from the Astonishing, Outrageous, Amazing, Incredible, Unbelievable Gary S. Paxton*. New Pax.
Evie Tornquist, *Mirror*. Word.

BEST GOSPEL PERFORMANCE, TRADITIONAL
• Oak Ridge Boys, "Have a Little Talk With Jesus." Rockland Road.
Blackwood Brothers, *Bill Gaither Songs*. Skylite.
Cathedral Quartet, *Then and Now*. Canaan.
LeFevres, *Till He Comes*. Canaan.
Rambos, *Naturally*. Heartwarming.
Speers, *Cornerstone*. Heartwarming.

BEST SOUL GOSPEL PERFORMANCE, CONTEMPORARY
• Edwin Hawkins & the Edwin Hawkins Singers, *Wonderful!* Birthright.
Danniebelle, *He Is King*. Light.
Jessy Dixon, "Born Again." Light.
Larnelle Harris, *More*. Word.
Mighty Clouds of Joy, "God Is Not Dead," track. ABC.

BEST SOUL GOSPEL PERFORMANCE, TRADITIONAL
• James Cleveland, *James Cleveland Live at Carnegie Hall*. Savoy.
James Cleveland & the Greater Metropolitan Church of Christ Choir, *The Lord Is My Life*. Savoy.
Rev. Cleavant Derricks & Family, *Satisfaction Guaranteed*. Canaan.
Five Blind Boys of Mississippi, "I'm Just Another Soldier." Jewel.
Savannah Choir & Rev. Isaac Douglas, *Stand Up for Jesus*. Creed.

BEST INSPIRATIONAL PERFORMANCE
• B.J. Thomas, *Home Where I Belong*. Myrrh/Word.
Salome Bey, Clinton Derricks-Carroll, Sheila Ellis, Delores Hall, William Hardy, Jr., Hector Jaime Mercado, Stanley Perryman, Mabel Robinson, William Thomas, Jr., *Your Arms Too Short to Box with God*. ABC.
Quincy Jones, James Cleveland conducting Wattsline Choir, "Oh Lord, Come By Here," track. A&M.
Carol Lawrence, *Tell All the World About Love*. Word.
Ray Price, *How Great Thou Art*. Word.

BEST ETHNIC OR TRADITIONAL RECORDING
• *Hard Again*, Muddy Waters. Blue Sky/CBS.
Blues Hit Big Town, Junior Wells. Delmark.
Right Place, Wrong Time, Otis Rush. Bullfrog.
Things That I Used to Do, Joe Turner. Pablo.
What Happened to My Blues, Willie Dixon. Ovation.

BEST LATIN RECORDING
• *Dawn*, Mongo Santamaria. Vaya.
Fire Works, Machito Orchestra with Lalo Rodriguez. Dutch Timeless.
La Leyenda, Tito Puente. Tico/Fania.
Muy Amigos/Close Friends, Eydie Gormé, Danny Rivera. Gala/ Coco.
Tomorrow: Barretto Live, Ray Barretto Band. Atlantic.

BEST INSTRUMENTAL ARRANGEMENT
• Harry Betts, Perry Botkin, Jr., Barry De Vorzon, "Nadia's Theme (*The Young and the Restless*)" (Barry De Vorzon). Arista.
Chick Corea, "Musicmagic" (Return to Forever). Columbia.
Crusaders, "Free as the Wind" (Crusaders), ABC.
Bob James, "Scheherezade" (Hubert Laws). CTI.
Herb Spencer, "*Roots* Mural Theme" (Quincy Jones). A&M.

BEST INSTRUMENTAL COMPOSITION
(Composer's Award)
• "Main Title from *Star Wars*," John Williams.
"Birdland," Joe Zawinul.
"Bond '77/*James Bond* Theme," Marvin Hamlisch.
"Gonna Fly Now (Theme from *Rocky*)," Bill Conti, Carol Connors, Ann Robbins.
"*Roots* Medley (Motherland, *Roots* Mural Theme)," Quincy Jones, Gerald Fried.

BEST ARRANGEMENT FOR VOICES
• Eagles, "New Kid in Town" (Eagles). Asylum.
Fleetwood Mac, "Go Your Own Way" (Fleetwood Mac). Warner Bros.
Heatwave, "All You Do Is Dial" (Heatwave). Epic.

BOSTON POPS

Grammy's biggest winner of the year, composer and conductor John Williams, earned three awards for Star Wars.

Quincy Jones, James Cleveland, John Mandel, "Oh Lord, Come By Here" (Quincy Jones). A&M.
Jim Seals, "Baby, I'll Give It to You" (Seals & Crofts). Warner Bros.

BEST INSTRUMENTAL ARRANGEMENT ACCOMPANYING VOCALIST(S)
• Ian Freebairn-Smith, "Love Theme from *A Star Is Born* (Evergreen)" (Barbra Streisand). Columbia.
Richard Carpenter, "Calling Occupants of Interplanetary Craft" (Carpenters). A&M.
Claus Ogerman, "Besame Mucho" (Joao Gilberto). Warner Bros.
Claus Ogerman, "Nature Boy" (George Benson). Warner Bros.
Seawind, "The Devil Is a Liar" (Seawind). CTI.

BEST CAST SHOW ALBUM
• *Annie*, Charles Strouse, Martin Charnin, composers. Larry Morton, Charles Strouse, producers. Columbia.
Guys and Dolls, Frank Loesser, composer, William Goldstein, producer. Motown.

I Love My Wife, Cy Coleman, Michael Stewart, composers. Cy Coleman, producer. Atlantic.

Starting Here, Starting Now, Richard Maltby, Jr., David Shire, composers. Jay David Saks, producer. RCA.

Your Arms Too Short to Box with God, Micki Grant, Alex Bradford, composers. Esmond Edwards, producer. ABC.

BEST ORIGINAL SCORE, MOTION PICTURE OR A TELEVISION SPECIAL
(Composer's Award)

• *Star Wars*, John Williams. 20th Century.

Rocky, Bill Conti. United Artists.

The Spy Who Loved Me, Marvin Hamlisch. United Artists.

A Star Is Born, Kenny Ascher, Alan & Marilyn Bergman. Rupert Holmes, Leon Russell, Barbra Streisand, Donna Weiss, Paul Williams, Kenny Loggins. Columbia.

You Light Up My Life, Joe Brooks. Arista.

BEST CLASSICAL ALBUM

• *Concert of the Century* (Recorded live at Carnegie Hall May 18, 1976), (solos: Leonard Bernstein, Vladimir Horowitz, Isaac Stern, Mstislav Rostropovich, Dietrich Fischer-Dieskau, Yehudi Menuhin, Lyndon Woodside). Thomas Frost, producer. Columbia.

Gershwin: Porgy & Bess, John De Main conducting Houston Grand Opera Production (solos: Dale, Smith, Shakesnider, Lane, Brice, Smalls). Thomas Z. Shepard, producer. RCA.

Haydn: Orlando Paladino, Antal Dorati conducting Orchestre de Chambre de Lausanne (solos: Auger, Ameling, Killebrew, Ahnsjo, Luxon, Trimarchi, Shirley). Erik Smith, producer. Philips.

Mahler: Symphony No. 9 in D Major, Carlo Maria Giulini conducting Chicago Symphony. Gunther Breest, producer. Deutsche Grammophon.

Parkening and the Guitar, (solo: Christopher Parkening). Patti Laursen, producer. Angel.

Ravel: Bolero; Debussy: La Mer & Apres Midi d'un Faune, Sir Georg Solti conducting Chicago Symphony. Ray Minshull, producer. London.

BEST CLASSICAL PERFORMANCE ORCHESTRA
(Conductor's Award)

• Carlo Maria Giulini conducting Chicago Symphony, *Mahler: Symphony No. 9 in D Major*. Gunther Breest, producer. Deutsche Grammophon.

Pierre Boulez conducting New York Philharmonic, *Bartók: The Wooden Prince*. Andrew Kazdin, producer. Columbia.

Herbert von Karajan conducting Berlin Philharmonic, *Bruckner: Symphony No. 8 in C Minor*. Hans Hirsch, producer. Deutsche Grammophon.

James Levine conducting Chicago Symphony, *Mahler: Symphony No. 3 in D Minor*. Thomas Z. Shepard, Jay David Saks, producers. RCA.

André Previn conducting London Symphony, *Tchaikovsky: Swan Lake*. Christopher Bishop, producer. Angel.

Sir Georg Solti conducting Chicago Symphony, *Ravel: Bolero*. Ray Minshuil, producer. London.

BEST CHAMBER MUSIC PERFORMANCE
(INSTRUMENTAL OR VOCAL)

• Juilliard Quartet, *Schönberg: Quartets for Strings (Complete)*. Columbia.

Emanuel Ax, Cleveland Quartet, *Dvorak: Quintet for Piano in A Major, Op. 81*. RCA.

Pezzo Elegiaco, Vladimir Horowitz, Isaac Stern, Mstislav Rostropovich, *Rachmaninoff: Sonata for Cello and Piano in G Minor, Op. 19, Andante; Tchaikovsky: Trio for Piano in A Minor, Op. 50*. Columbia.

Guarneri Quartet, *Bartók: Quartets for Strings (6)*. RCA.

David Munrow conducting Early Music Consort of London, *A Contemporary Elizabethan Concert* (works of Dowland, Williams, Purcell, etc.). Angel.

Prague String Quartet, *Dvorak: Quartets No. 8 in E Major, 0p. 80 & No. 10 in E Flat Major, Op. 51*. Deutsche Grammophon.

Ravi Shankar, Yehudi Menuhin, Jean-Pierre Rampal, Martine Geliot, Alla Rakha, *Improvisations, West Meets East, Album 3*. Angel.

BEST CLASSICAL PERFORMANCE, INSTRUMENTAL SOLOIST(S) (WITH ORCHESTRA)

• Itzhak Perlman, violin (Perlman conducting London Philharmonic), *Vivaldi: The Four Seasons*. Angel.

Lazar Berman, piano (Abbado conducting London Symphony), *Rachmaninoff: Concerto for Piano No. 3 in D Minor*. Columbia.

Alfred Brendel, piano (Haitink conducting London Philharmonic), *Beethoven: Concerti for Piano (5)*. Philips.

Jacqueline du Pre, cello (Barenboim conducting Philadelphia Orchestra), *Elgar: Concerto for Cello, Op. 85*. Columbia.

Alicia de Larrocha, piano (De Burgos conducting Royal Philharmonic), *Concertos from Spain (Surinach: Piano Concerto Montsalvage; Concerto Breve)*. London.

Maurizio Pollini, piano (Böhm conducting Vienna Philharmonic), *Beethoven: Concerto for Piano No. 4 in G Major*. Deutsche Grammophon.

Mstislav Rostropovich, cello (Bernstein conducting Orchestra National de France), *Schumann: Concerto for Cello & Orchestra in A Minor; Bloch: Schelomo*. Angel.

Solomon, piano (Dobrowen conducting

Classical Album of the Year Concert of the Century *was a tribute to Carnegie Hall conducted by Leonard Bernstein.*

Philharmonic), *Brahms: Concerto for Piano No. 2 in B Flat Major, Op. 83*. Vox.

BEST CLASSICAL PERFORMANCE, INSTRUMENTAL SOLOIST(S) (WITHOUT ORCHESTRA)

• Artur Rubinstein, piano, *Beethoven: Sonata for Piano No. 18 in E Flat Major, Op. 31 No. 3; Schumann: Fantasiestücke, Op. 12*. RCA.

Daniel Adni, piano, *Grainger: Piano Music of Percy Grainger*. Seraphim.

Michel Beroff, piano, *Messaien: 20 Regards de L'Enfant Jesus*. Connoisseur Society.

Alicia de Larrocha, piano, *Granados: Goyescas*. London.

Glenn Gould, piano, *Bach: The English Suites (Complete)*. Columbia.

Igor Kipnis, harpsichord, *Bach: Partitas for Harpsichord Nos. 1 in B Flat Major & 2 in C Minor*. Angel.

Itzhak Perlman, violin, *Itzhak Perlman Plays Fritz Kreisler: Album 2*. Angel.

BEST OPERA RECORDING

• *Gershwin: Porgy & Bess*, John De Main conducting Houston Grand Opera Production (solos: Albert, Dale, Smith, Shakesnider, Lane, Brice, Smalls). Thomas S. Shepard, producer. RCA.

Haydn: Orlando Paladino, Antal Dorati conducting Orchestre de Chambre de Lausanne (solos: Auger, Ameling, Killbrew, Ahnsjo, Luxon, Shirley, Trimarchi). Frik Smith, producer. Philips.

Janácek: Katya Kabanova, Charles Mackerras conducting Vienna Philharmonic (solos: Soderstrom, Kniplova). James Mallinson, producer. London.

Mussorgsky: Boris Godunov, Jerzy Semkow conducting Polish National Radio Symphony Orchestra & Chorus (solos: Talvela, Gedda). David Mottley, producer. Angel.

Puccini: Tosca, Colin Davis conducting Chorus and Orchestra of Royal Opera House, Covent Garden (solos: Caballe, Carreras, Wixell, Ramey). Erik Smith, producer Philips.

Wagner: Die Meistersinger von Nurnberg, Eugen Jochum conducting Deutsche Oper Berlin Orchestra & Chorus (solos: Fischer-Dieskau, Domingo, Ludwig, Ligendza). Gunther Breest, producer. Deutsche Grammophon.

Wagner: The Flying Dutchman, Sir Georg
Solti conducting Chicago Symphony
Orchestra & Chorus (solos: Bailey,
Martin, Talvela, Kollo, Krenn, Jones).
Ray Minshull, producer. London.
Weill: Threepenny Opera, Stanley Silver-
man conducting Original Cast of the-
New York Shakespeare Festival (solos:
Julia, Alexander, Greene). Larry Mor-
ton, producer. Columbia.

BEST CHORAL PERFORMANCE, OTHER THAN OPERA

• Sir Georg Solti, conductor, Margaret
Hillis, choral director, Chicago Sym-
phony Chorus and Orchestra, *Verdi:
Requiem*. RCA.
Serge Baudo conducting Stephen Caillat
Chorus and Orchestre de Paris, *Rous-
sel: Psalm 80*, for Tenor, Chorus, and
Orchestra. Connoisseur Society.
Colin Davis conducting John Alldis Choir;
London Symphony, *Berlioz: L'Enfance
Du Christ*. Philips.
Rafael Kubelik conducting Chorus of
Bavarian Radio & Bavarian Radio
Symphony), *Dvorak: Stabat Mater*.
Deutsche Grammophon.
Philip Ledger conducting King's College
Choir, Cambridge; Academy of St.
Martin-in-the-Fields, *Purcell: Funeral
Music for Queen Mary*. Angel.
Herbert von Karajan conducting Vienna
Singverein; Berlin Philharmonic,
Bruckner: Te Deum. Deutsche Gram-
mophon.
David Willcocks conducting King's Col-
lege Choir, Cambridge; Academy of
St. Martin-in-the-Fields, *Britten: Saint
Nicholas*. Seraphim.

BEST CLASSICAL VOCAL SOLOIST PERFORMANCE

• Janet Baker (Marriner conducting Acade-
my of St. Martin-in-the-Fields), *Bach:
Arias*. Angel.
Elly Ameling (de Waart conducting Rot-
terdam Philharmonic), *Schubert on
Stage*. Philips.
Dietrich Fischer-Dieskau (Ponti, accompa-
nist), *Ives: Songs*. Deutsche Gram-
mophon.
Donald Gramm (Hassard, accompanist),
But Yesterday Is Not Today (Songs by
Barber, Bowles, Copland, Chanler,
etc.). New World.

Luciano Pavarotti (Adler conducting
National Philharmonic), *Luciano
Pavarotti—O Holy Night*. London.
Elisabeth Söderström (Ashkenazy, accom-
panist), *Rachmaninoff: Songs, Volume
Two*. London.
Frederica von Stade (de Waart conducting
Rotterdam Philharmonic), *Rossini/
Mozart: Opera Arias*. Philips.
Gerard Souzay (Baldwin, accompanist),
Fauré: Songs (complete). Connoisseur
Society.
Galina Vishnevskaya, soprano, Mark
Reshetin, bass (Rostropovich conducting
Moscow Philharmonic), *Shostakovich:
Symphony No. 14*. Columbia.

BEST ENGINEERED RECORDING, CLASSICAL

• Kenneth Wilkinson, *Ravel: Bolero* (Solti
conducting Chicago Symphony). Lon-
don.
Paul Goodman, Anthony Salvatore, *Gersh-
win: Porgy & Bess* (De Main conduct-
ing Houston Grand Opera). RCA.
Bud Graham, Ray Moore, Milt Cherin,
Bartók: The Wooden Prince (Boulez
conducting New York Philharmonic).
Columbia.
Klaus Scheibe, *Mahler: Symphony No. 9 in
D Major* (Giulini conducting Chicago
Symphony). Deutsche Grammophon.
Heinz Wildhagen, *Mahler: Symphony No.
2 in C Minor ("Resurrection")*
(Abbado conducting Chicago Sympho-
ny). Deutsche Grammophon.
S.J.W. Witteveen, Dick van Dijk, *Berlioz:
L'Enfance du Christ* (Davis conducting
London Symphony). Philips.

BEST SPOKEN WORD, DOCUMENTARY, OR DRAMA RECORDING

• *The Belle of Amherst*, Julie Harris.
Credo.
*Alex Haley Tells the Story of his Search for
Roots*, Alex Haley. Warner Bros.
*For Colored Girls Who Have Considered
Suicide/When The Rainbow Is Enuf*
(Original Cast) Ntozake Shange, writ-
er. Buddah.
*J.R.R. Tolkien: The Silmarillion of Beren
and Luthien*, read by Christopher
Tolkien. Caedmon.
The Truman Tapes, Harry Truman speak-
ing with Ben Gradus. Caedmon.

BEST COMEDY RECORDING
• *Let's Get Small,* Steve Martin. Warner Bros.
Are You Serious??? Richard Pryor. Laff.
The Ernie Kovacs Album, Ernie Kovacs. Columbia.
On the Road, George Carlin. Little David.
Saturday Night Live, NBC's Saturday Night Live cast. Arista.

BEST RECORDING FOR CHILDREN
• *Aren't You Glad You're You*, Sesame Street Cast & Muppets. Sesame Street.
A Charlie Brown Christmas, Various (written by Charles M. Schulz). Charlie Brown Records.
Dope! The Dope King's Last Stand, Various artists (Lily Tomlin, Muhammad Ali, Pres. Jimmy Carter, etc.). Arthur Morrison, producer. Cornucopia.
Russell Hoban: The Mouse and his Child, read by Peter Ustinov. Caedmon.
The Sesame Street Fairy Tale Album, Jim Henson's Muppets. Sesame Street.

BEST ENGINEERED RECORDING, NON-CLASSICAL
• Roger Nichols, Elliot Scheiner, Bill Schnee, Al Schmitt, *Aja* (Steely Dan). ABC.
Ken Caillat, Richard Dashut, *Rumours* (Fleetwood Mac). Warner Bros.
Val Garay, *Simple Dreams* (Linda Ronstadt). Asylum.
Val Garay, *J T* (James Taylor). Columbia.
Bill Schnee, *Discovered Again!* (Dave Grusin). Sheffield Lab.

BEST ALBUM PACKAGE
(Art Director's Award)
• John Berg, *Love Notes* (Ramsey Lewis). Columbia.
Glen Christensen, *Hejira* (Joni Mitchell). Asylum.
Kosh, *Simple Dreams* (Linda Ronstadt). Asylum.
Kosh, *Singin'* (Melissa Manchester). Arista.
MPL/Hipgnosis, *Wings Over America* (Wings). Capitol.
Paula Scher, *Ginseng Woman* (Eric Gale). Columbia.
Paula Scher, *Yardbirds Favorites* (Yardbirds). Epic.
Abie Sussman, Bob Defrin, *Color as a Way of Life* (Lou Donaldson). Cotillion/Atlantic.

BEST ALBUM NOTES
(Annotator's Award)
• George T. Simon, *Bing Crosby: A Legendary Performer*. RCA.
Chris Albertson, *Stormy Blues* (Billie Holiday). Verve/Polydor.
Michael Brooks, *The Lester Young Story, Vol. I*. Columbia.
George T. Simon, *Guy Lombardo: A Legendary Performer*. RCA.
Patrick Snyder, *Jefferson Airplane—Flight Log* (Jefferson Airplane). Grunt/RCA.

PRODUCER OF THE YEAR
• Peter Asher. Columbia.
Bee Gees, Albhy Galuten, Karl Richardson. RSO.
Kenneth Gamble & Leon Huff. Philadelphia International.
Richard Perry. Atlantic.
Bill Szymczyk. Asylum.

Bee Gees Fever

"'Just call it Grammy Night with the Bee Gees,' sniffed a record company executive whose label does not handle that hot pop threesome who were expected to pull off a clean sweep," reported the *L.A. Herald Examiner*.

The Bee Gees entered the Grammy race with six nominations (compared to five for its nearest rival, Earth, Wind & Fire) and a triumphant air of invincibility. Disco now ruled supreme across America and the

"We're the happiest three brothers in the world!" said Barry Gibb (center) after the Bee Gees received five awards, including best LP, for Saturday Night Fever.

Australian-born Bee Gees were the undisputed kings of the new dance beat. Their music was also the centerpiece of the new best-selling LP of all time — the score to the blockbuster movie *Saturday Night Fever*, the story of a working-class teen, played by John Travolta, who lives for the weekends when he strives for glory on the dance floor of a New York disco. The album included six Bee Gees tunes, of which three reached number one on the charts: "Stayin' Alive" (nominated for Record and Song of the Year); the film's title number "Night Fever"; and "How Deep Is Your Love," which earned the vocal trio the best pop group singing award last year when it came out as a single prior to the movie and album release.

"'Stayin' Alive' should win the Grammy as the best record of 1978," wrote Robert Hilburn in the *L.A. Times*. "That's a prediction, and a value judg-

ment. The Bee Gee–dominated *Saturday Night Fever* soundtrack also should win a Grammy as the year's best album. That's just a prediction." Hilburn, like many other rock purists, was rooting instead for an LP that shocked everyone when it was included in the album competition — *Some Girls* by the Rolling Stones (called "the Stones at their raunchy best" by the *L.A. Times*) — marking the rebel group's first nomination ever. Also up for the album laurels was first-time nominee Jackson Browne for his now classic *Running on Empty*. Together these bids, said *Billboard*, represented "the most solid proof that, in their 21st year, the Grammys are more open to FM-oriented rock."

Despite such weighty competition, *Saturday Night Fever* took the Album of the Year award without a sweat, thus becoming only the second sound track (after *Peter Gunn* in 1958) and the first film score (and the only one to date) to hold the honor. It was also the first collaborative LP to win since *The Concert for Bangla Desh* in 1972. When the miniature gold gramophones were passed out to the winners, they were bestowed on 16 producers and a group of 10 artists comprised of some of the top disco talent of the day: the Bee Gees, Yvonne Elliman, K.C. & the Sunshine Band, Kool & the Gang, Ralph MacDonald, MFSB, Walter Murphy, Tavares, the Trammps, and David Shire. But just as the Bee Gees dominated the platter, they also dominated Grammy night. "Each mention of the group's name drew whoops of delight and shrieks from those sections of the balcony set aside for the general public," the *Times* observed.

Each mention of the Bee Gees' name "drew whoops of delight and shrieks from the balcony."

The Bee Gees earned one Grammy for the album prize, a second for being among its producers, and a third as the Best Producers of the Year, which they shared with coproducers Albhy Galuten and Karl Richardson. (Barry Gibb, Galuten, and Richardson were also behind the album to the other current hit John Travolta movie, *Grease*, that was contending for Album of the Year.) Two more Grammys followed: Best Arrangement for Voices (for "Stayin' Alive") and a repeat of the best pop group vocals award they reaped last year. Only four other artists had ever won five or more trophies in one year: Henry Mancini, Roger Miller, Paul Simon, and Stevie Wonder.

"It's just great — unbelievable!" Barry Gibb roared backstage. "We're the happiest three brothers in the world."

The Bee Gees were considered the front runners to nab the Record and Song of the Year awards, but were foiled by a spoiler who was not only not a disco maven, he wasn't even in attendance on Grammy night. The surprise winner of both prizes was Billy Joel, who was away in Paris. "Billy busted up the Bee Gees' year! I can't believe it!" producer Phil Ramone boomed to the *Herald Examiner*. "I was sitting there like a schnook when they announced Billy's song [Record of the Year 'Just the Way You Are']. I never thought we'd win."

Neither did just about anybody else. Joel was considered a long shot partly because of the enormous pre-Grammy hype over the Bee Gees, and also because his latest LP, *The Stranger*, was not a contender for Album of the Year.

After Joel's victories, the biggest shock on Grammy night was the winner of Best New Artist. "Either the Cars or Toto [seem] to be the most likely winner," said the *Times*, dismissing nominee Elvis Costello, who was the pick of one of its own music writers in a separate article. The choice turned out to be the disco band, A Taste of Honey, named after Herb Alpert's 1965 Grammy Record of the Year. The group would turn out to have only one hit, "Boogie Oogie Oogie," in its first incarnation, but its victory "served to emphasize the widespread appeal of disco music over the past year," said the *Herald Examiner*. (Stripped down from four members to two by the 1980s, A Taste of Honey would rebound with one more successful single, "Sukiyaki.") They were also only the second winners of the Best New Artist prize to be black (Natalie Cole preceded them in 1975). When asked about the latest color breakthrough backstage by a reporter for the *Times*, bass player and vocalist Hazel

Payne shot back, "Don't get us involved in a racial thing!" Keyboardist Perry Kibble added, "If we weren't exceptional, we wouldn't have won!"

Another Grammy shocker was lurking in the male pop vocal category. Given the preeminence of the Bee Gees this year, Jackson Browne was not expected to take Album of the Year for *Running on Empty*, but he *was* considered a shoo-in for the vocalist laurels. "Am I surprised at winning a Grammy for 'Copacabana'?" a victorious Barry Manilow said to reporters backstage after he pulled off an upset. "I sure am. I didn't even think it would be a hit single." "Copacabana (At the Copa)" was "a fluffy Latin-disco piece," according to the *Times*, from Manilow's triple-platinum contender for Album of the Year, *Even Now*.

Anne Murray had won a country vocalist Grammy in 1974 for her *Love Song* LP, but retired soon afterward in order to devote herself full-time to her recent marriage and newborn baby. By 1978, she was back in the business and in Grammy contention, too, for the Academy of Country Music's Song of the Year "You Needed Me." But she was competing in the Grammy's female pop vocalist category against some formidable nominees, all of whom already were, or would be, Grammy victors: Olivia Newton-John, Carly Simon, Barbra Streisand, and Donna Summer. When Murray prevailed, the *Times* said the win "came as something of a pleasant surprise over a field consisting entirely of soft-pop entries." Disco's reigning diva Donna Summer was the only one of the entries who hadn't won a Grammy yet, but she

Billy Joel halted a complete Bee Gees sweep by pulling off upsets in the Record and Song of the Year categories with "Just the Way You Are."

compensated for her loss to Murray — and further demonstrated disco's considerable pull — by picking up the r&b vocals honor over veterans Aretha Franklin and Natalie Cole (as well as aspiring divas Chaka Khan and Alicia Bridges). Summer's "Last Dance" was so popular that it was the year's only serious challenger to the status of the Bee Gees' "Night Fever" as the ultimate anthem of the disco set. In fact, "Last Dance" was actually part of the score to the *Saturday Night Fever* clone *Thank God It's Friday*, a film about a night at a fictitious Hollywood dance club aptly called Zoo Disco.

Instead of expressing joy or gratitude backstage after winning, though, Summer was visibly upset as she lobbied for the genre to have its own award. "Disco has sold millions and millions of records and has rejuvenated this industry," she ranted to reporters. "It's changing radio programming tremendously, as much as rock did in the late '60s. Winning the award was a thrill, but it would be even more of a thrill to win a Grammy in the first disco category." Next year Summer would see part of her wish fulfilled, with ironic consequences.

"Last Dance," written by Paul Jabara, was also the easy victor of Best Rhythm & Blues Song, even though it had its doubters. (Referring to the president of Casablanca Records, Jabara said fliply to the *Herald Examiner* reporter backstage, "Neil Bogart told me I probably wouldn't win. A lot he knows. Got a match?") Jabara's tune even beat the Bee Gees this year for Best Original Song at the Oscars, which caused some resentment among the *Saturday Night Fever* gang. (Ray Charles had served as the film's special musical material director and said after the Bee Gees' sweep at the N.A.R.A.S. awards, "I'm certainly glad that the Bee Gees and 'Stayin' Alive' were recognized by at least *some* professional academy.")

Earth, Wind & Fire was among the losers of Best R&B Song (for "Fantasy") and also lost its bid for the pop vocal group laurels to the Bee Gees, but nonetheless the group prevailed with its other three nominations: Best R&B Vocal Performance by a Group (*All 'n' All*), Best R&B Instrumental Performance ("Runnin'"), and an arrangement award for its founder, vocalist, drummer, and arranger, Maurice White. Some music on *All 'n' All* was used in another movie — the disastrous *Sgt. Pepper's Lonely Hearts Club Band*, a farfetched and overly fanciful dramatization of the Beatles' classic album that starred a host of celebrities, including members of Earth, Wind & Fire and the Bee Gees. The film was produced by Robert Stig-

wood, the same force behind *Saturday Night Fever* and *Grease*.

George Benson was the sole non-disco winner in the r&b lineup. He earned the male vocal award for his cover of the Drifters' hit "On Broadway," a single release from his *Weekend in L.A.* LP, a live recording made at Los Angeles's Roxy Theater in late 1977 where he also performed such songs as "It's All in the Game" and "The Greatest Love of All." The noted jazz guitarist only started singing on his records after he signed up with Warner Bros. in 1975. (He was rewarded the next year with Grammy's Record of the Year award for "This Masquerade.") Despite his success, however, jazz purists still resented his crossover pop performances as a singer. But Benson told *Billboard* about his work: "If kids can't hear it, I don't care how good it is. You can't sell it to them."

Jazz fusion vocal acrobat Al Jarreau (who can imitate the sound of horn, reed, and other instruments with uncanny precision) held onto the jazz singing slot for a second year in a row with his album *All Fly Home*, topping such name competitors as Ray Charles, Mel Tormé, and Sarah Vaughan. Among the nominees in the instrumental soloist category was a former Grammy champ who hadn't been heard from in some time — Stan Getz, who won both Album of the Year (*Getz/Gilberto*) and Record of the Year ("The Girl from Ipanema") in 1964. Getz hadn't even been nominated since 1967 when he lost to the Cannonball Adderley Quartet in the jazz group instrumental category. Now he was usurped for the soloist honors by last year's returning winner, Oscar Peterson, who was lauded for the album recording of his 1977 performance at Switzerland's Montreux Jazz Festival.

Getz, along with pianist Jimmy Rowles, was also up for this year's group instrumental award but lost to

1976 winner Chick Corea for *Friends*, on which Corea collaborated with drummer Steve Gadd, reed player Joe Farrell, and bassist Eddie Gomez. The big band prize went to a team that epitomized the genre's old-style traditions — the Thad Jones–Mel Lewis Orchestra — for *Live at Munich*, the last LP by the full 18-member group. Jones quit in 1978 to work with the Danish Radio Big Band in Copenhagen, while Lewis continued to lead the orchestra, as he had for the previous 20 years, in its weekly Monday night gigs at New York's Village Vanguard jazz club.

When Dolly Parton left Nashville in 1976 for a recording career in Hollywood, she tried to reassure her outraged c&w fans by telling them, "I'm not leaving country. I am just taking it with me." She had been nominated for a Grammy on 10 unsuccessful occasions in the past — last year in both the pop and country categories — but was given little chance of winning this year when she popped up again in the country category thanks to the negative attitudes perceived among Nashville voters. When she prevailed with her *Here You Come Again* album over last year's popular winner Crystal Gayle, however, *The New York Times* said the triumph proved "that Miss Parton has hardly lost her hold on her country fans for all her recent pop endeavors." Parton may have "gone Hollywood" recently, but she was nowhere in evidence at the Los Angeles Shrine Auditorium on Grammy night. "Eyes searched the hall when Dolly Parton won," noted the *Herald Examiner*, "but she didn't show."

Prior to his death in 1977, the only Grammys that Elvis Presley received were for three religious recordings, but he was now given one last chance at a secular prize when he was nominated posthumously as best male country vocalist for, ironically, a song called "Softly, As I Leave You." But the King was up against two formidable opponents: Willie Nelson and Johnny Paycheck. When Nelson won, Paycheck was observed in the audience waving an arm in the air and shouting, "Way to go, Willie!" even though Nelson was nowhere near enough to hear him. "Eyes searched the hall again," the *Herald Examiner* observed, "this time for Willie Nelson, who also stayed home." Nelson was honored for his rendition of "Georgia on My Mind," which last earned a Grammy in 1960 for Ray Charles.

Nelson was widely known as the reigning outlaw of country music, but he picked a poor time to dodge the ceremony for the music establishment's highest award. After Grammycast presenters Tanya Tucker and Glen Campbell sang the list of nominees for country's best vocal duo or group, the winners were revealed to be Nelson and Waylon Jennings for "Mammas, Don't Let Your Babies Grow Up

Comedy champ Steve Martin appeared at the podium with no trousers on.

to Be Cowboys," co-written and initially recorded by Ed Bruce in 1976. Bruce had actually composed the song for Nelson and Jennings, but, when he sensed a hit in the works, he wanted his own chance at stardom with it first. When his single failed, he finally passed the song on to Nelson and Jennings, who included it on their *Waylon and Willie* LP that spent more than three years on *Billboard*'s country album chart.

"Cowboys" and another country classic, "Take This Job and Shove It," were both up for Best Country Song, but they lost to "The Gambler," written by Don

Schlitz, who was a computer operator working the graveyard shift at Vanderbilt University in 1976 when he sold the tune to Capitol. The song hadn't yet been given its definitive performance by Kenny Rogers; like "Cowboys" co-composer Ed Bruce, its songwriter wanted to make the original recording. Shortly after it failed to make the country charts, Rogers took his rendition to the top of the rankings when he covered it and would go on to pick up the Grammy for best country vocal performance next year.

The Best Country Instrumental Performance category contained a number of "safe" choices, including Roy Clark and Doc Watson, but N.A.R.A.S. voters shocked Grammy watchers when they picked the controversial group Asleep at the Wheel for "One O'Clock Jump." Asleep at the Wheel members hailed originally from Berkeley, California, but moved to Austin, Texas, during the early part of their career to specialize in performing music they labeled country rock and western swing, the latter of which was defined by *Rolling Stone* as "hillbilly music's answer to jazz."

After losing 10 times in the past, Dolly Parton skipped this year's ceremony — and won.

In the line-up of six religious awards, winners included the returning 1975 champs Andrae Crouch & the Disciples for *Live in London*. Formed in 1965, the group specialized in combining gospel music with rock, jazz, and soul influences to achieve a mainstream sound enjoyed by Stevie Wonder, the Crusaders, and other artists who appeared on their albums. The religious awards had doubled in number over the past three years, welcoming victories in the new categories by a host of newcomers to the N.A.R.A.S. awards, including the Happy Goodman Family (*Refreshing*), Larry Hart ("What a Friend"), and the Mighty Clouds of Joy (*Live and Direct*).

The singer whose group trounced the Beatles in 1965 for the general group vocals award, causing one of the most spirited outcries in Grammy history — Anita Kerr — was up for Best Inspirational Performance 13 years later for *Precious Memories*. This time she took a trouncing herself when last year's winner B.J. Thomas proved invincible for *Happy Man*. Chicago bluesman Muddy Waters also reprised his 1977 victory for Best Ethnic or Traditional Recording for *I'm Ready*.

Last year Tito Puente was expected to prevail for Best Latin Recording, but he lost to his former band member from the 1950s, Mongo Santamaria. The famed multi-instrumentalist, composer, and bandleader now avenged the loss when he was honored for *Homenaje a Beny Moré*, his salute to the Cuban singer and bandleader Beny Moré that included vocals by Hector Lavoe and others. When the album proved to be a commercial success, Puente followed it up with a second hit volume in 1979 and a third in 1985.

Film score composer and conductor John Williams won his first Grammy for *Jaws* in 1975, then three more last year for *Star Wars*. He brought his total tally to an even half-dozen when he picked up two for his work on director Steven Spielberg's *Close Encounters of the Third Kind:* top film score and Best Instrumental Composition.

The *L.A. Times* said comedian Steve Martin ignited Grammy night with a real "spark" when he returned from last year to take the comedy laurels for *A Wild and Crazy Guy*. The LP showcased some of Martin's best work including his famous "King Tut" hit song, but it was his routine at the Grammycast when he accepted the prize that brought him the most laughs. He walked up to the podium, dressed appropriately in formal attire but without his tuxedo pants. After the audience laughter died down, he referred to the heavy use of four-letter words on his album, saying, "This is the pattern of my life. To win a Grammy for an album that was banned by K-Mart." A stage hand then appeared next to Martin and handed him his trousers, fully pressed and still draped over a hanger as if they had just arrived from the cleaners. "It's about time!" Martin fumed.

LONDON RECORDS

Violin virtuoso Itzhak Perlman shared the laurels for best classical album and best chamber music.

The choice of Classical Album of the Year was Brahms's *Concerto for Violin and Orchestra in D Major* performed by Itzhak Perlman and Carlo Maria Giulini conducting the Chicago Symphony Orchestra, both of whom also reaped Grammys last year. "There have been many distinguished recordings of the Brahms violin concerto," *High Fidelity* wrote, "but this one easily takes its place among the best. Conceptually, [Perlman's and Giulini's] is an extremely broad, majestic interpretation."

1978 could almost be called the year of Beethoven since three awards went to performances of his works. Perlman picked up an additional Grammy (best chamber music) for his rendering of Beethoven's sonatas for violin and piano with Vladimir Ashkenazy, which got mixed reviews (*High Fidelity* referred to both its "dragging tempos" and "radiant, sunny, gentle reading"). The same publication was more enthusiastic about the victor of the choral laurels: the Chicago Symphony and Chorus performance (under the direction of Sir Georg Solti and choral master Margaret Hillis) of *Missa Solemnis*: "[Solti's] vocal and instrumental forces are outstanding."

Herbert von Karajan once estimated that he and the Berlin Philharmonic had performed Beethoven's nine symphonies hundreds of times since he became the orchestra's conductor in 1955. In a published interview included with Deutsche Grammophon's eight-disc set of the complete works (a losing nominee for Classical Album of the Year that still took the orchestral honors), von Karajan mused on some of the different approaches he has used throughout his career. Referring to Symphony No. 7, the maestro said, "Of course, when we were young, the generation before us conducted it *much* slower. And I knew it was wrong, but I couldn't get out of this because of the inner content of the music .... Then both things were joined: the right tempo and the content of it."

Pianist Vladimir Horowitz picked up both soloist awards this year for recordings that celebrated the 50th anniversary of his American debut. *High Fidelity* referred to the "presumably studio-made Liszt B minor Sonata filled out with two late Fauré pieces (confusingly, even misleadingly, billed under the rubric *The Horowitz Concerts, 1977–78*) and a recording derived from his first performance with orchestra in 25 years, the Rachmaninoff Third Concerto featured in the New York Philharmonic's January 8 [1978] pension-fund concert .... On both records we are hearing the pianist still in the process of getting these fearsome works back into his fingers and his blood."

Critics generally applauded the orchestration work of the winning Best Opera Recording: excerpts from Lehar's *The Merry Widow* with Julius Rudel conducting the New York City Opera Chorus and Orchestra with Beverly Sills singing the lead role. Lambasted, though, were the new English lyrics such as "with girls in this oasis, I'm on a first name basis" and Sills's singing, which *High Fidelity* called "so tremulous as to be embarrassing." Sills was not nominated in the vocals category, which was claimed instead by Luciano

> *Orson Welles beat Richard Nixon for Best Spoken Word Recording.* **The Washington Post** *had actually been rooting for Nixon to win.*

Pavarotti for his *Hits from Lincoln Center*, topping other nominees Maria Callas, Marilyn Horne, and Dietrich Fischer-Dieskau.

The New York Times complained last year about production snafus and bad camera work at the Grammycast but hailed this year's show as a "tasteful, smoothly run affair." The *L.A. Herald Examiner* concurred, calling it "a large-scale opulent presentation that served as a vivid reminder of how huge the business of popular music has become .... The two-hour broadcast was crammed with 10 flashy production numbers."

Complaints came this year instead from *The Washington Post*, which took particular issue with host John Denver's singing of the top nominated songs ("he sang them all with no style at all"). It also noted that "an audible sigh of relief swept across the audience as Orson Welles beat out former president Richard Nixon in the Best Spoken Recording category." Welles was nominated for an LP recording of his timeless performance in the classic film *Citizen Kane,* whereas Nixon was up for the album release of his interviews with David Frost. The *Post* obviously had no love for the ex-president, having contributed to his downfall through its vigorous coverage of the Watergate scandal, and recently lampooned his N.A.R.A.S. nomination with an editorial that said: "If Mr. Nixon wins the Grammy, we fully expect to see television ads for *Richard Nixon's Greatest Hits.* There will be ... the classic non-swan song 'You Won't Have Richard Nixon to Kick Around Any More' ... or the heartwarming 'I Am Not a Crook,' televised live from Disneyland .... In short, the man is ready for stardom, and ready for his Grammy. May we say — for what must surely be the first time — we hope Mr. Nixon wins."

1978

The awards ceremony was broadcast on CBS from the Shrine Auditorium in Los Angeles on February 15, 1979, for the awards eligibility period of October 1, 1977, through September 30, 1978.

ALBUM OF THE YEAR
✓ • *Saturday Night Fever* (motion picture soundtrack), Bee Gees, David Shire, Yvonne Elliman, Tavares, Kool & the Gang, K.C. & the Sunshine Band, MFSB, Trammps, Walter Murphy, Ralph MacDonald. Bee Gees, Karl Richardson, Albhy Galuten, Freddie Perren, Bill Oakes, David Shire, Arif Mardin, Thomas J. Valentino, Ralph MacDonald, W. Walter, K.G. Productions, H.W. Casey, Richard Finch, Bobby Martin, Broadway Eddie, Ron Kersey, producers. RSO.
Even Now, Barry Manilow. Barry Manilow, Ron Dante, producers. Arista.
✓ *Grease* (original soundtrack), John Travolta, Olivia Newton-John, Frankie Valli, Frankie Avalon, Stockard Channing, Jeff Conaway, Cindy Bullens, Sha-Na-Na, Louis St. Louis. Barry Gibb, John Farrar, Louis St. Louis, Albhy Galuten, Karl Richardson, producers. Arista.
Running on Empty, Jackson Browne. Jackson Browne, producer. Asylum.
Some Girls, Rolling Stones. Glimmer Twins, producers.

RECORD OF THE YEAR
✓ • "Just the Way You Are," Billy Joel. Phil Ramone, producer. Columbia.
"Baker Street," Gerry Rafferty. Hugh Murphy, Gerry Rafferty, producers. United Artists.
"Feels So Good," Chuck Mangione. Chuck Mangione, producer. A&M.
✓"Stayin' Alive," Bee Gees. Bee Gees, Karl Richardson, Albhy Galuten, producers. RSO.
"You Needed Me," Anne Murray. Jim Ed Norman, producer. Capitol.

SONG OF THE YEAR
(Songwriter's Award)
✓ • "Just the Way You Are," Billy Joel.
✓"Stayin' Alive," Barry Gibb, Robin Gibb, Maurice Gibb.
"Three Times a Lady," Lionel Richie.

"You Don't Bring Me Flowers," Neil Diamond, Alan Bergman, Marilyn Bergman.
"You Needed Me," Randy Goodrum.

BEST NEW ARTIST
• A Taste of Honey. Capitol.
Cars. Elektra.
Elvis Costello. Columbia.
Chris Rea. United Artists.
Toto. CBS.

BEST POP VOCAL PERFORMANCE, MALE
✓• Barry Manilow, "Copacabana (At the Copa)." Arista.
Jackson Browne, *Running on Empty*. Asylum.
Dan Hill, "Sometimes When We Touch." 20th Century.
Gerry Rafferty, "Baker Street." United Artists.
Gino Vannelli, "I Just Wanna Stop." A&M.

BEST POP VOCAL PERFORMANCE, FEMALE
• Anne Murray, "You Needed Me." Capitol.
✓Olivia Newton-John, "Hopelessly Devoted to You." RSO.
Carly Simon, "You Belong to Me." Elektra.
Barbra Streisand, "You Don't Bring Me Flowers," solo version; track. Columbia.
✓Donna Summer, "MacArthur Park." Casablanca.

BEST POP VOCAL PERFORMANCE BY A DUO, GROUP, OR CHORUS
✓• Bee Gees, *Saturday Night Fever*. RSO.
Commodores, "Three Times a Lady." Motown.
✓Earth, Wind & Fire, "Got to Get You Into My Life." Columbia.
✓Roberta Flack, Donny Hathaway, "The Closer I Get to You." Atlantic.
✓Steely Dan, "FM (No Static at All)." MCA.

BEST POP INSTRUMENTAL PERFORMANCE
• Chuck Mangione, *Children of Sanchez*. A&M.
Chet Atkins, Les Paul, *Guitar Monsters*. RCA.

Donna Summer called winning an r&b prize for "Last Dance" a "thrill" but pressed hard for a new disco category.

Henry Mancini, *"The Pink Panther* Theme ('78)." United Artists.

Zubin Mehta conducting Los Angeles Philharmonic, *Star Wars and Close Enounters of the Third Kind.* London.

John Williams, *Close Encounters of the Third Kind* (original motion picture soundtrack). Arista.

BEST RHYTHM & BLUES SONG
(Songwriter's Award)

• "Last Dance," Paul Jabara.

"Boogie Oogie Oogie," Perry Kibble, Janice Johnson.

"Dance, Dance, Dance," Bernard Edwards, Kenny Lehman, Nile Rogers.

"Fantasy," Maurice White, Eddie de Barrio, Verdine White.

"Use Ta Be My Girl," Kenneth Gamble, Leon Huff.

BEST R&B VOCAL PERFORMANCE, MALE

• George Benson, "On Broadway." Warner Bros.

Peter Brown, "Dance With Me." T.K. Productions.

Ray Charles, "I Can See Clearly Now." Atlantic.

Teddy Pendergrass, "Close the Door." Philadelphia International.

Lou Rawls, *When You Hear Lou, You've Heard It All.* Philadelphia International/ Columbia.

BEST R&B VOCAL PERFORMANCE, FEMALE

• Donna Summer, "Last Dance." Casablanca.

Alicia Bridges, "I Love the Nightlife." Polydor.

Natalie Cole, "Our Love." Capitol.

Aretha Franklin, *Almighty Fire.* Atlantic.

Chaka Khan, "I'm Every Woman." Warner Bros.

BEST R&B VOCAL PERFORMANCE BY A DUO, GROUP, OR CHORUS

• Earth, Wind & Fire, *All 'n' All.* Columbia.

A Taste of Honey, "Boogie Oogie Oogie." Capitol.

Commodores, *Natural High.* Motown.

O'Jays, "Use Ta Be My Girl," track. Columbia.

Diana Ross, Michael Jackson, "Ease on Down the Road." MCA.

BEST R&B INSTRUMENTAL PERFORMANCE

• Earth, Wind & Fire, "Runnin'," track. Columbia.

Average White Band, "Sweet & Sour," track. Atlantic.

Brothers Johnson, "Streetwave," track. A&M.

Crusaders, *Images.* ABC.

Stanley Clarke, *Modern Man.* Nemperor.

BEST JAZZ VOCAL PERFORMANCE

• Al Jarreau, *All Fly Home.* Warner Bros.

Ray Charles, *True to Life.* Atlantic.

Eddie Jefferson, *The Main Man.* Inner City.

Irene Kral, *Gentle Rain.* Choice.

Mel Tormé, *Together Again, for the First Time.* Gryphon/Century.

Sarah Vaughan, *How Long Has This Been Going On.* Pablo.

BEST JAZZ INSTRUMENTAL PERFORMANCE, SOLOIST

• Oscar Peterson, *Montreux '77, Oscar Peterson Jam.* Pablo.

Al Cohn, *Heavy Love* (Al Cohn, Jimmy Rowles). Xanadu.

Stan Getz, *Stan Getz Gold.* Inner City.

Dexter Gordon, *Sophisticated Giant.* Columbia.

Woody Shaw, *Rosewood.* Columbia.

BEST JAZZ INSTRUMENTAL PERFORMANCE, GROUP
- Chick Corea, *Friends*. Polydor.
Al Cohn, Jimmy Rowles, *Heavy Love*. Xanadu.
Stan Getz, Jimmy Rowles, *The Peacocks*. Columbia.
Woody Shaw Concert Ensemble, *Rosewood*. Columbia.
Phil Woods Quintet, *Song for Sisyphus*. Gryphon/Century.

BEST JAZZ INSTRUMENTAL PERFORMANCE, BIG BAND
- Thad Jones, Mel Lewis, *Live in Munich*. Horizon/A&M.
Rob McConnell & the Boss Brass, *Big Band Jazz*. Umbrella.
Toshiko Akiyoshi–Lew Tabackin Big Band, *Insights*. RCA.
Dexter Gordon & Orchestra, *Sophisticated Giant*. Columbia.
Thad Jones, *Thad Jones Greetings & Salutations*. Biograph.

BEST COUNTRY SONG
(Songwriter's Award)
√ • "The Gambler," Don Schlitz.
√ "Every Time Two Fools Collide," Jan Dyer, Jeffrey Tweel.
"Let's Take the Long Way Around the World," Archie Jordan, Naomi Martin.
√ "Mammas, Don't Let Your Babies Grow Up to Be Cowboys," Ed & Patsy Bruce.
"Take This Job and Shove It," David A. Coe.

BEST COUNTRY VOCAL PERFORMANCE, MALE
√ • Willie Nelson, "Georgia on My Mind." Columbia.
Waylon Jennings, *I've Always Been Crazy*. RCA.
Ronnie Milsap, "Let's Take the Long Way Around the World." RCA.
Elvis Presley, "Softly, As I Leave You." RCA.
Johnny Paycheck, "Take This Job and Shove It." Epic.
Kenny Rogers, *Love or Something Like It*. United Artists.

BEST COUNTRY VOCAL PERFORMANCE, FEMALE
- *Here You Come Again*, Dolly Parton. RCA.
Crystal Gayle, "Talkin' in Your Sleep." United Artists.

Emmylou Harris, *Quarter Moon in a Ten Cent Town*. Warner Bros.
Barbara Mandrell, "Sleeping Single in a Double Bed." ABC.
Anne Murray, "Walk Right Back." Capitol.

BEST COUNTRY VOCAL PERFORMANCE BY A DUO OR GROUP
√ • Waylon Jennings, Willie Nelson, "Mammas, Don't Let Your Babies Grow Up to Be Cowboys." RCA.
Jim Ed Brown, Helen Cornelius, "If the World Ran Out of Love Tonight." RCA.
Oak Ridge Boys, "Cryin' Again." ABC.
Charlie Rich, Janie Fricke, "On My Knees." Epic.
√ Kenny Rogers, Dottie West, "Anyone Who Isn't Me Tonight." United Artists.
Statler Brothers, "Do You Know You Are My Sunshine." Mercury.

BEST COUNTRY INSTRUMENTAL PERFORMANCE
- Asleep at the Wheel, "One O'Clock Jump," track. Capitol.
Roy Clark, Buck Trent, *Banjo Bandits*. ABC.
Danny Davis & the Nashville Brass, *Cookin' Country*. RCA.
Roy Clark, "Steel Guitar Rag," track. Dot/ABC.
Doc Watson, Merle Watson, "Under the Double Eagle." United Artists.

Chick Corea teamed up with three Friends *to win the jazz group trophy.*

Best Gospel Performance, Contemporary or Inspirational

• Larry Hart, "What a Friend," track. Genesis.

Evie, *Come On, Ring Those Bells*. Word.

Imperials, *Imperials Live*. DaySpring.

Barry McGuire, *Cosmic Cowboy*. Sparrow.

Barry McGuire, *Destined to Be Yours*. Greentree.

Reba Rambo Gardner, *The Lady Is a Child*. Greentree/ Heartwarming.

Best Gospel Performance, Traditional

• Happy Goodman Family, *Refreshing*. Canaan.

Blackwood Brothers, *His Amazing Love*. Skylite Sing.

Cathedral Quartet, *Sunshine & Roses*. Canaan.

George Beverly Shea, *The Old Rugged Cross*. Word.

J.D. Sumner & the Stamps Quartet, *Elvis' Favorite Gospel Songs*. RCA.

Best Soul Gospel Performance, Contemporary

• Andrae Crouch & the Disciples, *Live in London*. Light.

Shirley Caeser, "Reach Out and Touch," track. Hob/Roadshow.

Danniebelle, Choralerna, *Danniebelle Live in Sweden with Choralerna*. Sparrow.

Walter Hawkins, *Love Alive II*. Light.

Highland Park Community Choir, Inc., "Because He's Jesus," track. Davida.

Loleatta Holloway, "You Light Up My Life." Gold Mine.

Best Soul Gospel Performance, Traditional

• Mighty Clouds of Joy, *Live and Direct*. ABC.

James Cleveland & the Charles Fold Singers, directed by Charles Fold, *Tomorrow*. Savoy.

James Cleveland & the Salem Inspirational Choir, directed by Doretha Wade, *I Don't Feel Noways Tired*. Savoy/ABC.

Rev. Isaac Douglas, featuring San Francisco Community Singers, 21st Century Singers, *Special Appearance*. Creed/Nashboro.

Gladys McFadden, Loving Sisters, " Amazing Grace," track. ABC.

Best Inspirational Performance

• B. J. Thomas, *Happy Man*. Myrrh.

Boones, *First Class*. Lamb & Lion.

Tennessee Ernie Ford, *He Touched Me*. Word.

Larry Hart, *Goin' Up in Smoke*. Genesis.

Anita Kerr, *Precious Memories*. Word.

Billy Preston, *Behold*. Myrrh.

Best Ethnic or Traditional Recording

• *I'm Ready*, Muddy Waters. Blue Sky.

Chicago Blues at Home, Louis Myers, John Littlejohn, Eddie Taylor, Jimmy Rogers, Johnny Shines, Homesick James Williamson, Bob Myers. Advent.

Clifton Chenier and His Red Hot Louisiana Band in New Orleans, Clifton Chenier. Dixieland/Jubilee.

I Hear Some Blues Downstairs, Fenton Robinson. Alligator.

U.S.A., Memphis Slim & His House Rockers, featuring Matt "Guitar" Murphy. Pearl.

Best Latin Recording

• *Homenaje a Beny Moré*, Tito Puente. Tico.

"Coro Miyare," track, Fania All Stars. Columbia.

La Raza Latina, Orchestra Harlow. Fania.

Laurindo Almeida Trio, Laurindo Almeida. Dobre.

Lucumi, Macumba, Voodoo, Eddie Palmieri. Epic.

Mongo à la Carte, Mongo Santamaria. Vaya.

Best Instrumental Arrangement

• Quincy Jones, Robert Freedman, "Main Title (Overture Part One)," *The Wiz* Original Soundtrack. MCA.

Alan Broadbent, "Aja" (Woody Herman Band). Century.

Chick Corea, "Mad Hatter Rhapsody" (Chick Corea). Polydor.

Joe Roccisano, "Green Earrings" (Woody Herman Band). Century.

Tom Tom 84, "Runnin'" (Earth, Wind & Fire). Columbia.

Best Arrangement for Voices

• Bee Gees, "Stayin' Alive" (Bee Gees). RSO.

Quincy Jones, Valerie Simpson, Nick Ashford, "Stuff Like That" (Quincy Jones). A&M.

Gene Puerling, "Cry Me a River" (Singers Unlimited). MPS/Capitol.

Ira Shankman, "High Clouds" (Vocal Jazz Incorporated). Grapevine.

McCoy Tyner, "Rotunda" (McCoy Tyner). Milestone.

BEST ARRANGEMENT ACCOMPANYING VOCALIST(S)

√• Maurice White, "Got to Get You Into My Life" (Earth, Wind & Fire). RSO.

Chick Corea, "Falling Alice" (Chick Corea). Polydor.

√ Tom Tom 84, "Fantasy" (Earth, Wind & Fire). Columbia.

Robert Freedman, "It Happens Very Softly" (Andrea Marcovicci). Take Home Tunes.

William Pursell, "We Three Kings" (Christmas Festival Chorale and Orchestra). National Geographic.

BEST INSTRUMENTAL COMPOSITION

• "Theme from *Close Encounters of the Third Kind*," John Williams.

"The Captain's Journey," Lee Ritenour.

"Consuelo's Love Theme," Chuck Mangione.

"End of the Yellow Brick Road," Quincy Jones, Nick Ashford, Valerie Simpson.

"Friends," Chick Corea.

BEST CAST SHOW ALBUM

• *Ain't Misbehavin'*, Thomas "Fats" Waller & others, composers. Thomas Z. Shepard, producer. RCA Red Seal.

The Best Little Whorehouse in Texas, Carol Hall, composer. John Simon, producer. MCA.

Beatlemania, John Lennon, Paul McCartney, George Harrison, Ringo Starr, composers. Sandy Yaguda, Kenny Laguna, producers. RCA Red Seal.

The King and I, Richard Rodgers, Oscar Hammerstein II, composers. Thomas Z. Shepard, producer. RCA Red Seal.

On the Twentieth Century, Adolph Green, Betty Comden, Cy Coleman, composers. Cy Coleman, producer. Columbia.

BEST ALBUM OF ORIGINAL SCORE WRITTEN FOR A MOTION PICTURE OR A TELEVISION SPECIAL

• *Close Encounters of the Third Kind*, John Williams. Arista.

Battlestar Galactica, Stu Phillip, John Tartaglia, Sue Collins, Glen Larson. MCA.

Holocaust: The Story of the Family Weiss, Morton Gould. RCA Red Seal.

Midnight Express, Giorgio Moroder, Chris Bennett, David Castle, William Hayes, Oliver Stone. Casablanca.

Revenge of the Pink Panther, Henry Mancini, composer, Leslie Bricusse, lyricist. United Artists.

ALBUM OF THE YEAR, CLASSICAL

• *Brahms: Concerto for Violin in D Major*, Carlo Maria Giulini conducting Chicago Symphony (solo: Itzhak Perlman). Christopher Bishop, producer. Angel.

Bach: Mass in B Minor, Neville Marriner conducting Academy of St. Martin-in-the-Fields. Vittorio Negri, producer. Philips.

Beethoven: Symphonies (9) Complete, Herbert von Karajan conducting Berlin Philharmonic. Michel Glotz, producer. Deutsche Grammophon.

Dvorak: Symphony No. 9 in E Minor "New World," Carlo Maria Giulini conducting Chicago Symphony. Gunther Breest, producer. Deutsche Grammophon.

Mahler: Symphony No. 4 in G Major, Claudio Abbado conducting Vienna Philharmonic. Rainer Brock, producer. Deutsche Grammophon.

Nielsen: Maskarade, John Frandsen conducting Danish Radio Symphony Orchestra and Chorus (solos: Hansen, Landy, Johansen, Plesner, Bastian, Sorens). Peter Willemoes, producer. Unicorn.

Rachmaninoff: Concerto No. 3 in D Minor for Piano (Horowitz Golden Jubilee), Vladimir Horowitz with Eugene Ormandy conducting New York Philharmonic. John F. Preiffer, producer. RCA.

Sibelius: Symphonies, Colin Davis conducting Boston Symphony. Philips.

DUETSCHE GRAMMOPHON

Best classical LP loser von Karajan won the orchestral honors for conducting all nine Beethoven symphonies.

BEST CLASSICAL ORCHESTRAL PERFORMANCE
(Conductor's Award)
• Herbert von Karajan conducting Berlin Philharmonic, *Beethoven: Symphonies (9) Complete*. Michel Glotz, producer. Deutsche Grammophon.

Claudio Abbado conducting Vienna Philharmonic, *Mahler: Symphony No. 9 in D Major*. Rainer Brock, producer. Deutsche Grammophon.

Pierre Boulez conducting New York Philharmonic, *Varese: Ameriques; Arcana; Ionisation (Boulez Conducts Varese)*. Andrew Kazdin, producer. Columbia.

Carlo Maria Giulini conducting Chicago Symphony, *Bruckner: Symphony No. 9 in D Minor*. Christopher Bishop, producer. Angel.

Neville Marriner conducting Concertgebouw Orchestra, *Holst: The Planets*. Vittorio Negri, producer. Philips.

Kurt Masur conducting Leipzig Gewandhaus Orchestra, *Mendelssohn: Symphonies (5) Complete*. Rainer Brock, producer. Vanguard.

Zubin Mehta conducting New York Philharmonic, *Stravinsky: Rite of Spring*. Andrew Kazdin, producer. Columbia.

André Previn conducting Chicago Symphony, *Shostakovich: Symphony No. 5*. Christopher Bishop, producer. Angel.

André Previn conducting London Symphony Orchestra, *Messiaen: Turangalila Symphony*. Christopher Bishop, producer. Angel.

Leonard Slatkin conducting St. Louis Symphony, *Rachmaninoff: Symphony No. 1 in D Minor*. Marc Aubort, Joanna Nickrenz, producers. Candide.

BEST CHAMBER MUSIC PERFORMANCE (INSTRUMENTAL OR VOCAL)
• Itzhak Perlman, Vladimir Ashkenazy, *Beethoven: Sonatas for Violin and Piano (Complete)*. London.

Melos Quartet with Mstislav Rostropovich, *Schubert: Quintet in C Major for Strings*. Deutsche Grammophon.

David Munrow conducting David Munrow Recorder Consort, Members of the Early Music Consort of London, *The Art of the Recorder*. Angel.

Itzhak Perlman, Pincas Zukerman, *Duets for Two Violins*. Angel.

Artur Rubinstein, Members of Guarneri Quartet, *Mozart: Quartets for Piano and Strings*. RCA.

Tokyo String Quartet, *Bartók: Quartet No. 2 for Strings, Op. 17, Quartet No. 6*. Deutsche Grammophon.

John Williams, Carlos Bonell, Brian Gascoigne, Morris Pert, Keith Marjoram, *John Williams & Friends*. Columbia.

BEST CLASSICAL PERFORMANCE, INSTRUMENTAL SOLOIST(S) (WITH ORCHESTRA)
• Vladimir Horowitz, piano (Ormandy conducting Philadelphia Orchestra), *Rachmaninoff: Concerto No. 3 in D Minor for Piano (Horowitz Golden Jubilee)*. RCA.

Emanuel Ax, piano (Ormandy conducting Philadelphia Orchestra), *Chopin: Concerto No. 2 in F Minor for Piano*. RCA.

Arnold Jacobs, tuba (Barenboim conducting Chicago Symphony), *Vaughan Williams: Concerto for Tuba*. Deutsche Grammophon.

Itzhak Perlman, violin (Giulini conducting Chicago Symphony), *Brahms: Concerto for Violin in D Major*. Angel.

Murray Perahia, piano (Perahia conducting English Chamber Orchestra), *Mozart: Concertos for Piano Nos. 21 in C Major & 9 in E Flat Major*. Columbia.

Mstislav Rostropovich, cello (Giulini conducting London Philharmonic), *Dvorak: Concerto for Cello in B Minor; Saint-Saëns: Concerto for Cello No. 1 in A Minor*. Angel.

BEST CLASSICAL PERFORMANCE, INSTRUMENTAL SOLOIST(S) (WITHOUT ORCHESTRA)

• Vladimir Horowitz, piano, *The Horowitz Concerts 1977-78*. RCA.

Claudio Arrau, piano, *Liszt: 12 Transcendental Etudes & 3 Etudes de Concert*. Philips.

Alfred Brendel, piano, *Bach: Italian Concerto; Choral Prelude; Prelude, S922; Chromatic Fantasy and Fugue; Fantasy and Fugue*. Philips.

Paul Jacobs, piano, *Debussy: Preludes for Piano, Books I & II*. Nonesuch.

Maurizio Pollini, piano, *Beethoven: The Late Piano Sonatas*. Deutsche Grammophon.

Charles Rosen, piano, *Beethoven: Variations on a Waltz by Diabelli*. Peters.

Rudolf Serkin, piano, *Rudolf Serkin on Television*. Columbia.

BEST OPERA RECORDING

• *Lehar: The Merry Widow*, Julius Rudel conducting New York City Opera Orchestra and Chorus (solos: Sills, Titus). George Sponhaltz, John Coveney, producers. Angel.

Charpentier: Louise, Julius Rudel conducting Chorus and Orchestra of Paris Opera (solos: Sills, Gedda). Christopher Bishop, producer. Angel.

Mozart: La Clemenza Di Tito, Colin Davis conducting Orchestra and Chorus of Royal Opera House, Covent Garden (solos: Baker, Popp, Minton, von Stade, Burrows). Philips.

Nielsen: Maskarade, John Frandsen conducting Danish Radio Symphony Orchestra and Chorus (solos: Hansen, Landy, Johansen, Plesner, Bastian, Sorensen). Peter Willemoes, producer. Unicorn.

Puccini: La Fanciulla del West, Zubin Mehta conducting Chorus and Orchestra of Royal Opera House, Covent Garden (solos: Neblett, Domingo, Milnes). Gunther Breest, producer. Deutsche Grammophon.

Shostakovich: The Nose, Gennady Rozhdestvensky conducting Chorus and Orchestra of Moscow Chamber Opera with soloists. Severin Pazukhin, producer. Columbia.

(R.) Strauss: Salome, Herbert von Karajan conducting Berlin Philharmonic (solos: Behrens, van Dam). Michel Glotz, producer. Angel.

Verdi: La Traviata, Carlos Kleiber conducting Bavarian State Opera Chorus and Orchestra (solos: Cotrubas, Domingo, Milnes). Dr. Hans Hirsch, producer. Deutsche Grammophon.

BEST CHORAL PERFORMANCE (OTHER THAN OPERA)

• Sir Georg Solti, conductor, Margaret Hillis, choral director, Chicago Symphony Orchestra and Chorus, *Beethoven: Missa Solemnis*. London.

Maurice Abravanel conducting Utah Chorale and Symphony Orchestra, *Bloch: Sacred Service*. Angel.

Leonard Bernstein, conductor, Joseph Flummerfelt, choral director, Westminster Choir and New York Philharmonic, *Haydn: Mass No. 9 in D Minor ("Lord Nelson Mass")*. Columbia.

Leonard Bernstein conducting Trinity Boys' Choir, English Bach Festival Chorus, English Bach Festival Orchestra, *Stravinsky: Les Noces & Mass*. Deutsche Grammophon.

Neville Marriner conducting Chorus and Academy of St. Martin-in-the-Fields, *Bach: Mass in B Minor*. Philips.

Riccardo Muti, conductor, Norbert Balatsch, choral director, New Philharmonia Chorus and Orchestra, *Vivaldi: Gloria in D Major & Magnificat*. Angel.

Leonard Slatkin, conductor, Thomas Peck, choral director, St. Louis Symphony Chorus and Orchestra, *Prokofiev: Alexander Nevsky*. Candide.

Sir Georg Solti, conductor, John Alldis, choral director, London Philharmonic Choir and Orchestra, *Walton: Belshazzar's Feast*. London.

Best Classical Performance, Vocal Soloist

• Luciano Pavarotti (various accompanists), *Luciano Pavarotti, Hits from Lincoln Center*. London.

Teresa Berganza (Asensio conducting English Chamber Orchestra), *Teresa Berganza, Favorite Zarzuela Arias*. Zambra.

Maria Callas (various conductors and orchestras), *Maria Callas/The Legend, the Unreleased Recordings*. Angel.

Dietrich Fischer-Dieskau (Kubelik conducting Bavarian Radio Orchestra), *Wagner: Arias*. Angel.

Marilyn Horne (Bernstein conducting Orchestre Nationale de France), *Ravel: Sheherazade*. Columbia.

Christa Ludwig (Böhm conducting Vienna Philharmonic), *Brahms: Alto Rhapsody*. Deutsche Grammophon.

Galina Vishnevskaya (Rostropovich conducting London Philharmonic), *Mussorgsky: Songs & Dances of Death*. Angel.

Best Engineered Recording, Classical

• Bud Graham, Arthur Kendy, Ray Moore, *Varese: Ameriques; Arcana; Ionisation (Boulez Conducts Varese)* (Boulez conducting New York Philharmonic). Columbia.

Marc Aubort, *Prokofiev: Alexander Nevsky* (Slatkin conducting St. Louis Symphony and Chorus). Candide.

Paul Goodman, *Berlioz: Symphonie Fantastique* (Ormandy conducting Philadelphia Orchestra). RCA.

Gunter Hermann, *Beethoven: Symphonies (9) Complete* (von Karajan conducting Berlin Philharmonic). Deutsche Grammophon.

Gunter Hermann, *Bruckner: Symphony No. 5 in B Flat Major* (von Karajan conducting Berlin Philharmonic). Deutsche Grammophon.

Chris Parker, *Messiaen: Turangalila Symphony* (Previn conducting London Symphony). Angel.

Jack Renner, *Fredrick Fennell, Cleveland Symphonic Winds*. Telarc.

Doug Sax, Bud Wyatt, *Wagner: Die Walkure: Ride of the Valkyries; Tristan: Prelude Act I; Götterdämmerüng: Siegfried's Funeral Music; Siegfried: Forest Murmurs* (Leinsdorf conducting Los Angeles Philharmonic). Sheffield Lab.

Bach: Mass in B Minor, Marriner conducting Chorus and Academy of St. Martin-in-the-Fields. Philips.

Holst: The Planets, Marriner conducting Concertgebouw Orchestra. Philips.

Best Comedy Recording

• *A Wild and Crazy Guy*, Steve Martin. Warner Bros.

The Rutles (All You Need Is Cash), Rutles. Warner Bros.

On Stage, Lily Tomlin. Arista.

Sex and Violins, Martin Mull. ABC.

The Wizard of Comedy, Richard Pryor. Laff.

Best Spoken Word Recording

• *Citizen Kane* (Original Motion Picture Soundtrack), Orson Welles. Mark 56.

John Steinbeck: The Grapes of Wrath (excerpts), read by Henry Fonda. Caedmon.

The Nixon Interviews with David Frost, Richard Nixon, David Frost. Polydor.

Roots (Original TV Soundtrack). Stan Cornyn, producer. Warner Bros.

Wuthering Heights, Dame Judith Anderson, Claire Bloom, James Mason, George Rose, Gordon Gould. Caedmon.

Best Recording for Children

• *The Muppet Show*, Muppets. Arista.

Charlie Brown's All-Stars (TV Special), Warren Lockhart, Jymn Magon, producers. Charlie Brown Productions.

The Hobbit (Soundtrack), Orson Bean, John Huston, Hans Conried. Buena Vista/ Disneyland.

Peter and the Wolf, David Bowie, Eugene Ormandy conducting Philadelphia Orchestra. RCA.

Sesame Street Fever, Muppets, Robin Gibb. Sesame Street.

BEST ENGINEERED RECORDING, NON-CLASSICAL

√ • Roger Nichols, Al Schmitt, "FM (No Static at All)" (Steely Dan). MCA.
George Massenberg, *All 'n' All* (Earth, Wind & Fire). Columbia.
John Neal, *Close Encounters of the Third Kind* (John Williams). Arista.
Alan Parsons, *Pyramid* (Alan Parsons Project). Arista.
Allen Sides, John Neal, *A Tribute to Ethel Waters* (Diahann Carroll). Orinda.
Bruce Swedien, *Sounds . . . and Stuff Like That* (Quincy Jones). A&M.

BEST ALBUM PACKAGE
(Art Director's Award)
• Johnny Lee, Tony Lane, *Boys in the Trees* (Carly Simon). Elektra.
John Berg, Paula Scher, *Heads* (Bob James). Columbia.
√ Ron Coro, *The Cars* (Cars). Elektra.
Ron Coro, Johnny Lee, *Out of the Woods* (Oregon). Elektra.
Gribbitt/Tim Bryant, *Last Kiss* (Fandango). RCA.
Tony Lane, *Bruce Roberts* (Bruce Roberts). Elektra.
Juni Osaki, *Children of Sanchez* (Chuck Mangione). A&M.
Barbara Wojirsch, *Non-Fiction* (Steve Kuhn). ECM.

BEST ALBUM NOTES
(Annotator's Award)
• Michael Brooks, *A Bing Crosby Collection, Vol. I & II.* (Bing Crosby). Columbia.
Irving Kolodin, Bill Bender, *Beethoven: Symphonies (9) Complete* (von Karajan conducting Berlin Philharmonic). Polydor.
Leonard Feather, *Ellington at Carnegie Hall 1943.* (Duke Ellington). Prestige.
Alan Lomax, *Georgia Sea Island Songs* (various artists). New World.
Dan Morgenstern, *The Individualism of Pee Wee Russell.* (Pee Wee Russell). Savoy.
Phil David Baker, R.D. Darrell, *Works of Carpenter/Gilbert/Weiss/Powell* (L.A. Philharmonic). New World.

BEST HISTORICAL REPACKAGE ALBUM
• *Lester Young Story Vol. 3.* Michael Brooks, producer. Columbia.
A Bing Crosby Collection, Vols. I & II. Michael Brooks, producer. Columbia.
The First Recorded Sounds 1888 to 1929 (Thomas Edison). George Garabedian, producer. Mark 56.
The Greatest Group of Them All (Ravens). Bob Porter, producer. Savoy.
La Divina (Maria Callas). Peter Andry, Walter Legge, producers. Angel.

BEST PRODUCER OF THE YEAR
• Bee Gees, Albhy Galuten, Karl Richardson
Peter Asher
Quincy Jones
Alan Parsons
Phil Ramone

Gotta Rock ... as Disco Rolls Out

Midway through the 1979 awards show, Grammy watchers couldn't believe their bugged-out eyes: There, at center stage, was rock & roll rebel leader Bob Dylan, dressed in a virgin white tuxedo, performing before the same music establishment that had all but snubbed him for the past decade and a half. Dylan did win a Grammy in 1972 for his contribution to the Album of the Year *The Concert for Bangla Desh*, but he never won one for any of his solo artistic accomplishments, which were considerable. That and the oversight of the Rolling Stones were two of the sacred rallying issues of Grammy bashers everywhere. Now, at the Grammy ceremony, the music establishment audience gave Dylan a standing ovation as he finished singing "Gotta Serve Somebody," a song that must have sounded to his fans like a surrender. The times, as Dylan had sung years earlier, were certainly a-changing.

So were the Grammys. N.A.R.A.S. — finally, said its critics — set up special awards for rock & roll music as well as disco, jazz fusion, and the classical producer of the year, bringing the year's awards to an all-time high of 57 categories. The inclusion of several new Grammys for rock marked an enormous battle won, though the victory was diminished by the fact that the new prizes would be bestowed off the air just prior to the Grammycast.

Ever since the awards were born in 1958, N.A.R.A.S. had failed to recognize the rock genre adequately. When the academy did make an occasional effort to recognize r&r with its own awards, as it did in 1959 and again from 1961 to 1966, the prizes often went astray. Nat "King" Cole won the "Top 40" artist statuette in 1959 (which was designated an r&r award till just a few weeks before the Grammy show) for a song that never even made the Top 40; the winner of Best Male Contemporary (R&R) Vocal Performance in 1965 was Roger Miller for "King of the Road." Finally, just after a prize went to a real rocker — Paul McCartney for his vocal performance of the Beatles' "Eleanor

"I didn't expect this," Bob Dylan said when won the new male rock vocalist award, "and I want to thank the Lord."

GLOBE PHOTO

Rigby" in 1966 — the category was dropped altogether. Now rock awards were not only back, but back in the right hands. The first new Best Male R&R Vocal Performance prize was bestowed to a grateful — and surprised — Bob Dylan. "I didn't expect this," the legendary rocker said, accepting it, "and I want to thank the Lord."

Dylan, born Jewish, declared himself a "born again" Christian at a time when an evangelical movement was sweeping the country. Even the current occupant of the White House, President Jimmy Carter, considered himself "saved." Dylan would lose his passion for Christianity after the early 1980s, but for now he embraced his new faith with public fervor. The "Somebody" he "gotta" serve in "Gotta Serve Somebody" was God. When the *L.A. Times* asked about the heavy emphasis on Christian messages on his latest album (*Slow Train Coming*), Dylan replied: "I know what some people have been saying, but this is no fad. It's the future. We're just laying the foundation."

Winner of the best female rock vocal award also claimed to be "born again" ("No less than seven times did Grammy recipients thank the Lord or Jesus or God" this year, noted *Billboard*), but was hardly a rocker in the same sense as Dylan. It was Donna Summer, who won for her "Hot Stuff" single from *Bad Girls*. Critics wondered: If the queen of the decadent disco movement was recently saved, too, could the movement's collapse be far behind?

Summer began the Grammy race with five nominations and was the clear front runner to take Album of the Year, as well as the new Best Disco Recording category — for which she lobbied heavily at last year's awards.

"All together, Summer had a single or album in the national Top 10 for 36 of 52 weeks in 1979," music columnist Robert Hilburn of the *L.A. Times* reported. "For 13 of those weeks, she had two singles in the Top 10 .... In a field of hit-makers, she was the biggest hit-maker. Plus, I may be idealistic, but I think Summer also has one other thing going for her: She made the best album."

Also up for Album of the Year was the artist who tied Summer in total nominations — Kenny Rogers, whose *The Gambler* and its title track were contenders for the LP honor and Record of the Year. Billy Joel's *52nd Street* was in the album race, too, but was considered a long shot since Joel won Record of the Year last year for "Just the Way You Are."

Some of Summer's most serious competition came from a group of old pros — also born again, in the professional sense. Wrote the *L. A. Herald Examiner*: "Although the Doobie Brothers have been a successful rock band for close to 15 years, it's only in the past few years, with the addition of songwriter-singer Michael McDonald, that the group has attained massive popularity by broadening their original hard-rock stance into a smoother, brisker romantic pop style." The Doobies had the most nominations in all — six: their *Minute by Minute* LP and title track up were up for Album and Song of the Year as well as the pop group vocals award; "What a Fool Believes" was contending for Record and Song of the Year plus Best Arrangement Accompanying Vocals.

The *L.A. Times* predicted that the Record of the Year winner would be "I Will Survive," the triumphant disco

N.A.R.A.S. — finally, said its critics — set up "permanent" awards for rock & roll.

standard that was also a comeback song for Gloria Gaynor, who was officially crowned "Queen of the Discos" at a coronation ceremony held in New York by the National Association of Discotheque Disc Jockeys for her debut album *Never Can Say Goodbye* in 1975. (Soon afterward, Gaynor's career went into decline as she was eclipsed by Donna Summer.) "I'm no disco fan," the *Times*'s Hilburn wrote about "I Will Survive," "but this *Rocky*-like slice of self-affirmation transcends that usually narrow genre. The only thing that worries me about its chances is the possibility of a disco backlash."

All of the top categories resulted in surprise choices.

Album of the Year turned out to be *52nd Street*, Billy's Joel's salute to the one-time "Tin Pan Alley" of New York, which included such powerful songs of self-reliance as "My Life" (a non-disco equivalent to "I Will Survive," said the critics). Joel's producer, Phil Ramone, "seemed just as stunned this time as he was last year when Joel walked off with the award for Record of the Year," observed the *L.A. Herald Examiner*. Ramone spoke again on behalf of his absent singer, saying, "I didn't feel we were going to win this year either. I'm proud of the album and I know Billy is, too — but this year, I'm shocked!" Joel also won a pop vocals prize for *52nd Street*.

The Record and Song of the Year honors went to the highly stylized, soul-rock ballad, "What a Fool Believes," about former lovers who run into each other by chance a few years later, trig-

> ## *"No funeral marches were played, but the death of disco was solemnly [observed]."*

gering old feelings of love and longing that were always stronger on his part than hers. The victories of "Fool" were hailed by the *Herald Examiner* as signalling "a return to normalcy" for rock music. They were also even hailed by normally cynical rock critics like Dave Marsh, who wrote, "For once the Grammys spent its accolades where they were deserved. Carefully crafted, gorgeously sung, beautifully arranged, and pristinely recorded, 'What a Fool Believes' holds up as one of the finest samples of seventies L.A. pop."

The Doobies also earned the arrangement and pop group vocals awards. "I speak for the band when I say that this is a form of acceptance we never got before," Doobie savior Michael McDonald told the press after the Grammycast, as he pushed his way through a sea of TV cameramen. "To be nominated was great. To be picked was even better." McDonald cowrote "Fool" with non-Doobie Kenny Loggins. Loggins remembered to reporters: "I met Michael at the front door of the house and we were writing from the first moment we met. I feel great about this."

Gloria Gaynor's "I Will Survive" picked up Best Disco Recording, topping Donna Summer's *Bad Girls* and even Michael Jackson's "Don't Stop 'Til You Get Enough," which had been produced by Quincy Jones and was considered another strong contender. Summer's loss was ironic — and somewhat tragic — considering the category was created, to a large extent, thanks to Summer's impassioned lobbying for it at last year's ceremony after she won an r&b award. Her victory this year, for a disco song in the rock & roll line-up instead of the disco slot, made the scenario even more bizarre. Worse, Gaynor's Best Disco Recording winner, "I Will Survive," would turn out to be the genre's death knell at the Grammys.

Disco may have been so influential just last year that *Saturday Night Fever* proved contagious at the Grammys, but this year the *Herald Examine*r reported "a real disco backlash." *The Washington Post* added: "No funeral marches were played, but the death of disco was solemnly commemorated. It was not that disco records didn't win any prizes, just that no fuss was made about them." Soon after the Grammycast, N.A.R.A.S. announced that the new disco category would be dropped.

When Michael Jackson ended up with Best R&B Male Vocal Performance, it marked the first victory for an artist who would one day win more Grammys in a year than anyone else (in 1983 for *Thriller*). "Don't Stop 'Til You Get Enough" was from the Jackson's first solo album (*Off the Wall*) since breaking away from his brothers' group act in 1978. "He wasn't at all sure that he could make a name for himself on his own," Jones told the French magazine *Actuel* about Jackson years later. The result nearly soared off the charts when *Off the Wall* sold nine million copies.

The "backlash" against disco helped to welcome back a number of past winners in the pop and r&b categories. Dionne Warwick hadn't won a Grammy since 1970 ("I'll Never Fall in Love Again") and hadn't had a hit record since 1974's "Then Came You." Now she reaped two Grammys in the same year for two comeback hits: the Barry

One critic described the Doobie Brothers' Record and Song of the Year "What a Fool Believes" as "carefully crafted, gorgeously sung, beautifully arranged."

Manilow–produced "I'll Never Love This Way Again" (Best Female Pop Vocal Performance) and "Déjà Vu" (Best Female R&B Vocal Performance). "Warwick's two awards," said the *Herald Examiner*, "restored this balladeer's place in the pop pantheon."

Herb Alpert hadn't been in the Hot 100 for five years and hadn't won a Grammy since 1966 when he snagged two for "What Now My Love." Now he was facing formidable opposition for Best Pop Instrumental Performance in the person of John Williams, whose latest super–film score composition was "Theme from *Superman* (Main Title)." Williams, who had recently picked up the baton at the Boston Pops, would win the film score honors again this year as well as Best Instrumental Composition for *Superman* (following up on his previous Grammy winners *Jaws*, *Star Wars*, and *Close Encounters of the Third Kind*), but he yielded to Alpert in the pop instrumental slot. Alpert's "Rise" was a dance number written by Randy Badazz, Alpert's cousin. It might have proven to be only a middling hit in the discos if it hadn't been adopted by the soap opera *General Hospital* to underscore some of the steamy scenes between the show's hot young couple, Luke and Laura. Thereafter, "Rise" rose fast to number one on the singles charts.

When Billy Joel's 52nd Street won the LP prize, his producer was just as "shocked" as last year.

Other returning Grammy greats included Earth, Wind & Fire for Best Rhythm & Blues Song "After the Love Is Gone," which peaked at number two on the weekly singles charts, and Paul McCartney's group Wings. McCartney was making news in 1979 by calling for a concert to benefit the victims of war-ravaged Cambodia. His fans thought that meant a Beatles reunion and began fueling a frenzy of speculation worldwide. It was something of an anticlimax then when McCartney and his Wings, instead of the old Fab Four, took center stage at London's Hammersmith Odeon Theater for the relief concert in December. There they performed the definitive version of "Rockestra Theme," earning them the Grammy for Best Rock Instrumental Performance.

The Eagles came back, too — but for their swan song at the Grammys and as a professional singing group. Their award was for Best Group Rock Vocal Performance for their last number one-ranked single, "Heartache Tonight." Soon thereafter the Eagles fell victim to the group's notorious inner feuding. "I knew the Eagles were over halfway through [the final album] *The Long Run*," bandmember Glenn Frey told the *L.A. Times*. The group had been working on the album during the 1977 Grammycast and refused to perform on the show, after agreeing to earlier, claiming they were busy and disapproved of competitions.

The Eagles beat out three of the five nominees also in line for Best New Artist: Dire Straits, the Knack, and the Blues Brothers (the comic duo formed by *Saturday Night Live*'s John Belushi and Dan Aykroyd). Dire Straits was considered a strong contender for top newcomer, but so were two other nominees — Rickie Lee Jones and comedian Robin Williams.

The media was rooting for singer/songwriter Rickie Lee Jones, who was

Montreal-born pianist Oscar Peterson (best jazz instrumental solo, Jousts*) has been called "the Liszt of jazz" by critics.*

considered a kind of Joni Mitchell for the dawning 1980s, "who celebrates the bohemian side of pop," added the *Herald Examiner*. Jones was up for four Grammys in all, including Song of the Year for her hit "Chuck E.'s in Love," but won only the Best New Artist prize. From a lover of beat poetry, Jones's acceptance remarks were fairly uninspired: "I thank my mother and my producer, my record company, my lawyer, my accountant, and you all."

The new award for Best Jazz Fusion Performance was claimed by a group that was used as a frequent example of talent overlooked because the category hadn't existed earlier: Weather Report, led by keyboardist Joe Zawinul and sax player Wayne Shorter, both of whom had once worked as sidemen for Miles Davis. Weather Report's *8:30* album was a two-disc set that included three sides of concert performances and one side of studio recordings that together chronicled the band's career since it was formed in 1971.

A loser in the new fusion category, Chick Corea, nonetheless proved a winner of the same award he and his band took last year, Best Group Instrumental Performance. This time he was teamed with vibraphonist Gary Burton on *Duet*. Among other jazz champs from last year, pianist Oscar Peterson reprised the soloist honors for *Jousts*. Ella Fitzgerald last won the vocals prize in 1976, but she came back again, topping talent such as Sarah Vaughan, for *Fine*

Grammy ceremony host Kenny Rogers lost his bids for Album and Record of the Year but still garnered the male country vocals statuette for "The Gambler."

CAPITOL RECORDS/ KRAGEN & CO.

and Mellow. Duke Ellington died in 1974 but was awarded a posthumous Grammy for recordings made of a performance he and his band gave at the Crystal Ballroom in Fargo, North Dakota, in 1940. Time-Life Records commemorated the 20th year since Billie Holliday's death by issuing some of her classic works and won Best Historical Reissue.

The title of 1979's Best Country Song almost contributed to it not getting recorded: "You Decorated My Life," by Debbie Hupp and Bob Morrison. Morrison told *Billboard*: "When Debbie and I finished it, a lot of people said, 'Decorated'? Come on, man!" Kenny Rogers was among the skeptical. He was set to record it, but resisted at first before finally caving in. Then the tune hit number one on the country chart and number seven on the pop line-up.

Rogers was at such a peak of success that he was asked to host the Grammy-cast, which he did to mixed notices. (*The Hollywood Reporter* was among those who applauded his handling of it; *The Washington Post* said his performance proved that more than disco was dead.) Of Rogers's five Grammy nods, including those for Album and Record of the Year, his only victory was for Best Male Country Vocal Performance for last year's Best Country Song "The Gambler." (The song and Rogers also reaped two Academy of Country Music Awards this year and three prizes from the Country Music Association.) Quincy Jones was expected to be named Producer of the Year for his work with Michael Jackson, but, in a major upset, Rogers's producer, Larry Butler, snatched the accolade instead.

> *Dionne Warwick's two awards "restored this balladeer's place in the pop pantheon."*

The female vocal honors went to Emmylou Harris exclusively despite the fact that her *Blue Kentucky Girl* LP also included vocals from two other country divas who, like Harris, moved to Hollywood recently — Dolly Parton and Linda Ronstadt.

The Charlie Daniels Band wasn't taken seriously as country talent in the early part of its career because of its crossover rock appeal, but when it added a heavy fiddle sound to "The Devil Went Down to Georgia," the band won the group vocal laurels, confirming their country status. (The band also added a second set of lyrics: The Methodists heard the line "son of a bitch"; the Baptists, "son of a gun.")

The father-son guitar-picking team of Doc and Merle Watson snagged the prize for instrumental performance (for "Big Sandy/Leather Britches"), which they last shared in 1974.

Given the importance that Christianity was playing at this year's Grammys, the religious awards took on a special priority. Host Kenny Rogers even told the audience of his belief that "Gospel is the backbone to all the music in our society."

The Mississippi-born gospel quartet the Blackwood Brothers won five awards between 1966 and 1973 but hadn't won since. Now they nabbed Best Traditional Gospel Performance for *Lift Up the Name of Jesus*. The Imperials won a religious prize for a third time in five years for *Heed the Call* (Best Contemporary or Inspirational Gospel Performance), and B.J. Thomas came back for a third year in a row in the category of Best Inspirational Performance with *You Gave Me Love (When No One Gave Me a Prayer)*.

The two soul gospel winners were also repeats from last year. N.A.R.A.S. voters again found the transcendental harmonies of the Mighty Clouds of Joy irresistible when they honored the group for *Changing Times*. The Clouds had enormous crossover appeal: They frequently shared a concert bill with an unlikely mix of talent that included Earth, Wind & Fire, the Rolling Stones, Andrae Crouch, and the artist the group beat twice this year to win the Grammy — double nominee the Rev. James Cleveland. Crouch won the contemporary soul gospel performance prize for *I'll Be Thinking of You*, a selection from which he performed on the Grammycast to rave reviews. Noted the *L.A. Herald Examiner*: "The other standout performance [other than Bob Dylan's] was given by gospel singer Andrae Crouch, whose genially passionate demeanor and electrifying delivery prompted a standing ovation."

Chicago bluesman Muddy Waters returned, too — for his third Grammy in a row for giving the Best Ethnic or Traditional Recording. His latest LP, *Muddy "Mississippi" Waters Live*, earned him the sixth — and last — Grammy of his career. Waters would reap no more before his death of a heart attack in 1983. Another three-year winning streak was marked in the children's recording category by Jim Henson's Muppets for their score to *The Muppet Movie*. (Curiously, it beat out three Sesame Street recordings, including *Sesame Disco!*, a follow-up to last year's losing — but hilarious — nominee *Sesame Street Fever*.) The Best Latin Recording was an eponymous album by Irakere, described by *The New York Times* as "the progressive pop-folk-jazz fusion ensemble from Cuba."

The Ages of Man won an Emmy in 1966 for being the Outstanding Single Dramatic Program of the Year and featured John Gielgud quoting Shakespearean verse on the advancing stages of growing old. Its transposition from TV to disc this year brought it the Grammy for Best Spoken Word Recording.

Had Robin Williams won his bid to be Best New Artist, he would have become only the second comedian to hold the honor (following Bob Newhart in 1960). Instead, he won a Grammy for Best Comedy Recording for his album *Reality ... What a Concept*, which showcased Williams doing what he does best: testing the limits of sanity and taste through rantings of improvisational humor.

The winner of Best Cast Show Album challenged the theatrical tastes of Broadway in 1979 in startling new ways. *Sweeney Todd* was Stephen Sondheim's bizarre and highly experimental musical, starring Len Cariou and Angela Lansbury, about a murderous barber in 19th-century London whose victims become the fillings of his girlfriend's meat pies. Since the show was also arguably an operetta, it won Best Engineered Classical Recording, but wasn't nominated for any other classical awards for which it should have been eligible, such as Best Opera Recording.

Sir Georg Solti and the Chicago Symphony Orchestra last won the Classical Album of the Year prize in 1975 for recording all nine Beethoven symphonies. This year they reclaimed the prize, as well as the orchestral honors, for tackling Brahms's four symphonic works, although they did not achieve the same critical praise that they did before from *High Fidelity*. The publication complained that the orchestra "everywhere sounds big" and blamed Solti's conducting and London Records' "gargantuan brass." It added: "The Chicago's recent Brahms series under James Levine sounds crisper, brighter" by comparison.

Solti conducted another work by Brahms to win the choral laurels with choral conductor Margaret Hillis and the Chicago Symphony Chorus. "Solti recorded the Brahms *German Requiem* once before," *High Fidelity* noted, "an early-Fifties Capitol album that constituted the sole commercial documentation of his tenure with the Frankfurt Opera .... The new version is also outstanding." James Mallinson, Solti's producer at London Records, was hailed as the first winner of the new Classical Producer of the Year award.

For a fourth year in a row Vladimir Horowitz reaped a soloist award for works he'd never recorded before: Liszt's *Mephisto Waltz*, Schumann's *Humoreske*, and Rachmaninoff's *Barcarolle* and *Humoresque*. The award for soloist with orchestral accompaniment went to Grammy newcomer Maurizio Pollini for Bartók's Concertos Nos. 1

and 2. *High Fidelity* said, "Musically, the new recording leaves nothing to be desired. Soloist and conductor are at one with each other and with the music." The chamber music prize went to Copland's *Appalachian Spring* by Dennis Russell Davies conducting the St. Paul Chamber Orchestra in a bravura performance that was recorded with superior electronic equipment.

High Fidelity wrote of the Best Opera Recording: Tenor "Jon Vickers' *Peter Grimes* [by Benjamin Britten] is the closest identification of an operatic performer and role in recent memory, and it's doubly fortunate that Philips has gotten it down on disc." Vickers failed to be nominated for best classical vocalist. Instead the award went to Luciano Pavarotti, who was emerging as a superstar in the late 1970s with a burdensome schedule of professional appearances. "The steady over-exploitation of Pavarotti's voice during the past few years," wrote *High Fidelity*, "has impaired its once considerable attractiveness and the ease with which he used to produce his brilliant high notes."

The Grammy show took place once again at the Shrine Auditorium in Los Angeles and proved, said the *Herald Examiner*, to be "an evening in which pop music vanquished both disco and country as the dominant force in current popular music." Presenters and performers included George Benson, Johnny Cash, the Charlie Daniels Band, the Doobie Brothers, Bob Dylan, James Galway, Kenny Loggins, Dionne Warwick, Debby Boone, George Burns, Natalie Cole, Deborah Harry, Isaac Hayes, Quincy Jones, and Kris Kristofferson. James Galway performed a flute solo. Sarah Vaughan and Joe Williams each sang a jazz song.

"The telecast did have its moments," *Billboard* said. "Neil Diamond and Barbra Streisand's performance of [Record of the Year nominee] 'You Don't Bring Me Flowers' was the classiest spot in the show. Not only was it well choreographed, but the level of emotion provided the only truly touching element of the show." The number was touching in more ways than one. "Streisand stroked Diamond's cheek at the climax of the song," noted the *Herald Examiner*, "to screams from their fans."

1979

The awards ceremony was broadcast on CBS from the Los Angeles Shrine Auditorium on February 27, 1980, for the eligibility period October 1, 1978, to September 30, 1979.

ALBUM OF THE YEAR
• *52nd Street,* Billy Joel. Phil Ramone, producer. Columbia.
Bad Girls, Donna Summer. Giorgio Moroder, Pete Bellotte, producers. Casablanca.
Breakfast in America, Supertramp. Supertramp, Peter Henderson, producers. A&M.
The Gambler, Kenny Rogers. Larry Butler, producer. United Artists.
Minute by Minute, Doobie Brothers. Ted Templeman, producer. Warner Bros.

RECORD OF THE YEAR
• "What a Fool Believes," Doobie Brothers. Ted Templeman, producer. Warner Bros.
"After the Love Has Gone," Earth, Wind & Fire. Maurice White, producer. ARC/CBS.
"The Gambler," Kenny Rogers. Larry Butler, producer. United Artists.
"I Will Survive," Gloria Gaynor. Dino Fekaris, Freddie Perren, producers. Polydor.
"You Don't Bring Me Flowers," Barbra Streisand, Neil Diamond. Bob Gaudio, producer. Columbia.

Song of the Year
(Songwriter's Award)
- "What a Fool Believes," Kenny Loggins, Michael McDonald.
- "After the Love Has Gone," David Foster, Jay Graydon, Bill Champlin.
- "Chuck E.'s in Love," Rickie Lee Jones.
- "Honesty," Billy Joel.
- "I Will Survive," Dino Fekaris, Freddie Perren.
- "Minute by Minute," Lester Abrams, Michael McDonald.
- "Reunited," Dino Fekaris, Freddie Perren.
- "She Believes in Me," Steve Gibb.

Best New Artist
- Rickie Lee Jones. Warner Bros.
- Blues Brothers. Atlantic.
- Dire Straits. Warner Bros.
- Knack. Capitol.
- Robin Williams. Casablanca.

Best Pop Vocal Performance, Male
- Billy Joel, *52nd Street*. Columbia.
- Robert John, "Sad Eyes." EMI-America.
- Kenny Rogers, "She Believes in Me." United Artists.
- Rod Stewart, "Do Ya Think I'm Sexy?" Warner Bros.
- James Taylor, "Up on the Roof." Columbia.

Best Pop Vocal Performance, Female
- Dionne Warwick, "I'll Never Love This Way Again." Arista.
- Gloria Gaynor, "I Will Survive," track. Polydor.
- Rickie Lee Jones, "Chuck E.'s in Love," track. Warner Bros.
- Melissa Manchester, "Don't Cry Out Loud." Arista.
- Donna Summer, *Bad Girls*. Casablanca.

Best Pop Performance by a Duo or Group with Vocal
- Doobie Brothers, *Minute by Minute*. Warner Bros.
- Commodores, "Sail On," track. Motown.
- Little River Band, "Lonesome Loser." Capitol.
- Barbra Streisand, Neil Diamond, "You Don't Bring Me Flowers." Columbia.
- Supertramp, *Breakfast in America*. A&M.

GLOBE PHOTO

Michael Jackson's first Grammy was for "Don't Stop 'Til You Get Enough." He would win eleven more by 1992.

Best Pop Instrumental Performance
- Herb Alpert, "Rise." A&M.
- Chuck Mangione, *An Evening of Magic*. A&M.
- Zubin Mehta, New York Philharmonic, *Manhattan* (film score music), Side 2. CBS.
- Frank Mills, "Music Box Dancer," track. Polydor.
- John Williams, "Theme from *Superman* (Main Title)," track. Warner Bros.

Best Rock Vocal Performance, Male
- Bob Dylan, "Gotta Serve Somebody." Columbia.
- Joe Jackson, "Is She Really Going Out With Him?" A&M.
- Robert Palmer, "Bad Case of Loving You (Doctor, Doctor)." Island/Warner Bros.

Rod Stewart , "Blondes (Have More
  Fun)," track. Warner Bros.
Frank Zappa, "Dancin' Fool." Zappa.

**BEST ROCK VOCAL PERFORMANCE,
FEMALE**
• Donna Summer, "Hot Stuff."
  Casablanca.
Cindy Bullens, "Survivor." United Artists.
Rickie Lee Jones, "The Last Chance
  Texaco," track. Warner Bros.
Bonnie Raitt , "You're Gonna Get What's
  Coming," track. Warner Bros.
Carly Simon, "Vengeance." Elektra.
Tanya Tucker, *TNT*. MCA.

**BEST ROCK PERFORMANCE BY A DUO
OR GROUP WITH VOCAL**
• Eagles, "Heartache Tonight." Asylum.
Blues Brothers, *Briefcase Full of Blues*.
  Atlantic.
Cars, *Candy-O*. Elektra.
Dire Straits, "Sultans of Swing." Warner
  Bros.
Knack, "My Sharona." Capitol.
Styx, *Cornerstone*. A&M.

**BEST ROCK INSTRUMENTAL
PERFORMANCE**
• Wings, "Rockestra Theme," track.
  Columbia.
Allman Brothers Band, "Pegasus," track.
  Capricorn.
Dixie Dregs, *Night of the Living Dregs*.
  Capricorn.
Neil Larsen, "High Gear." A&M.
Frank Zappa, "Rat Tomago," track. Zappa.

BEST RHYTHM & BLUES SONG
(Songwriter's Award)
• "After the Love Has Gone," David
  Foster, Jay Graydon, Bill Champlin.
"Ain't No Stoppin' Us Now," Gene
  McFadden, John Whitehead, Jerry
  Cohen.
"Déjà Vu," Isaac Hayes, Adrienne
  Anderson.
"Reunited," Dino Fekaris, Freddie Perren.
"We Are Family," Nile Rodgers, Bernard
  Edwards.

The Grammys' short-lived disco award
went to surprise winner "I Will Survive"
from Gloria Gaynor's Love Tracks LP.

**BEST RHYTHM & BLUES VOCAL
PERFORMANCE, MALE**
• Michael Jackson, "Don't Stop 'Til You
  Get Enough." Epic.
George Benson, "Love Ballad," track.
  Warner Bros.
Ray Charles, "Some Enchanted Evening."
  Atlantic.
Isaac Hayes, "Don't Let Go." Polydor.
Elton John, "Mama Can't Buy You Love."
  MCA.
Smokey Robinson, "Cruisin'." Motown.

**BEST RHYTHM & BLUES VOCAL
PERFORMANCE, FEMALE**
• Dionne Warwick, "Déjà Vu." Arista.
Natalie Cole, *I Love You So*. Capitol.
Minnie Ripperton, *Minnie*. Capitol.
Amii Stewart , "Knock on Wood." Ariola.
Donna Summer, "Dim All the Lights."
  Casablanca.
Anita Ward, "Ring My Bell." Juana.

**BEST RHYTHM & BLUES VOCAL
PERFORMANCE BY A DUO, GROUP,
OR CHORUS**
• Earth, Wind & Fire, "After the Love Has
  Gone." ARC/CBS.
Commodores, *Midnight Magic*. Motown.
McFadden & Whitehead, "Ain't No
  Stoppin' Us Now." Philips
  International.
Peaches & Herb, "Reunited." Polydor.
Sister Sledge, "We Are Family." Atlantic.

BEST RHYTHM & BLUES INSTRUMENTAL PERFORMANCE

• Earth, Wind & Fire, "Boogie Wonderland." ARC/CBS.
Herbie Hancock, "Ready or Not," track. Columbia.
Hubert Laws, "Land of Passion," track. Columbia.
Harvey Mason, "Wave," track. Arista.
Junior Walker, "Wishing on a Star," track. Whitfield/Warner Bros.

BEST DISCO RECORDING

• "I Will Survive," Gloria Gaynor. Dino Fekaris, Freddie Perren, producers. Polydor.
"Boogie Wonderland," Earth, Wind & Fire, Emotions. Maurice White, Al McKay, producers. ARC/CBS.
Bad Girls, Donna Summer. Giorgio Moroder, Pete Bellotte, producers. Casablanca.
"Do Ya Think I'm Sexy?" Rod Stewart. Tom Dowd, producer. Warner Bros.
"Don't Stop 'Til You Get Enough," Michael Jackson. Quincy Jones, producer. Epic.

BEST JAZZ FUSION PERFORMANCE, VOCAL OR INSTRUMENTAL

• Weather Report, *8:30*. ARC/CBS.
George Benson, *Livin' Inside Your Love*. Warner Bros.
Chick Corea Group, *Chick Corea/Secret Agent*. Polydor.
Don Sebesky with Jazz Quintet & Soloists and Symphony Orchestra, *Three Works for Jazz Soloists & Symphony Orchestra*. Gryphon.
Stanley Turrentine, *Betcha*. Elektra.

BEST JAZZ VOCAL PERFORMANCE

• Ella Fitzgerald, *Fine and Mellow*. Pablo.
Helen Humes, *Sneakin' Around*. Classic Jazz.
Eddie Jefferson, *The Live-liest*. Muse.
Sarah Vaughan, *I Love Brazil*. Pablo.
Joe Williams, *Prez and Joe*. GNP/Crescendo.

BEST JAZZ INSTRUMENTAL PERFORMANCE, SOLOIST

• Oscar Peterson, *Jousts*. Pablo.
Pepper Adams, *Reflectory*. Muse.
Paul Desmond, *Paul Desmond*. Artists House.
Dexter Gordon, *Manhattan Symphonie*. Columbia.

Zoot Sims, *Warm Tenor*. Pablo.

BEST JAZZ INSTRUMENTAL PERFORMANCE, GROUP

• Gary Burton, Chick Corea, *Duet*. ECM/Warner Bros.
Arnett Cobb, *Arnett Cobb and the Muse All Stars/Live at Sandy's*. Muse.
Bill Evans, Toots Thielemans, *Affinity*. Warner Bros.
Dizzy Gillespie, Count Basie, *The Gifted Ones*. Pablo.
Great Jazz Trio (Hank Jones, Buster Williams, Tony Williams), *Love for Sale*. Inner City.
Zoot Sims, *Warm Tenor*. Pablo.

BEST JAZZ INSTRUMENTAL PERFORMANCE, BIG BAND

• Duke Ellington, *At Fargo, 1940 Live*. Book of the Month Records.
Toshiko Akiyoshi–Lew Tabackin Big Band, *Kogun*. RCA.
Louie Bellson & the Explosion, *Note Smoking*. Discwasher.
Thad Jones, Mel Lewis, Umo, *Thad Jones/Mel Lewis & Umo*. RCA.
Mel Lewis & the Jazz Orchestra, *Naturally*. Telarc.

BEST COUNTRY SONG
(Songwriter's Award)

• "You Decorated My Life," Bob Morrison, Debbie Hupp.
"All the Gold in California," Larry Gatlin.
"Blue Kentucky Girl," Johnny Mullins.
"Every Which Way But Loose," Steve Dorff, Milton Brown, Snuff Garrett.
"If I Said You Have a Beautiful Body Would You Hold It Against Me," David Bellamy.

BEST COUNTRY VOCAL PERFORMANCE, MALE

• Kenny Rogers, "The Gambler." United Artists.
Willie Nelson, "Whiskey River." Columbia.
Charley Pride, *Burgers and Fries/When I Stop Leaving (I'll Be Gone)*. RCA.
Eddie Rabbitt, "Every Which Way But Loose." Elektra.
Hank Williams, Jr., *Family Tradition*. Elektra.

Best Country Vocal Performance, Female
- Emmylou Harris, *Blue Kentucky Girl*. Warner Bros.
- Crystal Gayle, *We Should Be Together*. United Artists.
- Brenda Lee, "Tell Me What It's Like." MCA.
- Barbara Mandrell, *Just for the Record*. MCA.
- Billie Jo Spears, "I Will Survive." United Artists.

Best Country Performance by a Duo or Group with Vocal
- Charlie Daniels Band, "The Devil Went Down to Georgia." Epic.
- Bellamy Brothers, "If I Said You Have a Beautiful Body Would You Hold It Against Me." Warner Bros.
- Larry Gatlin & the Gatlin Brothers Band, "All the Gold in California." Columbia.
- Willie Nelson, Leon Russell, "Heartbreak Hotel." Columbia.
- Kenny Rogers, Dottie West, "All I Ever Need Is You." United Artists.

Best Country Instrumental Performance
- Doc & Merle Watson, "Big Sandy/ Leather Britches," track. United Artists.
- Vassar Clements, Doug Jernigan, Jesse McReynolds, Buddy Spicher, *Nashville Jam*. Flying Fish.
- Floyd Cramer, *In Concert*. RCA.
- Lester Flatt's Nashville Grass, *Fantastic Pickin'*. CMH.
- Nashville Super Pickers, *Live from Austin City Limits*. Flying Fish.
- Osborne Brothers, *Bluegrass Concerto*. CMH.

Best Gospel Performance, Contemporary or Inspirational
- Imperials, *Heed the Call*. Dayspring.
- Andrus, Blackwood & Co., *Following You*. Greentree.
- Amy Grant, *My Father's Eyes*. Myrrh.
- Dan Peek, *All Things Are Possible*. MCA/Songbird.
- Evie Tornquist, *Never the Same*. Word.

Best Gospel Performance, Traditional
- Blackwood Brothers, *Lift Up the Name of Jesus*. Skylite.
- Dottie Rambo Choir, *A Choral Concert of Love*. Heartwarming.
- Mercy River Boys, *Breakout*. Canaan.
- Rex Nelon Singers, *Feelings*. Canaan.
- Cathedral Quartet, *You Ain't Heard Nothing Yet!* Canaan.

Best Soul Gospel Performance, Contemporary
- Andrae Crouch, *I'll Be Thinking of You*. Light.
- Cassietta George, *Cassietta in Concert*. Audio Arts.
- Rev. Jesse L. Jackson, Walter Hawkins & Family, Edwin Hawkins, Push Choir, Jackie Verdell, Danniebelle, Bili Thedford, Jessy Dixon, Andrae Crouch, *Push for Excellence*. Myrrh.
- Myrna Summers, *Give Me Something to Hold on To*. Savoy.
- Bili Thedford, *More Than Magic*. Good News.
- Kevin Yancy directing Fountain of Life Joy Choir, "Thank You." Gospel Roots.

Best Soul Gospel Performance, Traditional
- Mighty Clouds of Joy, *Changing Times*. Epic.
- Willie Banks & the Messengers, *For the Wrong I've Done*. HSE.
- James Cleveland & the Southern California Community Choir, *It's a New Day*. Savoy.
- James Cleveland & Triboro Mass Choir, Albert Jamison, director, *In God's Own Time*. Savoy.
- Troy Ramey & the Soul Searchers, *Try Jesus*. Nashboro.

Best Inspirational Performance
- B. J. Thomas, *You Gave Me Love (When Nobody Gave Me a Prayer)*. Myrrh.
- Pat Boone, *Just the Way I Am*. Lamb & Lion.
- Mike Douglas, *I'll Sing This Song for You*. Word.
- Willie Nelson, Leon Russell, "I Saw the Light," track. Columbia.
- Noel Paul Stookey, *Band and Bodyworks*. New World.

Best Ethnic or Traditional Recording
• *Muddy "Mississippi" Waters Live*, Muddy Waters. Blue Sky/CBS.
The Chieftains 7, Chieftains. Columbia.
Ice Pickin', Albert Collins. Alligator.
Laugh Your Blues Away, Uncle Dave Macon. Rounder.
Living Chicago Blues, Vol. 1, Jimmy Johnson Blues Band, Eddie Shaw & the Wolf Gang, Left Hand Frank & his Blues Band. Alligator.
Living Chicago Blues, Vol. 3, Lonnie Brooks Blues Band, Pinetop Perkins & Sons of the Blues. Alligator.
New England Traditional Fiddling. Paul F. Wells, producer. John Edwards Memorial Foundation.
New Orleans Jazz & Heritage Festival, Eubie Blake, Charles Mingus, Roosevelt Sykes, Clifton Chenier. Flying Fish.
So Many Roads, Otis Rush. Delmark.

Best Latin Recording
• *Irakere*, Irakere. Columbia.
Cross Over, Fania All Stars. Columbia.
Eternos, Celia Cruz, Johnny Pacheco. Vaya.
Touching You, Touching Me, Airto Moreira. Warner Bros.

Best Instrumental Composition
(Composer's Award)
• "Main Title Theme from *Superman*," John Williams.
"Ambiance," Marian McPartland.
"Angela (Theme from *Taxi*)," Bob James.
Central Park, Chick Corea.
Rise, Andy Armer, Randy Badazz.

Best Instrumental Arrangement
• Claus Ogerman, "Soulful Strut" (George Benson). Warner Bros.
Jeremy Lubbock, Harvey Mason, "Wave" (Harvey Mason). Arista.
Claus Ogerman, "Lazy Afternoon" (Freddie Hubbard). CBS.
Don Sebesky, "Sebastian's Theme" (Don Sebesky). Gryphon.
John Serry, "Sabotage" (John Serry). Chrysalis.

Recordings of Brahms's four symphonies and his German Requiem brought Sir Gorg Solti two more classical Grammys.

Best Album of Original Score Written for a Motion Picture or a Television Special
(Composer's Award)
• *Superman*, John Williams. Warner Bros.
Alien, Jerry Goldsmith. RCA.
Apocalypse Now, Carmine Coppola, Francis Coppola. Elektra.
Ice Castles, Alan Parsons, Eric Woolfson, Marvin Hamlisch, composers. Carole Bayer Sager, lyricist. Arista.
The Muppet Movie, Paul Williams, Kenny Ascher, composers/lyricists. Atlantic.

Best Cast Show Album
• *Sweeney Todd*, Stephen Sondheim, composer/lyricist. Thomas Z. Shepard, producer. RCA.
Ballroom, Billy Goldenberg, composer. Alan & Marilyn Bergman, lyricists. Larry Morton, producer. Columbia.
The Grand Tour, Jerry Herman, composer/lyricist. Mike Berniker, Jerry Herman, producers. Columbia.
I'm Getting My Act Together and Taking It On the Road, Gretchen Cryer, Nancy Ford, composers. Edward Kleban, producer. Columbia.

They're Playing Our Song, Marvin
  Hamlisch, composer. Carole Bayer
  Sager, lyricist. Brooks Arthur, Carole
  Bayer Sager, Marvin Hamlisch,
  producers. Casablanca.

**BEST ARRANGEMENT ACCOMPANYING
VOCALIST(S)**
• Michael McDonald, "What a Fool
  Believes" (Doobie Brothers). Warner
  Bros.
Jerry Hey, David Foster, "After the Love
  Has Gone" (Earth, Wind & Fire).
  ARC/CBS.
Byron Olson, "Everything Must Change"
  (Benard Ighner). Alfa.
Artie Butler, Barry Manilow, "I'll Never
  Love This Way Again" (Dionne
  Warwick). Arista.
Richard Evans, "'Round Midnight"
  (Richard Evans). Horizon.
Tom Tom 84, "September" (Earth, Wind
  & Fire). ARC/CBS.

BEST CLASSICAL ALBUM
• *Brahms: Symphonies (4) Complete*, Sir
  Georg Solti conducting Chicago
  Symphony Orchestra. James Mallinson,
  producer. London.
Britten: Peter Grimes, Colin Davis
  conducting Orchestra and Chorus of
  Royal Opera House, Covent Garden
  (solos: Vickers, Harper, Summers).
  Vittorio Negri, producer. Philips.
The Horowitz Concerts 1978/79 (solo:
  Vladimir Horowitz). John Pfeiffer,
  producer. RCA.
*Mussorgsky-Ravel: Pictures at an
  Exhibition; Stravinsky: The Firebird
  Suite*, Riccardo Muti conducting
  Philadelphia Orchestra. Christopher
  Bishop, producer. Angel.
Shostakovich: Lady Macbeth of Mtsensk,
  Mstislav Rostropovich conducting
  London Philharmonic; Ambrosian
  Opera Chorus (solos: Vishnevskaya,
  Gedda). Suvi Raj Grubb, producer.
  Angel.
*Webern: The Complete Works of Anton
  Webern, Volume I*, Pierre Boulez
  conducting Ensemble. Paul Myers,
  producer. Columbia.

*The Chicago Orchestra's best classical
recording of Brahms's four symphonies
"everywhere sounds big," said one critic.*

**BEST CLASSICAL ORCHESTRAL
RECORDING
(Conductor's Award)**
• *Brahms: Symphonies (4) Complete*, Sir
  Georg Solti conducting Chicago
  Symphony. James Mallinson, producer.
  London.
Holst: The Planets, Sir Georg Solti
  conducting London Philharmonic.
  James Mallinson, producer. London.
Ives: Three Places in New England,
  Dennis Russell Davies conducting St.
  Paul Chamber Orchestra. Tom Voegeli,
  producer. Sound 80.
Mahler: Symphony No. 4 in G Major,
  André Previn conducting Pittsburgh
  Symphony. Suvi Raj Grubb, producer.
  Angel.
*Rachmaninoff: Symphonies Nos. 2 in E
  Minor & 3 in A Minor*, Leonard Slatkin
  conducting St. Louis Symphony. Marc
  Aubort, Joanna Nickrenz, producers.
  Vox Box.
*Sibelius: Four Legends from the
  "Kalevala,"* Eugene Ormandy
  conducting Philadelphia Orchestra.
  John Willan, producer. Angel.
Zelenka: Orchestral Works (Complete),
  Alexander Van Wijnkoop conducting
  Camerata Bern. Dr. Andreas
  Holschneider, producer. Deutsche
  Grammophon.

BEST CHAMBER MUSIC PERFORMANCE (INSTRUMENTAL OR VOCAL)

• Dennis Russell Davies conducting St. Paul Chamber Orchestra, *Copland: Appalachian Spring*. Sound 80.

Pierre Boulez, Daniel Barenboim, Pinchas Zukerman/Pay & Ensemble Inter-Contemporain, *Berg: Chamber Concerto for Piano & Violin/Four Pieces for Clarinet & Piano*. Deutsche Grammophon.

Michael Debost, James Galway, *Telemann: 6 Sonatas for 2 Flutes*. Seraphim.

Fitzwilliam Quartet, *Shostakovich: Quartets Nos. 5 & 6*. L'Oiseau Lyre.

Yoshikazu Fukumura conducting Koto Flute, Ransom Wilson, New Koto Ensemble of Tokyo, *Vivaldi: Four Flute Concertos*. Angel.

Tokyo Quartet, *Debussy: Quartet in G Minor; Ravel: Quartet in F*. Columbia.

Itzhak Perlman, Lynn Harrell, Pinchas Zukerman, *Dohnanyi: Serenade, Op. 10; Beethoven: Serenade, Op. 8*. Columbia.

Pinchas Zukerman, Claude Bolling with Max Hediguer, Marcel Sabiani, *Bolling: Suite for Violin & Jazz Piano*. Columbia.

BEST CLASSICAL PERFORMANCE, INSTRUMENTAL SOLOIST(S) (WITH ORCHESTRA)

• Maurizio Pollini (Abbado conducting Chicago Symphony), *Bartók: Concertos for Piano Nos. 1 & 2*. Deutsche Grammophon.

Maurice Andre (Lopez-Cobos conducting London Philharmonic), *Trumpet Concertos by Haydn, Telemann, Albinoni & Marcello*. Angel.

James Galway (Gerhardt conducting National Philharmonic), *Annie's Song & Other Galway Favorites*. RCA.

Anne Sophie Mutter (von Karajan conducting Berlin Philharmonic), *Mozart: Concertos for Violin No. 3 in G Major & No. 5 in A Major*. Deutsche Grammophon.

Isaac Stern, Jean-Pierre Rampal (Jerusalem Music Center Chamber Orchestra), *Isaac Stern & Jean-Pierre Rampal Play Vivaldi & Telemann*. Columbia.

Barry Tuckwell (English Chamber Orchestra), *Horn Concertos by Joseph Haydn & Michael Haydn*. Angel.

Krystian Zimerman (Giulini conducting Los Angeles Philharmonic), *Chopin: Concerto for Piano No. 1 in E Minor*. Deutsche Grammophon.

BEST CLASSICAL PERFORMANCE, INSTRUMENTAL SOLOIST(S) (WITHOUT ORCHESTRA)

• Vladimir Horowitz, *The Horowitz Concerts 1978/79*. RCA.

Julian Bream, *Villa-Lobos: Etudes (12) & Suite Populaire Brasilienne*. RCA.

Glenn Gould, *Bach: Toccatas, Volume 1*. Columbia.

Paul Jacobs, *Debussy: Estampes, Images, Books 1 & 2*. Nonesuch.

Igor Kipnis, *Scarlatti: Sonatas (12)*. Angel.

Ursula Oppens, *Rzewski: The People United Will Never Be Defeated*. Vanguard.

Maurizio Pollini, *Boulez: Sonata for Piano No. 2*. Deutsche Grammophon.

Artur Rubinstein, *Franck: Prelude, Chorale & Fugue for Piano; Bach-Busoni: Chaconne; Mozart: Rondo in A Minor*. RCA.

Rosalyn Tureck, *Bach: Goldberg Variations*. Columbia.

BEST OPERA RECORDING

• *Britten: Peter Grimes*, Colin Davis conducting Orchestra and Chorus of Royal Opera House, Covent Garden (solos: Vickers, Harper, Summers). Vittorio Negri, producer. Philips.

Hindemith: Mathis der Maler, Rafael Kubelik conducting Bavarian Radio Symphony and Bavarian Radio Chorus (solos: Fischer-Dieskau, King). Friedrich Welz, John Willan, producers. Angel.

Shostakovich: Lady Macbeth of Mtsensk, Mstislav Rostropovich conducting London Philharmonic, Ambrosian Opera Chorus (solos: Vishnevskaya, Gedda). Suvi Raj Grubb, producer. Angel.

Verdi: Otello, James Levine conducting National Philharmonic (solos: Domingo, Scotto, Milnes). Richard Mohr, producer. RCA.

Verdi: Rigoletto, Julius Rudel conducting Philharmonia Orchestra and Ambrosian Opera Chorus (solos: Sills, Kraus, Milnes). John Fraser, producer. Angel.

BEST CHORAL PERFORMANCE, CLASSICAL (OTHER THAN OPERA)
• Sir Georg Solti, conductor, Margaret Hillis, choral director, Chicago Symphony and Chorus, *Brahms: A German Requiem*. London.

Maurice Abravanel, conductor, Newell B. Wright, choral director, Utah Chorale and Utah Symphony, *Stravinsky: Symphony of Psalms*. Angel.

Daniel Barenboim conducting Chorus of Orchestre de Paris and Orchestre de Paris, *Berlioz: La Damnation de Faust*. Deutsche Grammophon.

Leonard Bernstein conducting Radio Chorus of the N.O.S. Hilversum and Concertgebouworkest, *Beethoven: Missa Solemnis*. Deutsche Grammophon.

Lorin Maazel, conductor; Robert Page, choral director, Cleveland Orchestra & Chorus, *Berlioz: Requiem*. London.

John Oliver conducting Tanglewood Festival Chorus, *American Music for Chorus*. Deutsche Grammophon.

André Previn conducting London Symphony Chorus; Richard Hickox, chorus master, St. Clement Danes School Boys' Choir; Keith Walters, choral director, London Symphony, *Britten: Spring Symphony*. Angel.

Jerzy Semkow, conductor, Thomas Peck, choral director, St. Louis Symphony Chorus and Orchestra, *Beethoven: "Choral Fantasy," Elegiac Song, "Calm Sea and Prosperous Voyage."* Candide.

BEST CLASSICAL VOCAL SOLOIST PERFORMANCE
• Luciano Pavarotti (Bologna Orchestra), *O Sole Mio (Favorite Neapolitan Songs)*. London.

Elly Ameling (Dalton Baldwin, accompanist), *Mozart: Lieder*. Philips.

Victoria de los Angeles (Gerald Moore, accompanist), *Victoria de los Angeles in Concert*. Angel.

Dietrich Fischer-Dieskau (Sviatoslav Richter, accompanist), *Schubert: Lieder*. Deutsche Grammophon.

Jan de Gaetani (Dunkel, Anderson, Kalish, accompanists), *Ravel: Chansons Madecasses*. Nonesuch.

Yevgeny Nesterenko (Shenderovich, Krainev, accompanists), *Mussorgsky: Songs*. Columbia/Melodiya.

Leontyne Price (Garvey, accompanist), *Lieder by Schubert & Richard Strauss*. Angel.

Frederica von Stade (Katz, accompanist), *Frederica von Stade Song Recital*. Columbia.

BEST ENGINEERED RECORDING, CLASSICAL
• Anthony Salvatore, *Sondheim: Sweeney Todd*, Original Cast. RCA.

Marc Aubort, Joanna Nickrenz, *Rachmaninoff: Symphonies Nos. 2 & 3* (Slatkin conducting St. Louis Symphony). Vox Box.

Klaus Hiemann, *Bartók: Concertos for Piano Nos. 1 & 2* (Abbado conducting Chicago Symphony; solo: Pollini). Deutsche Grammophon.

Klaus Hiemann, *Prokofiev: Scythian Suite; Lt. Kije* (Abbado conducting Chicago Symphony). Deutsche Grammophon.

Tom Jung, *Copland: Appalachian Spring; Ives: Three Places in New England* (Davis conducting St. Paul Chamber Orchestra). Sound 80.

John Kurlander, *Hindemith: Concert Music for Strings & Brass; Symphonic Metamorphosis on Themes by Weber* (Ormandy conducting Philadelphia Orchestra). Angel.

John Kurlander, *Sibelius: Four Legends from the "Kalevala"* (Ormandy conducting Philadelphia Orchestra). Angel.

Vittorio Negri, *Britten: Peter Grimes* (Davis conducting Royal Opera House, Covent Garden; solos: Vickers, Harper, Summers). Philips.

Jack Renner, *Mussorgsky-Ravel: Pictures at an Exhibition* (Maazel conducting Cleveland Orchestra). Telarc.

Jack Renner, *Stravinsky: The Firebird Suite; Borodin: Prince Igor* (Shaw conducting Atlanta Symphony Orchestra and Chorus). Telarc.

Isao Tomita, *The Bermuda Triangle* (Isao Tomita). RCA.

CLASSICAL PRODUCER OF THE YEAR

• James Mallinson
Marc Aubort and Joanna Nickrenz
Andrew Kazdin
Paul Myers
Vittorio Negri
Thomas Z. Shepard
Robert Woods

BEST COMEDY RECORDING

• *Reality . . . What a Concept,* Robin
  Williams. Casablanca.
Comedy Is Not Pretty, Steve Martin.
  Warner Bros.
I Need Your Help, Barry Manilow, Ray
  Stevens. Warner Bros.
"Rubber Biscuit," track, Blues Brothers.
  Atlantic.
Wanted, Richard Pryor. Warner Bros.

BEST SPOKEN WORD, DOCUMENTARY OR DRAMA RECORDING

• *The Ages of Man (Readings from
  Shakespeare),* Sir John Gielgud.
  Caedmon.
Apocalypse Now, Original motion picture
  soundtrack. Elektra.
An American Prayer, Jim Morrison.
  Elektra.
The Ox-Bow Incident, Henry Fonda.
  Caedmon.
Stare with Your Ears, Ken Nordine. Snail.
Orson Welles/Helen Hayes at Their Best,
  Orson Welles, Helen Hayes. Mark 56.

BEST RECORDING FOR CHILDREN

• *The Muppet Movie*, Jim Henson, creator.
  Paul Williams, producer. Atlantic.
*Anne Murray Sings for the Sesame Street
  Generation*, Anne Murray. Sesame
  Street.
Sesame Disco! Jim Henson, creator. Joe
  Raposo, Michael DeLugg, producers.
  Sesame Street.
The Stars Come Out on Sesame Street, Jim
  Henson, creator. Jon Stone, producer,
  Jim Timmens, record editor. Sesame
  Street.
You're in Love, Charlie Brown, Jymn
  Magon, Lee Mendelson, producers.
  Charlie Brown.

BEST ENGINEERED RECORDING

• Peter Henderson, *Breakfast in America*
  (Supertramp). A&M.
Gary Loizzo, *Cornerstone* (Styx). A&M.
Alan Parsons, *Eve* (Alan Parsons Project).
  Arista.

Lee Herschberg, Lloyd Clifft, Tom Knox,
  Roger Nichols, *Rickie Lee Jones*
  (Rickie Lee Jones). Warner Bros.
Phil Edwards, *Just Friends* (LA-4).
  Concord Jazz.

BEST ALBUM PACKAGE
(Art Director's Award)

• Mike Doud, Mick Haggerty, *Breakfast in
  America* (Supertramp). A&M.
John Berg, *Ramsey* (Ramsey Lewis).
  Columbia.
Lynne Dresse Breslin, *With Sound Reason*
  (Sonny Fortune). Atlantic.
Ron Coro, Johnny Lee, *Near
  Perfect/Perfect* (Martin Mull). Elektra.
Peter Corriston, *Morning Dance* (Spyro
  Gyra). Infinity.
John Gillespie, *Fear of Music* (Talking
  Heads). Sire.
Hipgnosis, *In Through the Out Door* (Led
  Zeppelin). Swan Song.
Tony Lane, *Chicago 13* (Chicago).
  Columbia.
Michael Ross, *Look Sharp!* (Joe Jackson).
  A&M.

BEST ALBUM NOTES
(Annotator's Award)

• Bob Porter, James Patrick, *Charlie
  Parker: The Complete Savoy Sessions.*
  Savoy.
Melvin Maddocks, *Billie Holiday (Giants
  of Jazz).* Time-Life.
Dan Morgenstern, Stanley Dance, *Duke
  Ellington (Giants of Jazz).* Time-Life.
Dick Schory, *The Magical Music of Walt
  Disney.* Ovation.
Richard M. Sudhalter, *Hoagy Carmichael,
  A Legendary Performer and Composer.*
  RCA.

BEST HISTORICAL REISSUE

• *Billie Holiday (Giants of Jazz).* Jerry
  Korn, Michael Brooks, producers.
  Time-Life.
Duke Ellington (Giants of Jazz). Jerry
  Korn, producer. Time-Life.
The Magical Music of Walt Disney. Dick
  Schory, producer. Ovation.
*One Never Knows, Do One? The Best of
  Fats Waller.* George Spitzer, Chick
  Crumpacker, producers. Book of the
  Month Records.
A Tribute to E. Power Biggs. Andrew
  Kazdin, producer. Columbia.

PRODUCER OF THE YEAR
• Larry Butler
Mike Chapman
Quincy Jones
Ted Templeman
Maurice White

Cross Sails Away

"The only element of mystery or suspense" surrounding the Grammys, reported *Billboard*, "centered on which record industry legend — Sinatra or Streisand — would pick off the top awards."

Sinatra was tied with Stevie Wonder for having won the most Album of the Year prizes in the past (three), but now he was expected to be established as the supreme champ with a victory for *Trilogy*, a three-disc retrospective of his formidable career. Seventeen years had passed since Streisand last won the honor, and now she was back in contention for *Guilty*, her phenomenally successful duet with Barry Gibb. But more than anything, Streisand wanted her "Woman in Love" single to take the Record of the Year award, an honor that had eluded her on four occasions in the past. Her toughest competition was expected to be Sinatra's "Theme from *New York, New York*," a favorite because the Grammys were being held in Manhattan for the first time in five years. "New Yorkers are notoriously sentimental about their town," wrote the *L.A. Times*, "so you can imagine how wild the audience will go over Sinatra and that tune at New York's Radio City Music Hall."

Then came the biggest upset — and

Christopher Cross, at left, is the only artist to win all four top awards (with producer Michael Omartian, right). His multiple victories marked the biggest Grammy upset ever.

WIDE WORLD PHOTO

the most thorough sweep by a debut artist — in Grammy history.

As fans gathered in the cold, gusty air outside Radio City shortly before the show, no one seemed to notice the arrival of the 6-foot, 2-inch, 200-plus-pound Christopher Cross. ("The kids in the crowd seemed to be on the lookout for Barbra Streisand and Barry Gibb, who received the biggest screams of the evening," noted *The Los Angeles Herald Examiner*. Dionne Warwick, on the other hand, got "squeals.") Later on, as Cross began to pick up one Grammy and then another, he was still ignored back in the press room where the photographers and reporters waited restlessly for Streisand or Sinatra to burst into their midst with an armful of the golden gramophones, thereby giving them the page-one photos they needed for their newspapers back home. However, when

Cross, his eponymous album, and his hit song "Sailing" finally racked up wins for Best New Artist and Best Arrangement Accompanying Vocalist (which he shared with his producer/arranger Michael Omartian) as well as Record, Album, and Song of the Year, chaos erupted among the reporters as they scrambled to make up for previously lost photo and Q&A opportunities. "'Who the hell is this guy?' rang out more than once," reported *The Washington Post* about the press reaction to the artist who only a year earlier was playing a fraternity party in Austin, Texas.

Only twice before had anyone ever swept the "triple crown" of best record, album, and song awards: Paul Simon in 1970 and Carole King in 1971. Since both artists were established music names, neither qualified for Grammy's fourth highest honor of Best New Artist.

Christopher Cross pulled off the biggest sweep by a debut artist in Grammy history.

When Cross ended up claiming that prize, too, it was a grand slam that had never occurred before — and has not been repeated since.

Prior to making it big, Cross worked for 10 years in a band that played the latest hit music to Texas bar crowds. "When disco came in, we were a disco band," he told *The Washington Post*. "My material was in my guitar case, but people didn't want to hear it." Cross eventually got Warner Bros. executives to listen to it, though, after he sent them a demo tape. They, in turn, not only signed him up, but built him up — into an enormous star. Cross became the warm-up act at Fleetwood Mac and the Eagles concerts and was booked extensively on TV talk shows. The record company was rewarded with its best-selling album of the year (three million copies) and hit singles "Sailing" (which reached number one on the weekly charts), "Ride Like the Wind" (number two), and "Never Be the Same" (number nine).

What made his music so special? "I dunno," Cross told reporters at the Grammycast. "People just like it, I guess. It's a little bit of pop and a little bit of rock. Nothing really new." Critics were irate. Robert Hilburn of the *L.A. Times* was among those who claimed Cross's "music is so plain that it's a wonder N.A.R.A.S. voters even remembered his name" when it came time to vote. But the N.A.R.A.S. crowd not only knew their winner, they cheered him with a standing ovation as the rookie claimed his last prize of the night — Album of the Year — from music icon Diana Ross, who had failed again this year to win her first Grammy. Cross would be nominated for more awards next year for his partial contribution to the theme song to the hit film *Arthur*, (he'd lose the Grammy but win the Oscar). Soon thereafter he would fade from the pop charts — and from the Warner Bros. list of artists. Today he's trying to finance his albums independently. He told *TV Guide* in 1990, "I always feel a little left out when the Grammys come around. They've never asked me to come back or to present an award. These days, I don't even watch them."

The last singer to win Album of the Year for a debut LP was Barbra Streisand in 1963. This year the only Grammy she came up with was for best pop group vocal honors, which she shared with Barry Gibb for their "Guilty" single. Streisand had been considered a cinch to nab the female pop vocals award, but, as Christopher

Cross's victories foretold — it would be a night of endless upsets.

Streisand lost to 1973's Best New Artist, Bette Midler, who had a string of flop albums following her earlier Grammy victory but now saw her fate change in 1980 with "The Rose." Said the *L.A. Times*: "This Golden Globe-winning ballad from her smash dramatic film debut brought her back to the top."

The one award that Christopher Cross lost was the prize for best male pop vocal performance, which was snagged by Kenny Loggins for "This Is It." *Billboard* claimed the victory was "the biggest shock, outside of Cross's sweep" since Loggins also topped Sinatra, Kenny Rogers, and Grammycast host Paul Simon (who remarked, slyly, "Not to take anything away from Kenny Rogers, but Kenny was host of this show last year and won"). *Down Beat* complained that Loggins was nominated in both the pop and rock categories, but he lost his rock bid (for "I'm All Right") to 1979's winner of Album of the Year, Billy Joel, in yet another upset.

Joel won for *Glass Houses*, his musical statement that insisted he was a rock artist despite being pegged as a pop singer in recent years by critics. N.A.R.A.S. may have agreed with Joel by giving him the rock award, but few critics approved. The closest *Glass Houses* came to r&r, they argued, was the title (not the music) of its hit single "It's Still Rock & Roll to Me." Joel's win was also considered astonishing because he beat rock legend Paul McCartney, long-time loser Jackson Browne, and a never-before-nominated Bruce Springsteen, who was considered the front runner. Joel's producer Phil Ramone received the Producer of the Year prize, which caused even further controversy since it probably should have gone to him last year when Joel won Album of the Year. "Quincy Jones

was edged out for the third consecutive year," groused *Billboard*, "despite having been named the No. 1 pop producer of 1980 on *Billboard*'s year-end chart recaps."

The rest of the prizes went to bona-fide rockers but were still considered shockers. When Pat Benatar won the female vocal laurels for her *Crimes of Passion* LP, she was so stunned, she startled the audience by shrieking "Holy shit!" (Marianne Faithful was expected to win the prize for *Broken English*.) Benatar's acceptance remarks didn't have to be bleeped on TV, though, since, just like last year, the prizes were bestowed in an off-the-air ceremony held just hours before the prime-time Grammycast (a continuing sore point to sensitive rock fans since the awards were finally introduced on a permanent basis last year).

The group prize was supposed to be an overdue tribute to the British rockers Queen (for "Another One Bites the Dust"), but instead it went to those purveyors of hard rock tailored for America's hard-working blue-collar class — Bob Seger & the Silver Bullet Band (*Against the Wind*). British rock lovers had to be satisfied instead with the winners of the instrumental performance award — the Police, the trio once billed as "the Beatles of the 1980s." In their rookie years, the Police explored the combination of pop/rock sounds with reggae rhythm, which explained the title of their winning "Regatta de Blanc" ("White Reggae").

Diana Ross's startling loss of a Grammy in the r&b vocal category nonetheless had an element of justice to it. She was beaten by Stephanie Mills, whose first big break in show business came when, at the age of 15, she landed the role of Dorothy in the Broadway musical *The Wiz*. Mills played the part on stage for five years but was passed over for the film role in favor of superstar Ross (who was clearly more than 20 years too old for the part). Ross was considered the favorite to take the Grammy, too, because her song, "Upside Down," turned out to be the biggest solo hit of her career, ending up at number five in the year's Hot 100. If N.A.R.A.S. was finally going to give Ross a Grammy, award watchers reasoned, she might as well win it for her most successful single. But as good as

Stephanie Mills's shocking defeat of Diana Ross redressed an old score.

the tune was, it still wasn't as fine as Mills's "Never Knew Love Like This Before," which was written by Reggie Lucas and James Mtume, and also voted Best R&B Song over "Upside Down." On vinyl, Mills took the song to soaring emotional heights, too, far surpassing Ross's singsong delivery on "Upside Down."

Another loser of Best R&B Song, "Shining Star," ended up earning the r&b group vocals prize for the Manhattans. (This "Shining Star" was different from the song of the same name that brought Earth, Wind & Fire a Grammy in 1975, but it did have the same soulful sound executed in falsetto voice.) The remaining two r&b awards went to George Benson, whose best instrumental performance of "Off Broadway," a track from his *Give Me the Night* album (produced by Quincy Jones), also brought him the male vocal award. Jones may have lost the Producer of the Year prize to Phil Ramone, but he ended up winning a Grammy for Best Instrumental Arrangement, which he shared with Jerry Hey, for "Dinorah, Dinorah," a track from Benson's *Give Me the Night*.

Give Me the Night was one of the most critically acclaimed LPs of 1980, but while it failed to be named a contender for Album of the Year, it picked up an impressive fourth Grammy when Benson was hailed for giving the best male jazz vocal performance on its "Moody's Mood" track. (Some critics wondered: How could it compete as both an r&b *and* jazz LP?) The female jazz vocal prize was presented again to last year's winner, Ella Fitzgerald (for *A Perfect Match/Ella & Basie*), who now had a career total of 10. Count Basie got his own Grammy (his seventh) for best big band instrumental performance for *On the Road*.

"None of the jazz awards were given on stage," *Down Beat* grumbled. "The winners were merely run through, quickly and all but unintelligibly, within a list of 'other winners' (including the Best Recording for Children and Best Comedy Recording) by Harry Chapin and Judy Collins — both respected artists but neither known for their jazz chops." Time was reserved, however, for a performance by Chuck Mangione and the Manhattan Transfer of a medley of some of the fusion works contending for Grammys this year, including Mangione's "Give It All You Got" (which lost Best Instrumental Composition to John Williams's *The Empire Strikes Back*, also the winner of best film score) and the Manhattan Transfer's "Birdland," which won the new award for Best Jazz Fusion Performance, Vocal or Instrumental. "Birdland" also garnered Best Arrangement for Vocals.

When legendary jazz pianist Bill Evans died in 1980, he left behind two LPs with farewell titles that would both earn posthumous awards: *I Will Say Goodbye* (best soloist instrumental performance) and *We Will Meet Again* (best group instrumental performance).

Throughout his career, Evans liked to keep his groups to only two or three players, but he employed a quintet for *We Will Meet Again* that was comprised of bass, drums, his piano, and two horns. The horns marked a dramatic departure for Evans's trademark sound and it thrilled the critics.

The success of the latest John Travolta movie, *Urban Cowboy*, helped to popularize a number of country hits that also earned Grammys. In what *The New York Times* called "something of an upset," Anne Murray reaped the female vocal honors for "Could I Have This Dance," which was originally intended as a duet with Kenny Rogers to underscore the film's wedding scene. When negotiations with Rogers's managers dragged on too long, however, Murray recorded both the male and female parts herself and the producers liked the solo version enough to drop their talks with Rogers. *Urban Cowboy* was filmed at Gilley's, a Houston bar billed as "the largest honky tonk in the world" where patrons were prone to forget their woes by swilling Texas brew and riding the saloon's mechanical bull. The bar's owner, Mickey Gilley, and his "Urban Cowboy" Band won the instrumental performance prize for "Orange Blossom Special/Hoedown."

Texas talent ruled the rest of the country categories, too. Roy Orbison won his first Grammy (vocal duo honors, shared with two-time past winner Emmylou Harris) for "That Lovin' You Feelin' Again," which was also from a motion picture — *Roadie*, starring music artists Orbison, Meat Loaf, Blondie, and Hank Williams, Jr.

Another legendary Texan received his first Grammy this year when George Jones won the male vocal prize for "He Stopped Loving Her Today," about a man who dies early in life, leaving his sweetheart behind. The song's success marked "the climax to a stirring comeback year," according to *The New York Times*. Jones had recently triumphed over alcoholism and other personal problems but apparently did not expect a first Grammy to cap off his new good fortune. "He was already backstage with his tie off when the award was announced," *The Washington Post* noted. When he returned to the press room later on, award in hand, Jones told reporters, "I want to thank all the fans

Anne Murray received her best country vocals award for "Could I Have This Dance" from Rodney Dangerfield, winner of Best Comedy Recording for his No Respect LP.

and friends who stood by us. I also want to thank God. This has been the greatest year of my life."

Texan Willie Nelson had won three performance Grammys in the past, but none for composition prior to this year's acknowledgment for Best Coun-

Three-time Grammy-winning singer Willie Nelson was recognized as a songwriter for composing his classic Best Country Song "On the Road Again."

try Song "On the Road Again," which he wrote for the Sydney Pollack-produced film *Honeysuckle Rose* (later retitled *On the Road Again* for video release), in which he starred as a journeyman country crooner. Waylon Jennings once told *Billboard*: "I think Willie Nelson will go down as one of the greatest, if not *the* greatest, songwriter ever in country music. He can write the most complex song ... that will shoot over most people's heads and then he will turn around and write a little song like 'On the Road Again' that everyone can appreciate."

The religious awards welcomed back a host of talent from Grammy years past, including B.J. Thomas, Andrae Crouch, and others in an ensemble performance on the album *The Lord's Prayer*. The Blackwood Brothers returned from last year to reclaim the Best Traditional Gospel Performance prize for *We Come*

to Worship. The Rev. James Cleveland had won twice before but now shared his third with the Charles Gold Singers for *Lord, Let Me Be an Instrument.*

Last year a "born again" Bob Dylan looked out of place when he won a rock & roll Grammy for his religious song "Gotta Serve Somebody," but now he and his *Saved* LP were competing directly in the Best Inspirational Performance category where they belonged. Dylan lost, however, to Best New Artist of 1977, Debby Boone, for *With My Song I Will Praise Him.*

The recipient of the Best Latin Recording award was Cal Tjader and his sextet (for *La Onda va Bien*), an American known for his jazz work with the likes of Stan Getz and Charlie Byrd who also performed Latin music with such past Grammy champs as Eddie Palmieri and Mongo Santamaria.

Rodney Dangerfield got plenty of respect on Grammy night when his *No Respect* LP won Best Comedy Recording. The disc was a compilation of new material plus old one-liners that were recorded at his New York nightclub: "The other night I felt like having a few drinks. I went over to the bartender and said, 'Surprise me.' He showed me a naked picture of my wife .... Ain't got no sex life .... She cut me down to once a month. I'm lucky. Two guys I know she cut out completely." Dangerfield hammed it up at the Grammys, too. While up at the podium he clasped his first gold gramophone for dear life and explained his paranoia to the audience: "There's a guy in my neighborhood who's waiting to melt mine down."

1980

The prize for Best Cast Show Album became the source of a minor squabble when N.A.R.A.S. allowed theatrical revivals to compete. *Down Beat* was particularly irked that a new staging of the 1943 classic *Oklahoma!* was nominated. Andrew Lloyd Webber's *Evita*, starring Patti LuPone, won (over such stiff competition as *Barnum, One Mo' Time,* and *A Day in Hollywood/A Night in the Ukraine*) and earned Lloyd Webber two awards, as both its composer and coproducer.

Among the classical kudos, *Stereo Review* took issue with "the lopsided distribution ... with three awards going to the opera *Lulu* (best album, best opera, best engineering) and four to Itzhak Perlman (chamber music, soloist with orchestra twice — a tie with himself! — and soloist without orchestra). Yes, Perlman is undeniably a superb violinist and the Deutsche Grammophon recording of *Lulu* is a landmark of sorts, but weren't there some other fine classical recordings made during the year? There were, but they lacked the advantage of exposure: *Lulu* was broadcast on public television, and Perlman is a veteran TV talk-show guest who even appears on *Sesame Street*."

Deutsche Grammophon's *Lulu* was the first complete performance ever attempted of the opera by Alban Berg, who died in 1935. The production starred Teresa Stratas as Lulu and featured instrumental accompaniment by Pierre Boulez conducting the Paris Opera Orchestra. Berg's work also figured into the four Grammys awarded to Perlman, who was honored for performances of works by Shostakovich and Moszkowski, too. "Israeli-American violinist Itzhak Perlman may soon need an extension built onto his mantlepiece," *Billboard* said. "Perlman's Grammy Awards collection grew dramatically last week in the most impressive sweep by a classical artist in the ceremony's history."

Sir Georg Solti and the Chicago Symphony Orchestra won the orchestral honors for Bruckner's Sixth Symphony but took some heat from *High Fidelity*: "Solti has evinced a disturbing tendency to stress sound over content. Such is again the case: As virtuosic display, his Sixth is astounding; as music-making, it is appalling." The magazine also blasted Carlo Maria Giulini's conducting of the Philharmonia Orchestra in Mozart's *Requiem*, which was the recipient of the choral laurels for the Philharmonia's chorus and its master Norbert Balatsch. "Basses and timpani [are] the main offenders," it said about the orchestration. "The trombones are all over the place." The chorus, however, it noted, was "excellent."

Leontyne Price had been awarded ten Grammys between 1960 and 1974 but hadn't won another one since. Now she was back to claim the vocals prize for the fifth volume of her *Prima Donna* series.

Country star George Jones's victory marked "the climax to a stirring comeback."

High Fidelity wrote: "This program is an assertion that (at least in the recording studio) Leontyne Price can still sing damn near anything."

The 23rd Annual Grammy Awards "maintained a degree of elegance and were overall less gimmicky and hokey" than other ceremonies in the past, said *Billboard*. The musical performances included Patti LuPone giving a moving version of "Don't Cry for Me, Argentina" from *Evita*, Aretha Franklin wringing her heart in public with "Can't Turn You Loose," and winning country singer George Jones singing, noted the *Herald*

Examiner, "a verse of 'He Stopped Loving Her Today' that climaxed in a multiple-registered, goose-pimpling final note that even raised the hair on the back of *his* head." But the most moving aspect of the entire evening was what closed the Grammy telecast: host Paul Simon's eloquent tribute to fallen ex-Beatle John Lennon, who had been murdered at the entrance of his New York apartment building in December, 1980.

Once the formal ceremony was over, the informal partying began. *People* reported on the galas around town: "Paul Simon and five-statue winner Christopher ('Sailing') Cross chose the 'official' bash at the Hilton, where tickets ran from $75 to $175. So did Michael McDonald, Chuck Mangione, Kenny Loggins, and nearly 2,700 others. At CBS Records president Walter Yetnikoff's more intimate affair at the Four Seasons, Barbra Streisand liked the banana cheesecake so much she asked for a whole one to take home. Across town, Arista Records president Clive Davis had problems .... Aretha Franklin, the guest of honor at his party in the 48th floor Tower Suite, turned out to be afraid of heights. She couldn't bring herself to leave the elevator, so she turned around and went home. The $300 Grand Marnier-and-strawberry cake stayed in the fridge, while guests Chris Reeve, Jane Seymour, Rodney Dangerfield, and Mr. and Mrs. Bruce Sudano (a.k.a. Mrs. and Mr. Donna Summer) made do with poached bass and chocolate mousse."

1980

The awards ceremony was broadcast on CBS from New York's Radio City Music Hall on February 25, 1981, for the awards eligibility period of October 1, 1979, through September 30, 1980.

ALBUM OF THE YEAR
- *Christopher Cross*, Christopher Cross. Michael Omartian, producer. Warner Bros.
- *Glass Houses*, Billy Joel. Phil Ramone, producer. Columbia.
- *Guilty*, Barbra Streisand. Barry Gibb. Albhy Galuten, Karl Richardson, producers. Columbia.
- *Trilogy: Past, Present & Future*, Frank Sinatra. Sonny Burke, producer. Reprise.
- *The Wall*, Pink Floyd. Bob Ezrin, David Gilmour, Roger Waters, producers. Columbia.

RECORD OF THE YEAR
- "Sailing," Christopher Cross. Michael Omartian, producer. Warner Bros.
- "Lady," Kenny Rogers. Lionel Richie, Jr., producer. Liberty/United Artists.
- "The Rose," Bette Midler. Paul A. Rothchild, producer. Atlantic.
- "Theme from *New York, New York*," Frank Sinatra. Sonny Burke, producer. Reprise.

"Woman in Love," Barbra Streisand, Barry Gibb. Albhy Galuten, Karl Richardson, producers. Columbia.

SONG OF THE YEAR
(Songwriter's Award)
- "Sailing," Christopher Cross. Pop 'N' Roll Music, publisher.
- "Fame," Michael Gore, Dean Pitchford. MGM Affiliated Music, Inc., publishers.
- "Lady," Lionel Richie, Jr. Brockman Music, publisher.
- "Theme from *New York, New York*," John Kander, Fred Ebb. Unart, publisher.
- "The Rose," Amanda McBroom. Fox Fanfare Music, Inc., publisher.
- "Woman in Love," Barry Gibb, Robin Gibb. Stigwood Music, Inc., publisher.

BEST NEW ARTIST
- Christopher Cross. Warner Bros.
- Irene Cara. RSO.
- Robbie Dupree. Elektra.
- Amy Holland. Capitol.
- Pretenders. Sire.

BEST POP VOCAL PERFORMANCE, MALE
- Kenny Loggins, "This Is It," track from *Alive*. Columbia.
- Christopher Cross, *Christopher Cross*. Warner Bros.

Kenny Rogers, "Lady." Liberty/United
   Artists.
Paul Simon, "Late in the Evening."
   Warner Bros.
Frank Sinatra, "Theme from *New York,
   New York*." Reprise.

BEST POP VOCAL PERFORMANCE, FEMALE
• Bette Midler, "The Rose." Atlantic.
Irene Cara, "Fame." RSO.
Olivia Newton-John, "Magic." MCA.
Barbra Streisand, "Woman in Love."
   Columbia.
Donna Summer, "On the Radio."
   Casablanca.

**BEST POP PERFORMANCE
BY A DUO OR GROUP WITH VOCAL**
• Barbra Streisand, Barry Gibb, "Guilty,"
   track from *Guilty*. Columbia.
Ambrosia, "Biggest Part of Me." Warner
   Bros.
Pointer Sisters, "He's So Shy." Planet.
Kenny Rogers, Kim Carnes, "Don't Fall in
   Love With a Dreamer." United Artists.
Bob Seger & the Silver Bullet Band,
   "Against the Wind," track from *Against
   the Wind*. Capitol.

BEST POP INSTRUMENTAL PERFORMANCE
• Bob James, Earl Klugh, *One on One*.
   Columbia.
Herb Alpert, "Beyond." A&M.
Doobie Brothers, "South Bay Strut," track
   from *One Step*. Warner Bros.
Henry Mancini, "Ravel's *Bolero*." Warner
   Bros.
John Williams, London Symphony
   Orchestra, "Yoda's Theme," track from
   The Empire Strikes Back. RSO.

BEST ROCK VOCAL PERFORMANCE, MALE
• Billy Joel, *Glass Houses*. Columbia.
Jackson Browne, "Boulevard." Asylum.
Kenny Loggins, "I'm Alright, (Theme
   from *Caddyshack*)." Columbia.
Paul McCartney, "Coming Up (Live at
   Glasgow)." Columbia.
Bruce Springsteen, "Medley: Devil With
   the Blue Dress/Good Golly Miss
   Molly/Jenny Take a Ride," track from
   No Nukes. Asylum.

**BEST ROCK VOCAL PERFORMANCE,
FEMALE**
• Pat Benatar, *Crimes of Passion*.
   Chrysalis.
Joan Armatrading, *How Cruel*. A&M.

*"This Is It" Kenny Loggins sang to take
the pop vocals prize in an upset over
Christopher Cross and Frank Sinatra.*

Marianne Faithful, *Broken English*.
   Island.
Linda Ronstadt, "How Do I Make You."
   Asylum.
Grace Slick, *Dreams*. RCA.

**BEST ROCK PERFORMANCE BY A DUO
OR GROUP WITH VOCAL**
• Bob Seger & the Silver Bullet Band,
   Against the Wind. Capitol.
Blondie, "Call Me." Chrysalis.
Pink Floyd, *The Wall*. Columbia.
Pretenders, "Brass in Pocket (I'm Special)."
   Sire.
Queen, "Another One Bites the Dust." Elektra.

Vocal harmony group the Manhattan Transfer garnered the new jazz fusion performance award for "Birdland."

BEST ROCK INSTRUMENTAL PERFORMANCE
✓ • Police, "Regatta de Blanc," track from *Regatta de Blanc*. A&M.
Dixie Dregs, *Dregs of the Earth*. Arista.
Emerson, Lake & Palmer, "Peter Gunn." Atlantic.
Jean-Luc Ponty, "Beach Girl." Atlantic.
Pretenders, "Space Invader," track from *Pretenders*. Sire.

BEST RHYTHM & BLUES SONG
(Songwriter's Award)
• "Never Knew Love Like This Before," Reggie Lucas, James Mtume. Frozen Butterfly, publisher.
"Give Me the Night," Rod Temperton. Rodsongs, publisher.
"Let's Get Serious," Lee Garrett, Stevie Wonder. Jobete Music, Black Bull Music, publisher.
"Shining Star," Leo Graham, Paul Richmond. Content Music, publisher.
"Upside Down," Bernard Edwards, Nile Rodgers, publisher. Chic.

BEST R&B VOCAL PERFORMANCE, MALE
• George Benson, *Give Me the Night*. Warner Bros./Qwest.
Larry Graham, *One in a Million You*. Warner Bros.
Jermaine Jackson, "Let's Get Serious." Motown.
Al Jarreau, "Never Givin' Up." Warner Bros.

Stevie Wonder, "Master Blaster (Jammin')." Tamla/Motown.

BEST R&B VOCAL PERFORMANCE, FEMALE
• Stephanie Mills, "Never Knew Love Like This Before." 20th Century.
Roberta Flack, *Roberta Flack Featuring Donny Hathaway*. Atlantic.
Aretha Franklin, "Can't Turn You Loose," track from *Aretha*. Arista.
Minnie Riperton, *Love Lives Forever*. Capitol.
Diana Ross, "Upside Down." Motown.

BEST R&B PERFORMANCE BY A DUO OR GROUP WITH VOCAL
• Manhattans, "Shining Star." Columbia.
Commodores, *Heroes*. Motown.
Roberta Flack with Donny Hathaway, "Back Together Again." Atlantic.
Jacksons, *Triumph*. Epic.
Gladys Knight & the Pips, *About Love*. Columbia.
Spinners, "Cupid/I've Loved You for a Long Time." Atlantic.

BEST R&B INSTRUMENTAL PERFORMANCE
• George Benson, "On Broadway," track from *Give Me the Night*. Warner Bros./Qwest.
Brothers Johnson, "Smilin' on Ya," track from *Light Up the Night*. A&M.
Deodato, "Night Cruiser." Warner Bros.
B.B. King, "When I'm Wrong," track from *Now Appearing at Ole Miss*. MCA.
David Sanborn, "Anything You Want." Warner Bros.

JAZZ FUSION PERFORMANCE, VOCAL OR INSTRUMENTAL
• Manhattan Transfer, "Birdland." Atlantic.
Earl Klugh, *Dream Come True*. United Artists.
Chuck Mangione, *Fun and Games*. A&M.
Pat Metheny, *American Garage*. ECM.
Spyro Gyra, *Catching the Sun*. MCA.
Patrick Williams, *An American Concerto*. Columbia.

Best Jazz Vocal Performance, Male

- George Benson, "Moody's Mood," track from *Give Me the Night*. Warner Bros./Qwest.

Bill Henderson, *Street of Dreams*. Discovery.

Mark Murphy, *Satisfaction Guaranteed*. Muse.

Slam Stewart, "Sidewalks of New York," track from *New York, Sounds of the Apple*. Stash.

Mel Tormé, *Tormé/A New Album*. Gryphon.

Best Jazz Vocal Performance, Female

- Ella Fitzgerald, *A Perfect Match/Ella & Basie*. Pablo.

Betty Carter, *The Audience with Betty Carter*. Betcar.

Helen Humes, *Helen Humes and the Muse All Stars*. Muse.

Helen Merrill, *Chasin' the Bird*. Inner City.

Sarah Vaughan, *Sarah Vaughan: Duke Ellington Song Book One*. Pablo.

Best Jazz Instrumental Performance, Soloist

- Bill Evans, *I Will Say Goodbye*. Fantasy.

Pepper Adams (of the Helen Merrill Sextet), *Chasin' the Bird*. Inner City.

Hank Jones, *I Remember You*. Classic Jazz.

Jimmy Knapper, *Cunningbird*. Steeplechase.

Phil Woods, *The Phil Woods Quartet—Volume One*. Clean Cuts.

Best Jazz Instrumental Performance, Group

- Bill Evans, *We Will Meet Again*. Warner Bros.

Nick Brignola, *L.A. Bound*. Sea Breeze.

Heath Brothers, *Live at the Public Theatre*. CBS.

Hank Jones, *I Remember You*. Classic Jazz.

Bobby Shew, *Bobby Shew, Outstanding in His Field*. Inner City.

Phil Woods, *The Phil Woods Quartet—Volume One*. Clean Cuts.

Best Jazz Instrumental Performance, Big Band

- Count Basie and Orchestra, *On the Road*. Pablo.

Toshiko Akiyoshi–Lew Tabackin Big Band, *Farewell*. Ascent.

Louis Bellson Big Band, *Dynamite!* Concord Jazz.

Bob Florence Big Band, *Live at Concerts by the Sea*. Trend.

Mel Lewis & the Jazz Orchestra, *Bob Brookmeyer, Composer/Arranger*. Gryphon.

Rob McConnell & the Boss Brass, *Present Perfect*. Pausa.

Best Country Song (Songwriter's Award)

- "On the Road Again," Willie Nelson. Willie Nelson Music, publisher.

"He Stopped Loving Her Today," Bobby Braddock, Curly Putman. Tree International, publisher.

"I Believe in You," Roger Cook, Sam Hogin. Roger Cook Music/Cook House Music, publishers.

"Lookin' for Love," Bob Morrison, Wanda Mallette, Patti Ryan. Southern Nights, publisher.

"Drivin' My Life Away." Eddie Rabbitt, Even Stevens, David Malloy. Debdave Music, Briarpatch Music, publishers.

Best Country Vocal Performance, Male

- George Jones, "He Stopped Loving Her Today." Epic.

George Burns, "I Wish I Was Eighteen Again." Mercury.

Johnny Lee, "Lookin' for Love." Full Moon/Asylum.

Willie Nelson, "On the Road Again." Columbia.

Eddie Rabbitt, "Drivin' My Life Away." Elektra.

Best Country Vocal Performance, Female

- Anne Murray, "Could I Have This Dance." Capitol.

Crystal Gayle, "If You Ever Change Your Mind." Columbia.

Emmylou Harris, *Roses in the Snow*. Warner Bros.

Barbara Mandrell, "The Best of Strangers." MCA.

Sissy Spacek, "Coal Miner's Daughter." MCA.

Best Country Performance by a Duo or Group with Vocal

- Roy Orbison, Emmylou Harris, "That Lovin' You Feelin' Again." Warner Bros.

Charlie Daniels Band, *In America*. Epic.

Larry Gatlin & the Gatlin Brothers Band, "Take Me to Your Lovin' Place." Columbia.

Oak Ridge Boys, "Heart of Mine." MCA.

Tanya Tucker, Glen Campbell, "Dream Lover." MCA.

Best Country Instrumental Performance
• Gilley's Urban Cowboy Band, "Orange Blossom Special/Hoedown," track from *Urban Cowboy*. Full Moon/Asylum.

Chet Atkins, "Dance with Me." RCA.

Ry Cooder, *The Long Riders*. Warner Bros.

Floyd Cramer, *Dallas*. RCA.

Danny Davis & the Nashville Brass, "Cotton Eyed Joe." RCA.

Best Gospel Performance, Contemporary or Inspirational
• Reba Rambo, Dony McGuire, B.J. Thomas, Andrae Crouch, the Archers, Walter & Tramaine Hawkins, Cynthia Clawson, *The Lord's Prayer*. Light.

Andrae Crouch, "It's Gonna Rain." Light.

Amy Grant, *Never Alone*. Myrrh.

Imperials, *One More Song for You*. Dayspring.

Michael & Stormie Omartian, *The Builder*. Myrrh.

Best Gospel Performance, Traditional
• Blackwood Brothers, *We Come to Worship*. Voice Box.

Kenneth Copeland, *In His Presence*. KCP.

Rambos, *Crossin' Over*. Heartwarming.

Speers, *Interceding*. Heartwarming.

Jimmy Swaggart, *Worship*. Jim.

Lanny Wolfe Trio, *Make a Joyful Noise...* Impact.

Best Soul Gospel Performance, Contemporary
• Shirley Caesar, *Rejoice*. Word.

Rance Allen Group, *I Feel Like Going On*. Stax.

Dynamic Disciples, "You Don't Know What God Has Done for Me." L. Brown.

Tramaine Hawkins, *Tramaine*. Light.

Kristle Murden, *I Can't Let Go*. Light.

Best Soul Gospel Performance, Traditional
• James Cleveland & the Charles Fold Singers, *Lord, Let Me Be an Instrument*. Savoy.

James Cleveland & the Voices of Cornerstone, *A Praying Spirit*. Savoy.

Gospel Keynotes, *Ain't No Stopping Us Now*. Nashboro.

Dorothy Norwood, *God Can*. Savoy.

O'Neal Twins, *He Chose Me*. Savoy.

Albertina Walker with James Cleveland, *Please Be Patient With Me*. Savoy.

Best Inspirational Performance
• Debby Boone, *With My Song I Will Praise Him*. Lamb & Lion.

Commodores, "Jesus Is Love," track from *Heroes*. Motown.

Bob Dylan, *Saved*. Columbia.

Willie Nelson, *Family Bible*. Songbird.

B.J. Thomas, "Everything Always Works Out for the Best." Songbird.

Best Ethnic or Traditional Recording
• *Rare Blues*, Dr. Isaiah Ross, Maxwell Street Jimmy, Big Joe William, Son House, Rev. Robert Wilkins, Little Brother Montgomery, Sunnyland Slim. Norman Dayron, producer. Takoma.

Atlanta Blues: 1933, Blind Willie McTell, Curley Weaver, Buddy Moss. John Edwards Memorial Foundation.

Boil the Breakfast Early, Chieftains 9. Columbia.

Kidney Stew Is Fine, Eddie "Cleanhead" Vinson. Delmark.

Queen Ida & the Bon Temps Zydeco Band in New Orleans, Queen Ida. GNP/ Crescendo.

Best Latin Recording
• *La Onda va Bien*, Cal Tjader Sextet. Concord Jazz.

Dancemania '80, Tito Puente. Tico.

Hey, Julio Iglesias. Discos CBS International.

Irakere 2, Irakere. Columbia.

Rican/Struction, Ray Barretto. Fania.

Best Instrumental Arrangement
• Quincy Jones, Jerry Hey, "Dinorah, Dinorah," track from *Give Me the Night* (George Benson). Warner Bros.

Jorge Calandrelli, "Forget the Woman," track from *Morning Thunder* (Eddie Daniels). CBS.

Dave Grusin, "Marcosinho," track from *The Hawk* (Dave Valentin). GRP.

Bob Brookmeyer, "Skylark," track from *Bob Brookmeyer Composer/Arranger* (Mel Lewis). Gryphon.

Claus Ogerman, "Wave," track from *Terra Brasilis* (Antonio Carlos Jobim). Warner Bros.

BEST ARRANGEMENT FOR VOICES
• Janis Siegel, "Birdland," track from *Extensions* (Manhattan Transfer). Atlantic.

Joe Puerta, Burleigh Drummond, David Pack, "Biggest Part of Me" (Ambrosia). Warner Bros.

Rod Temperton, "Give Me the Night" (George Benson). Warner Bros./Qwest.

Gene Puerling, "Sweet Georgia Brown," track from *Friends* (Singers Unlimited). Pausa.

Alan Paul, Jay Graydon, "Twilight Zone/Twilight Tone," track from *Extensions* (Manhattan Transfer). Atlantic.

Andrew Lloyd Webber took two prizes as composer and coproducer of Evita.

BEST ARRANGEMENT ACCOMPANYING VOCALIST(S)
• Christopher Cross, Michael Omartian, "Sailing" (Christopher Cross). Warner Bros.

Don Costa, "Theme from *New York, New York*" (Frank Sinatra). Reprise.

David Cunningham, "Money" (Flying Lizards). Virgin.

Rob McConnell, "Tangerine," track from *the Singers Unlimited with Rob*

McConnell & the Boss Brass (Singers Unlimited). Pausa.

Joe Puerta, Burleigh Drummond, David Pack, "Biggest Part of Me" (Ambrosia). Warner Bros.

BEST INSTRUMENTAL COMPOSITION
• "The Empire Strikes Back," John Williams. Fox Fanfare Music, Inc., Bantha Music, publishers.

"An American Concerto," Patrick Williams. Keel One Music, publisher.

"Give It All You Got," Chuck Mangione. Gates Music, publisher.

"The Imperial March (Darth Vader's Theme)," John Williams. Fox Fanfare Music, Inc., Bantha Music, publisher.

"Yoda's Theme," John Williams. Fox Fanfare Music, Inc., Bantha Music, publishers.

BEST CAST SHOW ALBUM
• *Evita*, American recording. Andrew Lloyd Webber, composer. Tim Rice, lyrics. Andrew Lloyd Webber, Tim Rice, producers. MCA.

Barnum, Cy Coleman, composer. Michael Stewart, lyrics. Cy Coleman, Mike Berniker, producers. CBS Masterworks.

A Day in Hollywood/A Night in the Ukraine, Frank Lazarus, Jerry Herman, composers. Dick Vosburgh, Jerry Herman, lyrics. Hugh Fordin, producer. DRG.

Oklahoma! Richard Rodgers, composer. Oscar Hammerstein II, lyrics. Thomas Z. Shepard, producer. RCA.

One Mo' Time, songs by 27 different songwriters performed in early Black vaudeville days. Carl Seltzer, producer. Warner Bros.

BEST ALBUM OF ORIGINAL SCORE WRITTEN FOR A MOTION PICTURE OR A TELEVISION SPECIAL
• *The Empire Strikes Back*, John Williams. RSO.

Fame, Michael Gore, Anthony Evans, Paul McCrane, Dean Pitchford, Lesley Gore, Robert F. Colesberry. RSO.

One Trick Pony, Paul Simon. Warner Bros.

Stevie Wonder's Journey Through the Secret Life of Plants, Stevie Wonder, Michael Sembello, Stephanie Andrews, Yvonne Wright. Tamla/Motown.

√ *Urban Cowboy*, J.D. Souther, Boz Scaggs, David Foster, Jerry Foster, Bill Rice, Brian Collins, Robby Campbell, Joe Walsh, Bob Morrison, Johnny Wilson, Dan Fogelberg, Bob Seger, Wayland Holyfield, Bob House, Wanda Mallette, Patti Ryan. Full Moon/ Asylum.

BEST CLASSICAL ALBUM
• *Berg: Lulu*, Pierre Boulez conducting Orchestre de l'Opera de Paris (solos: Stratas, Minton, Mazura, Blankenheim). Guenther Breest, Michael Horwarth, producers. Deutsche Grammophon.
Bartók: Concerto for Violin and Orchestra, Zubin Mehta conducting Los Angeles Philharmonic (solo: Zukerman). Andrew Kazdin, producer. Columbia.
Berg: Concerto for Violin and Orchestra; Stravinsky: Concerto in D Major for Violin and Orchestra, Seiji Ozawa conducting Boston Symphony (solo: Perlman). Rainer Brock, producer. Deutsche Grammophon.
Bruckner: Symphony No. 6 in A Major, Sir Georg Solti conducting Chicago Symphony. Ray Minshull, producer. London.
Ruggles: Complete Music, Michael Tilson Thomas conducting Buffalo Philharmonic. Steven Epstein, producer. Columbia.

BEST CLASSICAL ORCHESTRAL RECORDING
(Conductor's Award)
• *Bruckner: Symphony No. 6 in A Major*, Sir Georg Solti conducting Chicago Symphony. Ray Minshull, producer. London.
Beethoven: Symphonies (9), Leonard Bernstein conducting Vienna Philharmonic. Hanno Rinke, producer. Deutsche Grammophon.
Respighi: Feste Romane/Fountains of Rome, Michael Tilson Thomas conducting Los Angeles Philharmonic. Steven Epstein, producer. Columbia.
Ruggles: Complete Music, Michael Tilson Thomas conducting Buffalo Philharmonic. Steven Epstein, producer. Columbia.
Shostakovich: Symphony No. 5, Leonard Bernstein conducting New York Philharmonic. John McClure, producer. Columbia.

BEST CHAMBER MUSIC PERFORMANCE (INSTRUMENTAL OR VOCAL)
• Itzhak Perlman, Pinchas Zukerman, *Music for Two Violins (Moszkowski: Suite for Two Violins; Shostakovich: Duets; Prokofiev: Sonata for Two Violins)*. Angel.
Daniel Barenboim, Luben Yordanoff, Albert Tetard, Claude Desurmont, *Messiaen: Quartet for the End of Time*. Deutsche Grammophon.
Cleveland Quartet, *Beethoven: Early Quartets, Op. 18*. RCA.
Juilliard Quartet, *Schubert: Quartet No. 15 in G Major, Op. 161*. Columbia.
Pinchas Zukerman, Marc Neikrug, *Debussy: Sonata No. 3 in G Minor for Violin & Piano; Fauré: Sonata in A Major for Violin and Piano*. Columbia.

BEST CLASSICAL PERFORMANCE, INSTRUMENTAL SOLOIST(S) (WITH ORCHESTRA) (Tie)
• Itzhak Perlman (Seiji Ozawa conducting Boston Symphony), *Berg: Concerto for Violin and Orchestra; Stravinsky: Concerto in D Major for Violin and Orchestra*. Deutsche Grammophon.
• Itzhak Perlman, Mstislav Rostropovich (Bernard Haitink conducting Concertgebouw Orchestra), *Brahms: Concerto in A Minor for Violin and Cello ("Double Concerto")*. Angel.
Maurice André (Maurice André conducting Franz Liszt Chamber Orchestra), *Bach for Trumpet*. Angel.
James Galway (I Solisti di Zagreb), *Telemann: Concertos in G & C for Flute; Suite in A Minor*. RCA.
Gerard Schwarz (Gerard Schwarz conducting Y Chamber Symphony of New York), *The Classic Trumpet Concerti of Haydn & Hummel*. Delos.
Pinchas Zukerman (Zubin Mehta conducting Los Angeles Philharmonic), *Bartók: Concerto for Violin and Orchestra*. Columbia.

BEST CLASSICAL PERFORMANCE, INSTRUMENTAL SOLOIST(S) (WITHOUT ORCHESTRA)
• Itzhak Perlman, *The Spanish Album*. Angel.
Glenn Gould, *Bach: Toccatas, Volume II*. Columbia.

Ruth Laredo, *Rachmaninoff: Music for Piano, Volume 7 (Sonatas Nos. 1 & 2)*. Columbia.

Joshua Rifkin, *Digital Ragtime, Music of Scott Joplin*. Angel.

Rudolf Serkin, *Brahms: Variations and Fugue on a Theme by Handel*. Columbia.

Leo Smit, *Copland: The Complete Music for Solo Piano*. Columbia.

BEST OPERA RECORDING

• *Berg: Lulu* (complete version), Pierre Boulez conducting Orchestre de l'Opera de Paris (solos: Stratas, Yvonne Minton, Mazura, Toni Blankenheim). Guenther Breest, Michael Horwarth, producers. Deutsche Grammophon.

Bartók: Bluebeard's Castle, Sir Georg Solti conducting London Philharmonic (solos: Sass, Kovats). Christopher Raeburn, producer. London.

Debussy: Pelleas et Melisande, Herbert von Karajan conducting Berlin Philharmonic (solos: von Stade, Stilwell). Michel Glotz, producer. Angel.

Puccini: La Bohéme, James Levine conducting National Philharmonic, Ambrosian Chorus (solos: Scotto, Kraus, Neblett, Milnes). John Mordler, producer. Angel.

Weill: Silverlake, Julius Rudel conducting New York City Opera Orchestra and Chorus (solos: Grey, Neill, Hynes, Harrold, Bonazzi). Eric Salzman, producer. Nonesuch.

BEST CHORAL PERFORMANCE, CLASSICAL (OTHER THAN OPERA)

• Norbert Balatsch, chorus master. Carlo Maria Giulini conducting Philharmonia Chorus and Orchestra, *Mozart: Requiem*. Angel.

Claudio Abbado conducting London Symphony Chorus and Orchestra, *Prokofiev: Alexander Nevsky*. Deutsche Grammophon.

Thomas Hilbish conducting University of Michigan Chamber Choir and Chamber Ensemble, *Menotti: The Unicorn, the Gorgon and the Manticore*. University of Michigan School of Music.

John Oliver, chorus master, Tanglewood Festival Chorus. Seiji Ozawa conducting Boston Symphony, *Schoenberg: Gurrelieder*. Philips.

Robert Shaw conducting Atlanta Symphony Chorus and Orchestra, *Boito: Prologue to Mefistofele*. Telarc.

BEST CLASSICAL VOCAL SOLOIST PERFORMANCE

• Leontyne Price (Henry Lewis conducting Philharmonic Orchestra), *Prima Donna, Volume 5, Great Soprano Arias from Handel to Britten*. RCA.

Elly Ameling (Jorg Demus, accompanist), *Mozart: Songs*. Seraphim.

Judith Blegen, (Pierre Boulez conducting New York Philharmonic), *Berg: Lulu Suite*. Columbia.

Kiri Te Kanawa (Andrew Davis conducting London Symphony), *(R.) Strauss: Four Last Songs and Orchestral Songs*. Columbia.

Jessye Norman (Pierre Boulez conducting New York Philharmonic), *Berg: Der Wein*, Concert Aria. Columbia.

Frederica von Stade (Andrew Davis conducting London Philharmonic), *Mahler: Songs of a Wayfarer and Ruckert Songs*. Columbia.

BEST ENGINEERED RECORDING, CLASSICAL

• Karl-August Naegler, *Berg: Lulu* (complete version), (Pierre Boulez conducting Orchestre de l'Opera de Paris; solos: Teresa Stratas, Yvonne Minton, Franz Mazura, Toni Blankenheim). Deutsche Grammophon.

Almeida: First Concerto for Guitar & Orchestra, (Laurindo Almeida, Elmer Ramsey conducting Los Angeles Orchestra de Camera). Concord Concerto.

Robert Norberg, Mitchell Tanenbaum, *Bach: The Six Brandenburg Concertos*, (Gerard Schwarz conducting Los Angeles Chamber Orchestra). Angel.

Bud Graham, Ray Moore, *Bartók: Concerto for Violin and Orchestra*, (Pinchas Zukerman, Zubin Mehta conducting Los Angeles Philharmonic). Columbia.

Michael Gray. *Brahms: Concerto in A Minor for Violin and Cello ("Double Concerto")*, (Itzhak Perlman, Mstislav Rostropovich, Bernard Haitink conducting Concertgebouw Orchestra). Angel.

John McClure, Ed Michalski. *Shostakovich: Symphony No. 5*, (Leonard Bernstein conducting New York Philharmonic). Columbia.

CLASSICAL PRODUCER OF THE YEAR
• Robert Woods
Steven Epstein
Andrew Kazdin
John McClure
Paul Myers

BEST COMEDY RECORDING
• *No Respect*, Rodney Dangerfield. Casablanca.
Contractual Obligation, Monty Python. Arista.
Holy Smoke, Richard Pryor. Laff.
Live at St. Douglas Convent, Father Guido Sarducci. Warner Bros.
Live from New York, Gilda Radner. Warner Bros.

BEST SPOKEN WORD, DOCUMENTARY, OR DRAMA RECORDING
• *Gertrude Stein, Gertrude Stein, Gertrude Stein*, Pat Carroll. Caedmon.
Adventures of Luke Skywalker, The Empire Strikes Back, original cast with narration. Pat Glasser, album producer. RSO.
A Curb in the Sky (James Thurber), Peter Ustinov. Caedmon.
I Sing Because I'm Happy, Volumes 1 & 2, Mahalia Jackson. Folkways.
Obediently Yours/Orson Welles, Orson Welles. Mark 56.

BEST RECORDING FOR CHILDREN
• *In Harmony/A Sesame Street Record*, Doobie Brothers, James Taylor, Carly Simon, Bette Midler, Muppets, Al Jarreau, Linda Ronstadt, Wendy Waldman, Libby Titus & Dr. John, Livingston Taylor, George Benson & Pauline Wilson, Lucy Simon, Kate Taylor & the Simon/Taylor Family. Lucy Simon, David Levine, producers. Sesame Street.

Big Bird's Birdtime Stories, Sesame Street Muppets and cast. Jim Henson, Muppets creator. Jim Timmens, album producer. Sesame Street.
Christmas Eve on Sesame Street, Muppets and Sesame Street cast. Jim Henson, Muppets creator. Dulcy Singer, Jon Stone, album producers. Sesame Street.
Love, Sesame Street Muppets and cast. Jim Henson, Muppets creator. Arthur Shimkin, album producer. Sesame Street.
The People in Your Neighborhood, Sesame Street Muppets. Jim Henson, Muppets creator. Jeffrey Moss, album producer. Sesame Street.

BEST ENGINEERED RECORDING
• James Guthrie, *The Wall* (Pink Floyd). Columbia.
Chet Himes, *Christopher Cross* (Christopher Cross). Warner Bros.
Bill Schnee, *Growing Up in Hollywood Town* (Lincoln Mayorga, Amanda McBroom). Sheffield Lab.
Bill Schnee, *New Baby* (Don Randi, Quest). Sheffield Lab.
Bruce Swedien. "Give Me the Night," track from *Give Me the Night* (George Benson). Warner Bros./Qwest.

BEST ALBUM PACKAGE
(Art Director's Award)
• Roy Kohara, *Against the Wind* (Bob Seger & the Silver Bullet Band). Capitol.
John Berg, *Chicago XIV* (Chicago). Columbia.
Ron Coro, Johnny Lee, *Cats*. Elektra.
Vigon Nahas Vigon, *Tusk* (Fleetwood Mac). Warner Bros.
Paula Scher, *One on One* (Bob James, Earl Klugh). Columbia.

BEST ALBUM NOTES
(Annotator's Award)
• David McClintock, *Trilogy: Past, Present & Future* (Frank Sinatra). Reprise.
David Evans, Bruce Bastin, *Atlanta Blues: 1933* (Blind Willie McTell, Curley Weaver, Buddy Moss). John Edwards Memorial Foundation.
Lorene Lortie, *Elvis Aaron Presley*. RCA.
John McDonough, Richard M. Sudhalter, *Lester Young (Giants of Jazz)*. Time Life.

Dan Morgenstern, *Chicago Concert, 1956* (Louis Armstrong). Columbia.

BEST HISTORICAL REISSUE ALBUM
• *Segovia, The EMI Recordings 1927–39.* Keith Hardwick, producer. Angel.
Early History of the Phonograph Record. George Garabedian, producer. Mark 56.
First Edition/The Golden Age of Broadway. C.E. Crumpacker, producer. RCA Special Production.
The Guitarists (Giants of Jazz), Jerry Korn, Michael Brooks, producers. Time Life.
Songs of the Depression: Happy Days Are Here Again, George Spitzer, Michael Brooks, producers. Book of the Month Records.

PRODUCER OF THE YEAR
• Phil Ramone
Quincy Jones
Michael Omartian
Queen, Mack
Stevie Wonder

"John Is with Us Here Tonight"

When John Lennon was gunned down in front of his New York City apartment building on a cold, dark morning in December, 1980, in many ways it really was the day the music died.

Among modern music visionaries, Lennon had been the keeper of rock's sacred flame. His music filled the public mind with lofty visions of a world without war ("Imagine," "Give Peace a Chance"), and continued to push rock's frontiers ever further in his newer work — even when it wasn't appreciated. "Once Lennon left the safety and prestige of the [Beatles], he was relegated to the mavericks," Robert Hilburn wrote in *The Los Angeles Times*. "After all, wasn't he the kook who went traipsing around with Yoko Ono looking like two 'gurus in drag'?"

"Gurus in drag" John Lennon and Yoko Ono: Ono's acceptance of the LP prize for Double Fantasy *after Lennon's death was one of Grammy's greatest dramas.*

Like most visionaries, Lennon had been misunderstood in his lifetime and, now that he was gone, the music industry clearly felt it owed his memory an overdue tribute. Lennon was the only member of the Beatles not to receive a Grammy since the Fab Four busted up in 1970. Worse, he'd never even been nominated. Now he and Ono had five nods for *Double Fantasy*, their eccentric valentine to each other that also included serious musings on how to right — or at least survive — a world gone mad. Hilburn and other critics applauded "the quiet wisdom of songs like Lennon's 'Watching the Wheels' or Ono's moving 'Hard Times Are Over.'" Smitten record-buyers turned tracks like "(Just Like) Starting Over" and "Woman" into hit singles. At the Grammys, "Starting Over" was up for Record of the Year, *Double Fantasy* for 1981's best album.

As the awards drama at the Shrine Auditorium in Los Angeles unfolded, Lennon and Ono lost their first three bids before the showdown came over Album of the Year. *Double Fantasy* was pitted against Kim Carnes's *Mistaken*

Identity in what critics were calling a close race, but even Carnes admitted she was rooting for the Lennons, weeping quietly in her seat as everyone waited for the announcement of the winner. ("How could you help not crying?" she later asked reporters, referring to the collective mood of mourning that engulfed the ceremony at that moment.) When *Double Fantasy* was named the winner, a thunderous standing ovation greeted Yoko Ono and Sean Lennon (Ono's and John Lennon's son) as they appeared on stage. The widow of rock's reigning martyr looked appropriately regal but emotionally racked. Fighting back tears, she told the crowd, "I think John is with us here tonight. John and I were always proud and happy that we were part of the human race, who made good music for the earth and for the universe."

It was, in the words of the *L.A. Times*, "one of the most dramatic moments in the 24-year history of the record industry competition."

Once Yoko and Sean resumed their seats, Kenny Loggins and Pat Benatar read through the list of contenders for Record of the Year. Once they "got to the fourth nominated record, Lennon's '(Just Like) Starting Over,' the television camera caught Ono crying," noted the *Times*. Again, Lennon and Ono's chief competition for the year's top Grammy was Carnes, whose "Bette Davis Eyes" was both a critical and commercial hit. The *L.A. Times* was among those that predicted "Eyes" would have it: "Over the past 23 years, the Record of the Year prize has gone to a No. 1 hit 15 times and to the No. 1 hit of the year 6 times. This wry, rock inflected smash could easily make that 16 and 7." When "Bette Davis Eyes" prevailed, the *Times* added, "It probably deserved to win. At the moment it was announced, though, Carnes's victory paled in comparison to Ono's loss."

"My mind was a little numb during the best-album award," Carnes told reporters backstage later. "But when I won best record, my head sort of exploded."

Carnes was a former New Christy Minstrel who, along with husband/ musician David Ellingson, also distinguished herself as a songwriter for Frank Sinatra, Barbra Streisand, Anne Murray, and other star talent. Her career as a singer was less noteworthy: Her husky voice often got her dismissed as "a female Rod Stewart" and, even as late as the mid-1980s, her best songs like "What About Me" always seemed to sell best when they were recorded by other artists, like Kenny Rogers and James Ingram. Ironically, "Bette Davis Eyes" — her biggest vocal hit and also winner of Song of the Year — was written by other tunesmiths: Donna Weiss and Jackie DeShannon. Reporters asked Weiss backstage what Bette Davis herself thought about the song. She answered: "Bette thanked us for making her part of the modern world. She says she's now a big hit with her grandson." After the single won Song of the Year, Davis sent roses to the artists.

> **When Record and Song of the Year "Bette Davis Eyes" became a hit, Davis said she became "part of the modern world."**

The Washington Post made a daring move this year when it polled a number of industry experts and asked them to handicap the top 16 awards. "There are only four shoo-ins," the group concluded: One was Carnes for best female pop vocal performance.

SECURITY PACIFIC COLLECTION/ L.A. PUBLIC LIBRARY

Lena Horne scored a stirring career comeback and a pop vocals prize for her Broadway LP The Lady and Her Music.

The winner in that category turned out to be an older music pro instead — Lena Horne. "It was a year for catching up with overlooked artists of the past," the *Post* said in the its wrap-up coverage. The *L.A. Herald Examiner* declared that this year's Grammys "belonged to the legends."

Horne began her career at age 17 when she was a crooner and hoofer at New York's famed Cotton Club. While still in her 20s, she performed at Carnegie Hall and began starring in a string of Hollywood films that would establish her as the first great black singing screen star — one with loads of class and talent. At the age of 64, Horne took her act to Broadway where a one-woman concert retrospective of her

work, *The Lady and Her Music,* was met by rave notices and sold-out audiences. "It's a lifetime achievement of a legend," said producer Quincy Jones as he picked up a Grammy for the LP's second award of the night: Best Cast Show Album.

But it was Jones himself — already a legend at 49 — who turned out to be the biggest winner of the night. His latest album, *The Dude,* which included contributions from singer James Ingram, scored a total of 11 nominations (although not all for him personally). Since Jones was also established as a leading producer of other artists' works, he had three additional nominations for non-*Dude* music such as Lena Horne's LP, as well as an accolade he finally won after being overlooked for the last three years: Producer of the Year.

"Jones finally received the kind of recognition befitting the studio genius he is," the *Herald Examiner* declared. "Jones, in fact, has been the best record producer in the world since George Martin's days of duty with the Beatles."

"If anyone owned the 24th annual Grammy Awards, it was Quincy Jones," the same paper said. Jones won five awards in all, the last three of which were for *The Dude*: the r&b group vocal performance award, an instrumental arrangement/accompanying vocals prize for *Dude* track "Ai No Corrida," and an instrumental arrangement trophy for "Velas." "You have to stay around a long time for moments like this," Jones said backstage later as he admired all five Grammys in his grasp. "Man, I've been nominated something like 60 times. I've seen four decades of change. Just my nominations had blown me away. But this," he added, holding up the golden statuettes with a smile, "this is something else. What a beautiful night. God bless."

The torrent of honors for Jones helped to contribute toward James

Ingram's victory for best r&b male vocal performance for a track from *The Dude* entitled "One Hundred Ways." (*The Washington Post* called the win "a mild upset" since Ingram was "a studio artist who doesn't even have his own record out.") Presenter James Brown (who at that time had never even been nominated for a Grammy) was more than mildly surprised by Ingram's victory, however. When he opened the envelope, the Godfather of Soul said, "and the award goes to ... Good God! I can't stand it!"

Ingram was also up for Best New Artist, but was considered a long shot thanks to another *Washington Post* "shoo-in" who actually came through: Sheena Easton.

Easton was one of the hip young singers vanquished by music's reigning "Lady" Lena Horne for the pop singing laurels. Easton lost to Horne for the same hit that made her seem so promising as Best New Artist: the title theme song to the latest James Bond flick *For Your Eyes Only*. The suddenly triumphant newcomer obviously felt she had paid her dues, though. "I wanted this *sooo* much," she said in her thick Scottish brogue while clutching her Grammy. "I'm glad at the party [afterward] I don't have to be gracious to everybody."

The rest of the pop singing honors were seized by artists who also struck gold in the jazz line-up. Vocal acrobat Al Jarreau had been well known in jazz circles for the previous half-dozen years, but now he was gaining a broader audience thanks to his best album nominee *Breakin' Away*, which earned him the pop male vocal award, plus the equivalent jazz prize for its "Blue Rondo à la Turk" track. The vocal quartet Manhattan Transfer won its first Grammy last year but now claimed two more: the jazz group vocal award for "Until I Met You (Corner Pocket)" and the group pop vocal honors for "Boy from New York City," both from their *Mecca for Moderns* LP. To win the pop prize, the Manhattan Transfer beat perennial loser Diana Ross, who was the odds-on favorite to prevail with her "Endless Love" duet with Lionel Richie, which was also considered a close contender for Record and Song of the Year.

Since this year's Grammys "belonged to the legends," Ella Fitzgerald's return for the third year in a row as recipient of the jazz female vocal award (for her performance at the Montreux Jazz Festival in Switzerland) seemed appropriate. Other artists honored for their recent work in the Alpine country were Chick Corea and Gary Burton, who had previously won the group instrumental prize in 1979, but now reprised their victory for a recording of a joint concert held in Zurich in 1979. The legendary sax player/composer/bandleader Gerry Mulligan had been prominent in the jazz field since the late 1940s when he worked with Miles Davis and Gene Krupa ("You feel as if you're listening to the past, present, and future of jazz all at one time," Dave Brubeck once said about Mulligan's music), but he received his first Grammy this year for *Walk on the Water*, a broad sampling of his original compositions. Tenor sax player John Coltrane died in 1967, but he received an instrumental award posthumously for *Bye Bye Blackbird*, the recording of a concert he performed in the mid-1960s that had not been released on disc earlier.

> *Pop singer and TV soap opera star Rick Springfield trounced "shoo-in" Bruce Springsteen.*

RCA

"I can't embroider or nothin' so I started writing songs," said Dolly Parton, winner of Best Country Song and a singing prize for "9 to 5."

Sax player/singer Grover Washington, Jr.'s bid for the jazz fusion award was another of *The Washington Post*'s "shoo-ins" that came out as predicted. His victorious *Winelight* LP contained the hit single "Just the Two of Us" that lost its bids to be Record and Song of the Year but nonetheless won as the year's Best Rhythm & Blues Song (it was written by Bill Withers, William Salter, and Ralph MacDonald).

"In the rock field, the female vocalist award is a tight battle between Pat Benatar (last year's winner in the same category) and Stevie Nicks (two-Grammy winner as part of Fleetwood Mac)," *The Washington Post* reported. "Bruce Springsteen, a non-winner despite platinum raves, may finally get a thank-you in the rock male category." Six out of the eight experts polled by *The Wash-*

ington Post said Springsteen was a cinch to get it for his LP *The River*.

Benatar ended up prevailing for a second year in a row (for "Fire & Ice" from her hit album *Precious Time*), while Springsteen was defeated by pop heart-throb Rick Springfield. *The New York Times* reported: "Springfield's victory over Bruce Springsteen and Rod Stewart in the rock vocal category was a characteristic example of the Grammys' tendency to reflect commercial performance — Mr. Springfield had a huge hit single with his 'Jessie's Girl' — more accurately than artistic accomplishment. Mr. Springsteen and Mr. Stewart both made their best albums in a number of years in 1981." Springfield was bolstered by his enormous popularity as an actor on the daytime soap opera *General Hospital* on which he played the character Dr. Noah Drake. "The record, you know, was just another record on the market," Springfield told reporters backstage. "But I really believe *General Hospital* gave it the hook, the kick in the rear."

The Police raided the last two rock categories, beating the Rolling Stones, who still hadn't gathered a single Grammy and were heavily favored to win finally for "Start Me Up" from *Tattoo You*. But with their critical and commercial success, *Zenyatta Mondatta*, the Police prevailed, taking the group vocal prize for the single "Don't Stand So Close to Me" and the instrumental performance laurels ("Behind My Camel"), which they retained from last year.

The Washington Post foretold only one of the country prizes correctly: "In the female country category, it's an acknowledged old-timer (Dolly Parton and '9 to 5') against a veteran who's just found success this year (Juice Newton and 'Queen of Hearts'). Look for a Parton victory."

Parton received four nominations for "9 to 5," three of them for composition. She started writing songs on a film set while she was bored just like Barbra Streisand did when she penned "Love Theme from *A Star Is Born* (Evergreen)." "The hardest thing was the long wait between shots," Parton once told *Billboard* about the filming of *9 to 5*, the movie in which she costarred with Jane Fonda and Lily Tomlin. "I can't embroider or nothin' like that, so I figured if I started writing songs, it would change my mood. I was amazed at how easily I could do it."

The outcome of her writing debut was so good that the tune was picked up as the film's official theme song and was competing at the Grammys for Song of the Year, Best Country Song, Best Female Country Vocal Performance, and best film score. It reaped both Best Country Song and the vocal performance trophy. (It lost Best Song at the Oscars to "Fame.") The film score honors went once again to John Williams, whose victorious *Raiders of the Lost Ark* score followed previous winners *Jaws* (1975), *Star Wars* (1977), *Close Encounters of the Third Kind* (1978), *Superman* (1979), and *The Empire Strikes Back* (1980).

The victory of "9 to 5" as Best Country Song was surprising considering that its chief challenger was "Elvira," sung by the Oak Ridge Boys, which had been the biggest-selling country song ever recorded in Nashville up to that point and had also been hailed as Single of the Year by both the Country Music Association and the Academy of Country Music. The Oak Ridge Boys had won four Grammys in the past, all for singing religious music, but when they netted one more for "Elvi-ra," it marked their first and only trophy for a country performance.

The Washington Post sized up the line-up for the male vocals accolade this way: "Eddie Rabbitt, who is basically a pop artist recording in Nashville, is a favorite as country male, though George Jones can't be discounted." *The Los Angeles Herald Examiner* called the whole category "a powerhouse line-up including Willie Nelson, George Jones, Eddie Rabbitt (well, he sells a lot of records), Ronnie Milsap, and — the most deserving and adventurous choice — John Anderson."

This year the Grammys "belonged to the legends."

The winner: Milsap, for his best-selling single "(There's) No Gettin' Over Me,"his third Grammy. It had been five years since Chet Atkins last snared the instrumental category, but he now reclaimed it with *After All These Years*, which gave him his seventh statuette in all.

Repeaters once again dominated the religious awards: Andrae Crouch (*Don't Give Up*, his fifth Grammy and fourth in a row), B.J. Thomas (*Amazing Grace*, his fifth consecutive award), and the Imperials (*Priority*, their fourth). Past Grammy victors J.D. Sumner and James Blackwood joined a number of other noted religious singers to take the traditional gospel performance prize for a talent roundup called *The Masters V*. Al Green would go on to win more than a half-dozen Grammys over the next decade, but he reaped his first for Best Traditional Soul Gospel Performance for *The Lord Will Make a Way*. Earlier in his career, Green had distinguished himself as a soul singer with such hits as "Let's Stay Together," but after he became a minister in the late 1970s, he would only perform gospel music.

B.B. King had won a Grammy back in 1970, and now he claimed a second for *There Must Be a Better World Somewhere* as Best Ethnic or Traditional Recording, "a curiously titled category usually reserved for blues artists" like King, noted *The New York Times*. Backstage, King told reporters that he was not a typical blues artist, which he described this way: "His pants are worn out and his shoes don't have laces and his cap is on backwards and he has a cigarette hanging out of the eastern corner of his lip.

"Now look at me," King added, pointing to his dapper tuxedo. "I rest my case."

"Guajira Pa La Jeva" reaped Best Latin Recording for Clare Fischer, who *The New York Times* said "is hardly a Latin musician, but Fischer has made a number of Latin-tinged pop-jazz albums over the years."

The Muppets continued to dominate the children's category when *Sesame Country* trounced those cartoon rockers the Chipmunks, who had not won a Grammy since 1960. The Muppets' latest winner featured a host of celebrity c&w singers such as Glen Campbell, Loretta Lynn, Tanya Tucker, and Crystal Gayle. The Chipmunks were also trounced for Best Comedy Recording by Richard Pryor, who dominated the category from 1974 to 1976, but hadn't scored another win since. This time he was honored for *Rev. Du Rite*, a spoof of how ministers use religious double-talk in sermons. "I come not here to plague you with the questions of the no answers," says Pryor as the Rev. Du Rite, "and you can't get to the left without the right ...." Most of Pryor's material on the LP was taped originally in 1976, which caused some critics to protest its eligibility. The race was also controversial because a track from Mel Brooks's film LP *History of the World — Part I* called "The Inquisition" was competing against its own album.

N.A.R.A.S. introduced a new category in 1981 that signaled a significant change in how music was being appreciated: Video of the Year. To be eligible, the music videos did not simply have to be shown on the new MTV cable channel or elsewhere on TV, but they had to be produced for the consumer home video market. In noting the first winner, *The Washington Post* gave away its own "Irony and Fair Warning Award to onetime Monkee Michael Nesmith for capturing the first-ever Video Grammy for 'Elephant Parts.' Nesmith, an industry maverick, has predicted that audio-only records will be obsolete within 10 years. He received a plaque rather than the traditional Victrola-shaped award."

Back in 1972, Sir Georg Solti and the Chicago Symphony won the Classical Album of the Year award for their rendition of Mahler's Symphony No. 8. In 1981, the honor was renamed Best Classical Album and went again to Solti and the Chicago Symphony for another work by Mahler — this time his second symphony — which also took the new prize for Best Classical Orchestra Recording (which replaced the earlier performance award). Solti had conducted the work earlier in his career using the London Symphony Orchestra, but this rendition was applauded by critics for being lighter. *High Fidelity* complained of some perceptible "impatience" on Solti's part, but added, "The orchestra plays magnificently and Sir Georg conducts brilliantly."

Itzhak Perlman won only half as many Grammys as he reaped in 1980 when he claimed two this year: for Best Chamber Music Performance with Vladimir Ashkenazy and Lynn Harrell for their Tchaikovsky Piano Trio in A Minor, and the soloist's (with orchestra) award for his participation in the salute to fellow violinist Isaac Stern on the occasion of Stern's 60th birthday, which was celebrated at the New York Philharmonic's 1980 opening night. *High Fidelity* predicted Perlman fans "will be ecstatic" over the birthday tribute, which also won Best Engineered Classical Recording.

The soloist award (without orchestral accompaniment) went to Vladimir Horowitz (*The Horowitz Concerts, 1979–80*), who lately spurned studio recordings in favor of concert performances, saying, "I could polish ... but I prefer the excitement." For the choral prize, Neville Marriner conducted the Chorus of the Academy of St. Martin-in-the-Fields in Haydn's *The Creation*, which they performed, said *High Fidelity*, with masterful "poise and buoyancy."

Throughout his conducting career, Sir Charles Mackerras had distinguished himself as one of the principal interpretors of works by Leos Janácek. For this year's Best Opera Recording, the first-time winner used some of the world's greatest Czech singers along with his Vienna Philharmonic orchestra to dramatize the composer's final opera, *From the House of the Dead*, which he based on Dostoevsky's recollections of his imprisonment in a Siberian labor camp. Soon after Janácek's death in 1928, the opera suffered considerable changes at the hands of two of his students who considered it unfinished. Mackerras's rendition was the first recording of the composer's original work. "At last it is possible to hear *House of the Dead* in all its spare, stark and uncompromising majesty,"

Vocal acrobat Al Jarreau proved dexterous enough to pull off wins in both the pop and jazz slots for Breakin' Away.

High Fidelity wrote, adding that Mackerras's conducting "is little short of brilliant and his stabbingly unsentimental interpretation penetrates right to the heart of the music." Mackerras's producer, James Mallinson, who also oversaw Solti's London recordings, was named Classical Producer of the Year.

Roundup celebrity concerts rarely get rave critical notices, but a notable exception occurred when Joan Sutherland, Marilyn Horne, and Luciano Pavarotti shared the stage at Lincoln Center and soon thereafter also shared the soloist's performance Grammy for singing excerpts from Verdi's *Otello*, Bellini's *Norma*, and Ponchielli's *La Gioconda*.

The Grammycast got good notices again this year, particularly for host John Denver, who, said *The Washington Post*, "was quite smooth, a far cry from the petrified Paul Simon last year." Entertainment included the Oak Ridge Boys singing "Elvira," Rick Springfield crooning "Jessie's Girl," and the Pointer Sisters singing the nominee list for Best New Artist ("and besting them all," added the *Post*).

The night had three notable losers,

though, including Diana Ross and Lionel Richie, whose "Endless Love" lost all four prizes for which it was nominated. For Richie, the night was even worse: He had three additional losing bids — two for his work with the Commodores and one as Producer of the Year.

Last year's big winner, Christopher Cross, was also in evidence this year competing for Record and Song of the Year plus Best Male Pop Vocal Perfor-mance. In addition to being the vocal artist, Cross shared the credit for writing "Arthur's Theme (Best That You Can Do)" with Peter Allen, Burt Bacharach, and Carole Bayer Sager, which was named Best Song at the Oscars. It failed to take any Grammys, and Cross — who last year became the only artist to win all four top prizes — vanished from all subsequent Grammy nominee lists from 1981 to today.

1981

The awards ceremony was broadcast on CBS from the Shrine Auditorium in Los Angeles on February 24, 1982, for the awards eligibility period of October 1, 1980, through September 30, 1981.

ALBUM OF THE YEAR
• *Double Fantasy*, John Lennon, Yoko Ono. John Lennon, Yoko Ono, Jack Douglas, producers. Geffen/Warner Bros.
Breakin' Away, Al Jarreau. Jay Graydon, producer. Warner Bros.
The Dude, Quincy Jones. Quincy Jones, producer. A&M.
Gaucho, Steely Dan. Gary Katz, producer. MCA.
Mistaken Identity, Kim Carnes. Val Garay, producer. EMI-America.

RECORD OF THE YEAR
• "Bette Davis Eyes," Kim Carnes. Val Garay, producer. EMI-America.
"Arthur's Theme (Best That You Can Do)," Christopher Cross. Michael Omartian, producer. Warner Bros.
"Endless Love," Diana Ross, Lionel Richie. Lionel Richie, producer. Motown.
"(Just Like) Starting Over," John Lennon. John Lennon, Yoko Ono, Jack Douglas, producers. Geffen/Warner Bros.
"Just the Two of Us," Bill Withers, Grover Washington, Jr. Grover Washington, Jr., Ralph MacDonald, producers. Elektra.

SONG OF THE YEAR
(Songwriter's Award)
• "Bette Davis Eyes," Donna Weiss, Jackie DeShannon.
"Arthur's Theme (Best That You Can Do)," Peter Allen, Burt Bacharach,

"I wanted this sooo *much," said Sheena Easton about her Best New Artist win.*

Carole Bayer Sager, Christopher Cross.
"Endless Love," Lionel Richie.
"Just the Two of Us," Bill Withers, William Salter, Ralph MacDonald.
"9 to 5," Dolly Parton.

BEST NEW ARTIST
• Sheena Easton. EMI-America.
Adam & the Ants. Epic/CBS.
Go-Go's. I.R.S.
James Ingram. A&M.
Luther Vandross. Epic/CBS.

Best Pop Vocal Performance, Male

- Al Jarreau, *Breakin' Away*. Warner Bros.
- Christopher Cross, "Arthur's Theme (Best That You Can Do)." Warner Bros.
- James Ingram, "Just Once," track. A&M.
- John Lennon, "Double Fantasy" (Lennon tracks only). Geffen/Warner Bros.
- Bill Withers, "Just the Two of Us," track. Elektra/Asylum.

Best Pop Vocal Performance, Female

- Lena Horne, *Lena Horne: The Lady and Her Music Live on Broadway*. Qwest/Warner Bros.
- Kim Carnes, "Bette Davis Eyes." EMI-America.
- Sheena Easton, "For Your Eyes Only." Liberty.
- Juice Newton, "Angel of the Morning." Capitol.
- Olivia Newton-John, "Physical." MCA.

Best Pop Performance by a Duo or Group with Vocal

- Manhattan Transfer, "Boy from New York City." Atlantic.
- Steely Dan, *Gaucho*. MCA.
- Daryl Hall, John Oates, *Private Eyes*. RCA.
- Pointer Sisters, "Slow Hand." Planet/Elektra/Asylum.
- Diana Ross, Lionel Richie, "Endless Love." Motown.

Best Pop Instrumental Performance

- Mike Post featuring Larry Carlton, "Theme from *Hill Street Blues*." Elektra/Asylum.
- Louis Clark conducting Royal Philharmonic Orchestra, *Hooked on Classics*. RCA.
- Quincy Jones, "Velas," track. A&M.
- Earl Klugh, *Late Night Guitar*. Liberty.
- Lee Ritenour, *Rit* (Side 2, Instrumentals). Elektra/Asylum.

Best Rock Vocal Performance, Male

- Rick Springfield, "Jessie's Girl." RCA.
- Rick James, "Super Freak." Gordy/Motown.
- Bruce Springsteen, *The River*. Columbia/CBS.
- Rod Stewart, "Young Turks." Warner Bros.
- Gary "U. S." Bonds, *Dedication*. EMI-America.

Best Rock Vocal Performance, Female

- Pat Benatar, "Fire and Ice." Chrysalis.
- Lulu, "Who's Foolin' Who," track. Alfa.
- Stevie Nicks, "Edge of Seventeen," track. Modern/Atlantic.
- Yoko Ono, "Walking on Thin Ice." Geffen/Warner Bros.
- Donna Summer, "Cold Love," track. Geffen/Warner Bros.

Best Rock Performance by a Duo or Group with Vocal

- Police, "Don't Stand So Close to Me." A&M.
- Foreigner, *4*. Atlantic.
- REO Speedwagon, *Hi Infidelity*. Epic/CBS.
- Stevie Nicks with Tom Petty & the Heartbreakers, "Stop Draggin' My Heart Around." Modern/Atlantic.
- Rolling Stones, *Tattoo You*. Rolling Stones/Atlantic.

Best Rock Instrumental Performance

- Police , "Behind My Camel," track. A&M.
- Dregs, *Unsung Heroes*. Arista.
- Robert Fripp, *The League of Gentlemen*. Polygram/Polydor.
- Kraftwerk, "Computer World," track. Warner Bros.
- Rush, "YYZ," track. Mercury.

Best Rhythm & Blues Song
(Songwriter's Award)

- "Just the Two of Us," Bill Withers, William Salter, Ralph MacDonald.
- "Ai No Corrida," Chas. Jankel, Kenny Young.
- "Lady (You Bring Me Up)," Harold Hudson, William King, Shirley King.
- "She's a Bad Mama Jama (She's Built, She's Stacked)," Leon Haywood.
- "When She Was My Girl," Marc Blatte, Larry Gottlieb.

Best R&B Vocal Performance, Male

- James Ingram, "One Hundred Ways," track from Quincy Jones's *The Dude*. A&M.
- Carl Carlton, "She's a Bad Mama Jama (She's Built, She's Stacked)." 20th Century.
- Rick James, *Street Songs*. Gordy/Motown.

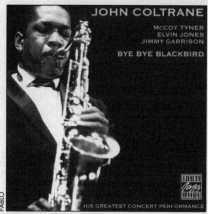

The late John Coltrane was remembered with a jazz award for Bye Bye Blackbird.

Teddy Pendergrass, "I Can't Live Without Your Love." Philadelphia International/CBS.
Luther Vandross, *Never Too Much*. Epic/CBS.

BEST R&B VOCAL PERFORMANCE, FEMALE
• Aretha Franklin, "Hold On, I'm Comin'," track. Arista.
Patti Austin, "Razzamatazz," track. A&M.
Chaka Khan, *What Cha' Gonna Do for Me*. Warner Bros.
Teena Marie, *It Must Be Magic*. Gordy/Motown.
Stephanie Mills, *Stephanie*. 20th Century.

BEST R&B PERFORMANCE BY A DUO OR GROUP WITH VOCAL
• Quincy Jones, *The Dude*. A&M.
Pointer Sisters, *Black & White*. Planet/Elektra/Asylum.
Stanley Clarke, George Duke, *The Clarke/Duke Project*. Epic/CBS.
Commodores, "Lady (You Bring Me Up)." Motown.
Earth, Wind & Fire, "Let's Groove." Arc/CBS.

BEST R&B INSTRUMENTAL PERFORMANCE
• David Sanborn, "All I Need Is You." Warner Bros.
Wilton Felder, *Inherit the Wind*. MCA.
Hiroshima, "Winds of Change (Henka Non Nagare)," track. Arista.
Ahmad Jamal, "You're Welcome, Stop on By," track. 20th Century.

Noel Pointer, "East St. Louis Melody," track. Liberty.

BEST JAZZ FUSION PERFORMANCE, VOCAL OR INSTRUMENTAL
• Grover Washington, Jr., *Winelight*. Elektra/Asylum.
Miles Davis, *The Man with the Horn*. Columbia/CBS.
Pat Metheny, Lyle Mays, *As Falls Wichita, So Falls Wichita Falls*. ECM.
Tom Scott, *Apple Juice*. Columbia/CBS.
Weather Report, *Night Passage*. ARC/CBS.

BEST JAZZ VOCAL PERFORMANCE, MALE
• Al Jarreau, "Blue Rondo à la Turk," track. Warner Bros.
Johnny Hartman, *Johnny Hartman Once in Every Life*. Bee Hive.
Jimmy Rowles, "Music's the Only Thing That's on My Mind," track. Progressive.
Mel Tormé, *Mel Tormé & Friends Recorded Live at Marty's New York City*. Finesse/CBS.
Joe Turner, *Have No Fear, Joe Turner Is Here*. Pablo.

BEST JAZZ VOCAL PERFORMANCE, FEMALE
• Ella Fitzgerald, *Digital III at Montreux*. Pablo Live.
Ernestine Anderson, *Never Make Your Move Too Soon*. Concord Jazz.
Helen Humes, *Helen*. Muse.
Etta Jones, *Save Your Love for Me*. Muse.
Janet Lawson, *The Janet Lawson Quintet*. Inner City/Music Minus One.

BEST JAZZ VOCAL PERFORMANCE, DUO, OR GROUP
• Manhattan Transfer, "Until I Met You (Corner Pocket)," track. Atlantic.
Clare Fischer's 2 + 2, *Clare Fischer & Salsa Picante Present 2 + 2*. Pausa.
Hi-Lo's, *Now*. Pausa.
Jackie & Roy, *East of Suez*. Concord Jazz.
Mel Tormé, Janis Ian, "Silly Habits," track. Finesse/CBS.

BEST JAZZ INSTRUMENTAL PERFORMANCE, SOLOIST
• John Coltrane, *Bye, Bye Blackbird*. Pablo.
Pepper Adams, *The Master ... Pepper Adams*. Muse.

Pete Christlieb, *Self Portrait*. Bosco 1.
Jimmy Rowles, *Music's the Only Thing on My Mind*. Progressive.
Ira Sullivan, *The Incredible Ira Sullivan*. Stash.

BEST JAZZ INSTRUMENTAL PERFORMANCE, GROUP
• Chick Corea, Gary Burton, *Chick Corea and Gary Burton in Concert, Zurich, October 28, 1979*. ECM.
Al Cohn, *Nonpareil*. Concord.
Vic Dickenson, *Vic Dickenson Quintet*. Storyville.
Red Rodney featuring Ira Sullivan, *Live at the Village Vanguard*. Muse.
Zoot Sims, *The Swinger*. Pablo.

BEST JAZZ INSTRUMENTAL PERFORMANCE, BIG BAND
• Gerry Mulligan & His Orchestra, *Walk on the Water*. DRG.
Toshiko Akiyoshi–Lew Tabackin Big Band, *Tanuki's Night Out*. Jazz America Marketing.
Panama Francis & the Savoy Sultans, *Panama Francis and the Savoy Sultans—Vol II*. Classic Jazz.
Rob McConnell & the Boss Brass, *Tribute*. Pausa.
Don Menza & his '80's Big Band, "Burnin' (Blues for Bird)," track. Realtime.

BEST COUNTRY SONG
(Songwriter's Award.)
• "9 to 5," Dolly Parton.
"Elvira," Dallas Frazier.
"I Was Country When Country Wasn't Cool," Kye Fleming, Dennis W. Morgan.
"Somebody's Knockin'," Ed Penney, Jerry Gillespie.
"You're the Reason God Made Oklahoma," Larry Collins, Sandy Pinkard.

BEST COUNTRY VOCAL PERFORMANCE, MALE
• Ronnie Milsap, "(There's) No Gettin' Over Me." RCA.
John Anderson, "I'm Just an Old Chunk of Coal (But I'm Gonna Be a Diamond Someday)." Warner Bros.
George Jones, "Still Doin' Time." Epic/CBS.
Willie Nelson, *Somewhere Over the Rainbow*. Columbia.

Eddie Rabbitt, "Step by Step." Elektra/Asylum.

BEST COUNTRY VOCAL PERFORMANCE, FEMALE
• Dolly Parton, "9 to 5." RCA.
Rosanne Cash, *Seven Year Ache*. Columbia/CBS.
Terri Gibbs, *Somebody's Knockin'*. MCA.
Barbara Mandrell, "I Was Country When Country Wasn't Cool." MCA.
Juice Newton, "Queen of Hearts." Capital.

COUNTRY PERFORMANCE, DUO OR GROUP WITH VOCAL
• Oak Ridge Boys, "Elvira." MCA.
Alabama, *Feels So Right*. RCA.
David Frizzell, Shelly West, "You're the Reason God Made Oklahoma." Warner Bros.
Emmylou Harris, Don Williams, "If I Needed You." Warner Bros.
Dottie West, Kenny Rogers, "What Are We Doin' in Love." Liberty.

BEST COUNTRY INSTRUMENTAL PERFORMANCE
• Chet Atkins, *Country, After All These Years*. RCA.
Chet Atkins, Doc Watson, *Reflections*. RCA.
Johnny Gimble, *The Texas Fiddle Collection*. CMH.
Barbara Mandrell, "Instrumental Medley: Mountain Dew, Fireball Mail, Old Joe Clark, Night Train, Uncle Joe's Boogie," track. MCA.
Merle Travis, *Travis Pickin'*. CMH.

BEST GOSPEL PERFORMANCE, CONTEMPORARY OR INSPIRATIONAL
• Imperials, *Priority*. Dayspring/Word.
Archers, *Spreadin' Like Wildfire*. Songbird/MCA.
Cynthia Clawson, *Finest Hour*. Triangle/Benson.
DeGarmo & Key, *This Ain't Hollywood*. Lamb & Lion/Benson.
Amy Grant, *In Concert*. Myrrh/Word.

BEST GOSPEL PERFORMANCE, TRADITIONAL
• J.D. Sumner/James Blackwood/Hovie Lister/Rosie Rozell/Jake Hess, *The Masters V*. Skylite.
Rusty Goodman, *Escape to the Light*. Canaan/Word.

Happy Goodman Family, *Goin' Higher*. Canaan/Word.

Rambos, *Rambo Reunion*. Heartwarming/Benson.

Lanny Wolfe Trio, *Can't Stop the Music*. Impact/Benson.

BEST SOUL GOSPEL PERFORMANCE, CONTEMPORARY

• Andrae Crouch, *Don't Give Up*. Warner Bros.

Al Green, "The Lord Will Make a Way," track. Hi-Myrrh/Word.

Edwin Hawkins, *Edwin Hawkins Live*. Myrrh/Word.

Walter Hawkins, *Walter Hawkins: The Hawkins Family*. Light.

Winans, *Introducing the Winans*. Light/Lexicon.

BEST SOUL GOSPEL PERFORMANCE, TRADITIONAL

• Al Green, *The Lord Will Make a Way*. Hi-Myrrh/Word.

Shirley Caesar, *Go*. Myrrh/Word.

James Cleveland & the Southern California Community Choir, *Where Is Your Faith*. Savoy.

Daniel Hawkins, *Daniel Hawkins*. Light/Lexicon.

Mighty Clouds of Joy, *Cloudbust*. Myrrh/Word.

BEST INSPIRATIONAL PERFORMANCE

• B.J. Thomas, *Amazing Grace*. Myrrh/Word.

Crusaders with Joe Cocker, "I'm So Glad I'm Standing Here Today," MCA.

Bob Dylan, *Shot of Love*. Columbia/CBS.

Barbara Mandrell, "In My Heart," track. MCA.

Donna Summer, "I Believe in Jesus," track. Geffen/Warner Bros.

Don Williams, "Miracles." MCA.

BEST ETHNIC OR TRADITIONAL RECORDING

• *There Must Be a Better World Somewhere*, B.B. King. MCA.

Blues Deluxe (Lonnie Brooks Blues Band, the Son Seals Blues Band, Mighty Joe Young, Muddy Waters, Koko Taylor & Her Blues Machine, Willie Dixon & the Chicago Blues All Stars). XRT/Alligator.

From the Heart of a Woman, Koko Taylor. Alligator.

Frozen Alive! Albert Collins. Alligator.

Living Chicago Blues Vol. IV, A.C. Reid & the Spark Plugs, Scotty & the Rib Tips, Lovie Lee with Carey Bell. Alligator.

BEST LATIN RECORDING

• "Guajira Pa La Jeva," track, Clare Fischer. Pausa.

Brazilian Soul, Laurindo Almeida, Charlie Byrd. Concord Jazz Picante.

Eddie Palmieri, Eddie Palmieri. Barbaro.

¡Gózame! Pero Ya ..., Cal Tjader. Concord Jazz Picante.

"Summertime," Digital at Montreux, 1980, Dizzy Gillespie, Mongo Santamaria. Pablo Live.

BEST INSTRUMENTAL COMPOSITION (Composer's Award)

• "Theme from *Hill Street Blues*," Mike Post.

Altered States, John Corigliano.

As Falls Wichita, So Falls Wichita Falls, Pat Metheny, Lyle Mays.

"For an Unfinished Woman," Gerry Mulligan.

"The Slaves," Jerry Goldsmith.

BEST ARRANGEMENT OF AN INSTRUMENTAL RECORDING

• Quincy Jones, "Velas" (Quincy Jones), track. Johnny Mandel, synthesizer & string arranger. A&M.

Toshiko Akiyoshi, "A Bit Byas'D" (Toshiko Akiyoshi–Lew Tabackin Big Band), track. Jazz America Marketing.

Jerry Goldsmith, "The Slaves" (Jerry Goldsmith), track. MCA.

Dave Grusin, "Mountain Dance" (Dave Grusin), track. GRP/Arista.

Billy May, "South Rampart Street Parade" (John Williams, Boston Pops), track. Philips.

BEST INSTRUMENTAL ARRANGEMENT ACCOMPANYING VOCAL(S)

• Quincy Jones, Jerry Hey, "Ai No Corrida" (Quincy Jones), track. A&M.

Greg Adams, "What Is Hip (Tower of Power)," track. Sheffield Lab.

Clare Fischer, "2 + 2 (Du, Du)," track. Pausa.

Arif Mardin, "And the Melody Still Lingers On (Night in Tunisia)" (Chaka Khan), track. Warner Bros.

Gino Vannelli, Joe Vannelli, Ross
Vannelli, "Living Inside Myself" (Gino
Vannelli), track. Arista.

BEST VOCAL ARRANGEMENT FOR TWO OR MORE VOICES

• Gene Puerling, "A Nightingale Sang in
Berkeley Square" (Manhattan
Transfer), track. Atlantic.
Clare Fischer, "2 + 2, (Du, Du)," (Clare
Fischer), track. Pausa.
Bernard Kafka, Jay Graydon, "Kafka"
(Manhattan Transfer), track. Atlantic.
Milcho Leviev, "(The Word of)
Confirmation" (Manhattan Transfer),
track. Atlantic.
Gene Puerling, "The Night We Called It a
Day" (Hi-Lo's), track. Pausa.

BEST CAST SHOW ALBUM

• Lena Horne: The Lady and Her Music
Live on Broadway, (Various composers
& lyricists). Quincy Jones, producer.
Qwest/Warner Bros.
Duke Ellington's Sophisticated Ladies,
(Duke Ellington & other composers &
lyricists). Thomas Z. Shepard, producer
RCA.
42nd Street, Harry Warren, composer. Al
Dubin, Johnny Mercer, Mort Dixon,
lyricists.Thomas Z. Shepard, producer.
RCA.
The Pirates of Penzance, Arthur Sullivan,
composer. William S. Gilbert, lyricist.
Peter Asher, producer. Elektra/Asylum.
Woman of the Year, John Kander,
composer. Fred Ebb, lyricist. John
McClure, producer. Arista.

BEST ALBUM OF ORIGINAL SCORE WRITTEN FOR A MOTION PICTURE OR A TELEVISION SPECIAL
(Composer's/Songwriter's Award)

• Raiders of the Lost Ark, John Williams.
Columbia/CBS.
The Elephant Man, John Morris. 20th
Century Fox.
Endless Love, Jonathan Tunick, Lionel
Richie, Thomas McClary.
Mercury/Polygram.
The Jazz Singer, Neil Diamond, Gilbert
Becaud, Alan Lindgren, Richard
Bennett, Doug Rhone. Capitol.
9 to 5, Charles Fox, Dolly Parton. 20th
Century Fox.

BEST CLASSICAL ALBUM

• Mahler: Symphony No. 2 in C Minor, Sir
Georg Solti conducting Chicago
Symphony Orchestra and Chorus
(solos: Buchanan, Zakai). James
Mallinson, producer. London.
The Horowitz Concerts 1979-80, Vladimir
Horowitz. John Preiffer, producer.
RCA.
Isaac Stern 60th Anniversary Celebration,
Zubin Mehta conducting New York
Philharmonic (solos: Stern, Perlman,
Zukerman). Andrew Kazdin, producer.
CBS.
Live from Lincoln Center: Sutherland,
Horne, Pavarotti, Richard Bonynge
conducting New York City Opera
Orchestra (solos: Joan Sutherland,
Marilyn Horne, Luciano Pavarotti).
Ray Minshull, producer. London.
The Unknown Kurt Weill, (solo: Teresa
Stratas). Eric Salzman, producer.
Nonesuch.

BEST CLASSICAL ORCHESTRAL RECORDING

• Mahler: Symphony No. 2 in C Minor, Sir
Georg Solti conducting Chicago
Symphony. James Mallinson, producer.
London.
Gershwin: Porgy & Bess (Symphonic
Picture); Cuban Overture and Second
Rhapsody, André Previn conducting
London Symphony. Suvi Raj Grubb,
producer. Angel.
Holst: The Planets, Simon Rattle
conducting Philharmonia Orchestra.
John Willan, producer. Angel.
Mahler: Symphony No. 10 (Deryck Cooke
Final Version), James Levine
conducting Philadelphia Orchestra. Jay
David Saks, producer. RCA.
Mozart: The Symphonies: Salzburg
1775-1783, Vol. 5, Christopher
Hogwood, Jaap Schroder, conductors,
Academy of Ancient Music. Morten
Winding, producer. L'Oiseau-Lyre.

BEST CHAMBER MUSIC PERFORMANCE
(INSTRUMENTAL OR VOCAL)

• Itzhak Perlman, Lynn Harrell, Vladimir
Ashkenazy, Tchaikovsky: Piano Trio in
A Minor. Angel.
Itzhak Perlman, Pinchas Zukerman,
Bartók: Duos for Two Violins. Angel.

Best Opera Recording From the House of the Dead *was a "majestic" reading by conductor Sir Charles Mackerras.*

Ray Still, Itzhak Perlman, Pinchas Zukerman, Lynn Harrell, *Oboe Quartets (Mozart, J.C. Bach, Karl Stamitz, Wanhal)*. Angel.

Toyko String Quartet, *Bartók: Quartets for Strings (6) Complete*. Deutsche Grammophon.

Guarneri Quartet, *The Complete String Quartets of Brahms & Schumann*. RCA.

BEST CLASSICAL PERFORMANCE, INSTRUMENTAL SOLOIST(S) (WITH ORCHESTRA)

• Isaac Stern, Itzhak Perlman, Pinchas Zukerman (Mehta conducting New York Philharmonic), *Isaac Stern 60th Anniversary Celebration*. CBS.

Emanuel Ax (Ormandy conducting Philadelphia Orchestra), *Chopin: Concerto for Piano No. 1 in E Minor*. RCA.

Stanley Drucker (Mehta conducting New York Philharmonic), *Corigliano: Concerto for Clarinet & Orchestra*. New World.

James Galway (Dutoit conducting Royal Philharmonic), *French Flute Concertos*. RCA.

Dylana Jenson (Ormandy conducting Philadelphia Orchestra), *Sibelius: Concerto for Violin in D Minor; Saint-Saëns: Introduction & Rondo Capriccioso*. RCA.

BEST CLASSICAL PERFORMANCE, INSTRUMENTAL SOLOIST(S) (WITHOUT ORCHESTRA)

• Vladimir Horowitz, *The Horowitz Concerts 1979-80*. RCA.

Itzhak Perlman (Samuel Sanders, accompanist), *Itzhak Perlman Plays Fritz Kreisler, Album 3*. Angel.

Murray Perahia, *Bartók: Sonata for Piano (1926); Improvisations on Hungarian Peasant Songs; Suite, Op. 14*. CBS.

Artur Rubinstein, *Artur Rubinstein, Schumann, Ravel, Debussy, Albeniz*. RCA.

Pinchas Zukerman (Marc Neikrug, accompanist), *Virtuoso Violin*. CBS.

BEST OPERA RECORDING

• *Janacek: From the House of the Dead*, Sir Charles Mackerras conducting Vienna Philharmonic (solos: Zahradnicek, Zitek, Zidek). James Mallinson, producer. London.

Berg: Wozzeck, Christoph von Dohnanyi conducting Vienna Philharmonic and Vienna State Opera Chorus (solos: Waechter, Silia). Christopher Raeburn, Michael Haas, producers. London.

Korngold: Violanta, Marek Janowski conducting Munich Radio Orchestra; Bavarian Radio Chorus (solos: Marton, Jerusalem). George Korngold, producer. CBS.

Monteverdi: Il Ritorno d'Ulisse in Patria, Raymond Leppard conducting London Philharmonic; Glyndebourne Chorus (solos: von Stade, Stillwell). David Mottley, producer. CBS.

Puccini: Le Villi, Lorin Maazel conducting National Philharmonic, Ambrosian Opera Chorus (solos: Scotto, Domingo, Nucci, Gobbi). Paul Myers, producer. CBS.

Rossini: L'Italiana in Algeri, Claudio Scimone conducting I Solisti Veneti, Chorus of Prague (solos: Horne, Ramey, Battle). Michel Gacin, producer. RCA.

Wagner: Parsifal, Herbert von Karajan conducting Berlin Philharmonic, Chorus of Deutsche Opera Berlin (solos: Hofmann, Veizovic, Moll, van Dam, Nimsgern, von Halem). Günther Breest, producer. Deutsche Grammophon.

BEST CHORAL PERFORMANCE, OTHER THAN OPERA
• Neville Marriner conducting Chorus of Academy of St. Martin-in-the-Fields, *Haydn: The Creation*. Philips.
Richard Cooke, choral conductor, London Symphony Orchestra Chorus. Eduardo Mata conducting London Symphony, *Orff: Carmina Burana*. RCA.
Thomas Peck, choral director, St. Louis Symphony Chorus. Leonard Slatkin, conducting St. Louis Symphony, *Prokofiev: Ivan the Terrible* from *Music From the Films*. Vox Cum Laude.
Robert Shaw, conductor, Atlanta Symphony Chorus, Atlanta Boy Choir, Atlanta Symphony, *Orff: Carmina Burana*. Telarc.
Richard Westenburg, choral conductor, Musica Sacra Chorus. Zubin Mehta conducting New York Philharmonic, *Verdi: Requiem*. CBS.

BEST CLASSICAL VOCAL SOLOIST PERFORMANCE
• Joan Sutherland, Marilyn Horne, Luciano Pavarotti (Richard Bonynge conducting New York City Opera Orchestra), *Live from Lincoln Center, Sutherland, Horne, Pavarotti*. London.
Elly Ameling (Dalton Baldwin, accompanist), *Think on Me*. CBS.
Barbara Hendricks (Sir Georg Solti conducting Chicago Symphony), *Del Tredici: Final Alice*. London.
Frederica von Stade (Seiji Ozawa conducting Boston Symphony), *Ravel: Sheherazade*; Cinq Melodies Populaires Grecques; Deux Melodies Hebraiques; Chansons Madecasses. CBS.
Teresa Stratas (Richard Woitach, accompanist), *The Unknown Kurt Weill*. Nonesuch.

BEST ENGINEERED RECORDING, CLASSICAL
• Bud Graham, Ray Moore, Andrew Kazdin, *Isaac Stern 60th Anniversary Celebration* (Zubin Mehta conducting the New York Philharmonic; solos: Isaac Stern, Itzhak Perlman, Pinchas Zukerman). CBS.
Michael Sheady, *Holst: The Planets* (Simon Rattle conducting Philharmonia Orchestra, Ambrosian Singers). Angel.

Paul Goodman, Jules Bloomenthal, Sydney Davis, Don Morrison, *Mahler: Symphony No. 10* (Deryck Cooke final version) (James Levine conducting Philadelphia Orchestra). RCA.
Michael Gray, Paul Goodman, *Orff: Carmina Burana* (Eduardo Mata conducting London Symphony; Richard Cooke conducting London Symphony Chorus; solos: Hendricks, Aler, Hagegård). RCA.
Jack Renner, Jules Bloomenthal, Sydney Davis, Jim Wolvington, *Orff: Carmina Burana*; *Hindemith: Symphonic Metamorphosis of Themes by Weber* (Robert Shaw conducting Atlanta Symphony Orchestra and Chorus, Atlanta Boys Choir; solos: Blegen, Brown, Hagegard). Telarc.

CLASSICAL PRODUCER OF THE YEAR
• James Mallinson. London
Steven Epstein. CBS.
Andrew Kazdin. CBS.
Jay David Saks. CBS.
Robert Woods. Telarc.

BEST COMEDY RECORDING
• *Rev. Du Rite*, Richard Pryor. Laff.
Airplane!, Lloyd Segal, album producer. Regency.
"The Inquisition," track, Mel Brooks. Warner Bros.
Mel Brooks' History of the World—Part I, Mel Brooks, Steve Barri, album producers. Warner Bros.
Urban Chipmunk (Chipmunks), Larry Butler, Janice Karman, Ross Bagdasarian, album producers. RCA.

BEST SPOKEN WORD, DOCUMENTARY, OR DRAMA RECORDING
• *Donovan's Brain*, Orson Welles. Radiola.
Justice Holmes' Decisions, Read by E.G. Marshall. Introductory commentary read by Louis Nizer. Caedmon.
The McCartney Interview (originally recorded for *Musician: Player & Listener* Magazine), Paul McCartney. Vic Garbarini, interviewer. Columbia.
"'Twas the Night Before Christmas," track, Ed McMahon. Livingsong.
Vladimir Nabokov: Lolita, James Mason. Caedmon.

Best Recording for Children

• *Sesame Country* (Muppets, Glen Campbell, Crystal Gayle, Loretta Lynn, Tanya Tucker), Jim Henson, Muppets creator. Dennis Scott, album producer. Sesame Street.

Ants'hillvania (Pat Boone & various artists), Jimmy Owens, Carol Owens, Cherry Boone O'Neill, writers. Dan Collins, producer. Birdwing/Sparrow.

Big Bird Discovers the Orchestra (Big Bird, Voices, and Orchestra), Jim Henson, creator. Arthur Shimkin, producer. Sesame Street.

A Chipmunk Christmas (Chipmunks & Santa Claus), Janice Karman, Ross Bagdasarian, writers & producers. RCA.

The Fox and the Hound (songs & dialogue from the original motion picture soundtrack featuring Pearl Bailey, Jack Albertson, Mickey Rooney), Elena Engel, producer. Disneyland.

Best Engineered Recording

• Roger Nichols, Elliot Scheiner, Bill Schnee, Jerry Garsza, *Gaucho* (Steely Dan). MCA.

Bruce Swedien, *The Dude* (Quincy Jones). A&M.

Mike Stone, Kevin Elson, *Escape* (Journey). Columbia/CBS.

Alan Parsons, *Turn of a Friendly Card* (Alan Parsons Project). Arista.

Nigel Gray, *Zenyatta Mondatta* (Police). A&M.

Best Album Package
(Art Director's Award)

• Peter Carriston, *Tattoo You* (Rolling Stones). Rolling Stones. Atlantic.

Carla Bley, Paul McDonough, *Social Studies* (Carla Bley). ECM.

Mike Doud, *Working Class Dog* (Rick Springfield). RCA.

Bush Hollyhead, *Positive Touch* (Undertones). Harvest/Capitol.

Kosh, *Eagles Live* (Eagles). Elektra/Asylum.

Best Album Notes
(Annotator's Award)

• Dan Morgenstern, *Erroll Garner: Master of the Keyboard*. Book-of-the-Month Records.

C. P. Crumpacker, *The Mario Lanza Collection*. RCA/Red Seal.

John McDonough, *Pee Wee Russell (Giants of Jazz)*. Time Life.

David Thomson, Philip W. Payne, *Fats Waller (Giants of Jazz)*. Time-Life.

Dick Wellstood with Willa Rouder, Frank Kappler, *James P. Johnson (Giants of Jazz)*. Time-Life.

Best Historical Album

• *Hoagy Carmichael: From "Star Dust" to "Ole Buttermilk Sky,"* (Hoagy Carmichael). George Spitzer, Michael Brooks, producers. Book-of-the-Month Records.

Birmingham Quartet Anthology (various). Doug Seroff, producer. Clanka/Lanka.

Miles Davis: Chronicle the Complete Prestige Recordings (Miles Davis). Orrin Keepnews, producer. Prestige.

The Quintet of the Hot Club of France (1936–1937) (Django Reinhardt, Stephane Grappelli). Kevin Yatarola, producer. Inner City/Music Minus One.

The Smithsonian Collection of Classic Country Music (various). Bill C. Malone, Bill Bennett, producers. Smithsonian.

Producer of the Year (Non-Classical)

• Quincy Jones
Val Garay
Robert John "Mutt" Lange, Mick Jones
Arif Mardin
Lionel Richie

Video of the Year

• *Michael Nesmith in Elephant Parts*, Michael Nesmith (VHS). Pacific Arts Video.

Eat to the Beat, Blondie (VHS). Chrysalis/WCI/RCA.

The First National Kidisc, various (videodisc). Bruce Seth Green, video producer. OPA/MCA.

One-Night Stand: A Keyboard Event, Eubie Blake, Kenny Barron, Arthur Blythe, Ron Carter, Stanley Clarke, George Duke, Charles Earland, Rodney Franklin, Herbie Hancock, Sir Roland Hanna, Bobby Hutcherson, Bob James, Hubert Laws, Buddy Williams (VHS). Richard Namm, video producer. CBS Video Enterprises.

Paul Simon, Paul Simon (disc). Pioneer Artists.

A Toto Surprise

Time magazine essayist Lance Morrow wrote after the 1982 awards show: "The crowd at the Grammy Awards looked as if it had just flown in from one of the moons of Saturn: glittering, snorting the intergalactic dust. Touches of the high crass mingled with a sort of metaphysical flash. Stevie Wonder, for example, wore a cumulously quilted white satin tuxedo whose upswept lapels formed great angel wings .... The American popular music industry was having its annual pageant."

Critics called Toto's workmanlike Record of the Year winner "Rosanna" a "bright, romantic reflection," but also blasted it for being "soulless" and "the w-r-e-c-k-o-r-d of the year."

WIDE WORLD PHOTO

On the occasion of Grammy's silver anniversary, it was the triumph of flash over substance in more ways than one. Just two years after N.A.R.A.S. let Christopher Cross sail off with the top awards for workmanlike music that will probably never earn him a Grammy Legends Award beside Quincy Jones, Smokey Robinson, and Billy Joel ... it did it again.

Toto, which led the Grammy contest from the outset with seven nominations, was a group comprised of polished L.A. session players who had worked with a broad range of music talent: Boz Scaggs, Steely Dan, Pink Floyd, Cheap Trick, Earth, Wind & Fire, and others. Prior to the Grammycast, the *L.A. Times*'s Robert Hilburn wrote, with some prophetic irony, "If everyone they've met in a studio during the last few years votes for them, it'll be a runaway, even though there's a disheartening lack of depth or daring to the group's music."

The accusation that their songs lacked depth plagued Toto, last contending for a Grammy in 1978 when the group lost its bid as Best New Artist to one of the safest pop groups of all — A Taste of Honey. Hilburn and other critics acknowledged that Toto's music possessed a certain "state-of-the-art professionalism." He even described their hit single "Rosanna" as a "bright, romantic reflection" that was "much admired in the industry," but added that it didn't seem to have "any aura of greatness about it." The *L.A. Herald Examiner* called the group "faceless." *The Washington Post* dismissed it as "soulless."

Hilburn considered the Record of the Year contest to be between Willie Nelson's "Always on My Mind" (his own choice) and Paul McCartney and Stevie Wonder's duet "Ebony & Ivory" (clearly, the viewing public's favorite). He predicted, however, that if Toto's *Toto IV* LP was named Album of the Year, a "Toto bandwagon" might be hard to stop. "If I were placing a bet" on the album contest, wrote Hilburn, "I'd be awfully tempted to go with Toto. As industry pros, N.A.R.A.S. members tend to judge music by what they know best: the mechanics. Remember Christopher Cross's sweep two years ago? Rather than search for artistic reach and sociological impact, they check the components, from engineering level to sales results, to see how well everyone did their job. Toto's album ranks high by these narrow standards."

> *"If everyone [Toto] met in a studio during the last few years votes for them, it'll be a runaway," the* **L.A. Times** *predicted.*

In a year in which some of the most critically acclaimed *and* commercially successful artists of the day such as Prince, Bruce Springsteen, and Elton John continued to go without a single Grammy, Toto picked up five: Record of the Year, Album of the Year (two prizes for each, as artists and producers), the separate Producer of the Year award, and Best Arrangement for Two or More Voices (for keyboardist David Paich).

Toto IV's engineers indeed did their job, garnering Best Engineered Recording, while various group members shared in two additional awards: Best Instrumental Arrangement Accompanying Vocals ("Rosanna") and Best Rhythm & Blues Song for "Turn Your Love Around," which Toto guitarist Steve Lukather wrote with Jay Graydon and Bill Champlin.

But the controversy occurring over Toto's success erupted specifically over two of the prizes. Toto's LP win, said Hilburn, "thwarted the hopes of Beatles fans for back-to-back album honors for John Lennon and Paul McCartney. Lennon's *Double Fantasy* was declared best LP last year, while McCartney's *Tug of War* was nominated in that category this time." Their victory with 1982's top single caused the *Herald Examiner* to quote "a longtime music industry observer" as saying, "'Rosanna'? Record of the Year? That's right, w-r-e-c-k-o-r-d of the year. This is award-winning music?"

Hilburn's choice of "Always on My Mind" did come through as Song of the Year, marking the first time since 1968 that a country tune took any of the high honors. ("Little Green Apples" was voted top song that year while Glen Campbell's *By the Time I Get to Phoenix* was named Album of the Year.) "Always" also swept the c&w awards: Best Country Song (for writers Johnny Christopher, Mark James, and Wayne Carson) and Best Male Country Vocal Performance for Willie Nelson. (It won the equivalent prizes at the Academy of Country Music and Country Music Association Awards, too.) For Nelson, it was the biggest hit in a career full of hits: "Always" spent two weeks on top of *Billboard*'s country chart and soared to number 5 in the weekly Hot 100.

The enormous success of Nelson's "Always" baffled music experts, though, because the song had been around for more than a decade and had failed to catch on earlier despite being recorded by a number of vocal greats. (Old songs were permitted to compete for Song of the Year as long as they had never been nominated before and there was a new recording released within the eligibility period.)

Brenda Lee was the first to release "Always" as a single in 1972. Elvis Presley took it to number 16 in the rankings the following year when it appeared at the "B" side to his "Separate Ways" platter. Several other versions followed, but it didn't click as a true country classic until a very reluctant Willie Nelson caved in to pleas from his wife and daughters to release his own version of it as a single. At the Grammycast, he performed it in a live piped-in broadcast from Texas that the *Herald Examiner* called one of the night's "fine and stirring performances."

The "rowdy" John Cougar (Mellencamp) failed to garner Album of the Year for American Fool *but rebounded with a rock award for "Hurts So Good."*

Aside from Nelson, most of the other top Grammys ended up in the hands of first-timers, like Toto, instead of the "legends" who dominated last year's show. The choice for Best New Artist was Men at Work, the Australian new wave quintet made famous by its funky videos. Men at Work had the number one–selling album of the year *Business As Usual*, which spawned such hits as "Who Can It Be Now?" and "Down Under" and also set a new record for a debut album spending the most time on top of the charts — 15 weeks — topping the Monkees' earlier record of 12. Men at Work performed on the Grammycast, but, as *The Washington Post* noted, sounded "tinny, stiff, and nervous."

Melissa Manchester began her career as one of Bette Midler's backup singers, the Harlettes. She had her first hit single in 1975 with "Midnight Blue," but failed to win a Grammy until she scored her biggest hit of all, "You Should Hear

How She Talks About You," which earned her the female pop vocals prize.

Lionel Richie was a leading contender for the male pop vocals award, but he almost didn't attend the Grammy show. "Having lost so many times" in the past, said the *L.A. Times*, "he didn't want to face another loss in person." Richie suffered an astounding seven defeats last year alone and only ended up attending the Grammys this year because his manager and wife talked him into it at the last minute. "I'm glad they did," Richie said later, holding his prize for "Truly," his first solo hit since leaving the Commodores in 1981. "If I had missed accepting my Grammy in person, I'd be kicking myself the rest of my life."

Joining the other first-time winners were Joe Cocker and Jennifer Warnes, recipients of the pop duo prize for "Up Where We Belong," the hit ballad from the smash movie *An Officer and a Gentleman* that won Best Song at the 1981 Oscars. "I was told it was the weirdest pairing ever," Warnes said backstage about her partnership with the notoriously wild Cocker. "But we did it and it turned out beautifully." More Oscar-winning music picked up Grammys when a dance version of the theme to the movie *Chariots of Fire* took the pop instrumental trophy. "This inspiring anthem may be what clinched the film's Oscar triumph last spring," wrote the *L.A. Times* after *Chariots* won both Best Picture and Best Film Score for 1981.

Willie Nelson's Song of the Year "Always on My Mind" marked the first time a country tune took a top honor since 1968.

Because of the differences in the eligibility periods for the Oscars and Grammys, the film score winner at the 1981 Oscars — John Williams's music for *E.T. The Extra-Terrestrial* — also picked up three Grammys this year: for best instrumental arrangement, Best Instrumental Composition, and best film score.

In the rock categories, the number-one single in the year's Hot 100 — "Eye of the Tiger" —ended up with the group vocals prize after Sylvester Stallone commissioned the Midwest rock group Survivor to write it for *Rocky III*, his latest sequel to his 1976 Oscar-winning Best Picture. A Flock of Seagulls, the British new wave group that took its name from the best-selling pop-philosophy book *Jonathan Livingston Seagull,* snagged the instrumental performance prize for "D.N.A."

John Cougar (who later went back to using his given name, Mellencamp) had recorded four LPs before hitting it big with *American Fool*, his Album of the Year contender that sold an impressive three million copies. The *L.A. Times* didn't think Cougar had a chance with the sedate N.A.R.A.S. crowd, though, claiming, "His rowdy rock approach is unlikely to get much support." But his "Hurts So Good" single did earn him the rock vocals award over an equally rowdy group of veterans that included Peter Gabriel, Don Henley, and Rod Stewart. The female vocals prize went to Pat Benatar for a third year in a row, this time for her "Shadows of the Night" single.

In the r&b lineup, the *L.A. Times* noted: "Critics point out that singer-songwriter Marvin Gaye — who received a standing ovation when he walked on stage during the telecast to sing 'Sexual Healing' — made some of the most acclaimed records of the '60s and '70s but had never won a Grammy." ("Politics, that's what it was, Hollywood games," Gaye once told biographer David Ritz to explain the oversight. "I refused to play those games and I suffered.") Now Gaye nabbed two Grammys for his comeback single that explored both sexual desire and spiritual feelings, but "received such recognition," Gaye said, "because of the sexual content." Holding his first Grammy backstage before a sea of reporters, he added, "This award is such an inspiration ... twenty-five years I've been waiting for it." Sadly, "Sexual Healing" would be Gaye's last hit: One year after his Grammy wins, he was shot to death by his father during a family squabble.

Dreamgirls, winner of the Grammy for Best Cast Show Album, also was responsible for the victor of the female r&b vocal prize: Jennifer Holliday. In the lavish Broadway musical, obviously based on the Supremes' climb to fame, the Tony Award-winning Holliday played the equivalent of real-life Florence Ballard, who was ousted from the "Dreams." Much of the show's material was written by composer Henry Krieger especially for Holliday, including her show-stopping "And I Am Telling You I'm Not Going," which she performed on the Grammycast last year. Her r&b award for the same song this year compensated her for the loss she suffered in the Best New Artist category.

There was a tie for the r&b group vocals category between the ultrafunk Cleveland group Dazz (short for "danceable jazz") Band for their one-hit wonder "Let It Whip" and Earth, Wind & Fire's "Wanna Be with You."

Mel Tormé's (right) triumph for his LP with George Shearing (left) was hailed as "a reason to rejoice."

Singer/guitarist/band leader Clarence "Gatemouth" Brown had been playing the blues since the 1940s and had received his share of critical approval along the way, but he failed to achieve superstar status. "Few paid attention when blues giant Clarence Gatemouth Brown came proudly yet humbly to meet the press and discuss his first-ever Grammy (for best traditional blues recording)," said the *Herald Examiner*. "In fact, there was only one reporter listening. 'It's a weird feeling,' said the 58-year-old Gatemouth, smiling. 'I've never even dreamed of this.'"

"The jazz awards left little or no cause for complaint," wrote the oft-critical jazz critic Leonard Feather in the *L.A. Times*. "There was particular reason to rejoice in both the vocal categories, since Sarah Vaughan and Mel Tormé, both of whom should have collected a roomful of Grammys by now, became winners for the first time.

"Ironically, Vaughan, who in the 25 years of the academy's history has made at least a dozen award-worthy albums of pure jazz, finally won with an LP that was not aimed at the jazz audience. *Gershwin Live!* is a classical album and should have been so classified." It would be the only Grammy Vaughan would win in a competitive category prior to her death in 1990. N.A.R.A.S. did gave her one more — a special Lifetime Achievement Award in 1989 for, N.A.R.A.S. said, her singing talent that "ranged all the way from jazz (where she was closely associated with the early bebop movement) to semi-classics, singing with small groups and classical orchestras and being equally at home with all."

"There was a touch of irony also in Tormé's victory," Feather claimed, "since last year he said, 'It is just not in the cards for me to win. How can you beat the power of a Warner Bros.?' Luckily for us and for him, block voting is by no means as potent a force as he believed." Singer Tormé won for what Feather called his "superb collaboration with [pianist] George Shearing," which was recorded on the Concord Jazz label. Most of Tormé's other competitors were likewise represented by small labels — except for Joe Williams's *8 to 5 I Lose*, which was recorded by Warner Bros.

The Washington Post called the bestowal of the rest of the jazz awards "fairly predictable": two-time past champ Phil Woods took the group instrumental prize for *"More" Live* by his quartet; Count Basie & His Orchestra scored an eighth career Grammy for Basie for *Warm Breeze* (best big band); and the Manhattan Transfer snagged their second-in-a-row group vocal award for "Route 66," thereby monopolizing the category since its inception. It was the ultra-hip, harmony-singing quartet's fourth Grammy in all. First-time winning jazz guitarist Pat Metheny and his group were among the front runners for the fusion award thanks to critical applause for their heavily synthesized sound and the variety of material on *Offramp*.

Miles Davis had won two Grammys earlier in his career (1960 and 1970), but in 1982 he hadn't made a recording in six years. In plotting his comeback, he took some chances: For his live *We Want Miles* album, Davis added guitarist Mike Stern and sax player Bill Evans. It was his own solo work on the LP, though, that earned him his first Grammy in 12 years — an honor that he may or may not have appreciated. As the *Herald Examiner* noted, Davis accepted it "without so much as a word or grimace of acknowledgment toward the industry that he professes to loathe."

For more than a half-dozen years beginning in the late 1960s, Roy Clark was the highest-paid performer in country music. He had also been named Entertainer of the Year by the Country Music Association in 1973, and was the host of the popular TV show *Hee Haw*, on which he often sang as he strummed his guitar or banjo. But as popular as Clark was, he had never before won a Grammy prior to his 1982 award for "Alabama Jubilee." Another big TV country star, Barbara Mandrell, who had had her own variety show on NBC, had hit songs dating back to the 1960s, too, but didn't win a Grammy prior to her Best Inspirational Performance trophy for *He Set My Life to Music*.

Country music's other big winners were less traditional country rockers. Juice Newton was expected to prevail in the female vocalist category last year but was upset by Dolly Parton. This time she eclipsed Parton with "Break It to Me Gently." The ultimate country rockers of the group Alabama won their first Grammy for what *Billboard* called "a modern country classic" — their album *Mountain Music*. It was an important time for Alabama: The group won the Academy of Country Music's awards for Top Vocal Group and Entertainer of the Year, and *Mountain Music* went platinum.

In an effort to counteract her sugar-sweet image, Olivia Newton-John made a point of adding lots of sexuality suggestive scenes to the video version of her 1981 hit song "Physical," which was taped in a fitness club. The result was an outcry from religious leaders — and a Video of the Year award at the Grammys.

Live on the Sunset Strip won Richard Pryor his fifth award for Best Comedy Recording. "Up-and-coming Eddie Murphy, star of *Saturday Night Live* and *48 Hours*, used the opportunity for a little mugging of his own," noted *The Washington Post* about the prize's presenter, who joked, "Rich won? I ain't leaving here without a Grammy. Seriously, folks, *somebody's* giving up their Grammy tonight."

The Best Classical Album category was a close contest won out by a recording of Bach's *Goldberg Variations*, nicknamed "The Gouldberg Variations" since the works were recorded more than once by the late pianist and posthumous winner Glenn Gould. "One of the most striking features of this landmark album is its unintentional aura of the memorial," *Fanfare* wrote, since the LP was released "almost simultaneously with Gould's death." Gould first taped the *Variations* in 1955, but wanted to give the sections more of an "arithmetical relationship," as he called it, complaining of "too much piano-playing going on" in pieces like "Variation 25." For his new interpretation, he garnered the additional award for best soloist performance without orchestra.

Among the losing contenders for best classical LP was the winner of the Best Classical Orchestra Recording prize: guest conductor James Levine and the Chicago Symphony for Mahler's Symphony No. 7 (*Song of the Night*). On two occasions in the previous 10 years (1972 and 1981), the Chicago Symphony was more successful at nabbing the top LP prize for renditions of Mahler symphonies by Solti. In this version, said *Fanfare*, Levine's "phrasing is outstanding."

The choral prize went to another loser of top LP award, *Berlioz: La Damnation de Faust*, with the Chicago Symphony performing this time under the baton of its resident director Sir Georg Solti. This was ninth year in a row that Solti had won an award, which established a new Grammy winning streak, surpassing Aretha Franklin's previous record of eight consecutive r&b prizes between from 1967 to 1974. (It was Solti's nineteenth over all.) "Kudos once more to Margaret Hillis," too, wrote *Fanfare* of

the Chicago symphony chorus's director, who won the same award three times in the late 1970s.

The soloist laurel for orchestral accompaniment was bestowed to Itzhak Perlman, who had won four other Grammys in the past five years. "Overtly spectacular does describe Itzhak Perlman's violin pyrotechnics" in this recording of Elgar's Concerto in B Minor for Violin and Orchestra, said *Fanfare*. The same publication applauded the winners of the chamber music prize, clarinetist Richard Stoltzman and pianist Richard Goode for their "expansive, clean-lined readings" of Brahms sonatas.

The Best Opera Recording prize went to 10-time past Grammy winner Pierre Boulez conducting the Bayreuth Festival Orchestra in Wagner's *Der Ring des Nibelungen*. Winning her twelfth award was Leontyne Price for her rendition of arias from Verdi operas called "sensational" and "Price at the peak of her form" by *Fanfare*.

Clutching his first Grammy proudly, Marvin Gaye said, "Twenty-five years I've been waiting for it!"

The Grammys ceremony, again broadcast on CBS from the Shrine Auditorium in Los Angeles, received virtually across-the-board bad reviews this year, on one hand because of the lack of excitement over the big winners like Toto, and on the other because there were fewer awards bestowed despite the fact that the ceremony had been stretched from two to three hours. That meant that there were "more generally dreadful musical numbers," said

The Washington Post, "as performed by such popular entertainers as Linda Ronstadt, Willie Nelson, Lena Horne, Kenny Rogers, the Spinners, Men at Work, Gladys Knight & the Pips, Bill Monroe, Leontyne Price, the Blackwood Brothers, Crystal Gayle, and Miles Davis." The L.A. Herald Examiner dismissed the "weirdness of Joan Baez singing 'Blowin' in the Wind' with [host] John Denver," while it applauded the medley performed by Ray Charles, Jerry Lee Lewis, Little Richard, and Count Basie as "an astonishing display of myth and muscle." The one-time rock hero Little Richard now considered himself "born again," however, and refused to sing songs without a religious message. In the medley with Basie, Charles, and Lewis, he changed a lyric of "What'd I Say" to:

"Found God in '74/ Don't sing rock & roll no more." "He was right," the Post commented. "Only the pencil mustache remains of the old fire."

The most damning review came from the Herald Examiner, which wrote: "The 25th annual Grammys was perhaps the single biggest artistic washout this ceremony has produced since its seminal days in the late '50s, when N.A.R.A.S. virtually disavowed significant rock & roll (and most significant jazz). With the exception of a few of the r&b and obligatory blues awards — the voters settled for the blandest, most prudent definition of pop music imaginable: not just massively popular pop, the kind certified by record sales and calculated accessibility — but pop that stands for technique over meaning, and smugness over courage."

1982

The awards ceremony was broadcast on CBS from the Shrine Auditorium in Los Angeles on February 23, 1983, for the awards eligibility period of October 1, 1981, through September 30, 1982.

ALBUM OF THE YEAR
√ • Toto IV, Toto. Toto, producer. Columbia/CBS.
√ American Fool, John Cougar. John Cougar Mellencamp, Don Gehman, producers. Riva/Polygram.
√ The Nightfly, Donald Fagen. Gary Katz, producer. Warner Bros.
The Nylon Curtain, Billy Joel. Phil Ramone, producer. Columbia/CBS.
√ Tug of War, Paul McCartney. George Martin, producer. Columbia.

RECORD OF THE YEAR
√ • "Rosanna," Toto. Toto, producer. Columbia.
√ "Always on My Mind," Willie Nelson. Chips Moman, producer. Columbia.
"Theme from Chariots of Fire," Vangelis. Vangelis, producer. Polydor.

√ "Ebony & Ivory," Paul McCartney, Stevie Wonder. George Martin, producer. Columbia.
√ "Steppin' Out," Joe Jackson. David Kershenbaum, Joe Jackson, producers. A&M.

SONG OF THE YEAR
(Songwriter's Award)
• "Always on My Mind," Johnny Christopher, Mark James, Wayne Thompson. Screen Gems, EMI Music Inc., Rose Bridge Music, publishers. CBS.
√ "Ebony & Ivory," Paul McCartney. MPL, publisher. Columbia/CBS .
"Eye of the Tiger," Frankie Sullivan, Jim Peterik. Holey Moley Music, Rude Music, Warner Bros. Music, Easy Action Music, publishers. Scotti Brothers/CBS.
√ "I.G.Y. (What a Beautiful World)," Donald Fagen. Freejunket Music, publisher. Warner Bros.
√ "Rosanna," David Paich, songwriter. Hudmar Publishing, publisher. Columbia/CBS.

BEST NEW ARTIST
• Men at Work.
  Columbia.
Asia. Geffen/Warner
  Bros.
Jennifer Holliday.
  Geffen/Warner Bros.
Human League. A&M.
Stray Cats. EMI-
  America.

BEST POP VOCAL PERFORMANCE, MALE
✓• Lionel Richie,
  "Truly." Motown.
✓ Donald Fagen, "I.G.Y.
  (What a Beautiful
  World)." Warner
  Bros.
✓ Joe Jackson, "Steppin'
  Out." A&M.
Elton John, "Blue Eyes." Geffen/Warner
  Bros.
Michael McDonald, "I Keep Forgetting
  (Everytime You're Near)." Warner
  Bros.
Rick Springfield, "Don't Talk to
  Strangers." RCA.

BEST POP VOCAL PERFORMANCE, FEMALE
• Melissa Manchester, "You Should Hear
  How She Talks About You." Arista.
Laura Branigan, "Gloria." Atlantic.
Juice Newton, "Love's Been a Little Bit
  Hard on Me." Capitol.
✓ Olivia Newton-John, "Heart Attack." MCA.
Linda Ronstadt, "Get Closer."
  Elektra/Asylum.

BEST POP PERFORMANCE BY A DUO OR GROUP WITH VOCAL
• Joe Cocker, Jennifer Warnes, "Up Where
  We Belong." Island.
✓ Chicago, "Hard to Say I'm Sorry." Full
  Moon/Warner Bros.
✓ Daryl Hall, John Oates, "Maneater." RCA.
✓ Paul McCartney, Stevie Wonder, "Ebony
  & Ivory." Columbia.
✓ Toto, "Rosanna." Columbia.

BEST POP INSTRUMENTAL PERFORMANCE
• Ernie Watts, "Chariots of Fire" (theme,
  dance version). Qwest/Warner Bros.
Louis Clark conducting Royal
  Philharmonic Orchestra, *Hooked on
  Classics*. RCA.
Earl Klugh, "Crazy for You."
  Liberty/Capitol.

*Jennifer Holliday wowed the Grammys show last year
with her r&b winner of 1982, "And I Am Telling You."*

David Sanborn, "As We Speak." Warner
  Bros.
John Williams, *E.T The Extra-Terrestrial*
  (Original motion picture soundtrack).
  MCA.

BEST ROCK VOCAL PERFORMANCE, MALE
✓• John Cougar, "Hurts So Good."
  Riva/Polygram.
Peter Gabriel, "Shock the Monkey."
  Geffen/Warner Bros.
Don Henley, "Dirty Laundry." Elektra.
Rick Springfield, "I Get Excited." RCA.
Rod Stewart, *Tonight I'm Yours*. Warner
  Bros.

BEST ROCK VOCAL PERFORMANCE, FEMALE
• Pat Benatar, "Shadows of the Night."
  Chrysalis.
Kim Carnes, "Voyeur." EMI-America.
Bonnie Raitt, "Green Light." Warner Bros.
Linda Ronstadt, "Get Closer."
  Elektra/Asylum.
Donna Summer, "Protection."
  Geffen/Warner Bros.

BEST ROCK PERFORMANCE BY A DUO OR GROUP WITH VOCAL
• Survivor, "Eye of the Tiger." Scotti
  Brothers/CBS.
✓ Asia, *Asia*. Geffen/Warner Bros.
✓ J. Geils Band, "Centerfold." EMI-America.
Kenny Loggins with Steve Perry, "Don't
  Fight It." Columbia/CBS.
✓ Frank & Moon Zappa, "Valley Girl."
  Barking Pumpkin.

Best Rock Instrumental Performance

- A Flock of Seagulls, "D.N.A." Jive/Arista.
Dregs, "Industry Standard." Arista.
Maynard Ferguson, "Don't Stop." Columbia.
King Crimson, "Requiem." EB/Warner Bros.
Van Morrison, "Scandinavia." Warner Bros.

Best Rhythm & Blues Song
(Songwriter's Award)

- "Turn Your Love Around," Jay Graydon, Steve Lukather, Bill Champlin. Garden Rake Music, Rehtakul Veets Music, JSH Music, publishers.
"Do I Do," Stevie Wonder. Jobete Music Co., Black Bull Music, publishers.
"It's Gonna Take a Miracle," Teddy Randazzo, Bobby Weinstein, Lou Staliman. Vogue Music, publisher.
"Let It Whip," Reggie Andrews, Leon "Ndugu" Chancler. Ujima Music, MacVacalac Music, publishers.
"Sexual Healing," Marvin Gaye, O. Brown. April Music, Inc, publisher.
"That Girl," Stevie Wonder. Jobete Music, Black Bull Music, publishers.

Best R&B Vocal Performance, Male

- Marvin Gaye, "Sexual Healing." Columbia/CBS.
George Benson, "Turn Your Love Around." Warner Bros.
Ray Parker, Jr., "The Other Woman." Arista.
Luther Vandross, "Forever, for Always, for Love." Epic/CBS.
Stevie Wonder, "Do I Do." Tamla/Motown.

Best R&B Vocal Performance, Female

- Jennifer Holliday, "And I Am Telling You I'm Not Going." Geffen/Warner Bros.
Aretha Franklin, "Jump to It." Arista.
Diana Ross, "Muscles." RCA.
Patrice Rushen, "Forget Me Nots." Elektra.
Donna Summer, "Love Is in Control (Finger on the Trigger)." Geffen/Warner Bros.
Deniece Williams, "It's Gonna Take a Miracle." Columbia.

Best Rhythm & Blues Performance by a Duo or Group with Vocal
(Tie)

- Dazz Band, "Let It Whip." Motown.
- Earth, Wind & Fire, "Wanna Be With You." ARC/CBS.
Crusaders with B.B. King, Josie James, "Street Life." MCA.
Paul McCartney, Stevie Wonder, "What's That You're Doing." Columbia/CBS.
Tavares, "A Penny for Your Thoughts." RCA.

Best R&B Instrumental Performance

- Marvin Gaye, "Sexual Healing." Columbia/CBS.
Eddie Murphy, "Boogie in Your Butt." Columbia/CBS.
Patrice Rushen, "Number One." Elektra/Asylum.
Spyro Gyra, "Stripes." MCA.
Grover Washington, Jr., "Come Morning." Elektra.

Best Jazz Fusion Performance, Vocal or Instrumental

- Pat Metheny Group, *Offramp*. ECM/Warner Bros.
David Sanborn, *As We Speak*. Warner Bros.
Tom Scott, *Desire*. Elektra/Musician.
Spyro Gyra, *Incognito*. MCA.
Weather Report, *Weather Report*. Columbia.

Best Jazz Vocal Performance, Male

- Mel Tormé, *An Evening with George Shearing and Mel Tormé*. Concord Jazz.
Dave Frisberg, *The Dave Frisberg Songbook, Volume I*. Omnisound Jazz.
Bill Henderson, *A Tribute to Johnny Mercer*. Discovery.
Mark Murphy, *Bop for Kerouac*. Muse.
Joe Williams, *8 to 5 I Lose*. Warner Bros.

Best Jazz Vocal Performance, Female

- Sarah Vaughan, *Gershwin Live!* CBS.
Ella Fitzgerald, *A Classy Pair*. Pablo Today.
Chaka Khan, *Echoes of an Era*. Elektra/Musician.
Cleo Laine, *Smilin' Through*. Finesse.
Maxine Sullivan, *Maxine Sullivan with the Ike Isaacs Quartet*. Audiophile/Jazzology.

Best Jazz Vocal Performance Duo or Group

- Manhattan Transfer, "Route 66." Atlantic.

Clare Fischer & Salsa Picante with 2 + 2, "One Night in a Dream." Discovery.

Jon Hendricks & Company, *Love*. Muse.

Jackie & Roy, "High Standards." Concord Jazz.

Singers Unlimited, "Easy to Love." Pausa.

Best Jazz Instrumental Performance, Soloist

- Miles Davis, *We Want Miles*. Columbia.

Tommy Flanagan, *The Magnificent Tommy Flanagan*. Progressive.

Wynton Marsalis, *Wynton Marsalis*. Columbia.

Jimmy Rowles, *Jimmy Rowles Plays Duke Ellington and Billy Strayhorn*. Columbia.

Ira Sullivan, *Night and Day*. Muse.

Best Jazz Instrumental Performance, Group

- Phil Woods Quartet, *"More" Live*. Adelphi.

Art Blakey & the Jazz Messengers, *Straight Ahead*. Concord Jazz.

Art Farmer Quartet, *A Work of Art*. Concord Jazz.

Tommy Flanagan Trio, *Giant Steps*. Enja/London.

Dizzy Gillespie with the Mitchell-Ruff Duo, *Dizzy Gillespie: Live with the Mitchell-Ruff Duo*. Book-of-the-Month Records.

Best Jazz Instrumental Performance, Big Band

- Count Basie & His Orchestra, *Warm Breeze*. Pablo Today.

Bob Florence Big Band, *Westlake*. Discovery.

Woody Herman Big Band, *The Woody Herman Big Band Live at the Concord Jazz Festival 1981*. Concord Jazz.

Mel Lewis & the Jazz Orchestra, *Make Me Smile & Other New Works by Bob Brookmeyer*. Finesse.

Rob McConnell & the Boss Brass, *Live in Digital*. Dark Orchid.

Best Country Song (Songwriter's Award)

- "Always on My Mind," Johnny Christopher, Wayne Thompson, Mark James. Screen Gems, EMI Music Inc., Rose Bridge Music, publishers.

"I'm Gonna Hire a Wino to Decorate Our Home," D. Blackwell. Peso Music, Wallet Music, publishers.

"Nobody," Kye Fleming, Dennis W. Morgan. Tom Collins Music Corp., publisher.

"Ring on Her Finger, Time on Her Hands," Don Goodman, Pam Rose, Mary Ann Kennedy. Tree Publishing Co. Inc., Love Wheel Music, publishers.

"She Got the Goldmine (I Got the Shaft)," Tim DuBois. House of Gold Music Inc., publisher.

Best Country Vocal Performance, Male

- Willie Nelson, "Always on My Mind." Columbia/CBS.

Ronnie Milsap, "He Got You." RCA.

Jerry Reed, "She Got the Goldmine (I Got the Shaft)." RCA.

Kenny Rogers, "Love Will Turn You Around." EMI/Liberty-Capitol.

Ricky Skaggs, "Heartbroke." Epic/CBS.

Best Country Vocal Performance, Female

- Juice Newton, "Break It to Me Gently." Capitol.

Rosanne Cash, "Ain't No Money." Columbia.

Emmylou Harris, *Cimarron*. Warner Bros.

Dolly Parton, "I Will Always Love You." RCA.

Sylvia, "Nobody." RCA.

Best Country Performance by a Duo or Group with Vocal

- Alabama, *Mountain Music*. RCA.

Waylon Jennings, Willie Nelson, "(Sittin' on) The Dock of the Bay." RCA.

Oak Ridge Boys, "Bobbie Sue." MCA.

Gram Parsons, Emmylou Harris, "Love Hurts." Sierra.

Whites, "You Put the Blue in Me." Elektra/Curb.

Al Green abandoned the pop charts in the 1970s to concencrate on singing only religious music like "Precious Lord," Best Traditional Soul Gospel Performance.

BEST COUNTRY INSTRUMENTAL PERFORMANCE

• Roy Clark, "Alabama Jubilee." Churchill.
Albert Coleman's Atlanta Pops Orchestra, *Just Hooked on Country*. Epic/CBS.
Joe Maphis, *The Joe Maphis Flat-Picking Spectacular*. CMH.
Poco, "Feudin'." MCA.
Doc & Merle Watson, "Below Freezing." Flying Fish.

BEST GOSPEL PERFORMANCE, CONTEMPORARY

• Amy Grant, *Age to Age*. Myrrh/Word.
Andrae Crouch, *My Tribute*. Light/Lexicon.
Imperials, *Stand By the Power*. Dayspring/Word.
Sandi Patti, *Lift Up the Lord*. Impact/Benson.
Reba Rambo, *Lady Live*. Light/Lexicon.

BEST GOSPEL PERFORMANCE, TRADITIONAL

• Blackwood Brothers, *I'm Following You*. Voice Box.
Cathedrals, *Something Special*. Canaan/Word.
Masters V, *O, What a Savior*. Skylite/Sing.
Rex Nelon Singers, *Feeling at Home*. Canaan/Word.
Dottie Rambo, *Makin' My Own Place*. HeartWarming/Benson.

BEST SOUL GOSPEL PERFORMANCE, CONTEMPORARY

• Al Green, "Higher Plane." Myrrh/Word.
Andrae Crouch, "Finally." Light/Elektra/Asylum.
Larnelle Harris, *Touch Me, Lord*. Impact/Benson.
Edwin Hawkins, *Edwin Hawkins Live with the Oakland Symphony Orchestra*. Myrrh/Word.
Mighty Clouds of Joy, *Miracle Man*. Myrrh/Word.

BEST SOUL GOSPEL PERFORMANCE, TRADITIONAL

• Al Green, "Precious Lord." Myrrh/Word.
Andrae Crouch, "We Need to Hear from You." Light/Elektra/Asylum.
Jessy Dixon, *Jesus Is Alive and Well*. Light/Lexicon.
Mighty Clouds of Joy, *Miracle Man*. Myrrh/Word.
Ben Moore, *He Believes in Me*. Priority/CBS.

BEST INSPIRATIONAL PERFORMANCE

• Barbara Mandrell, *He Set My Life to Music*. MCA/Songbird.
Kansas, "Crossfire." Kirshner/CBS.
Oak Ridge Boys, "Would They Love Him Down in Shreveport." MCA.
Leontyne Price, "God Bless America." RCA.
B.J. Thomas, "Miracle." Myrrh/Word.

Best Traditional Blues Recording
• *Alright Again*, Clarence "Gatemouth" Brown. Rounder.
Genuine Houserocking Music, Hound Dog Taylor & the House Rockers. Alligator.
He Was a Friend of Mine, Eddie "Cleanhead" Vinson, Roomful of Blues. Muse.
The New Johnny Otis Show, Johnny Otis. Alligator.
Sippie, Sippie Wallace. Atlantic.

Best Ethnic or Traditional Folk Recording
• *Queen Ida and the Bon Temps Zydeco Band on Tour*, Queen Ida. GNP Crescendo.
In the Tradition, Boys of the Lough. Flying Fish.
Live in America, John Renbourn Group. Flying Fish.
Metropolis, Klezmorim. Flying Fish.
Reggae Sunsplash '81: A Tribute to Bob Marley, various artists. Elektra.
Tennessee: Folk Heritage—The Mountains, various artists. Charles Wolfe, producer. Tennessee Folklore Society.

Best Latin Recording
• *Machito and his Salsa Big Band '82*, Machito. Timeless.
Rhythm of Life, Ray Barretto. Fania.
Canciones del Solar de los Aburidos, Willie Colon/Rubén Blades. Fania.
Escenas de Amor, José Feliciano. Motown Latino.
Momentos, Julio Iglesias. Disco CBS International.

Best Instrumental Composition
• "Flying (Theme from *E.T. The Extra-Terrestrial*)," John Williams. MCA, publisher.
"Adventure on Earth," John Williams. MCA, publisher.
"Are You Going with Me?" Pat Metheny, Lyle Mays. Pat-Meth Music, Lyle Mays Inc., publishers.
Desire, Tom Scott. Tomscot Music, publisher.
"In the Presence and Absence of Each Other, Parts 1, 2 & 3," Claus Ogerman. Gema/Ebony Musik Verlag, Gema, publishers.

Best Arrangement on an Instrumental Recording
• John Williams, "Flying (Theme from *E.T. The Extra-Terrestrial*)" (John Williams). MCA.
Les Hooper, "Pavane" (Les Hooper Big Band). Jazz Hounds.
Earl Klugh, Ronnie Foster, Clare Fischer, "Balladina" (Earl Klugh). EMI/Liberty.
Pat Metheny, Lyle Mays, "Are You Going With Me" (Pat Metheny Group). ECM.
Claus Ogerman, "Pavane pour une Infante Defunte" (Claus Ogerman featuring Jan Akkerman). Jazzman.

Best Arrangement for Voices
• David Paich, "Rosanna" (Toto). Columbia.
Al Capps, "Route 66" (Manhattan Transfer). Warner Bros.
Donald Fagen, "Ruby Baby" (Donald Fagen). Warner Bros.
Clare Fischer, "One Night (in a Dream)" (Clare Fischer & Salsa Picante with 2 + 2). Discovery.
Gene Puerling, "Lullaby of Birdland" (Singers Unlimited). Pausa.

Best Cast Show Album
• *Dreamgirls*, Henry Krieger, composer. Tom Eyen, lyricist. David Foster, producer. Geffen/Warner Bros.
Cats, Andrew Lloyd Webber, Richard Stilgoe, Trevor Nunn, composers. Poems by T.S. Eliot. Andrew Lloyd Webber, producer. Geffen/Warner Bros.
Joseph and the Amazing Technicolor Dreamcoat, Andrew Lloyd Webber, composer. Tim Rice, lyricist. Tim Rice, Roger Watson, producers. Chrysalis.
Merrily We Roll Along, Stephen Sondheim, composer and lyricist. Thomas Z. Shepard, producer. RCA.
Nine, Maury Yeston, composer and lyricist. Michael Berniker, producer. Columbia/CBS.

Best Album of Original Score Written for a Motion Picture or a Television Special
(Composer's/Songwriter's Award)
• *E.T. The Extra-Terrestrial*, John Williams, composer. MCA.
The French Lieutenant's Woman, Carl Davis, composer. DRG.

On Golden Pond, Dave Grusin, composer. MCA.

Ragtime, Randy Newman, composer. Elektra.

Victor/Victoria, Henry Mancini, composer. Leslie Bricusse, lyricist. MGM/Polygram.

BEST INSTRUMENTAL ARRANGEMENT ACCOMPANYING VOCAL(S)

✓ • Jerry Hey, David Paich, "Rosanna" (Toto). Columbia.

Les Hooper, "Easy to Love" (Singers Unlimited). Pausa.

✓ Rob Mounsey, Donald Fagen, "I.G.Y. (What a Beautiful World)" (Donald Fagen). Warner Bros.

Marty Paich, "Only a Miracle" (Kenny Loggins). Columbia.

Stevie Wonder, Paul Riser, "Do I Do" (Stevie Wonder). Tamla/Motown.

BEST CLASSICAL ALBUM

• *Bach: The Goldberg Variations*, Glenn Gould. Glenn Gould, Samuel Carter, album producers. CBS.

Berlioz: La Damnation de Faust, Sir Georg Solti conducting Chicago Symphony Orchestra and Chorus (solos: Frederica von Stade, Kenneth Riegel, Jose van Dam). James Mallinson, producer. London.

Debussy: La Mer; *Prelude a L'Apres-Midi d'un Faune*; *Danses Sacree et Profane*, Leonard Slatkin conducting St. Louis Symphony. Frances Tietov, harp. Robert Woods, producer. Telarc.

Mahler: Symphony No. 7 in E Minor ("Song of the Night"), James Levine conducting Chicago Symphony. Thomas Z. Shepard, Jay David Saks, producers. RCA.

Stravinsky: The Recorded Legacy, Igor Stravinsky, Robert Craft conducting various orchestras, ensembles, various solo artists. John McClure, producer. CBS.

BEST CLASSICAL ORCHESTRAL RECORDING
(Conductor's Award)

• *Mahler: Symphony No. 7 in E Minor ("Song of the Night")*, James Levine conducting Chicago Symphony. Thomas Z. Shepard, Jay David Saks, producers. RCA.

Debussy: La Mer; *Prelude a L'Apres-Midi d'un Faune*; *Danses Sacree et Profane*, Leonard Slatkin conducting Chicago Symphony. Robert Woods, producer. Telarc.

Holst: The Planets, Herbert von Karajan conducting Berlin Philharmonic. Günther Breest, Michel Glotz, producers. Deutsche Grammophon.

Mozart: Symphonies, Volume I (The Early Works), Christopher Hogwood conducting Academy of Ancient Music. Morton Winding, producer. L'Oiseau-Lyre.

R. Strauss: Death & Transfiguration; *Don Juan*; *Salome, Dance of the Seven Veils*, Eduardo Mata conducting Dallas Symphony. Jay David Saks, producer. RCA.

BEST CHAMBER MUSIC PERFORMANCE

• Richard Stoltzman, Richard Goode, *Brahms: The Sonatas for Clarinet & Piano, Op. 120*. London.

Cleveland Quartet with Pinchas Zuckerman, Bernard Greenhouse, *Brahms: The String Sextets (B Flat Major, Op. 18 & G Major, Op. 36)*. RCA.

James Galway, Kung-Wha Chung, Phillip Moll, Moray Welsh, *Bach: Trio Sonatas (BWV 1038, 1039, 1079)*. RCA.

Guarneri Quartet, *Borodin: Quartet No. 2 in D Major; Dohnanyi: Quartet No. 2 in D Flat Major, Op. 15*. RCA.

Lynn Harrell, Vladimir Ashkenazy, *Brahms: Sonatas for Cello & Piano No. 1 in E Minor, Op. 38 & No. 2 in F Major, Op. 99*. RCA.

BEST CLASSICAL PERFORMANCE, INSTRUMENTAL SOLOIST(S) (WITH ORCHESTRA)

• Itzhak Perlman (Daniel Barenboim conducting Chicago Symphony), *Elgar: Concerto for Violin in B Minor*. Deutsche Grammophon.

Vladimir Ashkenazy (Vladimir Ashkenazy conducting Philharmonia), *Mozart: Concerto for Piano No. 22 in E Flat Major, K 482 (Ashkenazy Plays & Conducts Mozart)*. London.

Alicia de Larrocha (Charles Dutoit
conducting Royal Philharmonic),
*Schumann: Concerto for Piano in A
Minor; Rachmaninoff: Concerto for
Piano No. 2 in C Minor, Op. 18.*
London.
Rudolf Serkin (Seiji Ozawa conducting
Boston Symphony), *Beethoven:
Concerto for Piano No. 4 in G Major,
Op. 58.* Telarc.
Joseph Silverstein (Seiji Ozawa
conducting Boston Symphony),
Vivaldi: The Four Seasons. Telarc.

BEST CLASSICAL PERFORMANCE,
INSTRUMENTAL SOLOIST(S)
(WITHOUT ORCHESTRA)
• Glenn Gould, *Bach: The Goldberg
Variations.* CBS.
Emanuel Ax, *Schumann: Humoreske, Op.
20; Fantasiestucke Op. 12.* RCA.
Vladimir Horowitz, *Horowitz at the Met
(Scarlatti, Chopin, Liszt,
Rachmaninoff).* RCA.
Ruth Laredo, *Barber: Sonata for Piano
Op. 26; Souvenirs, Op. 28; Nocturne,
Op. 33.* Nonesuch.
Alicia de Larrocha, *Granados: Danzas
Espanolas.* London.
Ronald Smith, *The Alkan Project (Etudes,
Op. 39, In All the Minor Keys).*
Arabesque.
Isao Tomita, *Grofe-Tomita: Grand
Canyon Suite; Anderson-Tomita:
Syncopated Clock.* RCA.

BEST OPERA RECORDING
Wagner: Der Ring des Nibelungen, Pierre
Boulez conducting Bayreuth Festival
Orchestra (solos: Jones, Altmeyer,
Wenkel, Hofmann, Jung, Jerusalem,
Zednik, McIntyre, Salminen, Becht)
Andrew Kazdin, producer. Philips.
Fauré: Penelope, Charles Dutoit
conducting Orchestre Philharmonique
de Monte Carlo (solos: Norman,
Vanzo, Huttenlocher). Pierre Tavoix,
producer. Erato.
Janácek: The Cunning Little Vixen, Sir
Charles Mackerras conducting Vienna
Philharmonic Orchestra and Vienna
State Opera Chorus (solos: Popp,
Randova, Jedlicka). James Mallinson,
producer. London.

Puccini: Tosca, James Levine conducting
Philharmonia Orchestra and Ambrosian
Opera Chorus (solos: Renata Scotto,
Domingo, Bruson). John Willan,
producer. Angel.
Puccini: Turandot, Herbert von Karajan
conducting Vienna Philharmonic
Orchestra, Vienna State Opera Chorus
and Vienna Boys' Choir (solos:
Domingo, Ricciarelli, de Palma,
Raimondi, Hendricks, Hornik). Günther
Breest, Michael Glotz, producers.
Deutsche Grammophon.
Weinberger: *Schwanda, The Bagpiper*,
Heinz Wallberg conducting Munich
Radio Orchestra, Bavarian Radio
Chorus (solos: Popp, Jerusalem. Prey,
Killebrew, Nimsgern). George
Krongold, producer. CBS.

BEST CHORAL PERFORMANCE
(OTHER THAN OPERA)
• Margaret Hillis, chorus master, Chicago
Symphony Orchestra Chorus. Sir
George Solti conducting Chicago
Symphony Orchestra, *Berlioz: La
Damnation de Faust.* London.
Norbert Balatsch, chorus master, Vienna
State Opera Chorus. Bernard Haitink
conducting Vienna Philharmonic
Orchestra (solos: Gundula Janowitz,
Tom Krause), *Brahms: German
Requiem.* Philips.
Nicholas Cleobury, chorus master, City of
Birmingham Symphony Orchestra
Chorus. Simon Rattle conducting City
of Birmingham Symphony Orchestra,
Janacek: Glagolitic Mass. Angel.
Laszlo Heltay, chorus master, Chorus of
Academy of St. Martin-in-the-Fields.
Neville Marriner conducting Academy
of St. Martin-in-the-Fields (solos:
Dietrich Fischer-Dieskau, Edith
Mathis, Siegfried Jerusalem), *Haydn:
The Seasons.* Philips.
Thomas Peck, chorus master, St. Louis
Symphony Chorus. Leonard Slatkin
conducting St. Louis Symphony
Orchestra, Rachmaninoff: "The Bells"
and "Russian Songs" (from album
Rachmaninoff Orchestral Music). Vox
Cum Laude.

Gerhard Schmidt-Gaden, choral conductor; Tolzer Knabenchor. Nikolaus Harnoncourt conducting Concentus Musicus Wien, *Bach: Cantatas Volume 30 (Nos. 120, 121, 122, 123)*. Telefunken.

Robert Shaw conducting Atlanta Symphony Orchestra Chorus and Atlanta Symphony Orchestra (solo: Sylvia McNair), *Poulenc: Gloria for Soprano, Choir and Orchestra (G Major)*. Telarc.

BEST CLASSICAL VOCAL SOLOIST PERFORMANCE
• Leontyne Price (Zubin Mehta conducting Israel Philharmonic), *Verdi: Arias (Leontyne Price Sings Verdi)*. London.

Elly Ameling (Dalton Baldwin, accompanist), *Fauré: La Bonne Chanson; Debussy: Chansons de Bilitis & Ariettes Oubliees*. CBS.

Kiri Te Kanawa (Gyorgy Fischer conducting Vienna Chamber Orchestra), *Mozart: Concert Arias (Andromeda, Il Burbero di Buon Core, Artaserse, Idomeneo, Cerere Placata)*. London.

Jessye Norman (Daniel Barenboim conducting Orchestre de Paris), *Berlioz: La Mort de Cleopatre*. Deutsche Grammophon.

Frederica von Stade (Martin Katz, accompanist), *Frederica von Stade Live!* CBS.

BEST ENGINEERED RECORDING, CLASSICAL
• Paul Goodman, *Mahler: Symphony No. 7 in E Minor ("Song of the Night")*, (James Levine conducting Chicago Symphony Orchestra). RCA.

Paul Goodman, *Dvorak: Symphony No. 9 in E Minor (From the New World)*, (James Levine conducting Chicago Symphony Orchestra). RCA.

Gunter Hermanns, *Holst: The Planets*, (Herbert von Karajan conducting Berlin Philharmonic). Deutsche Grammophon.

James Lock, Simon Eadon, *Berlioz: La Damnation de Faust*, (Sir Georg Solti conducting Chicago Symphony Orchestra and Chorus; solos: Frederica Von Stade, Kenneth Riegel, Jose van Dam). London.

Stan Tonkel, John Johnson, Ray Moore, Martin Greenblatt, Bud Graham, *Bach: The Goldberg Variations*, (solo: Glenn Gould). CBS.

CLASSICAL PRODUCER OF THE YEAR
• Robert Woods, Telarc.
Steven Epstein, CBS.
Glenn Gould, Samuel Carter. CBS.
James Mallinson, London.
Jay David Saks, RCA.

BEST SPOKEN WORD, DOCUMENTARY, OR DRAMA RECORDING
• *Raiders of the Lost Ark: The Movie on Record*. Tom Voegeli, producer. Columbia.

Charles Dickens' Nicholas Nickelby, read by Roger Rees. Caedmon.

Foundation's Edge, read by Isaac Asimov. Caedmon.

No Man's Island, Sir John Gielgud, Sir Ralph Richardson. Caedmon.

2010: Odyssey Two, read by Arthur C. Clarke. Caedmon.

BEST COMEDY RECORDING
• *Live on the Sunset Strip,* Richard Pryor. Warner Bros.

Eddie Murphy, Eddie Murphy. Columbia/CBS.

Great White North, Bob & Doug McKenzie. Mercury/Polygram.

A Place for My Stuff, George Carlin. Atlantic.

The Steve Martin Brothers, Steve Martin. Warner Bros.

BEST RECORDING FOR CHILDREN
• *In Harmony 2*, Billy Joel, Bruce Springsteen, James Taylor, Kenny Loggins, Carly and Lucy Simon, Teddy Pendergrass, Crystal Gayle, Lou Rawls, Deniece Williams, Janis Ian, Dr John. Lucy Simon, David Levine, producers. CBS.

Animals and Other Things, Candle with Agapeland Singers. Tony Salerno, producer. Birdwing/Sparrow.

Best of Friends, Smurfs. Frans Erkelens, producer. Sessions/Starland.

The Chipmunks Go Hollywood, Chipmunks. Janice Karman, Ross Bagdasarian, producers. RCA.

Here Comes Garfield, Lou Rawls, Desiree Goyette. CBS/Epic.

I Am God's Project, Birdwing Kids Korus. Billy Ray Hearn, Linda Gray, Frostie Gray, producers. Birdwing/Sparrow.

BEST ENGINEERED RECORDING (NON-CLASSICAL)
√ • Al Schmitt, Tom Knox, Greg Ladanyi, David Paich, Steve Porcaro, Dick Gall, Bruce Heigh, *Toto IV* (Toto). Columbia.
Neil Dorfsman, *Love Over Gold* (Dire Straits). Warner Bros.
√ Roger Nichols, Daniel Lazerus, Elliot Scheiner, *The Nightfly* (Donald Fagen). Warner Bros.
Alan Parsons, *Eye in the Sky* (Alan Parsons Project). Arista.
√ George Tutko, Don Gehman, Mark Stabbeds, *American Fool* (John Cougar). Riva/Polygram.

BEST ALBUM PACKAGE
(Art Director's Award)
• Kosh with Ron Larson, *Get Closer* (Linda Ronstadt). Elektra/Asylum.
Jules Bates, *Nothing to Fear* (Oingo Boingo). A&M.
Mick Haggerty, Ginger Canzoneri, *Vacation* (Go-Go's). IRS.
Denise Minobe, Ron Coro, *We Are One* (Pieces of a Dream). Elektra.
George Osaki, *Ongaku-Kai Live in Japan* (Crusaders). Crusaders/MCA.

BEST ALBUM NOTES
(Annotator's Award)
• John Chilton, Richard Sudhalter, *Bunny Berigan (Giants of Jazz)* (Bunny Berigan). Time-Life.
Gary Giddins, *Duke Ellington 1941* (Duke Ellington & His Orchestra). Smithsonian Collection.
Thornton Hagert, *An Experiment in Modern Music; Paul Whiteman at Aeolian Hall* (Paul Whiteman). Smithsonian Collection.

William Ivey, summary and glossary, *The Greatest Country Music Recordings of All Time*, (various artists). Franklin Mint Recording Society.
William Ivey, Bob Pinson, *60 Years of Country Music* (various artists). RCA.
Robert Palmer, *Young Blood* (Coasters). Atlantic/ Deluxe.

BEST HISTORICAL ALBUM
• *The Tommy Dorsey/Frank Sinatra Sessions Vols, 1, 2, 3* (Tommy Dorsey, Frank Sinatra). Alan Dell. RCA.
Bartók at the Piano, 1920–1945, (Béla Bartók). Dora Antal, producer. Hungaroton.
Bunny Berigan (Giants of Jazz) (Bunny Berigan). Michael Brooks, producer. Time-Life.
An Experiment in Modern Music: Paul Whiteman at Aeolian Hall (Paul Whiteman). Martin Williams, J.R. Taylor, producers. RCA.
Minstrels & Tunesmiths: The Commercial Roots of Early Country Music (various artists). John Edwards Memorial Foundation.

PRODUCER OF THE YEAR (NON-CLASSICAL)
• Toto
David Foster
Quincy Jones
Gary Katz
John Cougar Mellencamp, Don Gehman

VIDEO OF THE YEAR
• *Olivia Physical*, Olivia Newton-John. MCA Video.
Fun & Games, various artists. Margaret Murphy, producer. OPA/RCA Video.
The Tales of Hoffmann, Royal Opera conducted by George Pretre with Placido Domingo. Pioneer Artists.
The Tubes Video, Tubes. Pioneer Artists.
Visions: Elton John, Elton John. Embassy Home Entertainment.

The Michael Jackson Show

Grammy night was a genuine thriller in every way: The record that broke all existing records for album sales ended up setting a new awards precedent, too, when it won eight Grammys, the most ever.

Michael Jackson's *Thriller* spawned a national cult of Michaelmania, the likes of which had not been seen since Beatlemania swept America nearly 20 years earlier. Jackson, in fact, even *looked* like a Beatle as he entered the Shrine Auditorium for the Grammy show dressed in a sequined Sgt. Pepper commodore's coat (accessorized with a single sequined glove, a Jackson trademark). In another interesting Beatle allusion, one of the only four defeats Jackson would suffer among his staggering 12 nominations was for "The Girl Is Mine," his duet with Paul McCartney that was competing in the pop duo/group vocal category.

Jackson was at his professional apogee at the time of the 1983 awards. The artist, whose only previous Grammy was an r&b award for "Don't Stop 'Til You Get Enough" in 1979, now seemed to be taking that same advice to heart. *Thriller* became the number-one album of all time, selling more than 40 million copies worldwide, thereby topping the previous record of 25 million set by the Bee Gees et al. for Grammy's 1978 Album of the Year *Saturday Night Fever*. ("Everyone wants that record,"

Sixty million television viewers tuned in for a genuine Thriller *of a Grammycast to see Michael Jackson and Quincy Jones sweep up 12 awards between them.*

one record store manager told *The Washington Post* about *Thriller*'s phenomenal sales. "Kids, businessmen ... you'd be amazed.") Jackson's LP set another precedent, too, when it spawned seven Top 10 hits, three more than any album had ever launched before. As "The Gloved One," as press pundits nicknamed Jackson, took his seat in the front row of the auditorium for the Grammycast, 60 million Americans watched at home, a number surpassed that year only by the Super Bowl audience. Furthermore, viewers in more than 25 other countries watched, too.

The New York Times described Jackson as "a shy and wary little prince" as the show began, but that was hardly so. Jackson may have looked demure in the audience, but he proved to be a bold public presence in 1983. Even when the TV cameras cut away to commercials, there was Michael — in one of two hugely hyped advertisements for Pepsi that also touted his upcoming *Victory* tour with his brothers. The commercials had acquired their own share of fame — or infamy — when Jackson's hair caught fire during taping and he suffered second- and third-degree burns. (Interestingly, the accident occurred on the same stage where the Grammys were now being handed out.) Actor and presenter Mickey Rooney captured the spirit of the evening when he said early on in the ceremony, "It's a pleasure doing *The Michael Jackson Show*."

The previous record for winning the most Grammys in a year was held by Roger Miller, who nabbed six in 1965, most of them for "King of the Road." Jackson's eight were for Album of the Year, Record of the Year ("Beat It"), Best New Rhythm & Blues Song ("P.Y.T. [Pretty Young Thing]," which triumphed over two other Jackson songs), Producer of the Year (shared with last year's victor, Quincy Jones), Best Children's Recording (for an LP version of the hit movie *E.T. The Extra-Terrestrial*, also produced by Jones), and a never-before-seen sweep across three groups of categories. Jackson ended up with the male vocal performance awards for pop, rock, *and* r&b (for *Thriller*, "Beat It," and "Billie Jean," respectively). *Thriller* also won the prize for Best Engineered Recording.

"I just want to say thank you and I love you all," Jackson whispered when he picked up his first statuette. Later on, as his booty increased and he became increasingly emboldened by the supportive screams of his fans in the balcony, the "shy prince" assumed a kingly command of the ceremonies as he invited his sisters La Toya, Rebie, and Tricia up to the stage, and removed his sunglasses for the benefit of a legendary film star (and unlikely fan) watching at home, saying, "Katharine, this is for you." The gesture and remark were directed to Katharine Hepburn, who had recently admonished Jackson for wearing shades at the American Music Awards.

Jackson probably would have swept the two awards for music videos, too (increased from last year's one) since the videos for "Billie Jean," "Beat It," and "Thriller" were big hits on MTV, but they weren't qualified to compete this year because they hadn't been available for commercial sale before the eligibility cutoff period. Instead, Best Video, Short Form and Best Video Album were nabbed by Duran Duran "to no one's surprise," said *The Washington Post*, describing them as "MTV superstars."

When "Beat It" took Record of the Year, it beat the number-one song in the year's Hot 100, which was considered an equally strong contender: "Every Breath You Take" by the Police. "Every Breath" was written by the Police's lead vocalist, Sting, who in turn stung Jackson by copping the New Song of the Year award in what *The Washington Post* called an "upset that caught the experts by surprise." All the experts except one, that is. In an article written for the *L.A. Times*, *Billboard* columnist Paul Grein, who had an uncanny knack for calling these awards, predicted the winner correctly. He explained: "Ballads traditionally have an edge in this category. Besides, the presence of 'Billie Jean' and 'Beat It' may split the Jackson vote." Grein also foresaw the Police's seizure of the laurels for best rock group vocals for *Synchronicity*, but not the added prize it got for best pop group vocal performance ("Every Breath").

Jackson's impressive eight victories in one year set a new record.

That award, Grein believed, would go to Culture Club, which was virtually everyone's choice to nab Best New Artist. The British pop act was competing against four other British nominees. When it prevailed as expected, *Billboard* noted, "This marks the third year in a row that the award has gone to an international act." Culture Club was immensely popular and its victory was considered such a foregone conclusion that N.A.R.A.S. flew comedian Joan Rivers to London to interview the group and its outrageous cross-dressing lead singer Boy George (whose real name was George O'Dowd) for the U.S. TV audience. Early in the show, Rivers toyed with George playfully, saying, "You look like Brooke Shields on steroids!" George obviously enjoyed the ribbing and giggled in response. Later on, when his group won the rookie of the year prize, he tossed a kiss at the camera and said, "Thank you, America. You've got good taste, style, and you know a good drag queen when you see one!"

> *"Thank you, America!" Boy George said. "You've got good taste, style, and you know a good drag queen when you see one!"*

Irene Cara, who lost the Best New Artist award to Christopher Cross in 1980, came back strong this year with the music to the film *Flashdance*, which snagged nine nominations in all, the year's second biggest total. *Flashdance* starred Jennifer Beals as a factory welder by day who works as a sexy dancer by night. Its score was composed mostly by Giorgio Moroder, the renowned disco producer/songwriter. "The past year's dance music emphasis was seen not only in the *Thriller* sweep, but also in the strong showing made by *Flashdance*," *Billboard* reported, spotting a trend toward a renaissance of disco.

Flashdance's love theme brought Moroder the award for Best Instrumental Composition. Cara pulled off what *Billboard* called "the evening's biggest upset" when she reaped the female pop vocals prize for "Flashdance ... What a Feeling" over most pundits' (including Grein's) pick of Linda Ronstadt for her *What's New* LP. Co-writers Moroder, Keith Forsey, and singer/ colyricist Cara, whose "What a Feeling" was Best Song at the Oscars, also shared the prize for Grammy's best film score, along with a long list of other talent that included composer Michael Boddicker, who thanked Michael Jackson "for not writing a song for the movies." Among the competitors they did have to overcome was *Star Wars* and *Superman* composer John Williams, who had dominated the category for seven out of the previous eight years and was nominated this year for *Return of the Jedi*. The other prize for a show's score, Best Cast Show Album, went to the original Broadway cast recording of Andrew Lloyd Webber's *Cats*. The show's London cast recording had been nominated last year, but lost to Broadway's *Dreamgirls*.

Unlike Williams, singer Pat Benatar extended her winning streak by taking a fourth Grammy in a row for Best Female Rock Vocal Performance for "Love Is a Battlefield." (Grein called this category correctly with the caveat "unless Stevie Nicks pulls an upset.")

The last time that dance music was so big at the Grammys — in the late 1970s, when it wasn't yet a federal offense to call it "disco" — Chaka Khan was repeatedly passed over for prizes. This year she scored three of them, however, two for her eponymous album: best r&b vocal performance (topping last year's winner, who was expected to return: Jennifer Holliday) and for one of the LP's arrangements with Arif Mardin. In addition to her solo work, Khan was still a member of Rufus and so shared the r&b group vocal trophy for "Ain't Nobody," their last Top 10 hit together.

Disco's unexpected resurgence had an equally unexpected follower in jazz keyboardist and composer Herbie Hancock, who upset his purist fans when his dance-tinged "Rockit" soared up the charts and became one of the most popular videos on MTV. Hancock recorded it with members of the rock band Material and earned the Best R&B Instrumental Performance statuette. When he and the band performed the number on the Grammycast, *Variety* called the segment "particularly electrifying."

In the area of Best Traditional Blues Recording, two-time past winner B.B. King was hailed for his *Blues 'n' Jazz*, which *Rolling Stone* called "outstanding" because it "showcases some of King's finest vocal performances against exciting big-band arrangements." The Best Ethnic or Traditional Folk Recording award, which was traditionally claimed by blues artists, went to Clifton Chenier & His Red Hot Louisiana Band, known principally for fusing Cajun music with r&b sounds in works such as the group's victorious *I'm Here*.

The jazz line-up welcomed back a host of past winners such as the Pat Metheny Group, which held onto the fusion vocal prize they won last year for this year's *Travels*, a new two-disc set of live material. The velvet-voiced Mel Tormé reclaimed the male singing category with *Top Drawer*, while the Manhattan Transfer's "Why Not!" won the group the jazz vocal prize for a fourth year in a row. Ella Fitzgerald became

Culture Club beat out four other British groups to win as 1983's Best New Artist.

the seventh-most honored Grammy recipient when she picked up her twelfth, the female jazz vocal trophy for *The Best Is Yet to Come*. The Phil Woods Quartet made a comeback, too, in the group instrumental slot for its live recordings of performances at the Village Vanguard, New York's historic jazz club.

One of the few newcomers to the jazz awards was Wynton Marsalis, a 22-year-old trumpet virtuoso who pulled off a Grammy first by being nominated — and winning — in both the jazz and classical categories for *Think of One* (showcasing works by Thelonious Monk, Duke Ellington, and himself) and a separate album of music by Haydn, Mozart, and Hummel. The novelty of Marsalis being considered for both genres was enough for N.A.R.A.S. to invite him to perform on the show. When he won the jazz prize, Marsalis thanked his mother and father (noted jazz pianist Ellis Marsalis) "for putting up with me all these years practicing and making that noise on the trumpet" and his band members, who included his brother, saxophonist Branford.

The writer of the year's Best New Country Song, "Stranger in My House," was an unlikely hit songwriter: Mike Reid was a one-time tackle for the Cincinnati Bengals who got the idea for the song one day while having an argument with his wife. She worked nights; he worked days. "With our schedules, we weren't seeing a lot of each other," Reid told *Billboard*. "I told her, 'Living with you is like having a stranger in my house.' As soon as I said it, I thought, 'That's a great title for a song!' So I left the room and wrote it down. Then I went back and continued the argument."

Ronnie Milsap was nominated for the male vocals honors for his hit version of "Stranger" but lost to Lee Greenwood for "I.O.U." Greenwood was a relative newcomer to big-time country music. He finally had his first gold album, *Somebody's Gonna Love You*, just four days before the Grammycast. The Country Music Association voted Greenwood Male Vocalist of the Year.

The winner of the female vocal honors was Anne Murray for "A Little Good News," which celebrated a positive reading of the daily newspapers with lyrics like "Nobody O.D.-ed, nobody died in vain." The song got extraordinary media coverage when then Vice President George Bush referred to it in his political speeches. The C.M.A. named it Song of the Year.

For a second year in a row, Alabama (*The Closer You Get*) reaped the group

> **Presenter Joan Rivers was "thrilled to be part of the Emmys."**

vocals prize. "It all goes back to our fans," one band member told the press backstage. *The Washington Post* noted, with its usual (and sometimes refreshing) cynicism, that the group's "snakeskin boots complemented their black tuxes just fine."

Donna Summer lost her bid for best female pop vocals to Irene Cara, but made up for the loss by claiming Best Inspirational Performance for "He's a Rebel." With previous victories in the r&b lineup for "Last Dance" and in rock for "Hot Stuff," Summer joined Michael Jackson to become one of the few artists to win in three different award classifications.

Other religious slots welcomed such first-time champs as Sandra Crouch (twin sister of five-time past winner Andrae), who garnered the female soul gospel performance prize for *We Sing Praises*. Before Amy Grant branched out successfully into pop music in the early '90s, she recorded religious music almost exclusively and won her second of many Grammys for religious fare this year for "Ageless Medley." Al Green (*I'll Rise Again*) picked up his fourth award and third in a row, while Barbara Mandrell returned from last year to pick up a new trophy for her duet with Bobby Jones, "I'm So Glad I'm Standing Here Today."

A movement had been growing within N.A.R.A.S. in the recent past for more Latin categories. "So far the [single] prize has been dominated by tropical music," *Billboard* noted, "and one subcategory at that, Afro-Cuban Rhythms (salsa)." Now the former Best Latin Recording was scrapped in favor of three new performance categories: Latin Pop (claimed by José Feliciano, Grammy's Best New Artist of 1968, for *Me Enamore*), Mexican/American (going to the rock/ Tex-Mex fusion band Los Lobos of Los Angeles for "Anselma"), and Tropical Latin (won by 1978 Latin Grammy winner Tito Puente for *On Broadway*).

The winner of Best Comedy Recording was the target of protests from the gay community. On *Eddie Murphy Comedian*, the *Saturday Night Live* performer made jokes about AIDS, conjured up scenes of buggery between *The Honeymooners'* Jackie Gleason and Art Carney, and said to the audience, "Faggots are not allowed to look at my ass while I'm on stage. That's why I keep movin' while I'm up here." The award's presenters were Rodney Dangerfield, who won the prize in 1980, and Cyndi Lauper, next year's Best New Artist. Said *The Washington Post*: "Lauper, with her customized pink hair and wearing sequins on her face and clay fruits around her neck, squeaked and squealed like Betty Boop as Dangerfield told her, with utmost respect, 'You look like a rainbow, my dear.'"

Prior to the announcement of the winners of the classical awards, Sir Georg Solti was only one award shy of tying Henry Mancini's record for having the most total Grammys (20). Solti was in London on the night of the Grammycast where he waited eagerly by the phone for news of the voting results. "When the appointed hour had passed and no call came," according to *Grammy Pulse*, "he resigned himself to the idea of not winning and set about the task of consoling his children. 'I didn't expect I would win anything, but I was still very sad. I said to my children, "All right, papa didn't win anything. Bad luck, I can't win every year."' Three hours later, the news of his four new Grammy wins came over the BBC radio. 'You can imagine how tremendously happy I was.'" The next day, he said, he received a telegram from Mancini

that read, "I relinquish with pleasure my leadership to you."

Solti's wins marked the 10th year in a row that he had been Grammy-honored and established the longest winning streak in the awards' history.

Two of Solti's Grammys were for conducting Mahler's Symphony No. 9 in D Major, one marking the third time the maestro was honored with the prize for the year's top classical LP for a Mahler symphony (the others were for No. 8 in

Sting (left) of the Police shocked the experts when he won Song of the Year for "Every Breath You Take."

1972 and No. 2 in 1981). Solti's second trophy of 1983 was awarded for his orchestra's performance of Mahler's Ninth. (The same prize was awarded for the same work in 1977, when Carlo Maria Giulini acted as guest conductor of Solti's Chicago Symphony. The orchestra also played Mahler's Ninth with Solti holding the baton in 1967 in a performance called "brilliant" by some critics but dismissed by others as being too large and extroverted.) *Fanfare* called this version "praiseworthy" and "the best-played Ninth on records." It also won Best Engineered Recording.

Solti's third award was a choral Grammy for Haydn's *Creation*. His fourth accolade was in the category of Best Opera Recording, which resulted in a tie between Solti's reading of Mozart's

Wynton Marsalis scored a Grammy first by winning in jazz and classical categories. He thanked his parents "for putting up with me all those years practising."

The Marriage of Figaro (Le Nozzi de Figaro) — called "effervescent" by the critics — and the soundtrack to director Franco Zeffirelli's highly acclaimed 1982 film version of Verdi's *La Traviata* starring Teresa Stratas, Placido Domingo, and Cornell MacNeill, and with James Levine conducting the Metropolitan Opera Orchestra. Levine and the Met orchestra also performed for divas Leontyne Price and Marilyn Horne at their joint Met appearance that reaped them the vocal soloist honors.

Last year's winner of Best Classical Recording, the late pianist Glenn Gould, won the soloist (sans orchestra) prize for what *Gramophone* called his "masculine" and "sturdy" renditions of Beethoven sonatas that "may offend drawing-room susceptibilities." The chamber music award was shared by the exuberant Russian cellist Mstislav Rostropovich and the veteran Brahms pianist Rudolf Serkin for their Brahms sonatas. "There are times, especially in the E Minor Sonata, when these two temperaments mesh beautifully," said *Fanfare*. On the F Major Sonata, it added, "the collaboration is less successful."

Once again, the Grammys show was broadcast on CBS from the Shrine Auditorium in Los Angeles with John Denver acting as "the genial, efficient, and unflappable host," according to *The New York Times*. For the first time ever, music video clips were sometimes used in place of album covers or live shots of the performers when the nominees were announced.

Among the night's highlights was the bestowal of a Lifetime Achievement Award upon Chuck Berry, who performed on the show. He accepted the honor shouting, "Long live rock & roll!" and hugged his prize backstage, adding, "Man, I wouldn't give this up for anything. I'd kill for this."

Other musical numbers included Donna Summer singing "She Works Hard for the Money" ("She certainly does," commented the *Times*) and Annie Lennox of Eurythmics singing "Sweet Dreams" with "a pompadour and sideburns hair style which suggested," said *Variety*, "slender versions of Wayne Newton and Vegas-era Elvis Presley." Given the added prominence at the show of drag queen Boy George and a mascara-laden Michael Jackson, *The Washington Post* said, "Anyone tuning in without an awareness of The New Androgyny was in for a shock."

"The Grammys show had its failings, some unavoidable," the *Times* said. "Two major groups — the Police and Duran Duran — were not on hand to receive their awards. There were the inevitable momentary flubs. Miss Rivers allowed as how she was 'very thrilled to be part of the Emmys.' "

The awards ceremony was broadcast on CBS from the Shrine Auditorium in Los Angeles on February 28, 1984, for the awards eligibility period of October 1, 1982, through September 30, 1983.

ALBUM OF THE YEAR
- *Thriller*, Michael Jackson. Quincy Jones, Michael Jackson, producers. Epic/CBS.
- *Flashdance* (original soundtrack from the motion picture), Irene Cara, Shandi, Helen St. John, Karen Kamon, Joe Esposito, Laura Branigan, Donna Summer, Cycle V, Kim Carnes, Michael Sembello. Giorgio Moroder, producer. Casablanca/Polygram.
- *An Innocent Man*, Billy Joel. Phil Ramone, producer. Columbia.
- *Let's Dance*, Davie Bowie. David Bowie, Nile Rodgers, producers. EMI-America.
- *Synchronicity*, Police. Police, Hugh Padgham, producers. A&M.

RECORD OF THE YEAR
- "Beat It," Michael Jackson. Quincy Jones, Michael Jackson, producers. Epic/CBS.
- "All Night Long (All Night)," Lionel Richie. Lionel Richie, James Anthony Carmichael, producers. Motown.
- "Every Breath You Take," Police. Police, Hugh Padgham, producers. A&M.
- "Flashdance ...What a Feeling," Irene Cara. Giorgio Moroder, producer. Casablanca/Polygram.
- "Maniac," Michael Sembello. Phil Ramone, producer. Casablanca/Polygram.

NEW SONG OF THE YEAR
(Songwriter's Award)
- "Every Breath You Take," Sting. Magnetic Publishers (BMI), publisher.
- "All Night Long (All Night)," Lionel Richie. Brockman Music (ASCAP), publisher.
- "Beat It," Michael Jackson. Mijac Music (BMI), publisher.
- "Billie Jean," Michael Jackson. Mijac Music (BMI), publisher.
- "Maniac," Michael Sembello, Dennis Matkosky. Intersong Music, Famous Music Corp, WB Music Corp. (ASCAP), publishers.

BEST NEW ARTIST
- Culture Club. Epic/CBS.
- Big Country. Mercury/Polygram.
- Eurythmics. RCA.
- Men Without Hats. Backstreet/MCA.
- Musical Youth. MCA.

BEST POP VOCAL PERFORMANCE, MALE
- Michael Jackson, *Thriller*. Epic/CBS.
- Billy Joel, "Uptown Girl," track from *An Innocent Man*. Columbia.
- Prince, *1999*. Warner Bros.
- Lionel Richie, "All Night Long (All Night)." Motown.
- Michael Sembello, "Maniac." Casablanca/Polygram.

BEST POP VOCAL PERFORMANCE, FEMALE
- Irene Cara, "Flashdance ... What a Feeling." Casablanca/Polygram.
- Sheena Easton, "Telefone (Long Distance Love Affair)." EMI-America.
- Linda Ronstadt, *What's New*. Asylum.
- Donna Summer, "She Works Hard for the Money." Mercury.
- Bonnie Tyler, "Total Eclipse of the Heart." Columbia.

BEST POP PERFORMANCE BY A DUO OR GROUP WITH VOCAL
- Police, "Every Breath You Take." A&M.
- Culture Club, "Do You Really Want to Hurt Me." Virgin/Epic.
- James Ingram, Patti Austin, "How Do You Keep the Music Playing." Qwest/Warner Bros.
- Michael Jackson, Paul McCartney, "The Girl Is Mine." Epic/CBS.
- Kenny Rogers, Dolly Parton, "Islands in the Stream." RCA.

BEST POP INSTRUMENTAL PERFORMANCE
- George Benson, "Being With You," track from *In Your Eyes*. Warner Bros.
- Herb Alpert, "Blow Your Own Horn," instrumental tracks from album. A&M.
- Larry Carlton, *Friends*. Warner Bros.
- Joe Jackson, "Breakdown," track from *Mike's Murder*. A&M.
- Helen St. John, "Love Theme from *Flashdance*," track from *Flashdance*. Casablanca/Polygram.

BEST ROCK VOCAL PERFORMANCE, MALE
√ • Michael Jackson, "Beat It." Epic/CBS.
David Bowie, "Cat People (Putting Out
Fire)," track from *Let's Dance*. EMI
America.
Phil Collins, "I Don't Care Anymore,"
track from *Hello I Must Be Going*.
Atlantic.
Bob Seger, *The Distance*. Capitol.
Rick Springfield, "Affair of the Heart."
RCA.

BEST ROCK VOCAL PERFORMANCE, FEMALE
• Pat Benatar, "Love Is a Battlefield."
Chrysalis.
Joan Armatrading, *The Key*. A&M.
Kim Carnes, *Invisible Hands*. EMI-
America.
Stevie Nicks, *Stand Back*. Modern/Atlantic.
Bonnie Tyler, *Faster Than the Speed of
Night*. Columbia.

BEST ROCK PERFORMANCE BY A DUO OR GROUP WITH VOCAL
• Police, *Synchronicity*. A&M.
Big Country, "In a Big Country."
Mercury/Polygram.
√ Huey Lewis & the News, *Heart & Soul*.
Chrysalis.
√ Talking Heads, "Burning Down the
House." Sire/Warner Bros.
√ ZZ Top, *Eliminator*. Warner Bros.

BEST ROCK INSTRUMENTAL PERFORMANCE
• Sting, "Brimstone & Treacle," track from
Brimstone and Treacle. A&M.
Allan Holdsworth, "Road Games,"
instrumental tracks from *Road Games*.
Warner Bros.
Rainbow, "Anybody There."
Mercury/Polygram.
Pete Townshend, "Unused Piano:
Quadrophenia," track from *Scoop*.
Atlantic.
Stevie Ray Vaughan & Double Trouble,
"Rude Mood," track from *Texas Flood*.
Epic/CBS.

BEST NEW RHYTHM & BLUES SONG
(Songwriter's Award)
√ • "Billie Jean," Michael Jackson. Mijac
Music (BMI), publisher.
"Ain't Nobody," Hawk Wolinski. Overdue
Music (ASCAP), publisher.
"Electric Avenue," Eddy Grant.
Greenheart Music (ASCAP), publisher.

*Pat Benatar's "Love Is a Battlefield"
earned her a fourth rock prize in a row.*

√ "P.Y.T. (Pretty Young Thing)," James
Ingram, Quincy Jones. Eiseman Music
Co., Hen-Al Music, Kings Road (BMI),
Yellow Brick Road Music (ASCAP),
publishers.
√ "Wanna Be Startin' Somethin'," Michael
Jackson. Mijac Music (BMI), publisher.

BEST R&B VOCAL PERFORMANCE, MALE
• Michael Jackson, "Billie Jean." Epic/CBS.
Marvin Gaye, *Midnight Love*. Columbia.
James Ingram, "Party Animal."
Qwest/Warner Bros.
Jeffrey Osborne, *Stay with Me Tonight*.
A&M.
√ Prince, "International Lover," track from
1999. Warner Bros.

BEST R&B VOCAL PERFORMANCE, FEMALE
• Chaka Khan, *Chaka Khan*. Warner Bros.
Aretha Franklin, *Get It Right*. Arista.
Jennifer Holliday, *Feel My Soul*.
Geffen/Warner Bros.
Patti LaBelle, "The Best Is Yet to Come,"
track from Grover Washington, Jr.'s
The Best Is Yet to Come. Elektra.
Stephanie Mills, *Merciless*.
Casablanca/Polygram.
Deniece Williams, *I'm So Proud*.
Columbia.

Best R&B Performance by a Duo or Group with Vocal
- Rufus & Chaka Khan, "Ain't Nobody." Warner Bros.

DeBarge, *In a Special Way.* Gordy/Motown.

Earth, Wind & Fire, "Fall in Love with Me." Columbia.

Shalamar, "Dead Giveaway." Solar/Elektra/Asylum.

Weather Girls, "It's Raining Men." Columbia.

Best R&B Instrumental Performance
- Herbie Hancock, "Rockit." Columbia.

James Brown, "Today," track from *Bring It On.* Churchill.

Gap Band, "Where Are We Going?" track from *Gap Band V Jammin'.* Total Experience.

Quincy Jones, Jerry Hey, "Billie Jean" (instrumental version). Epic/CBS.

Kashif, "The Mood," track from *Kashif.* Arista.

Best Jazz Fusion Performance, Vocal or Instrumental
- Pat Metheny Group, *Travels.* ECM/Warner Bros.

Miles Davis, *Star People.* Columbia.

Spyro Gyra, *City Kids.* MCA.

Weather Report, *Procession.* Columbia.

Yellowjackets, *Mirage à Trois.* Warner Bros.

Best Jazz Vocal Performance, Male
- Mel Tormé, *Top Drawer* (album with George Shearing). Concord Jazz.

Mose Allison, *Lessons in Living.* Elektra/Musician.

Dave Frishberg, *The Dave Frishberg Songbook, Vol. 2.* Omnisound.

Jon Hendricks, *Cloudburst.* Enja/Polygram.

Jimmy Witherspoon, *Jimmy Witherspoon Sings the Blues with Panama Francis & the Savoy Sultans.* Muse.

Best Jazz Vocal Performance, Female
- Ella Fitzgerald, *The Best Is Yet to Come.* Pablo Today.

Ernestine Anderson, *Big City.* Concord Jazz.

Betty Carter, *Whatever Happened to Love?* Bet-Car.

Sue Raney, *Sue Raney Sings the Music of Johnny Mandel.* Discovery.

Sarah Vaughan, *Crazy and Mixed Up.* Pablo.

Best Jazz Vocal Performance, Duo or Group
- Manhattan Transfer, "Why Not!" track from *Bodies & Souls.* Atlantic.

Jackie Cain, Roy Kral, *A Stephen Sondheim Collection.* Finesse.

L.A. Jazz Choir, Gerald Eskelin, director, *Listen.* Mobile Fidelity Sound.

L.A. Voices, *Supersax & L.A. Voices.* Columbia.

Rare Silk, *New Weave.* Polydor.

Best Jazz Instrumental Performance, Soloist
- Wynton Marsalis, *Think of One.* Columbia.

Art Blakey, *Keystone 3.* Concord Jazz.

Chick Corea, *Trio Music.* ECM/Warner Bros.

Sonny Stitt, *Last Stitt Sessions, Vol. 1.* Muse.

Phil Woods, *At the Vanguard.* Antilles.

Best Jazz Instrumental Performance, Group
- Phil Woods Quartet, *At the Vanguard.* Antilles/Island.

Art Blakey & the Jazz Messengers, *Keystone 3.* Concord Jazz.

Herbie Hancock, *Quartet.* Columbia.

Philly Joe Jones/Dameronia, *To Tadd with Love.* Uptown.

Wynton Marsalis, *Think of One.* Columbia.

Red Rodney, Ira Sullivan Quintet, *Sprint.* Elektra/Musician.

Best Jazz Instrumental Performance, Big Band
- Rob McConnell & the Boss Brass, *All in Good Time.* Dark Orchid.

Count Basie Big Band, *Farmers' Market Barbecue.* Pablo.

Louie Bellson Big Band, *The London Gig.* Pablo.

Gil Evans, *Priestess.* Antilles/Island.

Bob Florence Limited Edition, *Soaring.* Bosco.

Best New Country Song
(Songwriter's Award)
- "Stranger in My House," Mike Reed. Lodge Hall Music Inc. (ASCAP), publisher.

"Baby I Lied," Deborah Allen, Rory Bourke, Rafe Van Hoy. Posey Music (BMI), Chappell Music (ASCAP), Unichappell Music/Van Hoy Music (BMI), publishers.

"I.O.U.," Kerry Chater, Austin Roberts. Vogue Music & the Welk Music Group, Chriswald Music, Hopi Sound Music, MCA Music, publishers.

✓ "Lady Down on Love," Randy Owen. Maypop Music/Buzzherb Music (BMI), publishers.

"A Little Good News," Tommy Rocco, Charlie Black, Rory Bourke. Welk/Chappell Music (ASCAP), publisher.

BEST COUNTRY VOCAL PERFORMANCE, MALE

• Lee Greenwood, "I.O.U." MCA.
Ray Charles, "Born to Love Me." Columbia.
Earl Thomas Conley, "Holding Her and Loving You." RCA.
Vern Gosdin, "If You're Gonna Do Me Wrong (Do It Right)." Compleat/Polygram.
Ronnie Milsap, "Stranger in My House." RCA.
✓ Kenny Rogers, "All My Life." Liberty.

BEST COUNTRY VOCAL PERFORMANCE, FEMALE

• Anne Murray, "A Little Good News." Capitol.
Deborah Allen, "Baby I Lied." RCA.
Crystal Gayle, "Baby What About You." Warner Bros.
Emmylou Harris, *Last Date*. Warner Bros.
Dolly Parton, *Burlap and Satin*. RCA.

BEST COUNTRY PERFORMANCE BY A DUO OR GROUP WITH VOCAL

• Alabama, *The Closer You Get*. RCA.
Larry Gatlin & the Gatlin Brothers Band, "Houston (Means I'm One Day Closer to You)." Columbia.
Merle Haggard, Willie Nelson, *Pancho and Lefty*. Epic/CBS.
Willie Nelson, Waylon Jennings, *Take It to the Limit*. Columbia.
Oak Ridge Boys, *American Made*. MCA.

BEST COUNTRY INSTRUMENTAL PERFORMANCE

• New South (Ricky Skaggs, Jerry Douglas, Tony Rice, J.D. Crowe, Todd Philips), "Fireball," track from *Bluegrass*. Sugar Hill.

Chet Atkins, "Tara Theme," track from *Work It Out with Chet Atkins*. Columbia.
Roy Clark, "Wildwood Flower." Churchill.
Albert Coleman's Atlanta Pops, "Classic Country I," track from *Classic Country*. Epic/CBS.
Earl Scruggs, "Roller Coaster," track from *Top of the World*. Columbia.
Doc & Merle Watson, *Doc & Merle Watson's Guitar Album*. Flying Fish.

BEST GOSPEL PERFORMANCE, MALE

• Russ Taff, *Walls of Glass*. Myrrh/Word.
Dion, *Chariots of Fire*. Light/Lexicon.
Dion, *I Put Away My Idols*. Dayspring/Word.
Phil Driscoll, *I Exalt Thee*. Sparrow/Birdwing.
Michael W. Smith, *Michael W. Smith Project*. Reunion/Word.

BEST GOSPEL PERFORMANCE, FEMALE

• Amy Grant, "Ageless Medley." Myrrh/Word.
Cynthia Clawson, "Come Celebrate Jesus," track from *Forever*. Priority.
Sandi Patti, "The Gift Goes On." Impact/Benson.
Michele Pillar, *Reign on Me*. Sparrow/Birdwing.
Sheila Walsh, *War of Love*. Sparrow/Birdwing.

BEST GOSPEL PERFORMANCE BY A DUO OR GROUP

• Sandi Patti, Larnelle Harris, "More Than Wonderful," track from *More Than Wonderful*. Impact/Benson.
Gaither Vocal Band, "No Other Name But Jesus," track from *Passin' the Faith Along*. Dayspring/Word.
Imperials, *Side by Side*. Myrrh/Word.
Mylon LeFevre & Broken Heart, *More*. Myrrh/Word.
Masters V, *The Masters V Featuring: Hovie Lister, J.D. Sumner, James Blackwood, Jake Hess, Shaun Neilsen*. Skylite.
White Heart, *White Heart*. Myrrh/Word.

BEST SOUL GOSPEL PERFORMANCE, MALE

• Al Green, *I'll Rise Again*. Myrrh/Word.
Solomon Burke, "Precious Lord, Take My Hand," track from *Take Me, Shake Me*. Savoy.
Morris Chapman, *Longtime Friends*. Myrrh/Word.

Thomas A. Dorsey, "Take My Hand, Precious Lord," track from *Say Amen Somebody*. DRG.

Leon Patillo, "Cornerstone," track from *Live Experience*. Myrrh/Word.

Best Soul Gospel Performance, Female

• Sandra Crouch, *We Sing Praises*. Light/Lexicon.

Vanessa Bell Armstrong, *Peace Be Still*. Onyx International/Benson.

Shirley Caesar, *Jesus, I Love Calling Your Name*. Myrrh/Word.

Tramaine Hawkins, *Determined*. Light/Lexicon.

Candi Staton, *Make Me an Instrument*. Beracah.

Albertina Walker, *God Is Able to Carry You Through*. Savoy.

Best Soul Gospel Performance by a Duo or Group

• Bobby Jones & New Life with Barbara Mandrell, "I'm So Glad I'm Standing Here Today," track from *Come Together*. Myrrh/Word.

Clark Sisters, *Sincerely*. New Birth/Benson.

Sandra Crouch, Andrae Crouch, "Glad I Heard Your Voice," track from *We Sing Praises*. Light/Lexicon.

Jean Johnson, Sandra Crouch, Linda McCrary, Andrae Crouch, "He's Worthy," track from *We Sing Praises*. Light/Lexicon.

Winans, *Long Time Comin'*. Light/Lexicon.

Best Inspirational Performance

• Donna Summer, "He's a Rebel," track from *She Works Hard for the Money*. Mercury/Polygram.

Linda Hopkins, "Precious Lord," track from *How Blue Can You Get*. Palo Alto.

Cristy Lane, "I've Come Back (To Say I Love You One More Time)," track from *Footprints in the Sand*. LS/Liberty.

Leontyne Price, *Noel! Noel!* London.

B.J. Thomas, *Peace in the Valley*. Myrrh/Word.

Best Traditional Blues Recording

• *Blues 'n' Jazz*, B.B. King. MCA.

Blues Train, Big Joe Turner & Roomful of Blues. Muse.

One More Mile, Clarence "Gatemouth" Brown. Rounder.

San Francisco '83, Albert King. Fantasy.

"Texas Flood," track from *Texas Flood*. Stevie Ray Vaughan & Double Trouble. Epic/CBS.

Best Ethnic or Traditional Folk Recording

• *I'm Here*, Clifton Chenier & His Red Hot Louisiana Band. Alligator.

The Grey Fox, Chieftains. DRG.

Raga Mishra Piloo, Ravi Shankar, Ali Akbar Khan. Angel.

Renaissance of the Celtic Harp, Alan Stivell. Rounder.

Synchro System, King Sunny Ade. Mango/Island.

Best Latin Pop Performance

• José Feliciano, *Me Enamore*. TPL.

Placido Domingo, "Besame Mucho," track from *My Life for a Song*. CBS Masterworks.

Lani Hall, *Lani*. A&M.

Menudo, *Una Aventura Llamada Menudo*. Raff.

José Luis Rodriguez, *Ven*. Discos CBS International.

Best Tropical Latin Performance

• Tito Puente & His Latin Ensemble, *On Broadway*. Concord Picante.

Ray Barretto, Celia Cruz, Adalberto Santiago, *Tremendo Trio*. Fania.

Rubén Blades, *El Que la Hace la Paga*. Fania-Vaya.

Willie Colon, *Corazon Guerrero*. Fania.

Mongo Santamaria, *Mongo Magic*. Roulette.

Best Mexican/American Performance

• Los Lobos, "Anselma," track from *... And a Time to Dance*. Slash.

Los Bukis, *Yo Te Necesito*. Profono.

Chelo, "A Cambio de Que," track from *Otro Mas*. Musart.

Vicente Fernandez, *La Diferencia*. CBS.

Juan Gabriel, *Todo*. Ariola.

Best Instrumental Composition

• "Love Theme from *Flashdance*," Giorgio Moroder, composer. ASCAP.

"An Actor's Life," Dave Grusin, composer. Golden Horizon Music Corp. (ASCAP), publisher.

Herbie Hancock gave an "electrifying" performance of his r&b winner "Rockit" at the Grammy ceremony.

"Dream Hunter," Michael Sembello, Dan Sembello, composers. Warner Bros. Music, Gravity Raincoat, Johdan Music, publishers.

"Rockit," Herbie Hancock, B. Laswell, M. Beinhorn, composers. Hancock Music/OAO Music, publishers.

"The Thorn Birds Theme," Henry Mancini, composer. Warner Bros. Music, publisher.

BEST INSTRUMENTAL ARRANGEMENT

• Dave Grusin, "Summer Sketches '82," track from *Dave Grusin & the N.Y./L.A. Dream Band* (Dave Grusin & the N.Y./L.A. Dream Band). GRP.

Toshiko Akiyoshi, "Remembering Bud," track from *European Memoirs* (Toshiko Akiyoshi–Lew Tabackin Big Band). Ascent.

Bob Florence, "Afternoon of a Prawn," track from *Soaring* (Bob Florence). Bosco.

Rob McConnell, "I Got Rhythm," track from *All in Good Time.* (Rob McConnell & the Boss Brass). Dark Orchid.

Patrick Williams, "Too Hip for the Room," track from *Dreams and Themes* (Patrick Williams). PCM.

BEST INSTRUMENTAL ARRANGEMENT ACCOMPANYING VOCAL(S)

• Nelson Riddle, "What's New," track from *What's New* (Linda Ronstadt). Asylum/Elektra.

David Foster, Jay Graydon, Jeremy Lubbock, "Mornin'," track from *Jarreau* (Al Jarreau). Warner Bros.

Jerry Hey, Al Jarreau, Tom Canning, Jay Graydon, "Step by Step," track from *Jarreau* (Al Jarreau). Warner Bros.

Arif Mardin, "Be Bop Medley," track from *Chaka Khan* (Chaka Khan). Warner Bros.

Lionel Richie, James Anthony Carmichael, "All Night Long (All Night)" (Lionel Richie). Motown.

BEST VOCAL ARRANGEMENT FOR TWO OR MORE VOICES

• Arif Mardin, Chaka Khan, "Be Bop Medley," track from *Chaka Khan* (Chaka Khan). Warner Bros.

Todd Buffa, "Red Clay," track from *New Weave* (Rare Silk). Polydor.

Jeremy Lubbock, "The Night That Monk Returned to Heaven," track from *Bodies and Souls* (Manhattan Transfer). Atlantic.

Alan Paul, "Code of Ethics," track from *Bodies and Souls* (Manhattan Transfer). Atlantic.

Janis Siegel, "Down South Camp Meetin'," track from *Bodies and Souls* (Manhattan Transfer). Atlantic.

BEST CAST SHOW ALBUM

• *Cats (Complete Original Broadway Cast Recording)*, Trevor Nunn, Richard Stilgoe, lyricists. Andrew Lloyd Webber, producer. Geffen/Warner Bros.

La Cage aux Folles, Jerry Herman, composer and lyricist. Thomas Z. Shepard, producer. RCA.

Little Shop of Horrors, Alan Menken, composer. Howard Ashman, lyricist. Phil Ramone, producer. Geffen/Warner Bros.

On Your Toes, Richard Rodgers, composer. Lorenz Hart, lyricist. Norman Newell, producer. Polydor/Polygram.

Zorba, John Kander, composer. Fred Ebb, lyricist. Thomas Z. Shepard, producer. RCA.

Best Album of Original Score Written for a Motion Picture or a Television Special

• *Flashdance*, Giorgio Moroder, Keith Forsey, Irene Cara, Shandi Sinnamon, Ronald Magness, Douglas Cotler, Richard Gilbert, Michael Boddicker, Jerry Hey, Phil Ramone, Michael Sembello, Kim Carnes, Duane Hitchings, Craig Krampf, Dennis Matkosky, songwriters. Casablanca/Polygram.

Gandhi, Ravi Shankar, George Fenton, composers. RCA.

Star Wars—Return of the Jedi, John Williams, composer. RSO/Polygram.

Stayin' Alive, Frank Stallone, Bruce Stephen Foster, R. Freeland, V. DiCola, T. Marolda, Joe Bean Esposito, Randy Bishop, Tommy Faragher, Barry Gibb, Maurice Gibb, Robin Gibb, songwriters. RSO/Polygram.

Tootsie—Original Motion Picture Sound Track, Dave Grusin, composer. Marilyn Bergman, Alan Bergman, songwriters. Warner Bros.

Best Classical Album

• *Mahler: Symphony No. 9 in D Major*, Sir Georg Solti conducting Chicago Symphony. James Mallinson, producer. London.

Haydn: Concerto for Trumpet & Orchestra in E Flat Major; Mozart: Concerto for Trumpet & Orchestra in D Major; Hummel: Concerto for Trumpet & Orchestra in E Flat Major, Raymond Leppard conducting National Philharmonic Orchestra (solo: Marsalis). Thomas Mowrey, producer. CBS.

Leontyne Price & Marilyn Horne in Concert at the Met, James Levine conducting Metropolitan Opera Orchestra (solo: Price, Horne). Jay David Saks, producer. RCA.

Verdi: Falstaff, Carlo Maria Giulini conducting Los Angeles Philharmonic and Los Angeles Master Chorale (solos: Bruson, Ricciarelli, Nucci, Hendricks, Terrani, Gonzalez, Boozer). Gunther Breest, Renate Kupfer, producers. Deutsche Grammophon.

Vivaldi: The Four Seasons & Concerto for 4 Violins, Op. 3, No. 10; Bach: Double Concerto BWV 1043; Mozart: Sinfonia Concertante, K.364, Zubin Mehta conducting Israel Philharmonic Orchestra (solos: Itzhak Perlman, Isaac Stern, Shlomo Mintz, Pinchas Zukerman, Ivry Gitlis, Ida Haendel). Steven Paul, producer. Deutsche Grammophon.

Best Classical Orchestral Recording
(Conductor's Award)

• *Mahler: Symphony No. 9 in D Major*, Sir Georg Solti conducting Chicago Symphony Orchestra. James Mallinson, producer. London.

Beethoven: Symphony No. 5 in C Minor, Op. 67, Carlo Maria Giulini conducting Los Angeles Philharmonic Orchestra. Gunther Breest, producer. Deutsche Grammophon.

Bernstein: West Side Story Symphonic Dances & Candide Overture; Barber: Adagio for Strings; Schuman: American Festival Overture, Leonard Bernstein conducting Los Angeles Philharmonic Orchestra. Hanno Rinke, producer. Deutsche Grammophon.

Del Tredici: In Memory of a Summer Day (Child Alice, Part One), Leonard Slatkin conducting St. Louis Symphony Orchestra. Marc J. Aubort & Joanna Nickrenz, producers. Nonesuch.

Mozart: The Symphonies, Vol. 6, Christopher Hogwood conducting Academy of Ancient Music (solo: Jaap Schroder). Morten Winding, producer. L'Oiseau-Lyre.

Best Chamber Music Performance

• Mstislav Rostropovich, Rudolf Serkin, *Brahms: Sonata for Cello & Piano in E Minor, Op. 38 & Sonata in F Major, Op. 99*. Deutsche Grammophon.

The Philip Glass Ensemble (Michael Riesman, conductor), *Glass: The Photographer*. CBS.

Nancy Allen & Tokyo String Quartet with Ransom Wilson & David Shifrin, *Ravel: Introduction & Allegro*. Angel.

Juilliard String Quartet, *Bartók: The String Quartets (6)*. CBS.

La Salle Quartet, *Zemlinsky: The String Quartets*. Deutsche Grammophon.

Itzhak Perlman, Lynn Harrell, Vladimir Ashkenazy, *Beethoven: "Archduke" Trio (Trio No. 6 in B Flat, Op. 97).* Angel.

BEST CLASSICAL PERFORMANCE, INSTRUMENTAL SOLOIST(S) (WITH ORCHESTRA)

• Wynton Marsalis (Leppard conducting National Philharmonic Orchestra), *Haydn: Concert for Trumpet & Orchestra in E Flat Major; Mozart: Concerto for Trumpet & Orchestra in D Major; Hummel: Concerto for Trumpet & Orchestra in E Flat Major.* CBS.

Leonard Bernstein (Bernstein conducting Los Angeles Philharmonic Orchestra), *Gershwin: Rhapsody in Blue.* Deutsche Grammophon.

Itzhak Perlman (Levine conducting Vienna Philharmonic), *Mozart: Concerto for Violin & Orchestra No. 3 in G Major, K. 216 & No. 5 in A Major, K. 219.* Deutsche Grammophon.

Rudolf Serkin (Ozawa conducting Boston Symphony Orchestra), *Beethoven: Concerto for Piano No. 3 in C Minor, Op. 37.* Telarc.

Simon Standage (Pinnock directing English Concert), *Vivaldi: The Four Seasons.* Archiv.

Isaac Stern, Pinchas Zukerman, Itzhak Perlman, Shlomo Mintz, Ivry Gitlis, Ida Haendel (Mehta conducting Israel Philharmonic Orchestra), *Vivaldi: The Four Seasons & Concerto for 4 Violins, Op. 3, No. 10.* Deutsche Grammophon.

Richard Stoltzman (Schneider conducting Mostly Mozart Festival Orchestra), *Weber: Concerto for Clarinet No. 1 in F Minor, Op. 73; Rossini: Theme & Variations for Clarinet & Orchestra; Mozart: Andante in C, K. 315* (transcribed for clarinet). RCA.

BEST CLASSICAL PERFORMANCE, INSTRUMENTAL SOLOIST(S) (WITHOUT ORCHESTRA)

• Glenn Gould, *Beethoven: Sonata No. 12 in A Flat Major, Op. 26 & No. 13 in E Flat Major, Op. 27, No. 1.* CBS.

Emil Gilels, *Beethoven: Sonata for Piano No. 15 in D Major, Op. 28 ("Pastoral") & No. 3 in C Major, Op. 2, No. 3.* Deutsche Grammophon.

Vladimir Horowitz, *Horowitz in London.* RCA.

Shlomo Mintz, *Paganini: Caprices (24).* Deutsche Grammophon.

Ivo Pogorelich, *Ravel: Gaspard de la Nuit; Prokofiev: Sonata for Piano No. 6 in A Major, Op. 82.* Deutsche Grammophon.

BEST OPERA RECORDING

• *Verdi: La Traviata (Original Soundtrack),* James Levine conducting Metropolitan Opera Orchestra and Chorus (solos: Teresa Stratas, Placido Domingo, Cornell MacNeill). Max Wilcox, Jay David Saks, producers. Elektra.

Mozart: Le Nozze di Figaro, Sir Georg Solti conducting London Philharmonic Orchestra (solos: Kiri Te Kanawa, Lucia Popp, Samuel Ramey, Thomas Allen, Kurt Moll, Frederica von Stade). Christopher Raeburn, producer. London.

Verdi: Aida, Claudio Abbado conducting La Scala Opera Orchestra and Chorus (solos: Katia Ricciarelli, Placido Domingo, Elena Obraztsova, Leo Nucci, Nicolai Ghiaurov, Ruggero Raimondi). Rainer Brock, producer. Deutsche Grammophon.

Verdi: Falstaff, Carlo Maria Giulini conducting Los Angeles Philharmonic and Los Angeles Master Chorale (solos: Renato Bruson, Leo Nucci, Katia Ricciarelli, Barbara Hendricks, Lucia Valentini Terrani). Gunther Breest, Renate Kupfer, album producers. Deutsche Grammophon.

Wagner: Tristan und Isolde, Leonard Bernstein conducting Chorus and Orchestra of the Bavarian Radio Symphony (solos: Peter Hoffman, Hildegard Behrens, Yvonne Minton). John McClure, producer. Philips.

Wagner: Tristan und Isolde, Carlos Kleiber conducting Dresden State Orchestra and Leipzig Radio Chorus (solos: Rene Kollo, Margaret Price, Brigitte Fassbaender). Dr. Hans Hirsch, producer. Deutsche Grammophon.

BEST CHORAL PERFORMANCE (OTHER THAN OPERA)

• Margaret Hillis, choral director, Chicago Symphony Orchestra Chorus. Sir Georg Solti conducting Chicago Symphony Orchestra, *Haydn: The Creation.* London.

Gunter Jena, choral conductor, North German Radio Chorus, Hamburg, *The Brahms Edition: Choral Works A Capella (Complete)*. Deutsche Grammophon.

Herbert von Karajan conducting Vienna Singverein and Vienna Philharmonic, *Haydn: The Creation*. Deutsche Grammophon.

Raymond Leppard conducting NDR Choir and Knabenchor Hannover; NDR Symphony Orchestra, *Bach: St. Matthew Passion*. Angel.

Trevor Pinnock conducting Choir of Westminster Abbey and English Concert, *Handel: Coronation Anthems*. Archiv.

Best Classical Vocal Soloist Performance

• Leontyne Price, Marilyn Horne (Levine conducting Metropolitan Opera Orchestra), *Leontyne Price & Marilyn Horne in Concert at the Met*. RCA.

Dietrich Fischer-Dieskau (Daniel Barenboim, accompanist), *The Brahms Edition: Lieder (Complete)*. Deutsche Grammophon.

Kiri Te Kanawa (Davis conducting London Symphony Orchestra), *Mozart Opera Arias*. Philips.

Jessye Norman (Daniel Barenboim, accompanist), *The Brahms Edition: Lieder*. Deutsche Grammophon.

Frederica von Stade (Jean-Philippe Collard, accompanist), *Fauré: Eighteen Songs*. Angel.

Best Engineered Recording, Classical

• James Lock, *Mahler: Symphony No. 9 in D Major* (Sir Georg Solti conducting Chicago Symphony Orchestra). London.

Marc J. Aubort, *Del Tredici: In Memory of a Summer Day (Child Alice, Part One)* (Leonard Slatkin conducting St. Louis Symphony Orchestra (solo: Bryn-Julson). Nonesuch.

Paul Goodman, William King. *Leontyne Price & Marilyn Horne in Concert at the Met* (James Levine conducting Metropolitan Opera Orchestra (solos: Price, Horne). RCA.

Gunter Hermanns, *R. Strauss: Metamorphoses; Death & Transfiguration* (Herbert von Karajan conducting Berlin Philharmonic). Deutsche Grammophon.

James Lock, John Dunkerley, *Haydn: The Creation* (Sir Georg Solti conducting Chicago Symphony Orchestra; Chicago Symphony Orchestra Chorus, Margaret Hillis, choral director). London.

Klaus Scheibe, *Verdi: Falstaff* (Carlo Maria Giulini conducting Los Angeles Philharmonic and Los Angeles Master Chorale (solos: Bruson, Nucci, Ricciareili, Hendricks, Valentini Terrani, Gonzalez, Boozer). Deutsche Grammophon.

Classical Producer of the Year

• Marc J. Aubort, Joanna Nickrenz. Nonesuch.

Andrew Cornall.

Steven Epstein. CBS.

Dr. Steven Paul. Deutsche Grammophon.

Jay David Saks. RCA.

Best Comedy Recording

• *Eddie Murphy: Comedian*, Eddie Murphy. Columbia.

Bill Cosby Himself, Bill Cosby. Motown.

Monty Python's The Meaning of Life, Monty Python. MCA.

Throbbing Python of Love, Robin Williams. Casablanca/Polygram.

What Becomes a Semi-Legend Most? Joan Rivers. Geffen/Warner Bros.

Best Spoken Word or Non-Musical Recording

• *Copland: Lincoln Portrait*, William Warfield. Mercury/Phillips.

Everything You Always Wanted to Know About Home Computers, Steve Allen, Jayne Meadows. Casablanca/Polygram.

Jane Fonda's Workout Record for Pregnancy, Birth and Recovery, Jane Fonda, Femmy De Lyser. Columbia.

Old Possum's Book of Practical Cats, Sir John Gielgud, Irene Worth. Caedmon.

The Robots of Dawn, Isaac Asimov. Caedmon.

Best Recording for Children

• *E.T. The Extra-Terrestrial* , Michael Jackson, narration & vocals. MCA.

Born to Add, Sesame Street Muppets. Christopher Cerf, producer. Jim Henson, Muppets creator. Sesame Street.

"Born to Add," track from *Born to Add*. Bruce Stringbean & the Sesame Street Band. Sesame Street.

The Music Machine Part II, Candle. Tony Salerno, Fletch Wiley, Ron Kreuger, producers. Birdwing/Sparrow.
Rocky Mountain Holiday, John Denver, Muppets. Jim Henson, Muppets creator. Sesame Street Records.

BEST ENGINEERED RECORDING
(NON-CLASSICAL)
• Bruce Swedien, *Thriller* (Michael Jackson). Epic/CBS.
Tommy Vicari, Thom Wilson, James Gallagher, Peter Chaiken, *Bossa Nova Hotel* (Michael Sembello). Warner Bros.
Jay Graydon, Ian Eales, Eric Prestis, *Jarreau* (Al Jarreau). Warner Bros.
Gary Loizzo, Will Rascati, Rob Kingsland, *Kilroy Was Here* (Styx). A&M.
Allan Sides, *Target* (Tom Scott). Atlantic.

BEST ALBUM PACKAGE
(Art Director's Award)
• Robert Rauschenberg, *Speaking in Tongues*, limited edition version (Talking Heads). Sire/Warner Bros.
✓ Bob Defrin, Lynn Dreese Breslin, *Records* (Foreigner). Atlantic.
Bill Levy, Murry Whiteman, *One Night With a Stranger* (Martin Briley). Mercury/ Polygram.
Michael Ross, *The Key* (Joan Armatrading). A&M.
Richard Seireeni, *Nothing But the Truth* (Mac McAnally). Geffen/Warner Bros.

BEST ALBUM NOTES
(Annotator's Award)
• Orrin Keepnews, *The "Interplay" Sessions* (Bill Evans). Milestone.
Lester Bangs, *The Fugs Greatest Hits Vol. 1* (Fugs). Adelphi.
Peter Guralnick, *The Okeh Sessions* (Big Maybelle). Epic/CBS.
Richard B. Hadlock, *Giants of Jazz: Joe Sullivan* (Joe Sullivan). Time Life.
John McDonough, *Seven Come Eleven* (Benny Goodman). Columbia.

BEST HISTORICAL ALBUM
• *The Greatest Recordings of Arturo Toscanini Symphonies Vol. 1*, Arturo Toscanini. Stanley Walker, Allan Steckler, producers. Franklin Mint.

Back in the Saddle Again: American Cowboy Songs, various country & western artists. Charlie Seemann, producer. New World.
The Complete Blue Note Recordings of Thelonious Monk, Thelonious Monk. Michael Cuscuna, producer. Mosaic.
Kings of New Orleans Jazz, Jelly Roll Morton, King Oliver, Sidney Bechet. Stanley Walker, Dan Morgenstern, producers. Franklin Mint.
The Motown Story: The First 25 Years, various artists. John Badeaux, producer. Motown.

PRODUCER OF THE YEAR
(NON-CLASSICAL)
• Quincy Jones, Michael Jackson
James Anthony Carmichael, Lionel Richie
Jay Graydon
Quincy Jones
Phil Ramone

BEST VIDEO, SHORT FORM
• *Girls on Film/Hungry Like the Wolf*, Duran Duran (VHS). EMI Music Video/Sony.
Bill Wyman, Bill Wyman (VHS). Sony/Ripple.
A Flock of Seagulls, A Flock of Seagulls (VHS/Beta). Arista/ Zomba/Sony.
Rod Stewart: Tonight He's Yours, Rod Stewart (VHS). Sony/Embassy Home Entertainment.
Videosyncracy, Todd Rundgren (VHS). Sony/Alchemedia.

BEST VIDEO ALBUM
• *Duran Duran*, Duran Duran. (VHS) Thorn EMI Video. Disc-Pioneer Artists.
Alice Cooper: "The Nightmare," Alice Cooper. (VHS) Warner Home Video.
Grace Jones: A One Man Show, Grace Jones. (VHS) Island Pictures/Vestron Video.
Olivia in Concert, Olivia Newton-John. (VHS) MCA Home Video.
Rolling Stones: Let's Spend the Night Together, Rolling Stones. (VHS) Embassy Home Entertainment.
Word of Mouth, Toni Basil. (Beta/VHS) Chrysalis.

Proud Tina's
Triumphant Return

It was "one of the most dramatic comebacks in music history," said *Variety*.

Back in the 1960s and '70s, Tina Turner's "wild, hip-shaking stance with the Ike and Tina Turner Revue ... helped define the concept of sex and soul," the *L.A. Times* once wrote. The singing couple got married in 1958, made their debut in *Billboard*'s Hot 100 in 1960 with "A Fool in Love," and followed up their early recording success with

Tina Turner capped off her dramatic career comeback with three awards, including best record. The excited LP champ Lionel Richie said, "It's heart attack time!"

numerous hits like "Proud Mary," which earned them an r&b Grammy in 1971.

But despite the dream-come-true quality of their professional life, Tina Turner later related in her autobiography that their private life was a hellish nightmare. Ike frequently beat her with shoe stretchers, telephones, and coat hangers, she said, resulting in broken bones and facial bruises that she had to cover up with heavy makeup before stepping out on stage to perform. She attempted suicide by taking 50 Valium in 1968 but was rescued in time and rushed to a nearby hospital where her stomach was pumped. Finally, on Independence Day, 1976, she left Ike after he beat her for the last time in the back of a limo in Dallas. Carrying only 36 cents and a gasoline credit card, she jumped out of the vehicle and at last struck out for a life on her own. But solo success was elusive. Turner struggled for years on the concert trail where she earned barely enough to retire old debts. Then came the release of her *Private Dancer* album, eight years after she jilted Ike, and suddenly she was a reigning star again. "Talk about hard climbs!" gasped the *L.A. Times*.

Private Dancer spent an impressive 71 weeks on the album charts and revealed the new Turner as proud and even defiant ("Better Be Good to Me"), cool and aloof ("What's Love Got to Do with It"), and even, at age 45, still sexy after all these years ("Private Dancer"). When all three songs became Top 10 hits, Turner was back in the headlines, too, and a surprise favorite on MTV for her saucy videos.

Turner's dramatic comeback was heralded by four Grammy triumphs, including three for Turner herself: Record of the Year and Best Female Pop Vocal Performance for "What's Love Got to Do

SECURITY PACIFIC COLLECTION/ L.A. PUBLIC LIRBARY

with It" plus Best Female Rock Vocal Performance for "Better Be Good to Me." The fourth award was also for "What's Love Got to Do It," hailed as Song of the Year and reaping gold for its songwriters, Graham Lyle and Terry Britten.

Described by *The New York Times* as "two sensational legs topped by an explosion of hair," Turner was greeted with several standing ovations throughout the Grammy night as she performed "What's Love" on the air and accepted the first two of her three prizes. Then came the presentation of the evening's highest honor, which was bestowed by a music superstar who still hadn't won a Grammy. "Diana Ross, swathed in a gown that looked like an enormous bow," noted the *Times*, presented "the Record of the Year award to Tina Turner, but the superstar was lost in the hustle and bustle of the occasion." A grateful Turner told the crowd gathered at Los Angeles's Shrine Auditorium, "I've been waiting so long for this!"

"Dancing in the Dark" finally brought Springsteen his first Grammy.

A minor controversy surrounded the fact that the number-one song in the year's Hot 100, Prince's "When Doves Cry," was missing from the line-up of Record of the Year nominees. But His Purpleness was still considered the front runner in the race for Album of the Year for the top-selling LP of 1984, the soundtrack to his movie *Purple Rain*, which became the biggest-grossing rock film ever made. Bruce Springsteen had been snubbed by the Grammys repeatedly in years past, but now he was in the running with *Born in the U.S.A.*, number one in *The Village Voice*'s annual Critics' Poll

of the year's top 100 LPs (*Purple Rain* came in at number two, *Private Dancer* at number five). *Private Dancer* was nominated, too, and certainly couldn't be discounted. Neither could Lionel Richie's *Can't Slow Down*, which appealed to the more conservative N.A.R.A.S. voters with hummable hits like Song of the Year nominee "Hello." The fifth contender was *She's So Unusual* by Cyndi Lauper, the odds-on favorite to nab Best New Artist. This was the most progressive line-up ever offered to Grammy voters and came about as a result of N.A.R.A.S.'s recent, highly successful drive to recruit more young members. "Richie is the kind of mainstream pop artist that Grammy voters have traditionally favored," said the *L.A. Times*, sizing up the contest, "but Prince has a narrow edge."

N.A.R.A.S.'s traditional contingent ended up prevailing on behalf of Richie's *Can't Slow Down* when the youth vote split between Prince and Springsteen. It was a long overdue triumph in a major category for one of pop's leading hitmakers. On three recent occasions, Richie had lost twin bids for Record and Song of the Year — in 1980, 1981, and 1983 — and had also lost twice as Producer of the Year. His defeat at the 1981 awards ceremony, in fact, was humiliating when *all seven* of his nominations proved fruitless. He finally won a pop vocals Grammy in 1984 for "Truly," but it was a modest victory compared to all his losses in the top categories. Vindication finally came with the LP laurels in 1984 and the added bonus of the Producer of the Year award, which he shared with James Anthony Carmichael — and also with Chicago's producer, David Foster, when the category experienced its first tie ever. Backstage, Richie told reporters, "It's heart attack time now. If you knew how many times I've sat out in that audience hearing the names of those other winners, wondering why — I don't want to wonder tonight. I just want to enjoy it."

It was considered such a foregone conclusion that Prince would dominate this year's awards that the *L.A. Times* wrote: "Memo to Prince: Call your tailor. Order a purple tux. Just as last year was Michael Jackson's year at the Grammys, this figures to be Prince's year .... Prince has never won a Grammy, but then he's never had an album stay at No. 1 for 24 weeks either. His Grammy time has come."

Prince won three awards in consolation for missing out in the top categories: the honors for best film score and group rock vocals for *Purple Rain* plus the prize for writing the Best New R&B Song "I Feel For You," which also earned Chaka Khan the award for best female r&b singing. Like he did at the American Music Awards, Prince performed on the Grammycast, rocking the Shrine Auditorium with an 8-and-a-half minute version of "Baby, I'm a Star" that ended with him making a dramatic exit down the hall's center aisle out to his purple limo waiting outside. "If he had won best album later in the show, he wouldn't have been there to accept it," the *L.A. Times* observed.

One prediction that did not go wrong was Cyndi Lauper's victory as Best New Artist, her only win of the night despite nominations for Album of the Year (*She's So Unusual*), Song of the Year ("Time After Time"), and Record of the Year ("Girls Just Want to Have Fun.") "I never really thought I could be anything," Lauper told the *L.A. Times* backstage later. "But I always thought if you really meant to do something and worked really hard that you could achieve anything. It's all a matter of what you have up here [pointing to her head] and in here [pointing to her

GLOBE PHOTO

Prince's "Grammy time has come," the pundits predicted before the show. His Purpleness ended up with three awards.

heart]." Soon afterward, the outrageous rocker ran into fellow winner Tina Turner backstage and told her "You're my idol!" She then gave Turner a kiss and asked her teasingly, "Was it as good for you as it was for me?"

While Springsteen had failed to be recognized by N.A.R.A.S. with a Grammy in the past, he proved he bore no ill will when he joined the record academy as a member of its New York chapter this year. Yet the big question remained: Would The Boss perform on the Grammycast? *The New York Times* reported: "Right up to air time, an element of suspense was generated over the question of whether Bruce Springsteen would compromise his artistic principles by becoming involved in such a glittering occasion. He didn't." Springsteen did show up in person, however, sporting long hair, sideburns and a long-ribboned bow tie to dress up his tux — and so was on hand to accept the prize for Best Male Rock Vocal Performance for

"Dancing in the Dark."

"It was so satisfying to finally see Springsteen receive his first Grammy that fans of the most acclaimed rock figure since Bob Dylan probably even forgave the recording academy for his loss three years ago to soap opera heartthrob Rick Springfield," commented the *L.A. Times.*

Throughout the night, as some awards redressed past oversights like Springsteen and Prince, and others recognized hot new artists, critics proclaimed that the Grammys at last were in tune with the front line music of the day. Phil Collins had his first solo number-one hit and his first Grammy (pop vocals) with "Against All Odds (Take a Look at Me Now)," the title song to the popular Jeff Bridges/Rachel Ward film about a man who goes to Mexico to track down a friend's runaway girlfriend. (Collins's victory seemed to come against all odds, too, when he topped such veteran co-nominees Kenny Loggins, Lionel Richie, and Stevie Wonder.) The theme to the box office smash movie *Ghostbusters* reaped Best Pop Instrumental Performance for Ray Parker, Jr. (again eclipsing Stevie Wonder). The British "classical rock" band Yes had been making hit records since 1968 but finally earned its first award for Best Rock Instrumental Performance of "Cinema," a track from *90125*. The Pointer Sisters had won their first Grammy for country music in 1974, but now they were ruling the pop charts with "Jump (For My Love)," which won them pop group vocals prize.

Trinidad-born Billy Ocean had a minor hit in 1976 with "Love Really Hurts Without You," but he came back strong in 1984 with "Caribbean Queen (No More Love on the Run)," which brought him the male r&b vocals trophy. (Ocean had recorded earlier versions using the titles "European Queen" and "African Queen" for the dance clubs.) Doobie Brother Michael McDonald became the first white to win in an r&b category since the Champs in 1958 when he shared this year's duo/group vocals award with 1981 Grammy champ James Ingram for "Yah Mo B There." Jazz keyboardist Herbie Hancock upset his diehard fans last year when he released one of his first dance-music albums, *Future Shock,* and won the r&b instrumental prize with its "Rockit" track. Now he reprised the victory with another r&b LP, *Sound-System.*

Jazz trumpeter Wynton Marsalis made Grammy history last year when he became the first artist to win awards in both classical and nonclassical categories. Shocking the experts this year, he did it again by taking the jazz solo instrumental laurels for *Hot House Flowers* (which failed to capture the same critical praise that his triumphant *Think of One* LP did last year) and the classical soloist's award (with orchestra) for performing works by Handel, Purcell, Torelli, Fasch, and Molter. For the third straight year, the group headed by 30-year-old jazz guitarist Pat Metheny held onto the fusion performance prize (*First Circle*), while the jazz slots welcomed a first-time winner when the band headed by drummer Art Blakey garnered the group instrumental honors for the track "New York Scene."

Jazz artists had performed on every Grammycast since 1977, but their omission this year triggered a heated revolt inside the record academy. Musician, composer, and critic Leonard Feather resigned from N.A.R.A.S. a week after the show. Other artists, reported the *L.A. Times,* "are tossing their $45 renewal notices in the nearest trash can." Feather wrote in the *Times*: "Last year, jazz managed to snare three-and-a-half minutes in a three-and-a-half hour program; this time around, not a single jazz nomi-

Count Basie died in 1984, but received a posthumous prize for 88 Basie Street.

nee got to play or sing a note. Not even Joe Williams, who at 66 won his long overdue first Grammy."

Williams won the only trophy given out this year for jazz vocals (for *Nothin' But the Blues*), since N.A.R.A.S. elected to recombine the three awards for male, female, and duo/group that had been given away over the previous three years. *The Times* noted, "Joe Williams appeared overjoyed at winning .... The veteran of the Count Basie Band dodged the perennial age question, saying with a grin, 'I'm old enough to enjoy this and young enough to want some more .... It feels marvelous. I'm glad it happened before the pipes went. I think I'll keep going as long as I can stay in tune.'"

The legendary (and eight-time past winner) Count Basie died in 1984, but he still proved to be a formidable presence at the Grammys when he snagged a final jazz award for the last album of his career, *88 Basie Street*, featuring works by Sammy Nestico as well as some of his own compositions such as "Contractor's Blues" and "Sunday at the Savoy." Basie also joined artists Chick Webb, Tommy Dorsey, and Benny Goodman on *Big Band Jazz*, winner of Best His-

torical Album and Best Album Notes. In addition, Basie's 1955 recording of "April in Paris" was inducted this year into the Hall of Fame, along with Gene Autry's "Rudolph, the Red-Nosed Reindeer" and other classics.

A posthumous prize was awarded in the country categories, too, to the winner of Best Country Song "City of New Orleans," writer Steve Goodman, who died of leukemia in September. Goodman had written it in the early 1970s about a Chicago train called "City of New Orleans" that was being shut down due to a shortage of riders. Arlo Guthrie recorded the first hit version of it in 1972 while Willie Nelson brought it to the upper rungs of the charts again in 1984. In what *Variety* called "one of the most touching moments" of the Grammy ceremony, Goodman's trophy was accepted on his behalf by his nine-and-a-half year old daughter Sarah.

Five-time past Grammy victor Nelson was nominated for best male vocals for "New Orleans" but lost to another country great, Merle Haggard, who scored his first win ever for "That's the Way Love Goes," a tune he'd recorded nearly a half-dozen times earlier in his career, but never before to his complete satisfaction. The mother-daughter team of Naomi and Wynonna Judd became first-time champs when they won the duo singing laurels for the song written for them by Kenny O'Dell, "Mama He's Crazy," which they called their "country foundation" since it became their first hit platter. (The song was also nominated for Best Country Song.)

Emmylou Harris had won three times in the past, but she returned for another for performing "In My Dreams." Ricky Skaggs took honors last year along with other name talent like Tony Rice billing themselves as the New South Group. He came back to claim a solo honor for his instrumental work on "Wheel Hoss," a track from *Country Boy*. Skaggs was being honored with multiple prizes in the early to mid-1980s. This was the third year in a row that he won the Country Music Association's instrumental award. Next year C.M.A. would named him Entertainer of the Year.

All of the following past winners for religious recordings returned with new prizes: Donna Summer ("Forgive Me"), Amy Grant ("Angels"), 1974's Best New Artist Debby Boone ("Keep the Flame Burning" with Phil Driscoll), Andrae Crouch ("Always Remember"), and Shirley Caesar and Al Green ("Sailin' on the Sea of Your Love"). Caesar claimed an additional Grammy for her *Sailin'* album version. On the Grammycast, host John Denver called gospel the root of most other forms of music and introduced a brief film that paid tribute to the genre. *Billboard* noted, "Crouch whisked the glitzy crowd away to a small Southern church during a well-produced gospel feature, an imaginary trip buoyed by stellar performances from pop staples, the Clark Sisters, the Rev. James Cleveland, and others."

Like the jazz line-up, the Latin categories became the focus of controversy when, noted *Variety*, "a group calling itself the Mexican-American Recording Artists handed out protest fliers outside the Shrine." At issue were the contenders for Best Mexican/American performance. "None of the nominees is Mexican-American (or Chicano)," reported the *L.A. Times*. "Brazilian Roberto Carolis sings in Portugese (although his nominated song is in Spanish); Raphael and Luis Miguel are from Spain; Sheena Easton is Scottish; Juan Gabriel and Yolanda Del Rio are Mexican citizens. None of the nominated songs by the performers is in English or even reflects the bilingual abilities of most Mexican-American performers." Furthermore, leading Mexican-American artists such as Vikki Carr and Santana had important album releases in 1984 but weren't nominated. The winner, noted the *L.A. Times*: "Sheena Easton, who has made news lately as the first performer to crack the top five in the pop, black, country and dance/disco charts, further demonstrated her range with a win in the category." She shared the award with Luis Miguel for "Me Gustas Tal Como Eres."

In the other Latin slots, two-time past winner Eddie Palmieri nabbed the tropical Latin laurels for "Palo Pa Rumba" and Placido Domingo took the pop category for "Always in My Heart." Like Wynton Marsalis, Domingo also pulled off a victory in the classical categories by winning a prize as a principal soloist for Best Opera Recording *Carmen*.

Winner of Best Ethnic or Traditional Folk Recording went to an artist who didn't begin performing professionally until the age of 60. Ninety-year-old singer and guitar player Elizabeth Cotten (*Elizabeth Cotten Live!*) was known for her unconventional method of plucking her instrument: Using two fingers of her left hand, she played her guitar upside down. "With her gray hair pulled back in a bun, she walked slowly into the press area, leaning heavily on a gnarled cane," noted the *L.A. Times*. "She was probably the first performer not asked what she thought of Prince. Asked how she learned her unusual left-handed gui-

"I'm old enough to enjoy this [Grammy] and young enough to want some more," said 66-year-old jazz singer Joe Williams.

tar technique, Cotten answered, 'Jesus showed me how. He taught me how to play guitar in a dream.'"

A new category was introduced this year for Best Reggae Recording, which was claimed by the vocal trio Black Uhuru (*Anthem*), called "the first important reggae group of the Eighties" by *Rolling Stone*.

During his sweepstakes victory last year, Michael Jackson failed to win a video award because none of his videos had been released commercially during the Grammy eligibility period. This year he made up for it by scoring Best Video Album for *Making Michael Jackson's "Thriller"* while David Bowie's eponymous video won him the short form prize. (Jackson's only other nomination this year was for a rhythm & blues Grammy for his duet with brother Jermaine, "Tell Me I'm Not Dreamin'"; the Jacksons' hugely successful *Victory* album came up with scratch in 1984.) "Weird Al" Yankovic reaped Best Comedy Recording for his parody of Jackson's "Beat It" called "Eat It," which conjured up a mother telling her child: "Just eat it/ Eat it/ Get yourself an egg and beat it ...." After winning, Yankovic was asked by reporters what he was going to do to celebrate. He responded, "I thought I'd get some free food and then go home and take a shower."

"Composer-conductor John Williams moved into a tie with Stevie Wonder for fifth place on the all-time list when he won his 15th Grammy" for his official score to the Olympic games held in Los Angeles, noted the *L.A. Times*. Williams tied for the Best Instrumental Composition award with Randy Newman for his score to the Robert Redford baseball film *The Natural*. Composer Stephen Sondheim picked up Grammy's Best Cast Show Album prize (his fifth) for his latest Broadway musical *Sunday in the Park with George*, which also earned a Pulitzer Prize.

Curiously, the winner of Best Classical Album was another show score — to the Oscars' Best Picture *Amadeus*. Mozart's music was brought to a wider-than-usual audience by Neville Marriner conducting the Academy of St. Martin-in-the-Fields, but the liberties taken with the composer's masterpieces in order to make them work in the context of a popular drama did not make its Grammy victory especially popular with classical music purists. The editing was necessary, though, the film and album's producer, John Strauss, told *Grammy Pulse*, so that Mozart's music could "reach beyond the normal classical music record-buying public."

A loser of the best classical album laurels rebounded when conductor Leonard Slatkin and the St. Louis Symphony won the orchestral honors for their recording of Prokofiev's Symphony No. 5 in B Flat, which also snagged the engineering award. Its critical reviews were schizophrenic. *Fanfare* called it "unconvincing" and added, "Slatkin makes us aware of his own interposition; he doesn't fix attention on the music, but on his manipulation of it." *High Fidelity* gave it the highest praise, calling the recording "one of the greatest this world has ever received."

Another loser of the best album prize turned up as winner of the choral awards: Brahms's *A German Requiem*, performed by the Chicago Symphony Orchestra and Chorus with conductor James Levine and choral director Margaret Hillis (earning her a sixth Grammy in the category). *High Fidelity* dismissed it as "melodramatically overwrought," however, and *Fanfare* said "Levine tends to extremes of tempo that tire with repeated hearings."

Cellist Yo-Yo Ma was gaining wide critical praise as of 1984 and capped it off with his first of many Grammys to

Fanfare *said tenor Placido Domingo's performance on Best Opera Recording* Carmen *was "dramatically responsive."*

come when he won the soloist trophy for a compilation of suites by Bach that the critics hailed for Ma's display of technical skill. The Juilliard Quartet reaped the chamber music prize for their final installment of all of Beethoven's quartets, which was cheered by *Fanfare* as "dramatic, often highly intense music-making."

Between 1960 and 1965, N.A.R.A.S. bestowed an award for new classical compositions but then dropped it, only to reintroduce the category in 1984. The new winner was Samuel Barber who had won once before, in 1964 for *Concerto*, and now was honored for his opera *Antony and Cleopatra*.

The year's Best Opera Recording marked a third victory in the category for Bizet's *Carmen*, which had been honored previously for recordings by Herbert von Karajan and the Vienna Philharmonic Orchestra and Chorus in 1964 and by Leonard Bernstein conducting the Metropolitan Opera Orchestra and Chorus in 1973. The 1984 winner was performed by Lorin Maazel conducting the French National Symphony Orchestra with soprano Julia Migenes Johnson in the lead and tenor Placido Domingo as Don José. *Fanfare* called this version far superior to the "strange, eccentric, unidiomatic one Maazel presided over in 1971," giving the credit to the new cast. Johnson, it said "makes deft, intelligent use of her small voice," while Domingo's performance was called "the most dramatically responsive and best sung of the three he has recorded." The album was the score to a 1984 French film that critic Leonard Maltin has called "overbaked and unbelievably inept," adding, "Still, opera buffs will enjoy the music — if they keep their eyes closed."

Neither Johnson nor Domingo was up for the vocal soloist accolade, which went to Jessye Norman, José van Dam, and Heather Hopper for *Songs of Maurice Ravel*, beating out Dame Janet Baker, Kathleen Battle, and Jessye Norman in her own separate bid. *Fanfare* was most appreciative of Norman, who, it said, "really cuts loose" on the Ravel album.

After the Grammy show concluded, the *L.A. Times* was among those applauding the record academy's new hipness. "The evening's main winner was the N.A.R.A.S.," it said. "After years of being ridiculed by pop and rock critics for being too conservative in its choices, the academy came up this year with its most impressive set of nominees and with a ceremony that clearly elevated rock performers to equal status with more mainstream artists. In fact, 1984 may go down as the year in which rock & roll was finally welcomed to the Grammy club — as such acclaimed rock figures as Prince, Bruce Springsteen, and Cyndi Lauper were almost constant subjects of attention during the three-hour-plus program."

The New York Times added: "Significantly, the show that once wouldn't recognize rock music opened up with the driving 'Heart of Rock & Roll' by Huey Lewis & the News, followed by a reminder from John Denver, once again the genial and unflappable host, that 30 years ago to the very month Bill Haley & the Comets altered the future of popular music with 'Rock Around the Clock.' It may have been a long time coming, but the Grammy Awards seem to have caught up with a bigger slice of reality. Maybe one of these years, they will even let the fans screaming in the balcony come downstairs and mingle with the power brokers and current idols.

"The production numbers covered an extraordinary range of music," the *Times* continued, "from Kenny Loggins and 'Footloose' to Julia Megenes Johnson slinking suggestively through an aria from Bizet's *Carmen* [and] a synthesizer session led by Stevie Wonder."

As part of the night's other entertainment, N.A.R.A.S. had also planned to invite the scores of headline artists who had recently recorded "We Are the World" as part of the U.S.A. for Africa benefit to raise money for the starving millions of drought-ridden Ethiopia, but since the record's release date was postponed a few weeks, the plans were scrapped. N.A.R.A.S. president Michael Melvoin told the L.A. Times, "They've assured me that since they expect it to be nominated next year, they think it would be proper to come back next year and stage a massive reunion on the Grammys .... Sounds fine to me."

1984

The awards ceremony was broadcast on CBS from the Shrine Auditorium in Los Angeles on February 26, 1985, for the awards eligibility period of October 1, 1983, to September 30, 1984.

ALBUM OF THE YEAR
- • *Can't Slow Down*, Lionel Richie. Lionel Richie, James Anthony Carmichael, producers. Motown.
- *Born in the USA*, Bruce Springsteen. Bruce Springsteen, Jon Landau, Chuck Plotkin, Steve Van Zandt, producers. Columbia/CBS.
- *Private Dancer*, Tina Turner. Rupert Hine, Terry Britten, Martyn Ware, Greg Walsh, Carter, track producers. Capitol.
- *Purple Rain—Music from the Motion Picture*, Prince & the Revolution. Prince & the Revolution, producers. Warner Bros.
- *She's So Unusual*, Cyndi Lauper. Rick Chertoff, producer. Portrait.

RECORD OF THE YEAR
- • "What's Love Got to Do with It," Tina Turner. Terry Britten, producer. Capitol.

"Dancing in the Dark," Bruce Springsteen. Bruce Springsteen, Jon Landau, Chuck Plotkin, Steve Van Zandt, producers. Columbia/CBS.
"Girls Just Want to Have Fun," Cyndi Lauper. Rick Chertoff, producer. Portrait.
"Hard Habit to Break," Chicago. David Foster, producer. Warner Bros.
"The Heart of Rock & Roll," Huey Lewis & the News. Huey Lewis & the News, producers. Chrysalis.

SONG OF THE YEAR
(Songwriter's Award)
- • "What's Love Got to Do with It," Graham Lyle, Terry Britten. Nyake Music, Ltd., administered by Chappell & Co., Inc. (ASCAP), Good Single Ltd., administered by Irving Music, Inc. (BMI), publishers.
"Against All Odds (Take a Look at Me Now)," Phil Collins. Golden Torch Music Corp. (ASCAP), Hit and Run Music Publishing Ltd. (PRS), Pun Music Inc. (ASCAP), publishers.
"Hello," Lionel Richie. Brockman Music (ASCAP), publisher.

Best New Artist Cyndi Lauper: "I never really thought I could be anything."

"I Just Called to Say I Love You," Stevie Wonder. Jobete Music Co., Inc., Black Bull Music, Inc. (ASCAP), publishers.
"Time After Time," Cyndi Lauper, Rob Hyman. Rella Music Co. (BMI), Dub Notes (ASCAP), publishers.

BEST NEW ARTIST
• Cyndi Lauper. Portrait.
Sheila E. Warner Bros.
Frankie Goes To Hollywood. Island.
Corey Hart. EMI-America.
Judds. RCA.

BEST POP VOCAL PERFORMANCE, MALE
• Phil Collins, "Against All Odds (Take a Look at Me Now)." Atlantic.
Kenny Loggins, "Footloose." CBS.
Lionel Richie, "Hello." Motown.
John Waite, "Missing You." EMI-America.
Stevie Wonder, "I Just Called to Say I Love You." Motown.

BEST POP VOCAL PERFORMANCE, FEMALE
• Tina Turner, "What's Love Got to Do With It." Capitol.
Sheila E., "The Glamorous Life." Warner Bros.
Sheena Easton, "Strut." EMI-America.
Cyndi Lauper, "Girls Just Want to Have Fun." Portrait.
Deniece Williams, "Let's Hear it for the Boy." Columbia/CBS.

BEST POP PERFORMANCE BY A DUO OR GROUP WITH VOCAL
• Pointer Sisters, "Jump (For My Love)." Planet.
Cars, "Drive." Elektra/Asylum.
Chicago, "Hard Habit to Break." Warner Bros.
Wham! "Wake Me Up Before You Go-Go." Columbia/CBS.
Yes, "Owner of a Lonely Heart." Atco.

BEST POP INSTRUMENTAL PERFORMANCE
• Ray Parker Jr., "Ghostbusters," track from *Ghostbusters* soundtrack. Arista.
Earl Klugh, *Nightsongs*. Capitol.
Steve Mitchell, Richard Perry, Howie Rice, "Jump (For My Love)." Planet.
Randy Newman, *The Natural*. Warner Bros.
Stevie Wonder, "I Just Called to Say I Love You." Motown.

BEST ROCK VOCAL PERFORMANCE, MALE
• Bruce Springsteen, "Dancing in the Dark." Columbia/CBS.
David Bowie, "Blue Jean." EMI-America.
Billy Idol, "Rebel Yell." Chrysalis.
Elton John, "Restless," track from *Breaking Hearts*. Geffen.
John Cougar Mellencamp, "Pink Houses." Riva.

BEST ROCK VOCAL PERFORMANCE, FEMALE
• Tina Turner, "Better Be Good to Me." Capitol.
Lita Ford, *Dancin' on the Edge*. Mercury.
Bonnie Tyler, "Here She Comes." CBS.
Wendy O. Williams, *Wow*. Passport/Jem.
Pia Zadora, "Rock It Out." MCA/Curb.

BEST ROCK PERFORMANCE BY A DUO OR GROUP WITH VOCAL
• Prince & the Revolution, *Purple Rain*— Music from the Motion Picture. Warner Bros.
Cars, *Heartbeat City*. Elektra.
Genesis, *Genesis*. Atlantic.
Van Halen, "Jump." Warner Bros.
Yes, *90125*. Atco.

BEST ROCK INSTRUMENTAL PERFORMANCE
• Yes, "Cinema," track from *90125*. Atco.
Genesis, "Second Home by the Sea," track from *Genesis*. Atlantic.
Lionel Hampton, "Vibramatic." Glad-Hamp.

Eddie Van Halen, "Donut City," track from *The Wild Life* sound track. MCA.
Stevie Ray Vaughan & Double Trouble, "Voodoo Chile (Slight Return)," track from *Couldn't Stand the Weather*. Epic. ✓

BEST NEW RHYTHM & BLUES SONG
(Songwriter's Award)
• "I Feel for You," Prince. Controversy Music (ASCAP), publisher.
"Caribbean Queen (No More Love on the Run)," Keith Diamond, Billy Ocean. Willesden Music (BMI), Zomba Entertainment, Inc. (ASCAP), publishers.
✓ "Dancing in the Sheets," Bill Wolfer, Dean Pitchford. Famous Music Corp. (ASCAP), Ensign Music Corp. (BMI), publishers.
"The Glamorous Life," Sheila E. Girl's Song Music (ASCAP), publisher.
"Yah Mo B There," James Ingram, Michael McDonald, Rod Temperton, Quincy Jones. Eiseman Music Co., Inc., Hen-A Publishing, Kings Road Music (BMI), Genevieve Music Rodsongs (PRS), Yellow Brick Road Music (ASCAP), publishers.

BEST R&B VOCAL PERFORMANCE, MALE
• Billy Ocean, "Caribbean Queen (No More Love on the Run)." Jive/Arista.
James Ingram, *It's Your Night*. Qwest.
Jeffrey Osborne, *Don't Stop*. A&M.
Jeffrey Osborne, "In the Name of Love," (on Ralph MacDonald recording). Polydor.
Stevie Wonder, "The Woman in Red," track from *Woman in Red* soundtrack. Motown.

BEST R&B VOCAL PERFORMANCE, FEMALE
• Chaka Khan, "I Feel for You." Warner Bros.
Patti Austin, *Patti Austin*. Qwest.
Shannon, *Let the Music Play*. Mirage.
✓ Tina Turner, "Let's Stay Together." Capitol.
✓ Deniece Williams, "Let's Hear It for the Boy." CBS.

BEST R&B PERFORMANCE BY A DUO OR GROUP WITH VOCAL
• James Ingram, Michael McDonald, "Yah Mo B There." Qwest.
Jermaine Jackson with Michael Jackson, "Tell Me I'm Not Dreamin' (Too Good to Be True)," track from *Jermaine Jackson*. Arista.

Kashif, Al Jarreau, "Edgartown Groove," track from *Send Me Your Love*. Arista.
Joyce Kennedy, Jeffrey Osborne, "The Last Time I Made Love." A&M.
Shalamar, "Dancing in the Sheets." Columbia/CBS.

BEST R&B INSTRUMENTAL PERFORMANCE
• Herbie Hancock, *Sound-System*. Columbia/CBS.
Stanley Clarke, "Time Exposure," track from *Time Exposure*. Epic.
Crusaders, *Ghetto Blaster*. MCA.
Sheila E., "Shortberry Strawcake," track from *The Glamorous Life*. Warner Bros.
Grover Washington, Jr., *Inside Moves*. Elektra.

BEST JAZZ FUSION PERFORMANCE, VOCAL OR INSTRUMENTAL
• Pat Metheny Group, *First Circle*. ECM.
Miles Davis, *Decoy*. Columbia/CBS.
Spyro Gyra, *Access All Areas*. MCA.
Earl Klugh, *Wishful Thinking*. Capitol.
David Sanborn, *Backstreet*. Warner Bros.

BEST JAZZ VOCAL PERFORMANCE
• Joe Williams, *Nothin' But the Blues*. Delos.
Lorez Alexandria, *Harlem Butterfly*. Discovery.
Carmen McRae, *You're Lookin' at Me*. Concord Jazz.
Sue Raney, *Ridin' High*. Discovery.
Mel Tormé, *An Evening at Charlie's*. Concord Jazz.

BEST JAZZ INSTRUMENTAL PERFORMANCE, SOLOIST
• Wynton Marsalis, *Hot House Flowers*. Columbia/CBS.
Pepper Adams, Kenny Wheeler, *Live at Fat Tuesday's*. Uptown.
Tommy Flanagan, *Thelonica*. Enja.
Zoot Sims, *Quietly There*. Pablo.
Ira Sullivan, *Ira Sullivan ... Does It All*. Muse.

BEST JAZZ INSTRUMENTAL PERFORMANCE, GROUP
• Art Blakey & the Jazz Messengers, "New York Scene." Concord Jazz.
Clare Fischer, *Whose Woods Are These*. Discovery.
Frank Foster, Frank Wess, *Two for the Blues*. Pablo.

Philly Joe Jones, *Dameronia; Look Stop Listen*. Uptown.

Phil Woods, Chris Swansen, *Piper at the Gates of Dawn*. Sea Breeze.

BEST JAZZ INSTRUMENTAL PERFORMANCE, BIG BAND

• Count Basie & His Orchestra, *88 Basie Street*. Pablo.

Toshiko Akiyoshi Jazz Orchestra, *Ten Gallon Shuffle*. Ascent.

Carla Bley Band, "Misterioso," track from *That's the Way I Feel Now*. A&M.

Bob Florence Limited Edition, *Magic Time*. Trend.

Woody Herman Big Band, *World Class*. Concord Jazz.

BEST COUNTRY SONG
(Songwriter's Award)

• "City of New Orleans," Steve Goodman. Buddah Music Inc., Turnpike Tom Music (ASCAP), publishers.

"All My Rowdy Friends Are Coming Over Tonight," Hank Williams Jr. Bocephus Music Inc. (BMI), publisher.

"Faithless Love," John David Souther. WB Music Corp., Golden Spread Music (ASCAP), publishers.

"God Bless the U.S.A.," Lee Greenwood. MCA, Sycamore Valley Music (BMI), publishers.

"Mama He's Crazy," Kenny O'Dell. Kenny O'Dell Music (BMI), publisher.

BEST COUNTRY VOCAL PERFORMANCE, MALE

• Merle Haggard, "That's the Way Love Goes." Epic.

Lee Greenwood, "God Bless the U.S.A." MCA.

Willie Nelson, "City of New Orleans." Columbia/CBS.

Ricky Skaggs, *Country Boy*. Epic.

Hank Williams, Jr., "All My Rowdy Friends Are Coming Over Tonight." Warner Bros./Curb.

BEST COUNTRY VOCAL PERFORMANCE, FEMALE

• Emmylou Harris, "In My Dreams." Warner Bros.

Janie Fricke, "Your Heart's Not in It." Columbia/CBS.

Crystal Gayle, "The Sound of Goodbye." Warner Bros.

Anne Murray, *Heart Over Mind*. Capitol.

Dolly Parton, "Tennessee Homesick Blues." RCA.

Country thrush and three-time past champ Emmylou Harris picked up a new vocalist Grammy for "In My Dreams."

BEST COUNTRY PERFORMANCE BY A DUO OR GROUP WITH VOCAL

• Judds, "Mama He's Crazy." RCA.

Alabama, "If You're Gonna Play in Texas (You Gotta Have a Fiddle in the Band)." RCA.

Barbara Mandrell, Lee Greenwood, "To Me." MCA.

Anne Murray with Dave Loggins, "Nobody Loves Me Like You Do." Capitol.

Willie Nelson, Julio Iglesias, "As Time Goes By," track from *Without a Song*. Columbia/CBS.

BEST COUNTRY INSTRUMENTAL PERFORMANCE

• Ricky Skaggs, "Wheel Hoss," track from *Country Boy*. Epic/CBS.

Chet Atkins, *East Tennessee Christmas*. Columbia/CBS.

Carlton Moody & the Moody Brothers, "Cotton-Eyed Joe." Lamon.

Doc & Merle Watson, "Twin Sisters," track from *Down South*. Sugar Hill.

Whites, "Move It On Over," track from *Forever You*. MCA.

Best Gospel Performance, Male
- Michael W. Smith, *Michael W. Smith 2*. Reunion/Word.

Bob Bailey, *I'm Walkin'*. Light/Lexicon.

Phil Driscoll, *Celebrate Freedom*. Sparrow.

Leon Patillo, "J.E.S.U.S.," track from *The Sky's the Limit*. Myrrh/Word.

Steve Taylor, *Meltdown*. Sparrow.

Best Gospel Performance, Female
- Amy Grant, "Angels," track from *Straight Ahead*. Myrhh/Word.

Debby Boone, *Surrender*. Lamb & Lion/Sparrow.

Sandi Patti, *Songs from the Heart*. Impact/Benson.

Michele Pillar, *Look Who Loves You Now*. Sparrow.

Kathy Troccoli, *Heart and Soul*. Reunion/Word.

Best Gospel Performance by a Duo or Group
- Debby Boone, Phil Driscoll, "Keep the Flame Burning," track from *Surrender*, Debby Boone album. Lamb & Lion/Sparrow.

Steve Camp, Michele Pillar, "Love's Not a Feeling," track from *Fire and Ice*, Steve Camp album. Sparrow.

Mylon LeFevre, Broken Heart, *Live Forever*. Myrrh/ Word.

New Gaither Vocal Band, *New Point of View*. Dayspring/Word.

Petra, *Not of this World*. Starsong/Word.

Best Soul Gospel Performance, Male
- Andrae Crouch, "Always Remember," track from *No Time to Lose*. Light/Lexicon.

Mel Carter, *Willing*. Onyx International/ Benson.

Rev. James Cleveland, "The Prayer," track from *I'm Giving My Life Up to You*. Savoy.

Jessy Dixon, *Sanctuary*. Power Disc/Benson.

Al Green, *Trust in God*. Myrrh/Word.

Best Soul Gospel Performance, Female
- Shirley Caesar, *Sailin'*. Myrrh.

Kristle Edwards, "Jesus, Come Lay Your Head on Me," track from *No Time to Lose*, Andrae Crouch album. Light.

Danniebelle Hall, *Unmistakably Danniebelle*. Onyx International.

Tata Vega, "Oh, It Is Jesus," track from *No Time To Lose*, Andrae Crouch album. Light.

Albertina Walker, *The Impossible Dream*. Savoy.

Best Soul Gospel Performance by a Duo or Group
- Shirley Caesar, Al Green, "Sailin' on the Sea of Your Love," track from *Sailin'*, (Shirley Caesar album). Myrrh.

Shirley Caesar, Anne Caesar Price, "Rejoice," track from *Sailin'* (Shirley Caesar album). Myrrh.

Edwin Hawkins, *Angels Will Be Singing*. Birthright/ Word.

Richard Smallwood Singers, *Psalms*. Onyx International/Benson.

BeBe & CeCe Winans, *Lord Lift Us Up*. PTL.

Best Inspirational Performance
- Donna Summer, "Forgive Me," track from *Cats Without Claws*. Geffen/ Warner Bros.

Philip Bailey, *The Wonders of His Love*. Myrrh/Word.

Pat Boone, *What I Believe*. Lamb & Lion/Sparrow.

Lisa Whelchel, *All Because of You*. Nissi.

Deniece Williams, "Whiter Than Snow," track from *Let's Hear It for the Boy*. CBS.

Best Ethnic or Traditional Folk Recording
- *Elizabeth Cotten Live!* Elizabeth Cotten. Arhoolie.

Good Rockin', Rocking Dopsie. GNP-Crescendo.

On a Saturday Night, Queen Ida. GNP-Crescendo.

100% Fortified Zydeco, Buckwheat Zydeco. Black Top/Rounder.

Open Road, Boys of the Lough. Flying Fish.

Best Traditional Blues Recording
- *Blues Explosion*, John Hammond, Stevie Ray Vaughan & Double Trouble, Sugar Blue, Koko Taylor & the Blues Machine, Luther "Guitar Junior" Johnson, J.B. Hutto & the New Hawks. Atlantic.

Guitar Slinger, Johnny Winter. Alligator.

I'm in a Phone Booth, Baby, Albert King. Fantasy.

Kansas City Here I Come, Joe Turner. Pablo.

You've Got Me Loving You, Bobby Bland.
MCA.

BEST LATIN POP PERFORMANCE
• Placido Domingo, *Always in My Heart
(Siempre en mi Corazón)*. CBS-
Masterworks.
Maria Conchita, *Maria Conchita*. A&M.
José Feliciano, *Como tu Quieres*. RCA.
Johnny, *Invítame*. RCA.
José José, *Secretos*. Ariola-America.
Menudo, *Evolución*. RCA.

BEST TROPICAL LATIN PERFORMANCE
• Eddie Palmieri, *Palo Pa Rumba*. Musica
Latina.
Rubén Blades, *Buscando America*. Elektra.
Willie Colon, *Criollo*. RCA.
El Gran Combo, *Breaking the Ice*.
Combo/Rico.
Poncho Sanchez, *¡Bien Sabroso!* Concord
Jazz.
Los Socios del Ritmo, *¡Y Ahora!
"Conniff."* Ariola.

BEST MEXICAN/AMERICAN PERFORMANCE
• Sheena Easton, Luis Miguel, "Me Gustas
Tal Como Eres." Top Hits.
Roberto Carlos, "Concavo y Convexo,"
track from *Roberto Carlos*. CBS
International.
Yolanda Del Rio, *Un Amor Especial*.
RCA.
Juan Gabriel, *Recuerdos II*. Ariola-
America.
Raphael, *Eternamente Tuyo*. CBS
International.

BEST REGGAE RECORDING
• *Anthem*, Black Uhuru. Island.
Captured Live, Peter Tosh. EMI-America.
King Yellowman, Yellowman.
Columbia/CBS.
"Reggae Night," Jimmy Cliff.
Columbia/CBS.
"Steppin' Out," Steel Pulse. Elektra.

BEST INSTRUMENTAL COMPOSITION
(Composer's Award—Tie)
• "The Natural," track from *The Natural*,
Randy Newman. TSP Music, Inc.
(ASCAP), publisher.
• "Olympic Fanfare and Theme," track
from *The Official Music of the XXIII
Olympiad at Los Angeles*, John
Williams. Warner Bros. Music (BMI),
publisher.

The A-Team, Mike Post, Peter Carpenter.
Darla, S.J.C., April, Marbo (ASCAP),
publishers.
Ghostbusters (Main Title Theme), Elmer
Bernstein. Golden Torch Music Corp.,
publisher.
Hot House Flowers, Wynton Marsalis.

BEST ARRANGEMENT ON AN INSTRUMENTAL
• Quincy Jones, Jeremy Lubbock, "Grace
(Gymnastics Theme)," track from *The
Official Music of the XXIII Olympiad at
Los Angeles* (Quincy Jones). CBS.
Stewart Copeland, "Brothers on Wheels,"
track from *Rumble Fish Soundtrack*
(Stewart Copeland). A&M.
Robert Freedman, "Stardust," track from
Hot House Flowers (Wynton Marsalis).
CBS.
Henry Mancini, "Cameo for Flute . . . for
James," track from *In the Pink* (James
Galway, Henry Mancini). RCA.
Don Sebesky, "Waltz for Debbie," track
from *Full Cycle* (Don Sebesky).
Crescendo.

BEST VOCAL ARRANGEMENT FOR TWO OR MORE VOICES
• Pointer Sisters, "Automatic," track from
Break Out (Pointer Sisters). Planet.
David Foster, "What About Me?" track
from *What About Me?* (Kenny Rogers,
Kim Carnes, James Ingram). RCA.
David Foster, Peter Cetera, "Hard Habit to
Break," track from *Chicago 17*
(Chicago). Full Moon/Warner Bros.
Richard Greene, Gunnar Madsen, "Helter
Skelter," track from *The Bobs* (Bobs).
Kaleidoscope.
Trevor Rabin, Chris Squire, "Leave It"
(Yes). Atco/Atlantic.

BEST CAST SHOW ALBUM
• *Sunday in the Park with George
(Original Cast Album)*, Stephen
Sondheim, composer and lyricist.
Thomas Z. Shepard, producer. RCA.
Doonesbury, Elizabeth Swados, composer.
Garry Trudeau, lyricist. Robert Liftin,
producer. MCA.
My One and Only, Ahmet Ertegun, Wally
Harper, producers. Atlantic.
A Stephen Sondheim Evening, Thomas Z.
Shepard, producer. RCA.

Sugar Babies, Jimmy McHugh, Arthur Malvin, Dorothy Fields, George Oppenheim, Harold Adamson, music and lyrics. Robert Sher, producer. Broadway Entertainment.

BEST ALBUM OF ORIGINAL SCORE WRITTEN FOR A MOTION PICTURE OR A TELEVISION SPECIAL
(Composer's/Songwriter's Award)
√• *Purple Rain*, Prince & the Revolution, John L. Nelson, Lisa & Wendy.
Against All Odds, Phil Collins, Stevie Nicks, Peter Gabriel, Stuart Adamson, Mike Rutherford, August Darnell, Michel Colombier, Larry Carlton.
√*Footloose*, Bill Wolfer, Dean Pitchford, Kenny Loggins, Tom Snow, Sammy Hagar, Michael Gore, Eric Carmen, Jim Steinman.
√*Ghostbusters*, Ray Parker Jr., Kevin O'Neal, Brian O'Neal, Bobby Alessi, David Immer, Tom Bailey, Graham Russell, David Foster, Jay Graydon, Diane Warren & the Doctor Mick Smiley, Elmer Bernstein.
Yentl, Michel Legrand, Alan Bergman, Marilyn Bergman.

BEST INSTRUMENTAL ARRANGEMENT ACCOMPANYING VOCAL(S)
√• David Foster, Jeremy Lubbock, "Hard Habit to Break" (Chicago). Full Moon/Warner Bros.
Laurie Anderson, "Gravity's Angel," track from *Mister Heartbreak* (Laurie Anderson). Warner Bros.
Thomas Dolby, "Mulu the Rain Forest," track from *The Flat Earth* (Thomas Dolby). Capitol.
Reggie Griffin, Arif Mardin, "I Feel for You," track from *I Feel for You* (Chaka Khan). Warner Bros.
Michel Legrand, "Papa, Can You Hear Me?" track from *Yentl*, original sound track (Barbra Streisand). CBS.

BEST CLASSICAL ALBUM
• *Amadeus (Original Soundtrack)*, Neville Marriner conducting Academy of St.-Martin-in-the-Fields; Ambrosian Opera Chorus; Choristers of Westminster Abbey; soloists. John Strauss, producer. Fantasy.
Beethoven: The 5 Piano Concertos, James Levine conducting Chicago Symphony (solo: Alfred Brendel). Volker Strauss, producer. Philips.

Brahms: A German Requiem, James Levine conducting Chicago Symphony Orchestra and Chorus (solos: Kathleen Battle, Hakan Hagegard). Thomas Z. Shepard, producer. RCA.
Prokofiev: Symphony No.5 in B Flat, Op. 100, Leonard Slatkin conducting St. Louis Symphony. Jay David Saks, producer. RCA.
Wynton Marsalis, Edita Gruberova: Handel, Purcell, Torelli, Fasch, Molter, Raymond Leppard conducting English Chamber Orchestra (solos: Wynton Marsalis, Edita Gruberova). Steven Epstein, producer. CBS.

BEST CLASSICAL ORCHESTRAL RECORDING
(Conductor's Award)
Prokofiev: Symphony No. 5 in B Flat, Op. 100, Leonard Slatkin conducting St. Louis Symphony. Jay David Saks, producer. RCA.
Amadeus (Original Soundtrack), Neville Marriner conducting Academy of St. Martin-in-the-Fields. John Strauss, producer. Fantasy.
Berlioz: Symphony Fantastique, Op. 14, Claudio Abbado conducting Chicago Symphony. Rainer Brock, producer. Deutsche Grammophon.
Gould: Burchfield Gallery & Apple Waltzes, Morton Gould conducting American Symphony. Thomas Frost, producer. RCA.
Mahler: Symphony No. 4 in G Major, Sir George Solti conducting Chicago Symphony. James Mallinson, producer. London.
Schubert: Symphony No. 9 in C Major ("The Great"), James Levine conducting Chicago Symphony. Dr. Steven Paul, producer. Deutsche Grammophon Archive.

BEST CHAMBER MUSIC PERFORMANCE
• Juilliard String Quartet, *Beethoven: The Late String Quartets*. CBS.
Cleveland Quartet with Emanuel Ax, *Brahms: Piano Quintet in F Minor, Op. 34*. RCA.
Chick Corea, Gary Burton, Ikwhan Bae, Carol Shive, Karen Dreyfus, Fred Sherry, *Corea: Lyric Suite for Sextet*. ECM.
Guarneri Quartet with Pinchas Zukerman, *Brahms: The String Quintets in F & G*. RCA.

Itzhak Perlman, Daniel Barenboim, *Mozart: Violin Sonatas, K. 301, 302, 303, 304*. Deutsche Grammophon.

Best Classical Performance, Instrumental Soloist(s) (with Orchestra)

- Wynton Marsalis, Edita Gruberova (Leppard conducting English Chamber Orchestra), *Wynton Marsalis, Edita Gruberova: Handel, Purcell, Torelli, Fasch, Molter*. CBS.
Emanuel Ax (Levine conducting Chicago Symphony), *Brahms: Piano Concerto No. 1 in D Minor*. RCA.
Julian Bream (Gardiner conducting Chamber Orchestra of Europe), *Rodrigo: Concierto de Aranjuez/ Invocation & Dance; Three Spanish Pieces (Music of Spain Vol. 8)*. RCA.
Alfred Brendel (Levine conducting Chicago Symphony), *Beethoven: The 5 Piano Concertos*. Philips.
Itzhak Perlman (Barenboim conducting Orchestre de Paris), *Wieniawski: Violin Concerto No. 2 in D Minor, Op. 22; Saint-Saëns: Violin Concerto No. 3 in B Minor, Op. 61*. Deutsche Grammophon.

Best Classical Performance, Instrumental Soloist(s) (without Orchestra)

- Yo-Yo Ma, *Bach: The Unaccompanied Cello Suites*. CBS.
Julian Bream, *Music of Spain, Vol. 7, "A Celebration of Andrés Segovia."* RCA.
Emil Gilels, *Beethoven: Piano Sonata No. 29 in B Flat Major, Op. 106 "Hammerklavier."* Deutsche Grammophon.
Glenn Gould, *R.Strauss: Glenn Gould Plays Strauss (Sonata; Five Pieces, Op. 3)*. CBS.
Alicia de Larrocha, *Schubert: Piano Sonata in B Flat Major, D. 960*. London.

Best Opera Recording

- *Bizet: Carmen (Original Soundtrack)*, Lorin Maazel conducting Orchestre National de France; Choeurs et Maitrise de Radio France (solos: Migenes Johnson, Esham, Domingo, Raimondi). Michel Glotz, producer. Erato.

Britten: The Turn of the Screw, Sir Colin Davis conducting members of Royal Opera House Orchestra, Covent Garden (solos: Donath, Harper, Tear). Erik Smith, producer. Philips.
Janácek: Jenufa, Sir Charles Mackerras conducting Vienna Philharmonic (solos: Soderstrom, Dvorsky, Ochman, Randova). James Mallinson, producer. London.
Mozart: Don Giovanni, Bernard Haitink conducting London Philharmonic; Glyndebourne Chorus (solos: Allen, Vaness, Van Allan, Ewing, Gale, Lewis, Rawnsley, Kavrakos). John Fraser, producer. Angel.
Verdi: Ernani, Riccardo Muti conducting Coro e Orchestra del Teatro alla Scala (solos: Domingo, Freni, Bruson, Ghiaurov). John Mordler, producer. Angel.

Best Choral Performance (Other Than Opera)

- Margaret Hillis, choral conductor, Chicago Symphony Chorus; James Levine conducting Chicago Symphony, *Brahms: A German Requiem*. RCA.
Riccardo Chailly conducting Cleveland Orchestra Chorus; Cleveland Orchestra, *Prokofiev: Alexander Nevsky, Op. 78*. London.
Riccardo Chailly conducting RSO Berlin Chorus; RSO Berlin Orchestra, *Orff: Carmina Burana*. London.
Christopher Hogwood conducting Westminster Cathedral Boys Choir; Chorus and Orchestra of the Academy of Ancient Music, *Mozart: Requiem*. L'Oiseau Lyre.
Simon Rattle conducting City of Birmingham Orchestra Chorus and Boys of Christ Church Cathedral, Oxford; City of Birmingham Symphony, *Britten: War Requiem*. Angel.

Best Classical Vocal Soloist Performance

- Jessye Norman, José van Dam, Heather Harper (Boulez conducting members of Ensemble Intercontemporain and BBC Symphony), *Ravel: Songs of Maurice Ravel*. CBS.

Dame Janet Baker (Geoffrey Parsons, accompanist), *Mahler's Songs of Youth.* Hyperion.

Hakan Hagegård, Kathleen Battle (James Levine, accompanist), *Brahms: Songs of Brahms.* RCA.

Kiri Te Kanawa (Solti conducting Chicago Symphony), *Mahler: Symphony No. 4 in G Major, 4th Movement.* London.

Jessye Norman (Maazel conducting Wiener Philharmonic), *Mahler: Symphony No. 2 in C Minor ("Resurrection").* CBS.

BEST NEW CLASSICAL COMPOSITION
(Composer's Award)

Antony and Cleopatra, Samuel Barber.
"Apple Waltzes," Morton Gould.
"Magabunda (Four Poems of Agueda Pizzaro)," Joseph Schwantner.
"The Perfect Stranger," Frank Zappa.
"Winter Cantata," Vincent Persichetti.

BEST ENGINEERED RECORDING, CLASSICAL

• Paul Goodman, *Prokofiev: Symphony No. 5 in B Flat, Op. 100* (Slatkin conducting St. Louis Symphony). RCA.

Tony Faulkner, Ray Moore, *Wynton Marsalis, Edita Gruberova: Handel, Purcell, Torelli, Fasch, Molter* (Leppard conducting English Chamber Orchestra; solo: Marsalis, Editz Gruberova). CBS.

Paul Goodman, *Brahms: A German Requiem* (Levine conducting Chicago Symphony Orchestra and Chorus; solos: Kathleen Battle, Hakan Hagegard). RCA.

Paul Goodman, *Brahms: Piano Concerto No. 1 in D Minor* (Levine conducting Chicago Symphony; solo: Ax). RCA.

James Lock, John Dunkerley, *Mahler: Symphony No. 4 in G Major* (Solti conducting Chicago Symphony; solo: Kiri Te Kanawa). London.

CLASSICAL PRODUCER OF THE YEAR

• Steven Epstein. CBS.
Marc Aubort, Joanna Nickrenz. Nonesuch.
Jay David Saks. RCA.
Robert E. Woods. Telarc.
Thomas Z. Shepard. RCA.

BEST COMEDY RECORDING

• "Eat It," track from *"Weird Al" Yankovic in 3-D*, "Weird Al" Yankovic. Rock 'n' Roll.

Here and Now, Richard Pryor. Warner Bros.

Hurt Me Baby, Make Me Write Bad Checks! Rick Dees. No-o-o Budget.

Rappin' Rodney, Rodney Dangerfield. RCA.

The 3 Faces of Al (Nick Danger), Fireside Theatre. Rhino.

BEST SPOKEN WORD OR NON-MUSICAL RECORDING

• *The Words of Gandhi*, Ben Kingsley. Caedmon.

Heart Play (Unfinished Dialogue), John Lennon, Yoko Ono. Polydor.

Our Time Has Come, Rev. Jesse Jackson. MCA.

The Real Thing (original cast recording), Jeremy Irons, Glenn Close. Nonesuch.

The Story of Indiana Jones and the Temple of Doom (narration, dialogue, and music from the original motion picture soundtrack), Jymn Magon, Ted Kryczko, album producers. Buena Vista.

BEST RECORDING FOR CHILDREN

• *Where the Sidewalk Ends*, Shel Silverstein. Ron Haffkine, producer. CBS.

Agapeland at Play With Holly Heart, Holly Heart. Billy Ray Hearn, Ken Pennell, producers. Birdwing/Sparrow.

Flashbeagle, starring Snoopy, Charlie Brown & the Whole Peanuts Gang. Lee Mendelson, Desiree Goyette, Ed Bogas, Jymn Magon, producers. Charlie Brown.

Jim Henson's Muppets Present Fraggle Rock, Jim Henson's Muppets. Jim Henson, Muppet creator. Philip Balsam, Don Gillis, producers. Muppet Music.

Kids Praise 4, Singsational Servants. Ernie Rettino, Debby Kerner, producers. Maranatha!/Word.

The Muppets Take Manhattan — The Original Soundtrack, the Muppets. Jim Henson, Muppet creator. Jeff Moss, producer. Warner Bros.

Best Engineered Recording
(Non-Classical)
• Humberto Gatica, *Chicago 17* (Chicago). Full Moon/Warner Bros.
Nigel Green, *Heartbeat City* (Cars). Elektra.
✓ Calvin Harris, *Can't Slow Down* (Lionel Richie). Motown.
Steven Miller, *Aerial Boundaries* (Michael Hedges). Windham Hill.
Phil Thornalley, *Into the Gap* (Thompson Twins). Arista.

Best Album Package
(Art director's Award)
✓ • Janet Perr, *She's So Unusual* (Cyndi Lauper). Portrait.
Bill Johnson, Virginia Team, Jeff Morris, *Willie Nelson* (Willie Nelson). CBS.
Bill Levy, *Every Man Has a Woman* (John Lennon, Harry Nilsson, Eddie Money, Rosanne Cash, others). Polydor.
Henry Marquez, *No Brakes* (John Waite). EMI-America.
Andy Summers, Michael Ross, *Bewitched* (Andy Summers, Robert Fripp). A&M.

Best Album Notes
(Annotator's Award)
• Gunther Schuller, Martin Williams, *Big Band Jazz* (Paul Whiteman, Fletcher Henderson, Chick Webb, Tommy Dorsey, Count Basie, Benny Goodman, others). Smithsonian.
Glenn Hinson, *Virginia Traditions Work Songs* (Field recordings 1936–1980, various artists). Blue Ridge.
Grover Sales, *Amadeus (Original Soundtrack Recording)* (Neville Marriner conducting Academy of St. Martin-in-the-Fields). Fantasy.
James Sundquist, *An Anthology of Sacred Carols for Classical Guitar* (James Sundquist). Eagle.
Z Factor, Lorene Lortie, *A Golden Celebration* (Elvis Presley). RCA.

Best Historical Album
• *Big Band Jazz* (Paul Whiteman, Fletcher Henderson, Chick Webb, Tommy Dorsey, Count Basie, Benny Goodman, others). J.R. Taylor, producer. Smithsonian.

Cotton Club Stars (various artists). Bernard Brightman, producer. Stash.
A Golden Celebration (Elvis Presley). Gregg Geller, Joan Deary, producers. RCA.
History Speaks: Franklin Delano Roosevelt (Franklin Delano Roosevelt, introduction by Clifton Fadiman). George Spitzer, producer. Book-of-the-Month Records.
World's First Entertainment Recordings 1889–1896 (various artists). George Garabedian, producer. Mark 56.

Producer of the Year
(Non-Classical)
(Tie)
• David Foster
• Lionel Richie, James Anthony Carmichael
Robert John "Mutt" Lange, Cars
Michael Omartian
Prince & the Revolution

Best Video, Short Form
• *David Bowie*, David Bowie. Sony/Picture Music.
Ashford & Simpson, Ashford & Simpson. Sony/Picture Music.
Phil Collins, Phil Collins. Sony/Philip Collins.
Rubber Rodeo Scenic Views, Rubber Rodeo. Sony/Polygram.
Thomas Dolby, Thomas Dolby. Sony/Picture Music.
Twist of Fate, Olivia Newton-John. MCA Home Video.

Best Video Album
• *Making Michael Jackson's Thriller*, Michael Jackson. Vestron Music Video.
Billy Joel Live from Long Island, Billy Joel. CBS/Fox Video.
Eurythmics Sweet Dreams, Eurythmics. RCA Video/Zoetrope.
Heartbeat City, Cars. Warner Home Video.
Serious Moonlight, David Bowie. Music Media.
We're All Devo, Devo. Pioneer Artist.

A "World"-Wide Victory

Not since Grammy's 1972 Album of the Year, *The Concert for Bangla Desh*, did America's music hierarchy rally for such an urgent and crucial cause. Drought-induced famine was killing millions in Africa and it was Harry Belafonte who initially sounded

Among the "all stars" who contributed to Record of the Year "We Are the World" were (from left) Dionne Warwick, Stevie Wonder, Quincy Jones, Michael Jackson, and Lionel Richie.

WIDE WORLD PHOTO

the call for help that would become an anthem rousing millions of record buyers to action. Belafonte had been inspired by Bob Geldof's success with "Do They Know It's Christmas?" — the Band Aid song that involved a host of British rock stars in famine relief.

"We Are the World" was written by Lionel Richie and Michael Jackson in only two and a half hours. ("We didn't really write this song. It came through us," Richie told reporters backstage at the Grammys. Jackson backed up his suggestion of divine intervention by claiming God chose him and Richie to write it.) For the USA for Africa project, producer Quincy Jones recruited 45 top music artists, a roster of rock royalty that included Paul Simon, Bruce Springsteen, Stevie Wonder, Bob Dylan, Hall & Oates, Diana Ross, Smokey Robinson, and Tina Turner. Immediately following the 1985 Ameri-

can Music Awards, Jones summoned them all to A&M's recording studios at 10 p.m. where he instructed them "to check [their] egos at the door" and get to work. By 8 o'clock the next morning, the job was done.

The effort, said *The Los Angeles Herald Examiner*, "seemed to embody the sort of positive social force that the pop music industry might achieve, given a semblance of community and conscience." The result was described by *The New York Times* as "an uplifting, all-star, Hollywood-produced ballad that was born to sweep the Grammys."

"We Are the World" became the biggest single in history, raised $60 million for famine relief, and won four awards: Record and Song of the Year, Best Group Pop Vocal Performance, and Best Short Form Music Video. In accepting the record award, Jones thanked "the generation that changed 'I, Me, My' to

'We, You, Us.'" Richie also singled out the music-buying public in his acceptance remarks, saying that "the most important thing was, when we called, you responded, and we thank you for it," then added, "We came here tonight to keep this message alive." Michael Jackson, dressed in a black military jacket studded with rhinestones, whispered into the podium microphone: "When you leave here, remember the children."

"*We Are the World*" *became the biggest-selling single ever and raised $60 million for African famine relief.*

Whereas the single version of "We Are the World" was considered the likely winner of its top honors, the also-nominated LP of the same name was not. Instead, the race for Album of the Year was considered a close contest between Phil Collins' *No Jacket Required*, Dire Straits' *Brothers in Arms,* and Sting's *The Dream of the Blue Turtles*. When Collins's *No Jacket* prevailed, *The Washington Post* said its success was due to being "the most accessible of the three," which therefore made it the most likely "to garner support from the conservative constituency that dominates N.A.R.A.S." Other sources thought its victory was deserved. Wrote *The New York Times*, "As both a songwriter and an instrumentalist, Collins is especially adept at sustaining a mood of suspense, often heavily tinged with menace. His shadowy song lyrics are suffused with lurking suspicion, dread, and the suggestion of passions so pent-up they could explode violently, though they never do." *No*

Jacket spun off five hits into the Hot 100, including "Don't Lose My Number" and "Sussudio," and spent seven weeks at number one on *Billboard*'s LP chart. It achieved that rank only four weeks after its release, which was less time than it took Michael Jackson's *Thriller* (Grammy's 1983 Album of the Year) to reach the same lofty height.

Collins won three Grammys in all, including Producer of the Year (with Hugh Padgham) and Best Male Pop Vocal Performance for *No Jacket Required*. At the Grammys, a jacket *was* recommended attire for men, even for superstar winners like Collins. "Am I glad I bought this tux!" he said early in the evening. By the time he picked up the Album of the Year award, the thrice-lauded Collins added, "I've run out of things to say, to be honest."

Dire Straits' music received the second-most nominations of the year: eight, compared to 12 for the Manhattan Transfer's *Vocalese*. The British rock band ended up with three awards, including an engineering prize and the laurels for rock group vocals for "Money for Nothing," which was a losing nominee for Record and Song of the Year. "Money" was somewhat controversial: Music critics and gay groups protested its disparaging reference to a "little faggot" in its lyrics, although Warner Bros. edited the phrase out of later releases. The third honor went to the group's founder/singer/guitarist Mark Knopfler, who shared the country instrumental laurels with guitarist Chet Atkins for "Cosmic Square Dance," a track from Atkins's *Stay Tuned*.

Former Eagle Don Henley's "The Boys of Summer" was another loser of Record and Song of the Year, but it garnered him the prize for best male rock singing as a consolation. Back in the press room, reporters plugged Henley with questions about the single described by *The Washington Post* as "angst-filled," but he seemed more eager to talk about the musical score he was writing for the Martin Scorsese film *The Color of Money* (sequel to *The Hustler*).

Tina Turner held on to the female rock vocal honors that she won last year ("Better Be Good to Me") for the song "One of the Living" from the film in which she also starred, *Mad Max: Beyond Thunderdome*. She triumphed over, among others, Pat Benatar, who had monopolized the category for four years straight before being ousted by Turner. As expected, the rock instrumental laurels went to U.K. guitarist Jeff Beck for "Escape," a track from his album *Flash*. Prior to his wild experiments with rock on *Flash* and other

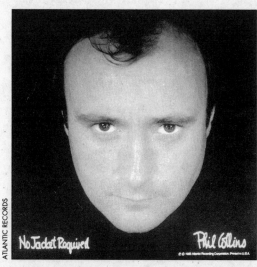

ATLANTIC RECORDS

Best LP No Jacket Required: *Phil Collins's music was full of suspense and "tinged with menace."*

recent LPs, Beck was known mostly for his mastery of r&b/pop music.

Also as expected, Sade (pronounced Shah-*day*) reaped the Best New Artist prize over such weak competition as John Lennon's son Julian and Katrina & the Waves. The Nigerian-born British pop star was red hot at Grammy time. She'd been dubbed the "Queen of Cool" in a recent cover story by *Time* magazine and already had two hit albums, *Diamond Life* and *Promise*, which sold a combined total of 12 million copies worldwide.

The Best New Artist line-up was considered weak in part because, in a controversial ruling, the even hotter former model Whitney Houston was barred from competing due to a technicality. A N.A.R.A.S. spokesman declared: "The rule that disqualified Whitney is perfectly clear .... An artist is not eligible if [he or she had a previous] label credit or album credit." Houston had made earlier minor contributions to albums by Jermaine Jackson and Teddy Pendergrass. In her defense, *Billboard* noted that former Best New Artist Carly Simon had recorded an album with her sister prior to her win for 1971 and asked, "Didn't last year's winner, Cyndi Lauper, receive credit as the lead singer on the Blue Angel album, for which she deserved, and got, considerable acclaim and attention?"

Houston, the daughter of famed gospel singer Cissy Houston, was a sudden pop superstar in 1985–86. Her eponymous album had two songs in the 1985's Hot 100 and was 1986's top-selling LP and a 1985 nominee for Grammy's Album of the Year. (It was also the biggest-selling debut album of all time.) As a consolation, one of those singles, "Saving All My Love for You," earned her the female pop vocals prize, which was presented by another relative of Houston's who was also a famous singing star — cousin Dionne Warwick. "Warwick bounced up and down in obvious delight as she read Whitney Houston's name as winner," noted the *Herald Examiner*. Houston said in her acceptance remarks, "Oh, my goodness. I must thank God, who makes it all possible for me!"

It was the number one–selling album of 1985 that brought Jan Hammer, a former keyboard artist for the Mahavishnu Orchestra, the honors for Best Instrumental Composition and Best Pop Instrumental Performance. Hammer's theme song to the hit TV detective series *Miami Vice* was the first all-instrumental number-one single hit since Vangelis's "Theme from *Chariots of Fire*," and the album spent the longest time ever at number one (11 weeks) for a score to a TV show, thereby surpassing the previous record set by Grammy's first Album of the Year winner, *The Music from Peter Gunn* (1958) by Henry Mancini. Hammer skipped the Grammy show because he was at his home in upstate New York "still working on this week's *Miami Vice* music," he said in a message passed on by his publicist.

When Rosanne Cash lost a Grammy in 1982, she wrote a song about her grief — and won an award for it this year.

Aretha Franklin had monopolized the female r&b vocals category for eight years between 1967 to 1974 but had only returned once since, in 1981, for "Hold On, I'm Coming." Now she was back with "Freeway of Love" (from her album *Who's Zoomin' Who*), which also nabbed Best Rhythm & Blues Song for writers Narada Michael Walden and Jeffrey Cohen. Stevie Wonder, who had reaped 15 Grammys in just four years during the mid-1970s but hadn't won a single golden statuette since, rebounded with the r&b male vocal award for *In Square Circle*. One of the album's biggest hits was "Part-Time Lover," which Wonder sang on the Grammy show in what the *Herald Examiner* called "a passionate performance."

When the Commodores snagged the r&b group vocals accolade for "Nightshift," *The Washington Post* called it "a particularly sweet victory [since] the veteran group had been virtually written off after the departure of Lionel Richie" in 1981. The *Herald Examiner* noted a group member's good humor about the split: "Lead singer J.D. Nicholas thanked, among others, former lead singer Lionel Richie for leaving the group so Nicholas could take his place."

Ever since 1973, jazz was the only music genre in which the nominations weren't determined by the N.A.R.A.S. membership. Instead, they were selected by craft committees. "The argument against the craft committee approach was that it was elitist and resulted in many of the same familiar names being nominated time and again," *Billboard* said. This year N.A.R.A.S. returned the vote to academy members on a one-year trial basis, resulting in bids for some unlikely jazz artists like Sting and Barry Manilow. *Billboard* complained, too, that "Manhattan Transfer is all over the place. A total of six selections from the group's star-studded *Vocalese* album, plus the album itself, are nominated in the male, female, and group vocal categories. Both Dizzie Gillespie and James Moody are nominated in the instrumental soloist category for their contributions to individual tracks."

The Manhattan Transfer ended up with the group vocals prize for itself plus the male singing honors for guest artists Jon Hendricks and Bobby McFerrin on its "Another Night in Tunisia" track. (The jazz singing awards were again broken down into male, female, and group categories after being combined into one prize last year.) McFerrin shared an additional award, for arrangement, with Cheryl Bentyne.

Despite the new voting procedure, familiar names among past winners continued to spring up: Alto sax player David Sanborn reaped the instrumental fusion accolade for *Straight to the Heart,* and trumpeter Wynton Marsalis returned to claim the both the solist and group instrumental awards for *Black Codes from the Underground.* Cleo Laine, the British-born singer of jazz, pop, classical, and show tune music, gave a historic appearance at Carnegie Hall in 1973, resulting in a best-selling, live two-disc album that reaped her a Grammy nomination for pop vocals in 1974. Laine returned 10 years later with *Cleo at Carnegie* and won the 1985 female jazz vocal prize. The soundtrack to the Francis Ford Coppola film *The Cotton Club*, filled mostly with masterworks by Duke Ellington, snagged the big band instrumental award for John Barry and Bob Wilber.

In an article in *Down Beat*, music critic Leonard Feather made reference to "the coast-to-coast brouhaha" that followed last year's omission of a jazz performance on the Grammycast. This year N.A.R.A.S. made up for the snub with an eight-minute segment described by the *Herald Examiner* as "a star-studded jazz jamboree that soared when horn players Dizzy Gillespie, Jon Faddis, Gerry Mulligan, and David Sanborn took the lead."

The country categories welcomed back a past Grammy star when songwriter Jimmy Webb won the prize for Best Country Song. *Billboard* remarked: "His 'Highwayman' was declared best country song 18 years after 'Up, Up and Away' [which he wrote] walked away with the Grammy for Song of the Year and 17 years after Webb's last Grammy, for arranging Richard Harris's 'MacArthur Park.'"

Another returning champ was three-time past winner Ronnie Milsap, who seized the male vocal laurels for what *The Washington Post* called "his smooth piece of nostalgia," "Lost in the Fifties Tonight (In the Still of the Night)," which lost its bid for Best Country Song, but did win the Song of the Year award from the Academy of Country Music. The tune was a tribute to the "doo-wop" era of country music in the 1950s and was based on "In the Still of the Nite" by Freddy Parris. The mother-daughter duo of Wynonna and Naomi Judd scored such success with their Grammy-winning performance of "Mama He's Crazy" last year that RCA gave them a full album project ("with a strong, midtempo groove," noted *Billboard*) in 1985 with *Why Not Me*, which earned them their second statuette.

When Johnny Cash's daughter Rosanne lost her bid for Best Female Country Vocal Performance at the 1982 awards, she left the Shrine Auditorium depressed. She told *Billboard*, "I was drivin' down Hollywood Boulevard and I was very tongue-in-cheek, saying, 'I got my new dress, I got my new shoes/I don't know why you don't want me,' just writing this little ditty and being very sarcastic. So when I went home and I showed Rodney [Crowell] what I had, he said, 'This is good enough to make into a real song. Why don't we write it together?' So we did." "I Don't Know Why You Don't Want Me" lost its bid for Best Country Song but at last won Cash the female vocal award for 1985. While accepting the trophy, she said, "I wrote it out of self-pity. How ironic to win with it!"

For the fourth year in a row Amy Grant (*Unguarded*) was awarded a Gospel Grammy, while other comeback veterans included Shirley Caesar ("Martin"), Larnelle Harris (two awards for tracks from *I've Just Seen Jesus*), and Jennifer Holliday ("Come Sunday"). A

After Lionel Richie left the Commodores in 1981, the group was "written off," but rallied to claim a Grammy for Nightshift*'s title track.*

A new category for Best Polka Recording was introduced this year and went to legendary polka artist and accordian player Frank Yankovic (no relation to "Weird Al"). "Yankovic, 70, thanked 'least but not last' all the musicians who helped him on his winning album, *70 Years of Hits*," said the *Herald Examiner*. The one-year-old award for Best Reggae Recording was bestowed for 1985 to singer Jimmy Cliff, noted for tinging his music with r&b influences and strong political messages. The purveyor of "swamp blues," Rockin' Sydney, was hailed for his Best Ethnic or Traditional Folk Recording, "My Toot Toot."

brother-sister duo that would come to sweep religious awards in future years, BeBe and CeCe Winans, took their first this year for *Tomorrow* plus while their brother Marvin garnered a trophy for the album's track "Bring Back the Days of Yea and Nay."

The category of Best Mexican/ American Performance caused a controversy last year when leading Mexican-American artists like Vikki Carr failed to be nominated over dubious other contenders. Carr, who had never won a Grammy before, finally prevailed this year for *Simplemente Mujer*.

"The award for Best Latin Pop Performance stayed distinctly within the family," commented the *Herald Examiner*. "It went to Lani Hall [*Es Facil Amar*], who received it from her husband, Herb Alpert, head of A&M Records, for which Hall records." There was a tie for the prize of Best Tropical Latin Performance between Eddie Palmieri (*Solito*) and Tito Puente & His Latin Ensemble (*Mambo Diablo*), but, in an embarrassing flub, only Puente was named as a winner on the Grammycast.

Soon after comedian Whoopi Goldberg was discovered by stage and screen director Mike Nichols, she was given her own Broadway show, the LP recording of which earned her the kudos for best comedy album. Going for strong gut reactions from her audience, Goldberg portrayed a series of down-and-out characters and brainless stereotypes in the show, including a junkie and an irritating California Valley Girl she called "Surfer Chick." "Surfer Chick" peppered her conversation with a grating amount of "you knows" and "OKs" while she described an abortion she gave herself using a coat hanger, saying, "You have to take the paper off because you never know where it's been."

Other Broadway shows were honored, too. August Wilson's dramatic tribute to a legendary American blues singer in *Ma Rainey's Black Bottom* snagged Best Spoken Word or Non-Musical Recording. When the score to a revival of *West Side Story* was named Best Cast Show Album over such newer competition as the Tony Award-winning *Big River* by Roger Miller, *High Fidelity* denounced its victory as "ludicrous."

West Side Story had won numerous prizes in the past, including jazz awards for André Previn in 1960 and Stan Kenton in 1961 as well as the 1961 honors for best film score. (The original Broadway production opened a year before the Grammys were inaugurated.) This year the film score laurels were awarded to the music from the Eddie Murphy comedy *Beverly Hills Cop*, beating out the music from *Back to the Future*, which was written in part by Huey Lewis. Huey Lewis & the News had four nominations in 1985, including Record of the Year nominee "The Power of Love," but reaped only one statuette, for their "Heart of Rock 'n' Roll" video (the song lost its bid for Record of the Year in 1984). "That puts the group in company with David Bowie and Duran Duran, who have also won Grammys for their videos, but not yet for their records," noted *Billboard*.

A storm of protest erupted over an accusation of bloc voting for the classical awards, which were denounced as "ridiculous" by *The Los Angeles Times* and "a bad joke" by *Billboard*. Writing a *Billboard* guest column, CBS Masterworks senior vice president Joseph Dash added: "N.A.R.A.S. was embarrassed by a stuff-the-ballot-box campaign that swung an incredible preponderance of classical Grammy nominations and awards of the Atlanta Symphony.

"In August, 1985, the Atlanta chapter of N.A.R.A.S. offered members of the Atlanta Symphony Orchestra and Chorus a 'pro-rated,' three-month N.A.R.A.S. membership for $10 that would enable them to cast Grammy ballots. With Atlanta chapter membership swelling 62 percent after the offer — from 265 to 430—those recordings received 12 Grammy nominations, including (according to published reports) four of the original five nominations for classical album of the year."

Robert Shaw conducting the Atlanta Symphony Orchestra and Chorus won three awards for their recording of Berlioz's *Requiem*: Best Classical Album, Best Classical Vocal Soloist Performance (for John Aler), and Best Choral Performance. The album was also named Best Engineered Recording. Shaw took the additional prize for Best Classical Orchestra Recording for Atlanta's reading of Fauré's *Palléas et Mélisande*.

When Sir Georg Solti set out to record Schöenberg's *Moses und Aron*, he told his musicians among the Chicago Symphony Orchestra and singers such as Franz Mazura (as Moses) and Philip Langridge (as Aaron) to "play and sing as if you were performing Brahms." The dynamic and highly romanticized version of the classic earned them the opera recording award, bringing Solti his 24th Grammy. (He had won continuously from 1972 to 1983 but failed to win in 1984.)

Cellist Yo-Yo Ma reaped two awards: for best soloist (with orchestra) for concertos by Elgar and and Best Chamber Music Performance for sonatas by Brahms. He shared the chamber music honors with pianist Emanuel Ax, who, critics complained, overpowered Yo-Yo Ma's playing. Still, reviewers applauded the Brahms LP for being one of the most truthful interpretations on record. Pianist Vladimir Ashkenazy had recorded Ravel works such as the "Pavane pour une Infante Defunte" earlier in his career, but showed much more artistic range in a new release that earned him the laurels for best soloist (without orchestra).

> *Accusations of bloc voting caused the classical awards to be dismissed as "a bad joke."*

GLOBE PHOTO

The Rolling Stones never won a Grammy but were given a Lifetime Achievement Award. "Thank you," Mick Jagger said, accepting it. "The joke is on you."

A new category was added this year for Best New Classical Artist (reminiscent of the Most Promising New Recording Artist award from the mid-1960s), which went to Chicago Pro Musica, a group composed of saxophonist Robert Black, pianist/composer Easley Blackwood, and nine members of the Chicago Symphony Orchestra. ("These people are good!" *Fanfare* roared). The category reinstated last year for new classical compositions was won by Andrew Lloyd Webber, who had snagged previous Grammys for his Broadway shows *Evita* in 1980 and *Cats* in 1983. His latest victory was for *Requiem*, a paean to his recently deceased father that featured music by the English Chamber Orchestra (with Lorin Maazel as conductor) and vocals by Lloyd Webber's then-wife Sarah Brightman, Placido Domingo, and the choir at Britain's Winchester Cathedral where the performance was recorded. Some critics dismissed the work as being derivative of Verdi and Fauré, while others called it the apogee of the composer's career.

Aptly, it was one of the vocalists on "We Are the World," Kenny Rogers, who acted as the Grammycast host at the Shrine Auditorium in Los Angeles despite having just had throat surgery. (Dionne Warwick was standing by ready to intercede on his behalf, in the event his pipes failed on the show.) Familiar complaints surfaced again, as when the *Herald Examiner* wrote: "Recognition for genuine rock 'n' roll continues to be the Grammys' biggest failing. For instance, the two hottest rock acts of 1985, Madonna and Bruce Springsteen, were ignored outside of nominations in two minor categories, and only a few rock performers made it to the stage as presenters, much less as performers."

The complaint was probably overblown, considering the music performances that were given by Sting, Huey Lewis & the News, and the Norwegian rock group a-ha, which was a losing nominee for Best New Artist. Whitney Houston's performance of "Saving All My Love for You" on the TV program was so hot that she won an Emmy Award for Outstanding Individual Performance in a Variety or Music Program. N.A.R.A.S. even made a special point this year of trying to redress a much older, embarrassing rock oversight when it bestowed a Lifetime Achievement Award on the Rolling Stones.

The *Herald Examiner* noted: "Although the Stones have been making popular music for more than 20 years, and have in fact made many of the most consequential works in all of rock 'n' roll, they had never before received a Grammy — and, given that this particular citation was something of a consolation prize, chances are they will never receive *another* one.

"If the Grammy folks were trying to apologize for the unconscionable way the band had been overlooked (if not purposely disregarded) in the past, it backfired on them. Mick Jagger and crew were wonderfully irreverent and vain — as if they knew that we knew how ludicrous this moment was, and all there was to do was to be mock-gracious about it.

"'Thank you,' said Jagger, 'to all the people who stood by us through the thick and thin over the years. And,' he added, using a vulgar British expression addressed to those who refused to take them seriously, 'the joke is on you.'"

1985

T he awards ceremony was broadcast on CBS from the Shrine Auditorium in Los Angeles on February 25, 1986, for the awards eligibility period of October 1, 1984, through September 30, 1985.

ALBUM OF THE YEAR
• *No Jacket Required*, Phil Collins. Phil Collins, Hugh Padgham, producers. Atlantic.
Brothers in Arms, Dire Straits. Mark Knopfler, Neil Dorfsman, producers. Warner Bros.
The Dream of the Blue Turtles, Sting. Sting, Pete Smith, producers. A&M.
We Are the World, USA for Africa/The Album, various. Columbia/CBS.
Whitney Houston, Whitney Houston. Arista.

RECORD OF THE YEAR
• "We Are the World," USA for Africa. Quincy Jones, producer. Columbia/CBS.
"Born in the U.S.A.," Bruce Springsteen. Bruce Springsteen, Jon Landau, Chuck Plotkin, Steve Van Zandt, producers. Columbia/CBS.
"The Boys of Summer," Don Henley. Don Henley, Danny Kortchmar, Greg Ladanyi, Mike Campbell, producers. Geffen.
"Money for Nothing," Dire Straits. Mark Knopfler, Neil Dorfsman, producers. Warner Bros.
"The Power of Love," Huey Lewis & the News. Huey Lewis & the News, producers. Chrysalis.

SONG OF THE YEAR
(Songwriter Award)
• "We Are the World," Michael Jackson, Lionel Richie. Mijac Music (BMI), Brockman Music (ASCAP), publishers.
"The Boys of Summer," Don Henley, Mike Campbell. Cass County Music, Wild Gator Music (ASCAP), publishers.
"Everytime You Go Away," Daryl Hall. UniChappell Music (BMI), Hot Cha Music, publishers.
"I Want to Know What Love Is," Mick Jones. Somerset Songs Publishing Inc., Evansongs Ltd. (ASCAP), publishers.
"Money for Nothing," Mark Knopfler, Sting. Chriscourt Ltd. administered by Almo Music Corp., Virgin Music, Inc. (ASCAP), publishers.

BEST NEW ARTIST
• Sade. Portrait/CBS.
a-ha. Warner Bros.
Freddie Jackson. Capitol.
Katrina & the Waves. Capitol.
Julian Lennon. Atlantic.

BEST POP VOCAL PERFORMANCE, MALE
• Phil Collins, *No Jacket Required*. Atlantic.
Glenn Frey, "The Heat Is On." MCA.
Sting, *The Dream of the Blue Turtles*. A&M.
Stevie Wonder, "Part-Time Lover." Tamla/Motown.
Paul Young, "Everytime You Go Away." Columbia/CBS.

BEST POP VOCAL PERFORMANCE, FEMALE
• Whitney Houston, "Saving All My Love for You." Arista.
Pat Benatar, "We Belong." Chrysalis.
Madonna, "Crazy for You." Geffen.
Linda Ronstadt, *Lush Life*. Elektra.
Tina Turner, "We Don't Need Another Hero (Thunderdome)." Capitol.

Best Pop Performance by a Duo or Group with Vocal
- USA for Africa, "We Are the World." Columbia/CBS.

Philip Bailey, Phil Collins, "Easy Lover." Columbia/CBS.

Foreigner, "I Want to Know What Love Is." Atlantic.

√ Huey Lewis & the News, "The Power of Love." Chrysalis.

Mr. Mister, "Broken Wings," track from *Welcome to the Real World*. RCA.

Best Pop Instrumental Performance
√ • Jan Hammer, "*Miami Vice* Theme." MCA.

Harold Faitermeyer, "Axel F." MCA.

David Foster, "Love Theme from *St. Elmo's Fire*." Atlantic.

Dave Grusin, Lee Ritenour, *Harlequin*. GRP.

Spyro Gyra, "Shake Down." MCA.

Best Rock Vocal Performance, Male
- Don Henley, "The Boys of Summer." Geffen.

Bryan Adams, *Reckless*. A&M.

John Fogerty, *Centerfield*. Warner Bros.

Mick Jagger, "Just Another Night." Columbia/CBS.

√ John Cougar Mellencamp, *Scarecrow*. Mercury.

Best Rock Vocal Performance, Female
- Tina Turner, "One of the Living." Capitol.

Pat Benatar, "Invincible (Theme from *The Legend of Billie Jean*)." Chrysalis.

Nona Hendryx, "Rock This House," track from *The Heat*. RCA.

Cyndi Lauper, "What a Thrill," track from *The Goonies* soundtrack. Epic/CBS.

Melba Moore, "Read My Lips," track from *Read My Lips*. Capitol.

Best Rock Performance by a Duo or Group with Vocal
√ • Dire Straits, "Money for Nothing." Warner Bros.

√ Bryan Adams, Tina Turner, "It's Only Love," track from *Restless* (Bryan Adams album). A&M.

Heart, *Heart*. Capitol.

Eurythmics, "Would I Lie to You?" RCA.

Starship, "We Built This City." Grunt.

Best Rock Instrumental Performance
- Jeff Beck, "Escape," track from *Flash*. Epic/CBS.

Jon Butcher Axis, "The Ritual," track from *Along the Axis*. Capitol.

Big Guitars from Texas, "Guitar Army," track from *Trash, Twang & Thunder*. Jungle.

Yngwie Malmsteen, *Rising Force*. Polydor.

Northern Star, "Back to Earth," track from *Northern Star I*. Dead Pidgeon.

Stevie Ray Vaughan & Double Trouble, "Say What!" track from *Soul to Soul*. Epic/CBS.

Best Rhythm & Blues Song
(Songwriter's Award)
- "Freeway of Love," Narada Michael Walden, Jeffrey Cohen. Gratitude Sky Music (ASCAP), Polo Grounds Music (BMI), publishers.

"New Attitude," Sharon Robinson, Jon Gilutin, Bunny Hull. Unicity Music Inc., Robinhill Music, Off Backstreet Music, Brassheart Music, Rockomatic Music (ASCAP-BMI), publishers.

"Nightshift," Walter Orange, Dennis Lambert, Franne Golde. Walter Orange Music, Tuneworks Co., Rightsong Music, Franne Golde Music, publishers.

"Through the Fire," David Foster, Tom Keane, Cynthia Weil. Dyad Music Ltd., Foster Frees Music, Neropub, Tom John Music (BMI), publishers.

"You Give Good Love," LaLa. New Music Group/MCA Music (BMI), publishers.

Best R&B Vocal Performance, Male
- Stevie Wonder, *In Square Circle*. Tamla/Motown.

Philip Bailey, *Chinese Wall*. Columbia/CBS.

Freddie Jackson, "You Are My Lady." Capitol.

Al Jarreau, "High Crime," track from *High Crime*. Warner Bros.

Luther Vandross, *The Night I Fell in Love*. Epic/CBS.

Alto reedman David Sanborn won the second jazz trophy of his career for his r&b-inflected LP Straight to the Heart.

BEST R&B VOCAL PERFORMANCE, FEMALE
• Aretha Franklin, "Freeway of Love." Arista.
Whitney Houston, "You Give Good Love." Arista.
Chaka Khan, *I Feel for You.* Warner Bros.
Patti LaBelle, "New Attitude." MCA.
Teena Marie, "Lovergirl," track from *Starchild.* Epic/CBS.

BEST R&B PERFORMANCE BY A DUO OR GROUP WITH VOCAL
• Commodores, "Nightshift." Gordy/Motown.
Ashford & Simpson, *Solid.* Capitol.
Eurythmics, Aretha Franklin, "Sisters Are Doin' It for Themselves," track from *Be Yourself Tonight* (Eurythmics album). RCA. Also track from *Who's Zoomin' Who?* (Aretha Franklin album). Arista.
Daryl Hall, John Oates with David Ruffin & Eddie Kendricks, "The Way You Do the Things You Do/My Girl." RCA.
Pointer Sisters, *Contact.* RCA.

BEST R&B INSTRUMENTAL PERFORMANCE
• Ernie Watts, *Musican.* Qwest.
Five Star, "First Avenue." RCA.
Paul Hardcastle, *Rain Forest.* Profile.
Jeff Lorber, "Pacific Coast Highway," track from *Step by Step.* Arista.
Barney Rachabane, "Caribbean Queen." Jive/Arista.
Sly & Robbie, "Bass & Trouble," track from *Language Barrier.* Island.
Dave Valentin, "Love Light in Flight," track from *Jungle Garden.* GRP.

BEST JAZZ VOCAL PERFORMANCE, MALE
• Jon Hendricks, Bobby McFerrin, "Another Night in Tunisia," track from *Vocalese* (Manhattan Transfer album). Atlantic.
George Benson, "Beyond the Sea (La mer)," track from *20/20.* Warner Bros.
David Frishberg, *Live at Vine Street.* Fantasy.
Mark Murphy, *Mark Murphy Sings Nat's Choice, The Nat "King" Cole Songbook, Volume I.* Muse.
Alan Paul, "Oh Yes, I Remember Clifford," track from *Vocalese* (Manhattan Transfer album). Atlantic.

BEST JAZZ VOCAL PERFORMANCE, FEMALE
• Cleo Laine, *Cleo at Carnegie the 10th Anniversary Concert.* DRG.
Cheryl Bentyne, "Meet Benny Bailey," track from *Vocalese* (Manhattan Transfer album). Atlantic.
Tania Maria, *Made in New York.* Manhattan.
Flora Purim, "20 Years Blue," track from *Humble People* (Flora Purim & Airto). George Wein Collection/Concord Jazz.
Janis Siegel, "Sing Joy Spring," track from *Vocalese* (Manhattan Transfer album). Atlantic.
Maxine Sullivan, *The Great Songs from the Cotton Club.* Stash.

BEST JAZZ VOCAL PERFORMANCE, DUO OR GROUP
• Manhattan Transfer, *Vocalese.* Atlantic.
Manhattan Transfer, Jon Hendricks, "Ray's Rockhouse," track from *Vocalese.* Atlantic.

Manhattan Transfer with the Four
Freshmen, "To You," track from
Vocalese. Atlantic.
Barry Manilow, Sarah Vaughan, "Blue,"
track from *2:00 A.M. Paradise Cafe*.
Arista.
Phil Mattson & the P.M. Singers, *Night in
the City*. Dark Orchid.
Rare Silk, *American Eyes*. Palo Alto.
University of Northern Colorado Vocal
Jazz I, *Hot IV*. Eaglear.

BEST JAZZ INSTRUMENTAL PERFORMANCE, SOLOIST
• Wynton Marsalis, *Black Codes from the
Underground*. Columbia/CBS.
Miles Davis, "Human Nature," track from
Unknown. Columbia/CBS.
Dizzy Gillespie, "Sing Joy Spring," track
from *Vocalese* (Manhattan Transfer
album). Atlantic.
Stanley Jordan, *Magic Touch*. Blue Note.
James Moody, "Meet Benny Bailey," track
from *Vocalese* (Manhattan Transfer
album). Atlantic.

BEST JAZZ INSTRUMENTAL PERFORMANCE, GROUP
• Wynton Marsalis Group, *Black Codes
from the Underground*. Columbia/CBS.
Chick Corea, Steve Kujala, *Voyage*. ECM.
Keith Jarrett, *Standards Vol. 2*. ECM.
Sting, "The Dream of the Blue Turtles,"
track from *The Dream of the Blue
Turtles*. A&M.
Various artists, *One Night with Blue Note*.
Michael Cuscuna, Mike Berniker,
producers. Blue Note.

BEST JAZZ INSTRUMENTAL PERFORMANCE, BIG BAND
• John Barry, Bob Wilber, *The Cotton
Club—Original Motion Picture
Soundtrack*. Geffen.
Toshiko Akiyoshi–Lew Tabackin Big
Band, *March of the Tadpoles*. Ascent.
Louie Bellson, *Don't Stop Now!* Bosco.
Lionel Hampton, *Ambassador at Large*.
Glad-Hamp.
George Russell & the Living Time
Orchestra, *The African Game*. Blue
Note.

BEST JAZZ FUSION PERFORMANCE, VOCAL OR INSTRUMENTAL
• David Sanborn, *Straight to the Heart*.
Warner Bros.
Miles Davis, *You're Under Arrest*.
Columbia/CBS.
Stanley Jordan Group, *Magic Touch*. Blue
Note.
Wayne Shorter, *Atlantis*. Columbia/CBS.
Spyro Gyra, *Alternating Currents*. MCA.
Weather Report, *Sportin' Life*.
Columbia/CBS.

BEST COUNTRY SONG
(Songwriter's Award)
• "Highwayman," Jimmy L. Webb. White
Oak Songs, publisher.
"Baby's Got Her Blue Jeans On," Bob
McDill. Hall-Clement Music
Publications, c/o Welk Music Group.
BMI, publishers.
"Desperados Waiting for a Train," Guy
Clark. Chappell Music, World Song
Publishing (ASCAP), publishers.
"Forty Hour Week (for a Livin')," Dave
Loggins, Lisa Silver, Don Schlitz.
Music Corp. of America, Inc. (BMI),
MCA Music, Leeds Music Corp.
(MCA), Patchwork Music, Don Schlitz
Music (ASCAP), publishers.
"I Don't Know Why You Don't Want
Me," Rosanne Cash, Rodney Crowell,
Chelcait Music, Atlantic Music Corp.
(BMI), Coolwell Music, Granite Music
Corp. (ASCAP), publishers.
"Lost in the Fifties Tonight (In the Still of
the Night)," Mike Reid, Troy Seals,
Fred Parris. Lodge Hall Music, Inc.,
Two Sons Music/Warner Bros. Music
Corp. (ASCAP), Lee Corp. (BMI),
publishers.
"Love Is Alive," Kent M. Robbins. Irving
Music Inc. (BMI), publisher.

BEST COUNTRY VOCAL PERFORMANCE, MALE
• Ronnie Milsap, "Lost in the Fifties
Tonight (In the Still of the Night)."
RCA.
Lee Greenwood, "I Don't Mind the Thorns
(If You're the Rose)." MCA.
Mel McDaniel, "Baby's Got Her Blue
Jeans On." Capitol.
Willie Nelson, "Forgiving You Was
Easy." Columbia/CBS.
Ricky Skaggs, "You Make Me Feel Like a
Man." Epic/CBS.

Best Country Vocal Performance, Female

- Rosanne Cash, "I Don't Know Why You Don't Want Me." CBS.
- Janie Fricke, "She's Single Again." Columbia/CBS.
- Emmylou Harris, *The Ballad of Sally Rose*. Warner Bros.
- Dolly Parton, *Real Love*. RCA.
- Juice Newton, "You Make Me Want to Make You Mine." RCA.

Best Country Performance by a Duo or Group with Vocal

- Judds, *Why Not Me*. RCA.
- √ Alabama, "Can't Keep A Good Man Down." RCA.
- Forester Sisters, *The Forester Sisters*. Warner Bros.
- Waylon Jennings, Willie Nelson, Johnny Cash, Kris Kristofferson, "Highwayman." Columbia/CBS.
- Marie Osmond, Dan Seals, "Meet Me in Montana." Capitol.
- √ Dolly Parton, Kenny Rogers, "Real Love," track from *Real Love* (Dolly Parton).RCA.

Best Country Instrumental Performance

- Chet Atkins, Mark Knopfler, "Cosmic Square Dance," track from *Stay Tuned* (Chet Atkins album). Columbia/CBS.
- Vassar Clements, John Hartford, Dave Holland, *Vassar Clements, John Hartford, Dave Holland*. Rounder.
- Charlie McCoy, "Lasso the Moon," track from *Rustlers' Rhapsody and Other Songs*. Warner Bros.
- Earl Scruggs, "Folsom Prison Blues," track from *American-Made, World-Played*. Columbia/CBS.
- Doc & Merle Watson, "Windy and Warm," track from *Pickin' the Blues*. Flying Fish.

Best Gospel Performance, Male

- Larnelle Harris, "How Excellent Is Thy Name," track from *I've Just Seen Jesus*. Benson.
- James Blackwood, *Fifty Golden Years*. Skylite/Sing.
- Phil Driscoll, *Power of Praise*. Sparrow.
- Steve Green, *He Holds the Keys*. Sparrow.
- Russ Taff, *Medals*. Myrrh/Word.

Best Gospel Performance, Female

- Amy Grant, *Unguarded*. Myrrh/Word.
- Debby Boone, *Choose Life*. Lamb & Lion/Sparrow.
- Sandi Patti, *Hymns Just for You*. Benson.
- Leslie Phillips, *Black and White in a Grey World*. Myrrh/Word.
- Sheila Walsh, *Don't Hide Your Heart*. Sparrow.

Best Gospel Performance by a Duo or Group

- Larnelle Harris, Sandi Patti, "I've Just Seen Jesus," track from *I've Just Seen Jesus*. Benson.
- De Garmo & Key, *Commander Sozo and the Charge of the Light Brigade*. Power Disc/Benson.
- Imperials, *Let the Wind Blow*. Myrrh/Word.
- Petra, *Beat the System*. Star Song.
- Randy Stonehill, Amy Grant, "I Could Never Say Goodbye." Myrrh/Word.

Best Soul Gospel Performance, Male

- Marvin Winans, "Bring Back the Days of Yea and Nay," track from *Tomorrow* (Winans album). Light.
- Howard McCrary, *So Good*. Good News.
- Douglas Miller, *Unspeakable Joy*. Light.
- Philip Nicholas, "Stop Your Searchin' (Try God!)," track from *Dedicated*. Command.
- Rev. Marvin Yancy, *Heavy Load*. Nashboro.

Best Soul Gospel Performance, Female

- Shirley Caesar, "Martin." Rejoice/Word.
- Vanessa Bell Armstrong, *Chosen*. Onyx International.
- Vernessa Mitchell, "Blessed Assurance," track from *This Is My Story*. Command.
- Dorothy Norwood, "Lift Him Up," track from *Lift Him Up*. Savoy.
- Deleon Richards, *Deleon*. Myrrh/Word.

Best Soul Gospel Performance by a Duo or Group

- Winans, *Tomorrow*. Light.
- Sandra Crouch & Friends, *We're Waiting*. Light.
- Sandra Crouch, Jean Johnson, "Completely Yes," track from *We're Waiting*. Light.
- Edwin Hawkins with Music & Arts Seminar Mass Choir, *Have Mercy*. Birthright.

Carvin Winans, Michael Winans, "Tomorrow," track from *Tomorrow*. Light.

BEST INSPIRATIONAL PERFORMANCE
• Jennifer Holliday, "Come Sunday," track from *Say You Love Me*. Geffen.
Pat Boone, *16,000 Faces*. B.P.I.
Glen Campbell, *No More Night*. Word.
Kool & the Gang, "You Are the One," track from *Emergency*. De-Lite.
Barbara Mandrell, *Christmas at Our House*. MCA.

BEST TRADITIONAL BLUES RECORDING
• B.B. King, "My Guitar Sings the Blues," track from *Six Silver Strings*. MCA.
Bobby Bland, *Members Only*. Malaco.
Roy Buchanan, *When a Guitar Plays the Blues*. Alligator.
Koko Taylor, *Queen of the Blues*. Alligator.
Big Joe Turner with Knocky Parker & His Houserockers, *Big Joe Turner with Knocky Parker and His Houserockers*. Southland.
Joe Turner, Jimmy Witherspoon, *Patcha, Patcha, All Night Long*. Pablo.
Johnny Winter, *Serious Business*. Alligator.

BEST ETHNIC OR TRADITIONAL FOLK RECORDING
• "My Toot Toot," Rockin' Sidney. Maison De Soul.
Live at the San Francisco Blues Festival, Clifton Chenier. Arhoolie.
Souvenirs, Dewey Balfa. Swallow.
Turning Point, Buckwheat Zydeco. Rounder.
Zydeco Gris Gris, Beausoleil. Swallow.

BEST LATIN POP PERFORMANCE
• Lani Hall, *Es Facil Amar*. A&M.
José Feliciano, *Yo Soy Tuyo*. RCA.
José Feliciano, José José, "Por Ella," track from *Yo Soy Tuyo*. RCA.
José José, *Reflexiones*. Ariola-America.
Lucia Mendez, *Solo una Mujer*. Ariola-America.

BEST TROPICAL LATIN PERFORMANCE
• Tito Puente & His Latin Ensemble, *Mambo Diablo*. Concord Jazz.
• Eddie Palmieri, *Solito*. Musica Latina International.
Rubén Blades, *Mucho Mejor*. Fania/Musica Latina International.

Bonny Cepeda y Orquestra, *Noche de Discotheque*. RCA.
Celia Cruz, Johnny Pacheco, *De Nuevo*. Vaya/Musica Latina International.
Mongo Santamaria & His Latin Jazz Orchestra, *Free Spirit, Espirito Libre*. Tropical Budda.

BEST MEXICAN/AMERICAN PERFORMANCE
• Vikki Carr, *Simplemente Mujer*. Discos CBS International.
Rocio Durcal, *Canta a Juan Gabriel*. Ariola-America.
Los Humildes, *13 Aniversario/13 Album/13 Exitos*. Profono Internacional.
Santiago Jiminez, Jr., *Santiago Strikes Again*. Arhoolie.
Maria de Lourdes, *Mujer Importante*. RCA.
Juan Valentin, *20 Exitos Romanticos con Juan Valentin*. Musart.

BEST REGGAE RECORDING
• Jimmy Cliff, *Cliff Hanger*. Columbia/CBS.
Blue Riddim Band, *Alive in Jamaica*. Flying Fish.
Burning Spear, *Resistance*. Heartbeat/Rounder.
Melody Makers featuring Ziggy Marley, *Play the Game Right*. EMI-America.
Judy Mowatt, *Working Wonders*. Shanachie.

BEST POLKA RECORDING
• *70 Years of Hits*, Frank Yankovic. Cleveland International/CBS.
Brass with Class, Brass Release. LeMans.
Polka Fireworks, Eddie Blazonczyk's Versatones. Bel-Aire.
Polskie Czucie Polish Feelings, L'il Wally & Orchestra. Jay Jay.
Simply Polkamentary, Lenny Gomulka & the Chicago Push. Chicago Polkas.

BEST ARRANGEMENT
ON AN INSTRUMENTAL
• Dave Grusin, Lee Ritenour, "Early A.M. Attitude," track from *Harlequin* (Dave Grusin, Lee Ritenour). GRP.
George Russell, *The African Game* (George Russell & the Living Time Orchestra). Blue Note.
Toshiko Akiyoshi, "March of the Tadpoles," track from *March of the Tadpoles* (Toshiko Akiyoshi–Lew Tabackin Big Band). Ascent.

Chip Davis, "Stille Nacht (Silent Night)," track from *Mannheim Steamroller Christmas* (Mannheim Steamroller). American Gramophone.

William D. Bruhn, "Suite of Dances from 'Pacific Overtures,'" track from *Sondheim* (Symphony Orchestra conducted by Paul Gemignani). Book-of-the-Month Records.

Best Instrumental Arrangement Accompanying Vocal(s)

• Nelson Riddle, "Lush Life," track from *Lush Life* (Linda Ronstadt). Asylum.

David Foster, "Through the Fire," (Chaka Khan). Warner Bros.

Frank Foster, Ralph Burns, "Beyond the Sea (La Mer)," track from *20/20* (George Benson). Warner Bros.

Dave Grusin, Lee Ritenour, "Harlequin," track from *Harlequin* (Dave Grusin, Lee Ritenour). GRP.

Peter Wolf, "Why Do People Fall in Love," track from *Copolin' Out* (Dennis Edwards, Thelma Houston). Gordy/Motown.

Best Vocal Arrangement for Two or more Voices

• Cheryl Bentyne, Bobby McFerrin, "Another Night in Tunisia" (Manhattan Transfer). Atlantic.

Dennis Lambert, "Nightshift" (Commodores). Motown.

Phil Mattson, "I Hear Music," track from *Night in the City* (Phil Mattson & the P.M. Singers). Dark Orchid.

Alan Paul, "Ray's Rockhouse," track from *Vocalese* (Manhattan Transfer). Atlantic.

Janis Siegel, Dennis Wilson, "Blee Biop Blues," track from *Vocalese* (Manhattan Transfer). Atlantic.

Best Instrumental Composition

✓ • *"Miami Vice* Theme," Jan Hammer, composer. MCA Music (ASCAP), publishers.

"Axel F," Harold Faltermeyer, composer. Famous Music Corp. (ASCAP), publishers.

"Back to the Future," Alan Silvestri.

"Love Theme from *St. Elmo's Fire*," David Foster, composer. Gold Horizon Music Corp., Foster Frees Music (BMI), publishers.

"With Bells On," Thad Jones, composer. Little Pumpkin, publisher.

Best Cast Show Album

• *West Side Story*, Stephen Sondheim, lyricist. Leonard Bernstein, composer & conductor. John McClure, producer. Deutsche Grammophon.

Big River, Roger Miller, composer & lyricist. Jimmy Bowen, producer. MCA.

Greatest Hits from "Leader of the Pack," Ellie Greenwich, Jeff Barry, Phil Spector, George "Shadow" Morton, songwriters. Bob Crewe, Ellie Greenwich, producers. Elektra.

The Tap Dance Kid, Robert Lorick, lyricist. Henry Krieger, composer. Martin Silvestri, producer. Polydor.

Very Warm for May, Oscar Hammerstein II, lyricist. Jerome Kern, composer. David Gooch, producer. AEI.

Best Album of Original Score Written for a Motion Picture or a Television Special
(Composer's/Songwriter's Award)

• *Beverly Hills Cop*, Sharon Robinson, John Gilutin, Bunny Hull, Hawk, Howard Hewett. Micki Free, Keith Forsey, Harold Faltermeyer, Allee Willis, Dan Sembello, Marc Benno, Richard Theisen. MCA.

Back to the Future, John Colla, Chris Hayes, Huey Lewis, Lindsey Buckingham, Alan Silvestri, Eric Clapton, Sean Hopper. MCA.

A Passage to India, Maurice Jarre. Capitol.

St. Elmo's Fire, David Foster, John Parr, Billy Squier, John & Dino Elefante, Jon Anderson, Fee Waybill, Steve Lukather, Richard Marx, Jay Graydon, Stephen A. Kipner, Peter Beckett, Cynthia Weil. Atlantic.

Witness, Maurice Jarre. Varese Sarabande.

Best Classical Album

• *Berlioz: Requiem*, Robert Shaw conducting Atlanta Symphony Orchestra & Chorus (solo: John Aler). Robert E. Woods, producer. Telarc.

*Berlioz: Les Nuits d'Et*e; Fauré: *Pelleas et Melisande*, Elly Ameling; Robert Shaw conducting Atlanta Symphony Orchestra. Robert E. Woods, producer. Telarc.

Dvorak: Symphony No. 7 in D Minor, James Levine conducting Chicago Symphony Orchestra. Jay David Saks, producer. RCA Red Seal.

Celebrated cellist Yo-Yo Ma won two accolades for his "truthful interpretations" of works by Brahms and Elgar.

Gershwin: Rhapsody in Blue; Second Rhapsody for Orchestra With Piano; Prelude for Piano; Short Story; Violin Piece; For Lily Pons; Sleepless Night; Promenade, Michael Tilson Thomas; Michael Tilson Thomas conducting Los Angeles Philharmonic Orchestra. Steven Epstein, producer. CBS Masterworks.

Handel: Messiah, Robert Shaw conducting Atlanta Symphony Orchestra and Chorus (solos: Erickson, McNair, Hodgson, Humphrey, Stilwell). Robert E. Woods, producer. Telarc.

Mahler: Symphony No. 7 in E Minor, Claudio Abbado conducting Chicago Symphony Orchestra. Rainer Brock, producer. Deutsche Grammophon.

Mozart: Violin & Piano Sonatas, K.296, 305, 306, (solos: Perlman, Barenboim). Dr. Steve Paul, producer. Deutsche Grammophon.

Prokofiev: Cinderella (Suite), Leonard Slatkin conducting St. Louis Symphony Orchestra. Jay David Saks, producer. RCA Red Seal.

Respighi: Pines of Rome; The Birds; Fountains of Rome, Louis Lane conducting Atlanta Symphony Orchestra. Robert E. Woods, producer. Telarc.

BEST CLASSICAL ORCHESTRAL RECORDING (Conductor's Award)

• *Fauré: Pelléas et Mélisande*, Robert Shaw conducting Atlanta Symphony Orchestra. Robert E. Woods, producer. Telarc.

Dvořák: Symphony No. 7 in D Minor, James Levine conducting Chicago Symphony Orchestra. Jay David Saks, producer. RCA Red Seal.

Liszt: A Faust Symphony, James Conlon conducting Rotterdam Philharmonic Orchestra, Michel Garcin, producer. Erato-Editions.

Prokofiev: Cinderella (Suite), Leonard Slatkin conducting St. Louis Symphony Orchestra. Jay David Saks, producer. RCA Red Seal.

Respighi: Pines of Rome; The Bird; Fountains of Rome, Louis Lane conducting Atlanta Symphony Orchestra. Robert E. Woods, producer. Telarc.

BEST NEW CLASSICAL ARTIST

• Chicago Pro Musica. Reference.

Sarah Brightman. Angel.

Rosalind Plowright. Deutsche Grammophon.

Esa-Pekka Salonen. Polygram Classics/Philips.

Brian Slawson. CBS Masterworks.

BEST CHAMBER MUSIC PERFORMANCE

• Emanuel Ax, Yo-Yo Ma, *Brahms: Cello and Piano Sonatas in E Major & F Major*. RCA.

Daniel Barenboim, Pinchas Zukerman, Jacqueline Dupré, *Tchaikovsky: Piano Trio in A Minor*. Angel.

Itzhak Perlman, Jorge Bolet, Juilliard String Quartet, *Chausson: Concerto for Violin, Piano & String Quartet, Op. 21*. CBS Masterworks.

Itzhak Perlman, Samuel Sanders, *Dvorak: Sonatina in G & Four Romantic Pieces; Smetana: From My Homeland*. Angel.

André Previn, Vienna Wind Soloists,
*Mozart: Piano & Wind Quintet in E
Flat; Beethoven: Piano & Wind
Quintet in E Flat*. Telarc.

BEST CLASSICAL PERFORMANCE, INSTRUMENTAL SOLOIST(S) (WITH ORCHESTRA)

• Yo-Yo Ma (Previn conducting London
Symphony Orchestra), *Elgar: Cello
Concerto, Op. 85; Walton: Concerto
for Cello & Orchestra*. CBS
Masterworks.

James Galway (Chung conducting Royal
Philharmonic Orchestra), *James
Galway Plays Khachaturian (Concerto
for Flute and Orchestra; Spartacus,
Masquerade & Gayaneh)*. RCA.

Itzhak Perlman (Mehta conducting Israel
Philharmonic Orchestra),
*Khachaturian: Violin Concerto in D
Minor*. Angel.

André Previn (Previn conducting
Pittsburgh Symphony Orchestra),
Gershwin: Rhapsody in Blue. Philips.

Andras Schiff (Dorati conducting
Concertgebouw Orchestra), *Schumann:
Piano Concerto in A Minor; Chopin:
Piano Concerto No. 2 in F Minor*.
London.

Michael Tilson Thomas (Thomas
conducting Los Angeles Philharmonic),
*Gershwin: Second Rhapsody for
Orchestra with Piano*. CBS
Masterworks.

BEST CLASSICAL PERFORMANCE, INSTRUMENTAL SOLOIST(S) (WITHOUT ORCHESTRA)

• Vladimir Ashkenazy, *Ravel: Gaspard de
la Nuit, Pavane pour une Infante
Defunte, Valses Nobles et
Sentimentales*. London.

Claudio Arrau, *Chopin: 4 Scherzi;
Polonaise, Fantaisie Op. 61*. Philips.

Julian Bream, *"Guitarra": The Guitar in
Spain*. RCA Red Seal.

Francois-Rene Duchable, *Chopin: Piano
Sonatas No. 2 in B Flat Minor & No. 3
in B Minor*. Erato-Editions.

Michael Tilson Thomas, *Gershwin:
Preludes for Piano; Short Story; Violin
Piece; For Lily Pons; Sleepless Night;
Promenade*. CBS Masterworks.

BEST OPERA RECORDING

• *Schoenberg: Moses und Aron*, Sir Georg
Solti conducting Chicago Symphony
Orchestra and Chorus (solos: Mazura,
Langridge). James Mallinson, producer.
London.

*Leoncavallo: Pagliacci (Original
Soundtrack)*, Georges Pretre
conducting Coro e Orchestra del Teatro
all Scala, Milano (solos: Stratas,
Domingo, Pons, Rinaldi, Andreolli).
Polygram Classics/Philips.

Puccini: Manon Lescaut, Giuseppe
Sinopoli conducting Philharmonia
Orchestra and Chorus of Royal Opera
House, Covent Garden (solos: Freni,
Domingo, Bruson, Rydi, Gambill).
Wolfgang Stengel, producer. Deutsche
Grammophon.

Stravinsky: The Rake's Progress, Riccardo
Chailly conducting London Sinfonietta
and London Sinfonietta Chorus (solos:
Langridge, Pope, Ramey, Walker,
Dobson). Andrew Cornall, producer.
London.

*Wagner: Der Fliegende Hollander (The
Flying Dutchman)*, Herbert von
Karajan conducting Berlin
Philharmonic Orchestra and Vienna
State Opera Chorus (solos: Jose Van
Dam, Dunja Vejzovic, Kurt Moll, Peter
Hofmann). Michael Glotz, producer.
Angel.

BEST CHORAL PERFORMANCE (OTHER THAN OPERA)

• Robert Shaw conducting Atlanta
Symphony Chorus and Orchestra (solo:
John Aler), *Berlioz: Requiem*. Telarc.

Daniel Barenboim conducting Choeurs et
Orchestre de Paris (solos: Murray,
Battle, Rendall, Salminen), *Mozart:
Requiem*. Angel.

Herbert von Karajan conducting
Konzertvereinigung Wiener
Staatsopernchor, Chor der Nationaloper
Sofia, Wiener Philharmoniker (solos:
Tomowa-Sintow, Baltsa, Carreras, Van
Dam), *Verdi: Requiem*. Deutsche
Grammophon.

Ton Koopman conducting Choeur "The Sixteen" and Amsterdam Baroque Orchestra (solos: Kweksilber, Bowman, Elliott, Reinhart), *Handel: Messiah*. Erato-Editions.

Lorin Maazel conducting English Chamber Orchestra and Winchester Cathedral Choir (Martin Neary, Dir.) (solos: Domingo, Brightman, Miles-Kingston), *Lloyd Webber: Requiem*. Angel.

BEST CLASSICAL VOCAL SOLOIST PERFORMANCE

• John Aler (Shaw conducting Atlanta Symphony Orchestra and Chorus), *Berlioz: Requiem*. Telarc.

Elly Ameling (Shaw conducting Atlanta Symphony Orchestra), *Berlioz: Les Nuits D'Ete*. Telarc.

Placido Domingo, Pilar Lorengar (Navarro conducting ORF Symphonieorchester), *Zarzuela Arias and Duets (Arias Only)*. CBS Masterworks.

Marilyn Horne (Foster conducting Orchestre Philharmonique de Monte Carlo), *Marilyn Horne Sings (Offenbach, Cherubini, Saint-Saëns, etc.)*. Erato-Editions.

Kiri Te Kanawa (Tate conducting English Chamber Orchestra), *Canteloube: Chants d'Auvergne, Vol. 2; Villa-Lobos: Bachianas Brasileiras, No. 5*. London.

Frederica von Stade (Ozawa conducting Boston Symphony Orchestra), *Berlioz: Les Nuites d'Ete; Debussy: La Damoiselle Elue*. CBS Masterworks.

BEST CONTEMPORARY COMPOSITION
(Composer's Award)

• *Requiem*, Andrew Lloyd Webber. Lorin Maazal conducting Winchester Cathedral Choir and English Chamber Orchestra (solos: Domingo, Brightman, Miles-Kingston). Really Useful Co., Ltd., publisher. Angel.

Harmonium for Large Orchestra and Chorus, John Adams. Edo De Waart conducting San Francisco Symphony Orchestra and Chorus. Associated Music, publisher. ECM.

Satyagraha, Philip Glass. Christopher Keene conducting New York City Opera Chorus and Orchestra (solo: Douglas Perry). Dunvagen Music, publisher. CBS Masterworks.

Serenade No. 3 for Piano and Chamber Orchestra, George Perle. Gerard Schwarz conducting Music Today Ensemble (solo: Richard Goode). Galaxy, publisher. Nonesuch.

Violin Concerto, Robert Starer. Seiji Ozawa conducting Boston Symphony Orchestra (solo: Itzhak Perlman). MCA Music, publisher. Angel.

BEST ENGINEERED RECORDING, CLASSICAL

• Jack Renner, *Berlioz: Requiem* (Shaw conducting Atlanta Symphony Orchestra and Chorus; solo: Aler). Telarc.

Paul Goodman, *Dvořák: Symphony No. 7 in D Minor* (Levine conducting Chicago Symphony Orchestra). RCA Red Seal.

Paul Goodman, Thomas MacCluskey, *Tchaikovsky: The Nutcracker (Complete)* (Slatkin conducting St. Louis Symphony Orchestra). RCA.

James Lock, *Mahler: Symphony No. 1 in D Major* (Solti conducting Chicago Symphony Orchestra). London.

Paul Goodman, *Prokofiev: Cinderella (Suite)* (Slatkin conducting St. Louis Symphony Orchestra). RCA Red Seal.

Jack Renner, *Berlioz: Les Nuits d'Ete*/Fauré: *Pelleas et Melisande* (Shaw conducting Atlanta Symphony Orchestra; solo: Ameling). Telarc.

Jack Renner, *Respighi: Pines of Rome; The Birds; Fountains of Rome* (Lane conducting Atlanta Symphony Orchestra). Telarc.

CLASSICAL PRODUCER OF THE YEAR

• Robert E. Woods. Telarc.
Steven Epstein. CBS Masterworks.
James Mallinson. London.
David Mottley.
Jay David Saks. RCA Red Seal.

BEST COMEDY RECORDING

• *Whoopi Goldberg (Original Broadway Show Recording)*, Whoopi Goldberg. Geffen.

"Born in East L.A.," Cheech & Chong. MCA.

Dare to Be Stupid, "Weird Al" Yankovic. Rock 'n' Roll/CBS.

"Honeymooners Rap," Joe Piscopo. Columbia/CBS.

"You Look Marvelous," Billy Crystal. A&M.

BEST SPOKEN WORD OR NON-MUSICAL RECORDING

• *Ma Rainey's Black Bottom* (Original Broadway Cast), Mike Berniker, producer. Manhattan.

The Adventures of Huckleberry Finn by Mark Twain, read by Dick Cavett. Listen for Pleasure.

Catch-22 by Joseph Heller, read by Alan Arkin. Listen for Pleasure.

The Spy Who Came in from the Cold by John Le Carré, read by John Le Carré. Listen for Pleasure.

Zuckerman Bound by Philip Roth, read by Philip Roth. Caedmon.

BEST RECORDING FOR CHILDREN

• *Follow That Bird (The Original Motion Picture Sound Track)*, Jim Henson's Muppets and Sesame Street cast. Jim Henson, Muppets creator. Steve Buckingham, producer. RCA.

Bullfrogs and Butterflies, Part II, Candle and the Agapeland Singers. Fletch Wiley, Ron Krueger, Frank Hernandez, producers. Birdwing/Sparrow.

E.T.A. Hoffman, Tchaikovsky, Nutcracker, Christopher Plummer, narrator. Michael Tilson Thomas conducting Philharmonia Orchestra. Ward Botsford, producer. Caedmon.

Prokofiev: Peter & the Wolf, Dudley Moore, John Williams & the Boston Pops Orchestra. John McClure, producer. Philips.

The Velveteen Rabbit, Meryl Streep, narrator. George Winston, piano. George Winston, Mark Sottnick, Clay Stites, producers. Dancing Cat.

We Are the World, Children of the World, George Duke, producer. Starborn.

BEST ENGINEERED RECORDING (NON-CLASSICAL)

• Neil Dorfsman, *Brothers in Arms* (Dire Straits). Warner Bros.

Jeff Hendrickson, *Crazy from the Heat* (David Lee Roth). Warner Bros.

Don Murray. *Harlequin* (Dave Grusin, Lee Ritenour). GRP.

Pete Smith, Jim Scott, *The Dream of the Blue Turtles* (Sting). A&M.

Paul Wickliffe, chief recording engineer. Chieli Minucci, Paul Wickliffe, mixers, *Modern Manners* (Special EFX). GRP.

BEST ALBUM PACKAGE (Art Director's Award)

• Kosh, Ron Larson, *Lush Life* (Linda Ronstadt). Asylum.

Jeffrey Kent Ayeroff, Jeri McManus, *Hunting High and Low* (a-ha). Warner Bros.

Renee Hardaway, Johnny Lee, *In Square Circle* (Stevie Wonder). Tamla/Motown.

Virginia Team, *Highwayman* (Waylon Jennings, Willie Nelson, Johnny Cash, Kris Kristofferson). Columbia/CBS.

Murry Whiteman, Bill Levy, Stan Watts, *Dangerous Moments* (Martin Briley). Mercury.

BEST ALBUM NOTES (Annotator's Award)

• Peter Guralnick, *Sam Cooke Live at the Harlem Square Club* (Sam Cooke). RCA.

Lenny Kaye, *Bleecker and MacDougal, The Folk Scene of the 1960's* (Judy Collins, Tom Paxton, Phil Ochs, others). Elektra.

Lenny Kaye, *Crossroads, White Blues in the 1960's* (Koener, Ray and Glover, Paul Butterfield Blues Band, Lovin' Spoonful, others). Elektra.

James R. Morris, J.R. Taylor, Dwight Blocker Bowers, *American Popular Song* (Fred Astaire, Bing Crosby, Judy Garland, Ella Fitzgerald, others). Smithsonian/CBS Special Products.

Neil Tesser, *The Girl from Ipanema, The Bossa Nova Years* (Stan Getz). Verve.

BEST HISTORICAL ALBUM

• *RCA/Met—100 Singers, 100 Years* (Melba, Schumann-Heink, Caruso, Price, Verrett, Domingo, 94 others). John Pfeiffer, producer. RCA Red Seal.

American Popular Song (Fred Astaire, Lena Horne, Nat "King" Cole, Sarah Vaughan, others). J.R. Taylor, producer. Smithsonian/CBS Special Products.

Bill Evans: The Complete Riverside Recordings (Bill Evans). Orrin Keepnews, producer. Riverside.

Billie Holiday on Verve 1946–1959 (Billie Holiday). Tohru Okamura, producer. Verve.

The Human Orchestra (Rhythm Quartets in the Thirties) (Mills Brothers, Ink Spots, Four Blackbirds, others). Doug Seroff, producer. Clanka Lanka.

PRODUCER OF THE YEAR (NON-CLASSICAL)
• Phil Collins, Hugh Padgham
David Foster
Don Henley, Danny Kortchmar, Greg Ladanyi
Mark Knopfler, Neil Dorfsman
Narada Michael Walden

BEST MUSIC VIDEO, SHORT FORM
• *We Are the World, The Video Event* (VHS/Beta), USA for Africa. Quincy Jones, producer. Tom Trbovich, video director. RCA/Columbia Pictures Home Video.

The Daryl Hall & John Oates Video Collection, 7 Big Ones (VHS/Beta), Daryl Hall & John Oates. Mick Haggerty, C.D. Taylor, video directors. RCA/Columbia Pictures Home Video.

Do They Know It's Christmas? (VHS), Band Aid. Trevor Horn, Midge Ure, record producers. Dave Bridges, Rob Wright, video directors. Vestron Video.

No Jacket Required (VHS), Phil Collins. Jim Vulcich, video director. Atlantic Video.

Private Dancer (VHS/Beta/Disc), Tina Turner. Brian Grant, video director. Sony/Pioneer.

BEST MUSIC VIDEO, LONG FORM
• *Huey Lewis & the News: The Heart of Rock & Roll* (VHS/Beta), Huey Lewis & the News. Bruce Gowers, video director. Warner Home Video.

The Police Synchronicity Concert (VHS/Beta), Police. Godley & Creme, video directors. A&M Video/I.R.S. Video.

Prince & the Revolution Live (VHS/Beta), Prince & the Revolution. Paul Becher, video director. Warner Music Video.

Tina Live, Private Dancer Tour (VHS/Beta), Tina Turner. David Mallet, video director. Sony/Picture Music/Capitol.

Wham! The Video (VHS), Wham! CBS/Fox Video.

Anthems Against AIDS and Apartheid

The 29th annual Grammys Awards show opened with Paul Simon and the Ladysmith Black Mambazo group performing "Diamonds on the Soles of Her Shoes," a number from Simon's album celebrating South African music, *Graceland*. "Mr. Simon then sat in the audience for more than three hours," observed *The New York Times*, "watching others beat him out in a number of awards categories."

But not in one of the biggest ones. At evening's close Simon heard presenters Whoopi Goldberg and Don Johnson call his name to ascend the stage again, this time to collect the gramophone trophy for Album of the Year. No doubt feeling vindicated for working so tirelessly to champion a controversial disc, Simon accepted the award by expressing his appreciation to his collaborators, who had valiantly survived, he said, "one of the most repressive regimes on the planet today."

Over all, it was a consciousness-raising night for other reasons, too. Winner of Song of the Year was "That's What Friends Are For," a fund-raising anthem for victims of AIDS that had raised nearly $1 million as of Grammy night. It was the second year in a row that a charitable song won the award ("We Are the World" scored in the same category last year). Also competing for various honors was "Sun City," a joint cry against apartheid by 45 artists that was orchestrated by Steve Van Zandt, but it received no awards.

Graceland was described by *The Washington Post* as "a mesmerizing mix of South African township rhythms and poetic vocals" and was the third Album

Paul Simon described his LP of the year winner Graceland *as "a motion toward helping" in the fight against apartheid.*

of the Year winner for Simon (following *Bridge Over Troubled Water* in 1970 and *Still Crazy After All These Years* in 1975), an accomplishment matched only by Frank Sinatra and Stevie Wonder in past years. To make the album, Simon had to buck some considerable foes, including the United Nations Committee Against Apartheid, which threatened to censure him for breaking the cultural boycott of South Africa. *The Village Voice* and other media also criticized him for his journey to Johannesburg to research the album material.

But Simon was actually a fellow critic of apartheid and supporter of the boycott, refusing, for instance, to perform while he was there. "This is a motion toward helping," he told *Esquire*. "It exposes a culture, a people .... I'm trying to be in the dialogue."

The Washington Post was among those predicting that *Graceland*'s title track would nab Song of the Year.

> **The United Nations had threatened to censure Simon for working in South Africa.**

"Other strong contenders include [Steve] Winwood's 'Higher Love,'" it added, "and [Peter] Gabriel's 'Sledgehammer,' a witty take on sexual double entendres that criminally failed to make the best music video category." Then the paper added as an afterthought, "If there's a left-field choice, it's the sentimental 'That's What Friends Are For.'"

"Friends" was written by Burt Bacharach and wife Carole Bayer Sager and was performed by Dionne Warwick, Elton John, Stevie Wonder, and Gladys Knight, winners of the group pop vocals award. It was the first Grammy for Elton John, who had been nominated 14 previous times since 1970. It was also first time Bacharach won Song of the Year despite five bids dating back to "Wives and Lovers" in 1963. "Friends" made friends again of Bacharach and Warwick, who had a falling out 10 years earlier after Warwick filed a lawsuit accusing the songwriter of breach of contract. Prior to that, Bacharach and partner Hal David were responsible for Warwick's reaching the pop charts an amazing 33 times.

It was Sager who patched things up between writer and artist — and she was also the one who suggested that the proceeds from their new joint effort go to AIDS research. Elizabeth Taylor, a noted AIDS activist, had dropped by the recording studio one day at the invitation of Stevie Wonder, thus giving Sager

the idea. While accepting the songwriter's prize, Bacharach said, "Of all the songs that I have written, it's the one song that, when I hear it on the radio or in performance, I still get a little teary."

Despite a career spanning 20 years, Steve Winwood had never been nominated for a Grammy before, but now he rallied by scoring the most nominations for 1986 (five — compared to four for second-placed Simon, Gabriel, and Wynton Marsalis). After being trounced in the Album and Song of the Year categories, Winwood managed to pull off what *Billboard* called "the biggest upset of the night" when he garnered Record of the Year for "Higher Love," his first number one–ranked single. The song also earned him the pop vocal honors, while its album, *Back in the High Life*, was named Best Engineered Recording. The artist, called a "rock survivor" by *Variety,* was nonplussed and even somewhat ungracious about the award. He told reporters: "I didn't care about winning a Grammy early in my career. When I first started out, I wouldn't even have come to the awards. The idea of approval by one's peers didn't matter to a 19-year-old singer. It still doesn't."

Peter Gabriel turned out to be the night's big loser when his four nods resulted in scratch. Janet Jackson had three bids, but she came up with the same result, including a loss, like Gabriel, in the race for Album of the Year for her multiplatinum *Control.* Jackson's producers, however, prevailed as Producers of the Year. *The New York Times* wrote: "Jimmy Jam and Terry Lewis looked almost mean and forbidding in their fedoras and shades, but turned out to be pussycats, quickly noting that 'we want to thank our moms, first of all.'"

Part of the reason for Jackson's defeat was reflected in *Variety*'s headline after the show: "Vets Dominate Grammy Awards." This year's ceremo-

Proceeds from best song "That's What Friends Are For," which featured singers, from left, Dionne Warwick, Stevie Wonder, and Gladys Knight, went to combat AIDS.

ny, agreed *The New York Times,* "provided a somewhat surprising picture of an industry drifting into middle age, if not already long there." Simon, Bacharach, Warwick, and Winwood were all part of music's new old guard and they were soon joined by another seasoned talent, Barbra Streisand. The 1963 Album of the Year winner was also among those who failed to win this year's LP laurels. Still, her nomination in the category was significant since it amounted to her seventh, thereby putting her in second place behind Frank Sinatra, leader of the *original* old guard, and his record-holding eight nods.

Streisand took the pop vocal laurels for a project that was considered chancy for any veteran artist trying to stay hip — *The Broadway Album* — a collection of her favorite show tunes, most of which were written by Stephen Sondheim (winner of this year's Best Cast Show Album, *Follies*). It was Streisand's eighth Grammy and it amounted to a shocking victory, since Madonna was expected to take the prize for "Papa Don't Preach." In her acceptance remarks, Streisand referred to the

trouble she had convincing her producers to let her record yet another LP of old show music. "It was a struggle to make this album," she said, and then said she was surprised people bought it. The platter's success, however, she added, was a "reaffirmation of the stature and quality of this timeless material." One of the reasons people bought the album was for its hauntingly beautiful rendition of *West Side Story*'s "Somewhere," which Streisand wanted rearranged to accommodate a new bridge she wanted near the end. The brilliant result earned its arranger, David Foster, a Grammy, too.

Among more fledgling talent, the winner of Best New Artist was no surprise. "This award should have Bruce Hornsby's name already engraved on it," *The Washington Post* said prior to the show of the lead artist of the Range, since the former pianist for Sheena Easton's band "has once again opened up radio to the sound of piano-powered pop .... Long shots here include the dreadful corporate rockers Glass Tiger, one-hit wonder Nu Shooz and Timbuk 3 (a clever Texas-based tech duo probably still in shock at having been nominated in the first place)." Accepting the award, Hornsby thanked "the large Hornsby clan out in Virginia" and "my big brother and our head cheerleader, Huey Lewis," who produced his hit single "The Way It Is."

In the rock categories, another one of the old pros, Tina Turner, proved her staying power by holding on to the female vocal laurels for a third year running for "Back Where You Started." (Turner and Pat Benatar had virtually monopolized the category since it was first minted in 1979.) The male honors went, as predicted, to the British white soul singer Robert Palmer for Record and Song of the Year nominee "Addicted to Love." Palmer wrote the tune after the melody came to him in his sleep one night and he woke up to hum it into a tape recorder. "In the morning, I listened to it and knew I'd caught one," he told *People*.

Eurythmics joined the Grammys in the past when Annie Lennox made a shocking gender-bending appearance at the 1983 awards show. Now they stunned Grammy watchers by pulling off an upset in the rock group vocals category for "Missionary Man" to win their only career trophy to date. The Fabulous Thunderbirds had been the odds-on favorite to take the prize for "Tuff Enuff," and their chief competition was expected to come from "Sun City."

> *Ronnie Milsap repeated his 1985 country vocals victory — for the same music.*

N.A.R.A.S. made a bold move this year to embrace more avant-garde works by introducing a category for New Age music that was claimed by Andreas Vollenweider for *Down to the Moon*. The only problem was that most of the artists nominated for it, like Vollenweider, noted *The Washington Post*, "reject the New Age tag as constrictive and misleading."

"The Art of Noise featuring Duane Eddy's 'Peter Gunn' won for best rock-instrumental performance," *Billboard* reported. "That is fitting, because [Henry] Mancini's original rendition of 'Peter Gunn' was a big winner at the first Grammy Awards ceremony in 1958."

"Oh, my Grammy! Oh, my Grammy!" Anita Baker shrieked backstage as she tried to calm down following her double upset in the r&b categories. Janet Jackson was supposed to grab the female vocals prize and Best Rhythm & Blues Song for "What Have You Done for Me Lately," but she was eclipsed for both by Baker, who prevailed for *Rapture* (with its hit single "Sweet Love") which quickly became a soul classic.

James Brown made a startling comeback when he snared the male r&b award 21 years after winning it the first time for the song that initially vaulted him to worldwide fame, "Papa's Got a Brand New Bag." *The Washington Post* was among those that predicted he'd get it again for his latest hit, "Living in America," while other sources such as *Billboard* foresaw a win by Luther Vandross ("Give Me the Reason"). After "Soul Brother Number 1" won, *Grammy Pulse* noted, "Brown couldn't make the Grammy show because he was in the middle of a European tour that took in a couple of Iron Curtain dates and Turkey!"

In the contest for group vocal honors, the Chicago Bears football team was given a presumably serious bid for "The Super Bowl Shuffle," a tongue-in-cheek promotion for their role in the biggest sports showdown of the year that proved funnier as a video than it was as a straightforward song. "If this wins [in r&b] and 'Sun City' doesn't [in the rock categories]," said the *Post*, "we'll know things haven't changed as much as some people have hoped." When Prince prevailed with "Kiss," he became the fourth artist — following Michael Jackson, Donna Summer, and Tina Turner — to win awards for both r&b and r&r. "The other three acts all won in r&b first and later in rock," observed *Billboard*.

GLOBE PHOTO

Twenty-one years after winning his first Grammy, James Brown returned with an r&b triumph for "Living in America."

"Prince did it the other way around."

Among the surprises in the jazz lineup was a victory by the creamy-voiced Diane Schuur, who would achieve jazz diva status by decade's end but won her first Grammy for 1986's *Timeless*. Benny Goodman died the previous June, but scored the first nomination of his career for *Let's Dance* in the big band category that ended up being claimed by the Tonight Show Band with Doc Severinsen for the group's eponymous LP. "No one hears the band play [on *The Tonight Show Starring Johnny Carson*] for more than 20 seconds at a time," Severinsen said. "This proves we can do it."

When the much-lauded trumpet wunderkind Wynton Marsalis entered the Grammy race with four bids, some critics predicted he'd finally get a public lesson in humility. He did on three of those four accounts, but still salvaged a win (best group instrumental prize) for *J Mood*. Marsalis shared one of his defeats

with his saxophonist brother Branford when the prize for best instrumental soloist was claimed by three-time past champ Miles Davis for *Tutu*.

1985 winner Bobby McFerrin turned out to be the star of the jazz prizes this year when he bested Mel Tormé and Joe Williams for the male vocals trophy and then gave a memorable acceptance speech. To win, McFerrin had performed what the *L.A. Herald Examiner* called some "sublime vocalizing" on the score to the celebrated jazz film *'Round Midnight* starring tenor sax player Dexter Gordon as a character loosely based on jazz greats Bud Powell and Lester Young. To express his thanks at the Grammy ceremony, McFerrin sang what the *Herald Examiner* called "some charming scat doodlings."

Controversy erupted in the country awards when Ronnie Milsap repeated his 1985 victory for male vocals — for the same music. Last year he won for the title track to *Lost in the Fifties Tonight*; this year he was hailed for the whole LP. (The single had been released in advance of the album and fell into an earlier Grammy eligibility period.) The victory was startling because the prize was expected to go instead to one of country music's young lions, Randy Travis. Travis and two other losing nominees, Steve Earle and Dwight Yoakam, performed on the Grammycast and together represented the new wave of talent that, according to the *Herald Examiner*, was "currently redefining the genre."

The female country vocals prize was bestowed on first-time champ Reba McEntire for "Whoever's in New England," her first number one–ranked single, from her first gold album. The song title refers to the musings of a jealous housewife whose husband takes frequent business trips to Boston.

The biggest winner in the country categories was "Grandpa (Tell Me 'Bout the Good Old Days)," the Judds' number one–ranked single that won them the best duo vocals prize for a third year in a row. It also won Best Country Song for tunesmith Jamie O'Hara, who, ironically, never knew his own grandparents. Like Robert Palmer's "Addicted to Love," "Grandpa" came to O'Hara in his sleep. "I woke up one morning and that's the song that came out," he told *Billboard*. "'Grandpa' was a gift that songwriters get every once in a while if you're putting in your work."

Best classical album Studio Recordings was "one of the high points" of Vladimir Horowitz's career.

Singer Deniece Williams was nominated for her first Grammy in the female pop vocals category in 1984 for "Let's Hear It for the Boy," from the film *Footloose*, but lost to Tina Turner. Now she won two gold gramophones in the religious categories, both for tracks from her album *So Glad I Know*. She shared one of the gospel prizes with Sandi Patti, with whom she performed "They Say," and who also reaped a second Grammy for *Morning Like This*.

The Latin awards were again the target of criticism when *Billboard* blasted the record academy for the failure of El Gran Combo to be nominated, calling the group "the undisputed tropical leader in popularity, record sales, and world geographical musical diffusion."

Still, the winners were less controversial than in past years: 1968's Best New Artist José Feliciano reaped the accolade for Best Latin Pop Performance for "Lelolai," a track from *Te Amare*, while the Mexican/American award went to Flaco Jimenez, the Tex-Mex accordionist and songwriter and son of Santiago Jimenez. Recipient of the tropical Latin prize was veteran singer Rubén Blades, who was certainly a tropical talent himself, being of Cuban-St. Lucian descent.

Albert Collins, Robert Cray, and Johnny Copeland shared the new prize for Best Traditional Blues Recording *Showdown!*, a reunion album for the trio. Prior to launching their solo careers, Cray and Copeland had been protégés of Collins, who was known as a "cold blues" singer because he was, in his own words, "like something cold in the ice box."

The new blues prize was a replacement in part for the old award for Best Ethnic or Traditional Folk Recording, which had usually gone to blues artists. Folk music was now given two new honors. Grammy's first Best Traditional Folk Recording was *Riding the Midnight Trail* by flat picker and three-time past winner Doc Watson. The equivalent kudos for a contemporary work went to a tribute LP to the late folk/country artist Steve Goodman by the likes of John Hartford, Richie Havens, the Nitty Gritty Dirt Band, and others.

There was a tie in the category introduced last year for polka: *Another Polka Celebration* by Eddie Blazonczyk's Versatones and *I Remember Warsaw* by Jimmy Sturr & His Orchestra. *Grammy Pulse* said the winners "had no problems about the tie. 'We've been friends for years,' said Sturr. 'People think there's a competition between Eddie and myself, but that's not so' .... Sturr said after the ceremony: 'These two Grammys will bring more unity to the polka field.'"

Bill Cosby once ruled the comedy category by winning eight Grammys over the nine years between 1964 and 1972 but thereafter scored none until this year. Now he rebounded with *Those of You with or without Children, You'll Understand.*

As a member of the Police, Sting lost the long-form video award last year to Huey Lewis & the News, but he came back to claim it for *Bring on the Night*, a compilation of excerpts from the critically acclaimed "rockumentary" film about his newest band. Dire Straits may have lost its bid for Album of the Year last year for *Brothers in Arms*, but the music now brought the rock group the short-form video prize, beating out works by Paul McCartney and the Pointer Sisters.

Vladimir Horowitz reigned over the classical categories when his *The Studio Recordings, New York 1985* reaped Best Classical Album, Best Engineered Recording, and the soloist's award, which now combined the two previously bestowed for artists performing with and without orchestral accompaniment.

Over the previous 12 years of his career, the 81-year-old Horowitz spurned recording in a studio in favor of tapes made during live performances and one done in the privacy of his home. His return caused some awkward problems, however, particularly when his piano was shipped to the studio after suffering what *Gramophone* called "a precarious descent from a second floor window." But the reviewer quickly added: "Let me say at once that the [album's] sound quality could scarcely be bettered."

The Studio Recordings, New York 1985 includes two sonatas each by Scarlatti and Liszt, a Scriabin étude, and works by Schubert and Schumann. *Stereo Review* said the outcome "can be described without hyperbole as one of the high points of his recording activity" while *Gramophone* called it "a graphic reminder of the last great believer in the divine right of keyboard kings." Horowitz's producer, Thomas Frost, was voted Classical Producer of the Year.

Losers in the best album competition included cellist Yo-Yo Ma and pianist Emanuel Ax, who nonetheless received the chamber music kudos (repeating their win of last year) for Beethoven's *Cello and Piano Sonata No. 4 in C Major*. Sir Georg Solti missed out last year, but returned to claim the orchestral prize for his Chicago Symphony Orchestra's performance of Liszt's *A Faust Symphony*. Critics hailed it as being superior even to Sir Thomas Beecham's 1959 recording with the Royal Philharmonic Orchestra, which had previously been considered the definitive reading.

James Levine headed up the Chicago Symphony Orchestra and Chorus for the year's Best Choral Performance: Orff's *Carmina Burana*. "As a performance, it is a satisfactory, rather than a memorable version," *Gramophone* wrote. The renowned 70-year-old Polish composer Witold Lutoslawski won Best Contemporary Composition for his Symphony No. 3, which he had been commissioned to write by the Chicago Symphony Orchestra and Sir Georg Solti. The Chicagoans performed it for the first time in September, 1983; its premiere recording came in 1986 by the Los Angeles Philharomic Orchestra under the baton of Esa-Pekka Salonen.

In Leonard Bernstein's *Candide* (which he called his "valentine to European music"), the composer heightened Voltaire's volly against the simpleminded optimism of 14th century France by satirizing the sacred operatic conventions that existed then and now. *Candide* bombed when it debuted on Broadway in 1956, mostly due to Lillian Hellman's ponderous book, but it was reworked in subsequent years, most successfully so in 1973 when director Hal Prince overhauled it for another New York production. John Mauceri served as the conductor for Prince's revision, but in 1982, he went to work editing the various versions into his own opera house rendition that stressed strong entertainment qualities and equally demonstrative vocals. Critics cheered it as the best of all possible recordings and, while *Candide* lost out as a Best Classical Album contender, it won Best Opera Recording.

Kathleen Battle's victory over Marilyn Horne, Luciano Pavarotti, Frederica von Stade, and Teresa Stratas for the vocalist's laurels was offset somewhat by the bad reviews she received for her triumphant roundup of Mozart arias. *Fanfare* did say that her singing was "superb," but blamed the "non-electric results of this recital [on André] Previn's lackluster conducting." *Gramophone* referred to her "fluent, silvery instrument" as sounding "rather thin and characterless."

Once again, the Grammy ceremony was held at Los Angeles's Shrine Auditorium, where the normally off-the-wall comic Billy Crystal proved to be a fairly tame host. Reviews of the show were mixed. *The Washington Post* called it a "sedate affair" while the *Herald Examiner* said it was "above average."

Entertainment included a rousing version of "God Bless the Child" by Anita Baker, a lackluster performance by Billy Idol (a losing nominee for Best Male Rock Vocal Performance), and, added the *Post*, "a wild blues summit involving guitarists Robert Cray, Kings Albert and B.B., singers Etta James and Koko Taylor, and a ragged but right supporting cast." Dionne Warwick, Stevie Wonder, and Gladys Knight hooked up for a version of "That's What Friends Are For" that the critics called even more soulful than the soulful recording.

The ceremony ended on a touching note — the production of "a particularly impassioned version" of "Stand by Me," according to the *Herald Examiner*, that was led by former Drifter Ben E. King and gathered momentum as more artists joined in. Eventually, more than 150 people swelled the stage, at which point, added the *Post*, "the song seemed to degenerate into 'Don't Stand So Close to Me,' or in a few instances, 'Don't Stand in Front of Me.'"

The *Herald Examiner* was less cynical: "It seemed as if we were witnessing something a bit more special than a mere star-studded grand finale — that, in fact, we were witnessing an invitation to take part in a heartfelt but risky experiment in fraternity — and with voices so lovely, and rhythms so undeniable, leading the way, who could resist such a call? With moments like these, clearly, the 29th Annual Grammys show set new standards against which its future performances will have to be judged."

1986

The awards ceremony was broadcast on CBS from the Shrine Auditorium in Los Angeles on February 24, 1987, for the awards eligibility period of October 1, 1985, to September 30, 1986.

ALBUM OF THE YEAR
✓ • *Graceland*, Paul Simon. Paul Simon, producer. Warner Bros.
✓ *Back in the High Life*, Steve Winwood. Russ Titelman, Steve Winwood, producers. Island.

The Broadway Album, Barbra Streisand. Barbra Streisand, Peter Matz, producers. Columbia/CBS.
Control, Janet Jackson. Jimmy Jam, Terry Lewis, producers. A&M.
✓ *So*, Peter Gabriel. Daniel Lanois, Peter Gabriel, producers. Geffen.

RECORD OF THE YEAR
✓ • "Higher Love," Steve Winwood. Russ Titelman, Steve Winwood, producers. Island.

Variety *called Record of the Year champ and best male pop singer Steve Winwood ("Higher Love") a "a rock survivor."*

"Addicted to Love," Robert Palmer. Bernard Edwards, producer. Island.
"The Greatest Love of All," Whitney Houston. Michael Masser, producer. Arista.
✓"Sledgehammer," Peter Gabriel. Daniel Lanois, Peter Gabriel, producers. Geffen.
"That's What Friends Are For," Dionne Warwick, Elton John, Gladys Knight, Stevie Wonder. Burt Bacharach, Carole Bayer Sager, producers. Arista.

SONG OF THE YEAR
(Songwriter's Award)
• "That's What Friends Are For," Burt Bacharach, Carole Bayer Sager. Carole Bayer Sager Music (BMI), New Hidden Valley Music (ASCAP), Warner Bros. Music Corp. (ASCAP), Warner-Tamerlane Publishing Corp., publishers.
"Addicted to Love," Robert Palmer. Bungalow Music N.V., Ackee Music (ASCAP), publishers.
✓"Graceland," Paul Simon. Paul Simon (BMI), publisher.

✓"Higher Love," Steve Winwood, Will Jennings. F.S. Limited PRS, Willin' David Music, Blue Sky Rider Songs (BMI), publishers.
✓"Sledgehammer," Peter Gabriel. Cliofine Ltd., Hidden Pun Music (BMI), publishers.

BEST NEW ARTIST
• Bruce Hornsby & the Range
Glass Tiger
Nu Shooz
Simply Red
Timbuk 3

BEST POP VOCAL PERFORMANCE, MALE
✓• Steve Winwood, "Higher Love." Island.
Peter Cetera, "Glory of Love (Theme from *The Karate Kid, Part II*)." Full Moon.
Kenny Loggins, "Danger Zone." Columbia/CBS.
Michael McDonald, "Sweet Freedom (Theme from *Running Scared*)." MCA.
✓Paul Simon, *Graceland*. Warner Bros.

BEST POP VOCAL PERFORMANCE, FEMALE
• Barbra Streisand, *The Broadway Album*. Columbia/CBS.
Cyndi Lauper, "True Colors." Portrait/CBS.
✓Madonna, "Papa Don't Preach." Sire.
Tina Turner, "Typical Male." Capitol.
Dionne Warwick, *Dionne & Friends*. Arista.

BEST POP PERFORMANCE BY A DUO OR GROUP WITH VOCAL
• Dionne Warwick, Elton John, Gladys Knight and Stevie Wonder, "That's What Friends Are For." Arista.
Peter Cetera, Amy Grant, "The Next Time I Fall." Warner Bros.
Patti LaBelle, Michael McDonald, "On My Own." MCA.
Mike & the Mechanics, "All I Need Is a Miracle." Atlantic.
✓Simply Red, "Holding Back the Years." Elektra.

BEST POP INSTRUMENTAL PERFORMANCE (ORCHESTRA, GROUP, OR SOLOIST)
• Harold Faltermeyer, Steve Stevens, "*Top Gun* Anthem," track from *Top Gun* motion picture soundtrack. Columbia/CBS.
Stanley Clarke, "Overjoyed," track from *Hideaway*. Epic/CBS.
David Foster, *David Foster*. Atlantic.

Genesis, "The Brazilian," track from *Invisible Touch*. Atlantic.

The Tonight Show Band with Doc Severinsen, "Johnny's Theme (*The Tonight Show* Theme)," track from *The Tonight Show Band with Doc Severinsen*. Amherst Records.

BEST ROCK VOCAL PERFORMANCE, MALE

- Robert Palmer, "Addicted to Love." Island.

John Fogerty, *Eye of the Zombie*. Warner Bros.

✓ Peter Gabriel, "Sledgehammer." Geffen.

Billy Idol, "To Be a Lover." Chrysalis.

Eddie Money, "Take Me Home Tonight." Columbia/CBS.

BEST ROCK VOCAL PERFORMANCE, FEMALE

- Tina Turner, "Back Where You Started," track from *Break Every Rule*. Capitol.

Pat Benatar, "Sex as a Weapon." Chrysalis.

Cyndi Lauper, "911," track from *True Colors*. Portrait/CBS.

Stevie Nicks, "Talk To Me." Modern.

Bonnie Raitt, "No Way to Treat a Lady." Warner Bros.

BEST ROCK PERFORMANCE BY A DUO OR GROUP WITH VOCAL

- Eurythmics, "Missionary Man." RCA.

Artists United Against Apartheid, "Sun City." Little Steven, Arthur Baker, producers. Manhattan.

Fabulous Thunderbirds, "Tuff Enuff." CBS Associated.

Rolling Stones, "Harlem Shuffle." Columbia/CBS.

ZZ Top, *Afterburner*. Warner Bros.

BEST ROCK INSTRUMENTAL PERFORMANCE (ORCHESTRA, GROUP OR SOLOIST)

- Art of Noise Featuring Duane Eddy, "Peter Gunn," track from *In Visible Silence*. China/Chrysalis.

Fabulous Thunderbirds, "Down at Antones," track from *Tuff Enuff*. CBS Associated.

Eric Johnson, "Zap," track from *Tones*. Reprise.

Alan Parsons Project, "Where's the Walrus?," track from *Stereotomy*. Arista.

Yes, "Amazing Grace," track from *90125 Live, The Solos*. Atlantic.

BEST RHYTHM & BLUES SONG (Songwriter's Award)

- "Sweet Love," Anita Baker, Louis A. Johnson, Gary Bias. Old Brompton Rd. (ASCAP) publisher, administered by Jobete Music.

"Give Me the Reason," Luther Vandross, Nat Adderley, Jr. April Music Inc., Uncle Ronnie's Music (ASCAP), Dillard Music (BMI), publishers.

✓ "Kiss," Prince & the Revolution. Controversy Music (ASCAP), publisher.

"Living in America," Dan Hartman, Charlie Midnight.

"What Have You Done For Me Lately," James Harris III, Terry Lewis, Janet Jackson. Flyte Tyme Tunes (ASCAP), publishers.

BEST RHYTHM & BLUES VOCAL PERFORMANCE, MALE

- James Brown, "Living in America." Scotti Brothers/CBS.

Al Jarreau, "Since I Fell for You," track from *Double Vision* (Bob James, David Sanborn album). Warner Bros.

Oran (Juice) Jones, "The Rain." DefJam/CBS.

Billy Ocean, "Love Zone." Jive/Arista.

Luther Vandross, "Give Me the Reason." Epic/CBS.

BEST RHYTHM & BLUES VOCAL PERFORMANCE, FEMALE

- Anita Baker, *Rapture*. Elektra.

Aretha Franklin, "Jumpin' Jack Flash." Arista.

Janet Jackson, *Control*. A&M.

Chaka Khan, *Destiny*. Warner Bros.

Patti LaBelle, *Winner in You*. MCA.

BEST RHYTHM & BLUES PERFORMANCE BY A DUO OR GROUP WITH VOCAL

✓ Prince & the Revolution, "Kiss." Paisley Park.

Ashford & Simpson, *Real Love*. Capitol.

Cameo, "Word Up." Atlanta Artists.

Chicago Bears Shufflin' Crew, "The Super Bowl Shuffle." Richard A. Tufo, Bobby Daniels, record producers. Red Label.

Run – D.M.C., *Raising Hell*. Profile.

Sade, *Promise*. Portrait/CBS.

First-time nominee Diane Schuur nabbed the female jazz vocals prize for Timeless.

BEST RHYTHM & BLUES INSTRUMENTAL PERFORMANCE (ORCHESTRA, GROUP, OR SOLOIST)
• Yellowjackets, "And You Know That," track from *Shades*. MCA.
Stanley Clarke, "The Boys of Johnson Street," track from *Hideaway*. Epic/CBS.
Billy Cobham, "Zanzibar Breeze," track from *Power Play*. GRP.
Kenny G., *Duotones*. Arista.
Kashif, "Movie Song," track from *Condition of the Heart*. Arista.

BEST JAZZ VOCAL PERFORMANCE, MALE
• Bobby McFerrin, "'Round Midnight," track from *'Round Midnight* soundtrack. Columbia/CBS.
Grady Tate, "She's Out of My Life," track from *Go for Whatcha Know*. Blue Note.
Mel Tormé, *An Elegant Evening*. Concord Jazz.
Joe Williams, *I Just Want to Sing*. Delos International.
Jimmy Witherspoon, *Midnight Lady Called the Blues*. Muse.

BEST JAZZ VOCAL PERFORMANCE, FEMALE
• Diane Schuur, *Timeless*. GRP.
Etta James, *Blues in the Night* (Etta James, Eddie "Cleanhead" Vinson album). Fantasy.
Flora Purim, "Esquinas," track from *The Magicians, Flora Purim and Airto*. Crossover.

Sue Raney, *Flight of Fancy*. Discovery.
Maxine Sullivan, *Uptown*. Concord Jazz.

BEST JAZZ VOCAL PERFORMANCE, DUO OR GROUP
• 2 + 2 Plus (Clare Fischer & His Latin Jazz Sextet), *Free Fall*. Discovery.
Jackie Cain, Roy Kral, *Bogie*. Fantasy.
Four Freshmen, *Fresh!* Pausa.
L.A. Jazz Choir (Gerald Eskelin, director), *From All Sides*. Pausa.
Arthur Prysock, Betty Joplin, "Teach Me Tonight," track from *A Rockin' Good Way*. Milestone.

BEST JAZZ INSTRUMENTAL PERFORMANCE, SOLOIST
• Miles Davis, *Tutu*. Warner Bros.
Eddie Daniels, *Breakthrough*. GRP.
Dizzy Gillespie, *Closer to the Source*. Atlantic.
Branford Marsalis, *Royal Garden Blues*. Columbia/CBS.
Wynton Marsalis, "Insane Asylum," track from *J Mood*. Columbia/CBS.

BEST JAZZ INSTRUMENTAL PERFORMANCE, GROUP
• Wynton Marsalis, *J Mood*. Columbia/CBS.
Art Blakey & the Jazz Messengers, *Art Blakey & the Jazz Messengers Live at Sweet Basil*. GNP Crescendo.
Gerry Mulligan, Scott Hamilton, *Soft Lights and Sweet Music*. Concord Jazz.
Keith Jarrett, Gary Peacock, Jack DeJohnette, *Standards Live*. ECM.
Teddy Wilson, Benny Carter, Red Norvo, Louis Bellson, Remo Palmier, George Duvivier, Freddie Green, *Swing Reunion*. Book-of-the-Month Records.

BEST JAZZ INSTRUMENTAL PERFORMANCE, BIG BAND
• The Tonight Show Band with Doc Severinsen, *The Tonight Show Band with Doc Severinsen*. Amherst.
Benny Goodman & His Orchestra, *Let's Dance*. Music-Masters.
Lionel Hampton & His Orchestra, *Sentimental Journey*. Atlantic.
Woody Herman & His Big Band, *50th Anniversary Tour*. Concord Jazz.
Mel Lewis Orchestra, *20 Years at the Village Vanguard*. Atlantic.

BEST JAZZ FUSION PERFORMANCE, VOCAL OR INSTRUMENTAL
• Bob James, David Sanborn, *Double Vision*. Warner Bros.
Chick Corea, *The Chick Corea Elektric Band*. GRP.
Lee Ritenour, *Earth Run*. GRP.
Clare Fischer & his Latin Jazz Sextet, *Free Fall*. Discovery.
Lyle Mays, *Lyle Mays*. Geffen.

BEST COUNTRY SONG
(Songwriter's Award)
• "Grandpa (Tell Me 'Bout the Good Old Days)," Jamie O'Hara. Cross Keys Publishing Co. Inc. (ASCAP). Tree Group, publisher.
"Daddy's Hands," Holly Dunn. Uncle Artie Music, publisher.
"Guitar Town," Steve Earle. Goldline Music Inc. (ASCAP), publisher.
"Guitars, Cadillacs," Dwight Yoakam. Coal Dust Music (BMI), publisher.
"Whoever's in New England," Quentin Powers, Kendall Franceschi. Silverline Music Inc., W.B.M. Music Corp. (BMI/SECAC), publishers.

BEST COUNTRY VOCAL PERFORMANCE, MALE
• Ronnie Milsap, *Lost in the Fifties Tonight*. RCA.
Steve Earle, *Guitar Town*. MCA.
✓ Randy Travis, "Diggin' Up Bones." Warner Bros.
Hank Williams, Jr., "Ain't Misbehavin'." Warner Bros.
Dwight Yoakam, *Guitars, Cadillacs, etc.*, *etc*. Reprise.

BEST COUNTRY VOCAL PERFORMANCE, FEMALE
• Reba McEntire, "Whoever's in New England." MCA.
Holly Dunn, "Daddy's Hands." MTM.
Crystal Gayle, "Cry." Warner Bros.
Emmylou Harris, "Today I Started Loving You Again." Warner Bros.
Kathy Mattea, "Love at the Five & Dime." Mercury.

BEST COUNTRY PERFORMANCE BY A DUO OR GROUP WITH VOCAL
• Judds, "Grandpa (Tell Me 'Bout the Good Old Days)," RCA.
✓ Alabama, "She and I." RCA.
Everly Brothers, *Born Yesterday*. Mercury.

Gatlin Brothers, "She Used to Be Somebody's Baby." Columbia/CBS.
Carl Perkins, Jerry Lee Lewis, Roy Orbison, Johnny Cash, *Class of '55*. America Record Corp.

BEST COUNTRY INSTRUMENTAL PERFORMANCE (ORCHESTRA, GROUP, OR SOLOIST)
• Ricky Skaggs, "Raisin' the Dickens," track from *Love's Gonna Get Ya*. Epic/CBS.
Jerry Douglas, *Under the Wire*. MCA Master Series.
Albert Lee, *Speechless*. MCA Master Series.
New Grass Revival, "Seven by Seven," track from *New Grass Revival*. EMI America.
Mark O'Connor, *Meanings Of*. Warner Bros.

BEST GOSPEL PERFORMANCE, MALE
• Philip Bailey, *Triumph*. Myrrh/Word.
Steve Green, *For God and God Alone*. Sparrow.
Larnelle Harris, *From a Servant's Heart*. Benson.
Michael W. Smith, *The Big Picture*. Reunion.
BeBe Winans, "It's Only Natural," track from *Kaleidoscope* (Keith Thomas album). Dayspring/ Word.

BEST GOSPEL PERFORMANCE, FEMALE
• Sandi Patti, *Morning Like This*. Word.
Cynthia Clawson, *Immortal*. Dayspring/Word.
Teri DeSario, *Voices in the Wind*. Dayspring/Word.
Sheila Walsh, *Shadowlands*. Myrrh/Word.
Deniece Williams, *So Glad I Know*. Sparrow.

BEST GOSPEL PERFORMANCE BY A DUO OR GROUP, CHOIR, OR CHORUS
• Sandi Patti, Deniece Williams, "They Say," track from *So Glad I Know*. Sparrow.
CeCe Winans, Carman, "Our Blessed Saviour Has Come," track from *A Long Time Ago... in a Land Called Bethlehem*. Benson.
DeGarmo & Key, *Street Light*. Power Disc/Benson.
First Call, *Undivided*. Dayspring/Word.
Petra, *Back to the Street*. Star Song/Word.

Best Soul Gospel Performance, Male
• Al Green, "Going Away." A&M.
Derrick Brinkley, *Glorious Day*. Tyscot.
Daryl Coley, *Just Daryl*. The First Epistle.
Rodney Friend, *Worthy*. Command.
Howard Smith, *Totally Committed*. Light.

Best Soul Gospel Performance, Female
• Deniece Williams, "I Surrender All," track from *So Glad I Know*. Sparrow.
Shirley Caesar, *Celebration*. Rejoice/Word.
Candi Staton, *Sing a Song*. Beracah.
Tramaine, *The Search Is Over*. A&M.
Albertina Walker, *Spirit*. Rejoice/Word.

Best Soul Gospel Performance by a Duo or Group, Choir, or Chorus
• Winans, *Let My People Go*. Qwest.
James Cleveland & the Southern California Community Choir, *James Cleveland & the Southern California Community Choir*. King James.
Dorothy Norwood, Rev. F.C. Barnes, Rev. Janice Brown, Albertina Walker, Rev. James Cleveland, *Dorothy Norwood & Friends*. AIR.
Albertina Walker, Shirley Caesar, *Jesus Is Mine*. Rejoice/Word.
Winans with Vanessa Bell Armstrong, "Choose Ye," track from *Let My People Go*. Qwest.

Best Traditional Blues Recording
• *Showdown*, Albert Collins, Robert Cray, Johnny Copeland. Alligator.
Jealous, John Lee Hooker. Pausa.
Live! Backstage Access, Willie Dixon. Pausa.
Live from Chicago, Mr. Superharp Himself!, James Cotton. Alligator.
Pressure Cooker, Clarence "Gatemouth" Brown. Alligator.

Best Traditional Folk Recording
• *Riding the Midnight Train*, Doc Watson. Sugar Hill.
Caught in the Act, Queen Ida. GNP/Crescendo.
Hot Steppin' with Rockin' Sidney, Rockin' Sidney. ZBC Records.
20th Anniversary Concert, New Lost City Ramblers with Elizabeth Cotton, Pete Seeger, the Highwood String Band. Flying Fish.

Waitin' for My Ya Ya, Buckwheat Zydecko. Rounder.

Best Contemporary Folk Recording
• *Tribute to Steve Goodman*, Arlo Guthrie, John Hartford, Richie Havens, Bonnie Koloc, Nitty Gritty Dirt Band, John Prine, others. Hank Neuberger, Al Bunetta, Dan Einstein, producers. Red Pajamas.
German Afternoons, John Prine. Oh Boy.
I'm Alright, Loudon Wainwright III. Rounder.
Last of the True Believers, Nanci Griffith. Philo.
No Easy Walk to Freedom, Peter, Paul & Mary. Gold Castle.

Best Latin Pop Performance
• José Feliciano, "Lelolai," track from *Te Amare*. RCA.
José José , "Pruebame." Ariola.
Pandora, "Como Te Va Mi Amor," track from *Pandora*. Odeon.
Danny Rivera, *Inolvidable Tito...a Mi Me Pasa Lo Mismo Que a Usted*. DNA/Puerto Rico.
Yuri, "Yo Te Pido Amor," track from *Yo Te Pido Amor*. Odeon.

Best Tropical Latin Performance
• Rubén Blades, *Escenas*. Elektra.
Mario Bauza, Graciela, *Afro-Cuban Jazz*. Caiman.
Willie Colon, *Especial No. 5*. Sonotone.
Celia Cruz, Tito Puente, *Homenaje á Beny More, Vol. III*. Vaya/ Musica Latina International.
Willie Rosario, *Nueva Cosecha*. Bronco.

Best Mexican/American Performance
• Flaco Jiminez, *Ay Te Dejo en San Antonio*. Arhoolie.
Rafael Buendia, *Y... ¡Zas!* Ariola.
Steve Jordan, *Turn Me Loose*. RCA.
Los Tigres del Norte, *El Otro Mexico*. Profono International.
Salvador Torres, "Unidos Cantemos." Mas.
Juan Valentin, *Juan Valentin*. Musart.
Los Yonics, "Corazón Vacio." Profono.

Best Reggae Recording
• *Babylon the Bandit*, Steel Pulse. Elektra.
Brutal, Black Uhuru. RAS.
"Club Paradise," Jimmy Cliff. Columbia/CBS.

Linton Kwesi Johnson in Concert with the Dub Band, Linton Kwesi Johnson & the Dub Band. Shanachie.
Rasta Philosophy, Itals. Nighthawk.

BEST POLKA RECORDING
• *Another Polka Celebration,* Eddie Blazonczyk's Versatones. Bel Aire.
• *I Remember Warsaw,* Jimmy Sturr & His Orchestra. Starr.
America's Favorites, Frank Yankovic. Smash.
By Special Request, Walter Ostanek (cassette). CBS/Select.
Thank You Dear and Give Her Roses, Hank Haller Ensemble. Haller.

BEST NEW AGE RECORDING
• *Down to the Moon,* Andreas Vollenweider. FM/CBS.
Canyon, Paul Winter. Living Music.
Rendezvous, Jean-Michel Jarre. Polydor-Dreyfus.
Windham Hill Records Sampler '86, various artists. Dawn Atkinson, Stewart Whitmore, producers. Windham Hill..
A Winter's Solstice, various artists. William Ackerman, Dawn Atkinson, producers. Windham Hill.

BEST INSTRUMENTAL COMPOSITION
(Composer's Award)
• *Out of Africa* (original motion picture soundtrack), John Barry, composer. MCA Inc., P.D., African Traditional/WB Inc., publishers.
Aliens (original motion picture soundtrack), James Horner, composer.
"Earth Run," track from *Earth Run,* Lee Ritenour, Dave Grusin, composers. Rit of Habeas Music (ASCAP), Roaring Fork Music (BMI), publishers.
"Elektric City," track from *The Chick Corea Elektric Band.* Chick Corea, composer. Not Bernie's Publishing Co. (BMI), publisher.
"J Mood," track from *J Mood,* Wynton Marsalis, composer. ASCAP.
"Top Gun Anthem," track from *Top Gun* motion picture soundtrack, Harold Faltermeyer, composer. Famous Music, publisher.
Young Sherlock Holmes (music from motion picture soundtrack), Bruce Broughton, composer. Famous Music, publisher.

BEST ARRANGEMENT ON AN INSTRUMENTAL
• Patrick Williams, "Suite Memories," track from *Someplace Else.* Soundwings.
Jorge Calandrelli, "The First Letter," track from *The Color Purple* soundtrack. Qwest.
Jorge Calandrelli, "Solfeggietto Metamorphosis," track from *Breakthrough.* GRP.
Bill Meyers, "AM/PM," track from *Images.* Spindletop.
Don Sebesky, "Cherokee," track from *Moving Lines.* Doctor Jazz.

BEST INSTRUMENTAL ARRANGEMENT ACCOMPANYING VOCAL(S)
• David Foster, "Somewhere," track from *The Broadway Album* (Barbra Streisand). Columbia/CBS.
Jorge Calandrelli, "Forget the Woman," track from *The Art of Excellence.* Columbia/CBS.
Clare Fischer, "Free Fall," track from *Free Fall.* Discovery.
Jeremy Lubbock, "A Time for Love," track from *Timeless.* GRP.
Rob McConnell, "Duke Ellington Medley," track from *Mel Tormé-Rob McConnell & the Boss Brass.* Concord Jazz.

BEST MUSICAL CAST SHOW ALBUM
• *Follies in Concert,* Stephen Sondheim, composer & lyricist. Thomas Z. Shepard, producer. RCA..
Me and My Girl, Douglas Furber, R. Butler, lyricists. Nod Gay, composer. Norman Newell, producer. Manhattan.
The Mystery of Edwin Drood (original Broadway cast recording), Rupert Holmes, composer & lyricist. Rupert Holmes, producer. Polydor.
Song & Dance, Andrew Lloyd Webber, composer. Don Black, Richard Maltby Jr., lyricists. Thomas Z. Shepard, producer. RCA..
Sweet Charity, Dorothy Fields, lyricist. Cy Coleman, composer. Cy Coleman, Mike Berniker, producers. EMI America.

BEST CLASSICAL ALBUM
• *Horowitz: The Studio Recordings, New York 1985,* Vladimir Horowitz. Thomas Frost, producer. Deutsche Grammophon.

Beethoven: Cello & Piano Sonata No. 4 in
C and variations, Yo-Yo Ma, Emanuel
Ax. James Mallinson, producer. CBS
Masterworks.

Beethoven: Symphony No. 9 in D Minor
(Choral), Robert Shaw conducting
Atlanta Symphony Orchestra and
Chorus (solos: Benita Valente, Jerry
Hadley, Florence Kopleff, John Cheek).
Thomas Frost, producer. Pro Arte.

Bernstein: Candide, John Manuceri
conducting New York City Opera
Chorus and Orchestra (solos: Erie
Mills, David Eisler, John Lankston,
Joyce Castle, Scott Reeve, Jack
Harrold, James Billings, Maris
Clement). Elizabeth Ostrow, producer.
New World.

Copland: Billy the Kid & Rodeo (Complete
Ballets), Leonard Slatkin conducting
St. Louis Symphony Orchestra. Marc
Aubort, Joanna Nickrenz, producers.
Angel.

Mendelssohn: Symphony No. 3 in A Minor
(Scottish); No. 4 in A (Italian), Sir
Georg Solti conducting Chicago
Symphony Orchestra. Andrew Cornall,
producer. London.

Pleasures of Their Company (Bach,
Gounod, Villa-Lobos), Kathleen Battle,
Christopher Parkening. Patti Laursen,
producer. Angel.

BEST CLASSICAL ORCHESTRAL
RECORDING
(Conductor's Award)

• Liszt: A Faust Symphony, Sir Georg Solti
conducting Chicago Symphony
Orchestra. Michael Haas, producer.
London.

Beethoven: Symphony No. 9 in D Minor
(Choral), Robert Shaw conducting
Atlanta Symphony Chorus and
Orchestra. Thomas Frost, producer. Pro
Arte.

Copland: Billy the Kid & Rodeo (Complete
Ballets), Leonard Slatkin conducting
St. Louis Symphony Orchestra. Marc
Aubort, Joanna Nickrenz, producers.
Angel.

Respighi: The Pines of Rome, The
Fountains of Rome, Roman Festivals,
Riccardo Muti conducting Philadelphia
Orchestra. John Willan, producer.
Angel.

Vaughan Williams: Sinfonia Antarctica,
Bernard Haitink conducting London
Philharmonic Orchestra. John Fraser,
producer. Angel.

BEST OPERA RECORDING

• Bernstein: Candide, John Mauceri
conducting New York City Opera
Chorus and Orchestra (solos: Mills,
Clement, Eisler, Lankston, Castle,
Reeve, Harrold, Billings). Elizabeth
Ostrow, producer. New World.

Mozart: The Marriage of Figaro, Sir
Neville Marriner conducting Academy
of St. Martin-in the-Fields (solos:
Hendricks, Raimondi, Popp, Baltsa,
Lloyd, Palmer, Baldin). Erik Smith,
producer. Phillips Classics.

Verdi: Don Carlos, Claudio Abbado
conducting La Scala Opera Chorus and
Orchestra (solos: Domingo, Ricciarelli,
Terrani, Raimondi, Ghiaurov). Rainer
Brock, producer. Deutsche
Grammophon.

Verdi: Otello, Lorin Maazel conducting
Orchestra e Coro del Teatro alla Scala
di Milano (solos: Domingo, Ricciarelli,
Diaz). James Mallinson, David Groves,
producers. Angel.

Verdi: Un Ballo in Maschera, Sir Georg
Solti conducting National Philharmonic
Orchestra (solos: Pavarotti, Price,
Bruson, Battle, Ludwig). Christopher
Raeburn, producer. London.

BEST CHAMBER MUSIC PERFORMANCE

• Yo-Yo Ma, Emanuel Ax, Beethoven:
Cello & Piano Sonata No. 4 in C and
variations. CBS Masterworks.

Benny Goodman, Berkshire String
Quartet, Fritz Maag, Leon Pammers,
Benny Goodman: Private Collection.
Musicmasters.

Lynn Harrell, Vladimir Ashkenazy,
Rachmaninoff: Cello & Piano Sonata.
London.

Members of Chicago Symphony Winds,
Vocalists, Mozart: Music for Basset
Horns (Divertimenti, Notturni,
Adagios). CBS Masterworks.

Itzhak Perlman, Vladimir Ashkenazy,
Brahms: Violin & Piano Sonatas. No. 1
in G; No. 2 in A; No. 3 in D Minor;
Hungarian Dances. Angel.

Best classical vocalist Kathleen Battle got mixed reviews for her Mozart arias.

BEST CLASSICAL PERFORMANCE, INSTRUMENTAL SOLOIST(S) (WITH OR WITHOUT ORCHESTRA)

- Vladimir Horowitz, *Horowitz: The Studio Recordings, New York 1985*. Deutsche Grammophon.

Claudio Arrau (Davis conducting Dresden State Orchestra), *Beethoven: Piano Concerto No. 5 in E Flat (Emperor)*. Philips Classics.

Dale Clevenger (Abbado conducting Chicago Symphony), *Mozart: Horn Concerti*. Deutsche Grammophon.

Adolph Herseth (Abbado conducting Chicago Symphony), *Haydn: Trumpet Concerto in E Flat*. Deutsche Grammophon.

Wynton Marsalis (Salonen conducting Philharmonia Orchestra), *Tomasi: Concerto for Trumpet and Orchestra; Jolivet: Concerto No. 2 for Trumpet; Concertino for Trumpet, String Orchestra and Piano*. CBS Masterworks.

Andras Schiff, *Bach: Well-Tempered Clavier Book I*. London.

BEST CHORAL PERFORMANCE (OTHER THAN OPERA)

- James Levine conducting Chicago Symphony Chorus and Orchestra; Margaret Hillis, choral director, *Orff: Carmina Burana*. Deutsche Grammophon.

John Eliot Gardiner conducting Monteverdi Choir and English Baroque Soloists, *Bach: Mass in B Minor*. Archiv.

Herbert von Karajan conducting Vienna Singverein and Wiener Philharmoniker; Heimuth Froschauer, chorus master, *Beethoven: Missa Solemnis*. Deutsche Grammophon.

Riccardo Muti conducting Westminster Choir and Philadelphia Orchestra; Joseph Flummerfelt, choral director, *Berlioz: Romeo et Juliet*. Angel.

Robert Shaw conducting Atlanta Symphony Chorus and Orchestra, *Choral Masterpieces*. Telarc.

BEST CLASSICAL VOCAL SOLOIST PERFORMANCE

- Kathleen Battle (Previn conducting Royal Philharmonic Orchestra), *Kathleen Battle Sings Mozart*. Angel.

Marilyn Horne (Davis conducting English Chamber Orchestra), *Beautiful Dreamer (The Great American Songbook)*. London.

Luciano Pavarotti (Chiaramello conducting Orchestra Del Teatro Communale di Bologna), *Passione Pavarotti (Favorite Neapolitan Love Songs)*. London.

Frederica von Stade (de Almeida conducting Royal Philharmonic Orchestra), *Canteloube: Chants D'Auvergne Vol. II; Triptyque*. CBS Masterworks.

Teresa Stratas (Schwarz conducting Chamber Symphony), *Stratas Sings Weill*. Nonesuch.

BEST CONTEMPORARY COMPOSITION (Composer's Award)

- *Symphony No. 3*, Witold Lutoslawski. Chester Music (ASCAP), publisher.

Septet, Chick Corea. Litha Music (ASCAP), publisher.

Company, Philip Glass. Dunvagen Music, publisher.

Mountain Songs (A Cycle of American Folk Music), Robert Beaser. European American Music, publisher.

Symphony No. 1, Ellen Taafe Zwilich. Margun Music Inc., publisher.

BEST ENGINEERED RECORDING, CLASSICAL
• Paul Goodman, *Horowitz: The Studio Recordings, New York 1985*, Vladimir Horowitz. Deutsche Grammophon.

Marc Aubort, *Copland: Billy the Kid & Rodeo (Complete Ballets)* (Slatkin conducting St. Louis Symphony Orchestra). Angel.

Paul Goodman, *Bernstein: Candide* (Mauceri conducting New York City Opera Chorus and Orchestra). New World.

James Lock, *Liszt: A Faust Symphony* (Solti conducting Chicago Symphony Orchestra). London.

Michael Sheady, *Respighi: The Pines of Rome, The Fountains of Rome, Roman Festivals* (Muti conducting Philadelphia Orchestra). Angel.

CLASSICAL PRODUCER OF THE YEAR
• Thomas Frost
Marc Aubort, Joanna Nickrenz
Steven Epstein
Jay David Saks
Robert Woods

BEST COMEDY RECORDING
• *Those of You With or Without Children, You'll Understand*, Bill Cosby. Geffen.

Bob and Ray: A Night of Two Stars Recorded Live at Carnegie Hall, Bob Elliott, Ray Goulding (cassette). Radioart.

I Have a Pony, Steven Wright. Warner Bros.

Mud Will Be Flung Tonight! Bette Midler. Atlantic.

Playin' with Your Head, George Carlin. Eardrum.

"Twist and Shout," Rodney Dangerfield, track from *Back to School* (original motion picture soundtrack). MCA.

BEST SPOKEN WORD OR NON-MUSICAL RECORDING
• *Interviews from the Class of '55, Recording Sessions*, Carl Perkins, Jerry Lee Lewis, Roy Orbison, Johnny Cash, Sam Phillips, Rick Nelson, Chips Moman. America Record Corp.

Gulliver, Sir John Gielgud (with Royal Philharmonic Orchestra). Soundwings.

Hardheaded Boys, Bill Cosby (featuring Double Force). Nicetown.

Interview with the Vampire, F. Murray Abraham (cassette). Random House Audiobooks.

The Stories of Ray Bradbury, Ray Bradbury (cassette). Random House Audiobooks.

BEST RECORDING FOR CHILDREN
• *The Alphabet*, Sesame Street Muppets. Kathryn King, Geri Van Rees, producers (cassette). Golden Books.

A Child's Gift of Lullabyes, Tanya Goodman. J. Aaron Brown, David R. Lehman, producers. JABA Records.

"Itsy Bitsy Spider," Carly Simon. Russ Kunkel, Bill Payne, George Massenburg, producers. Arista.

A Light in the Attic, Shel Silverstein. Ron Haffkine, producer. Columbia/CBS.

One-Minute Bedtime Stories, Shari Lewis. Stormy Sacks, Hal Sacks, producers. Caedmon.

BEST ENGINEERED RECORDING, NON-CLASSICAL
• Tom Lord Alge, Jason Corsaro, *Back in the High Life* (Steve Winwood). Island.

Humberto Gatica, *David Foster* (David Foster). Atlantic.

Mike Shipley, *Dog Eat Dog* (Joni Mitchell). Geffen.

Don Murray, *GRP Live in Session* (various artists).GRP.

Jason Corsaro, Eric (ET) Thorngren, *Riptide* (Robert Palmer). Island.

BEST ALBUM PACKAGE
(Art Director's Award)
• Eiko Ishioka, *Tutu*. Warner Bros.

Buddy Jackson, *Songs Unspoken*. Meadowlark.

Andrew Ellis, Colin Chambers, *Stereotom*. Arista.

Michael Hodgson, *True Stories*, Jeffrey Kent Ayeroff. Sire.

John Berg, *The Voice, The Columbia Years 1943–1952* (Frank Sinatra album). Columbia/CBS.

BEST ALBUM NOTES
(Annotator's Award)
• Gary Giddins, Wilfred Sheed, Jonathan Schwartz, Murray Kempton, Andrew Sarris, Cameron Crowe, *Biograph*. Columbia/CBS.

Richard Freed, Peter Eliot Stone, *Virtuosi.* Smithsonian.

David Hall, John Stratton, Tom Owen, Robert Tuggle, David Hamilton, *The Mapleson Cylinders*. Rodgers & Hammerstein Archives.

Stephen Holden, Frank Conroy, *The Voice, The Columbia Years 1943–1952* (Frank Sinatra album). Columbia/ CBS.

Lenny Kaye, *Elektrock the Sixties*. Elektra.

BEST HISTORICAL ALBUM

• *Atlantic Rhythm and Blues 1947–1974 Vols. 1–7*, various artists. Bob Porter, Aziz Goksel, producers. Atlantic.

Biograph, Bob Dylan. Jeff Rosen, producer. Columbia/CBS.

The Complete Keynote Collection (334 jazz performances from the 1940s). Kiyoshi Koyama, producer. Keynote.

The Mapleson Cylinders, various Metropolitan Opera artists. David Hamilton, Tom Owen, producers. Rodgers & Hammerstein Archives.

The Voice, The Columbia Years 1943–1952, Frank Sinatra. Joe McEwen, James Isaacs, producers. Columbia/CBS.

PRODUCER OF THE YEAR, NON CLASSICAL

• Jimmy Jam, Terry Lewis
David Foster
Michael Omartian
Paul Simon
Russ Titelman, Steve Winwood

BEST MUSIC VIDEO, SHORT FORM

• *Dire Straits Brothers in Arms*, Dire Straits (VHS). Various video directors. Warner Reprise Video.

Brother Where You Bound, Supertramp (VHS/Beta). Rene Daalder, video director. A&M Video.

Runaway, Louis Cardenas (VHS). Cayce B. Redding, video director. Allied Artists.

Rupert and the Frog Song, Paul McCartney (Disc). Various video directors. Pioneer Arists.

So Excited, Pointer Sisters (VHS/Beta). Richard Perry, video director. RCA/Columbia Pictures Home Video.

BEST MUSIC VIDEO, LONG FORM

• *Bring on the Night*, Sting (VHS/Beta/Disc). Michael Apted, video director. Karl-Lorimar Home Video.

Frank Sinatra: Portrait of an Album, Frank Sinatra (VHS). Emil G. Davidson, video director. MGM/UA Home Video.

90125 Live, Yes (VHS/Beta). Steven Soderbergh, video director. Atlantic Video.

Pete Townshend: White City, The Music Movie, Pete Townshend (VHS). Richard Lowenstein, video director. Vestron Music Video.

Sun City, Artists United Against Apartheid (VHS). Godley & Creme, Hart Perry, Jonathan Demme, video directors. Karl-Lorimar Home Video.

"A Night Loaded with Shockers"

Just four years after Michael Jackson made Grammy history for snaring the most awards in a single year (eight) for *Thriller*, he was back with five nominations for his latest megahit, *Bad*. His competition in the Album of the Year line-up, however, was fierce: Prince and Whitney Houston were both over-due for Grammys,

*Album of the Year champs U2 (*The Joshua Tree*) "seemed to be citizens of an alternative time frame," said* Time.

and he also faced a strong foe in the hot Irish rock band U2. When *Bad* turned out to have *really* bad luck with Grammy voters — winning only an engineering prize and nothing for Michael — *Billboard* called it "the biggest surprise of the night."

And that was saying something, considering *Variety* called it "a night loaded with shockers."

After Jackson's startling shut-out, the next biggest stunner came in who won the Record of the Year contest, in which he wasn't even nominated. The field included last year's winner Steve Winwood ("Back in the High Life Again"), the increasingly popular Suzanne Vega ("Luka"), the ultra-hot Los Lobos ("La Bamba," their cover of the Ritchie Valens song for the hit film of the same name), U2 at the top of its talents ("I Still Haven't Found What I'm Looking For"), and 1986's Album of the Year winner, Paul Simon, with a nomination that looked like it had gone astray from

last year. Since *Graceland*'s title track was released as a single after the eligibility period for 1986's nominations had passed, it was competing for 1987's top platter prize, even though the song was considered old news and its bid regarded as a fluke. Sizing up the contest, *Billboard* noted, "This is the first year that all five of the acts nominated in the Record of the Year category have rock credentials." U2 was favored. Vega was called the dark horse to watch.

Then came what *Variety* called the night's chief "jolt" — the winner was "Graceland," a song described by the *L.A. Times* as "a highly regarded reflection on the search for inner peace." Simon now had the most triumphs ever scored in the top category (three), following his previous victories in 1968 for "Mrs. Robinson" and in 1970 for "Bridge Over Troubled Water," both with his former partner Art Garfunkel. The reaction to the success of "Graceland" was hardly jubilant, however.

Calling the result "a major surprise," *The Washington Post* added, "Though widely admired as an album cut, the single never got off the ground. It peaked at No. 81 on the Hot 100, marking the first time that a Record of the Year winner has failed to crack the Top 40 .... Since Simon was in Brazil, his absence and the crowd's tepid response to the award sounded a disconcertingly sour note."

The fact that U2 was favored to take the prize was strange, considering that foreigners seldom did well in the top award categories. Nearly 90 percent of the past winners of Record, Song, or Album of the Year had been Americans. The sole exceptions over 30 years of Grammy history were the Beatles, Bee Gees, Sting, Phil Collins, Joao Gilberto, and Domenico Modugno. Now U2 joined their ranks by reaping the Album of the Year prize for *The Joshua Tree* as a consolation for its loss of Record of the Year — and also picked up the best rock group vocal performance laurels, too, for the LP.

Presenter Little Richard stunned the audience, ranting, "You never gave me no Grammys and I've been singing for years!"

Until recently, the former Irish pub band had been considered "the largest underground act in the world," according to its manager. *Time* magazine said in a 1987 cover story that its members seemed "to be citizens of some alternative time frame spliced from the ideal of the '60s and the musical free-for-all of the late '70s. Their songs have the phantom soul of the Band, the Celtic wonderment of their compatriot Van Morrison, and some of the assertiveness of punk, refined into lyrical morality plays." Their triumphant album *The Joshua Tree* (named after the California desert town where 1970s country rocker Gram Parsons died; the actual gnarled tree, like its Biblical namesake hero, is reputed to point the way to the Promised Land) received passionate critical praise and sold 4.5 million copies as of Grammy night. When U2 won its rock group trophy, it was "to thunderous applause," reported the *L.A. Herald Examiner*.

Then U2's The Edge [guitarist David Evans] grew solemn as he accepted the honor, the paper added, "thanking Bishop Tutu, Martin Luther King, and the alternative rock programming of college radio where U2 first received major airplay." The newspaper was only giving its readers a bit of Evans's "bit of a list." He also thanked, among others, Bob Dylan, Walt Disney, John the Baptist, Jimi Hendrix, Dr. Ruth Westheimer, Morris the Cat, Flannery O'Connor, Batman and Robin, "sumo wrestlers throughout the world, and, of course, Ronald Reagan."

"We set out to make music — soul music," Bono (vocalist Paul Hewson) added. "Soul music is not about being black or white or whether you use a drum machine. It's a decision to reveal and not conceal." He also made reference to the band's reputation for being politically outspoken, at first with a joke: "It really is hard to carry the weight of the world on your shoulders ... [saving] the whales ... organizing summit meetings between world leaders, but we enjoy our work." He then turned politically relevant: "It's hard, however, when 50 million people are watching not to take the opportunity to talk about things like South Africa, what's happening there."

U2 was also nominated for Song of

the Year but came up against another one of those shockers. "Also startling," said *Variety*, "was presentation of Song of the Year honors to 'Somewhere Out There,'" a tune from the animated film *An American Tail*, produced by Steven Spielberg, about 19th-century Russian mice immigrating to the U.S.A. "Somewhere" earned prizes for first-time winning songwriters James Horner, Barry Mann, and Cynthia Weil. The tune had recently lost its bid for the Oscar's Best Song of 1986 to *Top Gun*'s "Take My Breath Away," but made up for it with the additional Grammy for Best Song Written Specifically for a Motion Picture or Television. *The*

After being excluded from competing for Best New Artist in 1985 and losing best LP this year, Whitney Houston proved a winner as best female pop singer.

Washington Post observed a lack of enthusiasm over its chief victory as Song of the Year, though, over U2's "I Still Haven't Found What I'm Looking For," Suzanne Vega's "Luka," and others: "It didn't seem to be a popular choice with the crowd, which greeted the announcement with but a smattering of polite applause."

The biggest surprise of the night occurred when the often outrageous rock legend Little Richard joined Buster Poindexter (a.k.a. David Johansen, former member of the punk group the New York Dolls) as a presenter of the year's Best New Artist prize. After he opened the envelope and saw the winner's name, Little Richard delayed the news to tease the audience, saying, "And the winner is ... me!" He then launched into a tirade that was part playful and part serious, shouting, "I have never received nuthin'! You never gave me no Grammys and I've been singing for years! .... I am the *architect* of rock & roll! I am the *origi-*

nator!" Instead of a statuette, the Grammy crowd gave him a standing ovation and roared its approval. Backstage later, Little Richard said, "I am not bitter, but I would like to have one to look at."

The award's real winner turned out to be former *Soul Train* dancer Jody Watley, who was also the lead vocalist for Shalamar from 1977 to 1984 and now had such solo hits as "Looking for a New Love," which landed at number 20 in 1987's Hot 100. When she accepted the award, the *Post* noted that she "thanked God after her label MCA and her manager, but before her video director and her attorney."

Album of the Year loser Whitney Houston thanked "Almighty God" first of all when she accepted the trophy for best pop vocals for her fourth number-one single, "I Wanna Dance with Somebody (Who Loves Me)." She then mentioned her record company and its founder, Clive Davis. "I love you, Clive!" she cried. "I love you, Arista!"

Backstage, she made a sly reference to her current hit single when she told reporters, "I can't tell you how I feel. It's ... *so emotional*!" Her producer, Narada Michael Walden, who was also hailed as 1987's top producer on *Billboard*'s year-end chart, took the prize for Producer of the Year. Walden was such a popular choice that rival nominee Quincy Jones (for *Bad*) even told Walden that he'd voted for him, too.

Clips from Sting's critically acclaimed "rockumentary" *Bring on the Night* won a video award last year. Now the album release earned him the male pop singing statuette, although he was not present at the ceremony to accept it.

Winners of the duo or group singing kudos were on hand, however: former Righteous Brother Bill Medley and Jennifer Warnes for the Oscar-winning song of 1987 "(I've Had) The Time of My Life," from the film *Dirty Dancing*, about a spoiled teenage girl's love affair with a dancer while at a summer resort in the 1960s.

Warnes won this same Grammy in 1982 for her duet with Joe Cocker in the Oscar-winning "Up Where We Belong," which was used in the film *An Officer and a Gentleman*. *Grammy Pulse* reminded its readers: "Bill Medley was nominated (his only one until this year) for a Grammy Award in 1964 [Best Rock & Roll Recording]. Then he was one-half of the Righteous Brothers and their song was 'You've Lost That Lovin' Feeling' (written incidentally by Barry Mann and Cynthia Weill)," authors of Song of the Year "Somewhere Out There." When accepting his statuette, Medley thanked God, too, "for 26 wonderful years." Backstage, he told reporters: "It's been a long way back for me and I'm grateful. I had a lot of voice problems for about 10 years starting in the 1970s that kept me out of the business. Now I'd like to get back and do some rock & roll, some rhythm & blues ... jump back in the fast lane and get to work, pay the rent."

Springsteen fans were upset that his *Tunnel of Love* wasn't up for 1987's Album of the Year, but The Boss still snagged an impressive four nominations. When he ended up with one award, for best rock vocal for *Tunnel*, he became the first male artist to win twice in the rock categories since they were introduced in 1979. Strangely, there was no award bestowed this year for best female rock singing because N.A.R.A.S. said there weren't enough eligible entries.

One of Springsteen's three losing bids was for Best Rock Instrumental Performance, which was claimed by an electric rocker who loved to shock his fans with outrageous titles like "Why Does It Hurt When I Pee?" Frank Zappa's victorious work was *Jazz from Hell*, which he discussed with *The Cleveland Plain Dealer* one week before the Grammycast: "My nomination must have been an accident. Either that or a lot of people have a perverse sense of humor. I'm convinced that nobody ever heard [it]. I have no ambiguous feelings about the Grammys at all. I know they're fake. I find it difficult to believe that Whitney Houston is the answer to all of America's music needs."

Another veteran music great won his first Grammy when Smokey Robinson nabbed an r&b performance prize, thereby making up for having been overlooked — along with all other Motown artists, except the Temptations — by N.A.R.A.S. voters throughout the 1960s when he first gained fame with the Miracles. Robinson struck out on a solo career in 1972. He often wrote his own material, including the 1970 classic hit "Tears of a Clown," and was once called the best living poet in America by Bob Dylan. Ironically, Robinson earned his only Grammy to date for a single he didn't compose, "Just to See Her," a losing nominee for Best Rhythm & Blues Song written by Jimmy George and Lou Pardini. The victorious song turned out to be "Lean on Me" by Bill Withers — "15 years after it was first a hit," noted *Billboard*. (The song qualified for an award this year since it failed to be nominated for any in the past and there was a new recording this year, by Club Nouveau.) It was the third time Withers had won, setting a new Grammy record in the r&b category

Aretha Franklin set a new record, too, by becoming the female artist with the most Grammys (surpassing Leontyne Price's tally of 13) when she picked up two more for her album *Aretha* to bring her career total to 14. It was the eleventh time she won the female r&b slot, and a track she shared with George Michael, "I Knew You Were Waiting (for Me)," earned them both the duo/group prize. Michael had had the number one song in 1985's Hot 100 ("Careless Whisper") and again in 1987 ("Faith"), but his soul credits were dubious prior to his successful matchup with "Lady Soul." He said in a statement issued after the Grammycast: "Winning the r&b category with Aretha validates the tremendous influence r&b music has had on my music, songwriting, and creative process. Not bad for a Brit with soul."

Alto sax player David Sanborn had won three jazz Grammys in the past, but, like George Michael, also insisted that his music was heavily tinged with r&b. The proof came when he scored the r&b instrumental accolade for "Chicago Song."

Lots of jazz artists competed outside the jazz category this year. Sanborn, for example, beat fellow saxmen Stanley Turrentine and Najee to win in the r&b slot for "Chicago Song." Larry Carlton, noted *Billboard*, "is almost certainly the first musician in Grammy history to cop nominations in the jazz, fusion, and pop-instrumental categories in one year." (He ended up with the pop instrumental kudos for "Minute by Minute," topping fellow jazzmen Dave Grusin and Chick Corea.) The fusion award went to three-time past winner the Pat Metheny Group for *Still Life (Talking)*, over both Sanborn and Carlton. Trumpeter Wynton Marsalis came back, too, when *Marsalis Standard Time — Volume 1* brought him his eighth award in just five years.

Diane Schuur nabbed the female vocals award for a second consecutive year when she won for an album that had topped the jazz chart for nearly four months prior to Grammys night — *Diane Schuur & the Count Basie Orchestra*, also winner of an arrangement trophy. Mercer Ellington

Surprised rock contender Frank Zappa said, "My nomination must have been an accident."

and the Duke Ellington Orchestra seized the big band laurels for *Digital Duke*. Mercer had been the band's leader since his father's death in 1974.

At last year's Grammys, Bobby McFerrin won the male vocals award for his contribution to the film *'Round Midnight,* starring Dexter Gordon. A follow-up recording, *The Other Side of 'Round Midnight*, again rewarded McFerrin with the singing prize while Gordon himself was also honored with the instrumental soloist trophy. The album became the most lauded musical work of the year when it won a third award for composers Herbie Hancock, Wayne Shorter, Ron Carter, and Billy Higgins. *Billboard* objected to it early on when the full list of 1987's contenders was first announced: "The oddest nomination —

possibly of all time — for Best Instrumental Composition is 'Call Sheet Blues' from the *The Other Side of 'Round Midnight* soundtrack, which is not really a composition at all, but a spontaneously improvised blues [session]." *'Round Midnight* was the title of an original music work by Thelonious Monk, who died in 1982. Monk had recorded exclusively on the Riverside label between 1955 and 1961. The complete set of his Riverside recordings was named Best Historical Album and also won Best Album Notes.

The country categories welcomed "heathen" K.T. Oslin and Randy Travis, a surprise loser last year.

Reed player, composer, and teacher Yusef Lateef turned 76 this year and finally won his first Grammy. *Yusef Lateef's Little Symphony* was named Best New Age Performance instead of being honored in a jazz slot where some critics said it belonged. The nonjazz classification made some sense: Lateef's work was infused with strong Middle Eastern influences and he always objected to being labeled a jazzman despite his long career association with the genre and its greats, including Dizzy Gillespie and Cannonball Adderley. Accepting his prize, the veteran artist noted, "I've been at this 50 years this month!"

K.T. Oslin was described as a "veteran newcomer" by *The Washington Post* when the 45-year-old singer snagged the country vocals accolade for the title track to her debut album *80's Ladies*. (The LP features three types of women for the decade: "the smart one, the pretty one, and the borderline fool," in the words of one RCA official.) Prior to her solo LP, Oslin had worked on the periphery of the limelight doing backup vocals and other side work. Accepting her first Grammy, she invoked God and called herself "a heathen," saying, "He didn't have a lot of time to personally supervise me."

Though defeated last year, Randy Travis came back to claim the male singing laurels for *Always & Forever*, his megahit album that spent 43 weeks at the top of *Billboard*'s country LP chart and then became the first country album to crack the top 20 of the pop rankings since Kenny Rogers's *Eyes That See in the Dark* did so in 1983. Accepting his prize, the one-time Nashville cook and dishwasher said, "The Grammy was the farthest thing from my mind when I got into the music business. I never thought about winning one."

Travis was the artist who sang this year's Best Country Song, which was so popular that it was also hailed as Single of the Year by the Country Music Association and the Academy of Country Music: "Forever and Ever, Amen," by Paul Overstreet and Don Schlitz. Schlitz had won the same songwriting Grammy nine years earlier when he scripted "The Gambler," which became a standard for Kenny Rogers. Only two other songwriters had won the category twice: Roger Miller and Billy Sherrill.

Kenny Rogers hadn't won a Grammy

himself in eight years, but now he rallied to score a victory he shared with Ronnie Milsap in the new category of Best Duet Country Vocal Performance for "Make No Mistake, She's Mine." The tune was written by 1981 Record of the Year singer Kim Carnes ("Bette Davis Eyes"; Carnes and Rogers first worked together when they were both members of the New Christy Minstrels), who used "He's" instead of "She's" when she and Barbra Streisand recorded the original version in 1985. Soon thereafter, Rogers was touring with Milsap and needed a song they could sing together, so he picked "Mistake" and cleared the gender switch with Carnes.

"To no one's surprise, long-time-getting-around-to-that-project and longer-time friends Dolly Parton, Linda Ronstadt, and Emmylou Harris took the group vocal Grammy for *Trio*," reported *The Washington Post*, noting that the LP "also crossed over into the Album of the Year category." The *L.A. Times* described *Trio* as "a warm and endearing collection of country-flavored tunes."

Asleep at the Wheel had been asleep at the Grammys after 1978 when they last won the same award they took this year for "String of Pars" (best country instrumental). "It feels great. It feels amazing," band member Ray Benson said. "It's like you've been down 10 to nothing in the ninth inning — and winning. When we won our first Grammy [in 1978 for 'One O'Clock Jump'], we were working in a bar in Texas and hadn't got paid for the evening. Then the news came over the radio that we'd won. It's sometimes difficult keeping a band together. We are the Grateful Dead of country music."

The Grammys for religious performances went to a number of past winners, including Al Green ("Everything's Gonna Be Alright") and Larnelle Harris (*The Father Hath Provided*). Deniece Williams won two last year, but reaped only one in 1987 for "I Believe in You." Newcomers included Southern rocker Myron LeFevre & Broken Heart for *Crack the Sky*.

It was returning brother-sister champs, the Winans, who made the big news in the categories by scoring two victories, including the group soul gospel prize for the single "Ain't No Need to Worry," which was overseen by Grammy's Producer of the Year Narada Michael Walden and sung by the Winans along with Anita Baker. "They worked side by side kicking each other and just pushing it and made it happen," Walden told *Billboard* about their collaboration. When CeCe Winans also garnered the Grammy for female soul gospel vocals, she said,

> *"I've been at this 50 years this month!" said New Age winner Yusef Lateef.*

"Thank you, Jesus, number one. He is wonderful. He is my life."

"First of all, I thank God and then Paul Simon," said Joseph Shalalala, founder of the black South African a cappella group Ladysmith Black Mambazo, when he accepted the statuette for Best Traditional Folk Recording *Shaka Zulu*. Simon showcased the group on *Graceland* and produced *Shaka Zulu*.

Folk/county singer and guitarist Steve Goodman died of leukemia in 1984 (the same year he won Best Country Song for "City of New Orleans"), leaving behind *Unfinished Business*, which garnered Best Contemporary Folk Recording when it was released three years later. New Orleans music guru Professor Longhair passed away in 1980 but now won the traditional blues prize for *Houseparty New Orleans Style*.

Robert Cray shared the traditional blues award last year but now alone picked up the equivalent trophy for contemporary recordings for *Strong Persuader*. Jimmy Sturr & His Orchestra also tied for a Grammy last year, but claimed the Best Polka Recording trophy by themselves for *A Polka Just for Me*. "This is our 62nd album," Sturr said upon accepting it. "We started recording in Nashville 10 years ago. Before that we worked in New York and there's no question about it. Nashville helped our sound."

> *"Whoever thought anyone would feel sorry for Michael Jackson, especially at the Grammy Awards?"*

A third winner was honored posthumously when Peter Tosh's *No Nuclear War* was named Best Reggae Recording. Critics considered Tosh's music truer to the historic reggae sound than work by fellow Jamaican Bob Marley, although Tosh was frequently applauded for his daring fusion experiments like those on his triumphant LP .

The "Spanish Sinatra" Julio Iglesias had gained such an enormous worldwide following as of 1987 that he was listed in the *Guinness Book of World Records* as being the world's most popular recording artist, having sold 100 million copies of 60 albums in five languages. Iglesias proved popular with N.A.R.A.S. voters, too, when won his only career Grammy, Best Latin Pop Performance, for *Un Hombre Solo*. Los Tigres del Norte snared the Mexican/American laurels for *¡Gracias! America Sin Fronteras,* while five-time past winner Eddie Palmieri was hailed for Best Tropical Latin Performance (*La Verdad, The Truth*).

When the original Broadway version of *Les Miserables* was named Best Musical Cast Show Album, it was considered surprising for more than just the fact that critics had preferred a recording of the earlier London production: It beat odds-on favorite *The Phantom of the Opera* (London cast) by Andrew Lloyd Webber, who had won four previous Grammys. Also shocking was that 15-time past champ John Williams lost the film score laurels, as did fellow Grammy veteran Henry Mancini, to Ennio Morricone for his music to director Brian De Palma's film adaptation of the popular 1960s TV series *The Untouchables*.

Garrison Keillor had established himself as a superstar on the radio by spinning engaging yarns about the sleepy but sometimes scandalous goings-on in his fictitious Lake Wobegon, Minnesota. Keillor had recently canceled the show after 13 years on the air, but, when excerpts were collected onto a disc (and published in a bestselling book), *Lake Wobegon Day* was voted Best Spoken Word Recording.

Winner of 1979's Best Comedy Recording (*Reality ... What a Concept*) Robin Williams made a comeback with *A Night at the Met*. But Williams wasn't on hand to claim the statuette himself, so it was acceped for him by low-key comedian Steven Wright, who told the Grammy audience, "He couldn't be here, so we'll go look for him."

For the second year in a row, a recording by Vladimir Horowitz won both Classical Album of the Year and the laurels for best instrumental soloist. The pianist's latest victories were for *Horowitz in Moscow*, an historic recording of the virtuoso's triumphant return to the land of his birth after an absence of more than 60 years. When he also accepted a President's Special Merit Award from the academy, *The Washing-*

ton *Post* noted, "Horowitz looked somewhat dazed by his gaudy surroundings, saying in his still-thick Russian accent, 'Thank you, thank you very much. I am so very happy that classical music still has an appreciation.' When he won the album award, he simply smiled and carried it away, saying nothing."

"Horowitz's double victory brings his Grammy total to 22, a number topped only by one artist — Sir Georg Solti," *Billboard* noted. Solti picked up one more award this year, bringing his tally to 26, for *Beethoven: Symphony No. 9 in D Minor* as the year's Best Orchestral Recording. Solti and the Chicago Symphony gave the classic a slower-than-usual reading, which the critics applauded for its qualities of spaciousness.

Recordings taped over a five-year period of Beethoven's piano trios earned Itzhak Perlman, Lynn Harrel, and Vladimir Ashkenazy the chamber music prize. Perlman claimed a second Grammy when his *Mozart: Violin Concertos Nos. 2 and 4 in D* brought him the soloist award for orchestral accompaniment.

At the end of World War II, conductor Robert Shaw commissioned Paul Hindemith to compose a requiem for those who had died during the conflict. Taking his title from Walt Whitman's classic poem memorializing the slain Abraham Lincoln, Hindemith responded with *When Lilacs Last in the Dooryard Bloom'd (A Requiem for Those We Love)*, a performance of which earned Shaw and his Altanta Symphony Orchestra and Chorus the Grammy for Best Choral Performance.

Kathleen Battle won two awards when Richard Strauss's *Ariadne auf Naxos* was hailed as Best Opera Recording (Battle gave an "excellent" performance as Zerbinetta, said the critics) and her *Salzburg Recital* earned her the soloist vocal kudos.

The year's Best Contemporary Composition was Cello Concerto No. 2 by Polish composer Krzysztof Penderecki, who had recently "returned to melody," as he once put it, describing his break with the more avant-garde experimentations of his earlier years.

The Grammys returned to New York after a six-year absence for its 30th annual ceremony, which was held at Radio City Music Hall. Once again the Big Apple welcomed the gala with a warm reception that included a party for the nominees at the mayor's Gracie Mansion. Also, noted the *N.Y. Times*, "During the broadcast, the Spectacolor computerized billboard in Times Square flashed award winners' names moments after the onstage announcements. Police officers ringed the Music Hall as a red carpet was rolled up the Avenue of the Americas."

"The biggest surprise of the night," said *The Washington Post*, "was that Michael Jackson was shut out in all four categories in which he had been nominated." *Bad* nonetheless won Best Engineered Recording for its sound technicians and Jackson proved to be the night's most startling entertainment when he performed a blockbuster rendition of "Man in the Mirror." "For more than nine minutes of prime-time television, he revealed himself," the *L.A. Times* wrote. "Jackson moved with a sensual resolve and urgent desire that pleaded for approval and respect.

"Whoever thought anyone would feel sorry for Michael Jackson — especially at the Grammy Awards show?" the paper added. But "moments after being bathed in applause for one of the most striking performances ever by a pop performer on national television, Jackson, an intensely private person, had to sit in full view of millions as he suffered one humiliating defeat after another .... He couldn't have looked any more heartbroken if someone had just run away with his pet chimp."

The awards ceremony was broadcast on CBS from New York's Radio City Music Hall on March 2, 1988, for the awards eligibility period of October 1, 1986, to September 30, 1987.

ALBUM OF THE YEAR
• *The Joshua Tree*, U2. Daniel Lanois, Brian Eno, producers. Island.
Bad, Michael Jackson. Quincy Jones, Michael Jackson, producers. Epic.
Sign O' the Times, Prince. Prince, producer. Paisley Park.
Trio, Dolly Parton, Linda Ronstadt, Emmylou Harris. George Massenburg, producer. Warner Bros.
Whitney, Whitney Houston. Narada Michael Walden, producer. Arista.

RECORD OF THE YEAR
• "Graceland," Paul Simon. Paul Simon, producer. Warner Bros.
"Back in the High Life Again," Steve Winwood. Russ Titelman, Steve Winwood, producers. Island.
"I Still Haven't Found What I'm Looking For," U2. Daniel Lanois, Brian Eno, producers. Island.
"La Bamba," Los Lobos. Mitchell Froom, producer. Slash.
"Luka," Suzanne Vega. Steve Addabbo, Lenny Kaye, producers. A&M.

SONG OF THE YEAR
(Songwriter's Award)
• "Somewhere Out There," James Horner, Barry Mann, Cynthia Weil. MCA Music Publishing (ASCAP/BMI), publishers. MCA.
"Didn't We Almost Have It All," Michael Masser, Will Jennings. Prince Street Music (ASCAP), Willin' David Music (BMI), Blue Sky Riders Songs (BMI), publishers. Arista.
"I Still Haven't Found What I'm Looking For," U2. Chappell Music/U2 (ASCAP), publishers. Island.
"La Bamba," adapted by Ritchie Valens. Picture Our Music (BMI) c/o Warner-Tamerlane Publishing Corp. within the U.S. and Screen Gems-EMI Music Inc. (BMI) outside the U.S., publishers. A&M.
"Luka," Suzanne Vega. Waifersongs Ltd./AGF Music Ltd. (ASCAP), publishers. A&M.

SECURITY PACIFIC COLLECTION/ L.A. PUBLIC LIBRARY

Bruce Springsteen's second rock vocals Grammy was for his Tunnel of Love *LP.*

BEST NEW ARTIST
• Jody Watley
Breakfast Club
Cutting Crew
Terence Trent D'Arby
Swing Out Sister

BEST POP VOCAL PERFORMANCE, MALE
• Sting, *Bring on the Night*. A&M.
Michael Jackson, *Bad*. Epic.
Al Jarreau, *"Moonlighting* Theme." MCA.
Elton John, "Candle in the Wind." MCA.
Bruce Springsteen, "Brilliant Disguise." Columbia/CBS.

BEST POP VOCAL PERFORMANCE, FEMALE
• Whitney Houston, "I Wanna Dance With Somebody (Who Loves Me)." Arista.
✓ Belinda Carlisle, "Heaven Is a Place on Earth." MCA.
Carly Simon, *Coming Around Again*. Arista.
Barbra Streisand, *One Voice*. Columbia/CBS.
✓ Suzanne Vega, "Luka." A&M.

BEST POP PERFORMANCE BY A DUO OR GROUP WITH VOCAL
• Bill Medley, Jennifer Warnes, "(I've Had) The Time of My Life," track from *Dirty Dancing*. BMG Music/RCA.
✓ Heart, "Alone." Capitol.
Los Lobos, "La Bamba." Slash.
Linda Ronstadt, James Ingram, "Somewhere Out There." MCA.
Swing Out Sister, "Breakout." Mercury.

BEST POP INSTRUMENTAL PERFORMANCE
• Larry Carlton, "Minute by Minute." MCA.
Herb Alpert, *Keep Your Eye On Me* (instrumental tracks only). A&M.
Art of Noise, "Dragnet," track from *In No Sense? Nonsense!* China/Chrysalis.
Chick Corea Elektric Band, "Light Years," track from *Light Years*. GRP.
Dave Grusin, "It Might Be You," track from *Cinemagic*. GRP.

BEST ROCK VOCAL PERFORMANCE, SOLO
✓• Bruce Springsteen, *Tunnel of Love*. Columbia/CBS.
Joe Cocker, "Unchain My Heart." Capitol.
✓ Richard Marx, "Don't Mean Nothing." Manhattan.
Bob Seger, "Shakedown." MCA.
Tina Turner, "Better Be Good to Me," track from *The Prince's Trust 10th Anniversary Birthday Party*. A&M.

BEST ROCK PERFORMANCE BY A DUO OR GROUP WITH VOCAL
✓• U2, *The Joshua Tree*. Island.
Georgia Satellites, "Keep Your Hands to Yourself." Elektra.
✓ Heart, *Bad Animals*. Capitol.
Los Lobos, *By the Light of the Moon*. Slash.
Yes, *Big Generator*. Atco.

BEST ROCK INSTRUMENTAL PERFORMANCE (ORCHESTRA, GROUP, OR SOLOIST)
• Frank Zappa, *Jazz from Hell*. Barking Pumpkin.
Herbie Hancock, Dweezil Zappa, Terry Bozzio, "Wipe Out," track from *Back to the Beach* soundtrack. Columbia/CBS.
✓ Bruce Springsteen & the E Street Band, "Paradise by the 'C,'" track from *Live 1975–85*. Columbia/CBS.
Stevie Ray Vaughan, Dick Dale, "Pipeline." Columbia/CBS.
Stevie Ray Vaughan & Double Trouble, "Say What!" track from *Live Alive*. Epic.

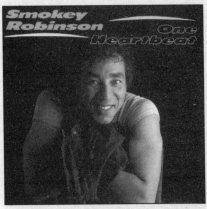

MOTOWN

Smokey Robinson's only Grammy so far was an r&b trophy for "Just to See Her."

BEST RHYTHYM & BLUES SONG
(Songwriter's Award)
• "Lean on Me," Bill Withers. Interior Music, publisher. King Jay/Warner Bros.
"Casanova," Reggie Calloway. Calloco Music, Hip Trip Music (BMI), publishers. Atlantic.
"Just to See Her," Jimmy George, Lou Pardini. Unicity Music Inc., Lucky Break Music, Lars Music (ASCAP), publishers. Motown.
"Skeletons," Stevie Wonder. Jobete Music Co. Inc., Black Bull Music Inc. (ASCAP), publishers. Motown.
✓ "U Got the Look," Prince. Controversy Music (ASCAP), publisher. Paisley Park.

Best Rhythm & Blues Vocal Performance, Male
• Smokey Robinson, "Just to See Her." Motown.
Jonathan Butler, "Lies." Jive.
Michael Jackson, "Bad." Epic.
Wilson Pickett, "In the Midnight Hour," track from *American Soul Man*. Motown.
Stevie Wonder, "Skeletons." Motown.

Best Rhythm & Blues Vocal Performance, Female
• Aretha Franklin, *Aretha*. Arista.
Natalie Cole, *Everlasting*. Manhattan.
Whitney Houston, "For the Love of You," track from *Whitney*. Arista.
✓ Jody Watley, "Looking for a New Love." MCA.
Nancy Wilson, *Forbidden Lover*. Columbia/CBS.

Best Rhythm & Blues Performance by a Duo or Group with Vocal
✓ • Aretha Franklin, George Michael, "I Knew You Were Waiting (for Me)," track from *Aretha*. Arista.
LeVert, *Casanova*. Atlantic.
Club Nouveau, "Lean on Me." King Jay/Warner Bros.
✓ Prince, Sheena Easton, "U Got the Look." Paisley Park.
Whispers, "Rock Steady." Solar/Elektra.

Best Rhythm & Blues Instrumental Performance (Orchestra, Group, or Soloist)
• David Sanborn, "Chicago Song." Warner Bros.
Herb Alpert, "Diamonds" instrumental version. A&M.
Jonathan Butler, "Going Home," track from *Jonathan Butler*. Jive.
Najee, *Najee's Theme*. EMI-America.
Stanley Turrentine, "Boogie on Reggae Woman," track from *Wonderland*. Blue Note.

Best Jazz Vocal Performance, Male
•Bobby McFerrin, "What Is This Thing Called Love," track from *The Other Side of 'Round Midnight*. Blue Note.
Billy Eckstine, *Billy Eckstine Sings with Billy Carter*. Emarcy.
Dave Frishberg, *Can't Take You Nowhere*. Fantasy.

Arthur Prysock, *This Guy's in Love with You*. Milestone.
Joe Williams, *Every Night*. Verve.

Best Jazz Vocal Performance, Female
• Diane Schuur, *Diane Schuur & the Count Basie Orchestra*. GRP.
Ella Fitzgerald, *Easy Living*. Pablo.
Carmen McRae, *Any Old Time*. Denon.
Janis Siegel, *At Home*. Atlantic.
Sarah Vaughan, *Brazilian Romance*. FM.

Best Jazz Instrumental Performance, Soloist
• Dexter Gordon, *The Other Side of 'Round Midnight*. GRP.
Michael Brecker, *Michael Brecker*. MCA/Impulse.
Eddie Daniels, *To Bird with Love*. GRP.
Branford Marsalis, "Cottontail," track from *Digital Duke* (Duke Ellington Orchestra album). GRP.
Wynton Marsalis, *Marsalis Standard Time, Vol. I*. Columbia/CBS.

Best Jazz Instrumental Performance, Group
• Wynton Marsalis, *Marsalis Standard Time, Volume I*. Columbia/CBS.
Michael Brecker, *Michael Brecker*. MCA/Impulse.
Larry Carlton, *Last Nite*. MCA.
Chick Corea, Miroslav Vitous, Roy Haynes, *Trio Music, Live in Europe*. FCM.
Eddie Daniels, *To Bird with Love*. GRP.

Best Jazz Instrumental Performance, Big Band
• Duke Ellington Orchestra conducted by Mercer Ellington, *Digital Duke*. GRP.
Louis Bellson & His Jazz Orchestra, *Louis Bellson & His Jazz Orchestra*. Musicmasters.
Woody Herman & His Big Band, *Woody's Gold Star*. Concord Jazz.
The Tonight Show Band with Doc Severinsen, *The Tonight Show Band with Doc Severinsen Volume II*. Amherst.
Patrick Williams's New York Band, *10th Avenue*. Soundwings.

BEST JAZZ FUSION PERFORMANCE, VOCAL, OR INSTRUMENTAL
• Pat Metheny Group, *Still Life (Talking)*. Geffen.
George Benson, Earl Klugh, *Collaboration*. Warner Bros.
Larry Carlton, *Discovery*. MCA.
David Sanborn, *A Change of Heart*. Warner Bros.
Yellowjackets, *Four Corners*. MCA.

BEST COUNTRY SONG
(Songwriter's Award)
✓• "Forever and Ever, Amen," Paul Overstreet, Don Schlitz. Writers Group Music, Scarlet Moon Music (BMI), MCA Publishing, Don Schlitz Music (ASCAP), publishers. Warner Bros.
✓ "All My Ex's Live in Texas," Sanger D. Shafer, Lyndia J. Shafer. Acuff-Rose-Opryland Music Inc. (BMI), publisher. MCA.
"80's Ladies," K.T. Oslin. Wooden Wonder Music (SESAC), publisher. BMG Music/RCA.
"I'll Still Be Loving You," Mary Ann Kennedy, Pat Bunch, Pam Rose. Todd Cerney (ASCAP), publisher. BMG Music/RCA.
"Tellin' Me Lies," Linda Thompson, Betsy Cook. Chappell Music (ASCAP), Firesign Music Ltd. (PRS), publishers. Warner Bros.

BEST COUNTRY VOCAL PERFORMANCE, MALE
• Randy Travis, *Always & Forever*. Warner Bros.
✓ George Strait, "All My Ex's Live in Texas." MCA.
Hank Williams Jr., *Born to Boogie*. Curb/Warner Bros.
Steve Earle, *Exit O*. MCA.
Dwight Yoakam, *Hillbilly Deluxe*. Reprise.

BEST COUNTRY VOCAL PERFORMANCE, FEMALE
• K.T. Oslin, "80's Ladies," track from *80's Ladies*. BMG Music/RCA.
Rosanne Cash, *King's Record Shop*. Columbia/CBS.
Emmylou Harris, *Angel Band*. Warner Bros.
Reba McEntire, "The Last One to Know." MCA.
Tanya Tucker, "Love Me Like You Used To." Capitol.

BEST COUNTRY PERFORMANCE BY A DUO OR GROUP WITH VOCAL
• Dolly Parton, Linda Ronstadt, Emmylou Harris, *Trio*. Warner Bros.
Desert Rose Band, *The Desert Rose Band*. MCA.
Judds, *Heartland*. BMG Music/RCA.
O'Kanes, "Can't Stop My Heart from Loving You." Columbia/CBS.
Restless Heart, "I'll Still Be Loving You," track from *Wheels*. BMG Music/RCA.

BEST COUNTRY VOCAL PERFORMANCE, DUET
✓• Ronnie Milsap, Kenny Rogers, "Make No Mistake, She's Mine." BMG Music/RCA.
Glen Campbell, Emmylou Harris, "You Are," track from *Still Within the Sound of My Voice*. MCA.
Glen Campbell, Steve Wariner, "The Hand That Rocks the Cradle." MCA.
Crystal Gayle, Gary Morris, "Another World." Warner Bros.
Michael Martin Murphey, Holly Dunn, "A Face in the Crowd." Warner Bros.

BEST COUNTRY INSTRUMENTAL PERFORMANCE (ORCHESTRA, GROUP, OR SOLOIST)
• Asleep at the Wheel, "String of Pars," track from *Asleep at the Wheel*. Epic.
Jerry Douglas, *Changing Channels*. MCA Master Series.
Stephane Grappelli, Vassar Clements, *Together at Last* (cassette). Flying Fish.
Albert Lee, *Gagged But Not Bound*. MCA.
Bill Monroe, "The Old Brown Country Barn," track from *Bluegrass '87*. MCA.

BEST GOSPEL PERFORMANCE, MALE
• Larnelle Harris, *The Father Hath Provided*. Benson.
Steve Green, *Joy to the World*. Sparrow.
Dallas Holm, *Against the Wind*. Dayspring/Word.
Leon Patillo, *Brand New*. Sparrow.
Wayne Watson, *Watercolour Ponies*. Dayspring/Word.

BEST GOSPEL PERFORMANCE, FEMALE
• Deniece Williams, "I Believe in You," track from *Water Under the Bridge*. Columbia/CBS.
Debby Boone, "The Name Above All Names," track from *Friends for Life*. Benson.

Terri Gibbs, "Turnaround." Canaan/Word.
Debbie McClendon, "Count It All Joy." Star Song.
Kathy Troccoli, "Images." Reunion.

BEST GOSPEL PERFORMANCE BY A DUO, GROUP, CHOIR, OR CHORUS

• Myron LeFevre & Broken Heart, *Crack the Sky*. Myrrh/Word.
Bill Gaither Trio, *Welcome Back Home*. Star Song.
Mr. Mister, "Healing Waters," track from *Go On*. BMG Music/RCA.
Petra, *This Means War!* Star Song.
Stryper, *To Hell with the Devil*. Enigma.

BEST SOUL GOSPEL PERFORMANCE, MALE

• Al Green, "Everything's Gonna Be Alright," track from *Soul Survivor*. A&M.
Jessy Dixon, *The Winning Side*. Power Disc/Benson.
Wintley Phipps, *Wintley Phipps*. Word.
Keith Pringle, *All to You*. Muscle Shoals.
BeBe Winans, "Call Me," track from *BeBe and CeCe Winans*. Sparrow.

BEST SOUL GOSPEL PERFORMANCE, FEMALE

• CeCe Winans, "For Always," track from *BeBe and CeCe Winans*. Sparrow.
Shirley Caesar, "The Lord Will Make a Way," track from *Her Very Best*. Rejoice/Word.
Della Reese, "You Gave Me Love," track from *Della Reese & Brilliance*. Air.
Lynette Hawkins Stephens, *Baby Sis*. Birthright.
Vickie Winans, *Be Encouraged*. Light.

BEST SOUL GOSPEL PERFORMANCE BY A DUO, GROUP, CHOIR, OR CHORUS

• Winans, Anita Baker, "Ain't No Need to Worry." Qwest.
Clark Sisters, *Heart and Soul*. Rejoice/Word.
Edwin Hawkins & the Music and Arts Seminar Mass Choir, *Give Us Peace*. Birthright.
BeBe and CeCe Winans, *BeBe and CeCe Winans*. Sparrow.
Winans, *Decisions*. Qwest.

BEST TRADITIONAL BLUES RECORDING

• *Houseparty New Orleans Style*, Professor Longhair. Rounder.
Cold Snap, Albert Collins. Alligator.
Live from Chicago, an Audience with the Queen, Koko Taylor. Alligator.

"Old Maid Boogie," Eddie "Cleanhead" Vinson, track from *The Late Show* (Etta James album). Fantasy.
Take Me Back, James Cotton. Blind Pig.

BEST CONTEMPORARY BLUES RECORDING

• *Strong Persuader*, Robert Cray Band. Mercury/Hightone.
After All, Bobby Bland. Malaco.
Glazed, Earl King, Roomful of Blues. Black Top/ Rounder.
On a Night Like This, Buckwheat Zydecko. Island.
"Standing on the Edge of Love," B.B. King, track from *The Color of Money* soundtrack. MCA.

BEST TRADITIONAL FOLK RECORDING

• *Shaka Zulu*, Ladysmith Black Mambazo. Warner Bros.
Belizaire the Cajun, Michael Doucet, Beausoleil. Arhoolie.
Celtic Wedding, Chieftains. Red Seal.
Mbube Roots, Zulu Choral Music from South Africa, Bantu Glee Singers, Crocodiles, Shooting Stars, others. Veit Erlmann, producer. Rounder.
Zulu Men's Singing Competition, various artists. Helen Kivnick, Gary Gardner, producers. Rounder.

BEST CONTEMPORARY FOLK RECORDING

• *Unfinished Business*, Steve Goodman. Red Pajamas.
Annual Waltz, John Hartford. MCA.
"Asimbonanga," track from *Recently*, Joan Baez. Gold Castle.
More Love Songs, Loudon Wainwright III. Rounder.
The Washington Squares, Washington Squares. Gold Castle.

BEST LATIN POP PERFORMANCE

• Julio lgiesias, *Un Hombre Solo*. Discos CBS International.
Maria Conchita Alonso, "Otra Mentira Mas." A&M.
Braulio, "En Bancarrota," track from *Lo Bello y Lo Prohibido*. Discos CBS International.
Emmanuel, *Solo*. BMG Music/RCA.
José José, *Siempre Contigo*. Ariola.
Lunna, *Lunna*. A&M.
Luis Miguel, *Luis Miguel '87, Soy Como Quiero Ser*. WEA Latina.
Yolandita Monge, *Laberinto de Amor*. Discos CBS International.
Danny Rivera, *Amar o Morir*. DNA.

Best Tropical Latin Performance
• Eddie Palmieri, *La Verdad, The Truth*. Fania/Musica Latina International.
Ray Barretto, *Aqui Se Puede*. Fania/Musica Latina International.
Rubén Blades, *Agua de Luna (Moon Water)*. Elektra.
Caribbean Express, *Caribbean Express*. A&M.
Celia Cruz, Willie Colon, *The Winners*. Vaya/Musica Latina International.
Hector Lavoe, *Strikes Back*. Fania/Musica Latina International.

Best Mexican/American Performance
• Los Tigres del Norte, *¡Gracias! America Sin Fronteras*. Profono International.
Antonio Aguilar, *15 Exitos con Tambora Vol. 2*. Musart.
Chavela y su Grupo Express, *El Rey del Barrio*. Profono International.
Los Diablos, *Celebración*. Discos CBS International.
Little Joe, *Timeless*. Discos CBS International.

Best Reggae Recording
• *No Nuclear War*, Peter Tosh. EMI America.
Hold on to Love, Third World. Columbia/CBS.
People of the World, Burning Spear. Slash.
UB40 CCCP (Live in Moscow), UB40. A&M.

Best Polka Recording
• Jimmy Sturr & His Orchestra, *A Polka Just for Me*. Starr.
Eddie Blazonczyk's Versatones, *Let's Celebrate Again*. Bel Aire.
Lenny Gomulka, Dick Pillar, *In Polka Unity*. Steljo.
Walt Groller & His Orchestra, *It's Polkamatic*. Chalet.
Kryger Brothers, *Polka Mania*. Starr.

Best New Age Performance
• Yusef Lateef, *Yusef Lateef's Little Symphony*. Atlantic.
Paul Horn, *Traveler*. Golden Flute/Global Pacific.
Kitaro, "The Field," track from *The Light of the Spirit*. Geffen.
Montreux, "Sweet Intentions," track from *Sign Language*. Windham Hill.
Patrick O'Hearn, *Between Two Worlds*. Private Music.

Liz Story, "Reconciliation," track from *Part of Fortune*. Novus.

Best Instrumental Composition
• "Call Sheet Blues," track from *The Other Side of 'Round Midnight*, Dexter Gordon, Wayne Shorter, Herbie Hancock, Ron Carter, Billy Higgins. Warner-Tamerlane Publishing Corp./WBM Music Corp. (BMI-SESAC), publishers. Blue Note.
"The Blues in Three," track from *The Glass Menagerie*, Henry Mancini. Northridge/Cineplex Odeon, publisher. MCA.
Bolling: Suite No. 2 for Flute and Jazz Piano Trio, Claude Bolling. Claude Bolling, France, publisher. FM.
"Jazz from Hell," track from *Jazz from Hell*, Frank Zappa. Munchkin Music (ASCAP), Pumpko Industries Ltd., publishers. Barking Pumpkin.
"Minuano (Six Eight)," track from *Still Life (Talking)*. Pat Metheny, Lyle Mays. Pat-Meth Music, Lyle Mays Inc. (BMI), publishers. Geffen.

Best Arrangement on an Instrumental
• Bill Holman, "Take the 'A' Train," track from *The Tonight Show Band with Doc Severinsen, Volume II*. Amherst.
Jorge Calandrelli, (strings arranged by Jorge Calandrelli, Dori Caymmi, Christian Chevalier), "Any Time, Any Season," track from *Any Time, Any Season*. Innovation.
Michael Convertino, "Main Title," track from *Children of a Lesser God*. GNP/Crescendo.
Dave Grusin, "The Heart Is a Lonely Hunter," track from *Cinemagic*. GRP.
Patrick Williams, "Jive Samba," track from *10th Avenue*. Soundwings.

Best Musical Cast Show Album
• *Les Miserables* (Broadway cast), Herbert Kretzmer, lyricist. Claude-Michel Schonberg, composer. Alain Boublil, Claude-Michel Schonberg, producers. Geffen.
Me and My Girl (Broadway cast), L. Arthur Rose, Douglas Furber, lyricists. Noel Gay, composer. Thomas Z. Shepard, album producer.

My Fair Lady (Kiri Te Kanawa, Jeremy Irons, others), Alan Jay Lerner, lyricist. Frederick Loewe, composer. Paul Myers, album producer. London.

The Phantom of the Opera (London cast), Charles Hart with Richard Stilgoe, lyricists. Andrew Lloyd Webber, composer. Andrew Lloyd Webber, producer. Polydor.

South Pacific (Kiri Te Kanawa, José Carreras, others), Oscar Hammerstein II, lyricist. Richard Rodgers, composer. Jeremy Lubbock, producer. FM.

BEST ALBUM OF ORIGINAL INSTRUMENTAL BACKGROUND SCORE WRITTEN FOR A MOTION PICTURE OR TELEVISION

• *The Untouchables* (motion picture soundtrack), Ennio Morricone, composer. Famous Music Corp. (ASCAP), publisher. A&M.

An American Tail (motion picture soundtrack), James Horner, composer. Various publishers. MCA.

The Glass Menagerie (motion picture soundtrack), Henry Mancini, composer. MCA.

The Princess Bride (motion picture soundtrack), Mark Knopfler, composer. Chariscourt Ltd., all rights administered by Almo Music Corp. (ASCAP), publisher. Warner Bros.

The Witches of Eastwick (motion picture soundtrack), John Williams, composer. Warner Tamerlane, publisher. John Williams, conductor. Warner Bros.

BEST SONG WRITTEN SPECIFICALLY FOR A MOTION PICTURE OR TELEVISION

• "Somewhere Out There" (from *An American Tail* soundtrack) James Horner, Barry Mann, Cynthia Weil. MCA Music Publishing (ASCAP/BMI), publishers. MCA.

"(I've Had) The Time of My Life" (from *Dirty Dancing* soundtrack), Frankie Previte, John Denicola, Donald Markowitz,. Knockout Music Inc., Jemava Music Corp., Donald Jay Music Ltd., R.U. Cyrius (ASCAP), publishers. BMG Music/RCA.

"*Moonlighting* Theme," Al Jarreau, Lee Holdridge. American Broadcasting Music, ABC Circle Music Inc. (ASCAP/BMI), publishers. MCA.

"Nothing's Gonna Stop Us Now" (from *Mannequin* soundtrack), Diane Warren, Albert Hammond. Realsongs/ Albert Hammond Music (admin. by WB Music Corp.) (ASCAP), publishers. Grunt.

"Who's That Girl?" (from *Who's That Girl?* soundtrack) Madonna, Patrick Leonard. WB Music Corp., Bleu Disque Music Co., Inc., Webb Girl Publishing Inc. by WB Music Corp. (ASCAP), Johnny Yumma Music (BMI), publishers. Sire.

When pianist Vladimir Horowitz won Best Classical Album "he simply smiled and carried it away, saying nothing."

BEST INSTRUMENTAL ARRANGEMENT ACCOMPANYING VOCAL(S)

• Frank Foster, "Deedles' Blues," track from *Diane Schuur & the Count Basie Orchestra.* GRP.

Randy Kerber, "Over the Rainbow," track from *One Voice.* Columbia/CBS.

Henry Mancini, "It Might as Well Be Spring," track from *The Hollywood Musicals.* Columbia/CBS.

Van Dyke Parks, Bill Ginn, "A Singer Must Die," track from *Famous Blue Raincoat.* Cypress.

Jack Walrath, "I'm So Lonesome I Could Cry," track from *Master of Suspense.* Blue Note.

Best Classical Album

• *Horowitz in Moscow*, Vladimir Horowitz. Thomas Frost, producer. Deutsche Grammophon.

Adams: The Chairman Dances; Christian Zeal and Activity; Two Fanfares for Orchestra; Tromba Iontana; Short Ride in a Fast Machine; Common Tones in Simple Time, Edo De Waart conducting San Francisco Symphony. Elektra/Nonesuch.

Beethoven: Symphony No. 9 in D Minor (Choral), Sir Georg Solti conducting Chicago Symphony Orchestra. Michael Haas, producer. London.

Fauré: Requiem, Op. 48; Durufle: Requiem, Op. 9, Robert Shaw conducting Atlanta Symphony Chorus and Orchestra. Robert Woods, producer. Telarc.

Hanson: Symphony No. 2 (Romantic); Barber: Violin Concerto, Leonard Slatkin conducting St. Louis Symphony. Marc Aubort, Joanna Nickrenz, producers. Angel.

Best Orchestral Recording
(Conductor's Award)

• *Beethoven: Symphony No. 9 in D Minor (Choral)*, Sir Georg Solti conducting Chicago Symphony Orchestra. Michael Haas, producer. London.

Berg/Webern/Schönberg: Orchestral Pieces, James Levine conducting Berlin Philharmonic. Werner Mayer, producer. Deutsche Grammophon.

Copland: Symphony No. 3; Quiet City, Leonard Bernstein conducting New York. Philharmonic. Hans Weber, producer. Deutsche Grammophon.

Hanson: Symphony No. 2 (Romantic), Leonard Slatkin conducting St. Louis Symphony. Marc Aubort, Joanna Nickrenz, producers. Angel.

Holst: The Planets, Charles Dutoit conducting Montreal Symphony Orchestra. Paul Myers, producer. London.

Best Chamber Music Performance
(Instrumental or Vocal)

• Itzhak Perlman, Lynn Harrell, Vladimir Ashkenazy, *Beethoven: The Complete Piano Trios*. Angel.

Beaux Arts Trio, *Dvorak: Piano Trio in E Minor (Dumky); Mendelssohn: Piano Trio in D Minor*. Philips Classics.

Kronos Quartet, *White Man Sleeps (Music by Volans, Ives, Hassell, Coleman, Johnson, Bartok)*. Elektra/Nonesuch.

Murray Perahia, members of the Amadeus Quartet, *Brahms: Piano Quartet No. 1 in G Minor*. CBS Masterworks.

Jean-Pierre Rampal, Isaac Stern, Salvatore Accardo, Mstislav Rostropovich, *Mozart: The Flute Quartets (K. 285, 285A, 285B, 298)*. CBS Masterworks.

Best Classical Performance, Instrumental Soloist(s) (with Orchestra)

• Itzhak Perlman (James Levine conducting Vienna Philharmonic), *Mozart: Violin Concertos Nos. 2 in D and 4 in D*. Deutsche Grammophon.

Dale Clevenger (Franz Liszt Chamber Orchestra), *Mozart: Horn Concertos No. 1–4, Rondo, Fragment*. CBS Masterworks.

Wynton Marsalis (Donald Hunsberger conducting Eastman Wind Ensemble, *Carnaval* (works by Arban, Clarke, Levy, Paganini, Rimskykorsakov, Bellstedt). CBS Masterworks.

Elmar Oliveira (Leonard Slatkin conducting St. Louis Symphony), *Barber: Violin Concerto, Op. 14*. Angel.

Murray Perahia (Bernard Haitink conducting Concertgebouw Orchestra), *Beethoven: Piano Concerto No. 5 in E Flat (Emperor)*. CBS Masterworks.

Best Classical Performance, Instrumental Soloist(s) (without Orchestra)

• Vladimir Horowitz, piano, *Horowitz in Moscow*. Deutsche Grammophon.

Itzhak Perlman, violin (Samuel Sanders, accompanist), *My Favorite Kreisler*. Angel.

Murray Perahia, *Beethoven: Piano Sonatas No. 17, Op. 31/18, Op. 31/26, Op. 81A*. CBS Masterworks.

Andras Schiff, piano, *Bach: The Well-Tempered Clavier, Book 2*. London.

Peter Serkin, piano, *Stravinsky, Wolpe, Lieberson* (Stravinsky: Serenade in A & Sonata; Wolpe: *Form IV, Broken Sequences, Pastorale, Pascaglia*; Lieberson: *Bagatelles*). New World.

Best Opera Recording

• *R. Strauss: Ariadne Auf Naxos*, James Levine conducting Vienna Philharmonic (solos: Tomowa-Sintow, Battle, Baltsa, Lakes, Prey). Cord Garben, producer. Deutsche Grammophon.

Mozart: Die Entfuhrung Aus Dem Serail, Sir Georg Solti conducting Vienna Philharmonic Orchestra and Chorus (solos: Gruberova, Battle, Winbergh, Zednik, Talvela). Christopher Raeburn, producer. London.

Mozart: Don Giovanni, Herbert von Karajan conducting Berlin Philharmonic Orchestra and Chorus (solos: Ramey, Tomowasintow, Baltsa, Battle, Winbergh, Furlanetto, Malta, Burchuladze). Michel Glotz, Werner Mayer, producers. Deutsche Grammophon.

Mozart: The Marriage of Figaro, Riccardo Muti conducting Vienna Philharmonic and Chorus (solos: Allen, Price, Battle, Hynninen, Murray, Rydl). James Mallinson, producer. Angel.

Verdi: Macbeth, Riccardo Chailly conducting Orchestra e Coro del Teatro Communale di Bologna (solos: Nucci, Verrett, Ramey, Luchetti, Barasorda). Andrew Cornall, producer. London.

Best Choral Performance (Other Than Opera)

• Robert Shaw conducting Atlanta Symphony Chorus and Orchestra, *Hindemith: When Lilacs Last in the Dooryard Bloom'd (A Requiem for Those We Love)*. Telarc.

John Eliot Gardiner conducting Monteverdi Choir and the English Baroque Soloists, *Bach:. St. John Passion*. Archiv.

Sir Charles Mackerras conducting Prague Philharmonic Chorus and Czech Philharmonic Orchestra. Lubomir Matl, chorus master, *Janacek: Glagolitic Mass*. Supraphon.

André Previn conducting Brighton Festival Chorus and Royal Philharmonic Orchestra. Laszlo Heltay, chorus master, *Tippett: A Child of Our Time*. RPO Records.

Klaus Tennstedt conducting London Philharmonic Choir and Orchestra, Richard Cooke, chorus master; Tiffin School Boys Choir, Neville Creed, chorus master, *Mahler: Symphony No. 8 in E Flat (Symphony of a Thousand)*. Angel.

Michael Tilson Thomas conducting Mormon Tabernacle Choir and Utah Symphony. Jerold D. Ottley, choral director, *Copland: Old American Songs; Canticle of Freedom; Four Motets*. CBS Masterworks.

Best Classical Vocal Soloist Performance

• Kathleen Battle (James Levine, accompanist), *Kathleen Battle, Salzburg Recital (Fauré, Handel, Mendelsohn, Mozart, Purcell, Strauss, Spirituals)*. Deutsche Grammophon.

Elly Ameling (Rudolf Jansen, accompanist), *Soire Francaise* (Debussy, Fauré, Poulenc, Franck, Cantelqube, Roussel, Chausson, Messiaen, etc.). Philips Classics.

Arleen Auger (The Yale Cellos of Aldo Parisot), *Villa-Lobos: Bachianas Brasileiras No. 5 for Soprano & Orchestra of Violincellos*. Delos Intl.

Marni Nixon (Keith Clark conducting members of Pacific Symphony Orchestra), *Copland: Eight Poems of Emily Dickinson*. Reference Recordings.

Jessye Norman (Geoffrey Parsons, accompanist), *R. Strauss: Lieder (including 'Malven')*. Philips Classics.

Best Contemporary Composition (Composer's Award)

• *Cello Concerto No. 2*, Krzysztof Penderecki (Krzysztof Penderecki conducting Philharmonia Orchestra; solo: Mstislav Rostropovich). Editions Schott, Mainz, publisher. Erato-Editions.

The Chairman Dances, John Adams (Edo De Waart conducting San Francisco Symphony). Associated Music Publishers (BMI), publisher. Elektra/Nonesuch.

Piano Concerto, Milton Babbitt (Alan
  Feinberg; Charles Wuorinen
  conducting American Composers
  Orchestra). C.F. Peters Corp.,
  publisher. New World.
A Sudden Rainbow, Joseph Schwanter
  (Leonard Slatkin conducting St. Louis
  Symphony Orchestra). Helicon Music
  Corp. (BMI), publisher.
  Elektra/Nonesuch.
Symphony No. 5, Roger Sessions
  (Christian Badea conducting Columbus
  Symphony Orchestra.) E.B. Marks,
  publisher. New World.
The Mask of Time, Michael Tippett
  (Andrew Davis conducting BBC
  Symphony Chorus and Orchestra).
  European American Music Distributors
  Corp., publishers. Angel.

BEST ENGINEERED RECORDING,
CLASSICAL
• Jack Renner, Fauré: Requiem, Op. 48;
  Durufle: Requiem, Op. 9 (Shaw
  conducting Atlanta Symphony Chorus
  and Orchestra; solos: Judith Blegen,
  James Morris). Telarc.
Thomas Frost, Horowitz in Moscow (solo:
  Vladimir Horowitz). Deutsche
  Grammophon.
John Pellowe, James Lock, Beethoven:
  Symphony No. 9 in D Minor (Choral)
  (Solti conducting Chicago Symphony
  Orchestra, solos). London.
John Pellowe, Tchaikovsky: 1812
  Overture; Romeo & Juliet; The
  Nutcracker Suite (Solti conducting
  Chicago Symphony Orchestra).
  London.
Jack Renner, Hindemith: When Lilacs Last
  in the Dooryard Bloom'd (A Requiem
  for Those We Love) (Shaw conducting
  Atlanta Symphony Orchestra and
  Chorus, Soloists). Telarc.

CLASSICAL PRODUCER OF THE YEAR
• Robert Woods
Steven Epstein
Thomas Frost
Michael Haas
Jay David Saks

BEST COMEDY RECORDING
• A Night at the Met, Robin Williams.
  Columbia/CBS.
The Best of Bob & Ray Vol. 1, Bob Elliott,
  Ray Goulding (cassette). Radioart.

THELONIOUS MONK
THE COMPLETE RIVERSIDE RECORDINGS

COMPACT DISC EDITION

RIVERSIDE

A collection of the late Thelonius Monk's
jazz works from 1955 to 1961 on the
Riverside label won best historical LP.

Polka Party! "Weird Al" Yankovic. CBS
  Associated/Rock 'n' Roll.
The World According to Me! Jackie
  Mason. Warner Bros.
Would Jesus Wear a Rolex? Ray Stevens.
  MCA.

BEST SPOKEN WORD OR NON-MUSICAL
RECORDING
• Lake Wobegon Days, Garrison Keillor
  (cassette). PHC.
Lauren Bacall by Myself, Lauren Bacall
  (cassette). Random House Audiobooks.
"Lincoln Portrait," Katharine Hepburn,
  track from Aaron Copland: Lincoln
  Portait & Other Works. Telarc.
Star Trek IV: The Voyage Home, read by
  Leonard Nimoy, George Takei (cas-
  sette). Simon & Schuster Audio Works.
Whales Alive, narration by Leonard
  Nimoy. Living Music.

BEST RECORDING FOR CHILDREN
• The Elephant's Child, Jack Nicholson,
  narration. Bobby McFerrin, music.
  Bobby McFerrin, Tom Bradshaw, Mark
  Sottnick, producers. Windham Hill.
Bullfrogs and Butterflies (Part III), Tony
  Salerno, Frank Hernandez, producers.
  Sparrow.
The Emperor and the Nightingale, Glenn
  Close, narration. Mark Isham, music.
  Mark Isham, Mark Sottnick, producers.
  Windham Hill.
Everything Grows, Raffi. Raffi, producer.
  Shoreline/A&M.

Lullaby for Teddy, Barbara Fairchild. J. Aaron Brown, David R. Lehman, Andy Tolbird, producers. Jaba.

BEST ENGINEERED RECORDING, NON-CLASSICAL
• Bruce Swedien, Humberto Gatica, *Bad*. Epic.
Don Murray, Keith Grant, engineers. Josiah Gluck, Dave Grusin, mixers, *Cinemagic* (cassette). GRP.
Ben Harris, Kyle Lehning, Joe Bogen, *Heart and Soul*. BMG Music/RCA.
Andrew Jackson, *A Momentary Lapse of Reason*. Columbia/CBS.
Tom Jung, *Neon* (cassette). Digital Music Projects.
Al Schmitt, *Reflections*. Soundwings.

BEST ALBUM PACKAGE
• Bill Johnson, *King's Record Shop*. Columbia/CBS.
Peter Barrett, *Shaka Zulu*. Warner Bros.
Bruce Licher, *Echelons*. Independent Project.
Ron Scarselli, *Document*. I.R.S.
Joe Stelmach, *Duke Ellington: The Webster Blanton Band*. BMG Music/RCA.

BEST ALBUM NOTES
• Orrin Keepnews, *Thelonius Monk, The Complete Riverside Recordings*. Riverside.
Peter Guralnick, *The Complete Sun Sessions*. BMG Music/RCA.
Nolan Porterfield, *Jimmie Rodgers on Record: America's Blue Yodeler*. Smithsonian Collection of Recordings.
Mark Tucker, *Singers and Soloists of the Swing Bands*. Smithsonian Collection of Recordings.
Charles K. Wolfe, *The Bristol Sessions*. Country Music Foundation.

BEST HISTORICAL ALBUM
• *Thelonius Monk, The Complete Riverside Recordings*, Thelonius Monk. Orrin Keepnews, album producer. Riverside.
The Bristol Sessions, Carter Family, Jimmie Rodgers, others. Bob Pinson, Kyle Young, historical album producers. Country Music Foundation.
The Gershwin Collection, Ella Fitzgerald, Johnny Mathis, Andy Williams, others. Paul Tannen, producer. Teledisc USSA.

The Otis Redding Story, Otis Redding. Kim Cooke, Bob Porter, Rob Bowman, producers. Atlantic.
Singers and Soloists of the Swing Bands, Louis Armstrong. Benny Goodman, Frank Sinatra, others. Margaret Robinson, producer. Smithsonian Collection of Recordings.

PRODUCER OF THE YEAR, NON-CLASSICAL
• Narada Michael Walden
Emilio & the Jerks
Quincy Jones, Michael Jackson
Daniel Lanois, Brian Eno
John Mellencamp, Don Gehman

BEST PERFORMANCE MUSIC VIDEO
• *The Prince's Trust All-Star Rock Concert*, David G. Croft, video director. Anthony Eaton, video producer. MGM Home Video.
Cyndi Lauper in Paris, Cyndi Lauper. Andy Morahan, video director. John Diaz, video producer. CBS Music Video Enterprises.
Horowitz in Moscow, Vladimir Horowitz. Brian Large, video director. Peter Gelb, video producer. Camivideo.
One Voice, Barbra Streisand. Dwight Hemion, video director. Gary Smith, Dwight Hemion, video producers. CBS/Fox Video Music.
Spontaneous Inventions, Bobby McFerrin. Bud Schaetzle, video director. Martin Fischer, video producer. PMI/HBO/Pioneer Artists.

BEST CONCEPT MUSIC VIDEO
• *Land of Confusion*, Genesis. John Lloyd, Jim Yukich, video directors. John Blair, video producer. Atlantic Video.
Control, The Videos, Part II, Janet Jackson. Dominic Sena, video director. Various video producers. A&M Video.
David Lee Roth, David Lee Roth. Pete Angelus/David Lee Roth, video directors. Various video producers. Warner Reprise Video.
Day In, Day Out, David Bowie. Julien Temple, video director. Amanda Perry, video producer. Picture Music International/Sony.
Kate Bush: The Whole Story, Kate Bush. Picture Music International/Sony Software.

All That Jazz

Commenting on the Record of the Year competition prior to the Grammycast, the *L.A. Times* wrote, "There will be considerable sentiment to give [Michael] Jackson the award to take some of the sting out of his Grammy shutout last year."

But when the night of the ceremony came, it turned out that an underrated fellow nominee named Bobby McFerrin had nothing to worry about. His "Don't Worry, Be Happy" not only triumphed for the top platter prize, it was also voted Song of the Year in addition to bringing McFerrin the laurels for pop vocal performance. McFerrin picked up a fourth Grammy when he snagged the jazz male vocals prize for "Brothers," a track from *Rob Wasserman's Duets*.

Bobby McFerrin wanted to create "something uplifting and jovial and funny" with his Record and Song of the Year "Don't Worry, Be Happy."

WIDE WORLD PHOTO

"The multiple triumph of Bobby McFerrin was at once surprising, gratifying, and puzzling," critic Leonard Feather wrote in the *L.A. Times*. "Here is an artist whose jazz credentials are impeccable, but who, over the past decade, has broadened his scope and his audience by developing into a unique entertainer and comedic personality."

McFerrin was known as a "vocal Cuisinart" in the jazz world for being able to combine piano, voice, and sometimes dance skills with his uncanny ability to imitate the sounds of an entire band. "McFerrin mixes playfulness and soul in his music in a way that gives his extraordinary voice free rein," wrote *The New York Times*, "but that also keeps his ideas rooted in one or another jazz or pop tradition."

"Don't Worry, Be Happy" was not only Grammy's Song of the Year, it was the bouncy, feel-good song of the year, selling 10 million single copies as of the awards night after being introduced on McFerrin's *Simple Pleasures* album and in the Tom Cruise movie *Cocktail*. (The upbeat song was so popular that Vice President George Bush even tried to appropriate it for his 1988 Presidential campaign, but was turned down by McFerrin.) Its biggest Grammy victory — for Record of the Year— marked the first time that a song from a film reaped the honor since Roberta Flack's "The First Time Ever I Saw Your Face" (featured in Clint Eastwood's *Play Misty for Me*) did so in 1972.

"I think it was so popular because it went to the spirit," McFerrin told reporters backstage about his song's broad success. "People wanted something uplifting and jovial and funny."

Leonard Feather wrote about his amazing Grammy romp: "McFerrin, a genuinely gifted artist, has crossed over the ghetto of jazz categories into the wider world of mass appeal." McFerrin's bold step, it turned out, was followed by a stampede of other jazz artists into more non-jazz victories, too. Feather added about the 1988 awards taking place in 1989: "It is possible that 1989 may be remembered in the music industry as the year of the great jazz Grammy crossover."

"Will the Beach Boys finally win their first Grammy for the light-hearted pop smash 'Kokomo'?" critic Paul Grein asked in the L.A. Times before the show. The Beach Boys were up for best group pop vocals for their comeback chart-topper "Kokomo" (also featured in *Cocktail*), but were overtaken by the Manhattan Transfer for *Brasil*. Frank Zappa was nominated again in the rock instrumental category, which he won last year, but got zapped by the Mexican-born, fusion guitarist Carlos Santana with *Blues for Salvador*. Mike Post (*Music from* L.A. *Law & Otherwise*) was the front runner for Best Pop Instrumental Performance, but he was surpassed by alto sax player David Sanborn (*Close Up*), the winner of three jazz Grammys in the past.

More jazz triumphs followed when six-time jazz honoree Chick Corea swept past five strong r&b contenders to

> *"Never before have so many jazz-related musicians been honored in so many nonjazz categories."*

claim that genre's instrumental category for *GRP Super Live in Concert*. Furthermore, Feather noted: "Roger Kellaway, a distinguished jazz composer, was a winner for best instrumental arrangement, another nonjazz department, for an album called *Memos from Paradise* by the jazz clarinetist Eddie Daniels .... [What these] victories add up to may well indicate a powerful trend .... Never before in the 31-year history of the Grammy Awards have two top divisions been won by a jazz artist, and never before have so many jazz-related musicians been honored in so many nonjazz categories."

Prior to the Grammycast, the *L.A. Times* sized up some of the top nonjazz contenders, saying, "This year's big surprise was the failure of British pop sensation George Michael to nab more than two nominations. Michael had figured to be among the leaders because his *Faith* album received generally favorable reviews and sold more than six million copies."

Michael ended up losing his bid for best male pop vocals to McFerrin, but topped the one-man-jazz-band for a bigger prize, Album of the Year, in a victory that signalled Michael's graduation from a one-time teen idol to a critically regarded musical talent. Michael got his start in the business as one half of the bubblegum pop group Wham! After his break with partner Andrew Ridgeley, he started hitting the charts solo, but, he told *Billboard*, "It's nerve-wracking. When you're given the freedom to do what you like because you're no longer part of a group, you're also given the freedom to make mistakes." Critics didn't think he was erring seriously, however. Stephen Holden of *The New York Times* wrote, "If asked to nominate the one contemporary pop star most likely to be as successful 10 years from now as today, I'd cast my vote for

George Michael. [He] has everything a pop star requires for longevity ... [including] extraordinary skills as a songwriter, arranger, and producer."

"Tracy Chapman could be headed for the biggest Grammy sweep ever by a new artist," predicted the *L.A. Times,* as well as several other Grammy authorities. "Chapman has an excellent chance of winning in all six categories [in which she's nominated] when the awards are handed out." Chapman's six nods were the most of the year (followed by five nominations for McFerrin), putting her in contention for Record, Album, and Song of the Year, in addition to Best New Artist, Best Female Pop Vocal Performance ("Fast Car"), and Best Contemporary Folk Recording (*Tracy Chapman*).

Prior to McFerrin's upset, "Fast Car" was thought to be in a dead-heat contest with Michael Jackson's "Man in the Mirror" for Record of the Year: It was a song strong on melody (a definite plus among older Grammy voters) and a hit video on MTV, too, thereby appealing to younger voters. It told the haunting tale of a impoverished young woman who works in a convenience store and lives in a shelter with her lover and their children. Yearning for escape, she sings to her lover: "You got a fast car/ And I got a plan to get us out of here ..../ You leave tonight or live and die this way." Its desperate message moved even the crustiest of critics. *The New York Times* called her work "resoundingly adult music, soft and temperate and literate." "If Chapman doesn't win [Best New Artist], the Grammys shouldn't even bother renting a hall," Grein wrote in the *L.A. Times.*

Chapman ended up with the trophies for pop vocals, folk recording, and Best New Artist. *Rolling Stone* gasped: "The Grammys seemed to be saluting the political, dangerous and — *gulp!* — hip."

Like the Grammyless Beach Boys,

*Best LP winner George Michael (*Faith*) "has everything a pop star requires for longevity," said* The New York Times.

Rod Stewart was hoping for his first victory when he was nominated for best rock vocalist for "Forever Young." Grammy voters, however, found white British soul singer Robert Palmer, just as his song title suggested, "Simply Irresistible." "Irresistible" was the third number one-ranked single of Palmer's career. His first, "Addicted to Love," brought him the same rock award in 1986. This time he also prevailed over a Grammyless Joe Cocker and one-time winner Eric Clapton, who shared in the 1972 Album of the Year Grammy for *The Concert for Bangla Desh* but had never won on his own. Clapton was nonetheless honored indirectly this year when the award for Best Historical Album was bestowed to the producer of his *Crossroads* LP, also winner of Best Album Notes.

With the exception of last year when the category was combined with the male vocal award, Tina Turner and Pat Benatar had virtually monopolized the female rock slot since it was reintroduced in 1979 and now were pitted against each other along with what the *L.A. Times* called "three hot, critically acclaimed newcomers": Toni Childs, Melissa Etheridge, and Sinéad O'Connor. When the vote for the newcomers split, Turner emerged triumphant for *Tina Live in Europe*.

Another past Grammy favorite proved strong when U2 returned from last year to take the rock instrumental category again, this time for "Desire," from the group's concert documentary film *U2: Rattle and Hum*. The Irish rockers also won Best Performance Music Video for "Where the Streets Have No Name," the lead song on their 1987 Album of the Year *The Joshua Tree*. "Weird Al" Yankovic snared the Best Concept Music Video award for *Fat*, his parody of Michael Jackson's *Bad*. Jackson's only nomination was for Record of the Year ("Man in the Mirror"), so he was shut out for a second year in a row.

"When the traditionally conservative recording academy decides to bestow an award upon it, heavy metal has clearly arrived," *Billboard* wrote, noting the addition of a new category for Best Hard Rock/Metal Performance. Metallica was widely expected to be the easy winner but was upset by what *The New York Times* called "the long-running, long-irrelevant band Jethro Tull," the British rock group named after the inventor of the steel drill. Lead singer Ian Anderson wasn't in attendance at the Grammy show to accept the prize, so *Rolling Stone* asked Metallica's James Hetfield what he thought of Tull's victory. "Maybe it would have excited me ten years ago," he answered.

Metallica was nevertheless invited to perform at the ceremony. "The thrash band Metallica emerged from a dry-ice cloud to perform a stunning version of 'One,'" *Rolling Stone* noted. "As Metallica leader James Hetfield sang the line 'Hold my breath as I wish for death,' the stodgy Grammy voters must have been nodding in agreement." The *L.A. Times* said Metallica "shook the Shrine Auditorium chandelier with a performance unlike anything ever seen or heard on a Grammy show."

The New Age award, introduced last year, was reaped by Shadowfax for *Folksongs for a Nuclear Village*. N.A.R.A.S. added a new prize this year for Best Rap Performance, which went to D.J. Jazzy Jeff & the Fresh Prince ("Parents Just Don't Understand"), who skipped the Grammycast.

D.J. Jazzy Jeff & the Fresh Prince had been invited to be presenters at the ceremony, but they joined three of their four rival nominees in a boycott because the new rap prize was being handed out at a separate, non-televised ceremony. A spokesman for the artists charged that rap music was being "treated like a stepchild" and "ghetto-ized." Grammycast producer Pierre Cossette countered: "The problem is arithmetic. When you have 76 categories and you only [have time] to put 12 on the air, you've got 64 unhappy groups of people." Only loser Kool Moe Dee agreed to accept the award, if he won. After both the on- and off-the-air ceremonies were over, winner the Fresh Prince (Will Smith) could be found at MTV's party at the L.A. club Cat & Fiddle where he told *Rolling Stone*, "They're giving us the award, but they're giving it to us under the table."

A curious coincidence occurred in the r&b lineup when Anita Baker repeated her dual victories of 1986 by again being named best female r&b vocalist and sharing in the writers' prize for Best R&B Song, "Giving You the Best That I Got," which was also a contender for

Record and Song of the Year. Gladys Knight & the Pips added to their previous Grammy stash (two in 1973 and a third for Knight's contribution to 1986 Song of the Year "That's What Friends Are For") by garnering the gold for best r&b group vocal performance.

"Will Luther Vandross win his first Grammy for best male r&b performance after being the premier male r&b singer for most of the eighties?" asked the *L.A. Times* before the show. Vandross had lost all six of his earlier bids (including one for 1981's Best New Artist) and now lost again — to a performer who lost Best New Artist last year: the hypersexed and overhyped Terence Trent D'Arby.

D'Arby was somewhat to blame for the surfeit of attention he was getting in the media, which was not all positive, thanks to how smugly he was behaving in public. Among other things, D'Arby was calling the album for which he won his Grammy, *Introducing the Hardline According to Terence Trent D'Arby*, "the most brilliant debut album from any artist this decade." He even said it was a better work than the Beatles' *Sgt. Pepper's Lonely Hearts Club Band* (winner of Grammy's 1967 Album of the Year). *Rolling Stone* came to his defense after the Grammycast, however, using the opportunity to bash N.A.R.A.S. voters one more time: "The victory of the one certifiably hip winner — Terence Trent D'Arby for best male, r&b vocal — can probably be attributed to the fact that he performed at last year's ceremony and thus was familiar to the constituents."

Losers of this year's Best New Artist prize, Take 6, still scored a dramatic coup by winning two other Grammys: a gospel award for their eponymous debut album and the jazz group vocals award for one of its tracks, "Spread Love." In "Spread Love," the young black sextet told listeners, "Spread love instead of spreading lies." Other tracks were more overtly religious, with titles such as "Get Away, Jordan" and "David and Goliath."

The jazz awards honored one of its greatest veterans for the first time when the female vocals prize went to Betty Carter (*Look What I Got!*), who was once called "the only real jazz singer" by fellow jazz diva Carmen McCrae. (McCrae, who had never won a Grammy either, was one of the nominees who lost to Carter. A duet LP, featuring both McCrae *and* Carter, lost the group vocals prize to Take 6.) Carter had been performing since the late 1940s when she toured with Lionel Hampton, but was not as widely known as McCrae, Ella Fitzgerald, Sarah Vaughan, and other queens of the genre since she seldom made recordings. She started her own label in 1971, Bet-Car, but issued only a few releases before signing with Verve in 1987.

The new hard rock/metal prize went to "the long-irrelevant" Jethro Tull.

For decades the Chicago blues scene was ruled by Muddy Waters, Howlin' Wolf, and Willie Dixon. Waters and Wolf died years ago, but Dixon was still going strong at age 72 and was hailed with his first Grammy (Best Traditional Blues Recording) for *Hidden Charms*.

Just prior to his death in 1988, Gil Evans, along with his Monday Night Orchestra, recorded a tribute to Bud Powell and Charlie "Yardbird" Parker — *Bud & Bird* — that earned them the big band jazz kudos. Sax legend and one-time Grammy winner John Coltrane had died two decades earlier, but *Blues for Coltrane: A Tribute to John Coltrane* now reaped the jazz group instrumental performance award for McCoy Tyner,

Pharaoh Sanders, David Murray, Cecil McBee, and Roy Haynes. The prize for best solo instrumental work was bestowed on fusion reedman Michael Brecker for *Don't Try This at Home*. Trumpet player Wynton Marsalis was nominated against both Brecker and the group paying homage to Coltrane, but he came up Grammyless for the first time since his winning streak began in 1983. Wynton's brother, sax player Branford, also lost in both competitions.

The Grammys' penchant for burying fallen music greats with laurels was shown in the country awards, too, when Roy Orbison, who died in 1988, was honored posthumously for his "Cryin'" duet with k.d. lang, which won them the new category of Best Country Vocal Collaboration.

The Grammyless Beach Boys lost both of their bids for "Kokomo."

After a three-year winning streak that ended in 1986, the mother-daughter duo, the Judds, staged a comeback in country music's duo/group vocal category for a track from their *Greatest Hits* album, "Give a Little Love." Also returning was Randy Travis (*Old 8 x 10*), who reclaimed the honors he won last year for best male vocalist. Another repeater from 1987 was the "western swing" band from Austin, Texas, Asleep at the Wheel, which held onto the country instrumental slot with "Sugarfoot Rag."

K.T. Oslin won her first Grammy last year, but surpassed that success by doing in the country categories exactly what Anita Baker did in the r&b lineup: She won both the female vocal honors and best song. Her triumph for "Hold Me," a track from *This Woman*, made Grammy history with two other, non-country victories. Never before had all three best song awards (Song of the Year, Best R&B Song, and Best Country Song) gone to the artists who both sang *and* wrote the work. Curiously, all three artists also won Grammys for their performances.

In addition to new categories for rap and heavy metal music, N.A.R.A.S. introduced a new slot for Best Bluegrass Recording, which was won by veteran singer, bandleader, and mandolin player Bill Monroe. The Kentucky native had been performing since the mid-1920s and was known as the father of bluegrass music, as *Rolling Stone* once noted, "not because he invented that variant of country & western, but because he was its most adventurous pioneer."

As usual, the religious categories welcomed back a chorus of past victors, including three four-time champs: Amy Grant (*Lead Me On*), Larnelle Harris (*Christmas*), and the Winans (*The Winans Live at Carnegie Hall*), who claimed the gospel prizes for, respectively, best female, male, and group performances. Last year CeCe Winans won her own Grammy. This year it was her brother BeBe's turn to claim the male soul gospel award for "Abundant Life." CeCe was nominated for the female soul gospel prize, but lost to Aretha Franklin (*One Lord, One Faith, One Baptism*), who bolstered her lead over all other female Grammy winners by bringing her total to 15 trophies.

Newcomer Roberto Carlos was the winner of Best Latin Pop Performance for his eponymous LP, while 1986 victor of the tropical Latin kudos, Ruben Blades, returned to reclaim the prize (*Antecedente*). Linda Ronstadt had previously won Grammys in both the pop and country fields, but now she crossed over into a third genre when she received the year's Best Mexican/American Performance award for *Canciones de mi Padre*.

Jimmy Sturr & His Orchestra held onto the Best Polka Recording accolade for a third year in a row with *Born to Polka*. Jamaica's native-music king, Bob Marley, died in 1981, but his legacy was continued by his son Ziggy, who won Best Reggae Recording for his album with the Melody Makers, *Conscious Party*.

Comedian Robin Williams scored two Grammy victories with prizes for the Best Recording for Children (*Pecos Bill*, which he narrated) and Best Comedy Recording (*Good Morning, Vietnam*, a collection of Williams's rantings and ravings from the hit movie in which he portrayed a wild army disc jockey). Composer Stephen Sondheim had won the award for Best Musical Cast Show Album four times in the past: *Company* (1970), *A Little Night Music* (1973), *Sweeney Todd* (1979), and *Sunday in the Park with George* (1984). Now he returned triumphant with *Into the Woods*, his hit Broadway show based loosely on the Grimms' fairy tales.

The trio of composing talent behind the Oscar's Best Picture *The Last Emperor* (Ryuichi Sakamoto, David Byrne, and Cong Su) prevailed over past winners John Williams and Maurice Jarre to reap the film score accolade.

Of the two songs from *Cocktail* considered for other Grammys this year (the Beach Boys' "Kokomo" and Record of the Year "Don't Worry, Be Happy"), only "Kokomo" was in the line-up for Best Song Written for a Motion Picture or Television. The Beach Boys lost again, however, when the trophy was snatched by 1985 Album of the Year winner Phil Collins for "Two Hearts," from the movie *Buster*, in which Collins made his film acting debut. He had previously acted professionally on the stage when his mother helped him to land the role of the Artful Dodger in a London production of *Oliver!* when Collins was 15 years old.

Serious discord erupted in the classical categories when Robert Shaw and the Atlanta Symphony Orchestra and Chorus won five awards, leading to accusations of bloc voting. (It was the fifth time in 10 years that Atlanta's producer Robert Woods was named Classical Producer of the Year.) "Insidious ... the question of bloc voting," *Billboard* commented. "Regional loyalties seem to be the functional culprit. There really is no other way to explain the lopsided Grammy results for the Atlanta Symphony Orchestra, its releasing labels, and producer. Does anyone doubt that the small but active Atlanta academy chapter [with 300 members] votes its municipal pride? Something is wrong."

"It takes very few votes to win a classical Grammy, because the number of people who vote is small," explained Joseph Dash, a CBS Masterworks executive. "N.A.R.A.S. should do something as soon as possible, before the value of a Grammy is reduced to zero."

Shaw and his team picked up three of their Grammys (Best Classical Album, the choral performance prize, and engineering laurels) — ironically, considering the uproar — for a work that critics considered one of their finest recordings: Verdi's *Requiem and Operatic Choruses*, featuring choruses from *Aida*, *Don Carlo*, and other classics. They also picked up the Best Orchestral Recording prize for *Ned Rorem's String Symphony; Sunday Morning; Eagles* in addition to the fifth Grammy awarded to producer Woods.

Vladimir Horowitz had won Best Classical Album the previous two years in a row and this year was a losing nominee (for *Horowitz Plays Mozart*), but at least he picked up the consolation prize of the soloist honors for orchestral accompaniment. Critics noted that the 85-year-old artist performed well on the

LP despite a noticeable decline of his powers due to age. The soloist's prize without orchestral backup was awarded to two-time past champ Alicia de Larrocha for works by Isaac Albéniz, which earned her rave reviews.

Sir Georg Solti nabbed two more awards to solidify his status as all-time Grammy champ, with 28 awards, for the year's Best Opera Recording (Wagner's *Lohengrin*) and the chamber music honors for a joint recording of works by Bartók and Brahms on which he played piano along with Murray Perahia.

"Longshot" Nixon in China by John Adams lost Best Opera Recording but won Best Contemporary Composition.

An album performance of John Adams's *Nixon in China* by the Orchestra of St. Luke's was "an inevitable nominee" for Best Opera Recording but also "a trendy longshot," according to the *L.A. Times*, correctly predicting its defeat. Still, *Nixon* earned its writer the consolation prize of Best Contemporary Composition. *Opera News* said of its recording,

"Though the opera itself is a media event, and the visual elements are sorely missed here, this is a brilliant execution of the score."

After its show in New York last year, the Grammycast returned to Los Angeles's Shrine Auditorium where Billy Crystal played host.

"The evening's most unusual moments were proved by female rock nominee Sinéad O'Connor, who performed wearing combat boots, ripped jeans, and black halter top to go with her shaven head, and rapper Kool Moe Dee, who chided the record academy in rhyme for not presenting the new rap award [on TV]," *Variety* said. *Rolling Stone* added: "When the show was over, everyone stumbled out of L.A.'s Shrine Auditorium and into their limousines (except for O'Connor, who refuses to ride in a limo) and took off to the parties."

Out on the town later on, Huey Lewis was overheard saying to Olivia Newton-John, "This year's awards just weren't that exciting."

Lewis may have been on to something. The Grammycast experienced its worst TV ratings ever. Just as bad, it was also the fourth time in the past five years that the ratings for the American Music Awards telecast surpassed those for the Grammys show.

1988

Winners were announced at the Shrine Auditorium, Los Angeles, on February 22, 1989, for the eligibility period of October 1, 1987, through September 30, 1988.

ALBUM OF THE YEAR
✓ • *Faith*, George Michael. George Michael, producer. Columbia/CBS.
✓ *...Nothing Like the Sun*, Sting. Sting, Neil Dorfsman, producers. A&M.
Roll with It, Steve Winwood. Steve Winwood, Tom Lord Alge, producers. Virgin.

Simple Pleasures, Bobby McFerrin. Linda Goldstein, producer. EMI/Manhattan.
✓*Tracy Chapman*, Tracy Chapman. David Kershenbaum, producer. Elektra.

RECORD OF THE YEAR
• "Don't Worry, Be Happy," Bobby McFerrin. Linda Goldstein, producer. EMI/Manhattan.
✓"Fast Car," Tracy Chapman. David Kershenbaum, producer. Elektra.
"Giving You the Best That I Got," Anita Baker. Michael J. Powell, producer. Elektra.

"Man in the Mirror," Michael Jackson. Michael Jackson, Quincy Jones, producers. Epic.

"Roll with It," Steve Winwood. Steve Winwood, Tom Lord Alge, producers. Virgin.

SONG OF THE YEAR
(Songwriter's Award)
- "Don't Worry, Be Happy," Bobby McFerrin. EMI.
✓ "Be Still My Beating Heart," Sting. A&M.
✓ "Fast Car," Tracy Chapman. Elektra.
"Giving You the Best That I Got," Anita Baker, Skip Scarborough, Randy Holland. Elektra.
"Piano in the Dark," Brenda Russell, Jeff Hall, Scott Cutler. A&M.

BEST NEW ARTIST
- Tracy Chapman. Elektra.
Rick Astley. RCA.
Toni Childs. A&M.
Take 6. Reprise.
Vanessa Williams. Polygram.

BEST POP VOCAL PERFORMANCE, MALE
- Bobby McFerrin, "Don't Worry, Be Happy." EMI/Manhattan.
Phil Collins, "A Groovy Kind of Love." Atlantic.
✓ George Michael, "Father Figure." Columbia.
✓ Sting, "Be Still My Beating Heart." A&M.
Steve Winwood, "Roll with It." Virgin.

BEST POP VOCAL PERFORMANCE, FEMALE
✓ - Tracy Chapman, "Fast Car." Elektra.
Taylor Dayne, *Tell It to My Heart*. Arista.
Whitney Houston, "One Moment in Time." Arista.
Joni Mitchell, *Chalk Mark in a Rain Storm*. Geffen.
Brenda Russell, *Get Here*. Elektra.

BEST POP VOCAL PERFORMANCE BY A DUO OR GROUP WITH VOCAL
- Manhattan Transfer, *Brasil*. Altantic.
✓ Beach Boys, "Kokomo." Elektra.
Escape Club, "Wild, Wild West." Atlantic.
✓ Gloria Estefan & the Miami Sound Machine, "Anything for You" (Spanish/English version). Epic.

N.A.R.A.S.'s choice of Tracy Chapman as Best New Artist was "political, dangerous and — gulp! — hip," said Rolling Stone.

Brenda Russell, Joe Esposito, "Piano in the Dark," track from *Get Here*. A&M.

BEST POP INSTRUMENTAL PERFORMANCE
- David Sanborn, *Close-Up*. Reprise.
Kenny G., *Silhouette*. Arista.
M/A/R/R/S, "Pump Up the Volume." 4th & Broadway/Island.
Mike Post, *Music from* L.A. Law & *Otherwise*. Polydor.
Joe Satriani, "Always With Me, Always With You." Relativity.

BEST ROCK VOCAL PERFORMANCE, MALE
- Robert Palmer, "Simply Irresistible." EMI/Manhattan.
✓ Eric Clapton, "After Midnight." Polydor.
Joe Cocker, *Unchain My Heart*. Capitol.
Robbie Robertson, *Robbie Robertson*. Geffen.
Rod Stewart, "Forever Young." Warner Bros.

BEST ROCK VOCAL PERFORMANCE, FEMALE
- Tina Turner, *Tina Live in Europe*. Capitol.
Pat Benatar, "All Fired Up." Chrysalis.

Toni Childs, "Don't Walk Away," track from *Union*. A&M.

Melissa Etheridge, "Bring Me Some Water," track from *Melissa Etheridge*. Island.

Sinéad O'Connor, *The Lion and the Cobra*. Chrysalis.

BEST ROCK PERFORMANCE BY A DUO OR GROUP WITH VOCAL
• U2, "Desire." Island.
✓ INXS, *Kick*. Atlantic.
Joan Jett & the Blackhearts, "I Hate Myself for Loving You." Blackheart.
Little Feat, *Let It Roll*. Warner Bros.
✓ Midnight Oil, "Beds Are Burning." Columbia/CBS.

BEST ROCK INSTRUMENTAL PERFORMANCE
• Carlos Santana, *Blues for Salvador*. Columbia/CBS.
Jeff Healey Band, "Hideaway," track from *See the Light*. Arista.
Jimmy Page, "Writes of Winter," track from *Outrider*. Geffen.
Joe Satriani, *Surfing with the Alien*. Relativity.
Frank Zappa, *Guitar*. Rykodisc.

BEST HARD ROCK/METAL PERFORMANCE, VOCAL OR INSTRUMENTAL
• Jethro Tull, *Crest of a Knave*. Chrysalis.
AC/DC, *Blow Up Your Video*. Atlantic.
Jane's Addiction, *Nothing's Shocking*. Warner Bros.
Metallica, *... And Justice for All*. Elektra.
Iggy Pop, "Cold Metal." A&M.

BEST RHYTHM & BLUES SONG
(Songwriter's Award)
• "Giving You the Best That I Got," Anita Baker, Skip Scarborough, Randy Holland. Elektra.
"Any Love," Luther Vandross, Marcus Miller. Epic.
"Don't Be Cruel," Babyface, L.A. Reid, Daryl Simmons. Solar/Epic.
"I'll Always Love You," Jimmy George. Arista.
"Just Got Paid," Johny Kemp, Gene Griffin. Columbia/CBS.

BEST RHYTHM & BLUES VOCAL PERFORMANCE, MALE
• Terence Trent D'Arby, *Introducing the Hardline According to Terence Trent D'Arby*. Columbia/ CBS.

Teddy Pendergrass, *Joy*. Elektra.
Al B. Sure, "Nite and Day." Warner Bros.
Luther Vandross, *Any Love*. Epic.
Stevie Wonder, *Characters*. Motown.

BEST RHYTHM & BLUES VOCAL PERFORMANCE, FEMALE
• Anita Baker, "Giving You the Best That I Got." Elektra.
Taylor Dayne, "I'll Always Love You." Arista.
Pebbles, "Girlfriend." MCA.
Karyn White, "The Way You Love Me." Warner Bros.
Vanessa Williams, "The Right Stuff." Wing.

BEST RHYTHM & BLUES PERFORMANCE BY A DUO OR GROUP WITH VOCAL
• Gladys Knight & the Pips, "Love Overboard." MCA.
Robert Cray Band, "Acting this Way," track from *Don't Be Afraid of the Dark*. Mercury.
E.U., "Da'Butt," track from *School Daze— Original Motion Picture Soundtrack*. EMI.
Jets, "Rocket 2 U." MCA.
New Edition, "If It Isn't Love." MCA.

BEST RHYTHM & BLUES INSTRUMENTAL PERFORMANCE
• Chick Corea, "Light Years," track from *GRP Super Live in Concert, Volumes I & II*. GRP.
Gerald Albright, "So Amazing." Atlantic.
Cornell Dupree & Who It Is, *Coast to Coast*. Antilles New Directions.
George Howard, *Reflections*. MCA.
Paul Jackson, Jr., *I Came to Play*. Atlantic.
Doc Powell, "What's Going On," track from *Love Is Where It's At*. Mercury.

BEST RAP PERFORMANCE
• D.J. Jazzy Jeff & the Fresh Prince, "Parents Just Don't Understand," track from *He's the DJ, I'm the Rapper*. Jive.
J.J. Fad, "Supersonic." Ruthless/Atlantic.
Kool Moe Dee, "Wild, Wild West," track from *How Ya Like Me Now*. Jive.
✓ L.L. Cool J, "Going Back to Cali." Columbia.
Salt-N-Pepa, "Push It." Next Plateau.

BEST JAZZ VOCAL PERFORMANCE, MALE
• Bobby McFerrin, "Brothers," track from *Rob Wasserman*'s *Duets*. MCA.
Mose Allison, *Ever Since the World Ended*. Blue Note.
Joao Gilberto, *Live in Montreux*. Elektra.
Mark Murphy, *September Ballads*. Milestone.
Mel Tormé, *A Vintage Year*. Concord Jazz.

BEST JAZZ VOCAL PERFORMANCE, FEMALE
• Betty Carter, *Look What I Got!* Verve.
Lena Horne, *The Men in My Life*. Three Cherries Records.
Rickie Lee Jones, "Autumn Leaves," track from *Rob Wasserman's Duets*. MCA.
Peggy Lee, *Miss Peggy Lee Sings the Blues*. Musicmasters.
Carmen McRae, *Fine and Mellow*. Concord Jazz.

BEST JAZZ VOCAL PERFORMANCE, DUO, OR GROUP
• Take 6, "Spread Love." Reprise.
Jackie Cain, Roy Krat, *One More Rose*. Audiophile.
Cunninghams, *Strings 'N' Swing "I Remember Bird."* Discovery.
Lena Horne, Joe Williams, "I Won't Leave You Again," track from *The Men in My Life*. Three Cherries Records.
Carmen McRae, Betty Carter, *The Carmen McRae–Betty Carter Duets*. Great American Music Hall.

BEST JAZZ INSTRUMENTAL PERFORMANCE, SOLOIST
• Michael Brecker, *Don't Try This at Home*. MCA-Impulse.
Miles Davis, *Music from Siesta*. Warner Bros.
Branford Marsalis, *Random Abstract*. Columbia/CBS.
Wynton Marsalis, *The Wynton Marsalis Quartet Live at Blues Alley*. Columbia/CBS.
Rob Wasserman, *Duets*. MCA.

BEST JAZZ INSTRUMENTAL PERFORMANCE, GROUP
• McCoy Tyner, Pharaoh Sanders, David Murray, Cecil McBee, Roy Haynes, *Blues for Coltrane: A Tribute to John Coltrane*. MCA-Impulse.
Chick Corea Elektric Band, "Amnesia," track from *Eye of the Beholder*. GRP.
Keith Jarrett Trio, *Still Live*. ECM.

Branford Marsalis Quartet, *Random Abstract*. Columbia/CBS.
Wynton Marsalis Quartet, *The Wynton Marsalis Quartet Live at Blues Alley*. Columbia/CBS.

BEST JAZZ INSTRUMENTAL PERFORMANCE, BIG BAND
• Gil Evans and the Monday Night Orchestra, *Bud & Bird*. Intersound.
Gene Harris All-Star Big Band, *Tribute to Count Basie*. Concord Jazz.
Woody Herman's Thundering Herd, *Ebony*. RCA Victor.
Bill Holman Band, *Bill Holman Band*. JVC.
Illinois Jacquet & His Big Band, *Jacquet's Got It!* Atlantic Jazz.

BEST JAZZ FUSION PERFORMANCE
• Yellowjackets, *Politics*. MCA.
David Benoit, *Every Step of the Way*. GRP.
Lyle Mays, *Sweet Dreams*. Geffen.
John Patitucci, *John Patitucci*. GRP.
Tom Scott, "Amaretto," track from *Streamlines*. GRP.

BEST COUNTRY SONG
(Songwriters Award)
• *Hold Me*, K.T. Oslin. RCA.
"Chiseled in Stone," Vern Gosdin, Max D. Barnes. Columbia.
"I Couldn't Leave You If I Tried," Rodney Crowell. Columbia/CBS.
"She's No Lady," Lyle Lovett. Curb/MCA.
"Streets of Bakersfield," Homer Joy. Reprise.

BEST COUNTRY VOCAL PERFORMANCE, MALE
• Randy Travis, *Old 8 x 10*. Warner Bros.
Rodney Crowell, *Diamonds & Dirt*. Columbia/CBS.
Lyle Lovett, *Pontiac*. MCA.
Dan Seals, "Addicted." Capitol.
Dwight Yoakam, *Buenas Noches from a Lonely Room*. Reprise.

BEST COUNTRY VOCAL PERFORMANCE, FEMALE
• K.T. Oslin, "Hold Me," track from *This Woman*. RCA.
Emmylou Harris, "Back in Baby's Arms," track from *Planes, Trains & Automobiles—Original Motion Picture Soundtrack*. MCA.

k.d. lang, "I'm Down to My Last Cigarette." Sire.

Reba McEntire, *Reba*. MCA.

Tanya Tucker, "Strong Enough to Bend." Capitol.

BEST COUNTRY VOCAL PERFORMANCE BY A DUO OR GROUP WITH VOCAL

• Judds, "Give a Little Love," track from *Greatest Hits*. RCA.

Forrester Sisters, *Sincerely*. Warner Bros.

Highway 101, *Highway 101—2*. Warner Bros.

Oak Ridge Boys, "Gonna Take a Lot of River." MCA.

Restless Heart, *Big Dreams in a Small Town*. RCA.

BEST COUNTRY VOCAL COLLABORATION

• Roy Orbison, k.d. lang, "Crying." Virgin.

Earl Thomas Conley, Emmylou Harris, "We Believe in Happy Endings," track from *The Heart of It All* (Earl Thomas Conley album). RCA.

Rodney Crowell, Rosanne Cash, "It's Such a Small World." Columbia/CBS.

k.d. lang, Brenda Lee, Loretta Lynn, Kitty Wells, "Honky Tonk Angels' Medley," track from *Shadowland* (k.d. lang album). Sire.

Dwight Yoakam, Buck Owens, "Streets of Bakersfield." Reprise.

BEST COUNTRY INSTRUMENTAL PERFORMANCE

• Asleep at the Wheel, "Sugarfoot Rag," track from *Western Standard Time*. Epic.

Johnny Gimble, "Still Fiddlin' Around." MCA.

Leo Kottke, "Busy Signal," track from *Regards from Chuck Pink*. Private Music.

Carlton Moody & the Moody Brothers, "The Great Train Song Medley," track from *Do the Sugar Foot Rag*. Lamon.

Mason Williams & Mannheim Steamroller, "Country Idyll," track from *Classical Gas*. American Gramaphone.

BEST GOSPEL PERFORMANCE, MALE

• Larnelle Harris, *Christmas*. Benson.

Steven Curtis Chapman, *Real Life Conversations*. Sparrow.

Steve Green, *Find Us Faithful*. Sparrow.

Michael W. Smith, *I 2 (Eye)*. Reunion.

Russ Taff, *Russ Taff*. Myrrh.

BEST GOSPEL PERFORMANCE, FEMALE

• Amy Grant, *Lead Me On*. A&M.

Margaret Becker, *The Reckoning*. Sparrow.

Sandi Patti, "Almighty God," track from *Make His Praise Glorious*. Word.

Deniece Williams, "Do You Hear What I Hear?" track from *Christmas — Various Artists*. Sparrow.

Delores Winans, "Precious Is the Name," track from *Ronald Winans Family & Friends Choir*. Selah Records.

BEST GOSPEL PERFORMANCE BY A DUO OR GROUP, CHOIR, OR CHORUS

• Winans, *The Winans Live at Carnegie Hall*. Qwest.

DeGarmo & Key, *D&K*. Power Disc/Benson.

First Call, *An Evening in December Vol. II*. Dayspring/Word.

Whites, *Doing It by the Book*. Canaan/Word.

BeBe & CeCe Winans, "Silent Night, Holy Night," track from *Christmas—Various Artists*. Sparrow.

BEST SOUL GOSPEL PERFORMACE, MALE

• BeBe Winans, "Abundant Life," track from *Ron Winans Family & Friends Choir*. Selah Records.

Walter Hawkins, solo tracks from *Special Gift*. Birthright.

Richard Smallwood, "You Did It All," track from *Visions*. Word.

Marvin Winans, "Dancin' in the Spirit," track from *Ron Winans Family & Friends Choir*. Selah Records.

Melvin Williams, *Back to the Cross*. Light.

BEST SOUL GOSPEL PERFORMANCE, FEMALE

• Aretha Franklin, *One Lord, One Faith, One Baptism*. Arista.

Vanessa Bell Armstrong, "Pressing On." Jive.

Shirley Caesar, *Live ... in Chicago*. Rejoice.

Tramaine Hawkins, *The Joy That Floods My Soul*. Sparrow.

CeCe Winans, "I Have a Father," track from *Ronald Winans Family & Friends Choir*. Selah Records.

Best Soul Gospel Performance by a Duo or Group, Choir, or Chorus
• Take 6, *Take 6*. Reprise
Clark Sisters, *Conqueror*. Rejoice/Word.
Aretha Franklin, Mavis Staples, "Oh Happy Day." Arista.
Edwin Hawkins, *That Name*. Birthright.
New Jersey Mass Choir, *Hold Up the Light*. Light.
Ronald Winans Family & Friends Choir, *Ronald Winans Family & Friends Choir*. Selah Records.

Best Traditional Folk Recording
• *Folkways: A Vision Shared — A Tribute to Woody Guthrie and Leadbelly*, Various artists. Don DeVito, Joe McEwen, Harold Leventhal, Ralph Rinzler, producers. Columbia/CBS.
Irish Heartbeat, Van Morrison, Chieftains. Mercury.
Journey of Dreams, Ladysmith Black Mambazo. Warner Bros.
Le Mystère des Voix Bulgares, Bulgarian State Radio & Television Female Vocal Choir. Elektra/Nonesuch.
"Pretty Boy Floyd," track from *Folkways: A Vision Shared*, Bob Dylan. Columbia/CBS.

Best Contemporary Folk Recording
• *Tracy Chapman*, Tracy Chapman. Elektra.
"Emergency," track from *Live at Carnegie Hall*, Sweet Honey in the Rock. Flying Fish.
Homeland—A Collection of Black South African Music, Various South African artists. Clive Risko, producer. Rounder.
John Prine Live, John Prine. Oh Boy.
Short Sharp Shocked, Michelle Shocked. Mercury.

Best Traditional Blues Recording
• *Hidden Charms*, Willie Dixon. Bug/Capitol.
Ain't Nothin' But a Party, Johnny Copeland. Rounder.
Live at Antone's Nightclub, James Cotton. Antone's Records.
Saturday Night Zydeco, Rockin' Dopsie. Maison de Soul.
The Story of My Life, Guitar Slim, Jr. Orleans.

Best Contemporary Blues Recording
• "Don't Be Afraid of the Dark," Robert Cray Band. Mercury.

Blues You Can Use, Bobby Bland. Malaco.
"Low-Commotion," track from *Get Rhythm*, Ry Cooder. Warner Bros.
Seven Year Itch, Etta James. Island.
Talk to Your Daughter, Robben Ford. Warner Bros.

Best Bluegrass Recording (Vocal or Instrumental)
• *Southern Flavor*, Bill Monroe. MCA.
Drive, Bela Fleck. Rounder.
Fifteenth Anniversary Celebration, Live at the Kennedy Center, Seldom Scene & Their Very Special Guests. Sugar Hill.
Home Is Where the Heart Is, David Grisman. Rounder.
New Moon Rising, Peter Rowan & the Nashville Bluegrass Band. Sugar Hill.

Best Latin Pop Performance
• Roberto Carlos, *Roberto Carlos*. Discos CBS International.
Dyango, *Cae la Noche*. EMI.
José José, *Soy Así*. Ariola.
José Luis Perales, *Sueno de Libertad*. Discos CBS International.
Raphael, *Las Apariencias Enganan*. Discos CBS International.

Best Tropical Latin Performance
• Rubén Blades, Son del Solar, *Antecedente*. Elektra.
Oscar D'Leon, *La Salsa Soy Yo*. TH-Rodven U.S.A.
Pete Escovedo, *Mister E*. Crossover.
Johnny Pacheco, Pete, "El Conde" Rodriguez, *Salsobita*. Fania.
Eddie Santiago, *Sigo Astrevido*. TH-Rodven U.S.A.

Best Mexican/American Performance
• Linda Ronstadt, *Canciones de mi Padre*. Elektra.
Bukis, *Si Me Recuerdas*. Melody.
Freddy's, *Vida Nueva*. EMI.
Flaco Jimenez, *Flaco's Amigos*. Arhoolie.
Jose Javier Solis, *No Me Olvidaras*. Profono.
Tigres Del Norte, *Idolos del Pueblo*. Fonovisa.
Pio Trevino & Majic, *Quiero Verte Otra Vez*. Discos CBS International.
Yonics, *Petalo y Espinas*. Fonovisa.

Best Reggae Recording
• *Conscious Party*, Ziggy Marley & the Melody Makers. Virgin.
"Breakfast in Bed," track from *UB40*. UB40, Chrissie Hynde. A&M.

Hanging Fire, Jimmy Cliff. Columbia/ CBS.

Toots in Memphis, Toots (Hibbert). Mango/ Island.

UB40, UB40. A&M.

BEST POLKA RECORDING

• *Born to Polka*, Jimmy Sturr & His Orchestra. Starr.

All Aboard It's Polka Time, Walter Ostanek & His Band. World Renowned Sounds.

Join the Polka Generation, Lenny Gomulka's Chicago Push. World Renowned Sounds.

Let's Have a Party, Stas Bulanda's Average Polka Band. Chicago Polkas.

Sounds from a Polka Party, Jimmy Weber & the Sounds. World Renowned Sounds.

BEST NEW AGE PERFORMANCE

• Shadowfax, *Folksongs for a Nuclear Village*. Capitol.

Suzanne Ciani, *Neverland*. Private Music.

Mark Isham, *Castalia*. Virgin.

Steve Khan, Rob Mounsey, *Local Color*. Denon.

Paul Winter, "Down in Belgorod," track from *Earthbeat*. Living Music.

BEST INSTRUMENTAL COMPOSITION

• "The Theme from *L.A. Law*," track from *Music from* L.A. Law *& Otherwise*, Mike Post (Mike Post). Polydor.

Central City Sketches (Side 2), Benny Carter composer and conducting American Jazz Orchestra. Musicmasters.

"Eternal Child," track from *Eye of the Beholder*, Chick Corea (Chick Corea Elektric Band). GRP.

"Olympic Spirit," track from 1988 Summer Olympics album *One Moment in Time*, John Williams (John Williams). Arista.

"Winter Games," track from *The Symphony Sessions*, David Foster (Vancouver Symphony). Atlantic.

BEST ARRANGEMENT ON AN INSTRUMENTAL

• Roger Kellaway, "Memos from Paradise," track from *Memos from Paradise* (Eddie Daniels). GRP.

David Balakrishnan, "A Night in Tunisia," track from *Turtle Island String Quartet* (Turtle Island String Quartet). Windham Hill.

Bill Barber, Bill Berg, Jimmy Johnson & Dick Oatts, "Jazz Patrol," track from *The Further Adventures of Flim & the BB's* (Flim & the BB's). DMP.

John Dankworth, "Caravan," track from *Misty* (John Dankworth conducting London Symphony Orchestra). Pro Arte.

Henry Mancini, "Suite from *The Thorn Birds*," track from *Premier Pops* (Henry Mancini & R.P.O. Pops). Denon.

BEST MUSICAL CAST SHOW ALBUM

• *Into the Woods*, Bernadette Peters, Joanna Gleason, Chip Zien, Tom Aldredge, Robert Westenberg. Stephen Sondheim, music and lyrics. Jay David Saks, producer. RCA.

Anything Goes, Patti LuPone, Bill McCutcheon, Howard McGillian, others. Cole Porter, composer & lyricist. Jay David Saks, producer. RCA.

Chess, David Carroll, Philip Casnoff, Judy Kuhn, others. Benny Andersson, Bjorn Ulvaeus, producers and composers. Tim Rice, lyricist. RCA Victor.

Of Thee I Sing/Let 'Em Eat Cake, Maureen McGovern, Larry Kert, Jack Gilford. Michael Tilson Thomas conducting New York Choral Artists & Orchestra of St. Luke's. Steven Epstein, producer. George & Ira Gershwin, composer and lyricist. CBS Records.

Show Boat, Frederica Von Stade, Jerry Hadley, Teresa Stratas, Nancy Culp, Lillian Gish, others. John McGlinn conducting London Sinfonietta. Jerome Kern, composer. Oscar Hammerstein, lyricist. John Fraser, producer. Angel.

BEST ALBUM OF ORIGINAL INSTRUMENTAL BACKGROUND SCORE WRITTEN FOR A MOTION PICTURE OR TELEVISION

• *The Last Emporer*, Ryuichi Sakamoto, David Byrne, Cong Su. Virgin.

Empire of the Sun, John Williams. Warner Bros.

Fatal Attraction, Maurice Jarre. GNP-Crescendo.

Tucker: The Man and His Dream, Joe Jackson. A&M.

Who Framed Roger Rabbit, Alan Silvestri. Walt Disney Records.

Best Song Written Specifically for a Motion Picture or Television

- "Two Hearts," track from *Buster*, Phil Collins, Lamont Dozier. Atlantic.
- "Century's End," track from *Bright Lights, Big City*, Donald Fagen. Warner Bros.
- "Cry Freedom," track from *Cry Freedom*, George Fenton, Jonas Gwangwa. MCA.
- ✓ "Kokomo," track from *Cocktail*, Mike Love, Terry Melcher, John Philips, Scott Mackenzie. Elektra.
- "One Moment in Time," track from 1988 Summer Olympics Album *One Moment in Time*, Albert Hammond, John Bettis. Arista.

Best Instrumental Arrangement Accompanying Vocal(s)

- Jonathan Tunick, "No One Is Alone," track from *Cleo Sings Sondheim* (Cleo Laine). RCA.
- Henry Mancini, "Volare," track from *Volare* (Luciano Pavarotti). London.
- Marcus Miller, "Funny," track from *Other Roads* (Boz Scaggs). Columbia/CBS.
- Mike Renzi, "I Wish I'd Met You," track from *Men in My Life* (Lena Horne, Sammy Davis Jr.). Three Cherries Records.
- Thomas Dolby & the Lost Toy People, "The Key to Her Ferrari," track from *Aliens Ate My Buick* (Thomas Dolby). EMI/Manhattan.

Best Classical Album

- *Verdi: Requiem and Operatic Choruses*; Robert Shaw conducting Atlanta Symphony Orchestra and Chorus. Robert Woods, producer. Telarc.
- *Horowitz Plays Mozart (Piano Concerto No. 23 in A & Piano Sonata No. 13 in B Flat)*, Vladimir Horowitz, piano. Carlo Maria Giulini conducting LaScala Opera Orchestra. Thomas Frost, producer. Deutsche Grammophon.
- *Mahler: Symphony No. 2 in C Minor "Resurrection,"* Leonard Berstein conducting New York Philharmonic. Hans Weber, producer. Deutsche Grammophon.
- *Rorem: String Symphony; Sunday Morning; Eagles*, Robert Shaw conducting Atlanta Symphony Orchestra for "String Symphony." Louis Lane conducting Atlanta Symphony Orchestra for "Sunday Morning," "Eagles." Robert Woods, producer. New World.

Bloc voting accusations again plagued the Atlanta Symphony and Classical Producer of the Year Robert Woods.

- *Wagner: Lohengrin*, Sir Georg Solti conducting Vienna State Opera Choir and Vienna Philharmonic (solos: Placido Domingo, Jessye Norman, Eva Randova, Siegmund Nimsgern, Hans Sotin, Dietrich Fischer-Dieskau). Christopher Raeburn, producer. London.

Best Orchestral Recording
(Conductor's Award)

- *Rorem: String Symphony*, Robert Shaw conducting Atlanta Symphony Orchestra; *Sunday Morning, Eagles*, Louis Lane conducting Atlanta Symphony. Robert Woods, producer. New World.
- *Beethoven: Symphony No. 9 in D Minor*, Roger Norrington conducting London Classical Players. David R. Murray, producer. Angel.
- *Bruckner: Symphony No. 7 in E*, Sir Georg Solti conducting Chicago Symphony Orchestra. Michael Haas, producer. London.

*Copland: Appalachian Spring (Complete);
Letter from Home; John Henry; Cortege
Macabre from Grohg*, Leonard Slatkin
conducting St. Louis Symphony
Orchestra. Joanna Nickrenz, producer.
Angel.

*Mahler: Symphony No. 2 in C Minor
("Resurrection").* Leonard Berstein
conducting New York Philharmonic.
Hans Weber, producer. Deutsche
Grammophon.

BEST CHAMBER MUSIC PERFORMANCE
(INSTRUMENTAL OR VOCAL)

• Murray Perahia, Sir George Solti, pianos.
David Corkhill, Evelyn Glennie,
percussion, *Bartók: Sonata for Two
Pianos and Percussion; Brahms:
Variation on a Theme by Joseph Haydn
for Two Pianos.* CBS Masterworks.

Guarneri Quartet, *Dvořák: String Quartet
in F ("American Quartet"); Smetana:
String Quartet in E Minor ("From My
Life").* Philips.

Kim Kashkashian, viola; Robert Levin,
piano, *Hindemith: Viola Sonatas (Op.
11/4; Op. 25/4 & Violin Sonatas,
1937).* ECM.

Gidon Kremer, violin; Martha Argerich,
piano, *Beethoven: Violin-Piano
Sonatas No. 4 in A, Op. 23 & No. 5 in
F, Op. 24.* Deutsche Grammophon.

James Levine, piano; Ensemble Wien-
Berlin, *Mozart: Quintet in E Flat for
Piano & Winds, K. 452; Beethoven:
Quintet in E Flat for Piano & Winds,
Op. 16.* Deutsche Grammophon.

BEST CLASSICAL PERFORMANCE,
INSTRUMENTAL SOLOIST(S) (WITH
ORCHESTRA)

• Vladimir Horowitz , piano (Carlo Maria
Giulini conducting LaScala Opera
Orchestra), *Mozart: Piano Concerto
No. 23 in A.* Deutsche Grammophon.

Gary Gray, clarinet (Harry Newstone
conducting Royal Philharmonic
Orchestra), *The Art of Gary Gray*
(Copland: Clarinet Concerto;
Lutoslawskiz: Dance Preludes for
Clarinet & Orchestra; Arnold: Clarinet
Concerto No. 1; etc.). Unicorn/
Kanchana Records.

Zoltan Kocsis, piano (Ivan Fischer
conducting Budapest Festival
Orchestra), *Bartók: Works for Piano &
Orchestra* (Concerto No. 1; Concerto
No. 2; Rhapsody for Piano &
Orchestra; etc.). Philips.

Wynton Marsalis, trumpet (Raymond
Leppard conducting English Chamber
Orchestra), *Baroque Music for
Trumpets (Vivaldi, Telemann,
Pachelbel, Haydn, Von Biber).* CBS
Masterworks.

Itzhak Perlman, violin (Zubin Mehta
conducting Israel Philharmonic
Orchestra), *Bruch: Scottish Fantasy &
Violin Concerto No. 2 in D Minor.*
Angel.

Isaac Stern, violin (Lorin Maazel
conducting Orchestra National de
France), *Dutilleux: L' Arbre Des
Songes—Concerto for Violin &
Orchestra.* CBS Masterworks.

Isaac Stern, violin; Yo-Yo Ma, cello
(Claudio Abbado conducting Chicago
Symphony Orchestra), *Brahms: Double
Concerto in A Minor, Op. 102.* CBS
Masterworks.

BEST CLASSICAL PERFORMANCE —
INSTRUMENTAL SOLOIST(S) (WITHOUT
ORCHESTRA)

• Alicia de Larrocha, piano, *Albéniz:
Iberia; Navarra; Suite Espagnola.*
London.

Alfred Brendel, piano, *Liszt: Annees De
Pelerinage, Second Year: Italy.* Philips.

Vladimir Horowitz, piano, *Mozart: Piano
Sonata No. 13 in B Flat, K. 333.*
Deutsche Grammophon.

Keith Jarrett, piano. *Bach: The Well-
Tempered Clavier, Book I.* ECM.

Maurizio Pollini, piano, *Schubert: The
Late Piano Sonatas (D. 958-959-960);
3 Piano Pieces, D. 946; Allegretto, D.
915.* Deutsche Grammophon.

BEST OPERA RECORDING

• *Wagner: Lohengrin*, Sir Georg Solti
conducting Vienna State Opera Choir
and Vienna Philharmonic (solos:
Placido Domingo, Dietrich Fischer-
Dieskau, Siegmund Nimsgern, Jessye
Norman, Eva Randova, Hans Sotin).
Christopher Raeburn, producer.
London.

Adams: Nixon in China,
Edo de Waart
conducting Orchestra of
St. Luke's (solos:
Sanford Sylvan, James
Maddalena, Thomas
Hammons, John
Duykers, Carolann
Page). Wilhelm
Hellweg, producer.
Elektra/Nonesuch.
Bellini: Norma, Richard
Bonynge conducting
Welsh National Opera
Orchestra and Chorus
(solos: Joan Sutherland,
Luciano Pavarotti,
Montserrat Caballé,
Samuel Ramey).
Andrew Cornall,
producer. London.

Luciano Pavarotti in Concert *brought the Italian tenor his fourth career Grammy for best classical vocalist.*

Berstein/Wadsworth: A Quiet Place,
Leonard Bernstein conducting Austrian
Radio Symphony (solos: Chester
Ludgin, Beverly Morgan, John
Brandstetter, Peter Kazaras, Jean Kraft,
Wendy White). Hans Weber, producer.
Deutsche Grammophon.
Mozart: Idomeneo, Sir John Pritchard
conducting Vienna Philharmonic
Orchestra & Chorus (solos: Luciano
Pavarotti, Agnes Baltsa, Lucia Popp,
Edita Gruberova, Leo Nucci).
Christopher Raeburn, producer.
London.
Puccini: La Bohème, Leonard Berstein
conducting Chorus and Orchestra of
Santa Cecilia (solos: Angelina Reaux,
Jerry Hadley, Barbara Daniels, Thomas
Hampson). Hans Weber, producer.
Deutsche Grammophon.

BEST CHORAL PERFORMANCE
(OTHER THAN OPERA)

• Robert Shaw conducting Atlanta
Symphony Orchestra and Chorus,
*Verdi: Requiem and Operatic
Choruses*. Robert Woods, producer.
Telarc.
Helmuth Froschauer, chorus master.
Herbert von Karajan conducting
Vienna Singverein and Vienna
Philharmonic, *Mozart: Requiem*.
Deutsche Grammophon.
John Eliot Gardiner conducting Monteverdi
Choir, English Baroque Soloists, *Bach:
Christmas Oratorio*. Archiv.

Margaret Hillis, choral director. Sir Georg
Solti conducting Chicago Symphony
Chorus and Orchestra, *Bach: St.
Matthew Passion*. London.
Trevor Pinnock conducting English
Concert Choir and English Concert,
*Vivaldi: Gloria; Scarlatti: Dixit
Dominus*. Archiv.

BEST CLASSICAL VOCAL SOLOIST
PERFORMANCE

• Luciano Pavarotti, tenor (Emerson
Buckley conducting Symphonic
Orchestra of Amelia Romagna "Arturo
Toscanini.") *Luciano Pavarotti in
Concert; (*Arias from *Lucia Di
Lammermoor, Rigoletto, La Bohème,
Fedora, Turandot*, etc.). CBS
Masterworks.
Arleen Auger, soprano (Dalton Baldwin,
accompanist), *Love Songs* (Copland, R.
Strauss, Poulenc, Mahler, Schumann,
Gounod, Schubert, etc.). Delos.
Jan DeGaetani, mezzo-soprano (Gilbert
Kalish, accompanist), *Songs of America*
(Stephen Foster, Elliott Carter, Ruth
Crawford, Milton Babbitt, George
Crumb, Carrie Jacobs-Bond, Irving
Fine, Sergius Kagen). Elektra/Nonesuch.
Christa Ludwig, soprano (James Levine,
accompanist), *Schubert: Winterreise*.
Deutsche Grammophon.
Jessye Norman, soprano (Geoffrey
Parsons, accompanist),
*Handel/Schubert/Schumann: Lieder
(Jessye Norman — Live at Hohenems)*.
Philips Classics.

Best Contemporary Composition
• John Adams, *Nixon in China* (Edo de Waart conducting Orchestra of St. Luke's). Elektra/Nonesuch.

Leonard Bernstein, Stephen Wadsworth, *A Quiet Place* (Leonard Berstein conducting Austrian Radio Symphony Orchestra; soloists). Deutsche Grammophon.

William Bolcom, *Symphony No. 4* (Slatkin conducting St. Louis Orchestra; Joan Morris, mezzo-soprano). New World.

Ned Rorem, *String Symphony* (Robert Shaw conducting Atlanta Symphony Orchestra). New World.

Karlheinz Stockhausen, *Amour* (Suzanne Stephens, clarinet). Deutsche Grammophon.

Best Engineered Recording, Classical
• Jack Renner, *Verdi: Requiem and Operatic Choruses* (Robert Shaw conducting Atlanta Symphony Chorus and Orchestra). Telarc.

Simon Eadon, *Bruckner: Symphony No. 7 in E* (Sir Georg Solti conducting Chicago Symphony Orchestra). London.

Cees Heijkoop, Willem van Leeuwen, Volker Strauss, *Beethoven: The Nine Symphonies (Complete)* (Bernard Haitink conducting Concertgebouw Orchestra). Philips Classics.

Jack Renner, *Beethoven: Missa Solemnis; Mozart: Great C Minor Mass* (Robert Shaw conducting Atlanta Symphony Chorus, Orchestra, Soloists). Telarc.

Klaus Scheibe, *Mahler: Symphony No. 2 ("Resurrection")* (Leonard Bernstein conducting New York Philharmonic). Deutsche Grammophon.

Classical Producer of the Year
• Robert Woods
Andrew Cornall
Steven Epstein
Thomas Frost
Joanna Nickrenz

Best Comedy Recording
• *Good Morning, Vietnam*, Robin Williams. A&M.

Even Worse, "Weird Al" Yankovic. Scotti Bros./Rock 'N' Roll Records.

Fontaine: Why Am I Straight? Whoopie Goldberg. MCA.

Jonathan Winters Finally Captured, Jonathan Winters. Dove Books on Tape.

What Am I Doing in New Jersey? George Carlin. Eardrum.

Best Spoken Word or Non-Musical Recording
• "Speech by Rev. Jesse Jackson, July 27," track from Aretha Franklin's *One Lord, One Faith, One Baptism*, Rev. Jesse Jackson. Arista.

A Christmas Carol (Charles Dickens), Sir John Gielgud. Bantam Audio Publishing.

A Prairie Home Companion: The 2nd Annual Farewell Performance, Garrison Keillor, various artists. Minnesota Public Radio.

The Screwtape Letters (C.S. Lewis), John Cleese. Audio Literature.

Winters' Tales (Jonathan Winters), Jonathan Winters. Sound Editions.

Best Recording for Children
• *Pecos Bill*, Robin Williams, narrator. Ry Cooder, music. Mark Sottnick, Ry Cooder, producers. Windham Hill.

The Bible: The Amazing Book. Tony Salerno, Ron Krueger, Frank Hernandez, producers. Sparrow.

The Legend of Sleepy Hollow, Glenn Close, narrator. Tim Story, music. Mark Sottnick, Tim Story, Robert Van Nutt, producers. Windham Hill.

Peter and the Wolf; Carnival of the Animals, Part II, "Weird Al" Yankovic, narrator. Wendy Carlos, music. Wendy Carlos, Al Yankovic, producers. Epic.

The Tailor of Gloucester, Meryl Streep, narrator. Chieftans, music. Mark Sottnick, producer. Windham Hill.

The Tale of Peter Rabbit . . ., Meryl Streep, narrator. Lyle Mays, music. Lyle Mays, Steve Cantor, Mark Sottnick, producers. Windham Hill.

Best Engineered Recording, Non-Classical
• Tom Lord Alge, *Roll With It* (Steve Winwood). Virgin.

John Archer, *Through the Lens* (Checkfield). American Gramaphone.

Ray Bardani, John Potoker, *Provision* (Scritti Politti). Warner Bros.

Mick Guzauski, *Facets* (Doc Severinsen). Amherst.

George Massenburg, *Let It Roll* (Little Feat). Warner Bros.

Elliot Scheiner, *Soul Searchin'* (Glenn Frey). MCA.

BEST ALBUM PACKAGE
• Bill Johnson, *Tired of the Runnin'* (O'Kanes). Columbia/CBS.
Andrew Reid, *Bete Noire* (Bryan Ferry). Reprise.
Jeri Heiden, *Brian Wilson* (Brian Wilson). Sire.
Bruce Licher, *Our Beloved Revolutionary Sweetheart* (Camper Van Beethoven). Virgin.
Henry Marquez, *Picture This* (the Valentine Brothers). EMI America.

BEST ALBUM NOTES
(Annotator's Award)
• Anthony DeCurtis, *Crossroads* (Eric Clapton). Polydor.
John Edward Hasse, *The Classic Hoagy Carmichael* (Hoagy Carmichael, others). Indiana Historical Society.
Miles Krueger, *Show Boat* (Frederica Von Stade, Jerry Hadley, Teresa Stratas, Nancy Culp, Lillian Gish, others; John McGlinn conducting London Sinfonietta). Angel.
Dan Morgenstern, *The Complete Commodore Jazz Recordings, Vol. 1* (Various artists). Mosaic.
Vaughn Webb, *Virginia Traditions: Southwest Virginia Blues* (Various folk artists). BRI.

BEST HISTORICAL ALBUM
• *Crossroads*, Eric Clapton. Bill Levenson, producer. Polydor.
The Classic Hoagy Carmichael, Hoagy Carmichael, others. John Edward Hasse, producer. Indiana Historical Society.
The Complete Commodore Jazz Recordings, Vol. 1, Various artists. Michael Cuscuna, producer. Mosaic.
Djangologie USA, Django Reinhartdt. Hugh Fordin, producer. Disques Swing.
The Erteguns' New York—New York Cabaret Music, Various artists. Bob Porter, producer. Atlantic.

PRODUCER OF THE YEAR, NON-CLASSICAL
• Neil Dorfsman
Thomas Dolby
David Kershenbaum
L.A. Reid, Babyface
Narada Michael Walden

BEST PERFORMANCE MUSIC VIDEO
• *Where the Streets Have No Name*, U2. Meiert Avis, video director. Michael Hamlyn, Ben Dossett, producers. Island.
Check It Out, John Cougar Mellencamp. Jonathon Dark, video director. Fay Greene, video producer. Polygram Music Video-U.S.
Glass Spider, David Bowie. David Mallet, video director. Anthony Eaton, video producer. MPI Home Video.
Stevie Nicks: Live at Red Rocks, Stevie Nicks. Marty Callner, video director. Rabia Dockray, video producer. Sony Video Software.
The Symphony Sessions, David Foster. Tony Greco, video director. Kris Mathur, video producer. Atlantic Records Video.

BEST CONCEPT MUSIC VIDEO
• *Fat*, "Weird Al" Yankovic. Jay Levey, video director. Susan Zwerman, video producer. Rock 'n' Roll/Epic.
Get a Job, Hampton String Quartet. Sara Nichols, video director. Warren Schatz, video producer. RCA.
Storytelling Giants, Talking Heads. David Byrne, video director. Alan Kleinberg, video producer. Warner Reprise Video.
This Note's for You, Neil Young. Julien Temple, video director. Lynn Rose-Higgins, video producer. Reprise/Warner Bros.
When We Was Fab, George Harrison. Godley & Creme, video directors. Lexi Godfrey, video producers. Warner Bros.

Bonnie Raitt's Comeback
in the *Nick of Time*

It was "a real miracle," Bonnie Raitt said of the outcome of the 32nd annual awards ceremony.

For 20 years, stardom had eluded the veteran country rock and blues artist who *The New York Times* once said "always seemed to be 'too good' a singer — too self-effacing, too subtle, too 'real' — to become a major pop star." The daughter of the noted Broadway singer John Raitt had quit college in 1969 to

"The impossible has happened," said the N.Y. Times *when Bonnie Raitt nabbed four Grammys, including best LP and a blues award she shared with John Lee Hooker (right).*

explore new musical directions in the small clubs of New York and Boston where she quickly developed a faithful following. Her albums sold well but never climbed higher than 25th in the pop charts, and she was dropped by Warner Bros. after 15 years while she battled alcoholism.

"Had I been asked three years ago to evaluate the chances of Ms. Raitt's winning four Grammy Awards with an album that would sell over two million copies, I would have shaken my head and said 'impossible,'" wrote critic Stephen Holden in the *N.Y. Times* after her sweep. "Now the impossible has happened. [But] Ms. Raitt's late-blooming success is anything but accidental. *Nick of Time* captures and defines a moment in her generation's self-awareness."

Nick of Time was the 40-year-old artist's first recording for her new label, Capitol, and expressed her disillusionments about love and getting older. While it sold a million copies prior to the Grammycast and marked what the *L.A. Times* called "a dramatic comeback" in her career, it was ranked only 40th on the LP charts at its highest and was considered "a l-o-n-g shot" for Album of the Year by Grammy seer/critic Paul Grein.

Grein had predicted in the *L.A. Times* that the Fine Young Cannibals' *The Raw & the Cooked* would prevail, while other seasoned Grammy watchers foresaw a romp by the eponymous album by the Traveling Wilburys, a group comprised of rock vets George Harrison, Bob Dylan, Jeff Lynne, Tom Petty, and Roy Orbison. But Raitt capped off her "dramatic" career ascendancy with what *Billboard* called "one of the biggest upsets in Grammy history."

Raitt scored a Grammy for each of her four nominations, becoming only the fourth female artist ever to win Album of the Year, following earlier triumphs by Judy Garland, Barbra Streisand, and Carole King. In addition, she won both the female rock and pop vocal awards and a prize for Best Traditional Blues Recording, which she shared with John Lee Hooker for "I'm in the Mood," a track from Hooker's *The Healer*. After her first few victories, Raitt told the viewing audience, "I'm so transported!" Finally stunned by her fourth win for the year's top LP, she said, "I can only take so much of this! Wake me when it's over!

"I'd like to thank God for bringing me to this at a time when I can really appreciate it," she added in a more somber voice, noting that *Nick of Time* was "my first sober album .... I made a lot of changes in my life, but I don't take responsibility for that." She credited "divine intervention" instead. Then she smiled proudly at the audience and said, "My sobriety means I'm going to feel *great* tomorrow!"

Soon after the show, one record store executive told *Billboard*, "Business absolutely exploded." Never before had the Grammys made such an impact on a winner's career. *Nick of Time* jumped to number 22 from 40th place in the trade paper's album chart, then up to number 6, then to first place for nearly a month, as the LP's pre-Grammy million in sales doubled. *The Washington Post* said her Grammy success proved "that good things happen to good people, although sometimes only in good time. Maybe that's why Raitt, 40, called her album *Nick of Time*."

Although he called the LP competition wrong, Paul Grein, a *Billboard* critic who often contributed articles to the *L.A. Times*, had previously demonstrated an uncanny knack for forecasting winners and even for predicting who would

be *nominated*. This year, when surveying the Record of the Year category in the *Times*, he openly addressed the artist he was sure would clinch it for "We Didn't Start the Fire," saying, "Billy Joel, get that tux pressed."

Joel was competing against Grammy's Best New Artist of 1973, Bette Midler, who was up for "Wind Beneath My Wings," a ballad that she'd sung in her hit movie *Beaches*. Grein said, "'Wind Beneath My Wings' is the kind of single that would have won hands-down in the early 1970s, but no longer." Regular *L.A. Times* music critic Robert Hilburn picked Don Henley's "The End of the Innocence" to win instead. "The worst case scenario," he wrote, "is a Midler or Joel victory." Hilburn, however, clearly didn't like either alternative. He added, "'Wind Beneath My Wings' is a hopelessly leaden melodrama, while 'We Didn't Start the Fire' is shallow and irritating. Either record on a jukebox should be enough to empty a room."

Never before had the Grammys made such an impact on a winner's career.

When Midler won, she told the audience, "I'm stunned and I'm flabbergasted," then roared, "Hey, Bonnie Raitt, I got one, too!" "Wind" swept the category of Song of the Year, too, for its writers Larry Henley and Jeff Silbar.

The biggest scandal in the history of the Grammys occurred after the naming of the year's Best New Artist — Milli Vanilli — a pop act from West Germany that had previously won the equivalent honor at the American Music Awards (plus two other prizes) and the 1989 Juno Award for Best International Album (*Girl You Know It's True*) bestowed by the Canadian Academy of Recording Arts and Sciences.

Milli's Grammy victory was ominous from the beginning. *The Washington Post* noted that the news of their win

Milli Vanilli was stripped of the Best New Artist prize when the duo was unmasked as lip-synching frontmen. They told the press they had "made a pact with the devil" for fame.

"played better in the balcony (where the fans sit) than it did in the mezzanine seats occupied by industry folk." When Milli Vanilli (translation: "positive energy" in Turkish) first hit the pop scene, *Time* magazine wrote, "Unheard of. Milli Vanilli, a dance-music duo that sounds like Alvin and the Chipmunks and speaks English like the two Teutonic muscleheads on *Saturday Night Live*, has done something boggling. The group, scorned by critics and adored by clubgoers and devotees of MTV, has scored three No. 1 singles off its debut album .... The Millis appear in their videos snazzily dressed, or half dressed, whirling like cotton candy around a spool .... Their lighter-than-airhead lyrics and freeze-dried hip-hop rhythms combine pop and pap in tunes for instant consumption and rapid oblivion."

Milli Vanilli was more than just the flavor of the week. *Girl* may have been fast food, but it sold just as briskly, rack-

ing up 7 million copies in sales in the U.S. and 12 million worldwide. Nothing seemed to dent the pair's enormous popularity, not even the results of *Rolling Stone*'s annual Critics' Picks Poll, which voted Milli the worst band of 1989 and *Girl* the worst album. ("We don't listen to what the critics say," Milli member Rob Pilatus told the *L.A. Times*. "It's not important what they think of us.") And not even the persistent rumor that the "dread-locked duo," as they were known in the press, didn't really sing their own music — which would be proven true. (Arista studio artists Johnny Davis, Brad Howell, and Charles Shaw really did the singing.) The rumor had considerable evidence behind it for those who didn't yet know the truth. *The New York Times* noted: "At a concert at Radio City Music Hall to benefit AIDS research, Mr. Pilatus and Mr. [Fabrice] Morvan ran offstage when there were technical difficulties with their tape. A few moments later their song boomed out, vocals and all."

Soon after their Grammy Awards triumph, the seemingly invincible Pilatus and Morvan, who had never sung professionally before, insisted that they do the vocals on their next album. When producer Frank Farian refused, they fired him. Then Farian retaliated by admitting the deception publicly and suddenly Milli Vanilli had to face the music.

The outcry that followed was horrific — and somewhat hilarious. "Milli Vanilli, Phony Baloney," screamed a headline in *The New York Post*. "For

Sham, Silli Vanilli!" countered a head-line in *The New York Daily News*. N.A.R.A.S. president Michael Greene said that the academy trustees "were just livid about the situation," adding, "It was fraud and we're appalled by it."

At a quickly called press conference in New York, Pilatus pleaded for sympa-thy. "We were living together in the pro-jects, with two other musicians in Munich," he told reporters, who acted more like sharks in a feeding frenzy. "We had nothing to eat, and we were unhappy. We wanted to be stars. And suddenly this guy [Farian] gave us a chance and we took it." Pitalus insisted that he and Morvan had informed Arista executives of the hoax early on (a charge denied by Arista) but also admitted they had "made a pact with the devil" for fame, which spawned new headlines the next day proclaiming "The Devil Made Them Do It." "But we don't understand that it's us, the two little guys from Ger-many, the victims, who have to play suddenly the role of the crooks," he added. The reporters present goaded the twosome into proving that they could really sing by insisting they perform "Girl You Know It's True" on the spot. "The performance, with their trademark dreadlocks shaking," noted *Time*, "only proved once more that looking good was what they did best."

Pitalus and Morvan might not have suffered such open scorn had it not been for remarks they made earlier in their career that were perceived as arrogant. "Musically, we are more talented than any Bob Dylan," Pilatus once boasted. "Musically, we are more talented than Paul McCartney. Mick Jagger, his lines are not clear. He don't know how he should produce a sound. I'm the new modern rock & roll. I'm the new Elvis." Shortly after the press confer-ence, N.A.R.A.S. ended the affair offi-cially by stripping Milli Vanilli of its award based on the fact that *Girl*'s album credits had been falsified.

Elsewhere in the pop field, Michael Bolton topped Prince, Billy Joel, Richard Marx, and Roy Orbison for the best male pop vocal Grammy for "How Am I Supposed to Live Without You." (Prince's nod was consid-ered an oddity because his *Bat-man* music was mostly instrumen-tal.) Bolton's career dated back to the late 1970s when he was the lead singer of the pop-rock group Blackjack before breaking away on a solo path in 1983. In his acceptance remarks, he acknowledged that his recent success made him seem like an overnight sensa-tion, but he added, "It was more like 3,642 nights."

> **The headlines were hilarious: "Milli Vanilli, Phony Baloney" and "For Sham, Silli Vanilli!"**

The British band Fine Young Canni-bals was expected to devour the pop group vocal laurels for "She Drives Me Crazy" but was upset by the U.S. duo of Aaron Neville, of the famed New Orleans r&b family, and Linda Ronstadt for "Don't Know Much," which they also sang on the Grammycast. (The per-formance was "quite good," opined *The Washington Post*.) "Don't Know Much" was a single from the Neville Brothers' *Yellow Moon*. Another track, "Healing Chant," earned all four brothers (Aaron, Arthur, Charles, and Cyril) the instru-mental trophy. In her acceptance speech, Ronstadt thanked her partner's mother, saying, "She gave us not only Aaron, but all the Neville Brothers, and that's a pretty great musical contribution." Ron-stadt's and the Nevilles' producer, Peter Asher, repeated his earlier 1977 victory as Producer of the Year.

Former Eagle Don Henley made up for his loss in the Record and Song of the Year categories by rallying to claim the Best Male Rock Vocal Performance honors for *The End of the Innocence*, which he won only moments after performing the title track on the show. "Great," he said smiling upon accepting the award. "You sing a song, you win an award."

The Traveling Wilburys rebounded from their defeat for Album of the Year, too, to receive the rock group accolade, giving Tom Petty and Jeff Lynne each their first Grammy. (Petty had been nominated seven times in previous years; Lynne, never). Critic Paul Grein was having a bad year trying to predict the winners. Referring to a potential sweep by the Traveling Wilburys in all contending categories, including the LP competition, he wrote about the rock group line-up, "The Rolling Stones should finally win their first Grammy unless sentiment for the Traveling Wilburys is overpowering."

> *"On the rap [music] front, it's smiles all around this year."*

Former Yardbird Jeff Beck had teamed up in the past with other artists such as Donovan, but now he earned the prize for Best Rock Instrumental Performance for *Jeff Beck's Guitar Shop with Terry Bozzio and Tony Hymas.*

Last year, when Metallica lost the prize for hard rock/ heavy metal in a shocking upset to Jethro Tull, the group nonetheless, said the *L.A. Times*, "shook the Shrine Auditorium chandelier with a performance unlike anything ever seen or heard on a Grammy show." The number Metallica staged for the 1988 awards, "One," now won the troupe the award for heavy metal music, which was now given its own category separate from hard rock.

Billboard was among the sources calling for N.A.R.A.S. to allow the winners of the hard rock kudos, the black rock group Living Colour, to compete for Best New Artist, which might have averted the Milli Vanilli scandal had the group won, but the academy refused on the basis that individual band members had made partial past contributions to works by other artists. Living Colour took its revenge on fellow nominees Guns 'N' Roses, Metallica, and Motley Crue with "Cult of Personality." Its victory over Guns 'N' Roses was particularly sensitive since, as *The Washington Post* noted, "Living Colour and Guns 'N' Roses [had] opened for the Rolling Stones in Los Angeles and exchanged harsh words both on and off the stage."

The *Post* also noted that Guns 'N' Roses was the target of another group at the Grammys: "Outside the auditorium, the Los Angeles chapter of the Guardian Angels protested the nomination of two groups they said promoted 'hate music.'" Public Enemy, the other band singled out, was competing for the Best Rap Performance award, which it lost to the British-born, New York City–raised Young MC for "Bust a Move." In sharp contrast to last year when four of the five nominees boycotted the awards show because the rap prize was bestowed off the telecast, the *L.A. Times* wrote, "On the rap front, it's smiles all around this year." The Grammycast even included time for a rap number, which was performed by last year's winners and this year's losing contenders D.J. Jazzy Jeff & the Fresh Prince.

The British soul-dance group Soul II Soul lost its Best New Artist bid to Milli Vanilli but garnered two awards in consolation: the r&b group vocal honors for "Back to Life," which they shared with vocalist Caron Wheeler, and the r&b

instrumental laurels for "African Dance." Winner of the male r&b vocals prize, Bobby Brown, had been labeled a "hot new act" by *The Washington Post* and was expected by some to be a likely Best New Artist contender, but N.A.R.A.S. disqualified him because of his previous work as a member of the New Edition.

"Anita Baker won the female r&b award for the third time in four years," said *Billboard*, "the most convincing domination of the category since Aretha Franklin's iron lock on the award in the '60s and '70s." Baker's victory over Franklin, Natalie Cole, Janet Jackson, and last year's Best New Artist nominee and dethroned Miss America Vanessa Williams was confusing to some, since Baker won this year for the album of the same name as the song that she won for in 1988, "Giving You the Best That I Got." But the single was released prior to the LP, causing the two to fall on different sides of the Grammys' eligibility periods for 1988 and 1989.

Confusion also reigned, albeit to a lesser extent, over the winner of Best R&B Song, "If You Don't Know Me By Now," which had been covered recently by Simply Red. *Billboard* explained: "The Grammy for Best R&B Song went to a recycled 1972 oldie for the second time in three years. Kenny Gamble and Leon Huff's 'If You Don't Know Me By Now' won this year; Bill Withers' "Lean On Me" won two years ago." Older songs were permitted to compete if they had never been nominated before and had new recordings made.

Last year jazz artists invaded traditionally nonjazz categories to score major triumphs, but the opposite happened to some degree in 1989. When Dr. John and 1979 Best New Artist Rickie Lee Jones won the duo/group jazz vocals award for "Makin' Whoopee," the *L.A. Times* pointed out that they were "two names more commonly associated with pop and rock."

The male jazz vocal winner was the source of some rumblings, too, when newcomer Harry Connick, Jr. — the young, Sinatra-styled miner of old gems by the likes of Cole Porter and Harold Arlen — prevailed over Dr. John, George Benson, and others for his score to the film *When Harry Met Sally ...*, which starred Billy Crystal and Meg Ryan. His songs included works by jazz greats George Gershwin and Duke Ellington as well as the Broadway composing team of Rodgers & Hart. Connick's victory, the *L.A. Times* predicted correctly, "is likely to stir criticism from the purist wing of the jazz community that has tended to think of Connick primarily as a cabaret or pop singer."

Another first-time champ emerged to claim the jazz kudos for show tunes when Ruth Brown was honored as best female vocalist for *Blues on Broadway,* besting the *L.A. Times*'s pick of Dianne Schuur for "The Christmas Song." Brown may have been known for decades in the jazz world as "Miss Rhythm," but she had never before been nominated despite a formidable career that included gigs with such greats as Thelonious Monk and Miles Davis. Trumpet legend Davis won two awards this year, too — for solo and big band instrumentals, both for *Aura* — in addition to being honored with N.A.R.A.S.'s coveted Lifetime Achievement Award.

In the group instrumental category, the *Times* observed, "It's brother against brother — Wynton vs. Branford Marsalis," but ended up picking the winner right when it forecasted a victory for the Chick Corea's Akoustic Band and its eponymous LP. The paper was less fortunate predicting the victor of the fusion prize when four-time past champ, the Pat Metheny Group, prevailed with *Letter from Home*. The *Times* had said,

"We see [Larry] Carlton's effort — his first since recovering from a gunshot assault outside his Hollywood Hills home — as the one left standing after this Grammy title fight."

The younger brother of blues guitarist Jimmie Vaughan, Stevie Ray Vaughan, distinguished himself at Switzerland's Montreux Jazz Festival in 1982. He reaped his first Grammy (over veteran nominee B.B. King) for *In Step*, which lost its bid for the Best Rock Instrumental Performance honors but was voted Best Contemporary Blues Recording.

Considering the country music credentials of Bonnie Raitt and the winners of Song of the Year (Larry Henley and Jeff Silbar), *Billboard* ran the following headline after this year's Grammy ceremony: "Nashville the Biggest Winner of All." The trade paper cited the Nashville roots of the recipients of the religious awards, too, such as the Winans clan. CeCe Winans won the female gospel prize for "Don't Cry"; brother BeBe reaped the male honors for "Meantime"; and another brother, Daniel, who was working with choir accompaniment, snagged the soul gospel group laurels for "Let Brotherly Love Continue." The young, black doo-wop sextet and double champs from last year, Take 6, took one more in 1989 for "The Savior Is Waiting." The only non-Nashville artist to win was Al Green ("As Long As We're Together"), who marked his seventh win over the past eight years.

Randy Travis's previous two-year reign over the male country vocals category came to an end when a double loser from last year, Lyle Lovett, rebounded with *Lyle Lovett and His Large Band*. k.d. lang shared the duet/group award in 1988 with the late Roy Orbison, but she now surpassed such past champs as Emmylou Harris and Dolly Parton to claim the female singing prize for *Absolute Torch and Twang*. The *Post* called

her triumph "something of a surprise," since, as *Billboard* put it, "the image lang projects scares the living hell out of country radio. She doesn't have her hair piled on top of her head. She doesn't look like the rest of them and that intimidates people."

The Nitty Gritty Dirt Band reaped two Grammys for its salute to country music Will the Circle Be Unbroken, Volume 2.

lang was teamed up with Dwight Yoakam for the vocal collaboration honors, but they lost to a duo with sentiment on its side. "Country legend Hank Williams, who died in 1953 — five years before the inception of the Grammys — shared a Grammy with his son, Hank Williams, Jr., on 'There's a Tear in My Beer,'" *Billboard* wrote, noting that the younger Hank achieved the task by singing along with an old tape of his dad crooning, too. "It was the first Grammy for both artists, though senior was awarded a Lifetime Achievement Award in 1987."

"There's a Tear in My Beer" was in the race for Best Country Song but lost to "After All This Time" by Rodney Crowell. Crowell began writing the tune about his relationship with wife Rosanne Cash in 1978, but didn't complete it until seven years later when he happened to come across some old notes for it. "It was as if five minutes had passed," he told *Billboard*, "so I finished the song."

A follow-up tribute to the broad heritage of country music swept the remaining two categories — instrumental music and duo/group vocals — for the Nitty Gritty Dirt Band's *Will the Circle Be Unbroken, Volume 2*. The band had recruited a host of country legends to perform on the first volume, including Ray Acuff, Merle Haggard, and Doc Watson. Virtually all of them returned for the sequel, which also snared Best Bluegrass Recording.

Jimmy Sturr & His Orchestra, which records in Nashville, stretched its monopoly over Best Polka Recording for a fourth consecutive year. Several other (non-Nashville) past champs came back for additional prizes, too, when 1968 Best New Artist José Feliciano was hailed for Best Latin Pop Performance (*Ceilito Lindo*) and the Tex-Mex/rock fusion band Los Lobos nabbed Best Mexican/American Performance (*La Pistola y el Corazón*), which it last won in 1983.

The veteran Afro-Cuban singer Celia Cruz, also known as the "Queen of Salsa," had contributed to Tito Puente's 1978 Best Latin Recording *Homenaje a Beny Moré*, but she didn't receive her own first Grammy until 1989 for her Best Tropical Latin Performance *Ritmo en el Corazon*. She shared the prize with Ray Barretto, the legendary Congo drummer, composer, arranger, and bandleader. Bob Marley's son, Ziggy, repeated his victory of last year when *One Bright Day* was named Best Reggae Recording.

Indigo Girls was a hot new singing and guitar-strumming duo act from Georgia that lost its bid for Best New Artist but won Best Contemporary Folk Recording for its eponymous debut LP.

A three-time past Grammy champ, composer and arranger Dave Grusin, picked up three more in 1989: an arrangement prize for "Suite from *The Milagro Beanfield War*" (a film directed by Robert Redford) and two more (best film score and another arranger's award) for his contributions to the Jeff Bridges–Beau Bridges–Michelle Pfeiffer film *The Fabulous Baker Boys*, about the travails of a gypsy lounge act. His previous victories included sharing the 1968 film score honors with Paul Simon for *The Graduate*.

Baker Boys pulled an upset over Danny Elfman's *Batman* score (and nominated works by John Williams and Peter Gabriel), but Elfman reaped the consolation for Best Instrumental Composition for "The *Batman* Theme." Prince lost both of his Grammy bids for *Batman*, but had contributed only a few songs to the blockbuster film starring Michael Keaton. Grammy's 1971 Best New Artist Carly Simon contributed only one song to director Mike Nichols' film *Working Girl*, but "Let the River Run" won both the Oscar and the Grammy as best film song.

> *"k.d. lang scares the living hell out of country radio,"* said **Billboard.** *"She doesn't have her hair piled on top of her head."*

The late *Saturday Night Live* comic Gilda Radner wasn't nominated for the comedy laurels this year but was hailed instead for *It's Always Something*, which was named Best Spoken Word or Non-Musical Recording. Radner had died in May of that year.

The winner of Best Comedy Recording became known in the music world as "Professor" Peter Schickele soon after the renowned composer began sharing his amusing thoughts on, and playful interpretations of, works by a great "Baroque master" on recording — *P.D.Q. Bach: 1712 Overture & Other Musical Assaults. The New York Times* called his work "the greatest comedy-in-music act before the public today."

"The video awards were strictly a family affair," the *L.A. Times* observed. Over the past two years, Michael Jackson had lost all of his nominations for his mega-hit *Bad* album, but this year at least he picked up Best Short Form Music Video for *Leave Me Alone.* His sister Janet nabbed the first Grammy of her career when she won the long-form video prize for *Rhythm Nation.*

"The classical Grammys produced a bumper crop of surprises this year," the *L.A. Times* reported. Following last year's accusations of bloc voting by the Atlanta Symphony Orchestra, an 11-member committee was established to come up with a final ballot instead of letting N.A.R.A.S. members determine the line-up as they had in the past. Missing were such usual Grammy favorites as Sir Georg Solti, Itzhak Perlman, and Luciano Pavarotti. "Last year the fat cats won in all categories," the *Times* reported. "This time around, the mix is so catholic that the outcome is hearteningly unclear."

Despite the procedural overhaul, Robert Shaw and the Atlanta Symphony Orchestra and Chorus ended up winning three awards, including a sixth Classical Producer of the Year prize for Robert Woods and two (Best Engineered Recording and Best Choral Performance) for the team's reading of Benjamin Britten's *War Requiem.* "Bloc voting from the Atlanta classical contingent no doubt contributed" to their sweep, said the *L.A. Times.* Britten him-self had been among the winners when *War Requiem* won the choral prize for its original 1963 recording.

"For the past two decades, the performance practice of the Bartók quartets has been defined by recordings of the Juilliard Quartet," *High Fidelity* wrote of the Juilliard recording that earned the quartet 1965 Grammy for best chamber music performance. Now a new and highly acclaimed version by the Emerson String Quartet reaped the same prize, plus Best Classical Album.

"It is against the Juilliard's standard that the Emerson Quartet must be measured," *High Fidelity* added, "and the Emerson fares so well that future recordings may well be judged against *it* ....The results are spectacular, yielding no less than a redefinition of the standards for Bartók quartet performance." The *L.A. Times* had called its chances for reaping best classical LP "tenuous" in a category usually "dominated by big-budget, big-name symphonies and operas" and predicted "the best album prize may go to Herbert von Karajan [*Bruckner: Symphony No. 8 in C Minor*], who in spite of being the most formidable (and best-selling) podium personage of our time, has never been a major player in the Grammy sweep-stakes. His chances are improved by the In Memoriam Factor (he recently died)."

Von Karajan was also competing for the orchestral laurels, but as the *L.A. Times* noted, "memorial sentiment did not help [his] final recording, nor did 25 weeks on the best-seller charts boost Gerard Schwarz and the Seattle Symphony past Leonard Bernstein's Mahler Third in the Orchestral category." Some critics blasted Bernstein and the New York Philharmonic's victorious interpretation as too exaggerated.

In the soloist (without orchestra) category, four of the five contenders were pianists and it was one of them, Andras

Schiff, who prevailed for his recording of Bach's English Suites, which was reviewed favorably for its ease of delivery. The competition for the soloist honors (with orchestra) was comprised of artists all performing works written in the twentieth century — a rare occurrence — and was won, as predicted, by cellist Yo-Yo Ma for his interpretations of works by Samuel Barber and Benjamin Britten. "Ma's celebrity, rather than his coupling of tough-nut concertos ... should make him the winner," the *Times* had forecast.

On two previous occasions, the Best Opera Recording Grammy was bestowed for performances of Wagner's *Ring* cycle: Sir Georg Solti and the Vienna Philharmonic won in 1966 for *Die Walküre* and Pierre Boulez and the Bayreuth Festival Orchestra were honored for their ambitious performance of the full cycle in 1982. This year's winner was *Die Walküre* with James Levine conducting the Metropolitan Opera Orchestra, starring Gary Lakes, Kurt Moll, James Morris, Jessye Norman, and Hildegard Behrens.

"The Met's *Walküre* is another mandatory purchase for Wagnerites, as well as an ideal set for those just starting a *Ring* collection," said *Stereo Review*. "This cast upsets the widespread notion that great Wagnerian voices disappeared with Birgit Nilsson and Jon Vickers .... Levine fuses these individual performances into a gripping representation of the opera as a whole." *The New York Times* added, "It ranks with the best this opera has received: grand yet exciting, pungent and full of character." Soprano Dawn Upshaw pulled an upset over Placido Domingo and Kathleen Battle to take the vocal soloist kudos. "Hers is a quintessentially American sound," said *Opera News*, "ideal for Samuel Barber's *Knoxville: Summer of 1915*, a classic of gentle nostalgia."

Winner of the year's Best Contemporary Composition was *Different Trains* by Steve Reich, a champion of minimalist style who preferred to write for small chamber-sized groups. "*Different Trains* represents the very apex of his creative output so far," commented *Hi-Fi News & Record Review*.

The Grammycast took place at the Shrine Auditorium in Los Angeles. *The Washington Post* commented, "Comedian Garry Shandling was harmless as host and, as always, the performances at the awards ceremony were uneven. The evening kicked off with Billy Joel's scintillating rendition of 'We Didn't Start the Fire,' featuring a single camera shot for the entire song, which could be a first in this age of frenetic visuals .... Performances by Ray Charles and Stevie Wonder during the McCartney tribute were curiously flat."

> *"The classical Grammys produced a bumper crop of surprises this year."*

The fact that Paul McCartney was being lauded with a Lifetime Achievement Award was announced weeks before the show, triggering the rumor that the Grammys would be the showcase for the long-awaited Beatles reunion since George Harrison was up for two awards, too, as part of the Traveling Wilburys. But Harrison declined to attend the ceremony and McCartney told the *L.A. Times* "flatly," "Rumors of a Beatles reunion are not possible because John is dead."

In a magnanimous gesture, the Grammys gave a Trustees Award to Dick Clark, the creator of the American Music Awards and former host of the TV show *American Bandstand*. Nat "King" Cole and Vladimir Horowitz were given posthumous Liftetime Achievement Awards.

Horowitz's widow, Wanda Toscanini Horowitz, didn't feel well enough to travel to California to accept the honor, so N.A.R.A.S. president Michael Greene flew to New York to present it to her at her brownstone on Manhattan's Upper East Side.

A curious writer for *The New Yorker* tagged along to record Mrs. Horowitz's reaction to the tribute. "You know, [Vladimir] used to say to me, 'I'm celebrated but not popular,'" she said. "He wanted to be popular. Not because he wanted to be a star, but because he wanted to know that he had really communicated with people.

"And my husband won more than Henry Mancini. He was proud of that."

1989

The awards ceremony was broadcast on CBS from the Shrine auditorium in Los Angeles on February 22, 1989, for the eligibility period of October 1, 1988, through September 30, 1989.

ALBUM OF THE YEAR
• *Nick of Time*, Bonnie Raitt. Don Was, producer. Capitol.
The End of the Innocence, Don Henley. Don Henley, Danny Kortchmar, producers. Geffen.
Full Moon Fever, Tom Petty. Jeff Lynne, Tom Petty, Mike Campbell, producers. MCA.
√ *The Raw & the Cooked*, Fine Young Cannibals. Fine Young Cannibals, producers. I.R.S./MCA.
Traveling Wilburys, Volume I, Traveling Wilburys. Jeff Lynne, George Harrison, producers. Wilbury.

RECORD OF THE YEAR
• "Wind Beneath My Wings," Bette Midler. Arif Mardin, producer. Atlantic.
"The End of the Innocence," Don Henley. Don Henley, Bruce Hornsby, producers. Geffen.
"The Living Years," Mike & the Mechanics. Christopher Neil, Mike Rutherford, producers. Atlantic.
√ "She Drives Me Crazy," Fine Young Cannibals. David Z., Fine Young Cannibals, producers. I.R.S./MCA.
√ "We Didn't Start the Fire," Billy Joel. Mick Jones, Billy Joel, producers. Columbia/CBS.

SONG OF THE YEAR
(Songwriter's Award)
• "Wind Beneath My Wings," Larry Henley, Jeff Silbar. Atlantic.
"Don't Know Much," Barry Mann, Cynthia Weil, Tom Snow. Elektra.
"The End of the Innocence," Don Henley, Bruce Hornsby. Geffen.
"The Living Years," Mike Rutherford, Brian A. Robertson. Atlantic.
√ "We Didn't Start the Fire," Billy Joel. Columbia/CBS.

BEST NEW ARTIST
• Milli Vanilli. Arista.
Neneh Cherry. Virgin.
Indigo Girls. Epic.
Soul II Soul. Virgin.
Tone Loc. Delicious Vinyl.

BEST POP VOCAL PERFORMANCE, MALE
• Michael Bolton, "How Am I Supposed to Live Without You." Columbia/CBS.
√ Billy Joel, "We Didn't Start the Fire." Columbia/CBS.
Richard Marx, "Right Here Waiting." EMI.
Roy Orbison, "You Got It." Virgin.
Prince, *Batman, Motion Picture Soundtrack*. Warner Bros.

BEST POP VOCAL PERFORMANCE, FEMALE
• Bonnie Raitt, "Nick of Time," track from *Nick of Time*. Capitol.
√ Paula Abdul, "Straight Up." Virgin.
√ Gloria Estefan, "Don't Wanna Lose You." Epic.
Bette Midler, "Wind Beneath My Wings." Atlantic.
Linda Ronstadt, *Cry Like a Rainstorm, Howl Like the Wind*. Elektra.

BEST POP VOCAL PERFORMANCE BY A DUO OR GROUP WITH VOCAL
- Linda Ronstadt, Aaron Neville, "Don't Know Much." Elektra.
- ✓ B-52's, "Love Shack." Reprise.
- ✓ Fine Young Cannibals, "She Drives Me Crazy." I.R.S./MCA.
- Mike & the Mechanics, "The Living Years." Atlantic.
- ✓ Simply Red, "If You Don't Know Me By Now." Elektra.

BEST POP INSTRUMENTAL PERFORMANCE
- Neville Brothers, "Healing Chant," track from *Yellow Moon*. A&M.
- Kenny G., "Breadline Blues," track from *Happy Anniversary, Charlie Brown*, (various artists). GRP.
- Earl Klugh, *Whispers and Promises*. Warner Bros.
- Paul Shaffer, "Late Night," track from *Coast to Coast*. Capitol.
- Andreas Vollenweider, "Dancing with the Lion." Columbia/CBS.

BEST ROCK VOCAL PERFORMANCE, MALE
- Don Henley, *The End of the Innocence*. Geffen.
- Joe Cocker, "When the Night Comes." Capitol.
- ✓ Tom Petty, "Free Fallin'," track from *Full Moon Fever*. MCA.
- Lou Reed, *New York*. Sire.
- Neil Young, *Freedom*. Reprise.

BEST ROCK VOCAL PERFORMANCE, FEMALE
- Bonnie Raitt, *Nick of Time*. Capitol.
- Pat Benatar, "Let's Stay Together." Chrysalis.
- Melissa Etheridge, *Brave and Crazy*. Island.
- Cyndi Lauper, "I Drove All Night." Epic.
- Tina Turner, *Foreign Affair*. Capitol.

BEST ROCK PERFORMANCE BY A DUO OR GROUP WITH VOCAL
- Traveling Wilburys, *Traveling Wilburys, Volume I*. Wilbury.
- Living Colour, "Glamour Boys." Epic.
- Rolling Stones, "Mixed Emotions." Rolling Stones/Columbia.
- U2, *Rattle and Hum*. Island.
- U2, B.B. King, "When Love Comes to Town." Island.

GLOBE PHOTO

"Hey, Bonnie Raitt, I got one, too!" Bette Midler said when "Wind Beneath My Wings" won Record of the Year.

BEST ROCK INSTRUMENTAL PERFORMANCE
- Jeff Beck, Terry Bozzio, Tony Hymas, *Jeff Beck's Guitar Shop with Terry Bozzio and Tony Hymas*. Epic.
- Steve Morse, *High Tension Wires*. MCA.
- Joe Satriani, "The Crush of Love," track from *Dreaming #11*. Relativity Records.
- Andy Summers, "A Piece of Time," track from *The Golden Wire*. Private Music.
- Stevie Ray Vaughan & Double Trouble, "Travis Walk," track from *In Step*. Epic.

BEST HARD ROCK PERFORMANCE, VOCAL OR INSTRUMENTAL
- Living Colour, "Cult of Personality." Epic.
- Aerosmith, "Love in an Elevator." Geffen.
- Great White, "Once Bitten, Twice Shy." Capitol.
- Guns 'N' Roses, *G 'N' R Lies*. Geffen.
- Motley Crue, "Dr. Feelgood." Elektra.

BEST METAL PERFORMANCE, VOCAL OR INSTRUMENTAL
• Metallica, "One." Elektra.
Dökken, *Beast from the East*. Elektra.
Faith No More, *The Real Thing*. Slash/Reprise.
Queensryche, "I Don't Believe in Love." EMI.
Soundgarden, *Ultramega O.K.* SST Records.

BEST RHYTHM & BLUES SONG
(Songwriter's Award)
✓• "If You Don't Know Me By Now," Kenny Gamble, Leon Huff. Elektra.
✓"Every Little Step," L.A. Reid, Babyface. MCA.
✓"Miss You Much," James Harris III, Terry Lewis. A&M.
"Superwoman," L.A. Reid, Babyface, Daryl Simmons. Warner Bros.
"When a Man Loves a Woman," Calvin Lewis, Andrew Wright. Scotti Bros./Epic.

BEST RHYTHM & BLUES VOCAL PERFORMANCE, MALE
✓• Bobby Brown, "Every Little Step." MCA.
Al Jarreau, *Heart's Horizon*. Reprise.
Prince, "Batdance." Warner Bros.
Smokey Robinson, "We've Saved the Best for Last." Arista.
Luther Vandross, "She Won't Talk to Me." Epic.

BEST RHYTHM & BLUES VOCAL PERFORMANCE, FEMALE
• Anita Baker, *Giving You the Best That I Got*. Elektra.
Natalie Cole, *Good to Be Back*. EMI.
Aretha Franklin, *Through the Storm*. Arista.
✓Janet Jackson, "Miss You Much." A&M.
Vanessa Williams, "Dreamin'," Wing/Polygram.

BEST RHYTHM & BLUES PERFORMANCE BY A DUO OR GROUP WITH VOCAL
• Soul II Soul, Caron Wheeler, "Back to Life." Virgin.
Aretha Franklin, James Brown, "Gimme Your Love." Arista.
Aretha Franklin, Whitney Houston, "It Isn't, It Wasn't, It Ain't Never Gonna Be." Arista.
Deniece Williams, Natalie Cole, "We Sing Praises," track from *Special Love*. Sparrow.

BeBe & CeCe Winans, "Celebrate New Life." Capitol.

BEST RHYTHM & BLUES INSTRUMENTAL PERFORMANCE
• Soul II Soul, "African Dance," track from *Keep on Movin'*. Virgin.
Gerald Albright, *Bermuda Nights*. Atlantic.
Babyface, "It's No Crime." Solar/Epic.
Omar Hakim, "Constructive Criticism," track from *Rhythm Deep*. GRP.
Stix Hooper, "I Can't Get Enough of Your Love," track from *Lay It on the Line*. Artful Balance.

BEST RAP PERFORMANCE
• Young MC, "Bust a Move." Delicious Vinyl.
De La Soul, "Me Myself and I." Tommy Boy.
D.J. Jazzy Jeff & the Fresh Prince, "I Think I Can Beat Mike Tyson." Jive/RCA.
Public Enemy, "Fight the Power." Motown.
Tone Loc, "Funky Cold Medina." Delicious Vinyl.

BEST JAZZ FUSION PERFORMANCE
• Pat Metheny Group, *Letter from Home*. Geffen.
Larry Carlton, *On Solid Ground*. MCA.
Terri Lyne Carrington, *Real Life Story*. Verve Forecast.
Miles Davis, *Amandla*. Warner Bros.
John Patitucci, *On the Corner*. GRP.
Joe Sample, *Spellbound*. Warner Bros.

BEST JAZZ VOCAL PERFORMANCE, MALE
• Harry Connick, Jr., *When Harry Met Sally ...* Columbia/CBS.
George Benson, *Tenderly*. Warner Bros.
Dr. John, *In a Sentimental Mood*. Warner Bros.
Lou Rawls, *At Last*. Blue Note/Capitol.
Joe Williams, *In Good Company*. Verve.

BEST JAZZ VOCAL PERFORMANCE, FEMALE
• Ruth Brown, *Blues on Broadway*. Fantasy.
Dee Dee Bridgewater, *Live in Paris*. Impulse.
Anita O'Day, *In a Mellow Tone*. Deutsche Grammophon.

Diane Schuur, "The Christmas Song,"
track from *GRP Christmas Collection.*
GRP.
Janis Siegel, *Short Stories (Janis Siegel,
Fred Hersch).* Atlantic.

BEST JAZZ VOCAL PERFORMANCE, DUO
OR GROUP
• Dr. John, Rickie Lee Jones, "Makin'
Whoopee." Warner Bros.
Ray Charles, Lou Rawls, "Save the Bones
for Henry Jones," track from *Just
Between Us.* Columbia/CBS.
James Moody, Dizzy Gillespie, "Get the
Booty," track from *Sweet and Lovely.*
Novus/RCA.
Take 6, "Like the Whole World's
Watching," track from *Steve Dorff &
Friends.* Reprise.
Joe Williams, Marlena Shaw, "Is You Is or
Is You Ain't My Baby," track from *In
Good Company.* Verve.

BEST JAZZ INSTRUMENTAL
PERFORMANCE, SOLOIST
(ON A JAZZ RECORDING)
• Miles Davis, *Aura.* Columbia/CBS.
Chick Corea, "Sophisticated Lady," track
from *Chick Corea Akoustic Band.*
GRP.
Wynton Marsalis, *The Majesty of the
Blues.* Columbia/CBS.
John Patitucci, "Bessie's Blues," track
from *Chick Corea Akoustic Band.*
GRP.
André Previn, *After Hours.* Telarc.

BEST JAZZ INSTRUMENTAL
PERFORMANCE, GROUP
• Chick Corea Akoustic Band, *Chick
Corea Akoustic Band.* GRP.
Branford Marsalis, *Trio Jeepy.*
Columbia/CBS.
Wynton Marsalis, *The Majesty of the
Blues.* Columbia/CBS.
André Previn, Joe Pass, Ray Brown, *After
Hours.* Telarc.
Yellowjackets, *The Spin.* MCA.

BEST JAZZ INSTRUMENTAL
PERFORMANCE, BIG BAND
• Miles Davis, *Aura.* Columbia/CBS.
Count Basie Orchestra conducted by Frank
Foster, *The Legend, The Legacy.*
Denon.
Duke Ellington Orchestra conducted by
Mercer Ellington, *Music Is My
Mistress.* MusicMasters.

Mel Lewis Jazz Orchestra, *The Definitive
Thad Jones.* MusicMasters.
McCoy Tyner Big Band,
Uptown/Downton. Milestone.

BEST COUNTRY SONG
(Songwriters Award)
• "After All This Time," Rodney Crowell.
Columbia.
√ A Better Man," Clint Black, Hayden
Nicholas. RCA.
"Luck in My Eyes," k.d. lang, Ben Mink.
Sire.
"She Don't Love Nobody," John Hiatt.
MCA/Curb.
"There's a Tear in My Beer," Hank
Williams, Sr. Curb.

BEST COUNTRY VOCAL PERFORMANCE,
MALE
• Lyle Lovett, *Lyle Lovett and His Large
Band.* MCA.
√ Clint Black, *Killin' Time.* RCA.
Rodney Crowell, "After All This Time."
Columbia.
Randy Travis, "It's Just a Matter of Time."
Warner Bros.
Keith Whitley, "I'm No Stranger to the
Rain." RCA.

BEST COUNTRY VOCAL PERFORMANCE,
FEMALE
• k.d. lang, *Absolute Torch and Twang.*
Sire.
Rosanne Cash, "I Don't Want to Spoil the
Party." Columbia.
Emmylou Harris, *Bluebird.* Reprise.
Kathy Mattea, *Willow in the Wind.*
Mercury.
Dolly Parton, "Why'd You Come in Here
Looking Like That." Columbia/CBS.

BEST COUNTRY VOCAL PERFORMANCE
BY A DUO OR GROUP WITH VOCAL
• Nitty Gritty Dirt Band, *Will the Circle Be
Unbroken, Volume 2.* Universal.
Desert Rose Band, "She Don't Love
Nobody." MCA/Curb.
Highway 101, "Honky Tonk Heart."
Warner Bros.
Judds, "Young Love." RCA.
Restless Heart, "Big Dreams in a Small
Town." RCA.

Best Country Vocal Collaboration

• Hank Williams, Jr., Hank Williams, Sr., "There's a Tear in My Beer." Curb.

Chris Hillman, Roger McGuinn, "You Ain't Goin' Nowhere." Universal.

Nitty Gritty Dirt Band with Johnny Cash, Roy Acuff, Ricky Skaggs, Levon Helm, Emmylou Harris, "Will the Circle Be Unbroken," track from *Will the Circle Be Unbroken, Vol. 2*. Universal.

Buck Owens, Ringo Starr, "Act Naturally." Capitol.

Dwight Yoakam, k.d. lang, "Sin City," track from *Just Lookin' for a Hit*. Reprise.

Best Country Instrumental Performance

• Randy Scruggs, Nitty Gritty Dirt Band, "Amazing Grace," track from *Will the Circle Be Unbroken Volume 2*. Universal.

Asleep at the Wheel, "Black and White Rag." Asleep at the Wheel Music.

Jerry Douglas, "If You've Got the Money (Honey, I've Got the Time)," track from *Plant Early*. MCA Master Series.

John Hartford, "All I Got Is Gone Away," track from *Down on the River*. Flying Fish.

New Grass Revival, "Big Foot," track from *Friday Night in America*. Capitol.

Best Gospel Performance, Male

• BeBe Winans, "Meantime," track from *Heaven* (BeBe and Cece Winans album). Capitol.

Eddie DeGarmo, *Feels Good to Be Forgiven*. Forefront/Benson.

Larnelle Harris, *I Can Begin Again*. Benson.

Wintley Phipps, *A Love Like This*. Coral/Word.

Michael W. Smith, "Holy, Holy, Holy," track from *Our Hymns* (various artists). Word.

Russ Taff, "Farther On," track from *The Way Home*. Myrrh/Word.

Best Gospel Performance, Female

• CeCe Winans, "Don't Cry," track from BeBe & CeCe Winans' *Heaven*. Capitol/Sparrow.

Margaret Becker, *Immigrant's Daughter*. Sparrow.

Debby Boone, *Be Thou My Vision*. Lamb & Lion/Benson.

Amy Grant, "'Tis So Sweet to Trust in Jesus," track from *Our Hymns* (various artists album). Word.

Sandi Patti, "Forever Friends." Word.

Deniece Williams, "Healing," track from *Special Love*. Sparrow.

Best Gospel Performance by a Duo or Group, Choir, or Chorus

• Take 6, "The Savior Is Waiting," track from *Our Hymns* (various artists album). Word.

First Call, "O Sacred Head Now Wounded," track from *Our Hymns* (various artists album). Word.

Mylon & Broken Heart, *Big World*. Star Song.

Petra, *On Fire!* Star Song.

BeBe & CeCe Winans, "Heaven." Capitol/Sparrow.

Best Soul Gospel Performance, Female or Male

• Al Green, "As Long as We're Together." A&M.

Albertina Walker, *My Time Is Not Over*. Word.

Beau Williams, *Wonderful*. Light.

Daniel Winans, "You Got a Choice to Make," track from *Brotherly Love*. Rejoice/Word.

Vickie Winans, *Total Victory*. Light.

Best Soul Gospel Performance by a Duo or Group, Choir, or Chorus

• Daniel Winans and Choir, "Let Brotherly Love Continue," track from *Brotherly Love*. Rejoice.

Rev. Milton Brunson & the Thompson Community Singers, *Available to You*. Rejoice.

Commissioned, *Will You Be Ready?* Light.

L.A. Mass Choir, *Can't Hold Back*. Light.

Minister Thomas Whitfield & the Thomas Whitfield Company, *And They Sang a Hymn*. Sound of Gospel/King James.

Best Traditional Folk Recording

• *Le Mystère Des Voix Bulgares, Volume II,* Bulgarian State Radio & Television Female Choir. Elektra/Nonesuch.

A la Veille Facon, Cajun Tradition. Swallow.

American Indian Dance Theatre, Various American Indian Tribes. Barbara Schwei, producer. Broadway Limited Records.

Blind Dog, Norman & Nancy Blake. Rounder.
Now That's a Good Tune, Masters of Traditional Missouri Fiddling. Grey Eagle Records.

BEST CONTEMPORARY FOLK RECORDING
• *Indigo Girls,* Indigo Girls. Epic.
"Bamboleo," Gipsy Kings. Elektra.
Bayou Cadillac, Beausoleil. Rounder.
Crossroads, Tracy Chapman. Elektra.
Old Friends, Guy Clark. Sugar Hill.

BEST TRADITIONAL BLUES RECORDING
• "I'm in the Mood," track from *The Healer* (John Lee Hooker album), Bonnie Raitt, John Lee Hooker. Chameleon Music Group.
Ginger Ale Afternoon, Willie Dixon. Varese Sarabande.
The Healer, John Lee Hooker. Chameleon Music Group.
"If I Can't Sell It, I'll Keep Sittin' on It," track from *Blues on Broadway,* Ruth Brown. Fantasy.
Memphis Blues, The Paris Sessions, Memphis Slim. Stash.

BEST CONTEMPORARY BLUES RECORDING
• *In Step,* Stevie Ray Vaughan & Double Trouble. Epic.
King of the Blues: 1989, B.B. King. MCA.
Live from Austin, Delbert McClinton. Alligator.
Midnight Run, Bobby Blue Bland. Malaco.
"Wang Dang Doodle," track from *Coast to Coast,* (Paul Shaffer album), Koko Taylor. Capitol.

BEST BLUEGRASS RECORDING
• "The Valley Road," track from *Will the Circle Be Unbroken Vol. 2,* Bruce Hornsby, Nitty Gritty Dirt Band. Universal.
At the Old Schoolhouse, Johnson Mountain Boys. Rounder.
Heartbreak Hotel, Doug Dillard Band. Flying Fish.
The Masters, Eddie Adcock, Kenny Baker, Josh Graves, Jesse McReynolds. CMH.
Bill Monroe & the Bluegrass Boys Live at the Opry, Bill Monroe & the Bluegrass Boys. MCA.
Two Highways, Alison Kraus, Union Station. Rounder.

BEST LATIN POP PERFORMANCE
• José Feliciano, "Cielito Lindo." EMI.
Chayanne, *Chayanne.* CBS Discos International.
Dyango, *Suspiros.* Capitol EMI Latin.
Miguel Gallardo, *America.* Philips/Polygram Latino.
José Luis Rodriguez, "Baila Mi Rumba." Mercury.

BEST TROPICAL LATIN PERFORMANCE
• Celia Cruz, Ray Barretto, *Ritmo en el Corazon.* Fania.
Ray Barretto, *Irresistible.* Fania.
Willie Colon, *Top Secrets/Altos Secretos.* Fania.
Eddie Palmieri, "Azucar," track from *Sueno.* Intuition/Capitol.
Wilfrido Vargas, *Animation.* Sonotone Music Corp.

BEST MEXICAN/AMERICAN PERFORMANCE
• Los Lobos, *La Pistola y el Corazon.* Warner Bros./Slash.
Narciso Martinez, *The Father of Tex-Mex Conjunto.* Folklyric.
Emilio Navaira & Rio Band, *Emilio Navaira & Rio Band.* CBS Discos International.
Peter Rubalcava, *Amanecer.* NALR.
Tigres del Norte, *Corridos Prohibidos.* Fonovisa, Inc.

BEST REGGAE RECORDING
• *One Bright Day,* Ziggy Marley & the Melody Makers. Virgin.
I.D., Wailers Band. Atlantic.
Liberation, Bunny Wailer. Shanachie.
Live in Paris, Burning Spear. Slash.
Serious Business, Third World. Mercury.

BEST POLKA RECORDING
• *All in My Love for You,* Jimmy Sturr & His Orchestra. Starr.
Any Time Is Polka Time, Walter Ostanek & His Band. World Renowned Sounds.
Moldie Oldie Golden Goodies, Gene Mendalski & the G-Men. Starr.
Penn Ohio Polka Pals Souvenir Edition, Penn Ohio Polka Pals. Marjon.
Polkaholic, Gordon Hartmann. HG Records.

BEST NEW AGE PERFORMANCE
• Peter Gabriel, *Passion* (Music from *The Last Temptation of Christ*). Geffen.
Enya, "Orinoco Flow (Sail Away)." Geffen.

Mark Isham, *Tibet*. Windham Hill.
Andreas Vollenweider, *Dancing with the Lion*. Columbia/CBS.
Paul Winter, "Icarus," track from *Wolf Eyes*. Living Music.

BEST INSTRUMENTAL COMPOSITION
• "The *Batman* Theme," Danny Elfman. Warner Bros.
"Field of Dreams," track from *Field of Dreams* soundtrack, James Horner. Novus.
"Letter from Home," track from *Letter from Home*, Pat Metheny. Geffen.
"Morning Sprite," track from *Chick Corea Akoustic Band*, Chick Corea. GRP.
"Suite from *The Milagro Beanfield War*," track from *Migration*, Dave Grusin . GRP.
"*Who Framed Roger Rabbit* Suite," track from *Screen Themes — Original Soundtracks and Themes*, Alan Silvestri. Varese Sarabande.

BEST ARRANGEMENT ON AN INSTRUMENTAL
• Dave Grusin, "Suite from *The Milagro Beanfield War*," track from *Migration* (Dave Grusin). GRP.
Frank Foster, "The Count Basie Remembrance Suite," track from *The Legend, The Legacy* (Count Basie Orchestra). Denon.
Les Hooper, "Anything Goes," track from *Anything Goes* (Les Hooper). ITI.
Thad Jones, "Three in One," track from *The Definitive Thad Jones* (Mel Lewis Jazz Orchestra). MusicMasters.
Maxine Roach, "Extensions," track from *Max Roach Presents the Uptown String Quartet* (Uptown String Quartet). Philips.

BEST MUSICAL CAST SHOW ALBUM
• *Jerome Robbins' Broadway*, Jason Alexander, Debbie Shapiro, Robert La Fasse, others. Jay David Saks, producer. RCA Victor.
Aspects of Love, Original London cast with Ann Crumb, Michael Ball, Kevin Olson, Kathleen Rowe McAllen. Andrew Lloyd Webber, producer & composer. Don Black, Charles Hart, lyricists. Polydor.

Broadway, The Hard Way, Frank Zappa, producer, composer, lyricist. Barking Pumpkin.
Sarafina! The Music of Liberation, Broadway cast. Mbongeni Ngema, Hugh Masekela, composers and lyricists. Mbongeni Ngema, producer. RCA Victor.
Sondheim: Pacific Overtures, James Holmes conducting English National Opera. John Yap, producer. RCA Victor.

BEST ALBUM OF ORIGINAL INSTRUMENTAL BACKGROUND SCORE WRITTEN FOR A MOTION PICTURE OR TELEVISION
• *The Fabulous Baker Boys*, Dave Grusin. GRP.
Batman, Danny Elfman (Sinfonia of London Orchestra). Warner Bros.
Field of Dreams, James Horner. Novus.
Indiana Jones and the Last Crusade, John Williams. Warner Bros.
*Passion (*Music for *The Last Temptation of Christ)*, Peter Gabriel. Geffen.

BEST SONG WRITTEN SPECIFICALLY FOR A MOTION PICTURE OR TELEVISION
• "Let the River Run," from the motion picture *Working Girl*, Carly Simon (Carly Simon). Arista.
"Angel of Harlem," from the motion picture *U2: Rattle & Hum*, Bono & U2 (U2). Island.
"The Girl Who Used to Be Me," from the motion picture *Shirley Valentine*, Alan & Marilyn Bergman, Marvin Hamlisch (Patti Austin). GRP.
"I Love to See You Smile," from the motion picture *Parenthood*, Randy Newman (Randy Newman). Reprise.
"Partyman," from the motion picture *Batman*, Prince (Prince). Warner Bros.

BEST INSTRUMENTAL ARRANGEMENT ACCOMPANYING VOCAL(S)
• Dave Grusin, "My Funny Valentine" from *The Fabulous Baker Boys* motion picture soundtrack (Michele Pfeiffer). GRP.
Frank Foster, "Bring on the Raindrops," track from *The Legend, The Legacy* (Carmen Bradford). Denon.
Janet Jackson , Terry Lewis, Jimmy Jam, "Rhythm Nation," track from *Rhythm Nation 1814* (Janet Jackson). A&M.

Don Sebesky, "Carlotta's Heart," track
from *Working Girl* motion picture
soundtrack (Carly Simon). Arista.

Marc Shaiman, "It Had to Be You," track
from *When Harry Met Sally ...* (Harry
Connick, Jr.). Columbia/CBS.

BEST CLASSICAL ALBUM
• *Bartók: 6 String Quartets*, Emerson
String Quartet. Wolf Erichson,
producer. Deutsche Grammophon.

Bruckner: Symphony No. 8 in C Minor,
Herbert von Karajan conducting
Vienna Philharmonic. Michel Glotz,
producer. Deutsche Grammophon.

*Busoni: Piano Concerto in C (with Male
Chorus)*, Christoph von Dohnanyi
conducting Cleveland Orchestra.
Garrick Ohlsson, piano. Robert Woods,
producer. Telarc.

*Hanson: Symphonies No. 1 in E Minor
("Nordic") and No. 2 ("Romantic");
Elegy in Memory of Serge
Koussevitsky*, Gerard Schwarz
conducting Seattle Symphony. Adam
Stern, producer. Delos International.

Wagner: Die Walküre, James Livein
conducting Meropolitan Opera Orchestra
(solos: Lakes, Moll, Morris, Norman,
Behrens, Ludwig). Cord Garben,
producer. Deutsche Grammophon.

BEST ORCHESTRAL PERFORMANCE
(Conductor's Award)
• Leonard Bernstein conducting New York
Philharmonic, *Mahler: Symphony No. 3
in D Minor*. Deutsche Grammophon.

Charles Dutoit conducting Montreal
Symphony Orchestra, *Bartók: Concerto
for Orchestra; Music for Strings,
Percussion and Celesta*. London.

Herbert von Karajan conducting Vienna
Philharmonic, *Bruckner: Symphony No.
8 in C Minor*. Deutsche Grammophon.

Orpheus Chamber Orchestra, *Copland:
Appalachian Spring; Short Symphony;
3 Latin American Sketches; Quiet City*.
Deutsche Grammophon.

Gerard Schwarz conducting Seattle
Symphony, *Hanson: Symphonies No. 1
in E Minor "Nordic" & 2 "Romantic";
Elegy in Memory of Serge Koussevitsky*.
Delos International.

BEST CHAMBER MUSIC PERFORMANCE
(INSTRUMENTAL OR VOCAL)
• Emerson String Quartet. *Bartók: 6 String
Quartets*. Deutsche Grammophon.

*The Emerson String Quartet "redefined"
Bartok's quartets and received two
awards, including Best Classical Album.*

Emanuel Ax, piano; Isaac Stern, violin;
Yo-Yo Ma, cello, *Shostakovich: Trio
No. 2 for Violin, Cello & Piano in E
Minor, Op. 67; Sonata for Cello &
Piano in D Minor*. CBS Masterworks.

Guarneri Quartet, *Beethoven: String
Quartet No. 13 in B Flat; Grosse Fuge
in B Flat*. Philips Classics.

Shlomo Mintz, violin; Yefim Bronfman,
piano, *Prokofiev: Violin Sonatas No. 1
in F Minor and No. 2 in D*. Deutsche
Grammophon.

Anne-Sophie Mutter, violin; Mstislav
Rostropovich, cello; Bruno Giuranna,
viola, *Beethoven: String Trios (E Flat,
Op. 3; Serenade in D, Op. 8; G, Op. 9
No. 1; D, Op. 9 No. 2; C, Op. 9 No. 3)*.
Deutsche Grammophon.

**BEST CLASSICAL PERFORMANCE —
INSTRUMENTAL SOLOIST (S)
(WITH ORCHESTRA)**
• Yo-Yo Ma, cello (David Zinman
conducting Baltimore Symphony
Orchestra), *Barber: Cello Concerto,
Op. 22; Britten: Symphony for Cello
and Orchestra, & Op. 68*. CBS
Masterworks.

Gidon Kremer, violin (Charles Dutoit conducting Boston Symphony), *Gubaidulina: Offertorium*. Deutsche Grammophon.

Robert McDuffie, violin (Leonard Slatkin conducting St. Louis Symphony Orchestra), *Schumann: Violin Concerto; Bernstein: Serenade for Violin, Strings & Percussion (After Plato's "Symposium")*. Angel.

Viktoria Mullova, violin (André Previn conducting Royal Philharmonic Orchestra), *Shostakovich: Violin Concerto No. 1; Prokofiev: Violin Concerto No. 2*. Philips Classics.

David Shifrin, clarinet (Gerard Schwarz conducting New York Chamber Symphony), *Copland: Clarinet Concerto*. Angel.

BEST CLASSICAL PERFORMANCE — INSTRUMENTAL SOLOIST(S) (WITHOUT ORCHESTRA)

• Andras Schiff, piano, *Bach: English Suites, BWV 806–11*. London.

Rudolf Firkusny, piano, *Martinu: Piano Sonata No. 1; Les Ritournelles; Fantasie et Toccata*. RCA Victor Red Seal.

Richard Goode, piano, *Beethoven: The Late Piano Sonatas (Opp. 101, 106, 109, 110, 111)*. Elektra/Nonesuch.

Janos Starker, cello (Shingeo Neriki, accompanist), *Popper: Romantic Cello Favorites*. Delos International.

Krystian Zimerman, piano, *Chopin: Four Ballades (Opp. 23, 38, 47, 52); Barcarolle, Op. 60; Fantasie, Op. 49*. Deutsche Grammophon.

BEST OPERA RECORDING

• *Wagner: Die Walküre*, James Levine conducting Metropolitan Opera Orchestra (solos: Lakes, Moll, Morris, Norman, Behrens, Ludwig). Cord Garben, producer. Deutsche Grammophon.

Berg: Wozzeck, Claudio Abbado conducting Vienna Philharmonic (solos: Grundheber, Raffeiner, Langridge, Zednik, Haugland, Behrens). Werner Mayer, Christopher Alder, producers. Deutsche Grammophon.

Gershwin: Porgy and Bess, Simon Rattle conducting London Philharmonic and Glyndebourne Chorus (solos: White, Haymon, Evans, Blackwell, Hubbard, Clarey, Baker). David R. Murray, producer. Angel.

R. Strauss: Elektra, Seiji Ozawa conducting Boston Symphony Orchestra (solos: Ludwig, Behrens, Secunde, Ulfung, Hynninen). Wilhelm Hellweg, producer. Philips Classics.

Tchaikovsky: Eugen Onegin, James Levine conducting Dresden State Orchestra (solos: Freni, von Otter, Lang, Allen, Shicoff, Burchuladze, Senechal). Cord Garben, producer. Deutsche Grammophon.

BEST CHORAL PERFORMANCE (OTHER THAN OPERA)

• Robert Shaw conducting Atlanta Symphony Orchestra and Chorus; Atlanta Boys Choir, *Britten: War Requiem*. Telarc.

Stephen Darlington conducting Christ Church Cathedral Choir, *Williams: Choral Music; Oxford Elegy, Flos Campi, etc*. Nimbus.

John Eliot Gardiner conducting Monteverdi Choir and English Baroque Soloists. *Handel: Jephtha*. Philips Classics.

Trevor Pinnock conducting English Concert Choir and English Concert. *Handel: Messiah*. Archiv.

Leonard Slatkin conducting London Philharmonic Choir and Orchestra. Richard Cooke, choral conductor. *Elgar: The Kingdom*. RCA Victor Red Seal.

BEST CLASSICAL VOCAL SOLOIST PERFORMANCE

• Dawn Upshaw, soprano (David Zinman conducting Orchestra of St. Luke's), *Knoxville: Summer of 1915* (music by Barber, Menotti, Harbison, Stravinsky). Elektra/Nonesuch.

Kathleen Battle, soprano (James Levine, accompanist), *Schubert: Lieder*. Deutsche Grammophon.

Placido Domingo, tenor (Julius Rudel, accompanist), *Puccini: The Unknown Puccini*. CBS Masterworks.

Placido Domingo, tenor; Kathleen Battle, soprano (James Levine conducting Metropolitan Opera Orchestra), *Live in Tokyo 1988*. Deutsche Grammophon.

William Sharp, baritone (Steven Blier, accompanist), *William Sharp, Baritone* (Works by Thomson, Bowles, Hoiby, Musto, etc.). New World.

BEST CONTEMPORARY COMPOSITION
• Steve Reich, *Different Train.* Elektra/Nonesuch.
Sofia Gubaidulina, *Offertorium.* Deutsche Grammophon.
Witold Lutoslawski, *Chain 2.* Deutsche Grammophon.
Witold Lutoslawski, *Partita.* Deutsche Grammophon.
Arvo Part, *Passio.* ECM.

BEST ENGINEERED RECORDING, CLASSICAL
• Jack Renner, *Britten: War Requiem* (Robert Shaw conducting Atlanta Symphony Orchestra and Chorus, Atlanta Boy's Choir, and Solos). Telarc.
John Dunkerley, *Bartók: Concerto for Orchestra; Music for Strings, Percussion and Celesta* (Charles Dutoit conducting Montreal Symphony Orchestra). London.
John Eargle, *Hanson: Symphonies No. 1 in E Minor ("Nordic") and No. 2 ("Romantic"); Elegy in Memory of Serge Koussevitsky* (Gerard Schwarz conducting Seattle Symphony). Delos International.
Wolfgang Mitlehner, *Wagner: Die Walküre* (James Levine conducting Metropolitan Opera Orchestra and Solos). Deutsche Grammophon.
Karl-August Naegler, Helmut Burk, *Mahler: Symphony No. 3 in D Minor* (Leonard Bernstein conducting New York Philharmonic; New York Choral Artists and Brooklyn Boys Chorus; solo: Ludwig). Deutsche Grammophon.

CLASSICAL PRODUCER OF THE YEAR
• Robert Woods
Wolf Erichson
Michael Haas
Patti Laursen
Elizabeth Ostrow

BEST COMEDY RECORDING
• *P.D.Q. Bach: 1712 Overture and Other Musical Assaults*, "Professor" Peter Schickele, Greater Hoople Area Off-Season Philharmonic. Telarc.
Dice, Andrew Dice Clay. Geffen.
Motherhood: The Second Oldest Profession, Erma Bombeck. McGraw-Hill-Areille Productions International.
"Wild Thing," Sam Kinison. Warner Bros.
Without You I'm Nothing, Sandra Bernhard. Enigma.

BEST SPOKEN WORD OR NON-MUSICAL RECORDING
• *It's Always Something*, Gilda Radner. Simon & Schuster Audio.
All I Really Need to Know I Learned in Kindergarten, Robert Fulghum. Sound Editions.
I Want to Grow Hair, I Want to Grow Up, I Want to Go to Boise, Erma Bombeck. Caedmon.
Sir John Gielgud Reads Alice in Wonderland, Sir John Gielgud. Nimbus.
The War of the Worlds 50th Anniversary Production, Jason Robards, Steve Allen, Douglas Edwards, others. Otherworld Media.

BEST RECORDING FOR CHILDREN
• *The Rock-a-Bye Collection, Volume I*, Tanya Goodman. Jaba Records.
Bullfrogs & Butterflies—I've Been Been Born Again, Various artists. Tony Salerno, Ron Kreuger, Frank Hernandez, producers. Anthony Paul Productions.
A Disney Spectacular (48 Favorite Disney Songs), Eric Kunzel conducting Cincinnati Pops Orchestra. Telarc.
Oliver & Company; Story & Songs from the Motion Picture, Various artists. Ted Kryczko, producer. Walt Disney Records.
Raffi in Concert with the Rise and Shine Band, Raffi. Shoreline/A&M.
Thumbelina, Kelly McGillis, narrator. Mark Isham, music. Windham Hill.

Best Engineered Recording, Non-Classical
• George Massenburg, *Cry Like a Rainstorm, Howl Like the Wind* (Linda Ronstadt). Elektra.
Bill Bottrell, *Like a Prayer* (Madonna). Sire.
Mike Campbell, Don Smith, Bill Botrell, *Full Moon Fever* (Tom Petty). MCA.
Neil Dorfsman, *Flowers in the Dirt* (Paul McCartney). Capitol.
Josiah Gluck, *Happy Anniversary, Charlie Brown* (Patti Austin, Dave Brubeck, Dave Grusin, Lee Ritenour.) GRP.
Don Murray, Ed Rak, *Migration* (Dave Grusin). GRP.

Best Album Package
(Art Director's Award)
• Roger Gorman, *Sound + Vision* (David Bowie). Rykodisc.
Bill Burks, Tommy Steele, *Foreign Affair* (Tina Turner). Capitol.
Tom Recchion, *Batman* (Prince). Warner Bros.
Tommy Steele, *Monster* (Fetchin Bones). Capitol.
Jimmy Wachtel, *World in Motion* (Jackson Browne). Elektra.

Best Album Notes
(Annotator's Award)
• Phil Schaap, *Bird: The Complete Charlie Parker on Verve* (Charlie Parker). Verve.
Dwight Blocker Bowers, *American Musical Theater—Shows, Songs and Stars* (Various artists). Smithsonian Collection.
Gene Lees, *The Complete Fantasy Recordings* (Bill Evans). Fantasy.
Howard Wright Marshall, Amy E. Skillman, *Now That's a Good Tune* (Masters of traditional Missouri fiddling). Grey Eagle Records.
Martin Williams, Dick Katz, Francis Davis, *Jazz Piano* (Various artists 1898–1964). Smithsonian Collection.

Best Historical Album
• *Chuck Berry — The Chess Box.* Andy McKaie, producer. Chess/MCA.
American Musical Theater—Shows, Songs and Stars (Various). Dwight Blocker Bowers, producer. Smithsonian Collection.
Blue Note 50th Anniversary Collection Volumes 1–5 1939–1989 (Various jazz artists). Michael Cuscuna, producer. Blue Note.

Jazz Piano (Various artists 1989–1964). Martin Williams, producer. Smithsonian Collection.
Nat King Cole & the King Cole Trio (Nat King Cole & the King Cole Trio). Will Freidwald, producer. Savoy Jazz.

Producer of the Year, Non-Classical
• Peter Asher
Emilio Estefan Jr., Jorge Casas, Clay Ostwald
Jimmy Jam, Terry Lewis, Janet Jackson
L.A. Reid, Babyface
Prince
Tears for Fears, David Bascombe

Best Music Video, Short Form
Leave Me Alone,, Michael Jackson. Jim Blashfield, video director. Frank DiLeo, Michael Jackson, Jim Blashfield, Jerry Kramer, video producers. Epic.
The Living Years, Mike & the Mechanics. Atlantic.
Orinoco Flow (Sail Away), Enya. Michael Geoghegan, video director. Paul McNally, video producer. Geffen.
Something to Hold On To, Trevor Rabin. Jeff Stein, video director. Julio Flores, video producer. Elektra.
There's a Tear in My Beer, Hank Williams Jr., Hank Williams, Sr. Ethan Russell, video director. Ethan Russell, Joanne Gardner, video producers. Warner Bros./Curb Records.

Best Music Video, Long Form
• *Rhythm Nation*, Janet Jackson. Dominic Sena, Jonathan Dayton, Valerie Faris, video directors. Avis McGarry, Jonathan Dayton, Valerie Faris, video producers. A&M.
Hangin' Tough, New Kids on the Block. Doug Nichol, video director. Bryan Johnson, video producer. CBS Music Video.
In Concert—Delicate Sound of Thunder, Pink Floyd. Wayne Isham, video director. Curt Marvis, video producer. CBS Music Video.
Moonwalker, Michael Jackson. Colin Chilvers, Jerry Kramer, video directors. Dennis Jones, Michael Jackson, Jerry Kramer, Frank DiLeo, video directors. CBS Music Video.
Savage, Eurythmics. Sophie Muller, video director. John Stewart, Billy Poveda, video producers. Virgin Video.

Keeping it Up: Quincy Jones

The man with the most friends, the most impressive career, and the most diverse talents in the music industry officially became the most honored pop artist in Grammy history when his *Back on the Block* swept up eight Grammys, sweeping him past Henry Mancini's record for having the most wins outside the classical categories. Of the LP's eight Grammys, six were for Jones personally, including Album of the Year, bringing his career tally to 25. Only Chicago Symphony conductor Sir Georg Solti, with 28, had more.

Quincy Jones became the second biggest winner in Grammy history, with 25 awards, when he reaped six for 1990 Album of the Year Back on the Block.

Quincy Jones had received his first Grammy for arranging jazz for Count Basie in 1963 and subsequently picked up, among others, prizes for jazz instrumental performance ("Walking in Space" in 1969), r&b group vocal performance (*The Dude* in 1981), and producing Michael Jackson's 1983 Album of the Year, *Thriller,* and the 1985 Record of the Year, "We Are the World."

Jones's career actually dates back to the early 1950s when he played trumpet for Lionel Hampton and Dizzy Gillespie. Ten years later he was leading the band for Frank Sinatra and soon thereafter, as a producer, was shepherding the careers of Lesley Gore, Roberta Flack, James Ingram, Chaka Khan, and others. He composed for films (*In the Heat of the Night*) and TV (*Sanford & Son*) and established himself as a successful record company executive with his own label,

Qwest. When Jones decided to put it all together and produce an album retrospective of great black music, the results were just as diverse — and amazing.

Back on the Block spanned four decades of black musical tradition, including bee-bop, soul, r&b, funk, hip-hop, and rap. Jones recruited an equally disparate array of talents for the task such as Sarah Vaughan, Ella Fitzgerald, Dizzy Gillespie, Ray Charles, George Benson, Chaka Khan, James Ingram, Siedah Garrett, Kool Moe Dee, and Ice-T. In the album notes, he writes, "These colleagues and I have taken a journey through every influence and everyone that I love in music ... and we've worked together to bridge generations and traverse musical boundaries."

"Pray for peace on earth," Jones said in his acceptance remarks, "and when we get peace on earth, let's take care of the earth."

In addition to the LP honors, *Back on the Block* earned Jones his third Producer of the Year award, Best Jazz Fusion Performance ("Birdland," with co-winners Dizzy Gillespie, Miles Davis, and others), Best Arrangement on an Instrumental ("Birdland," with co-winner Ian Prince and others), Best Group Rap Performance ("Back on the Block," with his son, Quincy Jones III, Melle Mel, etc.), and Best Instrumental Arrangement Accompanying Vocals ("The Places You Find Love," performed by Siedah Garrett, Chaka Kan, etc.). The half-dozen awards tied him with Roger Miller for having the second most victories in a single year. Miller earned his six in 1965 for "King of the Road" and *The Return of Roger Miller*. Michael Jackson surpassed Miller in 1983 with eight for his and Jones's *Thriller*.

> *Song of the Year "From a Distance" was a comfort to U.S. troops during the Desert Storm military engagement.*

Back on the Block also reaped an engineering trophy plus the r&b duo/group vocal award for Ray Charles and Chaka Khan as singers of "I'll Be Good to You." Khan had won four Grammys in the early 1980s. But, as Grammy watcher Paul Grein had written in the *L.A. Times* prior to the show, *"Everyone* will be rooting for Ray Charles to win his first Grammy in 15 years." They were not disappointed.

The most nominated artist of the year, Phil Collins, with eight bids, was a loser in the LP race for ... *But Seriously* and in six other categories, but he nonetheless took the highest prize, Record of the Year, for "Another Day in Paradise." The *L.A. Times* described the song as "a timely statement about social indifference in the homeless age, with a lush undisturbing arrangement that may be meant as irony."

Collins's consciousness-raising song was also up for Song of the Year, but lost to a ballad sung by Bette Midler that was considered potential trouble for "Paradise" in the record line-up, since, although Collins was seen as the early front runner, Midler won last year for "Wind Beneath My Wings."

"From a Distance" was written by Julie Gold and helped to calm the national spirit during the Operation Desert Storm military action just weeks prior to the Grammy ceremony when American troops joined United Nations forces in ousting the Iraqi soldiers of Saddam Hussein from Kuwait. The song was actually five years old and had also comforted warring Catholics and Protestants alike in Northern Ireland earlier when folk singer Nanci Griffith's first recording of it topped the Irish charts soon after it was penned. The *L.A. Times* described its appeal: "The philosophical reflection expresses a one-world sentiment, starting from the global perspective we've gained in the Space Age, and it seems perfect for a time in which ideologies overlap and right and wrong are not so black and white."

"I'm on top of the world, living a dream!" Gold gushed when she accepted her Grammy. "To our soldiers, we pray for your speedy return." Then she added, echoing Quincy Jones, "We pray for peace on earth."

Bette Midler was the favorite to snag the female pop vocal laurels for "From a Distance," but she lost to this year's Best New Artist, Mariah Carey, for "Vision of Love." Carey, a soul-pop singer and songwriter, noted the *Times*, "pulled off a rare parlay in the nominations" when she scored five, including nods for Record, Song, and Album of the Year. Prior to Carey, the only other artists ever nominated in all of Grammy's top four slots (including Best New Artist) were Tracy Chapman in 1988, who nabbed only the newcomer's kudos and Christopher Cross, who swept all four categories in 1980.

Mariah Carey lost her bids for Record, Album, and Song of the Year, but prevailed with Grammys for Best New Artist and Best Female Pop Vocal Performance ("Vision of Love").

Last year the *L.A. Times* told its readers, "This will be the Grammy voters' last chance to salute Roy Orbison [nominated for his last Top 10 hit "You Got It"], a classic pop vocalist whose only Grammys to date are in the country and spoken word fields." Orbison had died of a heart attack in 1988 and lost his posthumous Grammy bid of 1989 to Michael Bolton, but he prevailed this year when Virgin Records released a new, late recording of his 1964 classic, "Oh, Pretty Woman." Orbison beat Bolton this time and the rest of the stellar line-up that included Phil Collins, Billy Joel, James Ingram, and the still-Grammyless Rod Stewart.

Last year Linda Ronstadt and Aaron Neville pulled off an upset over Britain's Fine Young Cannibals to garner the duo/group pop vocals award. The pair now achieved another surprise victory with their latest hit "All My Life." The vanquished this time included Wilson Phillips, the hit pop group comprised of Carnie and Wendy Wilson (daughters of Beach Boy Brian Wilson) and Chynna Phillips (daughter of John

and Michelle Phillips of the Mamas & the Papas). Wilson Phillips had been viewed as the probable victor because the trio was also competing for Album and Song of the Year, in addition to Best New Artist.

The only Grammy that veteran rocker Eric Clapton ever won was for his partial contribution to 1972 Album of the Year *The Concert for Bangla Desh*. He'd been nominated on two other occasions (most recently losing to Robert Palmer in 1988) but finally prevailed all on his own by giving the year's Best Male Rock Vocal Performance in "Bad Love." Billy Idol had been expected to take the category with a large sympathy vote for "Cradle of Love," since he'd recently recovered from a serious motorcyle accident.

Yet another upset occurred when a Canadian newcomer to the pop charts slinked past the younger sister of Michael Jackson for the female rock honors. The *Times* had predicted a Janet Jackson victory, but Alannah Myles and her single "Black Velvet" managed to out do Jackson's "Black Cat," as well as six-time past winner Tina Turner and others. Jackson had been nominated seven times before, but the only award she'd won was last year for her *Rhythm Nation* video. Metallica won its first Grammy last year following its controversial defeat in 1988 by Jethro Tull. This year it repeated its Best Metal Performance victory for "Stone Cold Crazy," a track from Elektra Records' all-star album celebrating the label's 40th anniversary, *Rubaiyat*.

Like Rod Stewart, the Rolling Stones still hadn't won *any* Grammys, but were expected to prevail for the rock group laurels over the two dark-horse favorites, INXS and the Red Hot Chili Peppers. All three ended up being surpassed by an even darker horse when Aerosmith won for "Janie's Got a Gun." Its victory helped to make up for Aerosmith's loss last year in the hard rock category to Living Colour after having never before been nominated.

> *Sinéad O'Connor became the first artist ever to refuse a Grammy. She fumed, "I wouldn't want it near me."*

Aerosmith wasn't nominated for the hard rock prize, so Living Colour won easily for *Time's Up*. Guitarist Vernon Reid accepted the award by dedicating it to "all the bar bands, all the acts who are struggling to make it." *The New York Times* noted: "He was wearing a Sinéad O'Connor T-shirt, but his words suggested a willingness to participate in just the commercial process Ms. O'Connor professes to abhor."

What the *N.Y. Times* was talking about was a growing brouhaha over Irish rock singer Sinéad O'Connor, whom the *L.A. Times* called one of the two most dominant pop figures of the past year (the other being rap artist M.C. Hammer). The *L.A. Times* also called her hit cover of an old Prince song, "Nothing Compares 2 U," a nominee for Record of the Year, "the most compelling single in all of 1990."

O'Connor had four nominations but issued an announcement prior to the Grammycast saying that she wouldn't accept any awards if she won. When she ended up with the new prize for Best Alternative Music for her album, ironically titled *I Do Not Want What I Haven't Got* (which was not nominated for Album of the Year, to the surprise of many), she became the first artist in Grammy history to refuse an award.

O'Connor appeared on Arsenio Hall's late-night TV talk show shortly after making her announcement and elaborated, "I've said that if I win, I won't accept it and I wouldn't want it near me. As far as I'm concerned, it represents everything I despise about the music industry." In a separate interview with the *L.A. Times*, she accused N.A.R.A.S. of "false and materialistic values." The *Times* added: "She thinks the [Grammy] ceremony honors commercial success more than pop artistry." O'Connor said she wanted America's leading music artists to ignore the pop charts and concentrate instead on probing "the reasons why this world is now at war ... why [it] abuses its children ... and why people are homeless and are starving."

She had caused a controversy the previous summer when she refused to allow the national anthem to be played at one of her concerts and then suffered the ire of patriotic fans. Probably because the Gulf war was going on concurrently with the Grammy show and feelings of national pride were running particularly high, the backlash this time was stinging. Jeff Pollack, a leading radio and TV programmer, told the *Times*, "I think she must be from another planet. How she equates an awards ceremony with all the ills of the world is beyond my comprehension." California disc jockey Rick Dees reported a flood of telephone calls from listeners outraged by her stance. He told the *Times*, "I had no idea of the venom that is out there for this girl."

Critic Dave Marsh was more compassionate, writing, "I think it's an honorable thing to do, but not a helpful thing. I'd rather see her show up at the Grammys and make an anti-war statement."

O'Connor tried to cope with the growing chorus of denouncements by insisting that she was attacking the music industry in general and didn't mean to single out the Grammys. But she clearly had. She'd recently attended the MTV awards show as well as the American Music Awards ceremony, although she claimed she would boycott both in the future, too. The brouhaha finally died down soon after the Grammycast, which went on without her.

When that other leading pop artist of the year, M.C. Hammer, proved triumphant at the Grammys, too, he not only accepted the honors, he walked off with three of them, making him the second-biggest winner of the night, after Quincy Jones. Hammer lost his bids for Album and Record of the Year but made up for the defeats with the year's Best Rhythm & Blues Song ("U Can't Touch This," written with James Miller), Best Rap Solo Performance for the same song, and the Best Long Form Music Video for *Please Hammer Don't Hurt 'Em, The Movie. Please Hammer Don't Hurt 'Em* was the best-selling LP of the

year and was, commented the *L.A. Times*, "the album that made rap safe for mainstream America — and you don't get any more mainstream than Grammy voters. Eight million album buyers can't be wrong." In his acceptance remarks, Hammer mentioned the Persian Gulf crisis and dedicated his victories to the American soldiers who are "putting their lives on the line for us."

The creamy-voiced soul singer Luther Vandross had lost all of his previous nine Grammy bids dating back to 1981, but he finally snagged the r&b

Triple winner M.C. Hammer ("U Can't Touch This") "made rap safe for mainstream America."

male vocals accolade for "Here and Now." As she was for the female rock honors, Janet Jackson was favored to take the r&b female vocal kudos for "Alright" but was upset by Anita Baker (*Compositions*), who had now taken the category for the fourth time in five years.

The prize for Best New Age Recording ("New Age" was once defined as "mood music for Yuppies"), which went to one of its most popular artists, keyboardist Mark Isham, who had recorded with the Windham Hill label, one of the genre's biggest producers, since 1984.

After not having won a N.A.R.A.S. prize since 1983, the veteran Grammy queen Ella Fitzgerald, at age 72, made a triumphant comeback to claim the female jazz vocal laurels for *All That Jazz*, marking her 13th win. Pianist Oscar Peterson, now 65, hadn't won a Grammy since 1979, but he scored two this year for *The Legendary Oscar Peterson Trio Live at the Blue Note*: both the soloist and group jazz instrumental performance awards.

> *Kathy Mattea proved a double winner for her Best Country Song "Where've You Been."*

Second-time nominee Harry Connick, Jr., reprised his victory in the male jazz singing slot (for his best-selling *We Are in Love*, another controversial mix of jazz and show tunes), topping previous Grammy champs George Benson, Jon Hendricks, Bobby McFerrin, and Tony Bennett. Benson's album with the Count Basie Orchestra, *Big Boss Band*, won the big band instrumental trophy for conductor Frank Foster for its track "Basie's Bag."

Considering that Kathy Mattea had recently swept the Country Music Association Awards for the second year in a row, it was wasn't surprising when the young West Virginian thrush bested K.T. Oslin, Reba McEntire, and others for the female country vocals kudos for "Where've You Been," which was also hailed as Best Country Song, bringing laurels to its writers Jon Vezner and Don

Henry. After her victory, Mattea told *Entertainment Weekly*, "It's like, OK, what do you do now? Do you try to make these albums that sound like the other ones so you can keep winning these awards, or do you go for expressing your more artistic side?" She soon opted, the magazine added, "to follow her heart into more personal, seemingly less commercial territory" with her next album, *Time Passes By*, which would earn her another nomination next year.

Two songs popularized by Garth Brooks were close contenders for Best Country Song and one, "Friends in Low Places," was supposed to earn Brooks his first male vocal performance Grammy. The statuette ended up going to Vince Gill, though, for "When I Call Your Name," a song he wrote with Tim DuBois. Gill, now 34, had been working in near obscurity as a sideman and solo artist throughout the 1980s and then, as Gill told *Entertainment Weekly* about his career, "It went nuts in the last two years. I don't know why. It's the same four chords it's always been." The Country Music Association had just named him Country Male Vocalist of the Year and awarded him the Song of the Year prize for "When I Call Your Name."

The *L.A. Times* predicted the Judds would claim the duo/group performance category since, it said, "By now all the voters have learned of Naomi Judd's forced retirement from concerts due to health reasons." But the winner turned out to be the Kentucky Headhunters, ("the scariest things in country music," according to its rhythm guitarist Richard Young) for *Pickin' on Nashville*. *Time* magazine described the band thus: "The KenHeads blend whimsy, old-time picking and some refried hippie riffs with the dynamism of a rock band from some Ozark Olympus." More traditional talent won out in the vocal collaboration category when Chet

Atkins and Mark Knopfler scored with "Poor Boy Blues." They also picked up the instrumental performance honors for "So Soft, Your Goodbye," beating, among others, Asleep at the Wheel and David Grisman.

Despite her youth, 19-year-old upstart Alison Krauss took the laurels for Best Bluegrass Recording for *I've Got That Old Feeling. Time* magazine commented: "She's come a long way from being just another kid with a violin case. The bluegrass field has been tough for ladies, especially ones so young, but Krauss has had lots of practice. The old pro from Champaign, Illinois, recorded her first album at 14."

As usual, the religious awards were claimed by a host of returning veterans, including Take 6 (*So Much 2 Say*, Best Contemporary Soul Gospel Album), Sandi Patti (*Another Time ... Another Place*, Best Pop Gospel Album), and the Rev. James Cleveland, who died only a few weeks before the Grammy ceremony (*Having Church*, Best Gospel Album by a Choir or Chorus). Among the newcomers was the veteran Christian rock band Petra, which performed its own original material on recordings such as *Beyond Belief*, winner of Best Rock/ Contemporary Gospel Album.

The writers of the music used in the hit animated Disney film *The Little Mermaid* — Howard Ashman and Alan Menken — garnered two Grammys: Best Recording for Children for the movie soundtrack and the best film song award for the popular single "Under the Sea."

In the classical field, the special committee continued to select the nominees in order to prevent the threat of bloc voting. The target of those accusations in the past — the Atlanta Symphony Orchestra and Chorus — still received one Grammy this year, however, when the group was awarded the choral laurels for works by Walton and Bernstein.

But it turned out to be Leonard Bernstein's big year at the Grammys, as forecasted. "The recent passing of America's beloved, heart-on-sleeve, good-cause-associated, conductor-composer-educator — and [his Ives] recording's sheer beauty — will overwhelm the membership," the *L.A. Times* had predicted.

Bernstein and the New York Philharmonic garnered Best Classical Album for their recording of Charles Ives's Symphony No. 2 and other works such as "Central Park in the Dark," which were taped live during a performance at New York's Avery Fisher Hall.

Bernstein led the Chicago Symphony Orchestra in a recording of Shostakovich's Symphonies No. 1 and No. 7 and reaped the orchestral performance accolade over such competition as his own Best Classical Album and another Chicago Symphony recording with Grammy grabber Sir Georg Solti holding the baton. "Here Bernstein is in his element!" *American Record Guide* gushed over the Shostakovich program.

"Bernstein will also be the sentimental favorite for Best Contemporary Composition, with his *Arias and Barcarolles*," the *L.A. Times* predicted correctly, too. The work's strange title came from a comment once made by President Dwight Eisenhower after he heard Bernstein play a Mozart concerto. He said, "I like music with a theme, not all them arias and barcarolles."

The classical Grammys continued their memorial note when *The Last Recording* of the late Vladimir Horowitz, which contained works by Chopin, Haydn, Liszt, and Wagner, brought him the trophy for best soloist performance without orchestra. "Horowitz had an autumnal last period in which he was constantly looking at new literature and playing it in a relaxed, charming manner," *The New*

York Times commented on this LP. "Gone were the neuroticism and outsize dynamics that could surge into his playing. In this kind of performance he gives the feeling that now he is no longer out to prove anything, that he is merely having a good time playing the piano. His patented kind of electricity is still there."

Violinist Itzhak Perlman scored two awards, including the soloist (with orchestra) honors for works by Shostakovich and Glazunov. He also snagged the chamber music prize, sharing it with pianist Daniel Barenboim for three Brahms violin sonatas. The *L.A. Times* foresaw the latter victory, too, but said that the "thrilling" program of Bartók's *Contrasts* performed by Richard Goode and Richard and Lucy Stoltzman really *should* win instead.

The winner of Best Opera Recording was intimately related to last year's winner. Both were part of James Levine's first American production of Wagner's *The Ring of Nibelung*, which was staged at the Metropolitan Opera. *Die Walküre* won the 1989 kudos; this year it went to the *Das Rheingold* installment. "This is a gripping performance, both dramatically and musically," *Opera News* wrote.

Carreras, Domingo, Pavarotti in Concert, a recording commonly known as "The Three Tenors," brought the vocalist kudos to a triumvirate of talent: José Carreras, Placido Domingo, and Luciano Pavarotti. The *L.A. Times* did not approve, writing, "It finds Placido and Luciano bawling their golden lungs out and Carreras straining with his now-limited equipment to match their decibel output and endeavoring (with sporadic success) to sing on pitch. The recording has been declared a 'crossover hit.'"

The Grammy ceremony, hosted again by comedian Garry Shandling, was held in New York for the fifth time over all and the first time since 1988.

"Nielsen ratings appeared oblivious to the site change," *Variety* reported. "CBS won the 8 p.m. to 11 p.m. slot with an 18.8 rating and 31 share, almost identical to last year's 18.9/31."

Lifetime Achievement Awards were bestowed on Bob Dylan and the late John Lennon. The *L.A. Times* noted: "Dylan sang a blistering version of his old anti-war song 'Masters of War,' while Tracy Chapman sang Lennon's idealistic 'Imagine.'"

"Mr. Dylan made a characteristically enigmatic appearance," the *N.Y. Times* added. "He sang an unfamiliar song and then, after being handed an award by Jack Nicholson, Mr. Dylan said his father had told him: 'It's possible to be so defiled in this world that even your mother and father won't know you. But God will always believe in your own ability to mend your own ways.'"

1990

The awards ceremony was broadcast on CBS from Radio City Music Hall in New York City on February 20, 1991, for the eligibility period of October 1, 1989, through September 30, 1990.

ALBUM OF THE YEAR
• *Back on the Block*, Quincy Jones, Quincy Jones, producer. Qwest.
... *But Seriously*, Phil Collins. Phil Collins, Hugh Padham producers. Atlantic.

Mariah Carey, Mariah Carey. Various track producers only. Columbia/CBS.
Please Hammer Don't Hurt 'Em, M.C. Hammer. M.C. Hammer, producer. Capitol.
Wilson Phillips, Wilson Phillips. Glen Ballard, producer. SBK.

RECORD OF THE YEAR
- "Another Day in Paradise," Phil Collins. Phil Collins, Hugh Padham, producers. Atlantic.
- "From a Distance," Bette Midler. Arif Mardin, producer. Atlantic.
- "Nothing Compares 2 U," Sinéad O'Connor. Sinéad O'Connor, Nellee Hooper, producers. Ensign/Chrysalis.
- ✓ "U Can't Touch This," M.C. Hammer. M.C. Hammer, producer. Capitol.
- ✓ "Vision of Love," Mariah Carey. Rhett Lawrence, producer. Columbia/CBS.

SONG OF THE YEAR
(Songwriter's Award)
- "From a Distance," Julie Gold. Atlantic.
- "Another Day in Paradise," Phil Collins. Atlantic.
- ✓ "Hold On," Chynna Phillips, Glen Ballard, Carnie Wilson. SBK Records.
- "Nothing Compares 2 U," Prince. Ensign/Chrysalis.
- ✓ "Vision of Love," Mariah Carey, Ben Margulies. Columbia/CBS.

BEST NEW ARTIST
- Mariah Carey. Columbia/CBS.
- Black Crowes. Def American.
- Kentucky Headhunters. Mercury.
- Lisa Stansfield. Arista.
- Wilson Phillips. SBK.

BEST POP VOCAL PERFORMANCE, MALE
- Roy Orbison, "Oh Pretty Woman," track from *A Black & White Night Live*. Virgin.
- Michael Bolton, "Georgia on My Mind." Columbia/CBS.
- Phil Collins, "Another Day in Paradise." Atlantic.
- James Ingram, "I Don't Have the Heart." Warner Bros.
- Billy Joel, *Storm Front*. Columbia/CBS.
- Rod Stewart, "Downtown Train." Warner Bros.

BEST POP VOCAL PERFORMANCE, FEMALE
- ✓ Mariah Carey, "Vision of Love." Columbia/CBS.
- ✓ Whitney Houston, "I'm Your Baby Tonight." Arista.
- Bette Midler, "From a Distance." Atlantic.
- Sinéad O'Connor, "Nothing Compares 2 U." Ensign/Chrysalis.
- Lisa Stansfield, "All Around the World." Arista.

Eric Clapton shared the honors in 1972 for best LP Bangla Desh *but now won his first for solo work for "Bad Love."*

BEST POP PERFORMANCE BY A DUO OR GROUP WITH VOCAL
- Linda Ronstadt, Aaron Neville, "All My Life." Elektra.
- ✓ B-52's, "Roam." Reprise.
- ✓ Heart, "All I Wanna Do Is Make Love to You." Capitol.
- ✓ Bruce Hornsby & the Range, "Across the River." RCA.
- ✓ Wilson Phillips, "Hold On." SBK.
- ✓ Righteous Brothers, "Unchained Melody" (1990 re-recording). Curb.

BEST POP INSTRUMENTAL PERFORMANCE
- ✓ Angelo Badalamenti, *"Twin Peaks* Theme," track from *Twin Peaks Soundtrack*. Warner Bros.
- Phil Collins, "Saturday Night and Sunday Morning," track from *... But Seriously*. Atlantic.
- Kenny G, "Going Home," track from *Live*. Arista.
- Quincy Jones (various artists), "Setembro (Brazilian Wedding Song)," track from *Back on the Block*. Qwest.
- Stanley Jordan, "What's Goin' On," track from *Cornucopia*. Blue Note.

Aerosmith avenged its loss of last year in the hard rock category by winning the rock group prize ("Janie's Got a Gun").

BEST ROCK VOCAL PERFORMANCE, MALE
• Eric Clapton, "Bad Love." Reprise/Duck.
Joe Cocker, "You Can Leave Your Hat On." Capitol.
Billy Idol, "Cradle of Love." Chrysalis.
Jon Bon Jovi, "Blaze of Glory," track from *Blaze of Glory.* Mercury.
Neil Young, "Rockin' in the Free World." Reprise.

BEST ROCK VOCAL PERFORMANCE, FEMALE
• Alannah Myles, "Black Velvet." Atlantic.
Melissa Etheridge, "The Angels." Island.
√Janet Jackson, "Black Cat." A&M.
Stevie Nicks, "Whole Lotta Trouble." Modern/Atlantic.
Tina Turner, "Steamy Windows." Capitol.

BEST ROCK PERFORMANCE BY A DUO OR GROUP WITH VOCAL
√• Aerosmith, "Janie's Got a Gun." Geffen.
√INXS, "Suicide Blonde." Atlantic.
√Midnight Oil, *Blue Sky Mining.* Columbia/CBS
Red Hot Chili Peppers, "Higher Ground." EMI.
Rolling Stones, "Almost Hear You Sigh." Columbia/CBS.

BEST ROCK INSTRUMENTAL PERFORMANCE
• Vaughan Brothers, "D/FW," track from *Family Style.* Epic Associated.
Allman Brothers Band, "True Gravity," track from *Seven Turns.* Epic.
Eric Johnson, *Ah Via Musicom.* Capitol.

Joe Satriani, *Flying in a Blue Dream.* Relativity.
Steve Vai, *Passion and Warfare.* Relativity.

BEST HARD ROCK PERFORMANCE
• Living Colour, *Time's Up.* Epic.
AC/DC, *The Razors Edge.* Atco.
Faith No More, "Epic." Slash/Reprise.
Jane's Addiction, *Ritual de lo Habitual.* Warner Bros.
Motley Crue, "Kickstart My Heart." Elektra.

BEST METAL PERFORMANCE
• Metallica, "Stone Cold Crazy," track from *Rubaiyat* (Various artists album). Elektra.
Anthrax, *Persistence of Time.* Island.
Megadeth, *Rust in Peace.* Capitol.
Judas Priest, *Painkiller.* Columbia.
Sucidal Tenencies, *Lights ... Camera ... Revolution.* Epic.

BEST ALTERNATIVE MUSIC PERFORMANCE
• Sinéad O'Connor, *I Do Not Want What I Haven't Got.* Ensign/Chrysalis.
Laurie Anderson, *Strange Angels.* Warner Bros.
Kate Bush, *The Sensual World.* Columbia/CBS.
Replacements, *All Shook Down.* Sire/Reprise.
World Party, *Goodbye Jumbo.* Chrysalis/Ensign.

BEST RHYTHM & BLUES SONG
(Songwriter's Award)
√• "U Can't Touch This," James Miller, M.C. Hammer. Capitol.
√"Alright," Janet Jackson, James Harris III, Terry Lewis. A&M.
"Here and Now," Terry Steele, David L. Elliott. Epic.
"I'll Be Good to You," George Johnson, Louis Johnson, Sonora Sam. Qwest.
√"My, My, My," L.A. Reid, Babyface, Daryl Simmons. Motown.

BEST RHYTHM & BLUES VOCAL PERFORMANCE, MALE
• Luther Vandross, "Here and Now." Epic.
Babyface, "Whip Appeal." Solar/Epic.
√Tevin Campbell, "Round and Round." Warner Bros./Paisley Park.
√Johnny Gill, *Johnny Gill.* Motown.
Al B. Sure!, "Misunderstanding." Warner Bros.

Best Rhythm & Blues Vocal Performance, Female
- Anita Baker, *Compositions*. Elektra.

Regina Belle, "Make It Like It Was." Columbia/CBS.

√ Janet Jackson, "Alright." A&M.

Patti LaBelle, "I Can't Complain." MCA.

Pebbles, "Giving You the Benefit." MCA.

Best Rhythm & Blues Performance by a Duo or Group with Vocal
- Ray Charles, Chaka Khan, "I'll Be Good to You." Qwest.

After 7, "Can't Stop." Virgin.

Al B. Sure!, James Ingram, El DeBarge, Barry White, "The Secret Garden (Sweet Seduction Suite)." Qwest.

√ En Vogue, *Born to Sing*. Atlantic.

Was (Not Was), "Papa Was a Rolling Stone." Chrysalis.

Best Rap Solo Performance
√ • M.C. Hammer, "U Can't Touch This." Capitol.

Big Daddy Kane, "I Get the Job Done." Cold Chillin'/Reprise.

√ Monie Love, "Monie in the Middle." Warner Bros.

Queen Latifah, *All Hail the Queen*. Tommy Boy.

√ Vanilla Ice, "Ice Ice Baby." SBK.

Best Rap Performance by a Duo or Group
- Ice-T, Melle Mel, Big Daddy Kane, Kool Moe Dee, Quincy Jones III, "Back on the Block," track from Quincy Jones's *Back on the Block*. Warner Bros.

Digital Underground, "The Humpty Dance." Tommy Boy.

DJ Jazzy Jeff & the Fresh Prince, *And in This Corner ....* Jive/RCA.

Public Enemy, *Fear of a Black Planet*. Def Jam/Columbia.

West Coast Rap All-Stars, "We're All in the Same Gang." Warner Bros.

Best Jazz Vocal Performance, Male
- Harry Connick, Jr., *We Are in Love*. Columbia/CBS.

Tony Bennett, *Astoria: Portrait of the Artist*. Columbia/CBS.

George Benson, *Big Boss Band*. Warner Bros.

Jon Hendricks, *Freddie Freeloader*. Denon.

Bobby McFerrin, "Scrapple from the Apple," track from *The Many Faces of Bird*. Verve.

Best Jazz Vocal Performance, Female
- Ella Fitzgerald, *All That Jazz*. Pablo.

Betty Carter, *Droppin' Things*. Verve.

Peggy Lee, *The Peggy Lee Songbook — There'll Be Another Spring*. MusicMasters.

Carmen McRae, *Carmen Sings Monk*. Novus.

Dianne Reeves, "I Got It Bad and That Ain't Good," track from *Echos of Ellington Vol. #1*. Verve.

Best Jazz Instrumental Performance, Soloist
- Oscar Peterson, *The Legendary Oscar Peterson Trio Live at the Blue Note*. Telarc.

George Benson, "Basie's Bag," track from *Big Boss Band*. Warner Bros.

Miles Davis, *The Hot Spot*. Antilles.

Stan Getz, *Anniversary*. Emarcy.

Branford Marsalis, *Crazy People Music*. Columbia/CBS.

Best Jazz Instrumental Performance, Group
- Oscar Peterson Trio, *The Legendary Oscar Peterson Trio Live at the Blue Note*. Telarc.

Art Blakey, Dr. John, David "Fathead" Newman, *Bluesiana Triangle*. Windham Hill.

Branford Marsalis Quartet featuring Terence Blanchard, "Again Never," track from *Mo' Better Blues*. Columbia/CBS.

Wynton Marsalis (Group), *Standard Time Vol. 3 — The Resolution of Romance*. Columbia/CBS.

Max Roach, Dizzy Gillespie, *Max & Dizzy — Paris 1989*. A&M.

Best Jazz Instrumental Performance, Big Band
- Frank Foster, conductor, "Basie's Bag," track from *Big Boss Band* (George Benson album with the Count Basie Orchestra). Warner Bros.

Louie Bellson, *Airmail Special*. MusicMasters.

Bob Florence Limited Edition, *Treasure Chest*. USA Music Group.

GLOBE PHOTO

Seven-time past champ Johnny Cash (shown with wife June) was the recipient of an honorary Grammy Legends Award.

Lionel Hampton & His Big Band, *Cookin' in the Kitchen*. Glad Hamp.
Mel Lewis Jazz Orchestra, *The Definitive Thad Jones, Volume 2, Live from the Village Vanguard*. MusicMasters.

BEST JAZZ FUSION PERFORMANCE
• Quincy Jones, various artists, "Birdland," track from *Back on the Block*. Qwest.
Chick Corea Elektric Band, *Inside Out*. GRP.
Stan Getz, *Apasionado*. A&M.
Lee Ritenour, *Stolen Moments*. GRP
Spyro Gyra, *Fast Forward*. GRP.

BEST COUNTRY SONG
(Songwriter's Award)
• "Where've You Been," Jon Vezner, Don Henry. Mercury.
"Come Next Monday," K.T. Oslin, Rory Michael Bourke, Charlie Black. RCA.
√"The Dance," Tony Arata. Capitol/Nashville.
√"Friends in Low Places," DeWayne Blackwell, Earl Bud Lee. Capitol/Nashville.
"When I Call Your Name," Vince Gill, Tim DuBois. MCA.

BEST COUNTRY VOCAL PERFORMANCE, MALE
• Vince Gill, "When I Call Your Name." MCA.
√Garth Brooks, "Friends in Low Places." Capitol/Nashville.
Doug Stone, "I'd Be Better Off (in a Pine Box)." Epic.
√Randy Travis, "Hard Rock Bottom of Your Heart." Warner Bros.
√Dwight Yoakam, "Turn It On, Turn It Up, Turn Me Loose." Reprise.

BEST COUNTRY VOCAL PERFORMANCE, FEMALE
• Kathy Mattea, "Where've You Been." Mercury.
√Mary-Chapin Carpenter, "Quittin' Time." Columbia/CBS.
Carlene Carter, *I Fell in Love*. Reprise.
Reba McEntire, "You Lie." MCA.
K.T. Oslin, "Come Next Monday." RCA.

BEST COUNTRY PERFORMANCE BY A DUO OR GROUP WITH VOCAL
• Kentucky Headhunters, *Pickin' on Nashville*. Mercury.
√Alabama, "Jukebox in My Mind." RCA.
Judds, "Love Can Build a Bridge." Curb/RCA.
Restless Heart, "Fast Movin' Train." RCA.
Shenandoah, "Ghost in This House." Columbia/CBS.

BEST COUNTRY VOCAL COLLABORATION
• Chet Atkins, Mark Knopfler, "Poor Boy Blues." Columbia/CBS.
Waylon Jennings, Willie Nelson, Kris Kristofferson, Johnny Cash, *Highwayman 2*. Columbia/CBS.
Randy Travis, George Jones, "A Few Ole Country Boys." Warner Bros.
Randy Travis, B.B. King, "Waiting on the Light to Change," track from *Heroes & Friends*. Warner Bros.
Keith Whitley, Lorrie Morgan, "'Til a Tear Becomes a Rose." RCA.

BEST COUNTRY INSTRUMENTAL PERFORMANCE
• Chet Atkins, Mark Knopfler, "So Soft Your Goodbye," track from *Neck and Neck*. Columbia/CBS.
Asleep at the Wheel, "Pedernales Stroll," track from *Keepin' Me Up Nights*. Arista.
Foster & Lloyd, "Whoa," track from *Version of the Truth*. RCA-Victor.

David Grisman, *Dawg '90*. Acoustic Disc.
Wild Rose, "Wild Rose," track from
Breaking New Ground. Capitol.

BEST ROCK/CONTEMPORARY GOSPEL ALBUM
• *Beyond Belief*, Petra. Dayspring/Word.
Crank It Up, Myron LeFevre & Broken
Heart. Star Song.
Find Me in These Fields, Phil Keaggy.
Myrrh/Word.
Phase II, Eddie Degarmo.
Forefront/Benson.
The Secret of Time, Charlie Peacock.
Sparrow Records.

BEST POP GOSPEL ALBUM
• *Another Time ... Another Place*, Sandi
Patti. A&M/Word Inc.
Go West Young Man, Michael W. Smith.
Reunion.
God Is Good, First Call. Myrrh.
More to This Life, Steven Curtis Chapman.
Sparrow.
Warriors, Phil Driscoll. Word.

BEST SOUTHERN GOSPEL ALBUM
• *The Great Exchange*, Bruce Carroll.
Word.
He's Still in the Fire, Speers. Homeland.
Let the Redeemed Say So, Nelons.
Canaan/Word.
The Reunion, Happy Goodman Family.
Word/Epic.
Victory Road, J.D. Sumner & the Stamps.
River Song/Benson.

BEST TRADITIONAL SOUL GOSPEL ALBUM
• *Tramaine Hawkins Live*, Tramaine
Hawkins. Sparrow.
Bringing It Back Home, Clark Sisters.
Word/Word Inc.
I Remember Mama, Shirley Caesar.
Word/Word Inc.
Mom & Pop Winans, Mom & Pop Winans.
Sparrow.
*Ron Winans Presents Family & Friends
Choir II*, Ron Winans Family &
Friends Choir. Ronald Winans,
producer. Selah Records.

BEST CONTEMPORARY SOUL GOSPEL ALBUM
• *So Much 2 Say*, Take 6. Reprise.
Face to Face, Edwin Hawkins.
Lection/Polygram.
*He's Right on Time, Live from Los
Angeles*, Daryl Coley. Sparrow.

Portrait, Richard Smallwood Singers.
Word.
Return, Winans. Qwest.

BEST GOSPEL ALBUM BY A CHOIR OR CHORUS
• *Having Church*, Rev. James Cleveland &
the Southern California Community
Choir. Rev. James Cleveland, choir
director. Savoy.
He's Worthy, Dr. Jonathan Greer & the
Cathedral of Faith Choirs. Maurice
Culpepper, choir director. Savoy.
Hold On, Help Is on the Way, Georgia
Mass Choir, James Bignon, choir
director. Savoy.
Love Alive IV, Love Center Mass Choir.
Walter Hawkins, choir director. Malaco.
Open Our Eyes, Rev. Milton Brunson &
the Thompson Community Singers.
Rev. Milton Brunson, choir director.
Word/Word Inc.

BEST TRADITIONAL FOLK RECORDING
• *On Praying Ground*, Doc Watson. Sugar
Hill.
*Brazil Forro: Music for Maids and Taxi
Drivers*, Toinho de Alagoas, Duda da
Passira, Jose Orlando, Heleno Dos Oito
Baixos. Rounder.
Classic Tracks, Ladysmith Black
Mambazo. Shanachie.
Let's Get Cajun, Basin Brothers. Flying
Fish.
Old Time Duets, Whitstein Brothers.
Rounder.
*Partisans of Vilna: Songs of World War II
Jewish Resistance*, Various artists.
Flying Fish.

BEST CONTEMPORARY FOLK RECORDING
• *Steady On*, Shawn Colvin.
Columbia/CBS.
Days of Open Hand, Suzanne Vega.
A&M.
"Hammer and a Nail," track from *Nomads
- Indians - Saints*, Indigo Girls. Epic.
Helpless Heart, Maura O'Connell. Warner
Bros.

BEST TRADITIONAL BLUES RECORDING
• *Live at San Quentin*, B.B. King. MCA.
"Coming to Town," track from *The Hot
Spot*, John Lee Hooker, Earl Palmer,
Tim Drummond, Miles Davis, Roy
Rogers. Antilles.
Little Milton, *Too Much Pain* .... Malaco.

Standing My Ground, Clarence
"Gatemouth" Brown. Alligator.
"T'ain't Nobody's Bizness if I Do," track
from the *Black and Blue* cast
recording, Ruth Brown, Linda Hopkins.
Deutsche Grammophon.

BEST CONTEMPORARY BLUES RECORDING
• *Family Style*, Vaughan Brothers. Epic
Associated.
Jump for Joy, Koko Taylor. Alligator.
Midnight Stroll, the Robert Cray Band
featuring the Memphis Horns. Mercury.
"Red Hot & Blue," track from *Red, Hot
and Blue*, B.B. King, Lee Atwater.
Curb.
Stickin' to My Guns, Etta James. Island.

BEST BLUEGRASS RECORDING
• *I've Got that Old Feeling*, Alison Krauss.
Rounder.
The Boys Are Back in Town, Nashville
Bluegrass Band. Sugar Hill.
"Darlin' Boy," track from *Let it Fly*,
Dillards. Vanguard.
Grassroots to Bluegrass, Mac Wiseman.
CMH.
Take It Home, Hot Rize. Sugar Hill.

BEST LATIN POP PERFORMANCE
• José Feliciano, "Por Que Te Tengo Que
Olvidar?" track from *Nina*.
Capital/EMI Latin.
Duncan Dhu, *Autobiografia*. Sire/Warner
Bros.
Ana Gabriel, *Quien Como Tu*. CBS Discos
International.
Luis Miguel, *20 Anos*. WEA Latina.
Isabel Pantoja, "Se Me Enamora el Alma,"
track from *Se Me Enamora el Alma*.
RCA.

BEST TROPICAL LATIN PERFORMANCE
• Tito Puente, "Lambada Timbales," track
from *Goza mi Timbal*. Concord
Picante.
Willie Colon, *Color Americano*. CBS
Discos International.
Luis Enrique, "Amiga," track from *Los
Principes de la Salsa*. CBS Discos
International.
Tito Puente, Millie P., *Tito Puente
Presents Millie P*. RMM.
Poncho Sanchez, "Mama Guela," track
from *Chile con Soul*. Concord
Picante.

BEST MEXICAN/AMERICAN PERFORMANCE
• Texas Tornados, "Soy de San Luis,"
track from *Texas Tornados*. Reprise.
Los Diablos, *Nuestro Tiempo*. WEA
Latina.
Vicente Fernandez, *Las Clasicas de Jose
Alfredo Jimenez*. CBS Discos
International.
Santiago Jimenez, Jr., *Familia y Tradición*.
Rounder.
Mazz, "Amor con Amor," track from *No
Te Olvidare*. Capitol/EMI Latin.

BEST REGGAE RECORDING
• *Time Will Tell — A Tribute to Bob
Marley*, Bunny Wailer. Shanachie.
An Hour Live, Toots & the Maytals.
Sunsplash.
Make Place for the Youth, Andrew Tosh.
Tomato.
Mek We Dweet, Burning Spear.
Mango/Island.
Now, Black Uhuru. Mesa Records.

BEST POLKA RECORDING
• *When It's Polka Time at Your House*,
Jimmy Sturr & His Orchestra. Starr.
Everybody Polka, Eddie Blazonczyk's
Versatones. Bel-Aire.
Fiddle Faddle, Polka Family Band. Polka
Family Band.
Grand Illusion, Toledo Polkamotion.
World Renowned Sounds.
Sounds from the Heart, Jimmy Weber &
the Sounds. World Renowned Sounds.

BEST NEW AGE PERFORMANCE
• Mark Isham, *Mark Isham*. Virgin.
Acoustic Alchemy, "Caravan of Dreams,"
track from *Reference Point*. GRP.
Michael Hedges, *Taproot*. Windham Hill.
Mannheim Steamroller, *Yellowstone—The
Music of Nature*. American
Gramaphone.
Mysterious Voices of Bulgaria, *Balkan*.
Philippe Eidel, Arnaud Davis,
producers. Virgin.
Paul Winter, *Earth: Voices of a Planet*.
Living Music.

BEST INSTRUMENTAL COMPOSITION
• "Change of Heart," Pat Metheny.
Geffen.
"The Chief," Pat Metheny. GRP.
"Going Home," Kenny G., Walter
Aranasieff. Arista.

"One Last Pitch (Take Two)," Harry
Connick, Jr., Joe Livingston.
Columbia/CBS.
"The Sinister Minister," Bela Fleck.
Warner Bros.

BEST ARRANGEMENT
ON AN INSTRUMENTAL
• Quincy Jones, Ian Prince, Rod
Temperton, Jerry Hey, "Birdland,"
track from *Back on the Block* (Quincy
Jones, various artists). Qwest.
John Clayton, "Brush This," track from
The Groove Shop (Clayton-Hamilton
Jazz Orchestra). Capri.
Chick Corea, "Tale of Daring, Chapters
1–4," track from *Inside Out* (Chick
Corea Elektric Band). GRP.
Henry Mancini, "Monster Movie Music
Suite," track from *Mancini in
Surround—Mostly Monsters and
Murders* (Henry Mancini & the
Mancini Pops Orchestra). RCA Victor.
John Williams, "Born on the Fourth of
July" (John Williams). MCA.

BEST INSTRUMENTAL ARRANGEMENT
ACCOMPANYING VOCAL(S)
• Jerry Hey, Glen Ballard, Cliff Magness,
Quincy Jones, "The Places You Find
Love," track from Quincy Jones's *Back
on the Block* . Qwest.
Jorge Calandrelli, "Body and Soul," track
from *Astoria: Portrait of the Artist*
(Tony Bennett). Columbia/CBS.
George Duke, "Fumilayo," track from
Never Too Far (Dianne Reeves). EMI.
Mark Shaiman, Harry Connick, Jr.,
"Recipe for Love," track from *We Are
in Love* (Harry Connick, Jr.).
Columbia/CBS.
Mervyn Warren, Cedric Dent, "Come
Sunday," track from *Bigger World*
(Donna McElroy). Reprise.

BEST MUSICAL CAST SHOW ALBUM
• *Les Miserables, The Complete
Symphonic Recording*, Gary Morris,
Philip Quast, Kaho Shimada, Tracey
Shayne, and various casts. David
Caddick, album producer. Alain
Boublil, Herbert Kretzmer, lyricists.
Claude Michel Schonberg, composer.
Relativity Records.

Anything Goes, Kim Criswell, Cris
Groenendaal, Jack Gilford, Frederica
von Stade, and cast. John Foster, album
producer. Cole Porter, lyricist and
composer. Angel.
Black and Blue, Ruth Brown, Linda
Hopkins, and original Broadway cast.
Hugh Fordin, album producer. Various
lyricists and composers. Deutsche
Grammophon.
City of Angels, James Naughton, Gregg
Edelman, and original Broadway cast.
Cy Coleman, Mike Berniker, album
producers. Cy Coleman, composer.
David Zippel, lyrics. Columbia/CBS.
Gypsy, Tyne Daly, and Broadway cast.
John McClure, album producer.
Stephen Sondheim, lyricist. Jule Style,
composer. Elektra-Nonesuch.

BEST INSTRUMENTAL COMPOSITION
WRITTEN FOR A MOTION PICTURE
OR FOR TELEVISION
• *Glory*, James Horner. Virgin.
Dick Tracy Original Score, Danny Elfman.
Sire/Warner Bros.
"Driving Miss Daisy — End Titles," track
from *Driving Miss Daisy Original
Soundtrack*, Hans Zimmer. Varese
Sarabande.
*The Little Mermaid — Original Motion
Picture Soundtrack* (Instrumental score
portion of album), Alan Menken
(Various). Walt Disney.
"Theme from *Twin Peaks*," Angelo
Badalamenti (Angelo Badalamenti).
Warner Bros.

BEST SONG WRITTEN SPECIFICALLY
FOR A MOTION PICTURE OR TELEVISION
• "Under the Sea," track from *The Little
Mermaid Original Soundtrack*, Alan
Menken, Howard Ashman. Walt
Disney Records.
"Blaze of Glory," track from the motion
picture *Young Guns II*, Jon Bon Jovi.
Mercury.
"Kiss the Girl," track from *The Little
Mermaid — Original Motion Picture
Soundtrack*, Howard Ashman, Alan
Menken. Walt Disney.
"More," track from *Dick Tracy*, Stephen
Sondheim. Sire/Warner Bros.
"Sooner or Later," track from *I'm
Breathless* (Madonna album), Stephen
Sondheim. Sire/Warner Bros.

BEST CLASSICAL ALBUM

- *Ives: Symphony No. 2; The Gong on the Hook and Ladder (Fireman's Parade on Main Street); Central Park in the Dark; The Unanswered Question*, Leonard Bernstein conducting New York Philharmonic. Hans Weber, producer. Deutsche Grammophon.
- *Adams: Fearful Symmetries; The Wound-Dresser*, John Adams conducting Orchestra of St. Lukes (Sanford Sylvan, baritone). Elektra/Nonesuch.
- *Carreras, Domingo, Pavarotti in Concert*, José Carreras, Placido Domingo, Luciano Pavarotti, tenors. Zubin Mehta conducting Orchestra del Maggio Musicale Fiorentino and Orchestra del Teatro dell' Opera di Roma. Christopher Raeburn, producer. London.
- *Hanson: Symphonies 3 & 6; Fantasy Variations on a Theme of Youth*, Gerard Schwarz conducting Seattle Symphony and New York Chamber Symphony (Carol Rosenberger, piano). Adam Stern, producer. Delos International.
- *The Last Recording (Chopin, Haydn, Liszt, Wagner)*, Vladimir Horowitz, piano. Thomas Frost, producer. Sony Classical.
- *Rachmaninoff: Vespers*, Robert Shaw conducting Robert Shaw Festival Singers. Robert Woods, producer. Telarc.

BEST ORCHESTRAL PERFORMANCE
(Conductor's Award)

- Leonard Bernstein conducting Chicago Symphony Orchestra, *Shostakovich: Symphonies No. 1, Op. 10 and No. 7 ("Leningrad"), Op. 60.* Deutsche Grammophon.
- Leonard Bernstein conducting New York Philharmonic, *Ives: Symphony No. 2; The Gong on the Hook and Ladder (Fireman's Parade on Main Street); Central Park in the Dark; The Unanswered Question.* Deutsche Grammophon.
- Gerard Schwarz conducting Seattle Symphony Orchestra, *Hanson: Symphonies Nos. 3 & 6.* Delos International.
- Leonard Slatkin conducting St. Louis Symphony Orchestra, *Shostakovich: Symphony No. 8, Op. 65.* RCA Victor Red Seal.

Sir Georg Solti conducting Chicago Symphony Orchestra, *Beethoven: Symphonies No. 7 in A & No. 8 in F.* London.

BEST CHAMBER MUSIC OR OTHER SMALL ENSEMBLE PERFORMANCE

- Itzhak Perlman, violin. Daniel Barenboim, piano, *Brahms: The Three Violin Sonatas (No. 1, Op. 78; No. 2, Op. 100; No. 3, Op. 108).* Sony Classical.
- Mona Golabek, piano. Andres Cardenes, violin. Jeffrey Solow, cello, *Arensky: Piano Trio No. 2 in D Minor; Tchaikovsky: Piano Trio in A Minor.* Delos International.
- Juilliard String Quartet (solos: Benita Valente, Jan DeGaetani, Jon Humphrey, Thomas Paul) *Haydn: The Seven Last Words of Christ.* Sony Classical.
- Kronos Quartet, *Crumb: Black Angels; Tallis: Spem in Alium; Marta: Doom. A Sigh; Ives: They Are There!; Shostakovich: Quartet No. 8.* Elektra/Nonesuch.
- Richard Stoltzman, clarinet. Richard Goode, piano. Lucy Chapman Stoltzman, violin, *Bartók: Contrasts; Stravinsky: L'Histoire du Soldat — Suite; Ives: Largo, Songs.* RCA Victor Red Seal.

BEST CLASSICAL PERFORMANCE, INSTRUMENTAL SOLOIST(S) (WITH ORCHESTRA)

- Itzhak Perlman, violin (Zubin Mehta conducting Israel Philharmonic), *Shostakovich: Violin Concerto No. 1 in A Minor; Glazunov: Violin Concerto in A Minor, Op. 82.* Angel.
- Paul Crossley, piano (Esa-Pekka Salonen conducting London Sinfonietta), *Stravinsky: Works for Piano and Orchestra (Concerto for Piano & Orchestra; Capricco for Piano & Orchestra, etc.).* Sony Classical.
- Garrick Ohlsson, piano (Gerard Schwarz conducting Seattle Symphony), *Lazarof: Tableaux ("After Kandinsky") for Piano & Orchestra.* Delos International.
- Carol Rosenberger, piano (Gerard Schwarz conducting New York Chamber Symphony), *Hanson: Fantasy Variations on a Theme of Youth.* Delos International.

Rolf Smedvig, trumpet (Jahja Ling conducting Scottish Chamber Orchestra), *Trumpet Concertos (Haydn, Hummel, Tartini, Torelli, Bellini)*. Telarc.

BEST CLASSICAL PERFORMANCE — INSTRUMENTAL SOLOIST (WITHOUT ORCHESTRA)
• Vladimir Horwitz, piano, *The Last Recording* (Chopin, Haydn, Liszt, Wagner). Sony Classical.
Alicia de Larrocha, piano, *Mozart: Piano Sonatas K. 283, 331, 332, 333*. RCA Victor Red Seal.
Midori, violin, *Paganini: 24 Caprices for Solo Violin, Op. 1*. CBS Masterworks.
Ursula Oppens, piano, *Carter: Night Fantasies; Adams: Phrygian Gates*. Music & Arts Program of America, Inc.
Mitsuko Uchida, piano, *Debussy: 12 Piano Etudes*. Philips Classics.

BEST OPERA RECORDING
• *Wagner: Das Rheingold*, James Levine conducting Metropolitan Opera Orchestra (solos: Morris, Ludwig, Jerusalem, Wlaschiha, Moll, Zednik, Rootering). Cord Garben, producer. Deutsche Grammophon.
Mussorgsky: Boris Godunov, Mstislav Rostropovich conducting National Symphony Orchestra (solos: Raimondi, Vichnievskaia, Gedda, Plishka, Riegel, Tesarowicz). Michel Garcin, producer. Erato.
Prokofiev: The Love for Three Oranges, Kent Nagano conducting Orchestra of Opera de Lyon and Chorus (solos: Bacquier, Viala, Gautier, Dubosc, Bastin). Arend Prohmann, producer. Virgin Classics.
Verdi: Attila, Riccardo Muti conducting Orchestra e Coro del Teatro alla Scala Milano (solos: Ramey, Studer, Shicoff, Zancaro). David Groves, producer. Angel.
Weill: The Threepenny Opera, John Mauceri conducting RIAS Berlin Sinfonietta Berlin (solos: Lemper, Kollo, Milva, Adori, Denesch). Michael Haas, producer. London.

BEST CHORAL PERFORMANCE (OTHER THAN OPERA)
• Robert Shaw conducting Atlanta Symphony Orchestra Chorus and Orchestra, *Walton: Belshazzar's Feast; Bernstein: Chichester Psalms; Missa Brevis*. Telarc.
John Eliot Gardiner conducting Monteverdi Choir, London Oratory Junior Choir and English Baroque Soloists, *Bach: St. Matthew Passion*. Archive.
Bernard Haitink conducting London Philharmonic Choir and Orchestra, *Williams: Symphony No. 1 ("Sea Symphony")*. Angel.
Nicholas McGegan conducting U.C. Berkeley Chamber Chorus, Philip Brett, choral conductor and Philharmonia Baroque Orchestra, *Handel: Susanna*. Harmonia Mundi.
Robert Shaw conducting Robert Shaw Festival Singers, *Rachmaninoff: Vespers*. Telarc.

BEST CLASSICAL VOCAL PERFORMANCE
• José Carreras, Placido Domingo, Luciano Pavarotti, tenors (Zubin Mehta conducting Orchestra del Maggio Musicale Fiorentino and Orchestra del Teatro dell' Opera di Roma), *Carreras, Domingo, Pavarotti in Concert*. London.
Elly Ameling, soprano (Graham Johnson, accompanist), *Schubert: The Complete Songs — Volume 7*. Hyperion.
Jan DeGaetani, mezzo-soprano (David Effron conducting Eastman Chamber Ensemble), *Berlioz: Les Nuits D'Ete, Op. 7; Mahler: Five Wunderhorn Songs & Five Ruckert Songs*. Bridge.
Thomas Hampson, baritone (Geoffrey Parsons, accompanist), *Songs from des Knaben Wunderhorn* (Mahler, Brahms, Schumann, Loewe, Strauss, Zemlinsky, Von Weber). Teldec.
Sanford Sylvan, baritone (John Adams conducting Orchestra of St. Lukes), *Adams: The Wound-Dresser*. Elektra/Nonesuch.

BEST CONTEMPORARY COMPOSITION
• Leonard Bernstein, *Arias & Barcarolles*. William Sharp, baritone. Judy Kaye, soprano. Michael Barrett, Steven Blier, pianos. Koch International.

John Adams, *The Wound-Dresser*. Sanford
   Sylvan, baritone. John Adams
   conducting Orchestra of St. Luke's.
   Elektra/Nonesuch.
Henri Lazarof, *Tableaux (After Kandinsky)
   for Piano & Orchestra*. Garrick
   Ohlsson, piano. Gerard Schwarz
   conducting the Seattle Symphony.
   Delos International.
Terry Riley, *Salome Dances for Peace*.
   Kronos Quartet. Elektra/Nonesuch.
Ellen Taaffe Zwillich, *Symphony No.2*.
   Lawrence Leighton Smith conducting
   Louisville Symphony Orchestra.
   Louisville/First Edition Recordings.

BEST ENGINEERED RECORDING, CLASSICAL
• Jack Renner, *Rachmaninoff: Vespers*,
   Robert Shaw conducting Robert Shaw
   Festival Singers. Telarc.
Bud Graham, *Mahler: Symphony No. 8 in
   E Flat (Symphony of a Thousand)*,
   Lorin Maazel conducting Vienna
   Philharmonic; Vienna State Opera
   Chorus; Vienna Boys' Chorus; ORF
   Chorus & Arnold Schöenberg Choir.
   Sony Classical.
William Hoekstra, *Shostakovich:
   Symphony No. 8, Op. 65*, Leonard
   Slatkin conducting St. Louis Symphony
   Orchestra. RCA Victor Red Seal.
Karl-August Naegler, *Shostakovich:
   Symphonies No. 1, Op. 10 and No. 7
   ("Leningrad") Op. 60*, Leonard
   Bernstein conducting Chicago
   Symphony Orchestra. Deutsche
   Grammophon.
Judith Sherman, *Crumb: Black Angels;
   Tallis: Spem in Alium; Marta: Doom. A
   Sigh; Ives: They are There!;
   Shostakovich: Quartet No. 8*. Kronos
   Quartet. Elektra/Nonesuch.

CLASSICAL PRODUCER OF THE YEAR
• Adam Stern
Michael Fine
Judith Sherman
Hans Weber
Max Wilcox

BEST COMEDY RECORDING
• *P.D.Q. Bach: Oedipus Tex & Other
   Choral Calamities*, Professor Peter
   Schickele. Telarc.
*The Best of Bob & Ray: Selections from
   a Career Volume 4*, Bob Elliott, Ray
   Goulding. Radioart.

The Best of Comic Relief '90, Various
   artists. Rhino.
Jonathan Winters into the ... 90's,
   Jonathan Winters. Dove Books on
   Tape.
More News from Lake Wobegon, Garrison
   Keillor. PHC.

BEST SPOKEN WORD OR NON-MUSICAL RECORDING
• *Gracie: A Love Story*, George Burns.
   Simon & Schuster Audio.
*"Diane..." The Twin Peaks Tapes of Agent
   Cooper*, Kyle MacLachlan. Simon &
   Schuster Audio.
Jimmy Stewart and His Poems , Jimmy
   Stewart. Sound Editions.
*A Prairie Home Companion: The 4th
   Annual Farewell Performance*,
   Garrison Keillor. Minnesota Public
   Radio.
Profiles in Courage, John F. Kennedy, Jr.
   Harper Audio.

BEST RECORDING FOR CHILDREN
• *The Little Mermaid — Original Motion
   Picture Soundtrack* (songs and
   instrumental score), Howard Ashman,
   Alan Menken, composers. Walt
   Disney.
Doc Watson Sings Songs for Little Pickers,
   Doc Watson. Alacazam.
How the Leopard Got His Spots, Danny
   Glover, narrator. Ladysmith Black
   Mambazo, music. Windham Hill.
The Little Mermaid, Various artists &
   songs from the motion picture. Roy
   Dotrice, narrator. Dove Books on Tape.
*The Rock-A-Bye Collection — Volume
   Two*, Various artists. J. Aaron Brown,
   David R. Lehman, producers. Jaba
   Records.

BEST ENGINEERED RECORDING (NON-CLASSICAL)
• Bruce Swedien, *Back on the Block*
   (Quincy Jones). Qwest.
Steve Churchyard, Dan Marnien, *Bedtime
   Stories* (David Baerwald). A&M.
Scott Hendricks, *Holdin' a Good Hand*
   (Lee Greenwood). Capitol.
Don Murray, *Love Is Gonna Getcha*
   (Patti Austin). GRP.
Hugh Padgham, *... But Seriously*
   (Phil Collins). Atlantic.

BEST ALBUM PACKAGE
(Art Director's Award)
• Len Peltier, Jeffrey Gold, Suzanne Vega, *Days of Open Hand* (special edition hologram cover) (Suzanne Vega). A&M.
Carol Bobolts, Anita Baker, Jim Ladwig, *Compositions* (special edition blue binder cover) (Anita Baker). Elektra.
Jeri Heiden, *Behind the Mask* (Fleetwood Mac). Warner Bros.
Vaughan Oliver, *Bossanova* (Pixies). Elektra.
Tom Recchion, *Songs for Drella* (special edition black velvet cover) (Lou Reed, John Cale). Sire/Warner Bros.

BEST ALBUM NOTES
• Dan Morgenstern, *Brownie: The Complete Emarcy Recordings of Clifford Brown* (Clifford Brown). Emarcy.
Mary Katherine Aldin, Robert Palmer, *Muddy Waters — The Chess Box* (Muddy Waters). MCA/Chess.
Gary Giddons, *Art Pepper: The Complete Galaxy Recordings* (Art Pepper). Galaxy/Fantasy.
Robert Palmer, *Bo Diddley — The Chess Box* (Bo Diddley). MCA-Chess.
David Perry, *The Jack Kerouac Collection* (Jack Kerouac). Rhino.

BEST HISTORICAL ALBUM
• *Robert Johnson: The Complete Recordings*, Robert Johnson. Lawrence Cohn, producer. Columbia/CBS.
Beethoven: Symphonies 1–9 & Leonore Overture No. 3, Arturo Toscanini conducting NBC Symphony Orchestra. John Pfeiffer, producer. RCA Victor Gold Seal.
Brownie: The Complete Emarcy Recordings of Clifford Brown, Clifford Brown. Kiyoshi Koyama, producer. Emarcy.
The Jack Kerouac Collection, Jack Kerouac. James Austin, producer. Rhino.
Verdi: Aida, Falstaff, Requiem, Te Deum, Va, Pensiero, Hymn of the Nations, Arturo Toscanini conducting NBC Symphony Orchestra. John Pfeiffer, producer. RCA Victor Gold Seal.

PRODUCER OF THE YEAR
(NON-CLASSICAL)
• Quincy Jones
Glen Ballard
Phil Collins, Hugh Padgham
Mick Jones, Billy Joel
Arif Mardin

BEST MUSIC VIDEO, SHORT FORM
• *Opposites Attract,* Paula Abdul. Michael Patterson, Candice Reckinger, video directors. Sharon Oreck, video producer. Virgin.
All I Want, Lighting Seeds. Tarsem, video director. Lexi Godrey, video producer. MCA.
Another Day in Paradise, Phil Collins. Jim Yukich, video director. Paul Flattery, video producer. Atlantic.
Nothing Compares 2 U, Sinéad O'Connor. John Maybury, video director. Hugh Symonds, video producer. Chrysalis/Ensign Records.
Oh Father, Madonna. David Fincher, video director. Tim Clawson, video producer. Sire.

BEST MUSIC VIDEO, LONG FORM
• *Please Hammer Don't Hurt 'Em The Movie*, M.C. Hammer. Rupert Wainwright, video director. John Oetjen, video producer. Fragile Films.
Bernstein in Berlin, Beethoven: Symphony No. 9, Leonard Berstein. Humphrey Burton, video director. Deutsche Grammophon.
Live — Featuring the Rock Opera Tommy, the Who. Larry Jordan, video director. Michael Pillot, video producer. CMV Enterprises.
The Singles Collection, Phil Collins. Jim Yukich, video director. Paul Flattery, video producer. Atlantic.
We Too Are One Too, Eurythmics. Sophie Muller, video director. Arista.

An *Unforgettable* Sweep

It was, said virtually every press account the day after the Grammycast, an "unforgettable" night for Natalie Cole — and the Grammys, too.

The Best New Artist of 1975 made a triumphant return to the Grammy stage when her *Unforgettable* album and its title track brought Cole the awards for Album and Record of the Year in addition to the Song of the Year honors for its 77-year-old writer, Irving Gordon. Cole's victories marked only the eighth time in the Grammys' 34-year history that the record and album trophies went to the same artist or group and the fifth time that a woman reaped Album of the Year. *Unforgettable* also brought Cole the new award for Best Traditional Pop Performance and earned further prizes for engineering, arrangement, and Producer of the Year David Foster.

"I thank my dad [the late Nat 'King' Cole] for leaving me such a wonderful, wonderful legacy," said best record and album victor Natalie Cole.

Unforgettable had obvious artisty going for it, given Cole's considerable talents, but it also had enormous sentiment. Cole crafted it as a personal tribute to her late great father, Nat "King" Cole, who died of lung cancer in 1965 and was awarded a posthumous N.A.R.A.S. Lifetime Achievement Award 25 years later. She re-recorded 22 of his classic hits on the LP, giving them the same sort of dreamy quality her dad once did and, as she reached back through time, even managed to connect with his timeless spirit. On *Unforget-*

table's final — and title — track, Natalie joined her father in an intimate duet by splicing her 1991 version into the original tape of his Top 20 hit that was recorded exactly 40 years earlier. On the new tape, she yearned openly for him as together they sang the words "Unforgettable, that's what you are ...."

The unabashed sentimentality of the old-fashioned ballad made it an unlikely hit in the cynical rock era, but "Unforgettable" climbed to number 14 on *Billboard*'s singles chart and was considered irresistible by N.A.R.A.S.'s

WIDE WORLD PHOTO

conservative members at Grammy-voting time. When Natalie accepted the trophy for Record of the Year, she made reference to her new pop success, saying, "It's been an incredible, incredible time. I thank my dad for leaving me such a wonderful, wonderful legacy." Natalie had just recently bounced back from a long struggle with drug and alcohol abuse and also thanked her husband "for believing in me when I was having a hard time believing in myself."

Natalie's triumph was called "an outpouring of nostalgia for the days before rock & roll" by *The New York Times*, but it was one that came with a warning from the *L.A. Times*: "Although the series of awards [was] cheered by the Grammy audience, they — and other choices — are bound to renew grumbling by Grammy critics who believe N.A.R.A.S. tends to honor mainstream best sellers rather than the maverick forces that reshape pop music."

The fact that a 40-year-old ballad garnered Song of the Year also upset — and confused — some Grammy watchers, but N.A.R.A.S. rules allow *all* tunes to compete as long as new recordings were released within the eligibility period and the songs were never nominated before. Songwriter Irving Gordon took obvious pleasure in the victory of his pre-rock chesnut, saying as he accepted his statuette, "In a youth-oriented culture, it's nice to have a middle-aged song do something. It's nice to have a song come out that doesn't scream, yell, and have a nervous breakdown while it talks about tenderness. It's nice to have a song accepted where you don't get a hernia when you sing it."

The speech amounted to what the *L.A. Times* called "the worst nightmare of the progressive wing of the academy," not only for its slap at modern pop music, but because Gordon accepted his award from Michael Bolton, who had earlier sung a howling and impassioned rendition of his hit version of the classic Percy Sledge tune "When a Man Loves a Woman" for which he later won the laurels for Best Male Pop Vocal Performance. "I realized after I said it, what I had gotten myself into," Gordon told the *Times*. "I'm of a different generation, into a different kind of music." He apologized profusedly to Bolton as the singer escorted him off stage, but Bolton proved gracious, saying, "No, no, no ... I voted for you."

Backstage Bolton told reporters, "I happen to be very happy for him that he won. But as to how in touch Mr. Gordon is with today's music, I can't speak for him. I can say I don't get a hernia when I sing."

Natalie Cole's three victories were "an outpouring of nostalgia for the days before rock & roll."

According to *The New York Daily News*, the night's biggest "shocker" turned out to be the selection of Marc Cohn ("Walking in Memphis") as Best New Artist over the two leading contenders, C + C Music Factory and Boyz II Men. Cohn had three nominations in all but lost to Gordon in the Song of the Year category and to Bolton in the pop vocals performance contest. The introspective singer-songwriter and his 14-member band, the Supreme Court, were discovered, coincidentally, by Grammy's Best New Artist of 1971, Carly Simon, and subsequently given wide exposure when asked to perform at Caroline Kennedy's wedding reception.

For those who didn't expect Natalie Cole's amazing romp, the night was really supposed to be an unforgettable one for R.E.M., which had never been nominated before and now led all other contenders with seven bids, including ones for Record, Album, and Song of the Year. "The Georgia-based quartet, which blends enticing, folk-flavored rock-roots music with teasingly elusive lyrics, was the class of the alternative/college rock scene in the 1980s," the *L.A. Times* noted. *The Times* predicted that R.E.M. would win the top record award if Natalie Cole didn't, calling its hit song "Losing My Religion" "a masterful expression of anxiety and self-doubt."

"Losing My Religion" won R.E.M.

he was among those who believed "Losing My Religion" could beat Cole's "Unforgettable" for Record of the Year.

Most other Grammy watchers had considered a Bryan Adams song to be the strongest alternative to Natalie Cole's "Unforgettable" for the highest honors. Adams had the second largest number of nominations of the year (six), most of them for his blockbuster hit "(Everything I Do) I Do It for You," which was included in the film *Robin Hood: Prince of Thieves*, starring Kevin Costner, and proved to be the biggest-selling single since Grammy's 1985 Record of the Year winner, "We Are the World." The Canadian rocker pulled off only one victory, however, for "Everything" as best film song.

In third place with the most nods (five) was 1989 Grammy champ Bonnie Raitt, who ended up with three trophies, two of them (pop and rock vocals honors) for her bouncy "Something to Talk About." By the time the veteran country rocker picked up her third Grammy — the rock duo/group singing laurels, which she shared with Delbert McClinton for "Good Man, Good Woman" — she gasped while up at the podium, "Man, oh, man .... I've had enough already!"

A new category was added for Best Rock Song, which was claimed by four-time past Grammy winner Sting for "Soul Cages," who triumphed over considerable competition from Bryan Adams, Tom Petty, and Metallica. Metallica held onto the metal performance award for a surprising third year in a row, this time for its eponymous

GLOBE PHOTO

R.E.M. led this year's race with seven nods and nabbed three awards for "Losing My Religion" and Out of Time.

the short-form music video prize and the group pop vocals honors. *Out of Time*, the album that took the group to the top of the LP charts for the first time, reaped the new prize for Best Alternative Music Album. Considering that *Out of Time* was also up for Album of the Year, *The Washington Post* called the potential combination "a nice double, suggesting you can have your cake and eat it, too." *Out of Time*, however, was certainly an alternative choice compared to the eventual winner, *Unforgettable*, although Robert Hilburn of the *L.A. Times* grumbled about Grammy voters, "They should have saluted Nirvana." Hilburn was nonetheless a R.E.M. fan: Early on, album. "There was so much of a howl when tired rock warhorse Jethro Tull won over the infinitely more vital Metallica [for 1989], the year that the heavy metal category was introduced to the Grammy competition, that the academy voters seem afraid to vote for anyone other than Metallica for fear of making another mistake," said the *L.A. Times*.

In accepting the prize, drummer Lars Ulrich "couldn't resist having fun with the black-tie Radio City Music Hall audience" in New York, the *L.A. Times* added. Ulrich said, "I think the first thing we've got to do, obviously, is thank Jethro Tull for not putting out an album this year, right? ... Read between the lines .... You know what I mean."

Unlike Metallica, the veteran hard-rocking Van Halen (*For Unlawful Carnal Knowledge*) did pull off a Grammy victory on its first nomination, although not without hearing some complaints. "Guns 'N' Roses should have been the easy winner in the hard rock category," wrote the *L.A. Times*, "but voters went with Van Halen, a band that would have been considered too maverick at one time, but now seems a more established part of the musical community — at least when measured against Guns 'N' Roses." Eddie Van Halen said, as he accepted the trophy, "Over the years, we have not lost touch with fans. We've never second-guessed what they like. Our hearts are into this."

L.L. Cool J, the long-time rapper from Queens, New York, received his first Grammy when he snared the rap solo performance prize for "Mama Said Knock You Out." The *L.A. Times* took issue with the choice of the rap duo/group winner, the 1988 Grammy champs D.J. Jazzy Jeff & the Fresh Prince: "Public Enemy — far and away the most acclaimed, and sometimes most controversial, rap group — lost out to inconsequential D.J. Jazzy Jeff & the

Fresh Prince, probably because of the latter's wholesome image and TV success." The Fresh Prince (Will Smith) had a TV sitcom series, *The Fresh Prince of Bel Air*, which started in the fall of 1990 and was considered featherweight fare designed for his teenaged fans.

After having been overlooked on nine previous occasions, Luther Vandross won his first Grammy last year as 1990's best r&b singer and now scored two more victories. He repeated his win in the male r&b vocals category for *Power of Love*, also earning the Best Rhythm & Blues Song award for the album's title track. There was a tie for the female r&b vocals trophy between two first-time winners: Lisa Fischer ("How Can I Ease the Pain"), the Brooklyn-born artist who often toured with Vandross, and Patti LaBelle (*Burnin'*), one of the queens of r&b who had been performing professionally since the mid-1960s.

"Man, oh, man!" said triple winner Bonnie Raitt. "I've had enough already!"

Vandross, LaBelle, and such past Grammy favorites as Aretha Franklin, Prince, and Gladys Knight all lost in the r&b duo/group r&b line-up to Motown's newest stars and the losing nominee for Best New Artist, Boyz II Men (*Cooley-highharmony*). The four Boyz met at Philadelphia's High School of Creative and Performing Arts where they listened to "jazz, opera, classical, and everything — so that's what we sing," group member Nathan Morris told *Entertainment Weekly* soon after their victory. At the Grammycast, the Boyz squared off in what the magazine called "an a cappella duel" with the rival group Color Me

Badd, which they also trounced in the r&b category.

The jazz categories welcomed back lots of veteran champs, including four-time past victor Take 6 (Best Jazz Vocal Performance, *He Is Christmas*), seven-time past champ the Manhattan Transfer (contemporary jazz performance, "Sassy"), six-time past winner the Oscar Peterson Trio (jazz group instrumental, *Saturday Night at the Blue Note*), and the four-time recipient Stan Getz (solo instrumental, "I Remember You"), who had died of liver cancer in June. Dizzy Gillespie, still going strong at age 74, had won once before, in 1975, and now was hailed with the prize for large ensemble performance, which he shared with the United Nations Orchestra for their joint LP *Live at the Royal Festival Hall*.

B.B. "Blues Boy" King began his recording career in 1951 and was still going strong, too, 40 years later when he was lauded for the year's Best Traditional Blues Album *Live at the Apollo*. One of Chicago's leading bluesmen, Buddy Guy (actually born in Louisiana), nabbed the equivalent prize for contemporary LPs for *Damn Right, I've Got the Blues*.

One month before the Grammycast, Wynonna and Naomi Judd proved the amazing pull of country music when their pay-per-view TV special drew higher ratings than similar specials by the Rolling Stones and New Kids on the Block. This year the four-time past champs proved their considerable pull at the Grammys by scoring a double victory: the best country duo/group vocals award and the Best Country Song trophy for "Love Can Build a Bridge." Among the other songwriters they vanquished was the Washington, D.C.-born thrush Mary-Chapin Carpenter, who nonetheless won the female vocals accolade for her Best Country Song loser, "Down at the Twist and Shout."

Winner of the statuette for best male country crooner was the enormously popular, first-time recipient Garth Brooks for his history-making *Ropin' the Wind*. Prior to *Ropin'*'s release, no other country album had ever before

CAPITOL RECORDS

No one in the history of Nashville "has moved more albums with more velocity" than best country crooner Garth Brooks.

dawned on *Billboard*'s album chart at the number one position. "Since his recording debut a short three years ago, Brooks has moved more albums with more velocity than anyone else in the history of Nashville," *Entertainment Weekly* wrote, noting his impressive total of 16 million albums sold so far. The *L.A. Times* complained, "Grammy voters appear to have caved in to the enormous commercial success of Garth Brooks by giving him the best male singer award over Vince Gill, the superior vocalist. Brooks is a capable country singer, but his strength is the conviction and energy of his live show." Gill did win a Grammy for vocal collaboration, however, for his work with Steve Wariner and Ricky Scaggs ("Restless").

John Prine originally gained fame in the early 1970s when he sang the sad tale of a Vietnam vet, "Sam Stone," and received critical praise that labeled him "The New Dylan." By the early 1980s, he had trouble getting recorded but rallied by the decade's end and now picked up the Best Contemporary Folk Album Grammy for *The Missing Years*.

In the religious categories, a number of past winners returned for further glory, including Mighty Clouds of Joy (*Pray for Me*, Best Traditional Soul Gospel Album), which hadn't won a Grammy since 1979, and the brother-sister duo of BeBe and CeCe Winans (*Different Lifestyles*, Best Contemporary Soul Gospel Album). BeBe Winans accepted the latter award, saying, "Look out, music industry, gospel is here to stay!" New victors included the Sounds of Blackness, which won the prize for Best Gospel Album by a Choir or Chorus for *The Evolution of Gospel*. The statuette was accepted by band member Gary Hines, who thanked "The Father, Son, the Holy Ghost, and [producers] Jimmy Jam and Terry Lewis."

For the sixth year in a row, Jimmy Sturr & His Orchestra claimed the Best Polka Album statuette (*Live! At Gilley's*), leading to some controversy. *The New York Daily News* columnist David Hinckley wrote, "Polka fans are not happy that they have only one award and Jimmy Sturr always wins it."

The big news in the Latin awards was that pop star vocalist Vikki Carr at last won a Grammy Award after having been nominated only once before, in 1967, for her hit single "It Must Be Him." Twenty-four years after her initial loss, she rebounded with *Cosas del Amor*, which was hailed as Best Latin Pop Album. (Carr was born in Texas of Hispanic parents, who named her Florencia Bisenta de Casillas Martinez Cardona.)

Grateful Dead drummer Mickey Hart won the new award for Best World Music Album for *Planet Drum*. Reporting on Shabba Ranks's victory for *As Raw as Ever* as Best Reggae Album, *Time* magazine called him "the reigning monarch of reggae" and quoted Ranks as saying about *Raw*, "My type of work is ... energetic, you know? When you dance to my music, you get dizzy, get crazy." As he accepted his Grammy, he said, proudly, "I'm a star now."

Last year's homage to the late Leonard Bernstein in the classical categories continued this year when again he was given the honor for Best Classical Album posthumously. Conductor John Mauceri won the Grammy for Best Opera Recording in 1986 for his and director Hal Prince's "opera house" version of Bernstein's *Candide*, which was just one of many overhauls attempted following the original's disastrous reception on Broadway in 1956. Prior to his death, the composer made an ambitious effort to compile his own re-edited version, which he performed with the London Symphony Orchestra at the Barbican in London in 1989, and which earned him the top classical album honor when the recorded version was released two years later.

A losing contender for Best Classical Album, composer John Corigliano's *Symphony No. 1*, was hailed as Best Contemporary Composition and also garnered the orchestral award for conductor Daniel Barenboim and the Chicago Symphony Orchestra. Corigliano wrote the work as an elegy to fallen friends, three of whom had died of AIDS. Critics said Barenboim captured the composer's broad range of emotions — from expressions of quiet grief to outbursts of rage — with passionate sensitivity.

Another loser of the LP kudos was hailed with other awards when a recording of works by Samuel Barber earned the soloist (with orchestra) performance prize for pianist John Browning as well as the engineering prize. Pianist and three-time past Grammy champ Alicia de Larrocha returned for the soloist (without orchestra) trophy for her updated interpretations of works by Enrique Granados, which critics considered virtually equal in quality to versions she'd recorded more than a decade earlier. *American Record Guide* recommended the recording highly, calling it, "Music you may rightly call voluptuous, classic, richly colored. In the hands of this distinguished pianist, a native of Barcelona, the aura of Spain may overwhelm you."

The late Leonard Bernstein won Best Classical Album for his definitive overhaul of Candide.

Sir Georg Solti had won choral performance Grammys in the past for works by Berlioz, Haydn, Brahms, Beethoven, Verdi, and Mahler, and now scored one more for himself and the Chicago Symphony Orchestra and Chorus for Bach's *Mass in B Minor*, bringing the all-time Grammy champ to a career tally of 29. Quincy Jones remained in second place over all, with 25.

For the third year in a row, conductor James Levine dominated the Best Opera Recording category with installment recordings of his historic staging at the Metropolitan Opera of Wagner's full *The Ring of Nibelung*. This year he prevailed with *Götterdämmerung.* The vocal performance laurels were bestowed on 1989 victor Dawn Upshaw for a collection of works by Ravel, Stravinsky, and others.

Gospel-turned-pop star Amy Grant had won five Grammys for religious recordings between 1982 and 1988, but reaped no awards at all this year despite top bids in such secular categories as Record, Album and Song of the Year. Madonna had been passed up on four occasions in the past for nominations dating back to 1985, but she finally experienced her first victory when *Blonde Ambition World Tour Live* was hailed as Best Long Form Music Video.

The Grammycast emanated for a second consecutive year from Radio City Music Hall in New York and set a new record for length: four hours. Its disastrous TV ratings almost set another record, for the lowest viewership ever, but did slightly better — attaining a 16.2 rating — than the Grammys' worst showing, which occurred when the 1988 awards show garnered only a 16 point rating.

James Brown won the prize for Best Album Notes (*Star Time*), but also was the recipient of a Lifetime Achievement Award, which he accepted wordlessly before a standing ovation. When Barbra Streisand was given a Living Legends Award, she also was greeted with a standing ovation, but she acknowledged it with a brief speech during which she said, "In all honesty, I don't feel like a legend. I feel more like a work in progress."

The awards ceremony was broadcast on CBS from Radio City Music Hall in New York City on February 25, 1992, for the eligibility period of October 1, 1990, through September 30, 1991.

ALBUM OF THE YEAR
• *Unforgettable*, Natalie Cole. André Fischer, David Foster, Tommy Lipuma, producers. Elektra Entertainment.
Heart in Motion, Amy Grant. Keith Thomas, Brown Bannister, Michael Omartian, producers. A&M.
Luck of the Draw, Bonnie Raitt. Don Was, Bonnie Raitt, producers. Capital.
Out of Time, R.E.M. Scott Litt, R.E.M., producers. Warner Bros.
The Rhythm of the Saints, Paul Simon. Paul Simon, producer. Warner Bros.

RECORD OF THE YEAR
• "Unforgettable," Natalie Cole (with Nat "King" Cole). David Foster, producer. Elektra.
"Baby Baby," Amy Grant. Keith Thomas, producer. A&M.
"(Everything I Do) I Do It for You," Bryan Adams. Robert John "Mutt" Lange, producer. A&M
"Losing My Religion," R.E.M. Scott Litt, R.E.M., producers. Warner Bros.
"Something to Talk About," Bonnie Raitt. Don Was, Bonnie Raitt, producers. Capitol.

SONG OF THE YEAR
(Songwriter's Award)
• "Unforgettable," Irving Gordon.
"Baby Baby," Amy Grant, Keith Thomas.
"(Everything I Do) I Do For You," Bryan Adams, Robert John "Mutt" Lange, Michael Kamen..
"Losing My Religion," Bill Berry, Peter Buck, Mike Mills, Michael Stipe.
"Walking in Memphis," Marc Cohn.

BEST NEW ARTIST
• Marc Cohn. Atlantic.
Boyz II Men. Motown.
C + C Music Factory. Sony Music.
Color Me Badd. Giant.
Seal. Sire/Warner Bros.

BEST POP VOCAL PERFORMANCE, MALE
• Michael Bolton, "When a Man Loves a Woman." Columbia.
Bryan Adams, "(Everything I Do) I Do It for You." A&M.
Marc Cohn, "Walking in Memphis." Atlantic.
George Michael, "Freedom 90." Columbia.
Aaron Neville, *Warm Your Heart*. A&M.
Seal, "Crazy." Sire/Warner Bros.

BEST POP VOCAL PERFORMANCE, FEMALE
• Bonnie Raitt, "Something to Talk About." Capitol.
Oleta Adams, "Get Here." Fontana.
Mariah Carey, *Emotions*. Columbia.
Amy Grant, "Baby Baby." A&M.
Whitney Houston, "All the Man That I Need." Arista.

BEST POP PERFORMANCE BY A DUO OR GROUP WITH VOCAL
• R.E.M., "Losing My Religion." Warner Bros.
Commitments, *The Commitments— Original Motion Picture Soundtrack*. MCA.
Extreme, "More Than Words." A&M.
Jesus Jones, "Right Here, Right Now." SBK.
Wilson Phillips, "You're in Love." SBK

BEST TRADITIONAL POP PERFORMANCE
• Natalie Cole (with Nat "King" Cole), "Unforgettable." Elektra.
Harry Connick, Jr., *Blue Light, Red Light*. Columbia.
Johnny Mathis, *In a Sentimental Mood: Mathis Sings Ellington*. Columbia.
Diane Schuur, *Pure Schuur*. GRP.
Barbra Streisand, "Warm All Over," track from *Just for the Record*. Columbia.

BEST POP INSTRUMENTAL PERFORMANCE
• Michael Kamen conducting Greater Los Angeles Orchestra, *Robin Hood: Prince of Thieves*. Morgan Creek.
Candy Dulfer, *Saxuality*. Arista.
Kenny G., "Theme from *Dying Young*," track from *Dying Young* soundtrack. Arista.
Dave Grusin, *Havana*. GRP.
John Williams conducting Skywalker Symphony Orchestra, *John Williams Conducts John Williams/The Star Wars Trilogy*. Sony Classical.

BEST ROCK SONG
(Songwriter's Award)
√ • "Soul Cages," Sting. A&M.
"Been Caught Stealing," Jane's Addiction.
√ "Can't Stop This Thing We Started," Bryan Adams, Robert John "Mutt" Lange.
"Enter Sandman," James Hetfield, Lars Ulrich, Kirk Hammett.
√ "Learning to Fly," Tom Petty, Jeff Lynne.
"Silent Lucidity," Chris DeGarmo.

BEST ROCK VOCAL PERFORMANCE, SOLO
√ • Bonnie Raitt, *Luck of the Draw*. Capitol.
√ Bryan Adams, "Can't Stop This Thing We Started." A&M.
Eric Clapton, *24 Nights*. Reprise.
√ John Mellencamp, *Whenever We Wanted*. Mercury.
Robbie Robertson, *Storyville*. Geffen.
Bob Seger, *The Fire Inside*. Capitol.

BEST ROCK PERFORMANCE BY A DUO OR GROUP WITH VOCAL
√ • Bonnie Raitt, Delbert McClinton, "Good Man, Good Woman," track from *Luck of the Draw* (Bonnie Raitt album). Capitol.
Jane's Addiction, "Been Caught Stealing." Warner Bros.
Tom Petty & the Heartbreakers, *Into the Great Wide Open*. MCA.
Queensryche, "Silent Lucidity." EMI.
√ R.E.M., "Radio Song." Warner Bros.

BEST HARD ROCK PERFORMANCE WITH VOCAL
• Van Halen, *For Unlawful Carnal Knowledge*. Warner Bros.
AC/DC, "Moneytalks," track from *The Razors Edge*. Atco/Atlantic.

Alice in Chains, "Man in the Box." Columbia.
Guns 'N' Roses, *Use Your Illusion I*. Geffen.

BEST METAL PERFORMANCE WITH VOCAL
• Metallica, *Metallica*. Elektra.
Anthrax, *Attack of the Killer B's*. Island.
Soundgarden, *Badmotorfinger*. A&M.
Megadeth, "Hangar 18" (LP version). Capitol.
Motorhead, *1916*. WTG.

BEST ROCK INSTRUMENTAL PERFORMANCE
• Eric Johnson, "Cliffs of Dover." Capitol.
Allman Brothers Band, "Kind of Bird," track from *Shades of 2 Worlds*. Epic.
Danny Gatton, *88 Elmira Street*. Elektra.
Rush, "Where's My Thing?" track from *Roll the Bones*. Atlantic.
Yes, "Masquerade," track from *Union*. Arista.

BEST ALTERNATIVE MUSIC ALBUM
√ • *Out of Time*, R.E.M. Warner Bros.
Doubt, Jesus Jones. SBK.
Mighty Like a Rose, Elvis Costello. Warner Bros.
√ *Nevermind*, Nirvana. DGC.
Rumor and Sigh, Richard Thompson. Capitol.

BEST RHYTHM & BLUES SONG
(Songwriter's Award)
• "Power of Love/Love Power," Luther Vandross, Marcus Miller, Teddy Vann.
"Can You Stop the Rain," Walter Afanasieff, John Bettis.
"How Can I Ease the Pain," Narada Michael Walden, Lisa Fischer.
"I Wanna Sex You Up," Dr. Freeze.
"I'll Take You There," Alvertis Isbell.

BEST RHYTHM & BLUES VOCAL PERFORMANCE, MALE
• Luther Vandross, *Power of Love*. Epic.
James Brown, *Love Over-due*. Scotti Bros.
Peabo Bryson, "Can You Stop the Rain." Columbia.
Teddy Pendergrass, "How Can You Mend a Broken Heart." Elektra.
Keith Washington, "Kissing You." Qwest/Warner Bros.
Stevie Wonder, "Gotta Have You." Motown.

BEST RHYTHM & BLUES VOCAL PERFORMANCE, FEMALE
(Tie)
- Lisa Fischer, "How Can I Ease the Pain." Elektra.
- Patti LaBelle, *Burnin'*. MCA.

Aretha Franklin, *What You See Is What You Sweat*. Arista.

Gladys Knight, *Good Woman*. MCA.

Vanessa Williams, "Runnin' Back to You." Mercury.

BEST RHYTHM & BLUES PERFORMANCE BY A DUO OR GROUP WITH VOCAL
√ • Boyz II Men, *Cooleyhighharmony*. Motown.

Color Me Badd, "I Wanna Sex You Up." Giant.

Aretha Franklin, Luther Vandross, "Doctor's Orders," track from *What You See Is What You Sweat* (Aretha Franklin album). Arista.

Gladys Knight, Patti LaBelle, Dionne Warwick, "Superwoman." MCA.

√ Prince & the New Power Generation, "Gett Off." Paisley Park/Warner Bros.

BEST RAP SOLO PERFORMANCE
√ • L.L. Cool J, "Mama Said Knock You Out." Def Jam/Columbia.

Ice-T, "New Jack Hustler (Nino's Theme)." Giant.

√ M.C. Hammer, "Here Comes the Hammer (Version I)." Capitol.

√ Monie Love, "It's a Shame (My Sister)." Warner Bros.

Queen Latifah, "Fly Girl." Tommy Boy.

BEST RAP PERFORMANCE BY A DUO OR GROUP
- D.J. Jazzy Jeff & the Fresh Prince, "Summertime." Jive/RCA.

Heavy D. & the Boyz, "Now That We Found Love." Uptown/MCA.

Naughty by Nature, "O.P.P." Tommy Boy.

Public Enemy, *Apocalypse 91... The Enemy Strikes Black*. Def Jam/Columbia.

√ Salt-N-Pepa, "Let's Talk About Sex." Next Plateau.

BEST CONTEMPORARY JAZZ PERFORMANCE
(VOCAL OR INSTRUMENTAL)
- Manhattan Transfer, "Sassy," track from *The Offbeat of Avenues*. Columbia.

GLOBE PHOTO

Religious doo-wop group Take 6 won Grammy number five for He Is Christmas, *the year's Best Jazz Vocal Performance.*

Joe Sample, *Ashes to Ashes*. Warner Bros.

Claus Ogerman, Michael Brecker, *Claus Ogerman Featuring Michael Brecker*. GRP.

Bela Fleck, Flecktones, *Flight of the Cosmic Hippo*. Warner Bros.

Yellowjackets, *Greenhouse*. GRP.

Bobby McFerrin, *Medicine Music*. EMI.

BEST JAZZ VOCAL PERFORMANCE
- Take 6, *He Is Christmas*. Reprise.

Natalie Cole, "Long 'Bout Midnight," track from *Garfield — Various Artists*. GRP.

Shirley Horn, *You Won't Forget Me*. Verve.

Manhattan Transfer, *The Offbeat of Avenues*. Columbia.

Mel Tormé, "Ellington Medley," track from *Mel & George Do World War II*. Concord Jazz.

BEST JAZZ INSTRUMENTAL SOLO
- Stan Getz, "I Remember You," track from *Serenity*. Emarcy.

Dave Grusin, "How Long Has This Been Going On?" track from *The Gershwin Connection*. GRP.

David Sanborn, "Another Hand," track from *Another Hand*. Elektra-Musician.

Toots Thielemans, "Bluesette," track from *Cleo Laine's Jazz* (Cleo Laine album). RCA Victor.

Phil Woods, "All Bird's Children," track from *All Bird's Children*. Concord Jazz.

BEST JAZZ INSTRUMENTAL PERFORMANCE, GROUP

- Oscar Peterson Trio, *Saturday Night at the Blue Note*. Telarc.
- Chick Corea Akoustic Band, *Alive*. GRP.
- Dave Grusin, *The Gershwin Connection*. GRP.
- Lionel Hampton & the Golden Men of Jazz, *Lionel Hampton & the Golden Men of Jazz Live at the Blue Note*. Telarc.
- David Sanborn, *Another Hand*. Elektra-Musician.

BEST LARGE JAZZ ENSEMBLE PERFORMANCE

- Dizzy Gillespie & the United Nation Orchestra, *Live at the Royal Festival Hall*. Enja.
- Charlie Haden & the Liberation Music Orchestra, *Dream Keeper*. Blue Note.
- Rob McConnell & the Boss Brass, *The Brass Is Back*. Concord Jazz.
- Jay McShann, *Paris All-Star Blues (A Tribute to Charlie Parker)*. MusicMasters.
- Bob Mintzer, *Art of the Big Band*. Digital Music Products, Inc.
- Doc Severinsen & the Tonight Show Band, *Once More with Feeling*. Amherst.

BEST COUNTRY SONG
(Songwriter's Award)

- "Love Can Build a Bridge," Naomi Judd, John Jarvis, Paul Overstreet. RCA Records.
- "Don't Rock the Jukebox," Alan Jackson, Roger Murrah, Keith Stegall. Arista.
- "Down at the Twist and Shout," Mary-Chapin Carpenter. Columbia.
- "Eagle When She Flies," Dolly Parton. Columbia.
- "Here's a Quarter (Call Someone Who Cares)," Travis Tritt. Warner Bros.

BEST COUNTRY VOCAL PERFORMANCE, MALE

- Garth Brooks, *Ropin' the Wind*. Capitol.
- Billy Dean, "Somewhere in My Broken Heart." Capitol.
- Vince Gill, *Pocket Full of Gold*. MCA.
- Alan Jackson, *Don't Rock the Jukebox*. Arista.
- Travis Tritt, "Here's a Quarter (Call Someone Who Cares)." Warner Bros.

BEST COUNTRY VOCAL PERFORMANCE, FEMALE

- Mary-Chapin Carpenter, "Down at the Twist and Shout." Columbia.
- Kathy Mattea, *Time Passes By*. Mercury/Polygram.
- Reba McEntire, *For My Broken Heart*. MCA.
- Tanya Tucker, "Down to My Last Teardrop," track from *What Do I Do With Me*. Capitol.
- Trisha Yearwood, "She's in Love with the Boy." MCA.

BEST COUNTRY PERFORMANCE BY A DUO OR GROUP WITH VOCAL

- Judds, "Love Can Build a Bridge." RCA.
- Alabama, "Forever's as Far as I'll Go." RCA.
- Diamond Rio, "Meet in the Middle." Arista.
- Forrester Sisters, "Men," track from *Talkin' Bout Men*. Warner Bros.
- Kentucky Headhunters, *Electric Barnyard*. Mercury.
- Texas Tornados, *Zone of Our Own*. Reprise.

BEST COUNTRY VOCAL COLLABORATION

- Steve Wariner, Ricky Scaggs, Vince Gill, "Restless" track from *The New Nashville Cats* (Mark O'Connor album). Warner Bros.
- Lee Greenwood, Suzy Bogguss, "Hopelessly Yours," track from *A Perfect 10*. Capitol.
- Dolly Parton, Ricky Van Shelton, "Rockin' Years." Columbia.
- Roy Rogers, Clint Black, "Hold On Partner." RCA.
- Keith Whitley, Earl Thomas Conley, "Brotherly Love." RCA.

BEST COUNTRY INSTRUMENTAL PERFORMANCE

- Mark O'Connor, *The New Nashville Cats*. Warner Bros.
- Chet Atkins, Mark Knopfler, *Neck and Neck*. Columbia.
- Diamond Rio, "Poultry Promenade," track from *Diamond Rio*. Arista.
- Osborne Brothers, "Orange Blossom Special," track from *Hillbilly Fever*. CMH.
- Roy Rogers, Norton Buffalo, "Song for Jessica," track from *R&B*. Blind Pig.

BEST ROCK/CONTEMPORARY GOSPEL ALBUM
• *Under Their Influence,* Russ Taff. Myrrh.
Brave Heart, Kim Hill. Reunion.
Go to the Top, De Garmo & Key. Benson.
Nu Thang, D.C. Talk. Forefront/Benson.
Simple House, Margaret Becker. Sparrow.

BEST POP GOSPEL ALBUM
• *For the Sake of the Call,* Steven Curtis Chapman. Sparrow.
Larnelle Live (Psalms, Hymns and Spiritual Songs), Larnelle Harris. Benson.
The Me Nobody Knows, Marilyn McCoo. Warner Alliance.
Michael English, Michael English. Warner Alliance.
Shakin' the House ... Live, Carman and Commissioned (& the Christ Church Choir). Benson.

BEST SOUTHERN GOSPEL ALBUM
• *Homecoming,* Gaither Vocal Band. Star Song.
Hallelujah Time, Speers. Homeland.
Love Will, Talleys. Word.
Peace in the Valley, J.D. Sumner & the Stamps. River Song/Benson.
Shoulder to Shoulder, Mid-South Boys. Word.
Still Rollin', Chuck Wagon Gang. Associated Artists.

BEST TRADITIONAL SOUL GOSPEL ALBUM
• *Pray for Me,* Mighty Clouds of Joy. Word.
My Faith, Thomas Whitfield. Benson.
Thank You Mamma for Praying for Me, Jackson Southernaires. Malaco.
This Is Your Night, Williams Brothers. Blackberry.
The Truth About Christmas, Vanessa Bell Armstrong. Jive.

BEST CONTEMPORARY SOUL GOSPEL ALBUM
• *Different Lifestyles,* BeBe & CeCe Winans. Sparrow.
Look a Little Closer, Helen Baylor. Word.
Mean What You Say, Witness. Fixit/Star Song.
Phenomenon, Rance Allen Group. Bellmark.
The Promise, Ricky Dillard's New Generation Chorale. Muscle Shoals Sound Gospel.

BEST GOSPEL ALBUM BY A CHOIR OR CHORUS
• *The Evolution of Gospel,* Sounds of Blackness. Gary Hines, choir director. Perspective/A&M.
Above and Beyond, O'Landa Draper & the Associates. O'Landa Draper, choir director. Word.
Edwin Hawkins Music and Arts Seminar Chicago Mass Choir, Music and Arts Seminar Chicago Mass Choir. Edwin Hawkins, choir director. Lection/Polygram.
Hand in Hand, Christ Church Choir. Landy Gardner, choir director. Star Song.
Jesus Be Praised, Brooklyn Tabernacle Singers. Carol Cymbala, choir director. Word/Word Inc.
Rev. James Cleveland and the L.A. Gospel Messengers, L.A. Gospel Messengers. Rev. James Cleveland, choir director. Savoy.

BEST TRADITIONAL FOLK ALBUM
• *The Civil War (Original Soundtrack Recording),* Various artists. Elektra/Nonesuch.
Alligator Man, Jimmy C. Newman, Cajun Country. Rounder.
Le Mystere des Voix Bulgares, Vol. 3, Various Soloists and Choirs. Fontana.
My Dear Old Southern Home, Doc Watson. Sugar Hill.
Solo—Oldtime Country Music, Mike Seeger. Rounder.

BEST CONTEMPORARY FOLK ALBUM
• *The Missing Years,* John Prine. Oh Boy.
Back on the Bus, Y'all, Indigo Girls. Epic.
Cajun Conja, Beausoleil. RNA.
Interiors, Rosanne Cash. Columbia.
Jerry Garcia/David Grisman, Jerry Garcia, David Grisman. Acoustic Disc.

BEST TRADITIONAL BLUES ALBUM
• *Live at the Apollo,* B.B. King. GRP.
All My Life, Charles Brown. Bullseye Blues.
Johnnie B. Bad, Johnnie Johnson. Elektra/Nonesuch.
Mr. Lucky, John Lee Hooker. Charisma.
Mule Bone, Taj Mahal. Gramavision.

BEST CONTEMPORARY BLUES ALBUM
• *Damn Right, I've Got the Blues*, Buddy Guy. Silvertone.
Albert Collins, Albert Collins. Charisma.
Let Me In, Johnny Winter. Charisma.
Live—Simply the Best, Irma Thomas. Rounder.
Signature, Charlie Musselwhite. Alligator.

BEST BLUEGRASS ALBUM
• *Spring Training*, Carl Jackson, John Starling, Nash Ramblers. Sugar Hill.
Hillbilly Fever, Osborne Brothers. CMH.
Home of the Blues, Nashville Bluegrass Band. Sugar Hill.
Music Among Friends, Jim and Jesse McReynolds. Rounder.
Simple Pleasures, Alison Brown. Vanguard.

BEST LATIN POP ALBUM
• *Cosas del Amor*, Vikki Carr. Sony Discos International.
A Traves de Tus Ojos, Los Bukis. Fonovisa.
Amada Mas Que Nunca, Daniela Romo. Capitol/EMI Latin.
... Con Amor Eterno, Pandora. Capitol/EMI Latin.
Flor de Papel, Alejandra Guzman. Melody.

BEST TROPICAL LATIN ALBUM
• *Bachata Rosa*, Juan Luis Guerra 4.40. Karen.
Caminando, Ruben Blades. Sony Discos International.
Luces del Alma, Luis Enrique. Sony Discos International.
The Mambo King 100th LP, Tito Puente. RMM.
A Night at Kimball's East, Poncho Sanchez. Concord Picante.

BEST MEXICAN/AMERICAN ALBUM
• *16 de Septiembre*, Little Joe. Sony Discos International.
Para Adoloridos, Tigres del Norte. Fonovisa.
Para Nuestra Gente, Mazz. Capitol/EMI Latin.
Porque te Quiero, La Sombra. Fonovisa.

BEST REGGAE ALBUM
• *As Raw as Ever*, Shabba Ranks. Epic.
Gumption, Bunny Wailer. Shanachie.
Iron Storm, Black Uhuru. Mesa.
Jahmekya, Ziggy Marley & the Melody Makers. Virgin.
Victims, Steel Pulse. Elektra .
We Must Carry On, Rita Marley. Shanachie.

BEST POLKA ALBUM
• *Live! At Gilley's*, Jimmy Sturr & His Orchestra. Starr.
All Around the World, Eddie Blazonczyk's Versatones. Bel-Aire.
We Are Family, Polka Family Band. Polka Family Music.
When the Band Plays a Polka, Dynatones. World Renowned Sounds.
A Wonderful World of Polkas and Waltzs, Walter Ostanek. World Renowned Sounds.

BEST NEW AGE ALBUM
• *Fresh Aire 7*, Mannheim Steamroller. American Gramaphone.
Borrasca, Ottmar Liebert. Higher Octave Music.
Canyon Dreams, Tangerine Dream. Miramar.
Hotel Luna, Suzanne Ciani. Private Music.
In the Wake of the Wind, David Arkenstone. Narada.

BEST WORLD MUSIC ALBUM
• *Planet Drum*, Mickey Hart. Rykodisc, Inc.
Amen, Salif Keita. Mango/Island.
Brazilian Serenata, Dori Caymmi. Qwest.
Este Mundo, Gipsy Kings. Elektra/Musician.
Txai, Milton Nascimento. Sony Music.

BEST ARRANGEMENT
ON AN INSTRUMENTAL
• Dave Grusin, "Medley: Bess You Is My Woman/I Love You Porgy," track from *The Gershwin Connection* (Dave Grusin). GRP.
Peter Apfelbaum, "Candles and Stones," track from *Signs of Life* (Peter Apfelbaum & the Hieroglyphics Ensemble). Antilles.
Mike Bogle, "Got a Match?" track from *Lab 89* (University of North Texas One O'Clock Lab Band). North Texas Jazz.
Michael Kamen, "Maid Marian," track from *Robin Hood: Prince of Thieves — Original Soundtrack* (Michael Kamen conducting Greater Los Angeles Orchestra). Morgan Creek.
Henry Mancini, "The Untouchables," track from *Cinema Italiano* (Henry Mancini & Mancini Pops Orchestra). RCA Victor.

Best film song "(Everything I Do) I Do It for You" was from Bryan Adams's Neighbors *LP and the film* Robin Hood.

Ed Neumeister, "A Nightingale Sang in Berkeley Square," track from *To You — A Tribute to Mel Lewis* (Mel Lewis Jazz Orchestra album). MusicMasters.

BEST INSTRUMENTAL COMPOSITION
• "Basque," track from *The Wind Beneath My Wings*, Elton John. RCA Victor.
"Blu-Bop," track from *Flight of the Cosmic Hippo*, Bela Fleck, Howard Levy, Victor Wooten, Roy Wooten, composers. Warner Bros.
"Cliffs of Dover," Eric Johnson. Capitol.
"Corfu," track from *Claus Ogerman Featuring Michael Brecker*, Claus Ogerman. GRP.
"North on South Street," Herb Alpert, Greg Smith. A&M.

BEST MUSICAL SHOW ALBUM
• *The Will Rogers Follies (Original Broadway Cast Album)*, Keith Carradine & cast. Cy Coleman, Mike Berniker, album producers. Betty Comden, Adolph Green, lyricists. Cy Coleman, composer. Columbia.
Assassins, Jay David Saks, album producer. Stephen Sondheim, composer and lyricist. RCA Victor.

Into the Woods (Original London Cast Recording), Julia McKenzie, Imelda Staunton, Patsy Rowlands, Clive Carter. John A. Yap, album producer. Stephen Sondheim, composer and lyricist. RCA Victor.
Kiss Me Kate, John McGlinn, conductor (Josephine Barstow, Thomas Hampson, Kim Criswell). John Fraser, album producer. Cole Porter, composer and lyricist. Angel/EMI Classics.
The Music Man, Erich Kunzel conducting Cincinnati Pops Orchestra (Timothy Noble, Kathleen Brett, Doc Severinsen, others). Robert Woods, Elaine Martone, album producers. Meredith Willson, composer. Telarc.

BEST INSTRUMENTAL COMPOSITION WRITTEN FOR A MOTION PICTURE OR FOR TELEVISION
• *Avalon*, Randy Newman. Reprise.
Awakenings, Randy Newman. Reprise.
Dances with Wolves, John Barry. Epic.
Edward Scissorhands, Danny Elfman. MCA.
Havana, Dave Grusin. GRP.
Robin Hood: Prince of Thieves, Michael Kamen. Morgen Creek.

BEST SONG WRITTEN SPECIFICALLY FOR A MOTION PICTURE OR FOR TELEVISION
• "(Everything I Do) I Do It for You" from *Robin Hood: Prince of Thieves*, Bryan Adams, Robert John "Mutt" Lange, Michael Kamen. A&M.
"Gotta Have You," from *Jungle Fever*, Stevie Wonder. Motown.
"Somewhere in My Memory," main title track from *Home Alone* soundtrack, John Williams, Leslie Briscusse. CBS.
"You Can't Resist It," track from *Switch* soundtrack, Lyle Lovett. MCA.

BEST INSTRUMENTAL ARRANGEMENT ACCOMPANYING VOCAL(S)
• Marty Paich, "A Medley of: For Sentimental Reasons/Tenderly/Autumn Leaves," track from *Unforgettable* (Natalie Cole). Elektra.
Arthur Morton, "Alone in the World," track from *The Russia House — Motion Picture Soundtrack* (Patti Austin). MCA.

Harry Connick, Jr., "Blue Light, Red Light (Someone's There)," track from *Blue Light, Red Light* (Harry Connick, Jr.). Columbia.

√ Michel Legrand, "Nature Boy," track from *Unforgettable* (Natalie Cole). Elektra.

√ Johny Mandel, "Unforgettable" (Natalie Cole). Elektra.

BEST CLASSICAL ALBUM
• *Bernstein: Candide*, Leonard Bernstein conducting London Symphony Orchestra (solos: Hadley, Anderson, Ludwig, Green, Gedda, Jones, Ollmann). Hans Weber, producer. Deutsche Grammophon.

Barber: Symphony No. 1, Op. 9; Piano Concerto, Op. 38; Souvenirs, Op. 28, Leonard Slatkin conducting St. Louis Symphony Orchestra. John Browning, piano. Jay David Saks, producer. RCA Victor Red Seal.

Carter: The Four String Quartets; Duo for Violin & Piano, Juilliard String Quartet. Christopher Oldfather, piano. Gary Schultz, producer. Sony Classical.

Corigliano: Symphony No. 1, Daniel Barenboim conducting Chicago Symphony Orchestra. James Mallinson, John Corigliano, producers. Erato/Elektra International Classics.

Hanson: Symphony No. 4, Op. 34; Serenade, Op. 35; Lament for Beowulf, Op. 25; Pastorale, Op. 38; Merry Mount Serenade, Op. 35, Gerard Schwartz conducting Seattle Symphony Orchestra, New York Chamber Symphony ("Serenade" & "Paastorale"). Adam Stern, producer. Delos International.

Ives: Symphonies Nos. 1 & 4; Hymns, Michael Tilson Thomas conducting Chicago Symphony Orchestra and Chorus. Steven Epstein, producer. Sony Classical.

BEST ORCHESTRAL PERFORMANCE
(Conductor's Award)
• Daniel Barenboim conducting Chicago Symphony Orchestra, *Corigliano: Symphony No. 1*. Erato/Elektra International Classics.

Rafael Kubelik conducting Czech Philharmonic Orchestra, *Smetana: Ma Vlast*. Supraphon/Denon.

James Levine conducting Chicago Symphony Orchestra, *Holst: The Planets*. Deutsche Grammophon.

Leonard Slatkin conducting St. Louis Symphony Orchestra, *Copland: Symphony No. 3; Music for a Great City*. RCA Victor Red Seal.

Michael Tilson Thomas conducting Chicago Symphony Orchestra, *Ives: Symphonies Nos. 1 & 4*. Sony Classical.

BEST CHAMBER MUSIC PERFORMANCE
• Isaac Stern, Jamime Laredo, violins. Yo-Yo Ma, cello. Emanuel Ax, piano, *Brahms: Piano Quartets Opp. 25 & 6*. Sony Classical.

Arditti String Quartet, *Arditti II (Bartók: Quartet No. 4; Gubaidulina: Quartet No. 3; Schnittke: Quartet No. 2*. Gramavisions Records.

Hilliard Ensemble, *Gesualdo: Tenebrae*. ECM New Series.

Julliard String Quartet; Christopher Oldfather, piano, *Carter: The Four String Quartets; Duo for Violin & Piano*. Sony Classical.

Gidon Kremer, violin. Martha Argerich, piano, *Bartók: Violin Sonata No. 1; Janácek: Violin Sonata; Messiaen: Theme & Variations for Violin & Piano*. Deutsche Grammophon.

BEST CLASSICAL PERFORMANCE, INSTRUMENTAL SOLOIST(S) (WITH ORCHESTRA)
• John Browning, piano (Leonard Slatkin conducting St. Louis Symphony Orchestra), *Barber: Piano Concerto, Op. 38*. RCA Victor Red Seal.

Yuri Bashmet, viola (Mstislav Rostropovich conducting London Symphony Orchestra), *Schnittke: Viola Concerto*. RCA Victor Red Seal.

Stanley Drucker, clarinet (Leonard Bernstein conducting New York Philharmonic), *Copland: Clarinet Concerto*. Deutsche Grammophon.

Yo-Yo Ma, cello (Yuri Temirkanov conducting Leningrad Philharmonic Orchestra), *Tchaikovsky: Variations on a Rococo Theme, Op. 33*. RCA Victor Red Seal.

Mitsuko Uchida, piano (Jeffrey Tate conducting English Chamber Orchestra), *Mozart: Piano Concertos No. 15 in B Flat and No. 16 in D*. Phillips Classics.

Pinchas Zukerman, violin/viola (Leonard Slatkin conducting St. Louis Symphony Orchestra), *Bartók: Violin Concerto No. 2; Viola Concerto Op. Posth.; Violin Concerto No. 2 (Alternative Ending)*. RCA Victor Red Seal.

BEST CLASSICAL PERFORMANCE, INSTRUMENTAL SOLOIST (WITHOUT ORCHESTRA)

• Alicia de Larrocha, piano, *Granados: Goyescas; Allegro de Concierto; Danza Lenta*. RCA Victor Red Seal.

Alan Feinberg, piano, *The American Romantic (Beach, Gottschalk, Helps)*. Argo.

Rudolf Firkusny, piano, *Janácek: Piano Music (Sonata I.X.1905; On an Overgrown Path; In the Mist)*. RCA Victor Red Seal.

Evgeny Kissin, piano, *Evgeny Kissin: Carnegie Hall Debut Concert*. RCA Victor Red Seal.

Murray Perahia, piano, *The Aldeburgh Recital (Beethoven, Rachmaninoff, Schumann, Liszt)*. Sony Classical.

BEST OPERA RECORDING

• *Wagner: Götterdämmerung*, James Levine conducting Metropolitan Opera Orchestra and Chorus (solos: Behrens, Studer, Schwarz, Goldberg, Weikl, Wlaschiha, Salminen. Cord Garben, producer. Deutsche Grammophon.

Debussy: Pelleas et Melisande, Charles Dutoit conducting Orchestre Symphonique de Montreal (solos: Henry, Alliot-Lugaz, Thau, Cachemaille, Carlson, Golfier). Ray Minshull, producer. London.

Mozart: Idomeneo, John Eliot Gardiner conducting English Baroque Soloists (solos: Rolf-Johnson, Von Otter, McNair, Martinpelto). Karl-August Naegler, producer. Archiv.

Mussorgsky: Khovanshchina, Claudio Abbado conducting Vienna State Opera Orchestra and Concert Chorus (solos: Lipovsek, Atlantov, Burchuladze, Haugland, Kotscherga, Popov). Christopher Alder, producer. Deutsche Grammophon.

Schubert: Fierrabras, Claudio Abbado conducting Chamber Orchestra of Europe (solos: Studer, Mattila, Hampson). Christopher Alder, producer. Deutsche Grammophon.

R. Strauss: Elektra, Wolfgang Sawallisch conducting Bavarian Radio Orchestra and Chorus (solos: Studer, Weikl, Marton, Lipovsek, Winkler. Wilhelm Meister, producer. Angel/EMI Classics.

BEST PERFORMANCE OF A CHORAL WORK

• Sir Georg Solti conducting Chicago Symphony Chorus and Orchestra. Margaret Hillis, choral director, *Bach: Mass in B Minor*. London.

John Eliot Gardiner conducting Monteverdi Choir & English Baroque Soloists, *Beethoven: Missa Solemnis*. Archiv.

Krzysztof Penderecki conducting North German Radio Choir, Werner Hagen, chorus master; Bavarian Radio Chorus, Hans-Peter Rauscher, chorus master; and North German Radio Symphony Orchestra, *Penderecki: Polish Requiem*. Deutsche Grammophon.

Krzysztof Penderecki conducting Warsaw National Philharmonic Chorus and National Radio Symphony Orchestra, *Penderecki: St. Luke's Passion*. Argo.

Robert Shaw conducting Atlanta Symphony Chorus and Orchestra, *Janácek: Glagolitic Mass; Dvorák: Te Deum*. Telarc.

BEST CLASSICAL VOCAL PERFORMANCE

• Dawn Upshaw, soprano (Ensemble accompanist), *The Girl with Orange Lips* (De Falla, Ravel, Kim, Stravinsky, Delage). Elektra/Nonesuch.

Jan De Gaetani, mezzo-soprano (Lee Luvisi, piano; Lawrence Dutton, viola), *Jan De Gaetani in Concert Volume 2* (Brahms, Schumann, etc.). Bridge.

Thomas Hampson, baritone (Leonard Bernstein conducting Vienna Philharmonic), *Mahler: Songs of a Wayfarer; 5 Ruckert Lieder*. Deutsche Grammophon.

Samuel Ramey, baritone (Warren Jones, accompanist), *Copland: Old American Songs; Ives: Songs*. Argo.

Cheryl Studer, soprano (Sir Neville Marriner conducting Academy of St. Martin-in-the-Fields), *Mozart: Arias*. Philips Classics.

Sanford Sylvan, baritone (David Breitman, accompanist), *Beloved That Pilgrimage (Chanler: 8 Epitaphs; Barber: Hermit Songs; Copland: 12 Poems of Emily Dickinson)*. Elektra/Nonesuch.

Best Contemporary Composition
• John Corigliano, *Symphony No. 1* (Daniel Barenboim conducting Chicago Symphony Orchestra). Erato/Elektra International Classics.

Dominick Argento, *Te Deum* (Philip Brunelle conducting Plymouth Festival Chorus and Orchestra). Virgin Classics.

Elliot Carter, *Oboe Concerto* (Heinz Holliger, oboe; Pierre Boulez conducting Ensemble Intercontemporain). Erato/Elektra International Classics.

Nicholas Maw, *Odyssey* (Simon Rattle conducting City of Birmingham Symphony Orchestra). Angel.

Arvo Part, *Miserere*, (Hilliard Ensemble; Dennis Russell Davies conducting Orchester der Beethovenhalle Bonn). ECM.

Best Engineered Recording, Classical
• William Hoekstra, *Barber: Symphony No. 1, Op. 9; Piano Concerto, Op. 38; Souvenirs, Op. 28*, (Leonard Slatkin conducting St. Louis Symphony Orchestra; John Browning, piano). RCA Victor Red Seal.

Stanley Goodall, *Bartók: Music for Strings, Percussion & Celesta, etc.*, (Sir Georg Solti conducting Chicago Symphony Orchestra). London.

Gregor Zielinsky, *Bernstein: Candide*, (Leonard Bernstein conducting London Symphony Orchestra; solos: Hadley, Anderson, Ludwig, Green, Gedda, Jones, Ollmann). Deutsche Grammophon.

Lawrence Rock, *Corigliano: Symphony No. 1* (Daniel Barenboim conducting Chicago Symphony Orchestra). Erato/Elektra International Classics.

Wolfgang Mitlehner, *Wagner: Götterdämmerung*, (Levine conducting Metropolitan Opera Orchestra and Chorus; solos: Behrens, Studer, Schwarz, Goldberg, Weikl, Wlaschiha, Salminen). Deutsche Grammophon.

Classical Producer of the Year
• James Mallinson
Steven Epstein
Thomas Frost
Jay David Saks
Hans Weber

Best Comedy Album
• *P.D.Q. Bach: WTWP Classical Talkity-Talk Radio*, "Professor" Peter Schickele. Telarc.

Brand New, Jackie Mason. Columbia.

Local Man Moves to the City, Garrison Keillor. High Bridge.

Parental Advisory: Explicit Lyrics, George Carlin. Eardrum.

When You Look Like Your Passport Photo, It's Time to Go Home, Erma Bombeck. Harper Audio.

Best Spoken Word or Non-Musical Album
• *The Civil War (Geoffrey Ward with Rick Burns and Ken Burns)*, Ken Burns. Sound Editions.

The Hitchhiker's Guide to the Galaxy, Douglas Adams. Dove Audio.

A Life on the Road (Charles Kuralt), Charles Kuralt. Simon and Schuster Audioworks.

Me: Stories of My Life, Katharine Hepburn. Random House Audio.

Best Album for Children
• *A Cappella Kids*, Maranatha! Kids. Maranatha.

Brer Rabbit & the Wonderful Tar Baby, Danny Glover, narrator. Taj Mahal, music. Windham Hill.

The Emperor's New Clothes, Sir John Gielgud, narrator. Mark Isham, music. Windham Hill.

Paul Bunyan, Jonathan Winters, narrator. Leo Kottke, music. Windham Hill.

Prokofiev: Peter and the Wolf; A Zoo Called Earth/Gerald McBoing Boing, Dom De Luise, Peter Schickele, Carol Channing, narrators. Dino Anagnost, conductor. MusicMasters.

Best Engineered Album, Non-Classical
• Al Schmitt, Woody Woodruff, Armin Steiner, *Unforgettable* (Natalie Cole). Elektra.

Ed Cherney, *Luck of the Draw* (Bonnie Raitt). Capitol.

George Massenburg, *Warm Your Heart* (Aaron Neville). A&M.

Don Murray, *Havana* soundtrack (Dave Grusin). GRP.

Steve Nye, *Storyville* (Robbie Robertson). Geffen.

BEST ALBUM PACKAGE
(Art Director's Award)
- Vartan, *Billie Holiday, The Complete Decca Recordings* (Billie Holiday). GRP.

Geoff Gans, *Beat the Boots — Limited Edition Box Set* (Frank Zappa). FOO-EE/Rhino.

Jeff Gold, Kim Champagne, *Recycler* (special package) (ZZ Top). Warner Bros.

Gabrielle Raumberger, *Just for the Record* (Barbra Streisand). Columbia.

Dirk Walter, *Mighty Like a Rose* (special package) (Elvis Costello). Warner Bros.

BEST ALBUM NOTES
(Annotator's Award)
- James Brown, introduction. Cliff White, Harry Weinger, Nelson George, Alan M. Leeds, album notes writers, *Star Time* (James Brown). Polydor.

John Bauldie, *The Bootleg Series Volumes 1–3 (Rare & Unreleased) 1961–1991* (Bob Dylan). Columbia.

Rob Bowman, *The Complete Stax/Volt Singles 1959–1968* (Various artists). Atlantic.

Colin Escott, *The Original Singles Collection ... Plus* (Hank Williams). Polydor.

Robert Palmer, *The Birth of Soul* (Ray Charles). Atlantic.

BEST HISTORICAL ALBUM
- *Billie Holiday, The Complete Decca Recordings*, Billie Holiday. Steven Lasker, Andy McKaie, producers. GRP.

The Complete Caruso, Enrico Caruso. John Pfeiffer, producer. RCA Victor Gold Seal.

The Complete Stax/Volt Singles 1959–1968, Various artists. Steve Greenberg, producer. Atlantic.

The First 100 Years, Sir Georg Solti conducting Chicago Symphony Orchestra. Henry Fogel, producer. Chicago Symphony Orchestra.

Igor Stravinsky, The Recorded Legacy, Igor Stravinsky, others. John McClure, producer. Sony Classical.

PRODUCER OF THE YEAR, NON-CLASSICAL
- David Foster

Walter Afanasieff, Mariah Carey

Andre Fischer

Paul Simon

Keith Thomas

BEST MUSIC VIDEO, SHORT FORM
- *Losing My Religion*, R.E.M. Tarsem, video director. Dave Ramser, video line producer. Warner Bros.

Calling Elvis, Dire Straits. Steve Barron, video director. Adam Whitaker, video line producer. Warner Bros.

Series of Dreams, Bob Dylan. Meirt Avis, video director. Ben Dossett, video line producer. Columbia.

The Thunder Rolls, Garth Brooks. Bud Schaetzle, video director. Martin Fischer, video line producer. Capitol.

When You Wish Upon a Star, Billy Joel. Scott Garen, video director. Rhaz Zeisler, B.A. Robertson, video line producers. Walt Disney.

BEST MUSIC VIDEO, LONG FORM
- *Madonna: Blonde Ambition World Tour Live*, Madonna. David Mallet, Mark "Aldo" Miceli, video directors. Tony Eaton, video line producer. Pioneer LDCA, Inc.

Lifers Group World Tour Rahway Prison, That's It, Lifers Group. Penelope Spheeris, video director. Jessica Cooper, video line producer. Hollywood.

Live at Yankee Stadium, Billy Joel. Jon Small, video director and video line producer. Sony Music Video.

P.O.V., Peter Gabriel. Michael Chapman, Hart Perry, video directors. Sandy Lieberson, video line producer. Virgin Music Video.

Year of the Horse, Sinéad O'Connor. Sophie Mueller, video director. Steve Fargnoli, James Todd, video line producers. Chrysalis/Ensign.

Grammy Notes

How Grammy Award Winners Are Chosen

The Grammy Awards are decided by the 6,000 voting members of the National Academy of Recording Arts and Sciences who qualify to vote by virtue of having contributed creatively to at least six musical recordings. N.A.R.A.S. has 2,000 associate members as well, which include record firm executives, disc jockeys, publicists, and others, but they are only permitted to vote for nominees — not for the winners — since they are not involved in the creative side of the industry.

Special committees are set up to recommend nominees in the craft areas such as engineering, arranging, album notes, and album package. In the remaining 26 fields (jazz, reggae, polka, and Latin music, for example), the academy's full and associate members as well as record companies can recommend works to be considered. In most cases, singles and albums can compete against each other in the same categories. Record companies are permitted to suggest eight works or artists in each category.

Once the lists of potential nominees are compiled, N.A.R.A.S. members can pick one to five choices in up to 10 fields in which to vote, but they may vote for all the categories within each field, like jazz. Voters "are encouraged to limit their voting to fields in which they have considerable knowledge and expertise," according to N.A.R.A.S., but voters' credentials are not checked, which often leads to problems like accusations of winners being chosen because of their popularity or familiarity to voters. The ballots are tallied up by an accounting firm and then the five top vote-getters in each category become the nominees.

To determine winners on the final ballot, voters with full membership make their picks for Best Album, Record, and Song of the Year and Best New Artist and then are restricted to voting in nine fields. Again, the accounting firm tallies up the results and determines the winners.

Fast Grammy Facts

• Chicago Symphony conductor Sir Georg Solti has won more awards than anyone else: 29. Quincy Jones is the biggest winner outside the classical field, with 25 Grammys.

• Sir Georg Solti also has the longest winning streak in Grammy history, having won from 1974 to 1983 (10 years). Aretha Franklin has the second-longest victory streak, prevailing in the r&b categories for the eight years between 1967 and 1974. She is also the woman with the most awards (15).

• Michael Jackson holds the record for winning the most awards in a single year, which he did in 1983, claiming seven for Album of the Year *Thriller* and one for *E.T. The Extra-Terrestrial* as Best Recording for Children. The previous record was held by Roger Miller, who won six Grammys in 1965 for "King of the Road" and *The Return of Roger Miller*.

• Paul Simon has received Grammy's highest honor, Record of the Year, the most times (three) — for "Mrs. Robinson" in 1968, "Bridge Over Troubled Water" in 1970, and "Graceland" in 1987.

• Three artists are tied for winning Album of the Year the most times (three). Frank Sinatra won for *Come Dance with Me* in 1959, *September of My Years* in 1965, and *Sinatra: A Man and His Music* in 1966. Paul Simon won for *Bridge Over Troubled Water* in 1970, *Still Crazy After All These Years* in 1975, and *Graceland* in 1986. Stevie Wonder triumphed for *Innervisions* in 1973, *Fulfillingness' First Finale* in 1974, and *Songs in the Key of Life* in 1976.

• Only three artists have won Record Album and Song of the Year in one year: Paul Simon for his LP (with Art Garfunkel) and its title track *Bridge Over Troubled Water* in 1970, Carole King for "It's Too Late," *Tapestry*, and "You've Got a Friend" in 1971, and Christopher Cross for his eponymous album and "Sailing" in 1980. Cross also won Best New Artist, making him the only person to win all four of the top prizes.

• The only artist who has won Record of the Year twice in a row was Roberta Flack for "The First Time Ever I Saw Your Face" in 1972 and "Killing Me Softly with His Song" in 1973. Flack was also the first solo black artist to win in one of the top categories.

• The only artists to win Grammys in both the classical and non-classical fields were jazz trumpet player and bandleader Wynton Marsalis, who did so both in 1983 and 1984, and Placido Domingo, who won a Latin performance Grammy and an operatic award in 1984. (Marsalis has a total of six jazz awards in addition to his two classical prizes. Domingo has four classical Grammys plus his pop award.)

• Chet Atkins has won the most country awards (10), which he earned for instrumental performances like "The Entertainer" in 1975 and collaborative albums with Merle Travis, Les Paul, Jerry Reed and others. Roger Miller has won 11 Grammys, but only 9 of them were country prizes. In 1965, "King of the Road" won several c&w trophies, but it also scored in two "Contemporary (R&R)" categories.

• The biggest winner in the jazz field is Ella Fitzgerald with 13 Grammys, followed by Duke Ellington with 11. Bill Cosby has won the most (9) for Best Comedy Recording. Leontyne Price is the top-winning opera singer with 13 trophies.

• Michael Jackson is the only winner to prevail in the vocal performance categories for pop, rock, and r&b, which he did in 1983 during his *Thriller* sweep.

• Barbra Streisand was the youngest person ever to win a top award. She was just 22 when *The Barbra Streisand Album* was named 1963's best LP. (Stevie Wonder was 23 when he won 1973's Album of the Year award for *Innervisions.*)

• The only artist who has ever refused a Grammy was Sinéad O'Connor, who declined to accept her prize for Best Alternative Music Performance for *I Do Not Want What I Haven't Got* in 1990. She told Arsenio Hall on his TV talk show, "I've said that if I win, I won't accept it and I wouldn't want it near me. As far as I'm concerned, it represents everything I despise about the music industry."

• The only winner ever stripped of an award was Milli Vanilli, which lost its Best New Artist designation of 1989 after it was learned that the duo did not actually sing on its recordings.

• The Beatles never won Record of the Year, but they did claim the other three of Grammy's four top awards: Album of the Year (*Sgt. Pepper's Lonely Hearts Club Band,* 1967), Song of the Year ("Michelle," 1966), and Best New Artist (1964).

• The only Grammys Elvis Presley ever won were for albums in the religious categories: *How Great Thou Art* (Best Sacred Performance, 1967), *He Touched Me* (Best Inspirationsal Performance, 1972), and *How Great Thou Art* (live performance recording; Best Inspirational Performance, 1974).

All-Time Losers

The following artists have never won a Grammy Award in a competitive category, although many have been nominated. Some have received special or honorary prizes.

Roy Acuff*
Beach Boys
Chuck Berry
Jackson Browne
Byrds
Benny Carter*
Pablo Casals*
Cher
Patsy Cline
Sam Cooke
Elvis Costello
Creedence Clearwater Revival
Cream
Jim Croce
Bing Crosby*
Fats Domino*
Doors
Drifters
Four Tops
Peter Frampton
Benny Goodman*
Grateful Dead
Lionel Hampton
Jimi Hendrix
Jackson 5
Jefferson Airplane/Starship
Janis Joplin
Led Zeppelin
"Little Richard" Penniman
Mitch Miller
Van Morrison
Buck Owens
Pretenders
Queen
Ramones
Santana
Cat Stevens
Rolling Stones*
Diana Ross
Sex Pistols
Rod Stewart
Supremes
Talking Heads
Three Dog Night
Lawrence Welk
Kitty Wells*
Who
Hank Williams, Sr.

Lifetime Achievement Award honorees

Grammy Champs

Winners have received the highest number of awards:

Sir Georg Solti	29	Wynton Marsalis	8
Quincy Jones	25	Paul Simon*	8
Vladimir Horowitz	24	Frank Sinatra	8
Henry Mancini	20	Barbra Streisand	8
Stevie Wonder	17		
Aretha Franklin	15	Anita Baker	7
John Williams	15	Johnny Cash	7
Itzhak Perlman	14	Sir Colin Davis	7
Leonard Bernstein	14	Bill Evans	7
Ella Fitzgerald	13	Dave Grusin	7
Leontyne Price	13	Margaret Hillis	7
Robert Shaw	13	Oscar Peterson	7
		André Previn	7
Michael Jackson	12	Bonnie Raitt	7
		Phil Ramone	7
Pierre Boulez	11	Isaac Stern	7
Ray Charles	11	Tina Turner	7
Duke Ellington	11		
James Mallinson	11	Herb Alpert	6
Roger Miller	11	Bee Gees	6
Thomas Z. Shepard	11	Natalie Cole	6
		Phil Collins	6
Chet Atkins	10	Andrae Crouch	6
		Miles Davis	6
Artur Rubinstein	10	Earth, Wind & Fire	6
Robert Woods	10	José Feliciano	6
		5th Dimension	6
Count Basie	9	David Foster	6
Bill Cosby	9	Thomas Frost	6
Bobby McFerrin	9	Edward T. Graham	6
		Jerry Hey	6
George Benson	8	Robert M. Jones	6
Blackwood Brothers	8	B.B. King	6
Chick Corea	8	Pat Metheny	6
Al Green	8	Ronnie Milsap	6
Erich Leinsdorf	8	Ray Moore	6
James Levine	8	Linda Ronstadt	6
Manhattan Transfer	8	Stephen Sondheim	6
		Jimmy Sturr	6
		Muddy Waters	6
		Laurindo Almeida	5

Vladimir Ashkenazy	5	Carlo Maria Giulini	4
Beatles*	5	Glenn Gould	4
Shirley Caesar	5	Roy Halee	4
Glen Campbell	5	Marvin Hamlisch	4
Christopher Cross	5	Jake Hess	4
Placido Domingo	5	Imperials	4
Stan Getz	5	Al Jarreau	4
Amy Grant	5	Juilliard String Quartet	4
Emmylou Harris	5	Carole King	4
Larnelle Harris	5	Gladys Knight	4
Jim Henson	5	Alicia de Larrocha	4
Billy Joel	5	Lewis Layton	4
Judds	5	Andrew Lloyd Webber	4
Chaka Khan	5	Arif Mardin	4
Michel Legrand	5	Paul McCartney*	4
Yo-Yo Ma	5	Anne Murray	4
Dan Morgenstern	5	Vittorio Negri	4
Willie Nelson	5	Olivia Newton-John	4
Oak Ridge Boys	5	Dolly Parton	4
Roy Orbison	5	Prince	4
Eddie Palmieri	5	Tito Puente	4
Sandi Patti	5	Lionel Richie	4
Luciano Pavarotti	5	Mstislav Rostropovich	4
Peter, Paul & Mary	5	Lalo Schifrin	4
Police	5	Simon & Garfunkel*	4
Mike Post	5	Erik Smith	4
Richard Pryor	5	Donna Summer	4
Jack Renner	5	Swingle Singers	4
Jay David Saks	5	U2	4
David Sanborn	5	Stevie Ray Vaughan	4
Al Schmitt	5	Robin Williams	4
Sting	5	Phil Woods	4
Igor Stravinsky	5		
Take 6	5		
B.J. Thomas	5		
Toto	5		
Dionne Warwick	5		
Doc Watson	5		
Winans	5		
Burt Bacharach	4		
Pat Benatar	4		
John Berg	4		
Julian Bream	4		
Michael Brooks	4		
Rev. James Cleveland	4		
Eagles	4		
Roberta Flack	4		

* Individuals are listed separately from groups when their wins are distinguished from the group's wins. For example, where Paul Simon's number of prizes is given, it does not include those he won for being part of the Simon & Garfunkel team, although it does include his individual awards (such as for 1970 Song of the Year "Bridge Over Troubled Water") during his years with Art Garfunkel. Paul McCartney's number does not include his group prizes for the Beatles.

Lifetime Achievement
Award Honorees

When they were established in 1962, the Lifetime Achievement Awards acknowledged performers and nonperformers alike for outstanding career contributions to the music industry. After 1972, the awards were reserved for performers "who, during their lifetimes, have made creative contributions of outstanding artistic significance to the field of recordings." Recipients are chosen by two-thirds vote of the N.A.R.A.S. Board of Trustees and are given ebony and gold Grammy plaques.

Roy Acuff (1987)
Marian Anderson (1991)
Louis Armstrong (1972)
Fred Astaire (1989)
Irving Berlin (1968)
Leonard Bernstein (1985)
Chuck Berry (1984)
James Brown (1992)
Benny Carter (1987)
Enrico Caruso (1987)
Pablo Casals (1989)
Ray Charles (1987)
Dick Clark (1989)
Nat "King" Cole (1989)
John Coltrane (1992)
Bing Crosby (1962)
Miles Davis (1990)

Fats Domino (1987)
Bob Dylan (1991)
Duke Ellington (1966)
Ella Fitzgerald (1967)
John Birks "Dizzy" Gillespie (1989)
Benny Goodman (1986)
Jascha Heifetz (1989)
Jimi Hendrix (1992)
Woody Herman (1987)
Billie Holiday (1987)
Lena Horne (1989)
Vladimir Horowitz (1989)
Mahalia Jackson (1972)
B.B. King (1987)
John Lennon (1991)
Paul McCartney (1990)
Charlie Parker (1984)
Elvis Presley (1971)
Leontyne Price (1989)
Rolling Stones (1986)
Andrés Segovia (1986)
Frank Sinatra (1965)
Bessie Smith (1989)
Isaac Stern (1987)
Igor Stravinsky (1987)
Art Tatum (1989)
Arturo Toscanini (1987)
Sarah Vaughan (1989)
Muddy Waters (1992)
Kitty Wells (1991)
Hank Williams, Sr. (1987)

(Year of induction in parentheses)

Trustees and Living
Legends Awards

Trustees Awards are awarded by the N.A.R.A.S. Trustees "to individuals who have made such non-performing contributions of such broad scope that they do not fall within the framework of the annual Grammy Awards."

Grammy Living Legends Awards were introduced in 1989 and are bestowed by the N.A.R.A.S. Trustees "to individuals or groups for ongoing contributions and influence in the recording field."

Chris Albertson
Harold Arlen
Béla Bartók
Count Basie
Beatles
Emile Berliner
Dick Clark
Aaron Copland
John Culshaw
Walt Disney
Thomas A. Edison
Duke Ellington
Milt Gabler
George & Ira Gershwin
Berry Gordy
John Hammond
Larry Hiller
Eldridge R. Johnson
Quincy Jones
Jerome Kern
Goddard Lieberson
Johnny Mercer
Robert Moog
Les Paul
Krzystof Penderecki
Sam Phillips
Cole Porter
Richard Rodgers
Frank Sinatra
Sir Georg Solti
Leopold Stokowski
Billy Strayhorn
Paul Weston

Johnny Cash
Aretha Franklin
Billy Joel
Quincy Jones
Andrew Lloyd Webber
Liza Minnelli
Willie Nelson
Smokey Robinson
Barbra Streisand

Hall of Fame Awards

The Hall of Fame Awards were established in 1973 by the N.A.R.A.S. Board of Trustees to honor recordings and contributions to recordings released before the Grammy Awards were first given away for 1958. Certificates are bestowed upon persons who have contributed creatively to the works (including artists, songwriters,composers, arrangers, producers, and engineers) in addition to the original recording label.

"Ain't Misbehavin' "
Thomas "Fats" Waller. Released in 1929 by Victor.
Inducted, 1984.

"And the Angels Sing"
Benny Goodman & His Orchestra. Martha Tilton, vocal. Ziggy Elman, trumpet. Released in 1939 by RCA Victor.
Inducted, 1987.

"April in Paris"
Count Basie & His Orchestra. Released in 1955 by Clef.
Inducted, 1985.

"Artistry in Rhythm"
Stan Kenton & His Orchestra. Released in 1945 by Capitol.
Inducted, 1985.

"A-Tisket A-Tasket"
Chick Webb & His Orchestra with Ella Fitzgerald. Released in 1938 by Decca.
Inducted, 1986.

Bach: Goldberg Variations
Glenn Gould. Released in 1956 by Columbia.
Inducted, 1983.

Bach: Goldberg Variations for Harpsichord
Wanda Landowska. Released in 1945 by Victor.
Inducted, 1986.

Bach: Suites for Unaccompanied Cello (6)
Pablo Casals. Released in 1936–39 by RCA Victor.
Inducted, 1985.

Bach: The Well-Tempered Clavier (Complete)
Wanda Landowska. Released by 1949–54 by RCA Victor.
Inducted, 1977.

Bach-Stokowski: Toccata & Fugue in D Minor
Leopold Stokowski conducting Philadelphia Orchestra. Released in 1927 by Victrola.
Inducted, 1978.

Ballad for Americans
Paul Robeson. Released in 1940 by Victor.
Inducted, 1980.

Bartók: Contrasts for Violin, Clarinet & Piano
Béla Bartók, piano. Joseph Szigeti, violin. Benny Goodman, clarinet. Released in 1940 by Columbia.
Inducted, 1989.

Bartók: Quartets (6) (Complete)
Juilliard Quartet. Released in 1950
by Columbia.
Inducted, 1987.

*Beethoven: Concertos for Piano Nos. 1,
2, 3, 4, 5*
Artur Schnabel and Malcolm Sargent
conducting London Symphony (1, 5) and
London Philharmonic (2, 3, 4). Released
in 1955 by Victor.
Inducted, 1989.

Beethoven: Piano Sonatas (32)
Artur Schnabel. Released in 1932–38 by
Beethoven Sonata Society/HMV.
Inducted, 1975.

*Beethoven: Quartets for Strings (16)
(Complete)*
Budapest String Quartet. Released in 1952
by Columbia.
Inducted, 1981.

Beethoven: Symphonies (9)
Arturo Toscanini conducting NBC
Symphony Orchestra. Released in 1950-53
by RCA Victor.
Inducted, 1977.

"Begin the Beguine"
Artie Shaw & His Orchestra. Released
in 1938 by Bluebird.
Inducted, 1977.

Berg: Wozzeck
Dimitri Mitropoulos conducting New York
Philharmonic Orchestra, Mack Harrell,
Eileen Farrell. Released in 1952 by
Columbia.
Inducted, 1990.

Birth of the Cool
Miles Davis. Released in 1957
by Capitol.
Inducted, 1982.

"Black and Tan Fantasy"
Duke Ellington & His Orchestra. Released
in 1928 by Victor.
Inducted, 1981.

"Black, Brown and Beige"
Duke Ellington & His Famous Orchestra.
Released in 1944 by RCA Victor.
Inducted, 1990.

"Blue Yodel (T for Texas)"
Jimmie Rodgers. Released in 1928
by Victor.
Inducted, 1985.

"Blueberry Hill"
Fats Domino. Released in 1956
by Imperial.
Inducted, 1987.

"Body and Soul"
Coleman Hawkins & His Orchestra.
Released in 1939 by Bluebird.
Inducted, 1974.

"Blue Suede Shoes"
Carl Perkins. Released in 1956 by Sun.
Inducted, 1986.

"Call It Stormy Monday"
T-Bone Walker. Released in 1948
by Black & White.
Inducted, 1991.

Carnegie Hall Jazz Concert
Benny Goodman. Released in 1950
by Columbia.
Inducted, 1975.

Charlie Parker with Strings
Charlie Parker. Released in 1950
by Mercury.
Inducted, 1988.

"The Christmas Song"
Nat "King" Cole. Released in 1946
by Capitol.
Inducted, 1974.

"Cool Water"
Sons of the Pioneers. Released in 1941
by Decca.
Inducted, 1986.

"Empty Bed Blues"
Bessie Smith. Released in 1928
by Columbia.
Inducted, 1983.

"Four Brothers"
Woody Herman. Released in 1948 by
Columbia.
Inducted, 1984.

The Genius of Art Tatum,
Volumes 1–13
Art Tatum. Released in 1954–55 by Clef.
Inducted, 1978.

Gershwin: Porgy & Bess
Lehman Engel, conductor. Lawrence
Winters, Camilla Williams, others.
Released in 1951 by Columbia.
Inducted, 1976.

Gershwin: Porgy & Bess Highlights,
Volumes 1 & 2
Original cast and Broadway revival cast,
including Todd Duncan, Anne Brown,
others. Released in 1940 and 1942
by Decca.
Inducted, 1990.

Gershwin: Rhapsody in Blue
Oscar Levant, Eugene Ormandy conducting Philadelphia Orchestra. Released in
1945 by Columbia.
Inducted, 1990.

Gershwin: Rhapsody in Blue
Paul Whiteman with George Gershwin.
Released in 1927 by Victor.
Inducted, 1974.

"God Bless America"
Kate Smith. Released in 1939 by Victor.
Inducted, 1982.

"God Bless the Child"
Billie Holiday. Released in 1941 by Okeh.
Inducted, 1976.

"Hound Dog"
Elvis Presley. Released in 1956
by RCA Victor.
Inducted, 1988.

"How High the Moon"
Les Paul, Mary Ford. Released in 1951 by
Capitol.
Inducted, 1979.

I Can Hear It Now, Volumes 1–3
Edward R. Murrow. Released in 1948–50.
Inducted, 1978.

"I Can't Get Started"
Bunny Berigan & His Orchestra. Released
in 1937 by Victor.
Inducted, 1975.

"If I Didn't Care"
Ink Spots. Released in 1939 by Decca.
Inducted, 1987.

"I'll Never Smile Again"
Tommy Dorsey with Frank Sinatra and
Pied Pipers. Released in 1940 by Victor.
Inducted, 1982.

"In a Mist"
Bix Beiderbecke. Released in 1927
by Okeh.
Inducted, 1980.

"In the Mood"
Glenn Miller & His Orchestra. Released
in 1939 by Bluebird.
Inducted, 1984.

In the Wee Small Hours
Frank Sinatra. Released in 1955 by
Capitol.
Inducted, 1984.

"I've Got a Woman"
Ray Charles. Released in 1954 by Atlantic.
Inducted, 1990.

***Jelly Roll Morton: The Saga of
Mr. Jelly Lord***
(12 albums; Library of Congress
Recordings)
Ferdinand "Jelly Roll" Morton. Released
in 1949–50 by Circle Sound.
Inducted, 1980.

***Leoncavallo: Pagliacci, Act I: Vesti La
Giubba***
Enrico Caruso. Released in 1907 by Vic-
trola.
Inducted, 1975.

**"Lover Man (Oh, Where Can You
Be?)"**
Billie Holiday. Released in 1945 by Decca.
Inducted, 1989.

Mahler: Das Lied von der Erde
Bruno Walter conducting Vienna
Philharmonic Orchestra with Kathleen
Ferrier and Julius Patzak. Released in
1952 by London.
Inducted, 1981.

"Maybellene"
Chuck Berry. Released in 1955 by Chess.
Inducted, 1988.

"Misty"
Errol Garner Trio. Released in 1954 by
Mercury.
Inducted, 1991.

"Mood Indigo"
Duke Ellington & His Orchestra. Released
in 1931 by Brunswick.
Inducted, 1975.

"Moonlight Serenade"
Glenn Miller & His Orchestra. Released in
1939 by Bluebird.
Inducted, 1991.

"My Blue Heaven"
Gene Austin. Released in 1928 by Victor.
Inducted, 1991.

My Fair Lady
Original Broadway cast with Rex Harrison
and Julie Andrews. Released in 1956
by Columbia.
Inducted, 1977.

"Nobody"
Bert Williams. Released in 1906
by Columbia.
Inducted, 1981.

Oklahoma!
Original Broadway cast with Alfred Drake.
Orchestra and chorus directed by Jay
Blackton. Released in 1943 by Decca.
Inducted, 1976.

"One O'Clock Jump"
Count Basie & His Orchestra.
Released in 1937 by Decca.
Inducted, 1979.

"Ornithology"
Charlie Parker Sextet. Released in 1946
by Dial.
Inducted, 1989.

"Over the Rainbow"
Judy Garland. Released in 1939 by Decca.
Inducted, 1981.

"Pinetop's Boogie Woogie"
Pine Top Smith. Released in 1928 by
Vocalion.
Inducted, 1983.

Puccini: Tosca
Victor de Sabata conducting Orchestra and
Chorus of Teatro alla Scala, Milan, with
Maria Callas, Giuseppe DiStefano, and
Tito Gobbi. Released in 1953 by Angel.
Inducted, 1987.

Rachmaninoff: Piano Concerto No. 2 in C Minor
Sergei Rachmaninoff, piano, and Leopold Stokowski conducting Philadelphia Orchestra. Released in 1929 by Victrola.
Inducted, 1976.

Rachmaninoff: Rhapsody on a Theme of Paganini
Sergei Rachmaninoff, piano. Leopold Stokowski conducting Philadelphia Orchestra. Released in 1935 by Victor.
Inducted, 1979.

"Rock Around the Clock"
Bill Haley & the Comets. Released in 1955 by Decca.
Inducted, 1982.

"Roll Over Beethoven"
Check Berry. Released in 1956 by Chess.
Inducted, 1990.

"Rudolph, the Red-Nosed Reindeer"
Gene Autry. Released in 1949 by Columbia.
Inducted, 1985.

"September Song"
Walter Huston. Released in 1938 by Brunswick.
Inducted, 1984.

Show Boat
Paul Robeson, Helen Morgan, James Melton, Frank Munn, Countess Albani, Victor Young. Released in 1932 by Brunswick.
Inducted, 1991.

"Sing, Sing, Sing"
Benny Goodman. Released in 1937 by Victor.
Inducted, 1982.

"Singin' the Blues"
Frankie Trumbauer & His Orchestra with Bix Beiderbecke on cornet. Released in 1927 by Okeh.
Inducted, 1977.

South Pacific
Original Broadway cast with Mary Martin and Ezio Pinza. Released in 1949 by Columbia.
Inducted, 1987.

"Star Dust"
Artie Shaw & His Orchestra. Released in 1940 by RCA Victor.
Inducted, 1988.

"Strange Fruit"
Billie Holiday. Released in 1939 by Commodore.
Inducted, 1978.

"Take the 'A' Train"
Duke Ellington & His Orchestra. Released in 1941 by Victor.
Inducted, 1976.

"Tea for Two"
Art Tatum, piano solo. Released in 1939 by Decca.
Inducted, 1986.

"This Land Is Your Land"
Woody Guthrie. Released in 1947 by Asch.
Inducted, 1989.

Villa-Lobos: Bachianas Brasileras No. 5 — Aria
Bidu Sayao with Heitor Villa-Lobos conducting cello ensemble. Released in 1945 by Columbia.
Inducted, 1984.

Wagner: Tristan und Isolde
Wilhelm Furtwangler conducting
Philharmonia Orchestra, Chorus of Royal
Opera House, and soloists. Released in
1953 by RCA Victor.
Inducted, 1988.

"West End Blues"
Louis Armstrong & His Hot Five.
Released in 1928 by Okeh.
Inducted, 1974.

West Side Story
Original Broadway cast with Carol
Lawrence and Larry Kert. Released in
1957 by Columbia.
Inducted, 1991.

"White Christmas"
Bing Crosby. Released in 1942 by Decca.
Inducted, 1974.

"Your Cheating Heart"
Hank Williams, Sr. Released in 1953
by MGM.
Inducted, 1983.

Italic pages = Grammy victory or victories

Italic pages = Grammy victory or victories

Scotland, 263
Bagwell, Wendy, 173, 201, 230
Bailey, Bob, 401
Bailey, J.R., 199
Bailey, Pearl, 354
Bailey, Philip, 401-402, 416, *438*
Baird, Tom, 216
Baker, Anita, 430, 434, *436*, 458, 468, 472, *474*, 489, *496*, 509, *515*, 549
Baker, Janet, 122, 149, 176, 189, 204, 217-218, 233, *250*, 266, *283*, 405
Baker, Kenny, 499
Baker, LaVerne, 47, 56
Bakersfield Brass, 186
"Baker Street," 293
Balakrishnan, David, 478
Balatsch, Norbert, *335*, 369, 369
Baldwin, Marizona, 168
Balet, Jan, *96*
Balfa, Dewey, 420
Ballad for Americans, 553
Ballard, Glen, 513, *519*, 523
Ballard, Hank, 47
Band Aid, 426
Band on the Run, 228
Banks, Homer, 146
Banks, Willie, 314
Bantu Glee Singers, 458
"Baptism of Jesse Taylor, The," 230
Barber, Bill, 478
Barber, Samuel, 27, 81, 90, *94*, 396, *405*
Barbieri, Gato, 210, *215*
Barbra Streisand Album, The, 75, *78*, 84
Bare, Bobby, 75-76, *79*, 92-93, 107, 133, 230
Bare, Jr., Bobby, 230
Barefoot Jerry, 230
Barenboim, Daniel, 161, *264*-265, 318, 334, 404, 422-423, 512, 520, *538*
Barnes, Rev. F.C., 439
Barretto, Ray, 247, 332, 367, 383, 459, 491, 499
Barretto Band, Ray, 280
Barry, John, 94, 118, 120-121, 154, *160*, *418*, *440*, 537
Barry, Len, 105
Bart, Lionel, 67
Bartók, Bela, 108, 552-553
Bartók: Concerto No. 2 for Violin, 111
Bartók: Concerto for Orchestra, 216
Bartók: Contrasts for Violin, Clarinet & Piano, 553

Bartók: Quartets (6), 554
Bartók: 6 String Quartets, 501
Bascombe, David, 504
Bashmet, Yuri, 538
Basie, 25, 27-28, 37, 68
Basie, Count, 1-2, 13, 25, *27*-28, 37, 42, *46*, 47, 57, 68, 75, *79*, 118, 159, 185, 245, *262*, 273, *278*, 313, *331*, 360, 362, *365*, 381, 393, *400*, 497, *515*, 549, 552-553, 556
Basie & Zoot, 262
Basil, Toni, 388
Basin Brothers, 516
"Basque," *537*
Bass, Fontella, 106
Bass, Sid, 94
Bath Festival Orchestra, 108
Batman, 115, *500*
"Batman Theme," *120*
Battle, Kathleen, 405, 434, 441, *442*, 453, *462*, 502
"Battle Hymn of the Republic," 36
Battle of Kookamonga, The, *39*
"Battle of New Orleans, The," 33, *36*, 37
Baudo, Serge, 283
Bavarian Radio Chorus and Symphony, 110, 149, 352, 539
Baylor, Helen, 535
BBC Singers and Choral Society, 266
BBC Symphony Chorus, 249
BBC Tribute to John F. Kennedy, 97
B.C. & M. Choir, 201
Beach Boys, 118-119, 473, 479, 548
Beals, Carleton, *98*
Bean, Orson, 300
Beaser, Robert, 442
Beastie Boys, 11
"Beat It," *379*, 380
Beatles, 3, 8, 10-11, 13, 86-88, *91*, 92, 99, 100, 101, 104-106, 113-114, 118, 125-126, *130-131*, 134, 138-139, 144-145, 152, 157-158, 166, 171, 493, 547, 550
Beausoleil, 420, 458, 499, 535
"Beautiful Isle of Somewhere," 146
Beaux Arts Trio, 187, 461
"Be Bop Medley," 384
Becaud, Gilbert, 351
Beck, Jeff, 261, 409, *416*, 488, *495*
Becker, Margaret, 476, 498, 535

Bee, Molly, 107
Beecham, Sir Thomas, 43, 47, *48*
Bee Gees, 17, 184, 272, *277*, 284-286, *293*, *296*, *301*, 549
Beethoven: Concertos for Piano Nos. 1, 2, 3, 4, 5, 554
Beethoven: The Five Piano Concertos, 264
Beethoven: Piano Sonatas (32), 554
Beethoven: Quartets for Strings (16), 554
Beethoven: Symphonies (9) Complete, 248, 554
Beethoven: Symphony No. 9 in D Minor, 461
"Begin the Beguine," 554
"Behind Closed Doors," 210, 213-214, *215*
"Behind My Camel," 347
Beiderbecke, Bix, 555
"Being with You," 379
Beinhorn, M., 384
Belafonte, Harry, 28, 36, 37, 45, *46*, 69, 93, *107*
Belafonte at Carnegie Hall, 36
Belafonte Folk Singers, 46, 56-57
Belafonte Folk Singers at Home and Abroad, 57
Belafonte Returns to Carnegie Hall, 45
Belafonte Singers, 46
Belew, Carl, 107
Bell, Archie, 145
Bell, Thom, 172, 202, *235*
Bell, Vincent, 171
Bellamy, David, 313
Bellamy, Ralph, 50
Bellamy Brothers, 314
Bellavia, 264
Belle, Regina, 515
Bellson, Louie, 313, 331, 418, 456
Belvin, Jesse, 36, 37
Benatar, Pat, 323, *329*, 339, 342, 347, *363*, 374, *380*, 415-416, *436*, 473, *495*, 550
Bennett, Alan, 72
Bennett, Chris, 297
Bennett, Richard, 202, 351
Bennett, Robert Russell, 38
Bennett, Rodney, 247
Bennett, Tony, 4, 52, 62, *67*, 78, 91, 104-105, 515
Benoit, David, 475
Benson, George, 17, 200, 255, *260*, *261-262*, 288, *294*, 310, 313, 324, *330-331*,

Italic pages = Grammy victory or victories

Italic pages = Grammy victory or victories

Italic pages = Grammy victory or victories

Italic pages = Grammy victory or victories

Car Wash, 264
Casadesus, Gaby, 71
Casadesus, Robert, 71, 81
Casals, Pablo, 28, 548, 551, 553
Casas, Jorge, 504
Casey, Henry Wayne, 229, 245, 261
Cash, Johnny, 79, 92-93, 127-128, 133, 141-142, 146, 150, 151-152, 154-155, 157, 159, 164, 168, 172, 173, 186, 201, 246, 310, 419, 443, 498, 516, 549
Cash, Rosanne, 349, 365, 411, 418, 419, 457, 476, 497, 535
Cashman, Terry, 213
Cassidy, Shaun, 277
Castle, David, 297
"Cast Your Fate to the Winds," 68
"Cat, The," 92
"Catch a Falling Star," 26
Cathedral of Faith Choir, 517
Cathedral Quartet, 279, 296, 314
Cathedrals, 366
Catlin, Stanton, 98
Cato, Robert, 98, 137
Cats, 384
Cat Stevens, 548
Cavanaugh, Page, 79
Cavett, Dick, 425
Caymmi, Dori, 459, 536
Cecil, Malcolm, 220
Cello Concerto No. 2 (Penderecki), 462
Cepeda, Bonny, 420
Cetera, Peter, 402, 435
Chailly, Riccardo, 404, 423, 462
"Chain of Fools," 140-141, 145
Chaka Khan, 380
Chamberlain, Richard, 190
Chamberlin, Lee, 204
Champlin, Bill, 312, 364
Champs, 23, 28
Chancler, Leon "Ndugu," 364
"Change of Heart," 518
Changing Times, 314
Channing, Carol, 540
Channing, Stockard, 293
Chapin, Harry, 199, 228
Chapman, Edward, 82
Chapman, Mike, 320
Chapman, Morris, 382
Chapman, Steven Curtis, 517, 535
Chapman, Tracy, 467, 473, 477, 499
"Chariots of Fire," 362-363

Charles, Ray, 13, 42-43, 45-47, 54-56, 64, 67-68, 78-79, 116, 119, 130-131, 158, 200, 239, 245, 262, 294, 312, 362, 382, 493, 497, 505-506, 515, 549, 551, 556
Charles Singers, Ray, 46, 92, 131, 145, 158
Charlie Parker with Strings, 554
Charley Pride Sings Heart Songs, 200
Charnin, Martin, 280
Chase, 184
Chater, Kerry, 382
Chavela y su Grupo Express, 459
Chayanne, 499
Checker, Chubby, 14, 52, 56
Cheech & Chong, 190, 204, 210-211, 219, 234, 267, 424
Chelo, 383
Chenier, Clifton, 296, 315, 375, 383, 420
Cher, 184, 548
Cherin, Milt, 267
"Cherish," 119
Cherry, Neneh, 494
Chester & Lester, 262
Chevallier, Christian, 263
Chicago, 157, 170-171, 256, 260, 261, 283, 363, 397-398, 539
Chicago, 170
Chicago Bears Shufflin' Crew, 436
Chicago Blues Allstars, 350
Chicago Brass Ensemble, 161
Chicago Pro Musica, 413, 422
Chicago Push, 420
Chicago 17, 406
"Chicago Song," 456
Chicago Symphony Orchestra Chorus, 299, 318, 369, 387, 404, 442, 481
Chicago Symphony Winds, 441
Chicago X, 260, 268
Chick Corea and Gary Burton in Concert, Zurich, October 28, 1979, 347
Chieftains, 315, 332, 383, 458, 477
Chieftains 9, 332
Child of the 50's, 220
Children of Sanchez, 293
Children's Chorus of New England Conservatory, 176
Children of Truth, 201
Childs, Toni, 473-474
Chilton, John, 371

Chipmunks, 24, 110, 353-354, 370
"Chipmunk Song, The," 24, 26, 29, 30
Choeurs et Orchestre de Paris, 423
Choeur "The Sixteen," 424
Choir of King's College, 83
Choir of the Monks of Saint-Pierre de Solesmes Abbey, 266
Choir of Westminster Abbey, 387
"Chokin' Kind, The," 154, 158
Choralerna, 296
Chor der Nationaloper Sofia, 423
Chorus of Academy of St. Martin-in-the-Fields, 299, 353, 369
Chorus of Bavarian Radio, 283
Chorus of Deutsche Opera Berlin, 352
Chorus of La Scala, Milan, 266
Chorus of National Philharmonic Warsaw, 233
Chorus of Orchestre de Paris, 283, 318
Chorus and Orchestra of Washington Opera Society, 83
Chorus of Prague, 352
Chorus Pro Musica, 96
Chorus Viennesis, 162
Christ Church Cathedral Choir, 502, 535
Christlieb, Pete, 349
Christmas, 476
"Christmas Song, The," 554
Christoff, Boris, 96
Christopher, Johnny, 362, 365
Chuck Berry — The Chess Box, 504
"Chuck E.'s in Love," 311
Chuck Wagon Gang, 535
Chudd, Lew, 26
Chung, Kyung-Wha, 188, 232, 368
Ciani, Suzanne, 478, 536
Ciardi, John, 72
Ciccolini, Aldo, 188, 217
"Cielito Lindo," 499
"Cinema," 398
Citizen Caine, 300
City of Birmingham Symphony Orchestra Chorus, 369, 404
"City of New Orleans," 400
Civil War, The, 535, 540
Claire, Dom Jean, 266
Clancy Brothers, 57
Clapton, Eric, 192-193, 198,

Italic pages = Grammy victory or victories

467, 473, 483, 507, *514*,
   532
Clark, Cortelia, 115-116, 120
Clark, Dick, 2, 193, 493, 551-
   552
Clark, Guy, 418, 499
Clark, Kenny, 200
Clark, Louis, 347, 363
Clark, Petula, 14, 88, 91-*92*,
   101, 105, *106*, 130-131
Clark, Roy, 230, 295, 360,
   366, 382
Clark, Rudy, 199
Clark Sisters, 383, 458, 477,
   517
Clarke, Stanley, 263, 294, 398,
   435, 437
Clarke, Willie, *245*
"Class of '57," 201
"Classical Gas," 140, 145, *147*
Clawson, Cynthia, *332*, 349,
   382, 438
Clay, Cassius (Muhammad
   Ali), 76, 84, 268
Clay, Dice, 503
Clayton, John, 519
Clayton, Merry, 200
Clayton-Thomas, David, 152
Cleese, John, 482
Clement, Doris, 133
Clements, Vassar, 314, 419
Cleo at Carnegie: The 10th
   Anniversary Concert, 417
Cleva, Fausto, 39
Cleveland, Rev. James, 93,
   147, 160, 173, 201, 215,
   230, 246-247, 263, 274-
   275, *279*, 280, 296, 314,
   332, 350, 401, 439, 511,
   517, 535, 550
Cleveland Brass Ensemble,
   161
Cleveland Orchestra and
   Chorus, 318, 404
Cleveland Orchestra Chorus
   and Boys' Choir, *249*
Cleveland Quartet, 217, 334,
   368, 403
Clevenger, Dale, 442, 461
Cliff, Jimmy, 402, 412, *420*,
   439, 478
Cliff Hanger, 420
"Cliffs of Dover," 532
Cline, Patsy, 548
Clooney, Rosemary, 46
Close, Glenn, 405, 463, 482
Close Encounters of the Third
   Kind, 297
Closer You Get, The, 382
Close-Up, 473
Close to You, 166, 170-171
"Cloud Nine," 7, 140
Clouds, 155, 160

Coasters, 36, 37
Cobb, Arnett, 313
Cobb, Lee J., 123
Cobert, Robert, 160
Cobham, Billy, 437
Cochran, Hank, 56, 120
Cocker, Joe, 171, 350, 357,
   362, *363*, 455, 473, 495,
   514
Coe, David A., 295
Cohen, Jeffrey, 410, 416
Cohn, Al, 294-295, 349
Cohn, Marc, 525, *531*
Colder, Ben, 120
Cole, Nat "King," 10-12, 28,
   31, *36*, 37, 45, 56, 67, 493,
   504, 524, 531, 551, 554
Cole, Natalie, 10, 239, 243,
   244-245, 254, *261*, 278,
   294, 310, 312, 456, 496,
   524-525, *531*, 533, 549
Coleman, Albert, 366, 382
Coleman, Cy, 26, 199, *537*
Coleman Trio, Ornette, 119
Colesberry, Robert F., 333
Coley, Daryl, 517
Colla, John, 421
Collegiate Chorale, 82
Collegium Vocale of Cologne,
   190
Collins, Albert, 159, 315, 350,
   397, 432, 439, 458, 536
Collins, Brian, 334
Collins, Judy, 79, 133, *147*,
   160, 236-237, 245
Collins, Larry, 200
Collins, Phil, 380, 392, *398*,
   403, 406, 408, *415*, 416,
   426, 471, 473, *479*, 506,
   512-*513*, 523, 549-550
Collins, Sue, 297
Colombier, Michel, 187
Colon, Willie, 247, 367, 383,
   402, 439, 499, 518
Colorful Peter Nero, The , 69
"Color Him Father," 154, *158*
Color Me Badd, 531, 533
Color Me Barbra, 118
Colter, Jessi, 173, 246
Coltrane, John, 45, 106, 172,
   245, 278, 341, *348*, 551
Columbia Chamber Ensemble,
   170
Columbia Chamber Orchestra,
   122
Columbia Records Presents
   Vladimir Horowitz, 70
Colvin, Shawn, *517*
Comden, Betty, 39, *537*
Come Dance with Me, 31-32,
   36, *40*
Come Fly with Me, 22, 26
Come & Gone, 234

"Come Sunday," 420
Comets, 557
Commissioned, 498, 535
Commitments, 531
Commodores, 278, 293-294,
   311-312, 330, 332, 348,
   410, 412, *417*
Como, Perry, 13, 24, *26*, 184,
   213
Company, 173
Composers Quartet, 175
Compositions, 515
Comyn, Stan, 111
Conaway, Jeff, 293
Concentus Musicus, 189
Concentus Musicus Wien, 370
Concert for Bangla Desh, The,
   6, 8, 192-193, *198*
Concert of the Century, *281*
Conchita, Maria, 402
Concord Quartet, 249
Concord String Quartet, 217
Condie, Richard, 39
Confessions of a Broken Man,
   124
Conkling, Donna, 12
Conkling, Jim, 11, 13
Conley, Earl Thomas, 382,
   476, 534
Conlon, James, 422
Connick, Harry Jr., 489, *496*,
   510, *515*, 519, 531, 538
Conniff & Singers, Ray, 115,
   118, 145, 158
Connors, Carol, 280
Conreid, Hans, 39, 300
Conscious Party, 477
Conti, Bill, 277, 280-281
Control, 434
Conversations with Myself, 79
Convertino, Michael, 459
Cooder, Ry, 332, 477
Cook, Betsy, 457
Cook, Peter, 72, *234*
Cooke, Alistair, 251
Cooke, Sam, 68, 78-79, 92,
   106, 548
Cooley, Eddie, 26
Cooleyhighharmony, 533
Coolidge, Rita, 215, 230, 242,
   246
"Cool Water," 555
Cooper, Alice, 209, 212, 388
"Copacabana (at the Copa),"
   293
Copeland Singers, Alan, 118,
   145
Copeland, Kenneth, 332
Copeland, Johnny, 432, 439,
   477
Copeland, Stewart, 402
Copland, Aaron, 43, 47, *49*,
   70, 121, 232, 552

Italic pages = Grammy victory or victories

Copland: Lincoln Portrait,
387
Coppola, Carmine, 315
Coppola, Francis, 315
Corea, Chick, 214, 216, 245,
258, *262-263*, 264, 280,
289, *295-296*, 297, 307,
313, 315, 341, *349*, 381,
403, 438, 440, 442, 455,
456, 466, *474*, 475, 478,
489, 497, 500, 516, 519,
534, 549
Corigliano, John, 350, 529,
540
Cornall, Andrew, 387, 482
Cornelius, Helen, 295
Cornyn, Stan, *111*, *124*, 300
Corsaro, Jason, 443
"Cortelia Clark," 116
Cory, George, 67
Coryell, Larry, 185
Cosas del Amor, *536*
Cosby, Bill, 76-77, 84, 89, *97*,
101, *110*, 115, *123*, 129,
136, 142, *149*, 156-157,
163, 176, 182, *190*, *204*,
219, 267, 387, 432, *443*,
547, 549
Cossette, Pierre, 13, 486
Costa, Don, 107, 120, 333
Costello, Elvis, 293, 532, 548
Cotten, Elizabeth, 394, *401*,
439
Cotton, James, 439, 458, 477
Cotton Candy, 91
*Cotton Club, The — Original
Motion Picture
Soundtrack*, 418
Cougar, John (also see John
Cougar Mellencamp), 357-
358, 362
"Could I Have This Dance,"
331
Count Basie. *See* Basie, Count
*Country, After All These
Years*, 349
*Country Instrumentalist of the
Year*, 279
"Country Sunshine," 215
Court and Spark, 228
Covington, Warren, 27
Coward, Noel, 9-10
C + C Music Factory, 531
Crack the Sky, 458
Craft, Paul, 262
Cramer, Floyd, 160, 186, 230,
262, 279, 314, 332
Crane, Les, *190*
Cray, Robert, 432-433, *439*,
452
Cray Band, Robert, 458, 474,
477, 518
Cream, 144, 548

Creedence Clearwater Revival,
548
Cremona String Quartet, 148
Crespin, Regine, 81, 96, 117
Crest of a Knave, 474
Crimes of Passion, 329
Croce, Jim, 213, 548
Crocodiles, 458
Croft, David G., 464
Cronkite, Walter, 163, 190
Cropper, Steve, 141, 146
Crosby, Bing, 548, 551, 558
Crosby, David, 154, 157
Crosby, Stills & Nash, 154,
157, 158, 270, 277
Crosby, Stills & Nash, 152,
157
Crosby, Stills, Nash & Young,
170
Cross, Christopher, 3, 321-
323, *328*, 346-347, 546,
550
Cross, Douglass, 67
"Cross Country Suite," 27
Crossley, Paul, 520
Crossroads, *484*
Crouch, Andrae, 173, 215,
246, 263, 290, *296*, 308,
314, *332*, *350*, 366, 394,
401, 549
Crouch, Sandra, 376, *383*, 419
Crowell, Rodney, 418, 475-
476, 490, 497
Crusaders, 200, 214, 229, 262,
280, 294, 350, 399
Crutcher, Bettye, 146
Crutchfield, John, 133
Cruz, Celia, 315, 420, 439,
491, *499*
"Crying," 476
"Crying Time," 116, *119*
Crystal, Billy, 425, 434, 472
Cuba, Joe, 263
Culshaw, John, 552
"Cult of Personality," 495
Culture Club, 374-375, *379*
Cunningham, David, 333
Cunninghams, 475
Curtin, Phyllis, 189
Curtis, King, 119, *159*, 200,
215
Curzon, Clifford, 47
Cusack, Cyril, 136
Cutler, Scott, 473
Cutting Crew, 454
Cycle V, 379
Dale, Dick, 455
*Damn Right, I've Got the
Blues*, *536*
Damone, Vic, 52
Dana, Bill, 60, 117
Dance with Basie, 46
"Dancing in the Dark," 5,

397-398
Dancing Machine, 276
Dangerfield, Rodney, *336*,
377, 405, 443
"Dang Me," 89, *92-93*
Dang Me/Chug-a-Lug, 92
Daniels Band, Charlie, 308,
310, *314*, 331
Daniels, Dr. Stanley, 190
Daniels, Eddie, 437, 456
Dankworth, John, 478
Danna, Mrs. Jay, 12
Danniebelle, 279, 296
Danoff, Bill, 256, 261
Danoff, Taffy, 256
Darby, Ken, 34
D'Arby, Terence Trent, 454,
469, *474*
Darin, Bobby, 4, 6, 31-33, *36*,
38, *40*, 68, 88, 113, 119
Darion, Joe, 118
Darlington, Stephen, 502
Darren, James, 56
Dart, Thurston, 202
Dash, Joseph, 413
Dash, Michael M., 189
Dave Brubeck Quartet, 79
Dave Lambert Singers, 28
Davenport, Johnny, 26
Dave Pell Octet, 52
David, Hal, 78, 140, 157-158,
161, 167, 278
David, Mack, 69
David Bowie, *406*
Davie, Hutch, 133
Davies, Dennis Russell, 316
Davies, Hugh, *49*
Davies, Meridith, 218
Davis, Angela, 204
Davis, Billy Jr., 151-152, 257,
260, *261*
Davis, Carl, 367
Davis, Chip, 421
Davis, Clifton, 185
Davis, Clive, 447
Davis, Colin, 81, 121, 169,
174-175, 182, 187-188,
189, 197, 202-*203*, 227,
231, *233*, 243, *248*, 266,
282-283, 297, 299, 316,
317, 404, 549
Davis, Danny, 155, *160*, 172,
186, 201, 215, 230, 262,
279, 295, 332
Davis, Donald, 146, 261
Davis, Harold, 229
Davis, Herman, 172
Davis, Johnny, 486
Davis, Mac, 158, 199, 262
Davis, Meredith, 249
Davis, Miles, 25, *47*, 68, 76,
79, 92, 132, 146, 159, 167-
168, *172*, 173, 185, 348,

Italic pages = Grammy victory or victories

Italic pages = Grammy victory or victories

Italic pages = Grammy victory or victories

Index   569

English Bach Festival Chorus, 299
English Concert Choir, 502
Eno, Brian, 454, 464
Enrique, Luis, 518, 536
Ensemble Wien-Berlin, 480
"Entertainers, The," 246
Entremont, Philippe, 203
En Vogue, 515
Enya, 499, 504
Epstein, Steven, 36, 353, 387, *405*, 424, 443, 463, 482, 540
Erichson, Wolf, 503
Ervin, Sam, 234
"Escape," 416
Escape Club, 473
Es Facil Amar, 420
Esposito, Joe, 379, 473
Esquivel, 27, 37, 38, 46
Estefan, Emilio Jr., 504
Estefan, Gloria, 473, 494
Estes, George, *111*
Etheridge, Melissa, 474, 495, 514
E.U., 474
Eurythmics, 379, 406, 416-417, 430, 504, 523
Evans, Anthony, 333
Evans, Bill, 68, 76, 79, 119, 132, 142-144, 159, 168, *172*, 181, *185*, 230, *313*, 324-325, *331*, 549
Evans Trio, Bill, 56, 106, *146*, *185*, 262
Evans, Dale, 215
Evans, David, 446
Evans, Gil, 57, 68, 92, 107, 214, 381, 469, 475
Evans, Marion, 70, 80
Evans, Ray, 91
Evans, Richard, 316
Even Now, 293
Evening with Belafonte/Makeba, An, 107
Evening with George Shearing and Mel   Torme An, 364
Evening with Mike Nichols and Elaine May, An, 60
Everly Brothers, 27, 146, 438
"Everybody's Talkin'," 154, *157*
"Every Breath You Take," 373, 377, *379*
"Every Little Step," 496
"Every Man Wants to Be Free," 173
"(Everything I Do) I Do It for You," 526, 531, 537
"Everything Is Beautiful," 167, 171, 173
"Everything's Gonna Be Alright," 458

"Everytime I Feel the Spirit," *57*
"Everytime You Go Away," 415
Evie, 296
Evita, 333
Evolution of Gospel, The, 535
Exodus, 42, *45, 49*
Explosion, 313
Extreme, 531
Eyen, Tom, 367
"Eye of the Tiger," 362-363
Fabric, Bent (Bent Fabricus Bjerre), 14, 63, *68*
Fabulous Baker Boys, The, 500
Fabulous Thunderbirds, 436
Fad, J.J., 474
Fagen, Donald, 362-363, 367-368, 479
Fairchild, Barbara, 214, 464
"Fairytale," 230
Faith, 466, *472*
Faith, Percy, 13, 41, *45*-46, 50, 52, 80
Faithfull, Marianne, 329
Faith No More, 496, 514
Faltermeyer, Harold, 421, *435*, 440
"Fame," 328
Family Style, 518
Fania All-Stars, 247, 263, 296, 315
"Far East Suite," 128, 132
Fargo, Donna, 195, 197, *200*
Farina, Mimi and Richard, 120
Farmer Quartet, Art, 365
Farnon, Chris, 192
Farnon, Dennis, 11
Farnon, Robert, 69, 263
Farrell, Eileen, 29, 46, 49, 60, 65, *71*
Farrell, Joe, 200
"Fast Car," 467, 472-473
Fat, 483
Father Hath Provided, The, 457
Feather, Leonard, *85*, 144, 359-360, 392, 465-466
"Feelings," 244
"Feel Like Makin' Love," 228
"Feels So Good," 293
Feinberg, Alan, 539
Fekaris, Dino, 311
Felder, Don, 277
Felder, Wilton, 348
Feliciano, José, 18, 138, 140, 144, 367, *383*, 402, 432, *439*, 491, *499*, *518*, 549
Feliciano!, 140, *144*-145
Fender, Freddie, 246
Fenton, George, 385, 479
Ferguson, Maynard, 47, 185,

200, 277, 364
Fernandez, Vicente, 383, 518
Ferrante, Arthur, 160
Ferrante & Teicher, 42, 158
Ferrer, José, 30
Festival Quartet, 38
"Fever," 26
5th Dimension, 3, 9, 14, 125, 130, *131*, 151-152, *157*, *158*, 165, 183, 549
"50 Ways to Leave Your Lover," 260
52nd Street, 304, *310*, 311
Finch, Richard, *245, 261*
Fine, Michael, 522
Fine, Robert, 72, *84*
Finegan, Bill, 70
Fine and Mellow, 313
Fine Young Cannibals, 494-495
"Fireball," 382
Firebird, The, 65, 129
"Fire and Ice," 347
"Fire and Rain," 171
Fireside Theatre, 405
Firkusny, Rudolph, 58, 203, 502, 539
First Call, 438, 476, 498, 517
First Circle, 399
First Family, The, 62-63, *67*, 72, *198*
"First Time Ever I Saw Your Face, The," 5, 192-194, *199*
Fischer, André, 541
Fischer, Clare, 263, 348, *350*-351, 365, 367, 399, *437*, 438, 440
Fischer, Lisa, 527, 532, *533*
Fischer-Dieskau, Dietrich, 49, 71, 83, 96, 110, 122, 136, 149, 162, 169, *176*, 189, 217, 266, 275, 283, 300, 318, 387
Fitzgerald, Ella, 6, 12-13, 16, 24-26, *27-28*, 31, 33-34, *36, 37*, 42, 45, *46*, 56, 64, *67*, 114, 118, 257-258, *262*, 307, *313*, 324, *331*, 341, *348*, 364, 375, *381*, 456, 505, 510, *515*, 547, 549, 551, 553
Fitzgerald, Geraldine, 190
Fitzgerald & Pass ... Again, 262
Fitzwilliam Quartet, 265, 317
Five Blind Boys, 230
Five Blind Boys of Mississippi, 279
Fizdale, Robert, 81
Flack, Roberta, 3, 5, 179, 182, 185, 192-194, *198, 199*, 206-207, *213*, 221, 228,

Italic pages = Grammy victory or victories

Italic pages = Grammy victory or victories

Gary, John, 77-78
Gary Burton Quartet, 132
Gary McFarland Group, 106
Gascoigne, Brian, 298
Gatica, Humberto, *406*, 464
Gatlin, Larry, 258-259, *262*, 279, 313-314, 332, 382
Gatlin Brothers, 438
Gatlin Brothers Band, 314, 332, 382
Gatton, Danny, 532
Gaucho, 346
Gaye, Marvin, 132, 145, 185, 214, 229, 261-262, 278, 358, *364*, 380
Gayle, Crystal, 262, 274, 276-277, *279*, 295, 331, 354, 362, 382, 400, 438, 457
Gaynor, Gloria, 245, 304, 310-*313*
Gehman, Don, 371, 464
Geils, J., 363
Geliot, Martine, 281
Genesis, 398, 436, *464*
Genius of Art Tatum, The, 555
Genius + Soul = Jazz, 55
Genius of Ray Charles, 43, 45
Gentlemen of London Philharmonic Choir, 249
"Gentle on My Mind," 126, 130, *132-133*
Gentry, Bobbie, 125-127, *130*, *131*, 171
George, Cassietta, 160, 314
George, Chief Dan, 263
George, Jimmy, 455, 474
George Shearing Quintet, 68
Georgia Mass Choir, 517
"Georgia on My Mind," 42-43, 45-46, 289, 295
Georgia Satellites, 455
Gerry Mulligan Concert Jazz Band, 79
Gershwin, George, 260, 552
Gershwin, Ira, 552
Gershwin Live!, 16, 364
Gershwin: Porgy & Bess, *266*, *282*, 555
Gershwin: Porgy & Bess Highlights, 555
Gershwin: Rhapsody in Blue, 555
Gertrude Stein, Gertrude Stein, Gertrude Stein, *336*
Get Closer, 371
Getz, Stan, 14, 64, 67, *68*, 69, 87-88, *91*, 92, 106, 132, 288, 294-295, 515-516, 528, *533*, 550
Getz/Gilberto, 6, 14, *91*, 92
Ghiaurov, Nicolai, 108, 110
Ghosh, Shankar, 173
"Ghostbusters," 398

Giant Steps, 209, 214
Gibb, Andy, 277
Gibb, Barry, 293, 321-322, 328, *329*
Gibb, Maurice, 293
Gibb, Robin, 293, 300
Gibbs, Michael, 231
Gibbs, Terri, 349, 458
Gibson, Don, 27, 37, 160
Giddens, Gary, *443*
Gielgud, Sir John, 39, 50, *319*, 370, 387, 443, 482, 503, 540
"Gigi," 26
Gigi, 28
Gilbert, Carry, 278
Gilbert, Ken, 199
Gilberto, Astrud, 14, 87, 105
Gilberto, Joao, 87, 91, 278, 475
Gilels, Emil, 28, 162, 217, 404
Gil Evans Orchestra, 106
Gilford, Jack, 84
Gill, Johnny, 514
Gill, Vince, *516*, 528-529, *534*
Gillespie, Dizzy, 47, 57, 68, 106, 185, 241, *245*, 262, 313, 350, 365, 437, 497, 505, 528, *534*, 551
Gillespie, Jerry, 349
Gimble, Johnny, 349, 476
Gimbel, Norman, 105, *213*
Gingold, Hermione, 96, *267*
Ginn, Bill, 460
Gipsy Kings, 499
"Girl from Ipanema," 14, 87, *91*
Girls on Film/Hungry Like the Wolf, *388*
"Girls Just Want to Have Fun," 397
Girl with Orange Lips, The, 539
Girl You Know It's True, 485-486
Giuffre, Jimmy, 47
Giulini, Carol Maria, 94, 174, *188*, 275, *281*, 291, *297*, 385-386, 550
Giuranna, Bruno, 501
Give 'Em Hell Harry, *251*
"Give a Little Love," 476
Give Me the Night, 324, 330
"Giving You the Best that I Got," 472-473, *474*, 496
Glaser, Tompall, 120
Glaser Brothers, 132-133, 160, 186
Glass, Philip, 385, 442
Glass Houses, 328-329
Glazer, Tom, 84
Gleason, Joanna, 478

Glennie, Evelyn, *480*
Glory, *519*
Glover, Danny, 522, 540
Glyndebourne Opera Chorus, 203, 352
G-Men, 499
Gobbi, Tito, 29
"God Bless America," 555
"God Bless the Child," 555
Godfather, The, *202*
God Is in the House, 214
Godspell, *187*
Go-Go's, 346
"Going Away," 439
"Goin' Out of My Head," 116, 119
Golabek, Mona, 520
Gold, Arthur, & Robert Fizdale, 81
Gold, Ernest, 42, *45*, *49*
Gold, Jeffrey, *523*
Gold, Julie, 506, *513*
Gold, Marty, 80, 123
Goldberg, Whoopi, 427, 482
Golden Age Singers, 96
Golden Men of Jazz, 534
Golden Orchestra and Chorus, 190
Goldsboro, Bobby, 133, 139, 144, 145
Goldsmith, Jerry, 108, 231, 247, 264, 315, 350
Goldsmith's Choral Union, 249
Goldstein, Bob, 80
Golson, Benny, 231
Gomez, Eddie, 181
Gomulka, Lenny, 459
Gomulka's Chicago Push, Lenny, 478
Goode, Richard, 368, 502, 520
Good Evening, *234*
"Good Feelin'," *173*
Good King Bad, 262
"Good Life, The," 78
Goodman, Benny, 431, 437, 441, 548, 551, 553-554, 557
Goodman, Don, 365
Goodman, Paul, *370*, *405*
Goodman, Rusty, 349
Goodman, Steve, 393, *400*, 451, *458*
Goodman, Tanya, 443, *503*
"Good Man, Good Woman," 532
Good Morning, Vietnam, 482
Good Rockin', 401
Goodrum, Randy, 293
"Good Vibrations," 119
Goossens, Leon, 71
Gordon, Dexter, 278, 294, 313, *456*, *459*

Italic pages = Grammy victory or victories

Italic pages = Grammy victory or victories

Italic pages = Grammy victory or victories

Italic pages = Grammy victory or victories

Italic pages = Grammy victory or victories

Italic pages = Grammy victory or victories

Index   577

Italic pages = Grammy victory or victories

Italic pages = Grammy victory or victories

Index   579

Italic pages = Grammy victory or victories

Italic pages = Grammy victory or victories

Italic pages = Grammy victory or victories

Miller, Douglas, 419
Miller, Glenn, 37, 555-556
Miller, James, *514*
Miller, Jody, 100, *107*
Miller, Jonathan, 72
Miller, Marcus, 474, 479, *532*
Miller, Marvin, *110, 123*
Miller, Mitch, 548
Miller, Mrs., 123
Miller, Roger, 89, *92, 93*, 100, 104, *105, 106, 107*, 120, 146, 234, 546
Milli Vanilli, 6, 485-487, *494*, 547
Mills, Frank, 311
Mills, Mike, 531
Mills, Stephanie, 323-324, *330*, 348, 380
Milnes, Sherrill, 163, 233
Milsap, Ronnie, 225-226, *230*, 258, *262*, 276, 279, 343, *349*, 365, 382, 411, *418*, 430-431, *438*, 451, *457*, 549
Milstein, Nathan, 29, 38, 243, *250*, 265
Milt Jackson Quintet, 172
Mingus, Charlie, 25, 68, 76, 79, 315
Mink, Ben, 497
Minnelli, Liza, 552
Minton, Yvonne, 218
Mintz, Shlomo, 386, 501
Mintzer, Bob, 534
"Minute By Minute," 455
Minute By Minute, 310-311
"Missionary Man," 436
"Mission Impossible," *133-134*
"Mission Impossible/Norwegian Wood," 145
Mistaken Identity, 346
Mr. Mister, 416, 458
"Misty," 556
Mitchell, Howard, 50
Mitchell, Joni, 155, *160*, 221, 228, *231*, 261, 473
Mitchell, Steve, 398
Mitchell, Vernessa, 419
Mitchell-Ruff Duo, 365
Mitchell Trio, 120
Mitropoulos, Dimitri, 29, 554
Modern Jazz Quartet, 47, 56, 92
Modern Sounds in Country & Western Music, 67
Modugno, Domenico, 21-22, *26*
Moffo, Anna, 83, 110, 204
Molinari-Pradelli, Francesco, 134
Moll, Phillip, 368

Moman, Chips, *246*, 278, *443*
"Monday, Monday," 118-119
Monday Night Orchestra, *475*
Monie, Eddie, 436
Monie Love, 515, 533
"Money for Nothing," 415-416
Monge, Yolandita, 458
Monk, Thelonius, 25, 79, *464*
Monkees, 119, 131-132
Monroe, Bill, 362, 457, 470, *477*, 499
Montenegro, Hugo, 93, 133, 145, 147
Monteux, Pierre, 28, 38, 47
Monteverdi Choir, 442, 462, 481, 502, 539
Montgomery, Bob, 261
Montgomery, Little Brother, *332*
Montgomery, Wes, 106, 116, *119*, 145-146, 155, *159*, 201
Montreux '77, Oscar Peterson Jam, 294
"Mood Indigo," 556
Moods, 198
Moody, Carlton, 400, 476
Moody, James, 418, 497
Moody Brothers, 400, 476
"Moody's Mood," 331
Moog, Dr. Robert A., 156, 552
Moog Synthesizer, 162
"Moonlight Serenade, 556
"Moon River," 2, 53, *56*
Moore, Ben, 366
Moore, B.J., 107
Moore, Dorothy, 261, 278
Moore, Dudley, 72, *234*, 425
Moore, Melba, 171, 261, 416
Moore, Ray, *176, 267*, 300, *353*, 549
Moore, Rica Owen, 84
Moore, Sam, 128
Moorfoot, Colin, *250*
Moravec, Ivan, 122, 175
Moravian Festival Chorus, 48
"More," *80*
More Live, 365
More Music from Peter Gunn, 36
"More Than Wonderful," 382
Moreira, Airto, 315
Moreno, Rita, *204*
Morgan, Dennis W., 349, 365
Morgan, Helen, 557
Morgan, Lorrie, 516
Morgan, Misty, 173
Morganfield, McKinley, 181
Morgenstern, Dan, *220, 268*, *354, 523*, 550
Morini, Erica, 58
Mormon Tabernacle Choir, 12, 34, *36*, 78, 82, 122,

173, 462
Morning Like This, 438
Moroder, Giorgio, 297, 383, *385*
Morrell, Marty, 181
Morricone, Ennio, 147, 452, *460*
Morris, Gary, 457
Morris, Joan, 250
Morris, John, 351
Morrison, Bob, 307, *313*
Morrison, Jim, 151, 319
Morrison, Kathy, 146
Morrison, Van, 477, 548
Morse, Steve, 495
Morton, Arthur, 537
Morton, Ferdinand "Jelly Roll," 556
Morvan, Mr. [Fabrice], 486-487
Moscow Radio Chorus, 190
Moss, Buddy, 332
Moss, Jerry, 102
Motley Crue, 495, 514
Motorhead, 532
Motown, 7
Mottley, David, 424
Mottola, Tommy, 9
Mounsey, Rob, 368
Mountain Music, 365
Movements for Piano and Orchestra, 58
Mowatt, Judy, 420
Mozart: Cosi fan tutte, 148, 248
Mr. Lucky, 46
"Mrs. Robinson," 4, 138-139, *144*, 145
Mtume, James, *330*
Muddy "Mississippi" Waters Live, 315
Muddy Waters. *See* Waters, Muddy
Muddy Waters Woodstock Album, The, 247
Muhammad Ali (Cassius Clay) 76, 84
Muldaur, Maria, 228
Mull, Martin, 300
Muller, Franz, 266
Mulligan, Gerry, 25, 45-47, 57, 146, 200, 341, *349*, 350, 411, 437
Mullins, Johnny, 313
Mullova, Viktoria, 502
Munch, Charles, 28, *38*, 48, 55, *58*
Munrow, David, 260, 264, *265*, 281, 298
Muppet Movie, The, *319*
Muppets, 204, 284, 300, 309, 336, 344, 354, 387-388, 405

Italic pages = Grammy victory or victories

Italic pages = Grammy victory or victories

North, Alex, 80, 120-121, 264
Northern Star, 416
North German Radio Chorus, 387, 539
North Texas State University Lab Band, 246, 278
Norvo, Red, 37, 437
Norwood, Dorothy, 332, 419, 439
No Shortage, 246
No Strings, 69
Nothin' But the Blues, 399
"Nothing Compares 2 U," 513
Nu Shooz, 435
Nunn, Trevor, *384*
Oak Ridge Boys, 119, 132, 147, 160, 169, *173*, 186, 201, 215, *230, 263*, 274, 279, 295, 332, 343, 345, *349*, 365-366, 382, 476, 550
Oates, John, 347, 363, 417, 426
Oatts, Dick, 478
Oberlin, Russell, 96
Ocean, Billy, 392, 399, 436
O'Connell, Maura, 517
O'Connor, John J., 17
O'Connor, Mark, 438, 534
O'Connor, Norman, 113
O'Connor, Sinéad, 472, 508-509, 513, *514*, 523, 541, 547
O'Day, Anita, 496
"Ode to Billy Joe," 127, 130, 134
Ode to Billy Joe, 130
O'Dell, Kenny, *215*, 400
Odetta, 79
Offramp, 364
Ogdon, John, 81, 148
Ogerman, Claus, 80, 107, 119, 134, 263, 280, *315*, 333, 367, 537
"Oh Happy Day," 155
Oh Happy Day, 160
O'Hara, Jaimie, *438*
O'Hearn, Patrick, 459
Ohio Players, 245
Ohlsson, Garrick, 520
"Oh Pretty Woman," 513
Oistrakh, David, 70, 81, *175*, 188, 202-203, 227, *232*
O'Jays, 214, 229, 294
O'Kanes, *457*
Oklahoma!, 556
Old 8 x 10, 475
Oldfield, Mike, *231*
Oldham, Arthur, 211, *218, 266*
Oliveira, Elmar, 461
Oliver, 157
Oliver, John, 318, 335
Oliver, Tommy, 131

Olivia Physical, *371*
Oliviero, Nino, 80
Olson, Byron, 316
Omartian, Michael, 279, 321-322, 332, *333*, 336, 406, 444
Omartian, Stormie, 332
Omen, The, 264
"On Broadway," 294, 330
On Broadway, 383
On a Clear Day You Can See Forever, 108
"One," 488, 496
O'Neal, Brian, 403
O'Neal, Kevin, 403
O'Neal Twins, 332
One Bright Day, 499
One Flew Over the Cuckoo's Nest, 264
100% Fortified Zydeco, 401
100 Proof, 172
"One Hundred Ways," 347
O'Neill, Eugene, 84
"One of the Living," 416
One Lord, One Faith, One Baptism, 476
Only the Lonely, 22, 26, 30
"One O'Clock Jump," 556
One on One, 329
One of These Nights, 244
Ono, Yoko, 3, 9, 338-339, 346-347
On Praying Ground, 517
On the Road, 331
"On the Road Again," *331*
On a Saturday Night, 401
Open Road, 401
Oppens, Ursula, 317, 521
Opposites Attract, *523*
Orange, Walter, 278, 416
"Orange Blossom Special/Hoedown," 332
Orbison, Roy, 92, 325, *331*, *443*, 470, *476*, 494, 507, 550
Orchestra and Chorus of Paris National Opera, 135
Orchestra Harlow, 296
Orchestral Suite from Tender Land *Suite*, *49*
Oregon, 214
Orlando, Jose, 517
Orlando, Tony, 213
Ormandy, Eugene, 28, 47, 94, 121, 174, 188, 201-202, 217, 233, 316, 555
"Ornithology," 556
Orpheus Chamber Orchestra, 501
Ortolani, Riz, 80
Osborne, Jeffrey, 380, 399
Osborne Brothers, 534, 536
Oscar Peterson and Dizzy

Gillespie, 245
Oslin, K.T., 450, *457*, 470, *475*, 516
Osmond, Marie, 213-214, 419
Ostanek, Walter, 440, 478, 536
Ostrow, Elizabeth, 503
Ostwald, Clay, 504
O'Sullivan, Gilbert, 198-199
Other Side of 'Round Midnight, The, 449-450, 456
Otis, Johnny, 367
O'Toole, Peter, 97
Out of Africa, *440*
"Outa Space," 199
Out of Time, 531, *532*
"Over the Rainbow," 556
Overstreet, Paul, 450, *457*, 534
Owen, Randy, 382
Owens, A.L., 159
Owens, Buck, 79, 92-93, 476, 498, 548
Ozawa, Seiji, 148, 174, 188, 217, 248, 502
P., Millie, 518
Pacheco, Johnny, 263, 315, 420, 477
Pack, David, 333
Padgham, Hugh, 426, 523
Page, Gene, 216
Page, Jimmy, 474
Page, Robert, *249*
Paich, David, *261*, 362, *367-368*, 371
Paich, Marty, 70, 368, *537*
Palmer, Earl, 517
Palmer, Robert, 311, 430, 435, *436*, 467, *473*
Palmieri, Eddie, 241, *247*, *263*, 296, 350, 394, *402*, 412, 420, *459*, 550
Palo Pa Rumba, 402
Pammers, Leon, 441
Pandora, 439, 536
Pantoja, Isabel, 518
"Papa's Got a Brand New Bag," *106*
"Papa Was a Rolling Stone," 195, *199*, 200
Pardini, Lou, 456
Pareles, Jon, 15-16
Parkening, Christopher, 281, 441
Parker, Charlie "Yardbird," 224, *229*, 551, 554, 556
Parker, Dorothy, 60
Parker, Fess, 97
Parker, Knocky, 420
Parker, Ray Jr., 364, 392, *398*, 403
Parks, Van Dyke, 460
Parr, John, 421
Parris, Fred, 418

Italic pages = Grammy victory or victories

Italic pages = Grammy victory or victories

Ponchielli, Amilcare, 76
Poncia, Vini, *277*
Ponty, Jean-Luc, 330
"Poor Boy Blues," 516
Porcaro, Steve, 371
Porgy and Bess, *37*, 260
"Por Que Te Tengo Que
    Olvidar?" 518
Porter, Bob, *319*
Porter, Cole, *49*, 75, 552
Porterfield, Nolan, 464
Posey, Sandy, 118-119
Post, Mike, 245, *247*, *347*,
    350, 402, 473, *478*, 550
Potter, Brian, 252
Poulenc, Francois, 49, 58
Powell, Doc, 474
"Power of Love," 415
Power of Love, 532
"Power of Love/Love Power,"
    532
Powers, Quentin, 438
Prado, Perez, 27-28, 37, 46
Praeger, Stephan, 247
Prague Philharmonic Chorus,
    462
Prague String Quartet, 265,
    281
Prater, Dave, 128
Pray for Me, 535
"Precious Lord," 366
*Presenting the New Christy
    Minstrels*, 68
Presidents, 172
Presley, Elvis, 7-8, 22, 31, 34-
    38, 41, 45-46, 112-113,
    127, *132*, 146, 195, *201*,
    225-226, *230*, 269, 289,
    295, 547, 551, 555
Preston, Billy, 193-194, *198*,
    199, 201, 214-215, 228-
    229, 296
Pretenders, 328-330, 548
Pretre, Georges, 423
Previn, André, 12, 21, 27, *28*,
    34, 36-37, 42, 44-45, *47*,
    52, 54, *56*, 57, 77, 79-80,
    92, 121, 147-148, 204,
    211, 217, 232, 281, 298,
    316, 318, 351, 423, 462,
    497, 549
Previtali, Fernado, 39
Previte, Frankie, 460
Price, Leontyne, 44-45, *49*, 60,
    65, 77, *83*, 90, *96*, 104,
    110, 117, *122*, 129, *136*,
    143, 156, *162*, 176, 182-
    183, *189*, 204, 212, *218*,
    226-227, *233*, 250, 318,
    327, *335*, 362, 366, *370*,
    383, *387*, 547, 549, 551
Price, Margaret, 267
Price, Ray, 168, *172*, 186,

263, 279
Price, Vincent, 219
Pride, Charley, 120, 132-133,
    159, 173, 182, *186*, 197,
    200, 213-214, 230, 263,
    313
Prima, Louis, *27*
Prima Donna, 117
Prime Time, 278
Primrose, William, 28, 65, 70,
    148
Prince, 379-380, 391, 396-397,
    398, *399*, *403*, 406, 426,
    430-431, *436*, 454, 455,
    456, 494, 496, 500, 504,
    513, 533, 550
Prince, Ian, 519
Prince-Joseph, Bruce, 108
*Prince's Trust All-Star Rock
    Concert, The*, 464
Prine, John, 199, *439*, 477,
    529, *535*
Pringle, Keith, 458
Priority, 349
Pritchard, Sir John, 481
Private Dancer, 397
Procol Harum, 132
Professor Longhair, 452, *458*
Program of Song, A, 49
Prokofiev: Peter and the Wolf,
    60, 267
*Prokofiev: Symphony No. 5 in
    B Flat, Op. 100*, 403
Promises, Promises, 155, *161*
"Proud Mary," 185
Pryor, Richard, 226, *234*, 242,
    251, *267*, 284, 300, 336,
    344, 353, 360, *370*, 405,
    550
Prysock, Arthur, 437, 456
Public Enemy, 496, 515, 533
Puccini: Madame Butterfly,
    59, 60, 82, 83
Puccini: Tosca, 556
Puccini: Turandot, 45, *48*
Puckett & the Union Gap,
    Gary, 144-145
Puente, Tito, 280, *296*, 332,
    383, 412, *420*, 439, *518*,
    536, 550
Puerling, Gene, 216, 231, 247,
    263, 296, 333, *351*, 367
Puerte, Joe, 333
"Puff the Magic Dragon," 63
Pullins, Leroy, 120
Purim, Flora, 417, 437
Purify, Bobby, 119
Purify, James, 119
Purple, Dave, *190*
Purple Rain, 397-398, *403*
Pursell, William, 230, 297
Push Choir, 314
Putman, Curly, 146

"Put Your Hand in the Hand of
    the Man from Galilee,"
    182, 186
Puyana, Rafael, 203
Python, Monty, 251, 336, 387
Queen, 261, 329, 548
Queen Latifah, 515, 533
Queen and Mack, 337
"Queen of the House," 100,
    107
Queen Ida, 332, *367*, 439
*Queen Ida and the Bon Temps
    Zydeco Band on Tour*, 367
Queensryche, 496, 532
Quinn, Carmel, 110
Quire, 262
RCA Italiana Orchestra and
    Chorus, 82
*RCA/Met — 100 Singers, 100
    Years*, 425
R.E.M., 11, *531*, *532*, *541*
REO Speedwagon, 347
Rabbitt, Eddie, 313, 332
Rabin, Trevor, 402, 504
Rachabane, Barney, 417
Rachmaninoff, Sergei, 216,
    557
*Rachmaninoff Piano Concerto
    No. 2 in C Minor*, 557
*Rachmaninoff Piano Concerto
    No. 3*, 36
*Rachmaninoff: Rhapsody on a
    Theme of Paganini*, 557
Radcliffe Choral Society, 96
Radio Chorus of the N.O.S.
    Hilversum and
    Concertgebouworkest, 318
Radner, Gilda, 336, *503*
Rado, James, 140, 147
Rafferty, Gerry, 293
Raffi, 464, 503
Ragni, Gerome, 140, *147*
Raiders of the Lost Ark, *351*,
    370
Rainbow, 380
"Raindrops Keep Falling on
    My Head," 158
Rains, Claude, 72
Raisin, *231*
"Raisin' the Dickens," 438
Raitt, Bonnie, 4, 9, 312, 363,
    436, 484-485, 494, *499*,
    526, 531, *532*, 549
Rakha, Alla, 281
Ralke, Don, 94
Ralph Carmichael Singers and
    Orchestra, 107, 173
Ralph Hunter Choir, 37
Ram, 181
"Ramblin' Rose," 67
Rambo, Dottie, *147*, 186, 366
Rambo, Reba, *332*, 366
Rambos, 201, 332, 350

Italic pages = Grammy victory or victories

Italic pages = Grammy victory or victories

Italic pages = Grammy victory or victories

Index   589

Italic pages = Grammy victory or victories

Italic pages = Grammy victory or victories

363-364, 376, 378-379, *383*, 394, 550
"Summer in the City," 216
Summer of '42, 187
Summer Place, A, 41, *45*
Summers, Andy, 495
Summers, Myrna, 173, 314
"Summer Sketches '82," 384
Sumner, Don, 159
Sumner, J.D., 296, *349*, 517, 535
Sun of Latin Music, 247
Sunday in the Park with George, 402
Sunliters, 173, 201, 230
Sunnyland Slim, 201
Superman, 315
Supersax, 209, *214*, 230, 245
"Superstition," *214*
Supertramp, 310-311, 444
Supremes, 92, 99, 106
Sure, Al B., 474, 514-515
Survivor, 363
Sutherland, Joan, 49, 55, 58, *60*, 83, 96, *353*
Sutton, Glenn, 116, *120*, 168
Suzuki, Pat, 36
Sveshnikov, Aleksander, 233
Swaggart, Jimmy, 332
Swansen, Chris, 400
Swan Silvertones, 147, 215
Swe-Danes, 46
Swedien, Bruce, *388*, *464*, *522*
Sweeney Todd, 309, *315*
Sweet Baby James, 170
"Sweetest Sounds, The," 67
Sweet Honey in the Rock, 477
Sweet Inspiration, 146
"Sweet Love," *436*
Swift, Allen, 39
"Swing Dat Hammer," 46
Swingle, Ward Lamar, 76, *162*
Swingle Singers, 76, *78*, *92*, *105*, 118, 131, 156, 162, 550
Swingle Singers Go Baroque, The, 92
Swing Out Sister, 454
Switched-On Bach, 156, *161*, 162
Sykes, Roosevelt, 201, 315
Sylvan, Sanford, 521, 539
Sylvester, Robert, 189
Sylvia, 214, 365
Symphony No. 1 (Corigliano), *540*
Symphony No. 3 (Lutosławski), *442*
Symphony No. 4 (Ives), 108
Synchronicity, 379-380
Szell, George, 58, 80-81, 94, 121, 161, 174
Szeryng, Henryk, 38, 70, 162,

188, *232*, 242
Szigeti, Joseph, 71, 108, 553
Szymczyk, Bill, 284
TSOP (The Sound of Philadelphia), 224, *229*
Taff, Russ, *382*, 419, 476, 498, 535
Tjader Sextet, Cal, 332
Taj Mahal, 216
"Take the 'A' Train," 459, 557
"Take Five," 56
Takei, George, 463
Take Me Back, 246
Take 6, 469, 473, *475*, *477*, 490, 497, *498*, 511, *517*, 528, *533*, 550
"Talk About the Good Times," 173
Talking Heads, 380, 483, 548
Talleys, 535
Talvela, Martti, 218
Tangerine Dream, 536
Tanglewood Festival Chorus, 249, 318, 335
"Tapestry," 178, 184
Tapestry, *184*
Tarr Brass Ensemble, Edward, *148*
Tartaglia, John, 297
Tashi, 265
Taste of Honey, A, 6, 286, *293*, 294
"Taste of Honey, A," 4, 66, *69*, 102, *104*, 107
Tate, Grady, 437
Tattoo You, 354
Tatum, Art, 47, 209, *214*, 262, 551, 555, 557
Taupin, Bernie, 187
Tavares, *293*, 364
Taylor, Eddie, 296
Taylor, Gloria, 159
Taylor, Hound Dog, 263, 367
Taylor, James, 170-*171*, *179*, *184*, 272, 277, *311*, *336*, 370
Taylor, Johnnie, 145, 261
Taylor, KoKo, 350, *401*, 420, 434, 458, 499, 518
Taylor, Little Johnny, 79
Taylor, Steve, 401
Tchaikovsky: Concerto No. 1 in B Flat Minor, Op. 23, 26
Team, Virginia, 425
Tears for Fears, 504
"Tea for Two," 557
Tebaldi, Renata, *29*
Teicher, Lou, 160
Te Kanawa, Kiri, 335, 370, 387, 405, 424
Temperton, Rod, 330, 333, 399, 519
Temple University Choirs,

109, 135, 190, 233
Tempo, Nino, 14, 75, 78
Temptations, 7, 106, 140, *145*, 183, 195, *200*
Tender Land, The, 43
Tennstedt, Klaus, 462
"Tequila," 23, 28
Terrell, Tammi, 132
Terri, Salli, 29, 49
Terry, Clark, 92, 106, 246, 262
Tex, Joe, 92, 132, 200, 278
Texas Boys Choir, 149
Texas Tornados, *518*, 534
Tharpe, Sister Rosetta, 160
That Nigger's Crazy, *234*
"That Old Black Magic," 27
"That Was the Week That Was" cast, 97
"That's the Way Love Goes," 400
"That's What Friends Are For," 192, 427-428, *435*
Thedford, Bili, 314
Theilmans, Jean "Toots," 80
Thelonius Monk, The Complete Riverside Recordings, 464
Then and Now, 215
Theodorakis, Mikis, 108, 231
There Must Be a Better World Somewhere, *350*
"(There's) No Gettin' Over Me," 349
They Call Me Muddy Waters, 181, *187*
"They Say," 438
Thielemans, Toots, 313, 533
Think of One, 381
Third World, 459
"This Is It," 328
This Is a Recording, 190
"This Land Is Your Land," 557
"This Masquerade," 255, *260*, 261
This Time by Basie! Hits of the 50's and 60's, 79
"This Will Be," 245
Thomas, B.J., 158, 242, *279*, 290, *296*, 308, *314*, 332, *350*, 366, 383, 550
Thomas, Carla, 132
Thomas, Clifton, 146
Thomas, David Clayton, 158
Thomas, Edward, 146
Thomas, Irma, 536
Thomas, Jess, 95
Thomas, Keith, 531, 541
Thomas, Marlo, 220
Thomas, Michael Tilson, 174-175, 202, 248, 264-265, 334, 422-423, 462, 538
Thomas, Pat, 67
Thompson, Bob, 37
Thompson, Linda, 457

Italic pages = Grammy victory or victories

Italic pages = Grammy victory or victories

Italic pages = Grammy victory or victories

Ward, Anita, 312
Ward, Clara, 186, 201
Ware, Laverne, 185
Warfield, William, *387*
Wariner, Steve, 457, *534*
Waring & the Pennsylvanians, Fred, 68, 93
Warm Breeze, 365
Warnes, Jennifer, 357-358, 362-363, 448, *455*
Waronker, Lenny, 235, 268
Warren, Bobby, 160
Warren, Diane, 460
Warren, Mervyn, 519
War Requiem, 76, 80, 81
Warsaw National
· Philharmonic Chorus, 539
Warwick, Dionne, 14, 92, 131, 140, 143, *145*, 158-159, 167, *171*, 172, 228, 305, 310, *311-312*, 407, 409, 414, 428, 434, *435*, 550
Was (Not Was), 515
Washington, Carrol, 185
Washington, Dinah, 34, *37*
Washington, Ella, 145
Washington, Grover Jr., 342, 346, *348*, 364, 399
Washington, Keith, 532
Washington Squares, 458
Wasserman, Rob, 475
Waters, Muddy, 16, 47, 173, 181, *187*, *201*, 215, 231, 241, *247*, *280*, 290, *296*, 309, *315*, 350, 549, 551
Watley, Jody, 447, *455*, 456
Watrous, Bill, 246
Watson, Doc, 201, 210, 215, 231, *314*, 349, 366, 382, 400, 419. 432, 439, 517, 522, 535, 550
Watson, Johnny "Guitar," 278
Watson, Merle, *231*, *314*, 366, 382, 400, 419
Watson, Wayne, 457
Watts, Andre, 77, *81*, 82, 232, 266
Watts, Ernie, *363*, *417*
Watts 103rd Street Rhythm Band, 172
Watts, Stan, 425
Waylon and Willie, 289
Wayne, John, 219
Way We Were, The, 222, *228*, *231*
We Are in Love, 515
"We Are the World," 6, 192, 407-408, *415*, 416, *426*
We Come to Worship, 332
"We Didn't Start the Fire," 494
We Dig Mancini, 105
We Five, 100, 105

"We Got Us," 46
We Love You, Call Collect, *163*
We Want Miles, 365
We Will Meet Again, 331
Weatherly, Jim, 214
Weather Girls, 381
Weather Report, 16, 200, 307, *313*, 348, 364, 381, 418
Weaver, Curley, 332
Webb, Chick, 553
Webb, Jimmy, 125-126, *130*, *147*, 411, *418*
Webber, Andrew Lloyd, 327, *333*, *384*, 414, *424*, 550, 552
Weber, Hans, 522, 540
Weber, Jimmy, 478, 518
Webster, Francis, *105*
Webster, Margaret, 110
Webster, Paul, 36, 103, 105, 118
Weil, Cynthia, 416, 447, *454*, *460*, 494
Weill, Kurt, 27
Weisberg, Arthur, 188
Weiser, Norman, 84
Weiss, Donna, 281, *346*
Weissberg, Eric, *215*
Weissenberg, Alexis, 148, 175
Welch, Lenny, 79
Welk, Lawrence, 44, 57, 548
Weller Quartet, 121
Welles, Orson, 176, *267*, 319, 251, 292, *300*, 336, *353*
We'll Sing in the Sunshine, 93
Wells, Junior, 280
Wells, Kitty, 476, 548, 551
Wells, Mary, 68
Wells, Paul F., 315
Welsh, Moray, 368
We Sing Praises, 383
Wess, Frank, 399
Wess, Richard, 38
West, Bill, 93
West, Dottie, 89, 92, *93*, 107, 120, 132-133, 146, 160, 214, 230, 295, 314, 349
West, Tommy, 213
West Coast Rap All-Stars, 515
"West End Blues," 558
West Meets East, 135
West Side Story, 47, 56-57, *58*, *421*, 558
Westenburg, Richard, 353
Western Wind Vocal Ensemble, 217
Westminister Cathedral Boys Choir, 404
Westminister Choir, 59, 71, 96, 249, 299, 442
Weston, Paul, 11-12, 21, 26, *50*, 552

Weston, Randy, 214
Wexler, Jerry, 100
Wham!, 398, 426
"What Are You Doing the Rest of Your Life," 202
"What a Diff'rence a Day Makes," 37
"What a Fool Believes," 4, 17, 304, *310-311*, 316
"What a Friend," 296
"What Kind of Fool Am I," 62, 67
"What Now My Love," 115, 118, 120
What Now My Love, 118
"What's Love Got to Do With It," 5, 9, *397*, 398
"What's New," 384
Wheeler, Caron, 488
Wheeler, Kenny, 399
"Wheel Hoss," 400
Whelchel, Lisa, 401
When Harry Met Sally..., 496
"When a Man Loves a Woman," 531
"When I Call Your Name," 516
When It's Polka Time at Your House, 518
"When You're Hot, You're Hot," 186
"Where Is the Love," 194, 199, *245*
"Where the Soul Never Dies," 263
Where the Streets Have No Name, *483*
"Where've You Been," *516*
"While My Guitar Gently Weeps," 193
Whipped Cream and Other Delights, 104
Whispers, 456
White, Barry, 213-214, 231
White, Bukka, 231
White, Karyn, 474
White, Maurice, 264, 277, 294, *297*, 320
White, Verdine, 294
"White Christmas," 558
"White Dawn, The," 264
Whitehead, John, 199
White Heart, 382
Whiteman, Murray, 425
Whiteman, Paul, 555
Whites, 365, 400, 476
Whitfield, Norman, 146, 185, *199*, *264*
Whitfield, Thomas, 498, 535
Whiting, Margaret, 44, 77
Whitley, Keith, 516, 534
Whitmore, James, *251*
Whitmore, Ken, *111*, 190

Italic pages = Grammy victory or victories

Whitney, 454
Whitney Houston, 415
Who, 523, 548
"Who Can I Turn To," 91
"Whoever's in New England," 438
Who It Is, 474
Whoopi Goldberg (Original Broadway Show Recording), 424
Whorf, Christopher, *234*
Who's Afraid of Virginia Woolf?, 83
Why I Oppose the War in Vietnam, 176
Why Is There Air?, 101, 110
"Why Not!" 381
Wilber, Bob, 159, *418*
Wilbourne, Bill, 146
Wilcox, Harlow, 160
Wilcox, Max, 522
Wild Cherry, 260-261
Wild and Crazy Guy, A, 300
Wild Is Love, 45
Wilkes & Braun, Inc., 220
Wilkins, Robert, *332*
Wilkinson, Kenneth, *233, 283*
Willcocks, David, *82*, 218, 283
William, Big Joe, *332*
Williams, Andy, 24, 27, 56, 74, 78, 91, 118, 165, 197, 212, 243, 254
Williams, Arliene Nofchissey, 263
Williams, Beau, 498
Williams, Bert, 556
Williams, Big Joe, 332
Williams, Deniece, 364, *370*, 380, 398-399, 401, 432, *438-439*, 451, *457*, 476, 496, 498
Williams, Don, 350
Williams, Jr., Hank, 92, 93, 106, 313, 438, 457, 498, 504
Williams, Sr., Hank, 106, 490, 498, 504, 548, 551, 558
Williams, Joe, 310, 313, 364, 393, *399*, 437, 456, 475, 496
Williams, John, 122, 197, 202-203, 217, 232, 241, *247*, 250, 263, 273, *277, 280-281*, 290, 294, *297*, 298, 305-306, 311, *315*, 329, *333, 351*, 358, 363, *367*, 385, 395, 402, 425, 460, 478, 500, 519, 532, 537, 549
Williams, Kenny, 197
Williams, Marion, 69
Williams, Martin, *406*

Williams, Mason, 140, *145, 147*, 476
Williams, Milan, 278
Williams, Pat, 187, 230, *231*
Williams, Patrick, 330, 333, 384, *441*, 456, 459
Williams, Paul, 171, 228, 270, 277, 281, 315
Williams, Ralph, 185
Williams, Robin, 309, 311, *319*, 387, 452, *463*, 471, *482*, 550
Williams, Roger, 93, 120
Williams, Vanessa, 473-474, 496, 533
Williams, Wendy O., 398
Williams, William B., 66
Williams Brothers, 535
Williamson, Homesick James, 296
Williamson, James, 296
Willow Weep for Me, 155, 158
Will Rogers Follies, The, 537
Wills, Bob, 548
Wilson, August, 412
Wilson, Brian, 120
Wilson, Flip, 136, 149, 169, *176*, 190, 204
Wilson, Gerald, 80, 92
Wilson, Jackie, 47, 132
Wilson, Johnny, 334
Wilson, Meredith, 32
Wilson, Nancy, 90, *92*, 105, 456
Wilson, Norris, 215, *230*
Wilson, Stanley, 37
Wilson, Teddy, 437
Wilson Phillips, 512
Winans, 350, 383, 401, *419, 439*, 451, *458*, 470, *476*, 490, 517, 550
Winans, BeBe, 401, 411, 438, 458, 470, *476*, 490, 496, *498*, 529, *535*
Winans, Carvin, 420
Winans, CeCe, 401, 411, 438, 451, 458, 470, 476, 490, 496, *498*, 529, *535*
Winans, Daniel, 490, *498*
Winans, Delores, 476
Winans, Marvin, 411, *419*, 476
Winans, Michael, 420
Winans Family & Friends Choir, Ronald, 477, 517
Winans, Vickie, 458, 498
Winans Live at Carnegie Hall, The, 476
Winchell, Paul, *234*
"Winchester Cathedral," 114, 118, *119*
Winchester Cathedral Choir, 424

"Wind Beneath My Wings," 485
Winding, Kai, 80
Winelight, 348
Wings, 213, *228*, 306, *312*
Winnie the Pooh & Tigger Too, 234
Winstons, 154, 158
Winter, Edgar, 214, 216
Winter, Johnny, 401, 420, 536
Winter, Paul, 440, 478, 500, 518
Winterhalter, Hugo, 37
Winters, Jonathan, 50, 60, 72, 97, 482, 522, 540
Winwood, Steve, 4, *434*, 435, 444, 454, 472-473
Wiseman, Mac, 518
Wissert, Joe, 268
"Witchcraft," 22, 26
"Witch Doctor," 24
Withers, Bill, 180, 184, *185*, 346, *347, 455*
Witherspoon, Jimmy, 381, 420, 437
"Without You," 199
Witness, 535
"Wives and Lovers," 75, 78
Wiz, The, 247
Wold, Tommy, 79
Woldin, Judd, *231*
Wolf, Peter, 421
Wolfe, Charles K., 464
Wolfe, Lanny, 332
Wolfe Children's Chorus, Richard, 163, 190
Wolfe Trio, Lanny, 350
Wolfer, Bill, 399, 403
Wolinski, Hawk, 380
"Woman in Love," 328
Womenfolk, 107
Women's Chorus of Schola Cantorum, 71
Wonder, Stevie, 1, 4-5, 17, 119, 145, 172, 186, 206-209, *213-214*, 222-224, *228-229*, 235, 253-255, *260, 261*, 263-264, *268*, 321, 330, 333, 337, 363-364, 368, 397-399, 407-408, 415, *416*, 428, 434, *435, 455*, 456, 474, 493, 533, 537, 546-547, 549
Wonderfulness, 115, 123
Woodruff, Woody, 540
Woods, Phil, 185, 241, 245, *246*, 262, 273, *278*, 331, 360, 381, 400, 533, 550
Woods Quartet, Phil, *365, 375, 381*
Woods, Robert, 319, *336*, 353, *370*, 405, *424*, 443, 471, *482*, 492, *503*, 549

Italic pages = Grammy victory or victories

Index

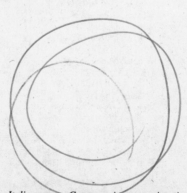

Italic pages = Grammy victory or victories